RICHARD HENRY DANA, JR.

RICHARD HENRY DANA, JR.

TWO YEARS BEFORE THE MAST
AND OTHER VOYAGES

Two Years Before the Mast
To Cuba and Back
Journal of a Voyage Round the World, 1859–1860

THE LIBRARY OF AMERICA

The text of *Journal of a Voyage Round the World* copyright © 1968 by
the Massachusetts Historical Society and copyright © 1968 by the
President and Fellows of Harvard College. Reprinted by permission.

The paper used in this publication meets the
minimum requirements of the American National Standard for
Information Sciences—Permanence of Paper for Printed
Library Materials, ANSI Z39.48—1984.

Distributed to the trade
in the United States by Penguin Putnam Inc.
and in Canada by Penguin Books Canada Ltd.

Library of Congress Catalog Number: 2005045094
For cataloging information, see end of Notes.
ISBN 1–931082–83–9

First Printing
The Library of America—161

Manufactured in the United States of America

THOMAS L. PHILBRICK
SELECTED THE TEXTS AND
WROTE THE NOTES FOR THIS VOLUME

Contents

Contents

TWO YEARS
BEFORE THE MAST

A Personal Narrative of Life at Sea

——Crowded in the rank and narrow ship,—
Housed on the wild sea with wild usages,—
Whate'er in the inland dales the land conceals
Of fair and exquisite, O! nothing, nothing,
Do we behold of that in our rude voyage.
COLERIDGE'S WALLENSTEIN.

Chapter I

I AM unwilling to present this narrative to the public without a few words in explanation of my reasons for publishing it. Since Mr. Cooper's Pilot and Red Rover, there have been so many stories of sea-life written, that I should really think it unjustifiable in me to add one to the number without being able to give reasons in some measure warranting me in so doing.

With the single exception, as I am quite confident, of Mr. Ames' entertaining, but hasty and desultory work, called "Mariner's Sketches," all the books professing to give life at sea have been written by persons who have gained their experience as naval officers, or passengers, and of these, there are very few which are intended to be taken as narratives of facts.

Now, in the first place, the whole course of life, and daily duties, the discipline, habits and customs of a man-of-war are very different from those of the merchant service; and in the next place, however entertaining and well written these books may be, and however accurately they may give sea-life as it appears to their authors, it must still be plain to every one that a naval officer, who goes to sea as a gentleman, "with his gloves on," (as the phrase is,) and who associates only with his fellow-officers, and hardly speaks to a sailor except through a boatswain's mate, must take a very different view of the whole matter from that which would be taken by a common sailor.

Besides the interest which every one must feel in exhibitions of life in those forms in which he himself has never experienced it; there has been, of late years, a great deal of attention directed toward common seamen, and a strong sympathy awakened in their behalf. Yet I believe that, with the single exception which I have mentioned, there has not been a book written, professing to give their life and experiences, by one who has been of them, and can know what their life really is. *A voice from the forecastle* has hardly yet been heard.

In the following pages I design to give an accurate and authentic narrative of a little more than two years spent as a common sailor, before the mast, in the American merchant service. It is written out from a journal which I kept at the time,

3

and from notes which I made of most of the events as they happened; and in it I have adhered closely to fact in every particular, and endeavored to give each thing its true character. In so doing, I have been obliged occasionally to use strong and coarse expressions, and in some instances to give scenes which may be painful to nice feelings; but I have very carefully avoided doing so, whenever I have not felt them essential to giving the true character of a scene. My design is, and it is this which has induced me to publish the book, to present the life of a common sailor at sea as it really is,—the light and the dark together.

There may be in some parts a good deal that is unintelligible to the general reader; but I have found from my own experience, and from what I have heard from others, that plain matters of fact in relation to customs and habits of life new to us, and descriptions of life under new aspects, act upon the inexperienced through the imagination, so that we are hardly aware of our want of technical knowledge. Thousands read the escape of the American frigate through the British channel, and the chase and wreck of the Bristol trader in the Red Rover, and follow the minute nautical manœuvres with breathless interest, who do not know the name of a rope in the ship; and perhaps with none the less admiration and enthusiasm for their want of acquaintance with the professional detail.

In preparing this narrative I have carefully avoided incorporating into it any impressions but those made upon me by the events as they occurred, leaving to my concluding chapter, to which I shall respectfully call the reader's attention, those views which have been suggested to me by subsequent reflection.

These reasons, and the advice of a few friends, have led me to give this narrative to the press. If it shall interest the general reader, and call more attention to the welfare of seamen, or give any information as to their real condition, which may serve to raise them in the rank of beings, and to promote in any measure their religious and moral improvement, and diminish the hardships of their daily life, the end of its publication will be answered.

R. H. D., Jr.

Boston, July, 1840.

Departure

THE fourteenth of August was the day fixed upon for the sailing of the brig Pilgrim on her voyage from Boston round Cape Horn to the western coast of North America. As she was to get under weigh early in the afternoon, I made my appearance on board at twelve o'clock, in full sea-rig, and with my chest, containing an outfit for a two or three years' voyage, which I had undertaken from a determination to cure, if possible, by an entire change of life, and by a long absence from books and study, a weakness of the eyes, which had obliged me to give up my pursuits, and which no medical aid seemed likely to cure.

The change from the tight dress coat, silk cap and kid gloves of an undergraduate at Cambridge, to the loose duck trowsers, checked shirt and tarpaulin hat of a sailor, though somewhat of a transformation, was soon made, and I supposed that I should pass very well for a jack tar. But it is impossible to deceive the practised eye in these matters; and while I supposed myself to be looking as salt as Neptune himself, I was, no doubt, known for a landsman by every one on board as soon as I hove in sight. A sailor has a peculiar cut to his clothes, and a way of wearing them which a green hand can never get. The trowsers, tight round the hips, and thence hanging long and loose round the feet, a super abundance of checked shirt, a low-crowned, well varnished black hat, worn on the back of the head, with half a fathom of black ribbon hanging over the left eye, and a peculiar tie to the black silk neckerchief, with sundry other minutiæ, are signs, the want of which betray the beginner, at once. Beside the points in my dress which were out of the way, doubtless my complexion and hands were enough to distinguish me from the regular *salt*, who, with a sun-burnt cheek, wide step, and rolling gait, swings his bronzed and toughened hands athwart-ships, half open, as though just ready to grasp a rope.

"With all my imperfections on my head," I joined the crew, and we hauled out into the stream, and came to anchor for the night. The next day we were employed in preparations for sea, reeving studding-sail gear, crossing royal yards, putting on chafing gear, and taking on board our powder. On the following night, I stood my first watch. I remained awake nearly all the first part of the night from fear that I might not hear when I was called; and when I went on deck, so great were my ideas of the importance of my trust, that I walked regularly fore and aft the whole length of the vessel, looking out over the bows and taffrail at each turn, and was not a little surprised at the coolness of the old salt whom I called to take my place, in stowing himself snugly away under the long boat, for a nap. That was a sufficient look-out, he thought, for a fine night, at anchor in a safe harbor.

The next morning was Saturday, and a breeze having sprung up from the southward, we took a pilot on board, hove up our anchor, and began beating down the bay. I took leave of those of my friends who came to see me off, and had barely opportunity to take a last look at the city, and well-known objects, as no time is allowed on board ship for sentiment. As we drew down into the lower harbor, we found the wind ahead in the bay, and were obliged to come to anchor in the roads. We remained there through the day and a part of the night. My watch began at eleven o'clock at night, and I received orders to call the captain if the wind came out from the westward. About midnight the wind became fair, and having called the captain, I was ordered to call all hands. How I accomplished this I do not know, but I am quite sure that I did not give the true hoarse, boatswain call of "A-a-ll ha-a-a-nds! up anchor, a-ho-oy!" In a short time every one was in motion, the sails loosed, the yards braced, and we began to heave up the anchor, which was our last hold upon Yankee land. I could take but little part in all these preparations. My little knowledge of a vessel was all at fault. Unintelligible orders were so rapidly given and so immediately executed; there was such a hurrying about, and such an intermingling of strange cries and stranger actions, that I was completely bewildered. There is not so helpless and pitiable an object in the world as a landsman beginning a sailor's life. At length those peculiar, long-drawn sounds, which denote that the crew are heaving at the windlass, began, and in a few moments we were under weigh. The noise of the water thrown from the bows began to be heard, the vessel leaned over from the damp night breeze, and rolled with the heavy ground swell, and we had actually begun our long, long journey. This was literally bidding "good night" to my native land.

Chapter II

T HE first day we passed at sea was the Sabbath. As we were
just from port, and there was a great deal to be done on
board, we were kept at work all day, and at night the watches
were set, and everything put into sea order. When we were
called aft to be divided into watches, I had a good specimen of
the manner of a sea captain. After the division had been made,
he gave a short characteristic speech, walking the quarter deck
with a cigar in his mouth, and dropping the words out between the puffs.

"Now, my men, we have begun a long voyage. If we get
along well together, we shall have a comfortable time; if we
don't, we shall have hell afloat. —All you've got to do is to
obey your orders and do your duty like men,—then you'll fare
well enough;—if you don't, you'll fare hard enough,—I can
tell you. If we pull together, you'll find me a clever fellow; if
we don't, you'll find me a *bloody* rascal. —That's all I've got to
say. —Go below, the larboard watch!"

I being in the starboard, or second mate's watch, had the
opportunity of keeping the first watch at sea. S——, a young
man, making, like myself, his first voyage, was in the same
watch, and as he was the son of a professional man, and had
been in a counting-room in Boston, we found that we had
many friends and topics in common. We talked these matters
over,—Boston, what our friends were probably doing, our
voyage, &c., until he went to take his turn at the look-out, and
left me to myself. I had now a fine time for reflection. I felt for
the first time the perfect silence of the sea. The officer was
walking the quarter deck, where I had no right to go, one or
two men were talking on the forecastle, whom I had little inclination to join, so that I was left open to the full impression
of everything about me. However much I was affected by the
beauty of the sea, the bright stars, and the clouds driven swiftly
over them, I could not but remember that I was separating
myself from all the social and intellectual enjoyments of life.
Yet, strange as it may seem, I did then and afterwards take

pleasure in these reflections, hoping by them to prevent my becoming insensible to the value of what I was leaving.

But all my dreams were soon put to flight by an order from the officer to trim the yards, as the wind was getting ahead; and I could plainly see by the looks the sailors occasionally cast to windward, and by the dark clouds that were fast coming up, that we had bad weather to prepare for, and had heard the captain say that he expected to be in the Gulf Stream by twelve o'clock. In a few minutes eight bells were struck, the watch called, and we went below. I now began to feel the first discomforts of a sailor's life. The steerage in which I lived was filled with coils of rigging, spare sails, old junk and ship stores, which had not been stowed away. Moreover, there had been no berths built for us to sleep in, and we were not allowed to drive nails to hang our clothes upon. The sea, too, had risen, the vessel was rolling heavily, and everything was pitched about in grand confusion. There was a complete "hurrah's nest," as the sailors say, "everything on top and nothing at hand." A large hawser had been coiled away upon my chest; my hats, boots, mattress and blankets had all *fetched away* and gone over to leeward, and were jammed and broken under the boxes and coils of rigging. To crown all, we were allowed no light to find anything with, and I was just beginning to feel strong symptoms of sea-sickness, and that listlessness and inactivity which accompany it. Giving up all attempts to collect my things together, I lay down upon the sails, expecting every moment to hear the cry of "all hands ahoy," which the approaching storm would soon make necessary. I shortly heard the rain-drops falling on deck, thick and fast, and the watch evidently had their hands full of work, for I could hear the loud and repeated orders of the mate, the trampling of feet, the creaking of blocks, and all the accompaniments of a coming storm. In a few minutes the slide of the hatch was thrown back, which let down the noise and tumult of the deck still louder, the loud cry of "All hands, ahoy! tumble up here and take in sail," saluted our ears, and the hatch was quickly shut again. When I got upon deck, a new scene and a new experience was before me. The little brig was close hauled upon the wind, and lying over, as it then seemed to me, nearly upon her beam ends. The heavy head sea was beating against her bows with the noise and force almost of a sledge hammer, and flying over the deck, drenching us completely through. The topsail haliards had been let go, and the great sails were filling out and backing against the masts with a noise like thunder. The wind was whistling through the rigging, loose ropes flying about; loud and, to me, unintelligible orders constantly given and rapidly executed, and the sailors "singing out" at the ropes in their hoarse and peculiar strains. In addition to all this, I had not got my "sea legs on," was dreadfully sick, with hardly strength enough to hold on to anything, and it was "pitch dark." This was my state when I was ordered aloft, for the first time, to reef topsails.

How I got along, I cannot now remember. I "laid out" on the yards and held on with all my strength. I could not have been of much service, for I remember having been sick several times before I left the topsail yard. Soon all was snug aloft, and we were again allowed to go below. This I did not consider much of a favor, for the confusion of everything below, and that inexpressible sickening smell, caused by the shaking up of the bilge-water in the hold, made the steerage but an indifferent refuge from the cold, wet decks. I had often read of the nautical experiences of others, but I felt as though there could be none worse than mine; for in addition to every other evil, I could not but remember that this was only the first night of a two years' voyage. When we were on deck we were not much better off, for we were continually ordered about by the officer, who said that it was good for us to be in motion. Yet anything was better than the horrible state of things below. I remember very well going to the hatchway and putting my head down, when I was oppressed by *nausea*, and always being relieved immediately. It was as good as an emetic.

This state of things continued for two days.

Wednesday, Aug. 20th. We had the watch on deck from four till eight, this morning. When we came on deck at four o'clock, we found things much changed for the better. The sea and wind had gone down, and the stars were out bright. I experienced a corresponding change in my feelings; yet continued extremely weak from my sickness. I stood in the waist on the weather side, watching the gradual breaking of the day, and the first streaks of the early light. Much has been said of the sun-rise at sea; but it will not compare with the sun-rise on shore. It wants the accompaniments of the songs of birds, the awakening hum of men, and the glancing of the first beams upon trees, hills, spires, and house-tops, to give it life and spirit. But though the actual *rise of the sun* at sea is not so beautiful, yet nothing will compare with the *early breaking of day* upon the wide ocean.

There is something in the first grey streaks stretching along the eastern horizon and throwing an indistinct light upon the face of the deep, which combines with the boundlessness and unknown depth of the sea around you, and gives one a feeling of loneliness, of dread, and of melancholy foreboding, which nothing else in nature can give. This gradually passes away as the light grows brighter, and when the sun comes up, the ordinary monotonous sea day begins.

From such reflections as these, I was aroused by the order from the officer, "Forward there! rig the head-pump!" I found that no time was allowed for day-dreaming, but that we must "turn-to" at the first light. Having called up the "idlers," namely carpenter, cook, steward, &c., and rigged the pump, we commenced washing down the decks. This operation, which is performed every morning at sea, takes nearly two hours; and I had hardly strength enough to get through it. After we had finished, swabbed down, and coiled up the rigging, I sat down on the spars, waiting for seven bells, which was the sign for breakfast. The officer, seeing my lazy posture, ordered me to slush the main-mast, from the royal-mast-head, down. The vessel was then rolling a little, and I had taken no sustenance for three days, so that I felt tempted to tell him that I had rather wait till after breakfast; but I knew that I must "take the bull by the horns," and that if I showed any sign of want of spirit or of backwardness, that I should be ruined at once. So I took my bucket of grease and climbed up to the royal-mast-head. Here the rocking of the vessel, which increases the higher you go from the foot of the mast, which is the fulcrum of the lever, and the smell of the grease, which offended my fastidious senses, upset my stomach again, and I was not a little rejoiced when I got upon the comparative terra firma of the deck. In a few minutes seven bells were struck, the log hove, the watch called, and we went to breakfast. Here I cannot but remember the advice of the cook, a simple-hearted African. "Now," says he, "my lad, you are well cleaned out; you have n't got a drop of your 'long-shore *swash* aboard of you. You must begin on a new tack,—pitch all your sweetmeats overboard, and turn-to upon good hearty salt beef and sea bread, and I'll promise you, you'll have your ribs well sheathed, and be as hearty as any of 'em, afore you are up to the Horn." This would be good advice to give to passengers, when they speak of the little niceties which they have laid in, in case of sea-sickness.

I cannot describe the change which half a pound of cold salt beef and a biscuit or two produced in me. I was a new being. We had a watch below until noon, so that I had some time to myself; and getting a huge piece of strong, cold, salt beef from the cook, I kept gnawing upon it until twelve o'clock. When we went on deck I felt somewhat like a man, and could begin to learn my sea duty with considerable spirit. At about two o'clock we heard the loud cry of "sail ho!" from aloft, and soon saw two sails to windward, going directly athwart our hawse. This was the first time that I had seen a sail at sea. I thought then, and have always since, that it exceeds every other sight in interest and beauty. They passed to leeward of us, and out of hailing distance; but the captain could read the names on their sterns with the glass. They were the ship Helen Mar, of New York, and the brig Mermaid, of Boston. They were both steering westward, and were bound in for our "dear native land."

Thursday, Aug. 21st. This day the sun rose clear, we had a fine wind, and everything was bright and cheerful. I had now got my sea legs on, and was beginning to enter upon the regular duties of a sea-life. About six bells, that is, three o'clock, P.M., we saw a sail on our larboard bow. I was very anxious, like every new sailor, to speak her. She came down to us, backed her main-top-sail, and the two vessels stood "head on," bowing and curvetting at each other like a couple of war-horses reined in by their riders. It was the first vessel that I had seen near, and I was surprised to find how much she rolled and pitched in so quiet a sea. She plunged her head into the sea, and then, her stern settling gradually down, her huge bows rose up, showing the bright copper, and her stem, and brest-hooks dripping, like old Neptune's locks, with the brine. Her decks were filled with passengers who had come up at the cry of "sail ho," and who by their dress and features appeared to be Swiss and French emigrants. She hailed us at first in French, but receiving no answer, she tried us in English. She was the ship "La Carolina," from Havre, for New York. We desired her to report the brig Pilgrim, from Boston, for the north-west coast of America, five days out. She then filled away and left us to plough on through our waste of waters. This day ended pleasantly; we had got into regular and comfortable weather, and into that routine of sea-life which is only broken by a storm, a sail, or the sight of land.

Chapter III

As we had now a long "spell" of fine weather, without any incident to break the monotony of our lives, there can be no better place to describe the duties, regulations, and customs of an American merchantman, of which ours was a fair specimen.

The captain, in the first place, is lord paramount. He stands no watch, comes and goes when he pleases, and is accountable to no one, and must be obeyed in everything, without a question, even from his chief officer. He has the power to turn his officers off duty, and even to break them and make them do duty as sailors in the forecastle. Where there are no passengers and no supercargo, as in our vessel, he has no companion but his own dignity, and no pleasures, unless he differs from most of his kind, but the consciousness of possessing supreme power, and, occasionally, the exercise of it.

The prime minister, the official organ, and the active and superintending officer, is the chief mate. He is first lieutenant, boatswain, sailing-master, and quarter-master. The captain tells him what he wishes to have done, and leaves to him the care of overseeing, of allotting the work, and also the responsibility of its being well done. *The* mate (as he is always called, *par excellence*) also keeps the log-book, for which he is responsible to the owners and insurers, and has the charge of the stowage, safe keeping, and delivery of the cargo. He is also, ex-officio, the wit of the crew; for the captain does not condescend to joke with the men, and the second mate no one cares for; so that when "the mate" thinks fit to entertain "the people" with a coarse joke or a little practical wit, every one feels bound to laugh.

The second mate's is proverbially a dog's berth. He is neither officer nor man. The men do not respect him as an officer, and he is obliged to go aloft to reef and furl the topsails, and to put his hands into the tar and slush, with the rest. The crew call him the "sailor's waiter," as he has to furnish them with spun-yarn, marline, and all other stuffs that they need in their work, and has charge of the boatswain's locker, which includes serving-boards, marline-spikes, &c. &c. He is expected by the captain to maintain his dignity and to enforce obedience, and still is kept at a great distance from the mate, and obliged to work with the crew. He is one to whom little is given and of whom much is required. His wages are usually double those of a common sailor, and he eats and sleeps in the cabin; but he is obliged to be on deck nearly all his time, and eats at the second table, that is, makes a meal out of what the captain and chief mate leave.

The steward is the captain's servant, and has charge of the pantry, from which every one, even the mate himself, is excluded. These distinctions usually find him an enemy in the mate, who does not like to have any one on board who is not entirely under his control; the crew do not consider him as one of their number, so he is left to the mercy of the captain.

The cook is the patron of the crew, and those who are in his favor can get their wet mittens and stockings dried, or light their pipes at the galley in the night watch. These two worthies, together with the carpenter and sailmaker, if there be one, stand no watch, but, being employed all day, are allowed to "sleep in" at night, unless all hands are called.

The crew are divided into two divisions, as equally as may be, called the watches. Of these the chief mate commands the larboard, and the second mate the starboard. They divide the time between them, being on and off duty, or, as it is called, on deck and below, every other four hours. If, for instance, the chief mate with the larboard watch have the first night-watch from eight to twelve; at the end of the four hours, the starboard watch is called, and the second mate takes the deck, while the larboard watch and the first mate go below until four in the morning, when they come on deck again and remain until eight; having what is called the morning watch. As they will have been on deck eight hours out of the twelve, while those who had the middle watch—from twelve to four, will only have been up four hours, they have what is called a "forenoon watch below," that is, from eight, A.M., till twelve, M. In a man-of-war, and in some merchantmen, this alternation of watches is kept up throughout the twenty-four hours; but our ship, like most merchantmen, had "all hands" from twelve o'clock till dark, except in bad weather, when we had "watch and watch."

An explanation of the "dog watches" may, perhaps, be of use to one who has never been at sea. They are to shift the watches each night, so that the same watch need not be on deck at the same hours. In order to effect this, the watch from *four* to *eight*, P.M., is divided into two half, or dog watches, one from four to six, and the other from six to eight. By this means they divide the twenty-four hours into *seven* watches instead of *six*, and thus shift the hours every night. As the dog watches come during twilight, after the day's work is done, and before the night watch is set, they are the watches in which everybody is on deck. The captain is up, walking on the weather side of the quarter-deck, the chief mate on the lee side, and the second mate about the weather gangway. The steward has finished his work in the cabin, and has come up to smoke his pipe with the cook in the galley. The crew are sitting on the windlass or lying on the forecastle, smoking, singing, or telling long yarns. At eight o'clock, eight bells are struck, the log is hove, the watch set, the wheel relieved, the galley shut up, and the other watch goes below.

The morning commences with the watch on deck's "turning-to" at day-break and washing down, scrubbing, and swabbing the decks. This, together with filling the "scuttled butt" with fresh water, and coiling up the rigging, usually occupies the time until seven bells, (half after seven,) when all hands get breakfast. At eight, the day's work begins, and lasts until sun-down, with the exception of an hour for dinner.

Before I end my explanations, it may be well to define a *day's work*, and to correct a mistake prevalent among landsmen about a sailor's life. Nothing is more common than to hear people say—"Are not sailors very idle at sea?—what can they find to do?" This is a very natural mistake, and being very frequently made, it is one which every sailor feels interested in having corrected. In the first place, then, the discipline of the ship requires every man to be at work upon *something* when he is on deck, except at night and on Sundays. Except at these times, you will never see a man, on board a well-ordered vessel, standing idle on deck, sitting down, or leaning over the side. It is the officers' duty to keep every one at work, even if there is nothing to be done but to scrape the rust from the chain cables. In no state prison are the convicts more regularly set to work, and more closely watched. No conversation is allowed among the crew at their duty, and though they frequently do talk when aloft, or when near one another, yet they always stop when an officer is nigh.

With regard to the work upon which the men are put, it is a matter which probably would not be understood by one who has not been at sea. When I first left port, and found that we were kept regularly employed for a week or two, I supposed that we were getting the vessel into sea trim, and that it would soon be over, and we should have nothing to do but to sail the ship; but I found that it continued so for two years, and at the end of the two years there was as much to be done as ever. As has often been said, a ship is like a lady's watch, always out of repair. When first leaving port, studding-sail gear is to be rove, all the running rigging to be examined, that which is unfit for use to be got down, and new rigging rove in its place: then the standing rigging is to be overhauled, replaced, and repaired, in a thousand different ways; and wherever any of the numberless ropes or the yards are chafing or wearing upon it, there "chafing gear," as it is called, must be put on. This chafing gear consists of worming, parcelling, roundings, battens, and service of all kinds—both rope-yarns, spun-yarn, marline and seizing-stuffs. Taking off, putting on, and mending the chafing gear alone, upon a vessel, would find constant employment for two or three men, during working hours, for a whole voyage.

The next point to be considered is, that all the "small stuffs" which are used on board a ship—such as spun-yarn, marline, seizing-stuff, &c. &c.—are made on board. The owners of a vessel buy up incredible quantities of "old junk," which the sailors unlay, after drawing out the yarns, knot them together, and roll them up in balls. These "rope-yarns" are constantly used for various purposes, but the greater part is manufactured into spun-yarn. For this purpose every vessel is furnished with a "spun-yarn winch;" which is very simple, consisting of a wheel and spindle. This may be heard constantly going on deck in pleasant weather; and we had employment, during a great part of the time, for three hands in drawing and knotting yarns, and making spun-yarn.

Another method of employing the crew is, "setting up" rigging. Whenever any of the standing rigging becomes slack, (which is continually happening,) the seizings and coverings must be taken off, tackles got up, and after the rigging is bowsed well taught, the seizings and coverings replaced; which is a very nice piece of work. There is also such a connection between different parts of a vessel, that one rope can seldom be touched without altering another. You cannot stay a mast aft by the back stays, without slacking up the head stays, &c. &c. If we add to this all the tarring, greasing, oiling, varnishing, painting, scraping, and scrubbing which is required in the course of a long voyage, and also remember this is all to be done in *addition to* watching at night, steering, reefing, furling, bracing, making and setting sail, and pulling, hauling and climbing in every direction, one will hardly ask, "What can a sailor find to do at sea?"

If, after all this labor—after exposing their lives and limbs in storms, wet and cold,

> "Wherein the cub-drawn bear would couch;
> The lion and the belly-pinched wolf
> Keep their furs dry;—"

the merchants and captains think that they have not earned their twelve dollars a month, (out of which they clothe themselves,) and their salt beef and hard bread, they keep them picking oakum—*ad infinitum*. This is the usual resource upon a rainy day, for then it will not do to work upon rigging; and when it is pouring down in floods, instead of letting the sailors stand about in sheltered places, and talk, and keep themselves comfortable, they are separated to different parts of the ship and kept at work picking oakum. I have seen oakum stuff placed about in different parts of the ship, so that the sailors might not be idle in the *snatches* between the frequent squalls upon crossing the equator. Some officers have been so driven to find work for the crew in a ship ready for sea, that they have set them to pounding the anchors (often done) and scraping the chain cables. The "Philadelphia Catechism" is,

> "Six days shalt thou labor and do all thou art able,
> And on the seventh—holystone the decks and scrape
> the cable."

This kind of work, of course, is not kept up off Cape Horn,

Cape of Good Hope, and in extreme north and south latitudes; but I have seen the decks washed down and scrubbed,
when the water would have frozen if it had been fresh; and all
hands kept at work upon the rigging, when we had on our
pea-jackets, and our hands so numb that we could hardly hold
our marline-spikes.

I have here gone out of my narrative course in order that
any who read this may form as correct an idea of a sailor's life
and duty as possible. I have done it in this place because, for
some time, our life was nothing but the unvarying repetition
of these duties, which can be better described together. Before
leaving this description, however, I would state, in order to
show landsmen how little they know of the nature of a ship,
that a *ship-carpenter* is kept in constant employ during good
weather on board vessels which are in, what is called, perfect
sea order.

Chapter IV

A FTER speaking the "Carolina," on the 21st August, nothing occurred to break the monotony of our life until

Friday, September 5th, when we saw a sail on our weather (starboard) beam. She proved to be a brig under English colors, and passing under our stern, reported herself as forty-nine days from Buenos Ayres, bound to Liverpool. Before she had passed us, "sail ho!" was cried again, and we made another sail, far on our weather bow, and steering athwart our hawse. She passed out of hail, but we made her out to be an hermaphrodite brig, with Brazilian colors in her main rigging. By her course, she must have been bound from Brazil to the south of Europe, probably Portugal.

Sunday, Sept. 7th. Fell in with the north-east trade winds. This morning we caught our first dolphin, which I was very eager to see. I was disappointed in the colors of this fish when dying. They were certainly very beautiful, but not equal to what has been said of them. They are too indistinct. To do the fish justice, there is nothing more beautiful than the dolphin when swimming a few feet below the surface, on a bright day. It is the most elegantly formed, and also the quickest fish, in salt water; and the rays of the sun striking upon it, in its rapid and changing motions, reflected from the water, make it look like a stray beam from a rainbow.

This day was spent like all pleasant Sabbaths at sea. The decks are washed down, the rigging coiled up, and everything put in order; and throughout the day, only one watch is kept on deck at a time. The men are all dressed in their best white duck trowsers, and red or checked shirts, and have nothing to do but to make the necessary changes in the sails. They employ themselves in reading, talking, smoking, and mending their clothes. If the weather is pleasant, they bring their work and their books upon deck, and sit down upon the forecastle and windlass. This is the only day on which these privileges are allowed them. When Monday comes, they put on their tarry trowsers again, and prepare for six days of labor.

To enhance the value of the Sabbath to the crew, they are

allowed on that day a pudding, or, as it is called, a "duff." This is nothing more than flour boiled with water, and eaten with molasses. It is very heavy, dark, and clammy, yet it is looked upon as a luxury, and really forms an agreeable variety with salt beef and pork. Many a rascally captain has made friends of his crew by allowing them duff twice a week on the passage home.

On board some vessels this is made a day of instruction and of religious exercises; but we had a crew of swearers, from the captain to the smallest boy; and a day of rest, and of something like quiet, social enjoyment, was all that we could expect.

We continued running large before the north-east trade winds for several days, until Monday—

September 22d; when, upon coming on deck at seven bells in the morning, we found the other watch aloft throwing water upon the sails; and looking astern, we saw a small clipper-built brig with a black hull heading directly after us. We went to work immediately, and put all the canvass upon the brig which we could get upon her, rigging out oars for studding-sail yards; and continued wetting down the sails by buckets of water whipped up to the mast-head, until about nine o'clock, when there came on a drizzling rain. The vessel continued in pursuit, changing her course as we changed ours, to keep before the wind. The captain, who watched her with his glass, said that she was armed, and full of men, and showed no colors. We continued running dead before the wind, knowing that we sailed better so, and that clippers are fastest *on* the wind. We had also another advantage. The wind was light, and we spread more canvass than she did, having royals and sky-sails fore and aft, and ten studding-sails; while she, being an hermaphrodite brig, had only a gaff topsail, aft. Early in the morning she was overhauling us a little, but after the rain came on and the wind grew lighter, we began to leave her astern. All hands remained on deck throughout the day, and we got our arms in order; but we were too few to have done anything with her, if she had proved to be what we feared. Fortunately there was no moon, and the night which followed was exceedingly dark, so that by putting out all the lights on board and altering our course four points, we hoped to get out of her reach. We had no light in the binnacle, but steered by the stars, and kept perfect silence through the night. At day-break there was no sign of anything in the horizon, and we kept the vessel off to her course.

Wednesday, October 1st. Crossed the equator in long. 24° 24' W. I now, for the first time, felt at liberty, according to the old usage, to call myself a son of Neptune, and was very glad to be able to claim the title without the disagreeable initiation which so many have to go through. After once crossing the line you can never be subjected to the process, but are considered as a son of Neptune, with full powers to play tricks upon others. This ancient custom is now seldom allowed, unless there are passengers on board, in which case there is always a good deal of sport.

It had been obvious to all hands for some time that the second mate, whose name was Foster, was an idle, careless fellow, and not much of a sailor, and that the captain was exceedingly dissatisfied with him. The power of the captain in these cases was well known, and we all anticipated a difficulty. Foster (called *Mr.* by virtue of his office) was but half a sailor, having always been short voyages and remained at home a long time between them. His father was a man of some property, and intended to have given his son a liberal education; but he, being idle and worthless, was sent off to sea, and succeeded no better there; for, unlike many scamps, he had none of the qualities of a sailor—he was "not of the stuff that they make sailors of." He was one of that class of officers who are disliked by their captain and despised by the crew. He used to hold long yarns with the crew, and talk about the captain, and play with the boys, and relax discipline in every way. This kind of conduct always makes the captain suspicious, and is never pleasant, in the end, to the men; they preferring to have an officer active, vigilant, and distant as may be, with kindness. Among other bad practices, he frequently slept on his watch, and having been discovered asleep by the captain, he was told that he would be turned off duty if he did it again. To prevent it in every way possible, the hen-coops were ordered to be knocked up, for the captain never sat down on deck himself, and never permitted an officer to do so.

The second night after crossing the equator, we had the watch from eight till twelve, and it was "my helm" for the last two hours. There had been light squalls through the night, and the captain told Mr. Foster, who commanded our watch, to keep a bright look-out. Soon after I came to the helm, I found that he was quite drowsy, and at last he stretched himself on the companion and went fast asleep. Soon afterwards, the captain came very quietly on deck, and stood by me for some time looking at the compass. The officer at length became aware of the captain's presence, but pretending not to know it, began humming and whistling to himself, to show that he was not asleep, and went forward, without looking behind him, and ordered the main royal to be loosed. On turning round to come aft, he pretended surprise at seeing the master on deck. This would not do. The captain was too "wide awake" for him, and beginning upon him at once, gave him a grand blow-up, in true nautical style—"You're a lazy, good-for-nothing rascal; you're neither man, boy, *soger*, nor sailor! you're no more than a *thing* aboard a vessel! you don't earn your salt! you're worse than a *Mahon soger*!" and other still more choice extracts from the sailor's vocabulary. After the poor fellow had taken this harangue, he was sent into his state-room, and the captain stood the rest of the watch himself.

At seven bells in the morning, all hands were called aft and told that Foster was no longer an officer on board, and that we might choose one of our own number for second mate. It is usual for the captain to make this offer, and it is very good policy, for the crew think themselves the choosers and are flattered by it, but have to obey, nevertheless. Our crew, as is usual, refused to take the responsibility of choosing a man of whom we would never be able to complain, and left it to the captain. He picked out an active and intelligent young sailor, born near the Kennebec, who had been several Canton voyages, and proclaimed him in the following manner: "I choose Jim Hall—he's your second mate. All you've got to do is, to obey him as you would me; and remember that he is *Mr.* Hall." Foster went forward into the forecastle as a common sailor, and lost *the handle to his name*, while young fore-mast Jim became Mr. Hall, and took up his quarters in the land of knives and forks and tea-cups

Sunday, October 5th. It was our morning watch; when, soon after the day began to break, a man on the forecastle called out, "Land ho!" I had never heard the cry before, and did not know what it meant, (and few would suspect what the words were, when hearing the strange sound for the first time,) but I soon found, by the direction of all eyes, that there was land stretching along on our weather beam. We immediately took in studding-sails and hauled our wind, running in for the land. This was done to determine our longitude; for by the captain's chronometer we were in 25° W., but by his observations we were much farther, and he had been for some time in doubt whether it was his chronometer or his sextant which was out of order. This land-fall settled the matter, and the former instrument was condemned, and becoming still worse, was never afterwards used.

As we ran in towards the coast, we found that we were directly off the port of Pernambuco, and could see with the telescope the roofs of the houses, and one large church, and the town of Olinda. We ran along by the mouth of the harbor, and saw a full-rigged brig going in. At two, P.M., we again kept off before the wind, leaving the land on our quarter, and at sundown, it was out of sight. It was here that I first saw one of those singular things called catamarans. They are composed of logs lashed together upon the water; have one large sail, are quite fast, and, strange as it may seem, are trusted as good sea boats. We saw several, with from one to three men in each, boldly putting out to sea, after it had become almost dark. The Indians go out in them after fish, and as the weather is regular in certain seasons, they have no fear. After taking a new departure from Olinda, we kept off on our way to Cape Horn.

We met with nothing remarkable until we were in the latitude of the river La Plata. Here there are violent gales from the south-west, called Pomperos, which are very destructive to the shipping in the river, and are felt for many leagues at sea. They are usually preceded by lightning. The captain told the mates to keep a bright look-out, and if they saw lightning at the south-west, to take in sail at once. We got the first touch of one during my watch on deck. I was walking in the lee gangway, and thought that I saw lightning on the lee bow. I told the second mate, who came over and looked out for some time. It was very black in the south-west, and in about ten minutes we saw a distinct flash. The wind, which had been south-east, had now left us, and it was dead calm. We sprang aloft immediately and furled the royals and top-gallant-sails, and took in the flying jib, hauled up the mainsail and trysail, squared the after yards, and awaited the attack. A huge mist capped with black clouds came driving towards us, extending over that quarter of the horizon, and covering the stars, which shone brightly in the other part of the heavens. It came upon us at once with a blast, and a shower of hail and rain, which almost took our breath from us. The hardiest was obliged to turn his back. We let the halyards run, and fortunately were not taken aback. The little vessel "paid off" from the wind, and ran on for some time directly before it, tearing through the water with everything flying. Having called all hands, we close reefed the topsails and trysail, furled the courses and jib, set the fore-top-mast staysail, and brought her up nearly to her course, with the weather braces hauled in a little, to ease her.

This was the first blow, that I had seen, which could really be called a gale. We had reefed our topsails in the Gulf Stream, and I thought it something serious, but an older sailor would have thought nothing of it. As I had now become used to the vessel and to my duty, I was of some service on a yard, and could knot my reef-point as well as anybody. I obeyed the order to lay* aloft with the rest, and found the reefing a very exciting scene; for one watch reefed the fore-topsail, and the other the main, and every one did his utmost to get his topsail hoisted first. We had a great advantage over the larboard watch, because the chief mate never goes aloft, while our new second mate used to jump into the rigging as soon as we began to haul out the reef-tackle, and have the weather earing passed before there was a man upon the yard. In this way we were almost always able to raise the cry of "Haul out to leeward" before them, and having knotted our points, would slide down the shrouds and back-stays, and sing out at the topsail halyards to let it be known that we were ahead of them. Reefing is the most exciting part of a sailor's duty. All hands are engaged upon it, and after the halyards are let go, there is

*This word "lay," which is in such general use on board ship, being used in giving orders instead of "go;" as, "*Lay* forward!" "*Lay* aft!" "*Lay* aloft!" &c., I do not understand to be the neuter verb *lie*, mispronounced, but to be the active verb *lay*, with the objective case understood; as, "Lay *yourselves* forward!" "Lay *yourselves* aft!" &c.

no time to be lost—no "sogering," or hanging back, then. If one is not quick enough, another runs over him. The first on the yard goes to the weather earing, the second to the lee, and the next two to the "dog's ears;" while the others lay along into the bunt, just giving each other elbow-room. In reefing, the yard-arms (the extremes of the yards) are the posts of honor; but in furling, the strongest and most experienced stand in the slings, (or, middle of the yard,) to make up the bunt. If the second mate is a smart fellow, he will never let any one take either of these posts from him; but if he is wanting either in seamanship, strength, or activity, some better man will get the bunt and earings from him; which immediately brings him into disrepute.

We remained for the rest of the night, and throughout the next day, under the same close sail, for it continued to blow very fresh; and though we had no more hail, yet there was a soaking rain, and it was quite cold and uncomfortable; the more so, because we were not prepared for cold weather, but had on our thin clothes. We were glad to get a watch below, and put on our thick clothing, boots, and south-westers. Towards sun-down the gale moderated a little, and it began to clear off in the south-west. We shook our reefs out, one by one, and before midnight had top-gallant sails upon her.

We had now made up our minds for Cape Horn and cold weather, and entered upon every necessary preparation.

Tuesday, Nov. 4th. At day-break, saw land upon our larboard quarter. There were two islands, of different size but of the same shape; rather high, beginning low at the water's edge, and running with a curved ascent to the middle. They were so far off as to be of a deep blue color, and in a few hours we *sank* them in the north-east. These were the Falkland Islands. We had run between them and the main land of Patagonia. At sun-set the second mate, who was at the mast-head, said that he saw land on the starboard bow. This must have been the island of Staten Land; and we were now in the region of Cape Horn, with a fine breeze from the northward, top-mast and top-gallant studding-sails set, and every prospect of a speedy and pleasant passage round.

Chapter V

Wednesday, Nov. 5th. The weather was fine during the previous night, and we had a clear view of the Magellan Clouds, and of the Southern Cross. The Magellan clouds consist of three small nebulæ in the southern part of the heavens, —two bright, like the milky-way, and one dark. These are first seen, just above the horizon, soon after crossing the southern tropic. When off Cape Horn, they are nearly over head. The cross is composed of four stars in that form, and is said to be the brightest constellation in the heavens.

During the first part of this day (Wednesday) the wind was light, but after noon it came on fresh, and we furled the royals. We still kept the studding-sails out, and the captain said he should go round with them, if he could. Just before eight o'clock (then about sun-down, in that latitude) the cry of "All hands ahoy!" was sounded down the fore scuttle and the after hatchway, and hurrying upon deck, we found a large black cloud rolling on toward us from the south-west, and blackening the whole heavens. "Here comes Cape Horn!" said the chief mate; and we had hardly time to haul down and clew up, before it was upon us. In a few moments, a heavier sea was raised than I had ever seen before, and as it was directly ahead, the little brig, which was no better than a bathing machine, plunged into it, and all the forward part of her was under water; the sea pouring in through the bow-ports and hawse-hole and over the knight-heads, threatening to wash everything overboard. In the lee scuppers it was up to a man's waist. We sprang aloft and double reefed the topsails, and furled all the other sails, and made all snug. But this would not do; the brig was laboring and straining against the head sea, and the gale was growing worse and worse. At the same time sleet and hail were driving with all fury against us. We clewed down, and hauled out the reef-tackles again, and close-reefed the fore-topsail, and furled the main, and hove her to on the starboard tack. Here was an end to our fine prospects. We made up our minds to head winds and cold weather; sent down the royal yards, and unrove the gear; but all the rest of the top hamper remained aloft, even to the sky-sail masts and studding-sail booms.

Throughout the night it stormed violently—rain, hail, snow, and sleet beating upon the vessel—the wind continuing ahead, and the sea running high. At day-break (about three, A.M.) the deck was covered with snow. The captain sent up the steward with a glass of grog to each of the watch; and all the time that we were off the Cape, grog was given to the morning watch, and to all hands whenever we reefed topsails. The clouds cleared away at sun-rise, and the wind becoming more fair, we again made sail and stood nearly up to our course.

Thursday, Nov. 6th. It continued more pleasant through the first part of the day, but at night we had the same scene over again. This time, we did not heave to, as on the night before, but endeavored to beat to windward under close-reefed topsails, balance-reefed trysail, and fore top-mast staysail. This night it was my turn to steer, or, as the sailors say, my *trick* at the helm, for two hours. Inexperienced as I was, I made out to steer to the satisfaction of the officer, and neither S—— nor myself gave up our tricks, all the time that we were off the Cape. This was something to boast of, for it requires a good deal of skill and watchfulness to steer a vessel close hauled, in a gale of wind, against a heavy head sea. "Ease her when she pitches," is the word; and a little carelessness in letting her ship a heavy sea, might sweep the decks, or knock the masts out of her.

Friday, Nov. 7th. Towards morning the wind went down, and during the whole forenoon we lay tossing about in a dead calm, and in the midst of a thick fog. The calms here are unlike those in most parts of the world, for there is always such a high sea running, and the periods of calm are so short, that it has no time to go down; and vessels, being under no command of sails or rudder, lie like logs upon the water. We were obliged to steady the booms and yards by guys and braces, and to lash everything well below. We now found our top hamper of some use, for though it is liable to be carried away or sprung by the sudden "bringing up" of a vessel when pitching in a chopping sea, yet it is a great help in steadying a vessel when rolling in a long swell; giving more slowness, ease, and regularity to the motion.

The calm of the morning reminds me of a scene which I forgot to describe at the time of its occurrence, but which I remember from its being the first time that I had heard the near breathing of whales. It was on the night that we passed between the Falkland Islands and Staten Land. We had the watch from twelve to four, and coming upon deck, found the little brig lying perfectly still, surrounded by a thick fog, and the sea as smooth as though oil had been poured upon it; yet now and then a long, low swell rolling over its surface, slightly lifting the vessel, but without breaking the glassy smoothness of the water. We were surrounded far and near by shoals of sluggish whales and grampuses, which the fog prevented our seeing, rising slowly to the surface, or perhaps lying out at length, heaving out those peculiar lazy, deep, and long-drawn breathings which give such an impression of supineness and strength. Some of the watch were asleep, and the others were perfectly still, so that there was nothing to break the illusion, and I stood leaning over the bulwarks, listening to the slow breathings of the mighty creatures—now one breaking the water just alongside, whose black body I almost fancied that I could see through the fog; and again another, which I could just hear in the distance —until the low and regular swell seemed like the heaving of the ocean's mighty bosom to the sound of its heavy and long-drawn respirations.

Towards the evening of this day, (Friday 7th,) the fog cleared off, and we had every appearance of a cold blow; and soon after sun-down it came on. Again it was clew up and haul down, reef and furl, until we had got her down to close-reefed topsails, double-reefed trysail, and reefed fore spenser. Snow, hail, and sleet were driving upon us most of the night, and the sea breaking over the bows and covering the forward part of the little vessel; but as she would lay her course the captain refused to heave her to.

Saturday, Nov. 8th. This day commenced with calm and thick fog, and ended with hail, snow, a violent wind, and close-reefed topsails.

Sunday, Nov. 9th. To-day the sun rose clear, and continued so until twelve o'clock, when the captain got an observation. This was very well for Cape Horn, and we thought it a little remarkable that, as we had not had one unpleasant Sunday during the whole voyage, the only tolerable day here should be a Sunday. We got time to clear up the steerage and forecastle, and set things to rights, and to overhaul our wet clothes a little. But this did not last very long. Between five and six—the sun was then nearly three hours high—the cry of "All starbowlines ahoy!" summoned our watch on deck; and immediately all hands were called. A true specimen of Cape Horn was coming upon us. A great cloud of a dark slate-color was driving on us from the south-west; and we did our best to take in sail, (for the light sails had been set during the first part of the day,) before we were in the midst of it. We had got the light sails furled, the courses hauled up, and the topsail reef-tackles hauled out, and were just mounting the fore-rigging, when the storm struck us. In an instant the sea, which had been comparatively quiet, was running higher and higher; and it became almost as dark as night. The hail and sleet were harder than I had yet felt them; seeming almost to *pin us down* to the rigging. We were longer taking in sail than ever before; for the sails were stiff and wet, the ropes and rigging covered with snow and sleet, and we ourselves cold and nearly blinded with the violence of the storm. By the time we had got down upon deck again, the little brig was plunging madly into a tremendous head sea, which at every drive rushed in through the bow-ports and over the bows, and buried all the forward part of the vessel. At this instant the chief mate, who was standing on the top of the windlass, at the foot of the spenser mast, called out, "Lay out there and furl the jib!" This was no agreeable or safe duty, yet it must be done. An old Swede, (the best sailor on board,) who belonged on the forecastle, sprang out upon the bowsprit. Another one must go: I was near the mate, and sprang forward, threw the downhaul over the windlass, and jumped between the knight-heads out upon the bowsprit. The crew stood abaft the windlass and hauled the jib down, while we got out upon the weather side of the jib-boom, our feet on the foot-ropes, holding on by the spar, the great jib flying off to leeward and *slatting* so as almost to throw us off of the boom. For some time we could do nothing but hold on, and the vessel diving into two huge seas, one after the other, plunged us twice into the water up to our chins. We hardly knew whether we were on or off; when coming up, dripping from the water, we were raised high into the air. John (that was the sailor's name) thought the boom would go, every moment, and called out to the mate to keep the vessel off, and haul down the staysail; but the fury of the wind and the breaking of the seas against the bows defied every attempt to make ourselves heard, and we were obliged to do the best we could in our situation. Fortunately, no other seas so heavy struck her, and we succeeded in furling the jib "after a fashion;" and, coming in over the staysail nettings, were not a little pleased to find that all was snug, and the watch gone below; for we were soaked through, and it was very cold. The weather continued nearly the same through the night.

Monday, Nov. 10th. During a part of this day we were hove to, but the rest of the time were driving on, under close-reefed sails, with a heavy sea, a strong gale, and frequent squalls of hail and snow.

Tuesday, Nov. 11th. The same.

Wednesday. The same.

Thursday. The same.

We had now got hardened to Cape weather, the vessel was under reduced sail, and everything secured on deck and below, so that we had little to do but to steer and to stand our watch. Our clothes were all wet through, and the only change was from wet to more wet. It was in vain to think of reading or working below, for we were too tired, the hatchways were closed down, and everything was wet and uncomfortable, black and dirty, heaving and pitching. We had only to come below when the watch was out, wring out our wet clothes, hang them up, and turn in and sleep as soundly as we could, until the watch was called again. A sailor can sleep anywhere—no sound of wind, water, wood or iron can keep him awake—and we were always fast asleep when three blows on the hatchway, and the unwelcome cry of "All starbowlines ahoy! eight bells there below! do you hear the news?" (the usual formula of calling the watch,) roused us up from our berths upon the cold, wet decks. The only time when we could be said to take any pleasure was at night and morning, when we were allowed a tin pot full of hot tea, (or, as the sailors significantly call it, "water bewitched,") sweetened with molasses. This, bad as it was, was still warm and comforting, and, together with our sea biscuit and cold salt beef, made quite a meal. Yet even this meal was attended with some uncertainty. We had to go ourselves to the galley and take our kid of beef and tin pots of tea, and run the risk of losing them before we could get below. Many a kid of beef have I seen rolling in the scuppers, and the bearer lying at his length on the decks. I remember an English lad who was always the life of the crew, but whom we afterwards lost overboard, standing for nearly ten minutes at the galley, with his pot of tea in his hand, waiting for a chance to get down into the forecastle; and seeing what he thought was a "smooth spell," started to go forward. He had just got to the end of the windlass, when a great sea broke over the bows, and for a moment I saw nothing of him but his head and shoulders; and at the next instant, being taken off of his legs, he was carried aft with the sea, until her stern lifting up and sending the water forward, he was left high and dry at the side of the longboat, still holding on to his tin pot, which had now nothing in it but salt water. But nothing could ever daunt him, or overcome, for a moment, his habitual good humor. Regaining his legs, and shaking his fist at the man at the wheel, he rolled below, saying, as he passed, "A man's no sailor, if he can't take a joke." The ducking was not the worst of such an affair, for, as there was an allowance of tea, you could get no more from the galley; and though the sailors would never suffer a man to go without, but would always turn in a little from their own pots to fill up his, yet this was at best but dividing the loss among all hands.

Something of the same kind befell me a few days after. The cook had just made for us a mess of hot "scouse"—that is, biscuit pounded fine, salt beef cut into small pieces, and a few potatoes, boiled up together and seasoned with pepper. This was a rare treat, and I, being the last at the galley, had it put in my charge to carry down for the mess. I got along very well as far as the hatchway, and was just getting down the steps, when a heavy sea, lifting the stern out of water, and passing forward, dropping it down again, threw the steps from their place, and I came down into the steerage a little faster than I meant to, with the kid on top of me, and the whole precious mess scattered over the floor. Whatever your feelings may be, you must make a joke of everything at sea; and if you were to fall from aloft and be caught in the belly of a sail, and thus saved from instant death, it would not do to look at all disturbed, or to make a serious matter of it.

Friday, Nov. 14th. We were now well to the westward of the Cape, and were changing our course to the northward as much as we dared, since the strong south-west winds, which prevailed then, carried us in towards Patagonia. At two, P.M., we saw a sail on our larboard beam, and at four we made it out to be a large ship, steering our course, under single-reefed topsails. We at that time had shaken the reefs out of our topsails, as the wind was lighter, and set the main top-gallant sail. As soon as our captain saw what sail she was under, he set the fore top-gallant sail and flying jib; and the old whaler—for such, his boats and short sail showed him to be—felt a little ashamed, and shook the reefs out of his topsails, but could do no more, for he had sent down his top-gallant masts off the Cape. He ran down for us, and answered our hail as the whale-ship, New-England, of Poughkeepsie, one hundred and twenty days from New York. Our captain gave our name, and added, ninety-two days from Boston. They then had a little conversation about longitude, in which they found that they could not agree. The ship fell astern, and continued in sight during the night. Toward morning, the wind having become light, we crossed our royal and skysail yards, and at daylight, we were seen under a cloud of sail, having royals and skysails fore and aft. The "spouter," as the sailors call a whaleman, had sent up his main top-gallant mast and set the sail, and made signal for us to heave to. About half-past seven their whale-boat came alongside, and Captain Job Terry sprang on board, a man known in every port and by every vessel in the Pacific ocean. "Don't you know Job Terry? I thought everybody knew Job Terry," said a green-hand, who came in the boat, to me, when I asked him about his captain. He was indeed a singular man. He was six feet high, wore thick, cowhide boots, and brown coat and trowsers, and, except a sun-burnt complexion, had not the slightest appearance of a sailor; yet he had been forty years in the whale trade, and, as he said himself, had owned ships, built ships, and sailed ships. His boat's crew were a pretty raw set, just out of the bush, and, as the sailor's phrase is, "hadn't got the hayseed out of their hair." Captain Terry convinced our captain that our reckoning was a little out, and, having spent the day on board, put off in his boat at sunset for his ship, which was now six or eight miles astern. He began a "yarn" when he came aboard, which lasted, with but little intermission, for four hours. It was all about himself, and the Peruvian government, and the Dublin frigate, and Lord James Townshend, and President Jackson, and the ship Ann M'Kim of Baltimore. It would probably never have come to an end, had not a good breeze sprung up, which sent him off to his own vessel. One of the lads who came in his boat, a thoroughly countrified-looking fellow, seemed to care very little about the vessel, rigging, or anything else, but went round looking at the live stock, and leaned over the pig-sty, and said he wished he was back again tending his father's pigs.

At eight o'clock we altered our course to the northward, bound for Juan Fernandez.

This day we saw the last of the albatrosses, which had been our companions a great part of the time off the Cape. I had been interested in the bird from descriptions which I had read of it, and was not at all disappointed. We caught one or two with a baited hook which we floated astern upon a shingle. Their long, flapping wings, long legs, and large, staring eyes, give them a very peculiar appearance. They look well on the wing; but one of the finest sights that I have ever seen, was an albatross asleep upon the water, during a calm, off Cape Horn, when a heavy sea was running. There being no breeze, the surface of the water was unbroken, but a long, heavy swell was rolling, and we saw the fellow, all white, directly ahead of us, asleep upon the waves, with his head under his wing; now rising on the top of a huge billow, and then falling slowly until he was lost in the hollow between. He was undisturbed for some time, until the noise of our bows, gradually approaching roused him, when, lifting his head, he stared upon us for a moment, and then spread his wide wings and took his flight.

Chapter VI

Monday, Nov. 19th. This was a black day in our calendar. At seven o'clock in the morning, it being our watch below, we were aroused from a sound sleep by the cry of "All hands ahoy! a man overboard!" This unwonted cry sent a thrill through the heart of every one, and hurrying on deck, we found the vessel hove flat aback, with all her studding-sails set; for the boy who was at the helm left it to throw something overboard, and the carpenter, who was an old sailor, knowing that the wind was light, put the helm down and hove her aback. The watch on deck were lowering away the quarter-boat, and I got on deck just in time to heave myself into her as she was leaving the side; but it was not until out upon the wide Pacific, in our little boat, that I knew whom we had lost. It was George Ballmer, a young English sailor, who was prized by the officers as an active and willing seaman, and by the crew as a lively, hearty fellow, and a good shipmate. He was going aloft to fit a strap round the main top-mast-head, for ringtail halyards, and had the strap and block, a coil of halyards, and a marline-spike about his neck. He fell from the starboard futtock shrouds, and not knowing how to swim, and being heavily dressed, with all those things round his neck, he probably sank immediately. We pulled astern, in the direction in which he fell, and though we knew that there was no hope of saving him, yet no one wished to speak of returning, and we rowed about for nearly an hour, without the hope of doing anything, but unwilling to acknowledge to ourselves that we must give him up. At length we turned the boat's head and made towards the vessel.

Death is at all times solemn, but never so much so as at sea. A man dies on shore; his body remains with his friends, and "the mourners go about the streets;" but when a man falls overboard at sea and is lost, there is a suddenness in the event, and a difficulty in realizing it, which give to it an air of awful mystery. A man dies on shore—you follow his body to the grave, and a stone marks the spot. You are often prepared for the event. There is always something which helps you to realize it when it happens, and to recall it when it has passed. A man is shot down by your side in battle, and the mangled body remains an *object*, and a *real evidence*; but at sea, the man is near you—at your side—you hear his voice, and in an instant he is gone, and nothing but a *vacancy* shows his loss. Then, too, at sea—to use a homely but expressive phrase—you *miss* a man so much. A dozen men are shut up together in a little bark, upon the wide, wide sea, and for months and months see no forms and hear no voices but their own, and one is taken suddenly from among them, and they miss him at every turn. It is like losing a limb. There are no new faces or new scenes to fill up the gap. There is always an empty berth in the forecastle, and one man wanting when the small night watch is mustered. There is one less to take the wheel, and one less to lay out with you upon the yard. You miss his form, and the sound of his voice, for habit had made them almost necessary to you, and each of your senses feels the loss.

All these things make such a death peculiarly solemn, and the effect of it remains upon the crew for some time. There is more kindness shown by the officers to the crew, and by the crew to one another. There is more quietness and seriousness. The oath and the loud laugh are gone. The officers are more watchful, and the crew go more carefully aloft. The lost man is seldom mentioned, or is dismissed with a sailor's rude eulogy —"Well, poor George is gone! His cruise is up soon! He knew his work, and did his duty, and was a good shipmate." Then usually follows some allusion to another world, for sailors are almost all believers; but their notions and opinions are unfixed and at loose ends. They say,—"God won't be hard upon the poor fellow," and seldom get beyond the common phrase which seems to imply that their sufferings and hard treatment here will excuse them hereafter,—"*To work hard, live hard, die hard, and go to hell after all, would be hard indeed!*" Our cook, a simple-hearted old African, who had been through a good deal in his day, and was rather seriously inclined, always going to church twice a day when on shore, and reading his Bible on a Sunday in the galley, talked to the crew about spending their Sabbaths badly, and told them that they might go as suddenly as George had, and be as little prepared.

Yet a sailor's life is at best but a mixture of a little good with much evil, and a little pleasure with much pain. The beautiful is linked with the revolting, the sublime with the commonplace, and the solemn with the ludicrous.

We had hardly returned on board with our sad report, before an auction was held of the poor man's clothes. The captain had first, however, called all hands aft and asked them if they were satisfied that everything had been done to save the man, and if they thought there was any use in remaining there longer. The crew all said that it was in vain, for the man did not know how to swim, and was very heavily dressed. So we then filled away and kept her off to her course.

The laws regulating navigation make the captain answerable for the effects of a sailor who dies during the voyage, and it is either a law or a universal custom, established for convenience, that the captain should immediately hold an auction of his things, in which they are bid off by the sailors, and the sums which they give are deducted from their wages at the end of the voyage. In this way the trouble and risk of keeping his things through the voyage are avoided, and the clothes are usually sold for more than they would be worth on shore. Accordingly, we had no sooner got the ship before the wind, than his chest was brought up upon the forecastle, and the sale began. The jackets and trowsers in which we had seen him dressed but a few days before, were exposed and bid off while the life was hardly out of his body, and his chest was taken aft and used as a store-chest, so that there was nothing left which could be called *his*. Sailors have an unwillingness to wear a dead man's clothes during the same voyage, and they seldom do so unless they are in absolute want.

As is usual after a death, many stories were told about George. Some had heard him say that he repented never having learned to swim, and that he knew that he should meet his death by drowning. Another said that he never knew any good to come of a voyage made against the will, and the deceased man shipped and spent his advance, and was afterwards very unwilling to go, but not being able to refund, was obliged to sail with us. A boy, too, who had become quite attached to him, said that George talked to him during most of the watch on the night before, about his mother and family at home, and this was the first time that he had mentioned the subject during the voyage.

The night after this event, when I went to the galley to get a light, I found the cook inclined to be talkative, so I sat down on the spars, and gave him an opportunity to hold a yarn. I was the more inclined to do so, as I found that he was full of the superstitions once more common among seamen, and which the recent death had waked up in his mind. He talked about George's having spoken of his friends, and said he believed few men died without having a warning of it, which he supported by a great many stories of dreams, and the unusual behavior of men before death. From this he went on to other superstitions, the Flying Dutchman, &c., and talked rather mysteriously, having something evidently on his mind. At length he put his head out of the galley and looked carefully about to see if any one was within hearing, and being satisfied on that point, asked me in a low tone—

"I say! you know what countryman 'e carpenter be?"

"Yes," said I; "he's a German."

"What kind of a German?" said the cook.

"He belongs to Bremen," said I.

"Are you sure o' dat?" said he.

I satisfied him on that point by saying that he could speak no language but the German and English.

"I'm plaguy glad o' dat," said the cook. "I was mighty 'fraid he was a Fin. I tell you what, I been plaguy civil to that man all the voyage."

I asked him the reason of this, and found that he was fully possessed with the notion that Fins are wizards, and especially have power over winds and storms. I tried to reason with him about it, but he had the best of all arguments, that from experience, at hand, and was not to be moved. He had been in a vessel at the Sandwich Islands, in which the sail-maker was a Fin, and could do anything he was of a mind to. This sail-maker kept a junk bottle in his berth, which was always just half full of rum, though he got drunk upon it nearly every day. He had seen him sit for hours together, talking to this bottle, which he stood up before him on the table. The same man cut his throat in his berth, and everybody said he was possessed.

He had heard of ships, too, beating up the gulf of Finland against a head wind, and having a ship heave in sight astern, overhaul and pass them, with as fair a wind as could blow, and all studding-sails out, and find she was from Finland.

"Oh ho!" said he; "I've seen too much of them men to want to see 'em 'board a ship. If they can't have their own way, they'll play the d——l with you."

As I still doubted, he said he would leave it to John, who was the oldest seaman aboard, and would know, if anybody did. John, to be sure, was the oldest, and at the same time the most ignorant, man in the ship; but I consented to have him called. The cook stated the matter to him, and John, as I anticipated, sided with the cook, and said that he himself had been in a ship where they had a head wind for a fortnight, and the captain found out at last that one of the men, whom he had had some hard words with a short time before, was a Fin, and immediately told him if he didn't stop the head wind he would shut him down in the fore peak. The Fin would not give in, and the captain shut him down in the fore peak, and would not give him anything to eat. The Fin held out for a day and a half, when he could not stand it any longer, and did something or other which brought the wind round again, and they let him up.

"There," said the cook, "what do you think o' dat?"

I told him I had no doubt it was true, and that it would have been odd if the wind had not changed in fifteen days, Fin or no Fin.

"Oh," says he, "go 'way! You think, 'cause you been to college, you know better than anybody. You know better than them as 'as seen it with their own eyes. You wait till you've been to sea as long as I have, and you'll know."

Chapter VII

W E continued sailing along with a fair wind and fine
weather until

Tuesday, Nov. 25th, when at daylight we saw the island of
Juan Fernandez, directly ahead, rising like a deep blue cloud
out of the sea. We were then probably nearly seventy miles
from it; and so high and so blue did it appear, that I mistook it
for a cloud, resting over the island, and looked for the island
under it, until it gradually turned to a deader and greener
color, and I could mark the inequalities upon its surface. At
length we could distinguish trees and rocks; and by the afternoon, this beautiful island lay fairly before us, and we directed
our course to the only harbor. Arriving at the entrance soon
after sun-down, we found a Chilian man-of-war brig, the only
vessel, coming out. She hailed us, and an officer on board,
whom we supposed to be an American, advised us to run in
before night, and said that they were bound to Valparaiso. We
ran immediately for the anchorage, but, owing to the winds
which drew about the mountains and came to us in flaws from
every point of the compass, we did not come to an anchor
until nearly midnight. We had a boat ahead all the time that we
were working in, and those aboard were continually bracing
the yards about for every puff that struck us, until about 12
o'clock, when we came-to in 40 fathoms water, and our anchor struck bottom for the first time since we left Boston—one
hundred and three days. We were then divided into three
watches, and thus stood out the remainder of the night.

I was called on deck to stand my watch at about three in the
morning, and I shall never forget the peculiar sensation which
I experienced on finding myself once more surrounded by
land, feeling the night breeze coming from off shore, and
hearing the frogs and crickets. The mountains seemed almost
to hang over us, and apparently from the very heart of them
there came out, at regular intervals, a loud echoing sound,
which affected me as hardly human. We saw no lights, and
could hardly account for the sound, until the mate, who had

been there before, told us that it was the "Alerta" of the Spanish soldiers, who were stationed over some convicts confined in caves nearly half way up the mountain. At the expiration of my watch I went below, feeling not a little anxious for the day, that I might see more nearly, and perhaps tread upon, this romantic, I may almost say, classic island.

When all hands were called it was nearly sunrise, and between that time and breakfast, although quite busy on board in getting up water-casks, &c., I had a good view of the objects about me. The harbor was nearly land-locked, and at the head of it was a landing-place, protected by a small breakwater of stones, upon which two large boats were hauled up, with a sentry standing over them. Near this was a variety of huts or cottages, nearly an hundred in number, the best of them built of mud and whitewashed, but the greater part only Robinson Crusoe like—of posts and branches of trees. The governor's house, as it is called, was the most conspicuous, being large, with grated windows, plastered walls, and roof of red tiles; yet, like all the rest, only of one story. Near it was a small chapel, distinguished by a cross; and a long, low, brown-looking building, surrounded by something like a palisade, from which an old and dingy-looking Chilian flag was flying. This, of course, was dignified by the title of *Presidio*. A sentinel was stationed at the chapel, another at the governor's house, and a few soldiers armed with bayonets, looking rather ragged, with shoes out at the toes, were strolling about among the houses, or waiting at the landing-place for our boat to come ashore.

The mountains were high, but not so overhanging as they appeared to be by starlight. They seemed to bear off towards the centre of the island, and were green and well wooded, with some large, and, I am told, exceedingly fertile valleys, with mule-tracks leading to different parts of the island.

I cannot here forget how my friend S—— and myself got the laugh of the crew upon us by our eagerness to get on shore. The captain having ordered the quarter-boat to be lowered, we both sprang down into the forecastle, filled our jacket pockets with tobacco to barter with the people ashore, and when the officer called for "four hands in the boat," nearly broke our necks in our haste to be first over the side, and had the pleasure of pulling ahead of the brig with a tow-line for a half an hour, and coming on board again to be laughed at by the crew, who had seen our manœuvre.

After breakfast the second mate was ordered ashore with five hands to fill the water-casks, and to my joy I was among the number. We pulled ashore with the empty casks; and here again fortune favored me, for the water was too thick and muddy to be put into the casks, and the governor had sent men up to the head of the stream to clear it out for us, which gave us nearly two hours of leisure. This leisure we employed in wandering about among the houses, and eating a little fruit which was offered to us. Ground apples, melons, grapes, strawberries of an enormous size, and cherries, abound here. The latter are said to have been planted by Lord Anson. The soldiers were miserably clad, and asked with some interest whether we had shoes to sell on board. I doubt very much if they had the means of buying them. They were very eager to get tobacco, for which they gave shells, fruits, &c. Knives also were in demand, but we were forbidden by the governor to let any one have them, as he told us that all the people there, except the soldiers and a few officers, were convicts sent from Valparaiso, and that it was necessary to keep all weapons from their hands. The island, it seems, belongs to Chili, and had been used by the government as a sort of Botany Bay for nearly two years; and the governor—an Englishman who had entered the Chilian navy—with a priest, half a dozen taskmasters, and a body of soldiers, were stationed there to keep them in order. This was no easy task; and only a few months before our arrival, a few of them had stolen a boat at night, boarded a brig lying in the harbor, sent the captain and crew ashore in their boat, and gone off to sea. We were informed of this, and loaded our arms and kept strict watch on board through the night, and were careful not to let the convicts get our knives from us when on shore. The worst part of the convicts, I found, were locked up under sentry in caves dug into the side of the mountain, nearly half way up, with mule-tracks leading to them, whence they were taken by day and set to work under task-masters upon building an aqueduct, a wharf, and other public works; while the rest lived in the houses which they put up for themselves, had their families with them, and seemed to me to be the laziest people on the face of the earth. They did nothing but take a *paseo* into the woods, a *paseo* among the houses, a *paseo* at the landing-place, looking at us and our vessel, and too lazy to speak fast; while the others were driving—or rather, driven—about, at a rapid trot, in single file, with burdens on their shoulders, and followed up by their task-masters, with long rods in their hands, and broad-brimmed straw hats upon their heads. Upon what precise grounds this great distinction was made, I do not know, and I could not very well know, for the governor was the only man who spoke English upon the island, and he was out of my walk.

Having filled our casks, we returned on board, and soon after, the governor, dressed in a uniform like that of an American militia officer, the *Padre*, in the dress of the grey friars, with hood and all complete, and the *Capitan*, with big whiskers and dirty regimentals, came on board to dine. While at dinner, a large ship appeared in the offing, and soon afterwards we saw a light whale-boat pulling into the harbor. The ship lay off and on, and a boat came alongside of us, and put on board the captain, a plain young Quaker, dressed all in brown. The ship was the Cortes, whaleman, of New Bedford, and had put in to see if there were any vessels from round the Horn, and to hear the latest news from America. They remained aboard a short time and had a little talk with the crew, when they left us and pulled off to their ship, which, having filled away, was soon out of sight.

A small boat which came from the shore to take away the governor and suite—as they styled themselves—brought, as a present to the crew, a large pail of milk, a few shells, and a block of sandal wood. The milk, which was the first we had tasted since leaving Boston, we soon despatched; a piece of the sandal wood I obtained, and learned that it grew on the hills in the centre of the island. I have always regretted that I did not bring away other specimens of the products of the island, having afterwards lost all that I had with me—the piece of sandal wood, and a small flower which I plucked and brought on board in the crown of my tarpaulin, and carefully pressed between the leaves of a book.

About an hour before sundown, having stowed our water-casks, we commenced getting under weigh, and were not a little while about it; for we were in thirty fathoms water, and in one of the gusts which came from off shore had let go our other bow anchor; and as the southerly wind draws round the mountains and comes off in uncertain flaws, we were continually swinging round, and had thus got a very foul hawse. We hove in upon our chain, and after stoppering and unshackling it again and again, and hoisting and hauling down sail, we at length tripped our anchor and stood out to sea. It was bright starlight when we were clear of the bay, and the lofty island lay behind us, in its still beauty, and I gave a parting look, and bid farewell, to the most romantic spot of earth that my eyes had ever seen. I did then, and have ever since, felt an attachment for that island, altogether peculiar. It was partly, no doubt, from its having been the first land that I had seen since leaving home, and still more from the associations which every one has connected with it in their childhood from reading Robinson Crusoe. To this I may add the height and romantic outline of its mountains, the beauty and freshness of its verdure, and the extreme fertility of its soil, and its solitary position in the midst of the wide expanse of the South Pacific, as all concurring to give it its peculiar charm.

When thoughts of this place have occurred to me at different times, I have endeavored to recall more particulars with regard to it. It is situated in about 33° 30′ S., and is distant a little more than three hundred miles from Valparaiso, on the coast of Chili, which is in the same latitude. It is about fifteen miles in length and five in breadth. The harbor in which we anchored (called by Lord Anson, Cumberland bay) is the only one in the island; two small *bights* of land on each side of the main bay (sometimes dignified by the name of bays) being little more than landing-places for boats. The best anchorage is at the western side of the bay, where we lay at about three cables' lengths from the shore, in a little more than thirty fathoms water. This harbor is open to the N.N.E., and in fact nearly from N. to E., but the only dangerous winds being the south-west, on which side are the highest mountains, it is considered very safe. The most remarkable thing perhaps about it is the fish with which it abounds. Two of our crew, who remained on board, caught in a few minutes enough to last us for several days, and one of the men, who was a Marblehead man, said that he never saw or heard of such an abundance. There were cod, breams, silver-fish, and other kinds whose names they did not know, or which I have forgotten.

There is an abundance of the best of water upon the island, small streams running through every valley, and leaping down from the sides of the hills. One stream of considerable size flows through the centre of the lawn upon which the houses are built, and furnishes an easy and abundant supply to the inhabitants. This, by means of a short wooden aqueduct, was brought quite down to our boats. The convicts had also built something in the way of a breakwater, and were to build a landing-place for boats and goods, after which the Chilian government intended to lay port charges.

Of the wood I can only say, that it appeared to be abundant; the island in the month of November, when we were there, being in all the freshness and beauty of spring, appeared covered with trees. These were chiefly aromatic, and the largest was the myrtle. The soil is very loose and rich, and wherever it is broken up, there spring up immediately radishes, turnips, ground apples, and other garden fruits. Goats, we were told, were not abundant, and we saw none, though it was said we might, if we had gone into the interior. We saw a few bullocks winding about in the narrow tracks upon the sides of the mountains, and the settlement was completely overrun with dogs of every nation, kindred, and degree. Hens and chickens were also abundant, and seemed to be taken good care of by the women. The men appeared to be the laziest people upon the face of the earth; and indeed, as far as my observation goes, there are no people to whom the newly-invented Yankee word of "loafer" is more applicable than to the Spanish Americans. These men stood about doing nothing, with their cloaks, little better in texture than an Indian's blanket, but of rich colors, thrown over their shoulders with an air which it is said that a Spanish beggar can always give to his rags; and with great politeness and courtesy in their address, though with holes in their shoes and without a sou in their pockets. The only interruption to the monotony of their day seemed to be when a gust of wind drew round between the mountains and blew off the boughs which they had placed for roofs to their houses, and gave them a few minutes' occupation in running about after them. One of these gusts occurred while we were ashore, and afforded us no little amusement at seeing the men look round, and if they found that their roofs had stood, conclude that they might stand too, while those who saw theirs blown off, after uttering a few Spanish oaths, gathered their cloaks over their shoulders, and started off after them. However, they were not gone long, but soon returned to their habitual *occupation* of doing nothing.

It is perhaps needless to say that we saw nothing of the interior; but all who have seen it, give very glowing accounts of it. Our captain went with the governor and a few servants upon mules over the mountains, and upon their return, I heard the governor request him to stop at the island on his passage home, and offer him a handsome sum to bring a few deer with him from California, for he said that there were none upon the island, and he was very desirous of having it stocked.

A steady, though light south-westerly wind carried us well off from the island, and when I came on deck for the middle watch I could just distinguish it from its hiding a few low stars in the southern horizon, though my unpractised eyes would hardly have known it for land. At the close of the watch a few trade-wind clouds which had arisen, though we were hardly yet in their latitude, shut it out from our view, and the next day,

Thursday, Nov. 27th, upon coming on deck in the morning, we were again upon the wide Pacific, and saw no more land until we arrived upon the western coast of the great continent of America.

Chapter VIII

As we saw neither land nor sail from the time of leaving
Juan Fernandez until our arrival in California, nothing of
interest occurred except our own doings on board. We caught
the south-east trades, and run before them for nearly three
weeks, without so much as altering a sail or bracing a yard. The
captain took advantage of this fine weather to get the vessel in
order for coming upon the coast. The carpenter was employed
in fitting up a part of the steerage into a trade-room; for our
cargo, we now learned, was not to be landed, but to be sold by
retail from on board; and this trade-room was built for the
samples and the lighter goods to be kept in, and as a place for
the general business. In the mean time we were employed in
working upon the rigging. Everything was set up taught, the
lower rigging rattled down, or rather rattled *up*, (according to
the modern fashion,) an abundance of spun-yarn and seizing-
stuff made, and finally, the whole standing-rigging, fore and
aft, was tarred down. This was my first essay at this latter business, and I had enough of it; for nearly all of it came upon my
friend S—— and myself. The men were needed at the other
work, and M——, the other young man who came out with
us, was laid up with the rheumatism in his feet, and the boy
was rather too young and small for the business; and as the
winds were light and regular, he was kept during most of the
daytime at the helm; so that nearly all the tarring came upon
us. We put on short duck frocks, and taking a small bucket of
tar and a bunch of oakum in our hands, went aloft, one at the
main royal-mast-head and the other at the fore, and began tarring down. This is an important operation, and is usually done
about once in six months in vessels upon a long voyage. It was
done in our vessel several times afterwards, but by the whole
crew at once, and finished off in a day; but at this time, as most
of it came upon two of us, and we were new at the business, it
took us several days. In this operation they always begin at the
mast-head and work down, tarring the shrouds, back-stays,
standing parts of the lifts, the ties, runners, &c., and go out to
the yard-arms, and come in, tarring, as they come, the lifts and

foot-ropes. Tarring the stays is more difficult, and is done by
an operation which the sailors call "riding down." A long piece
of rope—top-gallant-studding-sail halyards, or something of
the kind—is taken up to the mast-head from which the stay
leads, and rove through a block for a girt-line, or, as the sailors
usually call it, a *gant*-line; with the end of this a bowline is
taken round the stay, into which the man gets with his bucket
of tar and a bunch of oakum, and the other end being fast on
deck, with some one to tend it, he is lowered down gradually,
and tars the stay carefully as he goes. There he "swings aloft
'twixt heaven and earth," and if the rope slips, breaks, or is let
go, or if the bowline slips, he falls overboard or breaks his neck.
This, however, is a thing which never enters into a sailor's calculation. He only thinks of leaving no *holydays*, (places not
tarred,) for in case he should, he would have to go over the
whole again; or of dropping no tar upon deck, for then there
would be a soft word in his ear from the mate. In this manner
I tarred down all the head-stays, but found the rigging about
the jib-booms, martingale, and spritsail yard, upon which I
was afterwards put, the hardest. Here you have to hang on
with your eye-lids and tar with your hands.

This dirty work could not last forever, and on Saturday night
we finished it, scraped all the spots from the deck and rails,
and, what was of more importance to us, cleaned ourselves
thoroughly, rolled up our tarry frocks and trowsers and laid
them away for the next occasion, and put on our clean duck
clothes, and had a good comfortable sailor's Saturday night.
The next day was pleasant, and indeed we had but one unpleasant Sunday during the whole voyage, and that was off
Cape Horn, where we could expect nothing better. On Monday we commenced painting, and getting the vessel ready for
port. This work, too, is done by the crew, and every sailor who
has been long voyages is a little of a painter, in addition to his
other accomplishments. We painted her, both inside and out,
from the truck to the water's edge. The outside is painted by
lowering stages over the side by ropes, and on those we sat,
with our brushes and paint-pots by us, and our feet half the
time in the water. This must be done, of course, on a smooth
day, when the vessel does not roll much. I remember very well
being over the side painting in this way, one fine afternoon,

our vessel going quietly along at the rate of four or five knots, and a pilot-fish, the sure precursor of a shark, swimming alongside of us. The captain was leaning over the rail watching him, and we went quietly on with our work. In the midst of our painting, on

Friday, Dec. 19th, we crossed the equator for the second time. I had the feeling which all have when, for the first time, they find themselves living under an entire change of seasons; as, crossing the line under a burning sun in the midst of December, and, as I afterwards was, beating about among ice and snow on the fourth of July.

Thursday, Dec. 25th. This day was Christmas, but it brought us no holiday. The only change was that we had a "plum duff" for dinner, and the crew quarrelled with the steward because he did not give us our usual allowance of molasses to eat with it. He thought the plums would be a substitute for the molasses, but we were not to be cheated out of our rights in this way.

Such are the trifles which produce quarrels on shipboard. In fact, we had been too long from port. We were getting tired of one another, and were in an irritable state, both forward and aft. Our fresh provisions were, of course, gone, and the captain had stopped our rice, so that we had nothing but salt beef and salt pork throughout the week, with the exception of a very small duff on Sunday. This added to the discontent; and a thousand little things, daily and almost hourly occurring, which no one who has not himself been on a long and tedious voyage can conceive of or properly appreciate—little wars and rumors of wars,—reports of things said in the cabin,—misunderstanding of words and looks,—apparent abuses,—brought us into a state in which everything seemed to go wrong. Every encroachment upon the time allowed for rest, appeared unnecessary. Every shifting of the studding-sails was only to "*haze*"* the crew.

In the midst of this state of things, my messmate S—— and myself petitioned the captain for leave to shift our berths from

---

* *Haze* is a word of frequent use on board ship, and never, I believe, used elsewhere. It is very expressive to a sailor, and means to punish by hard work. Let an officer once say, "I'll *haze* you," and your fate is fixed. You will be "worked up," if you are not a better man than he is.

the steerage, where he had previously lived, into the forecastle. This, to our delight, was granted, and we turned in to *bunk* and mess with the crew forward. We now began to feel like sailors, which we never fully did when we were in the steerage. While there, however useful and active you may be, you are but a mongrel,—and sort of afterguard and "ship's cousin." You are immediately under the eye of the officers, cannot dance, sing, play, smoke, make a noise, or *growl*, (i. e. complain,) or take any other sailor's pleasure; and you live with the steward, who is usually a go-between; and the crew never feel as though you were *one of them*. But if you live in the forecastle, you are "as independent as a wood-sawyer's clerk," (nauticé,) and are a *sailor*. You hear sailors' talk, learn their ways, their peculiarities of feeling as well as speaking and acting; and moreover pick up a great deal of curious and useful information in seamanship, ship's customs, foreign countries, &c., from their long yarns and equally long disputes. No man can be a sailor, or know what sailors are, unless he has lived in the forecastle with them—turned in and out with them, eaten of their dish and drank of their cup. After I had been a week there, nothing would have tempted me to go back to my old berth, and never afterwards, even in the worst of weather, when in a close and leaking forecastle off Cape Horn, did I for a moment wish myself in the steerage. Another thing which you learn better in the forecastle than you can anywhere else, is, to make and mend clothes, and this is indispensable to sailors. A large part of their watches below they spend at this work, and here I learned that art which stood me in so good stead afterwards.

But to return to the state of the crew. Upon our coming into the forecastle, there was some difficulty about the uniting of the allowances of bread, by which we thought we were to lose a few pounds. This set us into a ferment. The captain would not condescend to explain, and we went aft in a body, with a Swede, the oldest and best sailor of the crew, for spokesman. The recollection of the scene that followed always brings up a smile, especially the quarter-deck dignity and eloquence of the captain. He was walking the weather side of the quarter-deck, and seeing us coming aft, stopped short in his walk, and with a voice and look intended to annihilate us, called out, "Well, what the d——l do you want now?" Whereupon we stated our grievances as respectfully as we could, but he broke in upon us, saying that we were getting fat and lazy, didn't have enough to do, and that made us find fault. This provoked us, and we began to give word for word. This would never answer. He clenched his fist, stamped and swore, and sent us all forward, saying, with oaths enough interspersed to send the words home,—"Away with you! go forward every one of you! I'll *haze* you! I'll work you up! You don't have enough to do! If you a'n't careful I'll make a hell of the ship! . . . . You've mistaken your man! I'm F—— T——, all the way from 'down east.' I've been through the mill, ground, and bolted, and come out a *regular-built down-east johnny-cake*, good when it's hot, but when it's cold, sour and indigestible;—and you'll find me so!" The latter part of this harangue I remember well, for it made a strong impression, and the "down-east johnny-cake" became a by-word for the rest of the voyage. So much for our petition for the redress of grievances. The matter was however set right, for the mate, after allowing the captain due time to cool off, explained it to him, and at night we were all called aft to hear another harangue, in which, of course, the whole blame of the misunderstanding was thrown upon us. We ventured to hint that he would not give us time to explain; it wouldn't do. We were driven back discomforted. Thus the affair blew over, but the irritation caused by it remained; and we never had peace or a good understanding again so long as the captain and crew remained together.

We continued sailing along in the beautiful temperate climate of the Pacific. The Pacific well deserves its name, for except in the southern part, at Cape Horn, and in the western parts, near the China and Indian oceans, it has few storms, and is never either extremely hot or cold. Between the tropics there is a slight haziness, like a thin gauze, drawn over the sun, which, without obstructing or obscuring the light, tempers the heat which comes down with perpendicular fierceness in the Atlantic and Indian tropics. We sailed well to the westward to have the full advantage of the north-east trades, and when we had reached the latitude of Point Conception, where it is usual to make the land, we were several hundred miles to the westward of it. We immediately changed our course due east, and sailed in that direction for a number of days. At length we began to heave-to after dark, for fear of making the land at night on a coast where there are no light-houses and but indifferent charts, and at day-break on the morning of

Tuesday, Jan. 13th, 1835, we made the land at Point Conception, lat. 34° 32′ N., long. 120° 06′ W. The port of Santa Barbara, to which we were bound, lying about sixty miles to the southward of this point, we continued sailing down the coast during the day and following night, and on the next morning,

Jan. 14th, 1835, we came to anchor in the spacious bay of Santa Barbara, after a voyage of one hundred and fifty days from Boston.

Chapter IX

CALIFORNIA extends along nearly the whole of the western coast of Mexico, between the gulf of California in the south and the bay of Sir Francis Drake on the north, or between the 22d and 38th degrees of north latitude. It is subdivided into two provinces—Lower or Old California, lying between the gulf and the 32d degree of latitude, or near it; (the division line running, I believe, between the bay of Todos Santos and the port of San Diego;) and New or Upper California, the southernmost port of which is San Diego, in lat. 32° 39′, and the northernmost, San Francisco, situated in the large bay discovered by Sir Francis Drake, in lat. 37° 58′, and called after him by the English, though the Mexicans call it Yerba Buena. Upper California has the seat of its government at Monterey, where is also the custom-house, the only one on the coast, and at which every vessel intending to trade on the coast must enter its cargo before it can commence its traffic. We were to trade upon this coast exclusively, and therefore expected to go to Monterey at first; but the captain's orders from home were to put in at Santa Barbara, which is the central port of the coast, and wait there for the agent who lives there, and transacts all the business for the firm to which our vessel belonged.

The bay, or, as it was commonly called, the *canal* of Santa Barbara, is very large, being formed by the main land on one side, (between Point Conception on the north and Point St. Buena Ventura on the south,) which here bends in like a crescent, and three large islands opposite to it and at the distance of twenty miles. This is just sufficient to give it the name of a bay, while at the same time it is so large and so much exposed to the south-east and north-west winds, that it is little better than an open roadstead; and the whole swell of the Pacific ocean rolls in here before a south-easter, and breaks with so heavy a surf in the shallow waters, that it is highly dangerous to lie near in to the shore during the south-easter season, that is, between the months of November and April.

This wind (the south-easter) is the bane of the coast of California. Between the months of November and April, (including a part of each,) which is the rainy season in this latitude, you are never safe from it, and accordingly, in the ports which are open to it, vessels are obliged, during these months, to lie at anchor at a distance of three miles from the shore, with slip-ropes on their cables, ready to slip and go to sea at a moment's warning. The only ports which are safe from this wind are San Francisco and Monterey in the north, and San Diego in the south.

As it was January when we arrived, and the middle of the south-easter season, we accordingly came to anchor at the distance of three miles from the shore, in eleven fathoms water, and bent a slip-rope and buoys to our cables, cast off the yard-arm gaskets from the sails, and stopped them all with rope-yarns. After we had done this, the boat went ashore with the captain, and returned with orders to the mate to send a boat ashore for him at sun-down. I did not go in the first boat, and was glad to find that there was another going before night; for after so long a voyage as ours had been, a few hours is long to pass in sight and out of reach of land. We spent the day on board in the usual avocations; but as this was the first time we had been without the captain, we felt a little more freedom, and looked about us to see what sort of a country we had got into, and were to spend a year or two of our lives in.

In the first place, it was a beautiful day, and so warm that we had on straw hats, duck trowsers, and all the summer gear; and as this was mid-winter, it spoke well for the climate; and we afterwards found that the thermometer never fell to the freezing point throughout the winter, and that there was very little difference between the seasons, except that during a long period of rainy and south-easterly weather, thick clothes were not uncomfortable.

The large bay lay about us, nearly smooth, as there was hardly a breath of wind stirring, though the boat's crew who went ashore told us that the long ground swell broke into a heavy surf on the beach. There was only one vessel in the port—a long, sharp brig of about 300 tons, with raking masts and very square yards, and English colors at her peak. We afterwards learned that she was built at Guayaquil, and named the "Ayacucho," after the place where the battle was fought that gave Peru her independence, and was now owned by a

Scotchman named Wilson, who commanded her, and was engaged in the trade between Callao, the Sandwich Islands, and
California. She was a fast sailer, as we frequently afterwards
perceived, and had a crew of Sandwich Islanders on board. Beside this vessel there was no object to break the surface of the
bay. Two points ran out as the horns of the crescent, one of
which—the one to the westward—was low and sandy, and is
that to which vessels are obliged to give a wide berth when
running out for a south-easter; the other is high, bold, and
well wooded, and, we were told, has a mission upon it, called
St. Buenaventura, from which the point is named. In the middle of this crescent, directly opposite the anchoring ground, lie
the mission and town of Santa Barbara, on a low, flat plain, but
little above the level of the sea, covered with grass, though entirely without trees, and surrounded on three sides by an amphitheatre of mountains, which slant off to the distance of
fifteen or twenty miles. The mission stands a little back of the
town, and is a large building, or rather collection of buildings,
in the centre of which is a high tower, with a belfry of five
bells; and the whole, being plastered, makes quite a show at a
distance, and is the mark by which vessels come to anchor. The
town lies a little nearer to the beach—about half a mile from
it—and is composed of one-story houses built of brown clay—
some of them plastered—with red tiles on the roofs. I should
judge that there were about an hundred of them; and in the
midst of them stands the Presidio, or fort, built of the same
materials, and apparently but little stronger. The town is certainly finely situated, with a bay in front, and an amphitheatre
of hills behind. The only thing which diminishes its beauty is,
that the hills have no large trees upon them, they having been
all burnt by a great fire which swept them off about a dozen
years before, and they had not yet grown up again. The fire
was described to me by an inhabitant, as having been a very
terrible and magnificent sight. The air of the whole valley was
so heated that the people were obliged to leave the town and
take up their quarters for several days upon the beach.

Just before sun-down the mate ordered a boat's crew ashore,
and I went as one of the number. We passed under the stern
of the English brig, and had a long pull ashore. I shall never
forget the impression which our first landing on the beach of

California made upon me. The sun had just gone down; it was getting dusky; the damp night wind was beginning to blow, and the heavy swell of the Pacific was setting in, and breaking in loud and high "combers" upon the beach. We lay on our oars in the swell, just outside of the surf, waiting for a good chance to run in, when a boat, which had put off from the Ayacucho just after us, came alongside of us, with a crew of dusky Sandwich Islanders, talking and hallooing in their out-landish tongue. They knew that we were novices in this kind of boating, and waited to see us go in. The second mate, how-ever, who steered our boat, determined to have the advantage of their experience, and would not go in first. Finding, at length, how matters stood, they gave a shout, and taking ad-vantage of a great comber which came swelling in, rearing its head, and lifting up the stern of our boat nearly perpendicular, and again dropping it in the trough, they gave three or four long and strong pulls, and went in on top of the great wave, throwing their oars overboard, and as far from the boat as they could throw them, and jumping out the instant that the boat touched the beach, and then seizing hold of her and running her up high and dry upon the sand. We saw, at once, how it was to be done, and also the necessity of keeping the boat "stern on" to the sea; for the instant the sea should strike upon her broad-side or quarter, she would be driven up broad-side on, and capsized. We pulled strongly in, and as soon as we felt that the sea had got hold of us and was carrying us in with the speed of a race-horse, we threw the oars as far from the boat as we could, and took hold of the gunwale, ready to spring out and seize her when she struck, the officer using his utmost strength to keep her stern on. We were shot up upon the beach like an arrow from a bow, and seizing the boat, ran her up high and dry, and soon picked up our oars, and stood by her, ready for the captain to come down.

Finding that the captain did not come immediately, we put our oars in the boat, and leaving one to watch it, walked about the beach to see what we could, of the place. The beach is nearly a mile in length between the two points, and of smooth sand. We had taken the only good landing-place, which is in the middle; it being more stony toward the ends. It is about twenty yards in width from high-water mark to a slight bank at which the soil begins, and so hard that it is a favorite place for running horses. It was growing dark, so that we could just distinguish the dim outlines of the two vessels in the offing; and the great seas were rolling in, in regular lines, growing larger and larger as they approached the shore, and hanging over the beach upon which they were to break, when their tops would curl over and turn white with foam, and, beginning at one extreme of the line, break rapidly to the other, as a long card-house falls when the children knock down the cards at one end. The Sandwich Islanders, in the mean time, had turned their boat round, and ran her down into the water, and were loading her with hides and tallow. As this was the work in which we were soon to be engaged, we looked on with some curiosity. They ran the boat into the water so far that every large sea might float her, and two of them, with their trowsers rolled up, stood by the bows, one on each side, keeping her in her right position. This was hard work; for beside the force they had to use upon the boat, the large seas nearly took them off their legs. The others were running from the boat to the bank, upon which, out of the reach of the water, was a pile of dry bullocks' hides, doubled lengthwise in the middle, and nearly as stiff as boards. These they took upon their heads, one or two at a time, and carried down to the boat, where one of their number stowed them away. They were obliged to carry them on their heads, to keep them out of the water, and we observed that they had on thick woollen caps. "Look here, Bill, and see what you're coming to!" said one of our men to another who stood by the boat. "Well, D——," said the second mate to me, "this does not look much like Cambridge college, does it? This is what I call '*head work*.'" To tell the truth, it did not look very encouraging.

After they had got through with the hides, they laid hold of the bags of tallow, (the bags are made of hide, and are about the size of a common meal bag,) and lifting each upon the shoulders of two men, one at each end, walked off with them to the boat, and prepared to go aboard. Here, too, was something for us to learn. The man who steered, shipped his oar and stood up in the stern, and those that pulled the after oars sat upon their benches, with their oars shipped, ready to strike out as soon as she was afloat. The two men at the bows kept their places; and when, at length, a large sea came in and floated her, seized hold of the gunwale, and ran out with her till they were up to their armpits, and then tumbled over the gunwale into the bows, dripping with water. The men at the oars struck out, but it wouldn't do; the sea swept back and left them nearly high and dry. The two fellows jumped out again; and the next time they succeeded better, and, with the help of a deal of outlandish hallooing and bawling, got her well off. We watched them till they were out of the breakers, and saw them steering for their vessel, which was now hidden in the darkness.

The sand of the beach began to be cold to our bare feet; the frogs set up their croaking in the marshes, and one solitary owl, from the end of the distant point, gave out his melancholy note, mellowed by the distance, and we began to think that it was high time for "the old man," as the captain is generally called, to come down. In a few minutes we heard something coming towards us. It was a man on horseback. He came up on the full gallop, reined up near us, addressed a few words to us, and receiving no answer, wheeled round and gallopped off again. He was nearly as dark as an Indian, with a large Spanish hat, blanket cloak or surreppa, and leather leggins, with a long knife stuck in them. "This is the seventh city that ever I was in, and no Christian one neither," said Bill Brown. "Stand by!" said Tom, "you haven't seen the worst of it yet." In the midst of this conversation the captain appeared; and we winded the boat round, shoved her down, and prepared to go off. The captain, who had been on the coast before and "knew the ropes," took the steering oar, and we went off in the same way as the other boat. I, being the youngest, had the pleasure of standing at the bow, and getting wet through. We went off well, though the seas were high. Some of them lifted us up, and sliding from under us, seemed to let us drop through the air like a flat plank upon the body of the water. In a few minutes we were in the low, regular swell, and pulled for a light, which, as we came up, we found had been run up to our trysail gaff.

Coming aboard, we hoisted up all the boats, and diving down into the forecastle, changed our wet clothes, and got our supper. After supper the sailors lighted their pipes, (cigars,

those of us who had them,) and we had to tell all we had seen
ashore. Then followed conjectures about the people ashore,
the length of the voyage, carrying hides, &c. &c., until eight
bells, when all hands were called aft, and the "anchor watch"
set. We were to stand two in a watch, and as the nights were
pretty long, two hours were to make a watch. The second
mate was to keep the deck until eight o'clock, and all hands
were to be called at daybreak, and the word was passed to keep
a bright look-out, and to call the mate if it should come on to
blow from the south-east. We had also orders to strike the bells
every half hour through the night, as at sea. My watchmate
was John, the Swedish sailor, and we stood from twelve to
two, he walking the larboard side, and I the starboard. At daylight all hands were called, and we went through the usual
process of washing down, swabbing, &c., and got breakfast at
eight o'clock. In the course of the forenoon, a boat went aboard
of the Ayacucho and brought off a quarter of beef, which
made us a fresh bite for dinner. This we were glad enough to
have, and the mate told us that we should live upon fresh beef
while we were on the coast, as it was cheaper here than the
salt. While at dinner, the cook called, "Sail ho!" and coming
on deck, we saw two sails coming round the point. One was a
large ship under top-gallant sails, and the other a small hermaphrodite brig. They both backed their topsails and sent
boats aboard of us. The ship's colors had puzzled us, and we
found that she was from Genoa, with an assorted cargo, and
was trading on the coast. She filled away again, and stood out;
being bound up the coast to San Francisco. The crew of the
brig's boat were Sandwich Islanders, but one of them, who
spoke a little English, told us that she was the Loriotte, Captain Nye, from Oahu, and was engaged in this trade. She was a
lump of a thing—what the sailors call a butter-box. This vessel,
as well as the Ayacucho, and others which we afterwards saw
engaged in the same trade, have English or Americans for officers, and two or three before the mast to do the work upon
the rigging, and to rely upon for seamanship, while the rest of
the crew are Sandwich Islanders, who are active, and very useful in boating.

The three captains went ashore after dinner, and came off
again at night. When in port, everything is attended to by the

chief mate; the captain, unless he is also supercargo, has little to do, and is usually ashore much of his time. This we thought would be pleasanter for us, as the mate was a good-natured man and not very strict. So it was for a time, but we were worse off in the end; for wherever the captain is a severe, energetic man, and the mate is wanting in both these qualities, there will always be trouble. And trouble we had already begun to anticipate. The captain had several times found fault with the mate, in presence of the crew; and hints had been dropped that all was not right between them. When this is the case, and the captain suspects that his chief officer is too easy and familiar with the crew, then he begins to interfere in all the duties, and to draw the reins taughter, and the crew have to suffer.

Chapter X

THIS NIGHT, after sundown, it looked black at the south-ward and eastward, and we were told to keep a bright look-out. Expecting to be called up, we turned in early. Waking up about midnight, I found a man who had just come down from his watch, striking a light. He said that it was beginning to puff up from the south-east, and that the sea was rolling in, and he had called the captain; and as he threw himself down on his chest with all his clothes on, I knew that he expected to be called. I felt the vessel pitching at her anchor, and the chain surging and snapping, and lay awake, expecting an instant summons. In a few minutes it came—three knocks on the scuttle, and "All hands ahoy! bear-a-hand up and make sail." We sprang up for our clothes, and were about half way dressed, when the mate called out, down the scuttle, "Tumble up here, men! tumble up! before she drags her anchor." We were on deck in an instant. "Lay aloft and loose the topsails!" shouted the captain, as soon as the first man showed himself. Springing into the rigging, I saw that the Ayacucho's topsails were loosed, and heard her crew singing-out at the sheets as they were hauling them home. This had probably started our captain; as "old Wilson" (the captain of the Ayacucho) had been many years on the coast, and knew the signs of the weather. We soon had the topsails loosed; and one hand remaining, as usual, in each top, to overhaul the rigging and light the sail out, the rest of us laid down to man the sheets. While sheeting home, we saw the Ayacucho standing athwart our bows, sharp upon the wind, cutting through the head sea like a knife, with her raking masts and sharp bows running up like the head of a grey-hound. It was a beautiful sight. She was like a bird which had been frightened and had spread her wings in flight. After the topsails had been sheeted home, the head yards braced aback, the fore-top-mast staysail hoisted, and the buoys streamed, and all ready forward, for slipping, we went aft and manned the slip-rope which came through the stern port with a turn round the timber-heads. "All ready forward?" asked the captain. "Aye, aye, sir; all ready," answered the mate. "Let go!" "All gone, sir;" and the iron cable grated over the windlass and through the hawse-hole, and the little vessel's head swinging off from the wind under the force of her backed head sails, brought the strain upon the slip-rope. "Let go aft!" Instantly all was gone, and we were under weigh. As soon as she was well off from the wind, we filled away the head yards, braced all up sharp, set the foresail and trysail, and left our anchorage well astern, giving the point a good berth. "Nye's off too," said the captain to the mate; and looking astern, we could just see the little hermaphrodite brig under sail standing after us.

It now began to blow fresh; the rain fell fast, and it grew very black; but the captain would not take in sail until we were well clear of the point. As soon as we left this on our quarter, and were standing out to sea, the order was given, and we sprang aloft, double reefed each topsail, furled the foresail, and double reefed the trysail, and were soon under easy sail. In these cases of slipping for south-easters, there is nothing to be done, after you have got clear of the coast, but to lie-to under easy sail, and wait for the gale to be over, which seldom lasts more than two days, and is often over in twelve hours; but the wind never comes back to the southward until there has a good deal of rain fallen. "Go below the watch," said the mate; but here was a dispute which watch it should be, which the mate soon however settled by sending his watch below, saying that we should have our turn the next time we got under weigh. We remained on deck till the expiration of the watch, the wind blowing very fresh and the rain coming down in torrents. When the watch came up, we wore ship, and stood on the other tack, in towards land. When we came up again, which was at four in the morning, it was very dark, and there was not much wind, but it was raining as I thought I had never seen it rain before. We had on oil-cloth suits and south-wester caps, and had nothing to do but to stand bolt upright and let it pour down upon us. There are no umbrellas, and no sheds to go under, at sea.

While we were standing about on deck, we saw the little brig drifting by us, hove to under her fore topsail double reefed; and she glided by like a phantom. Not a word was spoken, and we saw no one on deck but the man at the wheel. Toward morning the captain put his head out of the companion-way and told the second mate, who commanded our watch, to look out for a change of wind, which usually followed a calm and heavy rain; and it was well that he did; for in a few minutes it fell dead calm, the vessel lost her steerage-way, and the rain ceased. We hauled up the trysail and courses, squared the after yards, and waited for the change, which came in a few minutes, with a vengeance, from the north-west, the opposite point of the compass. Owing to our precautions, we were not taken aback, but ran before the wind with square yards. The captain coming on deck, we braced up a little and stood back for our anchorage. With the change of wind came a change of weather, and in two hours the wind moderated into the light steady breeze, which blows down the coast the greater part of the year, and, from its regularity, might be called a trade-wind. The sun came up bright, and we set royals, skysails, and studding-sails, and were under fair way for Santa Barbara. The little Loriotte was astern of us, nearly out of sight; but we saw nothing of the Ayacucho. In a short time she appeared, standing out from Santa Rosa Island, under the lee of which she had been hove to, all night. Our captain was anxious to get in before her, for it would be a great credit to us, on the coast, to beat the Ayacucho, which had been called the best sailer in the North Pacific, in which she had been known as a trader for six years or more. We had an advantage over her in light winds, from our royals and skysails which we carried both at the fore and main, and also in our studding-sails; for Captain Wilson carried nothing above top-gallant-sails, and always unbent his studding-sails when on the coast. As the wind was light and fair, we held our own, for some time, when we were both obliged to brace up and come upon a taught bowline, after rounding the point; and here he had us on fair ground, and walked away from us, as you would haul in a line. He afterwards said that we sailed well enough with the wind free, but that give him a taught bowline, and he would beat us, if we had all the canvass of the Royal George.

The Ayacucho got to the anchoring ground about half an hour before us, and was furling her sails when we came up to it. This picking up your cables is a very nice piece of work. It requires some seamanship to do it, and come to at your former moorings, without letting go another anchor. Captain Wilson was remarkable, among the sailors on the coast, for his skill in doing this; and our captain never let go a second anchor during all the time that I was with him. Coming a little to windward of our buoy, we clewed up the light sails, backed our main top-sail, and lowered a boat, which pulled off, and made fast a spare hawser to the buoy on the end of the slip-rope. We brought the other end to the capstan, and hove in upon it until we came to the slip-rope, which we took to the windlass, and walked her up to her chain, the captain helping her by backing and filling the sails. The chain is then passed through the hawse-hole and round the windlass, and bitted, the slip-rope taken round outside and brought into the stern port, and she is safe in her old berth. After we had got through, the mate told us that this was a small touch of California, the like of which we must expect to have through the winter.

After we had furled the sails and got dinner, we saw the Loriotte nearing, and she had her anchor before night. At sun-down we went ashore again, and found the Loriotte's boat waiting on the beach. The Sandwich Islander who could speak English, told us that he had been up to the town; that our agent, Mr. R——, and some other passengers, were going to Monterey with us, and that we were to sail the same night. In a few minutes Captain T——, with two gentlemen and one female, came down, and we got ready to go off. They had a good deal of baggage, which we put into the bows of the boat, and then two of us took the señora in our arms, and waded with her through the water, and put her down safely in the stern. She appeared much amused with the transaction, and her husband was perfectly satisfied, thinking any arrangement good which saved his wetting his feet. I pulled the after oar, so that I heard the conversation, and learned that one of the men, who, as well as I could see in the darkness, was a young-looking man, in the European dress, and covered up in a large cloak, was the agent of the firm to which our vessel belonged; and the other, who was dressed in the Spanish dress of the country, was a brother of our captain, who had been many years a trader on the coast, and had married the lady who was in the boat. She was a delicate, dark-complexioned young woman, and of one of the best families in California. I also found that we were to sail the same night. As soon as we got on board, the boats were hoisted up, the sails loosed, the windlass manned, the slip-ropes and gear cast off; and after about twenty minutes of heaving at the windlass, making sail, and bracing yards, we were well under weigh, and going with a fair wind up the coast to Monterey. The Loriotte got under weigh at the same time, and was also bound up to Monterey, but as she took a different course from us, keeping the land aboard, while we kept well out to sea, we soon lost sight of her. We had a fair wind, which is something unusual when going up, as the prevailing wind is the north, which blows directly down the coast; whence the northern are called the windward, and the southern the leeward ports.

Chapter XI

WE got clear of the islands before sunrise the next morning, and by twelve o'clock were out of the canal, and off Point Conception, the place where we first made the land upon our arrival. This is the largest point on the coast, and is an uninhabited headland, stretching out into the Pacific, and has the reputation of being very windy. Any vessel does well which gets by it without a gale, especially in the winter season. We were going along with studding-sails set on both sides, when, as we came round the point, we had to haul our wind, and took in the lee studding-sails. As the brig came more upon the wind, she felt it more, and we doused the sky-sails, but kept the weather studding-sails on her, bracing the yards forward so that the swinging-boom nearly touched the sprit-sail yard. She now lay over to it, the wind was freshening, and the captain was evidently "dragging on to her." His brother and Mr. R——, looking a little squally, said something to him, but he only answered that he knew the vessel and what she would carry. He was evidently showing off his vessel, and letting them know how he could carry sail. He stood up to windward, holding on by the backstays, and looking up at the sticks, to see how much they would bear; when a puff came which settled the matter. Then it was "haul down," and "clew up," royals, flying-jib, and studding-sails, all at once. There was what the sailors call a "mess"—everything let go, nothing hauled in, and everything flying. The poor Spanish woman came to the companion-way, looking as pale as a ghost, and nearly frightened to death. The mate and some men forward were trying to haul in the lower studding-sail, which had blown over the sprit-sail yard-arm and round the guys, while the topmast-studding-sail boom, after buckling up and springing out again like a piece of whalebone, broke off at the boom-iron. I sprang aloft to take in the main top-gallant studding-sail, but before I got into the top, the tack parted, and away went the sail, swinging forward of the top-gallant-sail, and tearing and slatting itself to pieces. The halyards were at this moment let go by the run; and such a piece of work I never had before, in taking in a sail. After great exertions I got it, or the remains of it, into the top, and was making it fast, when the captain, looking up, called out to me, "Lay aloft there, D——, and furl that main royal." Leaving the studding-sail, I went up to the cross-trees; and here it looked rather squally. The foot of the top-gallant-mast was working between the cross and trussel trees, and the royal-mast lay over at a fearful angle with the mast below, while everything was working, and cracking, strained to the utmost.

There's nothing for Jack to do but to obey orders, and I went up upon the yard; and there was a worse "mess," if possible, than I had left below. The braces had been let go, and the yard was swinging about like a turnpike-gate, and the whole sail having blown over to leeward, the lee leach was over the yard-arm, and the sky-sail was all adrift and flying over my head. I looked down, but it was in vain to attempt to make myself heard, for every one was busy below, and the wind roared, and sails were flapping in every direction. Fortunately, it was noon and broad daylight, and the man at the wheel, who had his eyes aloft, soon saw my difficulty, and after numberless signs and gestures, got some one to haul the necessary ropes taught. During this interval I took a look below. Everything was in confusion on deck; the little vessel was tearing through the water as if she were mad, the seas flying over her, and the masts leaning over at an angle of forty-five degrees from the vertical. At the other royal-mast-head was S——, working away at the sail, which was blowing from him as fast as he could gather it in. The top-gallant-sail below me was soon clewed up, which relieved the mast, and in a short time I got my sail furled, and went below; but I lost overboard a new tarpaulin hat, which troubled me more than anything else. We worked for about half an hour with might and main; and in an hour from the time the squall struck us, from having all our flying kites abroad, we came down to double-reefed top-sails and the storm-sails.

The wind had hauled ahead during the squall, and we were standing directly in for the point. So, as soon as we had got all snug, we wore round and stood off again, and had the pleasant prospect of beating up to Monterey, a distance of an hundred miles, against a violent head wind. Before night it began to rain; and we had five days of rainy, stormy weather, under close sail all the time, and were blown several hundred miles off the coast. In the midst of this, we discovered that our fore topmast was sprung, (which no doubt happened in the squall,) and were obliged to send down the fore top-gallant-mast and carry as little sail as possible forward. Our four passengers were dreadfully sick, so that we saw little or nothing of them during the five days. On the sixth day it cleared off, and the sun came out bright, but the wind and sea were still very high. It was quite like being at sea again: no land for hundreds of miles, and the captain taking the sun every day at noon. Our passengers now made their appearance, and I had for the first time the opportunity of seeing what a miserable and forlorn creature a sea-sick passenger is. Since I had got over my own sickness, the first two days from Boston, I had seen nothing but hale, hearty men, with their sea legs on, and able to go anywhere, (for we had no passengers;) and I will own there was a pleasant feeling of superiority in being able to walk the deck, and eat, and go about, and comparing one's self with two poor, miserable, pale creatures, staggering and shuffling about decks, or holding on and looking up with giddy heads, to see us climbing to the mast-heads, or sitting quietly at work on the ends of the lofty yards. A well man at sea has little sympathy with one who is sea-sick; he is too apt to be conscious of a comparison favorable to his own manhood.

After a few days we made the land at Point Pinos, (pines,) which is the headland at the entrance of the bay of Monterey. As we drew in, and ran down the shore, we could distinguish well the face of the country, and found it better wooded than that to the southward of Point Conception. In fact, as I afterwards discovered, Point Conception may be made the dividing line between two different faces of the country. As you go to the northward of the point, the country becomes more wooded, has a richer appearance, and is better supplied with water. This is the case with Monterey, and still more so with San Francisco; while to the southward of the point, as at Santa Barbara, San Pedro, and particularly San Diego, there is very litle wood, and the country has a naked, level appearance, though it is still very fertile.

The bay of Monterey is very wide at the entrance, being

about twenty-four miles between the two points, Año Nuevo at the north, and Pinos at the south, but narrows gradually as you approach the town, which is situated in a bend, or large cove, at the south-eastern extremity, and about eighteen miles from the points, which makes the whole depth of the bay. The shores are extremely well wooded, (the pine abounding upon them,) and as it was now the rainy season, everything was as green as nature could make it,—the grass, the leaves, and all; the birds were singing in the woods, and great numbers of wild fowl were flying over our heads. Here we could lie safe from the south-easters. We came to anchor within two cable lengths of the shore, and the town lay directly before us, making a very pretty appearance; its houses being plastered, which gives a much better effect than those of Santa Barbara, which are of a mud-color. The red tiles, too, on the roofs, contrasted well with the white plastered sides, and with the extreme greenness of the lawn upon which the houses—about an hundred in number—were dotted about, here and there, irregularly. There are in this place, and in every other town which I saw in California, no streets, or fences, (except here and there a small patch was fenced in for a garden,) so that the houses are placed at random upon the green, which, as they are of one story and of the cottage form, gives them a pretty effect when seen from a little distance.

It was a fine Saturday afternoon when we came to anchor, the sun about an hour high, and everything looking pleasantly. The Mexican flag was flying from the little square Presidio, and the drums and trumpets of the soldiers, who were out on parade, sounded over the water, and gave great life to the scene. Every one was delighted with the appearance of things. We felt as though we had got into a Christian (which in the sailor's vocabulary means civilized) country. The first impression which California had made upon us was very disagreeable:—the open roadstead of Santa Barbara; anchoring three miles from the shore; running out to sea before every south-easter; landing in a high surf; with a little dark-looking town, a mile from the beach; and not a sound to be heard, or anything to be seen, but Sandwich Islanders, hides, and tallow-bags. Add to this the gale off Point Conception, and no one can be at a loss to account for our agreeable disappointment in Monterey. Beside all this, we soon learned, which was of no small importance to us, that there was little or no surf here, and this afternoon the beach was as smooth as a duckpond.

We landed the agent and passengers, and found several persons waiting for them on the beach, among whom were some, who, though dressed in the costume of the country, spoke English; and who, we afterwards learned, were English and Americans who had married and settled in the country.

I also connected with our arrival here another circumstance which more nearly concerns myself; viz., my first act of what the sailors will allow to be seamanship—sending down a royal-yard. I had seen it done once or twice at sea, and an old sailor, whose favor I had taken some pains to gain, had taught me carefully everything which was necessary to be done, and in its proper order, and advised me to take the first opportunity when we were in port, and try it. I told the second mate, with whom I had been pretty *thick* when he was before the mast, that I would do it, and got him to ask the mate to send me up the first time they were struck. Accordingly I was called upon, and went up, repeating the operations over in my mind, taking care to get everything in its order, for the slightest mistake spoils the whole. Fortunately, I got through without any word from the officer, and heard the "well done" of the mate, when the yard reached the deck, with as much satisfaction as I ever felt at Cambridge on seeing a "*bene*" at the foot of a Latin exercise.

Chapter XII

T HE next day being Sunday, which is the liberty-day among merchantmen, when it is usual to let a part of the crew go ashore, the sailors had depended upon a day on land, and were already disputing who should ask to go, when, upon being called in the morning, we were turned-to upon the rigging, and found that the topmast, which had been sprung, was to come down, and a new one to go up, and top-gallant and royal-masts, and the rigging to be set up. This was too bad. If there is anything that irritates sailors and makes them feel hardly used, it is being deprived of their Sabbath. Not that they would always, or indeed generally, spend it religiously, but it is their only day of rest. Then, too, they are so often necessarily deprived of it by storms, and unavoidable duties of all kinds, that to take it from them when lying quietly and safely in port, without any urgent reason, bears the more hardly. The only reason in this case was, that the captain had determined to have the custom-house officers on board on Monday, and wished to have his brig in order. Jack is a slave aboard ship; but still he has many opportunities of thwarting and balking his master. When there is danger, or necessity, or when he is well used, no one can work faster than he; but the instant he feels that he is kept at work for nothing, no sloth could make less headway. He must not refuse his duty, or be in any way disobedient, but all the work that an officer gets out of him, he may be welcome to. Every man who has been three months at sea knows how to "work Tom Cox's traverse"—"three turns round the long-boat, and a pull at the scuttled-butt." This morning everything went in this way. "*Sogering*" was the order of the day. Send a man below to get a block, and he would capsize everything before finding it, then not bring it up till an officer had called him twice, and take as much time to put things in order again. Marline-spikes were not to be found; knives wanted a prodigious deal of sharpening, and, generally, three or four were waiting round the grindstone at a time. When a man got to the mast-head, he would come slowly down again to get something which he had forgotten; and

after the tackles were got up, six men would pull less than one
who pulled "with a will." When the mate was out of sight,
nothing was done. It was all up-hill work; and at eight o'clock,
when we went to breakfast, things were nearly where they
were when we began.

During our short meal, the matter was discussed. One proposed refusing to work; but that was mutiny, and of course was
rejected at once. I remember, too, that one of the men quoted
"Father Taylor," (as they call the seamen's preacher at Boston,)
who told them that if they were ordered to work on Sunday,
they must not refuse their duty, and the blame would not
come upon them. After breakfast, it leaked out, through the
officers, that if we would get through work soon, we might
have a boat in the afternoon and go a fishing. This bait was
well thrown, and took with several who were fond of fishing;
and all began to find that as we had one thing to do, and were
not to be kept at work for the day, the sooner we did it, the
better. Accordingly, things took a new aspect; and before two
o'clock, this work, which was in a fair way to last two days, was
done; and five of us went a fishing in the jolly-boat, in the direction of Point Pinos; but leave to go ashore was refused.
Here we saw the Loriotte, which sailed with us from Santa
Barbara, coming slowly in with a light sea-breeze, which sets
in towards afternoon, having been becalmed off the point all
the first part of the day. We took several fish of various kinds,
among which cod and perch abounded, and Foster, (the *ci-
devant* second mate,) who was of our number, brought up
with his hook a large and beautiful pearl-oyster shell. We afterwards learned that this place was celebrated for shells, and that
a small schooner had made a good voyage, by carrying a cargo
of them to the United States.

We returned by sundown, and found the Loriotte at anchor,
within a cable's length of the Pilgrim. The next day we were
"turned-to" early, and began taking off the hatches, overhauling the cargo, and getting everything ready for inspection.
At eight, the officers of the customs, five in number, came on
board, and began overhauling the cargo, manifest, &c. The
Mexican revenue laws are very strict, and require the whole
cargo to be landed, examined, and taken on board again; but
our agent, Mr. R——, had succeeded in compounding with

them for the two last vessels, and saving the trouble of taking the cargo ashore. The officers were dressed in the costume which we found prevailed through the country. A broad-brimmed hat, usually of a black or dark-brown color, with a gilt or figured band round the crown, and lined inside with silk; a short jacket of silk or figured calico, (the European skirted body-coat is never worn;) the shirt open in the neck; rich waistcoat, if any; pantaloons wide, straight, and long, usually of velvet, velveteen, or broadcloth; or else short breeches and white stockings. They wear the deer-skin shoe, which is of a dark-brown color, and, (being made by Indians,) usually a good deal ornamented. They have no suspenders, but always wear a sash round the waist, which is generally red, and varying in quality with the means of the wearer. Add to this the never-failing cloak, and you have the dress of the Californian. This last garment, the cloak, is always a mark of the rank and wealth of the owner. The "*gente de razón*," or aristocracy, wear cloaks of black or dark blue broadcloth, with as much velvet and trimmings as may be; and from this they go down to the blanket of the Indian; the middle classes wearing something like a large table-cloth, with a hole in the middle for the head to go through. This is often as coarse as a blanket, but being beautifully woven with various colors, is quite showy at a distance. Among the Spaniards there is no working class; (the Indians being slaves and doing all the hard work;) and every rich man looks like a grandee, and every poor scamp like a broken-down gentleman. I have often seen a man with a fine figure, and courteous manners, dressed in broadcloth and velvet, with a noble horse completely covered with trappings; without a *real* in his pockets, and absolutely suffering for something to eat.

Chapter XIII

THE next day, the cargo having been entered in due form, we began trading. The trade-room was fitted up in the steerage, and furnished out with the lighter goods, and with specimens of the rest of the cargo; and M——, a young man who came out from Boston with us, before the mast, was taken out of the forecastle, and made supercargo's clerk. He was well qualified for the business, having been clerk in a counting-house in Boston. He had been troubled for some time with the rheumatism, which unfitted him for the wet and exposed duty of a sailor on the coast. For a week or ten days all was life on board. The people came off to look and to buy—men, women, and children; and we were continually going in the boats, carrying goods and passengers,—for they have no boats of their own. Everything must dress itself and come aboard and see the new vessel, if it were only to buy a paper of pins. The agent and his clerk managed the sales, while we were busy in the hold or in the boats. Our cargo was an assorted one; that is, it consisted of everything under the sun. We had spirits of all kinds, (sold by the cask,) teas, coffee, sugars, spices, raisins, molasses, hard-ware, crockery-ware, tin-ware, cutlery, clothing of all kinds, boots and shoes from Lynn, calicoes and cottons from Lowell, crapes, silks; also, shawls, scarfs, neck-laces, jewelry, and combs for the ladies; furniture; and in fact, everything that can be imagined, from Chinese fire-works to English cart-wheels—of which we had a dozen pairs with their iron rims on.

The Californians are an idle, thriftless people, and can make nothing for themselves. The country abounds in grapes, yet they buy bad wine made in Boston and brought round by us, at an immense price, and retail it among themselves at a *real* (12½ cents) by the small wine-glass. Their hides too, which they value at two dollars in money, they give for something which costs seventy-five cents in Boston; and buy shoes (as like as not, made of their own hides, which have been carried twice round Cape Horn) at three and four dollars, and "chicken-skin" boots at fifteen dollars apiece. Things sell, on an average, at an advance of nearly three hundred per cent upon the Boston prices. This is partly owing to the heavy duties which the government, in their wisdom, with the intent, no doubt, of keeping the silver in the country, has laid upon imports. These duties, and the enormous expenses of so long a voyage, keep all merchants, but those of heavy capital, from engaging in the trade. Nearly two thirds of all the articles imported into the country from round Cape Horn, for the last six years, have been by the single house of Bryant, Sturgis & Co., to whom our vessel belonged and who have a permanent agent on the coast.

This kind of business was new to us, and we liked it very well for a few days, though we were hard at work every minute from daylight to dark; and sometimes even later.

By being thus continually engaged in transporting passengers with their goods, to and fro, we gained considerable knowledge of the character, dress, and language of the people. The dress of the men was as I have before described it. The women wore gowns of various texture—silks, crape, calicoes, &c.—made after the European style, except that the sleeves were short, leaving the arm bare, and that they were loose about the waist, having no corsets. They wore shoes of kid, or satin; sashes or belts of bright colors; and almost always a necklace and ear-rings. Bonnets they had none. I only saw one on the coast, and that belonged to the wife of an American sea-captain who had settled in San Diego, and had imported the chaotic mass of straw and ribbon, as a choice present to his new wife. They wear their hair (which is almost invariably black, or a very dark brown) long in their necks, sometimes loose, and sometimes in long braids; though the married women often do it up on a high comb. Their only protection against the sun and weather is a large mantle which they put over their heads, drawing it close round their faces, when they go out of doors, which is generally only in pleasant weather. When in the house, or sitting out in front of it, which they often do in fine weather, they usually wear a small scarf or neckerchief of a rich pattern. A band, also, about the top of the head, with a cross, star, or other ornament in front, is common. Their complexions are various, depending—as well as their dress and manner—upon their rank; or, in other words, upon the amount of

Spanish blood they can lay claim to. Those who are of pure Spanish blood, having never intermarried with the aborigines, have clear brunette complexions, and sometimes, even as fair as those of English women. There are but few of these families in California; being mostly those in official stations, or who, on the expiration of their offices, have settled here upon property which they have acquired; and others who have been banished for state offences. These form the aristocracy; intermarrying, and keeping up an exclusive system in every respect. They can be told by their complexions, dress, manner, and also by their speech; for, calling themselves Castilians, they are very ambitious of speaking the pure Castilian language, which is spoken in a somewhat corrupted dialect by the lower classes. From this upper class, they go down by regular shades, growing more and more dark and muddy, until you come to the pure Indian, who runs about with nothing upon him but a small piece of cloth, kept up by a wide leather strap drawn round his waist. Generally speaking, each person's caste is decided by the quality of the blood, which shows itself, too plainly to be concealed, at first sight. Yet the least drop of Spanish blood, if it be only of quatroon or octoon, is sufficient to raise them from the rank of slaves, and entitle them to a suit of clothes—boots, hat, cloak, spurs, long knife, and all complete, though coarse and dirty as may be,—and to call themselves Españolos, and to hold property, if they can get any.

The fondness for dress among the women is excessive, and is often the ruin of many of them. A present of a fine mantle, or of a necklace or pair of ear-rings, gains the favor of the greater part of them. Nothing is more common than to see a woman living in a house of only two rooms, and the ground for a floor, dressed in spangled satin shoes, silk gown, high comb, and gilt, if not gold ear-rings and necklace. If their husbands do not dress them well enough, they will soon receive presents from others. They used to spend whole days on board our vessel, examining the fine clothes and ornaments, and frequently made purchases at a rate which would have made a sempstress or waiting-maid in Boston open her eyes.

Next to the love of dress, I was most struck with the fineness of the voices and beauty of the intonations of both sexes. Every common ruffian-looking fellow, with a slouched hat, blanket cloak, dirty under-dress, and soiled leather leggins, appeared to me to be speaking elegant Spanish. It was a pleasure simply to listen to the sound of the language, before I could attach any meaning to it. They have a good deal of the Creole drawl, but it is varied with an occasional extreme rapidity of utterance, in which they seem to skip from consonant to consonant, until, lighting upon a broad, open vowel, they rest upon that to restore the balance of sound. The women carry this peculiarity of speaking to a much greater extreme than the men, who have more evenness and stateliness of utterance. A common bullock-driver, on horseback, delivering a message, seemed to speak like an ambassador at an audience. In fact, they sometimes appeared to me to be a people on whom a curse had fallen, and stripped them of everything but their pride, their manners, and their voices.

Another thing that surprised me was the quantity of silver that was in circulation. I certainly never saw so much silver at one time in my life, as during the week that we were at Monterey. The truth is, they have no credit system, no banks, and no way of investing money but in cattle. They have no circulating medium but silver and hides—which the sailors call "California bank notes." Everything that they buy they must pay for in one or the other of these things. The hides they bring down dried and doubled, in clumsy ox-carts, or upon mules' backs, and the money they carry tied up in a handkerchief;—fifty, eighty, or an hundred dollars and half dollars.

I had never studied Spanish while at college, and could not speak a word, when at Juan Fernandez; but during the latter part of the passage out, I borrowed a grammar and dictionary from the cabin, and by a continual use of these, and a careful attention to every word that I heard spoken, I soon got a vocabulary together, and began talking for myself. As I soon knew more Spanish than any of the crew, (who indeed knew none at all,) and had been at college and knew Latin, I got the name of a great linguist, and was always sent by the captain and officers to get provisions, or to carry letters and messages to different parts of the town. I was often sent to get something which I could not tell the name of to save my life; but I liked the business, and accordingly never pleaded ignorance. Sometimes I managed to jump below and take a look at my dictionary before going ashore; or else I overhauled some English resident on my way, and got the word from him; and then, by signs, and the help of my Latin and French, contrived to get along. This was a good exercise for me, and no doubt taught me more than I should have learned by months of study and reading; it also gave me opportunities of seeing the customs, characters, and domestic arrangements of the people; beside being a great relief from the monotony of a day spent on board ship.

Monterey, as far as my observation goes, is decidedly the pleasantest and most civilized-looking place in California. In the centre of it is an open square, surrounded by four lines of one-story plastered buildings, with half a dozen cannon in the centre; some mounted, and others not. This is the "Presidio," or fort. Every town has a presidio in its centre; or rather, every presidio has a town built around it; for the forts were first built by the Mexican government, and then the people built near them for protection. The presidio here was entirely open and unfortified. There were several officers with long titles, and about eighty soldiers, but they were poorly paid, fed, clothed and disciplined. The governor-general, or, as he is commonly called, the "general," lives here; which makes it the seat of government. He is appointed by the central government at Mexico, and is the chief civil and military officer. In addition to him, each town has a commandant, who is the chief military officer, and has charge of the fort, and of all transactions with foreigners and foreign vessels; and two or three alcaldes and corregidores, elected by the inhabitants, who are the civil officers. Courts and jurisprudence they have no knowledge of. Small municipal matters are regulated by the alcaldes and corregidores; and everything relating to the general government, to the military, and to foreigners, by the commandants, acting under the governor-general. Capital cases are decided by him, upon personal inspection, if he is near; or upon minutes sent by the proper officers, if the offender is at a distant place. No Protestant has any civil rights, nor can he hold any property, or, indeed, remain more than a few weeks on shore, unless he belong to some vessel. Consequently, the Americans and English who intend to reside here become Catholics, to a man;

the current phrase among them being,—"A man must leave his conscience at Cape Horn."

But to return to Monterey. The houses here, as everywhere else in California, are of one story, built of clay made into large bricks, about a foot and a half square and three or four inches thick, and hardened in the sun. These are cemented together by mortar of the same material, and the whole are of a common dirt-color. The floors are generally of earth, the windows grated and without glass; and the doors, which are seldom shut, open directly into the common room; there being no entries. Some of the more wealthy inhabitants have glass to their windows and board floors; and in Monterey nearly all the houses are plastered on the outside. The better houses, too, have red tiles upon the roofs. The common ones have two or three rooms which open into each other, and are furnished with a bed or two, a few chairs and tables, a looking-glass, a crucifix of some material or other, and small daubs of paintings enclosed in glass, and representing some miracle or martyrdom. They have no chimneys or fire-places in the houses, the climate being such as to make a fire unnecessary; and all their cooking is done in a small cook-house, separated from the house. The Indians, as I have said before, do all the hard work, two or three being attached to each house; and the poorest persons are able to keep one, at least, for they have only to feed them and give them a small piece of coarse cloth and a belt, for the males; and a coarse gown, without shoes or stockings, for the females.

In Monterey there are a number of English and Americans (English or "Ingles" all are called who speak the English language) who have married Californians, become united to the Catholic church, and acquired considerable property. Having more industry, frugality, and enterprise than the natives, they soon get nearly all the trade into their hands. They usually keep shops, in which they retail the goods purchased in larger quantities from our vessels, and also send a good deal into the interior, taking hides in pay, which they again barter with our vessels. In every town on the coast there are foreigners engaged in this kind of trade, while I recollect but two shops kept by natives. The people are naturally suspicious of foreigners, and

they would not be allowed to remain, were it not that they become good Catholics, and by marrying natives, and bringing
up their children as Catholics and Spaniards, and not teaching
them the English language, they quiet suspicion, and even
become popular and leading men. The chief alcaldes in Monterey and Santa Barbara were both Yankees by birth.

The men in Monterey appeared to me to be always on
horseback. Horses are as abundant here as dogs and chickens
were in Juan Fernandez. There are no stables to keep them in,
but they are allowed to run wild and graze wherever they
please, being branded, and having long leather ropes, called
"lassos," attached to their necks and dragging along behind
them, by which they can be easily taken. The men usually
catch one in the morning, throw a saddle and bridle upon him,
and use him for the day, and let him go at night, catching
another the next day. When they go on long journeys, they
ride one horse down, and catch another, throw the saddle and
bridle upon him, and after riding him down, take a third, and
so on to the end of the journey. There are probably no better
riders in the world. They get upon a horse when only four or
five years old, their little legs not long enough to come half
way over his sides; and may almost be said to keep on him
until they have grown to him. The stirrups are covered or boxed
up in front, to prevent their catching when riding through the
woods; and the saddles are large and heavy, strapped very tight
upon the horse, and have large pommels, or loggerheads, in
front, round which the "lasso" is coiled when not in use. They
can hardly go from one house to another without getting on a
horse, there being generally several standing tied to the door-
posts of the little cottages. When they wish to show their activity, they make no use of their stirrups in mounting, but
striking the horse, spring into the saddle as he starts, and
sticking their long spurs into him, go off on the full run. Their
spurs are cruel things, having four or five rowels, each an inch
in length, dull and rusty. The flanks of the horses are often sore
from them, and I have seen men come in from chasing bullock
with their horses' hind legs and quarters covered with blood.
They frequently give exhibitions of their horsemanship, in
races, bull-baitings, &c.; but as we were not ashore during any
holyday, we saw nothing of it. Monterey is also a great place

for cock-fighting, gambling of all sorts, fandangos, and every kind of amusement and knavery. Trappers and hunters, who occasionally arrive here from over the Rocky mountains, with their valuable skins and furs, are often entertained with every sort of amusement and dissipation, until they have wasted their time and their money, and go back, stripped of everything.

Nothing but the character of the people prevents Monterey from becoming a great town. The soil is as rich as man could wish; climate as good as any in the world; water abundant, and situation extremely beautiful. The harbor, too, is a good one, being subject only to one bad wind, the north; and though the holding-ground is not the best, yet I heard of but one vessel's being driven ashore here. That was a Mexican brig, which went ashore a few months before our arrival, and was a total wreck, all the crew but one being drowned. Yet this was from the carelessness or ignorance of the captain, who paid out all his small cable before he let go his other anchor. The ship Lagoda, of Boston, was there at the time, and rode out the gale in safety, without dragging at all, or finding it necessary to strike her top-gallant masts.

The only vessel in port with us was the little Loriotte. I frequently went on board her, and became very well acquainted with her Sandwich Island crew. One of them could speak a little English, and from him I learned a good deal about them. They were well formed and active, with black eyes, intelligent countenances, dark-olive, or, I should rather say, copper complexions, and coarse black hair, but not woolly like the negroes. They appeared to be talking continually. In the forecastle there was a complete Babel. Their language is extremely guttural, and not pleasant at first, but improves as you hear it more, and is said to have great capacity. They use a good deal of gesticulation, and are exceedingly animated, saying with their might what their tongues find to say. They are complete water-dogs, and therefore very good in boating. It is for this reason that there are so many of them on the coast of California; they being very good hands in the surf. They are also quick and active in the rigging, and good hands in warm weather; but those who have been with them round Cape Horn, and in high latitudes, say that they are useless in cold weather. In their dress they are precisely like our sailors. In addition to these Islanders, the vessel had two English sailors, who acted as boatswains over the Islanders, and took care of the rigging. One of them I shall always remember as the best specimen of the thorough-bred English sailor that I ever saw. He had been to sea from a boy, having served a regular apprenticeship of seven years, as all English sailors are obliged to do, and was then about four or five and twenty. He was tall; but you only perceived it when he was standing by the side of others, for the great breadth of his shoulders and chest made him appear but little above the middle height. His chest was as deep as it was wide; his arm like that of Hercules; and his hand "the fist of a tar—every hair a rope-yarn." With all this he had one of the pleasantest smiles I ever saw. His cheeks were of a handsome brown; his teeth brilliantly white; and his hair, of a raven black, waved in loose curls all over his head, and fine, open forehead; and his eyes he might have sold to a duchess at the price of diamonds, for their brilliancy. As for their color, they were like the Irishman's pig, which would not stay to be counted; every change of position and light seemed to give them a new hue; but their prevailing color was black, or nearly so. Take him with his well-varnished black tarpaulin stuck upon the back of his head; his long locks coming down almost into his eyes; his white duck trowsers and shirt; blue jacket; and black kerchief, tied loosely round his neck; and he was a fine specimen of manly beauty. On his broad chest he had stamped with India ink "Parting moments;"—a ship ready to sail; a boat on the beach; and a girl and her sailor lover taking their farewell. Underneath were printed the initials of his own name, and two other letters, standing for some name which he knew better than I did. This was very well done, having been executed by a man who made it his business to print with India ink, for sailors, at Havre. On one of his broad arms he had the crucifixion, and on the other the sign of the "foul anchor."

He was very fond of reading, and we lent him most of the books which we had in the forecastle, which he read and re-turned to us the next time we fell in with him. He had a good deal of information, and his captain said he was a perfect sea-man, and worth his weight in gold on board a vessel, in fair weather and in foul. His strength must have been immense, and he had the sight of a vulture. It is strange that one should be so minute in the description of an unknown, outcast sailor, whom one may never see again, and whom no one may care to hear about; but so it is. Some people we see under no remarkable circumstances, but whom, for some reason or other, we never forget. He called himself Bill Jackson; and I know no one of all my accidental acquaintances to whom I would more gladly give a shake of the hand than to him. Whoever falls in with him will find a handsome, hearty fellow, and a good shipmate.

Sunday came again while we were at Monterey, but, as before, it brought us no holyday. The people on shore dressed themselves and came off in greater numbers than ever, and we were employed all day in boating and breaking out cargo, so that we had hardly time to eat. Our ci-devant second mate, who was determined to get liberty if it was to be had, dressed himself in a long coat and black hat, and polished his shoes, and went aft and asked to go ashore. He could not have done a more imprudent thing; for he knew that no liberty would be given; and besides, sailors, however sure they may be of having liberty granted them, always go aft in their working clothes, to appear as though they had no reason to expect anything, and then wash, dress, and shave, after they have got their liberty. But this poor fellow was always getting into hot water, and if there was a wrong way of doing a thing, was sure to hit upon it. We looked to see him go aft, knowing pretty well what his reception would be. The captain was walking the quarter-deck, smoking his morning cigar, and Foster went as far as the break of the deck, and there waited for him to notice him. The captain took two or three turns, and then walking directly up to him, surveyed him from head to foot, and lifting up his fore finger, said a word or two, in a tone too low for us to hear, but which had a magical effect upon poor Foster. He walked forward, sprang into the forecastle, and in a moment more made his appearance in his common clothes, and went quietly to work again. What the captain said to him, we never could get him to tell, but it certainly changed him outwardly and inwardly in a most surprising manner.

Chapter XIV

AFTER a few days, finding the trade beginning to slacken, we hove our anchor up, set our topsails, ran the stars and stripes up to the peak, fired a gun, which was returned from the presidio, and left the little town astern, running out of the bay, and bearing down the coast again, for Santa Barbara. As we were now going to leeward, we had a fair wind and a plenty of it. After doubling Point Pinos, we bore up, set studding-sails alow and aloft, and were walking off at the rate of eight or nine knots, promising to traverse in twenty-four hours the distance which we were nearly three weeks in traversing on the passage up. We passed Point Conception at a flying rate, the wind blowing so that it would have seemed half a gale to us, if we had been going the other way and close hauled. As we drew near the islands off Santa Barbara, it died away a little, but we came-to at our old anchoring-ground in less than thirty hours from the time of leaving Monterey.

Here everything was pretty much as we left it—the large bay without a vessel in it; the surf roaring and rolling in upon the beach; the white mission; the dark town, and the high, treeless mountains. Here, too, we had our south-easter tacks aboard again,—slip-ropes, buoy-ropes, sails furled with reefs in them, and rope-yarns for gaskets. We lay here about a fortnight, employed in landing goods and taking off hides, occasionally, when the surf was not high; but there did not appear to be one half the business doing here that there was in Monterey. In fact, so far as we were concerned, the town might almost as well have been in the middle of the Cordilleras. We lay at a distance of three miles from the beach, and the town was nearly a mile farther; so that we saw little or nothing of it. Occasionally we landed a few goods, which were taken away by Indians in large, clumsy ox-carts, with the yoke on the ox's neck instead of under it, and with small solid wheels. A few hides were brought down, which we carried off in the California style. This we had now got pretty well accustomed to; and hardened to also; for it does require a little hardening, even to the toughest.

The hides are always brought down dry, or they would not be received. When they are taken from the animal, they have holes cut in the ends, and are staked out, and thus dried in the sun without shrinking. They are then doubled once, lengthwise, with the hair side usually in, and sent down upon mules or in carts, and piled above high-water mark; and then we take them upon our heads, one at a time, or two, if they are small, and wade out with them and throw them into the boat, which, as there are no wharves, we usually kept anchored by a small kedge, or keeleg, just outside of the surf. We all provided ourselves with thick Scotch caps, which would be soft to the head, and at the same time protect it; for we soon found that however it might look or feel at first, the "head-work" was the only system for California. For besides that the seas, breaking high, often obliged us to carry the hides so, in order to keep them dry, we found that, as they were very large and heavy, and nearly as stiff as boards, it was the only way that we could carry them with any convenience to ourselves. Some of the crew tried other expedients, saying that that looked too much like West India negroes; but they all came to it at last. The great art is in getting them on the head. We had to take them from the ground, and as they were often very heavy, and as wide as the arms could stretch and easily taken by the wind, we used to have some trouble with them. I have often been laughed at myself, and joined in laughing at others, pitching themselves down in the sand, trying to swing a large hide upon their heads, or nearly blown over with one in a little gust of wind. The captain made it harder for us, by telling us that it was "California fashion" to carry two on the head at a time; and as he insisted upon it, and we did not wish to be outdone by other vessels, we carried two for the first few months; but after falling in with a few other "hide droghers," and finding that they carried only one at a time, we "knocked off" the extra one, and thus made our duty somewhat easier.

After we had got our heads used to the weight, and had learned the true California style of *tossing a hide*, we could carry off two or three hundred in a short time, without much trouble; but it was always wet work, and, if the beach was stony, bad for our feet; for we, of course, always went barefooted on this duty, as no shoes could stand such constant wetting with salt water. Then, too, we had a long pull of three miles, with a loaded boat, which often took a couple of hours.

We had now got well settled down into our harbor duties, which, as they are a good deal different from those at sea, it may be well enough to describe. In the first place, all hands are called at daylight, or rather—especially if the days are short— before daylight, as soon as the first grey of the morning. The cook makes his fire in the galley; the steward goes about his work in the cabin; and the crew rig the head pump, and wash down the decks. The chief mate is always on deck, but takes no active part, all the duty coming upon the second mate, who has to roll up his trowsers and paddle about decks barefooted, like the rest of the crew. The washing, swabbing, squilgeeing, &c., lasts, or is made to last, until eight o'clock, when break-fast is ordered, fore and aft. After breakfast, for which half an hour is allowed, the boats are lowered down, and made fast astern, or out to the swinging booms, by geswarps, and the crew are turned-to upon their day's work. This is various, and its character depends upon circumstances. There is always more or less of boating, in small boats; and if heavy goods are to be taken ashore, or hides are brought down to the beach for us, then all hands are sent ashore with an officer in the long-boat. Then there is always a good deal to be done in the hold: goods to be broken out; and cargo to be shifted, to make room for hides, or to keep the trim of the vessel. In addition to this, the usual work upon the rigging must be going on. There is a good deal of the latter kind of work which can only be done when the vessel is in port;—and then everything must be kept taught and in good order; spun-yarn made; chafing gear repaired; and all the other ordinary work. The great difference between sea and harbor duty is in the division of time. Instead of having a watch on deck and a watch below, as at sea, all hands are at work together, except at meal times, from daylight till dark; and at night an "anchor-watch" is kept, which consists of only two at a time; the whole crew taking turns. An hour is allowed for dinner, and at dark, the decks are cleared up; the boats hoisted; supper ordered; and at eight, the lights put out, except in the binnacle, where the glass stands; and the anchor-watch is set. Thus, when at anchor, the crew have more time at night, (standing watch only about two hours,) but have no time to themselves in the day; so that reading, mending clothes, &c., has to be put off until Sunday, which is usually given. Some religious captains give their crews Saturday afternoons to do their washing and mending in, so that they may have their Sundays free. This is a good arrangement, and does much toward creating the preference sailors usually show for religious vessels. We were well satisfied if we got Sunday to ourselves, for, if any hides came down on that day, as was often the case when they were brought from a distance, we were obliged to bring them off, which usually took half a day; and as we now lived on fresh beef, and ate one bullock a week, the animal was almost always brought down on Sunday, and we had to go ashore, kill it, dress it, and bring it aboard, which was another interruption. Then, too, our common day's work was protracted and made more fatiguing by hides coming down late in the afternoon, which sometimes kept us at work in the surf by star-light, with the prospect of pulling on board, and stowing them all away, before supper.

But all these little vexations and labors would have been nothing,—they would have been passed by as the common evils of a sea-life, which every sailor, who is a man, will go through without complaint,—were it not for the uncertainty, or worse than uncertainty, which hung over the nature and length of our voyage. Here we were, in a little vessel, with a small crew, on a half-civilized coast, at the ends of the earth, and with a prospect of remaining an indefinite period, two or three years at the least. When we left Boston we supposed that it was to be a voyage of eighteen months, or two years, at most; but upon arriving on the coast, we learned something more of the trade, and found that in the scarcity of hides, which was yearly greater and greater, it would take us a year, at least, to collect our own cargo, beside the passage out and home; and that we were also to collect a cargo for a large ship belonging to the same firm, which was soon to come on the coast, and to which we were to act as tender. We had heard rumors of such a ship to follow us, which had leaked out from the captain and mate, but we passed them by as mere "yarns," till our arrival, when they were confirmed by the letters which we brought from the owners to their agent. The ship California, belonging to the same firm, had been nearly two years on the coast; had collected a full cargo, and was now at San Diego, from which port she was expected to sail in a few weeks for Boston; and we were to collect all the hides we could, and deposite them at San Diego, when the new ship, which would carry forty thousand, was to be filled and sent home; and then we were to begin anew, and collect our own cargo. Here was a gloomy prospect before us, indeed. The California had been twenty months on the coast, and the Lagoda, a smaller ship, carrying only thirty-one or thirty-two thousand, had been two years getting her cargo; and we were to collect a cargo of forty thousand beside our own, which would be twelve or fifteen thousand; and hides were said to be growing scarcer. Then, too, this ship, which had been to us a worse phantom than any flying Dutchman, was no phantom, or ideal thing, but had been reduced to a certainty; so much so that a name was given her, and it was said that she was to be the Alert, a well-known Indiaman, which was expected in Boston in a few months, when we sailed. There could be no doubt, and all looked black enough. Hints were thrown out about three years and four years;—the older sailors said they never should see Boston again, but should lay their bones in California; and a cloud seemed to hang over the whole voyage. Besides, we were not provided for so long a voyage, and clothes, and all sailors' necessaries, were excessively dear—three or four hundred per cent. advance upon the Boston prices. This was bad enough for them; but still worse was it for me, who did not mean to be a sailor for life; having intended only to be gone eighteen months or two years. Three or four years would make me a sailor in every respect, mind and habits, as well as body—nolens volens; and would put all my companions so far ahead of me that college and a profession would be in vain to think of; and I made up my mind that, feel as I might, a sailor I must be, and to be master of a vessel, must be the height of my ambition.

Beside the length of the voyage, and the hard and exposed life, we were at the ends of the earth; on a coast almost solitary; in a country where there is neither law nor gospel, and where sailors are at their captain's mercy, there being no American consul, or any one to whom a complaint could be made. We lost all interest in the voyage; cared nothing about the cargo, which we were only collecting for others; began to patch our clothes; and felt as though we were fixed beyond all hope of change.

In addition to, and perhaps partly as a consequence of, this state of things, there was trouble brewing on board the vessel. Our *mate* (as the first mate is always called, *par excellence*) was a worthy man;—a more honest, upright, and kind-hearted man I never saw; but he was too good for the mate of a merchant-man. He was not the man to call a sailor a "son of a b—h," and knock him down with a handspike. He wanted the energy and spirit for such a voyage as ours, and for such a captain. Captain T—— was a vigorous, energetic fellow. As sailors say, "he had n't a lazy bone in him." He was made of steel and whalebone. He was a man to "toe the mark," and to make every one else step up to it. During all the time that I was with him, I never saw him sit down on deck. He was always active and driving; severe in his discipline, and expected the same of his officers. The mate not being enough of a *driver* for him, and being perhaps too easy with the crew, he was dissatisfied with him, became suspicious that discipline was getting re-laxed, and began to interfere in everything. He drew the reins taughter; and as, in all quarrels between officers, the sailors side with the one who treats them best, he became suspicious of the crew. He saw that everything went wrong—that nothing was done "with a will;" and in his attempt to remedy the diffi-culty by severity, he made everything worse. We were in every respect unfortunately situated. Captain, officers, and crew, en-tirely unfitted for one another; and every circumstance and event was like a two-edged sword, and cut both ways. The length of the voyage, which made us dissatisfied, made the cap-tain, at the same time, feel the necessity of order and strict dis-cipline; and the nature of the country, which caused us to feel that we had nowhere to go for redress, but were entirely at the mercy of a hard master, made the captain feel, on the other hand, that he must depend entirely upon his own resources. Severity created discontent, and signs of discontent provoked severity. Then, too, ill-treatment and dissatisfaction are no "linimenta laborum;" and many a time have I heard the sailors say that they should not mind the length of the voyage, and the hardships, if they were only kindly treated, and if they could feel that something was done to make things lighter and easier. We felt as though our situation was a call upon our superiors to give us occasional relaxations, and to make our yoke easier. But the contrary policy was pursued. We were kept at work all day when in port; which, together with a watch at night, made us glad to turn-in as soon as we got below. Thus we got no time for reading, or—which was of more importance to us— for washing and mending our clothes. And then, when we were at sea, sailing from port to port, instead of giving us "watch and watch," as was the custom on board every other vessel on the coast, we were all kept on deck and at work, rain or shine, making spun-yarn and rope, and at other work in good weather, and picking oakum, when it was too wet for anything else. All hands were called to "come up and see it rain," and kept on deck hour after hour in a drenching rain, standing round the deck so far apart as to prevent our talking with one another, with our tarpaulins and oil-cloth jackets on, picking old rope to pieces, or laying up gaskets and robands. This was often done, too, when we were lying in port with two anchors down, and no necessity for more than one man on deck as a look-out. This is what is called "hazing" a crew, and "working their old iron up."

While lying at Santa Barbara, we encountered another south-easter; and like the first, it came on in the night; the great black clouds coming round from the southward, covering the mountain, and hanging down over the town, appearing almost to rest upon the roofs of the houses. We made sail, slipped our cable, cleared the point, and beat about, for four days, in the offing, under close sail, with continual rain and high seas and winds. No wonder, thought we, they have no rain in the other seasons, for enough seemed to have fallen in those four days to last through a common summer. On the fifth day it cleared up, after a few hours, as is usual, of rain coming down like a four hours' shower-bath, and we found ourselves drifted nearly ten leagues from the anchorage; and having light head winds, we did not return until the sixth day. Having recovered our anchor, we made preparations for getting under weigh to go down to leeward. We had hoped to go directly to San Diego, and thus fall in with the California before she sailed for Boston; but our orders were to stop at an intermediate port called San

Pedro, and as we were to lie there a week or two, and the California was to sail in a few days, we lost the opportunity. Just before sailing, the captain took on board a short, red-haired, round-shouldered, vulgar-looking fellow, who had lost one eye, and squinted with the other, and introducing him as *Mr.* Russell, told us that he was an officer on board. This was too bad. We had lost overboard, on the passage, one of the best of our number, another had been taken from us and appointed clerk, and thus weakened and reduced, instead of shipping some hands to make our work easier, he had put another officer over us, to watch and drive us. We had now four officers, and only six in the forecastle. This was bringing her too much down by the stern for our comfort.

Leaving Santa Barbara, we coasted along down, the country appearing level or moderately uneven, and, for the most part, sandy and treeless; until, doubling a high, sandy point, we let go our anchor at a distance of three or three and a half miles from shore. It was like a vessel, bound to Halifax, coming to anchor on the Grand Banks; for the shore being low, appeared to be at a greater distance than it actually was, and we thought we might as well have staid at Santa Barbara, and sent our boat down for the hides. The land was of a clayey consistency, and, as far as the eye could reach, entirely bare of trees and even shrubs; and there was no sign of a town,—not even a house to be seen. What brought us into such a place, we could not conceive. No sooner had we come to anchor, than the slip-rope, and the other preparations for south-easters, were got ready; and there was reason enough for it, for we lay exposed to every wind that could blow, except the north-west, and that came over a flat country with a range of more than a league of water. As soon as everything was snug on board, the boat was lowered, and we pulled ashore, our new officer, who had been several times in the port before, taking the place of steersman. As we drew in, we found the tide low, and the rocks and stones, covered with kelp and sea-weed, lying bare for the distance of nearly an eighth of a mile. Picking our way barefooted over these, we came to what is called the landing-place, at high-water mark. The soil was as it appeared at first, loose and clayey, and except the stalks of the mustard plant, there was no vegetation. Just in front of the landing, and immediately over

it, was a small hill, which, from its being not more than thirty
or forty feet high, we had not perceived from our anchorage.
Over this hill we saw three men coming down, dressed partly
like sailors and partly like Californians; one of them having on
a pair of untanned leather trowsers and a red baize shirt. When
they came down to us, we found that they were Englishmen,
and they told us that they had belonged to a small Mexican
brig which had been driven ashore here in a south-easter, and
now lived in a small house just over the hill. Going up this hill
with them, we saw, just behind it, a small, low building, with
one room, containing a fire-place, cooking-apparatus, &c.,
and the rest of it unfinished, and used as a place to store hides
and goods. This, they told us, was built by some traders in the
Pueblo, (a town about thirty miles in the interior, to which
this was the port,) and used by them as a storehouse, and also
as a lodging-place when they came down to trade with the vessels. These three men were employed by them to keep the
house in order, and to look out for the things stored in it.
They said that they had been there nearly a year; had nothing
to do most of the time, living upon beef, hard bread, and frijoles (a peculiar kind of bean very abundant in California). The
nearest house, they told us, was a Rancho, or cattle-farm, about
three miles off; and one of them went up, at the request of our
officer, to order a horse to be sent down, with which the
agent, who was on board, might go up to the Pueblo. From
one of them, who was an intelligent English sailor, I learned a
good deal, in a few minutes' conversation, about the place, its
trade, and the news from the southern ports. San Diego, he
said, was about eighty miles to the leeward of San Pedro; that
they had heard from there, by a Spaniard who came up on
horseback, that the California had sailed for Boston, and that
the Lagoda, which had been in San Pedro only a few weeks
before, was taking in her cargo for Boston. The Ayacucho was
also there, loading for Callao, and the little Loriotte, which
had run directly down from Monterey, where we left her. San
Diego, he told me, was a small, snug place, having very little
trade, but decidedly the best harbor on the coast, being completely land-locked, and the water as smooth as a duck-pond.
This was the depot for all the vessels engaged in the trade; each
one having a large house there, built of rough boards, in which

they stowed their hides, as fast as they collected them in their trips up and down the coast, and when they had procured a full cargo, spent a few weeks there taking it in, smoking ship, supplying wood and water, and making other preparations for the voyage home. The Lagoda was now about this business. When we should be about it, was more than I could tell; two years, at least, I thought to myself.

I also learned, to my surprise, that the desolate-looking place we were in was the best place on the whole coast for hides. It was the only port for a distance of eighty miles, and about thirty miles in the interior was a fine plane country, filled with herds of cattle, in the centre of which was the Pueblo de los Angelos—the largest town in California—and several of the wealthiest missions; to all of which San Pedro was the sea-port.

Having made our arrangements for a horse to take the agent to the Pueblo the next day, we picked our way again over the green, slippery rocks, and pulled aboard. By the time we reached the vessel, which was so far off that we could hardly see her, in the increasing darkness, the boats were hoisted up, and the crew at supper. Going down into the forecastle, eating our supper, and lighting our cigars and pipes, we had, as usual, to tell all we had seen or heard ashore. We all agreed that it was the worst place we had seen yet, especially for getting off hides, and our lying off at so great a distance looked as though it was bad for south-easters. After a few disputes as to whether we should have to carry our goods up the hill, or not, we talked of San Diego, the probability of seeing the Lagoda before she sailed, &c. &c.

The next day we pulled the agent ashore, and he went up to visit the Pueblo and the neighboring missions; and in a few days, as the result of his labors, large ox-carts, and droves of mules, loaded with hides, were seen coming over the flat country. We loaded our long-boat with goods of all kinds, light and heavy, and pulled ashore. After landing and rolling them over the stones upon the beach, we stopped, waiting for the carts to come down the hill and take them; but the captain soon settled the matter by ordering us to carry them all up to the top, saying that, that was "California fashion." So what the oxen would not do, we were obliged to do. The hill was low, but steep, and the earth, being clayey and wet with the recent

rains, was but bad holding-ground for our feet. The heavy barrels and casks we rolled up with some difficulty, getting behind
and putting our shoulders to them; now and then our feet
slipping, added to the danger of the casks rolling back upon
us. But the greatest trouble was with the large boxes of sugar.
These, we had to place upon oars, and lifting them up, rest the
oars upon our shoulders, and creep slowly up the hill with the
gait of a funeral procession. After an hour or two of hard work,
we got them all up, and found the carts standing full of hides,
which we had to unload, and also to load again with our own
goods; the lazy Indians, who came down with them, squatting
down on their hams, looking on, doing nothing, and when we
asked them to help us, only shaking their heads, or drawling
out "no quiero."

Having loaded the carts, we started up the Indians, who
went off, one on each side of the oxen, with long sticks, sharpened at the end, to punch them with. This is one of the means
of saving labor in California;—two Indians to two oxen. Now,
the hides were to be got down; and for this purpose, we
brought the boat round to a place where the hill was steeper,
and threw them down, letting them slide over the slope. Many
of them lodged, and we had to let ourselves down and set
them agoing again; and in this way got covered with dust,
and our clothes torn. After we had got them all down, we
were obliged to take them on our heads, and walk over the
stones, and through the water, to the boat. The water and the
stones together would wear out a pair of shoes a day, and as
shoes were very scarce and very dear, we were compelled to go
barefooted. At night, we went on board, having had the hardest and most disagreeable day's work that we had yet experienced. For several days, we were employed in this manner,
until we had landed forty or fifty tons of goods, and brought
on board about two thousand hides; when the trade began to
slacken, and we were kept at work, on board, during the latter part of the week, either in the hold or upon the rigging.
On Thursday night, there was a violent blow from the northward, but as this was off-shore, we had only to let go our other
anchor and hold on. We were called up at night to send down
the royal-yards. It was as dark as a pocket, and the vessel
pitching at her anchors. I went up to the fore, and my friend

S——, to the main, and we soon had them down "ship-shape and Bristol fashion;" for, as we had now got used to our duty aloft, everything above the cross-trees was left to us, who were the youngest of the crew, except one boy.

Chapter XV

FOR several days the captain seemed very much out of humor. Nothing went right, or fast enough for him. He quarrelled with the cook, and threatened to flog him for throwing wood on deck; and had a dispute with the mate about reeving a Spanish burton; the mate saying that he was right, and had been taught how to do it by a man *who was a sailor!* This, the captain took in dudgeon, and they were at sword's points at once. But his displeasure was chiefly turned against a large, heavy-moulded fellow from the Middle states, who was called Sam. This man hesitated in his speech, and was rather slow in his motions, but was a pretty good sailor, and always seemed to do his best; but the captain took a dislike to him, thought he was surly, and lazy; and "if you once give a dog a bad name"—as the sailor-phrase is—"he may as well jump overboard." The captain found fault with everything this man did, and hazed him for dropping a marline-spike from the main-yard, where he was at work. This, of course, was an accident, but it was set down against him. The captain was on board all day Friday, and everything went on hard and disagreeably. "The more you drive a man, the less he will do," was as true with us as with any other people. We worked late Friday night, and were turned-to, early Saturday morning. About ten o'clock the captain ordered our new officer, Russell, who by this time had become thoroughly disliked by all the crew, to get the gig ready to take him ashore. John, the Swede, was sitting in the boat alongside, and Russell and myself were standing by the main hatchway, waiting for the captain, who was down in the hold, where the crew were at work, when we heard his voice raised in violent dispute with somebody, whether it was with the mate, or one of the crew, I could not tell; and then came blows and scuffling. I ran to the side and beckoned to John, who came up, and we leaned down the hatchway; and though we could see no one, yet we knew that the captain had the advantage, for his voice was loud and clear—

"You see your condition! You see your condition! Will you

ever give me any more of your *jaw?*" No answer; and then
came wrestling and heaving, as though the man was trying to
turn him. "You may as well keep still, for I have got you," said
the captain. Then came the question, "Will you ever give me
any more of your jaw?"

"I never gave you any, sir," said Sam; for it was his voice that
we heard, though low and half choked.

"That's not what I ask you. Will you ever be impudent to
me again?"

"I never have been, sir," said Sam.

"Answer my question, or I'll make a spread eagle of you! I'll
flog you, by G–d."

"I'm no negro slave," said Sam.

"Then I'll make you one," said the captain; and he came to
the hatchway, and sprang on deck, threw off his coat, and
rolling up his sleeves, called out to the mate—"Seize that man
up, Mr. A——! Seize him up! Make a spread eagle of him! I'll
teach you all who is master aboard!"

The crew and officers followed the captain up the hatchway,
and after repeated orders the mate laid hold of Sam, who made
no resistance, and carried him to the gangway.

"What are you going to flog that man for, sir?" said John,
the Swede, to the captain.

Upon hearing this, the captain turned upon him, but
knowing him to be quick and resolute, he ordered the steward
to bring the irons, and calling upon Russell to help him, went
up to John.

"Let me alone," said John. "I'm willing to be put in irons.
You need not use any force;" and putting out his hands, the
captain slipped the irons on, and sent him aft to the quarter-
deck. Sam by this time was *seized up*, as it is called, that is,
placed against the shrouds, with his wrists made fast to the
shrouds, his jacket off, and his back exposed. The captain stood
on the break of the deck, a few feet from him, and a little
raised, so as to have a good swing at him, and held in his hand
the bight of a thick, strong rope. The officers stood round,
and the crew grouped together in the waist. All these preparations made me feel sick and almost faint, angry and excited
as I was. A man—a human being, made in God's likeness—
fastened up and flogged like a beast! A man, too, whom I had

lived with and eaten with for months, and knew almost as well
as a brother. The first and almost uncontrollable impulse was
resistance. But what was to be done? The time for it had gone
by. The two best men were fast, and there were only two beside myself, and a small boy of ten or twelve years of age. And
then there were (beside the captain) three officers, steward,
agent, and clerk. But beside the numbers, what is there for
sailors to do? If they resist, it is mutiny; and if they succeed,
and take the vessel, it is piracy. If they ever yield again, their
punishment must come; and if they do not yield, they are pirates for life. If a sailor resist his commander, he resists the law,
and piracy or submission, are his only alternatives. Bad as it
was, it must be borne. It is what a sailor ships for. Swinging the
rope over his head, and bending his body so as to give it full
force, the captain brought it down upon the poor fellow's back.
Once, twice,—six times. "Will you ever give me any more of
your jaw?" The man writhed with pain, but said not a word.
Three times more. This was too much, and he muttered something which I could not hear; this brought as many more as
the man could stand; when the captain ordered him to be cut
down, and to go forward.

"Now for you," said the captain, making up to John and
taking his irons off. As soon as he was loose, he ran forward to
the forecastle. "Bring that man aft," shouted the captain. The
second mate, who had been a shipmate of John's, stood still in
the waist, and the mate walked slowly forward; but our third
officer, anxious to show his zeal sprang forward over the windlass, and laid hold of John; but he soon threw him from him.
At this moment I would have given worlds for the power to
help the poor fellow; but it was all in vain. The captain stood
on the quarter-deck, bareheaded, his eyes flashing with rage,
and his face as red as blood, swinging the rope, and calling out
to his officers, "Drag him aft!—Lay hold of him! I'll *sweeten*
him!" &c. &c. The mate now went forward and told John
quietly to go aft; and he, seeing resistance in vain, threw the
blackguard third mate from him; said he would go aft of himself; that they should not drag him; and went up to the gangway and held out his hands; but as soon as the captain began
to make him fast, the indignity was too much, and he began to
resist; but the mate and Russell holding him, he was soon

seized up. When he was made fast, he turned to the captain, who stood turning up his sleeves and getting ready for the blow, and asked him what he was to be flogged for. "Have I ever refused my duty, sir? Have you ever known me to hang back, or to be insolent, or not to know my work?"

"No," said the captain, "it is not that that I flog you for; I flog you for your interference—for asking questions."

"Can't a man ask a question here without being flogged?"

"No," shouted the captain; "nobody shall open his mouth aboard this vessel, but myself;" and began laying the blows upon his back, swinging half round between each blow, to give it full effect. As he went on, his passion increased, and he danced about the deck, calling out as he swung the rope,—"If you want to know what I flog you for, I'll tell you. It's because I like to do it!—because I like to do it!—It suits me! That's what I do it for!"

The man writhed under the pain, until he could endure it no longer, when he called out, with an exclamation more common among foreigners than with us—"Oh, Jesus Christ! Oh, Jesus Christ!"

"Don't call on Jesus Christ," shouted the captain; "*he can't help you. Call on Captain T——. He's the man! He can help you! Jesus Christ can't help you now!*"

At these words, which I never shall forget, my blood ran cold. I could look on no longer. Disgusted, sick, and horror-struck, I turned away and leaned over the rail, and looked down into the water. A few rapid thoughts of my own situation, and of the prospect of future revenge, crossed my mind; but the falling of the blows and the cries of the man called me back at once. At length they ceased, and turning round, I found that the mate, at a signal from the captain, had cut him down. Almost doubled up with pain, the man walked slowly forward, and went down into the forecastle. Every one else stood still at his post, while the captain, swelling with rage and with the importance of his achievement, walked the quarter-deck, and at each turn, as he came forward, calling out to us,—"You see your condition! You see where I've got you all, and you know what to expect!"—"You've been mistaken in me—you didn't know what I was! Now you know what I am!"—"I'll make you toe the mark, every soul of you, or I'll flog you all, fore and aft, from the boy, up!"—"You've got a driver over you! Yes, a *slave-driver—a negro-driver*! I'll see who'll tell me he is n't a negro slave!" With this and the like matter, equally calculated to quiet us, and to allay any apprehensions of future trouble, he entertained us for about ten minutes, when he went below. Soon after, John came aft, with his bare back covered with stripes and wales in every direction, and dreadfully swollen, and asked the steward to ask the captain to let him have some salve, or balsam, to put upon it. "No," said the captain, who heard him from below; "tell him to put his shirt on; that's the best thing for him; and pull me ashore in the boat. Nobody is going to lay-up on board this vessel." He then called to Mr. Russell to take those two men and two others in the boat, and pull him ashore. I went for one. The two men could hardly bend their backs, and the captain called to them to "give way," "give way!" but finding they did their best, he let them alone. The agent was in the stern sheets, but during the whole pull—a league or more—not a word was spoken. We landed; the captain, agent, and officer went up to the house, and left us with the boat. I, and the man with me, staid near the boat, while John and Sam walked slowly away, and sat down on the rocks. They talked some time together, but at length separated, each sitting alone. I had some fears of John. He was a foreigner, and violently tempered, and under suffering; and he had his knife with him, and the captain was to come down alone to the boat. But nothing happened; and we went quietly on board. The captain was probably armed, and if either of them had lifted a hand against him, they would have had nothing before them but flight, and starvation in the woods of California, or capture by the soldiers and Indian blood-hounds, whom the offer of twenty dollars would have set upon them.

After the day's work was done, we went down into the forecastle, and ate our plain supper; but not a word was spoken. It was Saturday night; but there was no song—no "sweethearts and wives." A gloom was over everything. The two men lay in their berths, groaning with pain, and we all turned in, but for myself, not to sleep. A sound coming now and then from the berths of the two men showed that they were awake, as awake they must have been, for they could hardly lie in one posture a moment; the dim, swinging lamp of the forecastle shed its light over the dark hole in which we lived; and many and various reflections and purposes coursed through my mind. I thought of our situation, living under a tyranny; of the character of the country we were in; of the length of the voyage, and of the uncertainty attending our return to America; and then, if we should return, of the prospect of obtaining justice and satisfaction for these poor men; and vowed that if God should ever give me the means, I would do something to redress the grievances and relieve the sufferings of that poor class of beings, of whom I then was one.

The next day was Sunday. We worked as usual, washing decks, &c., until breakfast-time. After breakfast, we pulled the captain ashore, and finding some hides there which had been brought down the night before, he ordered me to stay ashore and watch them, saying that the boat would come again before night. They left me, and I spent a quiet day on the hill, eating dinner with the three men at the little house. Unfortunately, they had no books, and after talking with them and walking about, I began to grow tired of doing nothing. The little brig, the home of so much hardship and suffering, lay in the offing, almost as far as one could see; and the only other thing which broke the surface of the great bay was a small, desolate-looking island, steep and conical, of a clayey soil, and without the sign of vegetable life upon it; yet which had a peculiar and melancholy interest to me, for on the top of it were buried the remains of an Englishman, the commander of a small merchant brig, who died while lying in this port. It was always a solemn and interesting spot to me. There it stood, desolate, and in the midst of desolation; and there were the remains of one who died and was buried alone and friendless. Had it been a common burying-place, it would have been nothing. The single body corresponded well with the solitary character of everything around. It was the only thing in California from which I could ever extract anything like poetry. Then, too, the man died far from home; without a friend near him; by poison, it was suspected, and no one to inquire into it; and without proper funeral rites; the mate, (as I was told,) glad to have him out of the way, hurrying him up the hill and into the ground, without a word or a prayer.

I looked anxiously for a boat, during the latter part of the afternoon, but none came; until toward sundown, when I saw a speck on the water, and as it drew near, I found it was the gig, with the captain. The hides, then, were not to go off. The captain came up the hill, with a man, bringing my monkey jacket and a blanket. He looked pretty black, but inquired whether I had enough to eat; told me to make a house out of the hides, and keep myself warm, as I should have to sleep there among them, and to keep good watch over them. I got a moment to speak to the man who brought my jacket.

"How do things go aboard?" said I.

"Bad enough," said he; "hard work and not a kind word spoken."

"What," said I, "have you been at work all day?"

"Yes! no more Sunday for us. Everything has been moved in the hold, from stem to stern, and from the water-ways to the keelson."

I went up to the house to supper. We had frijoles, (the perpetual food of the Californians, but which, when well cooked, are the best bean in the world,) coffee made of burnt wheat, and hard bread. After our meal, the three men sat down by the light of a tallow candle, with a pack of greasy Spanish cards, to the favorite game of "treinta uno," a sort of Spanish "everlasting." I left them and went out to take up my bivouack among the hides. It was now dark; the vessel was hidden from sight, and except the three men in the house, there was not a living soul within a league. The coati (a wild animal of a nature and appearance between that of the fox and the wolf) set up their sharp, quick bark, and two owls, at the end of two distant points running out into the bay, on different sides of the hill where I lay, kept up their alternate, dismal notes. I had heard the sound before at night, but did not know what it was, until one of the men, who came down to look at my quarters, told me it was the owl. Mellowed by the distance, and heard alone, at night, I thought it was the most melancholy, boding sound I had ever heard. Through nearly all the night they kept it up, answering one another slowly, at regular intervals. This was relieved by the noisy coati, some of which came quite near to my quarters, and were not very pleasant neighbors. The next morning, before sunrise, the long-boat came ashore, and the hides were taken off.

We lay at San Pedro about a week, engaged in taking off hides and in other labors, which had now become our regular duties. I spent one more day on the hill, watching a quantity of hides and goods, and this time succeeded in finding a part of a volume of Scott's Pirate, in a corner of the house; but it failed me at a most interesting moment, and I betook myself to my acquaintances on shore, and from them learned a good deal about the customs of the country, the harbors, &c. This, they told me, was a worse harbor than Santa Barbara, for south-easters; the bearing of the headland being a point and a half more to windward, and it being so shallow that the sea broke often as far out as where we lay at anchor. The gale from which we slipped at Santa Barbara, had been so bad a one here, that the whole bay, for a league out, was filled with the foam of the breakers, and seas actually broke over the Dead Man's island. The Lagoda was lying there, and slipped at the first alarm, and in such haste that she was obliged to leave her launch behind her at anchor. The little boat rode it out for several hours, pitching at her anchor, and standing with her stern up almost perpendicularly. The men told me that they watched her till towards night, when she snapped her cable and drove up over the breakers, high and dry upon the beach.

On board the Pilgrim, everything went on regularly, each one trying to get along as smoothly as possible; but the comfort of the voyage was evidently at an end. "That is a long lane which has no turning"—"Every dog must have his day, and mine will come by-and-by"—and the like proverbs, were occasionally quoted; but no one spoke of any probable end to the voyage, or of Boston, or anything of the kind; or if he did, it was only to draw out the perpetual, surly reply from his shipmate— "Boston, is it? You may thank your stars if you ever see that place. You had better have your back sheathed, and your head coppered, and your feet shod, and make out your log for California for life!" or else something of this kind—"Before you get to Boston the hides will wear all the hair off your head, and you'll take up all your wages in clothes, and won't have enough left to buy a wig with!"

The flogging was seldom if ever alluded to by us, in the forecastle. If any one was inclined to talk about it, the others, with a delicacy which I hardly expected to find among them, always stopped him, or turned the subject. But the behavior of the two men who were flogged toward one another showed a delicacy and a sense of honor, which would have been worthy of admiration in the highest walks of life. Sam knew that the other had suffered solely on his account, and in all his complaints, he said that if he alone had been flogged, it would have been nothing; but that he never could see that man without thinking what had been the means of bringing that disgrace upon him; and John never, by word or deed, let anything escape him to remind the other that it was by interfering to save his shipmate, that he had suffered.

Having got all our spare room filled with hides, we hove up our anchor and made sail for San Diego. In no operation can the disposition of a crew be discovered better than in getting under weigh. Where things are done "with a will," every one is like a cat aloft: sails are loosed in an instant; each one lays out his strength on his handspike, and the windlass goes briskly round with the loud cry of "Yo heave ho! Heave and pawl! Heave hearty ho!" But with us, at this time, it was all dragging work. No one went aloft beyond his ordinary gait, and the chain came slowly in over the windlass. The mate, between the knight-heads, exhausted all his official rhetoric in calls of "Heave with a will!"—"Heave hearty, men!—heave hearty!" —"Heave and raise the dead!"—"Heave, and away!" &c. &c.; but it would not do. Nobody broke his back or his handspike by his efforts. And when the cat-tackle-fall was strung along, and all hands—cook, steward, and all—laid hold, to cat the anchor, instead of the lively song of "Cheerily, men!" in which all hands join in the chorus, we pulled a long, heavy, silent pull, and—as sailors say a song is as good as ten men—the anchor came to the cat-head pretty slowly. "Give us 'Cheerily!'" said the mate; but there was no "cheerily" for us, and we did without it. The captain walked the quarter-deck, and said not a word. He must have seen the change, but there was nothing which he could notice officially.

We sailed leisurely down the coast before a light, fair wind, keeping the land well aboard, and saw two other missions, looking like blocks of white plaster, shining in the distance; one of which, situated on the top of a high hill, was San Juan Campestrano, under which vessels sometimes come to anchor, in the summer season, and take off hides. The most distant one was St. Louis Rey, which the third mate said was only fifteen miles from San Diego. At sunset on the second day, we had a large and well wooded headland directly before us, behind which lay the little harbor of San Diego. We were becalmed off this point all night, but the next morning, which was Saturday, the 14th of March, having a good breeze, we stood round the point, and hauling our wind, brought the little harbor, which is rather the outlet of a small river, right before us. Every one was anxious to get a view of the new place. A chain of high hills, beginning at the point, (which was on our larboard hand, coming in,) protected the harbor on the north and west, and ran off into the interior, as far as the eye could reach. On the other sides, the land was low, and green, but without trees. The entrance is so narrow as to admit but one vessel at a time, the current swift, and the channel runs so near to a low stony point that the ship's sides appeared almost to touch it. There was no town in sight, but on the smooth sand beach, abreast, and within a cable's length of which three vessels lay moored, were four large houses, built of rough boards, and looking like the great barns in which ice is stored on the borders of the large ponds near Boston; with piles of hides standing round them, and men in red shirts and large straw hats, walking in and out of the doors. These were the hide-houses. Of the vessels: one, a short, clumsy, little hermaphrodite brig, we recognised as our old acquaintance the Loriotte; another, with sharp bows and raking masts, newly painted and tarred, and glittering in the morning sun, with the blood-red banner and cross of St. George at her peak, was the handsome Ayacucho. The third was a large ship, with top-gallant-masts housed, and sails unbent, and looking as rusty and worn as two years' "hide droghing" could make her. This was the Lagoda. As we drew near, carried rapidly along by the current, we overhauled our chain, and clewed up the topsails. "Let go the anchor!" said the captain; but either there was not chain enough forward of the windlass, or the anchor went down foul, or we had too much headway on, for it did not bring us up. "Pay out chain!"

shouted the captain; and we gave it to her; but it would not do. Before the other anchor could be let go, we drifted down, broadside on, and went smash into the Lagoda. Her crew were at breakfast in the forecastle, and the cook, seeing us coming, rushed out of his galley, and called up the officers and men.

Fortunately, no great harm was done. Her jib-boom ran between our fore and main masts, carrying away some of our rigging, and breaking down the rail. She lost her martingale. This brought us up, and as they paid out chain, we swung clear of them, and let go the other anchor; but this had as bad luck as the first, for, before any one perceived it, we were drifting on to the Loriotte. The captain now gave out his orders rapidly and fiercely, sheeting home the topsails, and backing and filling the sails, in hope of starting or clearing the anchors; but it was all in vain, and he sat down on the rail, taking it very leisurely, and calling out to Captain Nye, that he was coming to pay him a visit. We drifted fairly into the Loriotte, her larboard bow into our starboard quarter, carrying away a part of our starboard quarter railing, and breaking off her larboard bumpkin, and one or two stanchions above the deck. We saw our handsome sailor, Jackson, on the forecastle, with the Sandwich Islanders, working away to get us clear. After paying out chain, we swung clear, but our anchors were no doubt afoul of hers. We manned the windlass, and hove, and hove away, but to no purpose. Sometimes we got a little upon the cable, but a good surge would take it all back again. We now began to drift down toward the Ayacucho, when her boat put off and brought her commander, Captain Wilson, on board. He was a short, active, well-built man, between fifty and sixty years of age; and being nearly thirty years older than our captain, and a thorough seaman, he did not hesitate to give his advice, and from giving advice, he gradually came to taking the command; ordering us when to heave and when to pawl, and backing and filling the topsails, setting and taking in jib and trysail, whenever he thought best. Our captain gave a few orders, but as Wilson generally countermanded them, saying, in an easy, fatherly kind of way, "Oh no! Captain T——, you don't want the jib on her," or, "it isn't time yet to heave!" he soon gave it up. We had no objections to this state of things, for Wilson was a kind old man, and had an encouraging and pleasant way of speaking to us, which made everything go easily. After two or three hours of constant labor at the windlass, heaving and "Yo ho!"-ing with all our might, we brought up an anchor, with the Loriotte's small bower fast to it. Having cleared this and let it go, and cleared our hawse, we soon got our other anchor, which had dragged half over the harbor. "Now," said Wilson, "I'll find you a good berth;" and setting both the top-sails, he carried us down, and brought us to anchor, in hand-some style, directly abreast of the hide-house which we were to use. Having done this, he took his leave, while we furled the sails, and got our breakfast, which was welcome to us, for we had worked hard, and it was nearly twelve o'clock. After break-fast, and until night, we were employed in getting out the boats and mooring ship.

After supper, two of us took the captain on board the Lagoda. As he came alongside, he gave his name, and the mate, in the gangway, called out to the captain down the companion-way —"Captain T—— has come aboard, sir!" "Has he brought his brig with him?" said the rough old fellow, in a tone which made itself heard fore and aft. This mortified our captain a little, and it became a standing joke among us for the rest of the voyage. The captain went down into the cabin, and we walked forward and put our heads down the forecastle, where we found the men at supper. "Come down, shipmates! come down!" said they, as soon as they saw us; and we went down, and found a large, high forecastle, well lighted; and a crew of twelve or fourteen men, eating out of their kids and pans, and drinking their tea, and talking and laughing, all as independent and easy as so many "wood-sawyer's clerks." This looked like comfort and enjoyment, compared with the dark little fore-castle, and scanty, discontented crew of the brig. It was Satur-day night; they had got through their work for the week; and being snugly moored, had nothing to do until Monday, again. After two years' hard service, they had seen the worst, and all, of California;—had got their cargo nearly stowed, and expected to sail in a week or two, for Boston. We spent an hour or more with them, talking over California matters, until the word was passed—"Pilgrims, away!" and we went back with our captain. They were a hardy, but intelligent crew; a little roughened, and their clothes patched and old, from California wear; all able seamen, and between the ages of twenty and thirty-five. They inquired about our vessel, the usage, &c., and were not a little surprised at the story of the flogging. They said there were often difficulties in vessels on the coast, and sometimes knock-downs and fightings, but they had never heard before of a regular seizing-up and flogging. "Spread eagles" were a new kind of bird in California.

Sunday, they said, was always given in San Diego, both at the hide-houses and on board the vessels, a large number usually going up to the town, on liberty. We learned a good deal from them about curing and stowing of hides, &c., and they were anxious to have the latest news (seven months old) from Boston. One of their first inquiries was for Father Taylor, the seamen's preacher in Boston. Then followed the usual strain of conversation, inquiries, stories, and jokes, which one must always hear in a ship's forecastle, but which are perhaps, after all, no worse, nor, indeed, more gross, than that of many well-dressed gentlemen at their clubs.

Chapter XVI

T HE next day being Sunday, after washing and clearing decks, and getting breakfast, the mate came forward with leave for one watch to go ashore, on liberty. We drew lots, and it fell to the larboard, which I was in. Instantly all was preparation. Buckets of fresh water, (which we were allowed in port,) and soap, were put in use; go-ashore jackets and trowsers got out and brushed; pumps, neckerchiefs, and hats overhauled; one lending to another; so that among the whole each one got a good fit-out. A boat was called to pull the "liberty-men" ashore, and we sat down in the stern sheets, "as big as pay-passengers," and jumping ashore, set out on our walk for the town, which was nearly three miles off.

It is a pity that some other arrangement is not made in merchant vessels, with regard to the liberty-day. When in port, the crews are kept at work all the week, and the only day they are allowed for rest or pleasure is the Sabbath; and unless they go ashore on that day, they cannot go at all. I have heard of a religious captain who gave his crew liberty on Saturdays, after twelve o'clock. This would be a good plan, if shipmasters would bring themselves to give their crews so much time. For young sailors especially, many of whom have been brought up with a regard for the sacredness of the day, this strong temptation to break it, is exceedingly injurious. As it is, it can hardly be expected that a crew, on a long and hard voyage, will refuse a few hours of freedom from toil and the restraints of a vessel, and an opportunity to tread the ground and see the sights of society and humanity, because it is on a Sunday. It is too much like escaping from prison, or being drawn out of a pit, on the Sabbath day.

I shall never forget the delightful sensation of being in the open air, with the birds singing around me, and escaped from the confinement, labor, and strict rule of a vessel—of being once more in my life, though only for a day, my own master. A sailor's liberty is but for a day; yet while it lasts it is perfect. He is under no one's eye, and can do whatever, and go wherever, he pleases. This day, for the first time, I may truly say, in my whole life, I felt the meaning of a term which I had often heard—the sweets of liberty. My friend S—— was with me, and turning our backs upon the vessels, we walked slowly along, talking of the pleasure of being our own masters, of the times past, when we were free and in midst of friends, in America, and of the prospect of our return; and planning where we would go, and what we would do, when we reached home. It was wonderful how the prospect brightened, and how short and tolerable the voyage appeared, when viewed in this new light. Things looked differently from what they did when we talked them over in the little dark forecastle, the night after the flogging at San Pedro. It is not the least of the advantages of allowing sailors occasionally a day of liberty, that it gives them a spring, and makes them feel cheerful and independent, and leads them insensibly to look on the bright side of everything for some time after.

S—— and myself determined to keep as much together as possible, though we knew that it would not do to *cut* our shipmates; for, knowing our birth and education, they were a little suspicious that we would try to put on the gentleman when we got ashore, and would be ashamed of their company; and this won't do with Jack. When the voyage is at an end, you may do as you please, but so long as you belong to the same vessel, you must be a shipmate to him on shore, or he will not be a shipmate to you on board. Being forewarned of this before I went to sea, I took no "long togs" with me, and being dressed like the rest, in white duck trowsers, blue jacket and straw hat, which would prevent my going in better company, and showing no disposition to avoid them, I set all suspicion at rest. Our crew fell in with some who belonged to the other vessels, and, sailor-like, steered for the first grog-shop. This was a small mud building, of only one room, in which were liquors, dry and West India goods, shoes, bread, fruits, and everything which is vendible in California. It was kept by a Yankee, a one-eyed man, who belonged formerly to Fall River, came out to the Pacific in a whale-ship, left her at the Sandwich Islands, and came to California and set up a "Pulperia." S—— and I followed in our shipmates' wake, knowing that to refuse to drink with them would be the highest affront, but determining to slip away at the first opportunity. It is the universal custom with sailors for each one, in his turn, to treat the whole, calling for a glass all round, and obliging every one who is present, even to the keeper of the shop, to take a glass with him. When we first came in, there was some dispute between our crew and the others, whether the new comers or the old California rangers should treat first; but it being settled in favor of the latter, each of the crews of the other vessels treated all round in their turn, and as there were a good many present, (including some "loafers" who had dropped in, knowing what was going on, to take advantage of Jack's hospitality,) and the liquor was a *real* (12½ cents) a glass, it made somewhat of a hole in their lockers. It was now our ship's turn, and S—— and I, anxious to get away, stepped up to call for glasses; but we soon found that we must go in order—the oldest first, for the old sailors did not choose to be preceded by a couple of youngsters; and *bon gré, mal gré*, we had to wait our turn, with the twofold apprehension of being too late for our horses, and of getting *corned*; for drink you must, every time; and if you drink with one and not with another, it is always taken as an insult.

Having at length gone through our turns and acquitted ourselves of all obligations, we slipped out, and went about among the houses, endeavoring to get horses for the day, so that we might ride round and see the country. At first we had but little success, all that we could get out of the lazy fellows, in reply to our questions, being the eternal drawling "*Quien sabe?*" ("who knows?") which is an answer to all questions. After several efforts, we at length fell in with a little Sandwich Island boy, who belonged to Captain Wilson of the Ayacucho, and was well acquainted in the place; and he, knowing where to go, soon procured us two horses, ready saddled and bridled, each with a *lasso* coiled over the pommel. These we were to have all day, with the privilege of riding them down to the beach at night, for a dollar, which we had to pay in advance. Horses are the cheapest thing in California; the very best not being worth more than ten dollars apiece, and very good ones being often sold for three, and four. In taking a day's ride, you pay for the use of the saddle, and for the labor and trouble of catching the horses. If you bring the saddle back safe, they care but little what becomes of the horse. Mounted on our horses, which were spirited beasts, and which, by the way, in this country, are always steered by pressing the contrary rein against the neck, and not by pulling on the bit,—we started off on a fine run over the country. The first place we went to was the old ruinous presidio, which stands on a rising ground near the village, which it overlooks. It is built in the form of an open square, like all the other presidios, and was in a most ruinous state, with the exception of one side, in which the commandant lived, with his family. There were only two guns, one of which was spiked, and the other had no carriage. Twelve, half clothed, and half starved looking fellows, composed the garrison; and they, it was said, had not a musket apiece. The small settlement lay directly below the fort, composed of about forty dark brown looking huts, or houses, and two larger ones, plastered, which belonged to two of the "gente de razón." This town is not more than half as large as Monterey, or Santa Barbara, and has little or no business. From the presidio, we rode off in the direction of the mission, which we were told was three miles distant. The country was rather sandy, and there was nothing for miles which could be called a tree, but the grass grew green and rank, and there were many bushes and thickets, and the soil is said to be good. After a pleasant ride of a couple of miles, we saw the white walls of the mission, and fording a small river, we came directly before it. The mission is built of mud, or rather of the unburnt bricks of the country, and plastered. There was something decidedly striking in its appearance: a number of irregular buildings, connected with one another, and disposed in the form of a hollow square, with a church at one end, rising above the rest, with a tower containing five belfries, in each of which hung a large bell, and with an immense rusty iron cross at the top. Just outside of the buildings, and under the walls, stood twenty or thirty small huts, built of straw and of the branches of trees, grouped together, in which a few Indians lived, under the protection and in the service of the mission.

Entering a gate-way, we drove into the open square, in which the stillness of death reigned. On one side was the church; on another, a range of high buildings with grated windows; a third was a range of smaller buildings, or offices; and the fourth seemed to be little more than a high connecting wall. Not a living creature could we see. We rode twice round the square, in the hope of waking up some one; and in one circuit, saw a tall monk, with shaven head, sandals, and the dress of the Grey Friars, pass rapidly through a gallery, but he disappeared without noticing us. After two circuits, we stopped our horses, and saw, at last, a man show himself in front of one of the small buildings. We rode up to him, and found him dressed in the common dress of the country, with a silver chain round his neck, supporting a large bunch of keys. From this, we took him to be the steward of the mission, and addressing him as "Mayordomo," received a low bow and an invitation to walk into his room. Making our horses fast, we went in. It was a plain room, containing a table, three or four chairs, a small picture or two of some saint, or miracle, or martyrdom, and a few dishes and glasses. "Hay algunas cosas á comer?" said I. "Si, Señor!" said he. "Que gusta usted?" Mentioning frijoles, which I knew they must have if they had nothing else, and beef and bread, and a hint for wine, if they had any, he went off to another building, across the court, and returned in a few moments, with a couple of Indian boys, bearing dishes and a decanter of wine. The dishes contained baked meats, frijoles stewed with peppers and onions, boiled eggs, and California flour baked into a kind of macaroni. These, together with the wine, made the most sumptuous meal we had eaten since we left Boston; and compared with the fare we had lived upon for seven months, it was a regal banquet. After despatching our meal, we took out some money and asked him how much we were to pay. He shook his head, and crossed himself, saying that it was charity:—that the Lord gave it to us. Knowing the amount of this to be that he did not sell, but was willing to receive a present, we gave him ten or twelve *reals*, which he pocketed with admirable nonchalance, saying, "Dios se lo pague." Taking leave of him, we rode out to the Indians' huts. The little children were running about among the huts, stark naked, and the men were not much better; but the women had generally coarse gowns, of a sort of tow cloth. The men are employed, most of the time, in tending the cattle of the mission, and in working in the garden, which is a very large one, including several acres, and filled, it is said, with the best fruits of the climate. The language of these people, which is spoken by all the Indians of California, is the most brutish and inhuman language, without any exception, that I ever heard, or that could well be conceived of. It is a complete *slabber*. The words fall off of the ends of their tongues, and a continual *slabbering* sound is made in the cheeks, outside of the teeth. It cannot have been the language of Montezuma and the independent Mexicans.

Here, among the huts, we saw the oldest man that I had ever seen; and, indeed, I never supposed that a person could retain life and exhibit such marks of age. He was sitting out in the sun, leaning against the side of a hut; and his legs and arms, which were bare, were of a dark red color, the skin withered and shrunk up like burnt leather, and the limbs not larger round than those of a boy of five years. He had a few grey hairs, which were tied together at the back of his head; and he was so feeble that, when we came up to him, he raised his hands slowly to his face, and taking hold of his lids with his fingers, lifted them up to look at us; and being satisfied, let them drop again. All command over the lid seemed to have gone. I asked his age, but could get no answer but "Quien sabe?" and they probably did not know the age.

Leaving the mission, we returned to the village, going nearly all the way on a full run. The California horses have no medium gait, which is pleasant, between walking and running; for as there are no streets and parades, they have no need of the genteel trot, and their riders usually keep them at the top of their speed until they are tired, and then let them rest themselves by walking. The fine air of the afternoon; the rapid rate of the animals, who seemed almost to fly over the ground; and the excitement and novelty of the motion to us, who had been so long confined on shipboard, were exhilarating beyond expression, and we felt willing to ride all day long. Coming into the village, we found things looking very lively. The Indians, who always have a holyday on Sunday, were engaged at playing a kind of running game of ball, on a level piece of ground, near the houses. The old ones sat down in a ring, looking on, while the young ones—men, boys, and girls—were chasing the ball, and throwing it with all their might. Some of the girls ran like greyhounds. At every accident, or remarkable feat, the old people set up a deafening screaming and clapping of hands.

Several blue jackets were reeling about among the houses, which showed that the pulperias had been well patronized. One or two of the sailors had got on horseback, but being rather indifferent horsemen, and the Spaniards having given them vicious horses, they were soon thrown, much to the amusement of the people. A half dozen Sandwich Islanders, from the hide-houses and the two brigs, who are bold riders, were dashing about on the full gallop, hallooing and laughing like so many wild men.

It was now nearly sundown, and S—— and myself went into a house and sat quietly down to rest ourselves before going down to the beach. Several people soon collected to see "los Ingles marineros," and one of them—a young woman—took a great fancy to my pocket handkerchief, which was a large silk one that I had before going to sea, and a handsomer one than they had been in the habit of seeing. Of course, I gave it to her; which brought us into high favor; and we had a present of some pears and other fruits, which we took down to the beach with us. When we came to leave the house, we found that our horses, which we left tied at the door, were both gone. We had paid for them to ride down to the beach, but they were not to be found. We went to the man of whom we hired them, but he only shrugged his shoulders, and to our question, "Where are the horses?" only answered—"Quien sabe?" but as he was very easy, and made no inquiries for the saddles, we saw that he knew very well where they were. After a little trouble, determined not to walk down,—a distance of three miles—we procured two, at four *reals* apiece, with an Indian boy to run on behind and bring them back. Determined to have "the go" out of the horses, for our trouble, we went down at full speed, and were on the beach in fifteen minutes. Wishing to make our liberty last as long as possible, we rode up and down among the hide-houses, amusing ourselves with seeing the men, as they came down, (it was now dusk,) some on horseback and others on foot. The Sandwich Islanders rode down, and were in "high snuff." We inquired for our shipmates, and were told that two of them had started on horseback and been thrown or had fallen off, and were seen heading for the beach, but steering pretty wild, and by the looks of things, would not be down much before midnight.

The Indian boys having arrived, we gave them our horses, and having seen them safely off, hailed for a boat and went aboard. Thus ended our first liberty-day on shore. We were well tired, but had had a good time, and were more willing to go back to our old duties. About midnight, we were waked up by our two watch-mates, who had come aboard in high dispute. It seems they had started to come down on the same horse, double-backed; and each was accusing the other of being the cause of his fall. They soon, however, turned-in and fell asleep, and probably forgot all about it, for the next morning the dispute was not renewed.

Chapter XVII

THE next sound that we heard was "All hands ahoy!" and looking up the scuttle, saw that it was just daylight. Our liberty had now truly taken flight, and with it we laid away our pumps, stockings, blue jackets, neckerchiefs, and other go-ashore paraphernalia, and putting on old duck trowsers, red shirts, and Scotch caps, began taking out and landing our hides. For three days we were hard at work, from the grey of the morning until starlight, with the exception of a short time allowed for meals, in this duty. For landing and taking on board hides, San Diego is decidedly the best place in California. The harbor is small and land-locked; there is no surf; the vessels lie within a cable's length of the beach; and the beach itself is smooth, hard sand, without rocks or stones. For these reasons, it is used by all the vessels in the trade, as a depot; and, indeed, it would be impossible, when loading with the cured hides for the passage home, to take them on board at any of the open ports, without getting them wet in the surf, which would spoil them. We took possession of one of the hide-houses, which belonged to our firm, and had been used by the California. It was built to hold forty thousand hides, and we had the pleasing prospect of filling it before we could leave the coast; and toward this, our thirty-five hundred, which we brought down with us, would do but little. There was not a man on board who did not go a dozen times into the house, and look round, and make some calculation of the time it would require.

The hides, as they come rough and uncured from the vessels, are piled up outside of the houses, whence they are taken and carried through a regular process of pickling, drying, cleaning, &c., and stowed away in the house, ready to be put on board. This process is necessary in order that they may keep, during a long voyage and in warm latitudes. For the purpose of curing and taking care of these hides, an officer and a part of the crew of each vessel are usually left ashore; and it was for this business, we found, that our new officer had joined us. As soon as the hides were landed, he took charge of the house, and the captain intended to leave two or three of us with him, hiring Sandwich Islanders to take our places on board; but he could not get any Sandwich Islanders to go, though he offered them fifteen dollars a month; for the report of the flogging had got among them, and he was called "aole maikai," (no good,) and that was an end of the business. They were, however, willing to work on shore, and four of them were hired and put with *Mr.* Russell to cure the hides.

After landing our hides, we next sent ashore all our spare spars and rigging; all the stores which we did not want to use in the course of one trip to windward; and, in fact, everything which we could spare, so as to make room for hides: among other things, the pig-sty, and with it "old Bess." This was an old sow that we had brought from Boston, and which lived to get round Cape Horn, where all the other pigs died from cold and wet. Report said that she had been a Canton voyage before. She had been the pet of the cook during the whole passage, and he had fed her with the best of everything, and taught her to know his voice, and to do a number of strange tricks for his amusement. Tom Cringle says that no one can fathom a negro's affection for a pig; and I believe he is right, for it almost broke our poor *darky's* heart when he heard that Bess was to be taken ashore, and that he was to have the care of her no more during the whole voyage. He had depended upon her as a solace, during the long trips up and down the coast. "Obey orders, if you break owners!" said he. "Break *hearts*," he meant to have said; and lent a hand to get her over the side, trying to make it as easy for her as possible. We got a whip up on the main-yard, and hooking it to a strap round her body, swayed away; and giving a wink to one another, ran her chock up to the yard. "'Vast there! 'vast!" said the mate; "none of your skylarking! Lower away!" But he evidently enjoyed the joke. The pig squealed like the "crack of doom," and tears stood in the poor darky's eyes; and he muttered something about having no pity on a dumb beast. "*Dumb* beast!" said Jack; "if she's what you call a dumb beast, then my eyes a'n't mates." This produced a laugh from all but the cook. He was too intent upon seeing her safe in the boat. He watched her all the way ashore, where, upon her landing, she was received by a whole troop of her kind, who had been set ashore from the other vessels, and had multiplied and formed a large commonwealth. From the door of his galley, the cook used to watch them in their manœuvres, setting up a shout and clapping his hands whenever Bess came off victorious in the struggles for pieces of raw hide and half-picked bones which were lying about the beach. During the day, he saved all the nice things, and made a bucket of swill, and asked us to take it ashore in the gig, and looked quite disconcerted when the mate told him that he would pitch the swill overboard, and him after it, if he saw any of it go into the boats. We told him that he thought more about the pig than he did about his wife, who lived down in Robinson's Alley; and, indeed, he could hardly have been more attentive, for he actually, on several nights, after dark, when he thought he would not be seen, sculled himself ashore in a boat with a bucket of nice swill, and returned like Leander from crossing the Hellespont.

The next Sunday the other half of our crew went ashore on liberty, and left us on board, to enjoy the first quiet Sunday which we had had upon the coast. Here were no hides to come off, and no south-easters to fear. We washed and mended our clothes in the morning, and spent the rest of the day in reading and writing. Several of us wrote letters to send home by the Lagoda. At twelve o'clock the Ayacucho dropped her fore topsail, which was a signal for her sailing. She unmoored and warped down into the bight, from which she got under weigh. During this operation, her crew were a long time heaving at the windlass, and I listened for nearly an hour to the musical notes of a Sandwich Islander, called Mahannah, who "sang out" for them. Sailors, when heaving at a windlass, in order that they may heave together, always have one to sing out; which is done in a peculiar, high and long-drawn note, varying with the motion of the windlass. This requires a high voice, strong lungs, and much practice, to be done well. This fellow had a very peculiar, wild sort of note, breaking occasionally into a falsetto. The sailors thought that it was too high, and not enough of the boatswain hoarseness about it; but to me it had a great charm. The harbor was perfectly still, and his voice rang among the hills, as though it could have been heard for miles. Toward sundown, a good breeze having sprung up, she got under weigh, and with her long, sharp head cutting elegantly through the water, on a taught bowline, she stood directly out of the harbor, and bore away to the southward. She was bound to Callao, and thence to the Sandwich Islands, and expected to be on the coast again in eight or ten months.

At the close of the week we were ready to sail, but were delayed a day or two by the running away of Foster, the man who had been our second mate, and was turned forward. From the time that he was "broken," he had had a dog's berth on board the vessel, and determined to run away at the first opportunity. Having shipped for an officer when he was not half a seaman, he found little pity with the crew, and was not man enough to hold his ground among them. The captain called him a "soger,"* and promised to "ride him down as he would the main tack;" and when officers are once determined to "ride a man down," it is a gone case with him. He had had several difficulties with the captain, and asked leave to go home in the Lagoda; but this was refused him. One night he was insolent to an officer on the beach, and refused to come aboard in the boat. He was reported to the captain; and, as he came aboard, —it being past the proper hour,—he was called aft, and told that he was to have a flogging. Immediately, he fell down on deck, calling out—"Don't flog me, Captain T——; don't flog me!" and the captain, angry with him, and disgusted with his cowardice, gave him a few blows over the back with a rope's end and sent him forward. He was not much hurt, but a good deal frightened, and made up his mind to run away that very night. This was managed better than anything he ever did in his life, and seemed really to show some spirit and forethought. He gave his bedding and mattress to one of the Lagoda's crew, who took it aboard his vessel as something which he had bought, and promised to keep it for him. He then unpacked his

---

* *Soger* (soldier) is the worst term of reproach that can be applied to a sailor. It signifies a *skulk*, a *sherk*,—one who is always trying to get clear of work, and is out of the way, or hanging back, when duty is to be done. "Marine" is the term applied more particularly to a man who is ignorant and clumsy about seaman's work—a green-horn—a land-lubber. To make a sailor shoulder a handspike, and walk fore and aft the deck, like a sentry, is the most ignominious punishment that could be put upon him. Such a punishment inflicted upon an able seaman in a vessel of war, would break his spirit down more than a flogging.

chest, putting all his valuable clothes into a large canvass bag, and told one of us, who had the watch, to call him at midnight. Coming on deck at midnight, and finding no officer on deck, and all still aft, he lowered his bag into a boat, got softly down into it, cast off the painter, and let it drop down silently with the tide until he was out of hearing, when he sculled ashore.

The next morning, when all hands were mustered, there was a great stir to find Foster. Of course, we would tell nothing, and all they could discover was, that he had left an empty chest behind him, and that he went off in a boat; for they saw it lying up high and dry on the beach. After breakfast, the captain went up to the town, and offered a reward of twenty dollars for him; and for a couple of days, the soldiers, Indians, and all others who had nothing to do, were scouring the country for him, on horseback, but without effect; for he was safely concealed, all the time, within fifty rods of the hide-houses. As soon as he had landed, he went directly to the Lagoda's hide-house, and a part of her crew, who were living there on shore, promised to conceal him and his *traps* until the Pilgrim should sail, and then to intercede with Captain Bradshaw to take him on board the ship. Just behind the hide-houses, among the thickets and underwood, was a small cave, the entrance to which was known only to two men on the beach, and which was so well concealed that, though, when I afterwards came to live on shore, it was shown to me two or three times, I was never able to find it alone. To this cave he was carried before day-break in the morning, and supplied with bread and water, and there remained until he saw us under weigh and well round the point.

Friday, March 27th. The captain having given up all hope of finding Foster, and being unwilling to delay any longer, gave orders for unmooring ship, and we made sail, dropping slowly down with the tide and light wind. We left letters with Captain Bradshaw to take to Boston, and had the satisfaction of hearing him say that he should be back again before we left the coast. The wind, which was very light, died away soon after we doubled the point, and we lay becalmed for two days, not moving three miles the whole time, and a part of the second day were almost within sight of the vessels. On the third day, about noon, a cool sea-breeze came rippling and darkening

the surface of the water, and by sundown we were off St.
Juan's, which is about forty miles from San Diego, and is
called half way to San Pedro, where we were now bound. Our
crew was now considerably weakened. One man we had lost
overboard; another had been taken aft as clerk; and a third had
run away; so that, beside S—— and myself, there were only
three able seamen and one boy of twelve years of age. With
this diminished and discontented crew, and in a small vessel,
we were now to battle the watch through a couple of years of
hard service; yet there was not one who was not glad that
Foster had escaped; for, shiftless and good for nothing as he
was, no one could wish to see him dragging on a miserable life,
cowed down and disheartened; and we were all rejoiced to
hear, upon our return to San Diego, about two months afterwards, that he had been immediately taken aboard the Lagoda,
and went home in her, on regular seaman's wages.

After a slow passage of five days, we arrived, on Wednesday,
the first of April, at our old anchoring ground at San Pedro.
The bay was as deserted, and looked as dreary, as before, and
formed no pleasing contrast with the security and snugness of
San Diego, and the activity and interest which the loading and
unloading of four vessels gave to that scene. In a few days the
hides began to come slowly down, and we got into the old
business of rolling goods up the hill, pitching hides down, and
pulling our long league off and on. Nothing of note occurred
while we were lying here, except that an attempt was made to
repair the small Mexican brig which had been cast away in a
south-easter, and which now lay up, high and dry, over one
reef of rocks and two sand-banks. Our carpenter surveyed her,
and pronounced her capable of refitting, and in a few days the
owners came down from the Pueblo, and waiting for the high
spring tides, with the help of our cables, kedges, and crew, got
her off and afloat, after several trials. The three men at the
house on shore, who had formerly been a part of her crew, now
joined her, and seemed glad enough at the prospect of getting
off the coast.

On board our own vessel, things went on in the common
monotonous way. The excitement which immediately followed
the flogging scene had passed off, but the effect of it upon the
crew, and especially upon the two men themselves, remained.

The different manner in which these men were affected, corresponding to their different characters, was not a little remarkable. John was a foreigner and high-tempered, and though mortified, as any one would be at having had the worst of an encounter, yet his chief feeling seemed to be anger; and he talked much of satisfaction and revenge, if he ever got back to Boston. But with the other, it was very different. He was an American, and had had some education; and this thing coming upon him, seemed completely to break him down. He had a feeling of the degradation that had been inflicted upon him, which the other man was incapable of. Before that, he had a good deal of fun, and amused us often with queer negro stories,—(he was from a slave state); but afterwards he seldom smiled; seemed to lose all life and elasticity; and appeared to have but one wish, and that was for the voyage to be at an end. I have often known him to draw a long sigh when he was alone, and he took but little part or interest in John's plans of satisfaction and retaliation.

After a stay of about a fortnight, during which we slipped for one south-easter, and were at sea two days, we got under weigh for Santa Barbara. It was now the middle of April, and the south-easter season was nearly over; and the light, regular trade-winds, which blow down the coast, began to set steadily in, during the latter part of each day. Against these, we beat slowly up to Santa Barbara—a distance of about ninety miles—in three days. There we found, lying at anchor, the large Genoese ship which we saw in the same place, on the first day of our coming upon the coast. She had been up to San Francisco, or, as it is called, "chock up to windward," had stopped at Monterey on her way down, and was shortly to proceed to San Pedro and San Diego, and thence, taking in her cargo, to sail for Valparaiso and Cadiz. She was a large, clumsy ship, and with her topmasts stayed forward, and high poop-deck, looked like an old woman with a crippled back. It was now the close of Lent, and on Good Friday she had all her yards a'-cock-bill, which is customary among Catholic vessels. Some also have an effigy of Judas, which the crew amuse themselves with keel-hauling and hanging by the neck from the yard-arms.

Chapter XVIII

THE next Sunday was Easter Sunday, and as there had been no liberty at San Pedro, it was our turn to go ashore and misspend another Sabbath. Soon after breakfast, a large boat, filled with men in blue jackets, scarlet caps, and various colored under-clothes, bound ashore on liberty, left the Italian ship, and passed under our stern; the men singing beautiful Italian boat-songs, all the way, in fine, full chorus. Among the songs I recognised the favorite "O Pescator dell' onda." It brought back to my mind piano-fortes, drawing-rooms, young ladies singing, and a thousand other things which as little befitted me, in my situation, to be thinking upon. Supposing that the whole day would be too long a time to spend ashore, as there was no place to which we could take a ride, we remained quietly on board until after dinner. We were then pulled ashore in the stern of the boat, and, with orders to be on the beach at sundown, we took our way for the town. There, everything wore the appearance of a holyday. The people were all dressed in their best; the men riding about on horseback among the houses, and the women sitting on carpets before the doors. Under the piazza of a "pulperia," two men were seated, decked out with knots of ribands and bouquets, and playing the violin and the Spanish guitar. These are the only instruments, with the exception of the drums and trumpets at Monterey, that I ever heard in California; and I suspect they play upon no others, for at a great *fandango* at which I was afterwards present, and where they mustered all the music they could find, there were three violins and two guitars, and no other instruments. As it was now too near the middle of the day to see any dancing, and hearing that a bull was expected down from the country, to be baited in the presidio square, in the course of an hour or two, we took a stroll among the houses. Inquiring for an American who, we had been told, had married in the place, and kept a shop, we were directed to a long, low building, at the end of which was a door, with a sign over it, in Spanish. Entering the shop, we found no one in it, and the whole had an empty, deserted appearance. In a few minutes the man made his appearance, and apologized for having nothing to entertain us with, saying that he had had a fandango at his house the night before, and the people had eaten and drunk up everything.

"Oh yes!" said I, "Easter holydays!"

"No!" said he, with a singular expression to his face; "I had a little daughter die the other day, and that's the custom of the country."

Here I felt a little strangely, not knowing what to say, or whether to offer consolation or no, and was beginning to retire, when he opened a side door and told us to walk in. Here I was no less astonished; for I found a large room, filled with young girls, from three or four years of age up to fifteen and sixteen, dressed all in white, with wreaths of flowers on their heads, and bouquets in their hands. Following our conductor through all these girls, who were playing about in high spirits, we came to a table, at the end of the room, covered with a white cloth, on which lay a coffin, about three feet long, with the body of his child. The coffin was lined on the outside with white cloth, and on the inside with white satin, and was strewed with flowers. Through an open door we saw, in another room, a few elderly people in common dresses; while the benches and tables thrown up in a corner, and the stained walls, gave evident signs of the last night's "high go." Feeling, like Garrick, between tragedy and comedy, an uncertainty of purpose and a little awkwardness, I asked the man when the funeral would take place, and being told that it would move toward the mission in about an hour, took my leave.

To pass away the time, we took horses and rode down to the beach, and there found three or four Italian sailors, mounted, and riding up and down, on the hard sand, at a furious rate. We joined them, and found it fine sport. The beach gave us a stretch of a mile or more, and the horses flew over the smooth, hard sand, apparently invigorated and excited by the salt seabreeze, and by the continual roar and dashing of the breakers. From the beach we returned to the town, and finding that the funeral procession had moved, rode on and overtook it, about half way to the mission. Here was as peculiar a sight as we had seen before in the house; the one looking as much like a funeral procession as the other did like a house of mourning.

The little coffin was borne by eight girls, who were continually relieved by others, running forward from the procession and taking their places. Behind it came a straggling company of girls, dressed as before, in white and flowers, and including, I should suppose by their numbers, nearly all the girls between five and fifteen in the place. They played along on the way, frequently stopping and running all together to talk to some one, or to pick up a flower, and then running on again to overtake the coffin. There were a few elderly women in common colors; and a herd of young men and boys, some on foot and others mounted, followed them, or walked or rode by their side, frequently interrupting them by jokes and questions. But the most singular thing of all was, that two men walked, one on each side of the coffin, carrying muskets in their hands, which they continually loaded, and fired into the air. Whether this was to keep off the evil spirits or not, I do not know. It was the only interpretation that I could put upon it.

As we drew near the mission, we saw the great gate thrown open, and the pádre standing on the steps, with a crucifix in hand. The mission is a large and deserted-looking place, the out-buildings going to ruin, and everything giving one the impression of decayed grandeur. A large stone fountain threw out pure water, from four mouths, into a basin, before the church door; and we were on the point of riding up to let our horses drink, when it occurred to us that it might be consecrated, and we forbore. Just at this moment, the bells set up their harsh, discordant clang; and the procession moved into the court. I was anxious to follow, and see the ceremony, but the horse of one of my companions had become frightened, and was tearing off toward the town; and having thrown his rider, and got one of his feet caught in the saddle, which had slipped, was fast dragging and ripping it to pieces. Knowing that my shipmate could not speak a word of Spanish, and fearing that he would get into difficulty, I was obliged to leave the ceremony and ride after him. I soon overtook him, trudging along, swearing at the horse, and carrying the remains of the saddle, which he had picked up on the road. Going to the owner of the horse, we made a settlement with him, and found him surprisingly liberal. All parts of the saddle were brought back, and being capable of repair, he was satisfied with six reáls. We thought it would have been a few dollars. We pointed to the horse, which was now half way up one of the mountains; but he shook his head, saying, "No importe!" and giving us to understand that he had plenty more.

Having returned to the town, we saw a great crowd collected in the square before the principal pulperia, and riding up, found that all these people—men, women, and children— had been drawn together by a couple of bantam cocks. The cocks were in full tilt, springing into one another, and the people were as eager, laughing and shouting, as though the combatants had been men. There had been a disappointment about the bull; he had broken his bail, and taken himself off, and it was too late to get another; so the people were obliged to put up with a cock-fight. One of the bantams having been knocked in the head, and had an eye put out, he gave in, and two monstrous prize-cocks were brought on. These were the object of the whole affair; the two bantams having been merely served up as a first course, to collect the people together. Two fellows came into the ring holding the cocks in their arms, and stroking them, and running about on all fours, encouraging and setting them on. Bets ran high, and, like most other contests, it remained for some time undecided. They both showed great pluck, and fought probably better and longer than their masters would. Whether, in the end, it was the white or the red that beat, I do not recollect; but whichever it was, he strutted off with the true veni-vidi-vici look, leaving the other lying panting on his beam-ends.

This matter having been settled we heard some talk about "*caballos*" and "*carréra*," and seeing the people all streaming off in one direction, we followed, and came upon a level piece of ground, just out of the town, which was used as a race-course. Here the crowd soon became thick again; the ground was marked off; the judges stationed; and the horses led up to one end. Two fine-looking old gentlemen—Don Carlos and Don Domingo, so called—held the stakes, and all was now ready. We waited some time, during which we could just see the horses twisting round and turning, until, at length, there was a shout along the lines, and on they came—heads stretched out and eyes starting;—working all over, both man and beast. The steeds came by us like a couple of chain-shot—neck and neck; and now we could see nothing but their backs, and their hind hoofs flying in the air. As fast as the horses passed, the crowd broke up behind them, and ran to the goal. When we got there, we found the horses returning on a slow walk, having run far beyond the mark, and heard that the long, bony one had come in head and shoulders before the other. The riders were light-built men; had handkerchiefs tied round their heads; and were bare-armed and bare-legged. The horses were noble-looking beasts, not so sleek and combed as our Boston stable horses, but with fine limbs and spirited eyes. After this had been settled, and fully talked over, the crowd scattered again and flocked back to the town.

Returning to the large pulperia, we found the violin and guitar screaming and twanging away under the piazza, where they had been all day. As it was now sundown, there began to be some dancing. The Italian sailors danced, and one of our crew exhibited himself in a sort of West India shuffle, much to the amusement of the bystanders, who cried out, "Bravo!" "Otra vez!" and "Vivan los marineros!" but the dancing did not become general, as the women and the "gente de razón" had not yet made their appearance. We wished very much to stay and see the style of dancing; but, although we had had our own way during the day, yet we were, after all, but 'fore-mast Jacks; and having been ordered to be on the beach by sundown, did not venture to be more than an hour behind the time; so we took our way down. We found the boat just pulling ashore through the breakers, which were running high, there having been a heavy fog outside, which, from some cause or other, always brings on, or precedes a heavy sea. Liberty-men are privileged from the time they leave the vessel until they step on board again; so we took our places in the stern sheets, and were congratulating ourselves upon getting off dry, when a great comber broke fore and aft the boat, and wet us through and through, filling the boat half full of water. Having lost her buoyancy by the weight of the water, she dropped heavily into every sea that struck her, and by the time we had pulled out of the surf into deep water, she was but just afloat, and we were up to our knees. By the help of a small bucket and our hats, we bailed her out, got on board, hoisted the boats, eat our supper, changed our clothes, gave (as is usual) the whole history of our day's adventures to those who had staid on board, and having taken a night-smoke, turned-in. Thus ended our second day's liberty on shore.

On Monday morning, as an offset to our day's sport, we were all set to work "tarring down" the rigging. Some got girt-lines up for riding down the stays and back-stays, and others tarred the shrouds, lifts, &c., laying out on the yards, and coming down the rigging. We overhauled our bags and took out our old tarry trowsers and frocks, which we had used when we tarred down before, and were all at work in the rigging by sunrise. After breakfast, we had the satisfaction of seeing the Italian ship's boat go ashore, filled with men, gaily dressed, as on the day before, and singing their barcarollas. The Easter holydays are kept up on shore during three days; and being a Catholic vessel, the crew had the advantage of them. For two successive days, while perched up in the rigging, covered with tar and engaged in our disagreeable work, we saw these fellows going ashore in the morning, and coming off again at night, in high spirits. So much for being Protestants. There's no danger of Catholicism's spreading in New England; Yankees can't afford the time to be Catholics. American ship-masters get nearly three weeks more labor out of their crews, in the course of a year, than the masters of vessels from Catholic countries. Yankees don't keep Christmas, and ship-masters at sea never know when Thanksgiving comes, so Jack has no festival at all.

About noon, a man aloft called out "Sail ho!" and looking round, we saw the head sails of a vessel coming round the point. As she drew round, she showed the broadside of a full-rigged brig, with the Yankee ensign at her peak. We ran up our stars and stripes, and knowing that there was no American brig on the coast but ourselves, expected to have news from home. She rounded-to and let go her anchor, but the dark faces on her yards, when they furled the sails, and the Babel on deck, soon made known that she was from the Islands. Immediately afterwards, a boat's crew came aboard, bringing her skipper, and from them we learned that she was from Oahu, and was engaged in the same trade with the Ayacucho, Loriotte, &c., between the coast, the Sandwich Islands, and the leeward coast of Peru and Chili. Her captain and officers were Americans, and also a part of her crew; the rest were Islanders. She was called the Catalina, and, like all the other vessels in that trade, except the Ayacucho, her papers and colors were from Uncle Sam. They, of course, brought us no news, and we were doubly disappointed, for we had thought, at first, it might be the ship which we were expecting from Boston.

After lying here about a fortnight, and collecting all the hides the place afforded, we set sail again for San Pedro. There we found the brig which we had assisted in getting off, lying at anchor, with a mixed crew of Americans, English, Sandwich Islanders, Spaniards, and Spanish Indians; and though much smaller than we, yet she had three times the number of men; and she needed them, for her officers were Californians. No vessels in the world go so poorly manned as American and English; and none do so well. A Yankee brig of that size would have had a crew of four men, and would have worked round and round her. The Italian ship had a crew of thirty men; nearly three times as many as the Alert, which was afterwards on the coast, and was of the same size; yet the Alert would get under weigh and come-to in half the time, and get two anchors, while they were all talking at once—jabbering like a parcel of "Yahoos," and running about decks to find their cat-block.

There was only one point in which they had the advantage over us, and that was in lightening their labors in the boats by their songs. The Americans are a time and money saving people, but have not yet, as a nation, learned that music may be "turned to account." We pulled the long distances to and from the shore, with our loaded boats, without a word spoken, and with discontented looks, while they not only lightened the labor of rowing, but actually made it pleasant and cheerful, by their music. So true is it, that—

> "For the tired slave, song lifts the languid oar,
>   And bids it aptly fall, with chime
> That beautifies the fairest shore,
>   And mitigates the harshest clime."

We lay about a week in San Pedro, and got under weigh for San Diego, intending to stop at San Juan, as the south-easter season was nearly over, and there was little or no danger.

This being the spring season, San Pedro, as well as all the other open ports upon the coast, was filled with whales, that had come in to make their annual visit upon soundings. For the first few days that we were here and at Santa Barbara, we watched them with great interest—calling out "there she blows!" every time we saw the spout of one, breaking the surface of the water; but they soon became so common that we took little notice of them. They often "broke" very near us; and one thick, foggy night, during a dead calm, while I was standing anchor-watch, one of them rose so near, that he struck our cable, and made all surge again. He did not seem to like the encounter much himself, for he sheered off, and spouted at a good distance. We once came very near running one down in the gig, and should probably have been knocked to pieces and blown sky-high. We had been on board the little Spanish brig, and were returning, stretching out well at our oars, the little boat going like a swallow; our backs were forward, (as is always the case in pulling,) and the captain, who was steering, was not looking ahead, when, all at once, we heard the spout of a whale directly ahead. "Back water! back water, for your lives!" shouted the captain; and we backed our blades in the water and brought the boat to in a smother of foam. Turning our heads, we saw a great, rough, hump-backed whale, slowly crossing our fore foot, within three or four yards of the boat's stem. Had we not backed water just as we did, we should inevitably have gone smash upon him, striking him with our stem just about amidships. He took no notice of us, but passed slowly on, and dived a few yards beyond us, throwing his tail high in the air. He was so near that we had a perfect view of him, and, as may be supposed, had no desire to see him nearer. He was a disgusting creature; with a skin rough, hairy, and of an iron-grey color. This kind differs much from the sperm, in color and skin, and is said to be fiercer. We saw a few sperm whales; but most of the whales that come upon the coast are fin-backs, hump-backs, and right-whales, which are more difficult to take, and are said not to give oil enough to pay for the trouble. For this reason, whale-ships do not come upon the coast after them. Our captain, together with Captain Nye of the Loriotte, who had been in a whale-ship, thought of making an attempt upon one of them with two boats' crews, but as we had only two harpoons and no proper lines, they gave it up.

During the months of March, April, and May, these whales appear in great numbers in the open ports of Santa Barbara, San Pedro, &c., and hover off the coast, while a few find their way into the close harbors of San Diego and Monterey. They are all off again before midsummer, and make their appearance on the "off-shore ground." We saw some fine "schools" of sperm whales, which are easily distinguished by their spout, blowing away, a few miles to windward, on our passage to San Juan.

Coasting along on the quiet shore of the Pacific, we came to anchor, in twenty fathoms' water, almost out at sea, as it were, and directly abreast of a steep hill which overhung the water, and was twice as high as our royal-mast-head. We had heard much of this place from the Lagoda's crew, who said it was the worst place in California. The shore is rocky, and directly exposed to the south-east, so that vessels are obliged to slip and run for their lives on the first sign of a gale; and late as it was in the season, we got up our slip-rope and gear, though we meant to stay only twenty-four hours. We pulled the agent ashore, and were ordered to wait for him, while he took a circuitous way round the hill to the mission, which was hidden behind it. We were glad of the opportunity to examine this singular place, and hauling the boat up and making her well fast, took different directions up and down the beach, to explore it.

San Juan is the only romantic spot in California. The country here for several miles is high table-land, running boldly to the shore, and breaking off in a steep hill, at the foot of which the waters of the Pacific are constantly dashing. For several miles the water washes the very base of the hill, or breaks upon ledges and fragments of rocks which run out into the sea. Just where we landed was a small cove, or "bight," which gave us, at high tide, a few square feet of sand-beach between the sea and the bottom of the hill. This was the only landing-place. Directly before us, rose the perpendicular height of four or five hundred feet. How we were to get hides down, or goods up, upon the table-land on which the mission was situated, was more than we could tell. The agent had taken a long circuit, and yet had frequently to jump over breaks, and climb up steep places, in the ascent. No animal but a man or a monkey could get up it. However, that was not our look-out; and knowing that the agent would be gone an hour or more, we strolled about, picking up shells, and following the sea where it tumbled in, roaring and spouting, among the crevices of the great rocks. What a sight, thought I, must this be in a south-easter! The rocks were as large as those of Nahant or Newport, but, to my eye, more grand and broken. Beside, there was a grandeur in everything around, which gave almost a solemnity to the scene: a silence and solitariness which affected everything! Not a human being but ourselves for miles; and no sound heard but the pulsations of the great Pacific! and the great steep hill rising like a wall, and cutting us off from all the world, but the "world of waters!" I separated myself from the rest, and sat down on a rock, just where the sea ran in and formed a fine spouting horn. Compared with the plain, dull sand-beach of the rest of the coast, this grandeur was as refreshing as a great rock in a weary land. It was almost the first time that I had been positively alone—free from the sense that human beings were at my elbow, if not talking with me—since I had left home. My better nature returned strong upon me. Everything was in accordance with my state of feeling, and I experienced a glow of pleasure at finding that what of poetry and romance I ever had in me, had not been entirely deadened by the laborious and frittering life I had led. Nearly an hour did I sit, almost lost in the luxury of this entire new scene of the play in which I had been so long acting, when I was aroused by the distant shouts of my companions, and saw that they were collecting together, as the agent had made his appearance, on his way back to our boat.

We pulled aboard, and found the long-boat hoisted out, and nearly laden with goods; and after dinner, we all went on shore in the quarter-boat, with the long-boat in tow. As we drew in, we found an ox-cart and a couple of men standing directly on the brow of the hill; and having landed, the captain took his way round the hill, ordering me and one other to follow him. We followed, picking our way out, and jumping and scrambling up, walking over briers and prickly pears, until we came to the top. Here the country stretched out for miles, as far as the eye could reach, on a level, table surface; and the only habitation in sight was the small white mission of San Juan Campestrano, with a few Indian huts about it, standing in a small hollow, about a mile from where we were. Reaching the brow of the hill where the cart stood, we found several piles of hides, and Indians sitting round them. One or two other carts were coming slowly on from the mission, and the captain told us to begin and throw the hides down. This, then, was the way they were to be got down: thrown down, one at a time, a distance of four hundred feet! This was doing the business on a great scale. Standing on the edge of the hill and looking down the perpendicular height, the sailors,

> ——"That walked upon the beach,
> Appeared like mice; and *our* tall anchoring bark
> Diminished to her cock; her cock a buoy
> Almost too small for sight."

Down this height we pitched the hides, throwing them as far out into the air as we could; and as they were all large, stiff, and doubled, like the cover of a book, the wind took them, and they swayed and eddied about, plunging and rising in the air, like a kite when it has broken its string. As it was now low tide, there was no danger of their falling into the water, and as fast as they came to ground, the men below picked them up, and taking them on their heads, walked off with them to the boat. It was really a picturesque sight: the great height; the scaling of the hides; and the continual walking to and fro of the men, who looked like mites, on the beach! This was the romance of hide-droghing!

Some of the hides lodged in cavities which were under the bank and out of our sight, being directly under us; but by sending others down in the same direction, we succeeded in dislodging them. Had they remained there, the captain said he should have sent on board for a couple of pair of long halyards, and got some one to have gone down for them. It was said that one of the crew of an English brig went down in the same way, a few years before. We looked over, and thought it would not be a welcome task, especially for a few paltry hides; but no one knows what he can do until he is called upon; for, six months afterwards, I went down the same place by a pair of top-gallant studding-sail halyards, to save a half a dozen hides which had lodged there.

Having thrown them all down, we took our way back again, and found the boat loaded and ready to start. We pulled off; took the hides all aboard; hoisted in the boats; hove up our anchor; made sail; and before sundown, were on our way to San Diego.

Friday, May 8th, 1835. Arrived at San Diego. Here we found the little harbor deserted. The Lagoda, Ayacucho, Loriotte, and all, had left the coast, and we were nearly alone. All the hide-houses on the beach, but ours, were shut up, and the Sandwich Islanders, a dozen or twenty in number, who had worked for the other vessels and been paid off when they sailed, were living on the beach, keeping up a grand carnival. A Russian discovery-ship, which had been in this port a few years before, had built a large oven for baking bread, and went away, leaving it standing. This, the Sandwich Islanders took possession of, and had kept, ever since, undisturbed. It was big enough to hold six or eight men—that is, it was as large as a ship's forecastle; had a door at the side, and a vent-hole at top. They covered it with Oahu mats, for a carpet; stopped up the vent-hole in bad weather, and made it their head-quarters. It was now inhabited by as many as a dozen or twenty men, who lived there in complete idleness—drinking, playing cards, and carousing in every way. They bought a bullock once a week, which kept them in meat, and one of them went up to the town every day to get fruit, liquor, and provisions. Besides this, they had bought a cask of ship-bread, and a barrel of flour from the Lagoda, before she sailed. There they lived, having a grand time, and caring for nobody. Captain T—— was anxious to get three or four of them to come on board the Pilgrim, as we were so much diminished in numbers; and went up to the oven, and spent an hour or two trying to negotiate with them. One of them,—a finely built, active, strong and intelligent fellow,—who was a sort of king among them, acted as spokesman. He was called Mannini,—or rather, out of compliment to his known importance and influence, *Mr.* Mannini,—and was known all over California. Through him, the captain offered them fifteen dollars a month, and one month's pay in advance; but it was like throwing pearls before swine, or, rather, carrying coals to Newcastle. So long as they had money, they would not work for fifty dollars a month, and when their money was gone, they would work for ten.

"What do you do here, Mr. Mannini?"* said the captain.

"Oh, we play cards, get drunk, smoke—do anything we're a mind to."

"Don't you want to come aboard and work?"

"*Aole! aole make make makou i ka hana.* Now, got plenty money; no good, work. *Mamule*, money *pau*—all gone. Ah! very good, work!—*maikai, hana hana nui!*"

"But you'll spend all your money in this way," said the captain.

"Aye! me know that. By-'em-by money *pau*—all gone; then Kanaka work plenty."

This was a hopeless case, and the captain left them, to wait patiently until their money was gone.

We discharged our hides and tallow, and in about a week were ready to set sail again for the windward. We unmoored, and got everything ready, when the captain made another attempt upon the oven. This time he had more regard to the "mollia tempora fandi," and succeeded very well. He got Mr. Mannini in his interest, and as the shot was getting low in the locker, prevailed upon him and three others to come on board with their chests and baggage, and sent a hasty summons to me and the boy to come ashore with our things, and join the gang at the hide-house. This was unexpected to me; but anything in the way of variety I liked; so we got ready, and were pulled ashore. I stood on the beach while the brig got under weigh, and watched her until she rounded the point, and then went up to the hide-house to take up my quarters for a few months.

*The letter *i* in the Sandwich Island language is sounded like *e* in the English.

Chapter XIX

HERE was a change in my life as complete as it had been sudden. In the twinkling of an eye, I was transformed from a sailor into a "beach-comber" and a hide-curer; yet the novelty and the comparative independence of the life were not unpleasant. Our hide-house was a large building, made of rough boards, and intended to hold forty thousand hides. In one corner of it, a small room was parted off, in which four berths were made, where we were to live, with mother earth for our floor. It contained a table, a small locker for pots, spoons, plates, &c., and a small hole cut to let in the light. Here we put our chests, threw our bedding into the berths, and took up our quarters. Over our head was another small room, in which *Mr.* Russell lived, who had charge of the hide-house; the same man who was for a time an officer of the Pilgrim. There he lived in solitary grandeur; eating and sleeping alone, (and these were his principal occupations,) and communing with his own dignity. The boy was to act as cook; while myself, a giant of a Frenchman named Nicholas, and four Sandwich Islanders, were to cure the hides. Sam, the Frenchman, and myself, lived together in the room, and the four Sandwich Islanders worked and ate with us, but generally slept at the oven. My new messmate, Nicholas, was the most immense man that I had ever seen in my life. He came on the coast in a vessel which was afterwards wrecked, and now let himself out to the different houses to cure hides. He was considerably over six feet, and of a frame so large that he might have been shown for a curiosity. But the most remarkable thing about him was his feet. They were so large that he could not find a pair of shoes in California to fit him, and was obliged to send to Oahu for a pair; and when he got them, he was compelled to wear them down at the heel. He told me once, himself, that he was wrecked in an American brig on the Goodwin Sands, and was sent up to London, to the charge of the American consul, without clothing to his back or shoes to his feet, and was obliged to go about London streets in his stocking-feet three or four days, in the month of January, until the consul could have a pair of shoes *made for him*. His strength was in proportion to his size, and his ignorance to his strength—"strong as an ox, and ignorant as strong." He neither knew how to read nor to write. He had been to sea from a boy, and had seen all kinds of service, and been in every kind of vessels: merchantmen, men-of-war, privateers, and slavers; and from what I could gather from his accounts of himself, and from what he once told me, in confidence, after we had become better acquainted, he had even been in worse business than slave-trading. He was once tried for his life in Charleston, South Carolina, and though acquitted, yet he was so frightened that he never would show himself in the United States again; and I could not persuade him that he could never be tried a second time for the same offence. He said he had got safe off from the breakers, and was too good a sailor to risk his timbers again.

Though I knew what his life had been, yet I never had the slightest fear of him. We always got along very well together, and, though so much stronger and larger than I, he showed a respect for my education, and for what he had heard of my situation before coming to sea. "I'll be good friends with you," he used to say, "for by-and-by you'll come out here captain, and then you'll *haze* me well!" By holding well together, we kept the officer in good order, for he was evidently afraid of Nicholas, and never ordered us, except when employed upon the hides. My other companions, the Sandwich Islanders, deserve particular notice.

A considerable trade has been carried on for several years between California and the Sandwich Islands, and most of the vessels are manned with Islanders; who, as they, for the most part, sign no articles, leave whenever they choose, and let themselves out to cure hides at San Diego, and to supply the places of the men of the American vessels while on the coast. In this way, quite a colony of them had become settled at San Diego, as their head-quarters. Some of these had recently gone off in the Ayacucho and Loriotte, and the Pilgrim had taken Mr. Mannini and three others, so that there were not more than twenty left. Of these, four were on pay at the Ayacucho's house, four more working with us, and the rest were living at the oven in a quiet way; for their money was nearly gone, and they must make it last until some other vessel came down to employ them.

During the four months that I lived here, I got well acquainted with all of them, and took the greatest pains to become familiar with their language, habits, and characters. Their language, I could only learn orally, for they had not any books among them, though many of them had been taught to read and write by the missionaries at home. They spoke a little English, and by a sort of compromise, a mixed language was used on the beach, which could be understood by all. The long name of Sandwich Islanders is dropped, and they are called by the whites, all over the Pacific ocean, "Kanákas," from a word in their own language which they apply to themselves, and to all South Sea Islanders, in distinction from whites, whom they call "Haole." This name, "Kanaka," they answer to, both collectively and individually. Their proper names, in their own language, being difficult to pronounce and remember, they are called by any names which the captains or crews may choose to give them. Some are called after the vessel they are in; others by common names, as Jack, Tom, Bill; and some have fancy names, as Ban-yan, Fore-top, Rope-yarn, Pelican, &c. &c. Of the four who worked at our house, one was named "Mr. Bingham," after the missionary at Oahu; another, Hope, after a vessel that he had been in; a third, Tom Davis, the name of his first captain; and the fourth, Pelican, from his fancied resemblance to that bird. Then there was Lagoda-Jack, California-Bill, &c. &c. But by whatever names they might be called, they were the most interesting, intelligent, and kind-hearted people that I ever fell in with. I felt a positive attachment for almost all of them; and many of them I have, to this time, a feeling for, which would lead me to go a great way for the mere pleasure of seeing them, and which will always make me feel a strong interest in the mere name of a Sandwich Islander.

Tom Davis knew how to read, write, and cipher in common arithmetic; had been to the United States, and spoke English quite well. His education was as good as that of three quarters of the Yankees in California, and his manners and principles a good deal better, and he was so quick of apprehension that he might have been taught navigation, and the elements of many of the sciences, with the most perfect ease. Old "Mr. Bingham" spoke very little English—almost none, and neither knew how to read nor write; but he was the best-hearted old fellow in the world. He must have been over fifty years of age, and had two of his front teeth knocked out, which was done by his parents as a sign of grief at the death of Tamahamaha, the great king of the Sandwich Islands. We used to tell him that he ate Captain Cook, and lost his teeth in that way. That was the only thing that ever made him angry. He would always be quite excited at that; and say—"*Aole!*" (no.) "Me no eat Captain Cook! Me pikinini—small—so high—no more! My father see Captain Cook! Me—no!" None of them liked to have anything said about Captain Cook, for the sailors all believe that he was eaten, and that, they cannot endure to be taunted with.—"New Zealand Kanaka eat white man;—Sandwich Island Kanaka,— no. Sandwich Island Kanaka *ua like pu na haole*—all 'e same a' you!"

Mr. Bingham was a sort of patriarch among them, and was always treated with great respect, though he had not the education and energy which gave Mr. Mannini his power over them. I have spent hours in talking with this old fellow about Tamahamaha, the Charlemagne of the Sandwich Islands; his son and successor Riho Riho, who died in England, and was brought to Oahu in the frigate Blonde, Captain Lord Byron, and whose funeral he remembered perfectly; and also about the customs of his country in his boyhood, and the changes which had been made by the missionaries. He never would allow that human beings had been eaten there; and, indeed, it always seemed like an insult to tell so affectionate, intelligent, and civilized a class of men, that such barbarities had been practised in their own country within the recollection of many of them. Certainly, the history of no people on the globe can show anything like so rapid an advance. I would have trusted my life and my fortune in the hands of any one of these people; and certainly, had I wished for a favor or act of sacrifice, I would have gone to them all, in turn, before I should have applied to one of my own countrymen on the coast, and should have expected to have seen it done, before my own countrymen had got half through counting the cost. Their customs, and manner of treating one another, show a simple, primitive generosity, which is truly delightful; and which is often a reproach to our own people. Whatever one has, they all have. Money, food, clothes, they share with one another; even to the last piece of tobacco to put in their pipes. I once heard old Mr. Bingham say, with the highest indignation, to a Yankee trader who was trying to persuade him to keep his money to himself —"No! We no all 'e same a' you!—Suppose one got money, all got money. You;—suppose one got money—lock him up in chest.—No good!"—"Kanaka all e' same a' one!" This principle they carry so far, that none of them will eat anything in sight of others, without offering it all round. I have seen one of them break a biscuit, which had been given him, into five parts, at a time when I knew he was on a very short allowance, as there was but little to eat on the beach.

My favorite among all of them, and one who was liked by both officers and men, and by whomever he had anything to do with, was Hope. He was an intelligent, kind-hearted little fellow, and I never saw him angry, though I knew him for more than a year, and have seen him imposed upon by white people, and abused by insolent officers of vessels. He was always civil, and always ready, and never forgot a benefit. I once took care of him when he was ill, getting medicines from the ship's chests, when no captain or officer would do anything for him, and he never forgot it. Every Kanaka has one particular friend, whom he considers himself bound to do everything for, and with whom he has a sort of contract,—an alliance offensive and defensive,—and for whom he will often make the greatest sacrifices. This friend they call *aikane*; and for such, did Hope adopt me. I do not believe I could have wanted anything which he had, that he would not have given me. In return for this, I was always his friend among the Americans, and used to teach him letters and numbers; for he left home before he had learned how to read. He was very curious about Boston (as they call the United States); asking many questions about the houses, the people, &c., and always wished to have the pictures in books explained to him. They were all astonishingly quick in catching at explanations, and many things which I had thought it utterly impossible to make them understand, they often seized in an instant, and asked questions which showed that they knew enough to make them wish to go farther. The pictures of steamboats and railroad cars, in the columns of some newspapers which I had, gave me great difficulty to explain. The grading of the road, the rails, the construction of the carriages, they could easily understand, but the motion produced by steam was a little too refined for them. I attempted to show it to them once by an experiment upon the cook's coppers, but failed; probably as much from my own ignorance as from their want of apprehension; and, I have no doubt, left them with about as clear an idea of the principle as I had myself. This difficulty, of course, existed in the same force with the steamboats; and all I could do was to give them some account of the results, in the shape of speed; for, failing in the reason, I had to fall back upon the fact. In my account of the speed I was supported by Tom, who had been to Nantucket, and seen a little steamboat which ran over to New Bedford.

A map of the world, which I once showed them, kept their attention for hours; those who knew how to read pointing out the places and referring to me for the distances. I remember being much amused with a question which Hope asked me. Pointing to the large irregular place which is always left blank round the poles, to denote that it is undiscovered, he looked up and asked—"*Pau?*" (Done? ended?)

The system of naming the streets and numbering the houses, they easily understood, and the utility of it. They had a great desire to see America, but were afraid of doubling Cape Horn, for they suffer much in cold weather, and had heard dreadful accounts of the Cape, from those of their number who had been round it.

They smoke a great deal, though not much at a time; using pipes with large bowls, and very short stems, or no stems at all. These, they light, and putting them to their mouths, take a long draught, getting their mouths as full as they can hold, and their cheeks distended, and then let it slowly out through their mouths and nostrils. The pipe is then passed to others, who draw, in the same manner, one pipe-full serving for a half a dozen. They never take short, continuous draughts, like Europeans, but one of these "Oahu puffs," as the sailors call them, serves for an hour or two, until some one else lights his pipe, and it is passed round in the same manner. Each Kanaka on the beach had a pipe, flint, steel, tinder, a hand of tobacco, and a jack-knife, which he always carried about with him.

That which strikes a stranger most peculiarly is their style of singing. They run on, in a low, guttural, monotonous sort of chant, their lips and tongues seeming hardly to move, and the sounds apparently modulated solely in the throat. There is very little tune to it, and the words, so far as I could learn, are extempore. They sing about persons and things which are around them, and adopt this method when they do not wish to be understood by any but themselves; and it is very effectual, for with the most careful attention I never could detect a word that I knew. I have often heard Mr. Mannini, who was the most noted *improvisatore* among them, sing for an hour together, when at work in the midst of Americans and Englishmen; and, by the occasional shouts and laughter of the Kanakas, who were at a distance, it was evident that he was singing about the different men that he was at work with. They have great powers of ridicule, and are excellent mimics; many of them discovering and imitating the peculiarities of our own people, before we had seen them ourselves.

These were the people with whom I was to spend a few months; and who, with the exception of the officer, Nicholas the Frenchman, and the boy, made the whole population of the beach. I ought, perhaps, to except the dogs, for they were an important part of our settlement. Some of the first vessels brought dogs out with them, who, for convenience, were left ashore, and there multiplied, until they came to be a great people. While I was on the beach, the average number was about forty, and probably an equal, or greater number are drowned, or killed in some other way, every year. They are very useful in guarding the beach, the Indians being afraid to come down at night; for it was impossible for any one to get within half a mile of the hide-houses without a general alarm. The father of the colony, old Sachem, so called from the ship in which he was brought out, died while I was there, full of years, and was honorably buried. Hogs, and a few chickens, were the rest of the animal tribe, and formed, like the dogs, a common company, though they were all known and marked, and usually fed at the houses to which they belonged.

I had been but a few hours on the beach, and the Pilgrim was hardly out of sight, when the cry of "Sail ho!" was raised, and a small hermaphrodite brig rounded the point, bore up into the harbor, and came to anchor. It was the Mexican brig Fazio, which we had left at San Pedro, and which had come down to land her tallow, try it all over, and make new bags, and then take it in, and leave the coast. They moored ship, erected their tryworks on shore, put up a small tent, in which they all lived, and commenced operations. They made an addition to our *society*, and we spent many evenings in their tent, where, amid the Babel of English, Spanish, French, Indian, and Kanaka, we found some words that we could understand in common.

The morning after my landing, I began the duties of hide-curing. In order to understand these, it will be necessary to give the whole history of a hide, from the time it is taken from a bullock until it is put on board the vessel to be carried to Boston. When the hide is taken from the bullock, holes are cut round it, near the edge, by which it is staked out to dry. In this manner it dries without shrinking. After they are thus dried in the sun, they are received by the vessels, and brought down to the depot. The vessels land them, and leave them in large piles near the houses. Then begins the hide-curer's duty. The first thing is to put them in soak. This is done by carrying them down at low tide, and making them fast, in small piles, by ropes, and letting the tide come up and cover them. Every day we put in soak twenty-five for each man, which, with us, made an hundred and fifty. There they lie forty-eight hours, when they are taken out, and rolled up, in wheelbarrows, and thrown into the vats. These vats contain brine, made very strong; being sea-water, with great quantities of salt thrown in. This pickles the hides, and in this they lie forty-eight hours; the use of the sea-water, into which they are first put, being merely to soften and clean them. From these vats, they are taken, and lie on a platform twenty-four hours, and then are spread upon the ground, and carefully stretched and staked out, so that they may dry smooth. After they were staked, and while yet wet and soft, we used to go upon them with our knives, and carefully cut off all the bad parts:—the pieces of meat and fat, which would corrupt and infect the whole if stowed away in a vessel for many months, the large *flippers*, the ears, and all other parts which would prevent close stowage. This was the most difficult part of our duty; as it required much skill to take everything necessary off and not to cut or injure the hide. It was also a long process, as six of us had to clean an hundred and fifty, most of which required a great deal to be done to them, as the Spaniards are very careless in skinning their cattle. Then, too, as we cleaned them while they were staked out, we were obliged to kneel down upon them, which always gives beginners the back-ache. The first day, I was so slow and awkward that I cleaned only eight; at the end of a few days I doubled my number; and in a fortnight or three weeks, could keep up with the others, and clean my proportion—twenty-five.

This cleaning must be got through with before noon; for by that time they get too dry. After the sun has been upon them a few hours, they are carefully gone over with scrapers, to get off all the grease which the sun brings out. This being done, the stakes are pulled up, and the hides carefully doubled, with the hair side out, and left to dry. About the middle of the afternoon they are turned upon the other side, and at sundown piled up and covered over. The next day they are spread out and opened again, and at night, if fully dry, are thrown upon a long, horizontal pole, five at a time, and beat with flails. This takes all the dust from them. Then, being salted, scraped, cleaned, dried, and beaten, they are stowed away in the house. Here ends their history, except that they are taken out again when the vessel is ready to go home, beaten, stowed away on board, carried to Boston, tanned, made into shoes and other articles for which leather is used; and many of them, very probably, in the end, brought back again to California in the shape of shoes, and worn out in pursuit of other bullocks, or in the curing of other hides.

By putting an hundred and fifty in soak every day, we had the same number at each stage of curing, on each day; so that we had, every day, the same work to do upon the same number: an hundred and fifty to put in soak; an hundred and fifty to wash out and put in the vat; the same number to haul from the vat and put on the platform to drain; the same number to spread and stake out and clean; and the same number to beat and stow away in the house. I ought to except Sunday; for, by a prescription which no captain or agent has yet ventured to break in upon, Sunday has been a day of leisure on the beach for years. On Saturday night, the hides, in every stage of progress, are carefully covered up, and not uncovered until Monday morning. On Sundays we had absolutely no work to do, unless it was to kill a bullock, which was sent down for our use about once a week, and sometimes came on Sunday. Another good arrangement was, that we had just so much work to do, and when that was through, the time was our own. Knowing this, we worked hard, and needed no driving. We "turned out" every morning at the first signs of daylight, and allowing a short time, about eight o'clock, for breakfast, generally got through our labor between one and two o'clock, when we dined, and had the rest of the time to ourselves; until just before sundown, when we beat the dry hides and put them in the house, and covered over all the others. By this means we had about three hours to ourselves every afternoon; and at sundown we had our supper, and our work was done for the day. There was no watch to stand, and no topsails to reef. The evenings we generally spent at one another's houses, and I often went up and spent an hour or so at the oven; which was called the "Kanaka Hotel," and the "Oahu Coffee-house." Immediately after dinner we usually took a short *siésta* to make up for our early rising, and spent the rest of the afternoon according to our own fancies. I generally read, wrote, and made or mended clothes; for necessity, the mother of invention, had taught me these two latter arts. The Kanakas went up to the oven, and spent the time in sleeping, talking, and smoking; and my messmate, Nicholas, who neither knew how to read or write, passed away the time by a long *siésta*, two or three smokes with his pipe, and a *paséo* to the other houses. This leisure time is never interfered with, for the captains know that the men earn it by working hard and fast, and that if they interfered with it, the men could easily make their twenty-five hides apiece last through the day. We were pretty independent, too, for the master of the house—"capitan de la casa"—had nothing to say to us, except when we were at work on the hides, and although we could not go up to the town without his permission, this was seldom or never refused.

The great weight of the wet hides, which we were obliged to

roll about in wheelbarrows; the continual stooping upon those which were pegged out to be cleaned; and the smell of the vats, into which we were often obliged to get, knee-deep, to press down the hides; all made the work disagreeable and fatiguing;—but we soon got hardened to it, and the comparative independence of our life reconciled us to it; for there was nobody to *haze* us and find fault; and when we got through, we had only to wash and change our clothes, and our time was our own. There was, however, one exception to the time's being our own; which was, that on two afternoons of every week we were obliged to go off and get wood, for the cook to use in the galley. Wood is very scarce in the vicinity of San Diego; there being no trees of any size, for miles. In the town, the inhabitants burn the small wood which grows in thickets, and for which they send out Indians, in large numbers, every few days. Fortunately, the climate is so fine that they have no need of a fire in their houses, and only use it for cooking. With us, the getting of wood was a great trouble; for all that in the vicinity of the houses had been cut down, and we were obliged to go off a mile or two, and to carry it some distance on our backs, as we could not get the hand-cart up the hills and over the uneven places. Two afternoons in the week, generally Monday and Thursday, as soon as we had got through dinner, we started off for the bush, each of us furnished with a hatchet and a long piece of rope, and dragging the hand-cart behind us, and followed by the whole colony of dogs, who were always ready for the bush, and were half mad whenever they saw our preparations. We went with the hand-cart as far as we could conveniently drag it, and leaving it in an open, conspicuous place, separated ourselves; each taking his own course, and looking about for some good place to begin upon. Frequently, we had to go nearly a mile from the hand-cart, before we could find any fit place. Having lighted upon a good thicket, the next thing was to clear away the underbrush, and have fair play at the trees. These trees are seldom more than five or six feet high, and the highest that I ever saw in these expeditions could not have been more than twelve; so that, with lopping off the branches and clearing away the underwood, we had a good deal of cutting to do for a very little wood. Having cut enough for a "back-load," the next thing was to make it well fast with the rope, and heaving the bundle upon our backs, and taking the hatchet in hand, to walk off, up hill and down dale, to the hand-cart. Two good back-loads apiece filled the hand-cart; and that was each one's proportion. When each had brought down his second load, we filled the hand-cart, and took our way again slowly back to the beach. It was generally sundown when we got back, and unloading, covering the hides for the night, and getting our supper, finished the day's work.

These wooding excursions had always a mixture of something rather pleasant in them. Roaming about in the woods with hatchet in hand, like a backwoodsman, followed by a troop of dogs; starting up of birds, snakes, hares and foxes, and examining the various kinds of trees, flowers, and birds' nests, was, at least, a change from the monotonous drag and pull on shipboard. Frequently, too, we had some amusement and adventure. The coati, of which I have before spoken,—a sort of mixture of the fox and wolf breeds,—fierce little animals, with bushy tails and large heads, and a quick, sharp bark, abound here, as in all other parts of California. These, the dogs were very watchful for, and whenever they saw them, started off in full run after them. We had many fine chases; yet, although our dogs ran finely, the rascals generally escaped. They are a match for the dog,—one to one,—but as the dogs generally went in squads, there was seldom a fair fight. A smaller dog, belonging to us, once attacked a coati, single, and got a good deal worsted, and might perhaps have been killed, had we not come to his assistance. We had, however, one dog which gave them a good deal of trouble and many hard runs. He was a fine, tall fellow, and united strength and agility better than any dog that I have ever seen. He was born at the Islands, his father being an English mastiff, and his mother a greyhound. He had the high head, long legs, narrow body, and springing gait of the latter, and the heavy jaw, thick jowls, and strong fore-quarters of the mastiff. When he was brought to San Diego, an English sailor said that he looked, about the face, precisely like the Duke of Wellington, whom he had once seen at the Tower; and, indeed, there was something about him which resembled the portraits of the Duke. From this time he was christened "Welly," and became the favorite and bully of the beach. He always led the dogs by several yards in the chase, and had killed two coati at different times in single combats. We often had fine sport with these fellows. A quick, sharp bark from a coati, and in an instant every dog was at the height of his speed. A few moments made up for an unfair start, and gave each dog his relative place. Welly, at the head, seemed almost to skim over the bushes; and after him came Fanny, Bravo, Childers, and the other fleet ones,—the spaniels and terriers; and then, behind, followed the heavy corps,—bulldogs, &c.; for we had every breed. Pursuit by us was in vain, and in about half an hour a few of them would come panting and straggling back.

Beside the coati, the dogs sometimes made prizes of rabbits and hares, which are very plentiful here, and great numbers of which we often shot for our dinners. There was another animal that I was not so much disposed to find amusement from, and that was the rattlesnake. These are very abundant here, especially during the spring of the year. The latter part of the time that I was on shore, I did not meet with so many, but for the first two months we seldom went into "the bush" without one of our number starting some of them. The first that I ever saw, I remember perfectly well. I had left my companions, and was beginning to clear away a fine clump of trees, when, just in the midst of the thicket, not more than eight yards from me, one of these fellows set up his hiss. It is a sharp, continuous sound, and resembles very much the letting off of the steam from the small pipe of a steamboat, except that it is on a smaller scale. I knew, by the sound of an axe, that one of my companions was near, and called out to him, to let him know what I had fallen upon. He took it very lightly, and as he seemed inclined to laugh at me for being afraid, I determined to keep my place. I knew that so long as I could hear the rattle, I was safe, for these snakes never make a noise when they are in motion. Accordingly, I kept at my work, and the noise which I made with cutting and breaking the trees kept him in alarm; so that I had the rattle to show me his whereabouts. Once or twice the noise stopped for a short time, which gave me a little uneasiness, and retreating a few steps, I threw something into the bush, at which he would set his rattle agoing; and finding that he had not moved from his first place, I was easy again. In this

way I continued at my work until I had cut a full load, never
suffering him to be quiet for a moment. Having cut my load, I
strapped it together, and got everything ready for starting. I
felt that I could now call the others without the imputation
of being afraid; and went in search of them. In a few minutes
we were all collected, and began an attack upon the bush. The
big Frenchman, who was the one that I had called to at first,
I found as little inclined to approach the snake as I had been.
The dogs, too, seemed afraid of the rattle, and kept up a
barking at a safe distance; but the Kanakas showed no fear, and
getting long sticks, went into the bush, and keeping a bright
look-out, stood within a few feet of him. One or two blows
struck near him, and a few stones thrown, started him, and we
lost his track, and had the pleasant consciousness that he might
be directly under our feet. By throwing stones and chips in different directions, we made him spring his rattle again, and began another attack. This time we drove him into the clear
ground, and saw him gliding off, with head and tail erect,
when a stone, well aimed, knocked him over the bank, down a
declivity of fifteen or twenty feet, and stretched him at his
length. Having made sure of him, by a few more stones, we
went down, and one of the Kanakas cut off his rattle. These
rattles vary in number, it is said, according to the age of the
snake; though the Indians think they indicate the number of
creatures they have killed. We always preserved them as trophies, and at the end of the summer had quite a number. None
of our people were ever bitten by them, but one of our dogs
died of a bite, and another was supposed to have been bitten,
but recovered. We had no remedy for the bite, though it was
said that the Indians of the country had, and the Kanakas professed to have an herb which would cure it, but it was fortunately never brought to the test.

Hares and rabbits, as I said before, were abundant, and,
during the winter months, the waters are covered with wild
ducks and geese. Crows, too, were very numerous, and frequently alighted in great numbers upon our hides, picking
at the pieces of dried meat and fat. Bears and wolves are numerous in the upper parts, and in the interior, (and, indeed, a
man was killed by a bear within a few miles of San Pedro,
while we were there,) but there were none in our immediate

neighborhood. The only other animals were horses. Over a dozen of these were owned by different people on the beach, and were allowed to run loose among the hills, with a long lasso attached to them, and pick up feed wherever they could find it. We were sure of seeing them once a day, for there was no water among the hills, and they were obliged to come down to the well which had been dug upon the beach. These horses were bought at, from two, to six and eight dollars apiece, and were held very much as common property. We generally kept one fast to one of the houses every day, so that we could mount him and catch any of the others. Some of them were really fine animals, and gave us many good runs up to the presidio and over the country.

Chapter XX

AFTER we had been a few weeks on shore, and had begun to feel broken into the regularity of our life, its monotony was interrupted by the arrival of two vessels from the windward. We were sitting at dinner in our little room, when we heard the cry of "Sail ho!" This, we had learned, did not always signify a vessel, but was raised whenever a woman was seen coming down from the town; or a squaw, or an ox-cart, or anything unusual, hove in sight upon the road; so we took no notice of it. But it soon became so loud and general from all parts of the beach, that we were led to go to the door; and there, sure enough, were two sails coming round the point, and leaning over from the strong north-west wind, which blows down the coast every afternoon. The headmost was a ship, and the other, a brig. Everybody was alive on the beach, and all manner of conjectures were abroad. Some said it was the Pilgrim, with the Boston ship, which we were expecting; but we soon saw that the brig was not the Pilgrim, and the ship, with her stump top-gallant masts and rusty sides, could not be a dandy Boston Indiaman. As they drew nearer, we soon discovered the high poop and top-gallant forecastle, and other marks of the Italian ship Rosa, and the brig proved to be the Catalina, which we saw at Santa Barbara, just arrived from Valparaiso. They came to anchor, moored ship, and commenced discharging hides and tallow. The Rosa had purchased the house occupied by the Lagoda, and the Catalina took the other spare one between ours and the Ayacucho's, so that, now, each one was occupied, and the beach, for several days, was all alive. The Catalina had several Kanakas on board, who were immediately besieged by the others, and carried up to the oven, where they had a long pow-wow, and a smoke. Two Frenchmen, who belonged to the Rosa's crew, came in, every evening, to see Nicholas; and from them we learned that the Pilgrim was at San Pedro, and was the only other vessel now on the coast. Several of the Italians slept on shore at their hide-house; and there, and at the tent in which the Fazio's crew lived, we had some very good singing, almost every evening. The

Italians sang a variety of songs—barcarollas, provincial airs, &c.; in several of which I recognised parts of our favorite operas and sentimental songs. They often joined in a song, taking all the different parts; which produced a fine effect, as many of them had good voices, and all seemed to sing with spirit and feeling. One young man, in particular, had a falsetto as clear as a clarionet.

The greater part of the crews of the vessels came ashore every evening, and we passed the time in going about from one house to another, and listening to all manner of languages. The Spanish was the common ground upon which we all met; for every one knew more or less of that. We had now, out of forty or fifty, representatives from almost every nation under the sun: two Englishmen, three Yankees, two Scotchmen, two Welshmen, one Irishman, three Frenchmen (two of whom were Normans, and the third from Gascony), one Dutchman, one Austrian, two or three Spaniards, (from old Spain,) half a dozen Spanish-Americans and half-breeds, two native Indians from Chili and the Island of Chiloe, one Negro, one Mulatto, about twenty Italians, from all parts of Italy, as many more Sandwich Islanders, one Otaheitan, and one Kanaka from the Marquesas Islands.

The night before the vessels were ready to sail, all the Europeans united and had an entertainment at the Rosa's hide-house, and we had songs of every nation and tongue. A German gave us "Och! mein lieber Augustin!" the three Frenchmen roared through the Marseilles Hymn; the English and Scotchmen gave us "Rule Britannia," and "Wha'll be King but Charlie?" the Italians and Spaniards screamed through some national affairs, for which I was none the wiser; and we three Yankees made an attempt at the "Star-spangled Banner." After these national tributes had been paid, the Austrian gave us a very pretty little love-song, and the Frenchmen sang a spirited thing called "Sentinelle! O prenez garde a vous!" and then followed the *melange* which might have been expected. When I left them, the aquadiente and annisou was pretty well in their heads, and they were all singing and talking at once, and their peculiar national oaths were getting as plenty as pronouns.

The next day, the two vessels got under weigh for the

windward, and left us in quiet possession of the beach. Our numbers were somewhat enlarged by the opening of the new houses, and the *society* of the beach a little changed. In charge of the Catalina's house, was an old Scotchman, who, like most of his countrymen, had a pretty good education, and, like many of them, was rather pragmatical, and had a ludicrously solemn conceit. He employed his time in taking care of his pigs, chickens, turkeys, dogs, &c., and in smoking his long pipe. Everything was as neat as a pin in the house, and he was as regular in his hours as a chronometer, but as he kept very much by himself, was not a great addition to our society. He hardly spent a cent all the time he was on the beach, and the others said he was no shipmate. He had been a petty officer on board the British frigate Dublin, Capt. Lord James Townshend, and had great ideas of his own importance. The man in charge of the Rosa's house was an Austrian by birth, but spoke, read, and wrote four languages with ease and correctness. German was his native tongue, but being born near the borders of Italy, and having sailed out of Genoa, the Italian was almost as familiar to him as his own language. He was six years on board of an English man-of-war, where he learned to speak our language with ease, and also to read and write it. He had been several years in Spanish vessels, and had acquired that language so well, that he could read any books in it. He was between forty and fifty years of age, and was a singular mixture of the man-of-war's-man and Puritan. He talked a great deal about propriety and steadiness, and gave good advice to the youngsters and Kanakas, but seldom went up to the town, without coming down "three sheets in the wind." One holyday, he and old Robert (the Scotchman from the Catalina) went up to the town, and got so *cozy*, talking over old stories and giving one another good advice, that they came down, double-backed, on a horse, and both rolled off into the sand as soon as the horse stopped. This put an end to their pretensions, and they never heard the last of it from the rest of the men. On the night of the entertainment at the Rosa's house, I saw old Schmidt, (that was the Austrian's name) standing up by a hogshead, holding on by both hands, and calling out to himself—"Hold on, Schmidt! hold on, my good fellow, or you'll be on your back!" Still, he was an intelligent, good-natured old fellow, and had a chest-full of books, which he willingly lent me to read. In the same house with him was a Frenchman and an Englishman; the latter a regular-built "man-of-war Jack;" a thorough seaman; a hearty, generous fellow; and, at the same time, a drunken, dissolute dog. He made it a point to get drunk once a fortnight, (when he always managed to sleep on the road, and have his money stolen from him,) and to battle the Frenchman once a week. These, with a Chilian, and a half a dozen Kanakas, formed the addition to our company.

In about six weeks from the time when the Pilgrim sailed, we had got all the hides which she left us cured and stowed away; and having cleared up the ground, and emptied the vats, and set everything in order, had nothing more to do until she should come down again, but to supply ourselves with wood. Instead of going twice a week for this purpose, we determined to give one whole week to getting wood, and then we should have enough to last us half through the summer. Accordingly, we started off every morning, after an early breakfast, with our hatchets in hand, and cut wood until the sun was over the point,—which was our only mark of time, as there was not a watch on the beach—and then came back to dinner, and after dinner, started off again with our hand-cart and ropes, and carted and "backed" it down, until sunset. This, we kept up for a week, until we had collected several cords,—enough to last us for six or eight weeks—when we "knocked off" altogether, much to my joy; for, though I liked straying in the woods, and cutting, very well, yet the backing the wood for so great a distance, over an uneven country, was, without exception, the hardest work I had ever done. I usually had to kneel down and contrive to heave the load, which was well strapped together, upon my back, and then rise up and start off with it, up the hills and down the vales, sometimes through thickets,— the rough points sticking into the skin, and tearing the clothes, so that, at the end of the week, I had hardly a whole shirt to my back.

We were now through all our work, and had nothing more to do until the Pilgrim should come down again. We had nearly got through our provisions too, as well as our work; for our officer had been very wasteful of them, and the tea, flour, sugar, and molasses, were all gone. We suspected him of sending them up to the town; and he always treated the squaws with molasses, when they came down to the beach. Finding wheat-coffee and dry bread rather poor living, we clubbed together, and I went up to the town on horseback, with a great salt-bag behind the saddle, and a few reáls in my pocket, and brought back the bag full of onions, pears, beans, water-melons, and other fruits; for the young woman who tended the garden, finding that I belonged to the American ship, and that we were short of provisions, put in a double portion. With these we lived like fighting-cocks for a week or two, and had, besides, what the sailors call "a blow-out on sleep;" not turning out in the morning until breakfast was ready. I employed several days in overhauling my chest, and mending up all my old clothes, until I had got everything in order—patch upon patch, like a sand-barge's mainsail. Then I took hold of Bowditch's Navigator, which I had always with me. I had been through the greater part of it, and now went carefully through it, from beginning to end, working out most of the examples. That done, and there being no signs of the Pilgrim, I made a descent upon old Schmidt, and borrowed and read all the books there were upon the beach. Such a dearth was there of these latter articles, that anything, even a little child's story-book, or the half of a shipping calendar, appeared like a treasure. I actually read a jest-book through, from beginning to end, in one day, as I should a novel, and enjoyed it very much. At last, when I thought that there were no more to be got, I found, at the bottom of old Schmidt's chest, "Mandeville, a Romance, by Godwin, in five volumes." This I had never read, but Godwin's name was enough, and after the wretched trash I had devoured, anything bearing the name of a distinguished intellectual man, was a prize indeed. I bore it off, and for two days I was up early and late, reading with all my might, and actually drinking in delight. It is no extravagance to say that it was like a spring in a desert land.

From the sublime to the ridiculous—so, with me, from Mandeville to hide-curing, was but a step; for

Wednesday, July 18th, brought us the brig Pilgrim from the windward. As she came in, we found that she was a good deal altered in her appearance. Her short top-gallant masts were up; her bowlines all unrove (except to the courses); the quarter boom-irons off her lower yards; her jack-cross-trees sent down; several blocks got rid of; running-rigging rove in new places; and numberless other changes, of the same character. Then, too, there was a new voice giving orders, and a new face on the quarter-deck,—a short, dark-complexioned man, in a green jacket and a high leather cap. These changes, of course, set the whole beach on the *qui-vive*, and we were all waiting for the boat to come ashore, that we might have things explained. At length, after the sails were furled and the anchor carried out, the boat pulled ashore, and the news soon flew that the expected ship had arrived at Santa Barbara, and that Captain T—— had taken command of her, and her captain, Faucon, had taken the Pilgrim, and was the green-jacketed man on the quarter-deck. The boat put directly off again, without giving us time to ask any more questions, and we were obliged to wait till night, when we took a little skiff, that lay on the beach, and paddled off. When I stepped aboard, the second mate called me aft, and gave me a large bundle, directed to me, and marked "Ship Alert." This was what I had longed for, yet I refrained from opening it until I went ashore. Diving down into the forecastle, I found the same old crew, and was really glad to see them again. Numerous inquiries passed as to the new ship, the latest news from Boston, &c. &c. S—— had received letters from home, and nothing remarkable had happened. The Alert was agreed on all hands to be a fine ship, and a large one: "Larger than the Rosa"—"Big enough to carry off all the hides in California"—"Rail as high as a man's head"— "A crack ship"—"A regular dandy," &c. &c. Captain T—— took command of her, and she went directly up to Monterey; from thence she was to go to San Francisco, and probably would not be in San Diego under two or three months. Some of the Pilgrim's crew found old shipmates aboard of her, and spent an hour or two in her forecastle, the evening before she sailed. They said her decks were as white as snow—holystoned every morning, like a man-of-war's; everything on board "shipshape and Bristol fashion;" a fine crew, three mates, a sailmaker and carpenter, and all complete. "They've got a *man* for mate of that ship, and not a bloody *sheep* about decks!"—"A mate that knows his duty, and makes everybody do theirs, and won't be imposed upon either by captain or crew." After collecting

all the information we could get on this point, we asked something about their new captain. He had hardly been on board
long enough for them to know much about him, but he had
taken hold strong, as soon as he took command;—sending
down the top-gallant masts, and unreeving half the rigging,
the very first day.

Having got all the news we could, we pulled ashore; and as
soon as we reached the house, I, as might be supposed, proceeded directly to opening my bundle, and found a reasonable
supply of duck, flannel shirts, shoes, &c., and, what was still
more valuable, a packet of eleven letters. These I sat up nearly
all the night to read, and put them carefully away, to be read
and re-read again and again at my leisure. Then came a half a
dozen newpapers, the last of which gave notice of Thanksgiving, and of the clearance of "ship Alert, Edward H. Faucon,
master, for Callao and California, by Bryant, Sturgis & Co."
No one has ever been on distant voyages, and after a long absence received a newspaper from home, who cannot understand the delight that they give one. I read every part of them
—the houses to let; things lost or stolen; auction sales, and all.
Nothing carries you so entirely to a place, and makes you feel
so perfectly at home, as a newspaper. The very name of
"Boston Daily Advertiser" "sounded hospitably upon the ear."

The Pilgrim discharged her hides, which set us at work
again, and in a few days we were in the old routine of dry
hides—wet hides—cleaning—beating, &c. Captain Faucon
came quietly up to me, as I was at work, with my knife, cutting
the meat from a dirty hide, asked me how I liked California,
and repeated—"Tityre, tu patulæ recubans sub tegmine fagi."
Very apropos, thought I, and, at the same time, serves to show
that you understand Latin. However, a kind word from a captain is a thing not to be slighted; so I answered him civilly, and
made the most of it.

Saturday, July 11th. The Pilgrim set sail for the windward,
and left us to go on in our old way. Having laid in such a supply of wood, and the days being now long, and invariably
pleasant, we had a good deal of time to ourselves. All the duck
I received from home I soon made up into trowsers and
frocks, and displayed, every Sunday, a complete suit of my own
make, from head to foot, having formed the remnants of the

duck into a cap. Reading, mending, sleeping, with occasional excursions into the bush, with the dogs, in search of coati, hares and rabbits, or to encounter a rattlesnake, and now and then a visit to the presidio, filled up our spare time after hide-curing was over for the day. Another amusement, which we sometimes indulged in, was "burning the water" for craw-fish. For this purpose, we procured a pair of *grains*, with a long staff like a harpoon, and making torches with tarred rope twisted round a long pine stick, took the only boat on the beach, a small skiff, and with a torch-bearer in the bow, a steersman in the stern, and one man on each side with the grains, went off, on dark nights, to burn the water. This is fine sport. Keeping within a few rods of the shore, where the water is not more than three or four feet deep, with a clear sandy bottom, the torches light everything up so that one could almost have seen a pin among the grains of sand. The craw-fish are an easy prey, and we used soon to get a load of them. The other fish were more difficult to catch, yet we frequently speared a number of them, of various kinds and sizes. The Pilgrim brought us down a supply of fish-hooks, which we had never had before, on the beach, and for several days we went down to the Point, and caught a quantity of cod and mackerel. On one of these expeditions, we saw a battle between two Sandwich Islanders and a shark. "Johnny" had been playing about our boat for some time, driving away the fish, and showing his teeth at our bait, when we missed him, and in a few moments heard a great shouting between two Kanakas who were fishing on the rock opposite to us: "*E hana hana make i ka ia nui!*" "*E pii mai Aikane!*" &c. &c.; and saw them pulling away on a stout line, and "Johnny Shark" floundering at the other end. The line soon broke; but the Kanakas would not let him off so easily, and sprang directly into the water after him. Now came the tug of war. Before he could get into deep water, one of them seized him by the tail, and ran up with him upon the beach; but Johnny twisted round, turning his head under his body, and showing his teeth in the vicinity of the Kanaka's hand, made him let go and spring out of the way. The shark now turned tail and made the best of his way, by flapping and floundering, toward deep water; but here again, before he was fairly off, the other Kanaka seized him by the tail, and made a spring towards the beach, his companion at the same time paying away upon him with stones and a large stick. As soon, however, as the shark could turn, he was obliged to let go his hold; but the instant he made toward deep water, they were both behind him, watching their chance to seize him. In this way the battle went on for some time, the shark, in a rage, splashing and twisting about, and the Kanakas, in high excitement, yelling at the top of their voices; but the shark at last got off, carrying away a hook and line, and not a few severe bruises.

Chapter XXI

W E kept up a constant connection with the presidio, and by the close of the summer I had added much to my vocabulary, beside having made the acquaintance of nearly everybody in the place, and acquired some knowledge of the character and habits of the people, as well as of the institutions under which they live.

California was first discovered in 1536, by Cortes, and was subsequently visited by numerous other adventurers, as well as commissioned voyagers of the crown. It was found to be inhabited by numerous tribes of Indians, and to be in many parts extremely fertile; to which, of course, was added rumors of gold mines, pearl fishery, &c. No sooner was the importance of the country known, than the Jesuits obtained leave to establish themselves in it, to christianize and enlighten the Indians. They established missions in various parts of the country toward the close of the seventeenth century, and collected the natives about them, baptizing them into the church, and teaching them the arts of civilized life. To protect the Jesuits in their missions, and at the same time to support the power of the crown over the civilized Indians, two forts were erected and garrisoned, one at San Diego, and the other at Monterey. These were called Presidios, and divided the command of the whole country between them. Presidios have since been established at Santa Barbara and San Francisco; thus dividing the country into four large districts, each with its presidio, and governed by the commandant. The soldiers, for the most part, married civilized Indians; and thus, in the vicinity of each presidio, sprung up, gradually, small towns. In the course of time, vessels began to come into the ports to trade with the missions, and received hides in return; and thus began the great trade of California. Nearly all the cattle in the country belonged to the missions, and they employed their Indians, who became, in fact, their slaves, in tending their vast herds. In the year 1793, when Vancouver visited San Diego, the missions had obtained great wealth and power, and are accused of having depreciated the country with the sovereign, that they might be allowed to retain their possessions. On the expulsion of the Jesuits from the Spanish dominions, the missions passed into the hands of the Franciscans, though without any essential change in their management. Ever since the independence of Mexico, the missions have been going down; until, at last, a law was passed, stripping them of all their possessions, and confining the priests to their spiritual duties; and at the same time declaring all the Indians free and independent *Rancheros*. The change in the condition of the Indians was, as may be supposed, only nominal: they are virtually slaves, as much as they ever were. But in the missions, the change was complete. The priests have now no power, except in their religious character, and the great possessions of the missions are given over to be preyed upon by the harpies of the civil power, who are sent there in the capacity of *administradores*, to settle up the concerns; and who usually end, in a few years, by making themselves fortunes, and leaving their stewardships worse than they found them. The dynasty of the priests was much more acceptable to the people of the country, and, indeed, to every one concerned with the country, by trade or otherwise, than that of the administradores. The priests were attached perpetually to one mission, and felt the necessity of keeping up its credit. Accordingly, their debts were regularly paid, and the people were, in the main, well treated, and attached to those who had spent their whole lives among them. But the administradores are strangers sent from Mexico, having no interest in the country; not identified in any way with their charge, and, for the most part, men of desperate fortunes—broken down politicians and soldiers—whose only object is to retrieve their condition in as short a time as possible. The change had been made but a few years before our arrival upon the coast, yet, in that short time, the trade was much diminished, credit impaired, and the venerable missions going rapidly to decay. The external arrangements remain the same. There are four presidios, having under their protection the various missions, and pueblos, which are towns formed by the civil power, and containing no mission or presidio. The most northerly presidio is San Francisco; the next Monterey; the next Santa Barbara, including the mission of the same, St. Louis Obispo, and St. Buenaventura, which is the finest mission in the whole country, having very fertile soil and rich vineyards. The last, and most southerly, is San Diego, including the mission of the same, San Juan Campestrano, the Pueblo de los Angelos, the largest town in California, with the neighboring mission of San Gabriel. The priests in spiritual matters are subject to the Archbishop of Mexico, and in temporal matters to the governor-general, who is the great civil and military head of the country.

The government of the country is an arbitrary democracy; having no common law, and no judiciary. Their only laws are made and unmade at the caprice of the legislature, and are as variable as the legislature itself. They pass through the form of sending representatives to the congress at Mexico, but as it takes several months to go and return, and there is very little communication between the capital and this distant province, a member usually stays there, as permanent member, knowing very well that there will be revolutions at home before he can write and receive an answer; and if another member should be sent, he has only to challenge him, and decide the contested election in that way.

Revolutions are matters of constant occurrence in California. They are got up by men who are at the foot of the ladder and in desperate circumstances, just as a new political party is started by such men in our own country. The only object, of course, is the loaves and fishes; and instead of caucusing, paragraphing, libelling, feasting, promising, and lying, as with us, they take muskets and bayonets, and seizing upon the presidio and custom-house, divide the spoils, and declare a new dynasty. As for justice, they know no law but will and fear. A Yankee, who had been naturalized, and become a Catholic, and had married in the country, was sitting in his house at the Pueblo de los Angelos, with his wife and children, when a Spaniard, with whom he had had a difficulty, entered the house, and stabbed him to the heart before them all. The murderer was seized by some Yankees who had settled there, and kept in confinement until a statement of the whole affair could be sent to the governor-general. He refused to do anything about it, and the countrymen of the murdered man, seeing no prospect of justice being administered, made known that if nothing was done, they should try the man themselves. It chanced that, at this time, there was a company of forty trappers and hunters from Kentucky, with their rifles, who had made their head-quarters at the Pueblo; and these, together with the Americans and Englishmen in the place, who were between twenty and thirty in number, took possession of the town, and waiting a reasonable time, proceeded to try the man according to the forms in their own country. A judge and jury were appointed, and he was tried, convicted, sentenced to be shot, and carried out before the town with his eyes blindfolded. The names of all the men were then put into a hat, and each one pledging himself to perform his duty, twelve names were drawn out, and the men took their stations with their rifles, and firing at the word, laid him dead. He was decently buried, and the place was restored quietly to the proper authorities. A general, with titles enough for an hidalgo, was at San Gabriel, and issued a proclamation as long as the fore-top-bowline, threatening destruction to the rebels, but never stirred from his fort; for forty Kentucky hunters, with their rifles, were a match for a whole regiment of hungry, drawling, lazy half-breeds. This affair happened while we were at San Pedro, (the port of the Pueblo,) and we had all the particulars directly from those who were on the spot. A few months afterwards, another man, whom we had often seen in San Diego, murdered a man and his wife on the high road between the Pueblo and San Louis Rey, and the foreigners not feeling themselves called upon to act in this case, the parties being all natives, nothing was done about it; and I frequently afterwards saw the murderer in San Diego, where he was living with his wife and family.

When a crime has been committed by Indians, justice, or rather vengeance, is not so tardy. One Sunday afternoon, while I was at San Diego, an Indian was sitting on his horse, when another, with whom he had had some difficulty, came up to him, drew a long knife, and plunged it directly into the horse's heart. The Indian sprang from his falling horse, drew out the knife, and plunged it into the other Indian's breast, over his shoulder, and laid him dead. The poor fellow was seized at once, clapped into the calabozo, and kept there until an answer could be received from Monterey. A few weeks afterwards, I saw the poor wretch, sitting on the bare ground, in front of the calabozo, with his feet chained to a stake, and handcuffs about his wrists. I knew there was very little hope for him.

Although the deed was done in hot blood, the horse on which he was sitting being his own, and a great favorite, yet he was an Indian, and that was enough. In about a week after I saw him, I heard that he had been shot. These few instances will serve to give one a notion of the distribution of justice in California.

In their domestic relations, these people are no better than in their public. The men are thriftless, proud, and extravagant, and very much given to gaming; and the women have but little education, and a good deal of beauty, and their morality, of course, is none of the best; yet the instances of infidelity are much less frequent than one would at first suppose. In fact, one vice is set over against another; and thus, something like a balance is obtained. The women have but little virtue, but then the jealousy of their husbands is extreme, and their revenge deadly and almost certain. A few inches of cold steel has been the punishment of many an unwary man, who has been guilty, perhaps, of nothing more than indiscretion of manner. The difficulties of the attempt are numerous, and the consequences of discovery fatal. With the unmarried women, too, great watchfulness is used. The main object of the parents is to marry their daughters well, and to this, the slightest slip would be fatal. The sharp eyes of a dueña, and the cold steel of a father or brother, are a protection which the characters of most of them—men and women—render by no means useless; for the very men who would lay down their lives to avenge the dishonor of their own family, would risk the same lives to complete the dishonor of another.

Of the poor Indians, very little care is taken. The priests, indeed, at the missions, are said to keep them very strictly, and some rules are usually made by the alcaldes to punish their misconduct; but it all amounts to but little. Indeed, to show the entire want of any sense of morality or domestic duty among them, I have frequently known an Indian to bring his wife, to whom he was lawfully married in the church, down to the beach, and carry her back again, dividing with her the money which she had got from the sailors. If any of the girls were discovered by the alcalde to be open evil-livers, they were whipped, and kept at work sweeping the square of the presidio, and carrying mud and bricks for the buildings; yet a few reáls would generally buy them off. Intemperance, too, is a common vice among the Indians. The Spaniards, on the contrary, are very abstemious, and I do not remember ever having seen a Spaniard intoxicated.

Such are the people who inhabit a country embracing four or five hundred miles of sea-coast, with several good harbors; with fine forests in the north; the waters filled with fish, and the plains covered with thousands of herds of cattle; blessed with a climate, than which there can be no better in the world; free from all manner of diseases, whether epidemic or endemic; and with a soil in which corn yields from seventy to eighty fold. In the hands of an enterprising people, what a country this might be! we are ready to say. Yet how long would a people remain so, in such a country? The Americans (as those from the United States are called) and Englishmen, who are fast filling up the principal towns, and getting the trade into their hands, are indeed more industrious and effective than the Spaniards; yet their children are brought up Spaniards, in every respect, and if the "California fever" (laziness) spares the first generation, it always attacks the second.

Chapter XXII

Saturday, July 18th. This day, sailed the Mexican hermaphrodite brig, Fazio, for San Blas and Mazatlan. This was the brig which was driven ashore at San Pedro in a south-easter, and had been lying at San Diego to repair and take in her cargo. The owner of her had had a good deal of difficulty with the government about the duties, &c., and her sailing had been delayed for several weeks; but everything having been arranged, she got under weigh with a light breeze, and was floating out of the harbor, when two horsemen came dashing down to the beach, at full speed, and tried to find a boat to put off after her; but there being none on the beach, they offered a handful of silver to any Kanaka who would swim off and take a letter on board. One of the Kanakas, a fine, active, well-made young fellow, instantly threw off everything but his duck trowsers, and putting the letter into his hat, swam off, after the vessel. Fortunately, the wind was very light and the vessel was going slowly, so that, although she was nearly a mile off when he started, he gained on her rapidly. He went through the water leaving a wake like a small steamboat. I certainly never saw such swimming before. They saw him coming from the deck, but did not heave-to, suspecting the nature of his errand; yet, the wind continuing light, he swam alongside and got on board, and delivered his letter. The captain read the letter, told the Kanaka there was no answer, and giving him a glass of brandy, left him to jump overboard and find the best of his way to the shore. The Kanaka swam in for the nearest point of land, and, in about an hour, made his appearance at the hide-house. He did not seem at all fatigued, had made three or four dollars, got a glass of brandy, and was in fine spirits. The brig kept on her course, and the government officers, who had come down to forbid her sailing, went back, each with something like a flea in his ear, having depended upon extorting a little more money from the owner.

It was now nearly three months since the Alert arrived at Santa Barbara, and we began to expect her daily. About a half a mile behind the hide-house, was a high hill; and every afternoon, as soon as we had done our work, some one of us walked up to see if there were any sail in sight, coming down before the regular trades, which blow every afternoon. Each day, after the latter part of July, we went up the hill, and came back disappointed. I was anxious for her arrival, for I had been told by letter that the owners in Boston, at the request of my friends, had written to Captain T—— to take me on board the Alert, in case she returned to the United States before the Pilgrim; and I, of course, wished to know whether the order had been received, and what was the destination of the ship. One year more or less might be of small consequence to others, but it was everything to me. It was now just a year since we sailed from Boston, and at the shortest, no vessel could expect to get away under eight or nine months, which would make our absence two years in all. This would be pretty long, but would not be fatal. It would not necessarily be decisive of my future life. But one year more would settle the matter. I should be a sailor for life; and although I had made up my mind to it before I had my letters from home, and was, as I thought, quite satisfied; yet, as soon as an opportunity was held out to me of returning, and the prospect of another kind of life was opened to me, my anxiety to return, and, at least, to have the chance of deciding upon my course for myself, was beyond measure. Beside that, I wished to be "equal to either fortune," and to qualify myself for an officer's berth, and a hide-house was no place to learn seamanship in. I had become experienced in hide-curing, and everything went on smoothly, and I had many opportunities of becoming acquainted with the people, and much leisure for reading and studying navigation; yet practical seamanship could only be got on board ship; therefore, I determined to ask to be taken on board the ship when she arrived. By the first of August, we finished curing all our hides, stored them away, cleaned out our vats, (in which latter work we spent two days, up to our knees in mud and the sediments of six months' hide-curing, in a stench which would drive an Irishman from his breakfast,) and got in readiness for the arrival of the ship, and had another leisure interval of three or four weeks; which I spent, as usual, in reading, writing, studying, making and mending my clothes, and getting my wardrobe in complete readiness, in case I should go on board the ship; and in fishing, ranging the woods with the dogs, and in occasional visits to the presidio and mission. A good deal of my time was spent in taking care of a little puppy, which I had selected from thirty-six, that were born within three days of one another, at our house. He was a fine, promising pup, with four white paws, and all the rest of his body of a dark brown. I built a little kennel for him, and kept him fastened there, away from the other dogs, feeding and disciplining him myself. In a few weeks, I got him in complete subjection, and he grew finely, was very much attached to me, and bid fair to be one of the leading dogs on the beach. I called him *Bravo*, and the only thing I regretted at the thought of leaving the beach, was parting with him.

Day after day, we went up the hill, but no ship was to be seen, and we began to form all sorts of conjectures as to her whereabouts; and the theme of every evening's conversation at the different houses, and in our afternoon's *paséo* upon the beach, was, the ship—where she could be—had she been to San Francisco?—how many hides she would bring, &c. &c.

Tuesday, August 25th. This morning, the officer in charge of our house went off beyond the point a fishing, in a small canoe, with two Kanakas; and we were sitting quietly in our room at the hide-house, when, just before noon, we heard a complete yell of "Sail ho!" breaking out from all parts of the beach, at once,—from the Kanakas' oven to the Rosa's house. In an instant, every one was out of his house; and there was a fine, tall ship, with royals and skysails set, bending over before the strong afternoon breeze, and coming rapidly round the point. Her yards were braced sharp up; every sail was set, and drew well; the Yankee ensign was flying from her mizen-peak; and having the tide in her favor, she came up like a race-horse. It was nearly six months since a new vessel had entered San Diego, and of course, every one was on the *qui-vive*. She certainly made a fine appearance. Her light sails were taken in, as she passed the low, sandy tongue of land, and clewing up her head sails, she rounded handsomely to, under her mizen top-sail, and let go the anchor at about a cable's length from the shore. In a few minutes, the topsail yards were manned, and all three of the topsails furled at once. From the fore top-gallant yard, the men slid down the stay to furl the jib, and from the mizen top-gallant yard, by the stay, into the main-top, and thence to the yard; and the men on the topsail yards came down the lifts to the yard-arms of the courses. The sails were furled with great care, the bunts triced up by jiggers, and the jibs stowed in cloth. The royal yards were then struck, tackles got upon the yard-arms and the stay, the long-boat hoisted out, a large anchor carried astern, and the ship moored. Then the captain's gig was lowered away from the quarter, and a boat's crew of fine lads, between the ages of fourteen and eighteen, pulled the captain ashore. The gig was a light whale-boat, handsomely painted, and fitted up with cushions, &c., in the stern sheets. We immediately attacked the boat's crew, and got very thick with them in a few minutes. We had much to ask about Boston, their passage out, &c., and they were very curious to know about the life we were leading upon the beach. One of them offered to exchange with me; which was just what I wanted; and we had only to get the permission of the captain.

After dinner, the crew began discharging their hides, and, as we had nothing to do at the hide-houses, we were ordered aboard to help them. I had now my first opportunity of seeing the ship which I hoped was to be my home for the next year. She looked as well on board as she did from without. Her decks were wide and roomy, (there being no poop, or house on deck, which disfigures the after part of most of our vessels,) flush, fore and aft, and as white as snow, which the crew told us was from constant use of holystones. There was no foolish gilding and gingerbread work, to take the eye of landsmen and passengers, but everything was "ship-shape and Bristol fashion." There was no rust, no dirt, no rigging hanging slack, no fag ends of ropes and "Irish pendants" aloft, and the yards were squared "to a *t*" by lifts and braces. The mate was a fine, hearty, noisy fellow, with a voice like a lion, and always wide awake. He was "a man, every inch of him," as the sailors said; and though "a bit of a horse," and "a hard customer," yet he was generally liked by the crew. There was also a second and third mate, a carpenter, sailmaker, steward, cook, &c., and twelve, including boys, before the mast. She had, on board, seven thousand hides, which she had collected at the windward, and also horns and tallow. All these we began discharging, from both gangways at once, into the two boats, the second mate having charge of the launch, and the third mate of the pinnace. For several days, we were employed in this way, until all the hides were taken out, when the crew began taking in ballast, and we returned to our old work, hide-curing.

Saturday, Aug. 29th. Arrived, brig Catalina, from the windward.

Sunday, 30th. This was the first Sunday that the crew had been in San Diego, and of course they were all for going up to see the town. The Indians came down early, with horses to let for the day, and all the crew, who could obtain liberty, went off to the presidio and mission, and did not return until night. I had seen enough of San Diego, and went on board and spent the day with some of the crew, whom I found quietly at work in the forecastle, mending and washing their clothes, and reading and writing. They told me that the ship stopped at Callao in the passage out, and there lay three weeks. She had a passage of a little over eighty days from Boston to Callao, which is one of the shortest on record. There, they left the Brandywine frigate, and other smaller American ships of war, and the English frigate Blonde, and a French seventy-four. From Callao they came directly to California, and had visited every port on the coast, including San Francisco. The forecastle in which they lived was large, tolerably well lighted by bulls-eyes, and, being kept perfectly clean, had quite a comfortable appearance; at least, it was far better than the little, black, dirty hole in which I had lived so many months on board the Pilgrim. By the regulations of the ship, the forecastle was cleaned out every morning, and the crew, being very neat, kept it clean by some regulations of their own, such as having a large spit-box always under the steps and between the bits, and obliging every man to hang up his wet clothes, &c. In addition to this, it was holystoned every Saturday morning. In the after part of the ship was a handsome cabin, a dining-room, and a trade-room, fitted out with shelves and furnished with all sorts of goods. Between these and the forecastle was the "between-decks," as high as the gun deck of a frigate; being six feet and a half, under the beams. These between-decks were holystoned regularly, and kept in the most perfect order; the carpenter's bench and tools being in one part, the sailmaker's in another, and boatswain's locker, with the spare rigging, in a third. A part of the crew slept here, in hammocks swung fore and aft from the beams, and triced up every morning. The sides of the between-decks were clapboarded, the knees and stanchions of iron, and the latter made to unship. The crew said she was as tight as a drum, and a fine sea boat, her only fault being, that of most fast ships,—that she was wet, forward. When she was going, as she sometimes would, eight or nine knots on a wind, there would not be a dry spot forward of the gangway. The men told great stories of her sailing, and had great confidence in her as a "lucky ship." She was seven years old, and had always been in the Canton trade, and never had met with an accident of any consequence, and had never made a passage that was not shorter than the average. The third mate, a young man of about eighteen years of age, nephew of one of the owners, had been in the ship from a small boy, and "believed in the ship;" and the chief mate thought more of her than he would of a wife and family.

The ship lay about a week longer in port, when, having discharged her cargo and taken in ballast, she prepared to get under weigh. I now made my application to the captain to go on board. He told me that I could go home in the ship when she sailed (which I knew before); and, finding that I wished to be on board while she was on the coast, said he had no objection, if I could find one of my own age to exchange with me, for the time. This, I easily accomplished, for they were glad to change the scene by a few months on shore, and, moreover, escape the winter and the south-easters; and I went on board the next day, with my chest and hammock, and found myself once more afloat.

Chapter XXIII

Tuesday, Sept. 8th. This was my first day's duty on board the ship; and though a sailor's life is a sailor's life wherever it may be, yet I found everything very different here from the customs of the brig Pilgrim. After all hands were called, at daybreak, three minutes and a half were allowed for every man to dress and come on deck, and if any were longer than that, they were sure to be overhauled by the mate, who was always on deck, and making himself heard all over the ship. The headpump was then rigged, and the decks washed down by the second and third mates; the chief mate walking the quarterdeck and keeping a general supervision, but not deigning to touch a bucket or a brush. Inside and out, fore and aft, upper deck and between-decks, steerage and forecastle, rail, bulwarks, and water-ways, were washed, scrubbed and scraped with brooms and canvass, and the decks were wet and sanded all over, and then holystoned. The holystone is a large, soft stone, smooth on the bottom, with long ropes attached to each end, by which the crew keep it sliding fore and aft, over the wet, sanded decks. Smaller hand-stones, which the sailors call "prayer-books," are used to scrub in among the crevices and narrow places, where the large holystone will not go. An hour or two, we were kept at this work, when the head-pump was manned, and all the sand washed off the decks and sides. Then came swabs and squilgees; and after the decks were dry, each one went to his particular morning job. There were five boats belonging to the ship,—launch, pinnace, jolly-boat, larboard quarter-boat, and gig,—each of which had a coxswain, who had charge of it, and was answerable for the order and cleanness of it. The rest of the cleaning was divided among the crew; one having the brass and composition work about the capstan; another the bell, which was of brass, and kept as bright as a gilt button; a third, the harness-cask; another, the man-rope stanchions; others, the steps of the forecastle and hatchways, which were hauled up and holystoned. Each of these jobs must be finished before breakfast; and, in the mean time, the rest of the crew filled the scuttle-butt, and the cook scraped his kids (wooden tubs out of which the sailors eat) and polished the hoops, and placed them before the galley, to await inspection. When the decks were dry, the lord paramount made his appearance on the quarter-deck, and took a few turns, when eight bells were struck, and all hands went to breakfast. Half an hour was allowed for breakfast, when all hands were called again; the kids, pots, bread-bags, &c., stowed away; and, this morning, preparations were made for getting under weigh. We paid out on the chain by which we swung; hove in on the other; catted the anchor; and hove short on the first. This work was done in shorter time than was usual on board the brig; for though everything was more than twice as large and heavy, the cat-block being as much as a man could lift, and the chain as large as three of the Pilgrim's, yet there was a plenty of room to move about in, more discipline and system, more men, and more good will. Every one seemed ambitious to do his best: officers and men knew their duty, and all went well. As soon as she was hove short, the mate, on the forecastle, gave the order to loose the sails, and, in an instant, every one sprung into the rigging, up the shrouds, and out on the yards, scrambling by one another,—the first up the best fellow,—cast off the yard-arm gaskets and bunt gaskets, and one man remained on each yard, holding the bunt jigger with a turn round the tye, all ready to let go, while the rest laid down to man the sheets and halyards. The mate then hailed the yards— "All ready forward?"—"All ready the cross-jack yards?" &c. &c.; and "Aye, aye, sir!" being returned from each, the word was given to let go; and in the twinkling of an eye, the ship, which had shown nothing but her bare yards, was covered with her loose canvass, from the royal-mast-heads to the decks. Every one then laid down, except one man in each top, to overhaul the rigging, and the topsails were hoisted and sheeted home; all three yards going to the mast-head at once, the larboard watch hoisting the fore, the starboard watch the main, and five light hands, (of whom I was one,) picked from the two watches, the mizen. The yards were then trimmed, the anchor weighed, the cat-block hooked on, the fall stretched out, manned by "all hands and the cook," and the anchor brought to the head with "cheerily men!" in full chorus. The ship being now under weigh, the light sails were set, one after another, and she was under full sail, before she had passed the sandy point. The fore royal, which fell to my lot, (being in the mate's watch,) was more than twice as large as that of the Pilgrim, and, though I could handle the brig's easily, I found my hands full, with this, especially as there were no jacks to the ship; everything being for neatness, and nothing left for Jack to hold on by, but his eyelids.

As soon as we were beyond the point, and all sail out, the order was given, "Go below the watch!" and the crew said that, ever since they had been on the coast, they had had "watch and watch," while going from port to port; and, in fact, everything showed that, though strict discipline was kept, and the utmost was required of every man, in the way of his duty, yet, on the whole, there was very good usage on board. Each one knew that he must be a man, and show himself smart when at his duty, yet every one was satisfied with the usage; and a contented crew, agreeing with one another, and finding no fault, was a contrast indeed with the small, hard-used, dissatisfied, grumbling, desponding crew of the Pilgrim.

It being the turn of our watch to go below, the men went to work, mending their clothes, and doing other little things for themselves; and I, having got my wardrobe in complete order at San Diego, had nothing to do but to read. I accordingly overhauled the chests of the crew, but found nothing that suited me exactly, until one of the men said he had a book which "told all about a great highwayman," at the bottom of his chest, and producing it, I found, to my surprise and joy, that it was nothing else than Bulwer's Paul Clifford. This, I seized immediately, and going to my hammock, lay there, swinging and reading, until the watch was out. The between-decks were clear, the hatchways open, and a cool breeze blowing through them, the ship under easy way, and everything comfortable. I had just got well into the story, when eight bells were struck, and we were all ordered to dinner. After dinner came our watch on deck for four hours, and, at four o'clock, I went below again, turned into my hammock, and read until the dog watch. As no lights were allowed after eight o'clock, there was no reading in the night watch. Having light winds and calms, we were three days on the passage, and each watch below, during the daytime, I spent in the same manner, until I had finished my book. I shall never forget the enjoyment I derived from it. To come across anything with the slightest claims to literary merit, was so unusual, that this was a perfect feast to me. The brilliancy of the book, the succession of capital hits, lively and characteristic sketches, kept me in a constant state of pleasing sensations. It was far too good for a sailor. I could not expect such fine times to last long.

While on deck, the regular work of the ship went on. The sailmaker and carpenter worked between decks, and the crew had their work to do upon the rigging, drawing yarns, making spun-yarn, &c. as usual in merchantmen. The night watches were much more pleasant than on board the Pilgrim. There, there were so few in a watch, that, one being at the wheel, and another on the look-out, there was no one left to talk with; but here, we had seven in a watch, so that we had long yarns, in abundance. After two or three night watches, I became quite well acquainted with all the larboard watch. The sailmaker was the head man of the watch, and was generally considered the most experienced seaman on board. He was a thoroughbred old man-of-war's-man, had been to sea twenty-two years, in all kinds of vessels,—men-of-war, privateers, slavers, and merchantmen;—everything except whalers, which a thorough sailor despises, and will always steer clear of, if he can. He had, of course, been in all parts of the world, and was remarkable for drawing a long bow. His yarns frequently stretched through a watch, and kept all hands awake. They were always amusing from their improbability, and, indeed, he never expected to be believed, but spun them merely for amusement; and as he had some humor and a good supply of man-of-war slang and sailor's salt phrases, he always made fun. Next to him in age and experience, and, of course, in standing in the watch, was an Englishman, named Harris, of whom I shall have more to say hereafter. Then, came two or three Americans, who had been the common run of European and South American voyages, and one who had been in a "spouter," and, of course, had all the whaling stories to himself. Last of all, was a broad-backed, thick-headed boy from Cape Cod, who had been in mackerel schooners, and was making his first voyage in a square-rigged vessel. He was born in Hingham, and of course was called "Bucket-maker." The other watch was composed of about the same number. A tall, fine-looking Frenchman, with coal-black whiskers and curly hair, a first-rate seaman, and named John, (one name is enough for a sailor,) was the head man of the watch. Then came two Americans, (one of whom had been a dissipated young man of property and family, and was reduced to duck trowsers and monthly wages,) a German, an English lad, named Ben, who belonged on the mizen topsail yard with me, and was a good sailor for his years, and two Boston boys just from the public schools. The carpenter sometimes mustered in the starboard watch, and was an old seadog, a Swede by birth, and accounted the best helmsman in the ship. This was our ship's company, beside cook and steward, who were blacks, three mates, and the captain.

The second day out, the wind drew ahead, and we had to beat up the coast; so that, in tacking ship, I could see the regulations of the vessel. Instead of going wherever was most convenient, and running from place to place, wherever work was to be done, each man had his station. A regular tacking and wearing bill was made out. The chief mate commanded on the forecastle, and had charge of the head sails and the forward part of the ship. Two of the best men in the ship—the sailmaker from our watch, and John, the Frenchman, from the other, worked the forecastle. The third mate commanded in the waist, and, with the carpenter and one man, worked the main tack and bowline; the cook, *ex-officio*, the fore sheet, and the steward the main. The second mate had charge of the after yards, and let go the lee fore and main braces. I was stationed at the weather cross-jack braces; three other light hands at the lee; one boy at the spanker-sheet and guy; a man and a boy at the main topsail, top-gallant, and royal braces; and all the rest of the crew—men and boys—tallied on to the main brace. Every one here knew his station, must be there when all hands were called to put the ship about, and was answerable for every rope committed to him. Each man's rope must be let go and hauled in at the order, properly made fast, and neatly coiled away when the ship was about. As soon as all hands are at their stations, the captain, who stands on the weather side of the quarter-deck, makes a sign to the man at the wheel to put it down, and calls out "Helm's a lee'!" "Helm's a lee'!" answers the mate on the forecastle, and the head sheets are let go. "Raise tacks and sheets!" says the captain; "tacks and sheets!" is passed forward, and the fore tack and main sheet are let go. The next thing is to haul taught for a swing. The weather cross-jack braces and the lee main braces are each belayed together upon two pins, and ready to be let go, and the opposite braces hauled taught. "Main topsail haul!" shouts the captain; the braces are let go; and if he has taken his time well, the yards swing round like a top; but if he is too late, or too soon, it is like drawing teeth. The after yards are then braced up and be-layed, the main sheet hauled aft, the spanker eased over to lee-ward, and the men from the braces stand by the head yards. "Let go and haul!" says the captain; the second mate lets go the weather fore braces, and the men haul in to leeward. The mate, on the forecastle, looks out for the head yards. "Well, the fore topsail yard!" "Top-gallant yard's well!" "Royal yard too much! Haul in to windward! So! well *that!*" "Well *all!*" Then the starboard watch board the main tack, and the lar-board watch lay forward and board the fore tack and haul down the jib sheet, clapping a tackle upon it, if it blows very fresh. The after yards are then trimmed, the captain generally looking out for them himself. "Well the cross-jack yard!" "Small pull the main top-gallant yard!" "Well *that!*" "Well the mizen topsail yard!" "Cross-jack yards all *well!*" "Well all aft!" "Haul taught to windward!" Everything being now trimmed and in order, each man coils up the rigging at his own station, and the order is given—"Go below the watch!"

During the last twenty-four hours of the passage, we beat off and on the land, making a tack about once in four hours, so that I had a sufficient opportunity to observe the working of the ship; and certainly, it took no more men to brace about this ship's lower yards, which were more than fifty feet square, than it did those of the Pilgrim, which were not much more than half the size; so much depends upon the manner in which the braces run, and the state of the blocks; and Captain Wilson, of the Ayacucho, who was afterwards a passenger with us, upon a trip to windward, said he had no doubt that our ship worked two men lighter than his brig.

Friday, Sept. 11. This morning, at four o'clock, went below, San Pedro point being about two leagues ahead, and the ship going on under studding-sails. In about an hour we were waked up by the hauling of the chain about decks, and in a few minutes "All hands ahoy!" was called; and we were all at work, hauling in and making up the studding-sails, overhauling the chain forward, and getting the anchors ready. "The Pilgrim is there at anchor," said some one, as we were running about decks; and taking a moment's look over the rail, I saw my old friend, deeply laden, lying at anchor inside of the kelp. In coming to anchor, as well as in tacking, each one had his station and duty. The light sails were clewed up and furled, the courses hauled up, and the jibs down; then came the topsails in the buntlines, and the anchor let go. As soon as she was well at anchor, all hands lay aloft to furl the topsails; and this, I soon found, was a great matter on board this ship; for every sailor knows that a vessel is judged of, a good deal, by the furl of her sails. The third mate, sailmaker, and the larboard watch went upon the fore topsail yard; the second mate, carpenter, and the starboard watch upon the main; and myself and the English lad, and the two Boston boys, and the young Cape-Cod man, furled the mizen topsail. This sail belonged to us altogether, to reef and to furl, and not a man was allowed to come upon our yard. The mate took us under his special care, frequently making us furl the sail over, three or four times, until we got the bunt up to a perfect cone, and the whole sail without a wrinkle. As soon as each sail was hauled up and the bunt made, the jigger was bent on to the slack of the buntlines, and the bunt triced up, on deck. The mate then took his place between the knight-heads to "twig" the fore, on the windlass to twig the main, and at the foot of the main-mast, for the mizen; and if anything was wrong,—too much bunt on one side, clues too taught or too slack, or any sail abaft the yard,—the whole must be dropped again. When all was right, the bunts were triced well up, the yard-arm gaskets passed, so as not to leave a wrinkle forward of the yard—short gaskets with turns close together.

From the moment of letting go the anchor, when the captain ceases his care of things, the chief mate is the great man. With a voice like a young lion, he was hallooing and bawling, in all directions, making everything fly, and, at the same time, doing everything well. He was quite a contrast to the worthy, quiet, unobtrusive mate of the Pilgrim: not so estimable a man, perhaps, but a far better mate of a vessel; and the entire change in Captain T——'s conduct, since he took command of the ship, was owing, no doubt, in a great measure, to this fact. If the chief officer wants force, discipline slackens, everything gets out of joint, the captain interferes continually; that makes a difficulty between them, which encourages the crew, and the whole ends in a three-sided quarrel. But Mr. Brown (the mate of the Alert) wanted no help from anybody; took everything into his own hands; and was more likely to encroach upon the authority of the master, than to need any spurring. Captain T—— gave his directions to the mate in private, and except in coming to anchor, getting under weigh, tacking, reefing topsails, and other "all-hands-work," seldom appeared in person. This is the proper state of things, and while this lasts, and there is a good understanding aft, everything will go on well.

Having furled all the sails, the royal yards were next to be sent down. The English lad and myself sent down the main, which was larger than the Pilgrim's main top-gallant yard; two more light hands, the fore; and one boy, the mizen. This order, we always kept while on the coast; sending them up and down every time we came in and went out of port. They were all tripped and lowered together, the main on the starboard side, and the fore and mizen, to port. No sooner was she all snug, than tackles were got up on the yards and stays, and the long-boat and pinnace hove out. The swinging booms were then guyed out, and the boats made fast by geswarps, and everything in harbor style. After breakfast, the hatches were taken off, and all got ready to receive hides from the Pilgrim. All day, boats were passing and re-passing, until we had taken her hides from her, and left her in ballast trim. These hides made but little show in our hold, though they had loaded the Pilgrim down to the water's edge. This changing of the hides settled the question of the destination of the two vessels, which had been one of some speculation to us. We were to remain in the leeward ports, while the Pilgrim was to sail, the next morning, for San Francisco. After we had knocked off work, and cleared up decks for the night, my friend S—— came on board, and spent an hour with me in our berth between decks. The Pilgrim's crew envied me my place on board the ship, and seemed

to think that I had got a little to windward of them; especially
in the matter of going home first. S—— was determined to go
home in the Alert, by begging or buying; if Captain T——
would not let him come on other terms, he would purchase
an exchange with some one of the crew. The prospect of another year after the Alert should sail, was rather "too much of
the monkey." About seven o'clock, the mate came down into
the steerage, in fine trim for fun, roused the boys out of the
berth, turned up the carpenter with his fiddle, sent the steward
with lights to put in the between-decks, and set all hands to
dancing. The between-decks were high enough to allow of
jumping; and being clear, and white, from holystoning, made
a fine dancing-hall. Some of the Pilgrim's crew were in the
forecastle, and we all turned-to and had a regular sailor's shuffle, till eight bells. The Cape-Cod boy could dance the true
fisherman's jig, barefooted, knocking with his heels, and slapping the decks with his bare feet, in time with the music. This
was a favorite amusement of the mate's, who always stood at
the steerage door, looking on, and if the boys would not
dance, he hazed them round with a rope's end, much to the
amusement of the men.

The next morning, according to the orders of the agent, the
Pilgrim set sail for the windward, to be gone three or four
months. She got under weigh with very little fuss, and came so
near us as to throw a letter on board, Captain Faucon standing
at the tiller himself, and steering her as he would a mackerel
smack. When Captain T—— was in command of the Pilgrim,
there was as much preparation and ceremony as there would
be in getting a seventy-four under weigh. Captain Faucon was
a sailor, every inch of him; he knew what a ship was, and was as
much at home in one, as a cobbler in his stall. I wanted no better proof of this than the opinion of the ship's crew, for they
had been six months under his command, and knew what he
was; and if sailors allow their captain to be a good seaman, you
may be sure he is one, for that is a thing they are not always
ready to say.

After the Pilgrim left us, we lay three weeks at San Pedro,
from the 11th of September until the 2d of October, engaged
in the usual port duties of landing cargo, taking off hides, &c.
&c. These duties were much easier, and went on much more

agreeably, than on board the Pilgrim. "The more, the merrier," is the sailor's maxim; and a boat's crew of a dozen could take off all the hides brought down in a day, without much trouble, by a division of labor; and on shore, as well as on board, a good will, and no discontent or grumbling, make everything go well. The officer, too, who usually went with us, the third mate, was a fine young fellow, and made no unnecessary trouble; so that we generally had quite a sociable time, and were glad to be relieved from the restraint of the ship. While here, I often thought of the miserable, gloomy weeks we had spent in this dull place, in the brig; discontent and hard usage on board, and four hands to do all the work on shore. Give me a big ship. There is more room, more hands, better outfit, better regulation, more life, and more company. Another thing was better arranged here: we had a regular gig's crew. A light whale-boat, handsomely painted, and fitted out with stern seats, yoke, tiller-ropes, &c. hung on the starboard quarter, and was used as the gig. The youngest lad in the ship, a Boston boy about thirteen years old, was coxswain of this boat, and had the entire charge of her, to keep her clean, and have her in readiness to go and come at any hour. Four light hands, of about the same size and age, of whom I was one, formed the crew. Each had his oar and seat numbered, and we were obliged to be in our places, have our oars scraped white, our tholepins in, and the fenders over the side. The bow-man had charge of the boat-hook and painter, and the coxswain of the rudder, yoke, and stern-sheets. Our duty was to carry the captain and agent about, and passengers off and on; which last was no trifling duty, as the people on shore have no boats, and every purchaser, from the boy who buys his pair of shoes, to the trader who buys his casks and bales, were to be taken off and on, in our boat. Some days, when people were coming and going fast, we were in the boat, pulling off and on, all day long, with hardly time for our meals; making, as we lay nearly three miles from shore, from forty to fifty miles' rowing in a day. Still, we thought it the best berth in the ship; for when the gig was employed, we had nothing to do with the cargo, except small bundles which the passengers carried with them, and no hides to carry, besides the opportunity of seeing everybody, making acquaintances, hearing the news, &c. Unless the captain or agent were in the boat, we had no officer with us, and often had fine times with the passengers, who were always willing to talk and joke with us. Frequently, too, we were obliged to wait several hours on shore; when we would haul the boat up on the beach, and leaving one to watch her, go up to the nearest house, or spend the time in strolling about the beach, picking up shells, or playing hop-scotch, and other games, on the hard sand. The rest of the crew never left the ship, except for bringing heavy goods and taking off hides; and though we were always in the water, the surf hardly leaving us a dry thread from morning till night, yet we were young, and the climate was good, and we thought it much better than the quiet, hum-drum drag and pull on board ship. We made the acquaintance of nearly half California; for, besides carrying everybody in our boat,—men, women, and children,—all the messages, letters, and light packages went by us, and being known by our dress, we found a ready reception everywhere.

At San Pedro, we had none of this amusement, for, there being but one house in the place, we, of course, had but little company. All the variety that I had, was riding, once a week, to the nearest rancho, to order a bullock down for the ship.

The brig Catalina came in from San Diego, and being bound up to windward, we both got under weigh at the same time, for a trial of speed up to Santa Barbara, a distance of about eighty miles. We hove up and got under sail about eleven o'clock at night, with a light land-breeze, which died away toward morning, leaving us becalmed only a few miles from our anchoring-place. The Catalina, being a small vessel, of less than half our size, put out sweeps and got a boat ahead, and pulled out to sea, during the night, so that she had the sea-breeze earlier and stronger than we did, and we had the mor-tification of seeing her standing up the coast, with a fine breeze, the sea all ruffled about her, while we were becalmed, in-shore. When the sea-breeze died away, she was nearly out of sight; and, toward the latter part of the afternoon, the regular north-west wind set in fresh, we braced sharp upon it, took a pull at every sheet, tack, and halyard, and stood after her, in fine style, our ship being very good upon a taughtened bow-line. We had nearly five hours of fine sailing, beating up to windward, by long stretches in and off shore, and evidently gaining upon the Catalina, at every tack. When this breeze left us, we were so near as to count the painted ports on her side. Fortunately, the wind died away when we were on our inward tack, and she on her outward, so we were in-shore, and caught the land-breeze first, which came off upon our quarter, about the middle of the first watch. All hands were turned up, and we set all sail, to the skysails and the royal studding-sails; and with these, we glided quietly through the water, leaving the Catalina, which could not spread so much canvass as we, gradually astern, and, by daylight, were off St. Buenaventura, and our antagonist nearly out of sight. The sea-breeze, however, favored her again, while we were becalmed under the headland, and laboring slowly along, she was abreast of us by noon. Thus we continued, ahead, astern, and abreast of one another, alternately; now, far out at sea, and again, close in under the shore. On the third morning, we came into the great bay of Santa Barbara, two hours behind the brig, and thus lost the bet; though, if the race had been to the point, we should have beaten her by five or six hours. This, however, settled the relative sailing of the vessels, for it was admitted that although she, being small and light, could gain upon us in very light winds, yet whenever there was breeze enough to set us agoing, we walked away from her like hauling in a line; and in beating to windward, which is the best trial of a vessel, we had much the advantage of her.

Sunday, Oct. 4th. This was the day of our arrival; and somehow or other, our captain always managed not only to sail, but to come into port, on a Sunday. The main reason for sailing on the Sabbath is not, as many people suppose, because Sunday is thought a lucky day, but because it is a leisure day. During the six days, the crew are employed upon the cargo and other ship's works, and the Sabbath, being their only day of rest, whatever additional work can be thrown into Sunday, is so much gain to the owners. This is the reason of our coasters, packets, &c. sailing on the Sabbath. They get six good days' work out of the crew, and then throw all the labor of sailing into the Sabbath. Thus it was with us, nearly all the time we were on the coast, and many of our Sabbaths were lost entirely to us. The Catholics on shore have no trading and make no journeys on Sunday, but the American has no national religion, and likes to show his independence of priestcraft by doing as he chooses on the Lord's day.

Santa Barbara looked very much as it did when I left it five months before: the long sand beach, with the heavy rollers, breaking upon it in a continual roar, and the little town, imbedded on the plain, girt by its amphitheatre of mountains. Day after day, the sun shone clear and bright upon the wide bay and the red roofs of the houses; everything being as still as death, the people really hardly seeming to earn their sun-light. Daylight actually seemed thrown away upon them. We had a few visiters, and collected about an hundred hides, and every night, at sundown, the gig was sent ashore, to wait for the captain, who spent his evenings in the town. We always took our monkey-jackets with us, and flint and steel, and made a fire on the beach with the driftwood and the bushes we pulled from the neighboring thickets, and lay down by it, on the sand. Sometimes we would stray up to the town, if the captain was likely to stay late, and pass the time at some of the houses, in which we were almost always well received by the inhabitants. Sometimes earlier and sometimes later, the captain came down; when, after a good drenching in the surf, we went aboard, changed our clothes, and turned in for the night—yet not for all the night, for there was the anchor watch to stand.

This leads me to speak of my watchmate for nine months— and, taking him all in all, the most remarkable man I have ever seen—Tom Harris. An hour, every night, while lying in port, Harris and myself had the deck to ourselves, and walking fore and aft, night after night, for months, I learned his whole character and history, and more about foreign nations, the habits of different people, and especially the secrets of sailors' lives and hardships, and also of practical seamanship, (in which he was abundantly capable of instructing me,) than I could ever have learned elsewhere. But the most remarkable thing about him, was the power of his mind. His memory was perfect; seeming to form a regular chain, reaching from his earliest childhood up to the time I knew him, without one link wanting. His power of calculation, too, was remarkable. I called myself pretty quick at figures, and had been through a course of mathematical studies; but, working by my head, I was unable to keep within sight of this man, who had never been beyond his arithmetic: so rapid was his calculation. He carried in his head not only a log-book of the whole voyage, in which everything was complete and accurate, and from which no one ever thought of appealing, but also an accurate registry of all the cargo; knowing, precisely, where each thing was, and how many hides we took in at every port.

One night, he made a rough calculation of the number of hides that could be stowed in the lower hold, between the fore and main mast, taking the depth of hold and breadth of beam, (for he always knew the dimension of every part of a ship, before he had been a month on board,) and the average area and thickness of a hide; he came surprisingly near the number, as it afterwards turned out. The mate frequently came to him to know the capacity of different parts of the vessel, and he could tell the sailmaker very nearly the amount of canvass he would want for each sail in the ship; for he knew the hoist of every mast, and spread of every sail, on the head and foot, in feet and inches. When we were at sea, he kept a running account, in his head, of the ship's way—the number of knots and the courses; and, if the courses did not vary much during the twenty-four hours, by taking the whole progress, and allowing so many eighths southing or northing, to so many easting or westing; he would make up his reckoning just before the captain took the sun at noon, and often came wonderfully near the mark. Calculation of all kinds was his delight. He had, in his chest, several volumes giving accounts of inventions in mechanics, which he read with great pleasure, and made himself master of. I doubt if he ever forgot anything that he read. The only thing in the way of poetry that he ever read was Falconer's Shipwreck, which he was delighted with, and whole pages of which he could repeat. He knew the name of every sailor that had ever been his shipmate, and also, of every vessel, captain, and officer, and the principal dates of each voyage; and a sailor whom we afterwards fell in with, who had been in a ship with Harris nearly twelve years before, was very much surprised at having Harris tell him things about himself which he had entirely forgotten. His facts, whether dates or events, no one thought of disputing; and his opinions, few of the sailors dared to oppose; for, right or wrong, he always had the best of the argument with them. His reasoning powers were remarkable. I have had harder work maintaining an argument with him in a watch, even when I knew myself to be right, and he was only doubting, than I ever had before; not from his obstinacy, but from his acuteness. Give him only a little knowledge of his subject, and, certainly, among all the young men of my acquaintance and standing at college, there was not one whom I had not rather meet, than this man. I never answered a question from him, or advanced an opinion to him, without thinking more than once. With an iron memory, he seemed to have your whole past conversation at command, and if you said a thing now which ill agreed with something said months before, he was sure to have you on the hip. In fact, I always felt, when with him, that I was with no common man. I had a positive respect for his powers of mind, and felt often that if half the pains had been spent upon his education which are thrown away, yearly, in our colleges, he would have been a man of great weight in society. Like most self-taught men, he over-estimated the value of an education; and this, I often told him, though I profited by it myself; for he always treated me with respect, and often unnecessarily gave way to me, from an over-estimate of my knowledge. For the capacities of all the rest of the crew, captain and all, he had the most sovereign contempt. He was a far better sailor, and probably a better navigator, than the captain, and had more brains than all the after part of the ship put together. The sailors said, "Tom's got a head as long as the bowsprit," and if any one got into an argument with him, they would call out—"Ah, Jack! you'd better drop that, as you would a hot potato, for Tom will turn you inside out before you know it."

I recollect his posing me once on the subject of the Corn Laws. I was called to stand my watch, and, coming on deck, found him there before me; and we began, as usual, to walk fore and aft, in the waist. He talked about the corn laws; asked me my opinion about them, which I gave him; and my reasons; my small stock of which I set forth to the best advantage, supposing his knowledge on the subject must be less than mine, if, indeed, he had any at all. When I had got through, he took the liberty of differing from me, and, to my surprise, brought arguments and facts connected with the subject which were new to me, and to which I was entirely unable to reply. I confessed that I knew almost nothing of the subject, and expressed my surprise at the extent of his information. He said that, a number of years before, while at a boarding-house in Liverpool, he had fallen in with a pamphlet on the subject, and, as it contained calculations, had read it very carefully, and had ever since wished to find some one who could add to his stock of knowledge on the question. Although it was many years since he had seen the book, and it was a subject with which he had had no previous acquaintance, yet he had the chain of reasoning, founded upon principles of political economy, perfect in his memory; and his facts, so far as I could judge, were correct; at least, he stated them with great precision. The principles of the steam engine, too, he was very familiar with, having been several months on board of a steamboat, and made himself master of its secrets. He knew every lunar star in both hemispheres, and was a perfect master of his quadrant and sextant. Such was the man, who, at forty, was still a dog before the mast, at twelve dollars a month. The reason of this was to be found in his whole past life, as I had it, at different times, from himself.

He was an Englishman, by birth, a native of Ilfracomb, in Cornwall. His father was skipper of a small coaster, from Bristol, and dying, left him, when quite young, to the care of his mother, by whose exertions he received a common-school education, passing his winters at school and his summers in the coasting trade, until his seventeenth year, when he left home to go upon foreign voyages. Of this mother, he often spoke with the greatest respect, and said that she was a strong-minded woman, and had the best system of education he had ever known; a system which had made respectable men of his three brothers, and failed only in him, from his own indomitable obstinacy. One thing he often mentioned, in which he said his mother differed from all other mothers that he had ever seen disciplining their children; that was, that when he was out of humor and refused to eat, instead of putting his plate away, as most mothers would, and saying that his hunger would bring him to it, in time, she would stand over him and oblige him to eat it—every mouthful of it. It was no fault of her's that he was what I saw him; and so great was his sense of gratitude for her efforts, though unsuccessful, that he determined, at the close of the voyage, to embark for home with all the wages he should get, to spend with and for his mother, if perchance he should find her alive.

After leaving home, he had spent nearly twenty years, sailing upon all sorts of voyages, generally out of the ports of New York and Boston. Twenty years of vice! Every sin that a sailor knows, he had gone to the bottom of. Several times he had been hauled up in the hospitals, and as often, the great strength of his constitution had brought him out again in health. Several times, too, from his known capacity, he had been promoted to the office of chief mate, and as often, his conduct when in port, especially his drunkenness, which neither fear nor ambition could induce him to abandon, put him back into the forecastle. One night, when giving me an account of his life, and lamenting the years of manhood he had thrown away, he said that there, in the forecastle, at the foot of the steps—a chest of old clothes—was the result of twenty-two years of hard labor and exposure—worked like a horse, and treated like a dog. As he grew older, he began to feel the necessity of some provision for his later years, and came gradually to the conviction that rum had been his worst enemy. One night, in Havana, a young shipmate of his was brought aboard drunk, with a dangerous gash in his head, and his money and new clothes stripped from him. Harris had seen and been in hundreds of such scenes as these, but in his then state of mind, it fixed his determination, and he resolved never to taste another drop of strong drink, of any kind. He signed no pledge, and made no vow, but relied on his own strength of purpose. The first thing with him was a reason, and then a resolution, and the thing was done. The date of his resolution he knew, of course, to the very hour. It was three years before I knew him, and during all that time, nothing stronger than cider or coffee had passed his lips. The sailors never thought of enticing Tom to take a glass any more than they would of talking to the ship's compass. He was now a temperate man for life, and capable of filling any berth in a ship, and many a high station there is on shore which is held by a meaner man.

He understood the management of a ship upon scientific principles, and could give the reason for hauling every rope; and a long experience, added to careful observation at the time, and a perfect memory, gave him a knowledge of the expedients and resorts in times of hazard, which was remarkable, and for which I became much indebted to him, as he took the greatest pleasure in opening his stores of information to me, in return for what I was enabled to do for him. Stories of tyranny and hardship which had driven men to piracy;—of the incredible ignorance of masters and mates, and of horrid brutality to the sick, dead, and dying; as well as of the secret knavery and impositions practised upon seamen by connivance of the owners, landlords, and officers; all these he had, and I could not but believe them; for men who had known him for fifteen years had never taken him even in an exaggeration, and, as I have said, his statements were never disputed. I remember, among other things, his speaking of a captain whom I had known by report, who never handed a thing to a sailor, but put it on deck and kicked it to him; and of another, who was of the best connexions in Boston, who absolutely murdered a lad from Boston that went out with him before the mast to Sumatra, by keeping him hard at work while ill of the coast fever, and obliging him to sleep in the close steerage. (The same captain has since died of the same fever on the same coast.)

In fact, taking together all that I learned from him of seamanship, of the history of sailors' lives, of practical wisdom, and of human nature under new circumstances,—a great history from which many are shut out,—I would not part with the hours I spent in the watch with that man for any given hours of my life past in study and social intercourse.

Chapter XXIV

Sunday, Oct. 11th. Set sail this morning for the leeward; passed within sight of San Pedro, and, to our great joy, did not come to anchor, but kept directly on to San Diego, where we arrived and moored ship on

Thursday, Oct. 15th. Found here the Italian ship La Rosa, from the windward, which reported the brig Pilgrim at San Francisco; all well. Everything was as quiet here as usual. We discharged our hides, horns, and tallow, and were ready to sail again on the following Sunday. I went ashore to my old quarters, and found the gang at the hide-house going on in the even tenor of their way, and spent an hour or two, after dark, at the oven, taking a whiff with my old Kanaka friends, who really seemed glad to see me again, and saluted me as the *Aikane* of the Kanakas. I was grieved to find that my poor dog Bravo was dead. He had sickened and died suddenly, the very day after I sailed in the Alert.

Sunday was again, as usual, our sailing day, and we got under weigh with a stiff breeze, which reminded us that it was the latter part of the autumn, and time to expect south-easters once more. We beat up against a strong head wind, under reefed top-sails, as far as San Juan, where we came to anchor nearly three miles from the shore, with slip-ropes on our cables, in the old south-easter style of last winter. On the passage up, we had an old sea captain on board, who had married and settled in California, and had not been on salt water for more than fifteen years. He was astonished at the changes and improvements that had been made in ships, and still more at the manner in which we carried sail; for he was really a little frightened; and said that while we had top-gallant sails on, he should have been under reefed top-sails. The working of the ship, and her progress to windward, seemed to delight him, for he said she went to windward as though she were kedging.

Tuesday, Oct. 20th. Having got everything ready, we set the agent ashore, who went up to the mission to hasten down the hides for the next morning. This night we had the strictest orders to look out for south-easters; and the long, low clouds seemed rather threatening. But the night passed over without any trouble, and early the next morning, we hove out the long-boat and pinnace, lowered away the quarter-boats, and went ashore to bring off our hides. Here we were again, in this romantic spot; a perpendicular hill, twice the height of the ship's mast-head, with a single circuitous path to the top, and long sand beach at its base, with the swell of the whole Pacific breaking high upon it, and our hides ranged in piles on the overhanging summit. The captain sent me, who was the only one of the crew that had ever been there before, to the top, to count the hides and pitch them down. There I stood again, as six months before, throwing off the hides, and watching them, pitching and scaling, to the bottom, while the men, dwarfed by the distance, were walking to and fro on the beach, carrying the hides, as they picked them up, to the distant boats, upon the tops of their heads. Two or three boat-loads were sent off, until, at last, all were thrown down, and the boats nearly loaded again, when we were delayed by a dozen or twenty hides which had lodged in the recesses of the hill, and which we could not reach by any missiles, as the general line of the side was exactly perpendicular, and these places were caved in, and could not be seen or reached from the top. As hides are worth in Boston twelve and a half cents a pound, and the captain's commission was two per cent., he determined not to give them up; and sent on board for a pair of top-gallant studding-sail halyards, and requested some one of the crew to go to the top, and come down by the halyards. The older sailors said the boys, who were light and active, ought to go, while the boys thought that strength and experience were necessary. Seeing the dilemma, and feeling myself to be near the medium of these requisites, I offered my services, and went up, with one man to tend the rope, and prepared for the descent.

We found a stake fastened strongly into the ground, and apparently capable of holding my weight, to which we made one end of the halyards well fast, and taking the coil, threw it over the brink. The end, we saw, just reached to a landing-place, from which the descent to the beach was easy. Having nothing on but shirt, trowsers, and hat, the common sea-rig of warm weather, I had no stripping to do, and began my descent, by taking hold of the rope in each hand, and slipping down, sometimes with hands and feet round the rope, and sometimes breasting off with one hand and foot against the precipice, and holding on to the rope with the other. In this way I descended until I came to a place which shelved in, and in which the hides were lodged. Keeping hold of the rope with one hand, I scrambled in, and by the other hand and feet succeeded in dislodging all the hides, and continued on my way. Just below this place, the precipice projected again, and going over the projection, I could see nothing below me but the sea and the rocks upon which it broke, and a few gulls flying in mid air. I got down in safety, pretty well covered with dirt; and for my pains was told, "What a d—d fool you were to risk your life for a half a dozen hides!"

While we were carrying the hides to the boat, I perceived, what I had been too busy to observe before, that heavy black clouds were rolling up from seaward, a strong swell heaving in, and every sign of a south-easter. The captain hurried everything. The hides were pitched into the boats; and, with some difficulty, and by wading nearly up to our armpits, we got the boats through the surf, and began pulling aboard. Our gig's crew towed the pinnace astern of the gig, and the launch was towed by six men in the jolly-boat. The ship was lying three miles off, pitching at her anchor, and the farther we pulled, the heavier grew the swell. Our boat stood nearly up and down several times; the pinnace parted her tow-line, and we expected every moment to see the launch swamped. We at length got alongside, our boats half full of water; and now came the greatest difficulty of all,—unloading the boats, in a heavy sea, which pitched them about so that it was almost impossible to stand in them; raising them sometimes even with the rail, and again dropping them below the bends. With great difficulty, we got all the hides aboard and stowed under hatches, the yard and stay tackles hooked on, and the launch and pinnace hoisted, chocked, and griped. The quarter-boats were then hoisted up, and we began heaving in on the chain. Getting the anchor was no easy work in such a sea, but as we were not coming back to this port, the captain determined not to slip. The ship's head pitched into the sea, and the water rushed through the hawse-holes, and the chain surged so as almost to unship the barrel of the windlass. "Hove short, sir!" said the mate. "Aye, aye! Weather-bit your chain and loose the top-sails! Make sail on her, men—with a will!" A few moments served to loose the top-sails, which were furled with reefs, to sheet them home, and hoist them up. "Bear a hand!" was the order of the day; and every one saw the necessity of it, for the gale was already upon us. The ship broke out her own anchor, which we catted and fished, after a fashion, and stood off from the lee shore against a heavy head sea, under reefed top-sails, fore top-mast stay-sail and spanker. The fore course was given to her, which helped her a little; but as she hardly held her own against the sea which was setting her to leeward—"Board the main tack!" shouted the captain; when the tack was carried forward and taken to the windlass, and all hands called to the handspikes. The great sail bellied out horizontally as though it would lift up the main stay; the blocks rattled and flew about; but the force of machinery was too much for her. "Heave ho! Heave and pawl! Yo, heave, hearty, ho!" and, in time with the song, by the force of twenty strong arms, the windlass came slowly round, pawl after pawl, and the weather clue of the sail was brought down to the water-ways. The starboard watch hauled aft the sheet, and the ship tore through the water like a mad horse, quivering and shaking at every joint, and dashing from its head the foam, which flew off at every blow, yards and yards to leeward. A half hour of such sailing served our turn, when the clues of the sail were hauled up, the sail furled, and the ship, eased of her press, went more quietly on her way. Soon after, the fore-sail was reefed, and we mizen-top men were sent up to take another reef in the mizen top-sail. This was the first time I had taken a weather earing, and I felt not a little proud to sit astride of the weather yard-arm, pass the earing, and sing out, "Haul out to leeward!" From this time until we got to Boston, the mate never suffered any one but our own gang to go upon the mizen top-sail yard, either for reefing or furling, and the young English lad and myself generally took the earings between us.

Having cleared the point and got well out to sea, we squared away the yards, made more sail, and stood on, nearly before the wind, for San Pedro. It blew strong, with some rain, nearly all night, but fell calm toward morning, and the gale having gone over, we came-to,—

Thursday, Oct. 22nd, at San Pedro, in the old south-easter berth, a league from shore, with a slip-rope on the cable, reefs in the top-sails, and rope-yarns for gaskets. Here we lay ten days, with the usual boating, hide-carrying, rolling of cargo up the steep hill, walking barefooted over stones, and getting drenched in salt water.

The third day after our arrival, the Rosa came in from San Juan, where she went the day after the south-easter. Her crew said it was as smooth as a mill-pond, after the gale, and she took off nearly a thousand hides, which had been brought down for us, and which we lost in consequence of the south-easter. This mortified us; not only that an Italian ship should have got to windward of us in the trade, but because every thousand hides went toward completing the forty thousand which we were to collect before we could say good-by to California.

While lying here, we shipped one new hand, an Englishman, of about two or three and twenty, who was quite an acquisition, as he proved to be a good sailor, could sing tolerably, and, what was of more importance to me, had a good education, and a somewhat remarkable history. He called himself George P. Marsh; professed to have been at sea from a small boy, and to have served his time in the smuggling trade between Germany and the coasts of France and England. Thus he accounted for his knowledge of the French language, which he spoke and read as well as he did English; but his cutter education would not account for his English, which was far too good to have been learned in a smuggler; for he wrote an uncommonly handsome hand, spoke with great correctness, and frequently, when in private talk with me, quoted from books, and showed a knowledge of the customs of society, and particularly of the formalities of the various English courts of law and of Parliament, which surprised me. Still, he would give no other account of himself than that he was educated in a smuggler. A man whom we afterwards fell in with, who had been a shipmate of George's a few years before, said that he heard at the boarding-house from which they shipped, that George had been at a college, (probably a naval one, as he knew no Latin or Greek,) where he learned French and mathematics. He was by no means the man by nature that Harris was. Harris had made everything of his mind and character in spite of obstacles; while this man had evidently been born in a different rank, and educated early in life accordingly, but had been a vagabond, and done nothing for himself since. What had been given to him by others, was all that made him to differ from those about him; while Harris had made himself what he was. Neither had George the character, strength of mind, acuteness, or memory of Harris; yet there was about him the remains of a pretty good education, which enabled him to talk perhaps beyond his brains, and a high spirit and sense of honor, which years of a dog's life had not broken. After he had been a little while on board, we learned from him his remarkable history, for the last two years, which we afterwards heard confirmed in such a manner, as put the truth of it beyond a doubt.

He sailed from New York in the year 1833, if I mistake not, before the mast, in the brig Lascar, for Canton. She was sold in the East Indies, and he shipped at Manilla, in a small schooner, bound on a trading voyage among the Ladrone and Pelew Islands. On one of the latter islands, their schooner was wrecked on a reef, and they were attacked by the natives, and, after a desperate resistance, in which all their number except the captain, George, and a boy, were killed or drowned, they surrendered, and were carried bound, in a canoe, to a neighboring island. In about a month after this, an opportunity occurred by which one of their number might get away. I have forgotten the circumstances, but only one could go, and they yielded to the captain, upon his promising to send them aid if he escaped. He was successful in his attempt; got on board an American vessel, went back to Manilla, and thence to America, without making any effort for their rescue, or indeed, as George afterwards discovered, without even mentioning their case to any one in Manilla. The boy that was with George died, and he being alone, and there being no chance for his escape, the natives soon treated him with kindness, and even with attention. They painted him, tattoed his body, (for he would never consent to be marked in the face or hands,) gave him two or three wives; and, in fact, made quite a pet of him. In this way, he lived for thirteen months, in a fine climate, with a plenty to eat, half naked, and nothing to do. He soon, however, became tired, and went round the island, on different pretences, to look out for a sail. One day, he was out fishing in a small canoe with another man, when he saw a large sail to windward, about a league and a half off, passing abreast of the island and standing westward. With some difficulty, he persuaded the islander to go off with him to the ship, promising to return with a good supply of rum and tobacco. These articles, which the islanders had got a taste of from American traders, were too strong a temptation for the fellow and he consented. They paddled off in the track of the ship, and lay-to until she came down to them. George stepped on board the ship, nearly naked, painted from head to foot, and in no way distinguishable from his companion until he began to speak. Upon this, the people on board were not a little astonished, and having learned his story, the captain had him washed and clothed, and sending away the poor astonished native with a knife or two and some tobacco and calico, took George with him on the voyage. This was the ship Cabot, of New York, Captain Low. She was bound to Manilla, from across the Pacific, and George did seaman's duty in her until her arrival in Manilla, when he left her, and shipped in a brig bound to the Sandwich Islands. From Oahu, he came, in the British brig Clementine, to Monterey, as second officer, where, having some difficulty with the captain, he left her, and coming down the coast, joined us at San Pedro. Nearly six months after this, among some papers we received by an arrival from Boston, we found a letter from Captain Low, of the Cabot, published immediately upon his arrival at New York, and giving all the particulars just as we had them from George. The letter was published for the information of the friends of George, and Captain Low added, that he left him at Manilla to go to Oahu, and he had heard nothing of him since.

George had an interesting journal of his adventures in the Pelew Islands, which he had written out at length, in a handsome hand, and in correct English.

Chapter XXV

Sunday, November 1st. Sailed this day, (Sunday again) for Santa Barbara, where we arrived on the 5th. Coming round St. Buenaventura, and nearing the anchorage, we saw two vessels in port, a large full-rigged, and a small hermaphrodite brig. The former, the crew said must be the Pilgrim; but I had been too long in the Pilgrim to be mistaken in her, and I was right in differing from them; for, upon nearer approach, her long, low shear, sharp bows, and raking masts, told quite another story. "Man-of-war brig," said some of them; "Baltimore clipper," said others; the Ayacucho, thought I; and soon the broad folds of the beautiful banner of St. George,—white field with blood-red border and cross,—were displayed from her peak. A few minutes put it beyond a doubt, and we were lying by the side of the Ayacucho, which had sailed from San Diego about nine months before, while we were lying there in the Pilgrim. She had since been to Valparaiso, Callao, and the Sandwich Islands, and had just come upon the coast. Her boat came on board, bringing Captain Wilson; and in a half an hour the news was all over the ship that there was a war between the United States and France. Exaggerated accounts reached the forecastle. Battles had been fought, a large French fleet was in the Pacific, &c. &c.; and one of the boat's crew of the Ayacucho said that when they left Callao, a large French frigate and the American frigate Brandywine, which were lying there, were going outside to have a battle, and that the English frigate Blonde was to be umpire, and see fair play. Here was important news for us. Alone, on an unprotected coast, without an American man-of-war within some thousands of miles, and the prospect of a voyage home through the whole length of the Pacific and Atlantic oceans! A French prison seemed a much more probable place of destination than the good port of Boston. However, we were too salt to believe every yarn that comes into the forecastle, and waited to hear the truth of the matter from higher authority. By means of the supercargo's clerk, I got the amount of the matter, which was, that the governments had had a difficulty about the payment of a debt;

that war had been threatened and prepared for, but not actually declared, although it was pretty generally anticipated. This was not quite so bad, yet was no small cause of anxiety. But we cared very little about the matter ourselves. "Happy go lucky" with Jack! We did not believe that a French prison would be much worse than "hide-droghing" on the coast of California; and no one who has not been a long, dull voyage, shut up in one ship, can conceive of the effect of monotony upon one's thoughts and wishes. The prospect of a change is like a green spot in a desert, and the remotest probability of great events and exciting scenes gives a feeling of delight, and sets life in motion, so as to give a pleasure, which any one not in the same state would be entirely unable to account for. In fact, a more jovial night we had not passed in the forecastle for months. Every one seemed in unaccountably high spirits. An undefined anticipation of radical changes, of new scenes, and great doings, seemed to have possessed every one, and the common drudgery of the vessel appeared contemptible. Here was a new vein opened: a grand theme of conversation and a topic for all sorts of discussions. National feeling was wrought up. Jokes were cracked upon the only Frenchman in the ship, and comparisons made between "old horse" and "soup meagre," &c. &c.

We remained in uncertainty as to this war for more than two months, when an arrival from the Sandwich Islands brought us the news of an amicable arrangement of the difficulties.

The other vessel which we found in port was the hermaphrodite brig Avon, from the Sandwich Islands. She was fitted up in handsome style; fired a gun and ran her ensign up and down at sunrise and sunset; had a band of four or five pieces of music on board, and appeared rather like a pleasure yacht than a trader; yet, in connection with the Loriotte, Clementine, Bolivar, Convoy, and other small vessels, belonging to sundry Americans at Oahu, she carried on a great trade—legal and illegal—in otter skins, silks, teas, specie, &c.

The second day after our arrival, a full-rigged brig came round the point from the northward, sailed leisurely through the bay, and stood off again for the south-east, in the direction of the large island of Catalina. The next day the Avon got under weigh, and stood in the same direction, bound for San

Pedro. This might do for marines and Californians, but we knew the ropes too well. The brig was never again seen on the coast, and the Avon arrived at San Pedro in about a week, with a full cargo of Canton and American goods.

This was one of the means of escaping the heavy duties the Mexicans lay upon all imports. A vessel comes on the coast, enters a moderate cargo at Monterey, which is the only custom-house, and commences trading. In a month or more, having sold a large part of her cargo, she stretches over to Catalina, or other of the large uninhabited islands which lie off the coast, in a trip from port to port, and supplies herself with choice goods from a vessel from Oahu, which has been lying off and on the islands, waiting for her. Two days after the sailing of the Avon, the Loriotte came in from the leeward, and without doubt had also a snatch at the brig's cargo.

Tuesday, Nov. 10th. Going ashore, as usual, in the gig, just before sundown, to bring off the captain, we found, upon taking in the captain and pulling off again, that our ship, which lay the farthest out, had run up her ensign. This meant "Sail ho!" of course, but as we were within the point we could see nothing. "Give way, boys! Give way! Lay out on your oars, and long stroke!" said the captain; and stretching to the whole length of our arms, bending back again, so that our backs touched the thwarts, we sent her through the water like a rocket. A few minutes of such pulling opened the islands, one after another, in range of the point, and gave us a view of the Canal, where was a ship, under top-gallant sails, standing in, with a light breeze, for the anchorage. Putting the boat's head in the direction of the ship, the captain told us to lay out again; and we needed no spurring, for the prospect of boarding a new ship, perhaps from home, hearing the news, and having something to tell of when we got back, was excitement enough for us, and we gave way, with a will. Captain Nye, of the Loriotte, who had been an old whaleman, was in the stern-sheets, and fell mightily into the spirit of it. "Bend your backs and break your oars!" said he. "Lay me on, Captain Bunker!" "There she flukes!" and other exclamations, peculiar to whalemen. In the mean time, it fell flat calm, and being within a couple of miles of the ship, we expected to board her in a few moments, when a sudden breeze sprung up, dead ahead for the ship, and she braced up and stood off toward the islands, sharp on the larboard tack, making good way through the water. This, of course, brought us up, and we had only to "ease larboard oars; pull round starboard!" and go aboard the Alert, with something very like a flea in the ear. There was a light land-breeze all night, and the ship did not come to anchor until the next morning.

As soon as her anchor was down, we went aboard, and found her to be the whale-ship, Wilmington and Liverpool Packet, of New Bedford, last from the "off-shore ground," with nineteen hundred barrels of oil. A "spouter" we knew her to be as soon as we saw her, by her cranes and boats, and by her stump top-gallant masts, and a certain slovenly look to the sails, rigging, spars, and hull; and when we got on board, we found everything to correspond,—spouter fashion. She had a false deck, which was rough and oily, and cut up in every direction by the chimes of oil casks; her rigging was slack and turning white; no paint on the spars or blocks; clumsy seizings and straps without covers, and homeward-bound splices in every direction. Her crew, too, were not in much better order. Her captain was a slab-sided, shamble-legged Quaker, in a suit of brown, with a broad-brimmed hat, and sneaking about decks, like a sheep, with his head down; and the men looked more like fishermen and farmers than they did like sailors.

Though it was by no means cold weather, (we having on only our red shirts and duck trowsers,) they all had on woollen trowsers—not blue and ship-shape—but of all colors—brown, drab, grey, aye, and *green*, with suspenders over their shoulders, and pockets to put their hands in. This, added to guernsey frocks, striped comforters about the neck, thick cowhide boots, woollen caps, and a strong, oily smell, and a decidedly green look, will complete the description. Eight or ten were on the fore top-sail yard, and as many more in the main, furling the top-sails, while eight or ten were hanging about the forecastle, doing nothing. This was a strange sight for a vessel coming to anchor; so we went up to them, to see what was the matter. One of them, a stout, hearty-looking fellow, held out his leg and said he had the scurvy; another had cut his hand; and others had got nearly well, but said that there were plenty aloft to furl the sails, so they were sogering on the forecastle.

There was only one "splicer" on board, a fine-looking old tar, who was in the bunt of the fore top-sail. He was probably the only sailor in the ship, before the mast. The mates, of course, and the boat-steerers, and also two or three of the crew, had been to sea before, but only whaling voyages; and the greater part of the crew were raw hands, just from the bush, as green as cabbages, and had not yet got the hay-seed out of their heads. The mizen top-sail hung in the bunt-lines until everything was furled forward. Thus a crew of thirty men were half an hour in doing what would have been done in the Alert, with eighteen hands to go aloft, in fifteen or twenty minutes.

We found they had been at sea six or eight months, and had no news to tell us; so we left them, and promised to get liberty to come on board in the evening, for some curiosities, &c. Accordingly, as soon as we were knocked off in the evening and had got supper, we obtained leave, took a boat, and went aboard and spent an hour or two. They gave us pieces of whalebone, and the teeth and other parts of curious sea animals, and we exchanged books with them—a practice very common among ships in foreign ports, by which you get rid of the books you have read and re-read, and a supply of new ones in their stead, and Jack is not very nice as to their comparative value.

Thursday, Nov. 12th. This day was quite cool in the early part, and there were black clouds about; but as it was often so in the morning, nothing was apprehended, and all the captains went ashore together, to spend the day. Towards noon, the clouds hung heavily over the mountains, coming half way down the hills that encircle the town of Santa Barbara, and a heavy swell rolled in from the south-east. The mate immediately ordered the gig's crew away, and, at the same time, we saw boats pulling ashore from the other vessels. Here was a grand chance for a rowing match, and every one did his best. We passed the boats of the Ayacucho and Loriotte, but could gain nothing upon, and, indeed, hardly hold our own with, the long, six-oared boat of the whale-ship. They reached the breakers before us; but here we had the advantage of them, for, not being used to the surf, they were obliged to wait to see us beach our boat, just as, in the same place, nearly a year before, we, in the Pilgrim, were glad to be taught by a boat's crew of Kanakas.

We had hardly got the boats beached, and their heads out, before our old friend, Bill Jackson, the handsome English sailor, who steered the Loriotte's boat, called out that the brig was adrift; and, sure enough, she was dragging her anchors, and drifting down into the bight of the bay. Without waiting for the captain, (for there was no one on board but the mate and steward,) he sprung into the boat, called the Kanakas together, and tried to put off. But the Kanakas, though capital water dogs, were frightened by their vessel's being adrift, and by the emergency of the case, and seemed to lose their faculty. Twice, their boat filled, and came broadside upon the beach. Jackson swore at them for a parcel of savages, and promised to flog every one of them. This made the matter no better; when we came forward, told the Kanakas to take their seats in the boat, and, going two on each side, walked out with her till it was up to our shoulders, and gave them a shove, when, giving way with their oars, they got her safely into the long, regular swell. In the mean time, boats had put off from our ship and the whaler, and coming all on board the brig together, they let go the other anchor, paid out chain, braced the yards to the wind, and brought the vessel up.

In a few minutes, the captains came hurrying down, on the run; and there was no time to be lost, for the gale promised to be a severe one, and the surf was breaking upon the beach, three deep, higher and higher every instant. The Ayacucho's boat, pulled by four Kanakas, put off first, and as they had no rudder or steering oar, would probably never have got off, had we not waded out with them, as far as the surf would permit. The next that made the attempt was the whale-boat, for we, being the most experienced "beach-combers," needed no help, and staid till the last. Whalemen make the best boats' crews in the world for a long pull, but this landing was new to them, and notwithstanding the examples they had had, they slued round and were hove up—boat, oars, and men—all together, high and dry upon the sand. The second time, they filled, and had to turn their boat over, and set her off again. We could be of no help to them, for they were so many as to be in one another's way, without the addition of our numbers. The third time, they got off, though not without shipping a sea which drenched them all, and half filled their boat, keeping them baling, until they reached their ship. We now got ready to go off, putting the boat's head out; English Ben and I, who were the largest, standing on each side of the bows, to keep her "head on" to the sea, two more shipping and manning the two after oars, and the captain taking the steering oar. Two or three Spaniards, who stood upon the beach looking at us, wrapped their cloaks about them, shook their heads, and muttered, "Caramba!" They had no taste for such doings; in fact, the hydrophobia is a national malady, and shows itself in their persons as well as their actions.

Watching for a "smooth chance," we determined to show the other boats the way it should be done; and, as soon as ours floated, ran out with her, keeping her head on, with all our strength, and the help of the captain's oar, and the two after oarsmen giving way regularly and strongly, until our feet were off the ground, we tumbled into the bows, keeping perfectly still, from fear of hindering the others. For some time it was doubtful how it would go. The boat stood nearly up and down in the water, and the sea, rolling from under her, let her fall upon the water with a force which seemed almost to stave her bottom in. By quietly sliding two oars forward, along the thwarts, without impeding the rowers, we shipped two bow oars, and thus, by the help of four oars and the captain's strong arm, we got safely off, though we shipped several seas, which left us half full of water. We pulled alongside of the Loriotte, put her skipper on board, and found her making preparations for slipping, and then pulled aboard our own ship. Here Mr. Brown, always "on hand," had got everything ready, so that we had only to hook on the gig and hoist it up, when the order was given to loose the sails. While we were on the yards, we saw the Loriotte under weigh, and before our yards were mast-headed, the Ayacucho had spread her wings, and, with yards braced sharp up, was standing athwart our hawse. There is no prettier sight in the world than a full-rigged, clipper-built brig, sailing sharp on the wind. In a moment, our slip-rope was gone, the head-yards filled away, and we were off. Next came the whaler; and in a half an hour from the time when four vessels were lying quietly at anchor, without a rag out, or a sign of motion, the bay was deserted, and four white clouds were standing off to sea. Being sure of clearing the point, we stood off with our yards a little braced in, while the Ayacucho went off with a taught bowline, which brought her to windward of us. During all this day, and the greater part of the night, we had the usual south-easter entertainment, a gale of wind, variegated and finally topped off with a drenching rain of three or four hours. At daybreak, the clouds thinned off and rolled away, and the sun came up clear. The wind, instead of coming out from the northward, as is usual, blew steadily and freshly from the anchoring-ground. This was bad for us, for, being "flying light," with little more than ballast trim, we were in no condition for showing off on a taught bowline, and had depended upon a fair wind, with which, by the help of our light sails and studding-sails, we meant to have been the first at the anchoring-ground; but the Ayacucho was a good league to windward of us, and was standing in, in fine style. The whaler, however, was as far to leeward of us, and the Loriotte was nearly out of sight, among the islands, up the Canal. By hauling every brace and bowline, and clapping watch-tackles upon all the sheets and halyards, we managed to hold our own, and drop the leeward vessels a little in every tack. When we reached the anchoring-ground, the Ayacucho had got her anchor, furled her sails, squared her yards, and was lying as quietly as if nothing had happened for the last twenty-four hours.

We had our usual good luck in getting our anchor without letting go another, and were all snug, with our boats at the boom-ends, in half an hour. In about two hours more, the whaler came in, and made a clumsy piece of work in getting her anchor, being obliged to let go her best bower, and finally, to get out a kedge and a hawser. They were heave-ho-ing, stopping and unstopping, pawling, catting, and fishing, for three hours; and the sails hung from the yards all the afternoon, and were not furled until sundown. The Loriotte came in just after dark, and let go her anchor, making no attempt to pick up the other until the next day.

This affair led to a great dispute as to the sailing of our ship and the Ayacucho. Bets were made between the captains, and the crews took it up in their own way; but as she was bound to leeward and we to windward, and merchant captains cannot deviate, a trial never took place; and perhaps it was well for us that it did not, for the Ayacucho had been eight years in the

Pacific, in every part of it—Valparaiso, Sandwich Islands, Canton, California, and all, and was called the fastest merchantman that traded in the Pacific, unless it was the brig John Gilpin, and perhaps the ship Ann McKim of Baltimore.

Saturday, Nov. 14th. This day we got under weigh, with the agent and several Spaniards of note, as passengers, bound up to Monterey. We went ashore in the gig to bring them off with their baggage, and found them waiting on the beach, and a little afraid about going off, as the surf was running very high. This was nuts to us; for we like to have a Spaniard wet with salt water; and then the agent was very much disliked by the crew, one and all; and we hoped, as there was no officer in the boat, to have a chance to duck them; for we knew that they were such "marines" that they would not know whether it was our fault or not. Accordingly, we kept the boat so far from shore as to oblige them to wet their feet in getting into her; and then waited for a good high comber, and letting the head slue a little round, sent the whole force of the sea into the stern-sheets, drenching them from head to feet. The Spaniards sprang out of the boat, swore, and shook themselves, and protested against trying it again; and it was with the greatest difficulty that the agent could prevail upon them to make another attempt. The next time we took care, and went off easily enough, and pulled aboard. The crew came to the side to hoist in their baggage, and we gave them the wink, and they heartily enjoyed the half-drowned looks of the company.

Everything being now ready, and the passengers aboard, we ran up the ensign and broad pennant, (for there was no man-of-war, and we were the largest vessel on the coast,) and the other vessels ran up their ensigns. Having hove short, cast off the gaskets, and made the bunt of each sail fast by the jigger, with a man on each yard; at the word, the whole canvass of the ship was loosed, and with the greatest rapidity possible, everything was sheeted home and hoisted up, the anchor tripped and catheaded, and the ship under headway. We were determined to show the "spouter" how things could be done in a smart ship, with a good crew, though not more than half their number. The royal yards were all crossed at once, and royals and sky-sails set, and, as we had the wind free, the booms were run out, and every one was aloft, active as cats, laying out on the yards and booms, reeving the studding-sail gear; and sail after sail the captain piled upon her, until she was covered with canvass, her sails looking like a great white cloud resting upon a black speck. Before we doubled the point, we were going at a dashing rate, and leaving the shipping far astern. We had a fine breeze to take us through the Canal, as they call this bay of forty miles long by ten wide. The breeze died away at night, and we were becalmed all day on Sunday, about half way between Santa Barbara and Point Conception. Sunday night we had a light, fair wind, which set us up again; and having a fine sea-breeze on the first part of Monday, we had the prospect of passing, without any trouble, Point Conception,—the Cape Horn of California, where it begins to blow the first of January, and blows all the year round. Toward the latter part of the afternoon, however, the regular north-west wind, as usual, set in, which brought in our studding-sails, and gave us the chance of beating round the Point, which we were now just abreast of, and which stretched off into the Pacific, high, rocky and barren, forming the central point of the coast for hundreds of miles north and south. A cap-full of wind will be a bag-full here, and before night our royals were furled, and the ship was laboring hard under her top-gallant sails. At eight bells our watch went below, leaving her with as much sail as she could stagger under, the water flying over the forecastle at every plunge. It was evidently blowing harder, but then there was not a cloud in the sky, and the sun had gone down bright.

We had been below but a short time, before we had the usual premonitions of a coming gale: seas washing over the whole forward part of the vessel, and her bows beating against them with a force and sound like the driving of piles. The watch, too, seemed very busy trampling about decks, and singing out at the ropes. A sailor can always tell, by the sound, what sail is coming in, and, in a short time, we heard the top-gallant sails come in, one after another, and then the flying jib. This seemed to ease her a good deal, and we were fast going off to the land of Nod, when—bang, bang, bang—on the scuttle, and "All hands, reef top-sails, ahoy!" started us out of our berths; and, it not being very cold weather, we had nothing extra to put on, and were soon on deck. I shall never forget the fineness of the sight. It was a clear, and rather a chilly night; the stars were twinkling with an intense brightness, and as far as the eye could reach, there was not a cloud to be seen. The horizon met the sea in a defined line. A painter could not have painted so clear a sky. There was not a speck upon it. Yet it was blowing great guns from the north-west. When you can see a cloud to windward, you feel that there is a place for the wind to come from; but here, it seemed to come from nowhere. No person could have told, from the heavens, by their eyesight alone, that it was not a still summer's night. One reef after another, we took in the top-sails, and before we could get them hoisted up, we heard a sound like a short, quick rattling of thunder, and the jib was blown to atoms out of the bolt-rope. We got the top-sails set, and the fragments of the jib stowed away, and the fore top-mast stay-sail set in its place, when the great main-sail gaped open, and the sail ripped from head to foot. "Lay up on that main-yard and furl the sail, before it blows to tatters!" shouted the captain; and in a moment, we were up, gathering the remains of it upon the yard. We got it wrapped round the yard, and passed gaskets over it as snugly as possible, and were just on deck again, when, with another loud rent, which was heard throughout the ship, the fore top-sail, which had been double-reefed, split in two, athwartships, just below the reef-band, from earing to earing. Here again it was down yard, haul out reef-tackles, and lay out upon the yard for reefing. By hauling the reef-tackles chock-a-block, we took the strain from the other earings, and passing the close-reef earing, and knotting the points carefully, we succeeded in setting the sail, close-reefed.

We had but just got the rigging coiled up, and were waiting to hear "go below the watch!" when the main royal worked loose from the gaskets, and blew directly out to leeward, flapping, and shaking the mast like a wand. Here was a job for somebody. The royal must come in or be cut adrift, or the mast would be snapped short off. All the light hands in the starboard watch were sent up, one after another, but they could do nothing with it. At length, John, the tall Frenchman, the head of the starboard watch, (and a better sailor never stepped upon a deck,) sprang aloft, and, by the help of his long arms and legs, succeeded, after a hard struggle,—the sail blowing over the yard-arm to leeward, and the sky-sail blowing directly over his head,—in smothering it, and frapping it with long pieces of sinnet. He came very near being blown or shaken from the yard, several times, but he was a true sailor, every finger a fish-hook. Having made the sail snug, he prepared to send the yard down, which was a long and difficult job; for, frequently, he was obliged to stop and hold on with all his might, for several minutes, the ship pitching so as to make it impossible to do anything else at that height. The yard at length came down safe, and after it, the fore and mizen royal-yards were sent down. All hands were then sent aloft, and for an hour or two we were hard at work, making the booms well fast; unreeving the studding-sail and royal and sky-sail gear; getting rolling-ropes on the yards; setting up the weather breast-backstays; and making other preparations for a storm. It was a fine night for a gale; just cool and bracing enough for quick work, without being cold, and as bright as day. It was sport to have a gale in such weather as this. Yet it blew like a hurricane. The wind seemed to come with a spite, an edge to it, which threatened to scrape us off the yards. The mere force of the wind was greater than I had ever seen it before; but dark-ness, cold, and wet are the worst parts of a storm, to a sailor.

Having got on deck again, we looked round to see what time of night it was, and whose watch. In a few minutes the man at the wheel struck four bells, and we found that the other watch was out, and our own half out. Accordingly, the starboard watch went below, and left the ship to us for a couple of hours, yet with orders to stand by for a call.

Hardly had they got below, before away went the fore top-mast stay-sail, blown to ribands. This was a small sail, which we could manage in the watch, so that we were not obliged to call up the other watch. We laid out upon the bowsprit, where we were under water half the time, and took in the fragments of the sail, and as she must have some head sail on her, prepared to bend another stay-sail. We got the new one out, into the nettings; seized on the tack, sheets, and halyards, and the hanks; manned the halyards, cut adrift the frapping lines, and hoisted away; but before it was half way up the stay, it was blown all to pieces. When we belayed the halyards, there was nothing left but the bolt-rope. Now large eyes began to show themselves in the fore-sail, and knowing that it must soon go, the mate

ordered us upon the yard to furl it. Being unwilling to call up
the watch who had been on deck all night, he roused out the
carpenter, sailmaker, cook, steward, and other idlers, and, with
their help, we manned the fore-yard, and, after nearly half an
hour's struggle, mastered the sail, and got it well furled round
the yard. The force of the wind had never been greater than
at this moment. In going up the rigging, it seemed absolutely
to pin us down to the shrouds; and on the yard, there was
no such thing as turning a face to windward. Yet here was no
driving sleet, and darkness, and wet, and cold, as off Cape
Horn; and instead of a stiff oil-cloth suit, south-wester caps,
and thick boots, we had on hats, round jackets, duck trowsers,
light shoes, and everything light and easy. All these things make
a great difference to a sailor. When we got on deck, the man at
the wheel struck eight bells, (four o'clock in the morning,)
and "All starbowlines, ahoy!" brought the other watch up. But
there was no going below for us. The gale was now at its height,
"blowing like scissors and thumb-screws;" the captain was on
deck; the ship, which was light, rolling and pitching as though
she would shake the long sticks out of her; and the sails gaping
open and splitting, in every direction. The mizen top-sail,
which was a comparatively new sail, and close-reefed, split, from
head to foot, in the bunt; the fore top-sail went, in one rent,
from clew to earing, and was blowing to tatters; one of the
chain bobstays parted; the sprit-sail yard sprung in the slings;
the martingale had slued away off to leeward; and, owing to
the long dry weather, the lee rigging hung in large bights, at
every lurch. One of the main top-gallant shrouds had parted;
and, to crown all, the galley had got adrift, and gone over to
leeward, and the anchor on the lee bow had worked loose, and
was thumping the side. Here was work enough for all hands
for half a day. Our gang laid out on the mizen top-sail yard,
and after more than half an hour's hard work, furled the sail,
though it bellied out over our heads, and again, by a slat of the
wind, blew in under the yard, with a fearful jerk, and almost
threw us off from the foot-ropes.

Double gaskets were passed round the yards, rolling tackles
and other gear bowsed taught, and everything made as secure
as could be. Coming down, we found the rest of the crew just
laying down the fore rigging, having furled the tattered top-

sail, or, rather, swathed it round the yard, which looked like a broken limb, bandaged. There was no sail now on the ship but the spanker and the close-reefed main top-sail, which still held good. But this was too much after sail; and the order was given to furl the spanker. The brails were hauled up, and all the light hands in the starboard watch sent out on the gaff to pass the gaskets; but they could do nothing with it. The second mate swore at them for a parcel of "sogers," and sent up a couple of the best men; but they could do no better, and the gaff was lowered down. All hands were now employed in setting up the lee rigging, fishing the sprit-sail yard, lashing the galley, and getting tackles upon the martingale, to bowse it to windward. Being in the larboard watch, my duty was forward, to assist in setting up the martingale. Three of us were out on the martingale guys and back-ropes for more than half an hour, carrying out, hooking and unhooking the tackles, several times buried in the seas, until the mate ordered us in, from fear of our being washed off. The anchors were then to be taken up on the rail, which kept all hands on the forecastle for an hour, though every now and then the seas broke over it, washing the rigging off to leeward, filling the lee scuppers breast high, and washing chock aft to the taffrail.

Having got everything secure again, we were promising ourselves some breakfast, for it was now nearly nine o'clock in the forenoon, when the main top-sail showed evident signs of giving way. Some sail must be kept on the ship, and the captain ordered the fore and main spencer gaffs to be lowered down, and the two spencers (which were storm sails, bran new, small, and made of the strongest canvass) to be got up and bent; leaving the main top-sail to blow away, with a blessing on it, if it would only last until we could set the spencers. These we bent on very carefully, with strong robands and seizings, and making tackles fast to the clues, bowsed them down to the water-ways. By this time the main top-sail was among the things that have been, and we went aloft to stow away the remnant of the last sail of all those which were on the ship twenty-four hours before. The spencers were now the only whole sails on the ship, and being strong and small, and near the deck, presenting but little surface to the wind above the rail, promised to hold out well. Hove-to under these, and eased by having no sail above the tops, the ship rose and fell, and drifted off to lee-ward like a line-of-battle ship.

It was now eleven o'clock, and the watch was sent below to get breakfast, and at eight bells (noon), as everything was snug, although the gale had not in the least abated, the watch was set, and the other watch and idlers sent below. For three days and three nights, the gale continued with unabated fury, and with singular regularity. There were no lulls, and very little variation in its fierceness. Our ship, being light, rolled so as almost to send the fore yard-arm under water, and drifted off bodily, to leeward. All this time there was not a cloud to be seen in the sky, day or night;—no, not so large as a man's hand. Every morning the sun rose cloudless from the sea, and set again at night, in the sea, in a flood of light. The stars, too, came out of the blue, one after another, night after night, un-obscured, and twinkled as clear as on a still frosty night at home, until the day came upon them. All this time, the sea was rolling in immense surges, white with foam, as far as the eye could reach, on every side, for we were now leagues and leagues from shore.

The between-decks being empty, several of us slept there in hammocks, which are the best things in the world to sleep in during a storm; it not being true of them, as it is of another kind of bed, "when the wind blows, the cradle will rock;" for it is the ship that rocks, while they always hang vertically from the beams. During these seventy-two hours we had nothing to do, but to turn in and out, four hours on deck, and four be-low, eat, sleep, and keep watch. The watches were only varied by taking the helm in turn, and now and then, by one of the sails, which were furled, blowing out of the gaskets, and get-ting adrift, which sent us up on the yards; and by getting tack-les on different parts of the rigging, which were slack. Once, the wheel-rope parted, which might have been fatal to us, had not the chief mate sprung instantly with a relieving tackle to windward, and kept the tiller up, till a new one could be rove. On the morning of the twentieth, at daybreak, the gale had evidently done its worst, and had somewhat abated; so much so, that all hands were called to bend new sails, although it was still blowing as hard as two common gales. One at a time, and with great difficulty and labor, the old sails were unbent and sent down by the buntlines, and three new top-sails, made for the homeward passage round Cape Horn, and which had never been bent, were got up from the sail-room, and, under the care of the sailmaker, were fitted for bending, and sent up by the halyards into the tops, and, with stops and frapping lines, were bent to the yards, close-reefed, sheeted home, and hoisted. These were done one at a time, and with the greatest care and difficulty. Two spare courses were then got up and bent in the same manner and furled, and a storm-jib, with the bonnet off, bent and furled to the boom. It was twelve o'clock before we got through; and five hours of more exhausting labor I never experienced; and no one of that ship's crew, I will venture to say, will ever desire again to unbend and bend five large sails, in the teeth of a tremendous north-wester. Towards night, a few clouds appeared in the horizon, and as the gale moderated, the usual appearance of driving clouds relieved the face of the sky. The fifth day after the commencement of the storm, we shook a reef out of each top-sail, and set the reefed fore-sail, jib, and spanker; but it was not until after eight days of reefed top-sails that we had a whole sail on the ship; and then it was quite soon enough, for the captain was anxious to make up for leeway, the gale having blown us half the distance to the Sandwich Islands.

Inch by inch, as fast as the gale would permit, we made sail on the ship, for the wind still continued a-head, and we had many days' sailing to get back to the longitude we were in when the storm took us. For eight days more we beat to windward under a stiff top-gallant breeze, when the wind shifted and became variable. A light south-easter, to which we could carry a reefed top-mast studding-sail, did wonders for our dead reckoning.

Friday, December 4th, after a passage of twenty days, we arrived at the mouth of the bay of San Francisco.

Chapter XXVI

OUR place of destination had been Monterey, but as we were to the northward of it when the wind hauled a-head, we made a fair wind for San Francisco. This large bay, which lies in latitude 37° 58', was discovered by Sir Francis Drake, and by him represented to be (as indeed it is) a magnificent bay, containing several good harbors, great depth of water, and surrounded by a fertile and finely-wooded country. About thirty miles from the mouth of the bay, and on the south-east side, is a high point, upon which the presidio is built. Behind this, is the harbor in which trading vessels anchor, and near it, the mission of San Francisco, and a newly begun settlement, mostly of Yankee Californians, called Yerba Buena, which promises well. Here, at anchor, and the only vessel, was a brig under Russian colors, from Asitka, in Russian America, which had come down to winter, and to take in a supply of tallow and grain, great quantities of which latter article are raised in the missions at the head of the bay. The second day after our arrival, we went on board the brig, it being Sunday, as a matter of curiosity; and there was enough there to gratify it. Though no larger than the Pilgrim, she had five or six officers, and a crew of between twenty and thirty; and such a stupid and greasy-looking set, I certainly never saw before. Although it was quite comfortable weather, and we had nothing on but straw hats, shirts, and duck trowsers, and were barefooted, they had, every man of them, double-soled boots, coming up to the knees, and well greased; thick woollen trowsers, frocks, waist-coats, pea-jackets, woollen caps, and everything in true Nova Zembla rig; and in the warmest days they made no change. The clothing of one of these men would weigh nearly as much as that of half our crew. They had brutish faces, looked like the antipodes of sailors, and apparently dealt in nothing but grease. They lived upon grease; eat it, drank it, slept in the midst of it, and their clothes were covered with it. To a Russian, grease is the greatest luxury. They looked with greedy eyes upon the tallow-bags as they were taken into the vessel, and, no doubt, would have eaten one up whole, had not the officer kept watch over it. The grease seemed actually coming through their pores, and out in their hair, and on their faces. It seems as if it were this saturation which makes them stand cold and rain so well. If they were to go into a warm climate, they would all die of the scurvy.

The vessel was no better than the crew. Everything was in the oldest and most inconvenient fashion possible: running trusses on the yards, and large hawser cables, coiled all over the decks, and served and parcelled in all directions. The top-masts, top-gallant masts, and studding-sail booms were nearly black for want of scraping, and the decks would have turned the stomach of a man-of-war's-man. The galley was down in the forecastle; and there the crew lived, in the midst of the steam and grease of the cooking, in a place as hot as an oven, and as dirty as a pig-sty. Five minutes in the forecastle was enough for us, and we were glad to get into the open air. We made some trade with them, buying Indian curiosities, of which they had a great number; such as bead-work, feathers of birds, fur mocassins, &c. I purchased a large robe, made of the skins of some animal, dried and sewed nicely together, and covered all over on the outside with thick downy feathers, taken from the breasts of various birds, and arranged with their different colors, so as to make a brilliant show.

A few days after our arrival, the rainy season set in, and, for three weeks, it rained almost every hour, without cessation. This was bad for our trade, for the collecting of hides is managed differently in this port from what it is in any other on the coast. The mission of San Francisco, near the anchorage, has no trade at all, but those of San José, Santa Clara, and others, situated on large creeks or rivers which run into the bay, and distant between fifteen and forty miles from the anchorage, do a greater business in hides than any in California. Large boats, manned by Indians, and capable of carrying nearly a thousand hides apiece, are attached to the missions, and sent down to the vessels with hides, to bring away goods in return. Some of the crews of the vessels are obliged to go and come in the boats, to look out for the hides and goods. These are favorite expeditions with the sailors, in fine weather; but now, to be gone three or four days, in open boats, in constant rain, without any shelter, and with cold food, was hard service. Two of our men went up to Santa Clara in one of these boats, and were gone three days, during all which time they had a constant rain, and did not sleep a wink, but passed three long nights, walking fore and aft the boat, in the open air. When they got on board, they were completely exhausted, and took a watch below of twelve hours. All the hides, too, that came down in the boats, were soaked with water, and unfit to put below, so that we were obliged to trice them up to dry, in the intervals of sunshine or wind, upon all parts of the vessel. We got up tricing-lines from the jib-boom-end to each arm of the fore yard, and thence to the main and cross-jack yard-arms. Between the tops, too, and the mast-heads, from the fore to the main swifters, and thence to the mizen rigging, and in all directions athwart-ships, tricing-lines were run, and strung with hides. The head stays and guys, and the sprit-sail yard, were lined, and, having still more, we got out the swinging booms, and strung them and the forward and after guys, with hides. The rail, fore and aft, the windlass, capstan, the sides of the ship, and every vacant place on deck, were covered with wet hides, on the least sign of an interval for drying. Our ship was nothing but a mass of hides, from the cat-harpins to the water's edge, and from the jib-boom-end to the taffrail.

One cold, rainy evening, about eight o'clock, I received orders to get ready to start for San José at four the next morning, in one of these Indian boats, with four days' provisions. I got my oil-cloth clothes, south-wester, and thick boots all ready, and turned into my hammock early, determined to get some sleep in advance, as the boat was to be alongside before daybreak. I slept on till all hands were called in the morning; for, fortunately for me, the Indians, intentionally, or from mistaking their orders, had gone off alone in the night, and were far out of sight. Thus I escaped three or four days of very uncomfortable service.

Four of our men, a few days afterwards, went up in one of the quarter-boats to Santa Clara, to carry the agent, and remained out all night in a drenching rain, in the small boat, where there was not room for them to turn round; the agent having gone up to the mission and left the men to their fate, making no provision for their accommodation, and not even sending them anything to eat. After this, they had to pull thirty miles, and when they got on board, were so stiff that they could not come up the gangway ladder. This filled up the measure of the agent's unpopularity, and never after this could he get anything done by any of the crew; and many a delay and vexation, and many a good ducking in the surf, did he get to pay up old scores, or "square the yards with the bloody quill-driver."

Having collected nearly all the hides that were to be procured, we began our preparations for taking in a supply of wood and water, for both of which, San Francisco is the best place on the coast. A small island, situated about two leagues from the anchorage, called by us "Wood Island," and by the Spaniards "Isla de los Angelos," was covered with trees to the water's edge; and to this, two of our crew, who were Kennebec men, and could handle an axe like a plaything, were sent every morning to cut wood, with two boys to pile it up for them. In about a week, they had cut enough to last us a year, and the third mate, with myself and three others, were sent over in a large, schooner-rigged, open launch, which we had hired of the mission, to take in the wood, and bring it to the ship. We left the ship about noon, but, owing to a strong head wind, and a tide, which here runs four or five knots, did not get into the harbor, formed by two points of the island, where the boats lie, until sundown. No sooner had we come-to, than a strong south-easter, which had been threatening us all day, set in, with heavy rain and a chilly atmosphere. We were in rather a bad situation: an open boat, a heavy rain, and a long night; for in winter, in this latitude, it was dark nearly fifteen hours. Taking a small skiff which we had brought with us, we went ashore, but found no shelter, for everything was open to the rain, and collecting a little wood, which we found by lifting up the leaves and brush, and a few muscles, we put aboard again, and made the best preparations in our power for passing the night. We unbent the main-sail, and formed an awning with it over the after part of the boat, made a bed of wet logs of wood, and, with our jackets on, lay down, about six o'clock, to sleep. Finding the rain running down upon us, and our jackets getting wet through, and the rough, knotty logs rather indifferent couches, we turned out; and taking an iron pan which we brought with us, we wiped it out dry, put some stones around it, cut the wet bark from some sticks, and striking a

light, made a small fire in the pan. Keeping some sticks near, to
dry, and covering the whole over with a roof of boards, we
kept up a small fire, by which we cooked our muscles, and eat
them, rather for an occupation than from hunger. Still, it was
not ten o'clock, and the night was long before us, when one of
the party produced an old pack of Spanish cards from his
monkey-jacket pocket, which we hailed as a great windfall; and
keeping a dim, flickering light by our fagots, we played game
after game, till one or two o'clock, when, becoming really tired,
we went to our logs again, one sitting up at a time, in turn, to
keep watch over the fire. Toward morning, the rain ceased,
and the air became sensibly colder, so that we found sleep impossible, and sat up, watching for daybreak. No sooner was it
light than we went ashore, and began our preparations for
loading our vessel. We were not mistaken in the coldness of
the weather, for a white frost was on the ground, a thing we
had never seen before in California, and one or two little pud-
dles of fresh water were skimmed over with a thin coat of ice.
In this state of the weather, and before sunrise, in the grey of
the morning, we had to wade off, nearly up to our hips in
water, to load the skiff with the wood by arms-full. The third
mate remained on board the launch, two more staid in the
skiff, to load and manage it, and all the water-work, as usual,
fell upon the two youngest of us; and there we were, with frost
on the ground, wading forward and back, from the beach to
the boat, with arms-full of wood, barefooted, and our trowsers
rolled up. When the skiff went off with her load, we could only
keep our feet from freezing by racing up and down the beach
on the hard sand, as fast as we could go. We were all day at
this work, and toward sundown, having loaded the vessel as
deep as she would bear, we hove up our anchor, and made sail,
beating out of the bay. No sooner had we got into the large
bay, than we found a strong tide setting us out to seaward, a
thick fog which prevented our seeing the ship, and a breeze
too light to set us against the tide; for we were as deep as a sand-
barge. By the utmost exertions, we saved ourselves from being
carried out to sea, and were glad to reach the leewardmost
point of the island, where we came-to, and prepared to pass
another night, more uncomfortable than the first, for we were
loaded up to the gunwale, and had only a choice among logs

and sticks for a resting-place. The next morning, we made sail at slack water, with a fair wind, and got on board by eleven o'clock, when all hands were turned-to, to unload and stow away the wood, which took till night.

Having now taken in all our wood, the next morning a water-party was ordered off with all the casks. From this we escaped, having had a pretty good siege with the wooding. The water-party were gone three days, during which time they narrowly escaped being carried out to sea, and passed one day on an island, where one of them shot a deer, great numbers of which overrun the islands and hills of San Francisco Bay.

While not off, on these wood and water parties, or up the rivers to the missions, we had very easy times on board the ship. We were moored, stem and stern, within a cable's length of the shore, safe from south-easters, and with very little boating to do; and as it rained nearly all the time, awnings were put over the hatchways, and all hands sent down between decks, where we were at work, day after day, picking oakum, until we got enough to caulk the ship all over, and to last the whole voyage. Then we made a whole suit of gaskets for the voyage home, a pair of wheel-ropes from strips of green hide, great quantities of spun-yarn, and everything else that could be made between decks. It being now mid-winter and in high latitude, the nights were very long, so that we were not turned-to until seven in the morning, and were obliged to knock off at five in the evening, when we got supper; which gave us nearly three hours before eight bells, at which time the watch was set.

As we had now been about a year on the coast, it was time to think of the voyage home; and knowing that the last two or three months of our stay would be very busy ones, and that we should never have so good an opportunity to work for ourselves as the present, we all employed our evenings in making clothes for the passage home, and more especially for Cape Horn. As soon as supper was over and the kids cleared away, and each one had taken his smoke, we seated ourselves on our chests round the lamp, which swung from a beam, and each one went to work in his own way, some making hats, others trowsers, others jackets, &c. &c.; and no one was idle. The boys who could not sew well enough to make their own clothes, laid up grass into sinnet, for the men, who sewed for them in return. Several of us clubbed together and bought a large piece of twilled cotton, which we made into trowsers and jackets, and giving them several coats of linseed oil, laid them by for Cape Horn. I also sewed and covered a tarpaulin hat, thick and strong enough to sit down upon, and made myself a complete suit of flannel under-clothing, for bad weather. Those who had no south-wester caps, made them, and several of the crew made themselves tarpaulin jackets and trowsers, lined on the inside with flannel. Industry was the order of the day, and every one did something for himself; for we knew that as the season advanced, and we went further south, we should have no evenings to work in.

Friday, December 25th. This day was Christmas; and as it rained all day long, and there were no hides to take in, and nothing especial to do, the captain gave us a holyday, (the first we had had since leaving Boston,) and plum duff for dinner. The Russian brig, following the Old Style, had celebrated their Christmas eleven days before; when they had a grand blow-out, and (as our men said) drank, in the forecastle, a barrel of gin, ate up a bag of tallow, and made a soup of the skin.

Sunday, December 27th. We had now finished all our business at this port, and it being Sunday, we unmoored ship and got under weigh, firing a salute to the Russian brig, and another to the presidio, which were both answered. The commandant of the presidio, Don Guadaloupe Villego, a young man, and the most popular, among the Americans and English, of any man in California, was on board when we got under weigh. He spoke English very well, and was suspected of being favorably inclined to foreigners.

We sailed down this magnificent bay with a light wind, the tide, which was running out, carrying us at the rate of four or five knots. It was a fine day; the first of entire sunshine we had had for more than a month. We passed directly under the high cliff on which the presidio is built, and stood into the middle of the bay, from whence we could see small bays, making up into the interior, on every side; large and beautifully-wooded islands; and the mouths of several small rivers. If California ever becomes a prosperous country, this bay will be the centre of its prosperity. The abundance of wood and water, the extreme fertility of its shores, the excellence of its climate, which is as near to being perfect as any in the world, and its facilities for navigation, affording the best anchoring-grounds in the whole western coast of America, all fit it for a place of great importance; and, indeed, it has attracted much attention, for the settlement of "Yerba Buena," where we lay at anchor, made chiefly by Americans and English, and which bids fair to become the most important trading place on the coast, at this time began to supply traders, Russian ships, and whalers, with their stores of wheat and frijoles.

The tide leaving us, we came to anchor near the mouth of the bay, under a high and beautifully sloping hill, upon which herds of hundreds and hundreds of red deer, and the stag, with his high branching antlers, were bounding about, looking at us for a moment, and then starting off, affrighted at the noises which we made, for the purpose of seeing the variety of their beautiful attitudes and motions.

At midnight, the tide having turned, we hove up our anchor and stood out of the bay, with a fine starry heaven above us,— the first we had seen for weeks and weeks. Before the light northerly winds, which blow here with the regularity of trades, we worked slowly along, and made Point Año Nuevo, the northerly point of the Bay of Monterey, on Monday afternoon. We spoke, going in, the brig Diana, of the Sandwich Islands, from the North-west Coast, last from Asitka. She was off the point at the same time with us, but did not get in to the anchoring-ground until an hour or two after us. It was ten o'clock on Tuesday morning when we came to anchor. The town looked just as it did when I saw it last, which was eleven months before, in the brig Pilgrim. The pretty lawn on which it stands, as green as sun and rain could make it; the pine wood on the south; the small river on the north side; the houses, with their white plastered sides and red-tiled roofs, dotted about on the green; the low, white presidio, with its soiled, tri-colored flag flying, and the discordant din of drums and trumpets for the noon parade; all brought up the scene we had witnessed here with so much pleasure nearly a year before, when coming from a long voyage, and our unprepossessing reception at Santa Barbara. It seemed almost like coming to a home.

Chapter XXVII

THE only other vessel in the port was a Russian government bark, from Asitka, mounting eight guns, (four of which we found to be Quakers,) and having on board the ex-governor, who was going in her to Mazatlan, and thence over land to Vera Cruz. He offered to take letters, and deliver them to the American consul at Vera Cruz, whence they could be easily forwarded to the United States. We accordingly made up a packet of letters, almost every one writing, and dating them "January 1st, 1836." The governor was true to his promise, and they all reached Boston before the middle of March; the shortest communication ever yet made across the country.

The brig Pilgrim had been lying in Monterey through the latter part of November, according to orders, waiting for us. Day after day, Captain Faucon went up to the hill to look out for us, and at last, gave us up, thinking we must have gone down in the gale which we experienced off Point Conception, and which had blown with great fury over the whole coast, driving ashore several vessels in the snuggest ports. An English brig, which had put into San Francisco, lost both her anchors; the Rosa was driven upon a mud bank in San Diego; and the Pilgrim, with great difficulty, rode out the gale in Monterey, with three anchors a-head. She sailed early in December for San Diego and *intermedios.*

As we were to be here over Sunday, and Monterey was the best place to go ashore on the whole coast, and we had had no liberty-day for nearly three months, every one was for going ashore. On Sunday morning, as soon as the decks were washed, and we had got breakfast, those who had obtained liberty began to clean themselves, as it is called, to go ashore. A bucket of fresh water apiece, a cake of soap, a large coarse towel, and we went to work scrubbing one another, on the forecastle. Having gone through this, the next thing was to get into the head,—one on each side—with a bucket apiece, and duck one another, by drawing up water and heaving over each other, while we were stripped to a pair of trowsers. Then came the rigging-up. The usual outfit of pumps, white stockings, loose white duck trowsers, blue jackets, clean checked shirts, black kerchiefs, hats well varnished, with a fathom of black ribbon over the left eye, a silk handkerchief flying from the outside jacket pocket, and four or five dollars tied up in the back of the neckerchief, and we were "all right." One of the quarter-boats pulled us ashore, and we streamed up to the town. I tried to find the church, in order to see the worship, but was told that there was no service, except a mass early in the morning; so we went about the town, visiting the Americans and English, and the natives whom we had known when we were here before. Toward noon we procured horses, and rode out to the Carmel mission, which is about a league from the town, where we got something in the way of a dinner—beef, eggs, frijoles, tortillas, and some middling wine—from the mayordomo, who, of course, refused to make any charge, as it was the Lord's gift, yet received our present, as a gratuity, with a low bow, a touch of the hat, and "Dios se lo pague!"

After this repast, we had a fine run, scouring the whole country on our fleet horses, and came into town soon after sundown. Here we found our companions who had refused to go to ride with us, thinking that a sailor has no more business with a horse than a fish has with a balloon. They were moored, stem and stern, in a grog-shop, making a great noise, with a crowd of Indians and hungry half-breeds about them, and with a fair prospect of being stripped and dirked, or left to pass the night in the calabozo. With a great deal of trouble, we managed to get them down to the boats, though not without many angry looks and interferences from the Spaniards, who had marked them out for their prey. The Diana's crew,—a set of worthless outcasts, who had been picked up at the islands from the refuse of whale-ships,—were all as drunk as beasts, and had a set-to, on the beach, with their captain, who was in no better state than themselves. They swore they would not go aboard, and went back to the town, were stripped and beaten, and lodged in the calabozo, until the next day, when the captain bought them out. Our forecastle, as usual after a liberty-day, was a scene of tumult all night long, from the drunken ones. They had just got to sleep toward morning, when they were turned up with the rest, and kept at work all day in the water, carrying hides, their heads aching so that they could hardly stand. This is sailor's pleasure.

Nothing worthy of remark happened while we were here, except a little boxing-match on board our own ship, which gave us something to talk about. A broad-backed, big-headed Cape Cod boy, about sixteen years old, had been playing the bully, for the whole voyage, over a slender, delicate-looking boy, from one of the Boston schools, and over whom he had much the advantage, in strength, age, and experience in the ship's duty, for this was the first time the Boston boy had been on salt water. The latter, however, had "picked up his crumbs," was learning his duty, and getting strength and confidence daily; and began to assert his rights against his oppressor. Still, the other was his master, and, by his superior strength, always tackled with him and threw him down. One afternoon, before we were turned-to, these boys got into a violent squabble in the between-decks, when George (the Boston boy) said he would fight Nat, if he could have fair play. The chief mate heard the noise, dove down the hatchway, hauled them both up on deck, and told them to shake hands and have no more trouble for the voyage, or else they should fight till one gave in for beaten. Finding neither willing to make an offer of reconciliation, he called all hands up, (for the captain was ashore, and he could do as he chose aboard,) ranged the crew in the waist, marked a line on the deck, brought the two boys up to it, making them "toe the mark;" then made the bight of a rope fast to a belaying pin, and stretched it across the deck, bringing it just above their waists. "No striking below the rope!" And there they stood, one on each side of it, face to face, and went at it like two game-cocks. The Cape Cod boy, Nat, put in his double-fisters, starting the blood, and bringing the black and blue spots all over the face and arms of the other, whom we expected to see give in every moment: but the more he was hurt, the better he fought. Time after time he was knocked nearly down, but up he came again and faced the mark, as bold as a lion, again to take the heavy blows, which sounded so as to make one's heart turn with pity for him. At length he came up to the mark the last time, his shirt torn from his body, his face covered with blood and bruises, and his eyes flashing fire, and swore he would stand there until one or the other was killed, and set-to like a young fury. "Hurrah in the bow!" said the men, cheering him on. "Well crowed!" "Never say die, while there's a shot in the locker!" Nat tried to close with him, knowing his advantage, but the mate stopped that, saying there should be fair play, and no fingering. Nat then came up to the mark, but looked white about the mouth, and his blows were not given with half the spirit of his first. He was evidently cowed. He had always been master, and had nothing to gain, and everything to lose; while the other fought for honor and freedom, and under a sense of wrong. It would not do. It was soon over. Nat gave in; not so much beaten, as cowed and mortified; and never afterwards tried to act the bully on board. We took George forward, washed him in the deck-tub, complimented his pluck, and from this time he became somebody on board, having fought himself into notice. Mr. Brown's plan had a good effect, for there was no more quarrelling among the boys for the rest of the voyage.

Wednesday, January 6th. Set sail from Monterey, with a number of Spaniards as passengers, and shaped our course for Santa Barbara. The Diana went out of the bay in company with us, but parted from us off Point Pinos, being bound to the Sandwich Islands. We had a smacking breeze for several hours, and went along at a great rate, until night, when it died away, as usual, and the land-breeze set in, which brought us upon a taught bowline. Among our passengers was a young man who was the best representation of a decayed gentleman I had ever seen. He reminded me much of some of the characters in Gil Blas. He was of the aristocracy of the country, his family being of pure Spanish blood, and once of great importance in Mexico. His father had been governor of the province, and having amassed a large property, settled at San Diego, where he built a large house with a court-yard in front, kept a great retinue of Indians, and set up for the grandee of that part of the country. His son was sent to Mexico, where he received the best education, and went into the first society of the capital. Misfortune, extravagance, and the want of funds, or any manner of getting interest on money, soon eat the estate up, and Don Juan Bandini returned from Mexico accomplished, poor, and proud, and without any office or occupation, to lead the life of most

young men of the better families—dissolute and extravagant
when the means are at hand; ambitious at heart, and impotent
in act; often pinched for bread; keeping up an appearance of
style, when their poverty is known to each half-naked Indian
boy in the street, and they stand in dread of every small trader
and shopkeeper in the place. He had a slight and elegant figure, moved gracefully, danced and waltzed beautifully, spoke
the best of Castilian, with a pleasant and refined voice and accent, and had, throughout, the bearing of a man of high birth
and figure. Yet here he was, with his passage given him, (as I
afterwards learned,) for he had not the means of paying for it,
and living upon the charity of our agent. He was polite to
every one, spoke to the sailors, and gave four reáls—I dare say
the last he had in his pocket—to the steward, who waited
upon him. I could not but feel a pity for him, especially when
I saw him by the side of his fellow-passenger and townsman, a
fat, coarse, vulgar, pretending fellow of a Yankee trader, who
had made money in San Diego, and was eating out the very
vitals of the Bandinis, fattening upon their extravagance,
grinding them in their poverty; having mortgages on their
lands, forestalling their cattle, and already making an inroad
upon their jewels, which were their last hope.

Don Juan had with him a retainer, who was as much like
many of the characters in Gil Blas as his master. He called himself a private secretary, though there was no writing for him to
do, and he lived in the steerage with the carpenter and sailmaker. He was certainly a character; could read and write extremely well; spoke good Spanish; had been all over Spanish
America, and lived in every possible situation, and served in
every conceivable capacity, though generally in that of confidential servant to some man of figure. I cultivated this man's
acquaintance, and during the five weeks that he was with us,—
for he remained on board until we arrived at San Diego—I
gained a greater knowledge of the state of political parties in
Mexico, and the habits and affairs of the different classes of society, than I could have learned from almost any one else. He
took great pains in correcting my Spanish, and supplying me
with colloquial phrases, and common terms and exclamations
in speaking. He lent me a file of late newspapers from the city
of Mexico, which were full of the triumphal reception of Santa

Ana, who had just returned from Tampico after a victory, and with the preparations for his expedition against the Texians. "Viva Santa Ana!" was the by-word everywhere, and it had even reached California, though there were still many here, among whom was Don Juan Bandini, who were opposed to his government, and intriguing to bring in Bustamente. Santa Ana, they said, was for breaking down the missions; or, as they termed it—"Santa Ana no quiere religion." Yet I had no doubt that the office of administrador of San Diego would reconcile Don Juan to any dynasty, and any state of the church. In these papers, too, I found scraps of American and English news; but which were so unconnected, and I was so ignorant of everything preceding them for eighteen months past, that they only awakened a curiosity which they could not satisfy. One article spoke of Taney as Justicia Mayor de los Estados Unidos, (what had become of Marshall? was he dead, or banished?) and another made known, by news received from Vera Cruz, that "El Vizconde Melbourne" had returned to the office of "primer ministro," in place of Sir Roberto Peel. (Sir Robert Peel had been minister, then? and where were Earl Grey and the Duke of Wellington?) Here were the outlines of a grand parliamentary overturn, the filling up of which I could imagine at my leisure.

The second morning after leaving Monterey, we were off Point Conception. It was a bright, sunny day, and the wind, though strong, was fair; and everything was in striking contrast with our experience in the same place two months before, when we were drifting off from a north-wester under a fore and main spencer. "Sail ho!" cried a man who was rigging out a top-gallant studding-sail boom.—"Where away?"—"Weather beam, sir!" and in a few minutes a full-rigged brig was seen standing out from under Point Conception. The studding-sail halyards were let go, and the yards boom-ended, the after yards braced aback, and we waited her coming down. She rounded to, backed her main top-sail, and showed her decks full of men, four guns on a side, hammock nettings, and everything man-of-war fashion, except that there was no boatswain's whistle, and no uniforms on the quarter-deck. A short, square-built man, in a rough grey jacket, with a speaking-trumpet in hand, stood in the weather hammock nettings. "Ship ahoy!"—

"Hallo!"—"What ship is that, pray?"—"Alert."—"Where are you from, pray?" &c. &c. She proved to be the brig Convoy, from the Sandwich Islands, engaged in otter hunting, among the islands which lie along the coast. Her armament was from her being an illegal trader. The otter are very numerous among these islands, and being of great value, the government require a heavy sum for a license to hunt them, and lay a high duty upon every one shot or carried out of the country. This vessel had no license, and paid no duty, besides being engaged in smuggling goods on board other vessels trading on the coast, and belonging to the same owners in Oahu. Our captain told him to look out for the Mexicans, but he said they had not an armed vessel of his size in the whole Pacific. This was without doubt the same vessel that showed herself off Santa Barbara a few months before. These vessels frequently remain on the coast for years, without making port, except at the islands for wood and water, and an occasional visit to Oahu for a new outfit.

Sunday, January 10th. Arrived at Santa Barbara, and on the following Wednesday, slipped our cable and went to sea, on account of a south-easter. Returned to our anchorage the next day. We were the only vessel in the port. The Pilgrim had passed through the Canal and hove-to off the town, nearly six weeks before, on her passage down from Monterey, and was now at the leeward. She heard here of our safe arrival at San Francisco.

Great preparations were making on shore for the marriage of our agent, who was to marry Donna Anneta De G—— De N—— y C——, youngest daughter of Don Antonio N——, the grandee of the place, and the head of the first family in California. Our steward was ashore three days, making pastry and cake, and some of the best of our stores were sent off with him. On the day appointed for the wedding, we took the captain ashore in the gig, and had orders to come for him at night, with leave to go up to the house and see the fandango. Returning on board, we found preparations making for a salute. Our guns were loaded and run out, men appointed to each, cartridges served out, matches lighted, and all the flags ready to be run up. I took my place at the starboard after gun, and we all waited for the signal from on shore. At ten o'clock the bride went up with her sister to the confessional, dressed in deep black. Nearly an hour intervened, when the great doors of the mission church opened, the bells rang out a loud, discordant peal, the private signal for us was run up by the captain ashore, the bride, dressed in complete white, came out of the church with the bridegroom, followed by a long procession. Just as she stepped from the church door, a small white cloud issued from the bows of our ship, which was full in sight, the loud report echoed among the surrounding hills and over the bay, and instantly the ship was dressed in flags and pennants from stem to stern. Twenty-three guns followed in regular succession, with an interval of fifteen seconds between each, when the cloud cleared away, and the ship lay dressed in her colors, all day. At sundown, another salute of the same number of guns was fired, and all the flags run down. This we thought was pretty well—a gun every fifteen seconds—for a merchantman with only four guns and a dozen or twenty men.

After supper, the gig's crew were called, and we rowed ashore, dressed in our uniform, beached the boat, and went up to the fandango. The bride's father's house was the principal one in the place, with a large court in front, upon which a tent was built, capable of containing several hundred people. As we drew near, we heard the accustomed sound of violins and guitars, and saw a great motion of the people within. Going in, we found nearly all the people of town—men, women, and children—collected and crowded together, leaving barely room for the dancers; for on these occasions no invitations are given, but every one is expected to come, though there is always a private entertainment within the house for particular friends. The old women sat down in rows, clapping their hands to the music, and applauding the young ones. The music was lively, and among the tunes, we recognised several of our popular airs, which we, without doubt, have taken from the Spanish. In the dancing, I was much disappointed. The women stood upright, with their hands down by their sides, their eyes fixed upon the ground before them, and slided about without any perceptible means of motion; for their feet were invisible, the hem of their dresses forming a perfect circle about them, reaching to the ground. They looked as grave as though they were going through some religious ceremony, their faces as little excited as their limbs; and on the whole, instead of the spirited, fascinating Spanish dances which I had expected, I found the Californian fandango, on the part of the women at least, a lifeless affair. The men did better. They danced with grace and spirit, moving in circles round their nearly stationary partners, and showing their figures to great advantage.

A great deal was said about our friend Don Juan Bandini, and when he did appear, which was toward the close of the evening, he certainly gave us the most graceful dancing that I had ever seen. He was dressed in white pantaloons, neatly made, a short jacket of dark silk, gaily figured, white stockings and thin morocco slippers upon his very small feet. His slight and graceful figure was well calculated for dancing, and he moved about with the grace and daintiness of a young fawn. An occasional touch of the toe to the ground, seemed all that was necessary to give him a long interval of motion in the air. At the same time he was not fantastic or flourishing, but appeared to be rather repressing a strong tendency to motion. He was loudly applauded, and danced frequently toward the close of the evening. After the supper, the waltzing began, which was confined to a very few of the "gente de razón," and was considered a high accomplishment, and a mark of aristocracy. Here, too, Don Juan figured greatly, waltzing with the sister of the bride, (Donna Angustia, a handsome woman and a general favorite,) in a variety of beautiful, but, to me, offensive figures, which lasted as much as half an hour, no one else taking the floor. They were repeatedly and loudly applauded, the old men and women jumping out of their seats in admiration, and the young people waving their hats and handkerchiefs. Indeed, among people of the character of these Mexicans, the waltz seemed to me to have found its right place. The great amusement of the evening,—which I suppose was owing to its being carnival—was the breaking of eggs filled with cologne, or other essences, upon the heads of the company. One end of the egg is broken and the inside taken out, then it is partly filled with cologne, and the whole sealed up. The women bring a great number of these secretly about them, and the amusement is to break one upon the head of a gentleman when his back is turned. He is bound in gallantry to find out the lady and return the compliment, though it must not be done if the person sees you. A tall, stately Don, with immense grey whiskers, and a look of great importance, was standing before me, when I felt a light hand on my shoulder, and turning round, saw Donna Angustia, (whom we all knew, as she had been up to Monterey, and down again, in the Alert,) with her finger upon her lip, motioning me gently aside. I stepped back a little, when she went up behind the Don, and with one hand knocked off his huge *sombrero*, and at the same instant, with the other, broke the egg upon his head, and springing behind me, was out of sight in a moment. The Don turned slowly round, the cologne running down his face, and over his clothes, and a loud laugh breaking out from every quarter. He looked round in vain, for some time, until the direction of so many laughing eyes showed him the fair offender. She was his niece, and a great favorite with him, so old Don Domingo had to join in the laugh. A great many such tricks were played, and many a war of sharp manœuvering was carried on between couples of the younger people, and at every successful exploit a general laugh was raised.

Another singular custom I was for some time at a loss about. A pretty young girl was dancing, named, after what would appear to us the sacrilegious custom of the country—Espiritu Santo, when a young man went behind her and placed his hat directly upon her head, letting it fall down over her eyes, and sprang back among the crowd. She danced for some time with the hat on, when she threw it off, which called forth a general shout; and the young man was obliged to go out upon the floor and pick it up. Some of the ladies, upon whose heads hats had been placed, threw them off at once, and a few kept them on throughout the dance, and took them off at the end, and held them out in their hands, when the owner stepped out, bowed, and took it from them. I soon began to suspect the meaning of the thing, and was afterwards told that it was a compliment, and an offer to become the lady's gallant for the rest of the evening, and to wait upon her home. If the hat was thrown off, the offer was refused, and the gentleman was obliged to pick up his hat amid a general laugh. Much amusement was caused sometimes by gentlemen putting hats on the ladies' heads, without permitting them to see whom it was done by. This obliged them to throw them off, or keep them on at a venture, and when they came to discover the owner, the laugh was often turned upon them.

The captain sent for us about ten o'clock, and we went aboard in high spirits, having enjoyed the new scene much, and were of great importance among the crew, from having so much to tell, and from the prospect of going every night until it was over; for these fandangos generally last three days. The next day, two of us were sent up to the town, and took care to come back by way of Capitan Noriego's, and take a look into the booth. The musicians were still there, upon their platform, scraping and twanging away, and a few people, apparently of the lower classes, were dancing. The dancing is kept up, at intervals, throughout the day, but the crowd, the spirit, and the *elite*, come in at night. The next night, which was the last, we went ashore in the same manner, until we got almost tired of the monotonous twang of the instruments, the drawling sounds which the women kept up, as an accompaniment, and the slapping of the hands in time with the music, in place of castanets. We found ourselves as great objects of attention as any persons or anything at the place. Our sailor dresses—and we took great pains to have them neat and ship-shape—were much admired, and we were invited, from every quarter, to give them an American sailor's dance; but after the ridiculous figure some of our countrymen cut, in dancing after the Spaniards, we thought it best to leave it to their imaginations. Our agent, with a tight, black, swallow-tailed coat, just imported from Boston, a high stiff cravat, looking as if he had been pinned and skewered, with only his feet and hands left free, took the floor just after Bandini; and we thought they had had enough of Yankee grace.

The last night they kept it up in great style, and were getting into a high-go, when the captain called us off to go aboard, for, it being south-easter season, he was afraid to remain on shore long; and it was well he did not, for that very night, we slipped our cables, as a crowner to our fun ashore, and stood off before a south-easter, which lasted twelve hours, and returned to our anchorage the next day.

Chapter XXVIII

M onday, *Feb. 1st.* After having been in port twenty-one days, we sailed for San Pedro, where we arrived on the following day, having gone "all fluking," with the weather clue of the main-sail hauled up, the yards braced in a little, and the lower studding-sail just drawing; the wind hardly shifting a point during the passage. Here we found the Ayacucho and the Pilgrim, which last we had not seen since the 11th of September,—nearly five months; and I really felt something like an affection for the old brig which had been my first home, and in which I had spent nearly a year, and got the first rough and tumble of a sea-life. She, too, was associated in my mind with Boston, the wharf from which we sailed, anchorage in the stream, leave-taking, and all such matters, which were now to me like small links connecting me with another world, which I had once been in, and which, please God, I might yet see again. I went on board the first night, after supper; found the old cook in the galley, playing upon the fife which I had given him, as a parting present; had a hearty shake of the hand from him; and dove down into the forecastle, where were my old shipmates, the same as ever, glad to see me; for they had nearly given us up as lost, especially when they did not find us in Santa Barbara. They had been at San Diego last, had been lying at San Pedro nearly a month, and had received three thousand hides from the pueblo. These were taken from her the next day, which filled us up, and we both got under weigh on the 4th, she bound up to San Francisco again, and we to San Diego, where we arrived on the 6th.

We were always glad to see San Diego; it being the depot, and a snug little place, and seeming quite like home, especially to me, who had spent a summer there. There was no vessel in port, the Rosa having sailed for Valparaiso and Cadiz, and the Catalina for Callao, nearly a month before. We discharged our hides, and in four days were ready to sail again for the windward; and, to our great joy—*for the last time!* Over thirty thousand hides had been already collected, cured, and stowed away in the house, which, together with what we should collect, and the Pilgrim would bring down from San Francisco, would make out our cargo. The thought that we were actually going up for the last time, and that the next time we went round San Diego point it would be "homeward bound," brought things so near a close, that we felt as though we were just there, though it must still be the greater part of a year before we could see Boston.

I spent one evening, as had been my custom, at the oven with the Sandwich Islanders; but it was far from being the usual noisy, laughing time. It has been said, that the greatest curse to each of the South Sea islands, was the first man who discovered it; and every one who knows anything of the history of our commerce in those parts, knows how much truth there is in this; and that the white men, with their vices, have brought in diseases before unknown to the islanders, and which are now sweeping off the native population of the Sandwich Islands, at the rate of one fortieth of the entire population annually. They seem to be a doomed people. The curse of a people calling themselves Christian, seems to follow them everywhere; and even here, in this obscure place, lay two young islanders, whom I had left strong, active young men, in the vigor of health, wasting away under a disease, which they would never have known but for their intercourse with christianized Mexico and people from Christian America. One of them was not so ill; and was moving about, smoking his pipe, and talking, and trying to keep up his spirits; but the other, who was my friend, and *Aikane*—Hope, was the most dreadful object I had ever seen in my life: his eyes sunken and dead, his cheeks fallen in against his teeth, his hands looking like claws; a dreadful cough, which seemed to rack his whole shattered system, a hollow, whispering voice, and an entire inability to move himself. There he lay, upon a mat, on the ground, which was the only floor of the oven, with no medicine, no comforts, and no one to care for, or help him, but a few Kanakas, who were willing enough, but could do nothing. The sight of him made me sick and faint. Poor fellow! During the four months that I lived upon the beach, we were continually together, both in work, and in our excursions in the woods, and upon the water. I really felt a strong affection for him, and preferred him to any of my own countrymen there; and I believe there was nothing which he would not have done for me. When I came into the oven he looked at me, held out his hand, and said, in a low voice, but with a delightful smile, "*Aloha, Aikane! Aloha nui!*" I comforted him as well as I could, and promised to ask the captain to help him from the medicine-chest, and told him I had no doubt the captain would do what he could for him, as he had worked in our employ for several years, both on shore and aboard our vessels on the coast. I went aboard and turned into my hammock, but I could not sleep.

Thinking, from my education, that I must have some knowledge of medicine, the Kanakas had insisted upon my examining him carefully; and it was not a sight to be forgotten. One of our crew, an old man-of-war's-man, of twenty years' standing, who had seen sin and suffering in every shape, and whom I afterwards took to see Hope, said it was dreadfully worse than anything he had ever seen, or even dreamed of. He was horror-struck, as his countenance showed; yet he had been among the worst cases in our naval hospitals. I could not get the thought of the poor fellow out of my head all night; his horrible suffering, and his apparently inevitable, horrible end.

The next day I told the captain of Hope's state, and asked him if he would be so kind as to go and see him.

"What? a d——d Kanaka?"

"Yes, sir," said I; "but he has worked four years for our vessels, and has been in the employ of our owners, both on shore and aboard."

"Oh! he be d——d!" said the captain, and walked off.

This same man died afterwards of a fever on the deadly coast of Sumatra; and God grant he had better care taken of him in his sufferings, than he ever gave to any one else! Finding nothing was to be got from the captain, I consulted an old shipmate, who had much experience in these matters, and got from him a recipe, which he always kept by him. With this I went to the mate, and told him the case. Mr. Brown had been entrusted with the general care of the medicine-chest, and although a driving fellow, and a taught hand in a watch, he had good feelings, and was always inclined to be kind to the sick. He said that Hope was not strictly one of the crew, but as he was in our employ when taken sick, he should have the medicines; and he got them and gave them to me, with leave to go ashore at night. Nothing could exceed the delight of the Kanakas, when I came bringing the medicines. All their terms of affection and gratitude were spent upon me, and in a sense wasted, (for I could not understand half of them,) yet they made all known by their manner. Poor Hope was so much revived at the bare thought of anything's being done for him, that he was already stronger and better. I knew he must die as he was, and he could but die under the medicines, and any chance was worth running. An oven, exposed to every wind and change of weather, is no place to take calomel; but nothing else would do, and strong remedies must be used, or he was gone. The applications, internal and external, were powerful, and I gave him strict directions to keep warm and sheltered, telling him it was his only chance for life. Twice, after this, I visited him, having only time to run up, while waiting in the boat. He promised to take his medicines regularly until we returned, and insisted upon it that he was doing better.

We got under weigh on the 10th, bound up to San Pedro, and had three days of calm and head winds, making but little progress. On the fourth, we took a stiff south-easter, which obliged us to reef our top-sails. While on the yard, we saw a sail on the weather bow, and in about half an hour, passed the Ayacucho, under double-reefed top-sails, beating down to San Diego. Arrived at San Pedro on the fourth day, and came-to in the old place, a league from shore, with no other vessel in port, and the prospect of three weeks, or more, of dull life, rolling goods up a slippery hill, carrying hides on our heads over sharp stones, and, perhaps, slipping for a south-easter.

There was but one man in the only house here, and him I shall always remember as a good specimen of a California ranger. He had been a tailor in Philadelphia, and getting intemperate and in debt, he joined a trapping party and went to the Columbia river, and thence down to Monterey, where he spent everything, left his party, and came to the Pueblo de los Angelos, to work at his trade. Here he went dead to leeward among the pulperias, gambling rooms, &c., and came down to San Pedro, to be moral by being out of temptation. He had been in the house several weeks, working hard at his trade, upon orders which he had brought with him, and talked much of his resolution, and opened his heart to us about his past life. After we had been here some time, he started off one morning, in fine spirits, well dressed, to carry the clothes which he had been making to the pueblo, and saying he would bring back his money and some fresh orders the next day. The next day came, and a week passed, and nearly a fortnight, when, one day, going ashore, we saw a tall man, who looked like our friend the tailor, getting out of the back of an Indian's cart, which had just come down from the pueblo. He stood for the house, but we bore up after him; when, finding that we were overhauling him, he hove-to and spoke us. Such a sight I never saw before. Barefooted, with an old pair of trowsers tied round his waist by a piece of green hide, a soiled cotton shirt, and a torn Indian hat; "cleaned out," to the last reál, and completely "used up." He confessed the whole matter; acknowledged that he was on his back; and now he had a prospect of a fit of the horrors for a week, and of being worse than useless for months. This is a specimen of the life of half of the Americans and English who are adrift over the whole of California. One of the same stamp was Russell, who was master of the hide-house at San Diego, while I was there, and afterwards turned away for his misconduct. He spent his own money and nearly all the stores among the half-bloods upon the beach, and being turned away, went up to the presidio, where he lived the life of a desperate "loafer," until some rascally deed sent him off "between two days," with men on horseback, dogs, and Indians in full cry after him, among the hills. One night, he burst into our room at the hide-house, breathless, pale as a ghost, covered with mud, and torn by thorns and briers, nearly naked, and begged for a crust of bread, saying he had neither eaten nor slept for three days. Here was the great *Mr.* Russell, who a month before was "Don Tomàs," "Capitán de la playa," "Maéstro de la casa," &c. &c., begging food and shelter of Kanakas and sailors. He staid with us till he gave himself up, and was dragged off to the calabozo.

Another, and a more amusing specimen, was one whom we saw at San Francisco. He had been a lad on board the ship California, in one of her first voyages, and ran away and commenced *Ranchéro*, gambling, stealing horses, &c. He worked along up to San Francisco, and was living on a rancho near there, while we were in port. One morning, when we went ashore in the boat, we found him at the landing-place, dressed in California style,—a wide hat, faded velveteen trowsers, and a blanket cloak thrown over his shoulders—and wishing to go off in the boat, saying he was going to paseár with our captain a little. We had many doubts of the reception he would meet with; but he seemed to think himself company for any one. We took him aboard, landed him at the gangway, and went about our work, keeping an eye upon the quarter-deck, where the captain was walking. The lad went up to him with the most complete assurance, and raising his hat, wished him a good afternoon. Capt. T—— turned round, looked at him from head to foot, and saying coolly, "Hallo! who the h—— are you?" kept on his walk. This was a rebuff not to be mistaken, and the joke passed about among the crew by winks and signs, at different parts of the ship. Finding himself disappointed at head quarters, he edged along forward to the mate, who was overseeing some work upon the forecastle, and tried to begin a yarn; but it would not do. The mate had seen the reception he had met with aft, and would have no cast-off company. The second mate was aloft, and the third mate and myself were painting the quarter-boat, which hung by the davits, so he betook himself to us; but we looked at one another, and the officer was too busy to say a word. From us, he went to one and another of the crew, but the joke had got before him, and he found everybody busy and silent. Looking over the rail a few moments afterward, we saw him at the galley-door, talking with the cook. This was a great come-down, from the highest seat in the synagogue to a seat in the galley with the black cook. At night, too, when supper was called, he stood in the waist for some time, hoping to be asked down with the officers, but they went below, one after another, and left him. His next chance was with the carpenter and sailmaker, and he lounged round the after hatchway until the last had gone down. We had now had fun enough out of him, and taking pity on him, offered him a pot of tea, and a cut at the kid, with the rest, in the forecastle. He was hungry, and it was growing dark, and he began to see that there was no use in playing the *caballéro* any longer, and came down into the forecastle, put into the "grub" in sailor's style, threw off all his airs, and enjoyed the joke as much as any one: for a man must take a joke among sailors. He

gave us the whole account of his adventures in the country,—
roguery and all—and was very entertaining. He was a smart,
unprincipled fellow, was at the bottom of most of the rascally
doings of the country, and gave us a great deal of interesting
information in the ways of the world we were in.

Saturday, Feb. 13th. Were called up at midnight to slip for a
violent north-easter, for this rascally hole of San Pedro is unsafe in every wind but a south-wester, which is seldom known
to blow more than once in a half century. We went off with a
flowing sheet, and hove-to under the lee of Catalina island,
where we lay three days, and then returned to our anchorage.

Tuesday, Feb. 23d. This afternoon, a signal was made from the
shore, and we went off in the gig, and found the agent's clerk,
who had been up to the pueblo, waiting at the landing-place,
with a package under his arm, covered with brown paper and
tied carefully with twine. No sooner had we shoved off than
he told us there was good news from Santa Barbara. "What's
that?" said one of the crew; "has the bloody agent slipped off
the hooks? Has the old bundle of bones got him at last?"—
"No; better than that. The California has arrived." Letters,
papers, news, and, perhaps—friends, on board! Our hearts
were all up in our mouths, and we pulled away like good fellows; for the precious packet could not be opened except by
the captain. As we pulled under the stern, the clerk held up the
package, and called out to the mate, who was leaning over the
taffrail, that the California had arrived.

"Hurrah!" said the mate, so as to be heard fore and aft;
"California come, and news from Boston!"

Instantly there was a confusion on board which no one
could account for who has not been in the same situation. All
discipline seemed for a moment relaxed.

"What's that, Mr. Brown?" said the cook, putting his head
out of the galley—"California come?"

"Aye, aye! you angel of darkness, and there's a letter for you
from *Bullknop* 'treet, number two-two-five—green door and
brass knocker!"

The packet was sent down into the cabin, and every one
waited to hear of the result. As nothing came up, the officers
began to feel that they were acting rather a child's part, and
turned the crew to again; and the same strict discipline was

restored, which prohibits speech between man and man, while at work on deck; so that, when the steward came forward with letters for the crew, each man took his letters, carried them below to his chest, and came up again immediately; and not a letter was read until we had cleared up decks for the night.

An overstrained sense of manliness is the characteristic of seafaring men, or, rather, of life on board ship. This often gives an appearance of want of feeling, and even of cruelty. From this, if a man comes within an ace of breaking his neck and escapes, it is made a joke of; and no notice must be taken of a bruise or a cut; and any expression of pity, or any show of attention, would look sisterly, and unbecoming a man who has to face the rough and tumble of such a life. From this, too, the sick are neglected at sea, and whatever sailors may be ashore, a sick man finds little sympathy or attention, forward or aft. A man, too, can have nothing peculiar or sacred on board ship; for all the nicer feelings they take pride in disregarding, both in themselves and others. A thin-skinned man could not live an hour on shipboard. One would be torn raw unless he had the hide of an ox. A moment of natural feeling for home and friends, and then the frigid routine of sea-life returned. Jokes were made upon those who showed any interest in the expected news, and everything near and dear was made common stock for rude jokes and unfeeling coarseness, to which no exception could be taken by any one.

Supper, too, must be eaten before the letters were read; and when, at last, they were brought out, they all got round any one who had a letter, and expected to have it read aloud, and have it all in common. If any one went by himself to read, it was—"Fair play, there; and no skulking!" I took mine and went into the sailmaker's berth, where I could read it without interruption. It was dated August, just a year from the time I had sailed from home; and every one was well, and no great change had taken place. Thus, for one year, my mind was set at ease, yet it was already six months from the date of the letter, and what another year would bring to pass, who could tell? Every one away from home thinks that some great thing must have happened, while to those at home there seems to be a continued monotony and lack of incident.

As much as my feelings were taken up by my own intelligence from home, I could not but be amused by a scene in the steerage. The carpenter had been married just before leaving Boston, and during the voyage had talked much about his wife, and had to bear and forbear, as every man, known to be married, must, aboard ship; yet the certainty of hearing from his wife by the first ship, seemed to keep up his spirits. The California came; the packet was brought on board; no one was in higher spirits than he; but when the letters came forward, there was none for him. The captain looked again, but there was no mistake. Poor "Chips" could eat no supper. He was completely down in the mouth. "Sails" (the sailmaker) tried to comfort him, and told him he was a bloody fool to give up his grub for any woman's daughter, and reminded him that he had told him a dozen times that he'd never see or hear from his wife again.

"Ah!" said Chips, "you don't know what it is to have a wife, and"—

"Don't I?" said Sails; and then came, for the hundredth time, the story of his coming ashore at New York, from the Constellation frigate, after a cruise of four years round the Horn,— being paid off with over five hundred dollars,—marrying, and taking a couple of rooms in a four-story house,—furnishing the rooms, (with a particular account of the furniture, including a dozen flag-bottomed chairs, which he always dilated upon, whenever the subject of furniture was alluded to,)— going off to sea again, leaving his wife half-pay, like a fool,— coming home and finding her "off, like Bob's horse, with nobody to pay the reckoning;" furniture gone,—flag-bottomed chairs and all;—and with it, his "long togs," the half-pay, his beaver hat, white linen shirts, and everything else. His wife he never saw, or heard of, from that day to this, and never wished to. Then followed a sweeping assertion, not much to the credit of the sex, if true, though he has Pope to back him. "Come, Chips, cheer up like a man, and take some hot grub! Don't be made a fool of by anything in petticoats! As for your wife, you'll never see her again; she was 'up keeleg and off' before you were outside of Cape Cod. You've hove your money away like a fool; but every man must learn once, just as I did; so you'd better square the yards with her, and make the best of it."

This was the best consolation "Sails" had to offer, but it did not seem to be just the thing the carpenter wanted; for, during several days, he was very much dejected, and bore with difficulty the jokes of the sailors, and with still more difficulty their attempts at advice and consolation, of most of which the sailmaker's was a good specimen.

Thursday, Feb. 25th. Set sail for Santa Barbara, where we arrived on Sunday, the 28th. We just missed of seeing the California, for she had sailed three days before, bound to Monterey, to enter her cargo and procure her license, and thence to San Francisco, &c. Captain Arthur left files of Boston papers for Captain T——, which, after they had been read and talked over in the cabin, I procured from my friend the third mate. One file was of all the Boston Transcripts for the month of August, 1835, and the rest were about a dozen Daily Advertisers and Couriers, of different dates. After all, there is nothing in a strange land like a newspaper from home. Even a letter, in many respects, is nothing, in comparison with it. It carries you back to the spot, better than anything else. It is almost equal to *clairvoyance*. The names of the streets, with the things advertised, is almost as good as seeing the signs; and while reading "Boy lost!" one can almost hear the bell and well-known voice of "Old Wilson," crying the boy as "strayed, stolen, or mislaid!" Then there was the Commencement at Cambridge, and the full account of the exercises at the graduating of my own class. A list of all those familiar names, (beginning as usual with Abbot, and ending with W.,) which, as I read them over, one by one, brought up their faces and characters as I had known them in the various scenes of college life. Then I imagined them upon the stage, speaking their orations, dissertations, colloquies, &c., with the gestures and tones of each, and tried to fancy the manner in which each would handle his subject. *****, handsome, showy, and superficial; ****, with his strong head, clear brain, cool self-possession; *****, modest, sensitive, and underrated; B****, the mouth-piece of the debating clubs, noisy, vaporous, and democratic; and so following. Then I could see them receiving their A.Bs from the dignified, feudal-looking President, with his "auctoritate mihi commissâ," and walking off the stage with their diplomas in their hands; while, upon the very same day, their classmate was walking up and down California beach with a hide upon his head.

Every watch below, for a week, I pored over these papers, until I was sure there could be nothing in them that had escaped my attention, and was ashamed to keep them any longer.

Saturday, March 5th. This was an important day in our almanac, for it was on this day that we were first assured that our voyage was really drawing to a close. The captain gave orders to have the ship ready for getting under weigh; and observed that there was a good breeze to take us down to San Pedro. Then we were not going up to windward. Thus much was certain, and was soon known fore and aft; and when we went in the gig to take him off, he shook hands with the people on the beach, and said that he never expected to see Santa Barbara again. This settled the matter, and sent a thrill of pleasure through the heart of every one in the boat. We pulled off with a will, saying to ourselves (I can speak for myself at least)— "Good-by, Santa Barbara!—This is the last pull here!—No more duckings in your breakers, and slipping from your cursed south-easters!" The news was soon known aboard, and put life into everything when we were getting under weigh. Each one was taking his last look at the mission, the town, the breakers on the beach, and swearing that no money would make him ship to see them again; and when all hands tallied on to the cat-fall, the chorus of "Time for us to go!" was raised for the first time, and joined in, with full swing, by everybody. One would have thought we were on our voyage home, so near did it seem to us, though there were yet three months for us on the coast.

We left here the young Englishman, George Marsh, of whom I have before spoken, who was wrecked upon the Pelew Islands. He left us to take the berth of second mate on board the Ayacucho, which was lying in port. He was well qualified for this, and his education would enable him to rise to any situation on board ship. I felt really sorry to part from him. There was something about him which excited my curiosity; for I could not, for a moment, doubt that he was well born, and, in early life, well bred. There was the latent gentleman about him, and the sense of honor, and no little of the pride, of a young man of good family. The situation was offered him only a few hours before we sailed; and though he must give up returning to America, yet I have no doubt that the change from a dog's berth to an officer's, was too agreeable to his feelings to be declined. We pulled him on board the Ayacucho, and when he left the boat he gave each of its crew a piece of money, except myself, and shook hands with me, nodding his head, as much as to say,—"We understand one another," and sprang on board. Had I known, an hour sooner, that he was to leave us, I would have made an effort to get from him the true history of his early life. He knew that I had no faith in the story which he told the crew, and perhaps, in the moment of parting from me, probably forever, he would have given me the true account. Whether I shall ever meet him again, or whether his manuscript narrative of his adventures in the Pelew Islands, which would be creditable to him and interesting to the world, will ever see the light, I cannot tell. His is one of those cases which are more numerous than those suppose, who have never lived anywhere but in their own homes, and never walked but in one line from their cradle to their graves. We must come down from our heights, and leave our straight paths, for the byways and low places of life, if we would learn truths by strong contrasts; and in hovels, in forecastles, and among our own outcasts in foreign lands, see what has been wrought upon our fellow-creatures by accident, hardship, or vice.

Two days brought us to San Pedro, and two days more (to our no small joy) gave us our last view of that place, which was universally called the hell of California, and seemed designed, in every way, for the wear and tear of sailors. Not even the last view could bring out one feeling of regret. No thanks, thought I, as we left the sandy shores in the distance, for the hours I have walked over your stones, barefooted, with hides on my head;—for the burdens I have carried up your steep, muddy hill;—for the duckings in your surf; and for the long days and longer nights passed on your desolate hill, watching piles of hides, hearing the sharp bark of your eternal coati, and the dismal hooting of your owls.

As I bade good-by to each successive place, I felt as though

one link after another were struck from the chain of my servitude. Having kept close in shore, for the land-breeze, we
passed the mission of San Juan Campestráno the same night,
and saw distinctly, by the bright moonlight, the hill which I
had gone down by a pair of halyards in search of a few paltry
hides. "Forsitan et hæc olim," thought I, and took my last
look of that place too. And on the next morning we were under the high point of San Diego. The flood tide took us swiftly
in, and we came-to, opposite our hide-house, and prepared to
get everything in trim for a long stay. This was our last port.
Here we were to discharge everything from the ship, clean her
out, smoke her, take in our hides, wood, water, &c., and set
sail for Boston. While all this was doing, we were to lie still in
one place, and the port was a safe one, and there was no fear of
south-easters. Accordingly, having picked out a good berth, in
the stream, with a good smooth beach opposite, for a landing-
place, and within two cables' length of our hide-house, we
moored ship, unbent all the sails, sent down the top-gallant
yards and all the studding-sail booms, and housed the top-
gallant masts. The boats were then hove out, and all the sails,
the spare spars, the stores, the rigging not rove, and, in fact,
everything which was not in daily use, sent ashore, and stowed
away in the house. Then went all our hides and horns, and
we left hardly anything in the ship but her ballast, and this we
made preparation to heave out, the next day. At night, after we
had knocked off, and were sitting round in the forecastle,
smoking and talking and taking sailor's pleasure, we congratulated ourselves upon being in that situation in which we had
wished ourselves every time we had come into San Diego. "If
we were only here for the last time," we had often said, "with
our top-gallant masts housed and our sails unbent!"—and now
we had our wish. Six weeks, or two months, of the hardest
work we had yet seen, was before us, and then—"Good-by to
California!"

Chapter XXIX

WE turned-in early, knowing that we might expect an early call; and sure enough, before the stars had quite faded, "All hands ahoy!" and we were turned-to, heaving out ballast. A regulation of the port forbids any ballast to be thrown overboard; accordingly, our long-boat was lined inside with rough boards and brought alongside the gangway, but where one tub-full went into the boat, twenty went overboard. This is done by every vessel, for the ballast can make but little difference in the channel, and it saves more than a week of labor, which would be spent in loading the boats, rowing them to the point, and unloading them. When any people from the presidio were on board, the boat was hauled up and the ballast thrown in, but when the coast was clear, she was dropped astern again, and the ballast fell overboard. This is one of those petty frauds which every vessel practises in ports of inferior foreign nations, and which are lost sight of, among the countless deeds of greater weight which are hardly less common. Fortunately, a sailor, not being a free agent in work aboard ship, is not accountable; yet the fact of being constantly employed, without thought, in such things, begets an indifference to the rights of others.

Friday, and a part of Saturday, we were engaged in this work, until we had thrown out all but what we wanted under our cargo on the passage home; when, as the next day was Sunday, and a good day for smoking ship, we cleared everything out of the cabin and forecastle, made a slow fire of charcoal, birch bark, brimstone, and other matters, on the ballast in the bottom of the hold, calked up the hatches and every open seam, and pasted over the cracks of the windows, and the slides of the scuttles, and companion-way. Wherever smoke was seen coming out, we calked and pasted, and, so far as we could, made the ship smoke tight. The captain and officers slept under the awning which was spread over the quarter-deck; and we stowed ourselves away under an old studding-sail, which we drew over one side of the forecastle. The next day, from fear that something might happen, orders were given for no one to leave the ship, and, as the decks were lumbered up with everything, we could not wash them down, so we had nothing to do, all day long. Unfortunately, our books were where we could not get at them, and we were turning about for something to do, when one man recollected a book he had left in the galley. He went after it, and it proved to be Woodstock. This was a great windfall, and as all could not read it at once, I, being the scholar of the company, was appointed reader. I got a knot of six or eight about me, and no one could have had a more attentive audience. Some laughed at the "scholars," and went over the other side of the forecastle, to work, and spin their yarns; but I carried the day, and had the cream of the crew for my hearers. Many of the reflections, and the political parts, I omitted, but all the narrative they were delighted with; especially the descriptions of the Puritans, and the sermons and harangues of the Roundhead soldiers. The gallantry of Charles, Dr. Radcliffe's plots, the knavery of "trusty Tompkins,"—in fact, every part seemed to chain their attention. Many things which, while I was reading, I had a misgiving about, thinking them above their capacity, I was surprised to find them enter into completely.

I read nearly all day, until sundown; when, as soon as supper was over, as I had nearly finished, they got a light from the galley; and by skipping what was less interesting, I carried them through to the marriage of Everard, and the restoration of Charles the Second, before eight o'clock.

The next morning, we took the battens from the hatches, and opened the ship. A few stifled rats were found; and what bugs, cockroaches, fleas, and other vermin, there might have been on board, must have unrove their life-lines before the hatches were opened. The ship being now ready, we covered the bottom of the hold over, fore and aft, with dried brush, for dunnage, and having levelled everything away, we were ready to take in our cargo. All the hides that had been collected since the California left the coast, (a little more than two years,) amounting to about forty thousand, were cured, dried, and stowed away in the house, waiting for our good ship to take them to Boston.

Now began the operation of taking in our cargo, which kept us hard at work, from the grey of the morning till star-light, for six weeks, with the exception of Sundays, and of just time

to swallow our meals. To carry the work on quicker, a division
of labor was made. Two men threw the hides down from the
piles in the house, two more picked them up and put them on
a long horizontal pole, raised a few feet from the ground,
where they were beaten, by two more, with flails, somewhat
like those used in threshing wheat. When beaten, they were
taken from this pole by two more, and placed upon a platform
of boards; and ten or a dozen men, with their trowsers rolled
up, were constantly going, back and forth, from the platform
to the boat, which was kept off where she would just float,
with the hides upon their heads. The throwing the hides upon
the pole was the most difficult work, and required a sleight of
hand which was only to be got by long practice. As I was known
for a hide-curer, this post was assigned to me, and I continued
at it for six or eight days, tossing, in that time, from eight to
ten thousand hides, until my wrists became so lame that I gave
in; and was transferred to the gang that was employed in filling
the boats, where I remained for the rest of the time. As we
were obliged to carry the hides on our heads from fear of their
getting wet, we each had a piece of sheep-skin sewed into the
inside of our hats, with the wool next our heads, and thus were
able to bear the weight, day after day, which would otherwise
have soon worn off our hair, and borne hard upon our sculls.
Upon the whole, ours was the best berth; for though the
water was nipping cold, early in the morning and late at night,
and being so continually wet was rather an exposure, yet we
got rid of the constant dust and dirt from the beating of
the hides, and being all of us young and hearty, did not mind
the exposure. The older men of the crew, whom it would have
been dangerous to have kept in the water, remained on board
with the mate, to stow the hides away, as fast as they were
brought off by the boats.

We continued at work in this manner until the lower hold
was filled to within four feet of the beams, when all hands were
called aboard to commence *steeving*. As this is a peculiar operation, it will require a minute description.

Before stowing the hides, as I have said, the ballast is levelled
off, just above the keelson, and then loose dunnage placed
upon it, on which the hides rest. The greatest care is used in
stowing, to make the ship hold as many hides as possible. It is

no mean art, and a man skilled in it is an important character in California. Many a dispute have I heard raging high between professed "beach-combers," as to whether the hides should be stowed "shingling," or "back-to-back, and flipper-to-flipper;" upon which point there was an entire and bitter division of sentiment among the *savans*. We adopted each method at different periods of the stowing, and parties ran high in the forecastle, some siding with "old Bill" in favor of the former, and others scouting him, and relying upon "English Bob" of the Ayacucho, who had been eight years in California, and was willing to risk his life and limb for the latter method. At length a compromise was effected, and a middle course, of shifting the ends and backs at every lay, was adopted, which worked well, and which, though they held it inferior to their own, each party granted was better than that of the other.

Having filled the ship up, in this way, to within four feet of her beams, the process of steeving commenced, by which an hundred hides are got into a place where one could not be forced by hand, and which presses the hides to the utmost, sometimes starting the beams of the ship, resembling in its effects the jack-screws which are used in stowing cotton. Each morning we went ashore, and beat and brought off as many hides as we could steeve in the course of the day, and, after breakfast, went down into the hold, where we remained at work until night. The whole length of the hold, from stem to stern, was floored off level, and we began with raising a pile in the after part, hard against the bulkhead of the run, and filling it up to the beams, crowding in as many as we could by hand and pushing in with oars; when a large "book" was made of from twenty-five to fifty hides, doubled at the backs, and put into one another, like the leaves of a book. An opening was then made between two hides in the pile, and the back of the outside hide of the book inserted. Two long, heavy spars, called steeves, made of the strongest wood, and sharpened off like a wedge at one end, were placed with their wedge ends into the inside of the hide which was the centre of the book, and to the other end of each, straps were fitted, into which large tackles were hooked, composed each of two huge purchase blocks, one hooked to the strap on the end of the steeve, and the other into a dog, fastened into one of the beams, as far aft as it could be got. When this was arranged, and the ways greased upon which the book was to slide, the falls of the tackles were stretched forward, and all hands tallied on, and bowsed away until the book was well entered; when these tackles were nippered, straps and toggles clapped upon the falls, and two more luff tackles hooked on, with dogs, in the same manner; and thus, by luff upon luff, the power was multiplied, until into a pile in which one hide more could not be crowded by hand, an hundred or an hundred and fifty were often driven in by this complication of purchases. When the last luff was hooked on, all hands were called to the rope—cook, steward, and all—and ranging ourselves at the falls, one behind the other, sitting down on the hides, with our heads just even with the beams, we set taught upon the tackles, and striking up a song, and all lying back at the chorus, we bowsed the tackles home, and drove the large books chock in out of sight.

The sailors' songs for capstans and falls are of a peculiar kind, having a chorus at the end of each line. The burden is usually sung by one alone, and, at the chorus, all hands join in,—and the louder the noise, the better. With us, the chorus seemed almost to raise the decks of the ship, and might be heard at a great distance, ashore. A song is as necessary to sailors as the drum and fife to a soldier. They can't pull in time, or pull with a will, without it. Many a time, when a thing goes heavy, with one fellow yo-ho-ing, a lively song, like "Heave, to the girls!" "Nancy oh!" "Jack Crosstree," &c., has put life and strength into every arm. We often found a great difference in the effect of the different songs in driving in the hides. Two or three songs would be tried, one after the other, with no effect;—not an inch could be got upon the tackles—when a new song, struck up, seemed to hit the humor of the moment, and drove the tackles "two blocks" at once. "Heave round hearty!" "Captain gone ashore!" and the like, might do for common pulls, but on an emergency, when we wanted a heavy, "raise-the-dead" pull, which should start the beams of the ship, there was nothing like "Time for us to go!" "Round the corner," or "Hurrah! hurrah! my hearty bullies!"

This was the most lively part of our work. A little boating and beach work in the morning; then twenty or thirty men down in a close hold, where we were obliged to sit down and slide about, passing hides, and rowsing about the great steeves, tackles, and dogs, singing out at the falls, and seeing the ship filling up every day. The work was as hard as it could well be. There was not a moment's cessation from Monday morning till Saturday night, when we were generally beaten out, and glad to have a full night's rest, a wash and shift of clothes, and a quiet Sunday. During all this time,—which would have startled Dr. Graham—we lived upon almost nothing but fresh beef: fried beefsteaks, three times a day,—morning, noon, and night. At morning and night we had a quart of tea to each man; and an allowance of about a pound of hard bread a day; but our chief article of food was the beef. A mess, consisting of six men had a large wooden kid piled up with beefsteaks, cut thick, and fried in fat, with the grease poured over them. Round this we sat, attacking it with our jack-knives and teeth, and with the appetite of young lions, and sent back an empty kid to the galley. This was done three times a day. How many pounds each man ate in a day, I will not attempt to compute. A whole bullock (we ate liver and all) lasted us but four days. Such devouring of flesh, I will venture to say, was seldom known before. What one man ate in a day, over a hearty man's allowance, would make a Russian's heart leap into his mouth. Indeed, during all the time we were upon the coast, our principal food was fresh beef, and every man had perfect health; but this was a time of especial devouring; and what we should have done without meat, I cannot tell. Once or twice, when our bullocks failed and we were obliged to make a meal upon dry bread and water, it seemed like feeding upon shavings. Light and dry, feeling unsatisfied, and, at the same time, full, we were glad to see four quarters of a bullock, just killed, swinging from the fore-top. Whatever theories may be started by sedentary men, certainly no men could have gone through more hard work and exposure for sixteen months in more perfect health, and without ailings and failings, than our ship's crew, let them have lived upon Hygeia's own baking and dressing.

Friday, April 15th. Arrived, brig Pilgrim, from the windward. It was a sad sight for her crew to see us getting ready to go off the coast, while they, who had been longer on the coast than the Alert, were condemned to another year's hard service. I

spent an evening on board, and found them making the best
of the matter, and determined to rough it out as they might;
but my friend S—— was determined to go home in the ship, if
money or interest could bring it to pass. After considerable
negotiating and working, he succeeded in persuading my English friend, Tom Harris,—my companion in the anchor watch
—for thirty dollars, some clothes, and an intimation from Captain Faucon that he should want a second mate before the voyage was up, to take his place in the brig as soon as she was
ready to go up to windward.

The first opportunity I could get to speak to Captain Faucon, I asked him to step up to the oven and look at Hope,
whom he knew well, having had him on board his vessel. He
went to see him, but said that he had so little medicine, and
expected to be so long on the coast, that he could do nothing
for him, but that Captain Arthur would take care of him when
he came down in the California, which would be in a week or
more. I had been to see Hope the first night after we got into
San Diego this last time, and had frequently since spent the
early part of a night in the oven. I hardly expected, when I left
him to go to windward, to find him alive upon my return. He
was certainly as low as he could well be when I left him, and
what would be the effect of the medicines that I gave him, I
hardly then dared to conjecture. Yet I knew that he must die
without them. I was not a little rejoiced, therefore, and relieved, upon our return, to see him decidedly better. The medicines were strong, and took hold and gave a check to the
disorder which was destroying him; and, more than that, they
had begun the work of exterminating it. I shall never forget
the gratitude that he expressed. All the Kanakas attributed his
escape solely to my knowledge, and would not be persuaded
that I had not all the secrets of the physical system open to me
and under my control. My medicines, however, were gone,
and no more could be got from the ship, so that his life was
left to hang upon the arrival of the California.

Sunday, April 24th. We had now been nearly seven weeks in
San Diego, and had taken in the greater part of our cargo, and
were looking out, every day, for the arrival of the California,
which had our agent on board; when, this afternoon, some
Kanakas, who had been over the hill for rabbits and to fight

rattlesnakes, came running down the path, singing out, "Kail ho!" with all their might. Mr. H——, our third mate, was ashore, and asking them particularly about the size of the sail, &c., and learning that it was "*Moku—Nui Moku*," hailed our ship, and said that the California was on the other side of the point. Instantly, all hands were turned up, the bow guns run out and loaded, the ensign and broad pennant set, the yards squared by lifts and braces, and everything got ready to make a good appearance. The instant she showed her nose round the point, we began our salute. She came in under top-gallant sails, clewed up and furled her sails in good order, and came-to, within good swinging distance of us. It being Sunday, and nothing to do, all hands were on the forecastle, criticising the new-comer. She was a good, substantial ship, not quite so long as the Alert, and wall-sided and kettle-bottomed, after the latest fashion of south-shore cotton and sugar wagons; strong, too, and tight, and a good average sailer, but with no pretensions to beauty, and nothing in the style of a "crack ship." Upon the whole, we were perfectly satisfied that the Alert might hold up her head with a ship twice as smart as she.

At night, some of us got a boat and went on board, and found a large, roomy forecastle, (for she was squarer forward than the Alert,) and a crew of a dozen or fifteen men and boys, sitting around on their chests, smoking and talking, and ready to give a welcome to any of our ship's company. It was just seven months since they left Boston, which seemed but yesterday to us. Accordingly, we had much to ask, for though we had seen the newspapers that she brought, yet these were the very men who had been in Boston and seen everything with their own eyes. One of the green-hands was a Boston boy, from one of the public schools, and, of course, knew many things which we wished to ask about, and on inquiring the names of our two Boston boys, found that they had been school-mates of his. Our men had hundreds of questions to ask about Ann street, the boarding-houses, the ships in port, the rate of wages, and other matters.

Among her crew were two English man-of-war's-men, so that, of course, we soon had music. They sang in the true sailor's style, and the rest of the crew, which was a remarkably musical one, joined in the choruses. They had many of the latest sailor songs, which had not yet got about among our merchantmen, and which they were very choice of. They began soon after we came on board, and kept it up until after two bells, when the second mate came forward and called "the Alerts away!" Battle-songs, drinking-songs, boat-songs, love-songs, and everything else, they seemed to have a complete assortment of, and I was glad to find that "All in the downs," "Poor Tom Bowline," "The Bay of Biscay," "List, ye landsmen!" and all those classical songs of the sea, still held their places. In addition to these, they had picked up at the theatres and other places a few songs of a little more genteel cast, which they were very proud of; and I shall never forget hearing an old salt, who had broken his voice by hard drinking on shore, and bellowing from the mast-head in an hundred north-westers, with all manner of ungovernable trills and quavers— in the high notes, breaking into a rough falsetto—and in the low ones, growling along like the dying away of the boat-swain's "all hands ahoy!" down the hatchway, singing, "Oh no, we never mention him."

> "Perhaps, like me, he struggles with
> Each feeling of regret;
> But if he's loved as I have loved,
> He never can forget!"

The last line, being the conclusion, he roared out at the top of his voice, breaking each word up into half a dozen syllables. This was very popular, and Jack was called upon every night to give them his "sentimental song." No one called for it more loudly than I, for the complete absurdity of the execution, and the sailors' perfect satisfaction in it, were ludicrous beyond measure.

The next day, the California commenced unloading her cargo; and her boats' crews, in coming and going, sang their boat-songs, keeping time with their oars. This they did all day long for several days, until their hides were all discharged, when a gang of them were sent on board the Alert, to help us steeve our hides. This was a windfall for us, for they had a set of new songs for the capstan and fall, and ours had got nearly worn out by six weeks' constant use. I have no doubt that this timely reinforcement of songs hastened our work several days.

Our cargo was now nearly all taken in; and my old friend, the Pilgrim, having completed her discharge, unmoored, to set sail the next morning on another long trip to windward. I was just thinking of her hard lot, and congratulating myself upon my escape from her, when I received a summons into the cabin. I went aft, and there found, seated round the cabin table, my own captain, Captain Faucon of the Pilgrim, and Mr. R——, the agent. Captain T—— turned to me and asked abruptly—

"D——, do you want to go home in the ship?"

"Certainly, sir," said I; "I expect to go home in the ship."

"Then," said he, "you must get some one to go in your place on board the Pilgrim."

I was so completely "taken aback" by this sudden intimation, that for a moment I could make no reply. I knew that it would be hopeless to attempt to prevail upon any of the ship's crew to take twelve months more upon California in the brig. I knew, too, that Captain T—— had received orders to bring me home in the Alert, and he had told me, when I was at the hide-house, that I was to go home in her; and even if this had not been so, it was cruel to give me no notice of the step they were going to take, until a few hours before the brig would sail. As soon as I had got my wits about me, I put on a bold front, and told him plainly that I had a letter in my chest informing me that he had been written to, by the owners in Boston, to bring me home in the ship, and moreover that he had told me that I was to go in the ship.

To have this told him, and to be opposed in such a manner, was more than my lord paramount had been used to. He turned fiercely upon me, and tried to look me down, and face me out of my statement; but finding that that wouldn't do, and that I was entering upon my defence in such a way as would show to the other two that he was in the wrong,—he changed his ground, and pointed to the shipping papers of the Pilgrim, from which my name had never been erased, and said that there was my name,—that I belonged to her,—that he had an absolute discretionary power,—and, in short, that I must be on board the Pilgrim by the next morning with my chest and hammock, or have some one ready to go in my place, and that he would not hear another word from me. No court of star chamber could proceed more summarily with a poor devil, than this trio was about to do with me; condemning me to a punishment worse than a Botany Bay exile, and to a fate which would alter the whole current of my future life; for two years more in California would have made me a sailor for the rest of my days. I felt all this, and saw the necessity of being determined. I repeated what I had said, and insisted upon my right to return in the ship.

> I "raised my arm, and tauld my crack,
>   Before them a'."

But it would have all availed me nothing, had I been "some poor body," before this absolute, domineering tribunal. But they saw that I would not go, unless "vi et armis," and they knew that I had friends and interest enough at home to make them suffer for any injustice they might do me. It was probably this that turned the matter; for the captain changed his tone entirely, and asked me if, in case any one went in my place, I would give him the same sum that S—— gave Harris to exchange with him. I told him that if any one was sent on board the brig, I should pity him, and be willing to help him to that, or almost any amount; but would not speak of it as an exchange.

"Very well," said he. "Go forward about your business, and send English Ben here to me!"

I went forward with a light heart, but feeling as angry, and as much contempt as I could well contain between my teeth. English Ben was sent aft, and in a few moments came forward, looking as though he had received his sentence to be hung. The captain had told him to get his things ready to go on board the brig the next morning; and that I would give him thirty dollars and a suit of clothes. The hands had "knocked off" for dinner, and were standing about the forecastle, when Ben came forward and told his story. I could see plainly that it made a great excitement, and that, unless I explained the matter to them, the feeling would be turned against me. Ben was a poor English boy, a stranger in Boston, and without friends or money; and being an active, willing lad, and a good sailor for his years, was a general favorite. "Oh yes!" said the crew, "the captain has let you off, because you are a gentleman's son, and have got friends, and know the owners; and taken Ben, because he is poor, and has got nobody to say a word for him!" I knew that this was too true to be answered, but I excused myself from any blame, and told them that I had a right to go home, at all events. This pacified them a little, but Jack had got a notion that a poor lad was to be imposed upon, and did not distinguish very clearly; and though I knew that I was in no fault, and, in fact, had barely escaped the grossest injustice, yet I felt that my berth was getting to be a disagreeable one. The notion that I was not "one of them," which, by a participation in all their labor and hardships, and having no favor shown me, had been laid asleep, was beginning to revive. But far stronger than any feeling for myself, was the pity I felt for the poor lad. He had depended upon going home in the ship; and from Boston, was going immediately to Liverpool, to see his friends. Beside this, having begun the voyage with very few clothes, he had taken up the greater part of his wages in the slop-chest, and it was every day a losing concern to him; and, like all the rest of the crew, he had a hearty hatred of California, and the prospect of eighteen months or two years more of hide-droghing seemed completely to break down his spirit. I had determined not to go myself, happen what would, and I knew that the captain would not dare to attempt to force me. I knew, too, that the two captains had agreed together to get some one, and that unless I could prevail upon somebody to go voluntarily, there would be no help for Ben. From this consideration, though I had said that I would have nothing to do with an exchange, I did my best to get some one to go voluntarily. I offered to give an order upon the owners in Boston for six months' wages, and also all the clothes, books, and other matters, which I should not want upon the voyage home. When this offer was published in the ship, and the case of poor Ben was set forth in strong colors, several, who would not have dreamed of going themselves, were busy in talking it up to others, who, they thought, might be tempted to accept it; and, at length, one fellow, a harum-scarum lad, whom we called Harry Bluff, and who did not care what country or ship he was in, if he had clothes enough and money enough,— partly from pity for Ben, and partly from the thought he should have "cruising money" for the rest of his stay,—came forward, and offered to go and "sling his hammock in the bloody hooker." Lest his purpose should cool, I signed an order for the sum upon the owners in Boston, gave him all the clothes I could spare, and sent him aft to the captain, to let him know what had been done. The skipper accepted the exchange, and was, doubtless, glad to have it pass off so easily. At the same time he cashed the order, which was endorsed to him,* and the next morning, the lad went aboard the brig, apparently in good spirits, having shaken hands with each of us and wished us a pleasant passage home, jingling the money in his pockets, and calling out, "Never say die, while there's a shot in the locker." The same boat carried off Harris, my old watchmate, who had previously made an exchange with my friend S——.

I was sorry to part with Harris. Nearly two hundred hours (as we had calculated it) had we walked the ship's deck together, at anchor watch, when all hands were below, and talked over and over every subject which came within the ken of either of us. He gave me a strong gripe with his hand; and I told him, if he came to Boston again, not to fail to find me out, and let me see an old watchmate. The same boat brought on board S——, my friend, who had begun the voyage with me from Boston, and, like me, was going back to his family and to the society which we had been born and brought up in. We congratulated one another upon finding what we had long talked over and wished for, thus brought about; and none on board the ship were more glad than ourselves to see the old brig standing round the point, under full sail. As she passed abreast of us, we all collected in the waist, and gave her three loud, hearty cheers, waving our hats in the air. Her crew sprang into the rigging and chains, and answered us with three as loud, to which we, after the nautical custom, gave one in return. I took my last look of their familiar faces as they got over the rail, and saw the old black cook put his head out of the galley, and wave his cap over his head. The crew flew aloft to loose the top-gallant sails and royals; the two captains waved

---

*When the crew were paid off in Boston, the owners answered the order, but generously refused to deduct the amount from the pay-roll, saying that the exchange was made under compulsion. They also allowed S—— his exchange money.

their hands to one another; and, in ten minutes, we saw the last inch of her white canvass, as she rounded the point.

Relieved as I was to see her well off, (and I felt like one who had just sprung from an iron trap which was closing upon him) I had yet a feeling of regret at taking the last look at the old craft in which I had spent a year, and the first year, of my sailor's life—which had been my first home in the new world into which I had entered—and with which I had associated so many things,—my first leaving home, my first crossing the equator, Cape Horn, Juan Fernandez, death at sea, and other things, serious and common. Yet, with all this, and the feeling I had for my old shipmates, condemned to another term of California life, the thought that we were done with it, and that one week more would see us on our way to Boston, was a cure for everything.

Friday, May 6th, completed the taking in of our cargo, and was a memorable day in our calendar. The time when we were to take in our last hide, we had looked forward to, for sixteen months, as the first bright spot. When the last hide was stowed away, and the hatches calked down, the tarpaulins battened on to them, the long-boat hoisted in and secured, and the decks swept down for the night,—the chief mate sprang upon the top of the long-boat, called all hands into the waist, and giving us a signal by swinging his cap over his head,—we gave three long, loud cheers, which came from the bottom of our hearts, and made the hills and valleys ring again. In a moment, we heard three, in answer, from the California's crew, who had seen us taking in our long-boat, and—"the cry they heard—its meaning knew."

The last week, we had been occupied in taking in a supply of wood and water for the passage home, and in bringing on board the spare spars, sails, &c. I was sent off with a party of Indians to fill the water-casks, at a spring, about three miles from the shipping, and near the town, and was absent three days, living at the town, and spending the daytime in filling the casks and transporting them on ox-carts to the landing-place, whence they were taken on board by the crew with boats. This being all done with, we gave one day to bending our sails; and at night, every sail, from the courses to the sky-sails, was bent, and every studding-sail ready for setting.

Before our sailing, an unsuccessful attempt was made by one of the crew of the California to effect an exchange with one of our number. It was a lad, between fifteen and sixteen years of age, who went by the name of the "reefer," having been a midshipman in an East India Company's ship. His singular character and story had excited our interest ever since the ship came into the port. He was a delicate, slender little fellow, with a beautiful pearly complexion, regular features, forehead as white as marble, black hair, curling beautifully round it, tapering, delicate fingers, small feet, soft voice, gentle manners, and, in fact, every sign of having been well born and bred. At the same time, there was something in his expression which showed a slight deficiency of intellect. How great the deficiency was, or what it resulted from; whether he was born so; whether it was the result of disease or accident; or whether, as some said, it was brought on by his distress of mind, during the voyage, I cannot say. From his own account of himself, and from many circumstances which were known in connection with his story, he must have been the son of a man of wealth. His mother was an Italian woman. He was probably a natural son, for in scarcely any other way could the incidents of his early life be accounted for. He said that his parents did not live together, and he seemed to have been ill treated by his father. Though he had been delicately brought up, and indulged in every way, (and he had then with him trinkets which had been given him at home,) yet his education had been sadly neglected; and when only twelve years old, he was sent as midshipman in the Company's service. His own story was, that he afterwards ran away from home, upon a difficulty which he had with his father, and went to Liverpool, whence he sailed in the ship Rialto, Captain Holmes, for Boston. Captain Holmes endeavored to get him a passage back, but there being no vessel to sail for some time, the boy left him, and went to board at a common sailor's boarding-house, in Ann street, where he supported himself for a few weeks by selling some of his valuables. At length, according to his own account, being desirous of returning home, he went to a shipping-office, where the shipping articles of the California were open. Upon asking where the ship was going, he was told by the shipping-master that she was bound to California. Not knowing where that was, he told him that he wanted to go to Europe, and asked if California was in Europe. The shipping-master answered him in a way which the boy did not understand, and advised him to ship. The boy signed the articles, received his advance, laid out a little of it in clothes, and spent the rest, and was ready to go on board, when, upon the morning of sailing, he heard that the ship was bound upon the North-west Coast, on a two or three years' voyage, and was not going to Europe. Frightened at this prospect, he slipped away when the crew were going aboard, wandered up into another part of the town, and spent all the forenoon in straying about the common, and the neighboring streets. Having no money, and all his clothes and other things being in his chest, on board, and being a stranger, he became tired and hungry, and ventured down toward the shipping, to see if the vessel had sailed. He was just turning the corner of a street, when the shipping-master, who had been in search of him, popped upon him, seized him, and carried him on board. He cried and struggled, and said he did not wish to go in the ship, but the top-sails were at the mast-head, the fast just ready to be cast off, and everything in the hurry and confusion of departure, so that he was hardly noticed; and the few who did inquire about the matter were told that it was merely a boy who had spent his advance and tried to run away. Had the owners of the vessel known anything of the matter, they would have interfered at once; but they either knew nothing of it, or heard, like the rest, that it was only an unruly boy who was sick of his bargain. As soon as the boy found himself actually at sea, and upon a voyage of two or three years in length, his spirits failed him; he refused to work, and became so miserable, that Captain Arthur took him into the cabin, where he assisted the steward, and occasionally pulled and hauled about decks. He was in this capacity when we saw him; and though it was much better for him than the life in a forecastle, and the hard work, watching, and exposure, which his delicate frame could not have borne, yet, to be joined with a black fellow in waiting upon a man whom he probably looked upon as but little, in point of education and manners, above one of his father's servants, was almost too much for his spirit to bear. Had he entered upon this situation of his own free will, he could have endured it; but to have been deceived, and, in addition to that, forced into it, was intolerable. He made every effort to go home in our ship, but his captain refused to part with him except in the way of exchange, and that he could not effect. If this account of the whole matter, which we had from the boy, and which was confirmed by all the crew, be correct, I cannot understand why Captain Arthur should have refused to let him go, especially being a captain who had the name, not only with that crew, but with all whom he had ever commanded, of an unusually kind-hearted man. The truth is, the unlimited power which merchant captains have, upon long voyages on strange coasts, takes away a sense of responsibility, and too often, even in men otherwise well-disposed, substitutes a disregard for the rights and feelings of others. The lad was sent on shore to join the gang at the hide-house; from whence, I was afterwards rejoiced to hear, he effected his escape, and went down to Callao in a small Spanish schooner; and from Callao, he probably returned to England.

Soon after the arrival of the California, I spoke to Captain Arthur about Hope; and as he had known him on the voyage before, and was very fond of him, he immediately went to see him, gave him proper medicines, and, under such care, he began rapidly to recover. The Saturday night before our sailing, I spent an hour in the oven, and took leave of my Kanaka friends; and, really, this was the only thing connected with leaving California which was in any way unpleasant. I felt an interest and affection for many of these simple, true-hearted men, such as I never felt before but for a near relation. Hope shook me by the hand; said he should soon be well again, and ready to work for me when I came upon the coast, next voyage, as officer of the ship; and told me not to forget, when I became captain, how to be kind to the sick. Old "Mr. Bingham" and "King Mannini" went down to the boat with me, shook me heartily by the hand, wished us a good voyage, and went back to the oven, chanting one of their deep monotonous songs, the burden of which I gathered to be about us and our voyage.

Sunday, May 8th. This promised to be our last day in California. Our forty thousand hides, thirty thousand horns, besides several barrels of otter and beaver skins, were all stowed below, and the hatches calked down. All our spare spars were taken on board and lashed; our water-casks secured; and our live stock, consisting of four bullocks, a dozen sheep, a dozen or more pigs, and three or four dozen of poultry, were all stowed away in their different quarters: the bullocks in the long-boat, the sheep in a pen on the fore hatch, and the pigs in a sty under the bows of the long-boat, and the poultry in their proper coop, and the jolly-boat was full of hay for the sheep and bullocks. Our unusually large cargo, together with the stores for a five months' voyage, brought the ship channels down into the water. In addition to this, she had been steeved so thoroughly, and was so bound by the compression of her cargo, forced into her by so powerful machinery, that she was like a man in a strait jacket, and would be but a dull sailer, until she had worked herself loose.

The California had finished discharging her cargo, and was to get under weigh at the same time with us. Having washed down decks and got our breakfast, the two vessels lay side by side, in complete readiness for sea, our ensigns hanging from the peaks, and our tall spars reflected from the glassy surface of the river, which, since sunrise, had been unbroken by a ripple. At length, a few whiffs came across the water, and, by eleven o'clock, the regular north-west wind set steadily in. There was no need of calling all hands, for we had all been hanging about the forecastle the whole forenoon, and were ready for a start upon the first sign of a breeze. All eyes were aft upon the captain, who was walking the deck, with, every now and then, a look to windward. He made a sign to the mate, who came forward, took his station deliberately between the knight-heads, cast a glance aloft, and called out, "All hands, lay aloft and loose the sails!" We were half in the rigging before the order came, and never since we left Boston were the gaskets off the yards, and the rigging overhauled, in a shorter time. "All ready forward, sir!"—"All ready the main!"—"Cross-jack yards all ready, sir!"—"Lay down, all hands but one on each yard!" The yard-arm and bunt gaskets were cast off; and each sail hung by the jigger, with one man standing by the tie to let it go. At the same moment that we sprang aloft, a dozen hands sprang into the rigging of the California, and in an instant were all over her yards; and her sails, too, were ready to be dropped at the word. In the mean time our bow gun had been loaded and run out, and its discharge was to be the signal for dropping the sails. A cloud of smoke came out of our bows; the echoes of the gun rattled our farewell among the hills of California; and the two ships were covered, from head to foot, with their white canvass. For a few minutes, all was uproar and apparent confusion: men flying about like monkeys in the rigging; ropes and blocks flying; orders given and answered, and the confused noises of men singing out at the ropes. The top-sails came to the mast-heads with "Cheerily, men!" and, in a few minutes, every sail was set; for the wind was light. The head sails were backed, the windlass came round 'slip—slap' to the cry of the sailors;— "Hove short, sir," said the mate;—"Up with him!"—"Aye, aye, sir."—A few hearty and long heaves, and the anchor showed its head. "Hook cat!"—The fall was stretched along the decks; —all hands laid hold;—"Hurrah, for the last time," said the mate; and the anchor came to the cat-head to the tune of "Time for us to go," with a loud chorus. Everything was done quick, as though it were for the last time. The head yards were filled away, and our ship began to move through the water on her homeward-bound course.

The California had got under weigh at the same moment; and we sailed down the narrow bay abreast, and were just off the mouth, and finding ourselves gradually shooting ahead of her, were on the point of giving her three parting cheers, when, suddenly, we found ourselves stopped short, and the California ranging fast ahead of us. A bar stretches across the mouth of the harbor, with water enough to float common vessels, but, being low in the water, and having kept well to leeward, as we were bound to the southward, we had stuck fast, while the California, being light, had floated over.

We kept all sail on, in the hope of forcing over, but failing in this, we hove aback, and lay waiting for the tide, which was on the flood, to take us back into the channel. This was somewhat of a damper to us, and the captain looked not a little mortified and vexed. "This is the same place where the Rosa got ashore," observed our red-headed second mate, most mal-a-propos. A malediction on the Rosa, and him too, was all the answer he got, and he slunk off to leeward. In a few minutes, the force of the wind and the rising of the tide backed us into the stream, and we were on our way to our old anchoring-place, the tide setting swiftly up, and the ship barely manageable, in the light breeze. We came-to, in our old berth, opposite the hide-house, whose inmates were not a little surprised to see us return. We felt as though we were tied to California; and some of the crew swore that they never should get clear of the *bloody* coast.

In about half an hour, which was near high water, the order was given to man the windlass, and again the anchor was catted; but not a word was said about the last time. The California had come back on finding that we had returned, and was hove-to, waiting for us, off the point. This time we passed the bar safely, and were soon up with the California, who filled away, and kept us company. She seemed desirous of a trial of speed, and our captain accepted the challenge, although we were loaded down to the bolts of our chain plates, as deep as a sand-barge, and bound so taught with our cargo that we were no more fit for a race than a man in fetters;—while our antagonist was in her best trim. Being clear of the point, the breeze became stiff, and the royal masts bent under our sails, but we would not take them in until we saw three boys spring aloft into the rigging of the California; when they were all furled at once, but with orders to stay aloft at the top-gallant mast-heads, and loose them again at the word. It was my duty to furl the fore royal; and while standing by to loose it again, I had a fine view of the scene. From where I stood, the two vessels seemed nothing but spars and sails, while their narrow decks, far below, slanting over by the force of the wind aloft, appeared hardly capable of supporting the great fabrics raised upon them. The California was to windward of us, and had every advantage; yet, while the breeze was stiff, we held our own. As soon as it began to slacken, she ranged a little ahead, and the order was given to loose the royals. In an instant the gaskets were off and the bunt dropped. "Sheet home the fore royal!—Weather sheet's home!"—"Lee sheet's home!"—"Hoist away, sir!" is bawled from aloft. "Overhaul your clewlines!" shouts the mate. "Aye, aye, sir! all clear!"—"Taught leech! belay! Well the lee brace; haul taught to windward"—and the royals are set. These brought us up again; but the wind continuing light, the California set hers, and it was soon evident that she was walking away from us. Our captain then hailed, and said that he should keep off to his course; adding—"She is n't the Alert now. If I had her in your trim, she would have been out of sight by this time." This was good-naturedly answered from the California, and she braced sharp up, and stood close upon the wind up the coast; while we squared away our yards, and stood before the wind to the south-south-west. The California's crew manned her weather rigging, waved their hats in the air, and gave us three hearty cheers, which we answered as heartily, and the customary single cheer came back to us from over the water. She stood on her way, doomed to eighteen months' or two years' hard service upon that hated coast, while we were making our way to our home, which every hour and every mile was bringing us nearer to.

As soon as we parted company with the California, all hands were sent aloft to set the studding-sails. Booms were rigged out, tacks and halyards rove, sail after sail packed upon her, until every available inch of canvass was spread, that we might not lose a breath of the fair wind. We could now see how much she was cramped and deadened by her cargo; for with a good breeze on her quarter, and every stitch of canvass spread, we could not get more than six knots out of her. She had no more life in her than if she were water-logged. The log was hove several times; but she was doing her best. We had hardly patience with her, but the older sailors said—"Stand by! you'll see her work herself loose in a week or two, and then she'll walk up to Cape Horn like a race-horse."

When all sail had been set, and the decks cleared up, the California was a speck in the horizon, and the coast lay like a low cloud along the north-east. At sunset they were both out of sight, and we were once more upon the ocean, where sky and water meet.

Chapter XXX

AT eight o'clock all hands were called aft, and the watches set for the voyage. Some changes were made; but I was glad to find myself still in the larboard watch. Our crew was somewhat diminished; for a man and a boy had gone in the Pilgrim; another was second mate of the Ayacucho; and a third, the oldest man of the crew, had broken down under the hard work and constant exposure on the coast, and, having had a stroke of the palsy, was left behind at the hide-house, under the charge of Captain Arthur. The poor fellow wished very much to come home in the ship; and he ought to have been brought home in her. But a live dog is better than a dead lion, and a sick sailor belongs to nobody's mess; so he was sent ashore with the rest of the lumber, which was only in the way. By these diminutions, we were short-handed for a voyage round Cape Horn in the dead of winter. Beside S—— and myself, there were only five in the forecastle; who, together with four boys in the steerage, the sailmaker, carpenter, &c., composed the whole crew. In addition to this, we were only three or four days out, when the sailmaker, who was the oldest and best seaman on board, was taken with the palsy, and was useless for the rest of the voyage. The constant wading in the water, in all weathers, to take off hides, together with the other labors, is too much for old men, and for any who have not good constitutions. Beside these two men of ours, the second officer of the California and the carpenter of the Pilgrim broke down under the work, and the latter died at Santa Barbara. The young man, too, who came out with us from Boston in the Pilgrim, had to be taken from his berth before the mast and made clerk, on account of a fit of rheumatism which attacked him soon after he came upon the coast. By the loss of the sailmaker, our watch was reduced to five, of whom two were boys, who never steered but in fine weather, so that the other two and myself had to stand at the wheel four hours apiece out of every twenty-four; and the other watch had only four helmsmen. "Never mind—we're homeward bound!" was the answer to everything; and we should not have minded this, were it not for the thought that we should be off Cape Horn in the very dead of winter. It was now the first part of May; and two months would bring us off the Cape in July, which is the worst month in the year there; when the sun rises at nine and sets at three, giving eighteen hours night, and there is snow and rain, gales and high seas, in abundance.

The prospect of meeting this in a ship half manned, and loaded so deep that every heavy sea must wash her fore and aft, was by no means pleasant. The Alert, in her passage out, doubled the Cape in the month of February, which is mid-summer; and we came round in the Pilgrim in the latter part of October, which we thought was bad enough. There was only one of our crew who had been off there in the winter, and that was in a whale-ship, much lighter and higher than our ship; yet he said they had man-killing weather for twenty days without intermission, and their decks were swept twice, and they were all glad enough to see the last of it. The Brandywine frigate, also, in her passage round, had sixty days off the Cape, and lost several boats by the heavy seas. All this was for our comfort; yet pass it we must; and all hands agreed to make the best of it.

During our watches below we overhauled our clothes, and made and mended everything for bad weather. Each of us had made for himself a suit of oil-cloth or tarpaulin, and these we got out, and gave thorough coatings of oil or tar, and hung upon the stays to dry. Our stout boots, too, we covered over with a thick mixture of melted grease and tar, and hung out to dry. Thus we took advantage of the warm sun and fine weather of the Pacific to prepare for its other face. In the forenoon watches below, our forecastle looked like the workshop of what a sailor is,—a Jack at all trades. Thick stockings and drawers were darned and patched; mittens dragged from the bottom of the chest and mended; comforters made for the neck and ears; old flannel shirts cut up to line monkey-jackets; south-westers lined with flannel, and a pot of paint smuggled forward to give them a coat on the outside; and everything turned to hand; so that, although two years had left us but a scanty wardrobe, yet the economy and invention which necessity teaches a sailor, soon put each of us in pretty good trim for bad weather, even before we had seen the last of the fine. Even the cobbler's art was not out of place. Several old shoes were very decently repaired, and with waxed ends, an awl, and the top of an old boot, I made me quite a respectable sheath for my knife.

There was one difficulty, however, which nothing that we could do would remedy; and that was the leaking of the forecastle, which made it very uncomfortable in bad weather, and rendered half of the berths tenantless. The tightest ships, in a long voyage, from the constant strain which is upon the bowsprit, will leak, more or less, round the heel of the bowsprit, and the bitts, which come down into the forecastle; but, in addition to this, we had an unaccountable leak on the starboard bow, near the cat-head, which drove us from the forward berths on that side, and, indeed, when she was on the starboard tack, from all the forward berths. One of the after berths, too, leaked in very bad weather; so that in a ship which was in other respects as tight as a bottle, and brought her cargo to Boston perfectly dry, we had, after every effort made to prevent it, in the way of calking and leading, a forecastle with only three dry berths for seven of us. However, as there is never but one watch below at a time, by 'turning in and out,' we did pretty well. And, there being, in our watch, but three of us who lived forward, we generally had a dry berth apiece in bad weather.*

All this, however, was but anticipation. We were still in fine weather in the North Pacific, running down the north-east trades, which we took on the second day after leaving San Diego.

Sunday, May 15th, one week out, we were in latitude 14° 56' N., long. 116° 14' W., having gone, by reckoning, over thirteen hundred miles in seven days. In fact, ever since leaving San Diego, we had had a fair wind, and as much as we wanted of it. For seven days, our lower and top-mast studding-sails were set all the time, and our royals and top-gallant studding-sails, whenever she could stagger under them. Indeed, the captain had shown, from the moment we got to sea, that he was to have no boy's play, but that the ship had got to carry all she

*On removing the cat-head, after the ship arrived at Boston, it was found that there were two holes under it which had been bored for the purpose of driving treenails, and which, accidentally, had not been plugged up when the cat-head was placed over them. This was sufficient to account for the leak, and for our not having been able to discover and stop it

could, and that he was going to make up, by 'cracking on' to her, what she wanted in lightness. In this way, we frequently made three degrees of latitude, besides something in longitude, in the course of twenty-four hours.—Our days were spent in the usual ship's work. The rigging which had become slack from being long in port was to be set up; breast backstays got up; studding-sail booms rigged upon the main yard; and royal studding-sails got ready for the light trades; ring-tail set; and new rigging fitted and sails got ready for Cape Horn. For, with a ship's gear, as well as a sailor's wardrobe, fine weather must be improved to get ready for the bad to come. Our forenoon watch below, as I have said, was given to our own work, and our night watches were spent in the usual manner:—a *trick* at the wheel, a look-out on the forecastle, a nap on a coil of rigging under the lee of the rail; a yarn round the windlass-end; or, as was generally my way, a solitary walk fore and aft, in the weather waist, between the windlass-end and the main tack. Every wave that she threw aside brought us nearer home, and every day's observation at noon showed a progress which, if it continued, would, in less than five months, take us into Boston Bay. This is the pleasure of life at sea,—fine weather, day after day, without interruption,—fair wind, and a plenty of it,—and homeward bound. Every one was in good humor; things went right; and all was done with a will. At the dog watch, all hands came on deck, and stood round the weather side of the forecastle, or sat upon the windlass, and sung sea songs, and those ballads of pirates and highwaymen, which sailors delight in. Home, too, and what we should do when we got there, and when and how we should arrive, was no infrequent topic. Every night, after the kids and pots were put away, and we had lighted our pipes and cigars at the galley, and gathered about the windlass, the first question was,—

"Well, Tom, what was the latitude to day?"

"Why, fourteen, north, and she has been going seven knots ever since."

"Well, this will bring us up to the line in five days."

"Yes, but these trades won't last twenty-four hours longer," says an old salt, pointing with the sharp of his hand to leeward, —"I know that by the look of the clouds."

Then came all manner of calculations and conjectures as to

the continuance of the wind, the weather under the line, the south-east trades, &c., and rough guesses as to the time the ship would be up with the Horn; and some, more venturous, gave her so many days to Boston light, and offered to bet that she would not exceed it.

"You'd better wait till you get round Cape Horn," says an old croaker.

"Yes," says another, "you may see Boston, but you've got to 'smell hell' before that good day."

Rumors also of what had been said in the cabin, as usual, found their way forward. The steward had heard the captain say something about the straits of Magellan, and the man at the wheel fancied he had heard him tell the 'passenger' that, if he found the wind ahead and the weather very bad off the Cape, he should stick her off for New Holland, and come home round the Cape of Good Hope.

This passenger—the first and only one we had had, except to go from port to port, on the coast, was no one else than a gentleman whom I had known in my better days; and the last person I should have expected to have seen on the coast of California—Professor N——, of Cambridge. I had left him quietly seated in the chair of Botany and Ornithology, in Harvard University; and the next I saw of him, was strolling about San Diego beach, in a sailor's pea-jacket, with a wide straw hat, and barefooted, with his trowsers rolled up to his knees, picking up stones and shells. He had travelled over land to the North-west Coast, and come down in a small vessel to Monterey. There he learned that there was a ship at the leeward, about to sail for Boston; and, taking passage in the Pilgrim, which was then at Monterey, he came slowly down, visiting the intermediate ports, and examining the trees, plants, earths, birds, &c., and joined us at San Diego shortly before we sailed. The second mate of the Pilgrim told me that they had got an old gentleman on board who knew me, and came from the college that I had been in. He could not recollect his name, but said he was a 'sort of an oldish man,' with white hair, and spent all his time in the bush, and along the beach, picking up flowers and shells, and such truck, and had a dozen boxes and barrels, full of them. I thought over everybody who would be likely to be there, but could fix upon no one; when, the next day, just as we were about to shove off from the beach, he came down to the boat, in the rig I have described, with his shoes in his hand, and his pockets full of specimens. I knew him at once, though I should not have been more surprised to have seen the Old South steeple shoot up from the hide-house. He probably had no less difficulty in recognising me. As we left home about the same time, we had nothing to tell one another; and owing to our different situations on board, I saw but little of him on the passage home. Sometimes, when I was at the wheel of a calm night, and the steering required no attention, and the officer of the watch was forward, he would come aft and hold a short yarn with me; but this was against the rules of the ship, as is, in fact, all intercourse between passengers and the crew. I was often amused to see the sailors puzzled to know what to make of him, and to hear their conjectures about him and his business. They were as much puzzled as our old sailmaker was with the captain's instruments in the cabin. He said there were three:—the *chro*-nometer, the *chre*-nometer, and the *the*-nometer. (Chronometer, barometer, and thermometer.) The Pilgrim's crew christened Mr. N. "Old Curious," from his zeal for curiosities, and some of them said that he was crazy, and that his friends let him go about and amuse himself in this way. Why else a rich man (sailors call every man rich who does not work with his hands, and wears a long coat and cravat) should leave a Christian country, and come to such a place as California, to pick up shells and stones, they could not understand. One of them, however, an old salt, who had seen something more of the world ashore, set all to rights, as he thought,—"Oh, 'vast there!—You don't know anything about them craft. I've seen them colleges, and know the ropes. They keep all such things for cur'osities, and study 'em, and have men a' purpose to go and get 'em. This old chap knows what he's about. He a'n't the child you take him for. He'll carry all these things to the college, and if they are better than any that they have had before, he'll be head of the college. Then, by-and-by, somebody else will go after some more, and if they beat him, he'll have to go again, or else give up his berth. That's the way they do it. This old covey knows the ropes. He has worked a traverse over 'em, and come 'way out here, where nobody's ever been afore, and where they'll never think of coming." This explanation satisfied Jack; and as it raised Mr. N.'s credit for capacity, and was near enough to the truth for common purposes, I did not disturb it.

With the exception of Mr. N., we had no one on board but the regular ship's company, and the live stock. Upon this, we had made a considerable inroad. We killed one of the bullocks every four days, so that they did not last us up to the line. We, or, rather, they, then began upon the sheep and the poultry, for these never come into Jack's mess.* The pigs were left for the latter part of the voyage, for they are sailors, and can stand all weathers. We had an old sow on board, the mother of a

*The customs as to the allowance of "grub" are very nearly the same in all American merchantmen. Whenever a pig is killed, the sailors have one mess from it. The rest goes to the cabin. The smaller live stock, poultry, &c., they never taste. And, indeed, they do not complain of this, for it would take a great deal to supply them with a good meal, and without the accompaniments, (which could hardly be furnished to them,) it would not be much better than salt beef. But even as to the salt beef, they are scarcely dealt fairly with; for whenever a barrel is opened, before any of the beef is put into the harness-cask, the steward comes up, and picks it all over, and takes out the best pieces, (those that have any fat in them) for the cabin. This was done in both the vessels I was in, and the men said that it was usual in other vessels. Indeed, it is made no secret, but some of the crew are usually called to help in assorting and putting away the pieces. By this arrangement, the hard, dry pieces, which the sailors call 'old horse,' come to their share.

There is a singular piece of rhyme, traditional among sailors, which they say over such pieces of beef. I do not know that it ever appeared in print before. When seated round the kid, if a particularly bad piece is found, one of them takes it up, and addressing it, repeats these lines:

> 'Old horse! old horse! what brought you here?'
> —'From Sacarap' to Portland pier
> I've carted stone this many a year:
> Till, killed by blows and sore abuse,
> They salted me down for sailors' use.
> The sailors they do me despise:
> They turn me over and damn my eyes;
> Cut off my meat, and pick my bones,
> And pitch the rest to Davy Jones.'

There is a story current among seamen, that a beef-dealer was convicted, at Boston, of having sold old horse for ship's stores, instead of beef, and had been sentenced to be confined in jail, until he should eat the whole of it; and that he is now lying in Boston jail. I have heard this story often, on board other vessels beside those of our own nation. It is very generally believed, and is always highly commended, as a fair instance of retaliatory justice.

numerous progeny, who had been twice round the Cape of Good Hope, and once round Cape Horn. The last time going round, was very nearly her death. We heard her squealing and moaning one dark night, after it had been snowing and hailing for several hours, and, getting into the sty, we found her nearly frozen to death. We got some straw, an old sail, and other things, and wrapped her up in a corner of the sty, where she staid until we got into fine weather again.

Wednesday, May 18th. Lat. 9° 54′ N., long. 113° 17′ W. The north-east trades had now left us, and we had the usual variable winds which prevail near the line, together with some rain. So long as we were in these latitudes, we had but little rest in our watch on deck at night, for, as the winds were light and variable, and we could not lose a breath, we were all the watch bracing the yards, and taking in and making sail, and 'humbugging' with our flying kites. A little puff of wind on the larboard quarter, and then—"larboard fore braces!" and studding-booms were rigged out, studding-sails set alow and aloft, the yards trimmed, and jibs and spanker in; when it would come as calm as a duck-pond, and the man at the wheel stand with the palm of his hand up, feeling for the wind. "Keep her off a little!" "All aback forward, sir!" cries a man from the forecastle. Down go the braces again; in come the studding-sails, all in a mess, which half an hour won't set right; yards braced sharp up; and she's on the starboard tack, close hauled. The studding-sails must now be cleared away, and set up in the tops, and on the booms. By the time this is done, and you are looking out for a soft plank for a nap,—"Lay aft here, and square in the head yards!" and the studding-sails are all set again on the starboard side. So it goes until it is eight bells,— call the watch,—heave the log,—relieve the wheel, and go below the larboard watch.

Sunday, May 22d. Lat. 5° 14′ N., long. 166° 45′ W. We were now a fortnight out, and within five degrees of the line, to which two days of good breeze would take us; but we had, for the most part, what the sailors call 'an Irishman's hurricane,— right up and down.' This day it rained nearly all day, and being Sunday, and nothing to do, we stopped up the scuppers and filled the decks with rain water, and bringing all our clothes on deck, had a grand wash, fore and aft. When this was through, we stripped, to our drawers, and taking pieces of soap, with strips of canvass for towels, we turned-to and soaped, washed, and scrubbed one another down, to get off, as we said, the California dust; for the common wash in salt water, which is all that Jack can get, being on an allowance of fresh, had little efficacy, and was more for taste than utility. The captain was below all the afternoon, and we had something nearer to a Saturnalia than anything we had yet seen; for the mate came into the scuppers, with a couple of boys to scrub him, and got into a battle with them in heaving water. By unplugging the holes, we let the soap-suds off the decks, and in a short time had a new supply of rain water, in which we had a grand rinsing. It was surprising to see how much soap and fresh water did for the complexions of many of us; how much of what we supposed to be tan and sea-blacking, we got rid of. The next day, the sun rising clear, the ship was covered, fore and aft, with clothes of all sorts, hanging out to dry.

As we approached the line, the wind became more easterly, and the weather clearer, and in twenty days from San Diego,—

Saturday, May 28th, at about three P.M., with a fine breeze from the east-south-east, we crossed the equator. In twenty-four hours after crossing the line, which was very unusual, we took the regular south-east trades. These winds come a little from the eastward of south-east, and, with us, they blew directly from the east-south-east, which was fortunate for us, for our course was south-by-west, and we could thus go one point free. The yards were braced so that every sail drew, from the spanker to the flying-jib; and the upper yards being squared in a little, the fore and main top-gallant studding-sails were set, and just drew handsomely. For twelve days this breeze blew steadily, not varying a point, and just so fresh that we could carry our royals; and, during the whole time, we hardly started a brace. Such progress did we make, that at the end of seven days from the time we took the breeze, on

Sunday, June 5th, we were in lat. 19° 29' S., and long. 118° 01' W., having made twelve hundred miles in seven days, very nearly upon a taught bowline. Our good ship was getting to be herself again, had increased her rate of sailing more than one third since leaving San Diego. The crew ceased complaining of her, and the officers hove the log every two hours with evident satisfaction. This was glorious sailing. A steady breeze; the light trade-wind clouds over our heads; the incomparable temperature of the Pacific,—neither hot nor cold; a clear sun every day, and clear moon and stars each night; and new constellations rising in the south, and the familiar ones sinking in the north, as we went on our course,—"stemming nightly toward the pole." Already we had sunk the north star and the Great Bear in the northern horizon, and all hands looked out sharp to the southward for the Magellan Clouds, which, each succeeding night, we expected to make. "The next time we see the north star," said one, "we shall be standing to the northward, the other side of the Horn." This was true enough, and no doubt it would be a welcome sight; for sailors say that in coming home from round Cape Horn, and the Cape of Good Hope, the north star is the first land you make.

These trades were the same that, in the passage out in the Pilgrim, lasted nearly all the way from Juan Fernandez to the line; blowing steadily on our starboard quarter for three weeks, without our starting a brace, or even brailing down the skysails. Though we had now the same wind, and were in the same latitude with the Pilgrim on her passage out, yet we were nearly twelve hundred miles to the westward of her course; for the captain, depending upon the strong south-west winds which prevail in high southern latitudes during the winter months, took the full advantage of the trades, and stood well to the westward, so far that we passed within about two hundred miles of Ducie's Island.

It was this weather and sailing that brought to my mind a little incident that occurred on board the Pilgrim, while we were in the same latitude. We were going along at a great rate, dead before the wind, with studding-sails out on both sides, alow and aloft, on a dark night, just after midnight, and everything as still as the grave, except the washing of the water by the vessel's side; for, being before the wind, with a smooth sea, the little brig, covered with canvass, was doing great business, with very little noise. The other watch was below, and all our watch, except myself and the man at the wheel, were asleep under the lee of the boat. The second mate, who came out before the mast, and was always very *thick* with me, had been holding a yarn with me, and just gone aft to his place on the quarter-deck, and I had resumed my usual walk to and from the windlass-end, when, suddenly, we heard a loud scream coming from ahead, apparently directly from under the bows. The darkness, and complete stillness of the night, and the solitude of the ocean, gave to the sound a dreadful and almost supernatural effect. I stood perfectly still, and my heart beat quick. The sound woke up the rest of the watch, who stood looking at one another. "What, in the name of God, is that?" said the second mate, coming slowly forward. The first thought I had was, that it might be a boat, with the crew of some wrecked vessel, or perhaps the boat of some whale-ship, out over night, and we had run them down in the darkness. Another scream! but less loud than the first. This started us, and we ran forward, and looked over the bows, and over the sides, to leeward, but nothing was to be seen or heard. What was to be done? Call the captain, and heave the ship aback? Just at this moment, in crossing the forecastle, one of the men saw a light below, and looking down the scuttle, saw the watch all out of their berths, and afoul of one poor fellow, dragging him out of his berth, and shaking him, to wake him out of a nightmare. They had been waked out of their sleep, and as much alarmed at the scream as we were, and were hesitating whether to come on deck, when the second sound, coming directly from one of the berths, revealed the cause of the alarm. The fellow got a good shaking for the trouble he had given. We made a joke of the matter; and we could well laugh, for our minds were not a little relieved by its ridiculous termination.

We were now close upon the southern tropical line, and, with so fine a breeze, were daily leaving the sun behind us, and drawing nearer to Cape Horn, for which it behoved us to make every preparation. Our rigging was all examined and overhauled, and mended, or replaced with new, where it was necessary: new and strong bobstays fitted in the place of the chain ones, which were worn out; the sprit-sail yard and martingale guys and back-ropes set well taught; bran new fore and main braces rove; top-gallant sheets, and wheel-ropes, made of green hide, laid up in the form of rope, were stretched and fitted; and new top-sail clewlines, &c., rove; new fore top-mast back-stays fitted; and other preparations made, in good season, that the ropes might have time to stretch and become limber before we got into cold weather.

Sunday, June 12th. Lat. 26° 04′ S., long. 116° 31′ W. We had now lost the regular trades, and had the winds variable, principally from the westward, and kept on, in a southerly course, sailing very nearly upon a meridian, and at the end of the week,—

Sunday, June 19th, were in lat. 34° 15′ S., and long. 116° 38′ W.

Chapter XXXI

THERE began now to be a decided change in the appearance of things. The days became shorter and shorter; the sun running lower in its course each day, and giving less and less heat; and the nights so cold as to prevent our sleeping on deck; the Magellan Clouds in sight, of a clear night; the skies looking cold and angry; and, at times, a long, heavy, ugly sea, setting in from the southward, told us what we were coming to. Still, however, we had a fine, strong breeze, and kept on our way, under as much sail as our ship would bear. Toward the middle of the week, the wind hauled to the southward, which brought us upon a taught bowline, made the ship meet, nearly head-on, the heavy swell which rolled from that direction; and there was something not at all encouraging in the manner in which she met it. Being so deep and heavy, she wanted the buoyancy which should have carried her over the seas, and she dropped heavily into them, the water washing over the decks; and every now and then, when an unusually large sea met her fairly upon the bows, she struck it with a sound as dead and heavy as that with which a sledge-hammer falls upon the pile, and took the whole of it in upon the forecastle, and rising, carried it aft in the scuppers, washing the rigging off the pins, and carrying along with it everything which was loose on deck. She had been acting in this way all of our forenoon watch below; as we could tell by the washing of the water over our heads, and the heavy breaking of the seas against her bows, (with a sound as though she were striking against a rock,) only the thickness of the plank from our heads, as we lay in our berths, which are directly against the bows. At eight bells, the watch was called, and we came on deck, one hand going aft to take the wheel, and another going to the galley to get the *grub* for dinner. I stood on the forecastle, looking at the seas, which were rolling high, as far as the eye could reach, their tops white with foam, and the body of them of a deep indigo blue, reflecting the bright rays of the sun. Our ship rose slowly over a few of the largest of them, until one immense fellow came rolling on, threatening to cover her, and which I was sailor enough to know, by 'the feeling of her' under my feet, she would not rise over. I sprang upon the knight-heads, and seizing hold of the fore-stay with my hands, drew myself up upon it. My feet were just off the stanchion, when she struck fairly into the middle of the sea, and it washed her fore and aft, burying her in the water. As soon as she rose out of it, I looked aft, and everything forward of the main-mast, except the long-boat, which was griped and double-lashed down to the ring-bolts, was swept off clear. The galley, the pig-sty, the hen-coop, and a large sheep-pen which had been built upon the fore-hatch, were all gone, in the twinkling of an eye—leaving the deck as clean as a chin new-reaped—and not a stick left, to show where they had stood. In the scuppers lay the galley, bottom up, and a few boards floating about,—the wreck of the sheep-pen,—and half a dozen miserable sheep floating among them, wet through, and not a little frightened at the sudden change that had come upon them. As soon as the sea had washed by, all hands sprung up out of the forecastle to see what had become of the ship; and in a few moments the cook and Old Bill crawled out from under the galley, where they had been lying in the water, nearly smothered, with the galley over them. Fortunately, it rested against the bulwarks, or it would have broken some of their bones. When the water ran off, we picked the sheep up, and put them in the long-boat, got the galley back in its place, and set things a little to rights; but, had not our ship had uncommonly high bulwarks and rail, everything must have been washed overboard, not excepting Old Bill and the cook. Bill had been standing at the galley-door, with the kid of beef in his hand for the forecastle mess, when, away he went, kid, beef, and all. He held on to the kid till the last, like a good fellow, but the beef was gone, and when the water had run off, we saw it lying high and dry, like a rock at low tide—nothing could hurt *that*. We took the loss of our beef very easily, consoling ourselves with the recollection that the cabin had more to lose than we; and chuckled not a little at seeing the remains of the chicken-pie and pancakes floating in the scuppers. "This will never do!" was what some said, and every one felt. Here we were, not yet within a thousand miles of the latitude of Cape Horn, and our decks swept by a sea, not one half so high as we must expect to find there. Some blamed the captain for loading his ship so deep, when he knew what he must expect; while others said that the wind was always south-west, off the Cape, in the winter; and that, running before it, we should not mind the seas so much. When we got down into the forecastle, Old Bill, who was somewhat of a croaker,—having met with a great many accidents at sea—said that if that was the way she was going to act, we might as well make our wills, and balance the books at once, and put on a clean shirt. "'Vast there, you bloody old owl! you're always hanging out blue lights! You're frightened by the ducking you got in the scuppers, and can't take a joke! What's the use in being always on the look-out for Davy Jones?" "Stand by!" says another, "and we'll get an afternoon watch below, by this scrape;" but in this they were disappointed, for at two bells, all hands were called and set to work, getting lashings upon everything on deck; and the captain talked of sending down the long top-gallant masts; but, as the sea went down toward night, and the wind hauled abeam, we left them standing, and set the studding-sails.

The next day, all hands were turned-to upon unbending the old sails, and getting up the new ones; for a ship, unlike people on shore, puts on her best suit in bad weather. The old sails were sent down, and three new top-sails, and new fore and main courses, jib, and fore top-mast stay-sail, which were made on the coast, and never had been used, were bent, with a complete set of new earings, robands and reef-points; and reef-tackles were rove to the courses, and spilling-lines to the top-sails. These, with new braces and clewlines, fore and aft, gave us a good suit of running rigging.

The wind continued westerly, and the weather and sea less rough since the day on which we shipped the heavy sea, and we were making great progress under studding-sails, with our light sails all set, keeping a little to the eastward of south; for the captain, depending upon westerly winds off the Cape, had kept so far to the westward, that, though we were within about five hundred miles of the latitude of Cape Horn, we were nearly seventeen hundred miles to the westward of it. Through the rest of the week, we continued on with a fair wind, gradually, as we got more to the southward, keeping a more easterly course, and bringing the wind on our larboard quarter, until—

Sunday, June 26th; when, having a fine, clear day, the captain got a lunar observation, as well as his meridian altitude, which made us in lat. 47° 50′ S., long. 113° 49′ W.; Cape Horn bearing, according to my calculation, E.S.E. ½ E., and distant eighteen hundred miles.

Monday, June 27th. During the first part of this day, the wind continued fair, and, as we were going before it, it did not feel very cold, so that we kept at work on deck, in our common clothes and round jackets. Our watch had an afternoon watch below, for the first time since leaving San Diego, and having inquired of the third mate what the latitude was at noon, and made our usual guesses as to the time she would need, to be up with the Horn, we turned-in, for a nap. We were sleeping away 'at the rate of knots,' when three knocks on the scuttle, and "All hands, ahoy!" started us from our berths. What could be the matter? It did not appear to be blowing hard, and looking up through the scuttle, we could see that it was a clear day, overhead; yet the watch were taking in sail. We thought there must be a sail in sight, and that we were about to heave-to and speak her; and were just congratulating ourselves upon it—for we had seen neither sail nor land since we left port— when we heard the mate's voice on deck, (he turned-in 'all standing,' and was always on deck the moment he was called,) singing out to the men who were taking in the studding-sails, and asking where his watch were. We did not wait for a second call, but tumbled up the ladder; and there, on the starboard bow, was a bank of mist, covering sea and sky, and driving directly for us. I had seen the same before, in my passage round in the Pilgrim, and knew what it meant, and that there was no time to be lost. We had nothing on but thin clothes, yet there was not a moment to spare, and at it we went.

The boys of the other watch were in the tops, taking in the top-gallant studding-sails, and the lower and top-mast studding-sails were coming down by the run. It was nothing but "haul down and clew up," until we got all the studding-sails in, and the royals, flying-jib, and mizen top-gallant sail furled, and the ship kept off a little, to take the squall. The fore and main top-gallant sails were still on her, for the 'old man' did not mean to be frightened in broad daylight, and was determined to carry sail till the last minute. We all stood waiting for its coming, when the first blast showed us that it was not to be trifled with. Rain, sleet, snow, and wind, enough to take our breath from us, and make the toughest turn his back to windward! The ship lay nearly over upon her beam-ends; the spars and rigging snapped and cracked; and her top-gallant masts bent like whip-sticks. "Clew up the fore and main top-gallant sails!" shouted the captain, and all hands sprang to the clewlines. The decks were standing nearly at an angle of forty-five degrees, and the ship going like a mad steed through the water, the whole forward part of her in a smother of foam. The halyards were let go and the yard clewed down, and the sheets started, and in a few minutes the sails smothered and kept in by clewlines and buntlines.—"Furl 'em, sir?" asked the mate.—"Let go the top-sail halyards, fore and aft!" shouted the captain, in answer, at the top of his voice. Down came the top-sail yards, the reef-tackles were manned and hauled out, and we climbed up to windward, and sprang into the weather rigging. The violence of the wind, and the hail and sleet, driving nearly horizontally across the ocean, seemed actually to pin us down to the rigging. It was hard work making head against them. One after another, we got out upon the yards. And here we had work to do; for our new sails, which had hardly been bent long enough to get the starch out of them, were as stiff as boards, and the new earings and reef-points, stiffened with the sleet, knotted like pieces of iron wire. Having only our round jackets and straw hats on, we were soon wet through, and it was every moment growing colder. Our hands were soon stiffened and numbed, which, added to the stiffness of everything else, kept us a good while on the yard. After we had got the sail hauled upon the yard, we had to wait a long time for the weather earing to be passed; but there was no fault to be found, for French John was at the earing, and a better sailor never laid out on a yard; so we leaned over the yard, and beat our hands upon the sail, to keep them from freezing. At length the word came—"Haul out to leeward,"—and we seized the reef-points and hauled the band taught for the lee earing. "Taught band—Knot away," and we got the first reef fast, and were just going to lay down, when—"Two reefs—two reefs!" shouted the mate, and we had a second reef to take, in the same way. When this was fast, we laid down on deck, manned the halyards to leeward, nearly up to our knees in water, set the top-sail, and then laid aloft on the main top-sail yard, and reefed that sail in the same manner; for, as I have before stated, we were a good deal reduced in numbers, and, to make it worse, the carpenter, only two days before, cut his leg with an axe, so that he could not go aloft. This weakened us so that we could not well manage more than one top-sail at a time, in such weather as this, and, of course, our labor was doubled. From the main top-sail yard, we went upon the main yard, and took a reef in the main-sail. No sooner had we got on deck, than—"Lay aloft there, mizen-top-men, and close-reef the mizen top-sail!" This called me; and being nearest to the rigging, I got first aloft, and out to the weather earing. English Ben was on the yard just after me, and took the lee earing, and the rest of our gang were soon on the yard, and began to fist the sail, when the mate considerately sent up the cook and steward, to help us. I could now account for the long time it took to pass the other earings, for, to do my best, with a strong hand to help me at the dog's ear, I could not get it passed until I heard them beginning to complain in the bunt. One reef after another we took in, until the sail was close-reefed, when we went down and hoisted away at the halyards. In the mean time, the jib had been furled and the stay-sail set, and the ship, under her reduced sail, had got more upright and was under management; but the two top-gallant sails were still hanging in the buntlines, and slatting and jerking as though they would take the masts out of her. We gave a look aloft, and knew that our work was not done yet; and sure enough, no sooner did the mate see that we were on deck, than—"Lay aloft there, four of you, and furl the top-gallant sails!" This called me again, and two of us went aloft, up the fore rigging, and two more up the main, upon the top-gallant yards. The shrouds were now iced over, the sleet having formed a crust or cake round all the standing rigging, and on the weather side of the masts and yards. When we got upon the yard, my hands were so numb that I could not have cast off the knot of the gasket to have saved my life. We both lay over the yard for a few seconds, beating our hands upon the sail, until we started the blood into our fingers' ends, and at the next moment our hands were in a burning heat. My companion on the yard was a lad, who came out in the ship a weak, puny boy, from one of the Boston schools,—'no larger than a sprit-sail sheet knot,' nor 'heavier than a paper of lamp-black,' and 'not strong enough to haul a shad off a gridiron,' but who was now 'as long as a spare top-mast, strong enough to knock down an ox, and hearty enough to eat him.' We fisted the sail together, and after six or eight minutes of hard hauling and pulling and beating down the sail, which was as stiff as sheet iron, we managed to get it furled; and snugly furled it must be, for we knew the mate well enough to be certain that if it got adrift again, we should be called up from our watch below, at any hour of the night, to furl it.

I had been on the look-out for a moment to jump below and clap on a thick jacket and south-wester; but when we got on deck we found that eight bells had been struck, and the other watch gone below, so that there were two hours of dog watch for us, and a plenty of work to do. It had now set in for a steady gale from the south-west; but we were not yet far enough to the southward to make a fair wind of it, for we must give Terra del Fuego a wide berth. The decks were covered with snow, and there was a constant driving of sleet. In fact, Cape Horn had set in with good earnest. In the midst of all this, and before it became dark, we had all the studding-sails to make up and stow away, and then to lay aloft and rig in all the booms, fore and aft, and coil away the tacks, sheets, and halyards. This was pretty tough work for four or five hands, in the face of a gale which almost took us off the yards, and with ropes so stiff with ice that it was almost impossible to bend them. I was nearly half an hour out on the end of the fore yard, trying to coil away and stop down the top-mast studding-sail tack and lower halyards. It was after dark when we got through, and we were not a little pleased to hear four bells struck, which sent us below for two hours, and gave us each a pot of hot tea with our cold beef and bread, and, what was better yet, a suit of thick, dry clothing, fitted for the weather, in place of our thin clothes, which were wet through and now frozen stiff.

This sudden turn, for which we were so little prepared, was as unacceptable to me as to any of the rest; for I had been troubled for several days with a slight tooth-ache, and this cold weather, and wetting and freezing, were not the best things in the world for it. I soon found that it was getting strong hold, and running over all parts of my face; and before the watch was out I went aft to the mate, who had charge of the medicine-chest, to get something for it. But the chest showed like the end of a long voyage, for there was nothing that would answer but a few drops of laudanum, which must be saved for any emergency; so I had only to bear the pain as well as I could.

When we went on deck at eight bells, it had stopped snowing, and there were a few stars out, but the clouds were still black, and it was blowing a steady gale. Just before mid-night, I went aloft and sent down the mizen royal yard, and had the good luck to do it to the satisfaction of the mate, who said it was done "out of hand and ship-shape." The next four hours below were but little relief to me, for I lay awake in my berth, the whole time, from the pain in my face, and heard every bell strike, and, at four o'clock, turned out with the watch, feeling little spirit for the hard duties of the day. Bad weather and hard work at sea can be borne up against very well, if one only has spirit and health; but there is nothing brings a man down, at such a time, like bodily pain and want of sleep. There was, however, too much to do to allow time to think; for the gale of yesterday, and the heavy seas we met with a few days before, while we had yet ten degrees more southing to make, had convinced the captain that we had something before us which was not to be trifled with, and orders were given to send down the long top-gallant masts. The top-gallant and royal yards were accordingly struck, the flying jib-boom rigged in, and the top-gallant masts sent down on deck, and all lashed together by the side of the long-boat. The rigging was then sent down and coiled away below, and everything made snug aloft. There was not a sailor in the ship who was not rejoiced to see these sticks come down; for, so long as the yards were aloft, on the least sign of a lull, the top-gallant sails were loosed, and then we had to furl them again in a snow-squall, and *shin* up and down single ropes caked with ice, and send royal yards down in the teeth of a gale coming right from the south pole. It was an interesting sight, too, to see our noble ship, dismantled of all her top-hamper of long tapering masts and yards, and boom pointed with spear-head, which ornamented her in port; and all that canvass, which a few days before had covered her like a cloud, from the truck to the water's edge, spreading far out beyond her hull on either side, now gone; and she, stripped, like a wrestler for the fight. It corresponded, too, with the desolate character of her situation;—alone, as she was, battling with storms, wind, and ice, at this extremity of the globe, and in almost constant night.

Friday, July 1st. We were now nearly up to the latitude of Cape Horn, and having over forty degrees of easting to make, we squared away the yards before a strong westerly gale, shook a reef out of the fore top-sail, and stood on our way, east-by-south, with the prospect of being up with the Cape in a week or ten days. As for myself, I had had no sleep for forty-eight hours; and the want of rest, together with constant wet and cold, had increased the swelling, so that my face was nearly as large as two, and I found it impossible to get my mouth open wide enough to eat. In this state, the steward applied to the captain for some rice to boil for me, but he only got a—"No! d— you! Tell him to eat salt junk and hard bread, like the rest of them." For this, of course, I was much obliged to him, and in truth it was just what I expected. However, I did not starve, for the mate, who was a man as well as a sailor, and had always been a good friend to me, smuggled a pan of rice into the galley, and told the cook to boil it for me, and not let the 'old man' see it. Had it been fine weather, or in port, I should have gone below and lain by until my face got well; but in such weather as this, and short-handed as we were, it was not for me to desert my post; so I kept on deck, and stood my watch and did my duty as well as I could.

Saturday, July 2d. This day the sun rose fair, but it ran too low in the heavens to give any heat, or thaw out our sails and rigging; yet the sight of it was pleasant; and we had a steady 'reef-top-sail breeze' from the westward. The atmosphere, which had previously been clear and cold, for the last few hours grew damp, and had a disagreeable, wet chilliness in it; and the man who came from the wheel said he heard the captain tell 'the passenger' that the thermometer had fallen several degrees since morning, which he could not account for in any other way than by supposing that there must be ice near us; though such a thing had never been heard of in this latitude, at this season of the year. At twelve o'clock we went below, and had just got through dinner, when the cook put his head down the scuttle and told us to come on deck and see the finest sight that we had ever seen. "Where away, cook?" asked the first man who was up. "On the larboard bow." And there lay, floating in the ocean, several miles off, an immense, irregular mass, its top and points covered with snow, and its centre of a deep indigo color. This was an iceberg, and of the largest size, as one of our men said who had been in the Northern ocean. As far as the eye could reach, the sea in every direction was of a deep blue color, the waves running high and fresh, and sparkling in the light, and in the midst lay this immense mountain-island, its cavities and valleys thrown into deep shade, and its points and pinnacles glittering in the sun. All hands were soon on deck, looking at it, and admiring in various ways its beauty and grandeur. But no description can give any idea of the strangeness, splendor, and, really, the sublimity, of the sight. Its great size;—for it must have been from two to three miles in circumference, and several hundred feet in height;—its slow motion, as its base rose and sank in the water, and its high points nodded against the clouds; the dashing of the waves upon it, which, breaking high with foam, lined its base with a white crust; and the thundering sound of the cracking of the mass, and the breaking and tumbling down of huge pieces; together with its nearness and approach, which added a slight element of fear,—all combined to give to it the character of true sublimity. The main body of the mass was, as I have said, of an indigo color, its base crusted with frozen foam; and as it grew thin and transparent toward the edges and top, its color shaded off from a deep blue to the whiteness of snow. It seemed to be drifting slowly toward the north, so that we kept away and avoided it. It was in sight all the afternoon; and when we got to leeward of it, the wind died away, so that we lay-to quite near it for a greater part of the night. Unfortunately, there was no moon, but it was a clear night, and we could plainly mark the long, regular heaving of the stupendous mass, as its edges moved slowly against the stars. Several times in our watch loud cracks were heard, which sounded as though they must have run through the whole length of the iceberg, and several pieces fell down with a thundering crash, plunging heavily into the sea. Toward morning, a strong breeze sprang up, and we filled away, and left it astern, and at daylight it was out of sight. The next day, which was

Sunday, July 3d, the breeze continued strong, the air exceedingly chilly, and the thermometer low. In the course of the day we saw several icebergs, of different sizes, but none so near as the one which we saw the day before. Some of them, as well as we could judge, at the distance at which we were, must have been as large as that, if not larger. At noon we were in latitude 55° 12' south, and supposed longitude 89° 5' west. Toward night the wind hauled to the southward, and headed us off our course a little, and blew a tremendous gale; but this we did not mind, as there was no rain nor snow, and we were already under close sail.

Monday, July 4th. This was 'independent day' in Boston. What firing of guns, and ringing of bells, and rejoicings of all sorts, in every part of our country! The ladies (who have not gone down to Nahant, for a breath of cool air, and sight of the ocean) walking the streets with parasols over their heads, and the dandies in their white pantaloons and silk stockings! What quantities of ice-cream have been eaten, and what quantities of ice brought into the city from a distance, and sold out by the lump and the pound! The smallest of the islands which we saw to-day would have made the fortune of poor Jack, if he had had it in Boston; and I dare say he would have had no objection to being there with it. This, to be sure, was no place to keep the fourth of July. To keep ourselves warm, and the ship out of the ice, was as much as we could do. Yet no one forgot the day; and many were the wishes, and conjectures, and comparisons, both serious and ludicrous, which were made among all hands. The sun shone bright as long as it was up, only that a scud of black clouds was ever and anon driving across it. At noon we were in lat. 54° 27' S., and long. 85° 5' W., having made a good deal of easting, but having lost in our latitude by the heading of the wind. Between daylight and dark—that is, between nine o'clock and three—we saw thirty-four ice islands, of various sizes; some no bigger than the hull of our vessel, and others apparently nearly as large as the one that we first saw; though, as we went on, the islands became smaller and more numerous; and, at sundown of this day, a man at the mast-head saw large fields of floating ice, called 'field-ice,' at the south-east. This kind of ice is much more dangerous than the large islands, for those can be seen at a distance, and kept away from; but the field-ice, floating in great quantities, and covering the ocean for miles and miles, in pieces of every size —large, flat, and broken cakes, with here and there an island rising twenty and thirty feet, and as large as the ship's hull;— this, it is very difficult to sheer clear of. A constant look-out was necessary; for any of these pieces, coming with the heave of the sea, were large enough to have knocked a hole in the ship, and that would have been the end of us; for no boat (even if we could have got one out) could have lived in such a sea; and no man could have lived in a boat in such weather. To make our condition still worse, the wind came out due east, just after sundown, and it blew a gale dead ahead, with hail and sleet, and a thick fog, so that we could not see half the length of the ship. Our chief reliance, the prevailing westerly gales, was thus cut off; and here we were, nearly seven hundred miles to the westward of the Cape, with a gale dead from the eastward, and the weather so thick that we could not see the ice with which we were surrounded, until it was directly under our bows. At four, P.M. (it was then quite dark) all hands were called, and sent aloft in a violent squall of hail and rain, to take in sail. We had now all got on our 'Cape Horn rig'—thick boots, south-westers coming down over our neck and ears, thick trowsers and jackets, and some with oil-cloth suits over all. Mittens, too, we wore on deck, but it would not do to go aloft with them on, for it was impossible to work with them, and, being wet and stiff, they might let a man slip overboard, for all the hold he could get upon a rope; so, we were obliged to work with bare hands, which, as well as our faces, were often cut with the hail-stones, which fell thick and large. Our ship was now all cased with ice,—hull, spars, and standing rigging;—and the running rigging so stiff that we could hardly bend it so as to belay it, or, still worse, take a knot with it; and the sails nearly as stiff as sheet iron. One at a time, (for it was a long piece of work and required many hands,) we furled the courses, mizen top-sail, and fore top-mast stay-sail, and close-reefed the fore and main top-sails, and hove the ship to under the fore, with the main hauled up by the clewlines and

buntlines, and ready to be sheeted home, if we found it necessary to make sail to get to windward of an island. A regular
look-out was then set, and kept by each watch in turn, until
the morning. It was a tedious and anxious night. It blew hard
the whole time, and there was an almost constant driving of
either rain, hail, or snow. In addition to this, it was 'as thick as
muck,' and the ice was all about us. The captain was on deck
nearly the whole night, and kept the cook in the galley, with a
roaring fire, to make coffee for him, which he took every few
hours, and once or twice gave a little to his officers; but not a
drop of anything was there for the crew. The captain, who
sleeps all the daytime, and comes and goes at night as he
chooses, can have his brandy and water in the cabin, and his
hot coffee at the galley; while Jack, who has to stand through
everything, and work in wet and cold, can have nothing to wet
his lips or warm his stomach. This was a "temperance ship,"
and, like too many such ships, the temperance was all in the
forecastle. The sailor, who only takes his one glass as it is dealt
out to him, is in danger of being drunk; while the captain, who
has all under his hand, and can drink as much as he chooses,
and upon whose self-possession and cool judgment the lives of
all depend, may be trusted with any amount, to drink at his
will. Sailors will never be convinced that rum is a dangerous
thing, by taking it away from them, and giving it to the officers; nor that, that temperance is their friend, which takes from
them what they have always had, and gives them nothing in
the place of it. By seeing it allowed to their officers, they will
not be convinced that it is taken from them for their good; and
by receiving nothing in its place, they will not believe that it is
done in kindness. On the contrary, many of them look upon
the change as a new instrument of tyranny. Not that they prefer rum. I never knew a sailor, in my life, who would not
prefer a pot of hot coffee or chocolate, in a cold night, to all the
rum afloat. They all say that rum only warms them for a time;
yet, if they can get nothing better, they will miss what they
have lost. The momentary warmth and glow from drinking it;
the break and change which is made in a long, dreary watch by
the mere calling all hands aft and serving of it out; and the
simply having some event to look forward to, and to talk about;
give it an importance and a use which no one can appreciate

who has not stood his watch before the mast. On my passage round Cape Horn before, the vessel that I was in was not under temperance articles, and grog was served out every middle and morning watch, and after every reefing of top-sails; and though I had never drank rum before, and never intend to again, I took my allowance then at the capstan, as the rest did, merely for the momentary warmth it gave the system, and the change in our feelings and aspect of our duties on the watch. At the same time, as I have stated, there was not a man on board who would not have pitched the rum to the dogs, (I have heard them say so, a dozen times) for a pot of coffee or chocolate; or even for our common beverage—'water bewitched, and tea begrudged,' as it was.* The temperance reform is the best thing that ever was undertaken for the sailor; but when the grog is taken from him, he ought to have something in its place. As it is now, in most vessels, it is a mere saving to the owners; and this accounts for the sudden increase of temperance ships, which surprised even the best friends of the cause. If every merchant, when he struck grog from the list of the expenses of his ship, had been obliged to substitute as much coffee, or chocolate, as would give each man a pot-full when he came off the top-sail yard, on a stormy night;—I fear Jack might have gone to ruin on the old road.†

But this is not doubling Cape Horn. Eight hours of the night, our watch was on deck, and during the whole of that

---

*The proportions of the ingredients of the tea that was made for us, (and ours, as I have before stated, was a favorable specimen of American merchantmen) were, a pint of tea, and a pint and a half of molasses, to about three gallons of water. These are all boiled down together in the "coppers," and before serving it out, the mess is stirred up with a stick, so as to give each man his fair share of sweetening and tea-leaves. The tea for the cabin is, of course, made in the usual way, in a tea-pot, and drank with sugar.

†I do not wish these remarks, so far as they relate to the saving of expense in the outfit, to be applied to the owners of our ship, for she was supplied with an abundance of stores, of the best kind that are given to seamen; though the dispensing of them is necessarily left to the captain. Indeed, so high was the reputation of 'the employ' among men and officers, for the character and outfit of their vessels, and for their liberality in conducting their voyages, that when it was known that they had a ship fitting out for a long voyage, and that hands were to be shipped at a certain time;—a half hour before the time, as one of the crew told me, numbers of sailors were steering down the wharf, hopping over the barrels, like flocks of sheep.

time we kept a bright look-out: one man on each bow, another in the bunt of the fore yard, the third mate on the scuttle, one on each quarter, and a man always standing by the wheel. The chief mate was everywhere, and commanded the ship when the captain was below. When a large piece of ice was seen in our way, or drifting near us, the word was passed along, and the ship's head turned one way and another; and sometimes the yards squared or braced up. There was little else to do than to look out; and we had the sharpest eyes in the ship on the forecastle. The only variety was the monotonous voice of the look-out forward—"Another island!"—"Ice ahead!"—"Ice on the lee bow!"—"Hard up the helm!"—"Keep her off a little!" —"Stead-y!"

In the mean time, the wet and cold had brought my face into such a state that I could neither eat nor sleep; and though I stood it out all night, yet, when it became light, I was in such a state, that all hands told me I must go below, and lie-by for a day or two, or I should be laid up for a long time, and perhaps have the lock-jaw. When the watch was changed I went into the steerage, and took off my hat and comforter, and showed my face to the mate, who told me to go below at once, and stay in my berth until the swelling went down, and gave the cook orders to make a poultice for me, and said he would speak to the captain.

I went below and turned-in, covering myself over with blankets and jackets, and lay in my berth nearly twenty-four hours, half asleep and half awake, stupid, from the dull pain. I heard the watch called, and the men going up and down, and sometimes a noise on deck, and a cry of "ice," but I gave little attention to anything. At the end of twenty-four hours the pain went down, and I had a long sleep, which brought me back to my proper state; yet my face was so swollen and tender, that I was obliged to keep to my berth for two or three days longer. During the two days I had been below, the weather was much the same that it had been, head winds, and snow and rain; or, if the wind came fair, too foggy, and the ice too thick, to run. At the end of the third day the ice was very thick; a complete fog-bank covered the ship. It blew a tremendous gale from the eastward, with sleet and snow, and there was every promise of a dangerous and fatiguing night. At dark, the captain called all hands aft, and told them that not a man was to leave the deck that night; that the ship was in the greatest danger; any cake of ice might knock a hole in her, or she might run on an island and go to pieces. No one could tell whether she would be a ship the next morning. The look-outs were then set, and every man was put in his station. When I heard what was the state of things, I began to put on my clothes to stand it out with the rest of them, when the mate came below, and looking at my face, ordered me back to my berth, saying that if we went down, we should all go down together, but if I went on deck I might lay myself up for life. This was the first word I had heard from aft; for the captain had done nothing, nor inquired how I was, since I went below.

In obedience to the mate's orders, I went back to my berth; but a more miserable night I never wish to spend. I never felt the curse of sickness so keenly in my life. If I could only have been on deck with the rest, where something was to be done, and seen, and heard; where there were fellow-beings for companions in duty and danger—but to be cooped up alone in a black hole, in equal danger, but without the power to do, was the hardest trial. Several times, in the course of the night, I got up, determined to go on deck; but the silence which showed that there was nothing doing, and the knowledge that I might make myself seriously ill, for nothing, kept me back. It was not easy to sleep, lying, as I did, with my head directly against the bows, which might be dashed in by an island of ice, brought down by the very next sea that struck her. This was the only time I had been ill since I left Boston, and it was the worst time it could have happened. I felt almost willing to bear the plagues of Egypt for the rest of the voyage, if I could but be well and strong for that one night. Yet it was a dreadful night for those on deck. A watch of eighteen hours, with wet, and cold, and constant anxiety, nearly wore them out; and when they came below at nine o'clock for breakfast, they almost dropped asleep on their chests, and some of them were so stiff that they could with difficulty sit down. Not a drop of anything had been given them during the whole time, (though the captain, as on the night that I was on deck, had his coffee every four hours,) except that the mate stole a pot-full of coffee for two men to drink behind the galley, while he kept a look-out for the captain. Every man had his station, and was not allowed to leave it; and nothing happened to break the monotony of the night, except once setting the main top-sails to run clear of a large island to leeward, which they were drifting fast upon. Some of the boys got so sleepy and stupified, that they actually fell asleep at their posts; and the young third mate, whose station was the exposed one of standing on the fore scuttle, was so stiff, when he was relieved, that he could not bend his knees to get down. By a constant look-out, and a quick shifting of the helm, as the islands and pieces came in sight, the ship went clear of everything but a few small pieces, though daylight showed the ocean covered for miles. At daybreak it fell a dead calm, and with the sun, the fog cleared a little, and a breeze sprung up from the westward, which soon grew into a gale. We had now a fair wind, daylight, and comparatively clear weather; yet, to the surprise of every one, the ship continued hove-to. Why does not he run? What is the captain about? was asked by every one; and from questions, it soon grew into complaints and murmurings. When the daylight was so short, it was too bad to lose it, and a fair wind, too, which every one had been praying for. As hour followed hour, and the captain showed no sign of making sail, the crew became impatient, and there was a good deal of talking and consultation together, on the forecastle. They had been beaten out with the exposure and hardship, and impatient to get out of it, and this unaccountable delay was more than they could bear in quietness, in their excited and restless state. Some said that the captain was frightened,—completely cowed, by the dangers and difficulties that surrounded us, and was afraid to make sail; while others said that in his anxiety and suspense he had made a free use of brandy and opium, and was unfit for his duty. The carpenter, who was an intelligent man, and a thorough seaman, and had great influence with the crew, came down into the forecastle, and tried to induce the crew to go aft and ask the captain why he did not run, or request him, in the name of all hands, to make sail. This appeared to be a very reasonable request, and the crew agreed that if he did not make sail before noon, they would go aft. Noon came, and no sail was made. A consultation was held again, and it was proposed to take the ship from the captain and give the command of her to the mate, who had been heard to say that, if he could have his way, the ship would have been half the distance to the Cape before night,—ice or no ice. And so irritated and impatient had the crew become, that even this proposition, which was open mutiny, punishable with state prison, was entertained, and the carpenter went to his berth, leaving it tacitly understood that something serious would be done, if things remained as they were many hours longer. When the carpenter left, we talked it all over, and I gave my advice strongly against it. Another of the men, too, who had known something of the kind attempted in another ship by a crew who were dissatisfied with their captain, and which was followed with serious consequences, was opposed to it. S——, who soon came down, joined us, and we determined to have nothing to do with it. By these means, they were soon induced to give it up, for the present, though they said they would not lie where they were much longer without knowing the reason.

The affair remained in this state until four o'clock, when an order came forward for all hands to come aft upon the quarter-deck. In about ten minutes they came forward again, and the whole affair had been blown. The carpenter, very prematurely, and without any authority from the crew, had sounded the mate as to whether he would take command of the ship, and intimated an intention to displace the captain; and the mate, as in duty bound, had told the whole to the captain, who immediately sent for all hands aft. Instead of violent measures, or, at least, an outbreak of quarter-deck bravado, threats, and abuse, which they had every reason to expect, a sense of common danger and common suffering seemed to have tamed his spirit, and begotten something like a humane fellow-feeling; for he received the crew in a manner quiet, and even almost kind. He told them what he had heard, and said that he did not believe that they would try to do any such thing as was intimated; that they had always been good men, —obedient, and knew their duty, and he had no fault to find with them; and asked them what they had to complain of— said that no one could say that he was slow to carry sail, (which was true enough;) and that, as soon as he thought it was safe and proper, he should make sail. He added a few words about their duty in their present situation, and sent them forward, saying that he should take no further notice of the matter; but, at the same time, told the carpenter to recollect whose power he was in, and that if he heard another word from him he would have cause to remember him to the day of his death.

This language of the captain had a very good effect upon the crew, and they returned quietly to their duty.

For two days more the wind blew from the southward and eastward; or in the short intervals when it was fair, the ice was too thick to run; yet the weather was not so dreadfully bad, and the crew had watch and watch. I still remained in my berth, fast recovering, yet still not well enough to go safely on deck. And I should have been perfectly useless; for, from having eaten nothing for nearly a week, except a little rice which I forced into my mouth the last day or two, I was as weak as an infant. To be sick in a forecastle is miserable indeed. It is the worst part of a dog's life; especially in bad weather. The forecastle, shut up tight to keep out the water and cold air;—the watch either on deck, or asleep in their berths;—no one to speak to;—the pale light of the single lamp, swinging to and fro from the beam, so dim that one can scarcely see, much less read by it;—the water dropping from the beams and car-lines, and running down the sides; and the forecastle so wet, and dark, and cheerless, and so lumbered up with chests and wet clothes, that sitting up is worse than lying in the berth! These are some of the evils. Fortunately, I needed no help from any one, and no medicine; and if I had needed help, I don't know where I should have found it. Sailors are willing enough, but it is true, as is often said—No one ships for nurse on board a vessel. Our merchant ships are always under-manned, and if one man is lost by sickness, they cannot spare another to take care of him. A sailor is always presumed to be well, and if he's sick, he's a poor dog. One has to stand his wheel, and another his look-out, and the sooner he gets on deck again, the better.

Accordingly, as soon as I could possibly go back to my duty, I put on my thick clothes and boots and south-wester, and made my appearance on deck. Though I had been but a few days below, yet everything looked strangely enough. The ship was cased in ice,—decks, sides, masts, yards, and rigging. Two close-reefed top-sails were all the sail she had on, and every sail and rope was frozen so stiff in its place, that it seemed as though it would be impossible to start anything. Reduced, too, to her top-masts, she had altogether a most forlorn and crippled appearance. The sun had come up brightly; the snow was swept off the decks, and ashes thrown upon them, so that we could walk, for they had been as slippery as glass. It was, of course, too cold to carry on any ship's work, and we had only to walk the deck and keep ourselves warm. The wind was still ahead, and the whole ocean, to the eastward, covered with islands and field-ice. At four bells the order was given to square away the yards; and the man who came from the helm said that the captain had kept her off to N.N.E. What could this mean? Some said that he was going to put into Valparaiso, and winter, and others that he was going to run out of the ice and cross the Pacific, and go home round the Cape of Good Hope. Soon, however, it leaked out, and we found that we were running for the straits of Magellan. The news soon spread through the ship, and all tongues were at work, talking about it. No one on board had been through the straits, but I had in my chest an account of the passage of the ship A. J. Donelson, of New York, through those straits, a few years before. The account was given by the captain, and the representation was as favorable as possible. It was soon read by every one on board, and various opinions pronounced. The determination of our captain had at least this good effect; it gave every one something to think and talk about, made a break in our life, and diverted our minds from the monotonous dreariness of the prospect before us. Having made a fair wind of it, we were going off at a good rate, and leaving the thickest of the ice behind us. This, at least, was something.

Having been long enough below to get my hands well warmed and softened, the first handling of the ropes was rather tough; but a few days hardened them, and as soon as I got my mouth open wide enough to take in a piece of salt beef and hard bread, I was all right again.

Sunday, July 10th. Lat. 54° 10′, lon. 79° 07′. This was our position at noon. The sun was out bright; the ice was all left behind, and things had quite a cheering appearance. We brought our wet pea-jackets and trowsers on deck, and hung them up in the rigging, that the breeze and the few hours of sun might dry them a little; and, by the permission of the cook, the galley was nearly filled with stockings and mittens, hung round to be dried. Boots, too, were brought up; and having got a little tar and slush from below, we gave them a thick coat. After dinner, all hands were turned-to, to get the anchors over the bows, bend on the chains, &c. The fish-tackle was got up, fish-davit rigged out, and after two or three hours of hard and cold work, both the anchors were ready for instant use, a couple of kedges got up, a hawser coiled away upon the fore-hatch, and the deep-sea-lead-line overhauled and got ready. Our spirits returned with having something to do; and when the tackle was manned to bowse the anchor home, notwithstanding the desolation of the scene, we struck up "Cheerily ho!" in full chorus. This pleased the mate, who rubbed his hands and cried out—"That's right, my boys; never say die! That sounds like the old crew!" and the captain came up, on hearing the song, and said to the passenger, within hearing of the man at the wheel,—"That sounds like a lively crew. They'll have their song so long as there're enough left for a chorus!"

This preparation of the cable and anchors was for the passage of the straits; for, being very crooked, and with a variety of currents, it is necessary to come frequently to anchor. This was not, by any means, a pleasant prospect, for, of all the work that a sailor is called upon to do in cold weather, there is none so bad as working the ground-tackle. The heavy chain cables to be hauled and pulled about decks with bare hands; wet hawsers, slip-ropes, and buoy-ropes to be hauled aboard, dripping in water, which is running up your sleeves, and freezing; clearing hawse under the bows; getting under weigh and coming-to, at all hours of the night and day, and a constant look-out for rocks and sands and turns of tides;—these are some of the disagreeables of such a navigation to a common sailor. Fair or foul, he wants to have nothing to do with the ground-tackle between port and port. One of our hands, too, had unluckily fallen upon a half of an old newspaper which contained an account of the passage, through the straits, of a Boston brig, called, I think, the Peruvian, in which she lost every cable and anchor she had, got aground twice, and arrived at Valparaiso in distress. This was set off against the account of the A. J. Donelson, and led us to look forward with less confidence to the passage, especially as no one on board had ever been through, and the captain had no very perfect charts. However, we were spared any further experience on the point; for the next day, when we must have been near the Cape of Pillars, which is the south-west point of the mouth of the straits, a gale set in from the eastward, with a heavy fog, so that we could not see half of the ship's length ahead. This, of course, put an end to the project, for the present; for a thick fog and a gale blowing dead ahead are not the most favorable circumstances for the passage of difficult and dangerous straits. This weather, too, seemed likely to last for some time, and we could not think of beating about the mouth of the straits for a week or two, waiting for a favorable opportunity; so we braced up on the larboard tack, put the ship's head due south, and stuck her off for Cape Horn again.

Chapter XXXII

I N our first attempt to double the Cape, when we came up to the latitude of it, we were nearly seventeen hundred miles to the westward, but, in running for the straits of Magellan, we stood so far to the eastward, that we made our second attempt at a distance of not more than four or five hundred miles; and we had great hopes, by this means, to run clear of the ice; thinking that the easterly gales, which had prevailed for a long time, would have driven it to the westward. With the wind about two points free, the yards braced in a little, and two close-reefed top-sails and a reefed fore-sail on the ship, we made great way toward the southward; and, almost every watch, when we came on deck, the air seemed to grow colder, and the sea to run higher. Still, we saw no ice, and had great hopes of going clear of it altogether, when, one afternoon, about three o'clock, while we were taking a *siesta* during our watch below, "All hands!" was called in a loud and fearful voice. "Tumble up here, men!—tumble up!—don't stop for your clothes—before we're upon it!" We sprang out of our berths and hurried upon deck. The loud, sharp voice of the captain was heard giving orders, as though for life or death, and we ran aft to the braces, not waiting to look ahead, for not a moment was to be lost. The helm was hard up, the after yards shaking, and the ship in the act of wearing. Slowly, with the stiff ropes and iced rigging, we swung the yards round, everything coming hard and with a creaking and rending sound, like pulling up a plank which has been frozen into the ice. The ship wore round fairly, the yards were steadied, and we stood off on the other tack, leaving behind us, directly under our larboard quarter, a large ice island, peering out of the mist, and reaching high above our tops, while astern; and on either side of the island, large tracts of field-ice were dimly seen, heaving and rolling in the sea. We were now safe, and standing to the northward; but, in a few minutes more, had it not been for the sharp look-out of the watch, we should have been fairly upon the ice, and left our ship's old bones adrift in the Southern ocean. After standing to the northward a few hours, we wore ship, and, the wind having hauled, we stood to the southward and eastward. All night long, a bright look-out was kept from every part of the deck; and whenever ice was seen on the one bow or the other, the helm was shifted and the yards braced, and by quick working of the ship she was kept clear. The accustomed cry of "Ice ahead!"—"Ice on the lee bow!"—"Another island!" in the same tones, and with the same orders following them, seemed to bring us directly back to our old position of the week before. During our watch on deck, which was from twelve to four, the wind came out ahead, with a pelting storm of hail and sleet, and we lay hove-to, under a close-reefed fore top-sail, the whole watch. During the next watch it fell calm, with a drenching rain, until daybreak, when the wind came out to the westward, and the weather cleared up, and showed us the whole ocean, in the course which we should have steered, had it not been for the head wind and calm, completely blocked up with ice. Here then our progress was stopped, and we wore ship, and once more stood to the northward and eastward; not for the straits of Magellan, but to make another attempt to double the Cape, still farther to the eastward; for the captain was determined to get round if perseverance could do it, and the third time, he said, never failed.

With a fair wind we soon ran clear of the field-ice, and by noon had only the stray islands floating far and near upon the ocean. The sun was out bright, the sea of a deep blue, fringed with the white foam of the waves which ran high before a strong south-wester; our solitary ship tore on through the water as though glad to be out of her confinement; and the ice islands lay scattered upon the ocean here and there, of various sizes and shapes, reflecting the bright rays of the sun, and drifting slowly northward before the gale. It was a contrast to much that we had lately seen, and a spectacle not only of beauty, but of life; for it required but little fancy to imagine these islands to be animate masses which had broken loose from the "thrilling regions of thick-ribbed ice," and were working their way, by wind and current, some alone, and some in fleets, to milder climes. No pencil has ever yet given anything like the true effect of an iceberg. In a picture, they are huge, uncouth masses, stuck in the sea, while their chief beauty and grandeur, —their slow, stately motion; the whirling of the snow about their summits, and the fearful groaning and cracking of their parts,—the picture cannot give. This is the large iceberg; while the small and distant islands, floating on the smooth sea, in the light of a clear day, look like little floating fairy isles of sapphire.

From a north-east course we gradually hauled to the eastward, and after sailing about two hundred miles, which brought us as near to the western coast of Terra del Fuego as was safe, and having lost sight of the ice altogether,—for the third time we put the ship's head to the southward, to try the passage of the Cape. The weather continued clear and cold, with a strong gale from the westward, and we were fast getting up with the latitude of the Cape, with a prospect of soon being round. One fine afternoon, a man who had gone into the fore-top to shift the rolling tackles, sung out, at the top of his voice, and with evident glee,—"Sail ho!" Neither land nor sail had we seen since leaving San Diego; and any one who has traversed the length of a whole ocean alone, can imagine what an excitement such an announcement produced on board. "Sail ho!" shouted the cook, jumping out of his galley; "Sail ho!" shouted a man, throwing back the slide of the scuttle, to the watch below, who were soon out of their berths and on deck; and "Sail ho!" shouted the captain down the companion-way to the passenger in the cabin. Beside the pleasure of seeing a ship and human beings in so desolate a place, it was important for us to speak a vessel, to learn whether there was ice to the eastward, and to ascertain the longitude; for we had no chronometer, and had been drifting about so long that we had nearly lost our reckoning, and opportunities for lunar observations are not frequent or sure in such a place as Cape Horn. For these various reasons, the excitement in our little community was running high, and conjectures were made, and everything thought of for which the captain would hail, when the man aloft sung out—"Another sail, large on the weather bow!" This was a little odd, but so much the better, and did not shake our faith in their being sails. At length the man in the top hailed, and said he believed it was land, after all. "Land in your eye!" said the mate, who was looking through the telescope; "they are ice islands, if I can see a hole through a ladder;" and a few moments showed the mate to be right; and all our expectations fled; and instead of what we most wished to see, we had what we most dreaded, and what we hoped we had seen the last of. We soon, however, left these astern, having passed within about two miles of them; and at sundown the horizon was clear in all directions.

Having a fine wind, we were soon up with and passed the latitude of the Cape, and having stood far enough to the southward to give it a wide berth, we began to stand to the eastward, with a good prospect of being round and steering to the northward on the other side, in a very few days. But ill luck seemed to have lighted upon us. Not four hours had we been standing on in this course, before it fell dead calm; and in half an hour it clouded up; a few straggling blasts, with spits of snow and sleet, came from the eastward; and in an hour more, we lay hove-to under a close-reefed main top-sail, drifting bodily off to leeward before the fiercest storm that we had yet felt, blowing dead ahead, from the eastward. It seemed as though the genius of the place had been roused at finding that we had nearly slipped through his fingers, and had come down upon us with tenfold fury. The sailors said that every blast, as it shook the shrouds, and whistled through the rigging, said to the old ship, "No, you don't!"—"No, you don't!"

For eight days we lay drifting about in this manner. Sometimes,—generally towards noon,—it fell calm; once or twice a round copper ball showed itself for a few moments in the place where the sun ought to have been; and a puff or two came from the westward, giving some hope that a fair wind had come at last. During the first two days, we made sail for these puffs, shaking the reefs out of the top-sails and boarding the tacks of the courses; but finding that it only made work for us when the gale set in again, it was soon given up, and we lay-to under our close-reefs. We had less snow and hail than when we were farther to the westward, but we had an abundance of what is worse to a sailor in cold weather—drenching rain. Snow is blinding, and very bad when coming upon a coast, but, for genuine discomfort, give me rain with freezing weather. A snow-storm is exciting, and it does not wet through the clothes (which is important to a sailor); but a constant rain there is no escaping from. It wets to the skin, and makes all protection vain. We had long ago run through all our dry clothes, and as sailors have no other way of drying them than by the sun, we had nothing to do but to put on those which were the least wet. At the end of each watch, when we came below, we took off our clothes and wrung them out; two taking hold of a pair of trowsers,—one at each end,—and jackets in the same way. Stockings, mittens, and all, were wrung out also, and then hung up to drain and chafe dry against the bulkheads. Then, feeling of all our clothes, we picked out those which were the least wet, and put them on, so as to be ready for a call, and turned-in, covered ourselves up with blankets, and slept until three knocks on the scuttle and the dismal sound of "All star-bowlines ahoy! Eight bells, there below! Do you hear the news?" drawled out from on deck, and the sulky answer of "Aye, aye!" from below, sent us up again.

On deck, all was as dark as a pocket, and either a dead calm, with the rain pouring steadily down, or, more generally, a violent gale dead ahead, with rain pelting horizontally, and occasional variations of hail and sleet;—decks afloat with water swashing from side to side, and constantly wet feet; for boots could not be wrung out like drawers, and no composition could stand the constant soaking. In fact, wet and cold feet are inevitable in such weather, and are not the least of those little items which go to make up the grand total of the discomforts of a winter passage round the Cape. Few words were spoken between the watches as they shifted, the wheel was relieved, the mate took his place on the quarter-deck, the look-outs in the bows; and each man had his narrow space to walk fore and aft in, or, rather, to swing himself forward and back in, from one belaying pin to another,—for the decks were too slippery with ice and water to allow of much walking. To make a walk, which is absolutely necessary to pass away the time, one of us hit upon the expedient of sanding the deck; and afterwards, whenever the rain was not so violent as to wash it off, the weather-side of the quarter-deck, and a part of the waist and forecastle were sprinkled with the sand which we had on board for holystoning; and thus we made a good promenade, where we walked fore and aft, two and two, hour after hour, in our long, dull, and comfortless watches. The bells seemed to be an hour or two apart, instead of half an hour, and an age to elapse before the welcome sound of eight bells. The sole object was to make the time pass on. Any change was sought for, which would break the monotony of the time; and even the two hours' trick at the wheel, which came round to each of us, in turn, once in every other watch, was looked upon as a relief. Even the never-failing resource of long yarns, which eke out many a watch, seemed to have failed us now; for we had been so long together that we had heard each other's stories told over and over again, till we had them by heart; each one knew the whole history of each of the others, and we were fairly and literally talked out. Singing and joking, we were in no humor for, and, in fact, any sound of mirth or laughter would have struck strangely upon our ears, and would not have been tolerated, any more than whistling, or a wind instrument. The last resort, that of speculating upon the future, seemed now to fail us, for our discouraging situation, and the danger we were really in, (as we expected every day to find ourselves drifted back among the ice) 'clapped a stopper' upon all that. From saying—"*when* we get home"—we began insensibly to alter it to—"*if* we get home"—and at last the subject was dropped by a tacit consent.

In this state of things, a new light was struck out, and a new field opened, by a change in the watch. One of our watch was laid up for two or three days by a bad hand, (for in cold weather the least cut or bruise ripens into a sore,) and his place was supplied by the carpenter. This was a windfall, and there was quite a contest, who should have the carpenter to walk with him. As 'Chips' was a man of some little education, and he and I had had a good deal of intercourse with each other, he fell in with me in my walk. He was a Fin, but spoke English very well, and gave me long accounts of his country;—the customs, the trade, the towns, what little he knew of the government, (I found he was no friend of Russia,) his voyages, his first arrival in America, his marriage and courtship;—he had married a countrywoman of his, a dress-maker, whom he met with in Boston. I had very little to tell him of my quiet, sedentary life at home; and in spite of our best efforts, which had protracted these yarns through five or six watches, we fairly talked one another out, and I turned him over to another man in the watch, and put myself upon my own resources.

I commenced a deliberate system of time-killing, which

united some profit with a cheering up of the heavy hours. As soon as I came on deck, and took my place and regular walk, I began with repeating over to myself a string of matters which I had in my memory, in regular order. First, the multiplication table and the tables of weights and measures; then the states of the Union, with their capitals; the counties of England, with their shire towns; the kings of England in their order; and a large part of the peerage, which I committed from an almanac that we had on board; and then the Kanaka numerals. This carried me through my facts, and being repeated deliberately, with long intervals, often eked out the two first bells. Then came the ten commandments; the thirty-ninth chapter of Job, and a few other passages from Scripture. The next in the order, that I never varied from, came Cowper's Castaway, which was a great favorite with me; the solemn measure and gloomy character of which, as well as the incident that it was founded upon, made it well suited to a lonely watch at sea. Then his lines to Mary, his address to the jackdaw, and a short extract from Table Talk; (I abounded in Cowper, for I happened to have a volume of his poems in my chest;) "Ille et nefasto" from Horace, and Gœthe's Erl King. After I had got through these, I allowed myself a more general range among everything that I could remember, both in prose and verse. In this way, with an occasional break by relieving the wheel, heaving the log, and going to the scuttle-butt for a drink of water, the longest watch was passed away; and I was so regular in my silent recitations, that if there was no interruption by ship's duty, I could tell very nearly the number of bells by my progress.

Our watches below were no more varied than the watch on deck. All washing, sewing, and reading was given up; and we did nothing but eat, sleep, and stand our watch, leading what might be called a Cape Horn life. The forecastle was too uncomfortable to sit up in; and whenever we were below, we were in our berths. To prevent the rain, and the sea-water which broke over the bows, from washing down, we were obliged to keep the scuttle closed, so that the forecastle was nearly air-tight. In this little, wet, leaky hole, we were all quartered, in an atmosphere so bad that our lamp, which swung in the middle from the beams, sometimes actually burned blue, with a large circle of foul air about it. Still, I was never in better health than after three weeks of this life. I gained a great deal of flesh, and we all ate like horses. At every watch, when we came below, before turning-in, the bread barge and beef kid were overhauled. Each man drank his quart of hot tea night and morning; and glad enough we were to get it, for no nectar and ambrosia were sweeter to the lazy immortals, than was a pot of hot tea, a hard biscuit, and a slice of cold salt beef, to us after a watch on deck. To be sure, we were mere animals, and had this life lasted a year instead of a month, we should have been little better than the ropes in the ship. Not a razor, nor a brush, nor a drop of water, except the rain and the spray, had come near us all the time; for we were on an allowance of fresh water; and who would strip and wash himself in salt water on deck, in the snow and ice, with the thermometer at zero?

After about eight days of constant easterly gales, the wind hauled occasionally a little to the southward, and blew hard, which, as we were well to the southward, allowed us to brace in a little and stand on, under all the sail we could carry. These turns lasted but a short while, and sooner or later it set in again from the old quarter; yet at each time we made something, and were gradually edging along to the eastward. One night, after one of these shifts of the wind, and when all hands had been up a great part of the time, our watch was left on deck, with the main-sail hanging in the buntlines, ready to be set if necessary. It came on to blow worse and worse, with hail and snow beating like so many furies upon the ship, it being as dark and thick as night could make it. The main-sail was blowing and slatting with a noise like thunder, when the captain came on deck, and ordered it to be furled. The mate was about to call all hands, when the captain stopped him, and said that the men would be beaten out if they were called up so often; that as our watch must stay on deck, it might as well be doing that as anything else. Accordingly, we went upon the yard; and never shall I forget that piece of work. Our watch had been so reduced by sickness, and by some having been left in California, that, with one man at the wheel, we had only the third mate and three beside myself to go aloft; so that, at most, we could only attempt to furl one yard-arm at a time. We manned the weather yard-arm, and set to work to make a furl of it. Our lower masts being short, and our yards very square, the sail had a head of nearly fifty feet, and a short leach, made still shorter by the deep reef which was in it, which brought the clue away out on the quarters of the yard, and made a bunt nearly as square as the mizen royal-yard. Beside this difficulty, the yard over which we lay was cased with ice, the gaskets and rope of the foot and leach of the sail as stiff and hard as a piece of suction-hose, and the sail itself about as pliable as though it had been made of sheets of sheathing copper. It blew a perfect hurricane, with alternate blasts of snow, hail, and rain. We had to *fist* the sail with bare hands. No one could trust himself to mittens, for if he slipped, he was a gone man. All the boats were hoisted in on deck, and there was nothing to be lowered for him. We had need of every finger God had given us. Several times we got the sail upon the yard, but it blew away again before we could secure it. It required men to lie over the yard to pass each turn of the gaskets, and when they were passed, it was almost impossible to knot them so that they would hold. Frequently we were obliged to leave off altogether and take to beating our hands upon the sail, to keep them from freezing. After some time,—which seemed forever,—we got the weather side stowed after a fashion, and went over to leeward for another trial. This was still worse, for the body of the sail had been blown over to leeward, and as the yard was a-cock-bill by the lying over of the vessel, we had to light it all up to windward. When the yard-arms were furled, the bunt was all adrift again, which made more work for us. We got all secure at last, but we had been nearly an hour and a half upon the yard, and it seemed an age. It had just struck five bells when we went up, and eight were struck soon after we came down. This may seem slow work; but considering the state of everything, and that we had only five men to a sail with just half as many square yards of canvass in it as the main-sail of the Independence, sixty-gun ship, which musters seven hundred men at her quarters, it is not wonderful that we were no quicker about it. We were glad enough to get on deck, and still more, to go below. The oldest sailor in the watch said, as he went down,—"I shall never forget that main yard;—it beats all my going a fishing. Fun is fun, but furling one yard-arm of a course, at a time, off Cape Horn, is no better than man-killing."

During the greater part of the next two days, the wind was pretty steady from the southward. We had evidently made great progress, and had good hope of being soon up with the Cape, if we were not there already. We could put but little confidence in our reckoning, as there had been no opportunities for an observation, and we had drifted too much to allow of our dead reckoning being anywhere near the mark. If it would clear off enough to give a chance for an observation, or if we could make land, we should know where we were; and upon these, and the chances of falling in with a sail from the eastward, we depended almost entirely.

Friday, July 22d. This day we had a steady gale from the southward, and stood on under close sail, with the yards eased a little by the weather braces, the clouds lifting a little, and showing signs of breaking away. In the afternoon, I was below with Mr. H——, the third mate, and two others, filling the bread locker in the steerage from the casks, when a bright gleam of sunshine broke out and shone down the companion-way and through the sky-light, lighting up everything below, and sending a warm glow through the heart of every one. It was a sight we had not seen for weeks,—an omen, a god-send. Even the roughest and hardest face acknowledged its influence. Just at that moment we heard a loud shout from all parts of the deck, and the mate called out down the companion-way to the captain, who was sitting in the cabin. What he said, we could not distinguish, but the captain kicked over his chair, and was on deck at one jump. We could not tell what it was; and, anxious as we were to know, the discipline of the ship would not allow of our leaving our places. Yet, as we were not called, we knew there was no danger. We hurried to get through with our job, when, seeing the steward's black face peering out of the pantry, Mr. H—— hailed him, to know what was the matter. "Lan' o, to be sure, sir! No you hear 'em sing out, 'Lan' o?' De cap'em say 'im Cape Horn!"

This gave us a new start, and we were soon through our work, and on deck; and there lay the land, fair upon the larboard beam, and slowly edging away upon the quarter. All hands were busy looking at it,—the captain and mates from the quarter-deck, the cook from his galley, and the sailors from the forecastle; and even Mr. N., the passenger, who had kept in his shell for nearly a month, and hardly been seen by any-body, and who we had almost forgotten was on board, came out like a butterfly, and was hopping round as bright as a bird.

The land was the island of Staten Land, just to the eastward of Cape Horn; and a more desolate-looking spot I never wish to set eyes upon;—bare, broken, and girt with rocks and ice, with here and there, between the rocks and broken hillocks, a little stunted vegetation of shrubs. It was a place well suited to stand at the junction of the two oceans, beyond the reach of human cultivation, and encounter the blasts and snows of a perpetual winter. Yet, dismal as it was, it was a pleasant sight to us; not only as being the first land we had seen, but because it told us that we had passed the Cape,—were in the Atlantic,—and that, with twenty-four hours of this breeze, might bid de-fiance to the Southern ocean. It told us, too, our latitude and longitude better than any observation; and the captain now knew where we were, as well as if we were off the end of Long wharf.

In the general joy, Mr. N. said he should like to go ashore upon the island and examine a spot which probably no human being had ever set foot upon; but the captain intimated that he would see the island—specimens and all,—in—another place, before he would get out a boat or delay the ship one moment for him.

We left the land gradually astern; and at sundown had the Atlantic ocean clear before us.

Chapter XXXIII

IT IS usual, in voyages round the Cape from the Pacific, to keep to the eastward of the Falkland Islands; but as it had now set in a strong, steady, and clear south-wester, with every prospect of its lasting, and we had had enough of high latitudes, the captain determined to stand immediately to the northward, running inside the Falkland Islands. Accordingly, when the wheel was relieved at eight o'clock, the order was given to keep her due north, and all hands were turned up to square away the yards and make sail. In a moment, the news ran through the ship that the captain was keeping her off, with her nose straight for Boston, and Cape Horn over her taffrail. It was a moment of enthusiasm. Every one was on the alert, and even the two sick men turned out to lend a hand at the halyards. The wind was now due south-west, and blowing a gale to which a vessel close hauled could have shown no more than a single close-reefed sail; but as we were going before it, we could carry on. Accordingly, hands were sent aloft, and a reef shaken out of the top-sails, and the reefed fore-sail set. When we came to mast-head the top-sail yards, with all hands at the halyards, we struck up "Cheerily, men," with a chorus which might have been heard half way to Staten Land. Under her increased sail, the ship drove on through the water. Yet she could bear it well; and the captain sang out from the quarter-deck—"Another reef out of that fore top-sail, and give it to her!" Two hands sprang aloft; the frozen reef-points and earings were cast adrift, the halyards manned, and the sail gave out her increased canvass to the gale. All hands were kept on deck to watch the effect of the change. It was as much as she could well carry, and with a heavy sea astern, it took two men at the wheel to steer her. She flung the foam from her bows; the spray breaking aft as far as the gangway. She was going at a prodigious rate. Still, everything held. Preventer braces were reeved and hauled taught; tackles got upon the backstays; and each thing done to keep all snug and strong. The captain walked the deck at a rapid stride, looked aloft at the sails, and then to windward; the mate stood in the gangway, rubbing his hands, and talking aloud to the ship—"Hurrah, old bucket! the Boston girls have got hold of the tow-rope!" and the like; and we were on the forecastle, looking to see how the spars stood it, and guessing the rate at which she was going,—when the captain called out—"Mr. Brown, get up the top-mast studding-sail! What she can't carry she may drag!" The mate looked a moment; but he would let no one be before him in daring. He sprang forward,—"Hurrah, men! rig out the top-mast studding-sail boom! Lay aloft, and I'll send the rigging up to you!"—We sprang aloft into the top; lowered a girt-line down, by which we hauled up the rigging; rove the tacks and halyards; ran out the boom and lashed it fast, and sent down the lower halyards, as a preventer. It was a clear starlight night, cold and blowing; but everybody worked with a will. Some, indeed, looked as though they thought the 'old man' was mad, but no one said a word. We had had a new top-mast studding-sail made with a reef in it,—a thing hardly ever heard of, and which the sailors had ridiculed a good deal, saying that when it was time to reef a studding-sail, it was time to take it in. But we found a use for it now; for, there being a reef in the top-sail, the studding-sail could not be set without one in it also. To be sure, a studding-sail with reefed top-sails was rather a new thing; yet there was some reason in it, for if we carried that away, we should lose only a sail and a boom; but a whole top-sail might have carried away the mast and all.

While we were aloft, the sail had been got out, bent to the yard, reefed, and ready for hoisting. Waiting for a good opportunity, the halyards were manned and the yard hoisted fairly up to the block; but when the mate came to shake the catspaw out of the downhaul, and we began to boom-end the sail, it shook the ship to her centre. The boom buckled up and bent like a whip-stick, and we looked every moment to see something go; but, being of the short, tough upland spruce, it bent like whalebone, and nothing could break it. The carpenter said it was the best stick he had ever seen. The strength of all hands soon brought the tack to the boom-end, and the sheet was trimmed down, and the preventer and the weather brace hauled taught to take off the strain. Every rope-yarn seemed stretched to the utmost, and every thread of canvass; and with this sail added to her, the ship sprang through the water like a thing possessed. The sail being nearly all forward, it lifted her out of the water, and she seemed actually to jump from sea to sea. From the time her keel was laid, she had never been so driven; and had it been life or death with every one of us, she could not have borne another stitch of canvass.

Finding that she would bear the sail, the hands were sent below, and our watch remained on deck. Two men at the wheel had as much as they could do to keep her within three points of her course, for she steered as wild as a young colt. The mate walked the deck, looking at the sails, and then over the side to see the foam fly by her,—slapping his hands upon his thighs and talking to the ship—"Hurrah, you jade, you've got the scent!— you know where you're going!" And when she leaped over the seas, and almost out of the water, and trembled to her very keel, the spars and masts snapping and creaking,—"There she goes!—There she goes,—handsomely!—As long as she cracks she holds!"—while we stood with the rigging laid down fair for letting go, and ready to take in sail and clear away, if anything went. At four bells we hove the log, and she was going eleven knots fairly; and had it not been for the sea from aft which sent the chip home, and threw her continually off her course, the log would have shown her to have been going much faster. I went to the wheel with a young fellow from the Kennebec, who was a good helmsman; and for two hours we had our hands full. A few minutes showed us that our monkey-jackets must come off; and cold as it was, we stood in our shirt-sleeves, in a perspiration; and were glad enough to have it eight bells, and the wheel relieved. We turned-in and slept as well as we could, though the sea made a constant roar under her bows, and washed over the forecastle like a small cataract.

At four o'clock, we were called again. The same sail was still on the vessel, and the gale, if there was any change, had increased a little. No attempt was made to take the studding-sail in; and, indeed, it was too late now. If we had started anything toward taking it in, either tack or halyards, it would have blown to pieces, and carried something away with it. The only way now was to let everything stand, and if the gale went down, well and good; if not, something must go—the weakest stick or rope first—and then we could get it in. For more than an hour she was driven on at such a rate that she seemed actually to crowd the sea into a heap before her; and the water poured over the sprit-sail yard as it would over a dam. Toward daybreak the gale abated a little, and she was just beginning to go more easily along, relieved of the pressure, when Mr. Brown, determined to give her no respite, and depending upon the wind's subsiding as the sun rose, told us to get along the lower studding-sail. This was an immense sail, and held wind enough to last a Dutchman a week,—hove-to. It was soon ready, the boom topped up, preventer guys rove, and the idlers called up to man the halyards; yet such was still the force of the gale, that we were nearly an hour setting the sail; carried away the outhaul in doing it, and came very near snapping off the swinging boom. No sooner was it set than the ship tore on again like one that was mad, and began to steer as wild as a hawk. The men at the wheel were puffing and blowing at their work, and the helm was going hard up and hard down, constantly. Add to this, the gale did not lessen as the day came on, but the sun rose in clouds. A sudden lurch threw the man from the weather wheel across the deck and against the side. The mate sprang to the wheel, and the man, regaining his feet, seized the spokes, and they hove the wheel up just in time to save her from broaching to; though nearly half the studding-sail went under water; and as she came to, the boom stood up at an angle of forty-five degrees. She had evidently more on her than she could bear; yet it was in vain to try to take it in— the clewline was not strong enough; and they were thinking of cutting away, when another wide yaw and a come-to, snapped the guys, and the swinging boom came in, with a crash, against the lower rigging. The outhaul block gave way, and the top-mast studding-sail boom bent in a manner which I never before supposed a stick could bend. I had my eye on it when the guys parted, and it made one spring and buckled up so as to form nearly a half circle, and sprang out again to its shape. The clewline gave way at the first pull; the cleat to which the halyards were belayed was wrenched off, and the sail blew round the sprit-sail yard and head guys, which gave us a bad job to get it in. A half hour served to clear all away, and she was suffered to drive on with her top-mast studding-sail set, it being as much as she could stagger under.

During all this day and the next night, we went on under

the same sail, the gale blowing with undiminished force; two men at the wheel all the time; watch and watch, and nothing to do but to steer and look out for the ship, and be blown along;—until the noon of the next day—

Sunday, July 24th, when we were in latitude 50° 27′ S., longitude 62° 13′ W., having made four degrees of latitude in the last twenty-four hours. Being now to the northward of the Falkland Islands, the ship was kept off, north-east, for the equator; and with her head for the equator, and Cape Horn over her taffrail, she went gloriously on; every heave of the sea leaving the Cape astern, and every hour bringing us nearer to home, and to warm weather. Many a time, when blocked up in the ice, with everything dismal and discouraging about us, had we said,—if we were only fairly round, and standing north on the other side, we should ask for no more:—and now we had it all, with a clear sea, and as much wind as a sailor could pray for. If the best part of a voyage is the last part, surely we had all now that we could wish. Every one was in the highest spirits, and the ship seemed as glad as any of us at getting out of her confinement. At each change of the watch, those coming on deck asked those going below—"How does she go along?" and got for answer, the rate, and the customary addition— "Aye! and the Boston girls have had hold of the tow-rope all the watch, and can't haul half the slack in!" Each day the sun rose higher in the horizon, and the nights grew shorter; and at coming on deck each morning, there was a sensible change in the temperature. The ice, too, began to melt from off the rigging and spars, and, except a little which remained in the tops and round the hounds of the lower masts, was soon gone. As we left the gale behind us, the reefs were shaken out of the top-sails, and sail made as fast as she could bear it; and every time all hands were sent to the halyards, a song was called for, and we hoisted away with a will.

Sail after sail was added, as we drew into fine weather; and in one week after leaving Cape Horn, the long top-gallant masts were got up, top-gallant and royal yards crossed, and the ship restored to her fair proportions.

The Southern Cross we saw no more after the first night; the Magellan Clouds settled lower and lower in the horizon; and so great was our change of latitude each succeeding night, that we sank some constellation in the south, and raised another in the northern horizon.

Sunday, July 31st. At noon we were in lat. 36° 41′ S., long. 38° 08′ W.; having traversed the distance of two thousand miles, allowing for changes of course, in nine days. A thousand miles in four days and a half!—This is equal to steam.

Soon after eight o'clock, the appearance of the ship gave evidence that this was the first Sunday we had yet had in fine weather. As the sun came up clear, with the promise of a fair, warm day, and, as usual on Sunday, there was no work going on, all hands turned-to upon clearing out the forecastle. The wet and soiled clothes which had accumulated there during the past month, were brought up on deck; the chests moved; brooms, buckets of water, swabs, scrubbing-brushes, and scrapers carried down, and applied, until the forecastle floor was as white as chalk, and everything neat and in order. The bedding from the berths was then spread on deck, and dried, and aired; the deck-tub filled with water; and a grand washing begun of all the clothes which were brought up. Shirts, frocks, drawers, trowsers, jackets, stockings, of every shape and color, wet and dirty—many of them mouldy from having been lying a long time wet in a foul corner—these were all washed and scrubbed out, and finally towed overboard for half an hour; and then made fast in the rigging to dry. Wet boots and shoes were spread out to dry in sunny places on deck; and the whole ship looked like a back yard on a washing day. After we had done with our clothes, we began upon our own persons. A little fresh water, which we had saved from our allowance, was put in buckets, and, with soap and towels, we had what sailors call a fresh-water wash. The same bucket, to be sure, had to go through several hands, and was spoken for by one after another, but as we rinsed off in salt water, pure from the ocean, and the fresh was used only to start the accumulated grime and blackness of five weeks, it was held of little consequence. We soaped down and scrubbed one another with towels and pieces of canvass, stripping to it; and then, getting into the head, threw buckets of water upon each other. After this, came shaving, and combing, and brushing; and when, having spent the first part of the day in this way, we sat down on the forecastle, in the afternoon, with clean duck trowsers, and shirts on, washed, shaved, and combed, and looking a dozen shades lighter for it, reading, sewing, and talking at our ease, with a clear sky and warm sun over our heads, a steady breeze over the larboard quarter, studding-sails out alow and aloft, and all the flying kites abroad;—we felt that we had got back into the pleasantest part of a sailor's life. At sundown the clothes were all taken down from the rigging—clean and dry—and stowed neatly away in our chests; and our south-westers, thick boots, guernsey frocks, and other accompaniments of bad weather, put out of the way, we hoped, for the rest of the voyage, as we expected to come upon the coast early in the autumn.

Notwithstanding all that has been said about the beauty of a ship under full sail, there are very few who have ever seen a ship, literally, under all her sail. A ship coming in or going out of port, with her ordinary sails, and perhaps two or three studding-sails, is commonly said to be under full sail; but a ship never has all her sail upon her, except when she has a light, steady breeze, very nearly, but not quite, dead aft, and so regular that it can be trusted, and is likely to last for sometime. Then, with all her sails, light and heavy, and studding-sails, on each side, alow and aloft, she is the most glorious moving object in the world. Such a sight, very few, even some who have been at sea a good deal, have ever beheld; for from the deck of your own vessel you cannot see her, as you would a separate object.

One night, while we were in these tropics, I went out to the end of the flying-jib-boom, upon some duty, and, having finished it, turned round, and lay over the boom for a long time, admiring the beauty of the sight before me. Being so far out from the deck, I could look at the ship, as at a separate vessel; —and, there, rose up from the water, supported only by the small black hull, a pyramid of canvass, spreading out far beyond the hull, and towering up almost, as it seemed in the indistinct night air, to the clouds. The sea was as still as an inland lake; the light trade-wind was gently and steadily breathing from astern; the dark blue sky was studded with the tropical stars; there was no sound but the rippling of the water under the stem; and the sails were spread out, wide and high;—the two lower studding-sails stretching, on each side, far beyond the deck; the top-mast studding-sails, like wings to the top-sails; the top-gallant studding-sails spreading fearlessly out above them; still higher, the two royal studding-sails, looking like two kites flying from the same string; and, highest of all, the little sky-sail, the apex of the pyramid, seeming actually to touch the stars, and to be out of reach of human hand. So quiet, too, was the sea, and so steady the breeze, that if these sails had been sculptured marble, they could not have been more motionless. Not a ripple upon the surface of the canvass; not even a quivering of the extreme edges of the sail—so perfectly were they distended by the breeze. I was so lost in the sight, that I forgot the presence of the man who came out with me, until he said, (for he, too, rough old man-of-war's-man as he was, had been gazing at the show,) half to himself, still looking at the marble sails—"How quietly they do their work!"

The fine weather brought work with it, as the ship was to be put in order for coming into port. This may give a landsman some notion of what is done on board ship.—All the first part of a passage is spent in getting a ship ready for sea, and the last part in getting her ready for port. She is, as sailors say, like a lady's watch, always out of repair. The new, strong sails, which we had up off Cape Horn, were to be sent down, and the old set, which were still serviceable in fine weather, to be bent in their place; all the rigging to be set up, fore and aft; the masts stayed; the standing rigging to be tarred down; lower and top-mast rigging rattled down, fore and aft; the ship scraped, inside and out, and painted; decks varnished; new and neat knots, seizings and coverings to be fitted; and every part put in order, to look well to the owner's eye, on coming into Boston. This, of course, was a long matter; and all hands were kept on deck at work for the whole of each day, during the rest of the voyage. Sailors call this hard usage; but the ship must be in crack order, and "we're homeward bound" was the answer to everything.

We went on for several days, employed in this way, nothing remarkable occurring; and, at the latter part of the week, fell in with the south-east trades, blowing about east-south-east, which brought them nearly two points abaft our beam. These blew strong and steady, so that we hardly started a rope, until we were beyond their latitude. The first day of "all hands," one of those little incidents occurred, which are nothing in themselves, but are great matters in the eyes of a ship's company, as they serve to break the monotony of a voyage, and afford conversation to the crew for days afterwards. These small matters, too, are often interesting, as they show the customs and state of feeling on shipboard.

In merchant vessels, the captain gives his orders, as to the ship's work, to the mate, in a general way, and leaves the execution of them, with the particular ordering, to him. This has become so fixed a custom, that it is like a law, and is never infringed upon by a wise master, unless his mate is no seaman; in which case, the captain must often oversee things for himself. This, however, could not be said of our chief mate; and he was very jealous of any encroachment upon the borders of his authority.

On Monday morning, the captain told him to stay the fore top-mast plumb. He accordingly came forward, turned all hands to, with tackles on the stays and backstays, coming up with the seizings, hauling here, belaying there, and full of business, standing between the knight-heads to sight the mast,—when the captain came forward, and also began to give orders. This made confusion, and the mate, finding that he was all aback, left his place and went aft, saying to the captain—

"If you come forward, sir, I'll go aft. One is enough on the forecastle."

This produced a reply, and another fierce answer; and the words flew, fists were doubled up, and things looked threateningly.

"I'm master of this ship."

"Yes, sir, and I'm mate of her, and know my place! My place is forward, and yours is aft!"

"My place is where I choose! I command the *whole* ship; and you are mate only so long as I choose!"

"Say the word, Capt. T., and I'm done! I can do a man's work aboard! I didn't come through the cabin windows! If I'm not mate, I can be man," &c., &c.

This was all fun for us, who stood by, winking at each other, and enjoying the contest between the higher powers. The captain took the mate aft; and they had a long talk, which ended in the mate's returning to his duty. The captain had broken through a custom, which is a part of the common-law of a ship, and without reason; for he knew that his mate was a sailor, and needed no help from him; and the mate was excusable for being angry. Yet he was wrong, and the captain right. Whatever the captain does is right, ipso facto, and any opposition to it is wrong, on board ship; and every officer and man knows this when he signs the ship's articles. It is a part of the contract. Yet there has grown up in merchant vessels a series of customs, which have become a well understood system, and have almost the force of prescriptive law. To be sure, all power is in the captain, and the officers hold their authority only during his will; and the men are liable to be called upon for any service; yet, by breaking in upon these usages, many difficulties have occurred on board ship, and even come into courts of justice, which are perfectly unintelligible to any one not acquainted with the universal nature and force of these customs. Many a provocation has been offered, and a system of petty oppression pursued towards men, the force and meaning of which would appear as nothing to strangers, and doubtless do appear so to many " 'long-shore" juries and judges.

The next little diversion, was a battle on the forecastle, one afternoon, between the mate and the steward. They had been on bad terms the whole voyage; and had threatened a rupture several times. This afternoon, the mate asked him for a tumbler of water, and he refused to get it for him, saying that he waited upon nobody but the captain: and here he had the custom on his side. But in answering, he left off 'the handle to the mate's name.' This enraged the mate, who called him a "black soger;" and at it they went, clenching, striking, and rolling over and over; while we stood by, looking on, and enjoying the fun. The darkey tried to butt him, but the mate got him down, and held him, the steward singing out, "Let me go, Mr. Brown, or there'll be blood spilt!" In the midst of this, the captain came on deck, separated them, took the steward aft, and gave him a half a dozen with a rope's end. The steward tried to justify himself; but he had been heard to talk of spilling blood, and that was enough to earn him his flogging; and the captain did not choose to inquire any further.

Chapter XXXIV

THE same day, I met with one of those narrow escapes, which are so often happening in a sailor's life. I had been aloft nearly all the afternoon, at work, standing for as much as an hour on the fore top-gallant yard, which was hoisted up, and hung only by the tie; when, having got through my work, I balled up my yarns, took my serving-board in my hand, laid hold deliberately of the top-gallant rigging, took one foot from the yard, and was just lifting the other, when the tie parted, and down the yard fell. I was safe, by my hold upon the rigging, but it made my heart beat quick. Had the tie parted one instant sooner, or had I stood an instant longer on the yard, I should inevitably have been thrown violently from the height of ninety or an hundred feet, overboard; or, what is worse, upon the deck. However, "a miss is as good as a mile;" a saying which sailors very often have occasion to use. An escape is always a joke on board ship. A man would be ridiculed who should make a serious matter of it. A sailor knows too well that his life hangs upon a thread, to wish to be always reminded of it; so, if a man has an escape, he keeps it to himself, or makes a joke of it. I have often known a man's life to be saved by an instant of time, or by the merest chance,—the swinging of a rope,—and no notice taken of it. One of our boys, when off Cape Horn, reefing top-sails of a dark night, and when there were no boats to be lowered away, and where, if a man fell overboard, he must be left behind,—lost his hold of the reef-point, slipped from the foot-rope, and would have been in the water in a moment, when the man who was next to him on the yard caught him by the collar of his jacket, and hauled him up upon the yard, with—"Hold on, another time, you young monkey, and be d——d to you!"—and that was all that was heard about it.

Sunday, August 7th. Lat. 25° 59′ S., long. 27° 0′ W. Spoke the English bark Mary-Catherine, from Bahia, bound to Calcutta. This was the first sail we had fallen in with, and the first time we had seen a human form or heard the human voice, except of our own number, for nearly an hundred days. The very yo-ho-ing of the sailors at the ropes sounded sociably upon the ear. She was an old, damaged-looking craft, with a high poop and top-gallant forecastle, and sawed off square, stem and stern, like a true English "tea-wagon," and with a run like a sugar-box. She had studding-sails out alow and aloft, with a light but steady breeze, and her captain said he could not get more than four knots out of her; and thought he should have a long passage. We were going six on an easy bowline.

The next day, about three P.M., passed a large corvette-built ship, close upon the wind, with royals and sky-sails set fore and aft, under English colors. She was standing south-by-east, probably bound round Cape Horn. She had men in her tops, and black mast-heads; heavily sparred, with sails cut to a *t*, and other marks of a man-of-war. She sailed well, and presented a fine appearance; the proud, aristocratic-looking banner of St. George, the cross in a blood-red field, waving from the mizen. We probably were as fine a sight, with our studding-sails spread far out beyond the ship on either side, and rising in a pyramid to royal studding-sails and sky-sails, burying the hull in canvass, and looking like what the whalemen on the Banks, under their stump top-gallant masts, call "a Cape Horn-er under a cloud of sail."

Friday, August 12th. At daylight made the island of Trinidad, situated in lat. 20° 28′ S., long. 29° 08′ W. At twelve, M., it bore N.W. ½ N., distant twenty-seven miles. It was a beautiful day, the sea hardly ruffled by the light trades, and the island looking like a small blue mound rising from a field of glass. Such a fair and peaceful-looking spot is said to have been, for a long time, the resort of a band of pirates, who ravaged the tropical seas.

Thursday, August 18th. At three, P.M., made the island of Fernando Naronha, lying in lat. 3° 55′ S., long. 32° 35′ W.; and between twelve o'clock Friday night and one o'clock Saturday morning, crossed the equator, for the fourth time since leaving Boston, in long. 35° W.; having been twenty-seven days from Staten Land—a distance, by the courses we had made, of more than four thousand miles.

We were now to the northward of the line, and every day added to our latitude. The Magellan Clouds, the last sign of south latitude, were sunk in the horizon, and the north star, the

Great Bear, and the familiar signs of northern latitudes, were rising in the heavens. Next to seeing land, there is no sight which makes one realize more that he is drawing near home, than to see the same heavens, under which he was born, shining at night over his head. The weather was extremely hot, with the usual tropical alternations of a scorching sun and squalls of rain; yet not a word was said in complaint of the heat, for we all remembered that only three or four weeks before we would have given nearly our all to have been where we now were. We had a plenty of water, too, which we caught by spreading an awning, with shot thrown in to make hollows. These rain squalls came up in the manner usual between the tropics.—A clear sky; burning, vertical sun; work going lazily on, and men about decks with nothing but duck trowsers, checked shirts, and straw hats; the ship moving as lazily through the water; the man at the helm resting against the wheel, with his hat drawn over his eyes; the captain below, taking an afternoon nap; the passenger leaning over the taffrail, watching a dolphin following slowly in our wake; the sailmaker mending an old top-sail on the lee side of the quarter-deck; the carpenter working at his bench, in the waist; the boys making sinnet; the spun-yarn winch whizzing round and round, and the men walking slowly fore and aft with the yarns.—A cloud rises to windward, looking a little black; the sky-sails are brailed down; the captain puts his head out of the companion-way, looks at the cloud, comes up, and begins to walk the deck.—The cloud spreads and comes on;—the tub of yarns, the sail, and other matters, are thrown below, and the sky-light and booby-hatch put on, and the slide drawn over the forecastle.—"Stand by the royal halyards;"—the man at the wheel keeps a good weather helm, so as not to be taken aback.—The squall strikes her. If it is light, the royal yards are clewed down, and the ship keeps on her way; but if the squall takes strong hold, the royals are clewed up, fore and aft; light hands lay aloft and furl them; top-gallant yards clewed down, flying-jib hauled down, and the ship kept off before it,—the man at the helm laying out his strength to heave the wheel up to windward. At the same time a drenching rain, which soaks one through in an instant. Yet no one puts on a jacket or cap; for if it is only warm, a sailor does not mind a ducking; and the sun will soon be out again.

As soon as the force of the squall has passed, though to a common eye the ship would seem to be in the midst of it,—"Keep her up to her course, again!"—"Keep her up, sir," (answer);—"Hoist away the top-gallant yards!"—"Run up the flying-jib!"—"Lay aloft, you boys, and loose the royals!"—and all sail is on her again before she is fairly out of the squall; and she is going on in her course. The sun comes out once more, hotter than ever, dries up the decks and the sailors' clothes; the hatches are taken off; the sail got up and spread on the quarter-deck; spun-yarn winch set a whirling again; rigging coiled up; captain goes below; and every sign of an interruption is removed.

These scenes, with occasional dead calms, lasting for hours, and sometimes for days, are fair specimens of the Atlantic tropics. The nights were fine; and as we had all hands all day, the watch were allowed to sleep on deck at night, except the man at the wheel, and one look-out on the forecastle. This was not so much expressly allowed, as winked at. We could do it if we did not ask leave. If the look-out was caught napping, the whole watch was kept awake. We made the most of this permission, and stowed ourselves away upon the rigging, under the weather rail, on the spars, under the windlass, and in all the snug corners; and frequently slept out the watch, unless we had a wheel or a look-out. And we were glad enough to get this rest; for under the "all hands" system, out of every other thirty-six hours, we had only four below; and even an hour's sleep was a gain not to be neglected. One would have thought so, to have seen our watch, some nights, sleeping through a heavy rain. And often have we come on deck, and finding a dead calm and a light, steady rain, and determined not to lose our sleep, have laid a coil of rigging down so as to keep us out of the water which was washing about decks, and stowed ourselves away upon it, covering a jacket over us, and slept as soundly as a Dutchman between two feather beds.

For a week or ten days after crossing the line, we had the usual variety of calms, squalls, head winds, and fair winds;—at one time braced sharp upon the wind, with a taught bowline, and in an hour after, slipping quietly along, with a light breeze over the taffrail, and studding-sails out on both sides;—until we fell in with the north-east trade-winds; which we did on the afternoon of

Sunday, August 28th, in lat. 12° N. The trade-wind clouds had been in sight for a day or two previously, and we expected to take them every hour. The light southerly breeze, which had been blowing languidly during the first part of the day, died away toward noon, and in its place came puffs from the north-east, which caused us to take our studding-sails in and brace up; and, in a couple of hours more, we were bowling gloriously along, dashing the spray far ahead and to leeward, with the cool, steady north-east trades, freshening up the sea, and giving us as much as we could carry our royals to. These winds blew strong and steady, keeping us generally upon a bowline, as our course was about north-north-west; and sometimes, as they veered a little to the eastward, giving us a chance at a main top-gallant studding-sail; and sending us well to the northward, until—

Sunday, Sept. 4th, when they left us, in lat. 22° N., long. 51° W., directly under the tropic of Cancer.

For several days we lay 'humbugging about' in the Horse latitudes, with all sorts of winds and weather, and occasionally, as we were in the latitude of the West Indies,—a thunder storm. It was hurricane month, too, and we were just in the track of the tremendous hurricane of 1830, which swept the North Atlantic, destroying almost everything before it. The first night after the trade-winds left us, while we were in the latitude of the island of Cuba, we had a specimen of a true tropical thunder storm. A light breeze had been blowing directly from aft during the first part of the night, which gradually died away, and before midnight it was dead calm, and a heavy black cloud had shrouded the whole sky. When our watch came on deck at twelve o'clock, it was as black as Erebus; the studding-sails were all taken in, and the royals furled; not a breath was stirring; the sails hung heavy and motionless from the yards; and the perfect stillness, and the darkness, which was almost palpable, were truly appalling. Not a word was spoken, but every one stood as though waiting for something to happen. In a few minutes the mate came forward, and in a low tone, which was almost a whisper, told us to haul down the jib. The fore and mizen top-gallant sails were taken in, in the same silent manner; and we lay motionless upon the water, with an uneasy expectation, which, from the long suspense, became actually painful. We could hear the captain walking the deck, but it was too dark to see anything more than one's hand before the face. Soon the mate came forward again, and gave an order, in a low tone, to clew up the main top-gallant sail; and so infectious was the awe and silence, that the clewlines and buntlines were hauled up without any of the customary singing out at the ropes. An English lad and myself went up to furl it; and we had just got the bunt up, when the mate called out to us, something, we did not hear what,—but supposing it to be an order to bear-a-hand, we hurried, and made all fast, and came down, feeling our way among the rigging. When we got down we found all hands looking aloft, and there, directly over where we had been standing, upon the main top-gallant-mast-head, was a ball of light, which the sailors name a corposant (corpus sancti), and which the mate had called out to us to look at. They were all watching it carefully, for sailors have a notion that if the corposant rises in the rigging, it is a sign of fair weather, but if it comes lower down, there will be a storm. Unfortunately, as an omen, it came down, and showed itself on the top-gallant yard-arm. We were off the yard in good season, for it is held a fatal sign to have the pale light of the corposant thrown upon one's face. As it was, the English lad did not feel comfortably at having had it so near him, and directly over his head. In a few minutes it disappeared, and showed itself again on the fore top-gallant yard; and after playing about for some time, disappeared again; when the man on the forecastle pointed to it upon the flying-jib-boom-end. But our attention was drawn from watching this, by the falling of some drops of rain, and by a perceptible increase of the darkness, which seemed suddenly to add a new shade of blackness to the night. In a few minutes, low, grumbling thunder was heard, and some random flashes of lightning came from the south-west. Every sail was taken in but the top-sails; still, no squall appeared to be coming. A few puffs lifted the top-sails, but they fell again to the mast, and all was as still as ever. A moment more, and a terrific flash and peal broke simultaneously upon us, and a cloud appeared to open directly over our heads and let down the water in one body, like a falling ocean. We stood motionless, and almost stupified; yet nothing had been struck. Peal after peal rattled over our heads, with a sound which seemed actually to stop the breath in the body, and the "speedy gleams" kept the whole ocean in a glare of light. The violent fall of rain lasted but a few minutes, and was succeeded by occasional drops and showers; but the lightning continued incessant for several hours, breaking the midnight darkness with irregular and blinding flashes. During all which time there was not a breath stirring, and we lay motionless, like a mark to be shot at, probably the only object on the surface of the ocean for miles and miles. We stood hour after hour, until our watch was out, and we were relieved, at four o'clock. During all this time, hardly a word was spoken; no bells were struck, and the wheel was silently relieved. The rain fell at intervals in heavy showers, and we stood drenched through and blinded by the flashes, which broke the Egyptian darkness with a brightness which seemed almost malignant; while the thunder rolled in peals, the concussion of which appeared to shake the very ocean. A ship is not often injured by lightning, for the electricity is separated by the great number of points she presents, and the quantity of iron which she has scattered in various parts. The electric fluid ran over our anchors, top-sail sheets and ties; yet no harm was done to us. We went below at four o'clock, leaving things in the same state. It is not easy to sleep, when the very next flash may tear the ship in two, or set her on fire; or where the deathlike calm may be broken by the blast of a hurricane, taking the masts out of the ship. But a man is no sailor if he cannot sleep when he turns-in, and turn out when he's called. And when, at seven bells, the customary "All the larboard watch, ahoy!" brought us on deck, it was a fine, clear, sunny morning, the ship going leisurely along, with a good breeze and all sail set.

Chapter XXXV

FROM the latitude of the West Indies, until we got inside the Bermudas, where we took the westerly and south-westerly winds, which blow steadily off the coast of the United States early in the autumn, we had every variety of weather, and two or three moderate gales, or, as sailors call them, double-reef-top-sail breezes, which came on in the usual manner, and of which one is a specimen of all.—A fine afternoon; all hands at work, some in the rigging, and others on deck; a stiff breeze, and ship close upon the wind, and sky-sails brailed down.—Latter part of the afternoon, breeze increases, ship lies over to it, and clouds look windy. Spray begins to fly over the fore-castle, and wets the yarns the boys are knotting;—ball them up and put them below.—Mate knocks off work and clears up decks earlier than usual, and orders a man who has been em-ployed aloft to send the royal halyards over to windward, as he comes down. Breast backstays hauled taught, and tackle got upon the martingale back-rope.—One of the boys furls the mizen royal.—Cook thinks there is going to be 'nasty work,' and has supper ready early.—Mate gives orders to get supper by the watch, instead of all hands, as usual.—While eating supper, hear the watch on deck taking in the royals.—Coming on deck, find it is blowing harder, and an ugly head sea is running.—Instead of having all hands on the forecastle in the dog watch, smoking, singing, and telling yarns, one watch goes below and turns-in, saying that it's going to be an ugly night, and two hours' sleep is not to be lost. Clouds look black and wild; wind rising, and ship working hard against a heavy head sea, which breaks over the forecastle, and washes aft through the scuppers. Still, no more sail is taken in, for the captain is a driver, and, like all drivers, very partial to his top-gallant sails. A top-gallant sail, too, makes the difference be-tween a breeze and a gale. When a top-gallant sail is on a ship, it is only a breeze, though I have seen ours set over a reefed top-sail, when half the bowsprit was under water, and it was up to a man's knees in the lee scuppers. At eight bells, nothing is said about reefing the top-sails, and the watch go below, with orders to 'stand by for a call.' We turn-in, growling at the 'old man' for not reefing the top-sails when the watch was changed, but putting it off so as to call all hands, and break up a whole watch below. Turn-in 'all standing,' and keep ourselves awake, saying there is no use in going to sleep to be waked up again. —Wind whistles on deck, and ship works hard, groaning and creaking, and pitching into a heavy head sea, which strikes against the bows, with a noise like knocking upon a rock.— The dim lamp in the forecastle swings to and fro, and things 'fetch away' and go over to leeward.— "Doesn't that booby of a second mate ever mean to take in his top-gallant sails?—He'll have the sticks out of her soon," says old Bill, who was always growling, and, like most old sailors, did not like to see a ship abused.—By-and-by, an order is given;—"Aye, aye, sir!" from the forecastle;—rigging is heaved down on deck;—the noise of a sail is heard fluttering aloft, and the short, quick cry which sailors make when hauling upon clewlines.— "Here comes his fore top-gallant sail in!"—We are wide awake, and know all that's going on as well as if we were on deck.—A well-known voice is heard from the mast-head singing out to the officer of the watch to haul taught the weather brace.—"Hallo! There's S—— aloft to furl the sail!" —Next thing, rigging is heaved down directly over our heads, and a long-drawn cry and a rattling of hanks announce that the flying-jib has come in.— The second mate holds on to the main top-gallant sail until a heavy sea is shipped, and washes over the forecastle as though the whole ocean had come aboard; when a noise further aft shows that that sail, too, is taking in. After this, the ship is more easy for a time; two bells are struck, and we try to get a little sleep. By-and-by,—bang, bang, bang, on the scuttle—"All ha-a-ands, a ho-o-y!"—We spring out of our berths, clap on a monkey-jacket and south-wester, and tumble up the ladder.— Mate up before us, and on the forecastle, singing out like a roaring bull; the captain singing out on the quarter-deck, and the second mate yelling, like a hyena, in the waist. The ship is lying over half upon her beam-ends; lee scuppers under water, and forecastle all in a smother of foam.—Rigging all let go, and washing about decks; top-sail yards down upon the caps, and sails flapping and beating against the masts; and starboard watch hauling out the reef-tackles of the main top-sail.

Our watch haul out the fore, and lay aloft and put two reefs into it, and reef the fore-sail, and race with the starboard watch, to see which will mast-head its top-sail first. All hands tally-on to the main tack, and while some are furling the jib, and hoisting the stay-sail, we mizen-top-men double-reef the mizen top-sail and hoist it up. All being made fast—"Go below, the watch!" and we turn-in to sleep out the rest of the time, which is perhaps an hour and a half. During all the middle, and for the first part of the morning watch, it blows as hard as ever, but toward day-break it moderates considerably, and we shake a reef out of each top-sail, and set the top-gallant sails over them; and when the watch come up, at seven bells, for breakfast, shake the other reefs out, turn all hands to upon the halyards, get the watch-tackle upon the top-gallant sheets and halyards, set the flying-jib, and crack on to her again.

Our captain had been married only a few weeks before he left Boston; and, after an absence of over two years, it may be supposed he was not slow in carrying sail. The mate, too, was not to be beaten by anybody; and the second mate, though he was afraid to press sail, was afraid as death of the captain, and being between two fears, sometimes carried on longer than any of them. We snapped off three flying-jib booms in twenty-four hours, as fast as they could be fitted and rigged out; sprung the sprit-sail yard; and made nothing of studding-sail booms. Beside the natural desire to get home, we had another reason for urging the ship on. The scurvy had begun to show itself on board. One man had it so badly as to be disabled and off duty, and the English lad, Ben, was in a dreadful state, and was daily growing worse. His legs swelled and pained him so that he could not walk; his flesh lost its elasticity, so that if it was pressed in, it would not return to its shape; and his gums swelled until he could not open his mouth. His breath, too, became very offensive; he lost all strength and spirit; could eat nothing; grew worse every day; and, in fact, unless something was done for him, would be a dead man in a week, at the rate at which he was sinking. The medicines were all, or nearly all, gone; and if we had had a chest-full, they would have been of no use; for nothing but fresh provisions and terra firma has any effect upon the scurvy. This disease is not so common now as formerly; and is attributed generally to salt provisions, want of cleanliness, the free use of grease and fat (which is the reason of its prevalence among whalemen,) and, last of all, to laziness. It never could have been from the latter cause on board our ship; nor from the second, for we were a very cleanly crew, kept our forecastle in neat order, and were more particular about washing and changing clothes than many better-dressed people on shore. It was probably from having none but salt provisions, and possibly from our having run very rapidly into hot weather, after having been so long in the extremest cold.

Depending upon the westerly winds, which prevail off the coast in the autumn, the captain stood well to the westward, to run inside of the Bermudas, and in the hope of falling in with some vessel bound to the West Indies or the Southern States. The scurvy had spread no farther among the crew, but there was danger that it might; and these cases were bad ones.

Sunday, Sept. 11th. Lat. 30° 04′ N., long. 63° 23′ W.; the Bermudas bearing north-north-west, distant one hundred and fifty miles. The next morning, about ten o'clock, "Sail ho!" was cried on deck; and all hands turned up to see the stranger. As she drew nearer, she proved to be an ordinary-looking hermaphrodite brig, standing south-south-east; and probably bound out, from the Northern States, to the West Indies; and was just the thing we wished to see. She hove-to for us, seeing that we wished to speak her; and we ran down to her; boom-ended our studding-sails; backed our main top-sail, and hailed her—"Brig, ahoy!"—"Hallo!"—"Where are you from, pray?" —"From New York, bound to Curaçoa."—"Have you any fresh provisions to spare?"—"Aye, aye! plenty of them!" We lowered away the quarter-boat, instantly; and the captain and four hands sprang in, and were soon dancing over the water, and alongside the brig. In about half an hour, they returned with half a boat-load of potatoes and onions, and each vessel filled away, and kept on her course. She proved to be the brig Solon, of Plymouth, from the Connecticut river, and last from New York, bound to the Spanish Main, with a cargo of fresh provisions, mules, tin bake-pans, and other *notions.* The onions were genuine and fresh; and the mate of the brig told the men in the boat, as he passed the bunches over the side, that the girls had strung them on purpose for us the day he sailed. We had supposed, on board, that a new president had been chosen, the last winter, and, just as we filled away, the captain hailed and asked who was president of the United States. They answered, Andrew Jackson; but thinking that the old General could not have been elected for a third time, we hailed again, and they answered—Jack Downing; and left us to correct the mistake at our leisure.

It was just dinner-time when we filled away; and the steward, taking a few bunches of onions for the cabin, gave the rest to us, with a bottle of vinegar. We carried them forward, stowed them away in the forecastle, refusing to have them cooked, and ate them raw, with our beef and bread. And a glorious treat they were. The freshness and crispness of the raw onion, with the earthy taste, give it a great relish to one who has been a long time on salt provisions. We were perfectly ravenous after them. It was like a scent of blood to a hound. We ate them at every meal, by the dozen; and filled our pockets with them, to eat in our watch on deck; and the bunches, rising in the form of a cone, from the largest at the bottom, to the smallest, no larger than a strawberry, at the top, soon disappeared. The chief use, however, of the fresh provisions, was for the men with the scurvy. One of them was able to eat, and he soon brought him self to, by gnawing upon raw potatoes; but the other, by this time, was hardly able to open his mouth; and the cook took the potatoes raw, pounded them in a mortar, and gave him the juice to drink. This he swallowed, by the tea-spoonful at a time, and rinsed it about his gums and throat. The strong earthy taste and smell of this extract of the raw potato at first produced a shuddering through his whole frame, and after drinking it, an acute pain, which ran through all parts of his body; but knowing, by this, that it was taking strong hold, he persevered, drinking a spoonful every hour or so, and holding it a long time in his mouth; until, by the effect of this drink, and of his own restored hope, (for he had nearly given up, in despair) he became so well as to be able to move about, and open his mouth enough to eat the raw potatoes and onions pounded into a soft pulp. This course soon restored his appetite and strength; and in ten days after we spoke the Solon, so rapid was his recovery, that, from lying helpless and almost hopeless in his berth, he was at the mast-head, furling a royal.

With a fine south-west wind, we passed inside of the Bermudas; and notwithstanding the old couplet, which was quoted again and again by those who thought we should have one more touch of a storm before our voyage was up,—

> "If the Bermudas let you pass,
> You must beware of Hatteras—"

we were to the northward of Hatteras, with good weather, and beginning to count, not the days, but the hours, to the time when we should be at anchor in Boston harbor.

Our ship was in fine order, all hands having been hard at work upon her from daylight to dark, every day but Sunday, from the time we got into warm weather on this side the Cape.

It is a common notion with landsmen that a ship is in her finest condition when she leaves port to enter upon her voyage; and that she comes home, after a long absence,

> "With over-weathered ribs and ragged sails;
> Lean, rent and beggared by the strumpet wind."

But so far from that, unless a ship meets with some accident, or comes upon the coast in the dead of winter, when work cannot be done upon the rigging, she is in her finest order at the end of the voyage. When she sails from port, her rigging is generally slack; the masts need staying; the decks and sides are black and dirty from taking in cargo; riggers' seizings and overhand knots in place of nice seamanlike work; and everything, to a sailor's eye, adrift. But on the passage home, the fine weather between the tropics is spent in putting the ship into the neatest order. No merchant vessel looks better than an Indiaman, or a Cape Horn-er, after a long voyage; and many captains and mates will stake their reputation for seamanship upon the appearance of their ship when she hauls into the dock. All our standing rigging, fore and aft, was set up and tarred; the masts stayed; the lower and top-mast rigging rattled down, (or, up, as the fashion now is;) and so careful were our officers to keep the rattlins taught and straight, that we were obliged to go aloft upon the ropes and shearpoles with which the rigging was swifted in; and these were used as jury rattlins until we got close upon the coast. After this, the ship was scraped, inside and out, decks, masts, booms and all; a stage being rigged outside, upon which we scraped her down to the water-line; pounding the rust off the chains, bolts, and fastenings. Then, taking two days of calm under the line, we painted her on the outside, giving her open ports in her streak, and finishing off the nice work upon the stern, where sat Neptune in his car, holding his trident, drawn by sea horses; and re-touched the gilding and coloring of the cornucopia which ornamented her billet-head. The inside was then painted, from the sky-sail truck to the waterways—the yards black; mastheads and tops, white; monkey-rail, black, white, and yellow; bulwarks, green; plank-shear, white; waterways, lead color, &c. &c. The anchors and ring-bolts, and other iron work, were blackened with coal-tar; and the steward kept at work, polishing the brass of the wheel, bell, capstan, &c. The cabin, too, was scraped, varnished, and painted; and the forecastle scraped and scrubbed; there being no need of paint and varnish for Jack's quarters. The decks were then scraped and varnished, and everything useless thrown overboard; among which, the empty tar barrels were set on fire and thrown overboard, of a dark night, and left blazing astern, lighting up the ocean for miles. Add to all this labor, the neat work upon the rigging;— the knots, flemish-eyes, splices, seizings, coverings, pointings, and graffings, which show a ship in crack order. The last preparation, and which looked still more like coming into port, was getting the anchors over the bows, bending the cables, rowsing the hawsers up from between decks, and overhauling the deep-sea-lead-line.

Thursday, September 15th. This morning the temperature and peculiar appearance of the water, the quantities of gulf-weed floating about, and a bank of clouds lying directly before us, showed that we were on the border of the Gulf Stream. This remarkable current, running north-east, nearly across the ocean, is almost constantly shrouded in clouds, and is the region of storms and heavy seas. Vessels often run from a clear sky and light wind, with all sail, at once into a heavy sea and cloudy sky, with double-reefed top-sails. A sailor told me that on a passage from Gibraltar to Boston, his vessel neared the Gulf Stream with a light breeze, clear sky, and studding-sails out, alow and aloft; while, before it, was a long line of heavy, black clouds, lying like a bank upon the water, and a vessel

coming out of it, under double-reefed top-sails, and with royal
yards sent down. As they drew near, they began to take in sail
after sail, until they were reduced to the same condition; and,
after twelve or fourteen hours of rolling and pitching in a
heavy sea, before a smart gale, they ran out of the bank on the
other side, and were in fine weather again, and under their
royals and sky-sails. As we drew into it, the sky became cloudy,
the sea high, and everything had the appearance of the going
off, or the coming on, of a storm. It was blowing no more
than a stiff breeze; yet the wind, being north-east, which is
directly against the course of the current, made an ugly, chopping sea, which heaved and pitched the vessel about, so that
we were obliged to send down the royal yards, and to take in
our light sails. At noon, the thermometer, which had been repeatedly lowered into the water, showed the temperature to be
seventy; which was considerably above that of the air,—as is
always the case in the centre of the Stream. A lad who had
been at work at the royal mast-head, came down upon deck,
and took a turn round the long-boat; and looking very pale,
said he was so sick that he could stay aloft no longer, but was
ashamed to acknowledge it to the officer. He went up again,
but soon gave out and came down, and leaned over the rail, 'as
sick as a lady passenger.' He had been to sea several years, and
had, he said, never been sick before. He was made so by the irregular, pitching motion of the vessel, increased by the height
to which he had been above the hull, which is like the fulcrum
of the lever. An old sailor, who was at work on the top-gallant
yard, said he felt disagreeably all the time, and was glad, when
his job was done, to get down into the top, or upon deck. Another hand was sent to the royal mast-head, who staid nearly
an hour, but gave up. The work must be done, and the mate
sent me. I did very well for some time, but began at length to
feel very unpleasantly, though I had never been sick since the
first two days from Boston, and had been in all sorts of
weather and situations. Still, I kept my place, and did not come
down, until I had got through my work, which was more than
two hours. The ship certainly never acted so badly before. She
was pitched and jerked about in all manner of ways; the sails
seeming to have no steadying power over her. The tapering
points of the masts made various curves and angles against the

sky overhead, and sometimes, in one sweep of an instant, described an arc of more than forty-five degrees, bringing up with a sudden jerk which made it necessary to hold on with both hands, and then sweeping off, in another long, irregular curve. I was not positively sick, and came down with a look of indifference, yet was not unwilling to get upon the comparative terra firma of the deck. A few hours more carried us through, and when we saw the sun go down, upon our larboard beam, in the direction of the continent of North America, we had left the bank of dark, stormy clouds astern, in the twilight.

Chapter XXXVI

Friday, Sept. 16th. Lat. 38° N., long. 69° 00′ W. A fine south-west wind; every hour carrying us nearer in toward the land. All hands on deck at the dog watch, and nothing talked about, but our getting in; where we should make the land; whether we should arrive before Sunday; going to church; how Boston would look; friends; wages paid;—and the like. Every one was in the best spirits; and, the voyage being nearly at an end, the strictness of discipline was relaxed; for it was not necessary to order in a cross tone, what every one was ready to do with a will. The little differences and quarrels which a long voyage breeds on board a ship, were forgotten, and every one was friendly; and two men, who had been on the eve of a battle half the voyage, were laying out a plan together for a cruise on shore. When the mate came forward, he talked to the men, and said we should be on George's Bank before to-morrow noon; and joked with the boys, promising to go and see them, and to take them down to Marblehead in a coach.

Saturday, 17th. The wind was light all day, which kept us back somewhat; but a fine breeze springing up at nightfall, we were running fast in toward the land. At six o'clock we expected to have the ship hove-to for soundings, as a thick fog, coming up, showed we were near them; but no order was given, and we kept on our way. Eight o'clock came, and the watch went below, and, for the whole of the first hour, the ship was tearing on, with studding-sails out, alow and aloft, and the night as dark as a pocket. At two bells the captain came on deck, and said a word to the mate, when the studding-sails were hauled into the tops, or boom-ended, the after yards backed, the deep-sea-lead carried forward, and everything got ready for sounding. A man on the sprit-sail yard with the lead, another on the cat-head with a handful of the line coiled up, another in the fore chains, another in the waist, and another in the main chains, each with a quantity of the line coiled away in his hand. "All ready there, forward?"—"Aye, aye, sir!"— "He-e-ave!"—"Watch! ho! watch!" sings out the man on the sprit-sail yard, and the heavy lead drops into the water. "Watch!

ho! watch!" bawls the man on the cat-head, as the last fake of
the coil drops from his hand, and "Watch! ho! watch!" is
shouted by each one as the line falls from his hold; until it
comes to the mate, who tends the lead, and has the line in
coils on the quarter-deck. Eighty fathoms, and no bottom! A
depth as great as the height of St. Peters! The line is snatched
in a block upon the swifter, and three or four men haul it in
and coil it away. The after yards are braced full, the studding-
sails hauled out again, and in a few minutes more the ship had
her whole way upon her. At four bells, backed again, hove the
lead, and —soundings! at sixty fathoms! Hurrah for Yankee
land! Hand over hand, we hauled the lead in, and the captain,
taking it to the light, found black mud on the bottom. Studding-sails taken in; after yards filled, and ship kept on under
easy sail all night; the wind dying away.

The soundings on the American coast are so regular that
a navigator knows as well where he has made land, by the
soundings, as he would by seeing the land. Black mud is the
soundings of Block Island. As you go toward Nantucket, it
changes to a dark sand; then, sand and white shells; and on
George's Banks, white sand; and so on. Being off Block Island,
our course was due east, to Nantucket Shoals, and the South
Channel; but the wind died away and left us becalmed in a
thick fog, in which we lay the whole of Sunday. At noon of

Sunday, 18th, Block Island bore, by calculation, N.W. ¼ W.
fifteen miles; but the fog was so thick all day that we could see
nothing.

Having got through the ship's duty, and washed and shaved,
we went below, and had a fine time overhauling our chests,
laying aside the clothes we meant to go ashore in, and
throwing overboard all that were worn out and good for
nothing. Away went the woollen caps in which we had carried
hides upon our heads, for sixteen months, on the coast of California; the duck frocks, for tarring down rigging; and the
worn-out and darned mittens and patched woollen trowsers
which had stood the tug of Cape Horn. We hove them overboard with a good will; for there is nothing like being quit
of the very last appendages and remnants of our evil fortune.
We got our chests all ready for going ashore; ate the last 'duff'
we expected to have on board the ship Alert; and talked as

confidently about matters on shore as though our anchor were on the bottom.

"Who'll go to church with me a week from to-day?"

"I will," says Jack; who said aye to everything.

"Go away, salt water!" says Tom. "As soon as I get both legs ashore, I'm going to shoe my heels, and button my ears behind me, and start off into the bush, a straight course, and not stop till I'm out of the sight of salt water!"

"Oh! belay that! Spin that yarn where nobody knows your filling! If you get once moored, stem and stern, in old B——'s grog-shop, with a coal fire ahead and the bar under your lee, you won't see daylight for three weeks!"

"No!" says Tom, "I'm going to knock off grog, and go and board at the Home, and see if they won't ship me for a deacon!"

"And I," says Bill, "am going to buy a quadrant and ship for navigator of a Hingham packet!"

These and the like jokes served to pass the time while we were lying waiting for a breeze to clear up the fog and send us on our way.

Toward night a moderate breeze sprang up; the fog however continuing as thick as before; and we kept on to the eastward. About the middle of the first watch, a man on the forecastle sang out, in a tone which showed that there was not a moment to be lost,—"Hard up the helm!" and a great ship loomed up out of the fog, coming directly down upon us. She luffed at the same moment, and we just passed one another; our spanker boom grazing over her quarter. The officer of the deck had only time to hail, and she answered, as she went into the fog again, something about Bristol— Probably, a whaleman from Bristol, Rhode Island, bound out. The fog continued through the night, with a very light breeze, before which we ran to the eastward, literally feeling our way along. The lead was heaved every two hours and the gradual change from black mud to sand, showed that we were approaching Nantucket South Shoals. On Monday morning, the increased depth and deep blue color of the water, and the mixture of shells and white sand which we brought up, upon sounding, showed that we were in the channel, and nearing George's; accordingly, the ship's head was put directly to the northward, and we stood on, with perfect confidence in the soundings, though we had not taken an observation for two days, nor seen land; and the difference of an eighth of a mile out of the way might put us ashore. Throughout the day a provokingly light wind prevailed, and at eight o'clock, a small fishing schooner, which we passed, told us we were nearly abreast of Chatham lights. Just before midnight, a light land-breeze sprang up, which carried us well along; and at four o'clock, thinking ourselves to the northward of Race Point, we hauled upon the wind and stood into the bay, north-north-west, for Boston light, and commenced firing guns for a pilot. Our watch went below at four o'clock, but could not sleep, for the watch on deck were banging away at the guns every few minutes. And, indeed, we cared very little about it, for we were in Boston Bay; and if fortune favored us, we could all 'sleep in' the next night, with nobody to call the watch every four hours.

We turned out, of our own will, at daybreak, to get a sight of land. In the grey of the morning, one or two small fishing smacks peered out of the mist; and when the broad day broke upon us, there lay the low sand-hills of Cape Cod, over our larboard quarter, and before us, the wide waters of Massachusetts Bay, with here and there a sail gliding over its smooth surface. As we drew in toward the mouth of the harbor, as toward a focus, the vessels began to multiply, until the bay seemed actually alive with sails gliding about in every direction; some on the wind, and others before it, as they were bound to or from the emporium of trade and centre of the bay. It was a stirring sight for us, who had been months on the ocean without seeing anything but two solitary sails; and over two years without seeing more than the three or four traders on an almost desolate coast. There were the little coasters, bound to and from the various towns along the south shore, down in the bight of the bay, and to the eastward; here and there a square-rigged vessel standing out to seaward; and, far in the distance, beyond Cape Ann, was the smoke of a steamer, stretching along in a narrow, black cloud upon the water. Every sight was full of beauty and interest. We were coming back to our homes; and the signs of civilization, and prosperity, and happiness, from which we had been so long banished, were multiplying about us. The high land of Cape Ann and the rocks and shore of Cohasset were full in sight, the light-houses, standing like sentries in white before the harbors, and even the smoke from the chimneys on the plains of Hingham was seen rising slowly in the morning air. One of our boys was the son of a bucket-maker; and his face lighted up as he saw the tops of the well-known hills which surround his native place. About ten o'clock a little boat came bobbing over the water, and put a pilot on board, and sheered off in pursuit of other vessels bound in. Being now within the scope of the telegraph stations, our signals were run up at the fore, and in half an hour afterwards, the owner on 'change, or in his counting-room, knew that his ship was below; and the landlords, runners, and sharks in Ann street learned that there was a rich prize for them down in the bay: a ship from round the Horn, with a crew to be paid off with two years' wages.

The wind continuing very light; all hands were sent aloft to strip off the chafing gear; and battens, parcellings, roundings, hoops, mats, and leathers, came flying from aloft, and left the rigging neat and clean, stripped of all its sea bandaging. The last touch was put to the vessel by painting the sky-sail poles; and I was sent up to the fore, with a bucket of white paint and a brush, and touched her off, from the truck to the eyes of the royal rigging. At noon, we lay becalmed off the lower light-house; and it being about slack water, we made little progress. A firing was heard in the direction of Hingham, and the pilot said there was a review there. The Hingham boy got wind of this, and said if the ship had been twelve hours sooner, he should have been down among the soldiers, and in the booths, and having a grand time. As it was, we had little prospect of getting in before night. About two o'clock a breeze sprang up ahead, from the westward, and we began beating up against it. A full-rigged brig was beating in at the same time, and we passed one another, in our tacks, sometimes one and sometimes the other, working to windward, as the wind and tide favored or opposed. It was my trick at the wheel from two till four; and I stood my last helm, making between nine hundred and a thousand hours which I had spent at the helms of our two vessels. The tide beginning to set against us, we made slow work; and the afternoon was nearly spent, before we got abreast of the inner light. In the mean time, several vessels were coming down, outward bound; among which, a fine, large ship, with yards squared, fair wind and fair tide, passed us like a race-horse, the men running out upon her yards to rig out the studding-sail booms. Toward sundown the wind came off in flaws, sometimes blowing very stiff, so that the pilot took in the royals, and then it died away; when, in order to get us in before the tide became too strong, the royals were set again. As this kept us running up and down the rigging all the time, one hand was sent aloft at each mast-head, to stand-by to loose and furl the sails, at the moment of the order. I took my place at the fore, and loosed and furled the royal five times between Rainsford Island and the Castle. At one tack we ran so near to Rainsford Island, that, looking down from the royal yard, the island, with its hospital buildings, nice gravelled walks, and green plats, seemed to lie directly under our yard-arms. So close is the channel to some of these islands, that we ran the end of our flying-jib-boom over one of the out-works of the fortifications on George's Island; and had an opportunity of seeing the advantages of that point as a fortified place; for, in working up the channel, we presented a fair stem and stern, for raking, from the batteries, three or four times. One gun might have knocked us to pieces.

We had all set our hearts upon getting up to town before night and going ashore, but the tide beginning to run strong against us, and the wind, what there was of it, being ahead, we made but little by weather-bowing the tide, and the pilot gave orders to cock-bill the anchor and overhaul the chain. Making two long stretches, which brought us into the roads, under the lee of the Castle, he clewed up the top-sails, and let go the anchor; and for the first time since leaving San Diego,—one hundred and thirty-five days—our anchor was upon bottom. In half an hour more, we were lying snugly, with all sails furled, safe in Boston harbor; our long voyage ended; the well-known scene about us; the dome of the State House fading in the western sky; the lights of the city starting into sight, as the darkness came on; and at nine o'clock the clangor of the bells, ringing their accustomed peals; among which the Boston boys tried to distinguish the well-known tone of the Old South.

We had just done furling the sails, when a beautiful little pleasure-boat luffed up into the wind, under our quarter, and the junior partner of the firm to which our ship belonged, jumped on board. I saw him from the mizen top-sail yard, and knew him well. He shook the captain by the hand, and went down into the cabin, and in a few moments came up and inquired of the mate for me. The last time I had seen him, I was in the uniform of an under-graduate of Harvard College, and now, to his astonishment, there came down from aloft a 'rough alley' looking fellow, with duck trowsers and red shirt, long hair, and face burnt as black as an Indian's. He shook me by the hand, congratulated me upon my return and my appearance of health and strength, and said my friends were all well. I thanked him for telling me what I should not have dared to ask; and if—

> ——"the first bringer of unwelcome news
> Hath but a losing office; and his tongue
> Sounds ever after like a sullen bell—"

certainly I shall ever remember this man and his words with pleasure.

The captain went up to town in the boat with Mr. H——, and left us to pass another night on board ship, and to come up with the morning's tide under command of the pilot.

So much did we feel ourselves to be already at home, in anticipation, that our plain supper of hard bread and salt beef was barely touched; and many on board, to whom this was the first voyage, could scarcely sleep. As for myself, by one of those anomalous changes of feeling of which we are all the subjects, I found that I was in a state of indifference, for which I could by no means account. A year before, while carrying hides on the coast, the assurance that in a twelvemonth we should see Boston, made me half wild; but now that I was actually there, and in sight of home, the emotions which I had so long anticipated feeling, I did not find, and in their place was a state of very nearly entire apathy. Something of the same experience was related to me by a sailor whose first voyage was one of five years upon the North-west Coast. He had left home, a lad, and after several years of very hard and trying experience, found himself homeward bound; and such was the excitement of his feelings that, during the whole passage, he could talk and think of nothing else but his arrival, and how and when he should jump from the vessel and take his way directly home. Yet when the vessel was made fast to the wharf and the crew dismissed, he seemed suddenly to lose all feeling about the matter. He told me that he went below and changed his dress; took some water from the scuttle-butt and washed himself leisurely; overhauled his chest, and put his clothes all in order; took his pipe from its place, filled it, and sitting down upon his chest, smoked it slowly for the last time. Here he looked round upon the forecastle in which he had spent so many years, and being alone and his shipmates scattered, he began to feel actually unhappy. Home became almost a dream; and it was not until his brother (who had heard of the ship's arrival) came down into the forecastle and told him of things at home, and who were waiting there to see him, that he could realize where he was, and feel interest enough to put him in motion toward that place for which he had longed, and of which he had dreamed, for years. There is probably so much of excitement in prolonged expectation, that the quiet realizing of it produces a momentary stagnation of feeling as well as of effort. It was a good deal so with me. The activity of preparation, the rapid progress of the ship, the first making land, the coming up the harbor, and old scenes breaking upon the view, produced a mental as well as bodily activity, from which the change to a perfect stillness, when both expectation and the necessity of labor failed, left a calmness, almost of indifference, from which I must be roused by some new excitement. And the next morning, when all hands were called, and we were busily at work, clearing the decks, and getting everything in readiness for going up to the wharves,—loading the guns for a salute, loosing the sails, and manning the windlass—mind and body seemed to wake together.

About ten o'clock, a sea-breeze sprang up, and the pilot gave orders to get the ship under weigh. All hands manned the windlass, and the long-drawn "Yo, heave, ho!" which we had last heard dying away among the desolate hills of San Diego, soon brought the anchor to the bows; and, with a fair wind and tide, a bright sunny morning, royals and sky-sails set, ensign, streamer, signals, and pennant, flying, and with our guns firing, we came swiftly and handsomely up to the city. Off the end of the wharf, we rounded-to and let go our anchor; and no sooner was it on the bottom, than the decks were filled with people: custom-house officers; Topliff's agent, to inquire for news; others, inquiring for friends on board, or left upon the coast; dealers in grease, besieging the galley to make a bargain with the cook for his slush; 'loafers' in general; and last and chief, boarding-house runners, to secure their men. Nothing can exceed the obliging disposition of these runners, and the interest they take in a sailor returned from a long voyage with a plenty of money. Two or three of them, at different times, took me by the hand; remembered me perfectly; were quite sure I had boarded with them before I sailed; were delighted to see me back; gave me their cards; had a hand-cart waiting on the wharf, on purpose to take my things up; would lend me a hand to get my chest ashore; bring a bottle of grog on board if we did not haul in immediately,—and the like. In fact, we could hardly get clear of them, to go aloft and furl the sails. Sail after sail, for the hundredth time, in fair weather and in foul, we furled now for the last time together, and came down and took the warp ashore, manned the capstan, and with a chorus which waked up half the North End, and rang among the buildings in the dock, we hauled her in to the wharf. Here, too, the landlords and runners were active and ready, taking a bar to the capstan, lending a hand at the ropes, laughing and talking and telling the news. The city bells were just ringing one when the last turn was made fast, and the crew dismissed; and in five minutes more, not a soul was left on board the good ship Alert, but the old ship-keeper, who had come down from the counting-house to take charge of her.

Concluding Chapter

I TRUST that they who have followed me to the end of my narrative, will not refuse to carry their attention a little farther, to the concluding remarks which I here present to them.

This chapter is written after the lapse of a considerable time since the end of my voyage, and after a return to my former pursuits; and in it I design to offer those views of what may be done for seamen, and of what is already doing, which I have deduced from my experiences, and from the attention which I have since gladly given to the subject.

The romantic interest which many take in the sea, and in those who live upon it, may be of use in exciting their attention to this subject, though I cannot but feel sure that all who have followed me in my narrative must be convinced that the sailor has no romance in his every-day life to sustain him, but that it is very much the same plain, matter-of-fact drudgery and hardship, which would be experienced on shore. If I have not produced this conviction, I have failed in persuading others of what my own experience has most fully impressed upon myself.

There is a witchery in the sea, its songs and stories, and in the mere sight of a ship, and the sailor's dress, especially to a young mind, which has done more to man navies, and fill merchantmen, than all the pressgangs of Europe. I have known a young man with such a passion for the sea, that the very creaking of a block stirred up his imagination so that he could hardly keep his feet on dry ground; and many are the boys, in every seaport, who are drawn away, as by an almost irresistible attraction, from their work and schools, and hang about the decks and yards of vessels, with a fondness which, it is plain, will have its way. No sooner, however, has the young sailor begun his new life in earnest, than all this fine drapery falls off, and he learns that it is but work and hardship, after all. This is the true light in which a sailor's life is to be viewed; and if in our books, and anniversary speeches, we would leave out much that is said about 'blue water,' 'blue jackets,' 'open hearts,' 'seeing God's hand on the deep,' and so forth, and take this up like any other practical subject, I am quite sure we should do full as much for those we wish to benefit. The question is, what can be done for sailors, as they are,—men to be fed, and clothed, and lodged, for whom laws must be made and executed, and who are to be instructed in useful knowledge, and, above all, to be brought under religious influence and restraint? It is upon these topics that I wish to make a few observations.

In the first place, I have no fancies about equality on board ship. It is a thing out of the question, and certainly, in the present state of mankind, not to be desired. I never knew a sailor who found fault with the orders and ranks of the service; and if I expected to pass the rest of my life before the mast, I would not wish to have the power of the captain diminished an iota. It is absolutely necessary that there should be one head and one voice, to control everything, and be responsible for everything. There are emergencies which require the instant exercise of extreme power. These emergencies do not allow of consultation; and they who would be the captain's constituted advisers might be the very men over whom he would be called upon to exert his authority. It has been found necessary to vest in every government, even the most democratic, some extraordinary, and, at first sight, alarming powers; trusting in public opinion, and subsequent accountability, to modify the exercise of them. These are provided to meet exigencies, which all hope may never occur, but which yet by possibility may occur, and if they should, and there were no power to meet them instantly, there would be an end put to the government at once. So it is with the authority of the shipmaster. It will not answer to say that he shall never do this and that thing, because it does not seem always necessary and advisable that it should be done. He has great cares and responsibilities; is answerable for everything; and is subject to emergencies which perhaps no other man exercising authority among civilized people is subject to. Let him, then, have powers commensurate with his utmost possible need; only let him be held strictly responsible for the exercise of them. Any other course would be injustice, as well as bad policy.

In the treatment of those under his authority, the captain is amenable to the common law, like any other person. He is liable at common law for murder, assault and battery, and other offences; and in addition to this, there is a special statute of the United States which makes a captain or other officer liable to imprisonment for a term not exceeding five years, and to a fine not exceeding a thousand dollars, for inflicting any cruel punishment upon, withholding food from, or in any other way maltreating a seaman. This is the state of the law on the subject; while the relation in which the parties stand, and the peculiar necessities, excuses, and provocations arising from that relation, are merely circumstances to be considered in each case. As to the restraints upon the master's exercise of power, the laws themselves seem, on the whole, to be sufficient. I do not see that we are in need, at present, of more legislation on the subject. The difficulty lies rather in the administration of the laws; and this is certainly a matter that deserves great consideration, and one of no little embarrassment.

In the first place, the courts have said that public policy requires the power of the master and officers should be sustained. Many lives and a great amount of property are constantly in their hands, for which they are strictly responsible. To preserve these, and to deal justly by the captain, and not lay upon him a really fearful responsibility, and then tie up his hands, it is essential that discipline should be supported. In the second place, there is always great allowance to be made for false swearing and exaggeration by seamen, and for combinations among them against their officers; and it is to be remembered that the latter have often no one to testify on their side. These are weighty and true statements, and should not be lost sight of by the friends of seamen. On the other hand, sailors make many complaints, some of which are well founded.

On the subject of testimony, seamen labor under a difficulty full as great as that of the captain. It is a well-known fact, that they are usually much better treated when there are passengers on board. The presence of passengers is a restraint upon the captain, not only from his regard to their feelings and to the estimation in which they may hold him, but because he knows they will be influential witnesses against him if he is brought to trial. Though officers may sometimes be inclined to show themselves off before passengers, by freaks of office and authority, yet cruelty they would hardly dare to be guilty of. It is on long and distant voyages, where there is no restraint upon the captain, and none but the crew to testify against him, that sailors need most the protection of the law. On such voyages as these, there are many cases of outrageous cruelty on record, enough to make one heart-sick, and almost disgusted with the sight of man; and many, many more, which have never come to light, and never will be known, until the sea shall give up its dead. Many of these have led to mutiny and piracy,— stripe for stripe, and blood for blood. If on voyages of this description the testimony of seamen is not to be received in favor of one another, or too great a deduction is made on account of their being seamen, their case is without remedy; and the captain, knowing this, will be strengthened in that disposition to tyrannize which the possession of absolute power, without the restraints of friends and public opinion, is too apt to engender.

It is to be considered, also, that the sailor comes into court under very different circumstances from the master. He is thrown among landlords, and sharks of all descriptions; is often led to drink freely; and comes upon the stand unaided, and under a certain cloud of suspicion as to his character and veracity. The captain, on the other hand, is backed by the owners and insurers, and has an air of greater respectability; though, after all, he may have but a little better education than the sailor, and sometimes, (especially among those engaged in certain voyages that I could mention) a very hackneyed conscience.

These are the considerations most commonly brought up on the subject of seamen's evidence; and I think it cannot but be obvious to every one that here, positive legislation would be of no manner of use. There can be no rule of law regulating the weight to be given to seamen's evidence. It must rest in the mind of the judge and jury; and no enactment or positive rule of court could vary the result a hair, in any one case. The effect of a sailor's testimony in deciding a case must depend altogether upon the reputation of the class to which he belongs, and upon the impression he himself produces in court by his deportment, and by those infallible marks of character which always tell upon a jury. In fine, after all the well-meant and specious projects that have been brought forward, we seem driven back to the belief, that the best means of securing a fair administration of the laws made for the protection of seamen, and certainly the only means which can create any important change for the better, is the gradual one of raising the intellectual and religious character of the sailor, so that as an individual, and as one of a class, he may, in the first instance, command the respect of his officers, and if any difficulty should happen, may upon the stand carry that weight which an intelligent and respectable man of the lower class almost always does with a jury. I know there are many men who, when a few cases of great hardship occur, and it is evident that there is an evil somewhere, think that some arrangement must be made, some law passed, or some society got up, to set all right at once. On this subject there can be no call for any such movement; on the contrary, I fully believe that any public and strong action would do harm, and that we must be satisfied to labor in the less easy and less exciting task of gradual improvement, and abide the issue of things working slowly together for good.

Equally injudicious would be any interference with the economy of the ship. The lodging, food, hours of sleep, &c., are all matters which, though capable of many changes for the better, must yet be left to regulate themselves. And I am confident that there will be, and that there is now a gradual improvement in all such particulars. The forecastles of most of our ships are small, black, and wet holes, which few landsmen would believe held a crew of ten or twelve men on a voyage of months or years; and often, indeed in most cases, the provisions are not good enough to make a meal anything more than a necessary part of a day's duty;* and on the score of sleep, I

---

*I am not sure that I have stated, in the course of my narrative, the manner in which sailors eat, on board ship. There are neither tables, knives, forks, nor plates, in a forecastle; but the kid (a wooden tub, with iron hoops) is placed on the floor, and the crew sit round it, and each man cuts for himself with the common jack-knife or sheath-knife, that he carries about him. They drink their tea out of tin pots, holding little less than a quart each.

These particulars are not looked upon as hardships, and, indeed, may be considered matters of choice. Sailors, in our merchantmen, furnish their own eating utensils, as they do many of the instruments which they use in the ship's work, such as knives, palms and needles, marline-spikes, rubbers, &c. And considering their mode of life in other respects, the little time they would have for laying and clearing away a table with its apparatus, and the room it would take up in a forecastle, as well as the simple character of their meals, consisting

fully believe that the lives of merchant seamen are shortened by the want of it. I do not refer to those occasions when it is necessarily broken in upon; but, for months, during fine weather, in many merchantmen, all hands are kept, throughout the day, and, then, there are eight hours on deck for one watch each night. Thus it is usually the case that at the end of a voyage, where there has been the finest weather, and no disaster, the crew have a wearied and worn-out appearance. They never sleep longer than four hours at a time, and are seldom called without being really in need of more rest. There is no one thing that a sailor thinks more of as a luxury of life on shore, than a whole night's sleep. Still, all these things must be left to be gradually modified by circumstances. Whenever hard cases occur, they should be made known, and masters and owners should be held answerable, and will, no doubt, in time, be influenced in their arrangements and discipline by the increased consideration in which sailors are held by the public. It is perfectly proper that the men should live in a different part of the vessel from the officers; and if the forecastle is made large and comfortable, there is no reason why the crew should not live there as well as in any other part. In fact, sailors prefer the forecastle. It is their accustomed place, and in it they are out of the sight and hearing of their officers.

As to their food and sleep, there are laws, with heavy penalties, requiring a certain amount of stores to be on board, and safely stowed; and, for depriving the crew unnecessarily of food or sleep, the captain is liable at common law, as well as under the statute before referred to. Farther than this, it would not be safe to go. The captain must be the judge when it is necessary to keep his crew from their sleep; and sometimes a retrenching, not of the necessaries, but of some of the little niceties of their meals, as, for instance, *duff* on Sunday, may be a mode of punishment, though I think generally an injudicious one.

---

generally of only one piece of meat,—it is certainly a convenient method, and, as the kid and pans are usually kept perfectly clean, a neat and simple one. I had supposed these things to be generally known, until I heard, a few months ago, a lawyer of repute, who has had a good deal to do with marine cases, ask a sailor upon the stand whether the crew had "got up from table" when a certain thing happened.

I could not do justice to this subject without noticing one part of the discipline of a ship, which has been very much discussed of late, and has brought out strong expressions of indignation from many,—I mean the infliction of corporal punishment. Those who have followed me in my narrative will remember that I was witness to an act of great cruelty inflicted upon my own shipmates; and indeed I can sincerely say that the simple mention of the word flogging, brings up in me feelings which I can hardly control. Yet, when the proposition is made to abolish it entirely and at once; to prohibit the captain from ever, under any circumstances, inflicting corporal punishment; I am obliged to pause, and, I must say, to doubt exceedingly the expediency of making any positive enactment which shall have that effect. If the design of those who are writing on this subject is merely to draw public attention to it, and to discourage the practice of flogging, and bring it into disrepute, it is well; and, indeed, whatever may be the end they have in view, the mere agitation of the question will have that effect, and, so far, must do good. Yet I should not wish to take the command of a ship to-morrow, running my chance of a crew, as most masters must, and know, and have my crew know, that I could not, under any circumstances, inflict even moderate chastisement. I should trust that I might never have to resort to it; and, indeed, I scarcely know what risk I would not run, and to what inconvenience I would not subject myself, rather than do so. Yet not to have the power of holding it up *in terrorem*, and indeed of protecting myself, and all under my charge, by it, if some extreme case should arise, would be a situation I should not wish to be placed in myself, or to take the responsibility of placing another in.

Indeed, the difficulties into which masters and officers are liable to be thrown, are not sufficiently considered by many whose sympathies are easily excited by stories, frequent enough, and true enough, of outrageous abuse of this power. It is to be remembered that more than three fourths of the seamen in our merchant vessels are foreigners. They are from all parts of the world. A great many from the north of Europe, beside Frenchmen, Spaniards, Portuguese, Italians, men from all parts of the Mediterranean, together with Lascars, Negroes, and, perhaps worst of all, the off-casts of British men-of-war, and men from our own country who have gone to sea because they could not be permitted to live on land.

As things now are, many masters are obliged to sail without knowing anything of their crews, until they get out at sea. There may be pirates or mutineers among them; and one bad man will often infect all the rest; and it is almost certain that some of them will be ignorant foreigners, hardly understanding a word of our language, accustomed all their lives to no influence but force, and perhaps nearly as familiar with the use of the knife as with that of the marline-spike. No prudent master, however peaceably inclined, would go to sea without his pistols and handcuffs. Even with such a crew as I have supposed, kindness and moderation would be the best policy, and the duty of every conscientious man; and the administering of corporal punishment might be dangerous, and of doubtful use. But the question is not, what a captain ought generally to do, but whether it shall be put out of the power of every captain, under any circumstances, to make use of, even moderate, chastisement. As the law now stands, a parent may correct moderately his child, and the master his apprentice; and the case of the shipmaster has been placed upon the same principle. The statutes, and the common law as expounded in the decisions of courts, and in the books of commentators, are express and unanimous to this point, that the captain may inflict moderate corporal chastisement, for a reasonable cause. If the punishment is excessive, or the cause not sufficient to justify it, he is answerable; and the jury are to determine, by their verdict in each case, whether, under all the circumstances, the punishment was moderate, and for a justifiable cause.

This seems to me to be as good a position as the whole subject can be left in. I mean to say, that no positive enactment, going beyond this, is needed, or would be a benefit either to masters or men, in the present state of things. This again would seem to be a case which should be left to the gradual working of its own cure. As seamen improve, punishment will become less necessary; and as the character of officers is raised, they will be less ready to inflict it; and, still more, the infliction of it upon intelligent and respectable men, will be an enormity which will not be tolerated by public opinion, and by juries, who are the pulse of the body politic. No one can have a greater abhorrence of the infliction of such punishment than I have, and a stronger conviction that severity is bad policy with a crew; yet I would ask every reasonable man whether he had not better trust to the practice becoming unnecessary and disreputable; to the measure of moderate chastisement and a justifiable cause being better understood, and thus, the act becoming dangerous, and in course of time to be regarded as an unheard-of barbarity—than to take the responsibility of prohibiting it, at once, in all cases, and in whatever degree, by positive enactment?

There is, however, one point connected with the administration of justice to seamen, to which I wish seriously to call the attention of those interested in their behalf, and, if possible, also of some of those concerned in that administration. This is, the practice which prevails of making strong appeals to the jury in mitigation of damages, or to the judge, after a verdict has been rendered against a captain or officer, for a lenient sentence, on the grounds of their previous good character, and of their being poor, and having friends and families depending upon them for support. These appeals have been allowed a weight which is almost incredible, and which, I think, works a greater hardship upon seamen than any one other thing in the laws, or the execution of them. Notwithstanding every advantage the captain has over the seaman in point of evidence, friends, money, and able counsel, it becomes apparent that he must fail in his defence. An appeal is then made to the jury, if it is a civil action, or to the judge for a mitigated sentence, if it is a criminal prosecution, on the two grounds I have mentioned. The same form is usually gone through in every case. In the first place, as to the previous good character of the party. Witnesses are brought from the town in which he resides, to testify to his good character, and to his unexceptionable conduct when on shore. They say that he is a good father, or husband, or son, or neighbor, and that they never saw in him any signs of cruel or tyrannical disposition. I have even known evidence admitted to show the character he bore when a boy at school. The owners of the vessel, and other merchants, and perhaps the president of the insurance company, are then introduced; and they testify to his correct deportment, express their confidence in his honesty, and say that they have never seen anything in his conduct to justify a suspicion of his being capable of cruelty or tyranny. This evidence is then put together, and great stress is laid upon the extreme respectability of those who give it. They are the companions and neighbors of the captain, it is said,—men who know him in his business and domestic relations, and who knew him in his early youth. They are also men of the highest standing in the community, and who, as the captain's employers, must be supposed to know his character. This testimony is then contrasted with that of some half dozen obscure sailors, who, the counsel will not forget to add, are exasperated against the captain because he has found it necessary to punish them moderately, and who have combined against him, and if they have not fabricated a story entirely, have at least so exaggerated it, that little confidence can be placed in it.

The next thing to be done is to show to the court and jury that the captain is a poor man, and has a wife and family, or other friends, depending upon him for support; that if he is fined, it will only be taking bread from the mouths of the innocent and helpless, and laying a burden upon them which their whole lives will not be able to work off; and that if he is imprisoned, the confinement, to be sure, he will have to bear, but the distress consequent upon the cutting him off from his labor and means of earning his wages, will fall upon a poor wife and helpless children, or upon an infirm parent. These two topics, well put, and urged home earnestly, seldom fail of their effect.

In deprecation of this mode of proceeding, and in behalf of men who I believe are every day wronged by it, I would urge a few considerations which seem to me to be conclusive.

First, as to the evidence of the good character the captain sustains on shore. It is to be remembered that masters of vessels have usually been brought up in a forecastle; and upon all men, and especially upon those taken from lower situations, the conferring of absolute power is too apt to work a great change. There are many captains whom I know to be cruel and tyrannical men at sea, who yet, among their friends, and in their families, have never lost the reputation they bore in childhood. In fact, the sea-captain is seldom at home, and when he is, his stay is short, and during the continuance of it he is surrounded by friends who treat him with kindness and consideration, and he has everything to please, and at the same time to restrain him. He would be a brute indeed, if, after an absence of months or years, during his short stay, so short that the novelty and excitement of it has hardly time to wear off, and the attentions he receives as a visiter and stranger hardly time to slacken,—if, under such circumstances, a townsman or neighbor would be justified in testifying against his correct and peaceable deportment. With the owners of the vessel, also, to which he is attached, and among merchants and insurers generally, he is a very different man from what he may be at sea, when his own master, and the master of everybody and everything about him. He knows that upon such men, and their good opinion of him, he depends for his bread. So far from their testimony being of any value in determining what his conduct would be at sea, one would expect that the master who would abuse and impose upon a man under his power, would be the most compliant and deferential to his employers at home.

As to the appeal made in the captain's behalf on the ground of his being poor and having persons depending upon his labor for support, the main and fatal objection to it is, that it will cover every case of the kind, and exempt nearly the whole body of masters and officers from the punishment the law has provided for them. There are very few, if any, masters or other officers of merchantmen in our country, who are not poor men, and having either parents, wives, children, or other relatives, depending mainly or wholly upon their exertions for support in life. Few others follow the sea for subsistence. Now if this appeal is to have weight with courts in diminishing the penalty the law would otherwise inflict, is not the whole class under a privilege which will, in a degree, protect it in wrong-doing? It is not a thing that happens now and then. It is the invariable appeal, the last resort, of counsel, when everything else has failed. I have known cases of the most flagrant nature, where, after every effort has been made for the captain, and yet a verdict rendered against him, and all other hope failed, this appeal has been urged, and with such success that the punishment has been reduced to something little more than nominal; the court not seeming to consider that it might be made in almost every such case that could come before them. It is a little singular, too, that it seems to be confined to cases of shipmasters and officers. No one ever heard of a sentence, for an offence committed on shore, being reduced by the court on the ground of the prisoner's poverty, and the relation in which he may stand to third persons. On the contrary, it has been thought that the certainty that disgrace and suffering will be brought upon others as well as himself, is one of the chief restraints upon the criminally disposed. Besides, this course works a peculiar hardship in the case of the sailor. For if poverty is the point in question, the sailor is the poorer of the two; and if there is a man on earth who depends upon whole limbs and an unbroken spirit for support, it is the sailor. He, too, has friends to whom his hard earnings may be a relief, and whose hearts will bleed at any cruelty or indignity practised upon him. Yet I never knew this side of the case to be once adverted to in these arguments addressed to the leniency of the court, which are now so much in vogue; and certainly they are never allowed a moment's consideration when a sailor is on trial for revolt, or for an injury done to an officer. Notwithstanding the many difficulties which lie in a seaman's way in a court of justice, presuming that they will be modified in time, there would be little to complain of, were it not for these two appeals.

It is no cause of complaint that the testimony of seamen against their officers is viewed with suspicion, and that great allowance is made for combinations and exaggeration. On the contrary, it is the judge's duty to charge the jury on these points, strongly. But there is reason for objection, when, after a strict cross examination of witnesses, after the arguments of counsel, and the judge's charge, a verdict is found against the master, that the court should allow the practice of hearing appeals to its lenity, supported solely by evidence of the captain's good conduct when on shore, (especially where the case is one in which no evidence but that of sailors could have been brought against the accused,) and then, on this ground, and on the invariable claims of the wife and family, be induced to cut down essentially the penalty imposed by a statute made expressly for masters and officers of merchantmen, and for no one else.

There are many particulars connected with the manning of vessels, the provisions given to crews, and the treatment of them while at sea, upon which there might be a good deal said; but as I have, for the most part, remarked upon them as they came up in the course of my narrative, I will offer nothing further now, except on the single point of the manner of shipping men. This, it is well known, is usually left entirely to shipping-masters, and is a cause of a great deal of difficulty, which might be remedied by the captain, or owner, if he has any knowledge of seamen, attending to it personally. One of the members of the firm to which our ship belonged, Mr. S——, had been himself a master of a vessel, and generally selected the crew from a number sent down to him from the shipping-office. In this way he almost always had healthy, serviceable, and respectable men; for any one who has seen much of sailors can tell pretty well at first sight, by a man's dress, countenance, and deportment, what he would be on board ship. This same gentleman was also in the habit of seeing the crew together, and speaking to them previously to their sailing. On the day before our ship sailed, while the crew were getting their chests and clothes on board, he went down into the forecastle and spoke to them about the voyage, the clothing they would need, the provision he had made for them, and saw that they had a lamp and a few other conveniences. If owners or masters would more generally take the same pains, they would often save their crews a good deal of inconvenience, beside creating a sense of satisfaction and gratitude, which makes a voyage begin under good auspices, and goes far toward keeping up a better state of feeling throughout its continuance.

It only remains for me now to speak of the associated public efforts which have been making of late years for the good of seamen: a far more agreeable task than that of finding fault, even where fault there is. The exertions of the general association, called the American Seamen's Friend Society, and of the other smaller societies throughout the Union, have been a true blessing to the seaman; and bid fair, in course of time, to change the whole nature of the circumstances in which he is placed, and give him a new name, as well as a new character. These associations have taken hold in the right way, and aimed both at making the sailor's life more comfortable and creditable, and at giving him spiritual instruction. Connected with these efforts, the spread of temperance among seamen, by means of societies, called, in their own nautical language, Windward-Anchor Societies, and the distribution of books; the establishment of Sailors' Homes, where they can be comfortably and cheaply boarded, live quietly and decently, and be in the way of religious services, reading and conversation; also the institution of Savings Banks for Seamen; the distribution of tracts and Bibles;—are all means which are silently doing a great work for this class of men. These societies make the religious instruction of seamen their prominent object. If this is gained, there is no fear but that all other things necessary will be added unto them. A sailor never becomes interested in religion, without immediately learning to read, if he did not know how before; and regular habits, forehandedness (if I may use the word) in worldly affairs, and hours reclaimed from indolence and vice, which follow in the wake of the converted man, make it sure that he will instruct himself in the knowledge necessary and suitable to his calling. The religious change is the great object. If this is secured, there is no fear but that knowledge of things of the world will come in fast enough. With the sailor, as with all other men in fact, the cultivation of the intellect, and the spread of what is commonly called useful knowledge, while religious instruction is neglected, is little else than changing an ignorant sinner into an intelligent and powerful one. That sailor upon whom, of all others, the preaching of the Cross is least likely to have effect, is the one whose understanding has been cultivated, while his heart has been left to its own devices. I fully believe that those efforts which have their end in the intellectual cultivation of the sailor; in giving him scientific knowledge; putting it in his power to read everything, without securing, first of all, a right heart which shall guide him in judgment; in giving him political information, and interesting him in newspapers;—an end in the furtherance of which he is exhibited at ladies' fairs and public meetings, and complimented for his gallantry and generosity,—are all doing a harm which the labors of many faithful men cannot undo.

The establishment of Bethels in most of our own seaports, and in many foreign ports frequented by our vessels, where the gospel is regularly preached; and the opening of 'Sailors' Homes,' which I have before mentioned, where there are usually religious services and other good influences, are doing a vast deal in this cause. But it is to be remembered that the sailor's home is on the deep. Nearly all his life must be spent on board ship; and to secure a religious influence there, should be the great object. The distribution of Bibles and tracts into cabins and forecastles, will do much toward this. There is nothing which will gain a sailor's attention sooner, and interest him more deeply, than a tract, especially one which contains a story. It is difficult to engage their attention in mere essays and arguments, but the simplest and shortest story, in which home is spoken of, kind friends, a praying mother or sister, a sudden death, and the like, often touches the hearts of the roughest and most abandoned. The Bible is to the sailor a sacred book. It may lie in the bottom of his chest voyage after voyage; but he never treats it with positive disrespect. I never knew but one sailor who doubted its being the inspired word of God; and he was one who had received an uncommonly good education, except that he had been brought up without any early religious influence. The most abandoned man of our crew, one Sunday morning, asked one of the boys to lend him his Bible. The boy said he would, but was afraid he would make sport of it. "No!" said the man, "I don't make sport of God Almighty." This is a feeling general among sailors, and is a good foundation for religious influence.

A still greater gain is made whenever, by means of a captain who is interested in the eternal welfare of those under his command, there can be secured the performance of regular religious exercises, and the exertion, on the side of religion, of that mighty influence which a captain possesses for good, or for evil. There are occurrences at sea which he may turn to great account,—a sudden death, the apprehension of danger, or the escape from it, and the like; and all the calls for gratitude and faith. Besides, this state of things alters the whole current of feeling between the crew and their commander. His authority assumes more of the parental character; and kinder feelings exist. Godwin, though an infidel, in one of his novels, describing the relation in which a tutor stood to his pupil, says that the conviction the tutor was under, that he and his ward were both alike awaiting a state of eternal happiness or misery, and that they must appear together before the same judgment-seat, operated so upon his naturally morose disposition, as to produce a feeling of kindness and tenderness toward his ward, which nothing else could have caused. Such must be the effect upon the relation of master and common seaman.

There are now many vessels sailing under such auspices, in which great good is done. Yet I never happened to fall in with one of them. I did not hear a prayer made, a chapter read in public, nor see anything approaching to a religious service, for two years and a quarter. There were, in the course of the voyage, many incidents which made, for the time, serious impressions upon our minds, and which might have been turned to our good; but there being no one to use the opportunity, and no services, the regular return of which might have kept something of the feeling alive in us, the advantage of them was lost, to some, perhaps, forever.

The good which a single religious captain may do can hardly be calculated. In the first place, as I have said, a kinder state of feeling exists on board the ship. There is no profanity allowed; and the men are not called by any opprobrious names, which is a great thing with sailors. The Sabbath is observed. This gives the men a day of rest, even if they pass it in no other way. Such a captain, too, will not allow a sailor on board his ship to remain unable to read his Bible and the books given to him; and will usually instruct those who need it, in writing, arithmetic, and navigation; since he has a good deal of time on his hands, which he can easily employ in such a manner. He will also have regular religious services; and, in fact, by the power of his example, and, where it can judiciously be done, by the exercise of his authority, will give a character to the ship, and all on board. In foreign ports, a ship is known by her captain; for, there being no general rules in the merchant service, each master may adopt a plan of his own. It is to be remembered, too, that there are, in most ships, boys of a tender age, whose characters for life are forming, as well as old men, whose lives must be drawing toward a close. The greater part of sailors die at sea; and when they find their end approaching, if it does not, as is often the case, come without warning, they cannot, as on shore, send for a clergyman, or some religious friend, to speak to them of that hope in a Saviour, which they have neglected, if not despised, through life; but if the little hull does not contain such an one within its compass, they must be left without human aid in their great extremity. When such commanders and such ships, as I have just described, shall become more numerous, the hope of the friends of seamen will be greatly strengthened; and it is encouraging to remember that the efforts among common sailors will soon raise up such a class; for those of them who are brought under these influences will inevitably be the ones to succeed to the places of trust and authority. If there is on earth an instance where a little leaven may leaven the whole lump, it is that of the religious shipmaster.

It is to the progress of this work among seamen that we must look with the greatest confidence for the remedying of those numerous minor evils and abuses that we so often hear of. It will raise the character of sailors, both as individuals and as a class. It will give weight to their testimony in courts of justice, secure better usage to them on board ship, and add comforts to their lives on shore and at sea. There are some laws that can be passed to remove temptation from their way and to help them in their progress; and some changes in the jurisdiction of the lower courts, to prevent delays, may, and probably will be made. But generally speaking, more especially in things which concern the discipline of ships, we had better labor in this great work, and view with caution the proposal of new laws and arbitrary regulations, remembering that most of those concerned in the making of them must necessarily be little qualified to judge of their operation.

Without any formal dedication of my narrative to that body of men, of whose common life it is intended to be a picture, I have yet borne them constantly in mind during its preparation. I cannot but trust that those of them, into whose hands it may chance to fall, will find in it that which shall render any professions of sympathy and good wishes on my part unnecessary. And I will take the liberty, on parting with my reader, who has gone down with us to the ocean, and "laid his hand upon its mane," to commend to his kind wishes, and to the benefit of his efforts, that class of men with whom, for a time, my lot was cast. I wish the rather to do this, since I feel that whatever attention this book may gain, and whatever favor it may find, I shall owe almost entirely to that interest in the sea, and those who follow it, which is so easily excited in us all.

Twenty-Four Years After

I T WAS in the winter of 1835–6 that the ship Alert, in the prosecution of her voyage for hides on the remote and almost unknown coast of California, floated into the vast solitude of the Bay of San Francisco. All around was the stillness of nature. One vessel, a Russian, lay at anchor there, but during our whole stay not a sail came or went. Our trade was with remote Missions, which sent hides to us in launches manned by their Indians. Our anchorage was between a small island, called Yerba Buena, and a gravel beach in a little bight or cove of the same name, formed by two small, projecting points. Beyond, to the westward of the landing-place, were dreary sand-hills, with little grass to be seen, and few trees, and beyond them higher hills, steep and barren, their sides gullied by the rains. Some five or six miles beyond the landing-place, to the right, was a ruinous Presidio, and some three or four miles to the left was the Mission of Dolores, as ruinous as the Presidio, almost deserted, with but few Indians attached to it, and but little property in cattle. Over a region far beyond our sight there were no other human habitations, except that an enterprising Yankee, years in advance of his time, had put up, on the rising ground above the landing, a shanty of rough boards, where he carried on a very small retail trade between the hide ships and the Indians. Vast banks of fog, invading us from the North Pacific, drove in through the entrance, and covered the whole bay; and when they disappeared, we saw a few well-wooded islands, the sand-hills on the west, the grassy and wooded slopes on the east, and the vast stretch of the bay to the southward, where we were told lay the Missions of Santa Clara and San José, and still longer stretches to the northward and northeastward, where we understood smaller bays spread out, and large rivers poured in their tributes of waters. There were no settlements on these bays or rivers, and the few ranchos and Missions were remote and widely separated. Not only the neighborhood of our anchorage, but the entire region of the great bay, was a solitude. On the whole coast of California there was not a lighthouse, a beacon, or a buoy, and the charts were made up from old and disconnected surveys by British, Russian, and Mexican voyagers. Birds of prey and passage swooped and dived about us, wild beasts ranged through the oak groves, and as we slowly floated out of the harbor with the tide, herds of deer came to the water's edge, on the northerly side of the entrance, to gaze at the strange spectacle.

On the evening of Saturday, the 13th of August, 1859, the superb steamship Golden Gate, gay with crowds of passengers, and lighting the sea for miles around with the glare of her signal lights of red, green, and white, and brilliant with lighted saloons and staterooms, bound up from the Isthmus of Panama, neared the entrance to San Francisco, the great centre of a world-wide commerce. Miles out at sea, on the desolate rocks of the Farallones, gleamed the powerful rays of one of the most costly and effective light-houses in the world. As we drew in through the Golden Gate, another light-house met our eyes, and in the clear moonlight of the unbroken California summer we saw, on the right, a large fortification protecting the narrow entrance, and just before us the little island of Alcatraz confronted us,—one entire fortress. We bore round the point toward the old anchoring-ground of the hide ships, and there, covering the sand-hills and the valleys, stretching from the water's edge to the base of the great hills, and from the old Presidio to the Mission, flickering all over with the lamps of its streets and houses, lay a city of one hundred thousand inhabitants. Clocks tolled the hour of midnight from its steeples, but the city was alive from the salute of our guns, spreading the news that the fortnightly steamer had come, bringing mails and passengers from the Atlantic world. Clipper ships of the largest size lay at anchor in the stream, or were girt to the wharves; and capacious high-pressure steamers, as large and showy as those of the Hudson or Mississippi, bodies of dazzling light, awaited the delivery of our mails to take their courses up the Bay, stopping at Benicia and the United States Naval Station, and then up the great tributaries—the Sacramento, San Joaquin, and Feather Rivers—to the far inland cities of Sacramento, Stockton, and Marysville.

The dock into which we drew, and the streets about it, were densely crowded with express wagons and hand-carts to take luggage, coaches and cabs for passengers, and with men,—some looking out for friends among our hundreds of passengers,—agents of the press, and a greater multitude eager for newspapers and verbal intelligence from the great Atlantic and European world. Through this crowd I made my way, along the well-built and well-lighted streets, as alive as by day, where boys in high-keyed voices were already crying the latest New York papers; and between one and two o'clock in the morning found myself comfortably abed in a commodious room, in the Oriental Hotel, which stood, as well as I could learn, on the filled-up cove, and not far from the spot where we used to beach our boats from the Alert.

Sunday, August 14th. When I awoke in the morning, and looked from my windows over the city of San Francisco, with its storehouses, towers, and steeples; its court-houses, theatres, and hospitals; its daily journals; its well-filled learned professions; its fortresses and light-houses; its wharves and harbor, with their thousand-ton clipper ships, more in number than London or Liverpool sheltered that day, itself one of the capitals of the American Republic, and the sole emporium of a new world, the awakened Pacific; when I looked across the bay to the eastward, and beheld a beautiful town on the fertile, wooded shores of the Contra Costa, and steamers, large and small, the ferryboats to the Contra Costa, and capacious freighters and passenger-carriers to all parts of the great bay and its tributaries, with lines of their smoke in the horizon,—when I saw all these things, and reflected on what I once was and saw here, and what now surrounded me, I could scarcely keep my hold on reality at all, or the genuineness of anything, and seemed to myself like one who had moved in "worlds not realized."

I could not complain that I had not a choice of places of worship. The Roman Catholics have an archbishop, a cathedral, and five or six smaller churches, French, German, Spanish, and English; and the Episcopalians a bishop, a cathedral, and three other churches; the Methodists and Presbyterians have three or four each, and there are Congregationalists, Baptists, a Unitarian, and other societies. On my way to church, I met two classmates of mine at Harvard standing in a door-way, one a lawyer and the other a teacher, and made appointments for a future meeting. A little farther on I came upon another Harvard man, a fine scholar and wit, and full of cleverness and good-humor, who invited me to go to breakfast with him at the French house,—he was a bachelor, and a late riser on Sundays. I asked him to show me the way to Bishop Kip's church. He hesitated, looked a little confused, and admitted that he was not as well up in certain classes of knowledge as in others, but, by a desperate guess, pointed out a wooden building at the foot of the street, which any one might have seen could not be right, and which turned out to be an African Baptist meeting-house. But my friend had many capital points of character, and I owed much of the pleasure of my visit to his attentions.

The congregation at the Bishop's church was precisely like one you would meet in New York, Philadelphia, or Boston. To be sure, the identity of the service makes one feel at once at home, but the people were alike, nearly all of the English race, though from all parts of the Union. The latest French bonnets were at the head of the chief pews, and business men at the foot. The music was without character, but there was an instructive sermon, and the church was full.

I found that there were no services at any of the Protestant churches in the afternoon. They have two services on Sunday; at II A.M., and after dark. The afternoon is spent at home, or in friendly visiting, or teaching of Sunday Schools, or other humane and social duties.

This is as much the practice with what at home are called the strictest denominations as with any others. Indeed, I found individuals, as well as public bodies, affected in a marked degree by a change of oceans and by California life. One Sunday afternoon I was surprised at receiving the card of a man whom I had last known, some fifteen years ago, as a strict and formal deacon of a Congregational Society in New England. He was a deacon still, in San Francisco, a leader in all pious works, devoted to his denomination and to total abstinence,—the same internally, but externally—what a change! Gone was the downcast eye, the bated breath, the solemn, non-natural voice, the watchful gait, stepping as if he felt responsible for the balance of the moral universe! He walked with a stride, an uplifted open countenance, his face covered with beard, whiskers, and mustache, his voice strong and natural,—and, in short, he had put off the New England deacon and become a human being. In a visit of an hour I learned much from him about the religious societies, the moral reforms, the "Dashaways,"—total abstinence societies, which had taken strong hold on the young and wilder parts of society,—and then of the Vigilance Committee, of which he was a member, and of more secular points of interest.

In one of the parlors of the hotel, I saw a man of about sixty years of age, with his feet bandaged and resting in a chair, whom somebody addressed by the name of Lies.* Lies! thought I, that must be the man who came across the country from Kentucky to Monterey while we lay there in the Pilgrim in 1835, and made a passage in the Alert, when he used to shoot with his rifle bottles hung from the top-gallant studding-sail-boom-ends. He married the beautiful Doña Rosalía Vallejo, sister of Don Guadalupe. There were the old high features and sandy hair. I put my chair beside him, and began conversation, as any one may do in California. Yes, he was the Mr. Lies; and when I gave my name he professed at once to remember me, and spoke of my book. I found that almost—I might perhaps say quite—every American in California had read it; for when California "broke out," as the phrase is, in 1848, and so large a portion of the Anglo-Saxon race flocked to it, there was no book upon California but mine. Many who were on the coast at the time the book refers to, and afterwards read it, and remembered the Pilgrim and Alert, thought they also remembered me. But perhaps more did remember me than I was inclined at first to believe, for the novelty of a collegian coming out before the mast had drawn more attention to me than I was aware of at the time.

Late in the afternoon, as there were vespers at the Roman Catholic churches, I went to that of Notre Dame des Victoires. The congregation was French, and a sermon in French was preached by an Abbé; the music was excellent, all things airy and tasteful, and making one feel as if in one of the chapels in

*Pronounced *Leese*.

Paris. The Cathedral of St. Mary, which I afterwards visited, where the Irish attend, was a contrast indeed, and more like one of our stifling Irish Catholic churches in Boston or New York, with intelligence in so small a proportion to the number of faces. During the three Sundays I was in San Francisco, I visited three of the Episcopal churches, and the Congregational, a Chinese Mission Chapel, and on the Sabbath (Saturday) a Jewish synagogue. The Jews are a wealthy and powerful class here. The Chinese, too, are numerous, and do a great part of the manual labor and small shop-keeping, and have some wealthy mercantile houses.

It is noticeable that European Continental fashions prevail generally in this city,—French cooking, lunch at noon, and dinner at the end of the day, with *café noir* after meals, and to a great extent the European Sunday,—to all which emigrants from the United States and Great Britain seem to adapt themselves. Some dinners which were given to me at French restaurants were, it seemed to me,—a poor judge of such matters, to be sure,—as sumptuous and as good, in dishes and wines, as I have found in Paris. But I had a relish-maker which my friends at table did not suspect,—the remembrance of the forecastle dinners I ate here twenty-four years before.

August 17th. The customs of California are free; and any person who knows about my book speaks to me. The newspapers have announced the arrival of the veteran pioneer of all. I hardly walk out without meeting or making acquaintances. I have already been invited to deliver the anniversary oration before the Pioneer Society, to celebrate the settlement of San Francisco. Any man is qualified for election into this society who came to California before 1853. What moderns they are! I tell them of the time when Richardson's shanty of 1835—not his adobe house of 1836—was the only human habitation between the Mission and the Presidio, and when the vast bay, with all its tributaries and recesses, was a solitude,—and yet I am but little past forty years of age. They point out the place where Richardson's adobe house stood, and tell me that the first court and first town council were convened in it, the first Protestant worship performed in it, and in it the first capital trial by the Vigilance Committee held. I am taken down to the wharves, by antiquaries of a ten or twelve years' range, to identify the two points, now known as Clark's and Rincon, which formed the little cove of Yerba Buena, where we used to beach our boats,—now filled up and built upon. The island we called "Wood Island," where we spent the cold days and nights of December, in our launch, getting wood for our year's supply, is clean shorn of trees; and the bare rocks of Alcatraz Island, an entire fortress. I have looked at the city from the water, and at the water and islands from the city, but I can see nothing that recalls the times gone by, except the venerable Mission, the ruinous Presidio, the high hills in the rear of the town, and the great stretches of the bay in all directions.

To-day I took a California horse of the old style,—the run, the loping gait,—and visited the Presidio. The walls stand as they did, with some changes made to accommodate a small garrison of United States troops. It has a noble situation, and I saw from it a clipper ship of the very largest class, coming through the Gate, under her fore-and-aft sails. Thence I rode to the Fort, now nearly finished, on the southern shore of the Gate, and made an inspection of it. It is very expensive and of the latest style. One of the engineers here is Custis Lee, who has just left West Point at the head of his class,—a son of Colonel Robert E. Lee, who distinguished himself in the Mexican War.

Another morning I ride to the Mission Dolores. It has a strangely solitary aspect, enhanced by its surroundings of the most uncongenial, rapidly growing modernisms; the hoar of ages surrounded by the brightest, slightest, and rapidest of modern growths. Its old belfries still clanged with the discordant bells, and Mass was saying within, for it is used as a place of worship for the extreme south part of the city.

In one of my walks about the wharves, I found a pile of dry hides lying by the side of a vessel. Here was something to feelingly persuade me what I had been, to recall a past scarce credible to myself. I stood lost in reflection. What were these hides—what were they not?—to us, to me, a boy, twenty-four years ago? These were our constant labor, our chief object, our almost habitual thought. They brought us out here, they kept us here, and it was only by getting them that we could escape from the coast and return to home and civilized life. If it had not been that I might be seen, I should have seized one, slung it over my head, walked off with it, and thrown it by the old toss—I do not believe yet a lost art—to the ground. How they called up to my mind the months of curing at San Diego, the year and more of beach and surf work, and the steeving of the ship for home! I was in a dream of San Diego, San Pedro,—with its hill so steep for taking up goods, and its stones so hard to our bare feet,—and the cliffs of San Juan! All this, too, is no more! The entire hide-business is of the past, and to the present inhabitants of California a dim tradition. The gold discoveries drew off all men from the gathering or cure of hides, the inflowing population made an end of the great droves of cattle; and now not a vessel pursues the—I was about to say dear—the dreary, once hated business of gathering hides upon the coast, and the beach of San Diego is abandoned and its hide-houses have disappeared. Meeting a respectable-looking citizen on the wharf, I inquired of him how the hide-trade was carried on. "O," said he, "there is very little of it, and that is all here. The few that are brought in are placed under sheds in winter, or left out on the wharf in summer, and are loaded from the wharves into the vessels alongside. They form parts of cargoes of other materials." I really felt too much, at the instant, to express to him the cause of my interest in the subject, and only added, "Then the old business of trading up and down the coast and curing hides for cargoes is all over?" "O yes, sir," said he, "those old times of the Pilgrim and Alert and California, that we read about, are gone by."

Saturday, August 20th. The steamer Senator makes regular trips up and down the coast, between San Francisco and San Diego, calling at intermediate ports. This is my opportunity to revisit the old scenes. She sails to-day, and I am off, steaming among the great clippers anchored in the harbor, and gliding rapidly round the point, past Alcatraz Island, the light-house, and through the fortified Golden Gate, and bending to the southward,—all done in two or three hours, which, in the Alert, under canvas, with head tides, variable winds, and sweeping currents to deal with, took us full two days.

Among the passengers I noticed an elderly gentleman, thin, with sandy hair and a face that seemed familiar. He took off his glove and showed one shrivelled hand. It must be he! I went to him and said, "Captain Wilson, I believe." Yes, that was his name. "I knew you, sir, when you commanded the Ayacucho on this coast, in old hide-droghing times, in 1835-6." He was quickened by this, and at once inquiries were made on each side, and we were in full talk about the Pilgrim and Alert, Ayacucho and Loriotte, the California and Lagoda. I found he had been very much flattered by the praise I had bestowed in my book on his seamanship, especially in bringing the Pilgrim to her berth in San Diego harbor, after she had drifted successively into the Lagoda and Loriotte, and was coming into him. I had made a pet of his brig, the Ayacucho, which pleased him almost as much as my remembrance of his bride and their wedding, which I saw at Santa Barbara in 1836. Doña Ramona was now the mother of a large family, and Wilson assured me that if I would visit him at his rancho, near San Luis Obispo, I should find her still a handsome woman, and very glad to see me. How we walked the deck together, hour after hour, talking over the old times,—the ships, the captains, the crews, the traders on shore, the ladies, the Missions, the southeasters! indeed, where could we stop? He had sold the Ayacucho in Chili for a vessel of war, and had given up the sea, and had been for years a ranchero. (I learned from others that he had become one of the most wealthy and respectable farmers in the State, and that his rancho was well worth visiting.) Thompson, he said, hadn't the sailor in him; and he never could laugh enough at his *fiasco* in San Diego, and his reception by Bradshaw. Faucon was a sailor and a navigator. He did not know what had become of George Marsh (*ante*, pp. 195–97), except that he left him in Callao; nor could he tell me anything of handsome Bill Jackson (*ante*, pp. 82–83), nor of Captain Nye of the Loriotte. I told him all I then knew of the ships, the masters, and the officers. I found he had kept some run of my history, and needed little information. Old Señor Noriego of Santa Barbara, he told me, was dead, and Don Carlos and Don Santiago, but I should find their children there, now in middle life. Doña Angustia, he said, I had made famous by my praises of her beauty and dancing, and I should have from her a royal reception. She had been a widow, and remarried since, and had a daughter as handsome as herself. The descendants of Noriego had taken the ancestral name of De la Guerra, as they were nobles of Old Spain by birth; and the boy Pablo, who used to make passages in the Alert, was now Don Pablo de la Guerra, a Senator in the State Legislature for Santa Barbara County.

The points in the country, too, we noticed, as we passed them,—Santa Cruz, San Luis Obispo, Point Año Nuevo, the opening to Monterey, which to my disappointment we did not visit. No; Monterey, the prettiest town on the coast, and its capital and seat of customs, had got no advantage from the great changes, was out of the way of commerce and of the travel to the mines and great rivers, and was not worth stopping at. Point Conception we passed in the night, a cheery light gleaming over the waters from its tall light-house, standing on its outermost peak. Point Conception! That word was enough to recall all our experiences and dreads of gales, swept decks, topmast carried away, and the hardships of a coast service in the winter. But Captain Wilson tells me that the climate has altered; that the southeasters are no longer the bane of the coast they once were, and that vessels now anchor inside the kelp at Santa Barbara and San Pedro all the year round. I should have thought this owing to his spending his winters on a rancho instead of the deck of the Ayacucho, had not the same thing been told me by others.

Passing round Point Conception, and steering easterly, we opened the islands that form, with the main-land, the canal of Santa Barbara. There they are, Santa Cruz and Santa Rosa; and there is the beautiful point, Santa Buenaventura; and there lies Santa Barbara on its plain, with its amphitheatre of high hills and distant mountains. There is the old white Mission with its belfries, and there the town, with its one-story adobe houses, with here and there a two-story wooden house of later build; yet little is it altered,—the same repose in the golden sunlight and glorious climate, sheltered by its hills; and then, more remindful than anything else, there roars and tumbles upon the beach the same grand surf of the great Pacific as on the beautiful day when the Pilgrim, after her five months' voyage, dropped her weary anchors here; the same bright blue ocean, and the surf making just the same monotonous, melancholy roar, and the same dreamy town, and gleaming white Mission, as when we beached our boats for the first time, riding over the breakers with shouting Kanakas, the three small hide-traders lying at anchor in the offing. But now we are the only vessel, and that an unromantic, sail-less, spar-less, engine-driven hulk!

I landed in the surf, in the old style, but it was not high enough to excite us, the only change being that I was somehow unaccountably a passenger, and did not have to jump overboard and steady the boat, and run her up by the gunwales.

Santa Barbara has gained but little. I should not know, from anything I saw, that she was now a seaport of the United States, a part of the enterprising Yankee nation, and not still a lifeless Mexican town. At the same old house, where Señor Noriego lived, on the piazza in front of the court-yard, where was the gay scene of the marriage of our agent, Mr. Robinson, to Doña Anita, where Don Juan Bandini and Doña Angustia danced, Don Pablo de la Guerra received me in a courtly fashion. I passed the day with the family, and in walking about the place; and ate the old dinner with its accompaniments of frijoles, native olives and grapes, and native wines. In due time I paid my respects to Doña Angustia, and, notwithstanding what Wilson told me, I could hardly believe that after twenty-four years there would still be so much of the enchanting woman about her. She thanked me for the kind and, as she called them, greatly exaggerated compliments I had paid her; and her daughter told me that all travellers who came to Santa Barbara called to see her mother, and that she herself never expected to live long enough to be a belle.

Mr. Alfred Robinson, our agent in 1835–6, was here, with a part of his family. I did not know how he would receive me, remembering what I had printed to the world about him at a time when I took little thought that the world was going to read it; but there was no sign of offence, only a cordiality which gave him, as between us, rather the advantage in *status.*

The people of this region are giving attention to sheep-raising, wine-making, and the raising of olives, just enough to keep the town from going backwards.

But evening is drawing on, and our boat sails to-night. So, refusing a horse or carriage, I walk down, not unwilling to be a little early, that I may pace up and down the beach, looking off to the islands and the points, and watching the roaring, tumbling billows. How softening is the effect of time! It touches us through the affections. I almost feel as if I were lamenting the passing away of something loved and dear,—the boats, the Kanakas, the hides, my old shipmates! Death, change, distance, lend them a character which makes them quite another thing from the vulgar, wearisome toil of uninteresting, forced manual labor.

The breeze freshened as we stood out to sea, and the wild waves rolled over the red sun, on the broad horizon of the Pacific; but it is summer, and in summer there can be no bad weather in California. Every day is pleasant. Nature forbids a drop of rain to fall by day or night, or a wind to excite itself beyond a fresh summer breeze.

The next morning we found ourselves at anchor in the Bay of San Pedro. Here was this hated, this thoroughly detested spot. Although we lay near, I could scare recognize the hill up which we rolled and dragged and pushed and carried our heavy loads, and down which we pitched the hides, to carry them barefooted over the rocks to the floating long-boat. It was no longer the landing-place. One had been made at the head of the creek, and boats discharged and took off cargoes from a mole or wharf, in a quiet place, safe from southeasters. A tug ran to take off passengers from the steamer to the wharf, —for the trade of Los Angeles is sufficient to support such a vessel. I got the captain to land me privately, in a small boat, at the old place by the hill. I dismissed the boat, and, alone, found my way to the high ground. I say found my way, for neglect and weather had left but few traces of the steep road the hide-vessels had built to the top. The cliff off which we used to throw the hides, and where I spent nights watching them, was more easily found. The population was doubled, that is to say, there were two houses, instead of one, on the hill. I stood on the brow and looked out toward the offing, the Santa Catalina Island, and, nearer, the melancholy Dead Man's Island, with its painful tradition, and recalled the gloomy days that followed the flogging, and fancied the Pilgrim at anchor in the offing. But the tug is going toward our steamer, and I must awake and be off. I walked along the shore to the new landing-place, where were two or three store-houses and other buildings, forming a small depot; and a stage-coach, I found, went daily between this place and the Pueblo. I got a seat on the top of the coach, to which were tackled six little less than wild California horses. Each horse had a man at his head, and when the driver had got his reins in hand he gave the word, all the horses were let go at once, and away they went on a spring, tearing over the ground, the driver only keeping them from going the wrong way, for they had a wide, level pampa to run over the whole thirty miles to the Pueblo. This plain is almost treeless, with no grass, at least none now in the drought of mid-summer, and is filled with squirrel-holes, and alive with squirrels. As we changed horses twice, we did not slacken our speed until we turned into the streets of the Pueblo.

The Pueblo de los Angeles I found a large and flourishing town of about twenty thousand inhabitants, with brick side-walks, and blocks of stone or brick houses. The three principal traders when we were here for hides in the Pilgrim and Alert are still among the chief traders of the place,—Stearns, Temple, and Warner, the two former being reputed very rich. I dined with Mr. Stearns, now a very old man, and met there Don Juan Bandini, to whom I had given a good deal of notice in my book. From him, as indeed from every one in this town, I met with the kindest attentions. The wife of Don Juan, who was a beautiful young girl when we were on the coast, Doña Refugio, daughter of Don Santiago Argüello, the comman-dante of San Diego, was with him, and still handsome. This is one of several instances I have noticed of the preserving qual-ity of the California climate. Here, too, was Henry Mellus, who came out with me before the mast in the Pilgrim, and left the brig to be agent's clerk on shore. He had experienced varying fortunes here, and was now married to a Mexican lady, and had a family. I dined with him, and in the afternoon he drove me round to see the vineyards, the chief objects in this region. The vintage of last year was estimated at half a million of gallons. Every year new square miles of ground are laid down to vineyards, and the Pueblo promises to be the centre of one of the largest wine-producing regions in the world. Grapes are a drug here, and I found a great abundance of figs, olives, peaches, pears, and melons. The climate is well suited to these fruits, but is too hot and dry for successful wheat crops.

Towards evening, we started off in the stage-coach, with again our relays of six mad horses, and reached the creek before dark, though it was late at night before we got on board the steamer, which was slowly moving her wheels, under way for San Diego.

As we skirted along the coast, Wilson and I recognized, or thought we did, in the clear moonlight, the rude white Mission of San Juan Capistrano, and its cliff, from which I had swung down by a pair of halyards to save a few hides,—a boy who could not be prudential, and who caught at every chance for adventure.

As we made the high point off San Diego, Point Loma, we were greeted by the cheering presence of a light-house. As we swept round it in the early morning, there, before us, lay the little harbor of San Diego, its low spit of sand, where the water runs so deep; the opposite flats, where the Alert grounded in starting for home; the low hills, without trees, and almost without brush; the quiet little beach;—but the chief objects, the hide-houses, my eye looked for in vain. They were gone, all, and left no mark behind.

I wished to be alone, so I let the other passengers go up to the town, and was quietly pulled ashore in a boat, and left to myself. The recollections and the emotions all were sad, and only sad.

Fugit, interea fugit irreparabile tempus.

The past was real. The present, all about me, was unreal, unnatural, repellant. I saw the big ships lying in the stream, the Alert, the California, the Rosa, with her Italians; then the handsome Ayacucho, my favorite; the poor dear old Pilgrim, the home of hardship and hopelessness; the boats passing to and fro; the cries of the sailors at the capstan or falls; the peopled beach; the large hide-houses, with their gangs of men; and the Kanakas interspersed everywhere. All, all were gone! not a vestige to mark where one hide-house stood. The oven, too, was gone. I searched for its site, and found, where I thought it should be, a few broken bricks and bits of mortar. I alone was left of all, and how strangely was I here! What changes to me! Where were they all? Why should I care for them,—poor Kanakas and sailors, the refuse of civilization, the outlaws and beach-combers of the Pacific! Time and death seemed to transfigure them. Doubtless nearly all were dead; but how had they died, and where? In hospitals, in fever-climes, in dens of vice, or falling from the mast, or dropping exhausted from the wreck,—

> "When for a moment, like a drop of rain,
>   He sinks into thy depths with bubbling groan,
>   Without a grave, unknelled, uncoffined, and unknown."

The light-hearted boys are now hardened middle-aged men, if the seas, rocks, fevers, and the deadlier enemies that beset a sailor's life on shore have spared them; and the then strong men have bowed themselves, and the earth or sea has covered them.

Even the animals are gone,—the colony of dogs, the broods of poultry, the useful horses; but the coyotes bark still in the woods, for they belong not to man, and are not touched by his changes.

I walked slowly up the hill, finding my way among the few bushes, for the path was long grown over, and sat down where we used to rest in carrying our burdens of wood, and to look out for vessels that might, though so seldom, be coming down from the windward.

To rally myself by calling to mind my own better fortune and nobler lot, and cherished surroundings at home, was impossible. Borne down by depression, the day being yet at its noon, and the sun over the old point,—it is four miles to the town, the Presidio,—I have walked it often, and can do it once more,—I passed the familiar objects, and it seemed to me that I remembered them better than those of any other place I had ever been in;—the opening to the little cave; the low hills where we cut wood and killed rattlesnakes, and where our dogs chased the coyotes; and the black ground where so many of the ship's crew and beach-combers used to bring up on their return at the end of a liberty day, and spend the night *sub Jove.*

The little town of San Diego has undergone no change whatever that I can see. It certainly has not grown. It is still, like Santa Barbara, a Mexican town. The four principal houses of the gente de razon—of the Bandinis, Estudillos, Argüellos, and Picos—are the chief houses now; but all the gentlemen—and their families, too, I believe—are gone. The big vulgar shopkeeper and trader, Fitch, is long since dead; Tom Wrightington, who kept the rival pulpería, fell from his horse when drunk, and was found nearly eaten up by coyotes; and I can scarce find a person whom I remember. I went into a familiar one-story adobe house, with its piazza and earthen floor, inhabited by a respectable lower-class family by the name of Muchado, and inquired if any of the family remained, when a bright-eyed middle-aged woman recognized me, for she had heard I was on board the steamer, and told me she had married a shipmate of mine, Jack Stewart, who went out as second mate the next voyage, but left the ship and married and settled here. She said he wished very much to see me. In a few minutes he came in, and his sincere pleasure in meeting me was extremely grateful. We talked over old times as long as I could afford to. I was glad to hear that he was sober and doing well. Doña Tomasa Pico I found and talked with. She was the only person of the old upper class that remained on the spot, if I rightly recollect. I found an American family here, with whom I dined,—Doyle and his wife, nice young people, Doyle agent for the great line of coaches to run to the frontier of the old States.

I must complete my acts of pious remembrance, so I take a horse and make a run out to the old Mission, where Ben Stimson and I went the first liberty day we had after we left Boston (*ante*, pp. 109–16). All has gone to decay. The buildings are unused and ruinous, and the large gardens show now only wild cactuses, willows, and a few olive-trees. A fast run brings me back in time to take leave of the few I knew and who knew me, and to reach the steamer before she sails. A last look—yes, last for life—to the beach, the hills, the low point, the distant town, as we round Point Loma and the first beams of the light-house strike out towards the setting sun.

Wednesday, August 24th. At anchor at San Pedro by daylight. But instead of being roused out of the forecastle to row the long-boat ashore and bring off a load of hides before break-fast, we were served with breakfast in the cabin, and again took our drive with the wild horses to the Pueblo and spent the day; seeing nearly the same persons as before, and again getting back by dark. We steamed again for Santa Barbara, where we only lay an hour, and passed through its canal and round Point Conception, stopping at San Luis Obispo to land my friend, as I may truly call him after this long passage together, Captain

Wilson, whose most earnest invitation to stop here and visit him at his rancho I was obliged to decline.

Friday evening, 26th August, we entered the Golden Gate, passed the light-houses and forts, and clipper ships at anchor, and came to our dock, with this great city, on its high hills and rising surfaces, brilliant before us, and full of eager life.

Making San Francisco my head-quarters, I paid visits to various parts of the State,—down the Bay to Santa Clara, with its live oaks and sycamores, and its Jesuit College for boys; and San José, where is the best girls' school in the State, kept by the Sisters of Notre Dame,—a town now famous for a year's session of "The legislature of a thousand drinks,"—and thence to the rich Almaden quicksilver mines, returning on the Contra Costa side through the rich agricultural country, with its ranchos and the vast grants of the Castro and Soto families, where farming and fruit-raising are done on so large a scale. Another excursion was up the San Joaquin to Stockton, a town of some ten thousand inhabitants, a hundred miles from San Francisco, and crossing the Tuolumne and Stanislaus and Merced, by the little Spanish town of Hornitos, and Snelling's Tavern, at the ford of the Merced, where so many fatal fights are had. Thence I went to Mariposa County, and Colonel Fremont's mines, and made an interesting visit to "*the* Colonel," as he is called all over the country, and Mrs. Fremont, a heroine equal to either fortune, the salons of Paris and the drawing-rooms of New York and Washington, or the roughest life of the remote and wild mining regions of Mariposa,—with their fine family of spirited, clever children. After a rest there, we went on to Clark's Camp and the Big Trees, where I measured one tree ninety-seven feet in circumference without its bark, and the bark is usually eighteen inches thick; and rode through another which lay on the ground, a shell, with all the insides out, —rode through it mounted, and sitting at full height in the saddle; then to the wonderful Yo Semite Valley,—itself a stupendous miracle of nature, with its Dome, its Capitan, its walls of three thousand feet of perpendicular height,—but a valley of streams, of waterfalls, from the torrent to the mere shimmer of a bridal veil, only enough to reflect a rainbow, with their plunges of twenty-five hundred feet, or their smaller falls of eight hundred, with nothing at the base but thick mists, which form and trickle, and then run and at last plunge into the blue Merced that flows through the centre of the valley. Back by the Coulterville trail, the peaks of Sierra Nevada in sight, across the North Fork of the Merced, by Gentry's Gulch, over hills and through cañons, to Fremont's again, and thence to Stockton and San Francisco,—all this at the end of August, when there has been no rain for four months, and the air is clear and very hot, and the ground perfectly dry; windmills, to raise water for artificial irrigation of small patches, seen all over the landscape, while we travel through square miles of hot dust, where they tell us, and truly, that in winter and early spring we should be up to our knees in flowers; a country, too, where surface gold-digging is so common and unnoticed that the large, six-horse stage-coach, in which I travelled from Stockton to Hornitos, turned off in the high road for a Chinaman, who, with his pan and washer, was working up a hole which an American had abandoned, but where the minute and patient industry of the Chinaman averaged a few dollars a day.

These visits were so full of interest, with grandeurs and humors of all sorts, that I am strongly tempted to describe them. But I remember that I am not to write a journal of a visit over the new California, but to sketch briefly the contrasts with the old spots of 1835–6, and I forbear.

How strange and eventful has been the brief history of this marvellous city, San Francisco! In 1835 there was one board shanty. In 1836, one adobe house on the same spot. In 1847, a population of four hundred and fifty persons, who organized a town government. Then came the *auri sacra fames*, the flocking together of many of the worst spirits of Christendom; a sudden birth of a city of canvas and boards, entirely destroyed by fire five times in eighteen months, with a loss of sixteen millions of dollars, and as often rebuilt, until it became a solid city of brick and stone, of nearly one hundred thousand inhabitants, with all the accompaniments of wealth and culture, and now (in 1859) the most quiet and well-governed city of its size in the United States. But it has been through its season of Heaven-defying crime, violence, and blood, from which it was rescued and handed back to soberness, morality, and good government, by that peculiar invention of Anglo-Saxon Republican America, the solemn, awe-inspiring Vigilance

Committee of the most grave and responsible citizens, the last resort of the thinking and the good, taken to only when vice, fraud, and ruffianism have intrenched themselves behind the forms of law, suffrage, and ballot, and there is no hope but in organized force, whose action must be instant and thorough, or its state will be worse than before. A history of the passage of this city through those ordeals, and through its almost incredible financial extremes, should be written by a pen which not only accuracy shall govern, but imagination shall inspire.

I cannot pause for the civility of referring to the many kind attentions I received, and the society of educated men and women from all parts of the Union I met with; where New England, the Carolinas, Virginia, and the new West sat side by side with English, French, and German civilization.

My stay in California was interrupted by an absence of nearly four months, when I sailed for the Sandwich Islands in the noble Boston clipper ship Mastiff, which was burned at sea to the water's edge; we escaping in boats, and carried by a friendly British bark into Honolulu, whence, after a deeply interesting visit of three months in that most fascinating group of islands, with its natural and its moral wonders, I returned to San Francisco in an American whaler, and found myself again in my quarters on the morning of Sunday, December 11th, 1859.

My first visit after my return was to Sacramento, a city of about forty thousand inhabitants, more than a hundred miles inland from San Francisco, on the Sacramento, where was the capital of the State, and where were fleets of river steamers, and a large inland commerce. Here I saw the inauguration of a Governor, Mr. Latham, a young man from Massachusetts, much my junior; and met a member of the State Senate, a man who, as a carpenter, repaired by father's house at home some ten years before; and two more Senators from southern California, relics of another age,—Don Andres Pico, from San Diego; and Don Pablo de la Guerra, whom I have mentioned as meeting at Santa Barbara. I had a good deal of conversation with these gentlemen, who stood alone in an assembly of Americans, who had conquered their country, spared pillars of the past. Don Andres had fought us at San Pazqual and Sepulveda's rancho, in 1846, and as he fought bravely, not a common thing among the Mexicans, and, indeed, repulsed Kearney, is always treated with respect. He had the satisfaction, dear to the proud Spanish heart, of making a speech before a Senate of Americans, in favor of the retention in office of an officer of our army who was wounded at San Pazqual, and whom some wretched caucus was going to displace to carry out a political job. Don Andres's magnanimity and indignation carried the day.

My last visit in this part of the country was to a new and rich farming region, the Napa Valley, the United States Navy Yard at Mare Island, the river gold workings, and the Geysers, and old Mr. John Yount's rancho. On board the steamer, found Mr. Edward Stanley, formerly member of Congress from North Carolina, who became my companion for the greater part of my trip. I also met—a revival on the spot of an acquaintance of twenty years ago—Don Guadalupe Vallejo; I may say acquaintance, for although I was then before the mast, he knew my story, and, as he spoke English well, used to hold many conversations with me, when in the boat or on shore. He received me with true earnestness, and would not hear of my passing his estate without visiting him. He reminded me of a remark I made to him once, when pulling him ashore in the boat, when he was commandante at the Presidio. I learned that the two Vallejos, Guadalupe and Salvador, owned, at an early time, nearly all Napa and Sonoma, having princely estates. But they have not much left. They were nearly ruined by their bargain with the State, that they would put up the public buildings if the Capital should be placed at Vallejo, then a town of some promise. They spent $100,000, the Capital was moved there, and in two years removed to San José on another contract. The town fell to pieces, and the houses, chiefly wooden, were taken down and removed. I accepted the old gentleman's invitation so far as to stop at Vallejo to breakfast.

The United States Navy Yard, at Mare Island, near Vallejo, is large and well placed, with deep fresh water. The old Independence, and the sloop Decatur, and two steamers were there, and they were experimenting on building a despatch boat, the Saginaw, of California timber.

I have no excuse for attempting to describe my visit through the fertile and beautiful Napa Valley, nor even, what exceeded that in interest, my visit to old John Yount at his rancho, where I heard from his own lips some of his most interesting stories of hunting and trapping and Indian fighting, during an adventurous life of forty years of such work, between our back settlements in Missouri and Arkansas, and the mountains of California, trapping the Colorado and Gila,—and his celebrated dream, thrice repeated, which led him to organize a party to go out over the mountains, that did actually rescue from death by starvation the wretched remnants of the Donner Party.

I must not pause for the dreary country of the Geysers, the screaming escapes of steam, the sulphur, the boiling caldrons of black and yellow and green, and the region of Gehenna, through which runs a quiet stream of pure water; nor for the park scenery, and captivating ranchos of the Napa Valley, where farming is done on so grand a scale,—where I have seen a man plough a furrow by little red flags on sticks, to keep his range by, until nearly out of sight, and where, the wits tell us, he returns the next day on the back furrow; a region where, at Christmas time, I have seen old strawberries still on the vines, by the side of vines in full blossom for the next crop, and grapes in the same stages, and open windows, and yet a grateful wood fire on the hearth in early morning; nor for the titanic operations of hydraulic surface mining, where large mountain streams are diverted from their ancient beds, and made to do the work, beyond the reach of all other agents, of washing out valleys and carrying away hills, and changing the whole surface of the country, to expose the stores of gold hidden for centuries in the darkness of their earthy depths.

January 10th, 1860. I am again in San Francisco, and my revisit to California is closed. I have touched too lightly and rapidly for much impression upon the reader on my last visit into the interior; but, as I have said, in a mere continuation to a narrative of a sea-faring life on the coast, I am only to carry the reader with me on a revisit to those scenes in which the public has long manifested so gratifying an interest. But it seemed to me that slight notices of these entirely new parts of the country would not be out of place, for they serve to put in strong contrast with the solitudes of 1835–6 the developed interior, with its mines, and agricultural wealth, and rapidly filling population, and its large cities, so far from the coast, with their education, religion, arts, and trade.

On the morning of the 11th January, 1860, I passed, for the eighth time, through the Golden Gate, on my way across the delightful Pacific to the Oriental world, with its civilization three thousand years older than that I was leaving behind. As the shores of California faded in the distance, and the summits of the Coast Range sank under the blue horizon, I bade farewell—yes, I do not doubt, forever—to those scenes which, however changed or unchanged, must always possess an ineffable interest for me.

It is time my fellow-travellers and I should part company. But I have been requested by a great many persons to give some account of the subsequent history of the vessels and their crews, with which I had made them acquainted. I attempt the following sketches in deference to these suggestions, and not, I trust, with any undue estimate of the general interest my narrative may have created.

Something less than a year after my return in the Alert, and when, my eyes having recovered, I was again in college life, I found one morning in the newspapers, among the arrivals of the day before, "The brig Pilgrim, Faucon, from San Diego, California." In a few hours I was down in Ann Street, and on my way to Hackstadt's boarding-house, where I knew Tom Harris and others would lodge. Entering the front room, I heard my name called from amid a group of blue-jackets, and several sunburned, tar-colored men came forward to speak to me. They were, at first, a little embarrassed by the dress and style in which they had never seen me, and one of them was calling me *Mr.* Dana; but I soon stopped that, and we were shipmates once more. First, there was Tom Harris, in a characteristic occupation. I had made him promise to come and see me when we parted in San Diego; he had got a directory of Boston, found the street and number of my father's house, and, by a study of the plan of the city, had laid out his course, and was committing it to memory. He said he could go straight to the house without asking a question. And so he could, for I took the book from him, and he gave his course, naming each street and turn to right or left, directly to the door.

Tom had been second mate of the Pilgrim, and had laid up no mean sum of money. True to his resolution, he was going to England to find his mother, and he entered into the comparative advantages of taking his money home in gold or in bills,—a matter of some moment, as this was in the disastrous financial year of 1837. He seemed to have his ideas well arranged, but I took him to a leading banker, whose advice he followed; and, declining my invitation to go up and show himself to my friends, he was off for New York that afternoon, to sail the next day for Liverpool. The last I ever saw of Tom Harris was as he passed down Tremont Street on the sidewalk, a man dragging a hand-cart in the street by his side, on which were his voyage-worn chest, his mattress, and a box of nautical instruments.

Sam seemed to have got funny again, and he and John the Swede learned that Captain Thompson had several months before sailed in command of a ship for the coast of Sumatra, and that their chance of proceedings against him at law was hopeless. Sam was afterwards lost in a brig off the coast of Brazil, when all hands went down. Of John and the rest of the men I have never heard. The Marblehead boy, Sam, turned out badly; and, although he had influential friends, never allowed them to improve his condition. The old carpenter, the Fin, of whom the cook stood in such awe (*ante,* p. 38), had fallen sick and died in Santa Barbara, and was buried ashore. Jim Hall, from the Kennebec, who sailed with us before the mast, and was made second mate in Foster's place, came home chief mate of the Pilgrim. I have often seen him since. His lot has been prosperous, as he well deserved it should be. He has commanded the largest ships, and, when I last saw him, was going to the Pacific coast of South America, to take charge of a line of mail steamers. Poor, luckless Foster I have twice seen. He came into my rooms in Boston, after I had become a barrister and my narrative had been published, and told me he was chief mate of a big ship; that he had heard I had said some things unfavorable of him in my book; that he had just bought it, and was going to read it that night, and if I had said anything unfair of him, he would punish me if he found me in State Street. I surveyed him from head to foot, and said to him, "Foster, you were not a formidable man when I last knew you, and I don't believe you are now." Either he was of my opinion, or thought I had spoken of him well enough, for the next (and last) time I met him he was civil and pleasant.

I believe I omitted to state that Mr. Andrew B. Amerzene, the chief mate of the Pilgrim, an estimable, kind, and trustworthy man, had a difficulty with Captain Faucon, who thought him slack, was turned off duty, and sent home with us in the Alert. Captain Thompson, instead of giving him the place of a mate off duty, put him into the narrow between-decks, where a space, not over four feet high, had been left out among the hides, and there compelled him to live the whole wearisome voyage, through trades and tropics, and round Cape Horn, with nothing to do,—not allowed to converse or walk with the officers, and obliged to get his grub himself from the galley, in the tin pot and kid of a common sailor. I used to talk with him as much as I had opportunity to, but his lot was wretched, and in every way wounding to his feelings. After our arrival, Captain Thompson was obliged to make him compensation for this treatment. It happens that I have never heard of him since.

Henry Mellus, who had been in a counting-house in Boston, and left the forecastle, on the coast, to be agent's clerk, and whom I met, a married man, at Los Angeles in 1859, died at that place a few years ago, not having been successful in commercial life. Ben Stimson left the sea for the fresh water and prairies, settled in Detroit as a merchant, and when I visited that city, in 1863, I was rejoiced to find him a prosperous and respected man, and the same generous-hearted shipmate as ever.

This ends the catalogue of the Pilgrim's original crew, except for her first master, Captain Thompson. He was not employed by the same firm again, and got up a voyage to the coast of Sumatra for pepper. A cousin and classmate of mine, Mr. Channing, went as supercargo, not having consulted me as to the captain. First, Captain Thompson got into difficulties with another American vessel on the coast, which charged him with having taken some advantage of her in getting pepper; and then with the natives, who accused him of having obtained too much pepper for his weights. The natives seized him, one afternoon, as he landed in his boat, and demanded of him to sign an order on the supercargo for the Spanish dollars that they said were due them, on pain of being imprisoned on shore. He never failed in pluck, and now ordered his boat aboard, leaving him ashore, the officer to tell the supercargo to obey no direction except under his hand. For several successive days and nights, his ship, the Alciope, lay in the burning sun, with rain-squalls and thunder-clouds coming over the high mountains, waiting for a word from him. Toward evening of the fourth or fifth day he was seen on the beach, hailing for the boat. The natives, finding they could not force more money from him, were afraid to hold him longer, and had let him go. He sprang into the boat, urged her off with the utmost eagerness, leaped on board the ship like a tiger, his eyes flashing and his face full of blood, ordered the anchor aweigh, and the topsails set, the four guns, two on a side, loaded with all sorts of devilish stuff, and wore her round, and, keeping as close into the bamboo village as he could, gave them both broadsides, slam-bang into the midst of the houses and people, and stood out to sea! As his excitement passed off, headache, languor, fever, set in,—the deadly coast-fever, contracted from the water and night-dews on shore and his maddened temper. He ordered the ship to Penang, and never saw the deck again. He died on the passage, and was buried at sea. Mr. Channing, who took care of him in his sickness and delirium, caught the fever from him, but, as we gratefully remember, did not die until the ship made port, and he was under the kindly roof of a hospitable family in Penang. The chief mate, also, took the fever, and the second mate and crew deserted; and, although the chief mate recovered and took the ship to Europe and home, the voyage was a melancholy disaster. In a tour I made round the world in 1859–1860, of which my revisit to California was the beginning, I went to Penang. In that fairy-like scene of sea and sky and shore, as beautiful as material earth can be, with its fruits and flowers of a perpetual summer,—somewhere in which still lurks the deadly fever,—I found the tomb of my kinsman, classmate, and friend. Standing beside his grave, I tried not to think that his life had been sacrificed to the faults and violence of another; I tried not to think too hardly of that other, who at least had suffered in death.

The dear old Pilgrim herself! She was sold, at the end of this voyage, to a merchant in New Hampshire, who employed her on short voyages, and, after a few years, I read of her total loss at sea, by fire, off the coast of North Carolina.

Captain Faucon, who took out the Alert, and brought home the Pilgrim, spent many years in command of vessels in the Indian and Chinese seas, and was in our volunteer navy during the late war, commanding several large vessels in succession, on the blockade of the Carolinas, with the rank of lieutenant. He has now given up the sea, but still keeps it under his eye, from the piazza of his house on the most beautiful hill in the environs of Boston. I have the pleasure of meeting him often. Once, in speaking of the Alert's crew, in a company of gentlemen, I heard him say that that crew was exceptional; that he had passed all his life at sea, but whether before the mast or abaft, whether officer or master, he had never met such a crew, and never should expect to; and that the two officers of the Alert, long ago shipmasters, agreed with him that, for intelligence, knowledge of duty and willingness to perform it, pride in the ship, her appearance and sailing, and in absolute reliableness, they never had seen their equal. Especially he spoke of his favorite seaman, French John. John, after a few more years at sea, became a boatman, and kept his neat boat at the end of Granite Wharf, and was ready to take all, but delighted to take any of us of the old Alert's crew, to sail down the harbor. One day Captain Faucon went to the end of the wharf to board a vessel in the stream, and hailed for John. There was no response, and his boat was not there. He inquired, of a boatman near, where John was. The time had come that comes to all! There was no loyal voice to respond to the familiar call, the hatches had closed over him, his boat was sold to another, and he had left not a trace behind. We could not find out even where he was buried.

Mr. Richard Brown, of Marblehead, our chief mate in the Alert, commanded many of our noblest ships in the European trade, a general favorite. A few years ago, while stepping on board his ship from the wharf, he fell from the plank into the hold and was killed. If he did not actually die at sea, at least he died as a sailor,—he died on board ship.

Our second mate, Evans, no one liked or cared for, and I know nothing of him, except that I once saw him in court, on trial for some alleged petty tyranny towards his men,—still a subaltern officer.

The third mate, Mr. Hatch, a nephew of one of the owners, though only a lad on board the ship, went out chief mate the next voyage, and rose soon to command some of the finest clippers in the California and India trade, under the new order of things,—a man of character, good judgment, and no little cultivation.

Of the other men before the mast in the Alert, I know nothing of peculiar interest. When visiting, with a party of ladies and gentlemen, one of our largest line-of-battle ships, we were escorted about the decks by a midshipman, who was explaining various matters on board, when one of the party came to me and told me that there was an old sailor there with a whistle round his neck, who looked at me and said of the officer, "*he* can't show *him* anything aboard a ship." I found him out, and, looking into his sunburnt face, covered with hair, and his little eyes drawn up into the smallest passages for light,— like a man who had peered into hundreds of northeasters,— there was old "Sails" of the Alert, clothed in all the honors of boatswain's-mate. We stood aside, out of the *cun* of the officers, and had a good talk over old times. I remember the contempt with which he turned on his heel to conceal his face, when the midshipman (who was a grown youth) could not tell the ladies the length of a fathom, and said it depended on circumstances. Notwithstanding his advice and consolation to "Chips," in the steerage of the Alert, and his story of his runaway wife and the flag-bottomed chairs (*ante*, pp. 241-42), he confessed to me that he had tried marriage again, and had a little tenement just outside the gate of the yard.

Harry Bennett, the man who had the palsy, and was unfeelingly left on shore when the Alert sailed, came home in the Pilgrim, and I had the pleasure of helping to get him into the Massachusetts General Hospital. When he had been there about a week, I went to see him in his ward, and asked him how he got along. "Oh! first-rate usage, sir; not a hand's turn to do, and all your grub brought to you, sir." This is a sailor's paradise,—not a hand's turn to do, and all your grub brought to you. But an earthly paradise may pall. Bennett got tired of indoors and stillness, and was soon out again, and set up a stall, covered with canvas, at the end of one of the bridges, where he could see all the passers-by, and turn a penny by cakes and ale. The stall in time disappeared, and I could learn nothing of his last end, if it has come.

Of the lads who, beside myself, composed the gig's crew, I know something of all but one. Our bright-eyed, quick-witted little cockswain, from the Boston public schools, Harry May, or Harry Bluff, as he was called, with all his songs and gibes, went the road to ruin as fast as the usual means could carry him. Nat, the "bucket-maker," grave and sober, left the seas, and, I believe, is a hack-driver in his native town, although I have not had the luck to see him since the Alert hauled into her berth at the North End.

One cold winter evening, a pull at the bell, and a woman in distress wished to see me. Her poor son George,—George Somerby,—"you remember him, sir; he was a boy in the Alert; he always talks of you,—he is dying in my poor house." I went with her, and in a small room, with the most scanty furniture, upon a mattress on the floor,—emaciated, ashy pale, with hollow voice and sunken eyes,—lay the boy George, whom we took out a small, bright boy of fourteen from a Boston public school, who fought himself into a position on board ship (*ante*, pp. 224–25), and whom we brought home a tall, athletic youth, that might have been the pride and support of his widowed mother. There he lay, not over nineteen years of age, ruined by every vice a sailor's life absorbs. He took my hand in his wasted feeble fingers, and talked a little with his hollow, death-smitten voice. I was to leave town the next day for a fortnight's absence, and whom had they to see to them? The mother named her landlord,—she knew no one else able to do much for them. It was the name of a physician of wealth and high social position, well known in the city as the owner of many small tenements, and of whom hard things had been said as to his strictness in collecting what he thought his dues. Be that as it may, my memory associates him only with ready and active beneficence. His name has since been known the civilized world over, from his having been the victim of one of the most painful tragedies in the records of the criminal law. I tried the experiment of calling upon him; and, having drawn him away from the cheerful fire, sofa, and curtains of a luxurious parlor, I told him this simple tale of woe, of one of his tenants, unknown to him even by name. He did not hesitate; and I well remember how, in that biting, eager air, and at a late hour, he drew his cloak about his thin and bent form, and walked off with me across the Common, and to the South End, nearly two miles of an exposed walk, to the scene of misery. He gave his full share, and more, of kindness and material aid; and, as George's mother told me, on my return, had with medical aid and stores, and a clergyman, made the boy's end as comfortable and hopeful as possible.

The Alert made two more voyages to the coast of California, successful, and without a mishap, as usual, and was sold by Messrs. Bryant and Sturgis, in 1843, to Mr. Thomas W. Williams, a merchant of New London, Connecticut, who employed her in the whale-trade in the Pacific. She was as lucky and prosperous there as in the merchant service. When I was at the Sandwich Islands in 1860, a man was introduced to me as having commanded the Alert on two cruises, and his friends told me that he was as proud of it as if he had commanded a frigate.

I am permitted to publish the following letter from the owner of the Alert, giving her later record and her historic end,—captured and burned by the rebel Alabama:—

NEW LONDON, March 17, 1868.

RICHARD H. DANA, ESQ.:

Dear Sir,—I am happy to acknowledge the receipt of your favor of the 14th inst., and to answer your inquiries about the good ship Alert. I bought her of Messrs. Bryant and Sturgis, in the year 1843, for my firm of Williams and Haven, for a whaler, in which business she was successful until captured by the rebel steamer Alabama, September, 1862, making a period of more than nineteen years, during which she took and delivered at New London upwards of twenty-five thousand barrels of whale and sperm oil. She sailed last from this port, August 30, 1862, for Hurd's Island (the newly discovered land south of Kerguelen's), commanded by Edwin Church, and was captured and burned on the 9th of September following, only ten days out, near or close to the Azores, with thirty barrels of sperm oil on board, and while her boats were off in pursuit of whales.

The Alert was a favorite ship with all owners, officers, and men who had anything to do with her; and I may add almost all who heard her name asked if that was the ship the man went in who wrote the book called "Two Years before the Mast"; and thus we feel, with you, no doubt, a sort of sympathy at her loss, and that, too, in such a manner, and by wicked acts of our own countrymen.

My partner, Mr. Haven, sends me a note from the office this P.M., saying that he had just found the last log-book, and would send up this evening a copy of the last entry on it; and if there should be anything of importance I will enclose it to you, and if you have any further inquiries to put, I will, with great pleasure, endeavor to answer them.

Remaining very respectfully and truly yours,

THOMAS W. WILLIAMS.

P.S.—Since writing the above I have received the extract from the log-book, and enclose the same.

The last Entry in the Log-Book of the Alert.

"SEPTEMBER 9, 1862.

"Shortly after the ship came to the wind, with the main yard aback, we went alongside and were hoisted up, when we found we were prisoners of war, and our ship a prize to the Confederate steamer Alabama. We were then ordered to give up all nautical instruments and letters appertaining to any of us. Afterwards we were offered the privilege, as they called it, of joining the steamer or signing a parole of honor not to serve in the army or navy of the United States. Thank God no one accepted the former of these offers. We were all then ordered to get our things ready in haste, to go on shore,—the ship running off shore all the time. We were allowed four boats to go on shore in, and when we had got what things we could take in them, were ordered to get into the boats and pull for the shore,—the nearest land being about fourteen miles off,—which we reached in safety, and, shortly after, saw the ship in flames.

"So end all our bright prospects, blasted by a gang of miscreants, who certainly can have no regard for humanity so long as they continue to foster their so-called peculiar institution, which is now destroying our country."

I love to think that our noble ship, with her long record of good service and uniform success, attractive and beloved in her life, should have passed, at her death, into the lofty regions of international jurisprudence and debate, forming a part of the body of the "Alabama Claims";—that, like a true ship, committed to her element once for all at her launching, she perished at sea, and, without an extreme use of language, we may say, a victim in the cause of her country.

R. H. D., JR.

BOSTON, May 6, 1869.

TO CUBA AND BACK

A Vacation Voyage

To the Gentlemen of the SATURDAY CLUB,
this narrative of a short absence from home and
from their society, is dedicated.

CONTENTS.

Chapter I

SATURDAY, the twelfth day of February, 1859, is a dull, dark day in New York, with visitations of snow-squalls, as the United States Mail Steamer Cahawba swings at her pier, at the foot of Robinson-street—a pier crowded with drays and drivers, and a street of mud, snow and ice, and poor habitations. The steamer is to sail at one P.M.; and, by half-past twelve, her decks are full, and the mud and snow of the pier are well trodden by men and horses. Coaches drive down furiously, and nervous passengers put their heads out to see if the steamer is off before her time; and on the decks, and in the gangways, inexperienced passengers run against everybody, and mistake the engineer for the steward, and come up the same stairs they go down, without knowing it. In the dreary snow, the newspaper venders cry the papers, and the book venders thrust yellow covers into your face—"Reading for the voyage, sir—five hundred pages, close print!" And that being rejected, they reverse the process of the Sibyl,—with "Here's another, sir, one thousand pages, double columns." The great beam of the engine moves slowly up and down, and the black hull sways at its fasts. A motley group are the passengers. Shivering Cubans, exotics that have taken slight root in the hot-houses of the Fifth Avenue, are to brave a few days of sleet and cold at sea, for the palm-trees and mangoes, the cocoas and orange-trees, they will be sitting under in six days, at farthest. There are Yankee shipmasters going out to join their "cotton wagons" at New Orleans and Mobile, merchants pursuing a commerce that knows no rest and no locality; confirmed invalids advised to go to Cuba to die under mosquito-nets and be buried in a Potter's Field; and other invalids wisely enough avoiding our March winds; and here and there a mere vacation-maker, like myself.

Captain Bullock is sure to sail at the hour; and at the hour he is on the paddle-box, the fasts are loosed, the warp run out, the crew pull in on the warp on the port quarter, and the head swings off. No word is spoken, but all is done by signs; or, if a word is necessary, a low clear tone carries it to the listener.

There is no tearing and rending escape of steam, deafening and distracting all, and giving a kind of terror to a peaceful scene; but our ship swings off, gathers way, and enters upon her voyage, in a quiet like that of a bank or counting-room, almost under a spell of silence.

The house-tops and piers and hill-tops are lined with snow, the masts and decks are white with it, a dreary cold haze lies over the water, and we work down the bay, where few sails venture out, and but few are coming in; and only a strong monster of a Cunard screw-steamer, the Kangaroo, comes down by our side.

We leave city and suburbs, Brooklyn Heights, and the foggy outline of Staten Island, far behind us, and hurry through the Narrows, for the open sea. The Kangaroo crossed our hawse in a strange way. Is she steering wild, or what is it? Seeing two old unmistakable Yankee shipmasters, sitting confidentially together on two chairs, in affectionate proximity to the binnacle, I address myself to them, and my question, being put in proper nautical phrase, secures a respectful attention. I find they agree with me that the Kangaroo is a little wilful, and crosses our hawse on purpose, in some manœuvre to discharge her pilot before we do ours; and so thinks the quartermaster, who comes aft to right the colors. This manœuvering of the steamer and pilot vessel makes an incident for a few minutes' talk, and an opening for several acquaintances which will be voyage-long. The pilots are dropped into their little cock-boats, and their boats drop astern, and go bobbing over the seas, to the pilot schooner that lies to for them. The Kangaroo, with her mysterious submarine art of swimming without fins, stands due east for Liverpool, and we stand down the coast, southerly, for the regions of the Sun.

The Heights of Neversink are passed. The night closes in upon the sea, dreary, cold, and snowing; our signal lanterns, the red, the white, and the green, gleam out into the mist; the furnace fires throw a lurid light from the doors below, cheerful or fearful as may be the temper of mind of the looker-on; the long swell lifts and drops the bow and stern, and rolls the ship from side to side; the sea-bells begin to strike their strange reckoning of the half-hours; the wet and the darkness drive all below but the experts and the desperate, and our first night at sea has begun.

At six bells, tea is announced; and the bright lights of the long cabin table, shining on plates and cups and gleaming knives and hurrying waiters, make a cheerful and lively contrast with the dark, cold, deserted deck.

By night, I walk deck for a couple of hours with the young captain. After due inquiries about his family in Georgia, and due remembrance of those of his mother's line whom we loved, and the public honored, before the grave or the sea closed over them, the fascinating topic of the navy, the frigates and the line-of-battle ships and little sloops, the storms, the wrecks, and the sea-fights, fill up the time. He loves the navy still, and has left it with regret; but the navy does not love her sons as they love her. On the quarter-deck at fifteen, the first in rank of his year, favored by his commanders, with service in the best vessels, making the great fleet cruise under Morris, taking part in the actions of the Naval Brigade on shore in California, serving on the Coast Survey, a man of science as well as a sailor,—yet what is there before him, or those like him, in our navy? The best must continue a subaltern, a lieutenant, until he is gray. At fifty, he may be entitled to his first command, and that of a class below a frigate; and if he survives the African fevers and the Isthmus fevers, and the perils of the sea, he may totter on the quarter-deck of a line-of-battle ship when his skill is out of date and his capacity for further command problematical. And whatever may be the gallantry or the merit of his service, though he may cut off his right hand or pluck out his eye for the country's honor, the navy can give him no promotion, not even a barren title of brevet, nor a badge of recognition of merit, though it be but a star, or a half yard of blue ribbon. The most meritorious officers receive large offers from civil life; and then, it is home, family, society, education of children, and pecuniary competency on the one side, and on the other, only the navy, less and less attractive as middle life draws on.

The state-rooms of the Cahawba, like those of most American sea-going steamers, are built so high above the water that the windows may be open in all but the worst of weather, and good ventilation be ensured. I have a very nice fellow for my room-mate, in the berth under me; but, in a state-room, no room-mate is better than the best; so I change my quarters to a state-room further forward, nearer "the eyes of her," which the passengers generally shun, and get one to myself, free from the rattle of the steering gear, while the delightful rise and fall of the bows, and leisurely weather roll and lee roll, cradle and nurse one to sleep.

Chapter II

S UNDAY, FEBRUARY 13.—It is cold and rough, though not at all stormy, and those who are on deck wear thick coats and caps. There is no clergyman on board, and we have no religious service. Capt. Bullock used to read the Liturgy himself, but in these West India and New Orleans voyages there are many Roman Catholics, and those who are not Romanists are of so many denominations, that he received little encouragement in maintaining an official worship; and it is no longer held, unless there is a clergyman on board and a request is made by the passengers.

All day there has been no sail in sight, except the steamer Columbia, for Charleston, S.C.; and she soon disappeared below the horizon.

We are near Cape Hatteras. It is night, and soon the Light of Hatteras throws its bright, cheerful beam for thirty miles over a huge burial-ground of sailors. How many struggles with death, how many last efforts of the last resources of skill and courage, what floating wrecks of ships, what waste of life, has that light shone over! Under that reef, perished Bache, flying for harbor before the gale, in his little surveying brig. Every league has been and will be a field where lives and treasures are sown thick from the hand of Destruction,—one of those points on the earth's surface where, in the universal and endless struggle between life and death, preservation and destruction, the destroyers have the advantage.

Soon after 9 P.M. we stand out direct, to cross the Gulf Stream. A bucket is thrown over the side, and water drawn. Its temperature is at 42°. In fifteen minutes more, it is thrown again, and the water is at 72° 30′. We are in the Gulf Stream.

Monday, February 14.—Sea rather rough, and a good deal of sea-sickness. Several passengers have not been seen since we left the dock, and only about half appear at table. We are to the eastward of the Gulf Stream. The weather is clear, and no longer cold. At noon, we are in about the latitude of Charleston, S.C. No vessels in sight, all day. It is strange, and always excites the surprise and comment of sea-faring men, that in the great highway of nations, with the immense commerce that is perpetually running East and West, North and South, a steamer may make her three hundred miles a day, for day after day, and see no sails.

This is a truly glorious moonlight night. The seas and floods "in wavering morrice move;" the air is pure and not cold, the sky a deep blue, the sea a deep blue, the stars glisten, and the moon bathes all in a serene glory. It is hard to leave the deck and such a scene, for the small state-room and its sleeping-shelf. But there must be sleep for infirm human nature,—a nature that has even less self-sustaining power than a locomotive engine, and must not only be supplied with fuel and water at every stopping place, but must lie by, in a dark corner, in absolute repose and mere oblivion, for one quarter of its time, or it will wear out in a few days.

Tuesday, February 15.—A bright, sunny, cheerful day. Passengers have laid aside their thick coats and fur caps, the snow and ice are gone from the rigging and spars, the decks are dry, the sea is calm, and the steady-going engine alone, with easy exercise of power, drives the great hull, with its freight of cargo and provisions and human beings, over the placid sea, as fast as a furious gale could drive it, and leaves her long wake of foam on the sea, and her long wake of dark smoke in the sky.

The passengers are recovering from sea-sickness. The women sit on deck and sew and read, and the children play. That family of Creole children,—how sallow, how frail, what delicate limbs, yet not without life, and with no little grace! But they are petted, and the girls complain, and the boys are disposed to tyrannize over the other boys and the dogs. It is interesting to see, or to fancy we see the effect not only of climate, but of slavery, and of despotic institutions, on the characters of children. What career is there for Cuban youth of ambition or merit? and what must be their life without one?

I am feeling very much at home in the Cahawba. She is an excellent sea boat, and under the best of discipline. I hardly believed that her commander could,—that any commander could,—fully come up to all the praise that had been bestowed on him; but I think he weathers it all. The rule of quietness prevails, almost to the point of an English dinner-party. No order is given unless it be necessary, and none louder than is necessary for it to be heard. The reports are made in low voices, and the passengers are to see and hear as little as possible of the discipline of the ship. They do not know the quiet but certain means for ensuring the performance of every duty. They do not know that reports are made of the state of every part of the ship, and that, through the night, the cabins and passage ways and every place where fire can take, are watched, and that the watch reports every half hour. They have not learned the merits of sturdy, faithful Miller, the chief mate, or quick, plucky Porter, the second mate, who can hardly keep down his "Liner" training to the tone of the Mail Steamer, nor the thorough excellence of the Engineer. But they do know the capital qualities of Mr. Rodgers, the Purser, a grandson of the old Commodore, a nephew of Perry, and connected by blood or marriage with half the navy,—for his station and duties are among the passengers, and all become his personal friends.

The routine of the ship, as regards passengers, is this: a cup of coffee, if you desire it, when you turn out; breakfast at eight, lunch at twelve, dinner at three, tea at seven, and lights put out at ten.

Wednesday, February 16.—Beautiful, serene, summer sea! The thermometer is at 70°, awnings are spread, the ladies have their books and sewing on deck, the men read and play chess and smoke, and the children play. We have crossed the Gulf Stream again, and are skirting along the Coast of Florida, as near to shore as safety permits; and here the deep sea runs close to the land. All objects on shore are plainly discernible by the naked eye, from the deck. We are below St. Augustine, about half-way between that and Key West. The coast is an interminable reach of sand beach, with coral reefs before it and the Everglades behind it. There are three small white tents, on the green sward, close upon the beach, backed by a grove of trees, with signals flying. That is the station of the United States Coast Survey. Towards evening, we pass a rough camp which was one of the camps of "Billy Bowlegs," the famous Seminole warrior. There is the wreck of a bark, her lowermasts still standing, while the beach is strewn with casks and boxes. It is an old wreck, and they make no signal for aid.

After dark, a light is made on our starboard bow. It is Cape

Florida Light. At 11 P.M. we make the light on Carysfort Reef, the outermost and southernmost of the Florida lights; and, having given a good berth to the reef, stand out to sea again, to cross the Gulf Stream the third time.

What can exceed the beauty of these nights at sea—these moonlight nights, the still sea, those bright stars, the light, soft trade-wind clouds floating under them, the gentle air, and a feeling of tropical romance stealing over the exile from the snow and ice of New England! There is something in the clear blue warm sea of the tropics, which gives to the stranger a feeling of unreality. Where do those vessels come from, that rise out of the sea, in the horizon? Where do they go to, as they sink in the sea again? Are those blue spots really fast anchored islands, with men and children, and horses, and machinery, and schools, politics and newspapers on them, or are they afloat, and visited by beings of the air?

Chapter III

THURSDAY, FEBRUARY 17.—Again a beautiful, warm day. I wake, and the first glance out of my state-room window shows the sea and sky flushed with the red of a bright sunrise. Awnings are spread; straw-hats and linen coats are worn; sewing, reading, and chess-playing is going on among the elders, and the children are romping about the decks, beginning to feel entirely at home. There are boys from the Northern States, with fair skins and light hair, strong, loud-voiced, plainly dressed, in stout shoes, honest and awkward; and there are Cuban boys, with a mixed air of the passionate and the timorous, sallow, slender, small-voiced, graceful, but with the grace rather of girls than of boys, wearing slippers, ornamented waistcoats and jackets, and hats with broad bands of cord. What preternaturally black eyes those little Creole girls have! Are they really eyes, so out of proportion in size and effect to their small thin faces? Their mother is hale and full-fleshed, and probably they will come to the same favour at last.

Throughout the day, sailing down the outer edge of the Gulf Stream, we see vessels of all forms and sizes, coming in sight and passing away, as in a dioramic show. There is a heavy cotton droger from the Gulf, of 1200 tons burden, under a cloud of sail, pressing on to the northern seas of New England or Old England. Here comes a saucy little Baltimore brig, close-hauled and leaning over to it; and there, half down in the horizon, is a pile of white canvas, which the experienced eyes of my two friends, the passenger shipmasters, pronounce to be a bark, outward bound. Every passenger says to every other, how beautiful! how exquisite! That pale thin girl who is going to Cuba for her health, her brother travelling with her, sits on the settee, propped by a pillow, and tries to smile and to think she feels stronger in this air. She says she shall stay in Cuba until she gets well!

After dinner, Capt. Bullock tells us that we shall soon see the high lands of Cuba, off Matanzas; the first and highest being the Pan of Matanzas. It is clear over head, but a mist lies along the southern horizon, in the latter part of the day. The sharpest eyes detect the land, about 4 p.m., and soon it is visible to all. It is an undulating country on the coast, with high hills and mountains in the interior, and has a rich and fertile look. That height is the Pan, though we see no special resemblance, in its outline, to a loaf of bread. We are still sixty miles from Havana. We cannot reach it before dark, and no vessels are allowed to pass the Morro after the signals are dropped at sunset.

We coast the northern shore of Cuba, from Matanzas westward. There is no waste of sand and low flats, as in most of our southern states; but the fertile, undulating land comes to the sea, and rises into high hills as it recedes. "There is the Morro! and right ahead!" "Why, there is the city too! Is the city on the sea? We thought it was on a harbor or bay." There, indeed, is the Morro, a stately hill of tawny rock, rising perpendicularly from the sea, and jutting into it, with walls and parapets and towers on its top, and flags and signals flying, and the tall lighthouse just in front of its outer wall. It is not very high, yet commands the sea about it. And there is the city, on the sea-coast, indeed—the houses running down to the coral edge of the ocean. Where is the harbor, and where the shipping? Ah, there they are! We open an entrance, narrow and deep, between the beetling Morro and the Punta; and through the entrance, we see the spreading harbor and the innumerable masts. But the darkness is gathering, the sunset gun has been fired, we can just catch the dying notes of trumpets from the fortifications, and the Morro Lighthouse throws its gleam over the still sea. The little lights emerge and twinkle from the city. We are too late to enter the port, and slowly and reluctantly the ship turns her head off to seaward. The engine breathes heavily, and throws its one arm leisurely up and down; we rise and fall on the moonlit sea; the stars are near to us, or we are raised nearer to them; the Southern Cross is just above the horizon; and all night long, two streams of light lie upon the water, one of gold from the Morro, and one of silver from the moon. It is enchantment. Who can regret our delay, or wish to exchange this scene for the common, close anchorage of a harbor?

Chapter IV

FRIDAY, FEBRUARY 18.—We are to go in at sunrise, and few, if any, are the passengers that are not on deck at the first glow of dawn. Before us lie the novel and exciting objects of the night before. The steep Morro, with its tall sentinel lighthouse, and its towers and signal staffs and teeth of guns, is coming out into clear daylight; the red and yellow striped flag of Spain—blood and gold—floats over it. Point after point in the city becomes visible; the blue and white and yellow houses, with their roofs of dull red tiles, the quaint old Cathedral towers, and the almost endless lines of fortifications. The masts of the immense shipping rise over the headland, the signal for leave to enter is run up, and we steer in under full head, the morning gun thundering from the Morro, the trumpets braying and drums beating from all the fortifications, the Morro, the Punta, the long Cabaña, the Casa Blanca and the city walls, while the broad sun is fast rising over this magnificent spectacle.

What a world of shipping! The masts make a belt of dense forest along the edge of the city, all the ships lying head in to the street, like horses at their mangers; while the vessels at anchor nearly choke up the passage ways to the deeper bays beyond. There are the red and yellow stripes of decayed Spain; the blue, white and red—blood to the fingers' end—of La Grande Nation; the Union crosses of the Royal Commonwealth; the stars and stripes of the Great Republic, and a few flags of Holland and Portugal, of the states of Northern Italy, of Brazil, and of the republics of the Spanish Main. We thread our slow and careful way among these, pass under the broadside of a ship-of-the-line, and under the stern of a screw frigate, both bearing the Spanish flag, and cast our anchor in the Regla Bay, by the side of the steamer Karnac, which sailed from New York a few days before us.

Instantly we are besieged by boats, some loaded with oranges and bananas, and others coming for passengers and their luggage, all with awnings spread over their sterns, rowed by swarthy, attenuated men, in blue and white checks and straw

hats, with here and there the familiar lips and teeth, and vacant, easily-pleased face of the negro. Among these boats
comes one, from the stern of which floats the red and yellow
flag with the crown in its field, and under whose awning reclines a man in a full suit of white linen, with straw hat and red
cockade and a cigar. This is the Health Officer. Until he is satisfied, no one can come on board, or leave the vessel. Capt.
Bullock salutes, steps down the ladder to the boat, hands his
papers, reports all well,—and we are pronounced safe. Then
comes another boat of similar style, another man reclining
under the awning with a cigar, who comes on board, is clos-
eted with the purser, compares the passenger list with the passports, and we are declared fully passed, and general leave is
given to land with our luggage at the custom-house wharf.

Now comes the war of cries and gestures and grimaces
among the boatmen, in their struggle for passengers, increased
manifold by the fact that there is but little language in common between the parties to the bargains, and by the boatmen
being required to remain in their boats. How thin these boatmen look! You cannot get it out of your mind that they must
all have had the yellow fever last summer, and are not yet fully
recovered. Not only their faces, but their hands and arms and
legs are thin, and their low-quartered slippers only half cover
their thin yellow feet.

In the hurry, I have to hunt after the passengers I am to take
leave of who go on to New Orleans:—Mr. and Mrs. Benchley,
on their way to their intended new home in Western Texas, my
two sea-captains, and the little son of my friend, who is the
guest, on this voyage, of our common friend the captain, and
after all, I miss the hearty hand-shake of Bullock and Rodgers.
Seated under an awning, in the stern of a boat, with my trunk
and carpet-bag and an unseasonable bundle of Arctic overcoat
and fur cap in the bow, I am pulled by a man with an oar in
each hand and a cigar in mouth, to the custom-house pier.
Here is a busy scene of trunks, carpet-bags, and bundles; and
up and down the pier, marches a military grandee of about the
rank of a sergeant or sub-lieutenant, with a preposterous strut,
so out of keeping with the depressed military character of his
country, and not possible to be appreciated without seeing it.

If he would give that strut on the boards, in New York, he would draw full houses nightly.

Our passports are kept, and we receive a license to remain and travel in the island, good for three months only, for which a large fee is paid. These officers of the customs are civil and reasonably rapid; and in a short time my luggage is on a dray driven by a negro, and I am in a volante, managed by a negro postilion, and am driving through the narrow streets of this surprising city.

The streets are so narrow and the houses built so close upon them, that they seem to be rather spaces between the walls of houses than highways for travel. It appears impossible that two vehicles should pass abreast; yet they do so. There are constant blockings of the way. In some places awnings are stretched over the entire street, from house to house, and we are riding under a long tent. What strange vehicles these volantes are!— A pair of very long, limber shafts, at one end of which is a pair of huge wheels, and at the other end a horse with his tail braided and brought forward and tied to the saddle, an open chaise body resting on the shafts, about one third of the way from the axle to the horse; and on the horse is a negro, in large postilion boots, long spurs, and a bright jacket. It is an easy vehicle to ride in; but it must be a sore burden to the beast. Here and there we pass a private volante, distinguished by rich silver mountings and postilions in livery. Some have two horses, and with the silver and the livery and the long dangling traces and a look of superfluity, have rather an air of high life. In most, a gentleman is reclining, cigar in mouth; while in others, is a great puff of blue or pink muslin or calico, extending over the sides to the shafts, topped off by a fan, with signs of a face behind it. "Calle de los Officios," "Calle del Obispo," "Calle de San Ignacio," "Calle de Mercaderes," are on the little corner boards. Every little shop and every big shop has its title; but nowhere does the name of a keeper appear. Almost every shop advertises "por mayor y menor," wholesale and retail. What a Gil Blas, Don Quixote feeling the names of "posada," "tienda," and "cantina" give you!

There are no women walking in the streets, except negresses. Those suits of seersucker, with straw hats and red cockades, are soldiers. It is a sensible dress for the climate. Every third man, perhaps more, and not a few women, are smoking cigars or cigarritos. Here are things moving along, looking like cocks of new mown grass, under way. But presently you see the head of a horse or mule peering out from under the mass, and a tail is visible at the other end, and feet are picking their slow way over the stones. These are the carriers of green fodder, the fresh cut stalks and blades of corn; and my chance companion in the carriage, a fellow passenger by the Cahawba, a Frenchman, who has been here before, tells me that they supply all the horses and mules in the city with their daily feed, as no hay is used. There are also mules, asses, and horses with bananas, plantains, oranges and other fruits in panniers reaching almost to the ground.

Here is the Plaza de Armas, with its garden of rich, fragrant flowers in full bloom, in front of the Governor's Palace. At the corner, is the chapel erected over the spot where, under the auspices of Columbus, mass was first celebrated on the island. We are driven by a gloomy convent, by innumerable shops, by drinking places, billiard rooms, and the thick, dead walls of houses, with large windows, grated like dungeons, and large gates, showing glimpses of interior court-yards, sometimes with trees and flowers. But horses and carriages and gentlemen and ladies and slaves, all seem to use the same entrance. The windows come to the ground, and, being flush with the street, and mostly without glass, nothing but the grating prevents a passenger from walking into the rooms. And there the ladies and children sit sewing, or lounging, or playing. This is all very strange. There is evidently enough for me to see in the ten or twelve days of my stay.

But there are no costumes among the men, no Spanish hats, or Spanish cloaks, or bright jackets, or waistcoats, or open, slashed trowsers, that are so picturesque in other Spanish countries. The men wear black dress coats, long pantaloons, black cravats, and many of them even submit, in this hot sun, to black French hats. The tyranny of systematic, scientific, capable, unpicturesque, unimaginative France, evidently rules over the realm of man's dress. The houses, the vehicles, the vegetation, the animals, are picturesque; to the eye of taste

"Every prospect pleases, and only man is vile."

We drove through the Puerta de Monserrate, a heavy gateway of the prevailing yellow or tawny color, where soldiers are on guard, across the moat, out upon the "Paseo de Ysabel Segunda," and are now "estramuros," without the walls. The Paseo is a grand avenue running across the city from sea to bay, with two carriage-drives abreast, and two malls for foot passengers, and all lined with trees in full foliage. Here you catch a glimpse of the Morro, and there of the Presídio. This is the Teatro de Tacon; and, in front of this line of tall houses, in contrast with the almost uniform one-story buildings of the city, the volante stops. This is Le Grand's hotel.

Chapter V

To a person unaccustomed to the tropics or the south of Europe, I know of nothing more discouraging than the arrival at the inn or hotel. It is nobody's business to attend to you. The landlord is strangely indifferent, and if there is a way to get a thing done, you have not learned it, and there is no one to teach you. Le Grand is a Frenchman. His house is a restaurant, with rooms for lodgers. The restaurant is paramount. The lodging is secondary, and is left to servants. Monsieur does not condescend to show a room, even to families; and the servants, who are whites, but mere lads, have all the interior in their charge, and there are no women employed about the chambers. Antonio, a swarthy Spanish lad, in shirt sleeves, looking very much as if he never washed, has my part of the house in charge, and shows me my room. It has but one window, a door opening upon the veranda, and a brick floor, and is very bare of furniture, and the furniture has long ceased to be strong. A small stand barely holds up a basin and ewer which have not been washed since Antonio was washed, and the bedstead, covered by a canvas sacking, without mattress or bed, looks as if it would hardly bear the weight of a man. It is plain there is a good deal to be learned here. Antonio is communicative, on a suggestion of several days' stay and good pay. Things which we cannot do without, we must go out of the house to find, and those which we can do without, we must dispense with. This is odd, and strange, but not uninteresting, and affords scope for contrivance and the exercise of influence and other administrative powers. The Grand Seigneur does not mean to be troubled with anything; so there are no bells, and no office, and no clerks. He is the only source, and if he is approached, he shrugs his shoulders and gives you to understand that you have your chambers for your money and must look to the servants. Antonio starts off on an expedition for a pitcher of water and a towel, with a faint hope of two towels; for each demand involves an expedition to remote parts of the house. Then Antonio has so many rooms dependent on him, that every door is a Scylla, and every window a Charybdis, as he passes. A shrill, female voice, from the next room but one, calls "Antonio! Antonio!" and that starts the parrot in the court yard, who cries "Antonio! Antonio!" for several minutes. A deep, bass voice mutters "Antonio!" in a more confidential tone; and last of all, an unmistakably Northern voice attempts it, but ends in something between Antonio and Anthony. He is gone a good while, and has evidently had several episodes to his journey. But he is a good-natured fellow, speaks a little French, very little English, and seems anxious to do his best.

I see the faces of my New York fellow-passengers from the west gallery, and we come together and throw our acquisitions of information into a common stock, and help one another. Mr. Miller's servant, who has been here before, says there are baths and other conveniences round the corner of the street; and, sending our bundles of thin clothes there, we take advantage of the baths, with comfort. To be sure, we must go through a billiard-room, where the Creoles are playing at the tables, and the cockroaches playing under them, and through a drinking-room, and a bowling-alley; but the baths are built in the open yard, protected by blinds, well ventilated, and well supplied with water and toilet apparatus.

With the comfort of a bath, and clothed in linen, with straw hats, we walk back to Le Grand's, and enter the restaurant, for breakfast,—the breakfast of the country, at 10 o'clock. Here is a scene so pretty as quite to make up for the defects of the chambers. The restaurant with cool marble floor, walls twenty-four feet high, open rafters painted blue, great windows open to the floor and looking into the Paseo, and the floor nearly on a level with the street, a light breeze fanning the thin curtains, the little tables, for two or four, with clean, white cloths, each with its pyramid of great red oranges and its fragrant bouquet,—the gentlemen in white pantaloons and jackets and white stockings, and the ladies in fly-away muslins, and hair in the sweet neglect of the morning toilet, taking their leisurely breakfasts of fruit and claret, and omelette and Spanish mixed dishes, (ollas,) and café noir. How airy and ethereal it seems! They are birds, not substantial men and women. They eat ambrosia and drink nectar. It must be that they fly, and live in nests, in the tamarind trees. Who can eat a hot, greasy breakfast of cakes and gravied meats, and in a close room, after this?

I can truly say that I ate, this morning, my first orange; for I had never before eaten one newly gathered, which had ripened in the sun, hanging on the tree. We call for the usual breakfast, leaving the selection to the waiter; and he brings us fruits, claret, omelette, fish fresh from the sea, rice excellently cooked, fried plantains, a mixed dish of meat and vegetables (olla), and coffee. The fish, I do not remember its name, is boiled, and has the colors of the rainbow, as it lies on the plate. Havana is a good fish-market; for it is as open to the ocean as Nahant, or the beach at Newport; its streets running to the blue sea, outside the harbor, so that a man may almost throw his line from the curb-stone into the Gulf Stream.

After breakfast, I take a volante and ride into the town, to deliver my letters. Three merchants whom I call upon, have palaces for their business. The entrances are wide, the staircases almost as stately as that of Stafford House, the floors of marble, the panels of porcelain tiles, the rails of iron, and the rooms over twenty feet high, with open rafters, the doors and windows colossal, the furniture rich and heavy; and there sits the merchant or banker, in white pantaloons and thin shoes and loose white coat and narrow neck-tie, smoking a succession of cigars, surrounded by tropical luxuries and tropical defences. In the lower story of one of these buildings is an exposition of silks, cotton and linens, in a room so large that it looked like a part of the Great Exhibition in Hyde Park. At one of these counting-palaces, I met Mr. Theodore Parker and Dr. S. G. Howe, of Boston, who preceded me, in the Karnac. Mr. Parker is here for his health, which has caused anxiety to his friends lest his weakened frame should no longer support the strong intellectual machinery, as before. He finds Havana too hot, and will leave for Santa Cruz by the first opportunity. Dr. Howe likes the warm weather. It is a comfort to see him,— a benefactor of his race, and one of the few heroes we have left to us, since Kane died.

The Bishop of Havana has been in delicate health, and is out of town, at Jesus del Monte; and Miss M—— is not at home, and the Señoras F—— I failed to see this morning; but I find a Boston young lady, whose friends were desirous I should see her, and who was glad enough to meet one so lately from her home. A clergyman to whom, also, I had letters, is gone into the country, without much hope of improving his health. Stepping into a little shop to buy a plan of Havana, my name is called, and there is my hero's wife, the distinguished author and conversationist, whom it is an exhilaration to meet anywhere, much more in a land of strangers. Dr. and Mrs. Howe and Mr. Parker are at the Cerro, a pretty and cool place in the suburbs, but are coming in to Mrs. Almy's boarding-house, for the convenience of being in the city, and for nearness to friends, and the comforts of something like American or English housekeeping.

In the latter part of the afternoon, from three o'clock, our parties are taking dinner at Le Grand's. The little tables are again full, with a fair complement of ladies. The afternoon breeze is so strong that the draught of air, though it is hot air, is to be avoided. The passers-by almost put their faces into the room, and the women and children of the poorer order look wistfully in upon the luxurious guests, the colored glasses, the red wines, and the golden fruits. The Opera troupe is here, both the singers and the ballet; and we have Gazzaniga, Lamoureux, Max Maretzek and his sister, and others, in this house, and Miss Ada Phillips at the next door, and the benefit of a rehearsal, at nearly all hours of the day, of operas that the Habaneros are to rave over at night.

I yield to no one in my admiration of the Spanish as a spoken language, whether in its rich, sonorous, musical, and lofty style, in the mouth of a man who knows its uses, or in the soft, indolent, languid tones of a woman, broken by an occasional birdlike trill—

> "With wanton heed, and giddy cunning,
> The melting voice through mazes running"—

but I do not like it as spoken by the common people of Cuba, in the streets. Their voices and intonations are thin and eager, very rapid, too much in the lips, and, withal, giving an impression of the passionate and the childish combined; and it strikes me that the tendency here is to enfeeble the language, and take from it the openness of the vowels and the strength of the harder consonants. This is the criticism of a few hours' observation, and may not be just; but I have heard the same from persons who have been longer acquainted with it. Among the well educated Cubans, the standard of Castilian is said to be kept high, and there is a good deal of ambition to reach it.

After dinner, walked along the Paseo de Ysabel Segunda, to see the pleasure-driving, which begins at about five o'clock, and lasts until dark. The most common carriage is the volante, but there are some carriages in the English style, with servants in livery on the box. I have taken a fancy for the strange-looking two-horse volante. The postilion, the long, dangling traces, the superfluousness of a horse to be ridden by the man that guides the other, and the prodigality of silver, give the whole a look of style that eclipses the neat, appropriate English equipage. The ladies ride in full dress, décolletées, without hats. The servants on the carriages are not all negroes. Many of the drivers are whites. The drives are along the Paseo de Ysabel, across the Campo del Marte, and then along the Paseo de Tacon, a beautiful double avenue, lined with trees, which leads two or three miles, in a straight line, into the country.

At 8 o'clock, drove to the Plaza de Armas, a square in front of the governor's house, to hear the Retreta, at which a military band plays for an hour, every evening. There is a clear moon above, and a blue field of glittering stars; the air is pure and balmy; the band of fifty or sixty instruments discourses most eloquent music under the shade of palm-trees and mangoes; the walks are filled with promenaders, and the streets around the square lined with carriages, in which the ladies recline, and receive the salutations and visits of the gentlemen. Very few ladies walk in the square, and those probably are strangers. It is against the etiquette for ladies to walk in public in Havana.

I walk leisurely home, in order to see Havana by night. The evening is the busiest season for the shops. Much of the business of shopping is done after gas lighting. Volantes and coaches are driving to and fro, and stopping at the shop doors, and attendants take their goods to the doors of the carriages. The watchmen stand at the corners of the streets, each carrying a long pike and a lantern. Billiard-rooms and cafés are filled, and all who can walk for pleasure will walk now. This is also the principal time for paying visits.

There is one strange custom observed here in all the houses. In the chief room, rows of chairs are placed, facing each other, three or four or five in each line, and always running at right angles with the street wall of the house. As you pass along the street, you look up this row of chairs. In these, the family and the visitors take their seats, in formal order. As the windows are open, deep, and large, with wide gratings and no glass, one has the inspection of the interior arrangement of all the front parlors of Havana, and can see what every lady wears, and who is visiting her.

To-bed early, after so exciting a day as one's first day in the tropics.

Chapter VI

IF mosquito nets were invented for the purpose of shutting mosquitoes in with you, they answer their purpose very well. The beds have no mattresses, and you lie on the hard sacking. This favors coolness and neatness. I should fear a mattress, in the economy of our hotel, at least. Where there is nothing but an iron frame, canvas stretched over it, and sheets and a blanket, you may know what you are dealing with.

The clocks of the churches and castles strike the quarter hours, and at each stroke the watchmen blow a kind of boatswain's whistle, and cry the time and the state of the weather, which, from their name (serenos), should be always pleasant.

I have been advised to close the shutters at night, whatever the heat, as the change of air that often takes place before dawn is injurious; and I notice that many of the bedrooms in the hotel are closed, both doors and shutters, at night. This is too much for my endurance, and I venture to leave the air to its course, not being in the draught. One is also cautioned not to step with bare feet on the floor, for fear of the nigua (or chigua), a very small insect, that is said to enter the skin and build tiny nests, and lay little eggs that can only be seen by the microscope, but are tormenting and sometimes dangerous. This may be excessive caution, but it is so easy to observe, that it is not worth while to test the question.

Saturday, February 19.—There are streaks of a clear dawn; it is nearly six o'clock, the cocks are crowing, and the drums and trumpets sounding. We have been told of sea-baths, cut in the rock, near the Punta, at the foot of our Paseo. I walk down, under the trees, towards the Presidio. What is this clanking sound? Can it be cavalry, marching on foot, their sabres rattling on the pavement? No, it comes from that crowd of poor looking creatures that are forming in files in front of the Presidio. It is the chain-gang! Poor wretches! I come nearer to them, and wait until they are formed and numbered and marched off. Each man has an iron band riveted round his ankle, and another round his waist, and the chain is fastened, one end into each of these bands, and dangles between them, clanking with every movement. This leaves the wearers free to use their arms, and, indeed, their whole body, it being only a weight and a badge and a note for discovery, from which they cannot rid themselves. It is kept on them day and night, working, eating, or sleeping. In some cases, two are chained together. They have passed their night in the Presidio (the great prison and garrison), and are marshalled for their day's toil in the public streets and on the public works, in the heat of the sun. They look thoroughly wretched. Can any of these be political offenders? It is said that Carlists, from Old Spain, worked in this gang. Sentence to the chain-gang in summer, in the case of a foreigner, must be nearly certain death.

Farther on, between the Presidio and the Punta, the soldiers are drilling; and the drummers and trumpeters are practising on the rampart of the city walls.

A little to the left, in the Calzado de San Lázaro, are the Baños de Mar. These are boxes, each about twelve feet square and six or eight feet deep, cut directly into the rock which here forms the sea-line, with steps of rock, and each box having a couple of port-holes through which the waves of this tideless shore wash in and out. This arrangement is necessary, as sharks are so abundant that bathing in the open sea is dangerous. The pure rock, and the flow and reflow, make these bathing-boxes very agreeable, and the water, which is that of the Gulf Stream, is at a temperature of 72°. The baths are roofed over, and partially screened on the inside, but open for a view out, on the side towards the sea; and as you bathe, you see the big ships floating up the Gulf Stream, that great highway of the Equinoctial world. The water stands at depths of from three to five feet in the baths; and they are large enough for short swimming. The bottom is white with sand and shells. These baths are made at the public expense, and are free. Some are marked for women, some for men, and some "por la gente de color." A little further down the Calzado, is another set of baths, and further out in the suburbs, opposite the Beneficencia, are still others.

After bath, took two or three fresh oranges, and a cup of coffee, without milk; for the little milk one uses with coffee, must not be taken with fruit here, even in winter.

To the Cathedral, at 8 o'clock, to hear mass. The Cathedral,

in its exterior, is a plain and quaint old structure, with a tower
at each angle of the front; but within, it is sumptuous. There is
a floor of variegated marble, obstructed by no seats or screens,
tall pillars and rich frescoed walls, and delicate masonry of various colored stone, the prevailing tint being yellow, and a high
altar of porphyry. There is a look of the great days of Old Spain
about it; and you think that knights and nobles worshipped
here and enriched it from their spoils and conquests. Every
new eye turns first to the place within the choir, under that
alto-relief, behind that short inscription, where, in the wall of
the chancel, rest the remains of Christopher Columbus. Borne
from Valladolid to Seville, from Seville to San Domingo, and
from San Domingo to Havana, they at last rest here, by the
altar side, in the emporium of the Spanish Islands. "What is
man that thou art mindful of him!" truly and humbly says the
Psalmist; but what is man, indeed, if his fellow men are not
mindful of such a man as this! The creator of a hemisphere! It
is not often we feel that monuments are surely deserved, in
their degree and to the extent of their utterance. But when, in
the New World, on an island of that group which he gave to
civilized man, you stand before this simple monumental slab,
and know that all of him that man can gather up, lies behind it,
so overpowering is the sense of the greatness of his deeds, that
you feel relieved that no attempt has been made to measure it
by any work of man's hands. The little there is, is so inade-
quate, that you make no comparison. It is a mere finger-point,
the *hic jacet*, the *sic itur*.

The priests in the chancel are numerous, perhaps twenty or
more. The service is chanted with no aid of instruments, except once the accompaniment of a small and rather disordered
organ, and chanted in very loud and often harsh and blatant
tones, which reverberate from the marble walls, with a tiresome monotony of cadence. There is a degree of ceremony in
the placing, replacing, and carrying to and fro of candles and
crucifixes, and swinging of censers, which the Roman service
as practised in the United States does not give. The priests
seem duly attentive and reverent in their manner, but I cannot
say as much for the boys, of whom there were three or four,
gentlemen-like looking lads, from the college, doing service as
altar boys. One of these, who seemed to have the lead, was

strikingly careless and irreverent in his manner; and when he went about the chancel, to incense all who were there, and to give to each the small golden vessel to kiss, (containing, I suppose, a relic,) he seemed as if he were counting his playmates out for a game, and flinging the censer at them and snubbing their noses with the golden vessel.

There were only about half a dozen persons at mass, beside those in the chancel; and all but one of these were women, and of the women two were negroes. The women walk in, veiled, drop down on the bare pavement, kneeling or sitting, as the service requires or permits. A negro woman, with devout and even distressed countenance, knelt at the altar rail, and one pale-eyed priest, in cassock, who looked like an American or Englishman, knelt close by a pillar. A file of visitors, American or English women, with an escort of gentlemen, came in and sat on the only benches, next the columns; and when the Host was elevated, and a priest said to them, very civilly, in English, "Please to kneel down," they neither knelt nor stood, nor went away, but kept their seats.

After service, the old sacristan, in blue woollen dress, showed all the visitors the little chapel and the cloisters, and took us beyond the altar to the mural tomb of Columbus, and though he was liberally paid, haggled for two reals more.

In the rear of the Cathedral is the Seminario, or college for boys, where also men are trained for the priesthood. There are cloisters and a pleasant garden within them.

Chapter VII

BREAKFAST, and again the cool marble floor, white-robed tables, the fruits and flowers, and curtains gently swaying, and women in morning toilets. Besides the openness to view, these rooms are strangely open to ingress. Lottery-ticket venders go the rounds of the tables at every meal, and so do the girls with tambourines for alms for the music in the street. As there is no coin in Cuba less than the medio, 6¼ cents, the musicians get a good deal or nothing. The absence of any smaller coin must be an inconvenience to the poor, as they must often buy more than they want, or go without. I find silver very scarce here. It is difficult to get change for gold, and at public places notices are put up that gold will not be received for small payments. I find the only course is to go to one of the Cambios de Moneda, whose signs are frequent in the streets, and get a half doubloon changed into reals and pesetas, at four per cent. discount, and fill my pockets with small silver.

Spent the morning, from eleven o'clock to dinner-time, in my room, writing and reading. It is too hot to be out with comfort. It is not such a morning as one would spend at the St. Nicholas, or the Tremont, or at Morley's or Meurice's. The rooms all open into the court-yard, and the doors and windows, if open at all, are open to the view of all passers-by. As there are no bells, every call is made from the veranda rail, down into the court-yard, and repeated until the servant answers, or the caller gives up in despair. Antonio has a compeer and rival in Domingo, and the sharp voice of the woman in the next room but one, who proves to be a subordinate of the opera troupe, is calling out, "Do-meen-go! Do-meen-go!" and the rogue is in full sight from our side, making significant faces, until she changes her tune to "Antonio! Antonio! adonde está Domingo?" But as she speaks very little Spanish, and Antonio very little French, it is not difficult for him to get up a misapprehension, especially at the distance of two stories; and she is obliged to subside for a while, and her place is supplied by the parrot. She is usually unsuccessful, being either unreasonable, or bad pay. The opera troupe are rehearsing in the second flight, with doors and windows open. And throughout the hot middle day, we hear the singing, the piano, the parrot, and the calls and parleys with the servants below. But we can see the illimitable sea from the end of the piazza, blue as indigo; and the strange city is lying under our eye, with its strange blue and white and yellow houses, with their roofs of dull red tiles, its strange tropical shade-trees, and its strange vehicles and motley population, and the clangor of its bells, and the high pitched cries of the venders in its streets.

Going down stairs at about eleven o'clock, I find a table set in the front hall, at the foot of the great staircase, and there, in full view of all who come or go, the landlord and his entire establishment, except the slaves and coolies, are at breakfast. This is done every day. At the café round the corner, the family, with their white, hired servants, breakfast and dine in the hall, through which all the customers of the place must go to the baths, the billiard rooms, and the bowling-alleys. Fancy the manager of the Astor or Revere, spreading a table for breakfast and dinner in the great entry, between the office and the front door, for himself and family and servants!

Yesterday and to-day I noticed in the streets and at work in houses, men of an Indian complexion, with coarse black hair. I asked if they were native Indians, or of mixed blood. No, they are the Coolies! Their hair, full grown, and the usual dress of the country which they wore, had not suggested to me the Chinese; but the shape and expression of the eye make it plain. These are the victims of the trade, of which we hear so much. I am told there are 200,000 of them in Cuba, or, that so many have been imported, and all within seven years. I have met them everywhere, the newly arrived, in Chinese costume, with shaved heads, but the greater number in pantaloons and jackets and straw hats, with hair full grown. Two of the cooks at our hotel are Coolies. I must inform myself on the subject of this strange development of the domination of capital over labor. I am told there is a mart of Coolies in the Cerro. This I must see, if it is to be seen.

After dinner drove out to the Jesus del Monte, to deliver my letter of introduction to the Bishop. The drive, by way of the Calzada de Jesus del Monte, takes one through a wretched portion, I hope the most wretched portion, of Havana, by long lines of one story wood and mud hovels, hardly habitable even for negroes, and interspersed with an abundance of drinking shops. The horses, mules, asses, chickens, children, and grown people use the same door; and the back yards disclose heaps of rubbish. The looks of the men, the horses tied to the door-posts, the mules with their panniers of fruits and leaves reaching to the ground, all speak of Gil Blas, and of what we have read of humble life in Spain. The little negro children go stark naked, as innocent of clothing as the puppies. But this is so all over the city. In the front hall of Le Grand's, this morning, a lady, standing in a full dress of spotless white, held by the hand a naked little negro boy, of two or three years old, nestling in black relief against the folds of her dress.

Now we rise to the higher grounds of Jesus del Monte. The houses improve in character. They are still of one story, but high and of stone, with marble floors and tiled roofs, with court-yards of grass and trees, and through the gratings of the wide, long, open windows, I see the decent furniture, the double, formal row of chairs, prints on the walls, and well-dressed women manœuvering their fans.

As a carriage with a pair of cream-colored horses passed, having two men within, in the dress of ecclesiastics, my driver pulled up and said that was the Bishop's carriage, and that he was going out for an evening drive. Still, I must go on; and we drive to his house. As you go up the hill, a glorious view lies upon the left. Havana, both city and suburbs, the Morro with its batteries and lighthouse, the ridge of fortifications called the Cabaña and Casa Blanca, the Castle of Atares, near at hand, a perfect truncated cone, fortified at the top,—the higher and most distant Castle of Principe,

> "And, poured round all,
> Old Ocean's gray and melancholy waste"—

No! Not so! Young Ocean, the Ocean of to-day! The blue, bright, healthful, glittering, gladdening, inspiring Ocean! Have I ever seen a city view so grand? The view of Quebec from the foot of the Montmorenci Falls, may rival, but does not excel it. My preference is for this; for nothing, not even the St. Lawrence, broad and affluent as it is, will make up for the living sea, the boundless horizon, the dioramic vision of gliding, distant sails, and the open arms and motherly bosom of the harbor, "with handmaid lamp attending":—our Mother Earth, forgetting never the perils of that gay and treacherous world of waters, its change of moods, its "strumpet winds,"—ready is she at all times, by day or by night, to fold back to her bosom her returning sons, knowing that the sea can give them no drink, no food, no path, no light, nor bear up their foot for an instant, if they are sinking in its depths.

The regular episcopal residence is in town. This is only a house which the Bishop occupies temporarily, for the sake of his health. It is a modest house of one story, standing very high, with a commanding view of city, harbor, sea, and suburbs. The floors are marble, and the roof is of open rafters, painted blue, and above twenty feet in height; the windows are as large as doors, and the doors as large as gates. The mayordomo shows me the parlor, in which are portraits in oil of distinguished scholars and missionaries and martyrs.

On my way back to the city, I direct the driver to avoid the disagreeable road by which we came out, and we drive by a cross road, and strike the Paseo de Tacon at its outer end, where is a fountain and statue, and a public garden of the most exquisite flowers, shrubs, and trees; and around them are standing, though it is nearly dark, files of carriages waiting for the promenaders, who are enjoying a walk in the garden. I am able to take the entire drive of the Paseo. It is straight, very wide, with two carriage ways and two foot ways, with rows of trees between, and at three points has a statue and a fountain. One of these statues, if I recollect aright, is of Tacon; one of a Queen of Spain; and one is an allegorical figure. The Paseo is two or three miles in length; reaching from the Campo de Marte, just outside the walls, to the last statue and public garden, on gradually ascending ground, and lined with beautiful villas, and rich gardens full of tropical trees and plants. No city in America has such an avenue as the Paseo de Tacon. This, like most of the glories of Havana, they tell you they owe to the energy and genius of the man whose name it bears. —I must guard myself, by the way, while here, against using the words America and American, when I mean the United States and the people of our Republic; for this is America also; and they here use the word America as including the entire continent and islands, and distinguish between Spanish and English America, the islands and the main.

The Cubans have a taste for prodigality in grandiloquent or pretty names. Every shop, the most humble, has its name. They name the shops after the sun and moon and stars; after gods and goddesses, demi-gods and heroes; after fruits and flowers, gems and precious stones; after favorite names of women, with pretty, fanciful additions; and after all alluring qualities, all delights of the senses, and all pleasing affections of the mind. The wards of jails and hospitals are each known by some religious or patriotic designation; and twelve guns in the Morro are named for the Apostles. Every town has the name of an apostle or saint, or of some sacred subject. The full name of Havana, in honor of Columbus, is San Cristóbal de la Habana; and that of Matanzas is San Carlos Alcazar de Matanzas. It is strange that the island itself has defied all the Spanish attempts to name it. It has been solemnly named Juana, after the daughter of Ferdinand and Isabella; then Ferdinandina, after Ferdinand himself; then Santiago, and, lastly, Ave Maria; but it has always fallen back upon the original Indian name of Cuba. And the only compensation to the hyperbolical taste of the race is that they decorate it, on state and ceremonious occasions, with the musical prefix of "La siempre fidelísima Isla de Cuba."

At 7.30 P.M. went with my New York fellow-passengers to hear an opera, or, more correctly, to see the people of Havana at an opera. The Teatro de Tacon is closed for repairs. This is unfortunate, as it is said by some to be the finest theatre, and by all to be one of the three finest theatres in the world. This, too, is attributed to Tacon; although it is said to have been a speculation of a clever pirate, turned fish-dealer, who made a fortune by it. But I like well enough the Teatro de Villanueva. The stage is deep and wide, the pit high and comfortable, and the boxes light and airy and open in front, with only a light tracery of iron to support the rails, leaving you a full view of the costumes of the ladies, even to their slippers. The boxes are also separated from the passage ways in the rear, only by wide lattice work; so that the promenaders between the acts can see the entire contents of the boxes at one view; and the ladies dress and sit and talk and use the fan with a full sense that they are under the inspection of a "committee of the whole house." They are all in full dress, décolletées, without hats. It seemed, to my fancy, that the mature women were divisible into two classes, distinctly marked and with few intermediates, —the obese and the shrivelled. I suspect that the effect of time in this climate is to produce a decided result in the one direction or the other. But a single night's view at an opera is very imperfect material for an induction, I know. The young ladies had, generally, full figures, with tapering fingers and well rounded arms; yet there were some in the extreme contrast of sallow, bilious, sharp countenances, with glassy eyes. There is evidently great attention to manner, to the mode of sitting and moving, to the music of the voice in speaking, the use of the hands and arms, and, perhaps it may be ungallant to add, of the eyes.

The Governor-General, Concha, (whose title is, strictly, Capitan-General,) with his wife and two daughters, and two aides-de-camp, is in the Vice-regal box, hung with red curtains, and surmounted by the royal arms. I can form no opinion of him from his physiognomy, as that is rather heavy, and gives not much indication.

Between the acts, I make, as all the gentlemen do, the promenade of the house. All parts of it are respectable, and the regulations are good. I notice one curious custom, which I am told prevails in all Spanish theatres. As no women sit in the pit, and the boxes are often hired for the season, and are high-priced, a portion of an upper tier is set apart for those women and children who cannot or do not choose to get seats in the boxes. Their quarter is separated from the rest of the house by gates, and is attended by two or three old women, with a man to guard the entrance. No men are admitted among them, and their parents, brothers, cousins and beaux are allowed only to come to the door, and must send in refreshments, and even a cup of water, by the hands of the dueñas.

Military, on duty, abound at the doors and in the passage ways. The men to-night are of the regiment of Guards, dressed in white. There are enough of them to put down a small insurrection, on the spot. The singers screamed well enough, and the play was a poor one, Maria de Rohan, but the prima donna, Gazzaniga, is a favorite, and the excitable Cubans shout and scream, and throw bouquets, and jump on the benches, and, at last, present her with a crown, wreathed with flowers, and with jewels of value attached to it. Miss Adelaide Phillips is here, too, and a favorite, and has been crowned, they say; but she does not sing to-night.

Chapter VIII

To-morrow, I am to go, at eight o'clock, either to the church of San Domingo, to hear the military mass, or to the Jesuit church of Belen; for the service of my own church is not publicly celebrated, even at the British Consulate; no service but the Roman Catholic being tolerated on the island.

To-night there is a public mascara (mask ball) at the great hall, next door to Le Grand's. My only window is by the side of the numerous windows of the great hall, and all these are wide open; and I should be stifled if I were to close mine. The music is loud and violent, from a very large band, with kettle drums and bass drums and trumpets; and because these do not make noise and uproar enough, pistols are discharged, at the turns in the tunes. For sleeping, I might as well have been stretched on the bass drum. This tumult of noises, and the heat are wearing and oppressive beyond endurance, as it draws on past midnight, to the small hours; and the servants in the court of the hall seem to be tending at tables of quarrelling men, and to be interminably washing and breaking dishes. After several feverish hours, I light a match and look at my watch. It is nearly five o'clock in the morning. There is an hour to daylight,—and will this noise stop before then? The city clocks struck five; the music ceased; and the bells of the convents and monasteries tolled their matins, to call the nuns and monks to their prayers and to the bedsides of the sick and dying in the hospitals, as the maskers go home from their revels at this hideous hour of Sunday morning. The servants ceased their noises, the cocks began to crow and the bells to chime, the trumpets began to bray, and the cries of the streets broke in before dawn, and I dropped asleep just as I was thinking sleep past hoping for; when I am awaked by a knocking at the door, and Antonio calling, "Usted! Usted! Un caballero quiere ver Usted!" to find it half-past nine, the middle of the forenoon, and an ecclesiastic in black dress and shovel hat, waiting in the passage way, with a message from the bishop.

His Excellency regrets not having seen me the day before,

and invites me to dinner at three o'clock, to meet three or four gentlemen; an invitation which I accept with pleasure.

I am too late for the mass, or any other religious service, as all the churches close at ten o'clock. A tepid, soothing bath, at "Los baños públicos," round the corner, and I spend the morning in my chamber. As we are at breakfast, the troops pass by the Paseo, from the mass service. Their gait is quick and easy, with swinging arms, after the French fashion. Their dress is seersucker, with straw hats and red cockades: the regiments being distinguished by the color of the cloth on the cuffs of the coat, some being yellow, some green, and some blue.

Soon after two o'clock, I take a carriage for the bishop's. On my way out I see that the streets are full of Spanish sailors from the men-of-war, ashore for a holiday, dressed in the style of English sailors, with wide duck trowsers, blue jackets, and straw hats, with the name of their ship on the front of the hat. All business is going on as usual, and laborers are at work in the streets and on the houses.

The company consists of the bishop himself, the Bishop of Puebla de los Angelos in Mexico, Father Luch, the rector of the Jesuit College, who has a high reputation as a man of intellect, and two young ecclesiastics. Our dinner is well cooked, and in the Spanish style, consisting of fish, vegetables, fruits, and of stewed light dishes, made up of vegetables, fowls and other meats, a style of cooking well adapted to a climate in which one is very willing to dispense with the solid, heavy cuts of an English dinner.

The Bishop of Puebla wore the purple, the Bishop of Havana a black robe with a broad cape, lined with red, and each wore the Episcopal cross and ring. The others were in simple black cassocks. The conversation was in French; for, to my surprise, none of the company could speak English; and being allowed my election between French and Spanish, I chose the former, as the lighter infliction on my associates.

I am surprised to see what an impression is made on all classes in this country by the pending "Thirty Millions Bill" of Mr. Slidell. It is known to be an Administration measure, and is thought to be the first step in a series which is to end in an attempt to seize the island. Our steamer brought verbal intelligence that it had passed the Senate, and it was so announced in the Diario of the day after our arrival, although no newspaper that we brought so stated it. Not only with these clergymen, but with the merchants and others whom I have met since our arrival, foreigners as well as Cubans, this is the absorbing topic. Their future seems to be hanging in doubt, depending on the action of our government, which is thought to have a settled purpose to acquire the island. I suggested that it had not passed the Senate, and would not pass the House; and, at most, was only an authority to the President to make an offer that would certainly be refused. But they looked beyond the form of the act, and regarded it as the first move in a plan, of which, although they could not entirely know the details, they thought they understood the motive.

These clergymen were well informed as to the state of religion in the United States, the relative numbers and force of the various denominations, and their doctrinal differences; the reputations of Brownson, Parker, Beecher, and others; and most minutely acquainted with the condition of their own church in the United States, and with the chief of its clergy. This acquaintance is not attributable solely to their unity of organization, and to the consequent interchange of communication, but largely also to the tie of a common education at the Propaganda or St. Sulpice, the catalogues of whose alumni are familiar to the educated Catholic clergy throughout the world.

The subject of slavery, and the condition and prospects of the negro race in Cuba, the probable results of the Coolie system, and the relations between Church and State in Cuba, and the manner in which Sunday is treated in Havana, the public school system in America, the fate of Mormonism, and how our government will treat it, were freely discussed. It is not because I have any reason to suppose that these gentlemen would object to all they said being printed in these pages, and read by all who may choose to read it in Cuba, or the United States, that I do not report their interesting and instructive conversation; but because it would be, in my opinion, a violation of the universal understanding among gentlemen.

After dinner, we walked on the piazza, with the noble sunset view of the unsurpassed panorama lying before us; and I took my leave of my host, a kind and courteous gentleman of Old Spain, as well as a prelate, just as a few lights were beginning to sprinkle over the fading city, and the Morro Light to gleam on the untroubled air.

Made two visits in the city this evening. In each house, I found the double row of chairs, facing each other, always with about four or five feet of space between the rows. The etiquette is that the gentlemen sit on the row opposite to the ladies, if there be but two or three present. If a lady, on entering, go to the side of a gentleman, when the other row is open to her, it indicates either familiar acquaintance or boldness. There is no people so observant of outguards, as the Spanish race.

I notice, and my observation is supported by what I am told by the residents here, that there is no street-walking, in the technical sense, in Havana. Whether this is from the fact that no ladies walk in the streets,—which are too narrow for comfortable or even safe walking,—or by reason of police regulations, I do not know. From what one meets with in the streets, if he does not look farther, one would not know that there was a vice in Havana, not even drunkenness.

Chapter IX

MONDAY, FEBRUARY 2.—Rose before six, and walked as usual, down the Paseo, to the sea baths. How refreshing is this bath, after the hot night and close rooms! At your side, the wide blue sea with its distant sails, the bath cut into the clean rock, the gentle washing in and out of the tideless sea, at the Gulf Stream temperature, in the cool of the morning! As I pass down, I meet a file of Coolies, in Chinese costume, marching, under overseers, to their work or their jail. And there is the chain-gang! clank, clank, as they go, headed by officers with pistols and swords, and flanked by drivers with whips. This is simple wretchedness!

While at breakfast, a gentleman in the dress of the regular clergy, speaking English, called upon me, bringing me, from the bishop, an open letter of introduction and admission to all the religious, charitable, and educational institutions of the city, and offering to conduct me to the Belen (Bethlehem). He is Father B. of Charleston, S.C., temporarily in Havana, with whom I find I have some acquaintances in common, both in America and abroad. We drive together to the Belen. I say drive; for few persons walk far in Havana, after ten o'clock in the morning. The volantes are the public carriages of Havana; and are as abundant as cabs in London. You never need stand long at a street door without finding one. The postilions are always negroes; and I am told that they pay the owner a certain sum per day for the horse and volante, and make what they can above that.

The Belen is a group of buildings, of the usual yellow or tawny color, covering a good deal of ground, and of a thoroughly monastic character. It was first a Franciscan monastery, then a barrack, and now has been given by the Government to the Jesuits. The company of Jesuits here is composed of a rector and about forty clerical and twenty lay brethren. These perform every office, from the highest scientific investigations and instruction, down to the lowest menial offices, in the care of the children; some serving in costly vestments at the high altar, and others in coarse black garb at the gates. It is only three years since they established themselves in Havana, but in that time they have formed a school of two hundred boarders and one hundred day scholars, built dormitories for the boarders, and a common hall, restored the church and made it the most fully attended in the city; established a missionary work in all parts of the town, recalled a great number to the discipline of the Church, and not only created something like an enthusiasm of devotion among the women, who are said to have monopolized the religion of Cuba in times past, but have introduced among the men, and among many influential men, the practices of confession and communion, to which they had been almost entirely strangers. I do not take this account from the Jesuits themselves, but from the regular clergy of other orders, and from Protestants who are opposed to them and their influence. All agree that they are at work with zeal and success.

I met my distinguished acquaintance of yesterday, the rector, who took me to the boys' chapel, and introduced me to Father Antonio Cabre, a very young man of a spare frame and intellectual countenance, with hands so white and so thin, and eyes so bright, and cheek so pale! He is at the head of the department of mathematics and astronomy, and looks indeed as if he had outwatched the stars, in vigils of science or of devotion. He took me to his laboratory, his observatory, and his apparatus of philosophic instruments. These I am told are according to the latest inventions, and in the best style of French and German workmanship. I was also shown a collection of coins and medals, a cabinet of shells, the commencement of a museum of natural history, already enriched with most of the birds of Cuba, and an interesting cabinet of the woods of the island, in small blocks, each piece being polished on one side, and rough on the other. Among the woods were the mahoganies, the iron-wood, the ebony, the lignum vitæ, the cedar, and many others, of names unfamiliar to me, which admit of the most exquisite polish. Some of the most curious were from the Isla de Pinos, an island belonging to Cuba, and on its southern shore.

The sleeping arrangement for the boys here seemed to me to be new, and to be well adapted to the climate. There is a large hall, with a roof about thirty feet from the floor, and windows near the top, to give light and ventilation above, and small port-holes, near the ground, to let air into the passages. In this hall are double rows of compartments, like high pews, or, more profanely, like the large boxes in restaurants and chop-houses, open at the top, with curtains instead of doors, and each large enough to contain a single bed, a chair, and a toilet table. This ensures both privacy and the light and air of the great hall. The bedsteads are of iron; and nothing can exceed the neatness and order of the apartments. The boys' clothes are kept in another part of the house, and they take to their dormitories only the clothes that they are using. Each boy sleeps alone. Several of the Fathers sleep in the hall, in curtained rooms at the ends of the passage-ways, and a watchman walks the rounds all night, to guard against fire, and to give notice of sickness.

The boys have a playground, a gymnasium, and a riding-school. But although they like riding and fencing, they do not take to the robust exercises and sports of English school-boys. An American whom I met here, who had spent several months at the school, told me that in their recreations they were more like girls, and liked to sit a good deal, playing or working with their hands. He pointed out to me a boy, the son of an American mother, a lady to whom I brought letters and kind wishes from her many friends at the North, and told me that he had more pluck than any boy in the school.

The roof of the Belen is flat, and gives a pleasant promenade, in the open air, after the sun is gone down, which is much needed, as the buildings are in the dense part of the city.

The brethren of this order wear short hair, with the tonsure, and dress in coarse cassocks of plain black, coming to the feet, and buttoned close to the neck, with a cape, but with no white of collar above; and in these, they sweep like black spectres, about the passage-ways, and across the halls and court-yards. There are so many of them that they are able to give thorough and minute attention to the boys, not only in instruction, both secular and religious, but in their entire training and development.

From the scholastic part of the institution, I passed to the church. It is not very large, has an open marble floor, a gallery newly erected for the use of the brethren and other men, a sumptuous high altar, a sacristy and vestry behind, and a small altar, by which burned the undying lamp, indicating the presence of the Sacrament. In the vestry, I was shown the vestments for the service of the high altar, some of which are costly and gorgeous in the extreme, not probably exceeded by those of the Temple at Jerusalem in the palmiest days of the Jewish hierarchy. All are presents from wealthy devotees. One, an alb, had a circle of precious stones; and the lace alone on another, a present from a lady of rank, is said to have cost three thousand dollars. Whatever may be thought of the rightfulness of this expenditure, turning upon the old question as to which the alabaster box of ointment and the ordained costliness of the Jewish ritual "must give us pause," it cannot be said of the Jesuits that they live in cedar, while the ark of God rests in curtains; for the actual life of the streets hardly presents any greater contrast, than that between the sumptuousness of their apparel at the altar, and the coarseness and cheapness of their ordinary dress, the bareness of their rooms, and the apparent severity of their life.

The Cubans have a childish taste for excessive decoration. Their altars look like toy-shops. A priest, not a Cuban, told me that he went to the high altar of the cathedral once, on a Christmas day, to officiate, and when his eye fell on the childish and almost profane attempts at symbolism,—a kind of doll millinery,—if he had not got so far that he could not retire without scandal, he would have left the duties of the day to others. At the Belen there is less of this; but the Jesuits find or think it necessary to conform a good deal to the popular taste.

In the sacristy, near the side altar, is a distressing image of the Virgin, not in youth, but the mother of the mature man, with a sword pierced through her heart,—referring to the figurative prediction, "a sword shall pierce through thine own soul also." The handle and a part of the blade remain without, while the marks of the deep wound are seen, and the countenance expresses the sorest agony of mind and body. It is painful, and beyond all legitimate scope of art, and haunts one, like a vision of actual misery. It is almost the only thing in the church of which I have brought away a distinct image in my memory.

A strange, eventful history, is that of the Society of Jesus! Ignatius Loyola, a soldier and noble of Spain, renouncing arms and knighthood, hangs his trophies of war upon the altar of Monserrate. After intense studies and barefoot pilgrimages, persecuted by religious orders whose excesses he sought to restrain, and frowned upon by the Inquisition, he organizes, with Xavier and Faber, at Montmartre, a society of three. From this small beginning, spreading upwards and outwards, it overshadows the earth. Now, at the top of success, it is supposed to control half Christendom. Now, his order proscribed by State and Church alike and suppressed by the Pope himself, there is not a spot of earth in Catholic Christendom where the Jesuit can place the sole of his foot. In this hour of distress, he finds refuge in Russia, and in Protestant Prussia. Then, restored and tolerated, the order revives here and there in Europe, with a fitful life; and, at length, blazes out into a glory of missionary triumphs and martyrdoms in China, in India, in Africa, and in North America; and now, in these later days, we see it advancing everywhere to a new epoch of labor and influence. Thorough in education, perfect in discipline, absolute in obedience,—as yielding, as indestructible, as all-pervading as water or as air!

The Jesuits make strong friends and strong enemies. Many, who are neither the one nor the other, say of them that their ethics are artificial, and their system unnatural; that they do not reform nature, but destroy it; that, aiming to use the world without abusing it, they reduce it to subjection and tutelage; that they are always either in dangerous power, or in disgrace; and although they may labor with more enthusiasm and self-consecration than any other order, and meet with astonishing successes for a time, yet such is the character of their system that these successes are never permanent, but result in opposition, not only from Protestants, and moderate Catholics, and from the civil power, but from other religious orders and from the regular clergy in their own Church,—an opposition to which they are invariably compelled to yield, at last. In fine, they declare, that, allowing them all zeal, and all ability, and all devotedness, their system is too severe and too unnatural for permanent usefulness anywhere,—medicine and not food, lightning and not light, flame and not warmth.

Not satisfied with this moderated judgment, their opponents have met them, always and everywhere, with uniform and vehement reprobation. They say to them—the opinion of mankind has condemned you! The just and irreversible sentence of time has made you a by-word and a hissing, and reduced your very name, the most sacred in its origin, to a synonyme for ambition and deceit!

Others, again, esteem them the nearest approach in modern times to that type of men portrayed by one of the chiefest, in his epistle: "In much patience, in afflictions, in necessities, in distresses, in stripes, in imprisonments, in tumults, in labors, in watchings, in fastings; by pureness, by knowledge, by long-suffering; . . . by honor and dishonor; by evil report and good report; as deceivers and yet true; as unknown, and yet well known; as dying, and behold we live; as chastened, and not killed; as sorrowful, and yet always rejoicing; as poor, yet making many rich; as having nothing, and yet possessing all things."

Chapter X

A S THERE are no plantations to be seen near Havana, I determine to go down to Matanzas, near which the sugar plantations are in full tide of operation at this season. A steamer leaves here every night at ten o'clock, reaching Matanzas before daylight, the distance by sea being between fifty and sixty miles.

Took this steamer to-night. She got under way punctually at ten o'clock, and steamed down the harbor. The dark waters are alive with phosphorescent light. From each ship that lies moored, the cable from the bows, tautened to its anchor, makes a run of silver light. Each boat, gliding silently from ship to ship, and shore to shore, turns up a silver ripple at its stem, and trails a wake of silver behind; while the dip of the oar-blades brings up liquid silver, dripping, from the opaque deep. We pass along the side of the two-decker, and see through her ports the lanterns and men; under the stern of one frigate, and across the bows of another (for Havana is well supplied with men-of-war); and drop leisurely down by the Cabaña, where we are hailed from the rocks; and bend round the Morro, and are out on the salt, rolling sea. Having a day of work before me, I went early to my berth, and was waked up by the letting off of steam, in the lower harbor of Matanzas, at three o'clock in the morning. My fellow-passengers, who sat up, said the little steamer tore and plunged, and jumped through the water like a thing that had lost its wits. They seemed to think that the Cuban engineer had got a machine that would some day run away with him. It was, certainly, a very short passage.

We passed a good many vessels lying at anchor in the lower harbor of Matanzas, and came to anchor about a mile from the pier. It was clear, bright moonlight. The small boats came off to us, and took us and our luggage ashore. I was landed alone on a quay, carpet-bag in hand, and had to guess my way to the inn, which was near the water-side. I beat on the big, close-barred door; and a sleepy negro, in time, opened it. Mine host was up, expecting passengers, and after waiting on the very tardy movements of the negro, who made a separate journey to the yard for each thing the room needed, I got to bed by four o'clock, on the usual piece of canvas stretched over an iron frame, in a room having a brick floor, and windows without glass closed with big-bolted shutters.

Tuesday, February 22.—After coffee, walked out to deliver my letters to Mr. ——, an American merchant, who has married the daughter of a planter, a gentleman of wealth and character. He is much more agreeable and painstaking than we have any right to expect of one who is served so frequently with notice that his attentions are desired for the entertainment of a stranger. Knowing that it is my wish to visit a plantation, he gives me a letter to Don Juan C——, who has an ingenio (sugar plantation), called La Ariadne, near Limonar, and about twenty-five miles back in the country from Matanzas. The train leaves at 2.30 P.M., which gives me several hours for the city.

Although it is not yet nine o'clock, it is very hot, and one is glad to keep on the shady side of the broad streets of Matanzas. This city was built later and more under foreign direction than Havana, and I have been told, not by persons here however, that for many years the controlling influences of society were French, English, and American; but that lately the policy of the government has been to discourage foreign influence, and now Spanish customs prevail—bull-fights have been introduced, and other usages and entertainments which had had no place here before. Whatever may be the reason, this city differs from Havana in buildings, vehicles, and dress, and in the width of its streets, and has less of the peculiar air of a tropical city. It has about 25,000 inhabitants, and stands where two small rivers, the Yumuri and the San Juan, crossed by handsome stone bridges, run into the sea, dividing the city into three parts. The vessels lie at anchor from one to three miles below the city, and lighters, with masts and sails, line the stone quays of the little rivers. The city is flat and hot, but the country around is picturesque, hilly, and fertile. To the westward of the town, rises a ridge, bordering on the sea, called the Cumbre, which is a place of resort for the beauty of its views; and in front of the Cumbre, on the inland side, is the deep rich valley of the Yumuri, with its celebrated cavern. These I must see, if I can, on my return from the plantation.

In my morning walk, I see a company of Coolies, in the hot sun, carrying stones to build a house, under the eye of a task-master who sits in the shade. The stones have been dropped in a pile, from carts, and the Coolies, carry them, in files, to the cellar of the house. They are naked to the waist, with short-legged cotton trowsers coming to the knees. Some of these men were strongly, one or two of them powerfully built, but many seemed very thin and frail. While looking on, I saw an American face standing near me, and getting into conversation with the man, found him an intelligent shipmaster from New York, who had lived in Matanzas, for a year or two engaged in business. He told me, as I had heard in Havana, that the importer of the Coolies gets $400 a head for them from the purchaser, and that the Coolies are entitled from the purchaser to four dollars a month, which they may demand monthly if they choose, and are bound to eight years' service, during which time they may be held to all the service that a slave is subject to. They are more intelligent, and are put to higher labor than the negro. He said, too, it would not do to flog a Coolie. Idolaters as they are, they have a notion of the dignity of the human body, at least as against strangers, which does not allow them to submit to the indignity of corporal chastisement. If a Coolie is flogged, somebody must die; either the Coolie himself, for they are fearfully given to suicide, or the perpetrator of the indignity, or some one else, according to their strange principles of vicarious punishment. Yet such is the value of labor in Cuba, that a citizen will give $400, in cash, for the chance of enforcing eight years' labor, at $4 per month, from a man speaking a strange language, worshipping strange gods or none, thinking suicide a virtue, and governed by no moral laws in common with his master,—his value being yet further diminished by the chances of natural death, of sickness, accident, escape, and of forfeiting his services to the government, for any crime he may commit against laws he does not understand.

The Plaza is in the usual style,—an enclosed garden, with walks; and in front is the Government House. In this spot, so fair and so still in the noon-day sun, some fourteen years ago, under the fire of the platoons of Spanish soldiers, fell the patriot and poet, one of the few popular poets of Cuba, Gabriel de la Concepcion Valdez. Charged with being the head of that concerted movement of the slaves for their freedom which struck such terror into Cuba, in 1844, he was convicted and ordered to be shot. At the first volley, as the story is told, he was only wounded. "Aim here!" said he, pointing to his head. Another volley, and it was all over.

The name and story of Gabriel de la Concepcion Valdez are preserved by the historians and tourists of Cuba. He is best known, however, by the name of Placido, that under which he wrote and published, than by his proper name. He was a man of genius and a man of valor, but—he was a mulatto!

Chapter XI

Took the train for Limonar, at 2.30 P.M. There are three classes of cars, all after the American model, the first of about the condition of our first-class cars when on the point of being condemned as worn out; the second, a little plainer; and the third, only covered wagons with benches. The car I entered had "Davenport & Co., makers, Cambridgeport, Mass.," familiarly on its front, and the next had "Eaton, Gilbert & Co., Troy, N. York." The brakemen on the train are Coolies, one of them a handsome lad, with coarse, black hair, that lay gracefully about his head, and eyes handsome, though of the Chinese pattern. They were all dressed in the common shirt, trowsers and hat, and, but for their eyes, might be taken for men of any of the Oriental races.

As we leave Matanzas, we rise on an ascending grade, and the bay and city lie open before us. The bay is deep on the western shore, under the ridge of the Cumbre, and there the vessels lie at anchor; while the rest of the bay is shallow, and its water, in this state of the sky and light, is of a pale green color. The lighters, with sail and oar, are plying between the quays and the vessels below. All is pretty and quiet and warm, but the scene has none of those regal points, that so impress themselves on the imagination and memory in the surroundings of Havana.

I am now to get my first view of the interior of Cuba. I could not have a more favorable day. The air is clear, and not excessively hot. The soft clouds float midway in the serene sky, the sun shines fair and bright, and the luxuriance of a perpetual summer covers the face of nature. These strange palm-trees everywhere! I cannot yet feel at home among them. Many of the other trees are like our own, and though, tropical in fact, look to the eye as if they might grow as well in New England as here. But the royal palm looks so intensely and exclusively tropical! It cannot grow beyond this narrow belt of the earth's surface. Its long, thin body, so straight and so smooth, swathed from the foot—in a tight bandage of gray canvas, leaving only its deep-green neck, and over that its crest and plumage of deep-green leaves! It gives no shade, and bears no fruit that is valued by men. And it has no beauty to atone for those wants. Yet it has more than beauty,—a strange fascination over the eye and the fancy, that will never allow it to be overlooked or forgotten. The palm-tree seems a kind of *lusus naturæ,* to the northern eye—an exotic wherever you meet it. It seems to be conscious of its want of usefulness for food or shade, yet has a dignity of its own, a pride of unmixed blood and royal descent,—the hidalgo of the soil.

What are those groves and clusters of small growth, looking like Indian corn in a state of transmigration into trees, the stalk turning into a trunk, a thin soft coating half changed to bark, and the ears of corn turning into melons? Those are the bananas and plantains, as their bunches of green and yellow fruits plainly enough indicate, when you come nearer. But, that sad, weeping tree, its long yellow-green leaves drooping to the ground! What can that be? It has a green fruit like a melon. There it is again, in groves! I interrupt my neighbor's tenth cigarrito, to ask him the name of the tree. It is the cocoa! And that soft green melon becomes the hard shell we break with a hammer. Other trees there are, in abundance, of various forms and foliage, but they might have grown in New England or New York, so far as the eye can teach us; but the palm, the cocoa, the banana and plantain are the characteristic trees you could not possibly meet with in any other zone.

Thickets,—jungles I might call them—abound. It seems as if a bird could hardly get through them; yet they are rich with wild flowers of all forms and colors, the white, the purple, the pink, and the blue. The trees are full of birds of all plumage. There is one like our brilliant oriole. I cannot hear their notes, for the clatter of the train. Stone fences, neatly laid up, run across the lands;—not of our cold bluish-gray granite, the color, as a friend once said, of a miser's eye, but of soft, warm brown and russet, and well overgrown with creepers, and fringed with flowers. There are avenues, and here are clumps of the prim orange-tree, with its dense and deep-green polished foliage gleaming with golden fruit. Now we come to acres upon acres of the sugar-cane, looking at a distance like fields of overgrown broom-corn. It grows to the height of eight or ten feet, and very thick. An army could be hidden in it. This soil must be deeply and intensely fertile.

There, at the end of an avenue of palms, in a nest of shade-trees, is a group of white buildings, with a sea of cane-fields about it, with one high furnace-chimney, pouring out its volume of black smoke. This is a sugar plantation,—my first sight of an ingenio; and the chimney is for the steam works of the sugar-house. It is the height of the sugar season, and the untiring engine toils and smokes day and night. Ox carts, loaded with cane, are moving slowly to the sugar-house from the fields; and about the house, and in the fields, in various attitudes and motions of labor, are the negroes, men and women and children, some cutting the cane, some loading the carts, and some tending the mill and the furnace. It is a busy scene of distant industry, in the afternoon sun of a languid Cuban day.

Now these groups of white one-story buildings become more frequent, sometimes very near each other, all having the same character,—the group of white buildings, the mill, with its tall furnace-chimney, and the look of a distillery, and all differing from each other only in the number and extent of the buildings, or in the ornament and comfort of shade-trees and avenues about them. Some are approached by broad alleys of the palm, or mango, or orange, and have gardens around them, and stand under clusters of shade-trees; while others glitter in the hot sun, on the flat sea of cane-fields, with only a little oasis of shade-trees and fruit-trees immediately about the houses.

I now begin to feel that I am in Cuba; in the tropical, rich, sugar-growing, slave-tilled Cuba. Heretofore, I have seen only the cities and their environs, in which there are more things that are common to the rest of the world. The country life tells the story of any people that have a country life. The New England farm-house shows the heart of New England. The mansion-house and cottage show the heart of Old England. The plantation life that I am seeing and about to see, tells the story of Cuba, the Cuba that has been and that is.

As we stop at one station, which seems to be in the middle of a cane-field, the negroes and Coolies go to the cane, slash off a piece with their knives, cut off the rind, and chew the stick of soft, saccharine pulp, the juice running out of their mouths as they eat. They seem to enjoy it so highly, that I am tempted to try the taste of it, myself. But I shall have time for all this at La Ariadne.

These stations consist merely of one or two buildings, where the produce of the neighborhood is collected for transportation, and at which there are very few passengers. The railroad is intended for the carriage of sugar and other produce, and gets its support almost entirely in that way; for it runs through a sparse, rural population, where there are no towns; yet so large and valuable is the sugar crop that I believe the road is well supported. At each station, are its hangers-on of free negroes, a few slaves on duty as carriers, a few low whites, and now and then some one who looks as if he might be an overseer or mayoral of a plantation.

Limonar, appears in large letters on the small building where we next stop, and I get out and inquire of a squad of idlers for the plantation of Señor C——. They point to a group of white buildings, about a quarter of a mile distant, standing prettily under high shade-trees, and approached by an avenue of orange-trees. Getting a tall negro to shoulder my bag, for a real, I walk to the house. It is an afternoon of exquisite beauty. How can any one have a weather sensation, in such an air as this? There is no current of the slightest chill anywhere, neither is it oppressively hot. The air is serene and pure and light. The sky gives its mild assurance of settled fair weather. All about me is rich verdure, over a gently undulating surface of deeply fertile country, with here and there a high hill in the horizon, and, on one side, a ridge that may be called mountains. There is no sound but that of the birds, and in the next tree they may be counted by hundreds. Wild flowers, of all colors and scents, cover the ground and the thickets. This is the famous red earth, too. The avenue looks as if it had been laid down with pulverized brick, and all the dust on any object you see is red. Now we turn into the straight avenue of orange-trees,—prim, deep-green trees, glittering with golden fruit. Here is the one-story, high-roofed house, with long, high piazzas. There is a high wall, carefully whitewashed, enclosing a square with one gate, looking like a garrisoned spot. That must be the negroes' quarters; for there is a group of little negroes at the gate, looking earnestly at the approaching stranger. Beyond is the sugar-house, and the smoking chimney, and the ox carts, and the field hands. Through the wide, open door of the mansion, I see two gentlemen at dinner, an older and a younger,—the head of gray, and the head of black, and two negro women, one serving, and the other swinging her brush to disperse the flies. Two big, deep-mouthed hounds come out and bark; and the younger gentleman looks at us, comes out, and calls off the dogs. My negro stops at the path and touches his hat, waiting permission to go to the piazza with the luggage; for negroes do not go to the house door without previous leave, in strictly ordered plantations. I deliver my letter, and in a moment am received with such cordial welcome that I am made to feel as if I had conferred a favor by coming out to see them.*

*I have no right to introduce the public to the house of Mr. C——. But that has already been done. Many tourists, and last and most unreservedly of all, Miss Bremer, in her Homes of the New World, have already given it such publicity, that I have thought my lighter step would not be felt on the beaten way.

Chapter XII

AT SOME SEASONS, a visit may be a favor, on remote plantations; but I know this is the height of the sugar season,
when every hour is precious to the master. After a brief toilet,
I sit down with them; for they have just begun dinner. In five
minutes, I am led to feel as if I were a friend of many years.
Both gentlemen speak English like a native tongue. To the
younger it is so, for he was born in South Carolina, and his
mother is a lady of that State. The family are not here. They do
not live on the plantation, but in Matanzas. The plantation is
managed by the son, who resides upon it; the father coming
out occasionally for a few days, as now, in the busy season.

The dinner is in the Spanish style, which I am getting attached to. I should flee from a joint, or a sirloin. We have rice,
excellently cooked, as always in Cuba, eggs with it, if we choose,
and fried plantains, sweet potatoes, mixed dishes of fowl and
vegetables, with a good deal of oil and seasoning, in which a
hot red pepper, about the size of the barberry, prevails. Catalonia wine, which is pretty sure to be pure, is their table
claret, while sherry, which also comes direct from the mother-
country, is for dessert. I have taken them by surprise, in the
midst of the busiest season, in a house where there are no ladies;
yet the table, the service, the dress and the etiquette, are none
the less in the style of good society. There seems to be no
letting down, where letting down would be so natural and
excusable.

I suppose the fact that the land and the agricultural capital
of the interior are in the hands of an upper class, which does
no manual labor, and which has enough of wealth and leisure
to secure the advantages of continued intercourse with city and
foreign society, and of occasional foreign travel, tends to preserve throughout the remote agricultural districts, habits and
tone and etiquette, which otherwise would die out, in the
entire absence of large towns and of high local influences.

Whoever has met with a book called "Evenings in Boston,"
and read the story of the old negro, Saturday, and seen the
frontispiece of the negro fleeing through the woods of St.

Domingo, with two little white boys, one in each hand, will know as much of Mr. C——, the elder, as I did the day before seeing him. He is the living hero, or rather subject, for Saturday was the hero, of that tale. His father was a wealthy planter of St. Domingo, a Frenchman, of large estates, with wife, children, friends and neighbors. These were gathered about him in a social circle in his house, when the dreadful insurrection overtook them, and father, mother, sons and daughters were murdered in one night, and only two of the children, boys of eight and ten, were saved by the fidelity of Saturday, an old and devoted house servant. Saturday concealed the boys, got them off the island, took them to Charleston, South Carolina, where they found friends among the Huguenot families, and the refugees from St. Domingo. There Mr. C—— grew up; and after a checkered and adventurous early life, a large part of it on the sea, he married a lady of worth and culture, in South Carolina, and settled himself as a planter, on this spot, nearly forty years ago. His plantation he named El Labarinto, (The Labyrinth,) after a favorite vessel he had commanded, and for thirty years it was a prosperous cafetal, the home of a happy family, and much visited by strangers from America and Europe. The causes which broke up the coffee estates of Cuba, carried this with the others; and it was converted into a sugar plantation, under the new name of La Ariadne, from the fancy of Ariadne having shown the way out of the Labyrinth. Like most of the sugar estates, it is no longer the regular home of its proprietors.

The change from coffee plantations to sugar plantations,—from the cafetal to the ingenio, has seriously affected the social, as it has the economic condition of Cuba.

Coffee must grow under shade. Consequently the coffee estate was, in the first place, a plantation of trees, and by the hundred acres. Economy and taste led the planters, who were chiefly the French refugees from St. Domingo, to select fruit-trees, and trees valuable for their wood, as well as pleasing for their beauty and shade. Under these plantations of trees, grew the coffee plant, an evergreen, and almost an ever-flowering plant, with berries of changing hues, and, twice a year, brought its fruit to maturity. That the coffee might be tended and gathered, avenues wide enough for wagons must be carried through the plantations, at frequent intervals. The plantation was, therefore, laid out like a garden, with avenues and foot-paths, all under the shade of the finest trees, and the spaces between the avenues were groves of fruit-trees and shade-trees, under which grew, trimmed down to the height of five or six feet, the coffee plant. The labor of the plantation was in tending, picking, drying, and shelling the coffee, and gathering the fresh fruits of trees for use and for the market, and for preserves and sweetmeats, and in raising vegetables and poul-try, and rearing sheep and horned cattle and horses. It was a beautiful and simple horticulture, on a very large scale. Time was required to perfect this garden,—the Cubans call it paradise —of a cafetal; but when matured, it was a cherished home. It required and admitted of no extraordinary mechanical power, or of the application of steam, or of science, beyond the knowledge of soils, of simple culture, and of plants and trees.

For twenty years and more it has been forced upon the knowledge of the reluctant Cubans, that Brazil, the West India Islands to the southward of Cuba, and the Spanish Main, can excel them in coffee-raising. The successive disastrous hurri-canes of 1843 and 1845, which destroyed many and damaged most of the coffee estates, added to the colonial system of the mother-country, which did not give extraordinary protection to this product, are commonly said to have put an end to the coffee plantations. Probably, they only hastened a change which must at some time have come. But the same causes of soil and climate which made Cuba inferior in coffee-growing, gave her a marked superiority in the cultivation of sugar. The damaged plantations were not restored as coffee estates, but were laid down to the sugar-cane; and gradually, first in the western and northern parts, and daily extending easterly and southerly over the entire island, the exquisite cafetals have been prostrated and dismantled, the groves of shade and fruit trees cut down, the avenues and footpaths ploughed up, and the denuded land laid down to wastes of sugar-cane.

The sugar-cane allows of no shade. Therefore the groves and avenues must fall. To make its culture profitable, it must be raised in the largest possible quantities that the extent of land will permit. To attempt the raising of fruit, or of the or-namental woods, is bad economy for the sugar planter. Most of the fruits, especially the orange, which is the chief export, ripen in the midst of the sugar season, and no hands can be spared to attend to them. The sugar planter often buys the fruits he needs for daily use and for making preserves, from the neighboring cafetals. The cane ripens but once a year. Between the time when enough of it is ripe to justify beginning to work the mill, and the time when the heat and rains spoil its qualities, all the sugar making of the year must be done. In Louisiana, this period does not exceed eight weeks. In Cuba it is full four months. This gives Cuba a great advantage. Yet these four months are short enough; and during that time, the steam-engine plies and the furnace fires burn night and day.

Sugar making brings with it steam, fire, smoke, and a drive of labor, and admits of and requires the application of science. Managed with skill and energy, it is extremely productive. Indifferently managed, it may be a loss. The sugar estate is not valuable, like the coffee estate, for what the land will produce, aided by ordinary and quiet manual labor only. Its value is in the skill, and the character of the labor. The land is there, and the negroes are there; but the result is loss or gain, according to the amount of labor that can be obtained, and the skill with which the manual labor and the mechanical powers are applied. It is said that at the present time, in the present state of the market, a well-managed sugar estate yields from fifteen to twenty-five per cent. on the investment. This is true, I am inclined to think, if by the investment be meant only the land, the machinery, and the slaves. But the land is not a large element in the investment. The machinery is costly, yet its value depends on the science applied to its construction and operation. The chief item in the investment is the slave labor. Taking all the slaves together, men, women, and children, the young and the old, the sick and the well, the good and the bad, their market value averages above $1000 a head. Yet of these, allowing for those too young or too old, for the sick, and for those who must tend the young, the old and the sick, and for those whose labor, like that of the cooks, only sustains the others, not more than one half are able-bodied, productive laborers. The value of this chief item in the investment depends largely on moral and intellectual considerations. How unsatisfactory is it, then, to calculate the profits of the investment, when you leave out of the calculation the value of the controlling power, the power that extorts the contributions of labor from the steam and the engine and the fire, and from the more difficult human will. This is the "plus x" of the formula, which, unascertained, gives us little light as to the result.

But, to return to the changes wrought by this substitution of sugar for coffee. The sugar plantation is no grove, or garden, or orchard. It is not the home of the pride and affections of the planter's family. It is not a coveted, indeed, hardly a desirable residence. Such families as would like to remain on these plantations, are driven off for want of neighboring society. Thus the estates, largely abandoned by the families of the planters suffer the evils of absenteeism, while the owners live in the suburbs of Havana and Matanzas, and in the Fifth Avenue of New York. The slave system loses its patriarchal character. The master is not the head of a great family, its judge, its governor, its physician, its priest and its father, as the fond dream of the advocates of slavery, and sometimes, doubtless, the reality, made him. Middlemen, in the shape of administradores, stand between the owner and the slaves. The slave is little else than an item of labor raised or bought. The sympathies of common home, common childhood, long and intimate relations and many kind offices, common attachments to house, to land, to dogs, to cattle, to trees, to birds,—the knowledge of births, sicknesses, and deaths, and the duties and sympathies of a common religion,—all those things that may ameliorate the legal relations of the master and slave, and often give to the face of servitude itself precarious but interesting features of beauty and strength,—these they must not look to have.

This change has had some effect already, and will produce much more, on the social system of Cuba.

There are still plantations on which the families of the wealthy and educated planters reside. And in some cases the administrador is a younger member or a relative of the family, holding the same social position; and the permanent administrador will have his family with him. Yet, it is enough to say that the same causes which render the ingenio no longer a desirable residence for the owner, make it probable that the administrador will be either a dependent or an adventurer; a person from whom the owner will expect a great deal, and the slaves but little, and from whom none will get all they expect, and perhaps none all they are entitled to.

In the afternoon we went to the sugar-house, and I was initiated into the mysteries of the work. There are four agents: steam, fire, cane-juice, and negroes. The results are sugar and molasses. At this ingenio, they make only the Muscovado, or brown sugar. The processes are easily described, but it is difficult to give an idea of the scene. It is one of condensed and determined labor.

To begin at the beginning.—The cane is cut from the fields, by companies of men and women, working together, who use an instrument called a machete, which is something between a sword and a cleaver. Two blows with this slash off the long leaves, and a third blow cuts off the stalk, near to the ground. At this work, the laborers move like reapers, in even lines, at stated distances. Before them is a field of dense, high-waving cane; and behind them, strewn wrecks of stalks and leaves. Near, and in charge of the party, stands a driver, or more grandiloquently, a contra-mayoral, with the short, limber plantation whip, the badge of his office, under his arm.

Ox-carts pass over the field, and are loaded with the cane, which they carry to the mill. The oxen are worked in the Spanish fashion, the yoke being strapped upon the head, close to the horns, instead of being hung round the neck, as with us, and are guided by goads, and by a rope attached to a ring through the nostrils. At the mill, the cane is tipped from the carts into large piles, by the side of the platform. From these piles, it is placed carefully, by hand, lengthwise, in a long trough. This trough is made of slats, and moved by the power of the endless chain, connected with the engine. In this trough, it is carried between heavy, horizontal, cylindrical rollers, where it is crushed, its juice falling into receivers below, and the crushed cane passing off and falling into a pile on the other side.

This crushed cane, (bagazo) falling from between the rollers, is gathered into baskets, by men and women, who carry it on their heads into the fields and spread it for drying. There it is watched and tended as carefully as new-mown grass in haymaking, and raked into cocks or winrows, on an alarm of rain.

When dry, it is placed under sheds for protection against wet. From the sheds and from the fields, it is loaded into carts and drawn to the furnace doors, into which it is thrown by negroes, who crowd it in by the armful, and rake it about with long poles. Here it feeds the perpetual fires by which the steam is made, the machinery moved, and the cane-juice boiled. The care of the bagazo is an important part of the system; for if that becomes wet and fails, the fires must stop, or resort be had to wood, which is scarce and expensive.

Thus, on one side of the rollers is the ceaseless current of fresh, full, juicy cane-stalks, just cut from the open field; and on the other side, is the crushed, mangled, juiceless mass, drifting out at the draught, and fit only to be cast into the oven and burned. This is the way of the world, as it is the course of art. The cane is made to destroy itself. The ruined and corrupted furnish the fuel and fan the flame that lures on and draws in and crushes the fresh and wholesome; and the operation seems about as mechanical and unceasing in the one case as in the other.

From the rollers, the juice falls below into a large receiver, from which it flows into great, open vats, called defecators. These defecators are heated by the exhaust steam of the engine, led through them in pipes. All the steam condensed forms water, which is returned warm into the boiler of the engine. In the defecators, as their name denotes, the scum of the juice is purged off, so far as heat alone will do it. From the last defecator, the juice is passed through a trough into the first caldron. Of the caldrons, there is a series, or, as they call it, a train, through all which the juice must go. Each caldron is a large, deep, copper vat, heated very hot, in which the juice seethes and boils. At each, stands a strong negro, with long, heavy skimmer in hand, stirring the juice and skimming off the surface. This scum is collected and given to the hogs, or thrown upon the muck heap, and is said to be very fructifying. The juice is ladled from one caldron to the next, as fast as the office of each is finished. From the last caldron, where its complete crystallization is effected, it is transferred to coolers, which are large, shallow pans. When fully cooled, it looks like brown sugar and molasses mixed. It is then shovelled from the coolers into hogsheads. These hogsheads have holes bored in their bottoms; and, to facilitate the drainage, strips of cane are placed in the hogshead, with their ends in these holes, and the hogshead is filled. The hogsheads are set on open frames, under which are copper receivers, on an inclined plane, to catch and carry off the drippings from the hogsheads. These drippings are the molasses, which is collected and put into tight casks.

I believe I have given the entire process. When it is remembered that all this, in every stage, is going on at once, within the limits of the mill, it may well be supposed to present a busy scene. The smell of juice and of sugar-vapor, in all its stages, is intense. The negroes fatten on it. The clank of the engine, the steady grind of the machines, and the high, wild cry of the negroes at the caldrons to the stokers at the furnace doors, as they chant out their directions or wants—now for more fire, and now to scatter the fire—which must be heard above the din, "A-a-b'la! A-a-b'la!" "E-e-cha candela!" "Pu-er-ta!" and the barbaric African chant and chorus of the gang at work filling the cane-troughs;—all these make the first visit at the sugar-house a strange experience. But after one or two visits, the monotony is as tiresome as the first view is exciting. There is, literally, no change in the work. There are the same noises of the machines, the same cries from negroes at the same spots, the same intensely sweet smell, the same state of the work in all its stages, at whatever hour you visit it, whether in the morning, or evening, at midnight, or at the dawn of the day. If you wake up at night, you hear the "A-a-b'la! A-a-b'la!" "E-e-cha! E-e-cha!" of the caldron-men crying to the stokers, and the high, monotonous chant of the gangs filling the wagons or the trough, a short, improvisated stave, and then the chorus;—not a tune, like the song of sailors at the tackles and falls, but a barbaric, tuneless intonation.

When I went into the sugar-house, I saw a man with an unmistakably New England face in charge of the engine, with that look of intelligence and independence so different from the intelligence and independence of all other persons.

"Is not that a New England man?"

"Yes," said Mr. C——, "he is from Lowell; and the engine was built in Lowell."

When I found him at leisure, I made myself known to him, and he sat down on the brick work of the furnace, and had a

good unburdening of talk; for he had not seen any one from
the United States for three months. He talked, like a true
Yankee, of law and politics,—the Lowell Bar and Mr. Butler,
Mr. Abbott and Mr. Wentworth; of the Boston Bar and Mr.
Choate; of Massachusetts politics and Governor Banks; and of
national politics and the Thirty Millions Bill, and whether it
would pass, and what if it did.

This engineer is one of a numerous class, whom the sugar
culture brings annually to Cuba. They leave home in the autumn, engage themselves for the sugar season, put the machinery in order, work it for the four or five months of its
operation, clean and put it in order for lying by, and return to
the United States in the spring. They must be machinists, as
well as engineers; for all the repairs and contrivances, so necessary in a remote place, fall upon them. Their skill is of great
value, and while on the plantation their work is incessant, and
they have no society or recreations whatever. The occupation,
however, is healthful, their position independent, and their pay
large. This engineer had been several years in Cuba, and I
found him well informed, and, I think, impartial and independent. He tells me, which I had also heard in Havana, that
this plantation is a favorable specimen, both for skill and humanity, and is managed on principles of science and justice,
and yields a large return. On many plantations,—on most, I
suspect, from all I can learn—the negroes, during the sugar
season, are allowed but four hours for sleep in the twenty-four,
with one for dinner, and a half hour for breakfast, the night
being divided into three watches, of four hours each, the laborers taking their turns. On this plantation, the laborers are
in two watches, and divide the night equally between them,
which gives them six hours for sleep. In the day, they have half
an hour for breakfast and one hour for dinner. Here, too, the
very young and the very old are excused from the sugar-house,
and the nursing mothers have lighter duties and frequent intervals of rest. The women worked at cutting the cane, feeding
the mill, carrying the bagazo in baskets, spreading and drying
it, and filling the wagons; but not in the sugar-house itself, or
at the furnace doors. I saw that no boys or girls were in the
mill—none but full grown persons. The very small children do
absolutely nothing all day, and the older children tend the

cattle and run of errands. And the engineer tells me that in the long run this liberal system of treatment, as to hours and duties, yields a better return than a more stringent rule.

He thinks the crop this year, which has been a favorable one, will yield, in well-managed plantations a net interest of from fifteen to twenty-five per cent. on the investment; making no allowance, of course, for the time and skill of the master. This will be a clear return to planters like Mr. C——, who do not eat up their profits by interest on advances, and have no mortgages, and require no advances from the merchants.

But the risks of the investment are great. The cane-fields are liable to fires, and these spread with great rapidity, and are difficult to extinguish.* Last year Mr. C—— lost $7,000 in a few hours by fire. In the cholera season he lost $12,000 in a few days by deaths among the negroes.

According to the usual mode of calculation, I suppose the value of the investment of Mr. C—— to be between $125,000 and $150,000. On well-managed estates of this size, the expenses should not exceed $10,000. The gross receipts, in sugar and molasses, at a fair rate of the markets, cannot average less than between $35,000 and $40,000. This should leave a profit of between eighteen and twenty-two per cent. Still, the worth of an estimate depends on the principle on which the capital is appraised. The number of acres laid down to cane, on this plantation, is about three hundred. The whole number of negroes is one hundred, and of these not more than half, at any time, are capable of efficient labor; and there are twenty-two children below the age of five years, out of a total of one hundred negroes.

Beside the engineer, some large plantations have one or more white assistants; but here an intelligent negro has been taught enough to take charge of the engine when the engineer is off duty. This is the highest post a negro can reach in the mill, and this negro was mightily pleased when I addressed him as maquinista. There are, also, two or three white men

---

*While these sheets are in press, the newspapers report that a fire has spread over a section of country between Matanzas and Cardenas, not only destroying the standing cane, but burning up houses, sugar-mills, and the sugar and molasses stored for the market. Several lives were lost by the conflagration, which affected, more or less, above twenty plantations.

employed, during the season, as sugar masters. Their post is beside the caldrons and defecators, where they are to watch the work in all its stages, regulate the heat and the time for each removal, and oversee the men. These, with the engineer, make the force of white men who are employed for the season.

The regular and permanent officers of a plantation are the mayoral and mayordomo.

The mayoral is, under the master or his administrador, the chief mate or first lieutenant of the ship. He has the general oversight of the negroes, at their work or in their houses, and has the duty of exacting labor and enforcing discipline. Much depends on his character, as to the comfort of master and slaves. If he is faithful and just, there may be ease and comfort; but if he is not, the slaves are never sure of justice, and the master is sure of nothing. The mayoral comes, of necessity, from the middle class of whites, and is usually a native Cuban, and it is not often that a satisfactory one can be found or kept. The day before I arrived, in the height of the season, Mr. C—— had been obliged to dismiss his mayoral, on account of his conduct to the women, which was producing the worst results with them and with the men; and not long before, one was dismissed for conniving with the negroes in a wholesale system of theft, of which he got the lion's share.

The mayordomo is the purser, and has the immediate charge of the stores, produce, materials for labor, and provisions for consumption, and keeps the accounts. On well regulated plantations, he is charged with all the articles of use or consumption, and with the products as soon as they are in condition to be numbered, weighed, or counted, and renders his accounts of what is consumed or destroyed, and of the produce sent away.

There is also a boyero, who is the herdsman, and has charge of all the cattle. He is sometimes a negro.

Under the mayoral, are a number of contra-mayorales, who are the boatswain's mates of the ship, and correspond to the "drivers" of our southern plantations. One of them goes with every gang when set to work, whether in the field or elsewhere, and whether men or women, and watches and directs them, and enforces labor from them. The drivers carry under the arm, at all times, the short, limber plantation whip, the badge of their office and their means of compulsion. They are almost always negroes; and it is generally thought that negroes are not more humane in this office than the low whites. On this plantation, it is three years since any slave has been whipped; and that punishment is never inflicted here on a woman. Near the negro quarters, is a penitentiary, which is of stone, with three cells for solitary confinement, each dark, but well ventilated. Confinement in these, on bread and water, is the extreme punishment that has been found necessary for the last three years. The negro fears solitude and darkness, and covets his food, fire, and companionship.

With all the corps of hired white labor, the master must still be the real power, and on his character the comfort and success of the plantation depend. If he has skill as a chemist, a geologist, or a machinist, it is not lost; but, except as to the engineer, who may usually be relied upon, the master must be capable of overseeing the whole economy of the plantation, or all will go wrong. His chief duty is to oversee the overseers; to watch his officers, the mayoral, the mayordomo, the boyero, and the sugar masters. These are mere hirelings, and of a low sort, such as a slave system reduces them to; and if they are lazy, the work slackens; and if they are ill-natured, somebody suffers. The mere personal presence of the master operates as a stimulus to the work. This afternoon young Mr. C—— and I took horses and rode out to the cane-field, where the people were cutting. They had been at work a half hour. He stopped his horse where they were when we came to them, and the next half hour, without a word from him, they had made double the distance of the first. It seems to me that the work of a plantation is what a clock would be that always required a man's hand pressing on the main spring. With the slave, the ultimate sanction is force. The motives of pride, shame, interest, ambition, and affection may be appealed to, and the minor punishments of degradation in duty, deprivation of food and sleep, and solitary confinement, may be resorted to; but the whip which the driver always carries, reminds the slave that if all else fails, the infliction of painful bodily punishment lies behind, and will be brought to bear, rather than that the question be left unsettled. Whether this extreme be reached, and how often it be reached, depends on the personal qualities of the master. If he is lacking in self-control, he will fall into violence. If he has not the faculty of ruling by moral and intellectual power,—be he ever so humane, if he is not firm and intelligent, the bad among the slaves will get the upper hand, and he will be in danger of trying to recover his position by force. Such is the reasoning *à priori.*

At six o'clock, the large bell tolls the knell of parting day and the call to the Oracion, which any who are religious enough can say, wherever they may be, at work or at rest. In the times of more religious strictness, the bell for the Oracion, just at dusk, was the signal for prayer in every house and field, and even in the street, and for the benediction from parent to child, and master to servant. Now, in the cities, it tolls unnoticed, and on the plantations, it is treated only as the signal for leaving off work. The distribution of provisions is made at the storehouse, by the mayordomo, my host superintending it in person. The people take according to the number in their families; and so well acquainted are all with the apportionment, that in only one or two instances were inquiries necessary. The kitchen fires are lighted in the quarters, and the evening meal is prepared. I went into the quarters before they were closed. A high wall surrounds an open square, in which are the houses of the negroes. This has one gate, which is locked at dark; and to leave the quarters after that time, is a serious offence. The huts were plain, but reasonably neat, and comfortable in their construction and arrangement. In some were fires, round which, even in this hot weather, the negroes like to gather. A group of little negroes came round the strange gentleman, and the smallest knelt down with uncovered heads, in a reverent manner, saying, "Buenos dias Señor." I did not understand the purpose of this action, and as there was no one to explain the usage to me, I did them the injustice to suppose that they expected money, and distributed some small coins among them. But I learned afterwards that they were expecting the benediction,—the hand on the head, and the "Dios te haga bueno." It was touching to see their simple, trusting faces turned up to the stranger,—countenances not yet wrought by misfortune, or injury, or crime, into the strong expressions of mature life. None of these children, even the smallest, was naked, as one usually sees them in Havana. In one of the huts, a proud mother showed me her Herculean twin boys, sprawling in sleep on the bed. Before dark, the gate of the quarters is bolted, and the night is begun. But the fires of the sugar-house are burning, and half of the working people are on duty there for their six hours.

I sat for several hours with my host and his son, in the veranda, engaged in conversation, agreeable and instructive to me, on those topics likely to present themselves to a person placed as I was;—the state of Cuba, its probable future, its past, its relations to Europe and the United States, slavery, the Coolie problem, the free-negro-labor problem, and the agriculture, horticulture, trees and fruits of the island. The elder gentleman retired early, as he was to take the early train for Matanzas.

My sleeping-room is large and comfortable, with brick floor and glass windows, pure white bed linen and mosquito net, and ewer and basin scrupulously clean, bringing back, by contrast, visions of Le Grand's, and Antonio, and Domingo, and the sounds and smells of those upper chambers. The only moral I am entitled to draw from this is, that a well-ordered private house with slave labor, may be more neat and creditable than an ill-ordered public house with free labor. As the stillness of the room comes over me, I realize that I am far away in the hill country of Cuba, the guest of a planter, under this strange system, by which one man is enthroned in the labor of another race, brought from across the sea. The song of the negroes breaks out afresh from the fields, where they are loading up the wagons,—that barbaric undulation of sound:—

"Na-nu, A-ya,—Na-ne, A-ya:"

and the recurrence of here and there a few words of Spanish, among which "Mañana" seemed to be a favorite. Once, in the middle of the night, I waked, to hear the strains again, as they worked in the open field, under the stars.

Chapter XIII

WHEN I came out from my chamber this morning, the elder Mr. C—— had gone. The watchful negress brought me coffee, and I could choose between oranges and bananas, for my fruit. The young master had been in the saddle an hour or so. I sauntered to the sugar-house. It was past six, and all hands were at work again; amid the perpetual boiling of the caldrons, the skimming and dipping and stirring, the cries of the caldron-men to the firemen, the slow gait of the wagons, and the perpetual to-and-fro of the carriers of the cane. The engine is doing well enough, and the engineer has the great sheet of the New York Weekly Herald, which he is studying, in the intervals of labor, as he sits on the corner of the brickwork.

But a turn in the garden is more agreeable, among birds, and flowers, and aromatic trees. Here is a mignonette-tree, forty feet high, and every part is full and fragrant with flowers, as is the little mignonette in our flower-pots. There is the allspice, a large tree, each leaf strong enough to flavor a dish. Here is the tamarind-tree: I must sit under it, for the sake of the old song. My young friend joins me, and points out, on the allspice-tree, a chameleon. It is about six inches long, and of a pea-green color. He thinks its changes of color, which are no fable, depend on the will or on the sensations, and not on the color of the object the animal rests upon. This one, though on a black trunk, remained pale green. When they take the color of the tree they rest on, it may be to elude their enemies, to whom their slow motions make them an easy prey. At the corner of the house stands a pomegranate-tree, full of fruit, which is not yet entirely ripe; but we find enough to give a fair taste of its rich flavor. Then there are sweet oranges, and sour oranges, and limes, and cocoa-nuts, and pine-apples, the latter not entirely ripe, but in the condition in which they are usually plucked for our market, and abundance of fuschias, and Cape jasmines, and the highly prized night-blooming cereus.

The most frequent shade-tree here is the mango. It is a large, dense tree, with a general resemblance, in form and size,

468

to our lime or linden. Three noble trees stand before the door, in front of the house. One is a Tahiti almond, another a mango, and the third a cedar. And in the distance is a majestic tree, of incredible size, which is, I believe, a ceyba. When this estate was a cafetal, the house stood at the junction of four avenues, from the four points of the compass: one of the sweet orange, one of the sour orange, one of palms, and one of mangoes. Many of these trees fell in the hurricanes of 1843 and '45. The avenue which leads from the road, and part of that leading towards the sugar-house, are preserved. The rest have fallen a sacrifice to the sugar-cane; but the garden, the trees about the house, and what remains of the avenues, give still a delightful appearance of shelter and repose.

I have amused myself by tracing the progress, and learning the habits of the red ants, a pretty formidable enemy to all structures of wood. They eat into the heart of the hardest woods; not even the lignum vitæ, or ironwood, or cedar, being proof against them. Their operations are secret. They never appear upon the wood, or touch its outer shell. A beam or rafter stands as ever with a goodly outside; but you tap it, and find it a shell. Their approaches, too, are by covered ways. When going from one piece of wood to another, they construct a covered way, very small and low, as a protection against their numerous enemies, and through this they advance to their new labors. I think that they may sap the strength of a whole roof of rafters, without the observer being able to see one of them, unless he breaks their covered ways, or lays open the wood.

The course of life at the plantation is after this manner. At six o'clock, the great bell begins the day, and the negroes go to their work. The house servants bring coffee to the family and guests, as they appear or send for it. The master's horse is at the door, under the tree, as soon as it is light, and he is off on his tour, before the sun rises. The family breakfasts at ten o'clock, and the people,—la gente, as the technical phrase is for the laborers, breakfast at nine. The breakfast is like that of the cities, with the exception of fish and the variety of meats, and consists of rice, eggs, fried plantains, mixed dishes of vegetables and fowls, other meats rarely, and fruits, with claret or Catalonia and coffee. The time for the siesta or rest, is between breakfast and dinner. Dinner hour is three for the family, and two for the people. The dinner does not differ much from the breakfast, except that there is less of fruit and more of meat, and that some preserve is usually eaten, as a dessert. Like the breakfast, it ends with coffee. In all manner of preserves, the island is rich. The almond, the guava, the cocoa, the soursop, the orange, the lime, and the mamey apple, afford a great variety. After dinner, and before dark, is the time for long drives; and, when the families are on the estates, for visits to neighbors. There is no third meal; but coffee, and sometimes tea, is offered at night. The usual time for bed is as early as ten o'clock, for the day begins early, and the chief out-door works and active recreations must be had before breakfast.

In addition to the family house, the negro quarters, and the sugar-house, there is a range of stone buildings, ending with a kitchen, occupied by the engineer, the mayoral, the boyero, and the mayordomo, who have an old negro woman to cook for them, and another to wait on them. There is also another row of stone buildings, comprising the store-house, the penitentiary, the hospital, and the lying-in room. The penitentiary, I have described. The hospital and lying-in room are airy, well-ventilated, and suitable for their purposes. Neither of them had any tenants to-day. In the centre of the group of buildings, is a high frame, on which hangs the great bell of the plantation. This rings the negroes up in the morning, and in at night, and sounds the hours for meals. It calls all in, on any special occasion, and is used for an alarm to the neighboring plantations, rung long and loud, in case of fire in the cane-fields, or other occasions for calling in aid.

After dinner, to-day, a volante, with two horses, and a postilion in bright jacket and buckled boots and large silver spurs, the harness well-besprinkled with silver, drove to the door, and an elderly gentleman alighted and came to the house, attired with scrupulous nicety of white cravat and dress coat, and with the manners of the *ancien régime*. This is M. Bourgeoise, the owner of the neighboring, large plantation, Santa Catalina, one of the few cafetals remaining in this part of the island. He is too old, and too much attached to his plantation, to change it to a sugar estate; and he is too rich to need the change. He, too, was a refugee from the insurrection of St. Domingo, but older than M. C——. Not being able to escape, he was compelled to serve as aid-de-camp to Jacques Dessalines. He has a good deal to say about the insurrection and its results, of a great part of which he was an eye-witness. The sight of him brought vividly to mind the high career and sad fate of the just and brave Toussaint L'Ouverture, and the brilliant successes, and fickle, cruel rule, of Dessalines,—when French marshals were out-manœuvred by negro generals, and pitched battles were won by negroes and mulattoes against European armies.

This gentleman had driven over in the hope of seeing his friend and neighbor, Mr. C——, the elder. He remained with us for some time, sitting under the veranda, the silvered volante and its black horses and black postilion standing under the trees. He invited us to visit his plantation, which I was desirous to do, as a cafetal is a rarity now.

My third day at La Ariadne, is much like the preceding days: the early rising, the coffee and fruit, the walk, visits to the mill, the fields, the garden, and the quarters, breakfast, rest in-doors with reading and writing, dinner, out of doors again, and the evening under the veranda, with conversations on subjects now so interesting to me. These conversations, and what I had learned from other persons, open to me new causes for interest and sympathy with my younger host. Born in South Carolina, he has secured his rights of birth, and is a citizen of the United States, though all his pecuniary interests and family affections are in Cuba. He went to Paris at the age of nine, and remained there until he was nineteen, devoting the ten years to thorough courses of study in the best schools. He has spent much time in Boston, and has been at sea, to China, India, and the Pacific and California,—was wrecked in the Boston ship Mary Ellen, on a coral reef in the India seas, taken captive, restored, and brought back to Boston in another ship, whence he sailed for California. There he had a long and checkered experience, was wounded in the battle with the Indians who killed Lieut. Dale and defeated his party, was engaged in scientific surveys, topographical and geological, took the fever of the South Coast at a remote place, was reported dead, and came to his mother's door, at the spot where we are talking this evening, so weak and sunken that his brothers did not know him, thinking it happiness enough if he could reach his home, to die in his mother's arms. But home and its cherishings, and revived moral force, restored him; and now, active and strong again, when, in consequence of the marriage of his brothers and sisters, and the departure of neighbors, the family leave their home of thirty-five years for the city, he becomes the acting master, the administrador of the estate, and makes the old house his bachelor's hall.

An education in Europe or the United States must tend to free the youth of Cuba from the besetting fault of untravelled plantation-masters. They are in no danger of thinking their plantations and Cuba the world, or any great part of it. In such cases, I should think the danger might be rather the other way,—rather that of disgust and discouragement at the narrowness of the field, the entire want of a career set before them,—a career of any kind, literary, scientific, political, or military. The choice is between expatriation, and contentment in the position of a secluded cultivator of sugar by slave labor, with occasional opportunities of intercourse with the world and of foreign travel, with no other field than the limits of the plantation afford, for the exercise of the scientific knowledge, so laboriously acquired, and with no more exciting motive for the continuance of intellectual culture than the general sense of its worth and fitness.

Chapter XIV

I F THE MASTER of a plantation is faithful and thorough, will tolerate no misconduct or imposition, and yet is humane and watchful over the interests and rights, as well as over the duties of the negroes, he has a hard and anxious life. Sickness to be ministered to, the feigning of sickness to be counteracted, rights of the slaves to be secured against other negroes, as well as against whites, with a poor chance of getting at the truth from either; the obligations of the negro *quasi* marriage to be enforced against all the sensual and childish tendencies of the race; theft and violence and wanderings from home to be detected and prevented; the work to be done, and yet no one to be overworked; and all this often with no effectual aid, often with only obstructions, from the intermediate whites! Nor is it his own people only that are to be looked to. The thieving and violence of negroes from other plantations, their visits by night against law, and the encroachments of the neighboring free blacks and low whites, are all to be watched and prevented or punished. The master is a policeman, as well as an economist and a judge. His revolver and rifle are always loaded. He has his dogs, his trackers and seizers, that lie at his gate, trained to give the alarm when a strange step comes near the house or the quarters, and ready to pursue. His hedges may be broken down, his cane trampled or cut, or, still worse, set fire to, goats let into his pastures, his poultry stolen, and sometimes his dogs poisoned. It is a country of little law and order, and what with slavery and free negroes and low whites, violence or fraud are imminent and always formidable. No man rides far unarmed. The negroes are held under the subjection of force. A quarter-deck organization is established. The master owns vessel and cargo, and is captain of the ship, and he and his family live in the cabin and hold the quarter-deck. There are no other commissioned officers on board, and no guard of marines. There are a few petty officers, and under all, a great crew of negroes, for every kind of work, held by compulsion,—the results of a press-gang. All are at sea together. There are some laws, and civil authorities for the protection of each, but not very near, nor always accessible.

After dinner to-day, we take saddle-horses for a ride to Santa Catalina. Necessary duties in the field and mill delay us, and we are in danger of not being able to visit the house, as my friend must be back in season for the close of work and the distribution of provisions, in the absence of his mayoral. The horses have the famous "march," as it is called, of the island, an easy rapid step, something like pacing, and delightful for a quiet ride under a soft afternoon sky, among flowers and sweet odors. I have seen but few trotting horses in Cuba.

The afternoon is serene. Near, the birds are flying, or chattering with extreme sociability in close trees, and the thickets are fragrant with flowers; while far off, the high hills loom in the horizon; and all about us is this tropical growth, with which I cannot yet become familiar, of palms and cocoas and bananas. We amble over the red earth of the winding lanes, and turn into the broad avenue of Santa Catalina, with its double row of royal palms. We are in—not a forest, for the trees are not thick and wild and large enough for that—but in a huge, dense, tropical orchard. The avenue is as clear and straight and wide as a city mall; while all the ground on either side, for hundreds of acres, is a plantation of oranges and limes, bananas and plantains, cocoas and pine-apples, and of cedar and mango, mignonette and allspice, under whose shade is growing the green-leaved, the evergreen-leaved coffee plant, with its little dark red berry, the tonic of half the world. Here we have a glimpse of the lost charm of Cuba. No wonder that the aged proprietor cannot find the heart to lay it waste for the monotonous cane-field, and make the quiet, peaceful horticulture, the natural growth of fruit and berry, and the simple processes of gathering, drying, and storing, give place to the steam and smoke and drive and life-consuming toil of the ingenio!

At a turn in the avenue, we come upon the proprietor, who is taking his evening walk, still in the exact dress and with the exact manners of urban life. With truly French politeness, he is distressed, and all but offended, that we cannot go to his house. It is my duty to insist on declining his invitation, for I know that C—— is anxious to return. At another turn, we come upon a group of little black children, under the charge of a decent, matronly mulatto, coming up a shaded footpath, which leads among the coffee. C—— stops to give a kind word to them.

But it is sunset, and we must turn about. We ride rather rapidly down the avenue, and along the highway, where we meet several travellers, nearly all with pistols in their holsters, and one of the mounted police, with carbine and sword; and then cross the brook, pass through the little, mean hamlet of Limonar, whose inmates are about half blacks and half whites, but once a famed resort for invalids, and enter our own avenue, and thence to the house. On our way, we pass a burying-ground, which my companion says he is ashamed to have me see. Its condition is bad enough. The planters are taxed for it, but the charge of it is with the padre, who takes big fees for burials, and lets it go to ruin. The bell has rung long ago, but the people are waiting our return, and the evening duties of distributing food, turning on the night gang for night work, and closing the gates, are performed.

To-night the hounds have an alarm, and C—— is off in the darkness. In a few minutes he returns. There has been some one about, but nothing is discovered. A negro may have attempted to steal out, or some strange negro may be trying to steal in, or some prowling white, or free black, has been reconnoitering. These are the terms on which this system is carried on; and I think, too, that when the tramp of horses is heard after dark, and strange men ride towards the piazza, it causes some uneasiness.

The morning of the fourth day, I take my leave, by the early train for Matanzas. The hour is half-past six; but the habits of rising are so early that it requires no special preparation. I have time for coffee, for a last visit to the sugar-house, a good-by to the engineer, who will be back on the banks of the Merrimack in May, and for a last look into the quarters, to gather the little group of kneelers for "la bendicion," with their "Buenos dias, Señor." My horse is ready, the negro has gone with my luggage, and I must take my leave of my newly-made friend. Alone together, we have been more intimate in three days than we should have been in as many weeks in a full household. Adios! —may the opening of a new home on the old spot, which I hear is awaiting you, be the harbinger of a more cheerful life, and the creation of such fresh ties and interests, that the delightful air of the hill country of Cuba, the dreamy monotony of the day, the serenity of nights which seem to bring the stars down to your roof or to raise you half-way to them, and the luxuriance and variety of vegetable and animal life, may not be the only satisfactions of existence here.

A quiet amble over the red earth, to the station, in a thick morning mist, almost cold enough to make an overcoat comfortable; and, after two hours on the rail, I am again in Matanzas, among close-packed houses, and with views of blue ocean and of ships.

Chapter XV

INSTEAD of the posada by the water-side, I take up my quarters at a hotel kept by Ensor, an American, and his sister. Here the hours, cooking, and chief arrangements are in the fashion of the country, as they should be, but there is more of that attention to guests which we are accustomed to at home, than the Cuban hotels usually give.

The objects to be visited here are the Cumbre and the valley of the Yumurí. It is too late for a morning ride, and I put off my visit until afternoon. Gazzaniga and some of the opera troupe are here; and several Americans at the hotel, who were at the opera last night, tell me that the people of Matanzas made a handsome show, and are of opinion that there was more beauty in the boxes than we saw at the Villanueva. It appears, too, that at the Retreta, in the Plaza de Armas, when the band plays, and at evening promenades, the ladies walk about, and do not keep to their carriages as in Havana.

As soon as the sun began to decline, I set off for the Cumbre, mounted on a pacer, with a negro for a guide, who rode, as I soon discovered, a better nag than mine. We cross the stone bridges, and pass the great hospital, which dominates over the town. A regiment, dressed in seersucker and straw hats, is drilling, by trumpet call, and drilling well, too, on the green in front of the barracks; while we take our winding way up the ascent of the Cumbre.

The bay, town, and shipping lie beneath us; the Pan rises in the distance to the height of some 3,000 feet; the ocean is before us, rolling against the outside base of the hills; and, on the inside, lies the deep, rich, peaceful valley of the Yumurí. On the top of the Cumbre, commanding the noblest view of ocean and valley, bay and town, is the ingenio of a Mr. Jenkes, a merchant, bearing a name that would put Spanish tongues to their trumps to sound, were it not that they probably take refuge in the Don Guillermo, or Don Enrique, of his Christian name. The estate bears the name of La Victoria, and is kindly thrown open to visitors from the city. It is said to be a model establishment. The house is large, in a classic style, and costly, and the negro quarters, the storehouses, mechanic shops, and sugar-house are of dimensions indicating an estate of the first class.

On the way up from the city, several fine points of sight were occupied by villas, all of one story, usually in the Roman or Grecian style, surrounded by gardens and shade-trees, and with every appearance of taste and wealth.

It is late, but I must not miss the Yumurí; so we dive down the short, steep descent, and cross dry brooks and wet brooks, and over stones, and along bridle-paths, and over fields without paths, and by wretched hovels, and a few decent cottages, with yelping dogs and cackling hens and staring children, and between high, overhanging cliffs, and along the side of a still lake, and after it is so dark that we can hardly see stones or paths, we strike a bridle-path, and then come out upon the road, and, in a few minutes more, are among the gas-lights and noises of the city.

At the hotel, there is a New York company who have spent the day at the Yumurí, and describe a cave not yet fully explored, which is visited by all who have time,—abounding in stalactites, and, though much smaller, reminding one of the Mammoth Cave of Kentucky.

I cannot leave Matanzas without paying my respects to the family to whose kindness I owe so much. Mr. C—— lives in a part of the suburbs called Versailles, near the barracks, in a large and handsome house, built after the style of the country. There I spend an agreeable evening, at a gathering of nearly all the family, sons and daughters, and the sons-in-law and daughters-in-law. There is something strangely cosmopolitan in many of the Cuban families,—as in this, where are found French origin, Spanish and American intermarriage, education in Europe or the United States, home and property in Cuba, friendships and sympathies and half a residence in Boston or New York or Charleston, and three languages at command.

Here I learn that the Thirty Millions Bill has not passed, and, by the latest dates, is not likely to pass.

My room at Ensor's is on a level with the court-yard, and a horse puts his face into the grating as I am dressing, and I know of nothing to prevent his walking in at the door, if he chooses, so that the negro may finish rubbing him down by my looking-glass. Yet the house is neatly furnished and cared for, and its keepers are attentive and deserving people.

Chapter XVI

SATURDAY, FEBRUARY 28.—At eight o'clock this morning, I take my leave of Matanzas, by the railroad for Havana.

Although the distance to Havana, as the bird flies, is only sixty miles, the railroad, winding into the interior, to draw out the sugar freights, makes a line of nearly one hundred miles. This adds to the length of our journey, but also greatly to its interest.

In the cars are two Americans, who have also been visiting plantations. They give me the following statistics of a sugar plantation, which they think may be relied upon.

Lands, machinery, 320 slaves, and 20 Coolies, worth $500,000. Produce this year, 4,000 boxes of sugar and 800 casks of molasses, worth $104,000. Expenses, $35,000. Net, $69,000, or about 14 per cent. This is not a large interest on an investment so much of which is perishable and subject to deterioration.

The day, as has been every day of mine in Cuba, is fair and beautiful. The heat is great, perhaps even dangerous to a Northerner, should he be exposed to it in active exercise, at noon,—but, with the shade and motion of the cars, not disagreeable, for the air is pure and elastic, and it is only the direct heat of the sun that is oppressive. I think one notices the results of this pure air, in the throats and nasal organs of the people. One seldom meets a person that seems to have a cold in the head or the throat; and pocket handkerchiefs are used chiefly for ornament.

I cannot weary of gazing upon these new and strange scenes; the stations, with the groups of peasants and negroes and fruit-sellers that gather about them, and the stores of sugar and molasses collected there; the ingenios, glimmering in the heat of the sun, with their tall, furnace chimneys; the cane-fields, acres upon acres; the slow ox-carts carrying the cane to the mill; then the intervals of unused country, the jungles, adorned with little wild flowers, the groves of the weeping, drooping, sad, homesick cocoa; the royal palm, which is to trees what the camel or dromedary is among animals,—seeming to have strayed from Nubia or Mesopotamia; the stiff, close orange-tree, with its golden balls of fruit; and then the remains of a cafetal, the coffee plant growing untrimmed and wild under the reprieved groves of plantain and banana. How can this tire an eye that two weeks ago to-day rested on the midwinter snow and mud of the close streets of lower New York?

It is certainly true that there is such a thing as industry in the tropics. The labor of the tropics goes on. Notwithstanding all we hear and know of the enervating influence of the climate, the white man, if not laborious himself, is the cause that labor is in others. With all its social and political discouragements, with the disadvantages of a duty of about twenty-five per cent. on its sugars laid in the United States, and a duty of full one hundred per cent. on all flour imported from the United States, and after paying heavier taxes than any people on earth pay at this moment, and yielding a revenue, which nets, after every deduction and discount, not less than sixteen millions a year;—against all these disadvantages, this island is still very productive and very rich. There is, to be sure, little variety in its industry. In the country, it is nothing but the raising and making of sugar; and in the towns, it is the selling and exporting of sugar. With the addition of a little coffee and copper, more tobacco, and some fresh fruit and preserves, and the commerce which they stimulate, and the mechanic and trading necessities of the towns, we have the sum of its industry and resources. Science, arts, letters, arms, manufactures, and the learning and discussions of politics, of theology, and of the great problems and opinions that move the minds of the thinking world,—in these the people of Cuba have no part. These move by them, as the great Gulf Stream drifts by their shores. Nor is there, nor has there been in Cuba, in the memory of the young and middle-aged, debate, or vote, or juries, or one of the least and most rudimental processes of self-government. The African and Chinese do the manual labor; the Cubans hold the land and the capital, and direct the agricultural industry; the commerce is shared between the Cubans, and foreigners of all nations; and the government, civil and military, is exercised by the citizens of Old Spain. No Cuban votes, or attends a lawful political meeting, or sits on a jury, or sees a law-making assembly, except as a curiosity abroad, even in a municipality; nor has he ever helped to make, or interpret, or administer laws, or borne arms, except by special license of government granted to such as are friends of government. In religion, he has no choice, except between the Roman Catholic and none. The laws that govern him are made abroad, and administered by a central power, a foreign Captain-General, through the agency of foreign civil and military officers. The Cuban has no public career. If he removes to Old Spain, and is known as a supporter of Spanish royal power, his Creole birth is probably no impediment to him. But at home, as a Cuban, he may be a planter, a merchant, a physician, but he cannot expect to be a civil magistrate, or to hold a commission in the army, or an office in the police; and though he may be a lawyer, and read, sitting, a written argument to a Court of Judges, he cannot expect to be himself a Judge. He may publish a book, but the government must be the responsible author. He may edit a journal, but the government must be the editor-in-chief.

At the chief stations on the road, there are fruit-sellers in abundance, with fruit fresh from the trees: oranges, bananas, sapotes, and cocoas. The cocoa is eaten at an earlier stage than that in which we see it at the North, for it is gathered for exportation after it has become hard. It is eaten here when no harder than a melon, and is cut through with a knife, and the soft white pulp, mixed with the milk, is eaten with a spoon. It is luscious and wholesome, much more so than when the rind has hardened into the shell, and the soft pulp into a hard meat.

A little later in the afternoon, the character of the views begins to change. The ingenios and cane-fields become less frequent, then cease altogether, and the houses have more the appearance of pleasure retreats than of working estates. The roads show lines of mules and horses, loaded with panniers of fruits, or sweeping the ground with the long stalks of fresh fodder laid across their backs, all moving towards a common centre. Pleasure carriages appear. Next comes the distant view of the Castle of Atares, and the Principe, and then the harbor and the sea, the belt of masts, the high ridge of fortifications, the blue and white and yellow houses, with brown tops; and now we are in the streets of Havana.

It seems like coming home; and I feel as if I had been an age away, when it is only eight days since I first saw Cuba. Here are the familiar signs—Por mayor y menor, Posada y Cantina, Tienda, Panaderia, Relojeria, and the fanciful names of the shops, the high pitched falsetto cries of the streets, the long files of mules and horses, with panniers of fruit, or hidden, all but their noses and tails, under stacks of fresh fodder, the volantes, and the motley multitude of whites, blacks, and Chinese, soldiers and civilians, and occasionally priests,—negro women, lottery-ticket venders, and the girl musicians with their begging tambourines.

The same idlers are at the door of Le Grand's; a rehearsal, as usual, is going on at the head of the first flight; and the parrot is blinking at the hot, white walls of the court-yard, and screaming bits of Spanish. My New York friends have got back from the country a day before me. I am installed in a better room than before, on the house-top, where the sun is hot, but where there is air, and a view of the ocean.

Chapter XVII

THE WARM BATH round the corner, is a refreshment after a day's railroad ride in such heat; and there, in the front room, the man in his shirt sleeves is serving out liquor, as before, and the usual company of Creoles is gathered about the billiard tables. After a dinner in the handsome, airy restaurant of Le Grand's, I drive into the city in the evening, to the close streets of the Entramuros, and pay a visit to the lady whom I failed to see on my arrival. I am so fortunate as to meet her, and beside the pleasure to be found in her society, I am glad to be able to give her personal information from her attached and sympathizing friends, at the North.

While I am there, a tinkling sound of bells is heard in the streets, and lights flash by. It is a procession, going to carry the viaticum, the last sacrament, to a dying person.

From this house, I drove towards the water-side, past the Plaza de Armas, the old Plaza de San Francisco, with its monastery turned into an almazen (a storehouse of merchandise,) through the Calle de los Officios, to the boarding-house of Madame Almy, to call upon Dr. and Mrs. Howe. Mr. Parker left Havana, as he intended, last Tuesday, for Santa Cruz. He found Havana rather too hot for his comfort, and Santa Cruz, the most healthful and temperate of the islands, had always been his destination. He had visited a few places in the city, and among others, the College of Belen, where he had been courteously received by the Jesuits. I found that they knew his reputation as a scholar and writer, and a leading champion of modern Theism in America. Dr. Howe had called at Le Grand's, yesterday, to invite me to go with him to attend a trial, at the Audiencia, which attracted a good deal of interest among the Creoles. The story, as told by the friends of Señor Maestri, the defendant, is, that in the performance of a judicial duty, he discharged a person against whom the government was proceeding illegally, and that this led to a correspondence between him and the authorities, which resulted in his being deposed and brought to trial, before the Audiencia, on a charge of disrespect to the Captain-General. I have no means of learning the correctness of this statement, at present—

"I say the tale as 't was said to me."

The cause has, at all events, excited a deep interest among the Creoles, who see in it another proof of the unlimited character of the centralized power that governs them. I regret that I missed a scene of so much interest and instruction. Dr. Howe told me that Maestri's counsel, Señor Azcárate, a young lawyer, defended his friend courageously; but the evidence being all in writing, without the exciting conflicts and vicissitudes of oral testimony, and the written arguments being delivered sitting, there was not much in the proceedings to stimulate the Creole excitability. No decision was given, the Court taking time to deliberate. It seems to have been a Montalembert trial, on a small theatre.

To-night there is again a mascara at the next door, but my room is now more remote, and I am able to sleep through it. Once I awoke. It was nearly five o'clock. The music was still going on, but in softer and more subdued tones. The drums and trumpets were hushed, and all had fallen, as if by the magic touch of the approaching dawn, into a trance of sound, a rondo of constantly returning delicious melody, as nearly irresistible to the charmed sense as sound can be conceived to be,—just bordering on the fusing state between sense and spirit. It is a contradanza of Cuba. The great bells beat five, over the city; and instantly the music ceases, and is heard no more. The watchmen cry the hour, and the bells of the hospitals and convents sound their matins, though it is yet dark.

Chapter XVIII

A T BREAK of day, I am in the delightful sea-baths again, not ill-named Recreo and Elíseo. But the forlorn chain-gang are mustered before the Presidio. It is Sunday, but there is no day of rest for them.

At eight o'clock I present myself at the Belen. A lady, who was passing through the cloister, with head and face covered by the usual black veil, turned and came to me. It was Mrs. ——, whom I had seen last evening. She kindly took me to the sacristy, and asked some one to tell Father —— that I was there, and then went to her place in church. While waiting in the sacristy, I saw the robing and unrobing of the officiating priests, the preparation of altar ceremonials by boys and men, and could hear the voices and music in the church, on the other side of the great altar. The manner of the Jesuits is in striking contrast with that at the Cathedral. All is slow, orderly and reverential, whether on the part of men or boys. Instead of the hurried walk, the nod and duck, there is a slow march, a kneeling, or a reverential bow. At a small side altar, in the sacristy, communion is administered by a single priest. Among the recipients are several men of mature years and respectable position; and side by side with them, the poor and the negroes. In the Church, there is no distinction of race or color.

Father —— appears, is unrobed, and takes me to the gallery of the church, near the organ. From this, I looked down upon a sea of rich costumes of women, veiled heads, and kneeling figures, literally covering the floor of the church. On the marble pavement, the little carpets are spread, and on these, as close as they can sit or kneel, are the ladies of rank and wealth of Havana. A new comer glides in among them, seeking room for her carpet, or room of charity or friendship on a carpet already spread; and the kneelers or sitters move and gather in their wide skirts to let her pass. Here and there a servant in livery winds his way behind his mistress, bearing her carpet, and returns to the porch when it has been spread. The whole floor is left to women. The men gather about the walls and door-ways, or sit in the gallery, which is reserved for them. But among the women, though chiefly of rank and wealth, are some who are negroes, usually distinguished by the plain shawl, instead of the veil over the head. The Countess Villanueva, immensely rich, of high rank, and of a name great in the annals of Cuba, but childless, and blind, and a widow, is led in by the hand by her negro servant. The service of the altar is performed with dignity and reverence, and the singing, which is by the Jesuit Brothers themselves, is admirable. In the choir I recognized my new friends, the Rector and young Father Cabre, the professor of physics. The "Tantum ergo Sacramentum," which was sung kneeling, brought tears into my eyes, and kept them there.

After service, Mr. —— came to me, and made an engagement to show me the benevolent institutions on the Bishop's list, accepting my invitation to breakfast at Le Grand's, at eleven o'clock. At eleven he came, and after a quiet breakfast in a side room, we went to the house of Señor ——, whom he well knows, in the hope that he would go with us. The Señor was engaged to meet one of the Fathers at noon, and could not go, but introduced to me a relative of his, a young student of medicine in the University, who offered to take me to the Presidio and other places, the next day.

It occurred to us to call upon a young American lady, who was residing at the house of a Spanish lady of wealth and rank, and invite her to go with us to see the Beneficencia, which we thought she might do, as it is an institution under the charge of nuns, and she was to go with a Padre in full dress. But the customs of the country are rigid. Miss —— was very desirous to go, but had doubts. She consulted the lady of the house, who would know, if any one could, the etiquette of Havana. The Señora's reply was, "You are an American, and may do anything." This settled the matter in the negative, and we went alone. Now we drive to Don Juan ——'s. The gate is closed. The driver, who is a white, gets off and makes a feeble and timid rap at the door. "Knock louder!" says my friend, in Spanish. "What cowards they are!" he adds to me. The man makes a knock, a little louder. "There, see that! Peeking into the keyhole! Mean! An Englishman would beat the door down before he would do that." Don Juan is in the country,—so we fail of all our expected companions.

The Casa de Beneficencia is a large institution, for orphan and destitute children, for infirm old persons, and for the insane. It is admirably situated, bordering on the open sea, with fresh air and very good attention to ventilation in the rooms. It is a government institution, but is placed under charge of the Sisters of Charity, one of whom accompanied us about the building. Though called a government institution, it must not be supposed that it is a charity from the crown. On the contrary, it is supported by a specific appropriation of certain of the taxes and revenues of the island. In the building, is a church not yet finished, large enough for all the inmates, and a quiet little private chapel for the Sisters' devotions, where a burning lamp indicated the presence of the Sacrament on the small altar. I am sorry to have forgotten the number of children. It was large, and included both sexes, with a separate department for each. In a third department, are the insane. They are kindly treated and not confined, except when violent; but the Sister told us they had no medical treatment unless in case of sickness. (Dr. Howe told me that he was also so informed.) The last department is for aged and indigent women.

One of the little orphans clung to the Sister who accompanied us, holding her hand, and nestling in her coarse but clean blue gown; and when we took our leave, and I put a small coin into her little soft hand, her eyes brightened up into a pretty smile.

The number of the Sisters is not full. As none have joined the order from Cuba, (I am told literally none,) they are all from abroad, chiefly from France and Spain; and having acclimation to go through, with exposure to yellow fever and cholera, many of those that come here die in the first or second summer. And yet they still come, in simple, religious fidelity, under the shadow of death.

The Casa de Beneficencia must be pronounced by all, even by those accustomed to the system and order of the best charitable institutions in the world, a credit to the island of Cuba. The charity is large and liberal, and the order and neatness of its administration are beyond praise.

From the Beneficencia we drove to the Military Hospital. This is a huge establishment, designed to accommodate all the sick of the army. The walls are high, the floors are of brick and scrupulously clean, as are all things under the charge of the Sisters of Charity; and the ventilation is tolerable. The building suffered from the explosion of the magazine last year, and some quarters have not yet been restored for occupation. The number of sick soldiers now in hospital actually exceeds one thousand! Most of them are young, some mere lads, victims of the conscription of Old Spain, which takes them from their rustic homes in Andalusia and Catalonia and the Pyrenees, to expose them to the tropical heats of Cuba, and to the other dangers of its climate. Most had fevers. We saw a few cases of vomito. Notwithstanding all that is said about the healthfulness of a winter in Cuba, the experienced Sister Servant (which, I believe, is the title of the Superior of a body of Sisters of Charity) told us that a few sporadic cases of yellow fever occur in Havana, in all seasons of the year; but that we need not fear to go through the wards. One patient was covered with the blotches of recent smallpox. It was affecting to see the wistful eyes of these poor, fevered soldier-boys, gazing on the serene, kind countenances of the nuns, and thinking of their mothers and sisters in the dear home in Old Spain, and feeling, no doubt, that this womanly, religious care was the nearest and best substitute.

The present number of Sisters, charged with the entire care of this great hospital, except the duty of cooks and the mere manual and mechanic labor necessarily done by men, is not above twenty-five. The Sister Servant told us that the proper complement was forty. The last summer, eleven of these devoted women died of yellow fever. Every summer, when yellow fever or cholera prevails, some of them die. They know it. Yet the vacancies are filled up; and their serene and ever happy countenances give the stranger no indication that they have bound themselves to the bedside of contagious and loathsome diseases every year, and to scenes of sickness and death every day.

As we walked through the passage-ways, we came upon the little private chapel of the Sisters. Here was a scene I can never forget. It was an hour assigned for prayer. All who could leave the sick wards—not more than twelve or fourteen—were kneeling in that perfectly still, secluded, darkened room, in a double row, all facing to the altar, on which burned one taper, showing the presence of the Sacrament, and all in silent prayer.—That double row of silent, kneeling women, unconscious of the presence of any one, in their snow-white, close caps and long capes, and coarse, clean, blue gowns,—heroines, if the world ever had heroines, their angels beholding the face of their Father in heaven, as they knelt on earth!

It was affecting and yet almost amusing,—it would have been amusing anywhere else,—that these simple creatures, not knowing the ways of the world, and desirous to have soft music fill their room, as they knelt at silent prayer, and not having (for their duties preclude it) any skill in the practice of music, had a large music-box wound and placed on a stand, in the rear, giving out its liquid tones, just loud enough to pervade the air, without forcing attention. The effect was beautiful; and yet the tunes were not all, nor chiefly, religious. They were such as any music-box would give. But what do these poor creatures know of what the world marches to, or dances to, or makes love to? To them it was all music, and pure and holy!

Minute after minute we stood, waiting for, but not desiring, an end of these delightful sounds, and a dissolving of this spell of silent adoration. One of the Sisters began prayers aloud, a series of short prayers and adorations and thanksgivings, to each of which, at its close, the others made response in full, sweet voices. The tone of prayer of this Sister was just what it should be. No skill of art could reach it. How much truer than the cathedral, or the great ceremonial! It was low, yet audible, composed, reverent: neither the familiar, which offends so often, nor the rhetorical, which always offends, but that unconscious sustained intonation, not of speech, but of music, which frequent devotions in company with others naturally call out; showing us that poetry and music, and not prose and speech, are the natural expressions of the deepest and highest emotions.

They rose, with the prayer of benediction, and we withdrew. They separated, to station themselves, one in each ward of the hospital, there, aloud and standing, to repeat their prayers,— the sick men raising themselves on their elbows, or sitting in bed, or, if more feeble, raising their eyes and clasping their hands, and all who can or choose, joining in the responses.

Chapter XIX

DROVE OUT over the Paseo de Tacon to the Cerro, a height, formerly a village, now a part of the suburbs of Havana. It is high ground, and commands a noble view of Havana and the sea. Coming in, I met the Bishop, who introduced me to the Count de La Fernandina, a dignified Spanish nobleman, who owns a beautiful villa on this Paseo, where we walked a while in the grounds. This house is very elegant and costly, with marble floors, high ceilings, piazzas, and a garden of the richest trees and flowers coming into the court-yard, and advancing even into the windows of the house. It is one of the most beautiful villas in the vicinity of Havana.

There are several noblemen who have their estates and titles in Cuba, but are recognized as nobles of Spain;—in all, I should say, about fifty or sixty. Some of these have received their titles for civil or military services; but most of them have been raised to their rank on account of their wealth, or have purchased their titles outright. I believe there are but two grades, the marquis and the count. Among the titles best known to strangers are Villanueva, Fernandina, and O'Reilly. The number of Irish families who have taken rank in the Spanish service and become connected with Cuba, is rather remarkable. Beside O'Reilly, there are O'Donnel, O'Farrel, and O'Lawlor, descendants of Irishmen who entered the Spanish service after the battle of the Boyne.

Dr. Howe had seen the Presidio, the great prison of Havana, once; but was desirous to visit it again; so he joined me, under the conduct of our young friend, Señor ——, to visit that and the hospital of San Juan de Dios. The hospital we saw first. It is supported by the government,—that is to say, by Cuban revenues,—for charity patients chiefly, but some, who can afford it, pay more or less. There are about two hundred and fifty patients. This, again, is in the charge of the Sisters of Charity. As we came upon one of the Sisters, in a passage way, in her white cap and cape, and black and blue dress, Dr. Howe said, "I always take off my hat to a Sister of Charity," and we paid them all that attention, whenever we passed them. Dr.

Howe examined the book of prescriptions, and said that there was less drugging than he supposed there would be. The attending physician told us that nearly all the physicians had studied in Paris, or in Philadelphia. There were a great many medical students in attendance, and there had just been an operation in the theatre. In an open yard we saw two men washing a dead body, and carelessly laying it on a table, for dissection. I am told that the medical and surgical professions are in a very satisfactory state of advancement in the island, and that a degree in medicine, and a license to practise, carry with them proofs of considerable proficiency. It is always observable that the physical and the exact sciences are the last to suffer under despotisms.

The Presidio and Grand Carcel of Havana is a large building, of yellow stone, standing near the fort of the Punta, and is one of the striking objects as you enter the harbor. It has no appearance of a jail without, but rather of a palace or court; but within, it is full of live men's bones and of all uncleanness. No man, whose notions are derived from an American or English penitentiary of the last twenty years, or fifty years, can form an idea of the great Cuban prison. It is simply horrible. There are no cells, except for solitary confinement of "incommunicados," —who are usually political offenders. The prisoners are placed in large rooms, with stone floors and grated windows, where they are left, from twenty to fifty in each, without work, without books, without interference or intervention of any one, day and night, day and night, for the weeks, months or years of their sentences. The sights are dreadful. In this hot climate, so many beings, with no provision for ventilation but the grated windows,—so unclean, and most of them naked above the waist,—all spend their time in walking, talking, playing, and smoking; and, at night, without bed or blanket, they lie down on the stone floor, on what clothes they may have, to sleep if they can. The whole prison, with the exception of the few cells for the "incommunicados," was a series of these great cages, in which human beings were shut up. Incarceration is the beginning, middle and end of the whole system. Reformation, improvement, benefit to soul or body, are not thought of. We inquired carefully, both of the officer who was sent to attend us, and of a capitan de partido, who was there, and were positively assured that the only distinction among the prisoners was determined by the money they paid. Those who can pay nothing, are left to the worst. Those who can pay two reals (twenty-five cents) a day, are placed in wards a little higher and better. Those who can pay six reals (seventy-five cents) a day, have better places still, called the "Salas de distincion," and some privileges of walking in the galleries. The amount of money, and not the degree of criminality, determines the character of the punishment. There seems to be no limit to the right of the prisoners to talk with any whom they can get to hear them, at whatever distance, and to converse with visitors, and to receive money from them. In fact, the whole scene was a Babel. All that was insured was that they should not escape. When I say that no work was done, I should make the qualification that a few prisoners were employed in rolling tobacco into cigars, for a contractor; but they were very few. Among the prisoners was a capitan de partido (a local magistrate), who was committed on a charge of conniving at the slave-trade. He could pay his six reals, of course; and had the privileges of a "Sala de distincion" and of the galleries. He walked about with us, cigar in mouth, and talked freely, and gave us much information respecting the prison. My last request was to see the garrotte; but it was refused me.

It was beginning to grow dark before we got to the gate, which was duly opened to us, and we passed out, with a good will, into the open air. Dr. Howe said he was nowise reluctant to be outside. It seemed to bring back to his mind his Prussian prison, a little too forcibly to be agreeable. He felt as if he were in keeping again, and was thinking how he should feel if, just as we got to the gate, an officer were to bow and say, "Dr. Howe?" "Yes, sir." "You may remain here. There is a charge against you of seditious language, since you have been in the island." No man would meet such a danger more calmly, and say less about it, than he, if he thought duty to his fellow-beings called him to it.

The open air, the chainless ocean, and the ships freely coming and going, were a pleasant change to the eye, even of one who had never suffered bonds for conscience' sake. It seemed strange to see that all persons outside were doing as they pleased.

Chapter XX

A BULL-FIGHT has been advertised all over the town, at the Plaza de Toros. Shall we go? I would not, if it were only pleasure that I was seeking. As I am sure I expect only the contrary, and wish merely to learn the character of this national recreation, I will go.

The Plaza de Toros is a wooden amphitheatre, in the suburbs, open at the top,—a circle of rising seats, with the arena in the centre. I am late. The cries of the people inside are loud, sharp, and constant; a full band is blowing its trumpets and beating its drums; and the late stragglers are justling for their tickets. I go through at a low door,—find myself under benches filled with an eager, stamping, shouting multitude, make my way through a passage, and come out on the shady side, for it is a late afternoon sun, and take my place at a good point of view. A bull, with some blood about his fore-quarters, and two or three darts (bandarillas) sticking in his neck, is trotting harmlessly about the arena, "more sinned against than sinning," and seeming to have no other desire than to get out. Two men, each carrying a long, stout, wooden pole, pointed with a short piece of iron, not long enough to kill, but only to drive off and to goad, are mounted on two of the sorriest nags eyes ever beheld,—reprieved jades, whom it would not pay to feed and scarcely pay to kill, and who have been left to take their chances of death here. They could hardly be pricked into a trot, and were too weak to escape. I have seen horses in every stage of life and in every degree of neglect, but no New York negro hack-driver would have taken these for a gift, if he were obliged to keep them. The bull could not be said to run away from the horses, for they did not pursue; but when, distracted by sights and sounds, he came against a horse, the horse stood still to be gored, and the bull only pushed against him with his head, until driven off by the punching of the iron-pointed pole of the horseman.

Around the arena are sentry-boxes, each large enough to hold two men, behind which they can easily jump, but which the bull cannot enter; and from these, the cowardly wretches run out, flourish a red cloth at the bull, and jump back. Three or four men, with darts in hand, run before the bull, entice him by flapping their red cloths, and, as he trots up to them, stick bandarillas into his neck. These torment the bull, and he tries to shake them off, and paws the ground; but still he shows no fight. He trots to the gate, and snuffs to get out. Some of the multitude cry "Fuera el toro! Fuera el toro!" which means that he is a failure, and must be let out at the gate. Others are excited, and cry for the killer, the (matador); and a demoniacal scene follows, of yells and shouts, half drowned by twenty or thirty drums and trumpets. The cries to go on prevail; and the matador appears, dressed in a tight-fitting suit of green small-clothes, with a broad silver stripe, jerkin, and stockings,—a tall, light-complexioned, elegantly made, glittering man, bearing in one hand a long, heavy, dull black sword, and in the other a broad, red cloth. Now comes the harrying and dis-tracting of the bull by flags, and red cloths, and darts; the matador runs before, flings his cloth up and down; the bull trots towards it—no furious rush, or maddened dash, but a moderate trot,—the cloth is flashed over his face, and one skil-fully directed lunge of the sword into his back neck, and he drops instantly dead at the feet of the matador, at the very spot where he received the stab. Frantic shouts of applause follow; and the matador bows around, like an applauded circus-rider, and retires. The great gate opens, and three horses abreast are driven in, decked with ribbons, to drag the bull round the arena. But they are such feeble animals that, with all the flour-ish of music and the whipping of drivers, they are barely able to tug the bull along over the tan, in a straight line for the gate, through which the sorry pageant and harmless bull disappear.

Now, some meagre, hungry, swarthy, sweaty, mean-looking degenerates of Spain jump in and rake over the arena, and cover up the blood, and put things to rights again; and I find time to take a view of the company. Thankful I am, and cred-itable it is, that there are no women. Yes,—there are two mulatto women, in a seat on the sunny side, which is the cheap side. And there are two shrivelled, dark, Creole women, in a box; and there is one girl of eight or ten years, in full dress, with an elderly man. These are all the women. In the State Box, under the faded royal arms, are a few officials, not of high degree. The rest of the large company is a motley collection, chiefly of the middle or lower classes, mostly standing on the benches, and nearly all smoking.

The music beats and brays again, the great gates open, and another bull rushes in, distracted by sights and sounds so novel, and for a few minutes shows signs of power and vigor; but, as he becomes accustomed to the scene, he tames down; and after several minutes of flaunting of cloths and flags, and piercing with darts, and punching with the poles of the horsemen, he runs under the poor white horse, and upsets him, but leaves him unhurt by his horns; has a leisurely trial of endurance with the red horse, goring him a little with one horn, and receiving the pike of the driver,—the horse helpless and patient, and the bull very reasonable and temperate in the use of his power,—and then is enticed off by flags, and worried with darts; and, at last, a new matador appears,—a fierce-looking fellow, dressed in dark green, with a large head of curling, snaky, black hair, and a skin almost black. He makes a great strut and flourish, and after two or three unsuccessful attempts to get the bull head on, at length, getting a fair chance, plunges his black sword to the hilt in the bull's neck, —but there is no fall of the bull. He has missed the spinal cord, and the bull trots off, bleeding in a small stream, with a sword-handle protruding a few inches above the hide of his back-neck. The spectators hoot their contempt for the failure; but with no sign of pity for the beast. The bull is weakened, but trots about and makes a few runs at cloths, and the sword is drawn from his hide by an agile dart-sticker, (bandarillero,) and given to the black bully in dark green, who makes one more lunge, with no better success. The bull runs round, and reels, and staggers, and falls half down, gets partly up, lows and breathes heavily, is pushed over and held down, until a butcher dispatches him with a sharp knife, at the spinal cord. Then come the opened gates, the three horses abreast, decked with ribbons, the hard tug at the bull's body over the ground, —his limbs still swaying with remaining life, the clash and clang of the band, and the yells of the people.

Shall I stay another? Perhaps it may be more successful, and—if the new bull will only bruise somebody! But the new bull is a failure. After all their attempts to excite him, he only trots round, and snuffs at the gates; and the cry of "Fuera el toro!" becomes so general, with the significant triple beat of the feet, in time with the words, all over the house, that the gates are opened, and the bull trots through, to his quarters.

But the meanness, and cruelty, and impotency of this crowd! They cry out to the spear-men and the dart-men, and to the tormentors, and to the bull, and to the horses, and to each other, in a Babel of sounds, where no man's voice can possibly be distinguished ten feet from him, all manner of advice and encouragement or derision, like children at a play. One full grown, well-dressed young man, near me, kept up a constant cry to the men in the ring, when I am sure no one could distinguish his words, and no one cared to,—until I became so irritated that I could have throttled him.

But, such you are! You can cry and howl at bull-fights and cock-fights and in the pits of operas and theatres, and drive bulls and horses distracted, and urge gallant game-cocks to the death, and applaud opera singers into patriotic songs, and leave them to imprisonment and fines,—and you yourselves, cannot lift a finger, or join hand to hand, or bring to the hazard life, fortune, or honor, for your liberty and your dignity as men. Work your slaves, torture your bulls, fight your game-cocks, crown your dancers and singers,—and leave the weightier matters of judgment and justice, of fame by sea and land, of letters and arts and sciences, of private right and public honor, the present and future of your race and of your native land, to the care of others,—of a people of no better blood than your own, strangers and sojourners among you!

The next bull is treated to a refinement of torture, in the form of darts filled with heavy China crackers, which explode on the neck of the poor beast. I could not see that even this made him really dangerous. The light complexioned, green-and-silver matador dispatches him, as he did the first bull, with a single lunge, and—a fall and a quiver, and all is over!

The fifth bull is a failure and is allowed to go out of the ring. The sixth is nearly the same with the others, harmless if let alone, and goaded into short-lived activity, but not into anything like fury or even a dangerous animosity. He is treated to fire-crackers, and gores one horse a little,—the horse standing, side on, and taking it, until the bull is driven off by the punching of the spear; and runs at the other horse, and, to my delight, upsets the rider, but unfortunately without hurting him, and the black-haired matador in green tries his hand on him and fails again, and is hooted, and takes to throwing darts, and gets a fall, and looks disconcerted, and gets his sword again, and makes another false thrust; and the crippled and bleeding animal is thrown down and dispatched by the butcher with his short knife, and drawn off by the three poor horses. The gates close, and I hurry out of the theatre, in a din of shouts and drums and trumpets, the great crowd waiting for the last bull;—but I have seen enough.

There is no volante in waiting, and I have to take my seat in an omnibus, and wait for the end of the scene. The confusion of cries and shouts and the interludes of music still goes on, for a quarter of an hour, and then the crowd begins to pour out, and to scatter over the ground. Four faces in a line are heading for my omnibus. There is no mistaking that head man, the file leader. "Down East" is written legibly all over his face. Tall, thin, sallow, grave, circumspect! The others are not counterparts. They vary. But "New England" is graven on all.

"Wa-a-al!" says the leader, as he gets into the omnibus. No reply. They take their seats, and wipe their foreheads. One expectorates. Another looks too wise for utterance. "By," . . . . a long pause—How will he end it?—"Jingoes!" That is a failure. It is plain he fell short, and did not end as he intended. The sentiment of the four has not yet got uttered. The fat, flaxen-haired man makes his attempt. "If there is a new-milch cow in Vermont that wouldn't show more fight, under such usage, than them bulls, I'd buy her and make a present of her to Governor *Cunchy*,—or whatever they call him."—This is practical and direct, and opens the way to a more free interchange. The northern ice is thawed. The meanness and cruelty of the exhibition is commented upon. The moral view is not overlooked, nor underrated.—None but cowards would be so cruel. And last of all, it is an imposition. Their money has been obtained under false pretences. A suit would lie to recover it back; but the poor devils are welcome to the money. The coach fills up with Cubans; and the noise of the pavements drowns the further reflections of the four philanthropists, patriots and economists.

Chapter XXI

THE PEOPLE of Cuba have a mode of calling attention by a sound of the tongue and lips, a sort of "P—s—t!" after the fashion of some parts of the continent of Europe. It is universal here; and is used not only to servants and children, but between themselves, and to strangers. It has a mean sound, to us. They make it clear and penetrating; yet it seems a poor, effeminate sibilation, and no generous, open-mouthed call. It is the mode of stopping a volante, calling a waiter, attracting the attention of a friend, or calling the notice of a stranger. I have no doubt, if a fire were to break out at the next door, a Cuban would call "P—s—t!"

They beckon a person to come to them by the reverse of our motion. They raise the open hand, with the palm outwards, bending the fingers toward the person they are calling. We should interpret it to be a sign to go away.

Smoking is universal, and all but constant. I have amused myself, in the street, by seeing what proportion of those I meet have cigars or cigarettos in their mouths. Sometimes it has been one half, sometimes one in three. The cigar is a great leveller. Any man may stop another for a light. I have seen the poor porters, on the wharf, bow to gentlemen, strangers to them, and hold out a cigar, and the gentlemen stop, give a light, and go on,—all as of course.

In the evening, called on the Señoritas F——, at the house of Mr. B——, and on the American young lady at Señor M——'s, and on Mrs. Howe, at Mde. Almy's, to offer to take letters or packets.

At Mrs. Almy's, there is a gentleman from New York, Mr. G——, who is dying of consumption. His only wish is to live until the Cahawba comes in, that he may at least die at sea, if he cannot survive until she reaches New York. He has a horror of dying here, and being buried in the Potter's Field.—Dr. Howe has just come from his chamber.

I drove out to the bishop's, to pay my parting respects. It is about half-past eight in the evening. He has just returned from his evening drive, is dressed in a cool, cambric dressing-gown,

499

after a bath, and is taking a quiet cigar, in his high-roofed parlor. He is very cordial and polite, and talks again about the Thirty Millions Bill, and asks what I think of the result, and what I have seen of the island, and my opinion of the religious and charitable institutions. I praise the Belen and the Sisters of Charity, and condemn the prison, and he appears to agree with me. He appreciates the learning and zeal of the Brothers of Belen; speaks in the highest terms of the devotedness of the Sisters of Charity; and admits the great faults of the prison, but says it was built recently, at an enormous outlay, and he supposes the government is reluctant to be at the expense of abandoning it and building another. He charges me with messages of remembrance and respect to acquaintances we have in common. As I take my leave, he goes with me to the outer gate, which is kept locked, and again takes leave, for two leave-takings are the custom of the country, and returns to the solitude of his house.

Yesterday I drove out to the Cerro, to see the Coolie jail, or market, where the imported Coolies are kept for sale. It is a well-known place, and open to all visitors. The building has a fair-looking front; and through this I enter, by two porters, into an open yard in the rear, where, on the gravel ground, are squatting a double line of Coolies, with heads shaved, except a tuft on the crown, dressed in loose Chinese garments of blue and yellow. The dealer, who is a calm, shrewd, heartless looking man, speaking English as well as if it were his native tongue, comes out with me, calls to the Coolies, and they all stand up in a double line, facing inward, and we pass through them, preceded by a driver armed with the usual badge of the plantation driver, the short, limber whip. The dealer does not hesitate to tell me the terms on which the contracts are made, as the trade is not illegal. His account is this— The importer receives $340 for each Coolie, and the purchaser agrees to pay the Coolie four dollars per month, and to give him food, and two suits of clothes a year. For this, he has his services for eight years. The contract is reduced to writing before a magistrate, and two originals are made, one kept by the Coolie and one by the purchaser, and each in Chinese and Spanish.

This was a strange and striking exhibition of power. Two or three white men, bringing hundreds of Chinese thousands of miles, to a new climate and people, holding them prisoners, selling their services to masters having an unknown tongue and an unknown religion, to work at unknown trades, for inscrutable purposes!

The Coolies did not look unhealthy, though some had complaints of the eyes; yet they looked, or I fancied they looked,— some of them, unhappy, and some of them stolid. One I am sure had the leprosy; although the dealer would not admit it. The dealer did not deny their tendency to suicide, and the danger of attempting to chastise them, but alleged their great superiority to the negro in intelligence, and contended that their condition was good, and better than in China, having four dollars a month, and being free at the end of eight years. He said, which I found to be true, that after being separated and employed in work, they let their hair grow, and adopt the habits and dress of the country. The newly arrived Coolies wear tufts, and blue-and-yellow, loose, Chinese clothes. Those who have been here long are distinguishable from the whites only by the peculiar tinge of the cheek, and the form of the eye.

The only respect in which his account differed from what I heard elsewhere, was in the amount the importer receives, which has always been stated to me at $400.

While I am talking with him, a gentleman comes and passes down the line. He is probably a purchaser, I judge; and I leave my informant to follow what is more for his interest than talking with me.

The importation has not yet existed eight years. So the question, what will become of these men, exotics, without women or children, taking no root in the land, has not come to a solution. The constant question is—will they remain and mix with the other races? Will they be permitted to remain? Will they be able to go back?

So far as I can learn, there is no law in China regulating the contracts and shipment of Chinese Coolies, and none in Cuba regulating their transportation, landing, or treatment while here. The trade has grown up and been permitted and recognized, but not regulated. It is yet to be determined how far the contract is enforceable against either party. Those Coolies that are taken from the British East Indies to British islands, are taken under contracts, with regulations, as to their exportation and return, understood and enforced. Not so the Chinese Coolies. Their importers are *lege soluti*. Some say the government will insist on their being returned. But the prevailing impression is that they will be brought in debt, and bound over again for their debts, or in some other way secured to a life-long servitude.

Mr. ——, a very wealthy and intelligent planter, tells me he is to go over to Regla, tomorrow morning, to see a lot of slaves offered for sale to him, and asks me if I have ever seen a sale of slaves. I never have seen that sight, and accept his invitation. We are to leave here at half-past six, or seven, at the latest. All work is early here; I believe I have mentioned that the hour of 'Change for merchants is 7.30 A.M.

Chapter XXII

TUESDAY, MARCH 1.—Rise early, and walk to the sea-baths, and take a delightful float and swim. And refreshing it is, after a feverish night in my hot room, where I did not sleep an hour all night, but heard every quarter-hour struck, and the boatswain's whistle of the watchmen and their full cry of the hour and the weather, at every clock-strike. From the bath, I look out over the wall, far to the northeast, in the hope of catching a glimpse of the Cahawba's smoke. This is the day of her expected arrival. My New York friends and myself feel that we have seen Havana to our satisfaction, and the heat is becoming intense. We are beginning to receive advice against eating fruit after *café au lait*, or bananas with wine, and in favor of high crowned hats at noon to prevent congestion from heat, and to avoid fogs in the morning. But there is no Cahawba in sight, and I hear only the bray of trumpets and roll of drums from the Morro and Cabaña and Punta, and the clanking march of the chain-gang down the Paseo, and the march of the guard to trumpet and drum.

Mr. —— is punctual at seven, his son with him, and a man in a suit of white linen, who is the broker employed by Mr. ——. We take a ferry-boat and cross to the Regla; and a few minutes' walk brings us to a small nail factory, where all the workmen are Coolies. In the back yard of this factory is a line of low buildings, from which the slaves are brought out, to be shown. We had taken up, at the ferry-boat, a small, thin, sharp-faced man, who was the dealer. The slaves are formed in a semicircle, by the dealer and broker. The broker pushed and pulled them about in a coarse, careless manner, worse than the manner of the dealer. I am glad he is not to be their master. Mr. —— spoke kindly to them. They were fully dressed; and no examination was made except by the eye; and no exhibitions of strength or agility were required, and none of those offensive examinations of which we read so much. What examination had been made or was to be made by the broker, out of my presence, I do not know. The "lot" consisted of about fifty, of both sexes and of all ages; some being old, and some very young. They were not a valuable lot, and Mr. —— refused to purchase them all. The dealer offered to separate them. Mr. —— selected about half of them, and they were set apart. I watched the countenances of all,—the taken and the left. It was hard to decipher the character of their emotions. A kind of fixed hopelessness marked the faces of some, listlessness that of others, and others seemed anxious or disappointed, but whether because taken or rejected, it was hard to say. When the separation was made, and they knew its purpose, still no complaint was made and no suggestion ventured by the slaves that a tie of nature or affection was broken. I asked Mr. —— if some of them might not be related. He said he should attend to that, as he never separated families. He spoke to each of those he had chosen, separately, and asked if they had parent or child, husband or wife, or brother or sister among those who were rejected. A few pointed out their relations, and Mr. —— took them into his lot. One was an aged mother, one a wife, and another a little daughter. I am satisfied that no separations were made in this case, and equally satisfied that neither the dealer nor the broker would have asked the question.

I asked Mr. —— on what principle he made his selection, as he did not seem to me always to take the strongest. "On the principle of race," said he. He told me that these negroes were probably natives of Africa, (bozales,) except the youngest, and that the signs of the races were known to all planters. A certain race he named as having always more intelligence and ambition than any other; as more difficult to manage, but far superior when well managed. All of this race in the company, he took at once, whatever their age or strength. I think the preferred tribe was the Lucumí, but am not certain.

From this place, I made a short visit to the Almacen de azucar, in the Regla, the great storehouses of sugar. These are a range of one-story, stone warehouses, so large that a great part of the sugar crop of the island, as I am told, could be stored in them. Here the vessels go to load, and the merchants store their sugar here, as wine is stored in the London docks.

The Cubans are careful of the diet of foreigners, even in winter. I bought a couple of oranges, and young Mr. —— bought a sapote, a kind of sweet-sour apple, when the broker said "Take care! Did you not have milk with your coffee?" I inquired, and they told me it was not well to eat fresh fruit soon after taking milk, or to take bananas with wine, or to drink spirits. "But is this in winter, also?" "Yes; and it is already very hot, and there is danger of fever among strangers."

Went to La Dominica, the great restaurant and depot of preserves and sweetmeats for Havana, and made out my order for preserves to take home with me. After consultation, I am advised to make up my list as follows: guava of Peru, limes, mammey apples, soursop, cocoa-nut, oranges, guava jelly, guava marmalade, and almonds.

The ladies tell me there is a kind of fine linen sold here, called bolan, which it is difficult to obtain in the United States, and which would be very proper to take home for a present. On this advice, I bought a quantity of it, of blue and white, at La Diana, a shop on the corner of Calle de Obispo and San Ignacio.

Breakfasted with a wealthy and intelligent gentleman, a large planter, who is a native of Cuba, but of European descent. A very nice breakfast, of Spanish mixed dishes, rice cooked to perfection, fruits, claret, and the only cup of good black tea I have tasted in Cuba. At Le Grand's, we have no tea but the green.

At breakfast, we talked freely on the subject of the condition and prospects of Cuba; and I obtained from my host his views of the economical and industrial situation of the island. He was confident that the number of slaves does not exceed 500,000, to 200,000 free blacks, and 600,000 or 700,000 whites. His argument led him to put the number of slaves as low as he could, yet he estimated it far above that of the census of 1857, which makes it 375,000. But no one regards the census of slaves as correct. There is a tax on slaves, and the government has little chance of getting them stated at the full number. One planter said to a friend of mine a year or two ago, that his two hundred slaves were returned as one hundred. I find the best opinions put the slaves at 650,000, the free blacks at 200,000, and the whites at 700,000.

Havana is flooded with lottery-ticket venders. They infest every eating-house and public way, and vex you at dinner, in your walks and rides. They sell for one grand lottery,

established and guarantied by the government, always in operation, and yielding to the State a net revenue of nearly two
millions a year. The Cubans are infatuated with this lottery. All
classes seem to embark in it. Its effect is especially bad on the
slaves, who invest in it all they can earn, beg, or steal, allured
by the glorious vision of possibly purchasing their freedom,
and elevating themselves into the class of proprietors.

Some gentlemen at Le Grand's have been to a cock-fight. I
shall be obliged to leave the island without seeing this national
sport, for which every town, and every village has a pit, a Valle
de Gallos. They tell me it was a very exciting scene among the
spectators. Negroes, free and slave, low whites, Coolies, and
men of high condition, were all frantically betting. Most of the
bets were made by holding up the fingers and by other signs,
between boxes and galleries. They say I should hardly credit
the large sums which the most ordinary looking men staked
and paid.

I am surprised to find what an impression the Lopez expedition made in Cuba,—a far greater impression than is commonly supposed in the United States. The fears of the
government and hopes of sympathizers exaggerated the force,
and the whole military power of the government was stirred
against them. Their little force of a few hundred broken-down
men and lads, deceived and deserted, fought a body of eight
times their number, and kept them at bay, causing great
slaughter. The railroad trains brought the wounded into
Havana, car after car; rumors of defeat filled the city; artillery
was sent out; and the actual loss of the Spaniards, in killed and
wounded, was surprisingly large. On the front wall of the
Cabaña, plainly seen from the deck of every vessel that leaves
or enters the port, is a monument to the honor of those who
fell in the battle with the Filibusteros. The spot where Lopez
was garroted, in front of the Punta, is pointed out, as well as
the slope of the hill from the castle of Atares, where his sur-
viving followers were shot.

Chapter XXIII

To an American, from the free States, Cuba presents an object of singular interest. His mind is occupied and almost oppressed by the thought of the strange problems that are in process of solution around him. He is constantly a critic, and a philosophizer, if not a philosopher. A despotic civil government, compulsory religious uniformity, and slavery, are in full possession of the field. He is always seeking information as to causes, processes and effects, and almost as constantly baffled. There are three classes of persons in Cuba, from whom he receives contradictory and irreconcilable statements: the Cubans, the Spaniards, and foreigners of other nations. By Cubans, I mean the Criollos (Creoles), or natives of Cuba. By Spaniards, I mean the Peninsulares, or natives of Old Spain. In the third class, are comprised the Americans, English, French, Germans, and all other foreigners, except Spaniards, who are residents on the island, but not natives. This last class is large, possesses a great deal of wealth, and includes a great number of merchants, bankers and other traders.

The Spaniards, or Peninsulares, constitute the army and navy, the officers of the government in all departments, judicial, educational, fiscal and postal, the revenue and the police, the upper clergy, and a large and wealthy class of merchants, bankers, shopkeepers, and mechanics. The higher military and civil officers are from all parts of Spain; but the Catalans furnish the great body of the mechanics and small traders. The Spaniards may be counted on as opponents of the independence of Cuba, and especially of her annexation to the United States. In their political opinions, they vary. Some belong to the liberal, or Progresista party, and others are advocates of, or at least apologists for, the present order of things. Their force and influence is increased by the fact that the government encourages its military and civil officers, at the expiration of their terms of service, to remain in the island, still holding some nominal office, or on the pay of a retired list.

The foreign residents, not Spaniards, are chiefly engaged in commerce, banking, or trade, or are in scientific or mechanic employments. These do not intend to become citizens of Cuba. They strike no root into the soil, but feel that they are only sojourners, for purposes of their own. Of all classes of persons, I know of none whose situation is more unfavorable to the growth and development of sentiments of patriotism and philanthropy, and of interest in the future of a race, than foreigners, temporarily resident, for purposes of money-making only, in a country with which they have nothing in common, in the future or the past. This class is often called impartial. I do not agree to that use of the term. They are, indeed, free from the bias of feeling or sentiment; and from the bias generated by the combined action of men thinking and feeling alike, which we call political party. But they are subject to the attractions of interest; and interest will magnetize the mind as effectually as feeling. Planted in a soil where the more tender and delicate fibres can take no hold, they stand by the strong tap-root of interest. It is for their immediate advantage to preserve peace and the existing order of things; and even if it may be fairly argued that their ultimate interests would be benefited by a change, yet the process is hazardous, and the result not sure; and, at most, they would do no more than take advantage of the change, if it occurred. I should say, as a general thing, that this class is content with the present order of things. The island is rich, production is large, commerce flourishes, life and property are well protected, and if a man does not concern himself with political or religious questions, he has nothing to fear. Of the Americans in this class, many, doubtless, may be favorably inclined toward annexation, but they are careful talkers, if they are so; and the foreigners, not Americans, are of course earnestly opposed to it, and the pendency of the question tends to draw them towards the present government.

It remains only to speak of the Cubans. They are commonly styled Creoles. But as that word includes natives of all Spanish America, it is not quite definite. Of the Cubans; a few are advocates of the present government,—but very few. The far greater part are disaffected. They desire something approximating to self-government. If that can be had from Spain, they would prefer it. If not, there is nothing for them but independence, or annexation to some other power. Not one of them thinks of independence; and if it be annexation, I believe their present impulse is toward the United States. Yet on this point, among even the most disaffected of the Cubans, there is a difference of opinion. Many of them are sincere emancipationists, and fear that if they come in at the southern end of our Union, that question is closed forever. Others fear that the Anglo-Saxon race would swallow up the power and property of the island, as they have done in California and Texas, and that the Creoles would go to the wall.

It has been my fortune to see persons of influence and intelligence from each of these chief divisions, and from the subdivisions, and to talk with them freely. From the sum of their conflicting opinions and conflicting statements, I have endeavored to settle upon some things as certain; and, as to other things, to ascertain how far the debatable ground extends, and the principles which govern the debate. From all these sources, and from my own observations, I will endeavor to set down what I think to be the present state of Cuba, in its various interesting features, trusting to do it as becomes one whose acquaintance with the island has been so recent and so short.

POLITICAL CONDITION.

When the liberal constitutions were in force in Spain, in the early part of this century, the benefits of them extended to Cuba. Something like a provincial legislature was established; juntas, or advisory boards and committees, discussed public questions, and made recommendations; a militia was organized; the right to bear arms was recognized; tribunals, with something of the nature of juries, passed upon certain questions; the press was free, and Cuba sent delegates to the Spanish Cortes. This state of things continued, with but few interruptions or variations, to 1825. Then was issued the celebrated Royal Order of May 29, 1825, under which Cuba has been governed to the present hour. This Royal Order is the only constitution of Cuba. It was probably intended merely as a temporary order to the then Captain-General; but it has been found convenient to adhere to it. It clothes the Captain-General with the fullest powers, the tests and limit of which are as follows: ". . . . . fully investing you with the whole extent of power which, by the royal ordinances, is granted to the governors of besieged towns. In consequence thereof, His Majesty most amply and unrestrictedly authorizes your Excellency not only to remove from the island such persons, holding offices from government or not, whatever their occupation, rank, class, or situation in life may be, whose residence there you may believe prejudicial, or whose public or private conduct may appear suspicious to you . . . . ."

So that, since 1825, Cuba has been not only under martial law, but in a state of siege.

As to the more or less of justice or injustice, of honesty or peculation, of fidelity or corruption, of liberality or severity, with which these powers may have been exercised, a residence of a few days, the reading of a few books, and conversations with a few men, though on both sides, give me no right to pronounce. Of the probabilities, all can judge; especially when we remember that these powers are wielded by natives of one country over natives of another country.

Into the details and anecdotes, and the controversies respecting motives, I do not enter. Certain things we know. Since 1825, there has been no legislative assembly in Cuba, either provincial or municipal. The municipal corporations (ayuntamientos) were formerly hereditary, the dignity was purchasable, and no doubt the bodies were corrupt. But they exercised some control, at least in the levying and expending of taxes; and, being hereditary, were somewhat independent, and might have served, like those of Europe in the middle ages, as nuclei of popular liberties. These have lost the few powers they possessed, and the members are now mere appointees of the Captain-General. Since 1836, Cuba has been deprived of its right to a delegation in the Cortes. Since 1825, vestiges of anything approaching to popular assemblies, juntas, a jury, independent tribunals, a right of voting, or a right to bear arms, have vanished from the island. The press is under censorship; and so are the theatres and operas. When "I Puritani" is played, the singers are required to substitute Lealtà for Libertà, and one singer was fined and imprisoned for recusancy; and Facciolo, the printer of a secretly circulated newspaper, advocating the cause of Cuban independence, was garroted. The power of banishing, without a charge made, or a trial, or even a record, but on the mere will of the Captain-General, persons whose presence he thinks, or professes to think, prejudicial to the government, whatever their condition, rank, or office, has been frequently exercised, and hangs at all hours over the head of every Cuban. Besides, that terrible power which is restrained only by the analogy of a state of siege, may be at any time called into action. Cubans may be, and I suppose usually are, regularly charged and tried before judges, on political accusations; but this is not their right; and the judges themselves, even of the highest court, the Real Audiencia, may be deposed and banished, at the will of the military chief.

According to the strictness of the written law, no native Cuban can hold any office of honor, trust, or emolument in Cuba. The army and navy are composed of Spaniards, even to the soldiers in the ranks, and to the sailors at the guns. It is said by the supporters of the government that this order is not adhered to; and they point to a capitan-general, an intendente, and a chief of the customs, who were Cubans. Still, such is the written law; and if a few Cubans are put into office against the law, those who are so favored are likely to be the most servile of officers, and the situation of the rest is only the more degraded. Notwithstanding the exceptions, it may be said with substantial truth, that an independent Cuban has open to him no career, civil or military. There is a force of volunteers, to which some Cubans are admitted, but they hold their places at the will of the government; and none are allowed to join or remain with them unless they are acceptable to the government.

There are vexatious and mortifying regulations, too numerous and minute to be complied with or even remembered, and which put the people in danger of fines or extortion at every turn. Take, for instance, the regulation that no man shall entertain a stranger over night at his house, without previous notice to the magistrate. As to the absolute prohibition of concealed weapons, and of all weapons but the regulation sword and pistols,—it was no doubt introduced and enforced by Tacon as a means of suppressing assassinations, broils and open violence; and it has made life safer in Havana than it is in New York; yet it cannot be denied that it created a serious disability. In fine, what is the Spanish government in Cuba, but an armed monarchy, encamped in the midst of a disarmed and disfranchised people?

The taxes paid by the Cubans on their property, and the duties levied on their commerce, are enormous, making a net income of not less than $16,000,000 a year. Cuba pays all the expenses of its own government, the salaries of all officers, the entire cost of the army and navy quartered upon it, the maintenance of the Roman Catholic religion, and of all the charitable and benevolent institutions, and sends an annual remittance to Spain.*

The number of Spanish men-of-war stationed on the coast, varies from twenty-five to thirty. Of the number of soldiers of the regular army in Cuba, it is difficult to form an opinion. The official journal puts them at 30,000. The lowest estimate I heard, was 25,000; and the highest was 40,000. Judging from the number of sick I saw at the Hospital Militar, I should not be surprised if the larger estimate was nearer the truth.

Education is substantially in the hands of the government. As an instance of their strictness, no man can take a degree at the University, unless he makes oath that he does not belong to, has never belonged to, and will not belong to, any society not known to and permitted by the government.

But details are of little importance. The actual administration may be a little more or less rigid or lax. In its legal character, the government is an unmixed despotism of one nation over another.

RELIGION.

No religion is tolerated but the Roman Catholic. Formerly the church was wealthy, authoritative and independent, and checked the civil and military power by an ecclesiastical power wielded also by the dominant nation. But the property of the church has been sequestrated and confiscated, and the government now owns all the property once ecclesiastical, including the church edifices, and appoints all the clergy, from the bishop to the humblest country curate. All are salaried officers.

*Since my return, it has been officially announced that a commission is to be appointed to revise and reduce the tariffs of duties.

And so powerless is the church, that, however scandalous may be the life of a parish priest, the bishop cannot remove him. He can only institute proceedings against him before a tribunal over which the government has large control, with a certainty of long delays, and entire uncertainty as to the result. The bishopric of Havana was formerly one of the wealthiest sees in Christendom. Now the salary is hardly sufficient to meet the demands which custom makes in respect of charity, hospitality and style of living. It may be said, I think with truth, that the Roman Catholic Church has now neither civil nor political power in Cuba.

That there was a long period of time during which the morals of the clergy were excessively corrupt, I think there can be no doubt. Make every allowance for theological bias, or for irreligious bias, in the writers and tourists in Cuba, still, the testimony from Roman Catholics themselves is irresistible. The details, it is not worth while to contend about. It is said that a family of children, with a recognized relation to its female head, which the rule of celibacy prevented ever becoming a marriage, was general with the country priesthood. A priest who was faithful to that relation, and kept from cock-fighting and gambling, was esteemed a respectable man by the common people. Cuba became a kind of Botany Bay for the Romish clergy. There they seem to have been concealed from the eye of discipline. With this state of things, there existed, naturally enough, a vast amount of practical infidelity among the people, and especially among the men, who, it is said, scarcely recognized religious obligations at all.

No one can observe the state of Europe now, without seeing that the rapidity of communication by steam and electricity has tended to add to the efficiency of the central power of the Roman Catholic Church, and to the efficacy and extent of its discipline. Cuba has begun to feel these effects. Whether they have yet reached the interior, or the towns generally, I do not know; but the concurrent testimony of all classes satisfied me that a considerable change has been effected in Havana. The instrumentalities which that church brings to bear in such cases, are in operation: frequent preaching, and stricter discipline of confession and communion. The most marked result is in the number of men, and men of character and weight, who have become earnest in the use of these means. Much of this must be attributed, no doubt, to the Jesuits; but how long they will be permitted to remain here, and what will be the permanent effects of the movement, I cannot, of course, conjecture.

I do not enter into the old field of contest. "We care not," says one side, "which be cause and which effect;—whether the people are Papists, because they are what they are, or are as they are because they are Papists. It is enough that the two things coexist." The other side replies that no Protestant institutions have ever yet been tried for any length of time, and to any large extent, with southern races, in a tropical climate; and the question,—what would be their influence, and what the effect of surrounding causes upon them, lies altogether in the region of conjecture, or, at best, of faith.

Of the moral habits of the clergy, as of the people, at the present time, I am entirely unable to judge. I saw very little that indicated the existence of any vices whatever among the people. Five minutes of a street view of London by night, exhibits more vice, to the casual observer, than all Havana for a year. I do not mean to say that the social morals of the Cubans are good, or are bad; I only mean to say that I am not a judge of the question.

The most striking indication of the want of religious control, is the disregard of the Lord's Day. All business seems to go on as usual, unless it be in the public offices. The chain-gang works in the streets, under public officers. House-building and mechanic trades go on uninterrupted; and the shops are more active than ever. The churches, to be sure, are open and well filled in the morning; and I do not refer to amusements and recreations; I speak of public, secular labor. The Church must be held to some responsibility for this. Granted that Sunday is not the Sabbath. Yet, it is a day which, by the rule of the Roman Church, the English Church in England and America, the Greek Church and other Oriental Churches,—all claiming to rest the rule on Apostolic authority, as well as by the usage of Protestants on the continent of Europe,—whether Lutherans or Calvinists,—is a day of rest from secular labor, and especially from enforced labor. Pressing this upon an intelligent ecclesiastic, his reply to me was that the Church could not enforce the observance;—that it must be enforced by the civil authorities; and the civil authorities fall in with the selfishness and gratifications of the ruling classes. And he appealed to the change lately wrought in Paris, in these respects, as evidence of the consistency of his Church. This is an answer, so far as concerns the Church's direct authority; but it is an admission either of feeble moral power, or of neglect of duty in times past. An embarrassment in the way of more strictness as to secular labor, arises from the fact that slaves are entitled to their time on Sundays, beyond the necessary labor of providing for the day; and this time they may use in working out their freedom.

Another of the difficulties the church has to contend with, arises out of negro slavery. The Church recognizes the unity of all races, and allows marriage between them. The civil law of Cuba, under the interpretations in force here, prohibits marriage between whites and persons who have any tinge of the black blood. In consequence of this rule, concubinage prevails, to a great extent, between whites and mulattoes or quadroons, often with recognition of the children. If either party to this arrangement comes under the influence of the Church's discipline, the relation must terminate. The Church would allow and advise marriage; but the law prohibits it—and if there should be a separation, there may be no provision for the children. This state of things creates no small obstacle to the influence of the Church over the domestic relations.

SLAVERY.

It is difficult to come to a satisfactory conclusion as to the number of slaves in Cuba. The census of 1857 puts it at 375,000; but neither this census nor that of 1853 is to be relied upon, on this point. The Cubans are taxed for their slaves, and the government find it difficult, as I have said, to get correct returns. No person of intelligence in Cuba, however desirous to put the number at the lowest, has stated it to me at less than 500,000. Many set it at 700,000. I am inclined to think that 600,000 is the nearest to the truth.

The census makes the free blacks, in 1857, 125,000. It is thought to be 200,000, by the best authorities. The whites are about 700,000. The only point in which the census seems to agree with public opinion, is in the proportion. Both make the proportion of blacks to be about one free black to three slaves; and make the whites not quite equal to the entire number of blacks, free and slave together. As to the Coolies, it is impossible to do more than conjecture. In 1853, they were not noticed in the census; and in 1857, hardly noticed. The number imported may, to some extent, be obtained from the records and files of the Aduana, but not so as to be relied upon. I heard the number estimated at 200,000 by intelligent and well-informed Cubans. Others put it as low as 60,000. Certain it is that Coolies are to be met with everywhere, in town and country.

To ascertain the condition of slaves in Cuba, two things are to be considered: first, the laws, and secondly, the execution of the laws. The written laws, there is no great difficulty in ascertaining. As to their execution, there is room for opinion.

At this point, one general remark should be made, which I deem to be of considerable importance. The laws relating to slavery do not emanate from the slave-holding mind; nor are they interpreted or executed by the slave-holding class. The slave benefits by the division of power and property between the two rival and even hostile races of whites, the Creoles and the Spaniards. Spain is not slave-holding, at home; and so long as the laws are made in Spain, and the civil offices are held by Spaniards only, the slave has at least the advantage of a conflict of interests and principles, between the two classes that are concerned in his bondage.

The fact that one negro in every four is free, indicates that the laws favor emancipation. They do both favor emancipation, and favor the free blacks after emancipation. The stranger visiting Havana will see a regiment of one thousand free black volunteers, parading with the troops of the line and the white volunteers, and keeping guard in the Obra Pia. When it is remembered that the bearing arms and performing military duty as volunteers, is esteemed an honor and privilege, and is not allowed to the whites of Creole birth, except to a few who are favored by the government, the significance of this fact may be appreciated. The Cuban slave-holders are more impatient under this favoring of the free blacks, than under almost any other act of the government. They see in it an attempt, on the part of the authorities, to secure the sympathy and coöperation of the free blacks, in case of a revolutionary movement,—to set race against race, and to make the free blacks familiar with military duty, while the whites are growing up in ignorance of it. In point of civil privileges, the free blacks are the equals of the whites. In courts of law, as witnesses or parties, no difference is known; and they have the same rights as to the holding of lands and other property. As to their social position, I have not the means of speaking. I should think it quite as good as it is in New England, if not better.

So far as to the position of the blacks, when free. The laws also directly favor emancipation. Every slave has a right to go to a magistrate and have himself valued, and on paying the valuation, to receive his free papers. The valuation is made by three assessors, of whom the master nominates one and the magistrate the other two. The slave is not obliged to pay the entire valuation at once; but may pay it in instalments, of not less than fifty dollars each. These payments are not made as mere advances of money, on the security of the master's receipt, but are part purchases. Each payment makes the slave an owner of such a portion of himself, *pro parte indivisâ*, or as the Common Law would say, in tenancy-in-common, with his master. If the valuation be one thousand dollars, and he pays one hundred dollars, he is owned, one tenth by himself and nine tenths by his master. It has been said, in nearly all the American books on Cuba, that, on paying a share, he becomes entitled to a corresponding share of his time and labor; but, from the best information I can get, I think this is a mistake. The payment affects the proprietary title, but not the usufruct. Until all is paid, the master's dominion over the slave is not reduced, as respects either discipline, or labor, or right of transfer; but if the slave is sold, or goes by operation of law to heirs or legatees or creditors, they take only the interest not paid for, subject to the right of future payment under the valuation.

There is another provision, which, at first sight, may not appear very important, but which is, I am inclined to think, the best practical protection the slave has against ill treatment by his master: that is, the right to a compulsory sale. A slave may, on the same process of valuation, compel his master to transfer him to any person who will pay the money. For this purpose, he need establish no cause of complaint. It is enough if he desires to be transferred, and some one is willing to buy him. This operates as a check upon the master, and an inducement to him to remove special causes of dissatisfaction; and it enables the better class of slave-holders in a neighborhood, if cases of ill-usage are known, to relieve the slave, without contention or pecuniary loss.

In making the valuation, whether for emancipation or compulsory transfer, the slave is to be estimated at his value as a common laborer, according to his strength, age, and health. If he knows an art or trade, however much that may add to his value, only one hundred dollars can be added to the estimate for this trade or art. Thus the skill, industry and character of the slave, do not furnish an obstacle to his emancipation or transfer. On the contrary, all that his trade or art adds to his value, above one hundred dollars, is, in fact, a capital for his benefit.

There are other provisions for the relief of the slave, which, although they may make even a better show on paper, are of less practical value. On complaint and proof of cruel treatment, the law will dissolve the relation between master and slave. No slave can be flogged with more than twenty-five lashes, by the master's authority. If his offence is thought greater than that punishment will suffice for, the public authorities must be called in. A slave mother may buy the freedom of her infant, for twenty-five dollars. If slaves have been married by the Church, they cannot be separated against their will; and the mother has the right to keep her nursing child. Each slave is entitled to his time on Sundays and all other holidays, beyond two hours allowed for necessary labor, except on sugar estates during the grinding season. Every slave born on the island is to be baptized and instructed in the Catholic faith, and to receive Christian burial. Formerly, there were provisions requiring religious services and instruction on each plantation, according to its size; but I believe these are either repealed, or become a dead letter. There are also provisions respecting the food, clothing and treatment of slaves in other respects, and the providing of a sick room and medicines, &c.; and the government has appointed magistrates, styled Sindicos, numerous enough, and living in all localities, whose duty it is to attend to the petitions and complaints of slaves, and to the measures relating to their sale, transfer or emancipation.

As to the enforcement of these laws, I have little or no personal knowledge to offer; but some things, I think, I may treat as reasonably sure, from my own observation, and from the concurrent testimony of books, and of persons of all classes with whom I have conversed.

The rule respecting religion is so far observed as this, that infants are baptized, and all receive Christian burial. But there is no enforcement of the obligation to give the slaves religious instruction, or to allow them to attend public religious service. Most of those in the rural districts see no church and no priest, from baptism to burial. If they do receive religious instruction, or have religious services provided for them, it is the free gift of the master.

Marriage by the Church is seldom celebrated. As in the Roman Church marriage is a sacrament and indissoluble, it entails great inconvenience upon the master, as regards sales or mortgages, and is a restraint on the negroes themselves, to which it is not always easy to reconcile them. Consequently, marriages are usually performed by the master only, and of course, carry with them no legal rights or duties. Even this imperfect and dissoluble connection has been but little attended to. While the slave-trade was allowed, the planters supplied their stock with bozales (native Africans) and paid little attention, even on economic principles, to the improvement, or, speaking after the fashion of cattle-farms, to the increase of the stock on the plantation. Now that importation is more difficult, and labor is in demand, their attention is more turned to their own stock, and they are beginning to learn, in the physiology of increase, that canon which the Everlasting has fixed against promiscuous intercourse.

The laws respecting valuation, the purchase of freedom at once or by instalments, and the compulsory transfer, I know to be in active operation in the towns, and on plantations affording easy access to towns or magistrates. I heard frequent complaints from slave-holders and those who sympathized with them, as to the operation of these provisions. A lady in Havana had a slave who was an excellent cook; and she had been offered $1700 for him, and refused it. He applied for valuation for the purpose of transfer, and was valued at $1000 as a laborer, which, with the $100 for his trade, made a loss to the owner of

$600; and, as no slave can be subsequently sold for a larger sum than his valuation, this provision gave the slave a capital of $600. Another instance was of a planter near Matanzas, who had a slave taught as a carpenter; but after learning his trade, the slave got himself transferred to a master in the city, for the opportunity of working out his freedom, on holidays and in extra hours. So general is the enforcement of these provisions, that it is said to have resulted in a refusal of many masters to teach their slaves any art or trade, and in the hiring of the labor of artizans of all sorts, and the confining of the slaves to mere manual labor. I heard of complaints of the conduct of individuals who were charged with attempting to influence the credulous and too ready slaves to agree to be transferred to them, either to gratify some ill-will against the owner, or for some supposed selfish interest. From the frequency of this tone of complaint and anecdote, as well as from positive assertions on good authority, I believe these provisions to have considerable efficacy.

As to the practical advantage the slaves can get from these provisions in remote places; and as to the amount of protection they get anywhere from the special provisions respecting punishment, food, clothing, and treatment generally, almost everything lies in the region of opinion. There is no end to statement and anecdote on each side. If one cannot get a full and lengthened personal experience, not only as the guest of the slave-holder, but as the companion of the local magistrates, of the lower officers on the plantation, of slave-dealers and slave-hunters, and of the emancipated slaves, I advise him to shut his ears to mere anecdotes and general statements, and to trust to reasonable deductions from established facts. The established facts are, that one race, having all power in its hands, holds an inferior race in slavery; that this bondage exists in cities, in populous neighborhoods, and in remote districts; that the owners are human beings, of tropical races, and the slaves are human beings just emerging from barbarism; and that no small part of this power is exercised by a low-lived and low-minded class of intermediate agents. What is likely to be the effect on all the parties to this system, judging from all we know of human nature?

If persons coming from the North are credulous enough to

suppose that they will see chains and stripes and tracks of blood; and if, taking letters to the best class of slave-holders, seeing their way of life, and hearing their dinner-table anecdotes, and the breakfast-table talk of the ladies, they find no outward signs of violence or corruption, they will probably, also, be credulous enough to suppose they have seen the whole of slavery. They do not know that that large plantation, with its smoking chimneys, about which they hear nothing, and which their host does not visit, has passed to the creditors of the late owner, who is a bankrupt, and is in charge of a manager, who is to get all he can from it in the shortest time, and to sell off the slaves as he can, having no interest, moral or pecuniary, in their future. They do not know that that other plantation, belonging to the young man who spends half his time in Havana, is an abode of licentiousness and cruelty. Neither do they know that the tall hounds chained at the kennel of the house they are visiting, are Cuban bloodhounds, trained to track and to seize. They do not know that the barking last night was a pursuit and capture, in which all the white men on the place took part; and that, for the week past, the men of the plantation have been a committee of detective and protective police. They do not know that the ill-looking man who was there yesterday, and whom the ladies did not like, and all treated with ill-disguised aversion, is a professed hunter of slaves. They have never seen or heard of the Sierra del Cristal, the mountain-range at the eastern end of Cuba, inhabited by runaways, where white men hardly dare to go. Nor do they know that those young ladies, when little children, were taken to the city in the time of the insurrection in the Vuelta de Arriba. They have not heard the story of that downcast-looking girl, the now incorrigibly malignant negro, and the lying mayoral. In the cities, they are amused by the flashy dresses, indolence and good-humor of the slaves, and pleased with the respectfulness of their manners, and hear anecdotes of their attachment to their masters, and how they so dote upon slavery that nothing but bad advice can entice them into freedom; and are told, too, of the worse condition of the free blacks. They have not visited the slave-jails, or the whipping-posts in the house outside the walls, where low whites do the flogging of the city house-servants, men and women, at so many reals a head.

But the reflecting mind soon tires of the anecdotes of injustice, cruelty and licentiousness on the one hand, and of justice, kindness and mutual attachment, on the other. You know that all coexist; but in what proportion you can only conjecture. You know what slavery must be, in its effect on both the parties to it. You seek to grapple with the problem itself. And, stating it fairly, it is this,—Shall the industry of Cuba go on, or shall the island be abandoned to a state of nature? If the former, and if the whites cannot do the hard labor in that climate, and the blacks can, will the seven hundred thousand whites, who own all the land and improvements, surrender them to the blacks and leave the island, or will they remain? If they must be expected to remain, what is to be the relation of the two races? The blacks must do the hard work, or it will not be done. Shall it be the enforced labor of slavery, or shall the experiment of free labor be tried? Will the government try the experiment, and if so, on what terms and in what manner? If something is not done by the government, slavery will continue; for a successful insurrection of slaves in Cuba is impossible, and manumissions do not gain upon the births and importations.

As to the Coolie labor, I do not know that I have anything to add to what I have already incidentally stated. The Coolies are from China; and there is no law of China regulating or supervising their contracts there, or their shipment, or making any provisions for their security. Neither are there any specific laws of Cuba regulating their delivery here, or the relations between them and their masters. The Cuban authorities assume them to be free men, making voluntary contracts, and do no more. That they are kept in strict confinement until sold, and then kept to labor by force, there is no doubt. I suppose there is as little doubt that the form of a contract is gone through with, which binds them to all labor for eight years, at four dollars per month and their board and two suits of clothes annually. It is not yet eight years since their introduction; and it remains to be decided what this contract amounts to. That they can be forced into a servitude for life, if it is for the interest of their purchasers to force them to it, and the government does not interfere energetically, there can be as little doubt. It is known by all, I suppose, that no women or children are imported; and it is said that they do not amalgamate with the people of color. The tenure is so uncertain that their master has little motive to do more than keep them up to the labor point, so long as their labor is valuable, and to neglect them utterly, when it ceases to be so. They are deprived of all the sympathetic and humanizing influences and protections of home, family, common language, and common religion. They are idolaters; but no one seems enough interested in them to undertake their conversion. They are taught to labor, and taught nothing else. Their presence in Cuba adds another distressing element to the difficulties of the labor question, which hangs, like a black cloud, over all the islands of the West Indies.

MATERIAL RESOURCES. EDUCATION.

Cuba contains more good harbors than does any part of the United States south of Norfolk. Its soil is very rich, and there are no large wastes of sand, either by the sea or in the interior. The coral rocks bound the sea, and the grass and trees come down to the coral rocks. The surface of the country is diversified by mountains, hills and undulating lands, and is very well wooded, and tolerably well watered. It is interesting and picturesque to the eye, and abounds in flowers, trees of all varieties, and birds of rich plumage, though not of rich notes. It has mines of copper, and probably of iron, and is not cursed with gold or silver ore. There is no anthracite, but probably a large amount of a very soft, bituminous coal, which can be used for manufactures. It has also marble, and other kinds of stone; and the hard woods, as mahogany, cedar, ebony, ironwood, lignum-vitæ, &c., are in abundance. Mineral salt is to be found, and probably in sufficient quantities for the use of the island. It is the boast of the Cubans, that the island has no wild beasts or venomous reptiles. This has been so often repeated by tourists and historians, that I suppose it must be admitted to be true, with the qualification that they have the scorpion, and tarantula, and nigua; but they say that the bite of the scorpion and tarantula, though painful, is not dangerous to life. The nigua, (sometimes called chigua, and by the English corrupted into jigger,) is troublesome; and if it be permitted to lie long under the flesh, is ineradicable, and makes amputation necessary. With these exceptions, the claim to freedom from wild or venomous animals may be admitted. Their snakes are harmless, and the mosquitoes no worse than those of New England.

As to the climate, I have no doubt that in the interior, especially on the red earth, it is healthy and delightful, in summer as well as in winter; but on the river borders, in the low lands of black earth, and on the savannas, intermittent fever and fever-and-ague prevail. The cities have the scourge of yellow fever; and, of late years, also the cholera. In the cities, I suppose, the year may be divided, as to sickness, into three equal portions: four months of winter, when they are safe; four of summer, when they are unsafe; and four of spring and autumn, when they are passing from one state to the other. There are, indeed, a few cases of vomito in the course of the winter, but they are little regarded, and must be the result of extreme imprudence. It is estimated that twenty-five per cent. of the soldiers die of yellow fever the first years of their acclimation; and during the year of the cholera, sixty per cent. of the newly-arrived soldiers died. The mean temperature in winter is 70°, and in summer 83°, Fahrenheit. The island has suffered severely from hurricanes, although they are not so frequent as in others of the West India islands. They have violent thunderstorms in summer, and have suffered from droughts in winter, though usually the heavy dews keep vegetation green through the dry season.

That which has been to me, personally, most unexpected, is the industry of the island. It seems to me that, allowing for the heat of noon and the debilitating effect of the climate, the industry in agriculture and trade is rather striking. The sugar crop is enormous. The annual exportation is about 400,000 tons, or about 2,000,000 boxes, and the amount consumed on the island is very great, not only in coffee and in daily cooking, but in the making of preserves and sweetmeats, which are a considerable part of the food of the people. There is also about half a million hogsheads of molasses exported annually. Add to this, the coffee, tobacco and copper, and a general notion may be got of the industry and productions of the island. Its weak point is the want of variety. There are no manufactures of any consequence; the mineral exports are not great; and, in fact, sugar is the one staple. All Cuba has but one neck,—the worst wish of the tyrant.

As to education, I have no doubt that a good education in medicine, and a respectable course of instruction in the Roman and Spanish law, and in the natural sciences, can be obtained at the University of Havana; and that a fair collegiate education, after the manner of the Latin races, can be obtained at the Jesuit College, the Seminario, and other institutions at Havana, and in the other large cities; and the Sisters of the Sacred Heart have a flourishing school for girls at Havana. But the general elementary education of the people is in a very low state. The scattered life of planters is unfavorable to public day-schools, nay, almost inconsistent with their existence. The richer inhabitants send their children abroad, or to Havana: but the middle and lower classes of whites cannot do this. The tables show that of the free white children, not more than one in sixty-three attend any school, while in the British West India islands, the proportion is from one in ten to one in twenty. As to the state of education, culture and literary habits among the upper classes, my limited experience gives me no opportunity to judge. The concurrent testimony of tourists and other writers on Cuba is, that the habits of the Cuban women of the upper and middle classes are unintellectual.

To return to the political state and prospects of Cuba. As for those persons whose political opinions and plans are not regulated by moral principle, it may be safely said, that whatever their plans, their object will not be the good of Cuba, but their own advantage. Of those who are governed by principle, each man's expectation or plan will depend upon the general opinion he entertains respecting the nature of men and of society. This is going back a good way for a test; but I am convinced it is only going to the source of opinion and action. If a man believes that human nature in an unrestrained course, is good, and self-governing, and that when it is not so, there is a temporary and local cause to be assigned for the deviation; if he believes that men, at least in civilized society, are independent beings, by right entitled to, and by nature capable of, the exercise of popular self-government, and that if they have not this power in exercise, it is because they have been deprived of it by somebody's fraud or violence, which ought to be detected and remedied, as we abate a public nuisance in the highway; if a man thinks that overturning a throne and erecting a constitution will answer the purpose;—if these are his opinions as to men and society, his plan for Cuba, and for every other part of the world, may be simple. No wonder such an one is impatient of the inactivity of the governed masses, and is in a constant state of surprise that the fraud and violence of a few should always prevail over the rights and merits of the many—when they themselves might end their thraldom by a blow, and put their oppressors to rest—by a bare bodkin!

But if the history of the world and the observation of his own times have led a man to the opinion that, of divine right and human necessity, government of some sort there must be, in which power must be vested somewhere, and exercised somehow; that popular self-government is rather of the nature of a faculty than of a right; that human nature is so constituted that the actual condition of civil society in any place and nation, is, on the whole, the fair result of conflicting forces of good and evil—the power being in proportion to the need of power, and the franchises to the capacity for using franchises; that autocrats and oligarchs are the growth of the soil; and that every people has, in the main, and in the long run, a government as good as it deserves— If such is the substance of the belief to which he has been led or forced, he will look gravely upon the future of such a people as the Cubans, and hesitate as to the invention and application of remedies. If he reflects that of all the nations of the southern races in North and South America, from Texas to Cape Horn, the Brazilians alone, who have a constitutional monarchy, are in a state of order and progress; and if he further reflects that Cuba, as a royal province, with all its evils, is in a better condition than nearly all the Spanish republican states,—he may well be slow to believe that, with their complication of difficulties, and causes of disorder and weakness,—with their half million or more of slaves and quarter million or less of free blacks, with their Coolies, and their divided and hostile races of whites,—their Spanish blood, and their utter want of experience in the discharge of any public duties, the Cubans will work out successfully the problem of self-government. You cannot reason from

Massachusetts to Cuba. When Massachusetts entered into the Revolution, she had had one hundred and fifty years of experience in popular self-government; under a system in which the exercise of this power was more generally diffused among the people, and extended over a larger class of subjects, and more decentralized, than had ever been known before in any part of the world, or at any period of the world's story. She had been, all along, for most purposes, an independent republic, with an obligation to the British Empire undefined and seldom attempted to be enforced. The thirteen colonies were ships fully armed and equipped, officered and manned, with long sea experience, sailing as a wing of a great fleet, under the Admiral's fleet signals. They had only to pass secret signals, fall out of line, haul their wind, and sail off as a squadron by themselves; and if the Admiral with the rest of the fleet made chase and gave battle, it was sailor to sailor and ship to ship. But Cuba has neither officers trained to the quarter-deck, nor sailors trained to the helm, the yard, or the gun. Nay, the ship is not built, nor the keel laid, nor is the timber grown, from which the keel is to be cut.

The natural process for Cuba is an amelioration of her institutions under Spanish auspices. If this is not to be had, or if the connection with Spain is dissolved in any way, she will probably be substantially under the protection of some other power, or a part of another empire. Whatever nation may enter upon such an undertaking as this, should take a bond of fate. Beside her internal danger and difficulties, Cuba is implicated externally with every cause of jealousy and conflict. She has been called the key to the Gulf of Mexico. But the Gulf of Mexico cannot be locked. Whoever takes her is more likely to find in her a key to Pandora's box. Close upon her is the great island of Jamaica, where the experiment of free negro labor, in the same products, is on trial. Near to her is Hayti, where the experiment of negro self-government is on trial. And further off, separated, it is true, by the great Gulf Stream, and with the neighborhood of the almost uninhabited and uninhabitable sea-coast of Southern Florida, yet near enough to furnish some cause for uneasiness, are the slave-states of the Great Republic. She is an island, too; and as an island, whatever power holds or protects her, must maintain on the spot a sufficient army and navy, as it would not do to rely upon being able to throw in troops and munitions of war, after notice of need.

As to the wishes of the Cubans themselves, the degree of reliance they place, or are entitled to place, on each other, and their opportunities and capacity for organized action of any kind, I have already set down all I can be truly said to know; and there is no end to assertion and conjecture, or to the conflicting character of what is called information, whether received through men or books.

Chapter XXIV

ALL DAY there have been earnest looks to the northwest, for the smoke of the Cahawba. We are willing and desirous to depart. Our sights are seen, our business done, and our trunks packed. While we are sitting round our table after dinner, George, Mr. Miller's servant, comes in, with a bright countenance, and says "There is a steamer off." We go to the roof, and there, far in the N.W., is a small but unmistakable cloud of steamer's smoke, just in the course the Cahawba would take. "Let us walk down to the Punta, and see her come in." It is between four and five o'clock, and a pleasant afternoon, (there has been no rain or sign of rain in Cuba since we first saw it—twelve days ago,) and we saunter along, keeping in the shade, and sit down on the boards at the wharf, in front of the Presidio, near to where politicians are garroted, and watch the progress of the steamer, amusing ourselves at the same time, with seeing the negroes swimming and washing horses in the shallow water off the bank. A Yankee flag flies from the signal-post of the Morro, but the Punta keeps the steamer from our sight. It draws towards six o'clock, and no vessel can enter after dark. We begin to fear she will not reach the point in season. Her cloud of smoke rises over the Punta, the city clocks strike six, the Morro strikes six, the trumpets bray out, the sun is down, the signals on the Morro are lowering—"She'll miss it!"—"No—there she is!"—and, round the Punta comes her sharp black head, and then her full body, her toiling engine and smoking chimney and peopled decks, and flying stars and stripes— Good luck to her! and, though the signal is down, she pushes on and passes the forts without objection, and is lost among the shipping.

My companions are so enthusiastic that they go on board; but I return to my hotel and take a volante, and make my last calls, and take my last looks, and am ready to leave in the morning.

In half an hour, the arrival of the Cahawba is known over all Havana, and the news of the loss of her consort, the Black Warrior, in a fog off New York—passengers and crew, and specie safe. My companions come back. They met Capt. Bullock on the pier, and took tea with him in La Dominica. He sails at two o'clock to-morrow.

Wednesday, March 2, 1859.—I shall not see them again, but there they will be, day after day, day after day,—how long?— aye, how long?—the squalid, degraded chain-gang! The horrible prison!—profaning one of the grandest of sites, where city, sea and shore unite as almost nowhere else on earth! These were my thoughts as, in the pink and gray dawn, I walked down the Paseo, to enjoy my last refreshing in the rock-hewn sea-baths.

This leave-taking is a strange process, and has strange effects. How suddenly a little of unnoticed good in what you leave behind comes out, and touches you, in a moment of tenderness! And how much of the evil and disagreeable seems to have disappeared! Le Grand, after all, is no more inattentive and intractable than many others would become in his place; and he does keep a good table, and those breakfasts are very pretty. Antonio is no hydropathist, to be sure, and his ear distinguishes the voices that pay best; yet one pities him in his routine, and in the fear he is under, being a native of Old Spain, that his name will turn up in the conscription, when he will have to shoulder his musket for five years in the Cabaña and Punta. Nor can he get off the island, for the permit will be refused him, poor fellow!

One or two of our friends are to remain here, for they have pulmonary difficulties, and prefer to avoid the North in March. They look a little sad at being left alone, and talk of going into the country to escape the increasing heat. A New York gentleman has taken a great fancy to the volantes, and thinks that a costly one, with two horses, and silvered postilion in boots and spurs and bright jacket, would eclipse any equipage in the Fifth Avenue.

When you come to leave, you find that the strange and picturesque character of the city has interested you more than you think; and you stare out of your carriage to read the familiar signs, the names of streets, the Obra Pia, Lamparilla, Mercaderes, San Ignacio, Obispo, O'Reilly, and Officios, and the pretty and fantastic names of the shops. You think even the narrow streets have their advantages, as they are better shaded, and the awnings can stretch across them, though, to be sure, they keep out the air. No city has finer avenues than the Ysabel and the Tacon; and the palm-trees, at least, we shall not see at the North. Here is La Dominica. It is a pleasant place, in the evening, after the Retreta, to take your tea or coffee under the trees by the fountain in the court-yard, and meet the Americans and English;—the only public place, except the theatre, where ladies are to be seen out of their volantes. Still, we are quite ready to go; for we have seen all we have been told to see in Havana, and it is excessively hot, and growing hotter.

But no one can leave Cuba without a permit. When you arrive, the visé of your passport is not enough, but you must pay a fee for a permit to land, and remain in the island; and when you wish to return, you must pay four dollars to get back your passport, with a permit to leave. The custom-house officials were not troublesome in respect to our luggage, hardly examining it at all, and, I must admit, showed no signs of expecting private fees. Along the range of piers, where the bows of the vessels run in, and on which the labor of this great commerce is performed, there runs a high, wide roof, covering all from the intense rays of the sun. Before this was put up, they say that workmen used to fall dead with sun-strokes, on the wharves.

On board the Cahawba, I find my barrel of oranges from Yglesia, and box of sweetmeats from La Dominica, and boxes of cigars from Cabaña's, punctually delivered. There, once more, is Bullock, cheerful, and efficient; Rodgers, full of kindness and good-humor; and sturdy, trustworthy Miller, and Porter, the kindly and spirited; and the pleased face of Henry, the captain's steward; and the familiar faces of the other stewards; and my friend's son, who is well and very glad to see me, and full of New Orleans, and of last night, which he spent on shore in Havana. All are in good spirits, for a short sea voyage with old friends is before us; and then—home!

The decks are loaded and piled up with oranges:—oranges in barrels and oranges in crates, filling all the wings and gangways, the barrels cut to let in air, and the crates with bars just close enough to keep in the oranges. The delays from want of lighters, and the great amount of freight, keep us through the day; and it is nearly sundown before we get under way. All day the fruit boats are alongside, and passengers and crew lay in stocks of oranges and bananas and sapotes, and little boxes of sweetmeats. At length, the last barrel is on board, the permits and passenger-lists are examined, the revenue officers leave us, and we begin to heave up our anchor.

The harbor is very full of vessels, and the room for swinging is small. A British mail-steamer, and a Spanish man-of-war, and several merchantmen, are close upon us. Captain Bullock takes his second mate aft, and they have a conference, as quietly as if they were arranging a funeral. He is explaining to him his plan for running the warps and swinging the ship, and telling him beforehand what he is to do in this case, and what in that, and how to understand his signs, so that no orders, or as few as possible, need be given at the time of action. The engine moves, the warp is hauled upon, the anchor tripped, and dropped again, and tripped again, the ship takes the right sheer, clear of everything, and goes handsomely out of the harbor, the stars and stripes at her peak, with a waving of hats from friends on the Punta wharf. The western sky is gorgeous with the setting sun, and the evening drums and trumpets sound from the encircling fortifications, as we pass the Casa Blanca, the Cabaña, the Punta, and the Morro. The sky fades, the ship rises and falls in the heave of the sea, the lantern of the Morro gleams over the water, and the dim shores of Cuba are hidden from our sight.

After tea, all are on deck. It is a clear night, and no night or day has been else than clear at sea or on shore, since we first crossed the Gulf Stream, on our passage out. The Southern Cross is visible in the south, and the North Star is above the horizon in the north. No winter climate of Cuba, in mountain or on plain,—the climate of no land, can be compared with the ocean,—the clear, bracing, saline air of ocean! How one drinks it in! And, then, again, the rocking cradle that nurses one in sleep! Nothing but the necessity of sleep,—the ultimate necessity of self-preservation, can close one's eyes upon such a night as this, in the equinoctial seas.

Chapter XXV

THURSDAY, MARCH 3.—The open sea, fine weather, moderate breeze, and awnings spread, as it is still hot in the sun. The young gentleman who was at Mrs. Almy's, Mr. G——, survived to be brought on board. His friends say, that after one day's waiting, if the Cahawba had not arrived Tuesday night, he would not have lived till morning. He was brought on board in an arm-chair. The Purser, though a stranger to him, has given up his room to him; and the second mate, who knows his family, treats him like a brother. His first wish being accomplished, he now says that if he can live to see his home and to receive the sacrament, he will be content to meet his end, which he knows is soon to come.

Friday, March 4.—To-day, the sea is high and the vessel rolls and pitches, but the sky is clear and the air delightful. Awnings still up. Most of the passengers are seasick, and only one woman comes to dinner.

The body of the late Chief Justice Eustis, of Louisiana, is on board, about to be taken to his family tomb in Massachusetts. I wish we could, at least those of us who are from New England, in some proper way, testify our respect for the memory of a man of such learning and weight of character. But everything connected with the removal seems to be strictly private. The jumble of life has put on board Sheppard, the man who trained Morrissey for the famous fight with Heenan. He is a quiet, well-behaved man, among the passengers.

Glorious night. Walk deck with Captain Bullock until eleven o'clock. There is not an abuse in the navy, that we have not corrected, or a deficiency that we have not supplied. We have meted to each ship and hero in the war of 1812, with strictest justice, the due share of praise. We have given much better names to the new steam sloops-of-war, taking them from Indian rivers and lakes, and the battle-fields of the revolutionary war, than the names of towns where the leading politicians of the government party reside, which the sycophancy or vanity of those in office has selected.

Saturday, March 5.—Fine breeze, clear cool weather, fresh

blue sea, off the coast of North Carolina; but, as we keep in the Gulf Stream, we make no land. We are in the highway of the commerce of all the central part of America, yet, as before, how few vessels we see! Only one in three days!

A few ladies join a company gathered in the captain's state-room this evening, where all, who can, contribute their anec-dotes of sea life, of storms and wrecks, and of the traditions, notions, and superstitions of sailors, and snatches of sea-songs —Tom Bowline, Captain Kid, Bay of Biscay, and specimens of the less classical, but more genuine songs of the capstan and falls.

Sunday, March 6.—Cooler. Out of the Gulf Stream. Awnings taken down, clear sky, clear sea,—the finest, cheerfullest, wholesomest weather in the world! Poor G—— is still alive, and has hopes of getting in. We expect to be in by to-morrow noon. The sea is very smooth, and nearly all are relieved from sea-sickness. We pass a few vessels floating up the Gulf Stream, with wind and current,—a bark, an hermaphrodite brig, and a schooner; but no vessel of size or mark. As I pass G——'s room, at ten o'clock to-night, I see the faithful purser and sec-ond mate sitting, like brothers, by his bedside, relieving the young man who has come out to Havana from his father's counting-room, to bring him home. The sea is still, and all is favorable to the prolonging of life; yet he is very low, and wan-dering in his mind, and is talking of getting up a Sunday School.

Monday, March 7.—It is daybreak, the lights of Barnegat were made at four o'clock this morning, and now the heights of Neversink are visible; the long shore of New Jersey is open on our lee; the harbor of New York is but four or five hours off, where the ship may still her pulse, and rest, and friends meet friends. But death has visited us by night. G—— has passed away. He breathed his last before midnight, just as we were on the point of sighting the long wished for shore,—the haven where he would be.

So mixed and heterogeneous is the company of such a pas-senger ship, that few seem even to know that there has been a death, and fewer to remember it. The succession of events, the shore, the sails, the pilot, the news, the excitement and expec-tation, and the sights of home, are too engrossing.

On the low sand-beach of Long Island, are the bones of the Black Warrior, our consort. Far in the eastern horizon, just discernible, is the smoke of the Europa, due from Liverpool. The water far out to sea, twenty or thirty miles from the harbor, is dotted with little boats, fishing for the all-consuming market of New York; and steam-tugs, short and low, just breathing out a little steam, are watching, far out at sea, their chances for inward-bound vessels. On the larboard hand, are the twin lights of Neversink. We leave them astern, and are abreast of the low, white spit of Sandy Hook, when a pilot boat comes bobbing over the waves. We heave to, lower the steps, and the pilot jumps on board. In a few minutes, the news is over the ship—the Thirty Millions Bill withdrawn by Mr. Slidell, Congress adjourned, the five cent postage bill defeated, and the Sickles and Key tragedy. A few copies of New York papers are in the hands of the more eager passengers.

No harbor has a more beautiful and noble entrance than New York. The Narrows, Staten Island, the Heights of Brooklyn, the distant view of the Hudson River Highlands, the densely populous outskirts in all directions, the broad bay and its rich tributaries, on the north and the east,—and then, the tall spires and lofty warehouses of the city, and the long stretches, north and east and south and west, of the close-packed hulls and entangled spars of the shipping.

There is no snow to be seen over the landscape or on the house-tops, yet the leafless trees, the dry grass, the thick overcoats and furs, are in strange contrast with the palm-leaf hats, white linen coats, fluttering awnings, coveted shades, and the sun-baked harvests of five days ago.

We drew in to our dock as silently and surely as everything is done in the Cahawba. A crowd of New York hackmen is gathered on the pier, looking as if they had stolen their coaches and horses, and meant to steal our luggage. There are no policemen in sight. Everybody predicts a fight. The officers of the boat say that the police are of no use if present, for their indifference and non-intervention rather encourage the fighters.

For a few minutes, there is no other inconvenience than noise and crowding for passengers and luggage; but soon they press on the decks,—are ordered off,—hang back,—the crew try to force them ashore,—then comes a gathering about the

gangway—"I can fight if you can," says a quarter-master,—
and they are at it, blow for blow! As soon as the hackmen on
the wharf see the fight, they make a breach into the boat, and
the quarter-master is driven, with blows and curses, into the
engine-room,—the crew rally, and Rodgers jumps down into
the midst, spreads out his arms,—"Away with you all, out of
the ship!" Capt. Bullock steps down from the wheel-house, passengers gather round, and the hackmen fall back. Still, a few
resist, and one of them is knocked over the head by a marline-
spike, falls fainting, on the guards, and is lifted ashore by his
companions. The hackmen are slowly but firmly forced ashore.
But on the wharf, and leaning on the vessel's rail, they openly
threaten the lives of the crew, and especially of the man who
used the marlinespike, if they catch him on shore—"We'll wait
for you!"—"You *must* come, sooner or later! It will be the last
step you'll take! Your time is up!" etc., etc. The officers of the
boat are used to this, and expect to protect ship and passengers
by their own force, and at their own peril.

We had been talking high patriotism to some Cuban passengers; and all the comparisons, hitherto, had been favorable to
our country,—the style of the vessels, and the manner in which
the three boats, the health-boat, the revenue-boat, and the
news-boat, discharged their duties. But here was rather a
counterset. The strangers saw it in a worse light than we did.
We knew it was only a lawless fight for fares, and would end in
a few blows, and perhaps the loss of a bag or trunk or two. But
in their eyes, it looked like an insurrection of the lower orders.
They did not know where it would end. One elderly lady, in
particular, with great varieties of luggage, and speaking no
English, was in special trepidation, and could not be persuaded
to trust herself or her luggage to the chances of the conflict,
which she was sure would take place over it.

But it is the genius of our people to get out of difficulties, as
well as to get into them. The affair soon calms down; the
crowd thins off, as passengers select their coachmen, and leave
the boat; and in an hour or so after we touch the wharf, the
decks are still, the engine is breathing out its last, the ship has
done its stint in the commerce of the world, Bullock and
Rodgers are shaken by the hand, complimented and bade adieu

to by all, and our chance-gathered household of the last five days, not to meet again on earth or sea,—is scattered among the streets of the great city, to the snow-lined hills of New England, and over the wide world of the great West.

THE END.

JOURNAL OF A VOYAGE
ROUND THE WORLD
1859–1860

Voyage to the Pacific and Travels in California: July–September 1859

1859 July 20. Wed.   Sailed from N. York in the steam-ship Star of the West, Gray, commander, for Aspinwall. Between 4 & 500 passengers, (1st. & 2d. Cabin & Steerage).

Mr. Ripley, John Hodge & Capt. Bulloch of the Cahawba, down to take leave. Sailed at 1. P.M.

July 21 & 22d.   Very heavy weather, & great discomfort of passengers from seasickness & want of room. Three in my small stateroom, with three trunks, three valises, hat-box, guitar case, champagne basket &c.

Passengers—Capt. Poor U.S.N., going to take command of U.S. Sloop-of-War St. Louis, at Aspinwall, Lt. Myers & wife & child, going to Oregon, to join his Regt., 9th Infantry —Major Leonard & wife (a French woman) Qu. Master U.S. Army, Locke & Pope, merchants of S Fr., Miss Price of Cincinn., going to S. Fr. to marry a Mr. Lawler, Miss Dexter, niece of Rich. Hildreth, a Miss Payne of Me., going to marry in S. Fr., & a cousin of Capt. Poor, a Miss West, of Norfolk Va. A Miss Dana of Oswego N.Y., niece of A. H. Dana, of N.Y., & a Mrs. Gastner of S. Francisco. These are all I knew. Several Jews, who clanned together.

This ship was *filthy*. No care of water-rooms, poor ventilation, & no discipline over servants. We, at Capt.'s table, good attention—rest, little or none. Suffering of Steerage passengers, & 2d. Cabin passengers. In 1st cabin, no change of bed linen for whole passage—11 days—no cleaning out. Bad smell of dining-room, scarcely tolerable.

Hot weather begins, after passing Hatteras.

July 26.   At sundown make Morro Castle, & lie to all night.

27th.   At sunrise, enter Havana Harbor. Familiar scene, Morro, Cabaña, Ceasar Blanca, houses, palm-trees, boats & boatmen.

Breakfast at Le Grand's. Cordially received by Le Grand. (Domingo & Antonio also). Drive in volante. Guide of party. Cathedral, Mass, market, Dominica. On board at 10 o'ck, & sail out at noon.

Beautiful afternoon off coast of Cuba. Thunder storms over the island. Some yellow fever there, but not epidemic. One yellow fever man on board,—recovering.

Great heat from Havana to Aspinwall. No air, in state-rooms. Heat of mattresses. Up at day break ev. morning, & washed down by hose, refreshing bath, great use. Lie down on deck in shade.

Great deal of drinking, iced drinks, early & late. I drink nothing but tea & water, & am never thirsty.

Capt. Gray's chart-room, & our party gathering there, ev. evening.

Negro steward singing—

> "It may be for years,
> And it may be forever".

Steerage passengers always singing Nellie Gray—

> "Sweet Nellie Gray,
> They're taking me away,
> And I'll never see my darling any more".

Excep. hot & disagr. work selecting luggage from lower cabin.

No relig. service on board. I read the morn. service, Sunday, to abt. dos. persons in Chart-Room, the milit. people & a few others.

Aug. 1. Thursd.   Arrived at Aspinwall before day-break. Dismal place. Swamp, torrid marsh, hot, damp, a mist of vapors, like smoke, at sun-rise, all full of miasma. People on shore (whites) thin, shriveled, sallow,—effect of fever & ague. Negroes flourishing.

Find U.S. Frigate Roanoke, & Sloop St. Louis. Leave Capt.

Poor there. (He feels dismal at the prospect of 2 or 3 years in this region.) Aspinwall not intended to be lived in by whites. Worst place I ever saw. Rich fruits, oranges, limes, bananas, pears, &c. &c.

Take cars at 9 A.M. & are discharged at Panama in 3 hours. On my birth-day cross a Continent. In morning, afloat on Atlantic, in evening, afloat in Pacific. Aspinwall & Panama are in *South* America.

First half of passage across Isthmus is low swampy ground, decaying & growth of vegetation of richest character, going on at once. Very unhealthy. Population nearly all Negroes. Small Negro villages on the way. Negro women paddling in mud, with 4 flounces on white dresses, & barefooted! Latter half of passage across is hilly, mountainous, dry, picturesque. Grand view of Pacific Ocean. Picturesque character of Panama Bay— small mountainous islands, sprinkled over it. Ranges of mountains behind, connecting Andes & Cordilleras.

On board steam-ship Golden Gate, Whiting Master. Noble boat. Good regulations. Kept clean. Inspection of all parts daily.

Gossip & scandal in these boats. Passage long, & people not of highest style. Reputations often suffer, & sometimes justly, on these passages. So told by all, & believe it, from what I saw. Kept much by myself, & not intimate with any.

Picturesque character of all the Pacific Coast seen on this passage. Mountainous. Contrast with Atlantic, wh. is flat.

Sunday. Aug. 7. Acapulco, for coal. Best small harbor I ever saw—as good as possible. Breakfast ashore. Excellent Sp breakfast. Boat surrounded by boys swimming, naked in water, & diving for small coin. "Catch'ee one dime, Mistee". These boys dive & never failed to catch the coin thrown, & kept in water hours, without resting. Boats selling oranges, bananas &c.

Sat. Ev. Aug. 13th. Make headlands off San Francisco. Enter "Golden Gate" by moonlight. Lighthouses, large shipping, great Clippers at anchor, large city of 80,000 people. Contrast with the S. Fr. of 1836, in the Alert—not one house—a solitude.

Great crowd at landing. Little after midnight, reach Oriental Hotel.

Sunday. Aug. 14th. Walk in city. Church, morning service —large congregation. No afternoon service in any relig. soc. Most have service at 7½ P.M.,—but custom is mostly to go to but one service.

Meet Felton—Fabens. Called on by S. Adams, brother of Rev. N. Adams, D.D.

Dine with Felton, at Martin's. French Hs. Dinner as luxurious as in Paris. *Company*—Lt. Mowry, late of Army, now Del. elect fr. Arisona, Ex. Judge Parsons of a local court, Whitcomb, a lawyer, Judge Hagar. All are Northern men, with Southern, pro-slavery, duelling principles. Anecdotes of S. Fr. in early times. Judge Parsons' adjourning his Court to go & see the Morissey prise fight, on pretense of death of Judge McKinley of U.S. Supr. C't. Judges of Supreme C't. of Cal. attend opening of great gambling houses. Judiciary toasted, Ch. J. too drunk to reply, & Judge Wells gave "Success to Vice".

Dr. Hastings, Dr. Holman, Pringle, Wm. Duer, Bishop Kip, Hall McAllister, Bayley Peyton, &c.

Invitation to lecture before Mercantile Library. Ditto, to deliver the anniversary oration of Pioneer Society to celebrate the setlt. of S. Francisco. Decline both.

Offer fr. a liquor house to supply my side-board with best wines &c. during my stay, *gratis,*—declined of course. Attentions—interest shown in my revisit to California, notices in the newspapers &c.

Dine with Bishop Kip—present, B. & lady, Wm. Duer, Col. Turner, & Mr. Blanding, a lawyer, ex. U.S. Att'y., & Capt. in Palmetto Regt. in Mex. War.

Dine with Felton again—present, Parsons, Pringle, & Edmund Randolph, of Va., a leading lawyer here.

The Southern men, Blanding, Randolph, Pringle, &c. better than the N. men of S. principles I meet here.

Dine with Wm. Duer. Present, Mr. & Mrs. Duer, daughter & son, B'p. Kip & Baily Peyton. Anecdotes of early California life.

Visit U.S. Marine Hospital. Political jobbing, neglect of furniture for sick, failure of apparatus for heating &c., enormous money jobs, waste, & nothing done.

Visit City Hospital, not much better, but not so large expenses.

Deliver letter to Archb. Alemany. Large R.C. Church of St. Mary. Working Cath. clergy & sisterhoods. Gen. respect & popularity of Bsh. Alemany. Visit School & Orphan Hs. of Sisters of Charity. School of Presentation Nuns, & Hospital of Sisters of Mercy. All creditable institutions.

Went to R.C. Ch. on Fest. of Assumption. Sermon sd. was not article of Faith, but *gen. & pious* belief that the B.V.M. resumed her body, at death, & it was taken with her.

Windmills in gen. use here to raise water for irrigation & household purposes. More than 200 in the city.

Ch. R. Bond, assessor of taxes, attentive—takes me to ride. Go to the Mission. This looks like 1836, & is the only thing that does.

Felton takes me to San Mateo. Visit the fort, at entrance of harbor. Great work—not completed.

Ditto, the fortifications on Alcatrass Island.

Part of S. F. is built over the water on piles, streets, shops & all, the sea flowing under them. Part is on made land. Rest is on sand hills. No grass, no trees. Some flower gardens, with artif. irrigation in summer. Dreary sandhills form the background. Bay is capacious & grand.

Strong wind fr. sea, ev. day at abt. 11 o'ck., & blows until night—very strong,—dust. Climate cold, all summer. People wear woolen clothes, & thick flannel underclothes. Overcoats worn a good deal in afternoon. Thin clothes—never. Very healthy except for consumptives or rheumatics. Children strong & healthful.

From the testy of the best citisens, I think the Vigilence Committee was a necessity. It certainly was effectual. As a gen. rule, ev. good cit. is in its favor, & ev. bad citisen against it.

Jews & Chinese very numerous here. Jews, a business & political power. Chinese disfranchised, but very numerous—chiefly in the lighter labors & in trade. Signs in streets, of Chinese names. Generally, are under 5 year contracts with China companies & merchants, who pay them & employ & let them out. These contracts are legal & respected—I think.

Lawyers practice champerty & maintainance. Not illegal.

Injurious to the profession. Land-title lawyers been a curse to the city. Professional morals low—very low.

Sat. Aug. 20. Steamer Senator, for the leeward ports—to visit S. Diego, S. Barbara &c. Among passengers is Capt. John Wilson, who commanded the brig Ayacucho in 1835–6 (Two Years before Mast)—long talks over old times. He is now one of the richest & most respected rancheros in Cal. I was at his wedding, in S. Barbara—to Donña Ramona. He has large family—rancho in S. Luis Obispo.

Point Conception! What recollections associated with it! Now has lighthouse!

Aug. 21. Santa Barbara. The first place I saw in Cal. in 1835. Land in the surf, on the beach. Amphitheatre of mountains— Mission in the rear—islands on the sea side, & roaring surf! Call on Mr. Alfred Robinson. Lives at house of Noriego. Now (the children) called De la Guerra. Don Pablo de la Guerra, (Two Years &c.) receives me. Robinson's daughter, a belle.

Call on Donña Angustias, (Two Years &c. danced at Robinson's wedding) still a fine looking woman. My book gives her great celebrity, on the coast.

Judge Fernald, a young lawyer of S. Barbara, attentive. Grapes, olives, wine making, & sheep raising.

Aug. 22. San Pedro. The point—the beach—the hill! This was our hated spot—place of toil & exposure. There, too, is the Dead Man's Island.

Good deal of trade here—now Steamer to carry freight to an upper landing at head of creek. Phineas Banning, owner of the steamer & line of coaches to Los Angeles—very attentive to me. Coaches; six horses each, half wild,—run all the way. Level pampa for 30 miles to Los Angeles. Few trees, no grass, alive with squirrels. (Told that snake, squirrel & bird occupy the same hole.)

Los Angeles, prosperous, growing. All engaged in grape growing. Vineyards everywhere. Hot, but dry, & not unpleasant. Meet here Henry Mellus, my shipmate in Pilgrim, & his brother Frank, both settled here. Married sisters, Mex. women.

Dine with Mellus. Takes me to ride, to visit the vineyards. Grapes, olives, figs, peaches, pears & melons. Can raise fruits & flowers in ev. month in the year. Excellent climate for such, but too dry for wheat.

Of the people of Los Angeles of 1835–6, see John Temple, Stearns & Warner. Two former become immensely rich. At Stearns', met Don Juan Bandini (Two Years &c.) & his wife, Donña Refugio, still beautiful, daughter of Don Santiago Argüello, (then, 1836, Commandante of S. Diego.)

Meet here a brother of Geo. B. Emerson, who has been much abroad.

Return in P.M., on a run of 30 miles,—tearing rate—to San Pedro.

Tu. Aug. 23. San Diego. Familiar scenes. The great point (Loma), now Lighthouse on it, the little point, the beach, & the hills behind. All the hide houses gone! Also the Kanaka Oven. In their place, two or three shanties for use of people now there. In the stream, moored, a hulk, loaded with coal, to supply steamers in need—under charge of Capt.——& his boy Tom. Steamer went up to a place called New S. Diego, at head of Bay. Got her to put me ashore on the Beach. Landed alone, & spent 2 or 3 hours wandering on beach & hills, in meditation. Causes eno' for reflection. 23 years ago, curing hides, cutting wood—4 houses full of men—all gone—most dead. Found site of Kanaka oven, few bricks. Wandered over hills.

Walked up to the town, as so often before. "Black Ground". Village, familiar. Old adobe house of the Muchachos, large houses of Bandini & Estudillo & Arguello—Tomasa Pico still living. Estudillo dead. Bandini, I saw at Los Angeles.

Found here a shipmate of the Alert, Jack Stewart, now married & family—temperate & regular. Tom Wrightington, who kept the shop for Fitch, fell fr. his horse when drunk, & was found eaten by cayotes. Fitch dead. No one here but Stewart, that I remember.

Visit house of fellow passengers, in steamer, Doyle & wife. He is agent for mail coach line—nice people.

Horse, & ride to Mission. All gone to decay. Large gardens, —now only cactuses & willows & few olive trees. Aqueduct in ruins. Buildings delapidated. Barracks for U.S. troops close by, abandoned & in ruins. Full run back to town, as Ben S & I did, in 1835.

Took steamer in evening. Landed on Beach again & got shells, for memorials. One man fishing with Kanaka, on shores, who 5 years ago brot out large ship fr. Boston,—"Whisky did it.".

Steamed out of S. Diego—last look of Beach, hills, point &c.

Wed. 24. Aug.   S. Pedro again. Master set me ashore at the old landing, I to walk to the new. Searched out the old spots. The landing & hill nearly gone, by land-slides. Old house still standing. Stood on old spot where spent so many dreary hours —imagined little Pilgrim at anchor in offing, & old work, & shipmates.

Up to Los Angeles again. Breakfast with Banning—*present*, 2 Melluses, Capt. Hancock (U.S.A.) & wife, Lt. Merchant (?) U.S.A. just retd. fr. an exped. to the desert. (News of Major Armistead battle just come in.) Mr. Emerson, & others.

Lunch at Mellus'. Nearly same people—Wilson also. Down to S. Pedro in 3 hours—full run all the way. Ran one mile without lynch-pin.

Last looks at S. Pedro, at sundown.

Stopped at S. Barbara, for an hour. Judge Fernald sent me off box of S. B. wine.

Point Conception. Stopped at S. Luis Obispo & landed Wilson. Cordial invitation to visit him at his ranch—obliged to decline it. Passengers fr. S. Diego to S. Francisco, a Dr. Hoffman, intelligent man, & a German gentleman by name of——, a man of extr. acquirements & knowledge of Belles lettres & science, in all languages. His English is scientifically good. Valuable infn. fr. him as to history & condition of Calif.

Frid. Ev. 26. Aug.   Enter Golden Gate again. Fort, Light hs., Alcatrass Island, Angel Island, Sausolito Bay, clipper ships at anchor, town, opp. coast of Contra Costa. Oriental Hotel again.

Sat. Aug. 27.   After full consultn., start for the mines & Big Trees & Yosemite Falls. Steamer to Stockton. Almost perpetual fogs & chilly winds in S. Fr. Bay. Over coat necessary. Stop at Benicia—small place—a failure—sustained only by U.S. Barracks & drydock for Pan. Co.'s boats. Up the S. Joaquin to Stockton. At Stockton take coach for Bear Valley & Mariposa. All day fr. Stockton to little Sp mining town of Hornitos. Excep. hot & dusty, all day. Sometimes not see the horses fr. driver's seat. Miserable looking country—parched up. Thousand sq. miles of dust, struggling herbage, no trees, no grass, no flowers, no birds, no water! Windmills everywhere, to raise water—only mode—whether for house use or for irrigation. Artif. irrig. fr. May to October.

High country very healthy—but low lands about the river beds—called "River Bottoms" subject to fever & ague, & a bilious fever known as Tulare fever, fr. Tulare Lake, or Tule fever, fr. the *Tule*, a kind of reed that covers the low river lands of S. Joaquin &c. Cross the Stanislaus, the Tuolumne, & the Merced. The Stanislaus by a bridge built of timber brot fr. Puget Sound to S. Fr. & thence here. Cheaper than to get fr. mountains of Calif. (comment on timber of Cal.) At the Tuolumne, a ferry, & at the Merced a tavern known as Snelling's (?), a place of very bad repute—frequented by fighters, & murders very common. I mean *free-fight* killings. Three men killed here in fight, short time since. Later, was a fandango, & 3 men wounded—few words & revolvers & knives. If killed, only say "ought to have been in better luck".

Usual Calif. rig, out of cities, is belt with a revolver in holster & a knife in sheath, both suspended fr. belt. Every rider & most coach travellers so prepared.

Now in region of gold digging—placer diggings. Country *rooted up*, as by beaver, on all sides. Here & there men digging, or washing out, with washbowls & rockers &c. Stage coach & 6 horses & 18 passengers turn out, on highway, for a man digging gold in a trench!

Night at Hornitos—very hot. Chiefly Mex. & Chinese here.

Chief topic in Mariposa Co. is "*The* Col.". The Col.'s mines, & the Col.'s mill, & the Col.'s struggles with the Merced Co. Half the personable men are colonels, but "*the Col.*", fr. Stockton to the Sierra Nevada, is Frémont.

Breakfast at Bear Valley. Small & increasing village, created by Frémont's mining operations. F's house in the outskirts of the village. Here meet Col. —— a polit. & business friend of Frémont, & others. Take horse & ride to F.'s mines. Mountainous country, mountains nearly bare of grass & trees, except scrub oaks & small pines—a kind of chaporal. Dreary looking, but full of gold quartz, the famous Mariposa Grant, one of the 3 richest in the world. Meet Frémont on the mountain side, on a trail, just mounting his horse, wh. was tied to a bush. Introduced myself. Cordial welcome. Ride with him to his quartz mills, "Benton Mills". Has dammed the Merced River, & has two mills & building a 3d, & one steam mill.

Returned to his house & lunch. Mrs. Frémont, daughter, Miss Lilly, about 16, & sons, Charles, 8, Frank, 4, both bareheaded, sunburnt, hardy courageous boys—full of the speech & habits of the back woods. Frank rides mule to town. Before he cd. have a watermelon, was obliged to sing a song—

> "Oh don't you remember sweet Betsy fr. Pike.
> She came over the mountains with her brother Ike.
> She'd 2 shanghai roosters, & one spotted hog,
> A pair of brown heifers & one yellow dog.
> Tu ral lal &c. &c.

F.'s house beautifully situated, on slope, plenty water, well shaded with trees, only shaded house I've seen in Cal.,—view of Sierra Nevada, in distance.

Tu. 30th. Aug.   Started on horseback for the Sierra Nevada, with a guide—one Biddle Boggs, who knows the country—he also mounted, saddle bags, 2 blankets apiece. Very dusty & hot—downright beat of sun on head—dust in mouth & eyes & ears—cloud of dust after each horse. Dinner at Mariposa, Co. town, house of people named Hays (?) nice Massach people. Mariposa Gasette, Holmes editor,—2500 subscribers. Abt. 2 P.M. horses again. Even the trail in pine forest so dusty that ride far behind my guide—not like to follow a rabbit on a trail, for the dust lies thick under leaves or stones. At length, coveted shade of Pine Forest, mountain sides & streams of running water. Water grateful to man & horse. I drink no spirit —only cold tea in flask, or brook water. Stop at a lonely house, where only a shockingly deformed, hunch back young woman,

& get water melon—how refreshing! Graceful, unsurpassable manner in wh. she declines pay. Natural lady! American.

Grows dark, trail dim, no moon—lose trail, light match to find trail, obliged to stop—find nice running stream, the Can. . . , & little grass, & camp there. Tether the horses— build fire in stump of tree. Lie down, saddle bags for pillow, blankets, & look up into clear sky & stars. Delightful. No rain for 6 mos., earth dry, mountain air neither hot nor cold—& so very pure! Sleep sound.

Guide stupid, no prov. laid in, but bottle of quince preserves fr. Mrs. Frémont—eat that. Boggs' only topic is Col. Frémont, Mrs. Frémont, & the young ladies, & the trip they made to the Yosemite last May. Miss Nina & Miss Lilly &c.

Rose early, bath in the brook, horses, & on to Clark's. Clark an intellt. hunter & woodsman, who has camp here, near Big Trees, on South Fork of the Merced.

Breakfast with him. Indian Camp by his. Indians go off to get venison & trout for our dinner, & we go to the trees. Go on horseback, Clark our guide—abt. 5 miles off.

Measured one tree, bark gone—fr fire, & it measured 97 feet circ. If allow for bark, wd. be 103 f. or 104. Measured about 1 f. above ground, & clear of roots. Its lowest branch is about 160 f. fr. ground, & about 3 or 4 f. in diameter. One tree, lying on ground, inside all rotted out, bark & shell remaining, rode through it, sitting upright in saddle,—about 40 f. of trunk remaining, in length. Another tree, standing, burnt into, rode into the cavity, turned horse round & rode out. Names put on some trees. Dr. Gwin named one for himself, wh. a zealous Republican tore off, & substituted name of Horace Greeley. Agreed to name the 97 f. tree the "Giant Humboldt", & put up on it this card—"This tree is dedicated to the memory of Baron Humboldt, & is named the 'Giant Humboldt'—Aug. 31. 1859, Rich. H. Dana, Jr., Galen Clark, Biddle Boggs". To save it from sport of wits & politicians. Another fallen tree, 167 f. long, abt. 33 f. diameter at base, & 4 f. diameter at end— broken off—like stranded ship—named by Mrs. Frémont—the Fallen Monarch.

Big trees are of a species of the redwood, a soft porous wood, & soft dry bark—leaves like our white cedar,—evergreen.

The pine trees have a bark of pale chocolate color.

Supper at Clark's Camp. Indians brot in deer & trout. Indians lasy, sleep in open air, with fire & plain cooking on coals, & gather acorns & sugar-pine cones &c. Chief do servile work for Clark, to get food. Sleep under boughs. Bath at night & morning in the Merced, rapids over stones.

Breakfast, start for Yosemite. At Mountain Meadow, a camp of 2 brothers named Woodfall (?), & a China woman to cook. Been a grissley bear here last night & killed 3 pigs. The men been out after her.

Just before sundown, reached the high rocks that overhang the Yosemite Valley—"Inspiration Rock" &c. View of Valley beneath & Bride Veil Falls. Rocks over 2000 f. of perpend. height—bold, clear of trees, rising right from Valley.

Ride down into the Valley, slowly, sun-down, twilight, moonlight. Glorious views. One mountain, a bold perpend. bluff, white stone, abt. 2500 f. high, called El Capitan, but by the Indians—Tu-toch-a-nu-lah. Arrive at the camp, at abt. 8 o'ck. Supper—bright moonlight, star-light, in midst of mountain precipices—romantic in extreme. The Sisters, "Udola, Tulula"—very high.

Party of young mechanics fr. Stockton, camped near us, each a horse & blankets, a pack mule with cooking app. & stores—13 in all—sensible, well behaved men, making a sensible trip to see Falls, Big Trees &c.

Sep. 1.   Excursion up the Valley. The Vernal Falls & Nevada Falls. These are the Merced. The falls on sides of Valley, are snow falls, & all dry in summer, except the "Bridal Veil", wh. is small. Yosemite is dry now. In spring & winter, all the valley full of sound of falling water. Also visited a lake of green water, fr. wh. high mountains ascend almost perpendicularly.

Indians been out & speared trout, sold to us. Beautiful evening. Camp fires of whites & Indians. Indians gathering berries & acorns. Make a flour of the acorns.

Yosemite Valley is a long narrow valley, 12 or 15 miles long, & from ½ to ¼ miles wide, very rich & green, with the Merced winding thro' it, a deep green gentle stream, trees growing from the open ground without undergrowth, like Eng. park scenery, with the contrast of steep, awful cliffs rising on all sides directly to the sky. The most perfect valley possible. Some of the perpend. heights exceed 3000 & sev exceed 2000 f. & the falls vary fr. 800 to 2500 f. plunge.

Sep. 3. Left the valley early, wound round & over the mountain, & along the ridge, where are fine views of Valley & the highest peaks of Sierra Nevada. Rattlesnake crossed my path, jumped off horse & killed him with stones & stick, & saved his rattles. Seven in number.

Long & rather tedious day's ride—of 45 miles. At Deer Flat, a camp of mule train going to Walker's River, mules tethered, packs off, fires lighted, & people at supper. Dark, & go on by moon-light. Each of these days see tracks of brown bears— none of grissly. Go on until near 9 o'ck., & then reach North Fork of Merced, at place of man named ———. Here a collection of miners—one a Supervisor of the Co., all gambling & drinking. Drink, for everything. "Take a drink on it".

(Story of the member of Legisl. fr. the district, who carried round the head of Joaquin, the robber, & exhd for 2 bits apiece, & the head sold on exn. to pay his rent for rooms.)

(Frequent stories of fights, wh. are all with revolvers, among leading men, & the only qu seem to be wh. showed most pluck, & the qu. whether both are culpable is not raised.)

"Bit" is the univ. name for the 12½ or 10 cent piece.

Sep. 4. Bath in the N. Fork, & resume journey. Stop at a cave, a dome open at top, trees growing fr. the bottom, tops of branches just reaching the level of the ground. Leave the Coulterville trail on the right, and go over the ridge, the famous "Gantry's Gulch" on the left, & the ridges of Sierra Nevada beyond,—& before us—Mt. Bullion, & the hills of Frémont's Grant in Mariposa. (Gulch, is a narrow deep ravine.)

Reach Fremont's Mills at 3 P.M.—rest, & reach his house at a beautiful sunset. Delightfully refreshing warm bath & change of clothes—(my carpet bag brot up fr. Bear Valley Tavern). Supper & delightful ev.

(A woman here is cook who lived with me sev. months, named Mary *Collins* (?).

Sep. 5. Spend the day with Fremont, visiting his mines & shafts. Specimens of quartz.

Frémont's energy & industry—his own chemist & engineer—his conflict with the Merced Co., drawn up in battle array, for three days, revolvers & knives, & one word wd. put all into a blase of firearms. His courage & dogged resolution prevail. His victory over all obstacles. All the country accord to him these qualities in a remarkable degree.

Courage & spirit of Mrs. Frémont—her influence over people, & power of creating enthousiasm in all work.

Take even. coach for Hornitos. Hot, but much less dusty, as wind ahead. Night at Hornitos.

Sep. 6.   Coach at midnight for Stockton. Recross Merced, Tuolumne & Stanislaus & enter Stockton at 2 P.M.

All tell me that this dry, soil-less country, in the winter & spring is knee deep in grass & flowers—a garden. Miss Frémont gathered 21 diff. specimens of wild flowers in January.

Election in a few days. All the country placarded by advertisement bills of candidates—announcing themselves for diff. offices—posted on trees & houses, & along the trails.

Much of the placer mining done by Chinese. 2500 Chinese in Maraposa Co. alone.

Stockton, on a dead level, not on the S. Joaquin, but on a slue, or (set-up) fr the S. Joaquin, the banks & marshes filled with rank growth of tule. River & slue wind 7 miles in 1½. Called "City of Windmills", (fr. gr. number of windmills for raising water).

Steamer to S. Fr at 4 P.M. & reach S. Fr. next day, Sep. 7, early. Great change fr. extr. heat of interior to cold of the Bay. Change all clothing—danger of rheum. & fever if not change clothing. Mt. Diabolo & the islands of the Bay. Coast Range.

Oriental Hotel again. Mrs. Frémont & children there. Also Bayard Taylor & wife—he on a lecture excursion.

Dine with Felton again. *Present*, Judge McAllester of U.S. C. C't., his son Hall McAllester, Judge Baldwin of Supr., C't. of Cal., Mr. —— formerly M C fr. Ohio, Parsons & Whitcomb (Judge M.'s story of Webster & the "demurrer" to a Bill for an acct., by an old man, ag the B'k. of Geo.)

S. Fr. a great fruit & flower market. Glutted with fruits—peaches, pears, melons & grapes—of the largest richest & sweetest kind. Hortic. show, & great stories of the rapid growth

& productiveness of trees & shrubs & vines. Can raise fruits & flowers in open air in ev. m in the year. Great int. & pride in the cultivn. of fruits & flowers.

Since Vig. Commee. & triumph of "People's Party", S. Fr. a quiet & well governed city—been out all hours, & fewer signs of crime & dissipation than New York.

Election to-day. Good order at polls. Only want is a Reg Law, & all wd. be easy & peaceable. All business suspended, & best people make point to go to polls & give their day to it. Bad people wd. make a holiday anyhow—& best people must agree for one. Still, great amt. of drinking near the polls, at exp. of candidates & pol. parties.

Desire to see two things wh. must leave unseen for want of time. The Almeden Quicksilver mines, & the hydraulic mining in the North, near Folsom & Nevada. Seen almost all else.

European hours in S. F.—dine late, lunch.

Hawaii: September–December 1859

Sat. Sep. 10.   10 A.M. set sail, in the noble clipper ship "Mastiff" for Sandwich Islands. This ship is bound to Hong Kong, stops at the Islands to land mail & few passengers, & has 175 Chinese steerage passengers on board. Wm. O. Johnson, master. His wife on board. Cabin passengers—Geo. Clifford of S. F., merchant—(br. of Gov. Clifford of Mass.), Chas C. Harris, Esq., of Honolulu, a lawyer, young Mr. Jas. H. C. Richmond of N. Bedford, going to Honolulu to enter into business, & a Jew (?) named Shanburn. Ship of about 1200 tons, & said to be one of the best Am. ships afloat, & capt. a high reputation.

Beats out of harbor exceed. well. Quick in stays. Last view of S. Fr. hills, islands, forts, lighthouses, Golden Gate—& its fogs & strong N. E. winds.

First three days of passage; the coast fogs & cold hold on. Then clear, fair, Pacific Ocean weather, & light winds.

Enjoy highly life in a sailing vessel—so much better than a steamer. No noise, no smell of oil, no tremor, as still as country after city, & the int in the sails, winds, duties of seamen &c. Become intimate with Capt. Johnson. German by birth, well educated—a library on board wh. cost some 12 or $1500, & all other things to match—plate, cutlery, furniture, provisions &c. The ship his home & his idol & chief subject of conversation. He owns ¼ of her, & took her fr. the stocks, built in Donald McKay's best manner.

Chief Mate is —— Bailey of N. Bedford, Second Mate Johnson of Salem, 3d Mate a Frenchman, & crew of abt. 20 men. All newest fashions of rigging.

Capt. J. & wife very fond of animals—has on board a large Engl. mastiff, of 125 lbs. weight, "Watch", two Engl. spaniels, two spaniel pups, a King Charles spaniel—two tame Kangaroos, two walloughbees (?) a Java cat, pigeons, hens &c., a cow & calf, large number pigs &c. "Boy Tap" to take care of stock. "You Tap". "You Tap". "Kangaroos had no hay". "That dog no water". Constant attention to these animals. The mastiff follows Johnson everywhere, a perfect guard.

Interest myself & recall old times by watching working of

ship, & work on rigging. Songs of sailors. Go below. Chinese burn lamps & smoke—Capt. J. forbids it.

Thursday. Sep. 15. At abt. 5 P.M., quiet afternoon, good breese, all easy & happy, work going on. Capt. J. "Here, Mr. Bailey—fire in the ship!" Startled all. Smoke immediately pours up after ventilator & hatch. Call all hands aft. Rig hose to pump. Mates jump down the hatch aft, in the Lasarette (?) & smoke pours up in volumes, stifling. Officers spring up & report that between-decks all on fire, & hay taken fire in lower hold. Capt. J. immed. gives up all hope of saving ship, & stops pump & all hands go to work in clearing boats for lowering. "Is there powder on board?" "Yes". Capt. J. has gone below to get it. Magasine brot up & thrown overboard, & Capt. J. armed with revolver. Chinese are alarmed & rush for the boats —beat them back by belaying pins & threats, & presenting pistol. Steward shows presence of mind & stands by Capt. Gig is lowered first. Mrs. Johnson comes up, prepared to go in boat.

A British ship has been in sight the last 2 days, sailing with us. She is sev. miles astern. Set our ensign Union down, & half mast & back after yards. Capt. J. asks me to see his wife safely in boat. She goes over side on rope. Ch M & I help her in. Chinese rush for the boat—beaten back—take in Chinese women, Cabin passengers, & few Chinamen, who rush in. Excellent boat. 2d Mate takes command, 4 oars—& I help at one. Pull over 2 miles & put all safely on board the Engl. ship. Ship Achilles, bound to Sydney. Calmness of Mrs. Johnson.

Soon, 2 more boats come fr. the Mastiff, each full of Chinamen, one in charge of 3d Mate—other has no officer,—so I volunteer & take charge of the boat, with a steering oar. Pull for the Mastiff. Smoke pouring out, but flames not burst out yet. Put her alongside, & take in Chinese, hanging fr. the rails & ropes & chains. Great noise & attempts to get in, but as they cannot swim are afraid to jump in. Keep boat well off—& get her full. Men lie in bottom, & crouch down. Order 'em aft. Gentle, & ready to obey. Put them all safely on board the Achilles. My boat leaks & keep one hand bailing. Put off again for the Mastiff.

Five boats now employed—4 of Mastiff & one of the

Achilles, under charge of her 2d mate. These boats all flying to & fro. Remarkable that with the alarm, & so many (175) ignorant, useless men, not knowing our language, unaccustomed to boats—struggling for life—we should have launched every boat safely, none swamped or stove, & loaded, transported & put on board all—everyone—without an accident.

When got alongside last time found all the Chinese had been taken off. Boats now take off baggage of passengers & crew. We had taken none before, for afraid to leave the deck & boats, lest Chinese take them.

Steward saves all my luggage with trifling exceptions, as it was all in my room on deck & that was to windward. Nothing cd. be got from below or fr. lee side. Sailors house being on deck, save most of their clothes. Capt. J. saves the specie, $76,000, in gold, in boxes, & Ch M takes it to the Achilles, also 2 chronometers. The Capt. saves nothing of his own. Steward saves some trunks for him & for Mrs. Johnson. (Steward's name is Edw. Trofater.) Most of luggage in upper house is saved.

Now attempts to save the animals. The cat & one pup are smothered. Cow & one hog too large. The 2 wallabees are smothered. Save the two Kangaroos, all the large dogs, & number of poultry, pigs & pigeons. Capt. J. asks me to come on board & have a *calm conference* to see if anything more can be done. I do so. Very much fatigued by exertions in my boat, especially the steering oar, & head & lungs full of smoke. Capt. J. says all betw. decks a mass of fire, & will soon burst out thro' deck. Cannot get out longboat. Been trying it while we were in boats—too few men—& now of no use. All other boats out, & nothing more can be got fr. deck. Has been trying to get at the bread, but cannot cut thro' the deck. (Carpenter of no use—as seemed to lose his powers). Nor cd. it have been done—as too near fire. Nothing more can be done. My boat is full of luggage, & push off again—put all safely on board—2 boats remain by side of the Mastiff—& Capt. J., the Chief Mate, Steward, are the last to leave her—Not until ordered—Capt. last to leave.

Flames burst out thro' deck, at main mast. Now, nearly dark, & flames glow over the Ocean. Mrs. J. anxious lest her husband stay too long. Two figures on the quarter deck. Now disappear & the last two boats come off. Capt. J. comes on board, & the poor, noble Mastiff is abandoned.

Flames mount the rigging, catch the sails, & all a mass of fire. Main & missen mast fall. Foremast stands long, then drops, & only a burning hull.

Capt. Hart of the Achilles, a generous, frank British sailor, takes Capt. J. by hand. Now the excitement over & his duty done—the magnitude of the loss comes over him, & he says over & over—"My ship Mastiff! My ship Mastiff! Is it possible she is gone!" Like the mourning of David over Absalom.

All agree in a sense of the wonderful nature of our relief. Just 6.45 P.M. when Johnson leaves his ship. Not over 2 hours fr. time alarm first given, until she is an uninhabitable mass of fire—yet all saved. If no ship in sight, could not have been saved. Boats not hold half the people. (Was abt. 1000 lbs. bread & 6 bbls. water, on deck.) On delib. reflection believe that very doubtful if could have saved one life. Chinese wd. have been restrained with greater difficulty fr. the boats.

Place of fire was Lat. 30.46 N. Long. 128.35 West. Achilles gets under way again, & leaves the burning wreck of the poor Mastiff. For hours, we see the bright light over the Ocean.

All feel the kind Providence of God that we are saved fr. fearful suffering & death, & by common consent we have relig. service in the Cabin. I read passages fr. Scripture & portions of the Service. Thanksgivings & Prayers fr. the Service at sea. (Conv. with Capt. J. last night on board the Mastiff.)

Ascertained that one Chinaman is lost. He went below to save his box of money & was suffocated. All counted, & found only one missing.

Capt. Hart makes generous prov. for our comfort. He has his wife on board, & 3 passengers. Newman & wife, & Ryan— all Irish. Hart & wife are English.

Ch. Mate is Jarvis, Englishman from Essex, & 2d m. is Harley, Scotchman fr. Lanark. Capt. & both mates are good sailors, & solid, hardy men. Achilles a ship of 500 tons, fully loaded with wheat, betw. decks full, bound fr S. Fr. to Sydney Austr. Our crew go forward, & no place for the 174 Chinese but the open deck. Only 5 Chinese women, & they huddle together under the steps aft. Rest get on spars, boats, gratings &c., & what with blankets saved, & old sails wh. Hart gives them, make themselves as comf. as possible.

Very little rice on board, & give them boiled wheat, fr. the A.'s cargo, & bread, & allowance of water.

Hart agrees to bear off for S Islands.

Sepr. 18. Get the N.E. trades, & go on as fast as we can, lest get short of water or bread. All sails set.

Sep. 22. Thursd. One week since the fire. Still it is the only subject deep in our thoughts. Poor Johnson thinks & talks of scarcely anything but his poor ship, & a kind Providence that gave us a ship in sight,—wh. alone saved us. He fully feels that, & may also well pride himself on having saved ev life, all the money, without an accident or mishap.

We live very well on board the Achilles, the cooking good, provisions abundant, & the most cordial hospitality. All like Hart. In heavy seas & rain, Chinese get wet. Entertainment 3 times a day, to see water, bread & food served out to them. Queer old cove of a Chinaman, in Mr. Clifford's hat, whom we call "Clifford". The laughing girl & the small footed woman.

Tuesd. Sep. 27. At daylight, see island of Molokai, on port hand, & soon Oahu is right ahead. Land high, & often rising to mountains. Pass down Channel between Molokai & Oahu. Diamond Head, a bold picturesque point, at S.E. end of Honolulu Roads. Pilot boats, rowed by bare headed Kanakas. Come to anchor in outer roads. Coral reefs, with bright surf breaking over them, between us & shore. Go ashore in Kanaka boat. Lateen sail. Glorious surf each side of channel. Great many ships inside, chiefly whalers. Honolulu reminds me of S. Barbara, except the reefs, & the feature that the hills behind are rent by a deep valley, through wh. the trade winds blow. Town larger & more Am than I expected, abt. 14000 inhab. native & foreign. Lower part looks like any Am. seaport town.

Exn of crew before Judge Platt, Am. Consul. No suff proof of stealing ag any. Excitement in the town on our news.

Judge Harris takes me, Capt. J. & wife, & all the dogs but the K Ch spaniel, wh. was lost or stolen after landing, to his house, up the valley—fine prospect on seaward & landward.

Open sea, & high picturesque defile of valley. Delightful air, clear blue sky, trade wind clouds.

Wed. Sep. 28. Call & deliver letters of introduction. King is absent. Trouble about his shooting Mr. ———. Call on Prince Lot Kamehameha, his brother, who is Minister of Interior, Mr. Wylie, Min. of For. Affairs, Mr. Gregg, Min. of Finance, Mr. Bates, D. Att'y., Ch. Justice Allen, Judge Robertson, R. S. Davis, Rev. Mr. Damon, Seamen's Chaplain, Mr. Smith, Missionary, & some merchants.

Beautiful evenings, little showers, but not frequent, & otherwise *always* fine weather, except a few S. turns in winter. Thermometer even thro' the year.

Fruits—oranges, bananas, taro, cocoa nuts, breadfruit & guava, potatoes &c. Plenty of trees, flowers & grass. Contrast with S. Francisco.

Sunday. Oct. 2. Last 4 days busy aiding Capt. Johnson in his business, by friendly advice &c. Time for few calls. Call on Dr. Armstrong, Min. of Instruction, & on the R. Cath. Bishop. He & his clergy live in the Church yard, where all the mission buildings are. Contrast betw. this system, & that of Prot. missionaries in their families, at diff. houses—advantages & disadv. of each. Large R. Cath. Church of stone. Large Native Ch. of stone, abt. same sise. Attend service in Native Ch., Dr. Armstrong preaches in native tongue. Singular congregation. Sixty horses at door. Bonnets of all fashions of 60 years past— curiosity shop—natives awkward in shoes—only wear them Sundays. Look better bareheaded & barefooted, with flowers in hair, as on week days. Several chiefs in Church—but all wear the European dress. Women wear usually only one garment, a thin gown, not stiffened.

Week days women (except upper class) wear one gown, no shoes or bonnet, almost always wreaths on head. Men wear jacket & trowsers. Occasionally a man with only a malo round waist. Many young women very pretty. Many, especially older, walk like men.

All native women ride astride, with long flowing robes, & bare heads—look well. Upper class use side saddles. Almost every native seems to have a horse, whether man or woman— average cost of their horses $5. Many houses & walls are of

stone—coral. Color of ground is brown, agreeable to the eye
—so of the stone—like England. Roads hard, very little dust.
Am much interested in the people, like them. Climate perfect,
I should judge. Every day been delightful.

Sund. aftern., went to Bethel. Mr. Damon preached on the
loss of the Mastiff to a good congregation.

Spent an evening with a female chief, Pauwahe, married to
Mr. Bishop, an Am. merchant. She is an interesting, well educated & well bred woman of 27 years.

Called on Judge Borden, U.S. Commissioner. He & the
For. Sec. arranged for me a private interview with the King, for
Monday next. The King has shot a man, his private Sec., not
fatally—cause unknown—but people seem to sympathise with
the King, regretting his loss of temper. The King is considered
a man of superior intelligence & of honorable character.

Rode out to the Pali, a precipice, from wh. Kamehameha I
pitched his enemies. The scenery beautiful & picturesque.
About 5 miles from the town. Deep gorge in the mountains,
valley on each end, & blue sea on each end—the height of the
tops of the mountains 1800 & 2000 feet—very striking.

Honolulu Oct. 3, 1859.   One ev. last week called on Pauwahe
(Mrs. Bishop) a native female chief—well educated & well mannered & interesting—as dark as a mulatto. Husband a merchant—rich. She is treated with reverence by the natives, &
even whites treat her with some deference, in social circles.
Entitled to seat in House of Nobles. Her gr f was a naked savage. Called on Ch. J. Allen—laid up of the "Maui fever" or
"Boohoo fever"—a kind of short infl. rheumatic fever, wh. has
come in here within 5 or 6 years & attacks strangers almost
always. Not dangerous, but painful & depressing. The wife an
intelligent young lady fr. Bangor—talk over Prest. Woods of
Bowdoin, & the G. B. Emerson family &c.

Called on Rev. Mr. Smith, an Am. Missionary—very intell.
wife. (All say that the Missiony. wives, as gen. thing, more intellectual than the men).

Hardly a native man or woman but owns a horse—average
cost 4 & $5 each—& are constantly riding. Women bare
headed, flowers in hair, riding astride, with long strips of cloth
covering limbs, & coming nearly to ground.

Last battle ground betw. Kamehameha I & rebels, between the Pali & the falls—very pretty place.

Water brot in open runs, by road-side, from Nuuanu Valley.

Sunday morning early (Oct. 2) passing by a Missionary's house, heard the family, at prayers, singing one of the popular hymns of New England, wh. they introduced here. How it carried me back to the early hist. of the Am. Missions among these savages, & the changes now—, when Honolulu is a civilised place.

(In journal sent home) *Sund.* morn. to Native Church. 200 feet long (?) stone—full of people—elevated seat for the King, he not there. Curiosity shop of bonnets,—in ev. style of 60 years past. Natives look better bareheaded & barefooted than in shoes & bonnets—especially awkward in shoes. People take no part in the service. Music by small choir, prayers & sermon by preacher (Dr. Armstrong) & people sit & stand in prayer, at option, & sit all the rest of time. *Mere listeners.* No outward app of devotion—think it fault of clergy. As soon as benediction *began*, they begin a rush for doors, & minister turns directly round, & no effort is made to keep up any outward form or show of devotion. Confident that a liturgy & responsive service would take with these people. They must be *actors.*

Bethel—good congr. of leading whites. Wylie, Bates, &c. (Gregg is Catholic) & fair sermon on loss of Mastiff. Large Sunday School—well ordered, & plenty of books.

R. Cath. Cathedral large stone Ch. No seats, with plenty pictures &c. Great many Kanakas stay in the yard—all the recess. Two instructions & confessions in afternoon. Intellig. & respectable German priest, speaking English.

Kanaka women only one garment, often of thin material—must be more fav. to development than our tightened loads of clothing.

The washing is done in open streams, on stones—streams run along the outside of the village—lined with women washing—sometimes scarcely any dress on. Riding out to Pali, saw one woman bathing in a little pool, taking her bath, by road side—held her gown before her as we passed.

The King's schooner came in sight early Frid. morn. (Sep. 30) & he landed under salute & flags raised, but went privately to his palace. In retirement on acct. of his shooting Mr.

Neilson, his secretary. (Causes not known, but people disposed to uphold the King).

The libel suit by Hart for his salvage on the $83,000. Libel filed Thursd. Answ. filed Frid. morn., hearing Frid., & decision Saturday. Montgomery (Irishman) counsel for Hart, & Blair (½ br. of F.P.B.) for Johnson. Case very imperfectly managed, both on law & facts, by the counsel. Robertson, J, a sensible man, few words, & good kn of law; tho' never saw a law book until middle life—& been a common sailor. Gives ten per-cent for salvage, (Achilles in no *peril*, & no extr. service, & the owners of the money not to pay for the humanity &c.).

Mon. Oct. 3. By applic. of Judge Borden, & the intervention of sev. friends in office, King agrees to give me a private audience at 12.30 to-day. Go to palace—dress coat &c. House of Nobles in special session—in uniform, blue riband across breast & some in milit. dress. The Old Governor of Oahu ——, who once was a naked savage—dignified old man—Wylie, Gregg &c. & 3 or 4 Kanaka Chiefs. Hs. is mixed of Native Chiefs & Whites holding by appointment of King. (Bishop & Armstrong were added to the Nobles to-day).

The King, a tall, well made man of abt. 25, good looking, dignified & easy manners, & makes very agreeable impression both as to intellect & character. His friends say he is a true nobleman by nature. Speaks Engl. as native tongue. Interview of ½ hour. All stand when he comes in, & remain so until he asks us to sit. All the etiquette of royalty is observed. Guards at palace door &c. (Queen is at Maui.) Speaks of my book, of his visit to America & Europe, of the friendly aspect of U.S. Govt. &c. (Refers to Noah & Daniel, as the Websters of the anecdote.)

Palace very fair suites of rooms, high & well furnished. Contrast of few lasy Kanakas lying on ground, basking in sun, about the sides of the palace.

"Yankee" sails to-day (Oct. 3), Capt. & Mrs. Johnson & "Watch", & "Billy", kangaroos, the 2 Mates, "Tap" "Joe" &c.

Party this ev. at Mrs. Ch. Brewer's. Musical. Very good playing on piano & violin, & good singing. This musical soiree once a month. Great int. in it. Among performers, one half-caste lady, Mrs. Coady—rich & well educated. Sings well. Mrs. Bishop there. Mrs. Allen, Mrs. Gregg &c. &c.

Call on Lt. Reynolds U.S.N. laid up with bad leg, crutches &c. Here as U.S. Naval Store keeper.

A king is a king. The King here is a *power*, social as well as polil. Not only natives but the intell. & wealthy Engl. & Am. whites have an unconsc. loyalty. The *person of a king* is superior. My having a private interv. with him, at this time—when he is in retirement, has made an impression—and almost ev. leading man claims to have been instrumental in bringing it about—& even their wives intimate to me that, "my husband saw the King &c. &c." The King is an interesting spectacle—to any but a low mind, it is affecting & inspiring to see a young man struggling to maintain his Government & the supremacy of his race. It goes to your heart, & has an air of chivalry. Besides, the Govt. is a good one. Order & law are well preserved & administered—nowhere better, & education & charities sustained. Seamen are better regulated & protected ag. landsharks here than in any port in the U. States.

Visited Seaman's Home—Admirable institution. Good rooms, good table, reading room open to all Seamen—boarders or not—Shipping office attached. Stationary &c. furnished *gratis* to all seamen wishing to write home &c.

Pride of India trees planted freely here & grow fast. Tamarind trees, slow growth. Oranges plenty & sweet. Like the *taro* fried or boiled, but not the *poe*. Bananas excellent & wholesome. The Lahala tree with roots from the branches—species of *pandanus*. Dr. Armstrong, Min. of instruction, takes me to see the schools. The "Royal School" for natives, taught by Mr. Morris Beckwith & a Miss Cook. Beckwith is br of the principal of the Puna Ho College, & edd. at a N.E. college. 2 rooms—one for girls & one for boys—all Kanakas. Recite in geography, grammar, & arithmetic, with free use of blackboards. A girl of 15, half Kanaka & half Chinese is head scholar & assistant, a girl of intelligence & good character, named Rebecca. A very smart boy of 12 or so, full Kanaka, leads the boys class—his answers as quick as thought & face all alive. Kanakas generally find it hard to sit still, & attend—& assume very uncouth positions. Teacher says punctual in attendance.

Another school, in stone building, kept by Ingraham, for half-castes & a few whites. Mr. Armstrong says find it better to separate the full bloods fr. the half castes. Some fair drawings. Kanakas take to geography & drawing. Mimetic powers great. Yet, recitations in analysis of sentences in grammar very good —metaphysical trial.

Puna Ho. School of abt. 80 scholars, 60 or 70 of wh. are boarders, chiefly fr. the other islands. All but 4 are whites, children of missionaries, prof. men, & merchants. Very pretty spot, about 2 miles out of town, low buildings with verandahs, & well planted with trees. Day scholars come on horseback or in wagons. School of high character. About ½ girls. Girls live in building by themselves, but they recite in classes with the boys. Two daughters of Parker, the Missionary, clever girls, are teachers. Men teachers are all graduates of N.E. colleges. Beckwith, the principal, just left, with high reputation & much beloved. The boys are carried as far as the Sophomore studies. Heard a capital recitation in Horace, under Haskell,—the grammatical analysis as good as anywhere. Recitation in Greek, read by the printed accent & in Continental sound of vowels. This is a school of high character, & very attractive to the pupils.

Dined with Mr. Armstrong. Fine family of children & nice large house & grounds—all his trees grown in 8 years—as is chiefly the case in Honolulu (his great admiration of Charles Sumner & desire to see him.) Usual dinner hour here is late in afternoon, 4 or 5 o'ck., & the school keeps from 10 to 3 or 3½. So the Courts, from 9 or 10 to 3 or 4.

This ev. (Oct. 4) rode to Waititi, about 6 miles fr. Honolulu, on the beach, near Diamond Head, the site of the old Honolulu, where the first navigators came, & still many native huts there—also cottages occupied by whites for sea-bathing, in mid-summer. Entered sev. huts. Natives very cordial & kindly. Mostly have but one room, & all sleep on mats, some nearly naked & some with blankets, not much better than dogs in a kennel. Yet each hut had a Bible, their only book. These are the lower class, barefooted & bareheaded, but decently clothed by day, & owning horses. Riding by moonlight, under the tall cocoa nut palms, by the sea side of Oahu!

In Honolulu are several rich Chinese, some 15 or 20 who are

merchants of high standing & whose word is as good as their bond. They gave a ball to the King & Queen wh. cost $7000.

("Frisco", is the nickname of S. Francisco, among sailors & shipmasters, in the Pacific.)

Visited the prison. It is built of coral rock, well ventilated, & well adapted to the climate. The prisoners work on the public works, the roads, the reef &c. The Warden told me that the Chinese furnish far more than their quota of convicts, the foreigners (chiefly sailors) the next, & natives the least.

Attended Supr. C't. Allen C J & Robertson sitting, Bates arguing. Jury sit opp. the judges, & counsel sit on opp. sides of the space between.

Wed. Oct. 5, 1859. Sailed at 4 P.M. in the little sch. Mary, 80 tons, to visit island of Hawaii. 54 Kanakas on board, men & women, & sev. horses & dogs. Vessel very small & very slow & excess. disagreeable. Only cabin passengers are Capt. Mallett of Waimea (Hawaii), an Englishman, & a lad named Wm. Cornwell. Improve my time in learning Kanaka. Some natives intelligent & communicative. But Kanakas sleep on deck, lie about in heaps, eat poe with fingers fr. calabashes, & seem very much like half civilised Indians. Women like squaws. Yet, no drinking no quarreling. Every evening, just at dark, one makes a prayer, & all give respectful attention.

The mate of the sch. has a Kanaka wife on board, but she sleeps & eats with the other women, & like them, is a mere squaw. The best looking man among them, a young man, I found was of a Chief family—or chief-*ish,* as they use the adjective here.

Go to leeward of Laanai. Long calms, & vessel sails very slow. One blow & heavy sea, & feel seasick, for first time for long while—think it is chiefly the smells. Poe & fish the sole food of natives on board—drink is water.

On Laanai was a settlement of Mormons, nearly opp. Lahaina, but they failed of success & have left.

Oct. 8. Sat. Becalmed all day off Lahaini. Volcanic outlines of mountains behind Lahaina—extinct craters, & broken peaks —very picturesque.

On hill is Lahainaluna, the High School for Educ. of native youths, in Hawaiian. School of high repute, & great utility

—furnishes native teachers for native schools in all the islands. Founded by Am. B.C.F.M.

Going into Lahaina are sev. whale ships—& some are lying there.

(Last night dreamed of W. Cedar st., & all day full of strong impressions of my home there.)

Oct. 9.   Bay betw. E. & W. Maui, looks like 2 islands. East Maui is very mountainous, & green to summits. Highest is "Hale a ka Lá"—"House of the Sun". McGee's farm, rich, fertile spot. King goes there a great deal. Large extinct crater on Hale a ka Lá—sd. to be 30 miles in circumf.

Capt. Mallett & the mates, who are no friends of religion, admit the civilising influence of the Missionaries, & tell me that Sunday is very strictly observed in the islands—no cargo can be landed or recd. unless live stock, for humanity's sake. Also, the gen. extent of knowledge of reading & writing among the natives.

Oct. 10. Mond.   Reach Kawaihae, on N.W. side of Hawaii, early this morning. Last night, saw light of volcano on the side of Mauna Loa, which is running into the sea.

(Spent day at Macy's on shore. Whale Ship Europa of Edgertown, Manter, Master—only 200 bbls., young & excellent fellow, on first voyage as Master, good deal discouraged.)

Temple, or great altar, built to Louó by Kamehameha I, near the landing. Large extent—a great pile of coral stones, terraced down, & large flat area on top. Spent some time there, alone—said the Creed & Te Deum on the spot once consecrated to heathen rites. Sacrifices made here.

At night, took native canoe, for Kailua, to stop at the outflow of the lava into the sea.

Native canoes, built of one log, outrigger, Kanaka lies out to windward on outrigger. Paddles & sails.

Delightful motion—regulated by outrigger—wh. is a keel, 4 or 5 feet to windward.

3 Kanaka men, one woman & myself. Exquisite moonlight night, steady land breeze, bright stars, still water, floating along the coral reef, just clear of the surf, temperature.

About midnight, reach the outflow. The place where the lava flows into the sea, is 40 miles from the crater. The course fr. the crater is now nearly all covered over by crust of cold lava, & the stream runs under it, with here & there a vent. You see no stream of lava, until just before it reaches the sea. Place of outflow is abt. 2 miles wide. Not all flowing at once, but constantly changing. As the red hot lava plunges into the sea, it makes an explosion like a cannon, & a hissing of steam, & roar, as of surf, & clouds of steam rise up fr. the water. The sea is heated to a consid. distance. Felt it warm, to hand, & then hot. When as near as dared to go, found it as hot as cd. bear. Here, a little stream poured steadily in, there a wide thin sheet, then wd. come a large mass, breaking up all before it, & pitching into the sea, with roaring & hissing & clouds of steam. Then the places wd. cool over, the lava turn black, & the fiery mass burst out at another point. Yet the entire space is lava, black or fiery red. These changes added to the interest in watching it.

Natives a little afraid to go near—perhaps remains of superstitions. Peli, their goddess of wrath & vengeance, had her seat on the mountain, & these eruptions were her outbreaks of wrath. *Peli* is now the native word for volcano, & volcanic fires,—as our word comes fr. Vulcan.

After some 2 hours stay, released the natives fr. their unwelcome duty of keeping near the flow, & set sail for Kailua.

(My crackers saturated by smell of oil-skin in the tin boxes, sardines not to be opened by penknife, & tea with no sugar).

Sound sleep in the canoe. Its silence, & steady, quiet motion—air.

Tu. Oct. 11. Reach Kailua at about 10 A.M. Large open bay. On left, near the town, are remains of the great fort built by Kamehameha I, with number of cannon still mounted. Fort of coral, & large walls thick.

Small village now—once the residence of the king, & many great chiefs. Still, a large stone house, built by a chief called "Governor Adams", now hired by the King—who sometimes comes here for a few weeks bathing & fishing &c. Two large stone churches, nearly side by side, about same sise, Protestant & Catholic. Rev. Mr. Thurston, the Missionary, has charge, & is the only survivor, with his wife, of the first company of missionaries that came to the islands,—in 1820. Is the Nestor of the Missions. Letter to him. Find his house closed—he gone up to a small grass-house on the hill, where he raises coffee. (Go to the lodging house of one Travis. Find there Judge ——, circuit judge, just from a circuit in Kona & Kaú.)

Horse & ride up to Mr. Thurston's grass house, on the hill. Venerable old man, with long white beard. Mrs. Thurston, strong woman, masculine, rides astride & wears spurs. Led a life of strange vicissitudes. Found all savages here, & lived to see Xy. established & reigning, & to see children & gr. children about them, & all these now left them, & they alone. Lunched with them in their simple hut. Invited to take tea with them in their house in the village. From this hut, on hill side, can see that all between the hills & the beach is a lava formation, & still, in most places, mere bare lava. On hill sides, the lava is grown over with bushes, grass & trees, & has become extremely fertile. Chief trees are bread-fruit, orange, mango, cocoanut, other palms, & the castor oil bush, wh. is everywhere.

Large number of Kanakas loafing about town,—the King's boatmen & retainers, waiting his arrival. Stories here not favorable to the King's temperance & other morals. The Thurstons speak favorably of his natural qualities, & think the feeling of loyalty is strong towards him—his intelligence, impulses & manners good.

After noon, under shade of the R.C. Church, saw a priest walking, hot day, in well worn path. Introduced myself. He speaks only French. Few minutes, bell tolls for Vespers. Go in. Another priest, in Chancel, saying the service. From 10 to 15 kanakas, kneeling & singing the responses. Dim light of the Church—strange remoteness of place—universality of the worship—effect on the feelings & imagination. After service, walk with the priests under the shade of the walls. Both are intelligent men, & apparently good & sincere—at least, their countenances so express. They live in rear of the Church— what utter loneliness! Two men—no person for 800 miles knowing their language—only kanakas to talk with. Both well acqd. with state of the theol. questions in Europe & America. The church has no seats—but is matted over—people sit on mats, stand or kneel. Architecture good.

Walk up to Mr. Thurston's. Contrast of two systems. He has

3 grandchildren, walked down fr. their mother's—his daughter —Mrs. Taylor's, to spend night & next day, bringing fruits & presents—it being the 40th anniversary of the marriage of their gr. parents! Protestant clergy—have families, domestic circles & attachments—duties, pleasures, trials & experiences. Their homes & families are centres & fountains of civilisation to a barbarous neighborhood. Catholic clergy, unmarried, supported on little, free fr. cares of family, able to give all time to Church. Yet without the influences of the family, which meet natives at so many points.

Before going to Mr. T.'s to tea, walked to the fort of Kamehameha, the ruins of his house, & the spot, near the cocoa nut trees, where he died, & bathe in the sea, where he so often bathed, with all his chiefs, giving audience to foreigners, as he came up dripping from the water, with only a malo on.

Is a subterranean passage fr. Mr. Thurston's house to the beach, caused by very ancient volcanic action.

Wed. Oct. 12. Started early for Kealakekua. On horse, a Kanaka on foot carrying my luggage across his shoulders on a pole. Took the upper road. Passed Thurston's house, & saw him walking down to an early morning service. Passed Mrs. Taylor's house, in a high place on the hill-side, well wooded & pleasant—too early for a call.

This mountain road fr. Kailua to Kealakekua, is an earthly paradise. Never saw it exceeded. High & airy. Sea on one side. Mauna Loa on the other—rich soils, tropical denseness of foliage, road shaded by trees, air fragrant with flowers, & trees rich with fruit. One wishes to break out in praises to God for his works.

Breakfast at a Capt. Johnson's, an old Californian, who has a farm for sheep & bullocks. House shaded, & plenty of fruits— oranges, bananas, fresh figs, peaches, bread fruit. Also, raises coffee.

Ride on. Spend hour at house of Rev. Mr. Thurston's son— a young man, educated at Wms. College. Married a d. of Judge Andrews of Oahu, in feeble health—rather interesting for his high spirit—doomed to death.

Lunch at house of Mr. Thomas Paris. There meet young Thurston's wife, & her father, Judge Andrews. He (Judge A.)

is author of the Hawaiian dictionary & grammar, & is now employed on a larger dictionary.

Little further on, call on Rev. Mr. Paris, brother of Thomas. Fine situation, near brow of the *pali*, a steep hill above Kealakekua. Spend an hour there. Several children—one d. at school at Puna Ho.

Reached top of hill that overlooks the valley of Kealakekua & the sea. Beautiful view. Very rich & green, with stretches of black lava, & Kealakekua, looking more thoroughly Hawaiian than any place I have yet seen. Just as it does in the pictures in Cook's voyages, & there, across the Bay, under the cocoa nut trees, is the place where he fell.

Enter the little village of thatched huts. People look primitive & half barbarous. Yet, a church & school house, & am told a larger proportion can read & write than in the U. States. Men & children tumbling in the surf. Old man, grey hairs, comes dripping out of surf, to look at me, naked all but a little malo. Large proportion wear no trowsers, & some no shirts. Women all have a gown or chemise—barefooted & bareheaded, necklaces of beads or flowers, & garlands of flowers & berries, in hair. Many have very pretty expressions of countenance.

Only one white man here—a Capt. Cummings, a native of N. Hampshire, formerly master of whaler, has a Kanaka wife, & does all the business of the region of 20 miles round—is shop-keeper, collector, harbor master &c. Has good house, shop, wharf & tank. Only drawback here is want of water. None comes fr. above—land being porous & cavernous, fr. volcanic action. Must collect rain water in tanks. Is no trade here now, except occasionally a whaler comes in for potatoes & fresh fruits & water—for wh. C has a huge tank & hose.

Bathe in sea. Understand why Kanaka are so good swimmers, temperature of sea so delightful, & same through the year. Shd. live much in sea, if lived here. Amphibious.

Both Johnson & Cummings have native wives. J.'s did not come to table. C.'s did, but sat & ate awkwardly—rather pretty face, & graceful, when not forced into our fashions.

Thursd. Oct. 13.   So much pleased with Kealakekua (Ke ala ke Akua, the path of the Spirit) that stay all day. Take canoe &

am paddled over by natives to place where Cook was killed. Beach of lava & coral, grove of cocoa-nut trees, close to water, large flat rock, on wh. sea washes a little. Here he fell. There lay his boats, firing on the natives, who used stones & darts. Broke off piece of the rock. Just above the rock, is a stump of a tree, wh. the Br men of war have covered over with sheets of copper, to preserve it, with inscriptions in commemoration of Cook's death.

In the hill sides are little caves or openings where the natives used to bury their dead. Climbed up, & looked into them—saw skeletons.

Eat bread fruit at dinner. It is not eatable raw, but is boiled or baked. Taste is betw. bread & sweet potato. A native climbs up & gets me a cocoa nut. Milk is fresh & slightly tart. Taro is the great vegit. of these islands, for foreigners as well as natives—is to them what the potato is to Ireland. Foreigners use it boiled or baked, as vegetable, with meats. Natives chiefly as poe.

Hire a canoe & three men, to take me to Milorii. Start late in afternoon. Dripping natives, looking on. *Aloha.*

No trade winds felt on this side of the islands—but alternate land & sea breezes.

Grows dark & cloudy & wind ahead & moon not yet up. So natives land & beach the canoe, about 10 P.M., & go to a collection of huts, at a place called Kalaki-ki. People receive us well—gather round a calabash of poe & some fish. I begin to eat. No natives will eat. I ask them to. Look diffident, & one says must say Grace. Mortifies me. One native says grace, & all fall to. Give them my sardines. One very pretty native woman, (Tarahae) takes great pains to correct my pronunciation. Lie down on mats & sleep until moon is up—when take leave & go off in our canoe. (Before lying down kanakas have prayer & hymn to a familiar New England tune.)

In canoe all night. At daybreak, see canoes in groups of 5 to 10 each, fishing—great numbers of them before reach Milorii.

The three natives of the canoe are all religious—& nice fellows, kind & honest, & take pains for me.

At Milorii, are no white men. Go to hut of one Stephen—whom natives call Setepano, the nearest they can get to it. Go

to sleep on mat. My natives go back to Kealakekua, in their canoe. Learned my name, & call me *Dena*—(wh. gives our
sound), they having no term for Mr. Their highest chiefs have
no prefix or affix of honor, either men or women, but are addressed—as Pauwahe, Kaahumanu, &c.

One of them before leaving wakes me up & says—"Dena!
Dena! *hen*—you—by & by". "Do you want a hen?" "Aole.
Mamuli wahine get hen—oe—oe". That is—I am to have a
chicken for breakfast.

Had letter of introduction fr. Rev. Mr. Paris, to Setepano,
but he is *máo*, off. A kanaka goes off, & by noon gets me a
hoki—mule. But *hoki* kicks & won't be mounted. So kanaka
goes off for 3 hours more to get a horse. Mean time, I spend
the whole day in the hut with the women, except one bath in
the sea. Women stringing necklaces of yellow berries of pandanus tree, & sewing & ironing, all seated on mats. Managed
to have consid. conv. with them, betw. Hawaiian & signs. Have
got a pretty large vocabulary. In course of day other women
call in, to have a chat, & to see the haole. (One kanaka man's
description of one of these women, to her face, in simplicity,
in one word.) Probably a fair specimen of the native life &
customs.

Just before dark, Kanaka comes with horse. All sit down
again to poe & bananas. Am getting expert at eating poe with
my fingers.

Kanaka takes my luggage on pole, across his shoulders, &
walks off. My horse creeps after, & no whipping can get a trot
or fast walk out of him. It grows dark before we get 3 miles, &
at abt. 5 miles, we bring up at native house—large thatched
hut—with some 20 inmates, sitting or lying on mats around a
fire. Are well recd., but they have only poe & bananas. Before
lying down, one kanaka says a prayer. (So did my boatman, at
the other hut).

Sat. Oct. 15. Slept soundly until dawn. Here dismissed my
man, & engaged a new man & horse. Started at dawn, up the
lava streams, & across them, for Waiohinu. (The free & gross
conv. of some kanaka women, even in the good & well
ordered families. The last point that Xn. civilisation has to

carry with these people, is that wh. pertains to the relations of the sexes).

At both places, have entertained the natives very much by showing them the inside work of my watch.

Natives pronounce our proper names as near as they can, & in talking with them, we adopt their pronunciation. E. g. *Thurston*, is Kakini, Paris is Pareki, Lyman is Laimani, Stephen is Setepano &c.

From Milorii to Waiohinu, a distance of about forty miles, is a sea of lava. Some of this is smooth, hard lava, called *pahoehoe*, & the rest is rough, loose stones, *aa*. Imagine a blacksmith's heap of some thousand square miles, the shop closed for centuries, & you have it. All this has come from Mauna Loa. Desolation—Desolation.

Within abt. 7 miles of Waiohinu comes vegitation, grass & trees. Gradually the lava is lost—or rather time has grown it over.

Waiohinu is high land, some 1500 f. above the sea, but the sea in sight—long projecting points & the endless breaking of surf on the coral reefs in sight.

Very rich & fertile here. Trade winds are felt—being on the E. side of the island.

Call & deliver letters to Rev. Mr. Shipman. Mrs. S. so ill that refused to stay there, & am introduced to a young man named Gowen, from Maine, with young wife, just built little house here, shop, farm &c. Take my meals there, & sleep at Mr. Shipman's.

Had nothing but bananas for 20 hours. Shipman's a nice house—neatly furnished. Is comfort to undress & sleep betw. sheets—first time for 11 days.

Mr. Shipman & Mr. Gowen are the only white men betw. Hilo & Kealakehua a space of 120 or 150 miles. The physician comes fr. Kealakehua 80 miles, to see Mrs. S., & spends a week there. Also, at the house, a Mr. Frederick S. Lyman, son of Rev. D. B. Lyman of Hilo. He is tax collector for the district, & is on his tour of collection, a young man of about 21.

Dr. Herrick, very homely old man, a *granny*, is nurse & all, & gives emetics &c., in the true old style, to a poor feeble mother.

Gowen & wife, nice people of middle class, intelligent, interested in politics & literature, Republicans—been here little over a year, & married just before leaving home. Take the Weekly Tribune, Independent, & Atlantic Magasine. Have family prayers morning & evening, & are an acquisition to the mission.

Oct. 16. Sunday. First rain since came to the Islands. Rained all last night, & most of today. Went to the Native Meeting this morning. Tolerably full & good choir. Mrs. Shipman so ill that Mr. S. not preach. Service is conducted by a Kanaka, & becomingly. Singing good, to familiar old N. England tunes of Hebron, Dedham &c. wh. retain their names here, adapted to native life. Heberona, Dedahamai, &c. Old Hundred, being Haneii &c. The familiar words & tune of

> "The day is past & gone,
> The Evening shades appear;
> Oh may we ever bear in mind,
> The shades of death draw near".

is rendered—

"Ua hala keia la,	*hale*, gone; *keia*, this; *la*, day.
Ua uhi mai ka po;	*uhi mai*, veils over, *po*, night.
Pela, e malu koke mai,	*Pela*, thus. *Malu*, overshadows.
Ka make o kakou".	*kakou*, us all. *Make*, death.

The hymn sung to Hebron

A kau na la hoano nai;	A *kau*, and. *hoano*, praise & worship. *nai*, here, below.
He maha koe i ke ao,	*Maha koe*—to rest; *i ke ao*, as here
He la hoano ano e,	*ano e*, of a different kind.
He kapu maoli oia mau.	*Kapu*, sacred, *Maoli*, &c. eternal.

Noticed one man among the natives for his tall figure & dignified air, & learned that he was a chief.

I rode across the country with my California belt with revolver & knife—but told by all that no more need of weapons among these people than among children. All the property of this large district, & all its industry is in native hands, except the Mission & Mr. Gowen's.

Oranges sweet & plenty here. Also bananas.

Mond. Oct. 17. Mr. Shipman has a native school of about 70 scholars. His head teacher is a native, educated at Lahainluna —an intelligent man. Object is to carry on all the teachings in the native tongue—but desire of some to learn English is so strong that sev are taught it. Attended the school, & made them an address. Studies are reading, spelling, geography, grammar & arithmetic. Kanakas supple & active, & not like confinement, awkward & uneasy in formal positions, not stand straight or still. Difficulty with our consonants.

Leave of friends here, & start in co. with Mr. Lyman for the old crater of Kilauwea, & Hilo, a kanaka to carry my luggage, & a few pack oxen with Mr. L.'s goods.

Natives treading out wheat by horses—men & women mounted, & rather furious riding. Stop at chief's house.

Have eaten fresh figs at Waiohinu, & like them.

Journey is over volcanic country, lava fr. Manua Loa, but chiefly very old & well covered with vegitation. Sea is by our side, no harbors, but openings in coral reefs for boats, & little sand beaches, & where these are, you find knots of native houses. Surf breaks off 3 & 4 deep, on account of the steadiness of the trade winds, always in one direction. Here the old style of chiefs used to bathe, on surf-boards.

Spend night at a native house, at a little place called Keáwa, wh. Mr. Fr. Lyman has just bought, & where he intends to have a stock farm. Only natives in the house. Cook us a meat supper—also poe (pó-e, two syllables). Grace before supper, & prayers before turning in, in the native tongue, as matter of course.

Tuesd. Oct. 18. Up at daylight, & off for the crater, first breakfast & prayers. Grace before meat, & some prayer at morning & night are almost universal among the Kanakas— learned it from the Mission. families, who have been there first & often their only patterns of civilisation. While at prayers, felt a slight shock of earthquake.

The road up to the crater is very barren, no water, & chiefly *pahoehoe*. Crater is on a spur of Manua Loa, & abt. 4000 f.

above sea. Reach the rim of the crater at noon, go round two sides of it, to an uninhabited hut, where travelers stay. Lunch & start for the bottom of the crater. Smoke & steam coming up from it. Little openings in the rocks, by the roadside, where steam is coming up. For more than a mile beyond & outside of crater, these openings. Fire is under all the mountain, all about us. In rear of the hut, is a place where sulphur forms. Several small openings or cracks send up a warm steam of a sulphurous smell, & sulphur crystals form on the rocks, in large quantities.

Great Crater of Kilauwéa. Rim is nearly circular, & about ten miles in circumf. From the rim, the walls go down nearly perpendicular to the floor of the crater. The floor of the crater is about 700 f. below the rim. This floor has all, at some time been in action, emitting lava. But all except the centre is now hard floor of lava. The outskirts of this floor, near the walls, & especially on one side, are much grown over with fern bushes, & sometimes trees. Ferns grow up in cracks of hard lava. Greater part of floor of crater is lava, mere lava, sometimes *pahoehoe*, sometimes *aa*, generally nearly level. In centre of floor is a lake or pit, a crater within a crater. This is about 100 yards in diameter, nearly circular, & but little lower than the general floor of the crater. (In some parts of the floor, steam comes up through the cracks). Walked to the centre crater. It is all a mass of living lava, & in action. The lava quickly crusts over in cakes. Imagine a space of large cakes of ice, on a pond, with little spaces of water, the water in commotion & the cakes of ice, sometimes uniting & freesing together, & sometimes breaking up & tumbling over. The lava is black, or slate color. Under it is the sea of fire, or of red fiery molten lava. This breaks out, & is thrown up 18 or 20 feet, & breaks up the cakes of lava, & all is fire. Then, the fire subsides, & the black lava crusts over. Sometimes, nearly all the crater is a mass of fiery, boiling red lava, & sometimes it is here, & then there, all in violent action, but changing its place. Heat so that can hardly bear it on our faces. This is one of the mothers of lava wh. cover the country for 1000 sq. miles. *Swelling*, *throbbing*, & here & there bursting out—is this inner crater.

Return to hut, for night. Kanakas get supper, eat poe with fingers, (one-finger-poe & 2-finger-poe). Old kanaka makes prayer—"Makou, Makou—Akua, &c. pomaissai, pilikia &c.".

Start, by moonlight, at 2.30 A.M. Crater in full blast, & fire reddens the sky over it. Travel by moonlight, over the lava, & down the mountain. Manua Loa, & Manua Kea in full sight. Snow on top of Manua Kea. Manua Loa is abt. 14,000 f. high, twice the height of Mt. Washington.

Daylight. Clear day. Breakfast at native hut. Pretty faces of young native women—necklaces & garlands of berries or roses almost universal.

Some small trees of Sandalwood. The Sandalwood grows slowly, & must be very old before it gives odour. Old trade exhausted all the full grown trees, & is ended. Forests white with kukui trees, like the Amer. Chestnut in blossom. Guavas, sweet & sour are plenty. Guava tree is like quince tree, & guava like quince in form & color, seeds in middle ditto, tastes betw. insipid & sour. Last 7 miles before Hilo is rich, deeply fertile, luxuriant tropical growth, a *jungle* of flowers & trees, so thick that no animal can go through, (shd. think) except where road cut—yet not unwholesome, no miasma. Guavas, oranges, mangoes, kukui, pandanus, castor oil, bread fruit, banana, cocoa nut, papaia.

Open sea again, coral reefs, ships at anchor within them, & little town of Hilo. Streets straight, houses neat, fences neat, gardens, all shaded so thick that just see the houses. Prettiest town I have seen yet—tho' small.

Mr. Fred. Lyman invites me to his father's. Large, comfortable house, head of street, nice yard, full of flowers, shrubs & trees, like Wethersfield parsonage. Mr. Lyman, grey hairs, between 50 & 60 years, wife good figure & manners, matronly, kind, dignified, intelligent. Came here together in 1832, children all born here. Seen hardships & strange experiences— reared up excellent family. Eldest son, Henry Munson, took first honors at Wms. Coll., 1858, 2d is Fred., an excellent, serious, conscientious man, 3d David B. edd. at Puna Ho, is going to States to enter College, 4th, Ellen, at Puna Ho, 5th Rufus Anderson, at home, 6th Frank at Puna Ho, 7th Emma W. a nice girl of 10 years. Well ordered, intell. & well edd. family— all sing, & some play piano. My chamber like front chamber at Wethersfield, very comfortable & homelike. Capt. Brown, of Whaling bark, Belle, & wife are boarding with them.

Mr. Lyman keeps the native school of Hilo. School is

boarding-school solely, about 70 scholars, & free, i.e. $5 a year only paid. Is full & more applications than can receive. Is self supporting, scholars working & raising vegetables & fruits. Gives good practical education in arithmetic, grammar, geography, accounts, & music. Nearly all sing, & band of 8 or 10 who play flutes. Education is religious but liberal. All obliged to attend public worship, relig. lectures, catechism &c. Intended to be a Hawaiian language but some classes in English. Attended the school. Pupils live chiefly on poe & vegitables.

Mrs. Lyman taught school for native girls sev. years. At first, having no paper, used plantain leaf & wrote with style of fish-bone.

Oct. 20. Th. Rev. Mr. Coan, the clergyman, called & invited me to ride to the falls of Wai anuinui—or "rainbow water". No carriages here of any kind. All ride in saddle. Mrs. Coan went with us. River falls into a large chasm of stone, about 100 f. deep. Pretty scene & effect. Only about one mile from the village.

Returned & took tea at Mr. Coan's. Mrs. Coan is a woman of intellect & culture & very agreeable, & knows the ways of the world. Very large tamarind tree in Mr. Coan's yard, giving large shade.

The shades trees here are the tamarind, Mango, breadfruit & pandanus (puhalla) & papaia, & Pride of India.

Frid. Oct. 21. Called with Mr. Coan on the Governess of the island. She is half sister to the king, & perhaps the best repr I cd. see of the old chiefdom. She affects old usages & tries to revive the customs of chiefdom, keeps a large retinue of natives about her, who sit on the floor, or under trees all day, to await her leisure. She is very large, huge, & fat & indolent, but with a proud, domineering look. Her son, a chief of ancient line, with more of the chief blood in him than any one now living, a youth of 19, died a few weeks ago. She keeps his body in a lead coffin, in the large room of her house, behind a curtain, where it lies in State, & in the next room the natives keep up a dirge. It was uninterrupted, all the time of our visit. It sounded not unlike some of the dirges in the R. Cath. Church—low, & monotonous.

In the afternoon, went on a picknick, to a place across the

river Wailuku, called Puueo. All mounted—8 ladies, 9 gentlemen. Pretty spot. View of sea & mountains. (Just behind the town are three extinct craters, close together). Took lunch under pandanus tree—large, wide-spreading, & gives a deep, thick shade, perhaps the most complete I ever saw a tree give. Ladies have each a *re*, (garland of flowers) made up by the native women, who busy themselves at it.

Returning, crossing new chain suspension bridge, across the Wailuku, bridge breaks & falls, & the party are in great peril, thrown into the river, or in the wreck of the bridge, among kicking & struggling horses, & in deep water. Scene of consternation & dismay, for sev. minutes. Natives strip & plunge in—excellent swimmers, & very active in saving lives & extricating the horses. Two of Mr. Lyman's sons, Fredrick & David, distinguished themselves by their swimming, & successful efforts to save life. They swim like natives. Mrs. Henry Burdett, wife of Capt. Burdett of Boston, of ship Raduga, (who is son of H.B. that lived on Dana Hill, Cambridge) was in a great peril, & helped out by David Lyman & sustained until natives took her ashore. Fred. Lyman swam with Miss Pratt, sister of Mrs. Ch. Brewer of Honolulu to a point on the bridge where the natives took her. One lady, Mrs. Gulick of Honolulu, held to her horse's mane, until a native took her off. Miss Emma Lyman (10 years) was on a mule, & at the first sound of danger, the mule, with sure instinct, turned round & ran to the land, & carried her off just before the fall, not a second to spare—no horse or man did the like. Mrs. Austin, wife of Judge Austin (Stafford L. Austin of Hilo) was in the water, & helped out by a native, & her husband. None of the rest of the party fell with the bridge, being at the ends—except myself. I fell in the midst, at the worst part, keeping my seat in the saddle, & stirrup was crushed ag. timber & hurt my left foot. Horse involved in the wreck, & I left him & swam to bridge. This place broke down, & I swam to another. Held on upper rail by fingers. Got better hold & went ashore on the rail, hand over hand. Got there too late to do anything but help Mrs. Burdett up the bank, as she could not walk—fr. exhaustion—(but she was in a safe place, & left there by the natives & David, who went back to the wreck). Cd. hardly walk. Bone of little toe broken, & top of foot bruised.

Natives raised a *wail*, as soon as the bridge fell, wh. was heard all over town. The native women wailed over Emma Lyman, until they made her cry. The skill & fidelity & affection of the natives affecting. Kipi, the tax collector, a native, distinguished himself.

Bridge 200 f. long, rested on 2 chains, insufficient—about 8 or 10 f. above water, & water 25f. deep. Broke with a crack & then a tip, crash & fall. The crash was heard all over town, & drew all to the spot. Mrs. Lyman, who had three sons & a daughter in the party, remained in suspense some half hour, & prepared herself to resuscitate drowned persons, got out her book &c.

No one lost, & no one hurt (beyond mere bruises) but me. Wonderful escape. Seemed to me to be certain death to some, & maiming to most. Fall & crash of suspension bridge, 10 f. above deep water, & party of 10 or 12 men & women falling, with their horses!

Sund. Oct. 23.   Native worship in A.M. Mr. Coan officiated. Same want of reverence of action & manner. Fault of the *system*. Was no benediction. All sat in prayer & singing, & not even bend the head.

P.M. In the small chapel, service in English—about 50 persons. Returns thanks for the preservation of the party. (This party embraced about half the white residents & visitors in the place). Sermon in revival style, & fluent & rather effective—but too long. Congregational singing.

Little Emma Lyman, whom I like very much, wanted to be excused fr. sweeping out the chapel this morning, because it was so late, & people had to go in. But it was her task, & she did it—a little natural pride or shame. In the public service, this little child played the piano, (melodaian piano forte) for the singing.

Monday Oct. 24.   Took tea at Austin's. He is Circ. Judge, & Sec. to the Governess, being, in fact, Governor. Son of a lawyer in Buffalo. Mrs. A. is d. of Rev. Mr. Clark, of Honolulu, & her sister Mrs. Gulick, is with her.

Use arnica on my foot. Swelling goes down. Bone of little toe only, broken. Too small for splints. No pain, but keeps me still. Go out once a day on the horse, walking him. Dr. C. H. Wetmore, a fair physician & surgeon.

Mr. Miller U.S. Consul here.

Thursd. Oct. 27. Spent one ev. at house where Mrs. Burdett & Miss Pratt board. Mrs. B. plays piano very well—in this remote place it seems to me excellent playing. She is just married in Boston, abt. 20 years old, daughter of Tom Comer, an amiable, pretty woman, & very popular. Husband a good fellow, & consid. knowledge of music. His ship is Clipper, in merch. service—wife came out with him, & is good sailor.

Curious feature of life here is the number of whaling masters who bring their wives to the islands & leave them for the seasons, coming back in Spring & Fall. Many in Honolulu, some 40. Here are some 10 or 12. Half the foreign women here are whalers' wives. This is time for their return (October). Every day watching fr. housetops, & as ships come in, watch the whale boats coming ashore, & then the name flies—for no telegraph here. One ship brot news of death of a master whose wife was looking for him—killed by a whale in the Arctic.

Now, all the husbands have arrived but two. All the talk is of ships, the Arctic, the Ockotsk, the no. of barrels. The masters are rather a rough set, tho' two or three of them are well dressed, well bred men. Luck has been bad. Some have nothing, & few have paid their way.

Yesterday afternoon the flute band of native boys fr. the school came down & played for me. Eight flutes—played pretty well. Old fashioned tunes. Taught by a native in the upper class. Flute their favorite, as easy to learn, not get out of order, & can be carried anywhere. This disseminates music among the people.

Music at all fam. prayers here—& so generally, in the island. Custom to have prayers just after tea, & visitors who happen in, attend them. So, if you go out to tea—at Austin's &c.

Called on Mrs. Coan, spent hour. Also on Mrs. Burdett— plays piano. (The Whaling captains wives sing commonplace songs, negro melodies &c.—but seem to have a notion that Mrs. Burdett's style of music is superior.)

Temperature of Hilo is perfect. Thermometer between 70°

at night & 80° at noon. Never intensely hot, & never a chill. Not dry, but always perspiration, if needed. Nights always comfortable, & no mosquitoes—or few. In winter solstice, in worst weather, never below 60° or 50°. No bad weather except in four months. Rest of year, no storms. Only drawback is the frequent showers. In that respect, is like England in May & June. These, however, are weak showers, & keep everything delightfully green.

Century plant runs up a high thin stalk or trunk, to reach the sun. When has reached it, (gone to 40 feet) the plant fades & dies, exhausted.

Sugar cane grows wild & large, & is very sweet. All natives, Hawaiian & white, are fond of it. Two kinds of guavas—little-one, not much larger than plum, very pleasant. Larger, like quince, *ut supra*.

Read Macaulay's article on Wm. Pitt, fr. Encycl. Brittanica. Capital performance, discriminating, &, on the whole, just. Also some of Tennyson's best—his only good things—his earliest.

Kanakas make flutes from bamboo & play tolerably on them.

Frid. Oct. 28.   Sailed in whaling bark Favorite, of N. London, Smith, master, for Honolulu. Parting calls on Mr. & Mrs. Austin, Mr. & Mrs. Coan, Dr. & Mrs. Wetmore, & Mrs. Burdett & Miss Pratt. Dr. Wetmore refuses to receive compensation of his prof. services to me. Has visited me to bandage & ex my broken toe ev. day. Says the bridge accid. was a common calamity, & glad to aid the sufferers.

Left Hilo, good light breese. Fine view fr. the water—the 3 extinct craters behind the town, the sch. hs. & meeting hs., the land marks. North of the river, are the high cliffs, the streams running into the sea, the sugar plantations &c. The only running streams wh. reach the sea in all Hawaii, are the Wailukeu, & the streams betw. that & the N. E. point of the island. (All but one of the sugar estates are Chinese enterprises).

Before leaving Hilo, called on the R.C. priest. A French gentleman, very intelligent, well educated, good books, knows the state of theol. controversy in Europe, the theology of his own Ch., & has good manners. Very small building, & few disciples—seemed unwilling to tell me the number. Insisted on my accepting fr. him "Bossuet's Exposition de la doctrine Catholique".

The bark Belle, Brown, sails at same time. At night, Brown visits us in his boat. Long pulls of these whalers in boats. Some captains left their ships 20 miles fr. Hilo & pulled in.

Favorite, old bark, strong, fair sailer. Ch. mate, Sherman, good quiet fellow—14 boys fr. Capt.'s town. Are contented, tho' had bad luck.

In whaler, hours diff. fr. merch. & man of war—8 bells at 11 o'ck., & so on. Capt., 3 mates, 4 boatsteerers, cooper, blacksmith & some 26 men forward. Not over 300 tons. Ch. M. no watch unless near land or in bad place, or bad weather. Third M. stands his watch. On whaling ground, lie to, & stand in quarter watches, on boats' crews, headed by boatsteerers.

Accomm., cooking, very inferior. Dress of all hands not seamanlike, yet are hardy men, & good sailors, as far as working ship is concerned. Tends to that, yet not to discipline or neatness,—is not a neat calling—oil, grease &c. Men dress & look like a gang of soapboilers.

David Lyman is with me, bound to Honolulu, to fit for voyage to U. States, in the Raduga, where he is to enter college. Capt. Smith has been in the Alert, after she became a whaler. Says her reputation was made in that business by my book—& her captain proud of her as of a toy. Also, the 3d. M., Perkins, has been in her.

Sat. Oct. 29. At noon, are abt. 15 m. fr. Kawaihae, & high M'ts. of Maui in sight. Capt. leaves in boat for Kawaihae, to get potatoes &c. ready for us. All aftern. working in, with light breeses. Manua Loa, & the steam fr. the outflow of lava into sea.

Native pilot comes off. Introduces himself to me. Was a boy on board the Ayacucho, in 1835, 6. I remember him perfectly, & the face of the man of 40, recalls the boy of 16. Goes over the events of those times, for wh. he has a good memory. Says all the Kanakas on the beach are dead or unheard fr. except old "Mr. Bingham", who is at Kawai.

Whalers use boom-lances a great deal—if cannot get near eno' for hand lance. Iron lance about 6 inches long, charged with powder, & fuse abt. 6 inches more. Put in a hand grenade at boat's head. Discharge ignites the fuse. Lance goes into whale, & explodes in 11 seconds. Mr. Sherman says are excellent. Complicated outfit of a whale boat—officer, boatsteerer, 5 men, a sail & its rigging & mast, 6 oars, several harpoons & lances, the lines & tubs, 2 brlls. of water,—knives, boom-lances & gun & powder.

Little discipline. Officer of watch lies down on deck & reads, in light weather, or lies down in quarter boat—never obliged to walk deck—& holds long yarns with passengers. Galley is aft, by side of wheel. Crew not kept at work. Lie & stand about decks, & work ship when called upon. Very easy times. Yet, strong, hardy men, & masters & officers are excellent seamen, as to weather, handling a vessel &c., as constant experience, in all weathers & places, more than in merch. service,—often where no pilots or charts.

Sunday. Oct. 30.   Becalmed all day off E. Maui & Laanai. Deeply-gorged, volcanic outlines & surfaces of Maui. See sketch of Lahainaluna.

The boats are the favorite sitting places. More air & better view than on deck. Capt. & mates sit in the quarter boats, & the boat-steerers in the waist boats. Boat-steerers keep in waist, live in after steerage & eat at 2d table in cabin.

Mond. Oct. 31.   Becalmed great deal. Oahu in sight, & a rainbow spanning over it.

Crew sing a great deal, in dog watch. Some good voices among them. Sentimental songs are rather the favorites—one about harp on willow,—

> "If I had loved with a boyish love,
>   It would have been better for me".

And one called "The maid of Maui". Poor fellows, been 2 years out, & only 400 bbls., the vessel holding 2500 or 3000!

Tuesd. Nov. 1.   Off Honolulu at daylight. Several vessels going in, one the Josiah Bradlee, 170 days fr. Boston, the rest are whale ships.

Down boat & pull ashore, some 10 miles.

Honolulu again. Diamond Head, the valley, Waikiki, Punahou, the surf on the reefs, & the inner harbor now full of whale ships, 50 or more.

Am the guest of Mr. Bates, the lawyer—(Ashur D. Bates). He has a large, handsome house, up the valley, with good view of ocean, & well cultivated grounds. Again, the ringing hoofs of the fast riders on the valley road, the native women, riding astride, with long folds of yellow & striped cloth, & a garland on the head, & necklace of flowers or berries. Every person in Honolulu, man or woman, native or foreign, I should think, is on horseback once a day. Their calls are made so. Mr. & Mrs. Bishop (Pauwahi) canter up this evening. Judge Robertson &c. Each child in the family has a horse.

Mr. Bates' family is wife (now in U.S.), wife's sister, (who keeps house now), a deformed woman, sister of Dr. Judd, a son, Dudley, 21 yrs., a merchant, 2 boys of 8 or 10, a daughter, Lucilla, 13, & Mary, 6. House handsomely furnished, table well ordered & tended.

Ladies wear garlands of Cape Jessamines. The ginger of commerce bears a large flower, of exquisite fragrance. Mosquitoes so thick that no sleeping without nets. Even in Sailor's Home, have mosquito nets. No mosquitoes in Hilo.

Young Sleeper is dead—son of Sleeper of Roxbury, & brother of Mrs. Austin. He was ass. editor of the chief newspaper here.

No one here (in these islands) says "fine day", "pleasant morning", or the like, for they are matters of course. Only in midwinter is there any unpleasant weather, & not much then.

The Clipper ship Viking of Boston, is expected here from S. Francisco every day, & in her I hope to be able to get passage to China.

Thursd. Nov. 3. Salute fr. battery. King arrived, in his little sch., from Lahaina. Shown my foot to Dr. Ford. Bruise is healed & doing well. The fracture was simple, & cartelage is forming & will soon be strong eno' to admit of walking. At present, keep still, walking only as much as is necessary. Mr. Bates keeps a horse & chaise at my disposal all day.

The Ships are the life of this place, & their only means of communication with the world. Every child in Honolulu knows that the Viking is the next ship expected fr. S. Fr., & that she is going to China, & all watch the harbor for her, & for whalers.

Frid. Nov. 4. Dined at Allen's (Ch. Justice). Present—Allen *et ux.*, Judge Robertson, Harris, Bates, Lt. Reynolds (U. S. N.) et ux. Pleasant time. Like Robertson. Came here before the mast, learned all his law after 30, & is now a very satif. judge—good sense & industry. Knows the Hawaiian language well. Lt. Reynolds is an agreeable man, also. Mrs. Allen is well edd. & good manners. They have an eldest son, baby, whom people call the Prince of Kahoolawe, fr. a poor island the judge has leased.

Am told that the coolies brot here did not exceed 600 or 800, in all the group. They came intelligently & voluntarily, but as bound laborers for 5 or 8 years—to be used on plantations. Reason was that the natives were lured off to California & wd. not work at home. But coolies not do well under these contracts—as found themselves too valuable. The contracts ran out or were given up or bought out, & all Chinese here now are free laborers, & very good laborers, especially as house servants.

All the gentln. at table agree as to the mildness & gentleness of the natives, & also that they are grateful for what they consider to be real kindnessess—not for mere gifts, perhaps, for they think we have an abundance.

The worst said ag. the natives is that in times of wreck, danger of drowning &c. they wait for offers & insist of high pay before they go off, & stories are told of their letting people drown for want of suff. reward offered. I think these stories—(which are well vouched) are of the regular *beach-combers*, who live by diving & swimming, & not of others.

Sunday. Nov. 6. 9.30 A.M. went to a Native Ch. of wh. Rev. Mr. Smith is pastor. Services as usual in congr. societies, & the conduct of the people open to the ordinary objection, coming in at all times, no outward signs of reverence & scarcely of attention, & clergymen apparently indiff. to it. Mr. Smith preached in black sack coat & spurs,—this (spurs) is because all ride here, & he is not attentive eno' to externals to take them off. Yet, he is & has been for 20 years, a faithful laborer & teacher among the natives.

At 11 A.M. went to the R. Cath. Church. Well filled. Few chairs, &, in galleries, seats—but mostly sit down on mats on floor, & kneel. This is agreeable to the natives. Also, the native women here do not wear bonnets as in the Prot. Churches, & look better for it. The sea of bonnets is too ludicrous, in forms & colors. The natives enjoy the music, & many seem very devout in their private prayers & readings. A girl of about 18 was baptised, dressed in white, native sponsors &c.

The words used in all these islands are "Natives" & "foreigners", to distinguish the races. Whites born here are called foreigners. The natives called the first whites "haole"—foreigners, & they too have kept up that term for our race, irrespective of birth. "*Kanaka*" means "man", in their language & is not used except among sailors & by people out of the islands, California, in Atlantic States & in all ships, where it is the only term for the Polynesian race.

No afternoon services in any of the relig. soc. of Honolulu, but one at night. Went to the Fort St. Ch., the principal Ch. of the foreigners. Rev. Mr. Corwin preached. He is of Wms. College, formerly settled in S. José, Cal.—of the New School— H. W. Beecher style, good faculty for public speech, & quick mind.

Words in common use here—for a mem.

Yes—ai
No—aole
I—Wai
You—oe
He, she—ia
We—makou, kakou
Who?—owai
When?—ahéa
Where?—auhéa
What?—héaha
How much?—héaha ka uku
At what hour?—eka hora ehía
This—keia
That—kela
Here—manéi
There—maláila
Hither—mai
Thither—aku
Towards—ma, i

From (a place)—mai
Distant, away—máo
To-day—keia la
To-morrow—apópo
And—me, ame
But—aká
Be quick!—wiki viki
Done, finished—pau

Verbs

Bring, take—láawi
Bring here—laawi mai
Give—haáwi
Give me—haawi mai
Stop, wait—alía
Come—héle
Come here—hele mai
Go—hele
Go away, go off—hele áku

Talk, speak—olélo
Sleep—kiamoe
Die—make
Eat—ai
Take care—málama
Swim—aau
Pray—bule
Wish—make make
Conciliate, flatter—mavi mavi
Work—hana hana
Kill—hana maki
Make fast—hana pa
Sew—humi humi

Nouns

Water—wai
Wind—makáni!
Sea—kai
Rain—ua
Sun—la
Moon—mahína
Star —ukú
Day—la
Night—po
Week—hepedoma (for.)
Month—mahína, maláma
Year—makahiki
Fire—ahi
Canoe—waa
Boat—waapá
Vessel—moku
Fish—ia
Dog—ilío
Horse—lio
Mule—hoki

Baggage—ukána
Road, path—ala
Male—kane
Female—wahíni
Man—kanáka
Name—inóa
Foreigner, white man—haole
Light, lamp—kukúi
Spirit, God—Akúa
Child, offspring—keike
Father—makúa kane
Mother—makúa wahini
Trouble—pilikía
Church (the institution)—ekelésia (for.)
Church (the building)—hale pule
House—hale

Adjectives

Good—maikai
Bad—aole maikai
Fortunate, blessed—pomaikai
Skillful, clever—akamai
Large—nui
Small—uúku.
Afraid—makau
Ashamed—hila hila
Fast (secure)—pa
Solitary, alone—méha méha
Quick—wiki wiki
All—a páu
Land-ward—mauka
Sea-ward—makai

Mond. Nov. 7. To Punahou, with Mr. Corwin. He teaches Scripture History, but it is only the Old Test., long & diff. researches into obscure parts of Babalonian & Syrian history. They know nothing of the history of Apostolic times except what their own reading may give them. The old Judaising tendencies.

The whole school together. At request of Prof. made a short

address to the scholars, wh. was well received, in favor of classical studies & liberal, aesthetic culture.

Lunch at Mr. Corwin's. Nice wife & little children,—come fr. Orange Co. N.Y.

To the monthly musical society, at Dr. Guillon's. The usual company. Playing good—singing not so good as before. A sea captain introduced to me on ground that he was master of the Alert when she was in the whaling trade. Tells me she has always been a lucky ship & a favorite—is known in the whole whaling fleet as Dana's ship Alert.

Anderson, the magician, is here & astonishes the natives a good deal.

Very few birds on these islands—certainly very few in Oahu. Seldom hear a note.

Girls of 12 to 16 years ride on horseback here alone, to go to school, shopping, or to visit friends. Horses so cheap that most families have several,—4 or 5, & they feed like cows, in the fields.

Spent ev. at house of Mr. Castle, a trader, who came here as the secular, business man of the Mission. Honest & intelligent—but fearfully Yankee-country-deacon*ish*. Cd. not stand him long.

Wed. Nov. 9. Called on Dr. Ford. Says the bone has united, & that I shall be able to walk as usual in 2 or 3 days. This is cause of gratitude, indeed.

Called on Mr. Bishop—out; on the Halls, in; on the Allens, in,—long conv. on theology.

Many native words are in use among foreigners here, as certain French words with us. *Makai* & *mauka*, for landward & seaward, as to the position of houses, streets, lots &c.—*pilikía* for difficulty & trouble, *akamái* for clever, skillful, *pomaikai* for fortunate, *hu hu* for angry, *pau* & *pau voa* for done, ended &c., & the salutation *alóha* is in very general use, written in presentation books, & used in taking leave, it is so pretty.

Went to school of "Les Soeurs des Sacres Coeurs", a diff. order from that of the "Du Sacre Coeur", or a branch, perhaps, of that order. There are six teachers, & a school of 40 girls, all of foreign families—that is—whites. The sisters wear white gowns of some woolen fabrick, & white caps. They have been here only six months, & are all French or German-French.

All speak in high terms of Mr. Damon, the Seaman's Chaplain here. He is the right man in the right place, & has as much as he can do, in the whaling season. He buries all the poor outcast sailors, taking their shipmates to the grave, in the procession, giving hours to each. Saw him heading one yesterday, mounted, with umbrella, in the sun. He is an honest man & a good one.

Thursday. Nov. 10.   Calls on a Mr. & Mrs. Bishop, old people, missionaries, whose district is Ewa, beyond the Pali, but who live up the valley. Also on Mrs. Judge Allen, & a Mrs. Patsy, (whose husb. used to command the Don Quixote)—all these calls made with Mrs. Judd, senr., a very old & vigorous woman, a gr. gr. mother.

This evening Mr. Bates took Mr. & Mrs. Bishop,—not the old missionaries, but our friend, the Chief*ess* & her husband— & me to ride, by moonlight, to Waikiki, the sea-bathing place. Bright clear moon, cloudless sky, soft air. We sat an hour or so on the sand-beach; under the cocoa-nut trees. A native walking off into the water, before us, & swimming off out of sight, going to catch fish, just as if he had a boat. Funny notion that Pauwahi (Mrs. Bishop) would throw off her clothes & jump in & swim off to the reefs, into the surf. Her mother, certainly her gr. mother would have done it. She pretends she can't swim.

(Last ev. rode with Harris to the Manóa Valley, near Punahou).

This kingdom, the whole group of the Hawaiian islands, was held by a strictly feudal tenure. All the land belonged to the king. He allotted portions to his chiefs, who held on condition of rendering military service & giving certain returns of fruits &c. The chiefs made subinfeudations to the common people, who were mere tenants at will, also rendering similar services to the feudal lord. The analogy with the feudal style of Europe is exact, only it was not tempered by the aid of the judicial distinctions wh. in Europe created rights in the tenants.

Each district had its name, & so had each subdivision. For instance, Honolulu was the name of a small space, containing about ¼ of the present town. Muuanu was the upper part, Punahou the Eastern &c.

Lately the titles were arranged betw. the king & the chiefs, by a division, or partition, & now the chief holds absolute, allodial titles. The rights of the common people are secured in the lands they have held a certain number of years. But a great part of the common people are still tenants on chiefs' lands or the king's lands. But the operation of the direct tax system is to compel sales, for it is not income but principal that is taxed. The chiefs are taxed on the market value of their unimproved lands.

The families of chiefs are dying out. They do not increase. So of the common people. This is their own fault, or their misfortune wh. leads to fault. They ruin themselves in early life, & the women do not become mothers, or mothers of many children.

Frid. Nov. 11. Called, with Mrs. Judd senr., on Rev. Mr. Corwin & lady, Mr. Commissn. Borden & lady, a Mrs. Severance, Mrs. Dr. Smith, (née Patsy.)

Went to Punahou again. Heard some declamations, & at req. of teacher, addressed the scholars on subject of reading aloud, declamation, enunciation, pronunciation &c. Spent ev. at home of Mrs. Gulick, a missionary family, with 2 sons & a daughter at the school. Prof. Alexander & Mr. Haskell, a teacher, spent the ev. with us. Several girls of the school came in & spent ev. Their entertainment was to get me to describe persons, places & occurrences I had seen in England & U. States. They seemed interested. Among them were girls of the Hawaii families I had visited, Lyman, Coan & Paris; also a d. of Mr. Parker, the Missy at —— beyond the Pali, a superior girl, a sister of Prof. Alexander, &c.

Been warm South winds for sev. days, dog-day weather, & people complain, & sickness about. I have not felt it, & few foreigners do at first. All are longing for a return of the trade winds.

Sat. Nov. 12. Rain last night, & this morning the delightful, cool trades are blowing again.

Reading De Tocqueville's U. States. Very able book, especially on the Judiciary, & the *town system* of the North. Entirely wrong on the President's power,—a capital mistake, owing to his following the written constitution too much, & underrating the patronage & power over Congress.

Took tea at house of Clark, Post Master, son of the pastor of the King's Ch.

Sunday. Nov. 13. See that Mr. Bates is sensitive abt. my going to Ch. with his family. So go all day to Fort st. Sermon by Mr. Corwin. Impressive manner direct & earnest.

Pain in limbs all day, head ache & soreness of throat. Symptoms of Maui fever.

Wednesday Nov. 16. Last 3 days a-bed with Maui fever. Called a slight attack, but I think it rather severe, for a mere bilious derangement, tho' not for a fever. Kept abed & still, & obeyed orders. Was blessed by a quiet frame of mind—no glooms or despondencies, or home-sickness. Also, no trouble in my head except the bilious head ache,—I mean, no weight on it,—no congestion.

Last night, Yankee arrived, bringing Mrs. Bates, & a Miss Beals, a niece of the first Mrs. Bates. Mrs. B. has been in the U. States.

No clipper expected to touch here bound to China. Must return to S. Francisco. Great loss of time & money. My first serious disappointment. A vessel sails to-day, but all her berths are taken. Fear I must wait here a week or ten days longer, & then retrace my steps. But, shall I have good & not evil? I must be patient & grateful, for I have had much pleasure & been favored in every way. To-day, am up. No head ache.

Young Mr. Bates writes up that he has got me a passage in the bark Architect, wh. sails to-day for S. Francisco. This is better than nothing. Pack up my clothes, & go down in town. Just learned that a lumberman, bound from Puget Sound to Hong Kong, hove to off the reef for two hours, & landed her captain who goes to S. Fr. I am just too late. She has filled away & gone beyond the Point. Several persons knew this, but none in season to tell me. This confirms me in the opinion that I had better return to S. Fr., for even if a China-bound vessel comes here, she may be off before I can communicate with her. Take the advice of several merchants. All say that no certainty of a vessel for China, at this season. May have to wait here two months. To go to S. Fr. is a certain loss of five weeks, perhaps of more. To stay leaves all uncertain. I may get off in a day. I may not in two months. Determined to go.

Hurried leave of such persons as I meet. Mr. Bates comes to the dock, so Rev. Mr. Corwin, Harris & al. Had promised to speak at the anniversary of the opening of the Sailor's Home. It was due to Mr. Damon, & his excellent house & Mission. My sailing makes this impossible.

Wed. Nov. 16.   4 P.M. Sailed out of Honolulu harbor, in the bark Architect, bound to S. Fran. Last view of Muuanu Valley, Punch Bowl Hill, Punahou, & the Diamond Head.

Heavy blow & heavy sea. Double reefed topsails. My bilious derangement at Oahu affects me with sea-sickness, as badly as if it were my first trip at sea. For two days, I have been very sea-sick, or rather very sick, how much is owing to sea, & how much to Maui fever, I don't know; but I have a fair notion of what sea-sickness is, except that the motion is not disagreeable. There is no head-effect. It is merely a sickness of stomach, as one might have on shore. I like the motion, but am miserably weak & bilious—yet glad to find that I have no unpleasant sensations in the head, a proof that my head troubles of last summer are over.

After two days, got over my sickness, & am very well. Sleep & eat well, & keep in good spirits. Yet it is the dullest of voyages. Going right back over my track, & a loss of so much time in getting to China! Nor have I any desire to see Calif. again. Yet, I must have patience. I have had good fortune, & must expect some ill fortune.

Architect a bark of about 400 tons, & 4 years old, been a whaler, & just fr. the Arctic. Fitted up & sent to S. Fr. to be sold. Fish, of N. London, is master, Smith of N. L., Chief Mate, & a queer old duke named Brown, is 2d mate. All are whalemen. For cabin passengers, we have a Mrs. Palmer of N. Bedford, whose husband has just been killed by a whale in the Arctic, leaving her a widow with a boy of 5 years, & an infant of 11 mos., to find her way home. She has her children with her. She is in charge of a Capt. Blackmer, of Fair Haven, an *ex whale-master*, bound home over land. Next is a German, master of the Puget Sound lumberman, (suprá), name is Stege, a dull fellow. Then, two mates of whalemen, bound home over-land, Mellen & Sherman & a tall, N. Carolina sand-hiller, who has strangely strayed off whaling, before the mast, had enough of it, & written home for money, got it, procured his discharge & goes home overland. His name is Applewhite. The only one of this co. who is *talkable* is Blackmer. He is an intelligent, well informed man. Fish is a good fellow, & means well, but dull. Rest are nothing. All I can get from them is whaling anec-dotes. Have learned a good deal about the Arctic & Ochotsk whaling, among ice & walrus. Hundreds of our ships there from June to Oct. of every year. Whale a good deal in open boats, along the bays, sleeping on shore, & off from the ship for many days together.

Mrs. Palmer seems a worthy woman, & has rather a hard time with her infant & boy, with no servant. The children do not add agreeableness to the passage. Steward an odious man, & a little halfwitted cabin boy, the steward's serf,—the lowest depth to wh. human nature can fall—a cabin-boy in a whaler, under a bad steward. The boy seldom washes, & if he does, whose towel does he use? How idle he is, unless under the steward's eye, & then to hear his half-witted laugh, as he tries to enjoy the steward's talk & doings!

Sunday. Nov. 27.   Advent Sunday! What thoughts of home, & the church in Boston, & its service to-day,—its 15th anniver-sary! Went over all the service carefully.

Tuesd. Nov. 29.   Dull work. Adhere to strict routine, to pass my time. How well Kane learned that & expressed the truth. I must exclude reading, as part of my health regime,—so have little to aid me. Make up fictitious divisions of time. Rise at 6. Toilet of salt & fresh water. On deck, & at unobserved spot, stand & say over the morning service—(all that is appropr. to one person), & a few other prayers, varied by a chant, Te Deum or Gloria in Excelsis,—always beginning so beautifully & appropriately with—"From the rising of the Sun &c.", as it is always sun-rise at the moment. By this time is 7 o'ck. Walk deck until breakfast. After breakfast, walk deck until 10. At 10, read the Morning Lessons & Psalter. Then allow myself to read until 7 bells, 11.30, when go on deck, interest myself in the observations for altitude, & sometimes work up the latitude. Keep on deck until dinner, 1 o'ck. After dinner, allow myself to read or write until 3 o'ck. From 3 to nearly dark, on deck. Interest myself in the altitudes & time taken at 4 o'ck., & get out the chart, & mark our position, & speculate on winds & courses. Before dark, below & read the Ev. lessons & psalter. Walk deck until tea time. After tea, passengers are agreeable a while, if ever. But usually have to rely on walking deck until 8 o'ck. Blackmer often walks with me, & we talk everything threadbare. Sometimes Fish takes a few turns, but after the past, present & future winds are discussed, & the Ochotsk & Arctic are abandoned, he is out—*pau*. Soon after 8 o'ck., alone, on deck, go over the Ev. Service, & then turn in. I rather like this life, for a while. Pleasure in making the most of my resources.

My short reading times are given to Dr. Kane's Arctic Expeditions. This makes me well content in my own situation. An episode of heroism, is Kane's voyage.

(In my Hawaii journal, did I mention the *fleas?* In the native huts, they abound. Was bitten all over, yet can sleep with them —do not affect me badly. Clothes full of them, when got to Hilo.)

The sandhiller is full of dull stories about quarrels, fights & duels in Texas, where he spent two years, yet he is an amiable man, & spends sev. hours ev. day in tending Mrs. P.'s baby.

Head winds all the time. Only 20 h. of fair winds since we left Honolulu, 17 days.

Sat. Dec. 3. Wh bark Ripple, in sight. Capt. Fish & Capt. Blackmer go on board to "gam". Nearly calm. Capt. Morgan of the Ripple returns the compliment & stays until 11 P.M., & all but me are drinking in the cabin & making noise,—while we are losing a fair wind, the first for 10 days. Morgan is a "pious" man, speaks at prayer-meetings, & refuses to whale on Sundays, & bores awfully by exhibiting his religion to everyone, even strangers,—full of the conventional cant,—yet he got pretty tight last night. They had a smart lark, (on Blackmer's part) abt. a pig, wh. was carried to & fro in various attempts to get him fr. the Ripple, in wh. our side at last succeeded. Struggle for pig, & he fell down fore hatch.

Sunday. Dec. 4.   Fine day & good, fresh, fair wind. All in good spirits. Ripple alongside, Capt. Morgan comes on board to dinner, but no delay, as both vessels keep on. I keep clear of Morgan.

Mrs. Palmer improves on acq., & seems to have good plain educ., & good sense & feelings.

Wed. Dec. 7.   Make the land little below Monterey, some 75 or 80 miles S. of S. Francisco. Bad luck. Calm all day & night.

Calms & head-winds all Wed. Th. Fri. & Sat. Very hard to bear, & our port so near. I could be content no where, in such a case as this, but *at sea.*

Sat. night, strong wind & fair. Good progress.

California and the Pacific:
December 1859–March 1860

Sunday. Dec. 11. Arrive at S. Francisco. Pass "heads" at sunrise, beat in ag. strong head winds. Noble bay, & striking points—yet no wish to see it again. Land at noon. Tehama Hs., kept on European plan—more convenient & econom. for me. Comfort of dressing & washing & room eno'. In Architect, had no state-room, but slept in cabin, & no private place at all.

A good dinner, neat furniture, fresh meats & vegit., & excellent cooking, at French Restaurant. No one can conceive of the comfort of it, who has not been through a bad voyage at sea.

Landed too late for the A.M. Service. No aftern. service. At 7 P.M. went to vespers in R.C. Cathedral. Full, but not like the music. An Irish sermon. Said Scripture assures us that ¾ of the seed is lost. The parable says that three of the 4 *parts* are lost—but not wh. was the larger, or that were equal.

Mond. Dec. 12. Ride horse-back to Mission, before breakfast. Horses good & cheap. No vessel up for China. Fear long delay. Glorious weather here—like our warm October weather, & grapes, pears & apples in market, & flowers growing in open air. Dine tete-a-tete with Felton. Introduced to Judge Norton, thought to be the best judge in Cal.

Tuesd. Dec. 13. Ride to Cemetery, horse-back. Fine view fr. Cemetery of Pacific Ocean, Bay, City & Golden Gate. Site good, but no trees over 15 feet high—all scrub. Must be so here, I fear.

Dr. Morison, br. of Rev. of Milton, &c. takes me to ride to the beach. By far the grandest surf ever saw. Breakers break 8 or 9 deep, & the outer ones are fearfully high.

Dine with Felton, Abel Guy, the very rich banker, Koopmanschap, a German merchant who is aiding me to go to China, & a Mr. Liés, a lawyer of S. Barbara, French origin educated in Paris, speaks English perfectly, & is very clever, brilliant, drank rather too much & is a mere pleasure seeker. These are F.'s friends,—all too fast & too loose for my tastes. Edward Hoar, brother of Rockwood, left here the reputation of brilliant talents & reckless life,—the Sargent Prentiss of Young California.

Felton's first introduction to a Judge of the Supreme Court, Wells, a few days after his arrival here, in 1853. Wells was leaning ag. a wall, with a revolver in his hand, & inquiring for "that g—d—s—b—" that had told a story about him—gave his other hand to Felton.

Usual interest here, on good security is 2 percent a month, & that allowed to compound. Principal doubles in betw. 2 & 3 years.

Reasons given are (1) want of any system of credit, by wh. paper doubles & triples the actual specie (2) the risk there is as regards the value of all security, merchandise, fr. fluctuations in market, & real-estate from that cause & the doubts over all titles. Fluctuations in mdse. owing to being no market near here, & all goods sent here must be sold *here* or kept.

Wed. Dec.   Yesterday I returned my horse to wrong stable. They took it, thinking I meant to lodge him there. Called at the right stable to-day, & found they had been in alarm. Did not know me, even by name, & the owner had been censuring the hostler for letting a horse to a stranger without getting his name, & the hostler had just said "Well, if I could not trust that man, I could not trust my own father. If a man ever had an honest face, he had. He looked like one of our *first bankers*". I entered, just at the height of it, as they were about sending off for a search, & said—"I'll take that horse again, if he is in".

"He has not been here. He is not returned".

I insisted that I returned him, but on looking further, I saw I had gone to a stable just like it, at the next block, where the horse was quietly breakfasting. They were a good deal relieved.

Rode to a high hill, wh. gave grand view of Bay & entrance & town.

Bark Early Bird is up for Hong Kong—for Jan. 1st. This is probably the earliest vessel. Great loss of time. Yet, consolation is that I am in a healthful, invigorating climate, with nothing to trouble me, & suff. employt. to keep me fr. being dull. Shall employ interval in going to Sacramento, Almeden mines, Navy Yard, &c.

On board the Architect, after finishing Kane, found, in possession of a whaling mate, the fat, one vol. ed. of Byron's life, letters & poems, complete. Dealt out to myself Childe Harold, one canto a day. That done, began the letters. Read about 350 (say ½) of them, when voyage ended. Childe Harold a great production. Spots of highest genius, & nowhere poor, & always an easy mastery of versification. The letters of earlier life, before his return to England—not so good. Vain, egotistical, & not striking. Those written after he left England in 1816, fr. Germany, Switserland, & Italy, are extremely clever,—witty & often excellent thought as to poetry. He appreciated Crabbe fully. So he did Kean, as an actor, & came to appreciate Coleridge. His mind was less corrupted on the subject of poetry than on any other. It was the last citadel that fell. He was honest there. In a letter to Moore, he rather explains away what he says to Murray about Pope's superiority—yet it is not satisfactory. But what an unhappy wretch! I believe he had a conscience, after all, & that it haunted him & made him desperate at times.

Contrast his lines on his 36th birthday, with the words of St. Paul,—"I am now ready to be offered, & the time of my departure is at hand. I have fought a good fight, I have finished my course, I have kept the faith. Henceforth there is laid up for me &c."

How tired I got of hearing whaling stories. One man kept on, in a dull monotone, long stories, to me alone, the effect of wh. on my mind may be represented thus. "——whale——the whale——whales—the whale——the whale——."

Yet, the whaling in the Extreme North is a gallant service. Ev. year ships are lost in the ice, & men killed by whales & by bears. Whaling masters are the best of seamen, as regards working a ship & ground tackle, but not as regards the mechanic art of fitting rigging, & they have much less discipline, order & almost no etiquette. Without these, men alone, out of society & business, as in camp or at sea, soon degenerate & are demoralised. Poor Capt. Fish had none of those. His steward *snubbed* him, his cabin boy defied him, men did as they pleased, there were no *stations*, but all went by hap hasard. Whaling crews wear such hats, coats & trowsers as laboring men wear on shore, or loafers—seen them with green plaid pantaloons, Kossuth hats &c.—nothing shipshape.

Spent ev. at Bishop Kip's. Met a Mr. Olney, a R.I. man, who held high mil. command under the Vig Comm. Vig. Comm. had determined to destroy the U.S. ship John Adams, if she fired on the town. Olney says most of the naval & mil. officers sympathised with the Vig. Comm.

Meet, in street, Mr. Stien, of Brattleboro' Vt. He has come here to reside. Invited me to call upon his wife, & says her health is much better in California.

Thurs. Dec. 15.   Rode to Presidio. Troops target shooting. Clipper coming in under her fore & aft sails—pretty sight, hear song of sailors. Fine situation of Presidio.

Breakfast with Gov.-elect Latham, Judge Parsons, Felton, Liés, Hempstead, & Casserly—very pleasant—extravagant breakfast,—given by Parsons. Conv. clever, but on pers. topics, anecdotes &c., only. Stories of fights in Courts. Man drew pistol on Parsons. Two lawyers fought before Hagar J, in Court, & he let it go through. In another case, before Hagar J., this conversation took place:

Wilson (counsellor), "I desire a delay on account of absence of my client."

Blake (counsellor) "Of course she is absent. She is on a tour of f——n through the States".

Wilson. "You are a liar".

Blake "I claim the protection of the Court".

Hagar J. "I don't see that any injury has been done on either side, yet".

Letters home by overland mail of Dec. 16, to wife, Palfrey, Capt. Davis, & Barnum W. Field, & journal to Dec. 15.

Did I mention supra the anecdote of my returning a horse to the wrong stable, & going for him the next day & the man's trust in my looks?

Walk thro' the narrow alleys betw. Jackson & Pacific st. at night, where the Chinese live, in little rooms. These are coolies, under contracts, & kept at this business by their owners & importers.

Frid. Dec. 16. Visit camp of the "Digger Indians" in outskirts of the city. Several hundreds, captured & transported to a "Reserve" as thievish & predatory. Very ugly & rather squalid.

Call on Mrs. Major Lennard & Mrs. Lawler (Miss Price), & dine with latter. Nice little house, with view of harbor, bay & town, being on top of Telegr. Hill. Frankly says she has been perfectly happy in her marriage, & seems to be so, & Lawler says he shall always keep her so. Pleasant to see line begin in that way. She gave up a great deal for him.

Streets of S. Fr. covered with plank boards, & frequent "man-traps" & "horse-traps" in carriageways & side-walks. All S. Fr. is built on sand, what is not built on water, & hence the planking.

3d Artillery, Col. Merchant, at the Presidio. Calls fr. Drs. Holman & Hastings, Mr. Fred. Billings (lawyer), Bond, Capt. Thomas of J. Adams &c. &c.

Sat. Dec. 17. Attended Court to hear Judge Norton give his weekly batch of opinions. He is said by all classes, parties & callings, to be the best & ablest judge that ever sat in California. The confidence in his integrity & ability is unlimited. His great feat of memory consists in giving opinions in a long list of cases, having before him only the names of parties, referring to names, dates, places, amounts, points taken, cases relied upon, & his own reasons—all *ore tenus.* It is almost beyond belief. To-day, he gave about 10 or 15 opinions, all in that way. His language is concise & clear, & reasoning good. He decides about 1500 cases a year. In most cases, the parties have a choice of tribunals, among the District Courts, & Norton is such a favorite that the other Court is a sinecure.

Being the Sabbath, went, for the first time in my life, to a Jew. Synagogue. Found the clergyman there, Rev. H. A. Henry before service began, & got information fr. him, & present of a book of his for relig. instrn. of Hebrew youth. In middle is high box, where the clergyman reads & says all the service. Box is large eno' for 3 or 4 persons, cushioned desk for reading &c. At one end, opp. the door, is curtain, which, drawn, shows the 5 books of Moses, written on parchment & rolled on wooden rollers. I was too late for the morning service, & at the ev. service were only some 10 or 12 men & no women. All sit, with hats on, except that stand when curtain drawn & rolls taken out, & ditto when returned. All the service is in Hebrew, (wh. all Jews know, I presume) & all is chanted or intoned, even to the reading of the Scriptures. The parts, as in reading Scripture, the Clergyman reads alone, but the prayers & Psalms are chanted (or intoned) either responsively, or by clergym. & people together. They sit in prayer, with hats on, only occasionally bending heads. They talk in the intervals, & move about, & the whole seemed to me irreverend. A spectator wd. hardly know that it was a relig. service. It might be a school of adults.

Mr. Henry admits that they have lost the distinction of tribes, & the priesthood. The sacrifices are given up for two reasons, (1) because were to be offered only in Judea & (2) no High Priest. They divide the 10 Commandments in a diff. manner fr. both Catholics & Protestants. Their first is the mere declaration, in 20 Exodus 2d. Their second, is verses 3, 4, 5 & 6 united, as the R. Catholics unite them. The others follow as in all churches, to the 10th, which embraces verse 17. Protestants & Catholics do not treat verse 2 as a Commandment, therein differing fr. the Jews. Jews & Catholics agree in making one commandment of verses 3, 4, 5 & 6, therein differing from most Protestants. Jews & Protestants agree in making one commandment of verse 17, wh. Catholics divide into two. Swedenborgians unite verses 3–6, but whether they make their 10th by dividing the 17th or by adopting the 2d, I do not remember. The rabbi told me the Catholics were right in uniting the 3–6 verses, according to the mass. & traditions.

The countenances of the Jews at this service were intensely disagreeable,—indeed, are they not (the men, I mean) almost always so. The clergyman (rabbi?) was not disagreeable in expression, probably from not being in trade. Their worship is dull, formal & unhappy,—the worship of a disheartened people.

Did I mention that, in coming upon the coast, we had a mirage of the Light Hs. on Faroallon? The Light Hs. is a cone. By the mirage it looked an hour-glass,—two cones, one the actual building, & the other the inverted image, touching it?

To-day, in my morning's ride, saw men ploughing & others hoeing betw. rows of vegitables just coming up (Dec. 17th).

There has been no rain for more than two weeks, the finest of our Oct. weather—yet this is the rainy season.

Sunday. Dec. 18. Ride to Mission Dolores before breakfast. All building fitted into Chapel, & Mass saying there.

Trinity Church at 11 A.M. Rev. Mr. Thrall preaches. Fair congregation, rather *genteel,* no audible responses, excellent singing & playing, but choice of tunes & chants as bad as can be. No church like the Advent!

3 P.M. to Vespers at Notre Dame des Victoires, the French Church. The contrast betw. that & the Cathedral is that betw. a Paddy Church & a French Church. At Notre Dame des Victoires everything is as neat, clean, & orderly as it is possible to imagine. The vestments of priest & altar boys beautiful & in better taste than I ever saw in a R. Cath. Church, & the music excellent. Chanting, all Gregorian, slow & grave, & several beautiful hymns sung, in one of wh. I found myself shedding tears, mais pourquoi—je ne sais pas. What with the good taste, the neatness, the devout attention of the Congregation, the exquisite music, the odour of the incense, & the slow & reverent steps & genuflections of the priests,—the effect was better than ever saw in a R. Cath. Church. Short, familiar sermon, in French, by the Abbé Blaine.

7.30 P.M., to the Confirmation at Grace Church, with my friend Capt. Blanding, late U.S. Distr. Att., & Capt. in the Palmetto Regt., in the Mex. war,—an excellent fellow. Odd, that the two most religious, moral & gentlemanlike men I have met at the Bar here, should be from S. Carolina, Blanding & Pringle,—both are vestrymen of Grace Church. Church crowded, singing worse than at Trinity, i.e., voices & playing very good, selections of tunes abominable. They know absolutely nothing of the resources of music in the church, by way of chant & hymn,—sounded like second rate opera. Twenty six confirmed, & among them an *ex* M C & leading lawyer, & another lawyer, a reclaimed inebriate. Rest were young. The sermon & address by Bishop Kip.

Took tea with Blanding, at Martin's. He told me about the battles his regt. was in, from Vera Crus to Mexico City. He joined with 1100 men, & brot home 250. At Churubusco, more than half the Regt. on the ground was killed or wounded, including Col., Lt. Col. & Major. Quitman was the best vol. general, after Persifor Smith. Shields, rash & careless of lives, & not trustworthy as to truth, if his own reput. concerned.

Mond. Dec. 19.   Ride to Presidio. Warm, June morning & cloudless sky. So far, S. Fr. winter is delightful.

Tu. Dec. 20.   Sent journal & letters to wife & Mr. Parker, by steamer.

10 A.M. took steamer for Mare Island (Navy Yard). On board found Mr. Edw. Stanly, late M. C. fr. N. Car., now of Cal., on his way to his ranch, in Napa Valley, Gen. Vallejo (Don Guad. Mariano) & his son-in-law Frisbie, &, above all, old Mr. Yount, the famous pioneer & woodsman, the first white settler in Napa Valley. All invited, & insisted on my going to Napa. Glad to do it—as Napa Valley is the pride of Cal., & the Geysers one of its greatest curiosities, & old Yount is alone worth a journey there. Agreed to meet Stanly at Napa City tomorrow.

Landed at Navy Yard, Mare Island. Spent night at Com. Cunningham's, where met Miss West, fellow-passenger fr. N. York.

The Russian officers, fr. the 2 men-of-war steamers, were spending day there, Com. Popoff, 2 lieuts., & 8 or 10 middies, all young,—all spoke more or less Engl. & French, inquiring & polite. Com. P. & one lieut. were at Sebastopal.

Exd., with them, the docks. Russians lunched, waltsed & took leave early, to go back to S. Fr. (Old Com. C., alone at end of table, oblivious of all guests, barely knowing anything, sticking to his bottle after all left).

Com. C. takes the Naval Constructor, Hanscomb, & goes all over the new steamer, the Saginaw, with me. Neat boat, side wheel, light draft, first naval vessel built by us in Pacific. Go to Model Loft &c. Yard very large, & on a plan of magnif. proportions, if ever completed. Make acq. of Col. Turner, a Virginian, his wife d. of Key, the poet. He is Engineer, & a very kindly, hosp. & honorable man. Wife clever, & good children. Also Capt. McDougal, & Bissell, very civil & attentive, all.

Vessels here are Independence, 50, Receiving Ship, Decatur sloop of war, in ord., Saginaw, & 2 small steamers.

The off like the position of the Yard—healthy, safe fr. attack, remote fr. city & deep water. Use the native laurel for ship timber. Is very hard, cuts like lead, & fine polish.

Wed. Dec. 21. (Mare Island). Up early. Capt. McDougal waits on me, & sends me over to Vallejo in a yawl. At Vallejo, breakfast at Frisbie's, & meet Gen. Vallejo, & his younger d., La Señorita Josita, at school in S. Fr., & wives of Frisbie & his br., both d. of Vallejo. Frijoles for breakfast.

Gen. V. remembers me as a boy in the Alert's boat, in 1836. He repeats some of my conv. with him then. He was Comt. of Presidio.

The Vallejos, Guadaloupe & Salvador, owned nearly all Napa & Sonoma, having princely estates, but have little now, Guad., by bad management, & Salvador by that & gambling. Gen. V. got the capital placed here, on condition of putting up publ. b at his own exp. Did so, expended $100,000, but after 2 sessions was moved to S. Jose, & the town fell to pieces, the houses (wood) moved off &c. Within 5 years, has increased to 4 or 500 inh., & is promising. Doubt if V. gains by it, but Frisbie does, who owns most of the land here. All V's d are rather handsome, in the Mex. style, & are full blood whites.

Took coach for Napa City, wh. reached at noon. Ride up Napa Valley is beautiful. Never saw so much land under the plough in the same space, except in England. Great fields, level, rich, no undergrowth, fair sprinkling of large trees, & distances so great that the men are ploughing by flagstaffs, as a pilot would steer his ship. Peculiarity of valley is that is enclosed by high hills, river wandering through it, lands nearly level, & small hills, green to top, dotted over the valley, wh. can easily ride round or over—rising like artificial mounds.

Napa City, small town of say 1000 inhab., Co Hs., 2 or 3 churches, etc.

Stanley there with buggy & pair of mules. He has a ranch just below, sd. to be very valuable, $100,000 or so. Land here varies fr. 50 to $100 per acre. Rich in grains & fruits.

Napa Valley. Reached Yount's towards night. He has a principality here, of some 12000 acres, from mountain to mountain, & running length wise of the valley, the Napa Creek running thro' its centre. He owns a large mill, & has some 100 or so Indians encamped near his house, whom he employs. He lets his land at abt. $5 per acre a year—very much troubled with squatters. Lately married an intelligent middle aged woman, well educated &c., from N. York, who takes care of his affairs, keeps his accts., sees he is not cheated, & pays off his debts, for the old hunter has no business habits or knowledge. He had a former wife, & has children & gr. ch., but all have left him except a gr. d., Lilly Yount, abt. 12 yrs. old, at school at S. Fr., & now at home for Christmas—strong, hardy & fine looking girl. She owns 1000 acres of this land, wh. is a tol. fortune.

Old log house, modernised, one story, huge chimney & large logs & knee timbers burning on the fire. Hearty welcome.

In ev., old man tells us his Indians stories & his life. Born in N.C., Burke Co., in 1794, left home at 15, for Ky. (or Tenn.?), in war of 1812–14, joined mounted rifles & fought the Indians for 2 years, advanced to be lieut., & great reputation for courage & skill in woods & with rifle. After peace, takes to hunting & trapping, & engaged in it until 1843, incessantly, hunting over Arkansas, Texas, New Mexico &c., & trapping the Colorado, Gila &c. Frequent fights with Indians, & bears, panthers &c. Sev. times besieged in camp by Indians, & fights for days. Says, with gr. simplicity, that never killed an Indian for the sport of it, *for game*, but only in fight, when necessary.

He was the first white man that came into Napa Valley. It was then full of Indians & Grissly bears. Built log hut, & fought the Indians for sev. months. Once besieged in his hut for sev. days. Indians had only bows & arrows, & he had rifle & pistol. Usually he had 3 or 4 men, with him, whites or friendly Indians. Where house now stands, scene of sev. fights.

Grissly Bears ("Grisslies") has killed hundreds of. In one day, he & a Spaniard killed eight. Spaniards lasso them, & get a tree betw. them, & so the lasso holds the bear at distance, —always mounted. (Story of the Mexican who got lasso round bear's nose, & it came off.)

Yount's famous dream, is told by him to me.

He was living then in the valley, in 1843. He had never been over the mountains, by the N. route, but only by the Southern, & knew nothing of it. Dreamed that walking in strange place, large mountain, a white chalk rock, river & trees, all as plain as if been there, & came on large traveling party, men, women & children, "snowed up", starving to death, eaten their animals & begun to eat their own dead. Awoke, fell asleep, dreamed the same again. Troubled & after lying awake some time, fell asleep & dreamed it all a third time. So much impressed that believed it a Divine Revelation, went off to some hunters who knew this route, told them the dream & described the scene. They said they knew the place from his description. This confirmed him & them, & Yount gave $70, & others contributed, Gen. Vallejo &c., & party went out. At the very spot, as seen by him in his dream, (& they went by that) they found a party, just in that condition, & relieved & brought them in. This is known as the "Donner Party", & their story made a great impression on the public at the time. A large portion of them perished.

All I can say is that Yount believes what he tells, of this dream, thinks it was divinely sent, & the people in the Valley corroborate him so far as came to their kn, i.e., his telling the dream, with the minute description of the spot, the party going out on the faith of it & finding them there. Gen. Vallejo told me that it was true, so far as he knew of it. Yount is a man of unimpeachable integrity, & moderate & reasonable in his views, & does not exaggerate.

Yount's Ranch is called Caymas, an Indian name.

Th. Dec. 22. In this latitude, prob. 38° N., breakfasted open door, few remaining strawberries on vines, & some strawberries in blow, grapes still on vines, & fresh flowers in bloom. The creeping vines over the verandah are in luxuriant bloom. Best of weather, wood fires & open doors. This is Cal. winter.

Left for the geysers. Detained until noon by a pompous old half lawyer, Col. Fisher, who is drawing Y.'s Will, & wished Stanly to look at it. Glad he did.

Old man gave us bottle of wine of his own make. I like it. It has no spirit, but pure juice, pressed by hand. Better so. The skin & seeds of this grape shd. not go in.

Reached McDonald's at night, after delightful ride up valley. Above Yount's, on his land, is a white sulphur warm spring at tem. of 90°. As get higher, land is rougher, stones appear, few stone walls &c. Evergreen oak, & the common deciduous oak droops, almost like willows, with mistletoes & has long pendants of thin hanging grey moss, all among the leaves. Very pretty. Trees are large & come right out of the sod, as in Engl. parks. No clearing to be done, but put plough right in. The Napa Valley is Lake George, dried up, turned to rich soil, level, with little hills sprinkled over the level, & large trees alone & in clumps.

At McDonald's, large wood fire in stone chimney, sticks 4 f. long, & ½ dos. on at time. McD. is away, & his wife & 3 children, a hired man, a Norwegian, called Brady. Mrs. Mc. is neat, pretty & obliging, about 30 years old. Asked her how came to Cal., said, "Over the mountains". "Had hard time, then". She made no reply & did not wish to pursue the topic. Stanly & I both stuck with it, & asked Brady abt. it. Brady told us she was of the Donner Party, that Yount's party rescued. In that dreadful time, she lost father, mother (names were Graves) 2 sisters & br.-in-law, there, & a br. & sister died after they got in. She was then a young girl of about 15. The Graves fam. did not eat their dead, but some of the party did so. Her fam. were 11 in all, of whom 5 survived, all now living in Cal. & 2 married near her.

A Methodist Circuit rider spends night here. His first words, in dark, simple reply to Stanley's qu. how far came from to-day, "Well, Sir, from Clear Lake, only"—were uttered in so solemn a tone, as if were last he expected to utter in this life,— a rebuke, a warning, a final testament & benediction—all in one—revealed the Method. preacher.

Frid. Dec. 23. Started on horseback, (Stanly & I) with Brady for guide, for the Geysers. Fine mountain scenery, large trees. Little twinkling leaf of ev oak. Reach Geysers in 4 h. 45 m.

Spend 2½ hours wandering in the cañon & over the little hills. A space of ½ miles square, all devoted to hot springs, sulphur steam, coming fr. ground & rocks, & steam bursting out fr. hill sides, through little fissures, as big as steam boiler pipe, & with all the noise of escape steam in steam boat. Obliged to speak loud, when 200 feet off. Two cauldrons of stuff as black as ink, bubbling at boiling heat. Rest as color of water, more or less colored by green & yellow of sulphur. One pretty little cool spring of pure water, impregnated with sulphur & soda, pleasant to drink.

One cañon (ravine) is burnt over, & devoted like a Gehenna, to these fires, steam escapes & boiling discolored emissions. Through it all runs a quiet stream of pure water, over the rocks.

House stands prettily, & hot sulphur water conducted to baths in pipes. Scenery in neighb. is pretty, mountainous scenery.

Heavy fog sets in. Rain threatens. Start off at 2.30 P.M., with fear of being caught out in dark & rain. Push on at quick speed. At 5 o'ck., is pitch dark, heavy rain, & can see nothing. Single file, but can see neither Stanly nor his horse, nor can he see the guide or the guide's horse. Call out, at intervals, not to lose each other. Several streams to ford, & occ. a fallen tree. Guide loses the trail,—for we are on an Indian trail. He says he can follow the stream, & knows the hills,—wh. we can see ag. the sky, tho' we can see nothing ag. the ground. Only know we are in water by the splashing of horses' feet. Chance of spending night out in rain, in woods, rather gloomy. Cross stream again. Knows where he is. See light! It is McD.'s. Get lost in the yard, as cannot see fence, or barn or shed.

Glad to get to fire & lights & change of clothes & warm supper. Mrs. Mc. nearly given us up.

Rain hard, all night, pattering on roof. Not cold, not at freesing point, probably.

Sat. Dec. 24. Still heavy rain. Brady reports streams so swollen that cannot get buggy over. May have to stay here sev. days. Dreary prospect. Stanly lately married, sent wife to Sacramento, to spend Christmas with her br. Judge Baldwin, & he to meet her there to-day. She not know he has gone to Geysers. Must go on. Walk to house of one Keyes, ½ mile off. He knows of ford, not much over buggy floor. We go over on horses, & he drives over buggy. All right, on other side. But not off before noon. Cannot get to Napa in this state of roads, to-day.

Go on as best we can. Heavy rain, muddy roads & deep streams to ford. At dark, get to little shop, abt. 2 m. fr. Yount's. Must give up Yount's, as too dark, & large stream to cross. Neither of us knowing where. Wagon at door, wh. turns out to be from Yount's, & returning there. God-send. Follow it &

get in to Yount's at 7 P.M. Cordial welcome. Mrs. Yount we find to be an intell., well edd. woman, fr. New York, & very useful to Y. Miss Lilly there, too, the old man's favorite. There is a simple, natural courtesy in Y.'s manners, wh. is delightful. The receptions & leave-takings are models. He is a gentleman, roughened by 40 years' hardy adventure, & not a boor half polished.

His story of Glass, the hunter. Wounded by a grissly, shoulder torn, neck open, windpipe open, one flank gone. Major ——, Command. of the party, obliged to leave him, pd. man & boy $4.00 to stay with him & bury him when he died. Came in, after 2 days, reported dead & decently buried. Glass ate berries in reach, drank water, killed rattle snake, cut off head & tail, pounded up & ate rest. So, for 2 mos. Crawl a little, walk with cane. At last, got into fort. "How far to fort?" "Well, 200 miles, or so". Man & boy given up to him to punish. "If God forgive them, I will".

Next time, Glass wounded by arrow, companion cuts out the stone by rasor. Got well. Next time, betrayed into Indian Village, guns taken, Glass & six others, run for it. Pursued, 5 killed, "Bill" says last saw Old Glass run round rocks, & Indians soon after walking over 'em. Bill got in, & in few days in comes Glass. Next time, last seen making for thicket pursued by Indians. Gets in, nearly starved. Last of Glass, is that leaves a fort, to camp in open air, & is found on rock, killed by Indians.

All over Calif., the Americans hail from some state. All are emigrants. Men & fam. are described as fr. Va., Carolina, Missouri, Illinois, or from the New England states. State feeling very strong, yet the usual repugnancies of N. Engl. & the North ag. the South, & *vice versa*, are softened by intercourse, intermarriage, & tie of common int. in the new State.

State pride of Californians very strong. Remote. Severed by Ocean & Rocky Mountains fr. rest of world, & have a peculiar climate, & peculiar habits & history.

Pleasant night at Yount's. Still rains. Mrs. Y. just got home fr. below, tired, & no attempt at Xmas Eve.

Old man says "Gentn., I sort of believe in punishment", & goes on to say that some of the Donner Party had left a sick man to his fate—may have been their punishment. Inclined to believe in spiritual manifestations—"cannot limit power of spirit".

Sund. Dec. 25. Sund. & Christmas.   But Stanly must go on to Napa, & telegraph to his wife at Sacramento, or they will be in distress. Been so kind to me, & all on my account that came off here—so I accede to sugg., & our whole Xmas, is spent on a raining, muddy road. Afternoon, too late for Church, arrive at Napa City. Spend aft. & ev. in tavern bar-room, as no fire-place in any other room, where billiards are playing. But Stanly & I have some reas. & agreeable conv. All our journey, have had agreeab. conv. S. has anecdotes of Congr. life, politics &c. He is Republican, now, & opposed to ext. of slavery, a Churchman, communicant, Delegate to the late Gen. Conv. at Richmond (1859). He tells me he has seen the letters betw. John Randolph & his cousin Judith, after she had married Gouverneur Morris & had a son,—John writing an infamous letter to Morris, reviving her unf story. Morris knew it all, shewed her the letter, & she replied. He says if Jack did not bleed & blush, it was because he cd. not. He must have been crasy.

Mond. 26. Dec.   Steam Boat at Napa City, 10 A.M., for S. Fr. via Mare Isl., & Vallejo. At Mare Isl., shake hands with Comm. Cunningham, Capt. McDougal &c. on wharf, & Miss West goes to S. Fr., under charge of Com. C.'s son. (Don't like her manners. Attends to nothing but what relates to herself or her friends—so let her alone).

This is surely a grand basin, this bay, or series of bays. There is little Benicia, & now M. I. & V. are hidden. Here is Alcatras, & there the narrow Golden Gate! & there the town—yet a dreary fog lies over all.

Reach my rooms at Tehana Hs. before dark. This trip makes me less regret my revisit to Calif.

Tuesd.   Call on Mrs. Dr. Hastings & lunch there. Dine with B Kip, to meet the new Bishop of Br. Columbia, a delightful man, serious, well bred, & well toned, with a peculiarly pleasing voice. He preached at Ch. of Advent, in ev., an excellent

sermon, in agreeable, solemn, conv. manner, earnest, simple &
cultivated taste &c.—in fact he is worth the B. & all the clergy
of Cal. put together.

Ch. of Advent is Low Church, & a McAllister family affair,
with great pulpit in middle, no altar to he seen—but beautifully dressed with flowers & evergreens.

Th. Dec. 29. 1859.   Rose early. 8 A.M. took stage coach for
San José, to visit quicksilver mines &c. Seat with driver. Pass
old Mission Dolores & the San Bruno ranch, & go over the
new road out into Park by the side of the Bay. Rough country
& no trees until come to San Mateo. Here few large farms &
rich soil. Capt. Macondray's county hs. & farm in pretty place.
Public Hs. of San Mateo the best looking edif. out of S. Fr. I
have yet seen.

Now, all the way, rich, flat country—a large "land lake" as
Dr. Bushnell says. After rains is very muddy. Never saw mud
before, even in Cambridge—our soil is not deep eno'. Coast
Range in sight, with snow on its highest tops, across the Bay.

Redwood City, the Shire town of S. Mateo Co., is mere
mud hole, on a slough running up fr. the Bay, & forks there.
Trade in redwood timber.

Now comes Santa Clara valley. The live oak abounds here,
& the sycamore—the same as our sycamore or plane tree. As
far as eye reach, this land lake of rich, alluvial, with no undergrowth, & large trees timbered over it. Ranchos & farms abundant. Some, have pretty houses, & some rather approaching
the stately. All ranchos & large farms have names. These often
painted on the gate-way. The Spanish are the prettiest names
—but the land here is mostly held by Americans & British.
One is "Menlo Park".

Three men in field mounted. One rides toward us. "How
well that man rides—beautifully!" *Driver.* "Don't he? I'll bet!
He is one of the best riders in Cal". *I.* "Who is it?" *Driver.*
"Don Secundino Robles. He used to own most of this country
here, but has sold or lost most of it, & lives in that little hs.".

This is the way with most of the Old Spaniards.

Now come to pretty little town of Santa Clara, one of the
oldest of Missions, estbld. abt. 1770. There is the Mission, its
old adobe walls, its gardens & orchards, but in good order &

preservation, for it is the seat of the R. Cath. College. Additions have been made to it, & the effect of the whole is pleasing, the venerable & the active & useful. Wish had time & letters of introdn., & wd. stop & see the College. Driver says it is the best College or school in Calif., about 120 pupils. Town grows little, but San José eclipses it, in trade & pop., & is the Co. town of S. Clara Co.

In outskirts of S. Clara are the Agr. Fair Grounds, with Race Course &c. &c., well got up.

This is near head of the Bay. The vessels, steamers &c., stop at Alviso, some 6 miles fr. S. Clara & S. José.

The valley goes on to San Jose. This is a large thriving town. It was the second Puebla estbld. by the Spaniards, Los Angeles being the first. It was known in the North as "the puebla", as Los Angeles was in the South, & they were distinguished as the Upper Puebla & Lower Puebla. The Mission of S. José is some 12 or 14 miles off, on the W. side of the Bay.

The two large buildings in S. Jose are the Church & School. The Church was the old adobe church, wh. looked rather old & crumbling, but was solid, & the Spaniards were not willing to have it pulled down. So brick walls were built outside the adobe walls, a kind of veneering, making them some 7 feet thick, & two wings & a Chancel added, making a very large & fine looking building.

The School is kept by the Sisters of Notre Dame, for girls, & has nearly 200 scholars, & stands very high in public estemn. It is a large brick building, with large grounds enclosed by a wall.

Spent night at a French inn, where cooking was excellent, service as good as in Paris, & prices high. Large wood fire, in bar room, & all the frequenters are French. Great deal of talk round the fire, politics, Napoleon, Austriah, Les Anglais, Moriva, Espagne, Italy &c.

Young gentl. fr. Mr. Laurencel, comes over to spend the night & to drive me to the mines tomorrow.

Advertisement of Hamlet, to be played in the little theatre, Mr. & Mrs. W. C. Forbes. Go in & see 2d. & 3d. acts, & can stand no more. Yet interesting to see how this great play interests & affects an audience of farmers & traders & miners & their families, acted as badly as possible. In closet scene, when ghost comes in, Hamlet falls flat on floor, & is picked up by his mother. In the play scene, after hitching himself up to the king, in watching his countenance, fairly staring him out of countenance, when king springs up, & goes off, Hamlet seises him by the shoulders, shakes him, as he would a pickpocket he had detected,—amid great applause. In scene with Horatio, he hugs him in his arms at "as I do thee",—& when he disjoins, he says "Something too much of this"—& so on, & so on. Yet it is an attractive place, in their hands, in S. Fr., & Hamlet called twice before the curtain in one night.

Great French bed, 4 or 5 beds deep, curtains &c. & clean.

Frid. Dec. 30.   Up early, & off to the quicksilver mines. Leave the valley, & come to broken, hilly country.

One long vein runs across these hills, sev. miles in length, but held by diff. owners. The oldest & most Southerly mine is called the New Almeden. That is not in operation, being under an injunction, in suit by U.S. for possession, & they do not even permit any one to visit it. Ergo, do not go there, but to Mr. Laurencel's mine, the Enriquéta, named for his daughter. This is the name of the mine, village &c. Mr. L.'s family being in S. Fr., he boards at Enriquéta Hotel, a little place, but kept by Frenchmen, &, of course, well kept. Breakfast there, at 9 o'ck. Two intellig. gentlemen, besides L., speaking Fr. Sp. & Engl. & latter very fairly. In this little, remote place, we discuss Engl. & Fr. drama, Rachel, &c. They, though French, agree with us about the old Fr. drama.

The Frenchmen can make good bread anywhere, even in Boston. A Yankee can make good bread nowhere.

To the mine. High up the hill. Tunnels cut in, & shafts sunk. This mine only been in operation 6 or 8 mos. One shaft is 60 f. deep. Went down it, by candle lights, ladder,—a small timber, notches cut in it. The quicksilver ore is found only in the vermillion rock. These vermillion streaks run through the other formations. When pieces are broken & brot out to light, picked over by hand, & those that have the red streaks are accepted. These accepted pieces have from six to forty per cent of quicksilver in weight, the average being about 15 per cent.

These pieces are first crushed under stamps, moved by steam, then washed in troughs, shaken by steam, when the ore goes to the bottom & the earth is taken off,—then another washing & shaking, until the ore-bearing earth is pretty well separated. It is then dried, in large pans, & then put into furnaces, & kept in them four hours. In this heating process, the quicksilver evaporates, & ascends into retorts, collected, passed thro' water, in syphons, & then spit out drop by drop, into iron receivers. Then is bottled off in iron flask, with iron stoppers screwed in.

Most of the work men work on contract, by the job, or, as they say, tribute work. All the mines do the working in cos, & are paid by the weight of accepted stone, accounts being kept with each shaft.

Each shaft & tunnel has a name,—usually of a patron saint, & at entrance of it is a framed print of the Infant Jesus.

One year ago, not a house here. Now Enriquéta is a village of 40 or 50 houses, with Post off. &c.

Two or three miles below is another mine, just opened, & worked by a Balt Co., called Guadaloupe, & a village beginning. If these 3 mines, Almeden, Enriquéta & Guadaloupe, succeed as they promise now, there will be 10,000 people in these hills in a few years.

The quicksilver is carried by mules & wagons to Alviso, the head of the Bay, & shipped for S. Fr. San Jose is the market town of all these miners.

The discovery of the quicksilver mines was fr. inquiries made of the Indians as to where they got red paint for their faces &c. & they showed these rocks, with streaks of vermillion.

Lunch, & left my good friends, for San Jose, wh. reached at dark. Dined at my Fr house. Could not stand another night of the drama, & knowing no one, spent night in the bar-room, at the open fire. I like these French people. They are laborers or journeymen, yet are so polite, & more *civilised* than any other people in the same class of life. Drink very little, & smoke & talk.

Amusing, violent, theatr. dispute betw. 2 of them, & appeals to "amour propre" "parole d'honneur" &c. If it had been on stage, wd. have been vehement for Engl. or Am. tastes.

Sat. Dec. 31.   Stage coach early, for S. Fr., down the other side, the E. side, of the Bay.

East side of the Bay, San Jose Mission, San Lorenso, San Leandro, & the great grants of the Soto & Castro families, who own some three leagues of land apiece,—forms a glorious agricultural country—great land lake, between the Coast Range of Mountains & the Bay—some 4 to 10 miles wide, a perfect level, except at the foot of the hills, no undergrowth, & trees enough to make shade here & there. Houses well placed under the trees. Fine views of mountains & the great Bay. If the Napa Valley is Lake George, turned to land, this valley,—the Alameda Valley, is Lake Champlain ditto. Napa is more beautiful & picturesque, with better near views. This is on a larger scale with grander distant views. Napa has the great adv. of water, all summer. This is dry in summer, but not so dry as Sa. Clara Valley. The latter, in very dry seasons, loses its crops by drought.

Visit old Mission of San Jose. Church is standing, & in good order & is now in use. The orchard also. But the ruined adobe walls are all that show the rows of Indian huts, wh. the Xd. Indians held under these great mission principalities.

(Old Mr. Yount, by the way, spoke very favorably of the condition of these Missions & of their treatment of the Indians, when he came here first).

Oakland, in Contra Costa Co., is a large town, a populous suburb of S. Fr., & tho' only 6 or 8 miles off, across the Bay, has a diff. climate fr. S. Fr. (See Dr. Bushnell's reasonings on those facts). It is not so cold or windy in summer, & trees grow well there. It is, indeed, a grove of live oak, almost hiding the houses. Large steamers go fr. here to S. Fr. ev. few hours.

Reached my hotel, in S. Fr., at dark. Had neither dined, lunched nor breakfasted,—only cup of coffee, with bread dipped in, before left S. Jose.

Dined. Spent ev. at my room, & to bed early—tho' all the city is alive with New Year's Ev., balls, music, street processions, singing &c. Do not feel in humor for it. Feel too serious, away fr. home, end of a year, &c.

Sunday. Jan. 1, 1860. Auction rooms (night auctions) have drums & music & buffoons, to draw people in.

Signs here "Ici on parle Francais". "A qui so habla Espagnol" &c.

Cal. phrases.

Spondulics—Cash, ready money.

Dry up—stop, Hold one's tongue.

Gone in.—Dead, Given up.

You bet.—Certainly. Doubtless.

First rate.—used familiarly—for very well.

Ask a girl of 12 or 14 how she is, or how her mother is—she says "First rate, Sir". No paper money & no copper here. Smallest coin is ½ dime. Small prices go by *bits* i.e. York shillings, or 12½ cents, but a dime is always taken for a bit.

At restorants, dinner of canvass back duck is 50 cents, & of chicken is 75 cents, & eggs are 12½ cents apiece.

Monday. Jan. 2. Observed as holiday, for New Year's. Counting rooms & many other places closed. Calls on friends, as in N. York. All "receive", unless sickness or calamity, & then place basket on plate at door to receive cards. Called on *Mesdames*, Kip, Lawler, Blanding, Ewer, Morrison, Thompson, Hastings, Macondray & Holman.

Jan. 3. Tuesd. Took steamer "Queen City", 4 P.M., for Sacramento. S. is the capital, & the Leg. & Sup. C't. are in session there. Steamer is on Mississippi style, high pressure, one cabin running the whole length of the boat, uninterrupted by machinery, & makes great show. Prices are "high pressure", also. No accoms. for sleeping except state rooms, & those are $3 apiece, for one night, & not provided with anything but a bed; & for toilet, you must go to barber's shop & wash *coram omnibus*, & wipe on a roller. I made some complaint to clerk of boat, for wh. I suppose he set me down as a "bloated aristocrat".

After leaving the Bay, & getting into Sacramento River, country is low & level & stream full, as a passenger said, like the Mississippi. The Sacramento is growing shallow from the immense qu. of dirt thrown into its waters above by the gigantic hydraulic mining operations, wh. settles on bars below the city. The Steamers often ground on them, now, when 5 years ago here was water to spare. Marysville, on Feather River, is in danger of losing all its navigation by that cause.

Wed. Jan. 4. 1860.   At Sacramento. St. George Hotel, kept by Genl. Hutchinson, who has been Mayor of S., & is Genl. of Militia & vestryman of Grace Ch. &c. Large & first style hotel, excellently kept. Top full of politicians. A *sub.* in the Court Hs., a Mr. Jos. E. Lawrence, came up in boat to promote the int. of the Collector, Mr. Washington, as candidate for U.S. Senate. The election of Senator in Broderick's place, is the great thing now, & absorbs all attention. Every promt. man in the state is a candidate, & all are on the spot, making personal canvass, with their retinues. The S. Fr. Bulletin says that the Cust. Hs., Mint, Navy Agency, Post Off. &c. are removed to Sacr., *pro temp.*

No sooner got to hotel than a Boston client salutes me, one Hill, who has come here to dodge an order of Sup. C't. for custody of child. Then, a man comes "Is this Mr. Dana, of Boston?" "Yes, Sir." "You don't remember me. My name is Ryan". Still, I don't recall him. "I repaired your father's house, at Manchester, in 1846". "Oh Yes, you were the carpenter, &c.," & I began to inquire patronisingly after his success here, when he told me he was here as senator from Humboldt County! I had to come down sev. pegs. He was neatly dressed, carried himself erect & straight, & had quite an air, full of tongue, &, I suspect, a thorough going party hack, with none but Cal. scruples. I met him afterwards in the Governor's private rooms, full of importance.

To Supr. C't. room. In lobby, found Chief Just. Field. He is fr. Berkshire, br. of David Dudley F., &c. &c., also Baldwin & Cope J. J., & was introduced to numberless lawyers, who were all either *ex* judges or Cols., or Genls.—Crittenden, Campbell, McDougall, Williams, Hoag, &c. *Baldwin J.* is quick & fertile, but hasty, *Cope* J. is new & slow, but sensible. *Field C. Jus.* is the chief power. The Bench now is honest, learned & independent, &, for the first time, has public confidence. *Terry C. Jus.*, was the last of the ruffian & *buyable* order. Heard two questions argued, one touching the case of Terry, late Ch. Jus. indicted for killing Broderick.

Only diff. betw. manners of these judges & ours is in their

fam & free interc. with the bar, off the bench. At adjt., they come down into the Bar & talk with the members; & they sit & smoke in the lobby, with the members. This is wrong, & will die out, as all the tendencies in Cal. are in a conservative direction. I have been told by Field, Gov. Latham, the Gov. elect, & sev. leading democratic politicians, that the sentiment of the state is almost unanimous in favor of removing the Judiciary fr. polit. infl., of having the judges appointed by the Gov., instead of by pop. election, & giving them a life tenure; & that the Dem. party would take the respy of recommending these, if a Convention should be called. Sev. gentl. have told me the people would even sustain a system of retiring pensions for judges who have served for long periods.

Field tells me that the Reporter of their decisions makes dreadful work, being a polit. appointee, & the new Gov. is to recommend to Leg. to authorise the Court to appoint its own reporter. He thinks the last few vols. must be re-edited, & says they would give Horace Gray $20,000 to come out here & do it;—for he thinks Gray the model reporter.

A statute, drawn by Field, when he was in the Leg., provides that the usages & rules of the miners, in their several localities, shall be received in evidence, &, when not in conflict with the Const. & laws, shall govern. This is in lieu of a code of mining laws, & is far better; for the character of mining in different localities varies so much, & the needs & interests of the miners, that a gen. code would be impracticable. This system delights the miners, & the judges say that the rules & customs wh. have come before them are almost always sensible & just, though always verging on the severe & summary. When Magistrates were scarce, & before this statute, the miners in each region had their organisations, their written laws, their summary tribunals, & banished, flogged & hanged delinquents, without hesitation or scruple. Without this, they could not have lived. They still keep up their organisations & rules, & make prelim. inquiries, like gr. juries, but almost always take the delinquent into the nearest magistrate, & don't interfere afterwards, unless they have reason to think the magistr. releases him improperly,—in wh. case they still sometimes take him & try & punish him by their own tribunals,—but a decision of a *Court or jury* they always obey. The Supreme Court is very popular with the miners, as its decisions have sustained their rules, their water rights, & their investments, however rudely cared for by them.

Field tells me he was Alcalde of Marysville in 1850, before reg. organisation of counties & courts, had no definition or limit to his authority or jurisdiction, took unlimited jurisdiction over all cases brought before him (short of capital punishment), held the law in his own breast & declared it for each case, *pro re nata*, made novel writs, *in rem* or *in personam*, as he pleased, & the most curious judgments, but such as justice & the state of society required. Having no jails, & no houses but of canvas, & no jailors or sheriffs, no criminal could be confined longer than they could hold him in hand; so he used to order flogging, lashes on bare back, by installments, & where restitution was possible, or some important disclosures desirable, the lashes were to cease, at end of any installment when the required act was done. Under this system, order reigned in Marysville. Subsequently, he got his acts & records recognised by the Legisl., wh. protected him, & on them all the land titles of the town rest. He also told me that from 1849 to 1856, he never went into Court or the Leg. without a pair of Derringers in his pocket & a Bowie knife under his coat, & that he was advised to do so by the judges, who did the same—all men did. If a man was not ready to fight, either on the spot or by duel he could hardly live, certainly not tolerably, in Cal. Now, no man is armed, (except some rowdies who would be so anywhere) & a man may refuse a challenge on grounds of principle, if his life sustains him in the position.

Called on Miss Dana, my fellow-traveler from N. York, at the hs. of her br.-in-law, one Culver. Talked over the "Star of the West" &c. Nice, little helpless, innocent thing. Evg. at Field's rooms—anecdotes of Cal. life 1850-3,—almost incredible. *Inter alia*, he arrived at Marysville with 18 cents, & in 6 mos. made $60,000 by prof. practice & some lots bot on specn.—lost it in suits & pol. contests in a year more, & made another fortune at the bar.

Thursd. Jan. 5.   Rain & mud—all day & night.

Called on Rev. Mr. Hill, the Ep. clergyman. He complains of want of relig. interest, & of habits of Ch.—going—indifft., lax &c., but attentive & kind to him personally, & many good traits in the people.

Called on Rev. Mr. Beckwith, late Principal of Punahou School, whose wife is d. of Dr. Armstrong, the Missionary at Honolulu. He is in temp'y charge of a Preb. Soc. here. He left Punahou on acct. Mrs. B.'s health. Mrs. B. showed me Daguerrotypes of all the Punahou scholars, wh. were given to them, on their departure. Pleasant to see the faces of the Gulicks, Armstrongs, Parkers, Lymans, &c. &c.,—those excellent, intelligent kind young men & young women.

To the Legislature. State Hs. a long, brick building—one story in height. Assembl. & Senate Rooms well eno'. No bus. of conseq.

Long conv. with Don Pablo de la Guerra, who is senator fr. S. Barbara District. He saw S. Fr. twice destroyed by fire, a large city, of shanties & canvas houses chiefly, but large & full of goods & business, in the morning, & nothing standing at night, & rebuilding the next day. Thus, twice. Once, while fire raging, saw an old woman clearing off the coals & hot ashes & putting up a cloth tent with a board & a few bottles. His companion said "We ought to encourage such industry as that— let's take a drink". His anecdotes of early times—& impositions on the old Mex. holders of land—(wh. the judges tell me is true), they paying taxes & all their lands held by squatters whom no law wd. eject. Later decisions are restoring to them their rights. Don Pablo is an intelligent, cultivated man, & is a noble of Spain, by right of birth.

(An ign. judge in S. Fr., on a petn. for Hab. Corp. granted it ag. the petitioner for the amt. he owed the man who was illegally restraining him).

Dined at Gov. Latham's. L. a young man, clever, not more than ordinary in other resp., & a reg. politician. Mrs. L. the best mind of any woman I have met since I left home, & few better have I ever met, if any—ill health, pale, sallow. Is d. of Dr. Birdsall, now or late of the army. She is rich & so is L. *Ex* Lt. Gov. Purdy was present. After gents' left to look after the caucus, had long & intg. conv. with Mrs. L. on theological subjects, on wh. she perfectly understands herself.

Introdd. to Livingston, of the Alta, Gen. English ex Treasurer of Cal., &c.

Friday. Jan. 6.   Epiphany, &c, as I am a man of leisure, feel it my duty to go to Church. Found the only Episc. Ch. in the city locked—evidently the day forgotten or omitted (Mr. Hill complained of want of int., in his people). The only other church to keep the day, is, of course, the R. Cath., & I go there, where, in the rain & cold dull day, in a shell of a Church with bare brick walls on inside, mortar standing out, & holes not yet closed in the roof, was a congr. of not less than two hundred; & yet there had been an early service before this. I never saw a more still, attentive & (to all extern. appearance) devout congregation. One priest only,—the only one here. He has a day school for boys under the Church; & seven Sisters of Mercy, recently arrived, have a girls' school of abt. 200 scholars, also under the Ch. in a damp, dreary place, with bare walls. They have bought a lot for a school & convent, & will soon build. At the end of the side aisle was a reprn. of Our Lord, (being X'mas season) lying in the Manger,—a figure of the Virgin of the sise of life, standing before the child wh. is lying on the floor of the small place, & over it is a thatched roof, & grass lying about it,—all actual.

Congr. chiefly Irish, but some others.

To the Legislature. Met Mr. Billings of S. Fr., who introduced me to sev. members & notables. Don Pablo Dela Guerra & Don Andrés Pico are the only men of Sp. descent in a Senate of 40 members, in a country wh. was Mexican 13 years ago! In the Assembly, of 80, there is but one Mexican. Both branches very young men, mostly betw. 23 & 35, few over 35. Ryan sits reading his Newsp. & voting grandly on yeas & nays. My friend Dela Guerra is thot able & intelligent, & has the most of a patrician look of any man here.

Called on Mrs. McDougall. Her husb. is candidate for the U.S. Senate, so he is out. Mrs. McD. is in poor health, reminds me of Miss Wheaton, & is an intelligent, well educated woman. Met there the handsomest woman I have seen in Cal., wife of Mr. Stewart, a lawyer & member of Assembly, & d. of *ex* Senator Foote of Mississippi.

Sacramento is on a dead level & low, has been flooded sev. times & twice burned up. Now, a levee of 10 f. high is built round the city, & all the ground in occupation raised to that level, as they are now raising Chicago. It is laid out in regular rectangular blocks, like Philadelphia, the streets being wider. The streets parallel with the river are named by numbers, & the cross streets by letters. In some streets, trees are set out. More brick houses, in propn., than in San Fr., & all wooden houses are now prohibited. Awnings of wood, i.e. piassas, are built out to the whole width of the sidewalks, giving protection ag. sun & rain. These are generally made strong eno' for promenading on their tops from the windows of the second stories, wh. are used as parlors. The Episc. & one Presb. Ch. are handsome, of brick, with climbing roses, &c. The R.C. Ch. is a large shell, & there is a huge deformity of a Method. Church.

The statement that the rivers Sacramento, Feather & Yuba are badly filling up by the qu of earth sent down by the immense hydr. mining operations, is confirmed to me.

The city & Co. of Sacr. built a hall for State Agr. Fairs, in less than 60 days fr. first sod cut—a hall of brick, 140 x 100, the largest hall in U.S. unsupported by pillars. Inaugn. of Gov. Latham & Inaug. Ball to be there. (Obliged to buy a view of Sacr. fr. a young artist—sent it home by mail.)

Sat. Jan. 7. Rode out with two *ex* governors of Cal., Johnson & Purdy, to visit Sutter's Fort. Little of it remains—only the adobe angles & one adobe house.

Rode to house of Col. Zabriskie, f.-in-law of Gov. Johnson, where saw 3 fine looking women, Mrs. Z., & the 2 daughters, Mrs. Johnson, & Miss Annie. They have fine figures & classic features. The Col. a N. Jersey public man, of some note,—now in reduced circumstances. His hs. is on the only rising ground in the neighborhood of Sacramento.

Called on Mrs. Latham & Mrs. McDougall, & Mrs. Stewart. Latter is handsome & bright, but poverty of acquisitions & topics. Mrs. L. admits that the politics of Cal. are & have always been very corrupt, & that most of the votes in the Leg. are purchasable by office if not money—& that arrangements to give offices for votes are not concealed or thought dishonest by the greater number. She says polit. life is closed to any man who does not do such things.

Met two Demt. judges who doubt if the people wd. favor a judiciary for life by Executive appointment, at present; for politics are too corrupt to trust so long terms to the appt. of any governor, or any Convention—yet they think that is the true tenure, & shd. be aimed at. At present, all is too much tentative & fleeting—people, officers & laws.

All praise Don Pablo's speech, in 1855, on the extension of the stat. of limns. as to land titles. It was made in the Senate, in Spanish, & was a noble plea for the Old Californians & their rights, & carried the Senate & Legislature, & probably saved the State fr. the disgrace of a great robbery.

Met Major Gillespie, who was in active work here in the war of 1846,7, commanding at Los Angeles. He was beseiged there & capitulated, but with honors of war. He was present at the action of San Pasqual, where Don Andres Pico, with 70 men, defeated Gen. Kearny with sev. hundreds, & at sev. other actions where Pico distinguished himself. He says Pico was as brave as a lion, & the soul of honor. Pico is now in the Senate, sitting by the side of Don Pablo, the only repsves. of the old regime.

Sunday. Jan. 8. 1860.   To Church. Day reasonably pleasant, yet not above 40 persons in Church, of whom only 8 or 10 were women—very muddy, to be sure, but not raining. Yet a good sised Church, well furnished empty pews, &c. But I fear brother Hill is enough to provoke a good deal of staying at home—, "The bottamless-er-pii-at" (Bottomless pit) &c. *dégoûtant.*

Met Marshal Tukey in street, who saluted me.

Met a lawyer, partner & friend of Gov. Latham, who thinks Latham honest & capable &c., yet he boasted how in the Convention wh. nominated Latham (the contest being betw. him & Weller), he "traded Weller out of his boots",—got Cope, a lawyer fr. the mountains, to run for Supr. C't. judge, to be voted for by L.'s friends, & C's friends to go for L., & so on as to M. C.'s, State offices of all sorts—"Yes, Sir, Weller was 10 ahead on the first ballot, & before next morning Latham was 10 ahead. He worked it round by setting these offices & tickets ag. each other, & traded the Weller people out of their boots before they knew it". This lawyer is a reputable man, & does not think those things dishonest, so no money is paid down as a bribe.

(Telegraph, yesterday, that the "Early Bird" will not sail before Wednesday—so shall stay over the inauguration).

The univ. habit of "drinks" here, tells especially on the politicians. The candidate for Speaker had to be dropped because he got on a spree which lasted over the election day, & there was a drunken row at the Leg. caucus Frid. night. One member drew a knife on another, who drew a pistol, & instantly as many as 20 pistols were cocked. This stopped the fight. It was too serious. (The question is gravely discussed whether A. *did right* in drawing his knife, &c.) The best man among the Sen. candidates is J. A McDougall,—but his habits have been very bad, & his state is now critical,—wh., they say accounts for his wife's ill health. (Intemperance is the worst vice in a husband a woman can suffer from, for it is constant, public, & mortifying). So, the best two orators on the Repub. side, Judge Tracy & Col. Baker are the same way; & ex Gov. J. N. Johnson, my entertainer of yesterday, was "as tight as a peep" in the hotel the night before, & not quite straight yesterday, & he told me he was taking care of a young lawyer fr. the mining region, who could not get away unless a friend forced him off before the morning drinks began. While I was calling at Mrs. McD.'s, her husband came in rather boosey.

Joseph E. Lawrence, whom I supposed to be a N. York fast man & a mere Co. Hs. dem. politician, turns up a "spiritualist", in the techn. sense. He tells me he was a disbeliever in immortality &, of course, in X'y., & in all spiritual powers,—saw the rappings, mediums &c. (among good private circles at home), was led to think & read, & came to a belief in the immortality of the Soul, its active state after death, spiritual agency of angels & saints, miracles &c.,—thinks there shd. be prayers for the dead, invocation of saints &c., making the World of Spirits practical parts of our religion. How little we know of what is going on in men's minds! I had seen him here canvassing for his friend for the senate, & thought him a man that would laugh at the mere mention of a religious subject. So, I find that Mrs. Latham & Mrs. McDougall, in the whirl of bad politics, have given anxious attention & are now giving it, to the highest of subjects, & know their grounds. And *per contra*, how often men of good reputation & high profession have *no* religious or spiritual life or thoughts *whatever*. We are deceived both ways. Spent the ev. in Field's room. His wife has come,— a very pleasant & pretty young woman fr. Virginia, with cordial manners, & knows how to blush,—a lost art in California. They were in Berkshire in Sept. & gave me late news fr. my friends there.

Major Gillespie married a d. of Duane of Phil., has been unfortunate here, tried to be elected clerk of the Senate, but the Caucus set up another man, who, of course, would be elected, but Gillespie's old opponent in the war of 1847, Don Andrés Pico, made a speech in his favor, detailing, as a generous foe, his good conduct in the war, & expressing his astonishment that *Americans* shd. refuse to sustain a man who had shed his blood for his country's cause, & spoke so feelingly & well, that Gillespie recd. *every vote*.

There are three great interests in Cal., mining, agriculture & commercial. At present, I think that, in polit, & economical questions, the mining is the most powerful of these,—not in wealth or numbers probably, but by unity of interest. In questions touching their affairs, they are one man. (In this interest is included, of course, those who depend on them,—the mech. & traders in mining regions). Next is the agricultural, the richest & most numerous, but divided into various interests, grain growing, vine growing, cattle raising, &c., & large rancheros & small yeomen. The members of the Legislature are spoken of as from mining districts, or agric. districts. The comm. int. is almost solely San Francisco.

The practice of hailing from the state of previous residence is so general, that the state is put in the City Directory—thus: "Brown, John, druggist, 105 K. st., (Penn.) &c.", & new, permanent residents, are *introduced* as Mr. A. B. from Georgia, or Mass. &c.

Found out the member from Mendocino Co. & inquired about Canning Smith. He says Canning is Clerk of the Co., which is a good office. I inquired how he was succeeding, his character &c., as a relative,—he replied, being a Southern Chivalry man—"Well, Sir, him & me has had a difficulty, & I prefer to say nothing about him,—except that in his office he is thought an efficient man & good clerk".

Inauguration, in large Agr. Hall (120 x 100, instead of *140* x 100 as I said before). Three cos. of Militia. Gov. Weller introdd. Latham, & Latham, (previously sworn in, at the Leg. Hall) delivd. his inaug. address. No allusion to Nat. pol. Loud & pretty good voice. Large audience. Not order eno'. Boys making noise. Judges of Supr. C't., *ex* Gov. &c. on platform.

Don Pablo introduces me to Don Andrés Pico, who has old Spanish manners.

A humbug named Warren, editor of a paper here, has just been married, & told Mrs. Field he had married a woman who was "sound on all the progressive principles of the age".

The Chinese Chapel—a small brick building, arranged inside exactly like a Methodist Chapel, open pews, middle aisle, small square pulpit at head of the aisle. A few small tables about the pulpit were piled with pamphlets or unbound sheets, like tracts—in Chinese.

Inaug. Ball at the Agr. Hall. Complimentary ticket for me—including carriage. Arrangements of dressing rooms, supper room, &c. excellent. A hall of 120 x 100, no pillars, & very high roof, & the best dancing hall I ever saw. Large assembly, nearly all dance. Many fine looking women, & many very costly dresses. Mixed with them, the common rustics, with ungloved hands. *Ex* Gov. Weller & wife, Gov. Latham & wife, Lt. Gov. Downie & wife (a Mexican, cousin of Mrs. Henry Mellus), Ch. Jus. Field & wife, McDougall & wife, & innumerable ex governors, ex judges, &c. with wives & daughters.

Weller is a coarse, tobacco spitting man, with inattentive manners, & I had but few words with him.

Tuesd. Jan. 10. Parting calls, & took boat at 2 P.M. for S. Fr. Beautiful sail down the river. (Better site for city below, & reasons why failed). Felton on board. Tells me the secret that Latham is to be nomd. Senator to-night—all arranged—the word here is "combination", wh. means jobs, trades, &c. L. is as honest as any of them, & more free fr. trammels. Capt. of Steamer tells good stories of early Cal. life, the infamous, murderous *wag*, Ned McGowan &c. (Ned Mc's funny acct. of his man killing the Dutchman—'the only place he was mortal' &c. his *inf. machine* &c.). (Also, of Ned Marshall, & Senator

Foote—"That or *rain*"—fellow with window sash over his neck "running yet"—). The "same old drink".

At *S. Fr.*, 9 P.M., & my hotel & long night's rest.

Wed. Jan. 11. The Bark "Early Bird" sails to-night. Call on Mr. & Mrs. Stanly—letter fr. Frémont &c. Fine large French ship to sail for Hong Kong in 10 or 12 days. Shd. like to go in her, for advantage of speaking French—& wd. wait that time were I not already out of season in the East. Two weeks may make the diff. of my visiting or not visiting a country, escaping a quarantine or not &c.

To-night, I hope to see my last of California.

"A few short hours, & we will rise to give the morrow birth,
   And I shall hail the main & skies,—but not my Mother Earth".

The Capt. of the steamer came fr. Panama with Edm. D. Otis, & says he was a capital fellow, cheerful & full of fun & courage & the favorite of everybody. So, in S. Fr., but he fell away, & got to driving a job wagon, & was taken home by compassion, & died on the passage. Felton speaks very well of Bruce Upton, & says he was respected & liked here & his failure was owing to overconfidence.

Sunday. Jan. 15, 1860. At sea, on board bark "Early Bird", four days out fr. S. Francisco.

We sailed fr. S. Fr. Wed. night, Jan. 11th, about midnight. As this was my 8th time of passing the Golden Gate, I did not care to see it, & went on board, put state room in order & 'turned in', & waked up next day, (Thursd.) abt. 7 o'ck. with gentle rolling of the ship, to find myself at sea, the Golden Gate in sight, & the hills of the Coast Range. Calm or light winds all day. Next morning, Friday, out of sight of land, & glad am I to see the last of California, & to be on the broad Pacific, ev. hour bringing me nearer to China.

"Early Bird" is a neat, serviceable bark, of 500 tons, & a good sailer. Capt. M. H. Cook, Ch. M Cook (his brother), 2d. M. Fields.

What passengers are most concerned with, the cook & steward, are both excellent—cooking good, neat & with variety, & steward civil, neat & attentive. Voyage promises well, tho' we had no great expectations fr. it. Cabin small, but neat, no women or children in it, or cabin boy, & our passengers seem to be pleasant & intelligent men. The Capt. & Mate are sons of Cook of Hong Kong, a Highlander, an Engl. by birth,— they born in Delaware. My room-mate is a Mr. Williams, brother of S. Wells Williams of China, the author of The History of China. Another passenger is a young man named Robert Raymer, native of Hamburg, who speaks English perfectly, & French well enough, &, some Spanish. I have a rule with him, that we speak only French together,—for my benefit, as he speaks far better than I do. He has a great deal of information & is clever—going to China, on some mercantile business,—has been all over U.S., & in much of Europe & S. America. Another is Speidon, son of a purser in our Navy. He is Naval Storekeeper at Hong Kong. Another is a Capt. Williams, master of a lumberman trading betw. Puget Sound & China. (Large lumber trade fr. Puget Sound to China, Australia & S. Francisco. Chief export of Cal., is wheat to Australia). Also a Kittredge & Doland.

Nice breese set in Thursd. night & has kept up, to this time, smooth & gentle but fair, & we are making satisf. progress. We follow the Sun in his flight & ev. day lose some 10 or 12 minutes of time.

Sunday. Jan. 22. We are ten days out, in Lat. 24° 56' Long. 142.24, in the most delightful part of the most beautiful ocean, in the *blessed trade-winds,*—those strange winds that have blown in one direction, perhaps from the Creation, never falling away to a calm & never rising to a furious gale, with blue sea, soft, fleecy clouds, & clear sky. We have been fortunate in our weather, having had only one day or 36 hours of "doldrums" —(variables, just before we reached the trades—say fr. 28° to 32°), & 36 hours of heavy rolling sea & strong wind when we first took the trades—& then the *blessed trades* were a little too rough, & one night pitched us about, broke the furniture & dishes & lamps, & kept us awake.

Modern spiritualism, i.e. rappings & mediums has got among shipmasters. Have heard of several who believe in them. Capt. Randlett, Master of the celebrated clipper Surprise, believes that a woman crossed his deck one night in the China sea.

Curious, to see superstitions coming in at the cabin as they are going out of the forecastle!

Omitted to mention that we have two hundred & thirty Chinese passengers in the steerage, fifty more than we had in the Mastiff, a ship double the sise of this one. We have but one boat to lower on an emergency, & that too small for a high sea, & capable of holding only 4 or 5 persons; & have only two other boats on board, lashed on deck, & no doubt leaky, as they have not been in water for a long time—no long boat or pinnace. In fact, in case of disaster, we have *no resource.* Nor is there a breaker (small cask for water) on board. In case of fire, collision, or springing leak, we have nothing to look to. This is very wrong. Still, we are all in good spirits, & hope the best.

To-day—Jan. 22—is the Chinese New Year. The Chinese have been firing off crackers, suspended over the water by poles—for safety—, & throwing to the winds bits of gilt paper, as *ching-ching* (offerings) to the *Josh.* They chin-chined the Capt. by a box of stockings. The Chinese passengers always find their own food & cook for themselves,—the ship finding only firewood & water. They stow very close below, & have little ventilation; but are a quiet, peaceable, obedient people, & unquestionably intelligent. They have books among them, & read a good deal. Their books are printed on thin soft paper, mere tissue, made of bamboo or rice, & with paper covers. I have never seen one with a stiff cover. For musical instrument, they have a kind of banjo or guitar, with small body & very long neck, & three strings.

I have an unaccountable sense of happiness, on this voyage, as I lie on my berth, in my state-room, looking out on the sea, by moonlight, or starlight or sun light. It is not because I deserve it, or because my situation—away from all I love—makes me so, but, I suppose it is that my health must be good, & the air is pure, & I am free from care,—eating, wearing care, & have absolute leisure. But I believe that if there is nothing in one's circumstances to make one peculiarly happy or unhappy, his state will depend on so material & vulgar a thing as his *stomach.* Dyspepsia makes gloom. Digestion makes good spirits. No *place* is more favorable to cheerfulness than lying on a bunk, looking out one's window on a tropical sea, in fine weather, the ship gently bounding under you. I wonder at this sense of happiness,—that makes me ready to sing!

Kittredge is a N. H. boy, of good principles, with courteous manners, going to China, to engage in trade, determined to hold fast to integrity & temperance. Doland is a mechanic of Hong Kong, young & worldly, but well read & intelligent. Speidon is gentlemanlike & amiable. Raymer is engaged to a Miss Gardner of Salem, & is making a third effort to make money enough to marry, his efforts in the Western states & in S. America having failed—yet he has youth & spirits.

Wed. Jan. 25.   Said a little too much about the *blessed trades,* they have died away & left us in a calm yesterday, & to-day, the wind has been ahead, all day, & we are obliged to beat to windward. I knew that at & about the Sandw. Islands, in winter, the trades sometimes intermitted for a few days, & calms & S. winds set in; but I did not know that this intermission extended far out to sea. Capt. Williams, an old trader here, says that fr. Dec. to M'ch., there are intervals when you will sometimes lose the trades, for a few days, in certain latitudes, & S. & W. winds, calms & squalls intervene.

Calms & squalls (not heavy) all day & night.

Thursd. Jan. 26.   Last night, about midnight, after the winds had gone round the compass by way of W. & N., the trades set in again, & nothing can be more beautiful than this day—all sails set & drawing, studding sails full, freshening sea, clear sky. At noon, the Sand. Isl. abt. 250 miles off. Hope to *sight* them tomorrow.

Strange how I am able to spend my time. No *ennui,* no spare time, no weariness! Yet, my sanitary rules allow me not over 2 or 3 hours reading in the day. Called at 6½, washing &c. & on deck soon after 7. Breakfast at 8. On deck until 10. Reading or writing fr. 10 to 11½. On deck at 11½ & take observation for meridian altitude & work up the latitude. On deck 12 to 1. Dinner at 1. From dinner to 5 o'ck., talk, read & sleep. On deck 5 to 6. Tea at 6. On deck all the evening, walking or sitting. "Turn in" soon after 9. I suppose I walk deck an average of 5 hours a day. Ship, sea & sky are the same ev. day, & no news fr. without,—yet to me all is interest & variety, & no exhiln. is like a cracking breese & foaming sea. How much better is a sailing vessel than a dull, monotonous, steaming, smoking, greasy, oily steamer!

Frid. Jan. 27.   Fine weather & good winds. Went to topmast cross-trees to look for the islands. Not in sight. Glad to find that I can sit on cross-trees & look down on deck without any dissiness of head, as well as when I was a sailor boy. Am sure I could not have done this any time during the year before I left home. Regard it as proof of improved health.

Sat. Jan. 28.   Day of white chalk! "Land ho!" at day break. The island of Hawaii on our larboard bow. To mast head to look at it with glass. See the point & hill near which lies dear Hilo, &, over all, the summit of Mauna Kea, above the lower clouds, with patches of snow lying about it.

All day is passed delightfully, sailing through the channel betw. Hawaii & Maui, with Kawanawi & Lanai in sight. Could see the gullies & rivulets running to the sea, on Hawaii, & the mission of Rev. Mr. ——, & the point behind wh. lies Kawaihae, & the further point, off wh. I lay in my canoe to look at the out flow of the volcano. On Maui is the mountain, Hale a ka La, the bay where we were becalmed in the little sch. Mary, & the barren island Tahawarawe, where Judge Allen & Mr. Wylie feed their sheep. Can just see the slope, at the foot of wh. lies Lahaina.

The weather is exquisite, neither hot nor cold, sky & sea clear, & a steady trade blowing us rapidly along. How all enjoy it! Even the Chinese fire crackers & beat gongs to chin-chin the Josh for the fair wind. Delightful sunset & clear moonlight on the waters all night.

I do not believe I shall see, in my long journey, a place that will interest & charm me so much as this group of islands. It would delight me to land at Hilo & Honolulu, & spend a few hours, making flying calls among my friends, to see the native sights, & hear the native tongue. *Aloha! Aloha Nui!* Never, in all human probability shall I behold you again! The islands melt away in the golden sunset. As I walk the deck, I parody Byron's Farewell.

> "Adieu, Adieu, my island home
> Fades o'er the waters blue. . ."

Sund. Morn. Jan. 29. At sunrise, can just distinguish a dim outline of the highest points of Maui, & by noon, these are lost, & we have again an open horison.

Sund. night I always have a memorial of home, in singing to myself, on some spot on deck, alone, the chants & hymns of our Sund. nights at home—Venite, Bendictus, Benedia anima mea, Deus Misereatur, De Profundis & Adeste fideles.

Wed. Feb. 1, 1860. We are now well to Westward of the S. Islands, & farther to Westward than I have ever been before, wh. makes me feel that I am at last really on my way to China. But the trades have been very light since we left the islands, sometimes for hours almost a calm, & then rising to a 4 or 5 knot breese. This is discouraging, & deducts fr. my admiration of the trades, yet the winds are always fair, &—what can be more charming than these moonlight nights! Nothing but sea, sky, moon, stars, the deck, & the towering, white, silent sails! The passengers sit on deck, hour after hour, reluctant to go below.

I have a window in my state-room, just beside my berth, so that I can lie in it & look out upon the waves. Every morning, now, betw. 3 o'ck. & sunrise, I see the Southern Cross, gleaming in the Southern horison, just where my eye turns when I wake.

Last night, found a centipede in the cabin, & Raymer killed it. It was six inches long & as thick as my thumb. Mr. Williams, who we all think a little timid & splenetic, was not a little frightened at the thought of such animals being in the ship, & the Cap. & Speidon told him stories of their coming out in ships as you draw into warm weather. No sooner had he got to bed, than he sprang out, hurting his arm in the jump, thinking he felt one crawling over him.

I have adjusted the mate's quadrant successfully, by the rules in Bowditch, & take observations with it daily.

Capt. Cook is a quickwitted, entertaining, good natured, but profane, indolent, improvident, low toned fellow. Mate is better. Passengers hold out well. We are fortunate, on the whole in our chance gathered company of passengers. The ship is poorly provided except as regards the cabin table & the berth furniture, wh. are good. With over 200 Chinese steerage passengers, there is not one ventilator in the ship, nor a force pump, & only one little boat on the davits, & only two other boats, both lashed on deck. In case of necessity, we could not lower these boats in less than a ½ hour, & then they wd. not hold over 15 apiece. To put out a fire, we have only buckets.

Sund. Feb. 5. We have been disappointed in our trades. They have been very light, sometimes almost a calm, & never above 8 knots, & the last three days the winds have been from S. to S. W. But the weather has been exquisite.

One of the Chinese plays a kind of violin, with three strings, singing at the same time. This he keeps up by the 2 & 3 hours together, without intermission, with a downcast & doleful countenance, though the others seem entertained by it. Surprised to find so much neatness among the Chinese. Most have tooth brushes, & brush their teeth scrupulously, & most seem careful to wash, generally. I think they are neater than the same number of Irish wd. be, of the same class in life. As for myself, in these warm latitudes (18° N.), I take a salt water bath, by bucket & spunge ev. morning.

Have finished Williams' Hist. of China—a careful, elaborate, dull, ungenial book, & written in an inelegant but ambitious style, with prodigiously long & unusual words—"decollated" for "beheaded", "contracted a matrim. engagement" for "married", &c. My kn. of Latin, Greek & Fr. taxed to utmost to get at the meaning of some of his English words—must have a dict. in hand. He is a dry & narrow man, & repeats mere *phrases* about the Bible & Xn. Civilisation. Yet, is a good repository of facts.

Began Huc's Travels in China.

Wed. Feb. 8. The steward found two tarantulas, in the cabin—large hairy creatures, wh. disturbed the passengers not a little, but some say they are not poisonous.

The chronometer stopped to-day, the only one, & we are driven to dead reckoning & taking time by Mr. Speidon's watch. Our Chinese passengers play dominoes a great deal. Some play all night, by lanterns, & when the lanterns get dim, they hold the dom. up to them. Gambling & opium smoking are their chief amusements.

Friday. Feb. 10. To-day we perform the strange feat of skipping a day. Yesterday was Wed. Feb. 8th. To-day is Frid. Feb. 10th. Thursd. the 9th has no existence. Going round the globe with the sun, from E. to W., we lose a day. Of course, it makes no difference *where* we skip the day. Only we must do so before we get to port, as we should otherwise find ourselves one day in advance of the world. By this strange law, the indevout astronomers pussled the devout un-astronomers, & showed the Sabbatarians that if two Jews left Judea on their Sabbath, & went round the world different ways, when they met again one would be keeping Friday & the other Sunday instead of Saturday. It is a strange feeling—this annihilation of a day, when one comes actually to do it, notwithstanding your reason tells you that you have lost no time, but only added a little to each day of your voyage, by following the sun, until you make a total addition of 24 hours & must erase one day from your calendar, to be even with those who have stood still.

The crew would not be cheated of their duff day, so to-day is to be Thursd. in the galley, & the cook skips his Friday.

Sund. Feb. 12. It does seem strange to have Sunday come in six days. Some of the Chinese who had learned in California, to count by our days, were much pussled to find it Sunday.

I am struck with the good temper of these Chinese. They cook for themselves in two galleys on deck, the wood being served out to them by the pound, & they take their turns at the galleys, with their pots & pans, with little sticks of wood under them, over 200 of them, in messes, & yet there is no quarreling or crowding, but quietness & good order. Our women passengers, 5 or 6 in numbers, have very black hair, glossy, done up in our style, with handsome hair pins, & all have bracelets & ear-rings. The bracelets are said to be put on in childhood, & never removed.

Little bull dog pup on board—favorite with me—all yellow but a black face—came on board before his eyes were open.

Been examining Thoms' book on navigation. Think his explanation of the modes of ascertaining latitude & longitude are more intelligible to the unscientific than those of Bowditch. His explanations of Zenith, celestial equator, altitudes, declination, polar distance, mean time & apparent time, dip, asimuth, parallax &c. are excellent.

Tuesd. Feb. 14.   At 11 A.M., sailing along, in beautiful serene weather, & gentle breese,—"Land ho! Right ahead!"—"Keep her up—Keep her up North West. Brace the yards!" called us all on deck. We were going directly towards a low island, of coral reefs, just emerging above the water, & very near it, too. We could see the surf break upon it. Had we made it last night, we should probably have struck, the land is so low & the reefs extend out so far. Went into main top with glass. Island about 5 miles long, from S. E. to N. W., with heavy breakers on the N. W. end, a few trees & shrubs & grass, in parts. S. E. end has a grove of trees. We are in Lat. 19° 22′ N. & our Longitude is supposed to be 166° 28′ E., but as our chronometer has stopped we cannot be sure of the latter. Wake's Isl. is in 19° 10′ N. & Long. 166° 30′ E. by the general chart. It is, therefore, no doubt, Wake's Island. We strained our eyes to see if we could discover any signs of habitation, or signals fr. shipwrecked mariners, but could see none. Should have liked much to land on it, & search for fruits & berries & make sure that no one was on it.

Wed. Feb. 15.   We have now been out 34 days, & have had but 3 rainy or anywise unpleasant days, & taken in the royals only 3 or 4 times, & not reefed topsails once. Thermometer at 70° to 78° all the time, & the temp. of the sea about the same, at noon. No weather can be finer. Trades have been steady for the last week or 10 days, & moderate.

Travelling as I do gives one a strong notion as to the difference of races. The differences seem almost of the essence & ineradicable—Not to speak of the original unity, but of the present state of things. Mixtures of races seem doomed to extinction. There is a Chinese infant on board, born in Cal., but its little eyes are as Chinese, from the moment they were opened as any "oldest inhabitant". I do not believe the Kanakas can either increase & maintain themselves long as an equal race with the whites, or that a mixed race will multiply at all. These facts, & even that most striking one respecting the intermarriage of mulattoes, do not disprove the orig. unity, nor relieve the difficulties in the theory of orig. diversity.

Great disappointment in the steward. He turns out to be far from neat. In dress, habits, ways is rather disgusting—though civil eno' to us. Capt. Cook has no sensibilities, & is so incorrigibly careless & indifferent, that no hope of reformation of steward. Capt. smokes a pipe nearly all the time & drinks whiskey, & has no taste, & would not see it if the steward used a dishcloth for a napkin. We are all in a state of disgust, but there is no help for it. All depends on the Capt., at sea.

Frid. Feb. 17.   The water in the new casks is so bad that it made all the passengers sick yesterday. Could not drink it even in Chocolate. Mate exd & found all the casks the same. Gross negligence. Fortunately, the water in the tanks will last us in the cabin, & the Chinese boil their water & take it only in tea— rarely if ever drink water.

This is the third Am. ship I have been in since left the Mastiff, & the master of each has been a slovenly, careless man, with no discipline or system, & no care over his steward.

Finished Huc's China, narrative entertaining & descriptions as graphic as ever met with. He makes his reader a spectator & actor with him. His statements as to the religious, civil, social, polit. & econom. condition of China are more to the point & more intelligible than Williams', & in ¼ the space.

Also read Sir John Davis' China. Davis is a pedant & quotes inapplicable passages from Greek & Latin. Still, it is a fair work, & has been largely borrowed from by all writers since. Huc has the advantage of having lived in the interior of China 14 years, speaking the language &c. It is plain to me from Williams' own statements that the Am. Prot. Missions have, so far, done *nothing.* They never go into the interior, but only try to circulate books in the sea ports, & have hardly ten converts to show. He seems, himself, to be discouraged, & says that the random distribution of Bibles has been a failure, & worse.

Sunday. Feb. 19.   This day, 37 days out fr. S. Fr. Last four days very heavy rolling seas, wh. send sofas, trunks, chairs & dishes, lashed or unlashed, to & fro, & hardly let us sleep at night. Still, wind is fair & strong, & we make an average of 200 miles a day. If we had a neat steward, & a proper Capt. & it were not so late in the winter, (putting me out of season for

India) I shd. be very well content here. As it is, days are seasons to me, now. Fear I must give up Japan & India.

Attempt at a popular explanation of the mode of finding the latitude, at sea,—with which I have entertained myself—it is original, & made without referring to books.

I am at sea, & wish to ascertain how far I am from the Equator, or, my latitude. Suppose two lines to be drawn from the Earth's centre, the one to my position, & the other to the Equator at a point nearest to my position. The angle formed by these lines is my angular distance from the Equator, or my latitude. I cannot see the Equator, & cannot, therefore, measure this angle directly; but I can see the sun at noon. Suppose, then, the two lines to be extended. Suppose, for convenience, the Sun to be exactly on the Equator as it is twice a year. The line from the Earth's centre through the Equator will touch the Sun's centre, & the direction of the other, produced into the sky, is my zenith. The Sun's angle with my zenith is the Equator's angle with my position, or my latitude. I cannot fix the exact spot of my zenith for the purpose of an ordinary observation, but I know that my zenith is always 90°, or a quarter of a circle, from my horison. If, therefore, I measure the angle the Sun makes with my horison, I can obtain the angle it makes with my zenith. I measure, by a quadrant or sextant, the angle the Sun makes, at noon, with my horison, & find it to be, for example, 40°. As my horison & zenith form an angle of 90°, & the sun is between them, I deduct 40° from 90°, & get the angle the Sun makes with my zenith which is 50°. As the Sun is supposed to be on the Equator, this is also the angle the Equator makes with my zenith, or with my position, at its nearest point, which is my latitude. The reason I take the Sun's angle at noon, is that it is then nearest to my zenith, & thus gives the desired angle.

But, suppose the Sun is not on the Equator, but to the North of it. Suppose me to be also to the North of the Equator. I obtain the angle the Sun at noon makes with my zenith, as before. The books give me the angle the Sun makes with the Equator at the time of my observation, which is called its *declination*. As the Sun is between my zenith & the Equator, the angle it makes with my zenith, added to the angle it makes with the Equator, gives the angle my zenith makes with the

Equator. In other words, the Sun's zenith distance, added to its declination, gives the latitude. The principle & process are the same, if the sun & the observer are both South of the Equator. If one is North & the other South, then, as the Equator is between the zenith & the sun, I deduct the declination from the angle the Sun makes with my zenith, & obtain the angle of my zenith with the Equator, or my latitude.

This explanation is in general terms, merely to explain the principle. Several corrections must be made in details, for refraction of the atmosphere, the height of the observer above the earth's surface, &c., but the only correction necessary to be explained for a correct understanding of the foregoing, is that which is made for *parallax*. It will be observed that in measuring the angle the Sun makes with my horison, the angle is necessarily formed at my eye, on the Earth's surface, while the angle of the Sun with my zenith, & that of the horison with my zenith as referred to the Earth's centre. I must therefore make that angle equal to what it would have been if observed at the Earth's centre. This correction is given in the books, for every degree of altitude, & is called the correction Parallax.

Popular explanation of mode of ascertaining Longitude at sea. The time the Sun takes to go round the earth (to speak according to appearances), is divided into 24 hours, & the Earth's surface into 360 degrees of longitude. The sun, therefore, makes 15 degrees in an hour, one degree in four minutes & so on. We count our degrees of longitude from Greenwich. If at the ship's position the time differs one hour from the time at Greenwich, the ship is 15 degrees of longitude from Greenwich. If the time at the ship's position is later than that of Greenwich, she is to the Westward, & if earlier, to the Eastward of Greenwich. If, then, I can ascertain the exact time at the ship's position & at Greenwich at the same instant, I can get her longitude. Chronometers are set to Greenwich time, & what with their present accuracy & what with the means of ascertaining & making allowances for rates, the time at Greenwich can be sufficiently well ascertained for practical purposes. It then only remains to ascertain the time at the ship's position. The most convenient way would be to ascertain the exact moment of noon, that is, the moment the Sun passes the meridian of the ship's position, & note the time given by the Chronometer at that instant. But the sun rises & falls so little & so slowly at noon & seems to hang so long at about the same altitude, that no ordinary instruments can ascertain the exact moment of its passing meridian. The most usual method of ascertaining the time is to measure the altitude of the sun when it is rising or falling fast, that is, early in the forenoon or late in the afternoon. Certain formulae in the books enable us to learn, from this altitude, the exact time when the observation was made, as shown by the sun,—that is to say, how long time it was before or after the Sun's crossing the meridian of that place on that day. By noting the time by the Chronometer at the moment of the observation, we get the difference between the time at the ship's position & at Greenwich, and thus the longitude.

This is sufficient to explain the *principle*. An important correction must be made. The sun does not, in fact, go round the Earth in exactly 24 hours; and, consequently the difference between noon of one day & noon of another, as shown by the sun's crossing the meridian, is not exactly 24 hours. It slightly varies from that sum, & this variation is not always the same at all places & times, being sometimes more and sometimes less than 24 hours. Now, watches cannot be made to keep this varying time, so they are constructed upon an allowance of exactly 24 hours to a day, which is the average, or mean, of the Sun's days. The Sun's day, or the exact time as ascertained by the Sun's crossing the meridian at each place, is called the *apparent* time. The watch's day, of 24 hours between noon & noon, is called the *mean* time. The observation above described gives the *apparent* time, or the time as measured by the Sun's progress; while the Chronometer gives the *mean* time. This difference must be reconciled. A formula given in the books & called the Equation of Time, enables us to reduce the apparent time shown by the observation to mean time at that place. Having then the mean time at the ship's position & at Greenwich at the same instant, we obtain the exact difference of time, & thence the longitude.

Wed. Feb. 22.   This is Ash Wednesday of this year, & Washington's Birth Day, & the birth day of my little daughter. I must try to remember them all. I do love that little baby, & long to see her. As for Washington, the nation can take care of him to-day, & I confess I would rather kiss the baby, of the two, regimentals notwithstanding—"If that is treason, make the most of it." Lent, I shall not attempt to keep, as a bodily fast, at sea, for our meals, at best, are not too good for health & life.

Still fine weather, day & night, & fair, gentle trades, all the time. Read Hildreth's Japan. A dull & ill jointed arrangement of facts, yet of value, & mostly new to me.

Sund. Feb. 26. Forty four days out, & yet 1000 miles to go. The winds have been fair, but very light. Read the condensed narrative of Perry's expid. to Japan—well enough.

Mr. Doland, the sailmaker passenger, is a kind of John Halifax, gentleman. In point of manners, tact & general information, & knowl. of current Engl. literature, he is above the average of men one meets in good society.

Reading life of Charlotte Brontë. Very interesting. The best part is where one Lewis patronises her, & gives her advice as to novel writing, being himself an author, & she *uses him up* so on Miss Austen's novels, & the nature of poetry & sentiment. Emily Brontë's dog is a good point, & so is the end of the Chap. that describes the success of Jane Eyre. I lay in my berth, reading, & my girlish habit of crying at pathos or sentiment came over me. But my tears are few & short. The reservoir is low. It is only books that have that effect—actual cases not,—I think, so far as I recollect—which shows something wrong.

Winds being very light, a Chinese woman is burning four incense sticks & throwing overboard quantities of yellow strips of paper, with pin holes in them, as Chin-Chin. "By & bye catchee wind".

Sleepiness of Ch. mate, & long efforts of Fields to get him out. He is a spoiled child, selfish, indolent, sleeps on his watch, snubs his brother, the Capt., to his face, & it often takes ½ hour to get him out. Then he sits in a chair on deck & smokes a pipe, in his watch, &, if he is merry, dances a negro dance, in sight of the man at the wheel. His discipline is nothing but out breaks, & he always swears at the Chinese. *Per contra*, he read Mr. Everett's Address at founding of Dudley Observatory, was captivated by it, & has been trying to study astronomy ever since.

Wed. Feb. 29. We are near Formosa, & the trades have left us, & the Monsoon not reached us, so we have had three days of nearly entire calm. Hard to retain patience. Shall miss the steamer of M'ch. 5th fr. Hong Kong. Ev. day brings summer nearer, & so cuts me off more & more in my plans of Eastern travel.

Finish life of C. Bronte. Suspect that Mrs. Gaskell suppresses a little, or we shd. hear more of the opinions & thoughts of such a woman on the greatest of all questions. How lightly she takes Miss Martineau's atheism, yet quarrels with her for honestly telling her, when asked her opinion, that she thinks there are indelicacies in Shirley. Such a woman, with such a life & such experiences must have had something strong in the way either of faith or doubts. Where are they? Emily's bull dog is overworked—well the first time, but not bear three productions,— yet I'd rather have seen him than her, I fancy.

Ships with house on deck & lazeretto aft, & houses amidships, are not seamenlike. Were I an underwriter, I would object to them. Our crew might as well be in another ship, a-head, & the man at the wheel in a boat, astern.

Frid. Mch. 2. Six days of calm & light, very light breeses,— about half the time a dead calm, & the rest a 2 or 3 knot breese. Hard to bear. The steamer sails on the 5th & we shall lose it. Patience taxed, but holds out.

Yesterday a Chinaman dropped his wooden pillow on the head of a man below. What a row! Just such as Huc describes, all chattering & sticking out their skinny yellow fingers, & looking as if blows or scratches wd. come next, but no blow struck. *Debated* & settled.

Caught a shark. Great relief to monotony of a long dull day of calm. The 200 & odd Chinese, men & women, all on deck. Amusing to see them throw themselves upon him, knives in hand, when he was left to their mercies, on deck,—& such a chattering, squalling, bawling, & yet, with a dosen knives drawn & all the pushing & crowding, no one hurt. They cut him up for cooking. Our 2d M. got the head away fr. the whole of them.

Sat. Mch. 3.   Good breese all night, & steady fair wind all day. Passengers in better spirits. Are now within 600 miles of Hong Kong. But it is not the distance but the calms that trouble us.

Chinese difficulty, characteristic of them. Late in the evening, terrible chattering & yelling & crowding & sticking out of fingers & threatening with cleavers. Our men got away from them the man ag whom their attacks were directed, but such was the Babel that, what with that, & what with the bad English & bad interpreting, we could not ascertain whether the charge was that he had assaulted a woman "with intent &c.", or whether he had broken her teapot. In this state of things, the hearing was delayed until the next day, & the man stayed aft, sleeping on a settee on deck. Early in the morning there were messages to & fro, & negotiations, & it appeared that these born politicians had formed two parties, 19 in his favor & 190 odd ag. him, but terms were adjusted, & he went forward again. (Chinese are readers, talkers & traders, by habit of 4000 years).

We are now at the antipodes of home. It is noon here, midnight in Boston, day break in London, breakfast time in Calcutta, dinner time at Honolulu, & tea time in S. Francisco.

Mond. Mch. 5.   Sail ho! Larboard bow. Just visible. First sail we have seen since left S. Fr. We gain on her & she gradually drops astern. Never near eno' to see her colors by a glass.

Tu. Mch. 6.   Land ho!, at day break. Bashee Islands on our port bow, 4 miles off. Pass to Northward of the group. Small, bold, high, rocky & desolate looking islands. The Southernmost & largest is sd. to be inhabited, by people of Malay race. This is our Last stage. We are now in the Chinese sea, & we have the N. E. monsoons blowing us towards Hong Kong, the "loom of the land" over the S. end of the Island of Formosa.

The f t yard broke, (for 3 d. time) yard fell & struck man on the t rigging, & he fell to deck, distance of 50 or 60 feet—broke leg & badly cut. Great escape that not go overboard. If he had, cd. not have saved him, as high seas & hard blow & no proper boat. Took him to forecastle, where Capt. Williams, a passenger, assisted by Kittredge, whose father is a surgeon, set the leg, made splints & cradle. I helped as much as I could. Capt.

Cook did *nothing*, either by word or hand—not even to see that he was taken below. Man's name, George H. Plummer, of Portland Me.—been at sea 11 years, & from home 5 years. Young, intelligent, but a victim of bad habits which will retard his cure. Wonder not kill him. When sat by his berth, in the small, dirty forecastle, where 10 men burrow, hung round with wet clothes, & paved with chests & boots,—recurred to my own lot in my youth. Now I have seen forecastle life & sailor's life *from the cabin*, I begin to wonder how I endured it.

The moment we passed the Bashees, changed to heavy blow fr. N.E. & heavy sea, & 10 & 11 knots an hour.

Very bad night. Carried away main topgallant mast,—broken short off just above cross-trees, sail being set. All hands all night clearing the wreck. Capt. C. no more use than a child. The 2d mate did all, with the crew, who are excellent seamen— 4 or 5 of them as good as need be for any service. Hard work at mastheads, in heavy blow & sea, clearing rigging & sending down the wreck. In midst of it "Sail ho!", & saw a steamer, under fore & aft sails, beating up to windward, crossed our stern,—probably bound to Japan or North part of China. Crew behaved like men, & after 14 hours' work, when hoisted new topsail, gave us a jolly chorus of "Rando, boys, a-rando". Topsail tie broke again, & yard fell, for the fourth time. No one hurt.

Wed. Mch. 7.   Strong blow & heavy sea. Expect to make coast of China to-night. Capt. Williams & I visited sick man. W. loosened his bandages—man said all hands been so employed that no one had wet his bandage, & limb inflamed. Capt. C. not been near him, nor, so far as I know, even inquired for him.

China: March–April 1860

Th. Mch. 8.   Made land at midnight last night. At daybreak, are close in shore, just above entrance to Hong Kong. My first view of continent of Asia! Coast is line of bare rocky hills, & deep water. Chinese fishing boats. Excitement of Chinese passengers—some not seen home for 10 or 12 years. Hove-to for pilot. Chinese boat, bamboo sails, sharp bow, broad high stern, 4 men & 2 women & some children on board,—one woman working at ropes with baby strapped to her back. Families live in these pilot boats, having no other home. Managed her well in the sea & wind, though with great deal of noise— "too much bobbery"—(*Bobbery* is Pigeon for all kinds of trouble, row, fright & confusion.)

Pilot speaks no English—gave orders by signs—Hong Kong is an island, at mouth of Canton river, & harbor is the deep, wide passage, between it & the main. Called Limoon Passage. Passage winding—high, rocky hills each side, & bold shore, deep water. One turn more—Hong Kong in sight. Fleet of vessels at anchor, all flags, Engl., Amer., French, Spanish. Chinese junks & boats moving about by oar & sails—with all their families on board, babies strapped to back, little children with floats fastened to them, in case fall overboard,—bamboo sails. Engl., Fr. & Am. flags flying fr. large buildings on shore, Engl. man-of-war steamers, little fiery steam gunboats, & great hulks of superannuated & superceded line-of-battleships, for store ships & hospital ships. Drop anchor safely—& our voyage of 55 days is ended in safety. Reason for gratitude, for *if an exigency had occurred*, were unfit to meet it,—Capt. & mate quarreling, & both unfit, no discipline, no system, useless in an emergency, & no proper provision of boats, or spare spars, & short handed of men—with 220 passengers.

Hong Kong is built on a shelf between the high steep hills, & the sea, not more than wide enough for two parallel streets. Fine stone quay the length of the town, houses & stores large, high, & all of stone or brick,—some creeping up the hills,—hills dotted with evergreen trees,—looking like N. England, rather than tropical scenery. Ashore in Chinese boat, & deliver my letters in person to Russell & Co.—who make me their guest. At Russell & Co.'s, find letters from home, dated in Aug., Sep., Nov. & Dec., latest Dec. 6. Sat down to long enjoyment of them. No bad news, *laus Deo*, except death of Adele.

Also faithful file of Weekly Advertisers.

Mr. Warren Delano is here, just arrived, to take charge of the house of R. & Co., when Mr. Beckwith goes home.

All the business houses of the merchants here are large, high & stately. Rooms & entries as large as in Court Houses & like public buildings at home—long vistas of rooms & desks, at "magnificent distances". Crowd of coolies at the door, to do errands, & a comprador, in decent long robe of blue, in charge of them. Recd. by Delano & Beckwith with cordiality, & take me home, as guest. Each large merc. house here, Russell & Co., Aug. Hurd & Co. &c. &c. has a large palatial looking house, where the clerks & unmarried partners live. I have a room at Russell & Co.'s. Mr. Delano is there, his wife being at home. All dine together there, at 7 o'clock. Beckwith dines with us. A junior partner, Mr. Tyson, is there, & clerks, Torrey of Roxbury, (nephew of Sam. Torrey), King of Newport R.I., Frank Forbes, &c. &c., eight in all, live here—all New Engl. young men, training to Chinese business.

Handsome dinner, six Chinese servants & a Chinese butler, waiting on table—all so neat & clean. Cooking excellent—nice mutton, duck, rice & curry &c.

After dinner, call on Mrs. Beckwith, next door. Large handsome house. Beckwiths knew Ned in Heidelberg. B. thinks Ned one of the best conversers he ever met.

All houses (foreigners') are brick or stone, thick walls, large deep piassas, with blinds all round, at outside of piassas, making a kind of double house, large doors, windows & halls, & every possible contrivance to secure against heat in summer. This gives the town a look of patrician solidity & dignity.

Streets full of red coats & blue coats—English soldiers & seamen—1st Royals, 99th, 67th, 3d &c. Regiments, & numerous naval uniforms—& medals & clasps frequent. A sepoy regiment, black straight hair, regular features, jet black skins, mustaches,—as far as possible fr. Negro—, tall, straight & spirited looking fellows. Here & there Malays clothed all in white, with white turbans, & Parsees, in sombre colors, high hat of dark straw, without rim, grave & decorous. Europeans & Americans of all qualities, & all the rest Chinese.

Chinese coolies, or mere manual laborers, wear wide short trowsers, & loose sacks or tunics & barefooted. Superior classes, as traders, compradors, better shopkeepers &c. wear decent, grave long robes of blue or black, stockings & shoes of white or blue, like canoes.

What a hive of industry is a Chinese town! No industry is so minute, constant & infinitesimally divided. China is an ant hill. Shops with lacquered fronts are very pretty. What a reading or letter-using people they are! Words printed on every door post, & on masts of every boat or junk, & men reading in the streets & at the shops' counters their thin yellow paper books, with paper covers, wh. they roll up in their hands.

When Chinese build a house, they first erect a staging of bamboo to sustain a roof of straw, with projecting eaves, & under this they do all their work, protected ag. sun & rain.

All the Br. Govt. buildings are large, stately & strong. The streets are paved with stone, & a stone pier or quay runs the length of the town, the vessels lying at anchor in the stream; & only boats lying at the pier. From the pier, at intervals, are iron dants, as from a ship's side, to wh. the private boats of the foreigners are hoisted up.

(Understood, of course, that Hong Kong Island is Br. possession, ceded by treaty of 1843.)

Beckwith & Delano say, & so others have told me, that the peninsula opposite Hong Kong is a far better place for a town than Hong Kong—& they are very desirous that the Am. Govt. shd. get it by treaty. Tried to make Reed secure it but they speak contemptuously of Reed's course & capacity as a diplomatist. Two objections to Hong Kong. I. The high hills shut off the S.W. monsoons, which blow fr. May to Oct., & the town, at foot of hills, is exposed to a dead, sultry heat, all summer, & is very unhealthy then. II. There is not room enough betw. the hill & the water, for the trade & houses, & hill too steep for convenient use—& further, in typhoons, vessels obliged to go over to opp. shore to be safe. The opp. peninsula, Cowloon, is open to S.W. monsoons, & not so much exposed to typhoons, has hills of moderate height, & unlimited water front &c.

Frid. Mch. 9.   Quiet Chinese servant to brush clothes, black boots, &c., but think he meant to pocket a knife I left in pocket—found it when I insisted it was in pocket of coat when he took it.

My room is larger than my parlor at home, & I have a dressing room out of it, with bathing tub, &c., so that need not leave room for any purpose.

Russell & Co. has a breakfast at the business house, at 9 o'ck., where the same company, all the partners & clerks, sit down together. But, when we are called, at 7 o'ck., servant brings cup of excellent tea, with slice of toast. So they have two establishments, breakfast & lunch at the counting room, & dinner at the lodging house—& complete outfit of plate &c. for each. Same servants, I presume,—but very likely not.

Find that the Br. & Fr. embassadors, to whom I have letters, are at Shanghai, & the Bishop of Hong Kong is on a visit North, & Mr. Ward (Am. Min.) is at Canton, & Sir John Bowring has gone home. So my *grand* letters are useless here.

Tailors, shoemakers &c. come to your house, with their patterns &c., & take your orders & measures there. "Pigeon English"—or business English, is the intermediate language. *Walkee*, come, go; *talkee*, tell, say; *topside*, up, above; *downside*, down, below; *piecee*, number, as 2 *piecee man* 2 men—2 piecee chicken. Screw steamer, is *walkee inside*, & paddle-wheel is *Walkee outside. Pigeon*, is business, duty—"No my pigeon", not my duty.

This afternoon, visit fr. Capt. Wm. Ellery, whose ship, the "Starr King" is here.

Took R. & Co.'s 4 oared boat & rode about the harbor, & visit to the Early Bird. The 120 gun ship Princess Charlotte, a monster, is a hospital ship. So, the Minden, & others, all superceded by steam. Two or three neat Eng. & French steam frigates, & several little Engl. steam gun boats. These steam gun boats thought very serviceable in China. They are propellers, with 2 or 4 very large guns, & usually 3 masts, topsails & topg. sails at the fore, & only fore & aft sails at the missen. They have their numbers painted in huge letters on the quarter,— but have also names, I believe. The only Am. ship of war here, is the great useless Hartford, too big to go into most harbors.

No small vessels, to give our young officers commands, experience & knowledge of steam, or to protect our interests.

Labor so cheap in China, that each clerk of Russell & Co. keeps a sedan chair & two coolies, & that is not thought extravagant, beside his indoor servant, at his room. Rode home in Young Torrey's chair, wh. two small coolies, one not over 14 years old, bore on their shoulders, up the long hill, at a rapid walk, not stopping for breath. I think the Chinese laborers very strong, even when not large, but very broad shoulders are common.

Coolie, is the name given to the mere manual laborers in the open air,—the porters, errand runners, hod carriers &c. The indoor servants are a step higher. They never go errands out doors, or carry bundles—"not my pigeon". (*Pigeon*, is *business*.) Indoor servants of whatever age, are called "boys".

Indoor servants, like the traders & contracting mechanics, usually wear the long blue robe, stockings & shoes. The coolies & boat men, wear tunic, or sack, short wide trowsers, coming to knee, & are barefooted. They often strip to it, when at hard or hot work, having on only their trowsers.

Nothing can be more decent, neat & convenient than the dress of the women of the lower classes—Women of the upper classes are not seen abroad. Whatever the occupation or character of the women, they wear a loose tunic, reaching below the knee, with long sleeves, high neck, buttoned over the throat, & long loose trowsers. They think the dress of European women indecent. Nothing would induce even a girl from the "flower boats" to be seen abroad with low neck & short sleeves. If their lives are ever so polluted, they are decent & even carefully modest in their dress & manners.

At dinner, had dried lychee fruit. It has a stone, & is in shape & consistency like the prune, & very agreeable,—I think better than either prune or raisin.

Saturday Mch. 10. Took steamer Willamette for Canton, at 8 A.M. Commanded by Walcott, late of the Navy,—displaced for intemperance from the Navy, wh. reformed him.

My shipmate, Capt. Williams, on board, going up to join his ship at Whampoa. Two young British Officers, in scarlet loose sacks, buttons &c., going up to join their regiment,—3d (Buffs), hoping to go North, into action. Generally understood that a blow will be struck, North, soon, perhaps at Peiho. Sir Hope Grant is to come fr. India, to command in Chief. They are taking up ships at great prices, to carry troops & ammunition North.

Lower part of the Bay, about Hong Kong, & for sev. miles up is high & rocky & barren. As draw into the river, becomes lower, & richer, & cultivated.

The famous "Bogue forts", & Bocca Tigris & Tigre Island. These forts are large, long & well placed, on each side of the narrows, at the entrance to the river, & if well manned & served, could command it. They are nearly in ruins now from the English guns, & are abandoned. The Allies (Engl. & Fr. are allies in the *present* war) do not occupy them, & the Chinese dare not.

Tigre Island is a peculiar elevation of base granite rock, one looks like a dome. There are fancied resemblances to Tigre & Elephant in the rocks.

First sight of a pagoda. Some 10 or 12 stories high, octagonal (? polygon, at all events), with shrubs & flowers growing out from the balconies or little verandas that separate each story. Yet these are not planted. They are the growth from chance deposits of seeds & earth. They are striking & handsome objects. They multiply as we go on. Now, there are 3 & 4 in sight at a time. Rice fields, or *paddy* fields, (for it is called paddy until it is shelled) abound, & trees, & little close villages. Fear of robbers & pirates keeps them in close villages, as in the feudal times in Europe.

This river has been a scene of piracy, robbery & violence for years,—chiefly of Chinese on one another, but sometimes on foreigners. The master & mate of this steamer point out to me the spots where the most famous murders & robberies have taken place. They usually murder, if they rob. The steamers, even now, go armed. Two years ago, the Chinese Govt. offered a reward, & a large one, for every head of a foreigner. That is withdrawn, but the effect of it remains among the common people. Since the bombardment of Canton by the English in 1858, nothing but their military occupation keeps the Europeans safe here.

The famed anchorage of Lintin, a high rocky island, far off on the S. side of the Bay.

Whampoa—the anchorage of large ships trading at Canton. Large numbers of Am., Engl. & Fr. vessels there, & some men of war. The Hartford lies below Whampoa, to practice at target firing.

Boats, junks, of all kinds become thicker & thicker. How swift they go, by wind & tide, their huge single mat sail, with bamboo horisontal sticks across it! They reef by lowering only. This is quick & simple.

Now, the boat houses, anchored, in wh. thousands of the Cantonese live. The small boats are chiefly managed by women. They row & steer. Girls of 8, 10, & 12 years pull vigorously at the oars, & are very skillful in steering, & skill & quickness are required, in the crowds here. Our steamer goes slowly among them, bobbing them up & down in the heavy swell she makes, the boats just saving themselves fr. her paddles. But, how good natured the girls are! They pull away at the oars, & jump about, & laugh & show their white teeth—though they seem to be just on the point of upsetting, children, household goods & all, into the river. Now, we have passage boats, & cargo boats, & Mandarin boats, & sea-going junks, & river going junks, & anchored house-boats, & flower boats, & moving boats of all kinds, by the thousands, as thick as carriages & foot passengers together in the Strand. Some of the boats are very prettily fitted up, & you see the sacred fire & the incense of their rites, the worship of ancestors. (It is not prayer or invocation, but respectful, religious acts of veneration). Now we are in Canton! There are the ruins of the large stone buildings, & of the walls, in all directions, the effects of 36 hours of pitiless bombardment by the Engl. & Fr., not a shot being returned, & not one in 10,000 of the poor Chinese knowing what it was for.

Just before this, passed the "Barrier Forts" taken by our squadron under Com. Foote, the Portsmouth, Levant &c., & taken by the Eng. twice.

Came to anchor, & boats alongside, for freight & passengers. City on each side the river, wh. seems to me to be nearly as wide as the Thames,—but chief part on North side—small suburb only on South.

Russell & Co.'s Hong is on river bank, on S. side. Their boat comes off & takes me ashore. Mr. Orne, the partner here, receives me kindly, & room & servant assigned me.

The bombardment of 1858 & the occupation of Canton by the Allies since, have depressed trade here, & the burning of the foreign factories (agencies) have left the merchants only temporary places of refuge. Russell & Co. have only one partner & a clerk, (Sheppard, an Englishman) here, yet the house is large & there are some 10 or 12 indoor servants, & as many coolies for the boats & chairs.

How strange everything is! I am in the midst of China & Chinese, & from our windows & the balcony I look out upon this ancient river, literally alive with passing boats & junks, & cries as thick & fast as of birds in a forest!

Mr. Orne takes me out to visit the grounds preparing for the new factories. The site is much better than the old, being opposite the Macao Passage, wh. gives a sweep to the S. W. monsoons in summer. It is chiefly made-land, & will form an island of about 50 acres, separated from the city by a canal. It has a stone wall in building, & the coolies are filling in dirt in baskets, from little boats—50 acres by basket loads, on men's backs! What wd. the Back Bay Commnrs. say? The site for the new factories is called Shameen.

As we return, it is getting dusk, & the Chinese are lighting the lanterns in their boats. The river looks like a swamp of fire flies. Each boat, however small, has its little shrine, at wh. tapers or incense sticks are burned morning & night.

Call on Rev. Mr. Bonney, a Missionary of the Am. B.C.F.M. Mrs. Bonney has a school of Chinese girls—15 or 20 scholars, who board & lodge with them, & are indented to them for a term of years. They are taught Chinese, & not English. The effect of teaching Engl. to girls is said to be bad. The children said, or rather, *chanted*, the Lord's Prayer and sang a hymn, in Chinese, to an English tune, singing by note —"glory to Thee my God, this night".

Some conv. with Mrs. Bonney. She is daughter of Gen. Solomon V. Rensselaer of Albany, niece of the Patroon, & inquired after Mrs. N. Thayer, & Mrs. John E. Thayer of Boston, knows Mrs. Barnard, the Grangers &c. &c. & knew the Webbs (John & Hy), Mrs. Courtland V. Rensselaer &c. Mr. Bonney was a mechanic, with only a Lowe Sem. education—rather strange match—made by the Board, I fancy! She seems devoted to her work. Mr. Bonney is interpreter to the Am. Consulate, & is much respected here. He reads & speaks Chinese tolerably well. Their house is on the river bank, N. side, & our boat lay at their front door.

Called on Rev. Mr. Preston, missionary of Am. Presbyterian Board. He also lives on river. Wife from E. part of Conn.,—well enough—commonplace woman. Both these gent. offer me their services as *cicerones.*

Close by Mr. B.'s house, a fleet of boats is getting ready to sail with Chinese soldiers, up the river, to attack the robbers, who are in great force some 20 or 30 miles off. Robbers have taken sev. towns, & Canton wd. be in danger, but for the Allied occupation. The boats are gaudy with banners & devices & brave mottoes, & the soldiers have "victory" painted on their breasts. They are armed with spears & shields & a few matchlocks. It is said that not one in ten of them reaches the destination—they desert. There was a great beating on drums & gongs, & burning of incense sticks, & throwing to the winds of gilt paper, for a propitious voyage.

Returned, after dark, through this swamp of fire flies & jack o'lanterns, to Russell & Co.'s hong.

Dinner at 7 P.M. Mr. Orne & Mr. Sheppard appear in full dress of black dress coats, pantaloons & waistcoats, fresh shirts &c. This is the custom here & at Hong Kong, for dinner, & a good one, has a civilising effect on the young men. Only we three at dinner. Four servants wait at table. Excellent service, still, silent, clean men, & know their duties thoroughly—natural house servants. Orne tells me they are the best in the world, & trustworthy. Cooking excellent, such rice as we never get at home. Rice is steamed, here, dry, & each kernel separate. In-door servants all dress in long blue robes, white stockings & China shoes—heads & faces close shaved.

At night, watch the boats, from the balcony, & listen to the cries, & the broad field of moving & stationary lights.

Large sleeping room, open rafters, & mosquito nets—though cool weather—but heard no mosquito, yet.

When lie down to sleep, in the midst of this strange city, food enough for meditation & cause eno' for gratitude.

Sunday. Mch. 11, 1860. Up early. Chinese servant comes, takes away clothes, brushes & cleans them, folds up & places on chair, with boots blacked, as an Engl. servant does, & asks if have tea or fruit. As breakfast is late, take tea & toast,—tea a delight to smell or taste. Walk balcony, over river, until breakfast. See the families cooking, sewing & washing, in their little boats. These boats are covered over in stern & open in front. Here they sleep, cook, eat, wash & work. The girls row & steer, while the men are usually off at work as coolies, on shore, or in vessels. They pick up a living by carrying passengers (for there are no bridges across the river) & goods. Some of these boats are stationary, & only the houses of laboring men, but most are in motion. Such fleets of market garden boats, with meats, fruits & vegitables! Then shop-boats, & mechanic's boats, & large passenger boats going to & from the country (for a boat can go, by canals or rivers, all over China), & soldier-boats, & Mandrin-boats, & cargo boats, & the large, ornamented Hong-boats, the pleasure boats of the merchants.

Breakfast is of made dishes, rice & curry, eggs & omolettes, & fragrant tea. The tea this house uses costs *here* nearly $1 per pound. Tea must not be boiled. Pour upon the leaves boiling fresh water, as you need the tea. The water must not be allowed to stand in the kettle, simmering, but should be freshly boiled. Here, you can trust the Chinese to make it, but the merchants say that, at home, it should be made at table, tea in caddy, & water boiling at table.

After breakfast, go, by invitation, to hear (or rather see) Mr. Preston preach to the Chinese, in the open air, at one of their temples. Wonderful change wrought, here, by the Allied occupation. No foreigner has ever been inside the sacred walls of Canton, until now. In 1858, Engl. & Fr. took the city, stationed troops here, & established guard posts, & police & now foreigners can safely, by day, go all over the city. Engl. policemen, with neat blue dress & white band on hat, at corners of streets. In the suburbs, foreigners could hardly go beyond the factories without insult & risk, & the boys & all saluted them with the most odious appellations. Now, all is respect & deference. And so far is it carried, that the missionaries can safely &, even with pleasure, preach in the porches of their temples, while worship is going on within. (The missionaries differ as to the expediency of this, however, & the Catholics never do it).

Cross the river in the Hong boat of R. & Co. It is a long, wide boat, with a large covered part aft, large eno' for 4 persons to recline at length, furnished with Chinese pillows &c., & blinds—rowed by 5 men. Take two sedan chairs—each carried by 3 coolies, 2 before & 1 behind—Mr. Orne & I.

Now we pass the gate, in the city wall, a Fr. sentry one side & an Engl. the other, & are in the city—where in the world's history, no foreigner has been, with their knowledge, until now.

And, what a strange world, within! This long, narrow, winding alley,—not over 4 feet wide, from house to house, crammed, jammed, brimming, overflowing, shops, shops, shops, men, men, men,—a stream of life drifting up & drifting down,—cries & talking,—now & then a sedan chair, at a slow trot or fast walk, crying out to make way—make way! Little, minutest shops, crammed full of things to sell, & the grave shopmen behind their counters. Little bits of shops, full of little people working at the minutest work, with the minutest instruments! Coolies, in shirt & short trowsers, bare headed & bare footed. A better class, in long robes, skull-caps, shoes & long socks—women, in their sober comely dress of close necked tunic & long trowsers, some stepping free, with feet of natural sise, & some tottling on their little goat's feet, just able to get over the ground, in that mincing, swaying, tottling gait which they think so genteel. Close sedans, with ladies, behind closed blinds or curtains, or with a grave mandarin, or Chinese gentleman,—with pre-cursors & post-cursors, crying out to make way—& carrying, one his umbrella, another his fan & another his lantern & another his tablet of rank & office. Through all this, we drift along in our open chairs, at a jog trot, carefully navigating round the corners, &, if 2 chairs come abreast, making a dead stand, & edging sidewise into the shops. At some places, we stop, to see the vases & work. All is done in sight, & much in open air. At each open space, where there is a little more room, is a barber, with his chair & tools, & a cook with his portable furnace & little table of eatables, & a money changer, or a gambler, or a juggler. The compulsory shaving of the heads of all males, young & old, gives employment of numerous barbers. No Chinese wears hair on his face until he is 45 yrs. old, or is a gr. father, when he wears, or may wear, a moustache & beard or chin, but they never wear whiskers or long beards. The barbers not only shave heads & faces, but clean out the ears, & lifting the eyelids, run a piece of vine across the inside of the upper lid, to clean off the mucus. (This is thought to be one cause of the numerous opthalmic diseases here). There is a man bowing his head to a block, while the barber shaves & washes the crown, & there the barber is picking out an ear with a stick, delicately, & here he is nicely touching an upturned eyelid. In the shops are silk weavers, wood carvers, ivory cutters & carvers, seal cutters, spinners, lacquer workers,—an ant hill of industry! Everything done by hand & nothing by machinery. You might as well introduce steam into an ant-hill as into China. What would become of these 300,000,000 workers, each making the 9th part of the pin, & each getting enough to eat & to clothe himself!

Beside the modesty & neatness of the women's dress, they take nice care of their hair. It is always black, & usually abundant. They dress it in large bunches or ridges behind, with stone or glass ornaments & hair pins. They put no oil upon it, but plaster it with an extract of the slippery elm, which keeps it in place & makes it always look smooth, & yet does not make it greasy. Dishevelled or even rough hair, or curls are never seen. (I speak of the lower & middle classes, who walk the streets. The ladies, I have not yet seen).

Just as we reach the "Temple of 500 idols", we meet Mr. Preston coming away. We are late, & his preaching is over, & his crowd dispersed. He says he had a large & attentive audience, & told them their gods were wood & false, & could not do anything, & they rather assented to it.

Visited this Temple, or Pagoda. It is of the Buddhist (*pronounced* Bood-ist) religion. One large idol of Budda in the centre, & rows of little idols, (see infra, as to whether *idols*) each, however, about the sise of life, sitting, in long lines around the temple, & in the passage ways. These are said to be actually 500. They are of wood, gilded over. The gigantic central figure is Buddha (pronounced Boo-da), & he is of brass— a great, sleepy beast. Before him burn tapers, oil lamps & candles, & incense sticks, wh. consume slowly, without flame, like a slow match. On a large table before him, are offerings of fruits, meats & confectionary. The walls & door posts are covered with inscriptions in Chinese characters. The temple is of stone, with pagoda roof, the floors stone, the roofs tile. The grounds are extensive, with trees & grass, & long corridors & cloisters where the priests live;—for it is a Monastery as well as a temple. Sweep away the idols, & it would make a grave & venerable monastery or college of a Greek or R. Catholic Church. The stillness, the trees & the grass, the high roofs & high excluding walls are a relief from the streets (or lanes) of a Chinese city.

Return to lunch. Too late for the service of the Church of England, wh. is held in remote part. (Wherever there is a Br. consul in China, the Br. Govt. agree to give as much to sustain a Chaplain as the foreign residents will raise). Rev. Mr. Gray is Chaplain here, on those terms, $2000 a year in all. All speak well of him. On our way, call at Rev. Mr. Bonney's Chapel, wh. he has opened since the Allied occupation. Small, with seats for about 100, & a pulpit. He has a Chinese Chatachist, who addressed the people. The congr. consisted of Mr. B.'s school, —some 25 boys, & about 30 men—all Chinese. They sang "Jerusalem, My happy home" in Chinese, few joining except Mr. B. & the Chatachist & boys. Then he distributed copies of the Lord's Prayer & of the book of St. Mark. (They find it best to distribute the Bible in parts, a single gospel, they say).

Chinese have no weekly sacred day, but there are two sacred days in a month (lunar), which are somewhat observed as fasts & days of worship, but labor & trades go on.

Visit to the gardens of the great Hong merchant, Howqua. He is son of the great Howqua, who died a few years ago, worth, it is said, 30 millions of dollars. The gardens are his pleasure house & grounds, in the suburbs. Like everywhere else, you go to it by water. Here are some 20 acres of fish ponds, lakes, canals, stone bridges, grottoes, temples, pagoda roofs with stone pillars to shade the sitters at the beautiful tables of marble & ebony, grass plots, terraces, flowers in beds & flowers in pots, trees, shrubs, the lotus & the banyan, urns of flowers, the walks all paved with brick or large flags of stone, lines & lines of walls of open brick work with stone copings, some 2 or 3 feet high, on which rest thousands of flower pots with every kind of flower; & then there are singing birds,

cooing turtle doves, & falling gurgling waters. What an enormous outlay of expense! Worthy the Khan of an Oriental
Empire!

From this, we go to Puntinqua's gardens—(*pro.* Poon-tín-
qua) which are larger & richer than Howqua's. In the midst of
these gardens, is a private theatre. One house is for the guests,
& another, separated from it by a canal of some 12 f. wide, in
wh. swim fish & out of wh. grow creepers & shrubs, is for the
stage. It is luxury itself. The guests sit at open windows, in
large chairs, with tables before them, & look across the water
to the stage. Also, there is Puntinqua's summer house, full of
rooms, & furnished with chairs, tables, mirrors & bedsteads.
The favorite style of Chairs is to let in pieces of polished stone
for backs & seats, which have different colors, resembling
scenery. Some of the tablets, chairs & tables are extremely
costly. Some of the canals are large enough for large pleasure
boats, & one, almost dismantled, stands by the theatre.

Since the Br. occupation, these gardens are less cared for by
their owners, everything being unsettled in the state of things,
& incomes diminished.

The fish-ponds in the temple grounds as well as here, are
covered with a little green leaf, not larger than a mosquito, &
they tell me a few are thrown on the water, & they multiply
& cover its face, & the fish eat it.

Sam-pan is the name for the smaller boat, roofed over at the
after part, used to carry passengers short distances. Families live
in them. They are very neat. Each sampan has its little shrine,
where incense sticks or a taper burn twice a day. The boat-
people is the lowest class of Chinese, in morals & intelligence.
Yet the boat women are dressed in the same style of neatness
& modesty, do up their hair with the same care, & each little
boat has its looking glass. The sam-pans are mostly rowed &
steered by women, & in the melée of boats, amid all the
threatened collisions, & turnings & stoppings to avoid each,
they laugh & show their white teeth, & seem perfectly amiable. The babies are strapped to the backs of the mothers, but
the smallest children tottle about the little decks, tied by a
string to a stancheon or bench, & with little gourds tied to
their necks, as floats or buoys in case they fall overboard.

There starts a big passenger boat, for the interior, with some hundreds crowded on board, & tapers burning at the shrine, a gong beating, fireworks letting off, & gilt paper thrown to the winds, for propitiation of the appropriate divinities. There floats a big junk, a sea going junk, with an eye painted on each bow—"S'ppose no got eye, no can see. S'pose no can see, no can sa-vee; s'pose no can sa-vee (from French—*savoir*), no can make walk-ee all same so".

Coin. The Chinese have no coin except a base copper, with hole in middle, to string by, worth about a tenth part of a cent. They use the Sp. & Mex. dollar, ½ doll. & ¼ doll., but for less values they use bits of silver, uncoined, wh. go by weight, altogether. Indeed the Sp. & Mex. coins are taken by weight, so it is usual & as convenient to buy & sell in small sums by these broken bits of silver. For a dollar, you get a handful of them of all shapes & sises. Each shop & house has its scales, & each bit is weighed. The buyer as well as the seller has scales, in shopping & marketing. Almost everything is sold by weight— never I believe by measure,—sometimes by piece. Phrase is— children & chickens sold by the piece, all else by weight. The copper coin is called by Europeans, & in the Pigeon English, *cash*—so many cash, one cash, ten cash. Poor people seldom get silver, but buy & sell by the cash, in small sums. Gold does not pass in China. The great transactions of the foreign merchants are in Sp. dollars. The Chinese are very expert in counting dollars—I mean the bankers, brokers & clerks— weighing each on the finger, passing the good & throwing aside the light for subsequent weighing, & do this as fast as one can take up & drop them.

Great deal of sugar cane eaten. Bits for sale in the streets. Beetle nuts, to chew. Oranges excellent—& supply good, for 9 mos. in the year. Bananas, all the year. Chinese drink no water. Drink is tea, & grown persons occasionally wine, wh. they drink hot as they do tea.

Curious effect, going through the streets, to see a mechanic, in his shop, pegging away at an idol, pinching into his belly & chipping at his cheeks & shoulders.

March 12. Rev. Mr. Bonney breakfasts with us, & gives me his day. We have an open chair & 3 coolies each, but walk, for convenience & exercise, most of the time, coolies following.

He speaks the language & knows the habits of the people—so this is, in fact, my first real visit to the city—for any useful purpose.

We dive into the little streets, with their close jam of shops & people. A street in Canton is like an entry in the upper story & rear of a large country tavern, about as wide—doors as close together. They are all flagged with stone, & perfectly clean,—more easily kept so, as there are no horses or large animals in them. All is *foot work*. These little lanes are very gay, & even gaudy, with decorations, little flags & tablets & strips of cloth & paper, of all colors, with inscriptions in Chinese characters. These almost cover over the street, over head, from side to side. The houses are a story & a half high, the half story above for sleeping.

Each shop has its name, wh. is printed over the door,—indicating some quality claimed or desired. By this name, the shop is known & not by the name of its owner. (Even Howqua, is not the name of the gentleman, but of his hong, (counting-room, store-house); yet foreigners know him by no other name).

What a literary, or lettered people, these Chinese are! Over each door is an inscription, & over each inner door, & over each bench or oven, or anvil, or desk, or whatever place for working.

Meals are two a day, breakfast at 10 A.M., & dinner about 5 P.M. When they rise, they take a little tea or [   ].

Went into a shop where are made pottery, porcelain cups &c. The master & his long robed workmen were breakfasting at a table in the front room, & the coolies in a back room. Breakfast of Coolies was rice in abundance, tea, a made dish of vegitables, & some little cakes of flour or ground beans fried in oil. The table & plates were clean & neat, & their food well cooked & neatly set out. Their meal was neater & more wholesome than such as the poorer classes of Engl. & Am. get. Think of our grease & fat, & tough meat, bad bread, & worse hot cakes. I have seen something of the cooking of England, France, Sp. America & China,—& believe the worst cooking in the world is that of the middle & poorer classes in America. The Am. & Engl. are not *cooks*. The Fr. & Chinese are, & so are the Sp., to some extent. Think, too, of the great junks &

slices of heavy meat we all eat at home! Think of the head of a family, up to his elbows in blood, distributing half raw meat among his children, from fork & knife reeking with blood! Then a few waxy potatoes, clammy bread, & hard thick pie crust!

In this shop wh. is a fair specimen of all, over the front door is the usual inscription—"May rich customers enter here!". Over the steps up, a motto to the effect that all who ascend, shall bear in mind the elevation of virtue. Over the door to the hollow below,—"May all who go down remember humility" &c. So, over the oven, a call for good luck to what comes out, & over the work benches invocations & maxims & proverbs of virtue & industry. In a high place, hung with curtains, is a shrine with an idol, at which a taper is burning. The smaller shops have a little shrine at the door, in a niche. People of the shop very civil to us, rising from table, offering us tea & pipes, & making salutations as we come in & go out. Custom to make salutation when one enters or leaves a shop,—wishing good luck, excusing interruptions &c., in the florid style of Chinese politeness.

They are very fond of proverbs, maxims, mottoes &c. & cover their walls & door posts with them.

Visit Temple of Longevity. This covers large space of ground, in middle of the city, grass plots, trees, ponds of gold fish. The walks flagged with large, wide stones. It is also a monastery, & 200 priests reside here, in long cloistered ranges of one storied rooms. In centre is a large one story, pagoda roofed, temple. At door of temple, on each side, a huge ugly idol. In middle, a great image of Budda asleep. Around, are smaller images. Buddha is brass, rest are gilded. Howqua has ordered a daily service here for the long life of his mother, now 70 years old, for which he pays about $300. It is to last 49 days, & is now about half through. This service consists of prayers twice a day, for ½ hour each, & a perpetual burning of incense sticks & tapers. Before the idols stands a candelabra of 49 lamps, one for each day, & an incense stick before each lamp. Also, a large table on wh. are offered daily fruits, cakes &c.—wh. the priests eat, after they have been there a while. Mr. Bonney says (& so says Huc) that no intelligent Chinese think the God eats these things, or can, but they are offering to show willingness to part with goods &c.,—perhaps also, a notion of a *spiritual* partaking by the God, the things themselves, in their material form, being untouched.

Buddhist priests shave the entire head & wear cap. (Chinese laity, shave only front & top, & leave hair & long tail behind. This was not Chinese custom, but is compelled by the Tartars. Think of compelling 300 millions to shave heads & wear tails!)

A priest recognised Mr. Bonney. He had kept a shop, & Mr. B. had lent him Christian books & been kind to him. "Why become priest?" "Shop burned & all goods in it. No money to set up again. No friends to help. Very poor. Will starve. Now, have place to live & eno' to eat". He proceeded to say that Chr. books very good, & this religion not very good. This was to conciliate Mr. B., or rather a Chinese politeness, possibly he thought. A temple boy that stood by asked Mr. B. why he did not help the man, if he wanted him to be Christian. (This all in Chinese).

Pawn shops, very numerous. Pawn the smallest articles. Shops different times & rules of forfeiture. Went to one pawn shop & saw the system. Books carefully kept, & tickets given to each pawnor, & articles placed in store. The clerk wrote, or rather printed, (for they rather print or paint, than write their characters) very fast & handsomely. A handsome handwriting is highly valued by the Chinese,—& is very common. All writing is like printing of copper plate. They write with a brush of camel's hair, ground to a fine point, using India ink, which is placed on an ink-stone, by the writer's side. The operation is very neat & pretty. The clerk gave a pawn ticket, wh. he wrote out at Mr. B.'s request, for a hat, for 15 cents, (150 cash), with an indorsement in the corner, to show that it is of no value.

Met a detachment of coolies, under a Br. officer, each with a long bamboo pole. They are employed by the Br. army as porters & laborers, & are called, familiarly, the "Bamboo Rifles".

Quarters of the Tartar General—Chief of the Military. His old quarters battered by the bombardment & abandoned. Now, in smaller place.

Head quarters of the Allied Army. These are at the Yamún (pro. ya-moon—once for all, *a* is *ar*, *i* is *ee*, & *u* is *oo*), or palace of the Governor or Chief Magistrate, who is disposed by the

Allies. Large & regal place—broad stone walks, high roofed buildings, large grass plots & numerous trees. Found here Mr. Parkes, now one of the commissioners for China, & formerly Br. Consul at Hong Kong, a man of large experience. Spoke of my book on Cuba, in connexion with the Coolie trade, & said they had got valuable hints from it, in arranging their regulations here. He was in hurry, his wife leaving for England tomorow. Is to see me again on his return fr. Hong Kong.

Buddhist Temple & Pagoda, 1300 years old. Great ugly idols each side door, as usual, great brasen idol of Buddha in centre, & numerous other small idols. The Pagoda is 300 feet high, & more than ten centuries old, & delapidated. One cannot get above the third story, as the balconies (or whatever they are called) have fallen off.

Nearly all the temples & other large buildings in Canton suffered in the bombardment. One of the priests telling us of this, politely added,—they did not know they were our temples, or they would not have injured them.

Called on Rev. Mr. Graves, missionary of the Southern Bapt. Board. Found him dressed in suit of blue flannel, such as sailors & naval officers now wear. He has a small chapel & school, with a few scholars.

Time for *tiffen*, which is lunch, in all Br. India, China, & Australasia. Go to a China tea shop "True Abundance". Little tables, for 2 & 4 each, as in our eating houses. Place 2 cups on table, with tea leaves in each, turn hot water on them & cover the cups with saucers. Little cups to dip out tea & sip it. Tray, with 15 little plates, each holding diff. kinds of preserves & confection. Little cakes of black beans baked & ground to powder & mixed with little oil & scented, & covered with a crust of baked wheat flour—very good. Little preserved oranges, not larger than olives—excellent. Other confections of nice, quaint contrivance. All Chinese drink tea pure, without either milk or sugar. Milk not to be had. Sugar can be had if ordered. Drank it pure, *a la Chinoise*, & found it refreshing & agreeable. Nice little tiffen. Paid in silver bits, wh. they weighed at the counter, giving us cash for change.

Visit Temple to Confucius. (His Chinese name is Kong-Foo-Tze, which the Jesuits latinised to Con-fu-cius). Large grounds, walled in, silent groves, large trees, broad walks of flag stone,

& one large temple, in centre, one story, pagoda roof, high, stone floor. No idol or image in it, but simply a tablet to the honor of Confucius, on a kind of high dais, with an inscription over it "Sacred to the Spirit of Kong-Foo-Tze, the most sacred teacher. None such have been before him, nor since". In another place "the teacher of 1000 generations".

On the sides of the temple are tablets to the great pupils of Confucius,—the chief of whom is Mencius (Men-Tze'). There are no priests or preachers or teachers of the Confucians. He established no religion, no system, no sacrifices, & pretended to no revelation. He was simply a philosopher, teaching only moral philosophy, political economy, the social duties, manners & ceremonies in public & private life, the duties & rites arising out of the social system &c.,—with maxims, proverbs, rules & parables. On these his fame is founded. They do not elevate him above a human being, but venerate his memory & pay honors to his spirit,—not by prayers or sacrifices, but by creating temples or monuments, by tablets, & 2 or 3 times a year by a great procession of all the dignitaries, reverential salutations &c. &c. A scholar who resides at the temple—for it is a kind of refuge for poor scholars, told us he had been through five of the annual examinations, but had failed each time. "Why so?" "My poor exercises were not thought good enough". "Shall you try again?" "Yes. I have nothing else to do".

The system of competitive literary examinations has always prevailed in China. All social & official rank (except the military, which is rather looked down upon) depends on these examinations. Without a degree, no civil office is open to any one. A second degree, called by foreigners Master of Arts—opens higher offices, & the third degree, the highest of all. The examinations are in writing (chirography, I mean) composition in prose & verse, in the Classics—i.e. Confucius, Mencius &c. &c. The ex. are held in every district, for the first degree, & thousands present themselves, & it lasts sev. weeks. Candidates are locked into little rooms, each day, hardly large eno' to turn round in, with only paper & ink stone. Not over 1 in 10 gets a degree. Those who have a first degree may be afterwards exd. for the 2d, & so on. China is full of poor *plucked* men, whom the dignity of scholars will not allow to labor or trade, & the want of a degree keeps from civil office.

They are the copyists, & smaller pedagogues. One rejected friend looked rather weak & simple. I cd. not but pity him.

On our way, dropped into a little school of 12 boys, under one teacher. Mr. Bonney asked him if he had a degree. Not yet. Not able to pass—therefore, he teaches this little school, for very small pay. The boys sit, as Chinese boys probably have for 2000 years, on just such seats & at just such benches as Engl. & Am. boys. They study aloud. When they recite, they turn back to teacher, & rattle off, swaying the body to & fro They are taught to read & write, & then they commit to memory passages from the Classics, which they do not understand. A bright little boy of 12, stood up, back to teacher & said off his day's lesson, *memoriter*, wh. was a passage from Confucius, of about 12 mo. page, entirely unintelligible to him.

Thence, to the Foundling Hospital—a Chinese institution, but so run down after the Allied occupation that Allies have been obliged to aid it. The Engl. support here 50 nurses, & the French about 20, the rest by Chinese. There are about 100 nurses & 200 foundling infants. Yet the institution will accomodate 1000, if there were nurses eno'. They are all wet nurses, & the children are sent away when weaned. There are some 8 head women, or matrons, all of whom presented themselves to us. Lanes of little rooms, brick walls & earth floors, each with a nurse or 2 & a quota of babies.

Went to top of the city wall, where the Fr. & Engl. garrisons chiefly are. The Engl. are Marines, the 3d Buffs, & 67th. The French are only Marines. But in French navy, there is no difference betw. marines & sailors—all are sailors & all are drilled to the musket & drum. To make them into marines, they tuck their wide bottomed blue trowsers into white gaiters, & strap a belt round them with sword & pistol &c. The rest of their dress is sailor. The Engl. marines are soldiers only, with red coats.

Before leaving the Hospital, we made a call upon the resident physician, a Chinese. He is an M.D., & has two degrees in the public examinations, & wore a gilt button. The general supervising officer, a higher mandarin than he, was paying him a visit. There they sat, these two Chinese gentlemen, in long robes, black skull-caps topped with the button of literary & official rank, each with his long pipe & his tobacco box, with two servants in waiting, having a quiet talk, fanning themselves & looking out on the trees,—wh. I suppose is the sum of the official inspection. Each rose, clasped his hands together & bowed low, in the Chinese fashion, & had seats brought to us, & the servants brot us tea & pipes. Declined the latter but took the tea,—wh., as every where here, is made as you use it, a cup with a great spoonful of leaves, water poured on it, cup covered & left to stand about three minutes. Mr. Bonney had a long talk with them. The Dr. inquired after an Engl. work on anatomy wh. had been translated into Chinese, & Mr. B. gave him a note of introduction to the person who had it for sale. When the note was finished, a Chinese envelope was produced, highly ornamented, open at an end instead of the side as with us. "Then they have envelopes here". "They had them before we had them in Europe".

What did not this wonderful people have before us? Gunpowder, printing, mariners' compass,—& now, *envelopes!* And how exquisite is their politeness! Their motions are slow, their eyes fixed on you with an expression of interest & affection—the hypocrites—not exceeded by that of a young belle seeking to make her first conquest, & if they hand or take anything, it is with a bow & a careful place of the thing in your convenient reach. They are trained, & have been trained in the *rites* since the time of Confucius. When we take leave, they press their hands together & bow low, at the door, follow us to the outer door & repeat the performance there, with a look mingled of delight at having had such a pleasure & pain at losing it so soon.

The next place we visit, is the Hall of Examination. This is a large building where the examiners sit, & around it is a large area of some 6 or 8 acres, with bricked passageways lined with one story sheds or cabins, each large enough for a big Newfoundland dog to kennel in, which are the rooms in wh. the candidates are shut up, each to prepare their writings & theses. There are no less than 7000 of these. Think of 7000 candidates, in one district, & the chance for a degree not more than one in ten! But these buildings suffered so in the bombardment that they have been allowed to go to ruin, & the last two examinations have been held at a large temple in the country.

Here is the parade ground of the Chinese, in the day of

power, where the soldiers practiced their gymnastics, for they were little else, & shot their arrows. Now buffaloes are feeding upon it. The buffalo is the principal beef & milk animal here. It is what is called "Water buffalo", & differs from the Am. bison. It is fond of water, & lives in it, in warm weather.

The Br. have a telegraph to & fr. each military station in the city, but it is under ground, as the Chinese would cut it, were it in the air. They have also a post-office & parcels delivery,— but only for the Military. With all the civilisation of the Chinese, they never had a post, for public use, but only Govt. couriers.

The last place of our visit to-day is the "Execution Ground". Here, for centuries, the capital punishments of the city have been inflicted. Here thousands & tens of thousands have been beheaded, & the soil is saturated with human blood. Nor is this all. Tortures the most frightful have been inflicted here, such as it can hardly enter into the mind to conceive, & the air has been rended with shrieks & cries of the ultimate agonies of men.

Yet, the ground is small & obscure, with no indication of its purpose, being merely an open space or yard, behind a row of humble dwelling houses, some half acre or more in extent, without any public building, or other mark of a public character to it. Broken pottery lies about it, & people pass & repass over it, & when not in use for executions, it is used as a rubbish yard by the neighborhood. Mr. Bonney told me he saw 15 men beheaded there not long ago. The convicts are tied hand & foot, made to stand in rows, facing all one way, with heads bent over, & 2 or 3 executioners, each with a sharp cleaver, goes along & lops off their heads, with one blow to each, the head rolls off, the body starts up & falls over, & a very few minutes does the whole work. Sometimes 200 have been beheaded here at a time. Last week two were beheaded. They were to have been flayed alive, wh. is the favorite process, but the Br. officers forbade it, & the judicial mandarins had to content themselves with lopping off the heads.

A gentleman, Mr. Owen of the Br. Co. House, told me he was here once at an exn., & saw them begin their cutting up of a live man, but was obliged to leave, it was so dreadful. They began, with their very sharp cleavers, to cut slices off his cheeks & breasts & thighs & to lop off fingers & toes. The decree of the Court orders death by a certain number of cuttings, & the skill of the executioners is shown by getting all his cuts, his 20, 50 or 100, before the man is fully dead. This miserable dirty undesignated back-yard of a place has been for centuries the scene of these horrors.

As we are going home, towards dark, the shops are lighting up their shrines. In the larger shops, large lamps or candles burn before the large idol in his curtained shrine, in the rear, while the bits of shops, mere front counters, have their bits of niches at the door posts, in which the doll idol sits, & before it burns the bit candle. The candles & sticks burn abt. 15 or 30 minutes, for this ev. oblation.

Stop at the door of a large house, of a mandarin whom Mr. B. knows, in hope of seeing the interior. But the very polite door keeper says the owner has taken a wife, & the marriage fête is not concluded, & he has friends at dinner &c. &c. The front door is open, & through it we see a hall brilliantly illuminated with Chinese lanterns, & hurrying servants, & walls tapestried with red paper inscribed all over with characters in honor of the event, the family & the Gods. At the door sit four minstrels, a drummer, a cymbal striker, & 2 guitar players. They play a salute to each guest, when he enters or leaves. I spoke to Mr. B. & pointed to the minstrels, & they, thinking it an order to play, gave us a salute as we left.

Dined at Mr. Bonney's. Mr. & Mrs. B. feel very favorably to the English Army of occupation. They tell me the Eng. officers are very polite to the missionaries, often make contributions, offer them aid & protection in anything they undertake, & absolutely know no difference betw. Am. & English in their attentions & protection. So it is, they tell me, as to all Am. here. They are protected by the Allies equally with the Engl. residents. Mr. B. tells me that the Fr. troops are not so popular with the Chinese as the English. Mr. Preston confirms this statement.

Messers. Russell & Co. sent their great Hong-boat for me, & it was kept waiting from 6 o'ck. to 9. But that was thought nothing of. The coolies *live* in the boat, & may as well be here as at R. & Co.'s wharf.

"Old Head", the boat-master of Russell & Co., is an old

Chinaman, known to all Am. who have been in Canton the last 30 & even 40 years. He knew Mr. John P. Cushing & inquired of me about him, & Mr. C. must have left here more than 30 years ago. This nick-name of "Old Head" he is proud of, & the Chinese call him by it. He has charge of all the boats & boat-coolies of the house, & also owns sev. boats on the river. (Funny story of Old Head's being cheated in buying a boy, in the market).

Tuesd. Mch. 13. To-day, the Rev. Mr. Preston is to be my guide. Boat down to his house, wh. is on the river side & near the Gate of Eternal Purity. Start off, on foot, at abt. 10 A.M. for a ramble thro' the city.

Small door, curtain before it—"That is an opium shop. Go in!" Went in. Two rows of sleeping tables, with mats & pillows, to hold 2 or 3 persons each—& lamps & opium pipes. Smoker reclines at length, head on the hard pillow, & a servant loads the pipe with opium, puts it to his mouth, & tends it for him. Mode is to put little of the opium, in a soft gum form, into the small hole of the bowl, & put bowl to the lamp & inhale, swallow the smoke into the lungs. This was a low class shop, & poor people attended it. They come in & get a pipe or two & go off. Some, the confirmed topers, smoke until they are stupefied.

To the "Ten Thousand ages Temple", or "Temple of the Emperor"—for "10,000 ages", is a title of the Emperor. This is a large building, standing in an extensive enclose, planted with evergreen trees. It is a mere temple of honor. On the Emperor's birth day, on New Year's days, & on the 1st & 15th of ev. month, there are services here in his honor, burning of incense & lamps, & prostrations of the people before his tablet. I believe they bow the head, touching the forehead to the earth 9 times

Large Mahommedan Mosque, outside the walls, in the Eastern suburb. It is in the Chinese style of architecture, & has no sign of the crescent about it, or anything else to distinguish its religion, except the absence of all idols or images of any kind. At middle of one wall, opposite the door, is a recess, with curtains. Over it are Arabic characters, & the posts & columns are lined with Arabic, & there are tablets of the same. The floor is matted all over. There are no seats, & from the ceiling hang Chinese lanterns & European chandeliers,—but these are used for lighting & not for worship.

Temple of the God of War. Walled in, & large yard, grass plots, evergreen trees (chiefly a kind of bastard Banyan), flagged walks, large Chinese building of one story. This temple is confined to rich & superior people, who alone worship there —it being, I believe, their property. Consequently, it is not much frequented. Usually, it is a complete solitude. The idols are as usual, large & small, some of brass & some gilded, some hideous, some merely funny, & some grave & proper. There is one tablet here given by the unfortunate Commissioner Yeh.

A Buddhist Monastery. Quiet enclosed spot of several acres, standing in midst of city. Long rows of rooms for the priests & scholars, with cloisters, like the old monastic institutions of Europe. It has an open temple, in wh. the people go—freely to worship. Several women worshipping there. Before each idol incense sticks as usual & tapers. Each worshipper buys her sticks & tapers at stalls in the temple, also all her other offerings. The temple, like that at Jerusalem, is a place for sale of everything used in the worship, & of refreshments. There are more buyers & sellers than worshippers. One woman touches her forehead to the pavement 9 times, with her open hands reverently placed together, & then throws up two bits of wood & as they come down is good luck or bad luck. She is either seeking a lucky day, or a lucky place for a house or shop, or a lucky name for something or somebody, or a prophecy of good or ill luck on some proposed enterprise. She repeats the operation several times. Another woman, after prayers & prostrations, draws an incense stick from a number, examines its mark & goes to an old priest, who examines his tables & tells her whether it is good or ill luck. Before the great idol, is a large table with offerings of fruits & confectionary. The women also burn gilt paper, & paper-money. This paper money is of slight value, if any, but answers as well as money for the spirit of deity to which it is offered.

Great numbers of book shops & book stalls. Stop at one of the best of the shops. Mr. Preston knows the man, & says he has many valuable books. Showed me some books of Confucius & Mencius, & the four classics. No Chinese book is ever a stiff cover. The books are laid away on shelves as we put away note paper. Printing is on a yellow colored paper with very black ink.

Next visited the Governor's College. This is an institution for the education of youth already advanced in their studies, like the fellowships & scholarships of England.

The Treasury—a truly magnificent building—long vistas of avenues under trees, with broad flagged pavement, & large buildings of Chinese architecture, of stone & brick, with highly ornamented tile roofs—all in the usual gay & gaudy style of Chinese edifices. It is now occupied by the French officials & troops.

Now in the Tartar quarter. All the Tartar women have three earings, while Chinese women have one, & the Tartar women never cramp their feet. The Tartars are the dominant race— that is to say, the imperial fam. is Tartar, & so are the military commanders, (all, or nearly all) & a portion of all civil officers. But here there are Tartars of the lower class. They have taller & larger figures than the Chinese, with a more manly carriage & air, noses larger & more acquiline—the Chinese being usu- ally small & flat—, & eyes more like the European. They wear the shaven front & tail behind. But the Tartar is not suited for the quiet industry of the city. He must be a soldier, or a moun- taineer, or herdsman—either the open country, or at least, command & leisure in a city. Consequently, the Tartar quarter contrasts very unfavorably with the Chinese. There is some- thing approaching the city Irish of America about the quarter —though not one half so bad—the women neater & the chil- dren neater & better clad, & the men more civilised far, than our city Irish. Still, they are not so neat as the Chinese—there is little trade or business in the quarter, the houses have little furniture & often are dilapidated, & there is a look of im- pending bankruptcy about the whole region.

Called at French Mission. Delivd. my gen. letters fr. Bhp. Hughes & Fitzpatrick. B'p. of Canton a tall, slender, middle- aged French gentleman of agreeable manners & mild voice. A Fr. priest with him who has suffered fr. imprisonment, want of food & clothing, in the interior, & fears he has consumption— rather an interesting man. Whole number of priests in the dio- cese, 10, of wh. 2 are Chinese, educated at Macao. No sisters, of any order. Thinks there are 2000 Chinese professed Catholics in the city, including the families of professors. Am to call again to see school. Rooms very plain. Since the Allied occupation, not built or made any permanent arrangements as things uncertain. The European priests no longer wear the Chinese costume & tail &c., while in the city. Did so, in the interior, & do now, wherever for. dress is objectionable.

Saw juggler practicing his tricks in an open square, with crowd round him. No police there, & no disorder. Tricks were of the usual sort that we see at home.

Famous temple known among foreigners as the "Temple of Horrors"—not its Chinese name. Large seated image of God of judgment & punishment—same in each chamber, & 4 or 6 chambers on each side. In each chamber he is represented as sentencing a poor creature to some punishment for his sins in this life,—the dreadful executioners standing round. The figures are about the sise of life. In one, the man is standing upright in a wooden box & two men are sawing him in two, from the head downwards, with a two handled saw. In another, he is lying down & beaten with great bamboo sticks. In another, he is put into a mill, & they are grinding him up. In another, the victim is standing, & the executioners are lowering over him a large red-hot bell.

Amid all these horrors, the people are busily buying & selling, in the Temple Court, & some are worshipping at shrines, & throwing up the bits of wood, to learn the luck. These bits are flat on one side, & convex on the other, & if they fall in diff. ways it is good luck, if alike, bad luck. The luck of every day & place must be ascertained. The advertisements of houses to let, represent them as lucky, built on lucky days &c. One shrine in this temple is for all prayers &c. relating to children, & another for ancestors.

As we pass out, we see a room, near the temple—not of it— where a story teller is entertaining his company. He has a large room, with plain wooden benches, where his audience sit, he sitting on a raised platform. We take our seats, & Mr. Preston interprets the story. It is of a young scholar—scholars are the heroes of Chinese novels & stories, & not soldiers—learned & beautiful. He walks into the open country, & this country is described. Then reaches a mountain, finds a cave in it, enters, goes on, comes to another open, secret place. This he describes minutely—the trees, flowers, birds &c., & an exquisite palace & gardens. At a window of the palace, a beautiful lady, looking into the garden. She sees him, closes ½ the window, looks at him secretly with one eye. He is enchanted, lingers, grows late, a messenger comes fr. her to warn him off, as in danger, he replies how can he leave such a place & such a lady. Messenger says gate will be shut. It grows twilight, she leaves window, & he obliged to return thro' the gate & mountain to the city. Such a simple, harmless story as this holding a chance crowd in a large city! I doubt if N. York or London wd. be content with anything so harmless. The story teller has an animated, but dignified & simple manner, with rather graceful gestures, & Mr. P. says his language is good. His paragraphs are marked by striking on the table a small bit of wood, like a chequer man. Each auditor contributes a few cash, & there is tobacco for sale, for the smokers. Some idlers spend hours here, smoking & listening. The story teller has no book or notes before him.

A temple to the God of Medicine, with very elaborate figures.

Temple of the "Five Genii",—one of the most famous in the city. It belongs to the sect of the Taope, or Rationalists, a sect founded by Lao-tze, about 600 years B.C. This is the first Taos temple I have seen. It is very large, in the same style with the others, & has numerous images. It has the famous foot of Buddha, a stone which marks its form. (I forget whether it is an image of the foot, or merely its impression,—last or a shoe). The 5 genii sit on 5 thrones, & before each is a little insignificant block of stone. The tradition is that each genius had a ram, & each ram was turned into these very blocks of stone.

Great Temple to Confucius. Like the others I saw, it is a silent solitude in the midst of this great city. The grounds are walled in & embrace some 6 acres or more, with avenues under trees, grass plots, flower bed, flower pots on low brick walls, & several large buildings. In centre is a large tablet to his honor, before wh. the scholars prostrate themselves sev. times a year. The front gate has never been opened, they say, since the tablet was carried thro' it, & Mr. Preston doubts if even the Emperor wd. be thought worthy to have it opened for him. This temple is now chiefly used as the place where the candidates for degrees assemble after their examination is over, to hear the result. The names of the successful candidates are written on large pieces of paper, & pasted to the wall of a certain avenue, at the side. Some parts of the papers are on the wall still. This is the spot of triumph or defeat to thousands every year. In front of the chiefly building, in the Court Yard is an avenue flagged with stones, which crosses a small canal by a handsome stone bridge, arched & on some 20 f. in length. This place is called the "Scholars' Pool" & "Scholars' Bridge", for all scholars cross it to receive their degrees. To cross the Scholars' Pool, is the phrase for obtaining a degree.

Next, we visit a Mahommedan Mosque, in the old city. It is in the Chinese style, & not distinguishable from a college or exn. hall, except by the Arabic Characters upon it. In a little room, in the Purlies of the temple, a poor Chinese scholar, a Mahommedan, has school of some 20 Chinese boys, the children of Chinese Mahommedans, whom he is teaching the Arabic. I presume all the Mahommedans learn it. Whether the Mahommedans here are descendants of the Mongols & others who came to China centuries ago, or of their Chinese converts, I do not know—perhaps they do not. Mahommedanism has always been tolerated in China, but not spread much. We make an appointment to attend worship here Friday at 1 o'ck., —the Mahom. Sabbath.

So ends my second most interesting & instructive day of examination of this strange city & people.

Wed. Mch. 14, 1860.   The Chinese watchmen are required to beat on a hollow piece of bamboo, as they walk the streets at night, to show that they are awake. One hears this continual *thung, thung,* every waking hour, & the boatmen's cries on the river never cease.

To-day saw a lorcha. It was a long, sharp three masted schooner-rigged vessel, of about 3 or 400 tons, with duck or cotton sails. At each mast a large fore-&-aft lug sail, (by wh. I mean a sail that goes forward of the mast as well as abaft) & at the main a square topsail & t. g. sail. The junks have also lug sails, very large, of fine matting, with bamboo horisontal sticks each of wh. acts as a boom when the sail is lowered to it. While we sit at breakfast, in the room on the river, a shade passes over us as if the sun were eclipsed, & looking up we see the huge sail of a junk covering up our whole patch of sky.

Went out with Mr. Orne to see the shops for working in lacquer & ivory. The work is exquisitely neat & minute, & all done by hand. Every form & color of the lacquer tables & chairs & stands is the touch of a pencil by hand. A silent company is this little low room full of lacquer workers, each at his seat pencil in hand, & colors at his side. The patterns are on paper, & lie open before the workers. The outline is transferred to the table by pricks of needle points in the paper, thro' wh. a powder is spread.

In the ivory shop, I saw a nest of 21 ivory open-work balls, each so open that could see through the 20 to the little inner ball, not larger than a pea.

The master of the ivory shop has a nephew who is practicing gymnastics to fit himself for a mandarin soldier. There is an exn. for this office, as for the literary degrees, but all that is required for the military art is strength & agility. We went to the little room where the candidate was practicing. He is a small, thin man, with small hands & legs & skinny fingers, but very strong. His feats were equal to the Acrobats. A weight I could scarcely tip on end, he lifted, put on his breast & bending backwards sustained it there for sev. seconds. He is also required to practice with bow & arrow. At the last exn. he passed in the bow & arrow, but failed in the gymnastics. He will try again this year.

To the Honám Temple, at 5 P.M., to see the priests worship. This is by far the largest temple & grounds in Canton. These priests were men of large ideas. The grounds & structures are stately & generous. On entering the gate, a long vista of wide, straight flagged avenue, with tall evergreen trees on each side, terminates at the main temple. But there are numerous smaller temples, & a *town* of cloisters & dormitories, running in even lines, right & left. One could easily be lost in them. Then there are sev. small gardens & grass plots, & one large garden, beautifully laid out comprising sev. acres, reaching out to the suburbs of the city. In this garden is a brick structure where they burn the bones of the deceased priests, another where the ashes are temporarily placed, & a third, a large handsome sarcophagus, wh. is their final resting place, & on wh. appear the inscriptions of their names & with the appropriate mottoes & invocations. The chief trees are banyans & olives—I mean the chief that we recognise. The worship began just at dusk. There was 28 priests, probably the whole number now occupying this once populous monastery. They kneeled on the matted floor, facing one way, towards the shrine of Buddha, joined their hands by touching their fingers together & not by clasping them, & occasionally touched the foreheads 3 times to the floor. These kneelings & prostrations, with the continual repeating in unison, in a sort of droning chant, some sounds of words, once having a signification, in the land this worship came from, centuries ago, but now unknown to the Chinese, —traditionary sounds of more than a thousand years—these constituted the worship. This was continued about half an hour. Then they filed into line, headed by the chief priest, & made the circuit of the temple, inside, three times, their hands reverently meeting before them, & droning over a chant, the words of which were nearly these—Ma Ma Hominy For—Ma Ma Hominy For. Then another prostration, & it ended. All the while tapers & incense sticks are burning before the Chief & the smaller shrines.

I must say that the manner of the priests was grave, slow, reverential & dignified. The old oriental tradition of manner, —& much better than that at the Cathedral at Havannah, wh. it a good deal resembled. If the idols had been removed, & the furniture of the Cathedral put in their place, I could have recommended these boys & men as patterns to the boys & men of the Havana Cathedral. The close resemblance of the Buddhist worship to the R. Cath. has been noticed by all writers & travelers. It is so striking, that some of the early Jesuits in China ascribed it to the work of the Devil, counterfeiting true religion. Some will attribute it to a common element of idolatry & formalism, & others to the common traditions of the Patriarchal ages;—as the temple worship at Jerusalem, with its bloody rites, its altars, its priestly vestments, its images of Cherubim over the Mercy Seat, its brasen oxen, & its memorials of Moses & Aaron, differed not much *to the eye* from that of the surrounding heathen nations. But one was to the Most High, & the others to idols.

Visited the ancestral temple of the Howqua family. It stands by itself, in enclosed grounds, is large & costly, with porcelain tiles in the ceiling, & the walls covered with tablets in honor of the different ancestors. Before these, incense sticks are continually burning. Wealthy families have the separate temples, for their ancestral halls. Others have a room set apart in their houses, & the poorest have a little shrine with a tablet or two in the corner of the chief room. (See the account of this ancestral worship, its nature, whether idolatrous or not, in Williams' China, Davis' China & Huc).

Thursday. Mch. 15, 1860. Take a coolie & go alone into the city, to call on the R. Cath. bishop & see his institutions. It is a long walk—say 2½ miles from the boat landing. Saw the same priests as before. Showed me an orphan asylum, in wh. are 70 orphan boys. Chinese, with 2 Chinese teachers, priests—educated at Macao. When I go in, each Chinese priest comes forward, stands before me, puts his hands together, bends one knee—not quite to the ground, to make his salutation. I answered it the best I could, by bowing low & taking off my hat. The latter is known to be our usage, but is not that of the Chinese, who keep on the hat,—sitting bare headed being a familiarity. The boys learn Chinese & a little Latin—the latter in the Roman Characters—for it is not possible to write a foreign language in the Characters of an ideographic alphabet.

They have also a small hospital, wh. I did not see. The priest who went with me, a Frenchman, asked me if I was not struck with the resemblance of the Buddhist worship to their own.

Chinese tiffen. Very good—tea pure (without milk or sugar) &, as before, a tray with exactly 15 little plates with two pieces of confectionary or preserve on each. Preserved oranges, about sise of Sp. olive, excellent.

A great city without a sound of carriage wheels or the hoofs of horses! Only the human voice & the human footfall strikes the ear!

Canton seems to be one great one-storied house, with its entries & long passage ways, with doors each side, crammed with people, with an occasional glimpse of sky at openings in the roof, & here & there an open Court Yard. As you go through the streets, the shops seem to have no front, but to be open on that side, like a booth, but they have movable shutters wh. they put up at night.

Called on Rev. Mr. Gray, the Br. civil chaplain. He is too ill to go about with me, which he very much regrets. He says the 500 images in the Temple are not of gods or demi-gods, but of sages, the supposed pupils of Buddha, to wh. these honors are paid.

Among the gates of Canton are Eternal Purity, Eternal Joy, Tranquil Sea.

Frid. Mch. 16. To the Mahomm. Mosque at 1.30 P.M., with Mr. & Mrs. Preston. Called at house of a Chinese Mahommmedan. The people in the street saw Mrs. P. get out of her chair at the door, & crowded into the gentleman's house, to inspect a European lady. Mr. P. tells me the people of the street take great liberties in the outer courts of private houses. They thronged round Mrs. P., chiefly children, but as the news spread, some Chinese ladies, of the better class came in. Such a jabber as they kept up! The old Chinese gent. was powerless to get them out.

Went to the Mosque, under his wing, the crowd following. Let in at a side gate &, upon our distinct promise not to step inside the Mosque during worship, (wh. is an abomination unto the Mahommedans), we were led to the open door. The floor of the Mosque is open, covered with matting, & without seats. Only men were present.—men & boys—whole number some 60 or 70. They sat down on the mats, in rows, all facing one way—wh. doubtless was towards Mecca, & in that direction is the pulpit & a niche, like a shrine, but with no image or picture—for the Mahom. allow none. They pray kneeling, & mostly in silence, with hands joined, & occasionally bend forward & touch the forehead to the floor. This motion, though reverential enough, presents a curious spectacle when long rows of men are seen from behind. Some 8 or 10, who seemed to be leaders in the worship, wore white turbans. The rest wore skull caps, going up to a point in the middle, like a minareted dome. The chief officiator, at one point, went into the pulpit & chanted a long piece, whether it was from the Koran, or a sermon I do not know. Each man took off his shoes at the door, & a long line of strange looking shoes was ranged against the wall, inside. From here they took them by hand to the door. They all wore some kind of sock.

Desirous of seeing the interior of a Chinese gentleman's house, we called on a gentleman whose name is spelt by Europeans Hu, but pronounced Huf-y. He is a friend of Mr. Preston. He is the head of one of the most wealthy & distinguished families in the province; &, "China fashion", the whole family, brothers, uncles, nephews & first cousins, live under the roof—or rather, in the same enclosure, for there is a little village of houses & court yards & passage ways constituting the establishment. It is said that 2 or 300 persons form the household, including servants. There are no less than three schools for the children of different ages. The ancestral hall is a small temple, standing by itself, with tablets to centuries of ancestors, before wh. lamps continually burn, & around which are grouped the standards of the various offices they have held. Room after room, court after court, open ranges of flower pots & bird cages, garden plots, furniture of ebony with variegated polished stone backs, profusions of lanterns, 20 sedan chairs standing in the halls, & the flitting of long-robed upper servants & short-tuniced Coolies indicated the wealth & consequence of our host. The man himself, we found in one of his smallest & plainest rooms, in a plain dress. He received us with the usual courtesy of his nation, & made the usual minute inquiries they think so polite, after our age, our families, our health &c. He is a little over 30, & has but one wife. He is a scholar, & over his front door is inscribed his second degree of Master of Arts. We found him engaged with a galvanic battery, wh. he had imported from New York. He was in the habit of giving electric shocks to his friends, & offered us one. He had had two steel plates made in the horse shoe form, & was trying to get them magnetised, but had not succeeded as yet. Mr. Preston offered to introduce to him the Br. officer of Engineers, who has charge of the underground magn. telegraph betw. the military posts in the city. Mr. P. says he is a man of intelligence, but, excepting these little curiosity matters, is wasting his life with opium. He was smoking tobacco from a long water pipe, wh. a servant ever & anon prepared, put to his mouth & took it away again. He offered us tea, wh. we accepted—also what he called wine, wh. I drank fr. curiosity. It was as colorless as water, was made fr. rice, & was, in fact, not wine but spirit. Going out, we passed under a gate way the inscription on wh. showed that it was built by one of his ancestors by special permission of the Emperor.

Our last visit to-day was to a festive temple, a temporary erection of bamboo poles, covered with richly painted cloth & matting, set up by vol. contrib. of the neighborhood, in honor of the fact that the city had not been entirely destroyed by the Allies. Each person in the neighborhood contributed a sum equal to one month's rent of his place of business. The interior was very showy with lanterns, & suspended strips of cloth & paper of brilliant colors, with shrines & idols, & tables of fruits & flowers. It was to stand but three days. The place was also decorated with furniture, paintings & other works of Chinese art, lent by their owners. Entrance free to all, & perfect order prevailing. This is, certainly, rather a liberal contribution for a mere temp. & occas. offering of thanks. The presiding deity of the Temple is called the Queen of Heaven.

This evening, went to visit the famous Flower Boats. For safety, & to prevent all misconstruction as to purposes, took Mr. Orne & Mr. Sheppard, "Old Head" & an escort of Coolies with lanterns. It seems the custom is to let a boat for the night, with its contents & appurtenances, & the Chinese invite their friends to dine with them there. One cannot see them, as a mere visitor, without intruding upon some one's party. Still, as the doors & windows are wide open, it is not unusual or unexpected. We selected one wh. seemed a good specimen, & introduced ourselves, in Pigeon English, to the man who was giving the entertainment. He received us politely, & offered us tea & pipes. His company consisted of three friends. A Chinese dinner was about being served to them, on separate stands, in their little saucers, & all were smoking. Four young girls, with hair most extravagantly extended behind & dressed with flowers, with faces conspicuously rouged, but modest in dress & manners, denisens of the boat, were of their company, & there were two musicians & several waiters. Mr. Orne told our host that I was a foreign gentleman, that I had never smoked an opium pipe, & was desirous to do so. He courteously ordered a servant to prepare one, & directed me how to lie down & take the pipe to my mouth—for they always smoke opium reclining. The servant loaded the pipe, & I drew the smoke, swallowed as much as I could into my lungs, puffed out the rest, & got a good notion of the taste, though not enough, of course (I was not willing to risk it) to get the effect of a sleep, or indeed any effect on the consciousness. The taste is acrid & not pleasant. It remained in my mouth all night. We asked for music & the grave gentleman placed a stand between his legs, with a box upon it covered with hide, on which he beat with two sticks, while the two musicians played on their stringed instruments,—one like a guitar & one like a banjo, a kind of music between that of the bagpipes & the banjo, to a monotonous song like the genuine negro plantation chants. I cannot see in their music, so far, the signs of a tolerable civilisation,—to be sure, I have heard only that of the lower classes.

Our whole stay was only about 15 m. & we were bowed out of the boat, our host glad eno' to be rid of us, & left the gaudy, illuminated flower-boat, for a pull back, against the tide, on the dark river, glittering but not lighted by its fire-fly boat lights.

All our passing about involves boats, as we are on the Honan side of the river; & Russell & Co.'s hong, has its ret-inue of boats & boatmen, as well as of other coolies. I have become so much at home here, that I take no coxwain, but steer the gig among the junks & boats, by day or by night. But the sampans & the hong-boats provide their helms*man*, who is usually a woman. Most large vessels are propelled in part, by a long large scull at the stern, formed of two pieces of timber lashed together, which requires 2, 4 & sometimes 6 persons to work. It is surprising to see with what ease & grace a woman will manage the sculling oar of her boat, often with one hand. It is rather a graceful motion, in their easy dress.

Saturday. Mch. 17. This day, by Mr. Bonney's kindness, is given to an expedition to the White Cloud Mountain. This is a hill, about the height, I judge, of Blue Hill, Milton, lying about six miles to the N.E. of the N.E. gate of the city. We hired two chairs, with 3 coolies to each, to carry us there & back, to the summit if we required it, for two dollars in all—one dollar for a chair & 3 bearers for all day! As we went thro' the city, Mr. B. pointed out certain places for my observation. Several small academies, for the instruction of advanced scholars. These, he says, are very common, &, before the capture of the city, were very well attended. One large place enclosed by a high wall of open brick work, through wh. we could see the grass & trees & a large building—that is the ancestral hall of a clan or tribe; for the Chinese keep up their clans like the Highlanders, & the ancestral hall for the common ancestors binds the clans together. Over the entrance to one, are five papers, for the Five Filicities.

As we go out, beyond the walls, we come upon a party of the Buffs & 67th, target shooting, with English rifles, at 600 yards.

We leave behind us the venerable walls of the city—more than 800 years old, grass grown, shrub grown & even tree grown, on their perpendicular sides. They are perpendicular faces of brick, outside, & sloping earth mounds inside.

As we get out into the country, we see something of Chinese horticulture & agriculture. Large paddy fields, low & wet, where the rice is sown & nursed, & from which, when it has reached a height of 6 inches, it is taken up & set out by hand in open rows, in wider spaces, in the drier fields. Next are tea fields, where the tea shrub, with dark green leaves, & looking like a close clipped hawthorne hedge, is growing. Then there are sweet potato fields, & olive fields, where the tall, thin olive tree grows, with dark green leaves.

Now we leave the low country & ascend the hills. These hills are rocky & entirely barren of trees & vegetation, except in the little valleys or cañons, where the water flows over rocky bottoms in the wet season, edging them with rich green grass & shrubs & trees. But these barren hills are cities of the dead! Not one hill, or one field, but every hill, every high field is a cemetary, a necropolis. The tombs of the wealthier classes are large & stately, not high, never towering into obelisks or arches, but far extended curves of ornamental walls within walls, centering & culminating in the portal of the tomb, over which is the inscription of the name, age & office of the deceased. Sometimes these costly structures are tombs for a family, sometimes sacred to the remains of one person. The tombs & graves of the less wealthy, have simple head stones, as with us, with the name & date of birth & death of the occupant.

Indeed, a Chinese cemetary differs not from one of our own except in the style of the more costly structures, &, (as to this region at least) in that they are not enclosed spaces, like Mt. Auburn & Greenwood, but the entire region of barren hills, for miles, without enclosure or landmark, are given up to them.

This is possible in a country like China, for here people cannot live sparsely about the country. It is not safe. As soon as you have passed the walls, & the close suburbs nestling under them, you see no houses; but only towns or villages, built as close as the centre of Canton, where the people herd, even if they have no walls, for the advantage of common vigilance & strength. Some of these tombs were built, as their inscriptions indicate, more than a thousand years ago.

In a charming green valley, amid olive trees & banyan trees & running water, with a view over the city & river & country below, secluded yet commanding a beautiful prospect, beautiful to look at & to look from, lies a Buddhist monastery. It is new,—that is, not more than 50 or 60 years old. It is built of dark bricks, with tiled roofs, in several buildings separated by ports & cloistered passages. It is out of our way, & as there are several more to be seen, we do not stop.

Here is a little close village, stifling & stinking with its narrows streets—less clean than Canton.

Now, out on the open hill our path leads directly through the open Court Yard of another monastery. It is silent, our knockings at the great door meet with no response. The monks —there are but 2 or 3 here now—are out either begging or buying at the village or the city.

The tombs & graves follow us all the way up to the very summit of the White Cloud Mountain, & the finest sites, commanding the nobler views, but always on high & dry ground, the tombs are built. And every step of the ascent, from the first leaving of the low ground to the top of the mountain, the broad walk is paved with wide flag stones, &, in the ascents, these stones are laid in stairs. The expense of this may be estimated when it is remembered that these stones are carried by men, slung from their shoulders, two by two, & that the stones for the tombs are also mostly brought far by wind & tide.

Now we are nearly at the top, & here, in one of the most delightful spots conceivable, stands, or rather lies, & nestles, the monastery of the White Cloud. It is built in a little valley wh. opens wide at the lower end, disclosing a view of the river, city & distant country, while the site has the advantage of perfect quietness, seclusion, a look of entire repose, the shades of trees & rocks & hill sides, the fall of water & the singing of birds. And how exquisite is the note of that bird, in that deep green tree just over the farther roof! We stand & listen, & catch it again & again. It is a new note to me. As liquid as falling water—& so rich & soft in melody.

Our chairs & coolies we leave at the monastery, & climb to the top of the hill, but the cloud is too thick to give us the full view. Our chairs, by the way, we got out of, as soon as we began the ascent, not only fr. regard to the coolies, but because we preferred the walk.

Above the monastery, at the top, or very near the top of the hill, is a large tomb, erected by a pious son & gr. son to their mother, who was buried there. Their name is Fang. It is a costly structure, every stone brought from a distance to Canton, & carried up the hill by hand. It has 2 lions, of the sise of life, & 2 high stone columns. Over the numerous ravines, thro' which, in the rainy season the water pours, handsome stone bridges are built, with a perfect arch span, & stone railings on either side, as good as any in England. Yet they are very old. The arch is no special tradition or local invention, but something to which all cultivated knowledge & experience would lead.

Return to the monastery. Its architecture is as noble as its situation. How lofty, how spacious, how airy, how strong, is everything! A noble stone bridge, a noble platform of stone— such spacious halls & passages & courts,—& all so solid & so ancient! To be purified from its Buddhist idols, & transformed to a Christian College, school, or monastery, is all that it needs. How I would delight to come here, in the heat of summer & spend a few weeks of leisure, with books & nature!

The old abbot (if one may so call him) held a long conference with Mr. B., over our lunch, in wh. he could not be persuaded to join, but wh. he had set out for us in his best hall. He says the monastery is now poor—very poor, & one of the brothers who has an ulcer, cannot get money enough to put himself under the charge of Dr. Kerr, in Canton.

In a lower court is a stone well, of the sweetest & purest & softest of water. People send all the way from Canton for it. The abbot offered Mr. B. leave to send for it at all time (it would take a coolie all day to get 2 buckets full). The well is not deep,—about 10 f., full nearly to the top, clear bottom, & always the water running in & out. It is, indeed, a stone pool, in a running underground stream. Over it grows a large olive tree.

The chief idol in this monastery is the Water Dragon King. But Buddha is its divinity. In one shrine, are tablets on wh. are engraved the names of the founders & chief benefactors of the monastery, & before the tablets tapers & incense are always burning.

Take our leave of the courteous solitaries; & resume our walk down the stone steps, & down the miles of nicely laid flag-stones, towards the level country. About ½ way down—another road from the one we came up—we stop at a very pretty monastery, prettily situated. It, is of the Taos, or Rationalist religion. We find only one priest there. He is alone, in a small room, reading, in Chinese, an English tract against the use of opium. He receives us politely, & praises the tract. Mr. B. gave him a copy of the Gospel of St. Mark. How dull & lonely this place & this life is! The Taos priests wear the long queu wh. the Buddhists do not. This Taos priest is from the upper provinces, & talks what is called the Mandarin dialect (Anglicé for Mandarin is not a Chinese word).

Between the White Cloud Monastery & the city, by this route, are 3 monasteries, 2 Taos & 1 Buddhist. We stopped a while at each. At the Buddhist, is a large image of Buddha, wh. represents him as a fat, jolly god, with a huge paunch, & fat laughing eyes. "Yes", said the priest, "he does not trouble himself about anything. He is always happy & easy. Your God does concern himself with everything—Buddha does not. But, you see he is happy to see you". "Yes", said I "& equally so to see us go away". "Yes, Yes, he cares for nothing". How much of this is sincere confession, & how much is Chinese politeness?

How scarce fuel must be in Canton! Here are poor people about among the hills scratching up dried grass to burn under their pots.

Between the city walls & the top of Mt. White Cloud are

nothing but monasteries, close villages & tombs. There is a party of 3 Chinese, of good condition, selecting a spot for a tomb. Yet, little doubt, they will, sensible as they are, consult the luck sticks or some other device, in the Temple.

On the ground, at intervals, are bits of paper cut in curious forms, dropped as they go by funeral processions.

The last thing on our way in, is the village devoted to the lepers,—the Leper Village. What associations of ancient story does the very name recall! We turn aside & enter it. I may well say enter it, for it is as close & compact as a fortress, though without a wall. And how filthy it is! The main street is straight, & flagged, about 10 f. wide. From this the side streets run off at right angles, mere dirty passage ways betw. houses, & not over four feet wide.

A respectable looking man, the best dressed, comes forward, & offers to be our guide. He is not a leper. He says he is of a younger branch of the Howqua family. He lives here because his wife is a leper. Not one in ten of the people we see, including children, are lepers. They are the children of parents, one or both of whom may be lepers, or they are husbands or near relatives of lepers sent here, whom they have faithfully followed. Some, not lepers, remain here, because they were born & have always lived here, & have property here. They do not seem to think leprosy contagious or infectious. The lepers are not white, as I supposed. On the contrary, their skin is red & blotched & swelled, like a spot just recovering from being frosen, &, in some cases, the hands & feet dwindle away & fall off. Even here, the all pervading Chinese literature extends itself. Here, at the end of a dirty passage, is a school, of some 20 boys. Not one of the boys is a leper. Perhaps the leper boys are kept apart,—though in the streets & at the little temple they all sit & walk together & in the temple porch we saw four men playing cards, 2 of whom were lepers & 2 not. In one corner of the school room, in a square part set off to him, was a pig! He was clean enough to be sure, but a pig in a stye, & close against him, not 4 feet off, sat a boy of ten studying Confucius! (The smallest boys that can read, read the great classics & commit them to memory, without understanding more than a few words).

The whole population of this village is about one thousand.

A little temple & god & shrine & lepers, of course, at the head of the main street. It is a dreadful, piteous little den. The people, young & old, come out to see us. I suppose a foreign visitor is a very rare thing among them.

Now, to the walls again, into our chairs, through the gates, along the narrow, close, gaily decorated, intensely alive & industrious streets, two or three miles, & then the river, the sampan girls crying out recommendations of their respective boats & smiling at us, showing their white teeth—we select one that has a little earnest boy of 8 or 10, clamoring for us,—& are landed at the Russell & Co.'s. Hong—wh. the boat-people call "Lussel-y Hong", as near as they can get to it—at exactly 5 P.M., in time to get ready for our dinner at the house of Yung Ting, the nephew of the great Howqua. There are four visiting cards from Yung Ting, on our table, one for each of his expected guests. These cards are pieces of red paper, about 4 in. by 2, with the name written on them. These visiting cards they had, too, in China before Europe learned to write.

Reach the house at 6 o'ck. Received at the door by an upper servant. Yung Ting soon appears,—a man of about 35, dressed in plain grey silk high necked long robe, with black skull-cap. None of the Chinese show or wear any white linen or cotton. We are led to an open room, opening into a Court, & take seats. Yung Ting inquires with anxious solicitude the name & age & residence of each guest, & seems struggling to keep all in mind. (The guests, are Mr. Delano, Mr. Orne, Rev. Mr. Preston, who is also interpreter, & myself). Tea is brot as soon as we are seated. When he is called out by his steward for an instant, he apologises all around & places his little boy, who is formally introduced to each of us, a boy not over ten years old, in his chair, to do the honors in his absence,—tho' it is but for a moment. The little boy looks as composed & grave as a mandarin, with no boyish awkwardness. Then Yung Ting re-appears, dinner is announced, & we are led to another room. Here is a table for six, for the boy sits at the foot, grave & silent for 3 hours, eating little, but never faltering or moving fr. his upright, respectful position, & never speaking.

The room is brilliantly lighted with Chinese lanterns & European chandeliers. There are some six or eight servants waiting on the table. It is set with fruits & flowers, & some 10 or 12 dishes of preserves, but the preserves are no more offered to us to eat than the flowers. Our seats have no backs, which is tiring to us, unused to that since school days. There is European wine & Chinese. Which will we have. Of course, we choose the Chinese. This is always served hot, from little china tea-pots, in very small porcelain cups, not over 2 thimble-fulls to a cup, but when your host drinks with you, you must exhaust the cup & turn it upside down, in proof of your fidelity to the *rites.*

Now begins the series of courses. I did not count them, I am sorry I did not. We agreed that they must have been between 20 & 30. And such strange compositions, fins of sharks, sinews of dolphins, berries of the lotus, the most recherché & improbable things are the most prised. He told us fairly that many of them had no other merit, & were made eatable by condiments only. I ate too much of the first courses, not expecting so many, & the courses began to pall. But, I did not like to refuse. I *tasted* of each, & our host required ever so many little bumpers of us all, & I feared we were all overcharged with food & liquid—not that the wine was at all intoxicating, for it is weak, & we did not take enough for that, but it is sweet & palls on the taste.

A course consists of one dish, & that is given to each guest. There is no helping from large plates to small, but to each guest is brought a large tea-cup or deep saucer full of what he is to eat, seasoned & mixed with its vegitables & sauce, & covered to keep it hot. Sometimes there is a second dish, for the sauce or seasoning. Chop sticks, of ivory! It is my first attempt, but I resolve to do or starve & after frequent failures get the nack of them pretty well. For the liquids,—for some courses are soups—we have porcelain spoons. The last course is tea, wh. is always a signal to go. Our dinner took about three & a half hours—& all devoted to the courses, with little intervals. This style is very favorable to conversation, as there is no helping & offering or requesting of things to eat,—the bane of an ill-served dinner at home.

But, how exquisite is the politeness of Yung Ting. He exhausts ingenuity in framing inquiries to show his unspeakable interest in each of us—our ages, if married, how many children, & of what sex & ages, how came here, if had pleasant passage, how many days, was the boat crowded, was the weather good,—& at each question he bends his eyes on you anxious for your answer, & if your ship was crowded or the weather bad he is distressed, & if it was good he is relieved & delighted. Then, when you speak to him or answer his questions, he never allows himself an abstracted look, but fixes his eyes on you, & gives frequent emissions of guttural sounds, to denote his attention & interest & varying emotions. Indeed, he knows nothing but the pleasure of his guests. To that everything bends. Now, all this is from the books of rites, which educated Chinese study from early boyhood,—books written 2000 years before Chesterfield was born!

From dinner, we adjourn to another room, where tea is offered again. (I forgot to name, as an instance of the freaks of fashion, that the dishes he took most pride in placing before us were European porcelain, when many of his plates & cups would be worth their weight in gold in Paris or London, among connoiseurs). Now he invites us to walk round his house, & we are shown through a series of rooms for sitting & rooms for sleeping—no women's apartments, however are ever shown to men, nor can Madame Howqua or Yung Ting be seen on any terms—& a library, wh., being of unbound books, looks like a paper shop, &c. &c., & one shrine, with tapers & incense sticks. His ancestral hall is, I suppose, that of the Howquas. (By the way, How-qua, is the personal name, & not the family name, nor, as I have said *ante*, the hong name of the great merchant of world wide renown. But it is given as a family name by foreigners, and the son & successor of the great Howqua, is known as Howqua by all foreigners & in all his relations with the allies).

When we rise to depart, our host says he has chairs for each of us. He bows low & takes impressive leave of each of us at the door, & again at outer door, & we go home, through the narrow streets, a flashing train of lanterns,—Chinese lanterns —2 or 3 hung to each chair, & lantern bearers before & behind our train.

So ends my first Chinese dinner.

Sunday. M'ch. 18, 1860. Rise early, & after a cup of tea & slice of toast in my room, go, with my coolie guide—whom

the Russell hong call "Chesterfield", from his politeness, to the
7 o'ck. Mass of the French mission. It is a long walk, of 2 or 2½
miles, thro' the heart of the city. There were about 200 Chinese, at the mass, all sitting on the matted floor & kneeling.
They had mass-books in Chinese, & seemed to enter intelligently into the service. The chief portions usually sung by
choirs, were chanted by the Chinese,—the Lord's Prayer,
Creed, Confiteor &c. in the Chinese. They do much better with
chants than with metrical hymns. There were two Chinese
priests in the Chancel, with two Europeans, & six Chinese altar boys, dressed in Chinese costume (as, indeed, the Chinese
priests were) with red skull-caps.

Returned to breakfast, walking back. At 11 A.M. went to the
English Consular Chapel, where we had the English service,
with a congregation of about fifty English & Americans, with a
very fair choir. I was very grateful to take part in this service
after more than two months deprivation of it. Mrs. Bonney
was there. The American Prot. Missionaries have no service in
English on Sunday, only a kind of Sunday ev. Prayer Meeting
at one of their houses. (I suspect that the Bonneys both rather
incline towards our church).

Called on Mr. H. S. Parkes, this afternoon, taking a third
long walk. Staid at home, read & wrote.

Monday. M'ch. 19. What with the Chinese dinner, & what
with the three long walks—but I admit it was the 20 or 30
courses—I had a tossing feverish night, with extravagant &
erring dreams. To-day, better, but rather tender, & keep at
home, in order to be well eno' to dine with Parkes this
evening. Parkes promised to send an Orderly sarjeant & chair
for me, as the gates would be closed at 6½ P.M.

Find myself feeling pretty well at night, & having had no
tenderness about the head, which is good sign. At about 6 ½,
coolie comes to door—"One piece-y Sojer-man downside
talky you", & there is the striped Orderly with band on hat &
military salute, to conduct me to Mr. Parkes. Boat to the
Allies' Landing, where a chair waits. The great gate is closed,
but opens its ponderous & *iron* jaws to the potency of the
Commissioner's pass, & I am taken to the Yamun. Had hoped
to see Parkes alone, to get his views of the Engl. side of all

these questions, as he knows the history better than any official now here. But there was company—for Sir Hope Grant, the new Commander in Chief for China arrived in the city this evening, &, among others, one of his staff, Major Taylor, is staying with Parkes. Major Taylor was at the 2d relief of Lucknow by Sir C. Campbell, & in the war since, seen service, has clasps & medals—a young man, with a soft voice & gentle manner, but with a long head. There is something taking in this life of the officer in an army like the British, now a few years in India, under the eye of the world, & now in China, in great operations,—epoch of history, & such opportunities for learning human nature & the ways of the world. This young man had been preparing himself, by reading Huc, &c. He tells me that the Highlanders, in the Indian campaigns, fought in the bonnet & kilt, in full costume.

At 11 o'ck., took leave, & headed by the Orderly, my little procession of lantern bearers & sedan bearers traversed the dark narrow streets. Few were abroad except the watchmen, each with his lantern & two bits of bamboo, wh. he beats together. These gay shops have their fronts closed in by shutters. At the great gate of the Wall, the guard are turned out to unlock it, & the chains grate & bars fall, & the lanterns shine on the red coats of these foreigns possessors—a strange & unwelcome sight to the poor Chinese, who thought themselves lords of the tributary earth. So, each street is closed & locked, at its end, & at each we make a few minutes stop. The water side is reached, I dismiss my orderly & suite, & take a sampan for the hong. A whole sleeping family are turned out from the little covered cuddy to make room for me & row me up to my place—Lussel-y Hong.

(At Parkes', one waiter at table was a thin, tall black, silent sepoy, dressed in white from head to foot, turban robe & all. The rest were Chinese. Have I mentioned, too, that there is a regiment of sepoys in the city. How England has subdued nations & races to her use! The Scotch & Irish fight the E. Indians in the Oudh, & the Sikhs & Sepoys are carried to China to fight the Chinese!)

Parkes says that Howqua is squeesed by the Chinese Government, on every pretext. It is thought that he lately was obliged to make a *donation* of $50,000.

Tuesd. Mch. 20.   Dinner, or rather *tiffen*, at Howqua's at 2 P.M. Mr. Delano, Orne & myself. His house in the old city, within the walls. Howqua, who is son & representative of the great Hong merchant sev. years dead, is about 50 years old, pale & thin, dressed in blue robe, black quilted silk tunic over it, edged with blue collar, & skull-cap. He has bot the right to wear red button, & is of the highest attainable rank.

First, sit few minutes at round table & take tea. Then dinner announced. Dinner much as at Yung Ting's, except that D. & O. say was better cooked. Sit on stools without backs, & each guest has, on floor, by his side, a china jar to put anything in off his plate. Wine both European & Chinese. The plate, of the richest & most exquisite old china make, very rare. Table set with 16 kinds of preserve & confectionary, & fruits & flowers—all untouched. Twelve courses, first being the celebrated Bird's Nest, & the 2d, Shark's fins, & the 3d lotus berries &c. &c., the Key Lung's eggs, (a fruit) &c. Then 14 dishes of more solid *food,* handed round in order to each guest,—making, in fact 26 courses, only that the last 14 are handed for a choice. Now we rise & retire to the reception room, for an interval, with the intimation that dinner is not done. Quarter hour in *this* room, walking & talking, dinner announced again, & we return to a table with 6 kinds of confectionary, & 12 of cakes, all at our choice. After these, tea, wh. is a signal of end. Then to the reception room again, where the little round table is set with tea again, wh. we only play with. Then take leave. Howqua is a grave, polite man, & kept up the same course of inquiries, polite listenings for answers, & apparent devotion to our happiness as his nephew. At the latter part of dinner, his son joins us,—a man of 22 or 23, who has recd. a second degree—pale, sallow, physically feeble, as nearly all Chinese of the upper, unlaboring classes seem to be—for they take no exercise, not even walking if they can be carried. The Chinaman does not live who has ever taken a constitutional walk. Mr. Preston was again a guest, & interpreter. Howqua is well informed as to position & gen. character of Engl. Fr. & America, our rail roads, telegraphs, commerce, &c.

To-night sit on piassa, over river, looking at the flitting boat-lights, & listening to the strained cries of the Chinese boat-people—those who had something to sell, on the water to be heard more than a mile up the river.

("Mak-y-larn-boy"—make-learn-boy, a boy who lives at a hong, without wages, to learn English &c. "Nias-kee" never mind, no matter. "Man-man", stop, wait. "Go up stairs & show this gentleman my two guns". "Walk-y topside, make see this gentleman two piece-y my gun". &c. Pigeon English).

Wednesday, Afternoon, M'ch. 21. At Macao. Talk of palaces —I have never seen in any Engl. gentl. or noblemen's house such chambers as there are in this house, where I am lodged, the guest of Mr. Ward, our Minister! My chamber is 19 paces long & 12 paces wide, & about 20 feet high. The walls are 2½ f. thick. It is a palace. It was built by one of the wealthy old Portuguese families, & bought by Augustine Heard & Co., who still own it. As they live & do all their business in Hong Kong, they use it only as an occasional place of resort for a pleasure trip. Yet, this gives an idea of the style of these Anglo-Chinese merchants, that they maintain such a palace, for old associations sake, & a little present convenience. Heard & Co. put the house at the disposal of Mr. Ward, during his sojourn in Macao, & he invites me to be his guest. Mr. John Heard, of the firm, is also here for a day or two. And we three gentle-men, each living *en garcon*, wander about these huge lofty rooms, with their echoing bare floors, & under the shaded piassas. In one side of my room is a bed, a portion of which I occupy with sheets & blankets of the usual width, leaving sev-eral feet of waste land on each side. One gets exercise enough in walking from the toilet table to the wash stand,—a chamber of magnificent distances.

But, how came I here? I left Canton at 7.30 A.M., in the little steamer Spark, taking grateful leave of Delano, Orne & Sheppard, & "Old Head" (who desired his remembrances to Mr. J. P. Cushing, Messrs. Forbes &c.) & steamed down among the tossing & tumbling sampans & hong boats, banging ag. each other under our paddle-surf, but the laughing girls never losing their temper, & men reaching poles on board with letters attached at the last moment, after we are under way,— & we pass the now familiar grounds of the Old Factories & the

Dutch Folly, & pass the great junks with their preposterously gaudy banners & red scarfs tied to the mussle of each gun,—& now the ruins of the Barrier Forts, & now the tall pagoda on the hill top, & are clear of the city & down in the wide Estuary. There lies the Fr. steam frigate, & there the Br. Admiral's tender, the Coromandel, & there the Br. gun-boat "89", & here is steaming slowly up with a leadsman in the chains, gunboat "87", both "walk-y insides" & rigged with 3 masts, with fore & aft sails & a square topsail at the fore.

At Whampoa are some 30 merchant vessels at anchor, not counting the junks & schooners. Here, too, is a stone dry-dock, for vessels of the largest class, & 2 or 3 mud docks. Rice fields, Pagodas on hills, a few close villages, like sections taken from the centre of a city, & now the Bogue Forts, & the widening estuary, & the low fields rise in high picturesque hills, & the country becomes rough & granity. The outline of country on all sides of the great opening, between Macao & Hong Kong, below, & the Bogue Forts above, is picturesque with high receding distant hills, & impending cliffs.

There lies Macao, open to the sea, its half moon beach, its stone sea-wall, its broad flagged sea-walk, & its old, very old Portuguese forts & churches & convents, & its palatial private houses & gardens. And such crowds of little boats, hurrying off to us, & the chattering, crowding, struggling boats & boatmen & boat-women, urging their boats under our very wheels, to secure the first passengers. Land, & Mr. Heard sends my luggage to his house.

Mr. Ward (his Excellency, John E. Ward, Min. &c.) is here, & a very pleasant, manly, intelligent person, he seems to be, & so all report him. He is of Savannah Geo., but educated in N. Engl.,—2 years at Cambr. Law School, 1836,7, & married Olivia Sullivan. Unfortunately, Mrs. Ward is not here, but in Europe, with her children.

Dine with Mr. Nye, at 7 o'ck. Present, Nye, Ward, Heard, Capt. Devens, (Charlestown), & Mr. —— Gassett, of Boston. Nye was a dashing merchant, failed for 2½ millions, paying 5 per cent, & now lives in retirement at Macao, but in a palace of a house, with suites of elegantly furnished rooms. Says he was introduced to my father in New York, heard his lectures there, & my father went to his house to see his picture gallery. Gassett talks of my father's tales & poems, & has a favorite copy here with him. Devens is the deft. in the suit that Butler of Lowell tried so often. Gassett has been a R. Catholic, became so at Singapore years ago, but has renounced that Church. Tells me he has the highest admiration for the self devotion of the clergy in this part of the world,—that there is nothing beyond it in history, & respects the piety & faith of the devout members of the Church,—but his difficulty was in the necessity of surrendering private judgement entirely, not only as to the great doctrines,—wh. was not a serious difficulty with him —but as to the conduct of life. He says it is an iron system, & the devout man (& such he says he was for some years, following all the discipline) is required to follow his spiritual director in all things of a moral or religious character, as the voice of God. This he could not do. He reviewed the grounds, & renounced the Church. But he says he sees no middle ground. Without the authority of the Church, there is no revelation, & with the Church falls the "mythology" of Christianity. He is a Theodore Parker man, now.

Thursday. M'ch. 22. Walk with Mr. Heard & Mr. Nye to the Peña, a hill on wh. a building, formerly a convent, stands. Here is a beautiful view. The situation of Macao is almost without an equal. Before it is the open sea, with the distant mountains across the wide expanse, the surf breaking on the half-moon beach, close to wh. the solid yellow stone houses stand. Behind the town, is a large but land-locked bay, called the Inner Harbor. Between them is a second passage to the China Sea, & beyond these a fourth bay. Macao is a peninsula, with two passages to the sea, & two large bays. The peninsula is diversified, in a picturesque manner, with hills, & every wind has a fair sweep, making this the most salubrious place in China. Were it not that a bar keeps all vessels drawing over 16 feet out in the open roads, 4 or 6 miles off,—it would be the favorite business place also. As it is, betw. this disadvantage & the disadvantage of Portuguese rule, it is chiefly a pleasure & health resort. Rents are low, & labor very cheap. (Washing & ironing of the nicest kind is $2 for 100 pieces). Its history is most interesting, going back to the heroic age of navigators & missionaries.

Called, with Mr. Ward, on the Governor of Macao. Dom Isadoro Guimaiaes. He is a perfectly well bred man, of the simple but high manner, speaks English pretty well, & is thought a man of entire honor & more than usual capacity. What a beautiful foot he has! He is recently married. La Senora is a native, Portuguese, very large, very dark, very sallow, & rather stately,—love affair.

Called, with Ward, on Mrs. Endicott, wife of Mr. Jas. P. Endicott (Salem) our consul here. An incredibly spacious house, with a street of piassa lined with flower pots, & open to the sea. Mrs. E. rather a pretty English woman. Afterwards, to a place Mr. E. has bought, intending to build on it. It is one of the noblest sites possible, commanding the 4 bays & town.

Mr. Hunter calls. Go with him (Ward & I) to Camoens' garden & grotto. The garden is the private property of a wealthy & ancient Portug. family, who have owned it over 200 years. It is the garden of their house, & under lock & key, but is opened to all who send in their cards. I think it is the most beautiful garden I ever saw. Excellent taste has been shown in dealing with nature, for the garden is a rocky, broken ground, with boulders & large trees, yet interspersed with the nicest arrangements of horticulture. At the top of one of the hills, commanding the full sea-view, is the grotto, where Camoens used to sit to read & to compose his Lusiad. And how it is honored! A kind of temple built over it, & a pedestal surmounted by a terra cotta head of Camoens, & several tablets erected by the voluntary gift of admirers. Next this garden, is the Protestant burying ground, a beautiful spot, filled with graves, the stones & monuments over wh. are in the highest degree creditable to the liberality of the Engl. & Am. residents here, as well as to the piety of the friends of the dead. One is of Dr. Morrison, & there are others of his family. Several to Engl. & Am. naval officers, among others to Mr. Waldron, Lt. Brooke, &c., Ld. H. Churchill, &c. &c.

This ground is full & closed. But a new one, almost, but not quite as beautiful is opened. Mr. Hunter tells me that the Portuguese authorities & people are liberal & kind, in the highest degree, to foreigners & Protestants. He thinks there is no place on earth where there is less bigotry of religion & nation.

To the Temple of Wanghia (*pro.* Wong-yor), where the first treaty betw. America & China was signed, that of Mr. Cushing, in 1844. (By the way, all persons, merchants, diplomatists, & residents of leisure—all agree that that was a most excellent treaty,—perhaps the best ever made by any body with China, & much better than Reed's. They only wish Reed had let it alone. We lost by the change. Poor Reed! Nobody speaks well of him. The—yes, contempt—felt for him by *all* Americans in China—I have seen no exception, is sad to think of. They say he was a quiddling Philad. lawyer, a mere toady, to Lord Elgin, thinking only of the honor of his position, the passage out in a frigate, & the passage home thro' Europe. *Here,* he did nothing, or worse. I can't find a man to speak patiently of him. All agree that Elgin is a man of extraordinary sagacity, firmness, perseverance & pluck.)

Extraordinary & anomalous state of things betw. Engl. & China. At Canton Engl. & Chinese officers meet & dine together & inquire the news from the North. Whether there has been a battle, & which got the victory,—& the Br. fleet & army are going up to fight, & a battle was fought at the Peiho,—yet all the time, the Br. are collecting the Custom House duties for the Chinese Govt., in all the free ports, as the agents of that Government, & paying the money over to the Chinese treasury!

Pigeon. In America there are a great many ships. "America-side, too much piecey ship, have got".

Went to Nye's to see his pictures—one ¾ length of William 1st, Pr. of Orange. The face is very like it in Motley's book, wh. tends confirm the correctness of both. Also one of Chinnery portraits, Sir Andrew Ljungstedt. Went to Temple of Ama Kok, dedicated by some survivors of a wrecked junk, centuries ago. Curious scene of a quarrel betw. two women, each on her knees, knocking her forehead on the pave, before the idol, each telling Josh the story, interrupting each other, & the men of the two families standing by the side & backing the women —precisely as if they were before a Justice of the Peace, all jabbering fiercely. I doubt if the poor Josh could have understood it, if he had had ears. Offerings of fans & a pair of boots made to the God, or to some spirit.

Visit to Ap-pong, one of the wealthiest Chinese here. House very large, with sev. foreign pictures & engravings. Conversation with him in Pigeon English.

Visit to house of Wo Lung, another leading merchant. His is a new house & very beautifully furnished, with European pictures, & a piano. His son, a nice looking youth of 14, received us. This family are Christians, & it was a comfort to see a house without the idols & Josh sticks. In place of them, was a handsome private Chapel. The lad speaks Spanish, being educated in Manilla. He told me there were about 500 Chinese Christians—all Catholics—in Macao.

(Go-down, a corruption of some E. Indian word, is the universal Engl. word in the Eastern world for a store-house).

Spent the ev. at a party at the Governor's. Present, his lady, & his sister Mrs. Cate, Hunter, the Endicotts, Count Klyskowski, the Fr. Sec. of Legation in China, Mr. Ward, & the Capt. of a Portug. man-of-war, who is here. The ladies all speak English.

Pop. of Macao is about 60,000, of wh. 50,000 are Chinese, & the rest chiefly a mixed race of Portuguese with the people fr. Malabar. There is consid. mixed Portug. & Chinese blood, but the mixture is chiefly the former.

Saturday. Mch. 24.   Pick-nick at Pak Shan temple, a place some 10 miles fr. Macao; one of those exquisite spots, like the White Cloud Monastery, wh. the Buddhist priest here selected with so much taste. It is on high ground, yet sheltered, with evergreen pines about it, & pure mountain water, with a view over Macao Bay terminating in the high hills of pale stone. Our party was Ward, Hunter, Nye, Mr. & Mrs. Endicott, Count Klyskowski, Ch. Sec. of the Fr. Legation, & 2 or 3 others. Mrs. E. was the moving spirit. We had a train of 10 sedans & about 40 servants. An excellent lunch. At the Temple, some of the servants laid out their "cash" in buying tapers & incense sticks & after due worship tried their luck with the Josh sticks. They shake them up, & the one that falls out is their luck. This has a number, wh. is compared or professed to be compared, with printed paper. Mrs. E. & some of our party prevailed on the men to try luck for them. The answers are vague, general & written in characters capable of different interpretations. Yet this consultation of the oracles is the prevalent custom of China—but so it was of Rome & Athens, in their best days.

The buffalo, as it is called, is the ox & cow of China. There is two kinds. One is more like our bison, has a short sharp horn & a large hump. The other, the water-buffalo, has horns turned back upon the head, *a La 'Imperatrice*, & its skin has a good deal the look of an aquatic animal.

There are large coolie barracoons in Macao, one of wh. we saw fr. the Camoens garden.

Sunday Morn. Mch. 25.   The U.S. frigate Hartford has come over from Hong Kong & I am invited, by Mr. Ward, to return to Hong Kong in her. Would like it much,—but fear that must go over to-day, to be in season for the mail steamer up the coast. No service in the Engl. Chapel, so went to High Mass at the Cathedral, but could not understand or follow it at all, so left early. Walk round the pits &c. with Mr. Ward. Crowds of Parsees, Chinese, Portuguese, mixed races, & some Engl. & Americans in streets.

Cathedral is large, & open floor, but tawdry & not rich—imitations, all.

The village of Pak Shan, wh. we visited yesterday, is composed entirely of people of one clan or family, by whom it was settled 700 years ago. The men marry without, but no man is allowed to settle there from without. The population is now about 4000.

Parting calls, this evening, on Governor & lady, the Endicotts, Hunter, Case & lady & Gassett.

Mond. Mch. 26.   Hartford too late for us. Obliged, after all, to take the mail steamer Feima, & reach Hong Kong at II A.M. Steamers for North sail this afternoon & tomorrow.

Recd. a kind letter from Jona. Russell, at Manilla, inviting me there. By this learn the death of Mrs. Russell.

This place is full English soldiers & sailors, ships of war & troop-ships, bound up the coast, to strike a blow if terms are not made with the Chinese. I fear these poor Chinese are more sinned against than sinning. And if they err through ignorance or wilfulness, yet they are visited with terrible punishments for small mistakes or misconduct. A young officer came over with us from Macao who had the Victoria Cross, & medals for

Sevastopol, Delhi, Lucknow &c. &c.—yet he cannot be more than 25 years old.

Walking thro' the streets of Hong Kong with Mr. Delano yesterday, a Chinaman came up to me, with beaming countenance, & with that practical equality wh. marks their common society, said "Ah! How you do? My glad see you!" & held out his hand. I shook hands with him, but could not remember him, as all Chinese look alike, at first. "My in ship, burn up. You savee—you have got". "Oh yes. The Mastiff". "Yes. Very good—very good". And he told me he came in the Elisa & Ella from Oahu to H. Kong. The good fellow seemed truly glad to see me.

Tuesd. Mch. 27.   Sailed in P.&O. steamer Pekin, for Shanghai, 9.30 A.M. Left the shelf on the hill-side on wh. Hong Kong stands,—its flying flags of all nations afloat & ashore, its men-of-war & its merchantmen, & steamed thro' the high hills & bold shores, & frequent islands, steep & bold, into the open sea. Opposite to Hong Kong, on the peninsula of Kowloon, are the tents of the 44th Reg., which has taken possession of it,—a most important movement in the history of China, for if the Br. hold it, it will probably surpass Hong Kong.

Passage fr. H. K. to Shanghai, a sail of 4 or 5 days, is $95 dollars. The P.&O. Co. keep up the unjust custom of making all pay for the liquors drank.

Frid. M'ch. 30.   Yesterday we were off Amoy, to-day we are off Fu-Chau. No incidents. Few passengers, large vessel, plenty of room, large state room to myself, & good table. Chief interest in the vessel is as an exponent to Br. power & the Br. system in the East.

This ship is built by Br. art & capital at home, owned by Br. capital, & officered by Br. subjects, engaged in the trade of the East, & manned by the practically subjected nations of Asia. The captain & mates, the engineer & his assistants, the purser, Steward & under steward are English. All the rest are Asiatics, six Secunneys are the helmsmen, three mixed Portuguese & Malays are quarter-masters, a surang (boatswain), two tindals (boatswain's mates) & 40 Lascars, are the sailors. There is a boat's crew of 6 Chinese. A Harildan (corporal) & three Sepoys in red coats do soldier's duty on the quarter-deck, some 20 Lascars & Malays & Chinese work under the engineers, & the cabin servants are turbaned Bengalese & Malays. How thin & black they are! And that Bengalese, in the maroon colored long robe, when he is sea-sick, vomits a dark yellow bile drawn fr. 4000 years of tropical life. The British is the dominating race of the Oriental world. They have eclipsed us in steam, far more decidedly than we have them in canvass. Our merchant sailing-vessels are faster & finer than theirs, but in both navy & merchant service, & in all their numerous steam Co. services, they have left all the world behind them in steam.

It is a comfort to exchange the disorder, negligence & close quarters of the Early Bird, for the strict, almost military discipline & etiquette, the neatness & thoroughness of this ship,— where every man has his place & his uniform or badge of office, where the officer of the deck is not allowed to speak to a passenger or to sit down or lean ag. anything, & where there is always a quarter-master at the Conn.

The Chinese are as industrious on the sea, as on the land. For 10 & 20 miles off all the great ports, Canton, Macao, H. Kong, Amoy, &c. the fishing boats are to be counted not by scores but by hundreds. They go out from 2 & 3 to 10 & 15 miles fr. shore, & cast drag nets, two vessels to a net, & lie, as if at anchor, moored to their drifting nets, tossing about in the heavy sea, some of them with families of women & children on board. There could not have been less than 500 in sight at one time yesterday morning.

(By the way, Dominick Lynch, Adele's brother, though something of a brag, has a high reputation here for pluck & seamanship. He has conducted enterprises ag. pirates, rather desperate in their character, with success, & recd. large compensation for them). Last night, in the crowd of fishing boats, we unfortunately ran over one. The companion boat went to its help, & there was great halloing, & we hope no one was killed or drowned. They were all either drowned or saved before we cd. have got back to them.

Sunday. April 1, 1860. For two days we have had weather very rough, cold & rainy. To-day, we had snow & sleet. Three days before, in H. Kong, prudent people were walking under double umbrellas, to keep off the sun. It is piteous to see the lascars & Bengalese shivering in their cottons & linens, for this boat does not belong to this line, but to that betw. H. Kong & Bombay, & is here, for the *nonce*, & the poor fellows are un-provided. Capt. Brooks does his best for them.

As an off-set to running over a boat to-day we rescued a boat full. It was a little open boat with 22 men in it, whose junk had sunk in the gale, & who had been drifting about helpless for two days. They were very grateful, & chin-chinned, & kow-towed at a great rate, especially when the kind hearted Capt. sent them two great pots of hot tea & some rice. Chinese like, they squatted down on deck, & patiently kept their places all day & night, & were covered over in line, at night, by a strip of canvas.

Our passengers are Count Klyskowski, the Fr. Chief Sec. of Legation, a Russian naval captain going to join his ship in Japan, a Master in the Br. navy, a stupid Belgian-French-Pole coming to China for a civil office, & a few Engl. travelling & mercantile snobs.

The peculiarity of the Br. marine system is the great number of steam companies it has all over the world, Atlantic, Baltic, E. Indies, W. Indies, S. America, Australia, India, & Africa. These are now chiefly screws, with full sails, like their men of war. They are officered by a class of men betw. the commis-sioned officers of the Navy & the common merchantmen,— the same class that make the masters & master's mates in the Navy,—like those of the old E. India Co.

In the thick mist & snow we see a Chinese boat with bam-boo sails, & pilots flag, & she comes alongside, & a smart un-mistakable Yankee pilot springs on board. Sev. of the pilots of the Yang Tse Kiang are Yankee, & they use Chinese boats of choice. This pilot tells me they are the best.

All the afternoon we are at the mouth of the great Yang Tze Kiang, the great river of China. It is here about 20 miles wide. The Br. steam corvette Furious has lately ascended it 800 miles.

Monday. April. 2.   At anchor at Woon Sung, to discharge opium, & we go up to Shanghai in small boats, I in one of

Jardine & Co.'s. At Woon Sung lie the opium receiving ships, stored with this curse of China. They are very large ships, well armed & manned.

Shanghai lies on a river, or arm of the sea, that makes up from the Yang Tze Kiang. The country around is flat, liable to inundation & protected by a levee, called Bund, wh. extends hundreds of miles. The city is only on one side of the river, so there is none of that *boat life* you see in Canton. The Bund lines the river, being here some 50 or 60 feet wide, & is the pier for commerce. The vessels lie at anchor in the stream, opposite the Bund, & boats carry to & fro mdse. & people. On the Bund, at the E. end, are the great Commercial houses, the Consulates, the Legations, & the residences of the chief foreigners, wh. are stately solid buildings. That of Russell & Co., their lodging house, is said to be the best private house this side the Cape of Good Hope. Then there are Heard & Co., Jardine, Watteson & Co., Dent & Co., &c. &c., and the "flags of all nations" from Consulates, & those of the "Treaty Powers" from the Legations. The Br. men of war, the noble frigate Imperiuse, the beautiful corvette Cruiser, & the Furious & Roebuck, & a few gun boats, (all steamers), lie among the shipping close to the Bund.

Installed at Russell & Co.'s, with two rooms & a coal fire, a servant &c., & Mr. Walsh (the partner) very attentive. Breakfast at 11. (You call for tea & toast in your room when you please, before that). Another guest is the French Col. of the Commissariat, a monster, with grey hair & beard & three decorations & blood-red trowsers—name is Du But.

Called on Hon. Mr. Bruce, the Br. Minister. He looks something between his brother Ld. Elgin & Thackeray. Talk about coolie trade here, & in Cuba. He has quoted my book in his despatches. Dine with him tomorrow. Call on Heard & Co., & M. de Bourbulon the Fr. Minister. Spend the evening at the latter. M. de B. speaks English perfectly & was Sec. of Leg. at Washington several years. Mde. de B. is Miss Kate McLeod, niece of those Inglis-McLeods that used to be in Boston, Mde. Calderon &c., & looks like them. Am to dine there Wed., if do not sooner sail for Japan.

Walked about the city this afternoon,—the European part, or Concessions, as they are called. This part is level, regularly laid out, & built with large, solid houses. Shanghai is to be the great port of China. It is the centre of the Silk trade & has as good & perhaps even a better chance for the tea trade than Canton.

Coolies here are larger & fuller in face than those of Southern China. As they trot along under their burdens, they keep up an unvarying grunt or cry, at every step, so that the crowd of them in the close streets, sounds like a drove of cattle going through our streets to Brighton fair. What a caprice is custom! There is none of this sound in Canton, & here it is universal, & yet they are the same people, doing the same work, in the same manner.

Visited the mud dock for ships. It is like our stone dry docks, only the walls are mud, kept back by piles,—needing constant repair. The ground does not admit of stone, they say.

I believe I omitted to speak of the climate, in Southern China. At H. Kong, Canton & Macao, when the wind was Northerly, it was cool & good out-door weather, & if there was also rain, a coal fire was agreeable. When the wind was Southerly, or calm, it was warm & rather close, & the direct rays of the sun it was best to avoid. Umbrellas & pith hats were then worn, or common hats with folds of crape, turban-wise, on the outside. This was fr. M'ch. 8 to 27th. Here it is cool, & fires are used. But warm weather is expected.

Tuesd. April 3.   Called on Bishop Boone. He has a promising institution conducted in proper style. He is its head & all the clergy & teachers, men & women, are working under him; —they all live together, the unmarried in his house, & the married in houses adjoining, & the Chapel & schools are in the grounds. Conv. with him about the diff. missionary plans & theories. After long experience here, he has come to the conclusion, & acts upon it, that a random distribution of the Scriptures or of parts of them, does more harm than good. As to mere preaching, without more,—it is useful only as a mode of inviting the Chinese to come & learn. He has no confidence in any mode but that of thorough *instruction, ab origine.* He begins with the Creed, & instructs them in it, article at a time, requiring them to commit it to memory as they go on. For instance, the first article "God the Father, Almighty" is an unknown idea to them, & must be thoroughly instilled first. Then, the second—respecting Our Saviour, & so on. After they are taught, & as they can understand it, Scripture is given to them to read, in selected parts, & some to commit to memory, & then they are taught the Liturgy, the greater part of wh. they come to know by heart, by reason of the wonderful Chinese power of memory. He has sev. blind Chinese, who know almost the entire liturgy, especially the Communion Office. They also learn the Canticles, & chant them. He spoke of the notion some have that putting the Scriptures into the hand of an intelligent heathen is a promised means of grace, as bibliolotry. Every Chinese is treated as a Catechumen, & the Creed is taught *as truth*. His Government also is thoroughly Episcopal. He is head & ruler. Nothing is submitted to vote. He confers & consults with his clergy, but he says they do not believe, nor does he, that a *majority* is "set over them as the Lord". His corps consists as follows—4 American presbyters, 2 Chinese deacons, 3 Chinese candidates for orders, studying in his house, 3 Chinese male teachers, 4 American ladies (unmarried) teachers, & 2 American men with their wives, training as teachers. There are 2 boarding schools, one for boys & one for girls, each limited to 40, & always full, & with innumerable applicants. No scholars is recd. as boarders unless the parents bind them, as apprentices are bound, by indentures to the Bishop for ten years,—anything less than that is not worth while.

Mrs. Boone is a sister of Bishop Elliott, of Georgia. Took the address of the R. Cath. Bishop's residence, wh. is at the other end of the city, & with a chair & 4 coolies, started to make it a visit. It seems there are two R.C. institutions, one at Ton Ka Du, wh. is the Cathedral, & another at Tse Ka Wae, wh. is a college, & is some 6 or 8 miles in the country. By some mistake of mine, or in the direction given me, my coolie started off for Tse Ka Wae. I knew the Cathedral was in the city, & I found they were taking me into the country, among rice fields & peasants' cabins, & along the tow-paths, of canals & creeks, with a pagoda in the distance. But explanation was out of the question, as none of them could speak a word even of pigeon English. I made up my mind to let them go on until 5 o'ck., & then if they came to no stop to make them turn back. At this moment, I saw four men coming along the tow-path, in full Chinese costume, tails & all, dressed after the decent manner of Chinese scholars, when, just as they passed me, I caught a word of French. I stopped & spoke, & they answered in French, & fortunately they proved to be four Jesuit scholars, & said they had been at Tse Ka Wae, & were returning to Ton Ka Du; so I got out & walked with them, after a hubbub of explanation among the coolies. These were Frenchmen, young, candidates for orders, & are here, dressing eating & talking & reading as Chinese, as do all the R.C. priests in this part of China. (I was some four miles out of my way).

Ton Ka Du is a large collection of buildings, of wh. the cathedral is the chief, on the water's edge, composed of schools & lodging rooms for priests & scholars. Delivered my letters to the Bishop, M. de Bornier, who, with his vicar, received me with true Fr. politeness, & showed me the Church, dedicated to St. Francis Xavier, the largest in China, with a portrait of St. Francis over the altar, & the school &c. In the school, the pupils (Chinese) are taught latin. The statistics he gave me are as follows—1 Bishop, 29 European priests, 10 Chinese priests, 270 scholars in the college at Tse Ka Wae, & 480 Chinese girls in the girls school. In the entire province, the pop. of wh. is abt. 10 millions, they reckon 75000 Catholic Chinese, & 5000 scholars in all the Catholic Schools. Return thro' the city, at candle lighting. Difficult to realise that I am in the centre of a strange Chinese city,—I a Boston lawyer, with large family & clients!

Dinner at Mr. Bruce's. Present, Admiral Jones, R. N., Capt. Jones R. N., Mr. Parkes, Br. Commr. at Canton, Dent, the merchant &c. &c. A young nob named Wyndham, who talked in the extreme style of Punch's Engl. fash. youth—*aw-fellaw-clevaw* &c. Bruce has humor & more than ever reminds me of Thackeray. He spoke with earnestness & even with emotion of Commodore Tattnall, his aide at the Peiho, & especially his despatch to the U.S. Govt., wh. Bruce thinks so magnanimous, & so modest. Tattnall went thro' the thickest fire to visit Adm. Hope, when he heard he was wounded, & his coxwain was killed by his side.

Wed. Apr. 4.   Spent morning at Bishop Boone's. Exd his

schools. The 40 boys are taught by 3 Chinese men & one Am. lady, Miss Fay. Miss F. is great admirer of father's poetry & prose, & quoted it to me & has his 2 vols. A class of boys demonstrated difficult problems in spherical geometry, respecting sections of pyramids. They read fr. Mencius & Confucius, as well as fr. Engl. books translated into Chinese. The girls have two Am. ladies, (one a d. of Gen. Walter Jones of Wash. D.C.) & one Chinese man, for teachers. They chaunted the *Venite* in Chinese, to our familiar chant. Neither boys nor girls are taught English, except in special cases, where the Bishop feels entire confidence in their religious character. The effect is always bad, on the poorer classes. Good judgement is shown, in making no attempt to change their customs. The girls are dressed in the comely & modest Chinese costume, & the boys have the tail & tonsure, & all the native dress. They eat with chopsticks, & use only Chinese cookery. The girls are all employed in housework & sewing &c. in turn, to fit them for humble spheres of life, & even the cramped feet are allowed to go on, if the parents insist upon it,—for it affects their social position, chance of marriage &c. The girls looked fat & happy. Here, as elsewhere, I see the difference betw. the N. & S. of China. Here there is more flesh & color,—a kind of brunette.

At 2 P.M., Rev. Mr. Lyles, one of the longest resident here of B Boone's clergy, called, to take me to see the city. He speaks Chinese well & is very kind, as well as duly inquisitive into everything Chinese. Rev. Mr. Smith, a new comer, accompanied him. We gave five hours to a very interesting exn. of the city.

Shanghai has about 500,000 inhab., ⅔ of whom live within the walls. The streets are as narrow as those of Canton, & here, as there, there are no horses or carriages, & only human foot-falls. There is less wealth & style here, & the people do not seem so neat, & the city arrangements are not so good. The temples, ancestral halls, yamuns &c. bear no comparison with those of Canton. It is like comparing Limerick with Dublin.

We were fortunate in our day. It was a Sacred day, the Spring Festival of Tzing Ning, 14th day of 3d mo., & the tutelary-gods were carried about in processions, in large sedan chairs, looking like so many gaudy Mandarins, with long lines of men bearing umbrellas, lanterns, boards with inscriptions, & great beatings of gongs. People who have been sick & made vows in their sickness, & recover, pay their vows on this day. These devotees are dressed in Scarlet & were frequent. Some very small children were dressed out in red, babies, whose parents had vowed for them. Some of the vows are explained to Mr. Lyles by the parties; were of rather a trifling character,—as, to wear a kind of wooden manacle all day,—while some were painful.

This is also one of the days of ancestral worship, & the streets were crowded with people bearing strings of silver paper money,—this is a cheap silver-foiled paper, made in form of dollars, several hundreds of wh. can be bought for a cent. The poorest burn a string of these, & the rich burn incredible quantities of the foolish stuff. We passed coolies bearing large basket loads of it. It is sold in the shops, hung out in strings like onions at a green grocers. They are thought, when burned at the shrines, to be worth their *face*, their nominal amount, in the Spirit Land.

Baptist Chapel, with a high tower fr. wh. is best view of the city. For 90 miles in all directions is dead level. For 3 or 4 miles, a level of tile roofs & beyond that a level of rice fields, & vegitable fields, intersected by dull canals. Interior of Bapt. Chapel is plain, & like their Chapels at home. Built by Engl. Baptists.

Calendering of cloth done by rolling a huge stone over it, to & fro, weighing 1000 lbs., & moved by men's feet.

Just in time to see the return of an idol to his temple, fr. his procession thro' the city. Great crowd before the temple door, but no confusion or violence,—an orderly, self-regulating populace. Long procession, on a fast trot, as draw near the temple, & the great sedan chair is hurried into the temple, with its upright sitting figure of an idol. Then the chief men in the processions, make circuits thro' the crowd, coming back to the front, &, as soon as they come in sight of the idol, they are supposed to be so inspired that they break into a run, & trot in a quick run to the idol, & prostrate themselves before him. Yet it is to be observed that in none of their rites is there anything bloody or obscene,—the purest & simplest of idolatries the world has ever seen. After the procession was dismissed, we went into the temple, & poked about into all the secret places, even to the *sanctum sanctorum*—where the idol is enshrined.

There it was, rather oppressive, with close air, burning incense, dark & damp passages, with grim effigies of attendant deities, & the bedisened idol himself. It is to be noticed that the utmost freedom is allowed, not only to Chinese, but to foreigners, to go into all parts of the temple, & without fee; & so I have found it everywhere in China.

Coming out, we found a Missionary of the London Miss. Soc., addressing a crowd of auditors, on the folly & wickedness of their idolatry, & the necessity of worshipping the one true God. He had a considerable audience, & there was no sign of opposition or dislike. They are eminently a reasoning people, & think ev. man entitled to a hearing.

Went to a tea-shop, in wh. some 500 Chinese, men, women & children, were taking their public evening meal of tea with a few cakes, vegetables & confections. We had cups of *red tea,* with pea nuts to eat. This is their best tea here, & is very good. This, too, is an orderly & quiet multitude—yet it is a great fête day. A man must have sharp sight & a knowing turn, who can see any external signs of vice in a Chinese city. I have not yet seen even a drunken man.

Here is a juggler, naked to the waist, with a crowd about him, swallowing swords & stones, & doing very strange things, with extraordinary ingenuity,—more surprising from his being without sleeves or any places of concealment, & no trap-doors, or accomplices,—a half naked man, in the open air, with a crowd pressing upon him. And here is a fortune teller, at his tables, & there is a man throwing bubbles from a stick, in the most incomprehensible way,—filling the air with them. At this shop, I bought a Chinese pencil, ink, ink stone, & paper, the sacred articles, which by their liberal system, pass all custom houses & excises duty free. Gamblers & gambling shops are frequent—but there is no violence or anything to shock one, & the risks are not large. But the taste for gambling is universal. A boy, who wishes to buy a cake with 6 cash, will put down 3, & by the turn of the die, get the cake for ½ price, or lose his money. Opium shops, too, with their close drawn curtains over the front door, are in every street. We go into one. There are 6 or 8 men lying at length on the mats, each with his pillow & pipe,—& seedy, jaundiced, weak eyed looking wretches they are. One told Mr. Lyles he had a trouble in his bowels, &

took opium for it. "Yes", said Mr. L., "that is always the story —medical advice. It relieves the difficulty the first time, but when it comes again, there is no strength to meet it with, & the habit has become too strong". There was one dreadfully haggard looking woman, but whether a customer or an attendant, I could not tell.

Now to the Chapel, in the city. It is a respectable building, is of brick, rather of the Gothic type, but without tower or spire, & capable of seating 3 or 400 people. It was built at the expense of Mr. William Appleton of Boston, costing $5000. A creditable building. It is used chiefly as a preaching place. It is in a public street, in the centre of population, & here, every afternoon, one of Bishop Boone's clergy comes, & the doors are opened & people invited to come in. He preaches to them, addressing them on any subject he pleases, calculated to draw them from their idols, & interest them in the Christian religion, & after the address, he asks them to stand reverently, while he prays to God for them, & then he offers a prayer, in their behalf. Then he invites any who are interested & desire to know more of the matter, to remain & see him in the vestry. There the clergy talk with them, take their names & address (to guard against impositions) give a few tracts, & engage them to come again. In this way out of hundreds & thousands, they occasionally get a catechumen or a child out of a family for a school. They have to guard especially ag. their coming under pretence of learning in order to get assistance. Their charities are very sparing & cautious, on that account—yet without charity to the distressed, they will not be respected.

The catechumens are taught in the way I have stated, by instruction founded on the Creed, & the Creed committed to memory, as they go on, & Scripture dealt out, as they can understand it, the Ten Commandments & the chief parts of the service gradually learned—baptism administered when they have come to a reasonable understanding of the faith & desire to obey the law. Then Confirmation & Communion, as they are fitted. Of course, no attempt is made to perform the Church Service regularly at the preaching places in the city, as our Service is intended for the common worship of a company of Christians. There is, however, a day school at the Chapel, & occasionally, I believe ev. Sunday, the Service is performed there in the morning, to the Christians. The offices for Communion, Baptism & Confirmation, & the morning & evening prayer are translated & taught, & lately the Litany. They agree that the Liturgy is invaluable, with these converts. Their interest in it & knowledge of it grows daily,—& it is a rock of defense & support.

This evening, dined at French Legation, with M. & Mde. de Bourbulon. *Present*, a Fr. Admiral & Colonel, Count Klyskowski, & a few others. Service handsome, & cooking good, being French. After dinner, Mde. de B. sang some Fr. songs. Can anything be more meagre than a Fr. song? & then two Spanish songs—& what a contrast! A grace, a charm, a spirit indeed! The Sp. song of Maria Dolores—the "Mulatto,—Mulattito" song, was fascinating—guitars & troubadors & contradansas combined!

Thursd. April 5. Spent two hours on board H.B.M. steam frigate Furious, by invitation of Capt. Jones. Capt. J., a post-captain, is not much over 40, his first lieut. is about 24, & his second lieut. only 19. In our Navy they would all be midshipmen except Capt. J., & he a lieut., with chance of being Commander at 50, & post captain at 60. Saw them furl sails. The whole crew are Britons, & a fine manly, seamanlike set of fellows they are—the boatswain & his mates, & the quartermasters &c., especially. Now, seamen are degraded to 2d class for gross & frequent misconduct, & only 2d class men can be flogged, & that only by the Capt., after inquiry & exn. of witnesses, & an interval of 24 hours for *cooling time.*

All agree, here, American, Fr. & Br., that the Br. Navy on the coast of China, is in fine condition. The officers are all on the start for work & adventure, like the Greek athlete;—for promotion & decorations follow every act of distinguished good conduct, & their fleet of small vessels gives junior officers chances for command, experience & distinction. Our poor Navy is in a deplorable state,—no chance for young officers, no promotion or orders or decorations for good conduct, & a deadness over all,—minds becoming inane over ward-room gossip.

Called on Rev. Dr. Bridgman, A.B.C.F.M. Large house & comfortable, but in the room, three women & a baby that they all *mam maed* to, & one man in a white chokey cravat that they all *wived* to, & things were so muxy & uninteresting that I soon left them. Dr. B. seemed rather an old granny.

Called on the Bishop of Victoria, the Br. Bishop who has jurisdiction over all Br. Church people in China. He is rather ditto to Dr. Bridgman, & his talk was of externals, & not deep in them.

Called on Dent & Co., A. Heard & Co., & a Russian Commodore who is staying with Heard & Co. The Dents have a palace. It is sumptuous. In their grounds are a small pack of Chinese & Japanese deer, an aviary of tropical birds, &c. &c. Among the birds, the Japanese pheasant exceeds in grace of action & richness of colors any bird I ever saw. The Russian Commodore speaks English very well, cannot be more than 30 years of age, had read my Two Years &c., & has soft, pleasant manners. Visit Russell & Co.'s *go-downs*,—large store houses, lighted by clerestories, & looking like our rail-road depots, & full of teas & silks.

Walsh (Russell & Co.) gave me a dinner party. Company were Meadows, author of a big work on China, Wade, formerly Capt. in Br. Army & now Chinese Sec. to the Br. Legation, Major Fisher of the R. Engineers, Davis, a Br. Magistrate & barrister &c. Wade & Meadows are thought to be the best Chinese scholars in the country. Davis is a man of various information, & an A. M. of Cambridge, Eng. Wade told some excellent stories about Sir John Browning, Chisholm Austey & the H. Kong Bar. Wade & Meadows both oppose & discourage the plan of putting Chinese in Roman letters, wh. Bishop Boone has adopted.

To-day great pleasure & advantage of an offer of a passage to Japan, in Dent & Co.'s steamer Yiang Tze, in wh. Mr. Dent is to make an excursion to Japan, on a partly business & partly pleasure trip. He has invited, besides me, the B. of Victoria, & Mr. Parkes. It is a great opportunity. But for this, I should have to wait here indefinitely, perhaps 2 or 3 weeks. They sail Saturday, 7th. Sorry for that, as Sunday is Easter.

Frid. April 6.   Good Friday.   At 9 A.M. went to the Chinese Service, at Bishop Boone's Chapel. This is a simple building, in the Gothic style, with a tower in the middle of the front, &

well proportioned, & in every way Ecclesiastical in its style. Surprised to find a full company, of some 200 Chinese, men & women, including the 80 children of the school. These are nearly all communicants or catechumen, or, at least, advanced enough to take part in the service. The singing, responses, Creed &c. were joined in very generally & heartily. Having an Engl. Prayer Book, I could follow the services perfectly well, not knowing a word of Chinese, & say the same things in Engl. that these poor converts or half converts said in Chinese. A Chinese clergyman, in full canonicals, distinguished only by his tonsure, tail & skull-cap, officiated with B. Boone.

At 11 A.M. Litany & Communion, in English. Company of about 20 persons,—chiefly the mission family. The Br. & Am. *public*, who go to church at all Good Friday, go to the large Engl. Church, near the middle of the Br. Concession. This is only a mission & school Chapel. But very interesting to join with these earnest people, in their little chapel, in our bond of Common Service, in wh. this day millions in all parts of the world are uniting. And beyond the Engl. & American communities,—all, R. Catholic, Greek, American, the Eastern Christians, Lutherans—all commemorate the Central Fact of the Christian Faith,—& the Jews, the world over, on this day keep their Passover.

This afternoon Dr. Bridgman called. He appeared better. Says there are only two missionaries of the A.B.C.F.M. in Shanghai, & Mrs. B. is the only Am. teacher. There is one boarding school of 22 scholars, & 2 or 3 day schools, wh. Mrs. B. visits & supervises, taught by older Chinese pupils. They also make no attempt to interfere with the dress or mode of eating of the pupils. Dr. B. confines his labors to a translation of the Scriptures, wh. has been on for sev. years. Spend rest of day quietly, at home. Weather cool & bracing.

Japan: April 1860

Saturd. Apr. 7.   Steamer Yang Tse, for Japan. It is a large Am. built steamer, commanded & officered by Americans. Parkes does not go. So our company consists of Ld. Bishop of Victoria & myself, as guests, Mr. Dent, his partner, Mr. Webb, Mr. Ashton, a merchant, & a small staff of clerks & interpreters. Get underway at noon. Pass the Fr. frigate Forban, the Eng. men of war Furious, Roebuck & Nimrod, & the fleet of merchantmen, & the great transport wh. last night brot up Sir Hope Grant & staff, & the fleet of junks, with their great eyes & gaudily painted sides & scarfed cannon & are out in the great river. The Yang Tse Kiang, tho' so large, is shallow in parts, with shoals & banks, & is very difficult of navigation. Toward the mouth of the river, we pass the Pei Ho, going up, having on board the Fr. Gen. Montauban & his staff. (The Fr. Govt. bot this steamer of Russell & Co. for $200,000, cash).

Sund. Apr. 8. Easter.   The bishop is sea-sick, & keeps his bed; —so we have no service. It is a dull, rainy, rolling & pitching day,—as dull an Easter as I had Christmas in the Nappa hotel.

The commander of this boat is a Capt. Dearborn, a N.H. man, who commanded Boston ships for sev. years on this coast, & Forbes' brig, the Antelope, for sev. years, & has commanded this boat for three years. He is a man of character & experience. Conversed with him about our navy. He is a patriot, but says our navy on this coast is, & has always been, in a deplorable state. The officers idle & often scandalously dissipated, & their minds set on trading in *curios* & on getting home. The discipline slack, & no spirit or energy. He named two or three ships wh. were exceptions to this; but it is the rule. He says the British navy is, & for years has been, in the highest practicable condition, full of work, energy & emulation, young officers employed & encouraged, promotion, prise-money & honors accessible to all, the mess expenses low, & dissipation among officers rare, & gross cases rendering them liable to public disgrace & suspension fr. command. He thinks them far before the Fr., as seamen.

Capt. Dearborn mentioning the "Mary Ellen", I inquired & he told me he commanded her when she was lost, & remembered Chantrand (See "Cuba & back"), & says C. was very intelligent & active, & that his quickness in learning words of the Malay language, & the favor he got into with Malay families, were the chief causes of their getting along as well as they did.

(Did I mention that Mde. de Bourbulon smokes a genuine cigar, after dinner—no cigarrito, but a full Manilla cigar? She reminds me of Mrs. S. G. Ward, & affects to speak Engl. with a foreign accent).

Monday. Apr. 9.   Land of Japan in sight. Cape Gotto, some 80 miles fr. Nagasaki. Run close in. Land is bold & rocky, but with more trees than that of the Southern coast of China,—evergreens, pines &c.,—& patches of rich green. There is no sandy & flat spots. All is bold, hilly, rocky, & well sprinkled with trees. My first view of Japan!

We are heading, the Capt. tells us, for the entrance to Nagasaki, but it cannot be seen. There is no sign of an opening of a harbor, but only bold hills, with green valleys. Vessels have been known to cruise here 2 & 3 days without finding it. Round a little point we go, & behind an island, where there seems no room, & we open a narrow, deep channel. Here a fort, & there a few houses;—& how very prettily that little village lies on the slope! There is a Japanese boat, with a dark blue jib & a white mainsail. Now, as we pass rapidly along the shore, cultivated spots, groups of houses increase. The distribution of hills & valleys, trees, rocks, green spots & houses is beautiful, & the bay is completely land-locked. Here, on the left, as we enter, is the famous Mount of Martyrs, where the early Missionaries & Japanese Christians were martyred. Here, in 1597, 26 Franciscans & Jesuits were crucified. And, for nearly a century afterwards, the executions of persistent Christians, foreign & Japanese, took place, until it became a place of terror at times, & at times a place of pious pilgrimage by Christians, & gained its name of Holy Mount, or Mount of Martyrs.

Now we open the shipping. There are 8 or 10 ships, chiefly Am. whalemen, lying at anchor, & beyond, a fleet of Japanese junks. There, in that boat that is coming off to us, is my first sight of a Japanese. Three men row the boat. They are strong, large men, darker & less yellow than the Chinese, more silent & less decently clad. They scull the boats, both at the sides & stern, & never pull the oars, as we do.

How beautifully the town lies, at the foot of the many topped gently sloping hills! And the harbor is landlocked, like an interior lake, more so even than Acapulco. And how pretty are these numerous little bays, or havens, that make up on all sides, with the cluster of houses at the head of each. There is an appearance of considerable cultivation, on shore, & trees are frequent, shading the outlying groups of houses. We come to anchor, near the shore, among the ships, one of wh. is a Dutch man-of-war.

And this is Nagasaki, famous in the history of the long attempted contact of East with West. Three hundred years ago, Nagasaki was solely a Christian city, its prince, its nobles, its people were all professed Catholics, & no other places of worhip existed here. Here the Catholics had churches & colleges, & this was the seat of the Chief Labors of Father Valignano, not the first but the most distinguished & longest resident of the missionaries. This was made the centre of the persecutions, until, after a struggle of a century, & after the endurance of incredible trials & tortures, the Catholic religion was exterminated, & at the beginning of the 18th century not a church nor college nor even the ruins of one could be seen, & even the graves & tombs of the Christians were dug up & their bones scattered, so that not a sign of them remained. Along with this, came the ignominious career of the Dutch merchants, who were tolerated on the understanding of their not being Christians, & who, it is even said, conformed to the ceremony of trampling on the Cross, required of all resident foreigners & all suspected Christians, & made the most debasing concessions to retain the trade, & lost it after all. There is the little peninsula of Desima, in the centre of the city, to wh. the Dutch were so long limited. For 150 years, no Christian, known to be such, has been allowed to live here. But, now, under the late treaties, they can live here, & may hire houses, but cannot own land or build. There fly the consular flags of Gr. Britain, the U. States, France & Holland, & now, some 10 or 20 merchants, chiefly Engl., American, & Dutch reside here, attempting to open a trade, & there is one missionary, & only one, a Mr. Williams, one of B. Boone's clergy. The B. of Victoria goes ashore, to be his guest. Boats come off to us, bringing all the Europeans of the place, for letters & news. Among them are agents of Dent & Co., Jardine & Co., Mr. Walsh, who I suppose acts for Russell & Co., & some small traders, Jews & Parsees. But it is late in the afternoon & we dine, & put off our visit on shore until tomorrow. While we are at dinner, a company of Japanese officials enter the cabin, each with his two swords, to make official inquiries & to get some cognac or Curacoa to drink. But we put them off, as we are dining, & they quietly go ashore,—rather a sign, I think, of their declining power, in competition with the advancing European race.

Tuesd. Apr. 10.   Beautiful morning, & nothing can be more lovely than the scene fr. the deck of our steamer. There are patches of granite rock, with evergreen shrubs & trees about them, as on the coast off Beverly & Manchester, & patches of cultivated land. Above Nagasaki, the land is terraced, on the hill sides by walls of stone, & well cultivated, & among the stones & over the walls is a thick growth of creepers, like the Engl. ivy & lichen.

Go ashore. Call on Am. Consul, Mr. Walsh, br. of Walsh of Shanghai, & get my permit to change money. For foreigners can only change a limited quantity of money into Japanese coin, & that only on a consular permit. A passenger is allowed to change $3 a day, wh. he must do at the Custom House, & have each entered on his permit. For each dollar, I got 3 itsbus, (or inchebus), a oblong square silver coin, very prettily devised. For an itsbu, you get four itsus, silver of same shape of the itsbu, but smaller, or 2 nitsus, wh. are itsus, a little gilded. The Co. Hs. officers were squatting on mats, each wearing two swords, one with a book & writing materials, & one with the counting board of China on wh. they count by balls on wires, on the decimal principle.

Met the Bishop of Victoria, with Rev. Mr. Williams, & went with them to call on the Br. Consul, who is a son of the celebrated Morrison, & a gentlemanlike man. Thence walked thro' the city, to Mr. Williams' hs., where I staid & lunched. It is a Japanese house of dark wood, with sliding screen doors everywhere, by wh. rooms may always be thrown into one. Mr. Williams tells me there is only one clergyman here besides himself, a Mr. Verbeck, of the Dutch Refd. Ch.; but neither of them is permitted to preach or teach in the Japanese, & they are consequently mere students of Japanese. There are no Cath. Missionaries, & it is said none will be sent until they are permitted to act as Missionaries. Called on Rev. Mr. Verbeck, who offers to go about with me tomorrow & show me the curiosities of the town,—Mr. Wms. being engaged with the Bishop.

After this, finding it almost impossible to lose my way, betw. the hills & the harbor, I wandered about by myself, for 3 or 4 hours. Among other places, I got to a theatre, where a play was going on, before a very large audience, promiscuous, of men women & children, crowded, jammed in together, under a roof of bamboo & grass. The play consisted, as in our lowest style of farces, of practical jokes of falling & pushing & striking with fans & brushes, & high sharp unnatural tones of voice. At the side of the stage, was seated on a mat, a man who seemed to me to act a chorus, occasionally speaking & singing. The singing, like that I have heard in the streets, is deeper toned than the Chinese, &, even with the women, a kind of unnatural barytone seems to be the fashion.

The streets are wider than those of Chinese cities, full twice as wide, & well flagged with broad stones, & neater than the Chinese. Here, also, there are no carriages,—only human foot-falls—& curious foot-falls they are. For all wear the sandal, the heel of wh. is not tied up, but flaps at every step, slip-slap, slip-slap, so that there is a perpetual clatter of heels in the streets,—indeed, the only sound to be heard, but those of human voices. I am told that only persons of high rank are permitted to ride on horseback, & they seldom do it. Occasionally a bullock is used as a beast of burden, in the streets, but loads are carried by coolies (Japanese) with sticks, as in China, & they usually grunt & chant as they go along, like those of Shanghai.

Walking at random thro' the streets, thro' an open window I saw one of those public warm baths, of wh. so much has been written, & wh. tell the tale of Japanese life so fully. They were open to sight of all who chose to stop & look at them, & the bathers seemed shameless. A woman sat on a platform, by the window, mending the clothes she was going to put on, heedless of the passers by. In the bath were some 8 or 10 men & women, as close as they could well stow, while others were wiping themselves on the platform, in a condition tolerable only before the Fall. Yet, there was nothing improper in their *conduct*. For aught one could guess, the secret might be that they knew no evil; but the fact is known to be that they know more evil than any other people. All foreigners here agree in their testimony, that, in one respect, the Japanese are the most shamelessly immoral people on earth.

A large tract, on the water, has been allotted to foreigners here, & is in process of filling up, like that at Canton, & the work is done by the basket full, on the shoulders of coolies. Yet there are some thousands of them, & the work goes on pretty well. Near the ground, saw a large house of thatch & bamboo, where were tables set for some 1000 coolies, a tea cup & plate to each.

Dined with Mr. Walsh. He has a wife, who is a Canadian lady of the name of Church. She & Mrs. Verbeck, are the only foreign women in this part of Japan, & are very lonely. Especially good fish at dinner, & Japanese oranges. (Excellent fish market, & this morn. Capt. Dearborn went ashore early & bot fish eno' for 70 persons—all hands—for one dollar).

Walsh & his br. in law, Church, speak well of the Japanese in some respects. They say they are full as intelligent as the Chinese, & more manly. It seems to me they are less civilised, more of the savage in their dress, or want of dress, stronger, more willful, & not so excessively rooted, in their ways & opinions, to antiquity. But one day is little ground for a generalisation.

Passed the night on board the Yang Tse.

Wed. Ap. 11. The steamer Aroff is in, fr. Kenagawa, bound to Shanghai. As we leave for Kenagawa tomorrow morning, I close this journal, to send by the Aroff. She brings such news of civil war in Yeddo as makes my chance of visiting it very slight.

The Japanese have less of the pale yellow complexion than the Chinese, & are both darker & fairer, some a clear dark, & some a brunette. The little children are often fair brunettes, & so are many of the grown women. But the women rouge a great deal. The married women, & unmarried women who has reached middle life color their teeth black. This is considered an elegance, & girls are eager for the time when they can do it. The men shave the front of the head & bring the hair up to the top, in a small cue, of 4 or 5 inches long. The women draw their hair to the top where it is kept in place by gilt or silvered pins & combs, & by a thin paste or glue. The men wear a loose robe, wh. opens in front, tied at the waist by a belt, & the lower classes wear nothing else. The better dressed wear trowsers. The women wear robes, less careful & proper than the Chinese,—and indeed, those are not national ideas. No attempts to Christianise the Japanese have been made for 150 years, since the Catholics were exterminated, & none are making, or permitted, now.

Wed. Apr. 11. Nagasaki, Japan. (Sent journal to Apr. 11, fr. Nagasaki, by steamer Aroff for Shanghai.) This is a great relig. festival day, among the people. The temples are thronged, the women & children are dressed in their best, simple arches of bamboo dressed with leaves are thrown across the chief streets, lanterns are suspended fr. every available place, & transparencies prepared for the evening. Rev. Mr. Verbeck's to dine, at 1 o'ck. Mrs. V. is from Troy N.Y. a pleasant & rather pretty young woman, with exact manners. A Japanese pheasant, roasted, tastes like our partridge. After dinner, Mr. V. & I make an excursion thro' the city, on foot. There are no sedan chairs in Japan, the only conveyance being a close box, fitted with complicated slides, on the floor of wh. you have to sit. These are rare. I have seen but one in the city.

Our first visit is to a Temple, the principal one. It is on the hillside, with broad flights of stone steps leading up to it, &, at the foot, on the street, two large columns of copper, supporting a cornice of the same. The Temple itself is plainer than those in China, but in good condition. The site is one of the best in the city, commanding a noble view of the city, harbor & hills beyond. Next we went to a temple where worship was going on. This was Buddhist, & like the worship in China. The entire floor of the temple was filled with sitting & kneeling persons, chiefly women. The interior is gaudy with gilding &

lacquer work, the shrine is overloaded with ornaments, tapers burn & incense smokes before it, long robed & shaven priests kneel, & a choir sing a long hymn, accompanied by an instrument that sounds like a comb & paper,—the singing being in a thin, high, sharp key. Saw some persons at the door, who could not get in, throwing little pieces of copper at persons who were kneeling, hitting them in the neck & on the head. At first, we thought this was sport, & irreverent, but we noticed that they looked grave in doing it, & those whom the pieces hit took it gravely & picked them up, not intermitting their prayers. Mr. Verbeck suggested that the pieces thrown were a substitute for the presence of those who could not get in,—a vicarious or symbolical attendance. This is a mere guess, but it receives confirmation from the fact that absent people send their cards to the temple, by servants, who paste them on a table before the shrine. We saw a girl bring her mistress' card & paste it there, where there were already some hundreds. The only difference I could notice in the worship fr. that of China, is that in prayer the people rub the palms of their hands slowly together. Rosaries are in use among them. The priests file in before the altar, kneel, prostrate themselves, &, at the end of the service, file out at a side door, as in the R. Cath. worship. Indeed, there is no striking difference betw. the Buddhist & R. Cath. worship, in the externals.

To another temple of the ancient religion of Japan, wh. prevailed before the introduction of Buddhism. (Mr. V. thinks this has assimilated itself to the Buddhist. There is no conflict between the two sects). This temple was chiefly frequented by children, who played freely about its most sacred places, & over its nicely matted floors, but without undue noise or any rudeness.

There is a street in Nagasaki known as the Street of Temples. One side of it is occupied by the grounds of various temples, extending fr. ½ a mile to a mile in length. These grounds are all on the hill-side, with flights of stone steps & terraced grounds. The beggars are innumerable, importunate & sometimes offensive. Probably these are more numerous to-day, it being a festival. Some are begging monks or friars, & are respectfully treated. They are known by their dress & a little bell they beat, hung at their stomachs. Some seemed well & hearty, & must be begging by some heriditary or official right. The children of the poorer class often hold out their hands for coin.

The Japanese children are very pretty & engaging. They look happy, as if they were well treated & well fed. I am told that the parental rule is gentle. I think in two days, I have not seen or heard a crying child. They have very bright eyes, white teeth, & clear brown complexions. The young girls, too, are pretty. Low broad foreheads, of the Greek type, thick black hair, white teeth & intelligent ardent eyes are common. But as soon as they come to the age of blackened teeth, they are hideous. They keep their mouths open, to exhibit these black teeth, surrounded by highly rouged lips, wh. gives them a look of toothless fatuity, as if of extreme old age. Beside the rouge, wh. is so common on the lips & cheeks, they often whiten the rest of the face & the neck, to the hue of the palest Northern complexion. A Japanese married woman is this—black teeth, rouged lips & cheeks, neck & rest of the face whitened, & black hair dressed on the top of the head with ornamented combs & pins & stiffened by a wash of thin paste. The dress of all women is a wrapper, gathered by a belt at the waist. Of wrappers, they wear one, two, three, or more, according to their taste & wealth, & the state of the weather. In cold weather, one will be quilted. The poor usually wear but one. But whatever the number of garments, they are all wrappers. The under wrappers are of rich silk. The men also wear wrappers, but trowsers are also worn by a portion of the men. The babies seem to live out of doors, being carried everywhere by the women, sometimes on the back, as in China, but usually in front, lodged in the loose folds of the wrapper above the girdle. (The women nurse their babies, in the most open manner, in the streets, theatres, temples & all public places, & often go with entire open fronts, the whole field of the infant's labors being open to view. This, however, is nothing. For, when it is warm, the women of the lower classes leave off all clothing above the waist, & the men have nothing either above the waist or below it).

This day, we were told, was for the worship of the middle & poorer classes. The upper classes have a separate day. Here, as in China, the names of benefactors to a temple or shrine, are engraved on tablets & conspicuously placed. The Japanese bell is of copper, struck with a heavy stick of soft wood, wh. is swung by machinery, & strikes at the end, giving a soft deep tone. The bells do not bulge or flare out at the bottom, like ours, but are shaped like a thimble.

The hills wh. surround the city are covered with tombs. The city of the dead is above, & the city of the living is below. The tombs are in the Chinese style, surrounded by low walls, terraced, & some 2 or 3 feet high, wh. go about the tomb a little after the manner of the child's "Walls of Troy". The stone used here is a kind of dark granite, a good color.

The combined moisture & warmth of the climate of Japan, give rise to a growth of creeping plants, with tiny leaves, like the clover, but of a thick, evergreen texture, like the ivy. The plant grows out of the joints of stone walls, & even from the tiled roofs of old houses, & so dense is it, that some times you can hardly tell whether the structure before you is a stone wall or a bank. This gives great beauty to the terrace walls, the temples & large stone enclosures, public & private.

Mr. Verbeck (whose initials are G. F.) took me to pay a visit to a Japanese gentleman of the middle class, a two sworded man. He has a house on the hill-side, commanding a fine view. The temple grounds,—the range of them, lie beneath him. He received us courteously. The Japanese salute is to join your hands before you, & bow profoundly once or twice. The only diff, in the Chinese is that they shake their joined hands, as if they were shaking props. The Japanese gentleman gave us tea & some nice spunge cake, just such as Mrs. Nichols makes. He sat on his mat, & the servant brought him the teapot, hot water, portable fire apparatus, tea cups & tea caddy, & he made the tea himself. I noticed that he heated the cups with water first, á la R. H. Dana Senr. The tea was ground fine as flour, & of a bronse color. This he said was rare & nice. He also made us some from the leaf, wh. I like better. The Japanese tea is not prepared, like most of the Chinese, for a long sea voyage. The leaf seems to be simply dried. It is soft & tender, & the beverage has a taste of weak green tea. (*Mem.* the professed tea-tasters in China, who buy for the merchants, rub the tea in the hand, blow upon it, & put it to the nose. If it stands this test, it is afterwards subjected to boiling water).

Our host inquired whether the Japanese embassy had reached the United States. Mr. V. says he understood the difference between America, & the great nations of Europe.

The Japanese wear handsome colors of silks. It seems to me they have more varieties of colors & more taste in them than the Chinese. The Chinese wear chiefly blue, white, black & brown. Here they have beautiful tints of purple & lilac, & a kind of checked grey, or grey & lilac, wh. is very pretty.

On our way down fr. the old gentleman's house, we passed a tree,—a small tree or large shrub—covered & filled deep with beautiful pink flowers, small & close together. Laid upon the ground, it would have made "a bed of heaped Elysian flowers". Mr. V. did not know its name. I believe I have mentioned the double flowering cherry tree, wh. has no fruit, & the Camelias Japonicas, single & double, wh. are so rich & so common.

The manners of all the people, young & old, are civil. The little children are becoming accustomed to foreigners, & at every step meet us with the pretty salutation—Ohio—pronounced exactly as we pronounce the name of the State. The chief amusement here, of young & old, now, is the flying of kites. They are of all shapes, & beautifully colored & figured. An amusement & mischief is to cut the string of another kite by drawing across it. To do this, they put upon a portion of the string fine particles of glass, by a kind of glue or paste.

Currency. As well as I can make it out, the chief silver coin is properly called a *bu* (pronounced *boo*), worth about 35 cents, an oblong square of silver. *Ichi* is Japanese for *one,* & one of these is called ichibu, whence the name for the coin among foreigners has become ichibu, & we speak of 2 & 3 ichibus. The *shu* is a silver coin of the same shape, worth about eight cents. One of these is called an *ishu,* wh. is a contraction for ichi shu. Whence foreigners call this coin also the *ishu.* The *ishu* gilded, or of nikle, doubles its value, & is called a *nishu,* wh. means two *shus.* Then they have a copper coin, flat, of an oval shape, as large as the longitudinal section of an egg, with a square hole in the middle. This is the *tempo,* sixteen *tempo* go to the *ichibu,* which makes it about two cents. They have also the little copper *seni,* or *kas* or *kash,* of China, getting out of circulation, & worth about 2 or 3/10 of a cent. Of all these, I have specimens. The gold, I have not yet learned. The *tael* like the English pound, is not coined. It is the sum by wh. all reckonings are made, & represents here, as in China, about $1.30. The iron *zeni* is worth about 1/50 of a cent!

There are two little mountain streams that run thro' Nagasaki, crossed by high arched bridges of dark granite. On one of these I saw a water wheel, of full sise, in operation. Mr. Verbeck gives me a Japanese map of Nagasaki.

On board again, at night, as we start for Kenagawa at daybreak. Take my leave of Nagasaki by its bright lights seen from the steamer's deck.

Thursd. April 12. At sea, again, going round the South coast of Japan, bound to Kenagawa. Mr. Dent tells me that about one & a half million of dollars worth of silk has been exported fr. Japan in the last nine months, wh. is pretty well for the beginning of a trade. Also, considerable vegitable wax, sapan wood, for a die. The tea has not yet been prepared for a sea voyage, & its adaptation to the European market is not settled. The trade to Japan is something, especially in edeble seaweed. But the Japanese take nothing in return. They have never either imported or exported anything! They have produced & consumed, by themselves, independently of the rest of the world.

Mr. Dent also tells me that the Russians are introducing their woolens into China, by overland trade, & undersell the English & Americans, who are limited to cottons.

Mr. Verbeck tells me the best he can learn as to the women of Japan, is this. The virtue of the wife is strictly guarded, & a failure punished severely. So, of the unmarried daughters of men of the upperclasses. Men seem to be under no particular control in that respect, more than is the case of drinking,— excess or publicity is to be avoided. The licensed public brothels, are the peculiarity of Japan. The daughters of the poorer classes are placed there, freely, & indented to the keepers. In them, they get a better education than they can get at home. The mistress is bound to teach them reading & writing, music, manners & accomplishments. From these places they marry, & often marry well. It seems to be considered an advance in the condition of a poor girl, but would be a disgrace to one of the upper classes. To carry out the anomaly, the master of one of these houses, though recognised by law, loses caste, & however rich, is regarded a little as the Southern planter regards the slave-dealer. He thinks the concubines are mostly serfs & vassals,—for, all know that the feudal system prevails in full vigor in Japan. The concubine is protected & has rights, for herself & her children, but is not a wife. There is but one *wife*, which is substantially the law of China.

Frid. Apr. 13.   Very heavy sea all last night, & all to-day. None but a strong vessel could stand it, Capt. Dearborn, who has been 30 years at sea, & is a moderate talker, tells me it is the most dangerous sea he ever saw. It comes fr. all directions. It stove in our larboard box & swamped a boat wh. was above the hurricane deck. All-day 8 men are employed driving the water off decks. It comes pouring over all parts of the ship. The Capt. thought at one time it would carry off everything. The seas off Japan have the reputation of being the worst in the world. The Chinese servants were all fastened below, under battened hatches, all sea-sick. There was something bewildering in the effect of the seas, as they tossed about, & broke over us, & we tore through them with the power of our great engines. It is a wonder to me that the complicated machinery of steamboats holds out so well.

Yesterday was a calm, beautiful day, & the picturesque coast of Japan, blue in the distance, passed by our sides, mountains, hills & vales. At night, it was so dark that, on deck, I could not see the passage down, & had to grope, like a blind man, & the sea was all alive with phospherescent light. I thought something was going to happen. Roll, pitch, plunge, bang, splash, swash—all day long,—a dreary time. I read Oliphant's China & Japan, but not with pleasure, & those who are not sea sick are rather grouty.

Sat. Apr. 14.   All cleared off. Fine day, & sea almost smooth. All hands bright again, & the Canary birds are singing.

Monday. Apr. 16.   At Yokahama, the sea port of Yeddo, in the centre of the kingdom of Japan! On shore, at the house of a kind friend, walking in the country among groves & plantations & temples & the huts of the poor, by hill sides & rivulets, & examining the rich trees & foliage & flowers of this wonderful country. Have I not every reason to be thankful for the success that attends my steps?

But, to go back to my voyage here. All day Saturday, we were out of sight of land, & at sundown none was to be seen, but no sooner was it dark than first one volcano, then another, & at length four were to be seen, now fading almost out of sight, & now brightening up into a steady glare, through the darkness. They must have been very distant. Coming among islands, our Capt. whose charts, the best to be had here, were 30 miles out of the way here, putting us at noon some 20 miles in the country, on a mountain,—hove us to under short head of steam until daylight of Sunday, & all Sunday morning we were on deck, watching with delight these beautiful shores, as we passed up the great bay of Yeddo. The shores are as beautiful as the Isle of Wight, the best points of Staten Island, or of the North of England. No sand, no flats, no rugged bare hills, nor merely a rolling country,—but such a disposition of hills, valleys, slopes, small plains, occasional rocks, half concealed by evergreens, & the whole sprinkled over with trees, sometimes sparse & sometimes in groves, & signs of the most elaborate cultivation, terraced gardens, the deep green of the rice fields & the brilliant yellow of the rape seed. Then this magnificent bay, as open as the sea, 20 & 30 miles across, seems all alive with boats fishing for the great market of Yeddo, & the daily wants of the dwellers on its shores. To count these boats is out of the question. They dot the horison as thick as an artist could put them on his canvas. I have no doubt that 2000 could be seen from our decks. Meat is scarce with these people. Fish & rice are their subsistence.

While we are looking at the shores, through our glasses, I see a large cloud, close to the horison, singularly regular in its shape. It is broad at the base, very high, & cut sharp off at the top. "Do you see Fusiama?" "No". "There, just where you are looking". "That. No. Impossible, that is a cloud—all snow white—too high for a mountain". Is it a cloud or a mountain? That is the question. John Bull proposes to take a bet on it. As we draw nearer, spots, then strips of dark green are disclosed on its sides, low down, but all its upper half, at least, is pure white, the white of snow,—for the great mountain, volcano, of Fusiama, it certainly is.

Now comes in sight the shipping at anchor, in front of the double town of Yokahama & Kenagawa, H.B.M. brig Camilla, a raking bark from the Sandwich Islands, the Zoe, a pretty little herm brig fr. S. Francisco, the Ida Rogers, & a bit of a topsail sch. from S. Fr., the Page, & Dent & Co.'s great receiving ship loading a ship alongside of her, & a Dutch bark, & a Br. ship, & there, up the bay, out of sight, lies the mysterious inapproachable city of Yeddo. We are soon at anchor, & boarded. Three Custom Hs. officers, each with two swords, go into the cabin & take notes in strange characters of the Capt.'s report & drink their Curacoa, & a midshipman from the Camilla, for letters & newspapers, & some half dosen Am. & Engl. come in sampans. Among them is Dr. Bates, son of my kind host at Honolulu, established here as a physician, & soon Dr. Hall comes on board, to whom I have letters, & invites me ashore to be his guest.

Dr. Hall, (George R.) is a Mass. man, married a d. of Mr. Beal of Kingston, knows the Severs, Lt. James Dana, & our Plymouth friends, especially Marston Watson. He has been in China sev. years, & in Japan six mos., in mercantile pursuits, partner of Walsh & Co. He has just finished a plain house of wood, but well furnished, & installs me in a good room, with many of the comforts of life. He has begun a little plantation of shrubs & trees about his house, wh. I examine with him. Here are camelia Japonicas, white & red, single & double, double flowering cherry & peach, & evergreens of the most beautiful varieties, some closely resembling our hemlock & cedar, yet with differences. One with very graceful weeping branches, called the weeping pine, for it is a white pine. The yew grows to great height here, & bears its red berries. There is also the ground pine, the savin, the juniper, the pitch pine & the English holly. Then there is the Cryptomeria Japonica, a celebrated evergreen among Naturalists. Of all these, he has small growing specimens, while they are in sight, in full growth, on the neighboring hills. The privet, used here for hedges, is in abundance. Probably Japan is the best country in the world for varieties of evergreens.

By the Treaties, the 3 ports opened to foreigners, are Nagasaki, Kenagawa & Hakodadi. But the Japanese insisted that Yokahama, adjoining Kenagawa, should be the place for the residence of foreigners. As it is more convenient for commerce, having deeper water, the foreigners have gladly accepted it, but the foreign officials, to preserve the treaty, enter their protest, & fix the Consulates at Kenagawa. They are about three miles apart, but Yokahama will be the place of foreign trade & residence. A large, liberal allotment, or concession of land has been made for the foreign settlement, with the waterfront of about five thousand feet, & embracing, in all, some one hundred acres. Here are to be the houses, offices & "go-downs" of the foreign residents. This allotment was made only a little over a year ago. Twelve months ago, there was not a house upon it. Now, houses & offices & godowns are going up in all directions. Heard & Co.'s is nearly done, Dent & Co.'s in progress, Walsh & Co.'s nearly done, & numerous others, just completed, in progress or planned out, for the various Dutch, British, American & Russian merchants who have flocked here, among whom is the usual proportion of Jews. The foreign Concession is regularly laid out in wide streets & enclosed within a stockade, at the gates of which the Japanese military keep guard, not to shut in the foreigners, for the treaties give them a range of about 20 miles into the country, in one direction, & seven in the direction of Yeddo, but to guard them against robbers & assasins. This is not unneeded. Not long ago, (about 6 mos.) a Russian officer & two seamen were attacked & butchered, just at dusk, in the open streets of the Concession, & only 3 or 4 weeks ago, two masters of Dutch merchant vessels, said to be steady & respectable men, were set upon & cut to pieces, at about the same hour & place. Since the last event, the foreign consuls have issued an order, advising all foreigners to go armed, & not be out unnecessarily after dark, & the Japanese guards are strictly kept. No clue can be found to either of the murders. The common report among the Japanese is that they were done by retainers of some great neighboring princes, known to be hostile to foreigners & to the powers at Yeddo. My California belt comes into play now, & is a convenience.

In the afternoon, Dr. Hall takes me a delightful walk into

the country, for a mile or so. I cannot cease admiring the picturesque beauty of the disposition—the *lay*—of the land, in this world of Japan. The hills are just high enough, they are of every shape & form, the valleys & levels lie delightfully among them, & the trees shade everything, & every wall, every stone, every big trunk of a tree has its "garniture & screen" of ivy & other creeping vine. The ivy is that of England, without poison & an evergreen hue. There are sturdy oaks, too, for it to grow upon.

The hill sides are always terraced, where they are cultivated at all. This, Dr. Hall tells me, is to prevent the washing down of the soil. Acres & acres are laid down to paddy fields, from wh. they are now just beginning to draw off & pump off the water. Rice is the staff of life here, & its exportation is prohibited.

The houses are tiled on the roofs, & to resist the force of the typhoons, & to give tenacity to the roof, there is a plantation of the *fleurs de lis* at the ridge of every roof. This produced a singular, but pleasing effect. The yards are lined, & the walks are lined with hedges, close cut, as in England,—their own invention, centuries old. These hedges are of privet, & various evergreen thorn bushes, & of the yew. The rasberry abounds here, & is in full blow, now, & the little, simple violet, "wee, modest", but world known, violet, sprinkles over all the warm banks.

Before an old temple, wh. we visit, stands an ancient oak, an old gingo tree, & several of the Cryptomeria Japanica; and in the court of a Jap. gentleman's house, is the curiosity of a pitch pine tree,—or, what ought to have been a tree—150 years old, grown to the height of about four feet, & then spread out over a flat surface, 15 feet square, supported by a trellis. The Japanese, like the Chinese, delight in torturing trees into grotesque shape, imitations of birds & beasts. In that respect they have not much more taste than a Dutchman. We made a call upon a dignitary, who was holding a court of conciliation, at which sat, or squatted, some half dosen litigants & witnesses, & there was ever so much writing, in big books. They gave us cups of hot saki, a wine made of rice, the chief drink of the country, & a pleasant confection of bean. (You cannot call on a Chinese or

Japanese, without an offer of tea, or wine, & tobacco, & some little cake or confection).

Returning through the Japanese village, we saw one of those institutions of the country, the public bath, where, as at Nagasaki, men & women were bathing & making their toilets. These are as open to the street as a barber's shop. Dr. Hall thinks the water is not changed all day, & that the better class bathe early. At the Guard House were a file of Japanese soldiers, squatting on mats. Behind them was a row of musquets, with percussion caps & bayonets, made by native workmen. The Japanese make minie rifles & Colt's pistols. They have none of the obstinate Chinese nonsense of matchlocks & bows & arrows. Saw some exquisite red porcelain cups. Dr. Hall says their colors, in their silks, are not fast, tho' pretty.

Calls & returns from Habersham (formerly Lieut. in U.S. Navy, author &c.) Stearns, Brower, & Knight, merchants here, & Dorr, the U.S. Consul.

Went with Dr. Bates, in his boat, to Kenagawa. It is about 3 miles across. (Dr. Bates hires four boatmen, to be always by the boat, & to find themselves, & gives for the four $12 a month. Manual labor is worth about 50 or 60 cents a week). Kenagawa is a village, lying along the Imperial high road, Tekaido, wh. runs through the realm to & fr. Yeddo, & wh. skirts between the hill & the water. Called on Rev. Mr. Brown, Missionary of A.B.C.F.M., but he & all his family, & Dr. Hepburn, the Miss. phys., were gone on a day's excursion. These families occupy a temple, & live among the idols. How did they get it?

Speaking of missionaries, Mr. Williams, at Nagasaki, said that when he gave a Chinese Bible to a native, it was sent back the next day, with a message fr. the Governor, that if it was done again, it would bring both parties into trouble. And Mr. Verbeck told me that a Japanese, who had bought a translation of an Engl. work on history, came to him for an explanation of the words "God" & "Jesus Christ", & that he felt obliged to decline his request. The consequence to the Missionary, might be banishment or such restrictions & annoyances as would make his life there useless, & *to* the native might be very serious if not fatal. This can hardly be called Missionary work!

In truth, the few Missionaries in Japan are simply what the Chinese call "Makeelarn boys",—learning the language & customs.

Called on Mr. Dorr, the U.S. Consul. He lives in a temple, on the high ground above the village, fr. wh. flies the Am. ensign. This is a large & beautiful temple, with grounds laid out in the usual taste of the Bonses (Buddhist priests). The gods are screened off, by a paper wall, but all the rest of the temple is for his use, assigned to him as the official residence. He tells me it is the best residence that any foreigner has in Japan, better than the foreign ministers have at Yeddo. Dorr, (E. W.) is a Boston man, & is said to be a generous fellow. He presses on me an invitation to visit him at his temple, wh. I shall accept. Yesterday, he sent to Mr. Harris, our Minister, at Yeddo, my application for permission to go to Yeddo. By the treaty it is not to be opened to Americans or any foreigners until 1862, except those connected with the Embassy. But he thinks I can go, notwithstanding. In his grounds are Camelia Japanicas (or, is it *Camilla*?) fifty feet high, with deep crimson flowers to their very tops. The haliards that hoist the Am. ensign on the flag staff are made fast round the chin of an idol! The oddity of this is extreme, & perhaps it is a portent. In part of his grounds are the tombs of the priests, & in another, the place where the dead are burned. This latter is still in use. Dorr tells me that they only burn off the flesh, & bury the skeleton entire.

Mr. Dorr tells me that the report of the assassination of the Prince Regent by emissaries of the Prince of Mito, is true, (The Emperor is a boy of 16). The Prince of Mito is a great feudal chief, who is bitterly opposed to the foreigners, to the treaties recently made, & to the party in power, which is supposed to favor foreigners. Immediately on the assassination, the Prince of Mito withdrew to his country, in the mountains, & has been levying a large force. Civil war is apprehended. The Japanese authorities have told Mr. Dorr that they cannot protect him in Kenagawa, if the Prince of Mito comes this way, & advise him to withdraw to Yokahama, but he refuses, believing it to be a dodge to remove the Consulate.

The view of the Bay, from the terrace of Mr. Dorr's temple, he compared to views on the Isle of Wight. The same thing struck me.

Returned to Yokahama. (I believe the Japanese authorities, contend, under the treaty, that Yokahama is part of Kenagawa). Dorr opened his collection of ancient Japanese coins, & gave me several. One, a *koban*, gold, some 200 years old, worth, intrinsicaly about $4.85. Another, a gold *ichibu*, of the value of $2, & one of the old silver ichibus. He says that the unit of their coinage is the *zene*, (Chinese *kas* or kash), a small iron coin, with square hole in middle. Of these, there are about 1600 to an ichibu. The smallest silver coin is the *ishu*, equal to 400 zene, or ¼ ichibu. The *ishu* made of nickle wh. is called the *nishu*, is worth two *ishu*, or 800 zene. The large, oval copper piece, with the hole in it, is the tempo & is worth 100 zene, or ¼ *ishu*. Small transactions are measured by *ichibu* & *tempo*.

This afternoon, went with Dr. Hall to inspect the Gankero. There is a large section of ground set apart especially for this purpose by the government. It is separated by a creek & bridge fr. the rest of the town. Licenses are given to persons to build houses & maintain them there, for the purpose of prostitution, on the Japanese system, of wh. I have spoken. A year ago there was not a foreigner here, & no trade & few inhabitants. It was opened to foreigners & trade on 4 July last, & now it has grown so, chiefly in Japanese, of course, that the place, the Gankero, has sprung up as in a night. Most of the houses now are but partly built, & the utmost industry prevails,—carpenters, painters, tilers &c. The chief establishment looked like a temple, it is so large & handsome. Within are parlors, reception rooms, dining rooms, a dancing hall, a theatre, &c. &c. The chief rooms were beautifully carved & elaborately painted. The chief artists of Yeddo contributed each a panel, for the walls & ceiling. Lacquered furniture & screens abound, & great neatness everywhere. It is not yet occupied, being in the finishers' hands. It has a court yard, planted with trees & shrubs, where is to be a fountain.

Next we visited some of the other establishments, a specimen of each class. Those of the 2d & 3d class were large houses, well ventilated, with bathing rooms & kitchens & sleeping rooms, & each a large reception room. These were occupied & in full operation. The women, being all unmarried, have white teeth, are painted white & red, especially the lips, & have their hair dressed in the most elaborate style, with large puffs, hair pins & combs, stiffened by thin glue; & some of them wore huge head dresses of cheap finery. These girls belong to the establishment, almost like slaves. They are sold, or apprenticed by their parents. They are usually taken very young & are taught. We saw some practicing instrumental music & singing. One girl Dr. Hall thought could not be over 10 or 12 years old. One was a new comer, & was in the hands of the barber, a woman, who was dressing her hair in the most artistic manner, with brushes in the glue or paste, combs, pins &c., decking the poor victim. The lowest class of houses were what the foreigners call the stalls. Here are rows of stalls, each about 8 feet by 4, with a sliding door in front, & each occupied by a woman. We passed through them. In some, the women were asleep, in others they stood at their doors to entice the passers by. We had to dodge, to avoid being seised by them. This was the lowest & most distressing view of all. I cannot think the whole number of public courtesans in the entire Gankero, can be less than a thousand. Yet the entire population of the town does not exceed 3 or 4000. But the town is a place of constant resort for traders, travellers & sight-seers from the interior, as well as of sailors fr. the ships. The Govt. undertakes the police regulation of the Gankero, & Dr. Hall thinks there are Japanese physicians employed there. But venereal disease is almost universal. Not one in ten is clear of it. Mr. Habersham dined with us—a man of good manners, but ill reported of in the Navy.

Tuesd. Apr. 17. Go again to Kenagawa. Short call on Dorr. Call on the Browns. Rev. is off with the Consul, but see Mrs. Brown. Who should she turn up to be but a daughter of Rev. Shubael Bartlett of E. Windsor, Conn. She & Mr. B. were 8 years in China, left on account of her health, spent 12 years at home, & have been in Japan some 6 or 8 mos. They have handsome quarters, in the Jobúchichi temple.

All the Protestant Missionaries I have seen, whether in China, Japan or the S Islands, live in respectable, comfortable quarters, with servants, on equal social relations with the wealthy classes, & are able to give time & attention to visitors. Their position is an advance in social position & comforts of life to many of them. They do not live as well, with as much leisure and as many servants in the grade of life many of them come from. They live better than the families of the poorer country clergymen at home. If this is known & understood, it is not to be complained of. It is their policy to present themselves to the natives as well ordered, dignified Christian families. Many have ridiculed them & sneered at them for their sedans, & coolies & cooks &c. But the poorest foreigners keep servants, & labor is cheap, while labor might be injurious to their health & position. Their position is that of fairly salaried Congregational clergymen's families in our larger New Engl. towns. If they claim to be making sacrifices, beyond such as are implied in a residence in such places, they claim too much. Beyond what is necessarily implied in residing in such places, a Missionary life in S. Islands, China & Japan is no sacrifice to any but a person coming from the "upper 10,000" of society. I speak of the missionaries of the Am. Board, the Ep. Ch., Presb. & Dutch Refd. Churches.

Met a funeral procession, with drums, gongs & all sorts of banners & devices, & four women in white, either mourners or Buddhist nuns. Streets are full of Major Fonblanque's horses, he has been buying for the Engl. army.

Went on board the Japanese hulk. It is a ship of 6 or 800 tons, built entirely by the Japanese, some 30 years ago, unfortunately from the model of a very old Dutch ship. She is laid up useless, in the present state of naval architecture. It is creditable to them, still. Now they have 5 steamers, all commanded & engineered by themselves.

The Japanese language has more vowels than the Chinese. It has, occasionally a little of the sound of the rougher Spanish. Instead of the Hwangs, Kongs, Chungs of China, they have Kenagáwa, Yokoháma, Yeddo, Meto &c., & the pretty salutation of *Ohio*, & the *alingáto* for thank you.

They have the lotus here, in abundance, & the Oleander all the year. The wheat gives a deep green to the fields.

Young Talbot, of Olyphant & Co. is here. Oliphant & Co. are one of the great Am. Merc. houses of China, next after Russells and Heards.

Japanese Words

So, yes	*San ny*, three
Ny, no	*Sii my*, four
Ohio, good day	*Go my*, five
Arlingato, thank you	*Rook my*, six
Yuroski, very well	*Stii my*, seven
Ichi, one	*Hachi my*, eight
Nii my, two	*Ku my*, nine
	To, ten

The proper spelling of the city is *Yedo*, with one *d*. The Japanese scarcely sound the *Y*; & the d goes with the last syllable, Yé-do. The volcano is Fusi Yama, Matchless Mountain.

Thursd. Apr. 19.   Called on M. de Bellecour, the Fr. Consul Gen. He is a most elab. polite man. Dined & spent the ev. with Mr. Brown the Missionary. He is of the D Refd. Board, & not the A.B.C.F.M. Great variety of evergreens in their yard & garden. They call the Temple "The Evergreens",—the Japanese name is *Yobúchichi*. They have pitch pine, white pine, cedars of various kinds, ground pine, a delicate weeping pine, something resembling the hemlock, the arbor vita, the yew, the holly, juniper, savin, & the box tree, wh. grows to the full height of a tree, with leaves like our low box. The box is used here for hedges, & makes a thick hedge of full height. Mr. B. is a man of learning & good sense. He is studying the Japanese, under a native teacher. Gave me his views as to the Chinese & Jap. languages & characters. Thinks the Chinese characters were made for the purpose of representing the word or sound attached by usage to the thing, & that the ideographic or figurative character was adopted for its fitness, convenience & ease in being remembered. These characters being established, the *sound* of each must be taught by tradition. Abstract ideas were represented by characters somewhat arbitrary, & therefore purest phonetic, in principle, but often in fact also, & somewhat ideographic, on principles of mnemonics. The characters have now come to be substantially phonetic, & differ from our system in this, that each character represents an entire word. The fact that diff, provinces will recognise a character & its *idea*, & give it diff.w words & the same meaning, (as the Eur. nations will the sign V, for five, or cinq, or fünf) is historical merely—that is, the sounds have changed, or, the character has been taught, under a sound, like V, X, &c. in numerals. He thinks the Japanese had no writing, until taught by the Chinese. The Chinese teachers used their own characters for their appropriate meanings, & taught them to the Japanese, who gave them the Japanese sound, as the Am. missionary teaches the Kanaka to use the sign V, & tells him he must call it *alima*, while we call it *five*. The Japanese afterward constructed a system of letters or characters, more on the principle of an alphabet, i.e., or rather, *syllabarium*, phonetic purely. They adopted the basis of Chinese characters, but used only a few of them. This is the running hand of Japan, & resembles our written style. Then they adopted another alphabet of square characters. The former is in chief use. The latter is used for annotations chiefly. They also use the Chinese characters sometimes alone, & oftener interspersed with their own. Consequently, a Japanese scholar must know three systems of writing. A great many Chinese words are introduced, modified by the Japanese tongue, wh. requires more vowels. They count in two sets of words, the pure Japanese, & the Chino-Japanese. I rarely saw a Japanese writing that was not sprinkled with Chinese characters.

The Browns have a piano, probably the only one in Japan. Miss Julia Brown, the d. has pressed some leaves & flowers for Mrs. Dana, in a book. There is a newly arrived Baptist missionary here, Goble & wife. He was a marine in one of our vessels, & seems a dull, unlearned & unteachable man. He speaks Engl. so indistinctly that I cannot always understand him, & has no breeding—one of those to whom it is a social advance to be a Missionary, & have a servant, & do no labor, & be called *Rabbi, Rabbi*. There are 2 Missy phys. here, with their wives— Dr. Simmons & Hepburn—just saw the latter a moment.

Did I mention that Wednesday, I moved over fr. Yokoháma to Kanagáwa, & am the guest of Mr. Dorr, at the Consulate, the Temple Hōngáskugí? Here is a Mr. Henderson, of N.Y., who assists Dorr, & Davenport, son of Rev. Mr. D., once an Ep. clergyman, & now Irvingite,—used to visit at our house. Young D. came here before the mast, & was wrecked on the coast of Japan, in the bark Nymph. He tells me the Japanese were very kind to them, treated them hospitably, sent them to

Kanagawa in a junk, & stole nothing. The Jap. authorities made an inventory of everything saved fr. the vessel, even to old paint-brushes, & insisted on restoring everything acc. to the inventory, & wd. not allow them to give away, or even throw away anything—from fear of suspicions or other trouble. D. thinks it was not so much superior honesty in the common people, as fear of the Government's thoroughness & severity.

This (Th. 19th) afternoon, storm of wind & rain—very heavy. Some vessels drag at their anchors. I staid at Mr. Brown's until late. He offered me a lantern & a soldier to light & guard me home. But as I could see my way, & had my revolver & bowie knife on an outside belt, I declined both, & went to the Consulate alone. It was rather dark, & a few men were in the street. I kept the middle, with hand on pistol. When got in, both Dorr & Henderson said it was too great a risk. Dorr intended to send a guard for me. It seems the Jap. authorities have advised foreigners not to go out after dark unless with guards, armed, & with lanterns. I did not know *so* much danger was attached to it, or I should have accepted the guard. What a *bore* it must be to the Japanese, who have got on well enough by themselves for 20 centuries, to have us come in here, & be obliged to find us guards at our houses, & in the streets, & give us privileges, & yield up their customs to us!

But, how it did blow through the great trees around the Temple, to-night! Then, too, the officials came round & doubled the guard; for there were reports that a gang of bad fellows were in the neighborhood. Beside the gen. risk of robbers, it is generally believed or feared, that there are emissaries about of those princes who are hostile to foreigners, sent to make trouble with us, if they can. It is the gen. opinion that the murders of foreigners that have taken place, were by these last. Some, however, think these fears & notions groundless.

Frid. Apr. 20. Beautiful, still day, warm—hot,—the bay stilled down like a lake. Very hot at noon. Japanese boys running stark naked down the Tokaido, from their swimming—leaving their clothes at home. Women sit at their doors, letting all drop, to their waists, & the men of the laboring class, have next to nothing on,—not decent. I do not see how a foreign woman can live here. The men of the better class—soldiers, officials—wear trowsers, shoes & tunics.

The chief object of my visit here, has been to go to Yedo. It seems, Mr. Harris, our Minister, puts a strict construction upon the treaty,—that no Am. can go to Yedo unless he has business with the Embassy that cannot be conveniently transacted elsewhere. Had I known this, I could have obtained some official rank or business to bring me within the rule. As it was, I sent him my letter from Mr. Ward, & my request for permit to visit the city. He replied, in complimentary terms,—would make an exception in my case if he could in any, &c. &c., but must stand to his rule or admit all who applied,—wh. wd. be a violation of the treaty.

At the same time, the Br. Minister, who takes a more liberal view of the treaty, invited Messers. Dent & Webb; & the latter went to Yedo. On Harris' asking expln. fr. the Br. Minister, Alcock, he said that Dent was an official at H. Kong, & Webb a Portug. Consul at Shanghai. But as neither of these offices gave them any relations or business with the Embassy, it amounts to this,—Harris admits none unless on necess. official business at Yedo, while Alcock exercises a discretion, according to the pers. claims of the applicant. The Fr. Minister does the same. Mr. H. may be right & they wrong in the course, but it places Americans at a disadvantage. I own it was rather provoking to see a mere Br. merch. going to Yedo, & an Am. gentleman, travelling for information, shut out, when that merchant at home could no more approach the Society I visit in England than he could read Greek. The Fr. Minister, Bellecour, to whom I bore a despatch fr. the Fr. Legation, was unfortunately at Kanagawa, & I did not feel at liberty to keep it back until he should go to Yedo. M. de Bellecour deprecated Harris' construction, & said if I were not a citisen of a country wh. had an embassador at Yedo, he would give me a permit. To wh. I replied that this was the first time I had ever felt inconvenience fr. being an Am. citisen. The Americans here seemed mortified at the result, & Dorr talked large & did nothing.

Crossed to Yokohama, to do a little shopping. Young man, named Richards, fr. Roxbury, Mass., who speaks Jap. a little &

knows the habits of the people & the value of their goods, went round with me. The shops are neatness itself, the floors covered with white mats, & every table & shelf looking as if it were lacquered or veneered. The Jap. take off their sandals at the doors of their houses. At shops, there is usually a row of sandals at the door, standing like carriages at a fash. shop in London. Bought a small cabinet of rattan inlaid & silver, lacquered,—intended as a present to Miss Porter,—½ dos. ver-million tea cups & saucers, & a piece of silk for a thin coat, & a *puckeny-Japonica*, as I call it,—a hat turban for hot weather. Dr. Hall made me several presents,—wh. I value highly—a Japanese official sword, with its little *hari kari* dagger at-tached, & a Jap. dagger with white shark's skin handle, two in-laid card cases (one for Mrs. Dana) & ½ dos. vermillion tea cups & saucers of child's sise, for one of my daughters. Mr. Dorr was profuse in his presents, so that I had to stop him. He has given me a gold *koban*, about 200 years old, of an intrinsic value of about $4.85, 2 gold *ichibus*, worth about $2 apiece, 3 or 4 little pieces of carved figures,—the Dragon of Japan &c. &c., & 2 crystals, & one large piece of unwrought crystal, & a gold charm (essence bottle), & a beaten out koban, for a clasp. Mr. Dent has given me—very old ⅓ koban, gold.

While shopping, saw the Governor of Yokohama go by, in his box. He was preceeded & followed by guards with lances & swords, & all the people dropped on their knees & bowed their foreheads to the ground, as he passed. This is always done for great officials. For the lesser, the people bow low as they walk. Henderson tells me he saw the Prince of Satsuma go thro' Kanagáwa, on his way to Yedo, with a train of fr. 4 to 6000 persons, soldiers, civil & mil. officers, & servants. This is the usual retinue of the daimios, or great princes, when they travel in state.

The Jap. have built 2 moles in the harbor, for the accomn. of the foreign commerce, entirely of their own engineering, wh. look well, & are said to be very strong.

The horses are usually shod with shoes of straw. The people, —especially women, in wet weather, wear clogs—pieces of board, raised 2 or 3 inches by blocks, & fastened round the naked foot by straw thongs. On these, they get over the ground fast. Sometimes I have turned round thinking a horse was coming upon me, & found it a girl on a fast run. The upper classes have ornamented clogs. Before the mole, the Jap. have driven piles, to keep off the heavy seas, but it is said that the worms eat up a pile in a year. This is a pity, as this port, Yokohama-Kanagawa, is a mere open roadstead, & the mole exposed to typhoons.

Tho' the Japanese have a literature, & a large proportion of the people know how to read, yet they are by no means as literary as the Chinese. I saw few or no mottoes, proverbs & quotations, inscribed on their doors & walls.

By the rule, foreigners change dollars here daily at the Co. Hs. into ichibus, fr. 10 to $15 a day. This gives a profit to the changer of 20%. My host made about $3 a day on my name, as I did not use the ichibus. This is a gratifn. to a visitor, to be sure that he costs nothing.

Dined with Dorr. Thunder storm. Cleared up by 10 o'ck. P.M., & as we start at 4 A.M., must go on board to-night. We went down in a grand procession, 2 large Jap. lanterns in front, & 2 behind, each painted with the stars & stripes, & ½ dos. soldiers with 2 swords each, & Dorr & I, arm in arm, & 2 more Americans, all with revolvers,—thro' the great st., to the Consular boat, & off in the boat with our lanterns & men, to the steamer.

Saturday. Apr. 21. Steamer Yang Tse, at sea, off entrance of Yedo Bay. Fusi Yama (Matchless Mountain) in plain sight, early this morning,—its huge cone of snow piercing the sky. The coast to the N. of Yedo Bay is rather more rugged than at the Southland, yet it is green, among the hills. The countless boats! And we are 10 to 20 miles fr. the coast!

Sund. Ap. 22. Capt. Dearborn says the Engl. chart is as bad to the Nd. as to Sd. of Yedo. A large bay is omitted, & a headland is 30 miles too far out at sea. Last night, at 2 A.M., Capt. D. saw a ledge of rocks, with breakers, nearly a-head, abt. ½ m. off, we being 50 miles from the land. This is down on no chart. Perry's Chart, true as far as it goes, is professedly imperfect & partial. No regular survey has ever been made of the coast.

Mem. The Jap. officers on guard at the Am. Consul's temple, take down a note of ev. person who goes in or out.

Sin Syn is the ancient Jap. faith, & *sintoo* is the name given

to the believers. The spiritual emperor, the Mikado, is believed
to be of divine descent. The temporal Emperor, Tycoon, was
first a civil & mil. chief under the Mikado, but is now the real
head of affairs.

The Fr. priest at Yedo is not, as I said, a bishop, but only an
abbe. The dogs are numerous in Jap. villages, with wolf heads,
bark much, cowardly, sometimes bite the heels,—Oliphant
thinks them handsome—I do not. The Japanese build fire-
proof houses of a kind of clay, wh. they lay on the walls to the
thickness of 2 & 3 feet, the walls being furred out, interlaced
with lines of rope. This process requires long time for hardening, but answers its purpose. The Europeans have their
store-houses built in this way. Country too volcanic, too much
danger of earthquake for brick or stone.

On board the Yang Tse, the officers give orders in Malay—
as all the crew are Malays, & the Europ. & Am. officers here
soon learn it. It seems full of r's & vowels.

Mond. Ap. 23, 1860.   Made the mouth of the Straits of Sangar, wh. lie betw. Nipon & Yeso, & in the ev. are at anchor in
Hakodadi. The hills are covered with snow at the tops, &
patches of snow lie about them, almost to the foot. It is weather
for over-coats & thick gloves. No small change in 3 days!

Hakodadi lies on a peninsula, & has a good, landlocked harbor, but so wide as to give great range to the Northerly winds,
making holding a little insecure. The peninsula is hilly, one
peak being about 1000 f. high. There are small groves of firs &
pines, but trees are scarce,—cut down, I fancy, for firewood, as
coal is scarce, & the weather cold. The town lies at the foot &
on the lower slope of the hills.

Three Jap. officials come off, two-sworded men, & sit in the
cabin & take notes of name & tonnage of the steamer, departure, objects &c. Polite in their manner. One speaks Engl. intelligibly. Drink a good deal of Curacoa. Leave an inf officer
on board, who first makes an effort to get quarters in the
cabin, but subsides into the steerage, & then diplomatises for a
seat at our table, but acquieces in his fate.

Tuesd. Ap. 24.   Landed. The town is like Kanagawa. Streets
of fair width, clear eno', & pretty well watered,—wh. is done
by pails & dippers. Great many shops. I believe everybody in

China & Japan keeps a shop, & they live by buying fr. each other. Lacquers, carvings, & other *curios* for sale, but inferior. Small sweet oranges, with loose skins, large acid oranges, large tasteless pears, dried persimmons, & all kinds of confectionary & cakes, but rather for poorer people.

Called on the Am. Consul, a huge man, named Rice, 6 f. 5 & covered with hair, a loud talker. Has no salary, & not much in fees, & is also a merchant. This is wrong in our Govt. A Consul shd. never be a merchant, for 2 reasons—1st he becomes often a party in questions submitted to him, & 2d he has advantages over other merchants, by knowl. of their affairs officially derived. In Japan, there is a 3d reason,—that merchants are looked down upon, as an inferior class.

Call on Capt. Fletcher, I believe the only other Am. here. His wife is here, an intelligent English woman. F. is a merchant here. Mrs. F. likes the Japanese—says she has some most faithful & intellig. servants fr. among them. (Her story of her servant who took a wife on trial, in case *Mrs. F.* liked her,— otherwise to be returned). Met there, a Mrs. Grinnell, wife of a whaling Capt., a delicate, pleasant woman, who has been two Arctic seasons in the ship, & is going a third. She had met some of the whaling madams who were at Hilo, & heard of our Bridge accident. She had spent a season at Hilo, knew the Lymans, Coans, Austins, &c. At the Am. Consuls', met some ½ dos. whaling masters, all of whom knew of my having been at the Islands, the Mastiff, & bridge accidents &c., & were very attentive to me, & desirous to talk & make my acquaintance.

There are, in port, 8 Am. whaleships, 1 Am. merchant ship, 1 Russian war steamer, 2 Japanese war schooners, & the Yang Tse. The schooners were built by the Japanese, & are well modelled, well looking vessels, like our Baltimore Clippers.

Called on the Abbé Mermet, the only R. Cath. missionary in Japan, except the Abbé Girard at Yedo. He is a young man, with intellig. countenance & very agreeable manners— thoroughly polite. Tells me he is not allowed to preach or teach. His mission is to learn the language, history, religions &c. of Japan, & to make acquaintances & remove prejudices. He is very popular with the natives as well as foreigners, & is thought to have influence with the authorities. His quarters are very plain & poor,—bitter cold, he says, in winter, but how the presence of one man of intellect, culture & high breeding, illumines a humble room! He is of the Mission Etrangère, a French order. He tells me there are no memorials or relics of the ancient Christians in Japan—utter extinction of everything, not even a sign to denote a sacred spot. Hakodadi was never a seat of missions. This island, Yeso, is a conquest of the Japanese (Niponese), from the Ainoes, or wild hairy men,—a few of whom still live in the remote parts, tributaries,—whom the Japanese, in their pictures, represent as being as hairy as baboons. Mermet tells me that the bridge wh. connected the Decima with the city of Nagasaki had the cross inlaid in it, & the Dutch were obliged to step upon the Cross whenever they passed, & when the later Europeans came, & went round it, the Jap. said—"See, they are not Dutch"—("Hollander" is the Jap. word). By the way, everywhere in Japan they distinguish Am. fr. Engl., & as soon as they hear us speak, even in the little shops, they ask if "Americani" or "Ingelesi". Our flag is the favorite in Japan.

At Mermet's met a young Japanese, who is son of one of the physicians of the Tycoon. He speaks English well, & French pretty well. His uncle & brother are in the Embassy to America. It is hard to conceive of a gentleman without linen—but all the Japanese, of whatever rank, wear the cotton or dark silk wrappers about their bodies, with open necks, & no relief. The Chinese wear no linen or cotton, but have a kind of collar of blue silk, that is some relief. Imagine a swarthy man, just coming fr. a bath, with only pantaloons & a dark cotton wrapper, & you have the middle class of Japanese. Ditto, without the pantaloons, is the laboring man, in cool weather; & with neither, is the laborer in hot weather.

Heard the dull, stern beating of a gong, & followed it into a small temple. The priest on his knees, before the shrine, is beating the gong & chanting the same 3 or 4 words, over & over, & the worshipper, a woman, who has paid for the performance, is kneeling there too, rubbing the palms of her hands together, swaying her body a little, occasionally touches her forehead to the floor, & telling the beads on her rosary, a bead at each repitition of the words by the priest, who is tired, & looks out the corner of his eye to see if she is near the end of her string. Mrs. Fletcher tells me that the Jap. women are frequent & regular in their attendance at the temples, at the morning service, which is soon after dawn. Little idols & rosaries & incense sticks are for sale in the shops,—the rosaries of stone, crystal or carved wood. There are no signs of decay, neglect or disorder in the Japanese temples.

The Jap. Govt. is building a fort here. The masonry is very well done, to my eye, & so say others. They are their own engineers. (The war steamer they have sent to California is navigated by themselves).

Where we landed, this morning, at the Custom Hs., in a small enclosure, was an affecting sight. The little enclosure was fairly floored over with the bodies of supplicants, on their knees, with foreheads to the earth, before the Magistrate, who sat within the door, waiting their turn to be examined & receive permits, either to journey or to sojourn here, I forget which. But the bending attitude before the Magistrate is not so significant here as it would at first seem, for polite men bend to each other, almost to the ground, in meeting in the street, & quite so in their houses. And all servants & laboring men do so, in coming into the houses of their employers.

Wed. Apr. 25. Ashore at 6 A.M. Called on Mermet. He has finished his private mass & prayers, in his little chapel—(open to foreigners on Sundays) & is ready to see me. I told him how Bishop Boone proceeded, & he says that is the way the Catholics have always done, on principle; & intimated that B. Boone's course was a violation of the Prot. principle. Take tea & toast with him.

Worshippers coming fr. the temples, & sound of dull gongs. After a breakfast on board, walk, alone, to the summit of the Peak. Enjoyment of a lonely walk in the country, to a man who has been long on ship board! Always found it so, in Cal. & elsewhere. View good—rather desolate, the foggy ocean & the rugged peninsula. On the way up & down the Peak, in little hollows, & where the paths meet, are little shrines, with carved figures, on slabs of stone,—as in the times of the "Ages of Faith" in Europe, & they are as well covered with inscriptions & votive offerings. Beside the Shrines, there are sev. little temples, wh. have signs of being in use. One seemed to be for mariners, as it was plastered with pictures of ships in various conditions of peril. I wanted to take one away, but thought some poor devil might miss his offering & think himself coming to grief. Stopped & ate snow, in the hollows. Counted the vessels at anchor in the Bay—180 junks, 10 Am. Ships, 1 Am. steamer, 1 Russian war steamer, & 2 Jap. war schooners.

On the side of the hill are superficial quarries of rock, wh. they are getting out to build the fort. Stopped & talked with the laborers—or rather tried signs with them—with more or less success. They all seemed polite & pleasant. Even these common laborers could read & write, & one got out his paper (wh. ev. man seems to carry in his bosom) & wished me to write my name on it. Pipe & pouch, paper, pen & ink stone, almost ev. man carries on his person.

At the foot of the hill, is the Russian Consul's new house, built of the mud walls, in the native fashion, colored on the surface. It is a large & handsome house, designed by the Russians, but built by Japanese.

Walking thro' the streets, heard noise of children in school, followed the sound, & came to a humble little house, in the porch of wh. was a collection of sandals, straw & wood, & inside some 40 boys, fr. 6 to 10 years of age, sitting on benches at little tables, each with a book before him, swaying their bodies to & fro, & all reading or repeating at the very top of their voices, making a horrid din, in this little, dark low-roofed room. The grave old teacher sat in the midst, keeping a good eye over them. Here, as in China, the boys study aloud, & the reason is said to be that the teacher may hear the sounds they give to the characters,—for a character does not indicate its sound, but the sound must be taught. As the teacher & I had no language in common, I learned nothing fr. him. The boys looked very lively & happy—a contrast with the stupor of an 8 year old school, when I was of that age.

I fully agree with the Japanese travellers in their opinion of the cheerfulness & happiness of the children. It is obvious. They sing as they go along in the streets, sometimes 3 or 4 hand in hand, & the discipline seems easy. Parents seem to be affectionate & equable with them, & so their elder sisters, who lug them on their backs. Saw two little girls, some 5 years old, sitting on a bench, before a door—& singing & beating sticks in time. They looked so pretty & good that I gave them a silver ishu, (worth about 8 cents)—a fortune to them. They bowed their little foreheads to the bench, in adoration, & would not raise them up until I was out of sight.

The roofs are mostly covered with stones, to keep them steady in the high winds. Mr. Rice, the Consul, gave me 2 silver coins, which will soon be rare. They were issued by the Jap. Govt. 8 July 1859, to pass for a half dollar each, being actually of that weight. They were stamped with characters signifying that they were for use in dealings betw. foreigners & natives. The Am. & Br. Ministers repudiated them, & the coinage is stopped. It was called 2 ishu, or ½ itsibu.

Thursd. Apr. 26. Sailed fr. Hakodadi, at day-break, through the Straits of Sangar, & at 8 o'ck. were out in the Japan sea. So we shall circumnavigate Nipon.

We take on board a new passenger, a Dr. Lindau, a Prussian, by birth, & a Swiss Comm. envoy who has been sev. months in Japan, & collected a good deal of information. His great treasure is a duplicate of the colored drawings of the birds, reptiles, insects & flowers of Japan, made by the celebrated Japanese savant, Dr. Kusimoto Tzuiken, the chief physician to the Tycoon. This morning, he exhibited them to us, on the cabin table. I was amased. They are as good as Audubon, possibly better. I do not see how they could be exceeded. They are all done by hand, & copied. Kusimoto Tzuiken has let Dr. Lindau have them for the purpose of getting them published in Europe, under his name, for the honor he expects to gain by it. Dr. L. is to have the credit of the scientific arrangement, wh. the Jap. Dr. cannot make. The attitudes of the birds are full of spirit, & every *hair* is painted. The silver hues are so well given that they seem to quiver in the air. The insects are done with exquisite taste & finish. The pencil is as fine as the cobweb. They interested & pleased me more than anything of the kind I ever saw before. These people are not to be treated as un-civilised, when, unknown to the world, unaided, uninfluenced fr. abroad, they produce such works.

Dr. L. says the college at Yedo has faculties of med. & belles lettres, & gives degrees, as in China, & that a kn. of reading & writing is almost universal.

At Hakodadi there are several jorogas, as at the other places we have visited, but having seen fair specimens at the Gangero of Yokohama, I did not care to enter them. They looked neat without, & one was the largest & best looking private house in the town. This is said to be a Govt. affair, & the Am. Consul told me that one of the Govt. officials came to him to ask him to remove the prohibition upon Am. seamen coming on shore after dark, as it diminished the receipts of the joroga.

In sev. houses in Hakodadi I noticed that certain places wh. with us are in the rear are here at the front door, just inside, & open.

Great complaints are made here & at Kanagawa of the conduct of the officers of the Mississippi & Powhatan, in trading & taking adv. of their position to speculate in itsebus. It is said that they took up itsebus, under the Cu. Hs. privilege, so largely that the merchants could not get enough for their purposes. They took them up by the thousands, & some officers are said to have made sev. thousands of dollars by it. They also bought up large quantities of articles, as mdse., to sell in China, turning the ships into mere traders, & having no freight, duties or commissions to pay, could undersell the merchants.

The Japanese use wood cuts, & it is said, have begun to engrave on copper plates.

Sat. Ap. 29.   Last night, being 30 miles off by our reckoning, came near running upon an island of the Oke group, a current having set us 30 miles to the S. E., in 15 hours. The bright look out always kept here, saved us. Capt. D had been told that the current here was the other way. Perhaps it is changeable.

> I'm on the sea. I'm on the Sea,
> I am where I would ever be!

Not quite so—but the abundance of fresh air & exercise, the regularity of hours, the simplicity of food, the abundance of sleep, & the freedom from cares & duties have great value & charm.

China: April–June 1860

Mond. Ap. 30. Coast of China in sight, off mouth of Yang Tse Kiang. Shall be in Shanghai to-night. Had a most delightful voyage, successful throughout—& seen all in an unprecedentedly short time. Mr. Dent refuses all compensation. It is his party of pleasure—I mean Dent & Co.'s.

(Contrast betw. the steamers that steer forward & those that steer aft. The quiet, order & watchfulness of this vessel. Excellent sea-boat. Excellent qualities of Capt. Dearborn.)

Yellow water of the Yang Tse' Kiang, far out at sea. Light ship. At Woonsung, the French fleet. The Renommée, Vice Admiral's, & a rear admiral, & the Entreprenante, 80 guns, full of troops, la vivandière, looking over the rail. At anchor, in Shanghai, before dark. Mr. Grew kindly comes on board, to see me ashore. All inquire for news. The *ultimatum* of the Allies is refused, & preparations for an attack at the Peiho. The Br. have taken possession of Chusan, & all their troops & ships (except the Furious) are there. Lord Elgin & Baron Gros are to come out by next steamer. Yet, so anomalous is this war, that whole regiments of coolies are hired as laborers, & on the other side, Br. & Fr. ships pay duties here, & they are still collected by the Treaty Powers, on the Emperor's acct.

Here I am, again, in my sumptuous rooms, at Russell & Co.'s, with all my luggage safe & in its old places, my bed, my books, a good fire (for it is cool at night) & a file of Boston papers, & tea, & so many kind & attentive friends, & myself brot back in life & health, after a delightful & instructive voyage to a new Empire! If one has not a heart of stone, here is a time & place for gratitude! And, I felt it, when I sat down in my chair, & looked about me & reflected.

Wed. May 2. Called on Bruce. He has very handsome eyes. Professes to think his brother's superceding him is good policy. Then, to M. & Mde. de Bourbulon. M. is evidently annoyed by being superceded by Baron Gros. Met there Genl. Montauban, Com. in Chief of the Fr. army in China. (Conversation about the horses the Fr. have imported fr. Japan, & the

General's curious question thro' M. de B.). Then, called on Meadows & Wade, the Chinese scholars, & on Dent & Dearborn & Webb & Ashton. (Gilman & Co. is *Tay Ping,* or Lasting Peace. Russell & Co. is *Ki Chong,* or Long Flag).

Thursd. May. 3.   Mr. Grew drove me to the Races. Horses all owned & ridden by the Engl. here, & no jockeys allowed. One good run betw. Cammabert & Cheerful. The white top boots & small clothes are a becoming dress—manly.

Tea with Rev. Mr. Lyle, Smith & wife, Dr. & Mrs. ——. Most of them been in Boston, & had good Boston talk, for a change.

Frid. May. 4.   Dined with Bishop Boone. He says Chinese eating rats is very rare, & denied by them. He never, in 17 years, known a case. The man in the street, with rats on his pole, & bell, is not selling them, but they are his sign as a *rat-killer.* This has misled foreigners. So, as to dogs. Very rare. Doubts Cushing's "bow-wow" story. Severe on Bayard Taylor's book on China. Thinks him prejudiced & ignorant of the subject—*full* of mistakes.

Sat. May. 5.   Walk to Ti Ka Wei, about 6 miles out. Priest receives us kindly, on my letter of introduction. Here are 94 pupils, boys, all Chinese, & children of Xn. parents. There are three priests now, 2 French & 1 Italian, & several Chinese teachers. One room for drawing, painting & sculpture, & sev. youths at work. Another for music. In that was a choir of a piano, violin, base viol, clarionet, 2 flutes & nine voices—performing a Kyrie Eleison, & very creditably. Rooms neat. Gardens & play-grounds. Boys are taught Chinese literature, with our sciences, history &c. No attempt to Europeanise them, but to be educated as *Chinese* Christians. The priests dress in Chinese costume. Gave us (Grew was my companion) a tiffin of cake, dried fruit & claret wine. Large chapel, dressed with flowers, for May, in honor of La Sainte Vierge. Return thro' the city.

Dinner at Ashton's. Present, Dr. Lindau, Meadows, Compton (Ed. of North China Herald) & al. All in best style. Each guest, as it is raining, comes in his sedan, & all the coolies wait

at the house until we are ready to return,—3 or 4 hours—&
take us home with lanterns.

Omitted to mention that on our way fr. Ti Ka Wei, we
stopped at a small obelisk, wh. is called the "Baby Tower" by
foreigners. Said that Chinese throw into it their living female
infants, when they want to be rid of them. *Quien Sabe?*

Sund. May 6. At the Fr Chapel at 9 A.M. Fr. & Engl. soldiers & Chinese. Mass for Br at 9 & for Fr. at 10. Genl. Montauban & brilliant staff present. Sermon to the Br. soldiers. At
11, to the Engl. Church, where we had sermon & Communion. Start to-night for Suchau.

Having a few hours of leisure before dark, strolled off into
the city, alone. Enjoyed my stroll, stopping at shops, buying a
few cakes &c. to taste their street cookery. Passed Gen. Montauban & his 2d in command, also on a stroll. Passed near a
temple, & hearing a noise & seeing a crowd, went in. A play
going on. Dense crowd in the area, & 2 galleries, one for men
& one for women—so different from the indiscriminate Japanese huddle. Wished to get into the gallery, wh. seemed to be
reserved for select persons, & went into rear of the temple, behind the idol, to a side door. Keeper, an old bonze, shut it
against me, but opening it to let out a person, I went in, & he
consented to show me up—all this by signs. So, I got a front
seat in the gallery.

Actors all men, & mostly bonzes. Two dressed as women—
for women never play in public here. Of the characters, one
seemed to be an absurd pompous magistrate, & one was the
fun-maker, who made dum show to the audience, ridiculing
the others. After the play was over, I went to the door leading
behind the scenes, &, by quiet perseverance & bowing, succeeded in getting in, & saw the actors undress, & wash off
paint. They were civil & amused.

The audience never clap or stamp or cheer. Nor did I hear
them cry out at all. Except by laughing, they give no audible
approval.

Trip to Suchau. Started from Shanghai this ev., May 6th, on
an expedition, by boat, to Suchau,—the famous city—the
"Paris of China". Doubtful if any foreigners will be admitted
now, as late visitors have been refused; but, if not, the trip will

show me the interior of China. We have three boats, one for cooks & chow-chow, & 2 for passengers. Mr. Walsh & Dr. Lindau in one, Rev. Messers. Lyle & Smith & I in the other. And a beautiful start off we have! Full moon, fair tide, clear sky & exquisite weather. The river, the bridges, the gliding boats give it a fairy-like air.

At the first bridge is a gate, & there was a characteristic row of Chinese officials, wh. ended in our giving a few cash for leave to pass. Stay up until 11 o'ck., delighted with our voyaging.

Our boats have settees, on wh. we sleep, & tables, book-racks & other conveniences, & we are entirely comfortable. Each boat has a crew of six boat-men, a boy to wait on each of us, & a cook & butler.

May 7th.   Settled our regime—to rise early & take tea & toast, & walk until breakfast, wh. is to be at 9. Dinner at 4. Betw. br. & dinner, keep under cover. Walk again towards evening. The walk this morning was very interesting, along the track path, through little villages, stopping at temples, under groves of trees, & amid the fields of wheat, rice & vegetables wh. mark the endless industry of this people. Verily, there is no end to it. Every square foot is under cultivation, & laborers are everywhere. How the manuring is attended to! They dig up the mud & other sediment fr. the rivers, place it in pits, add all they can get to it, to make a compost, & cover their lands, wh. in this way give two crops a year, one of wheat & one of rice. They fish the mud up fr. the river by a machine wh. one man works, on the principle of a pair of snuffers.

At almost every house people are weaving cotton cloth, sometimes indoors, by a small loom, & sometimes in the open air, on warps nearly as long as a rope walk. Numerous little pits, in wh. they make indigo. The frequent little tributaries compel us to walk back into the country, to find bridges, wh. we always find not far off—& always of stone, neatly arched. All the bridges across the Suchau Creek are of stone, neatly built, high & arched. That at Wang Du, is the largest we have yet seen. A few pagodas in sight, & groups of small gates or arches, to the honor of persons who have been noted for virtue, especially to young widows who have refused remarriage.

Pass the bridge of the "Literary Star". Most of these bridges are segments of circles, say 220 degrees. No windmills in China, so far as I can learn.

Hill & city of Khsoun San. Passed the city & hill of Khsoun San. Pagoda on hill, in centre of city.

Tuesd. May 8. Early this morning, reached the city of Su Chau. For sev. hours, we passed along the suburbs, & halted at the great gate, & made the boats fast, & had our conference as to how we should assault the city. One plan was to take chairs, close them up, & go by the gate unseen. Another was, to try to take our boats thro' the watergate, keeping in the cabins. But came to conclusion to try the open course of presenting ourselves at the gate. At the gate Zi Mung, 2 or 3 mandarins came out & we were stopped, & a crowd soon gathered. Mr. Lyle, who is interpreter & cicerone, got into a conference with the head officer, wh. resulted in our being invited into the office. Here we were ceremoniously seated, & general conversation began. The chief politely, with smiles & bows, inquires the ages, names & occupations of each, & writes them down. How Chinese was the scene! As ceremonious & dignified as the Chinese officials are, yet the people crowd in & take part in everything. We had some friends among them. The official said—"No. Very sorry. Fixed rule. No foreigners could be admitted". Mr. Lyle knew eno', & we had read eno', of Chinese character, to be quiet & persevering. We kept our seats, talked, spoke of the great reputation of the city, our desire to see it, our disappointment &c., & at last the official confers, & says the rule is strict, but admits of one exception. If a *few* foreigners, 5 or 6, come *early in the morning*, before great crowd assembles, the officer has a discretion to let them in. We say we will take a soldier, who can keep us out of trouble &c., & pay for him. "Oh, No. You are welcome to two soldiers, & no pay". So, two rather forlorn soldiers, with white badges on their breast, go, one before & one behind us, instructed to show the great places to the distinguished foreigners, & we take a ceremonious leave, with great bowings & tsing-tsingings, & go on our way.

Su Chau is much like the cleaner parts of Canton & Shanghai. We were early, & the streets were not so thronged as I have usually seen them in those cities. Our first visit is to an old, dim, smoky pagoda-built temple, dedicated to Sau Tsing, the Three Pure Ones. It is 4 or 5 stories in height, each with its idols, shrines & tapers. One great idol has the name of Shang Ti, wh. Mr. Lyle tells me the first Protestant translations of the Scriptures unfortunately adopted for God, very much as if the Evangelists had taken Zeus (Jupiter), from the Greeks.

Next visit is to the famous Nine Storied Pagoda. All the way, we are followed by a crowd of hundreds of men & boys, & as we go thro' the narrow streets, all come to their windows & doors to stare at us. A foreigner is a rare sight in Su Chau, most of the people have never seen one, & now, foreigners have no right here, & are only admitted by special courtesy. But at the Pagoda, the crowd must stop; for we pay $2 for our admission, & we do not choose to invite the crowd. (But, in the Temple, there is no exclusion, & they pressed on our heels even up to the feet of the idols, & saw our familiar way of tapping them with our canes, without objection. Indeed, the crowd, tho' intensely curious, was civil & well deported).

The pagoda is in good repair. Each story has its gallery entire, on wh. we can walk, & wooden stairs lead fr. story to story, inside. The upper story gives us the view of the great city & suburbs. Su Chau is said to contain two millions of people. The suburbs are very large, & the walls on one side enclose large spaces of unoccupied land, some of wh. is used for wheat, & none of it arranged for pleasure grounds or walks for the people,—mere wastes. On the walls,—wh. are high, in good repair & moated, & in places ivy grown, are numerous banners & a few soldiers. Name of Pagoda is Vok Tss' Tah,—(*tah* is pagoda, *Vok*, divining, &c., *Tss'* monastery).

The Chinese are not free fr. our vanity of writing names on walls, & the stories of the pagoda are covered over with names & sentiments. Visit the institution for the poor. It is not a house, but streets of small houses, all within a wall, & all under rule. There are 900 paupers here. They live 4, 8 or 10 in each small house. It is a public charity. Not clean, bad smells, no drainage, & very little care. The paupers seem to take care of their own houses. Saw among them sev. cases of ophthalmia & elephantiasis.

Return to our boats to breakfast. We pay our guides a reasonable sum, & immediately the officer appears, looking very grave & distressed, & asks how we could think of giving them money, & begs us to take it back, but Mr. L. thinks it will do if we apologise & leave it with them, wh. we do, & then come the bowings, & smiles & wishes for good voyage.

After breakfast, walk thro' the great Northern suburb, built on the Grand Canal of China. This is beautiful. The canal is wide, lined with trees, good houses, pretty shops, & open spaces behind walls, indicating residences of wealthy people. The bridges are stately, & always of stone, usually with arches, most of wh. are more than half circles, & canals run across the main canal, making a Chinese Venice of this city. A long line of people follow us along the bank, as we drop down the canal, exhibiting ourselves sitting in chairs on the front of our boats, the Am. ensign floating fr. the masthead, & each bridge is covered with gasers.

Now we get out & walk among the shops. A crowd presses on us all the time, but almost always civil. A few cases of bad words to us, but when Mr. L. turns & rebukes them gently, the crowd takes his part. We do some shopping, & I buy a box of Japanese dominoes for 80 cash,—8 cents. The most attractive are the flower shops wh. are very numerous, & filled with beautif. flowers in pots, & dwarfed trees. In most cases, we are invited to the gardens in the rear, where these flowers are growing. Graffing is in high fashion. We buy some flowers, cheap eno',—I mean plants in pots, to ornament our boat. The great number of these flower shops indicates a good taste among the people.

Lastly we visit the celebrated pagoda & pleasure grounds of Hu Chau Tah. (*Hu Chau,* is Tiger district, & *tah* is pagoda). The Pagoda is on a hill, & the grounds are made up of artificial piles of rocks, groves & lines of trees, plateaus of smooth rocks, stairs in rocks, roofs for shade, groups of flowers &c., &, at frequent intervals, houses for refreshment. In one of these, wh. looks out over the whole city of Su Chau & the country for miles about it, we took a refreshment of tea, cakes & confectionary, & bought out a confectioners' entire waiter full for .75 cents, & distributed it among the boys that had followed us.

These grounds are the favorite resort, day & night, of the people of leisure in Su Chau, & Su Chau is said to have more such people than any city of China.

In the pagoda, in a dim room, among grim idols, was a school of some 30 or 40 boys, reading at the tops of their voices, under the usual half starved, disappointed looking teacher,— the disappointee of a dosen examinations for degrees.

Returned to our boats to late dinner, after a day of great interest & pleasure,—with the triumph of entering Su Chau, fr. wh. nearly all foreigners are excluded, & into which none entered before 1857.

After dinner, we sit out on the deck, in chairs, smoking & talking, & looking at the never ending varieties of boats, bridges, towns, gasing people, evening lanterns, & lighted houses.

At about 9 o'ck., we reach a gate wh. shuts across the Grand Canal, & blocks all progress after dark. Here is another case for diplomacy. Mr. Lyle & I go ashore, & seek out the Custom House, presenting ourselves, on our way, before the astonished eyes of the *sanctum sanctorum* Chinamen, at the counters of their quiet shops, at this late hour, in a central city of China. Here, at the Custom Hs. we meet the chief official, who has charge of the gate, & assures us that no boats can pass after it is closed for the night. There is something interesting in the appearance of this gentleman, for *gentleman* he was, if ever there was one. He is young, say 2 or 3 & 20, with a countenance of great intelligence, frankness & gentleness, with every appearance of integrity, & a charm of manner, wh. wd. have carried off the prise in a competitive exn. of manners, I doubt not.

The refusal being positive, there is nothing to do but to sit down quietly, & wait for a change of policy. So, we seated ourselves, & Mr. Lyle had a gen. convn. on topics of interest, & our friend inquired about Dr. Hobson's work on anatomy, wh. has been translated into Chinese, & for other books of history & geography, some of wh. he possessed. He had spent sev. dollars in buying our books, & Mr. Lyle offered to get him others. We then invited him on board our boat, & as he accepted the invitation, we had hopes. In our little cabin we offered him cigars & wine. He tasted the wine, but politely intimated that he was not strong eno' to drink such wine, & smoked only a part of the cigar. At length, signs of concession appeared, & soon the order was given to open the gate. Mr.

Lyle asked him to distribute some money among the men who had been set to work at this unusual hour,—wh. was as near to an offer of money as Mr. L. liked to go. His refusal was a master-piece. It could not have been better done. It was deprecatory. It seemed to say,—*how could you think of money?* He looked hurt, yet superior, & waved it off, & gently placed his hand on Mr. Lyle's shoulder to seat him again, & passed directly to another subject, as you would hurry by a bad smell in the street. Nor was it acting. He was in earnest. Mr. Lyle gave him a translation of St. Luke's Gospel, a brief catechism, & 2 or 3 other small tracts, & a lead pencil (always acceptable to Chinese, who have only ink) & as it rained, we insisted on his taking an umbrella, wh. we wd. not hear of his returning. Indeed, he became such a favorite, that we should soon have given him half we had. He remained on board until we reached the end of the city, & then took his leave with many professions of esteem of each side. I never saw, in any country, or society, better manners,—self-possessed, gentle, dignified, & giving the impression of a single eye to the pleasure & convenience of others. By his kindness we saved an entire day, in one town; for thus, by traveling all night, we reached our next place of visit at early morning, instead of late in the afternoon.

(Our friend's name is *Oo* or *U*).

Wed. May. 9. Our next point is the city of Pu Si'. This is a large city, on the Grand Canal, surrounded by very high, moated & ivy grown walls, with populous suburbs. We stopped our boats, & walked to the gate, &, as usual, were refused admittance. Here was another sit down, another long talk, another most gracious & special yielding, & a walk through the town under guidance of a soldier. This is a poor town,—at least the parts we went thro',—except that the Yamun, (the seat of the city Government) is the largest & finest official building I have seen since leaving Canton. It is stately, with spacious grounds, walks, trees &c. But near the gate, on a stone platform, under a little roof of tiles, at a kind of Market Cross, lay 3 or 4 beggars, in their rags, piteous objects, one *dead*. He had died in the night, & no one had yet removed him.

Boats & late breakfast, & stop at the village at the foot of the Wei San, the famous range of hills, the highest in this region.

San is hill, & *Tsung* is village. The village, Wei San Tsung, is beautiful. It has a sheet of water, an artificial basin, lined with trees, covered with lotus leaves, & ending in a stone coping fr. wh. pours a stream of pure water.

From the village, we ascended the series of hills, each (except the highest) having its temple. At the highest we stop, & spend an hour or two in delighted viewing of the broad landscape. The cities of the great plain, lie beneath us. A boundless plain it is, appearing to us perfectly level, & so green with fields of wheat & rice, & cultivated everywhere. No fences. No roads. No feeding cattle. But rivers, canals, bridges, & endless, endless fields of grain, & mites of men at work, & mites of boats floating up & down, & the whole studded over with hamlets of 3 & 4, or 20 & 30 houses each, standing under groups of trees, & looking like islands in the green sea. The industry, & the populousness of China! It has not been overrated. Large cities, of 20, 50 & 100,000 inhabitants, occur at not long intervals, & villages like ant hills, while the country is alive with laborers, tracking boats, dredging for the muck heaps, fishing, sowing, transplanting, & digging & spinning in the open air. The Grand Canal, in a long silver thread runs thro' the plain, to the Northward, & there, just seen in the horison, is the broader sheet of the Great River. And in that direction, not in sight, but not far off, lies the former capital of China, the Southern Capital, Nan King,—now in possession of the rebels —the long haired men. That collection of white tents, at the foot of our hill, is the Imperialist camp, for the protection of this region. Bounding the whole Western horison, filling up a quarter of the circle, is the Great Lake, Ta Hu, looking like the sea coast, with no land visible across its waters. The air is so pure, the day so fine, the view so limitless, that we can hardly leave it in time for our descent. The laboriousness of the Chinese has furnished a brick & stone walk, from the highest temple quite to the low land, sometimes in steps, sometimes on a slanting plane. On an inclined plane, they lay each brick with narrow side up, & horisontal, so as to form ridges. This prevents slipping.

In all this interior of China, where foreigners are everywhere rarely, & in some places never, seen,—we cannot move without a retinue of boys & men, some of them well dressed &

decent persons. We left the village with 100 or more, wh. fell off at every stage of ascent, leaving us alone on the highest hill. Now, as we descend, they join us again, & we troop thro' the village & the rooms of the temple, & to the tea garden. The latter is the usual rockery, with water covered with lotus leaves, & deep shades of trees, & rows of flower pots on low brick walls, & climbing roses, & ivy grown walls, & little grottoes, & little roofed polygons, in wh. are polished tables, & solemn Chinese with pipes & tea cups.

On the whole, this village, Wei San Tsung, is a choice place, —a place of retreat for people in good circumstances, & adorned & kept in order accordingly. One private estate has large rich gardens, & several ancestral halls dignify the suburbs.

After dinner, drop down to visit the Camp. Just before we reach it, at a handsome polygonal building with pagoda roof, our boat is stopped—& our boatmen report that "No can", & a prodigious hubbub of voices ashore, & an over seeing military Mandarin, with pale yellow button & peacock's tail, comes to know *how we could possibly think of going to the camp.* So, Mr. Lyle comes into requisition again, & we ask leave at least to pay our respects to the Chief, in the big house. This is right, & we go ashore & enter the great hall, & the chief receives us at the door, most graciously, & begs us to be seated; & tea is brought, & he has a long conversation with Mr. Lyle. Here, again, is this singular development of Chinese life. Awful as the great Mandarin is, the common crowd come into the room, filling up all but the little space about the chairs, listening to all that is said, & signifying their interest, or approval of each thing by unmistakable signs. The officer thinks it quite eno', if the crowd gives us space about the chairs. Mr. Lyle says that most of this Mandarin's talk was to exhibit his importance & knowledge to the crowd,—his acquaintance with foreign affairs & great people, & to magnify his condescension in allowing us to enter the camp,—wh. of course he eventually did, giving us two officers to guide us.

The military are not distinguishable by their clothes, which are those of civil life. This Mandarin had three plumes, one a peacock's tail & the others of fox' fur, hanging behind his hat from the button. The officers had the fur plumes without the peacock's tail, & the common soldiers had only a piece of white cotton on the breast of their tunics, on wh. is inscribed the name of their corps, with a character signifying "brave", or "valiant".

But, the poor camp! The miserable camp, that looked so gay at a distance, with white tents & numberless banners of every hue! It is a mud hole, in low ground, hardly drained at all, enclosed by a breast-work, on which is one gingall, & from wh. flutter the gayest banners, I should think one to each man, almost—while 2 or 300 miserable lowest caste men, unarmed & undisciplined, lie about in the tents, or stroll over the ground. I did not see a pistol or gun, & only 2 or 3 swords, & not a spear in the entire camp. It looked as if the troops were away, & the loafers had taken possession. We asked to see a lance exercise, but the lances were on board the junks. The crowd of common soldiers followed us & crowded about the officers, & got up on the platform with them, without any appearance of discipline or etiquette. Still, the tents were new, clean & white, & the first thing that my eye fell upon, on entering the camp, was the words "Lowell, Massachusetts", "Amoskeag N. H." on the white surface of the tents. They were all of Massachusetts drillings. The floors, too, were matted, & clean, & so far as the tents & their *con-tents* were concerned, the Government had made good provision, but there seems to be an entire ignorance of what a camp should be, either in a military or a sanitary point of view. These were, however, the Militia, & no Tartars among them.

Did I mention that Mr. Lyle put his melodeon (?) windpiano, on board? We have music every evening. He & Dr. Lindau, both play, & decent singing is got up among us. Lindau has a large répertoire of German songs—among wh. we have Lützow, Mide ven vege ne jag', Das leben lange Tag, gaudeamus igitur, Edete bibite, Vedrai Casino, & passages fr. operas, waltses & a few religious pieces, & Mr. Lyle has Moore, & Scotch ballads &c. We spend the early ev. very pleasantly in this way. Indeed, our life in the boats is delightful—all agree that it is so. We go ashore & walk when we please, in town or country, stop & go on as we please. We have books & music, conversation, an excellent table, good servants & plenty of them, convenient places to sleep, wash, read or write, fine weather, neither hot nor cold, & new objects of interest every day,—& we are free from the noise & dust of a road, the steam, smoke, & oil & din of a steamer, & the rolling & pitching of the sea. We are floating, on even keel, through towns, between fields, & past temples, pagodas & hamlets.

On one Chinese boat, as we pass, in the dusk of the evening, a woman is on the roof, crying out, with strange cries. "What is it, Mr. Lyle?" Mr. Lyle listens. She is calling home the spirit of her child. The child is in the boat below, unconscious, or delirious. The spirit of the child has wandered off, & the mother goes on the roof & cries out to call it home. Now the attendant below says it is right, the child is itself again, the spirit has found its way back, & the mother comes down. In another boat is a wail for the dead, whose coffin is borne along in it.

It is funny to see our cook take his charcoal out of the barrel with chopsticks; yet it is a clean way of doing it. All his cooking is done with bits of charcoal, in small pots, yet we have soup, rice & curry, fish, meat, vegetables, & pudding ev. day.

Thursday. May 10. Walk for 1½ hour, along the canal, before breakfast. After breakfast, pass the town of Mok Tok, the Bridge of the Winds, & towards noon, reach the point of our destination in this direction,—the beautiful hill, Ling Nga, San. We mount the hill & from the temple at the top, (the *Tsung Pau*) have the most exquisite view any of us have seen in China. It is not so high, & therefore the view not quite so extensive as that from Wei San, but it has more variety, & more striking points, & the great city of Su Chau with its tall pagoda lies beneath us, while the close view, the scene where we stand, is exquisite—a grove of evergreens, ivy grown walls, a half ruined Seven Storied pagoda, a venerable temple full of courts & passage-ways & cloisters, once an imperial residence, enough for a monastery & college of hundreds of pupils,—all but entirely deserted, & terraces with walls of brick & stone, grown over with creepers, overlooking precipices at the foot of wh. lie the immense plains, teeming with people, boats, & hamlets, & covered with the verdure of increasing cultivation. This is the sea mark of our utmost sail, & we are satisfied! It is enough.

As we go slowly down the hill, we see a wall, & two men beckoning to us from it, & pointing to a ladder they have placed against it. Behind the wall are roofs of a group of buildings, all lying nestling in a most romantic spot. No one but Mr. Smith is with me, & the rest of our party have gone round the hill. I am for following the signal, & Mr. Smith agrees to it, so we go up the ladder, where two Chinamen on the wall help us down, & we find ourselves in a most romantic spot, grottoes, deep shades, terraces, opening vistas, & a group of handsome buildings in the best repair; &, as we follow our guides, we come to an open court, roofed over, where, at little tables, some dosen or more Chinese, well dressed men, of the upper class, are taking tea & pipes & sweetmeats. They rise & with the urbanity of 30 centuries request us to join them, & our tea & sweetmeats are brought us, but not a word can we say. In a few minutes a man comes in & makes signs to us that there are three men on the path, & to know if they belong to our party. We make signs that they do, & we should like to have them join us; so they are sent for, & are soon brought in, astonished at the discovery of this enchanted scene,—Arabian Nights, Aladdin—Open Sesame, & what not. Mr. Lyle gets into conversation with the elder & apparently chief man of the party, whose long silk robe, of beautiful purple hue & graceful shape, & rich lining, fascinates us all, & learns that this place is the ancestral hall of the Tsiang family, who allow it to be used as a summer resort for people from the town below, & an old dependent of the family makes a penny by supplying tea & cakes. An hour more must be spent in rambling about the delightful spot, where Chinese taste has fallen in with & not interfered with the natural beauties.

We invited the chief man of the company, the fascinating silk robe, to visit us in our boat, & he spent a half hour with us, Mr. Lyle playing for him on the melodion & giving him some tracts & St. Luke's gospel. He was a little senile & dull, but we respected his exterior.

(*San*, hill; *Ta'h*, pagoda; *Miau*, temple; *Yuen*, garden; *ka*, family; *Sz'*, monastery; *Nan*, South; *Pe*, North; *King*, capital.)

Frid. May 11. Another walk before breakfast, of an hour or so. At noon, reach the city of Khwun San. It is celebrated as having a high hill & pagoda on its top enclosed within the compass of its walls. We find the city rather a mean one, with few objects of interest. From the hill top, we see that the walls enclose a space entirely unused, equal in extent to the whole city. Either the city has fallen away to ½ its original sise, or it was walled in on a notion of increase that has not been answered.

The silence of a Chinese city is surprising. Two cities we have passed, under the walls, just after night-fall, & they were as silent as cities of the dead. So is it, even with this city, at high noon. No wheels, & no shod hoofs, & the city gives out no sound. In the town, we saw a man standing at the temple gate, in a *cangue*. His offense was that he had concealed his property from arrest. He seemed quiet & content eno', & could walk about. The cangue is only a square piece of board, perhaps 3 f. sq., with a hole for the neck. Inside the Yamun, we saw some boxes, like cattle racks, in wh. men are placed standing, & left to die of starvation & fatigue. Behind the temple were tea gardens, of the usual pattern, lakes & lotus flowers, grottoes, trees, benches, roofed courts, tables, & a few tea-sipping & pipe-puffing, contemplative, *farnienti* Chinese.

Late dinner, conversation, music & bed.

Saturday. May 12. Early up—tea & toast, walk along the banks, & through the town of Wong Du, where we examined an oil factory,—pressing of oil from the bean, commonly called the Shanten bean. This is a great article of trade, in the Province, the oil being used for cooking & lights. Mr. Walsh says the trade in it is enormous. We sit on a high stone bridge & await our boats, with a crowd about us. This is our last landing. At 2 A.M., within 12 miles of Shanghai, get aground in narrow bend, & cannot move until full tide. Heavy rain & mud, so cannot walk home. Spend afternoon & night pleasantly on board, in conversation, reading & music, &, starting at daybreak, reach Shanghai Sund. morning at 9½ o'ck., & am again in my quarters at Russell & Co.'s. No news, but the arrival of U.S. steam gun-boat Saganaw from S. Francisco, via Honolulu & H. Kong. Mail fr. home not arrived.

So ends a delightful & instructive trip into interior of China.

Through the kindness of my friend Capt. Oliver J. Jones, of the Furious, I recd. an invitation from Capt. Francis Marten, of the Roebuck, to make a passage with him to Chusan. Dr. Lindau is also of the party. The Roebuck sailed Tuesd. ev. May

15th. I first called on Mr. Bruce, who gave me a letter of introduction to Mr. Hughes, the British Commissioner at Chusan, & Count Klyskowski gave me one to De Meritens, the Fr. Commissioner. It seems Chusan is taken possn. of by the Allies, jointly, & a Commn. appointed, as in Canton, for regn of all civil affairs.

The Roebuck is a screw sloop-of-war, used now as a Despatch boat, & is going to Chusan with the mail for the Allies, & despatches. Our quarters in the small cabin, where we all (Capt., Lindau & I) sleep in cots or on the lockers, & have one place for washing. The fleet here is so short of officers that the 1st lieut. is a mate, acting as lieut., a youth of 20, & the only other officer is a midshipman of 17, Ellis, who acts as a lieut., & keeps a watch & commands a division. There is also a Master, a man of experience,—but in the Br. Navy the masters are not in the line of promotion. Marten, however, does all his own work, & is 1st lieut., master & all,—on deck nearly all the time, & giving orders directly to the men.

Fine looking crew. No better looking men than the petty officers—qu. masters, b's mates, gunner's mates, Capts. of tops &c. Some of these men were with Sir Wm. Peel at Lucknow &c.

Anchored Tu. night near Wosung. All Wed. were steaming down the Yang Tse', & across to Chusan, & Wed. night anchored off the group, & Thursd. morn came in sight of Chusan. The Corvette, Scout, lay off, & signalled us to the Admiral, & in an hour more we were at anchor at Ting Hae—the port of Chusan. Here lie the Imperieuse, Admiral Jones' flag ship, Capt. Maguire, 51 guns, the corvette Pearl, 21, Capt. Borlase, two gun boats, a French gunboat, & outside, the corvette Scout, 21. Ashore, the two flags are flying on the Fort, & red coats & red trowsers fill the streets.

I like Marten much. He is a handsome, spirited, gallant fellow, and an excellent seaman. Want of interest at home has kept him back fr. a post capt's. commission, & he feels it, but loves the service, & wd. not leave it, tho' younger men go over his head ev. day, without merit or service. Yet, in the Am. Navy a man of 46 would hardly think himself slighted that he had not been a post captain sev. years. The Midshipman, Ellis, is an Hon., a son of Lord Howard de Walden, & gr. son of the

Duke of Portland. It is interesting to see his soft, delicate manners, blushing face, & drawing-room voice, giving orders to the great rough seamen. I spent an hour in the ward-room, & I thought the seniors,—the lieut., Master, Surgeon &c., were too rough & hard upon him, & certainly his birth & connexions are entirely disregarded there. The engineer, who is merely a mechanic, ranks above him, & Ellis has to defer to him,—but Ellis is the only *gentleman* in the ward-room,—the others are roughs.

Chusan is an archepelago, a group of almost innumerable islands, if we include the rocks. The chief island, commonly called Chusan, has a small but safe harbor, Ting Hae. Here is a town of about 20,000 inhabitants, with walls, a high fort, gates &c. It surrendered, without attempt at resistance, a month ago, & is now garrisoned by some 2000 Engl. & 200 French. The Engl. have the 99th & 67th, Marines & Artillery.

Delivered my letter to Mr. Hughes & am invited to stay at his Yamun. The Commissioners have a large Yamun, & subdivide it, the Br. one end, & the French the other. Call on Meritens, the Fr. Commn.

Ting Hae is walled, & has a citadel, called, sometimes the Fort of Horrors, because of some little figures representing the punishments of the wicked, but on small scale, making the name ridiculous. Walked there with Mr. Hughes. Outside are the graves of the soldiers who died here during the Br. occupation in 1843 (?), in such numbers. It was then very sickly.

Mr. Hughes takes me to two tea gardens, one a private residence. As usual, rock-work, flowers, trees, water, bridges, & roofed seats. Called on the Chief Mandarin of Chusan, the military commander, a red button, but sadly shorn of his beams, as the Br. garrison has taken possessn. of his Yamun, leaving him only a few rooms. Yet his manner is stately, & his politeness unabated.

A police of Br. & Fr. soldiers, acting under the Allied Commissnrs., control the city, & Martial law reigns. There have been many outrages by the Br. soldiers, mostly when drunk, for wh. they are severely punished. Of 50 cases brot before the Court, all were British, & none French,—so the Fr. Commn. told Lindau.

The Br. commander, Col. Reeves, of the 99th, is an old ass, —almost brainless—an amiable man, but tiresome, loud-laughing, & unamenable to logic. Spent a half hour with him.

In our walk, met a Chinese albino.

Did I mention, in my trip to Su Chau, the boats with the fishing cormorants, 6 or 4 on each side, trained to catch fish? *Vide* Huc.

This ev. (Thursday) dined with Admiral Jones, on board the Imperieuse. Present, Lady & Adm. Jones, Capt. Maguire, Capt. John Borlase, of the Pearl, Capt. Marten of the Roebuck, Lts. Jones & Robertson, & Dr. Lindau. Band to play, for an hour or so. Noble ship, 51 guns, & large quarters. Singing & guitar in the ward-room. Marten gave me his gig to go ashore, & as it was dark, & I had never seen the harbor by night, & the men mistook the outer hill for the citadel, we pulled half round it before was found the landing. Walked to Yamun, challenged by sentries &c., all in due style.

Friday. May 18.   To the French Mission. It is at Uku San, about 2 miles out of town. Here is one European priest, Père Montagneux, a Lasarist. He has 2 Chinese priests with him, & 6 Chinese lads who are Seminarists, to become priests. He has a small school, of 20 boys or so, & there is another for orphans in the city. This is a recent institution, not over 6 years old. The Chapel is proper, & of good sise. The père is polite & ready to inform me. His Chinese priests speak Latin, but neither Fr. nor Engl. It was curious to hear them talking in Latin about sending a Coolie to find Père Montagneux.

At the citadel, found a genuine young Irish officer, of the Charles Lever novels stamp, from Galway—sweet voiced, warm hearted, careless, dashing fellow, lacking in that controlling self respect & propriety that marks the English;—but you pity & like him.

No one could point out the Cameronian Hill, so called from the great number of the Cameronians, 36th, that are buried there.

The Commissioners hope to make Chusan more healthy, by regulations, than it was in 1843, but the stagnant water of the paddy fields must be hasardous, always in summer,—& a Chinese city is always nasty & full of smells, & nuisances.

Ting Hae is overrun with camp followers, who have opened shops & put up signs here, to attract the foreigners. These are both Chinese & foreigners. Tailors advertise themselves as fr. Paris & London, & confectioners, & even take great London & Paris shop names, in their wretched little hovels—"Stults, tailor, fr. London".

Major Gen. Sir Robert Napier arrived unexpectedly, in the Granada, to take command of Chusan. He came to our Ya-mun, with his staff, a set of showy, handsome young dogs, in their scarlet & gold & clattering swords. Napier is a tall, hand-some man of about 5 & 40.

Dined with the Commissioners, vis: Mr. Hughes, Capt. Gibson & Baron Meritens, & the chief of police, a young Capt. Clayton, & a Fr. Capt. Dabry, a very pleasant man, said to be of note in literature & science.

My lodgings are in the room once sacred to various idols, & passing along the passage, by night, with a single candle, I light up a part of the dim temple, revealing huge threatening & smiling idols, of colossal forms. But one gets used to gods in this part of the world, & sleeps & eats & reads among them without thought.

Saturday. May 19.   Dr. Lindau & I sailed this morning, in a Chinese junk, for Ning Po. The passage lies through the Chu-san Archipelago, famous for pirates, who infest it now even more than formerly, for they are driven from other places. "Flapped in the bay the pirate's sheet". Recently, one of their leaders, an Englishman named Ferguson, was killed by some of his gang. The Dr. & I had our revolvers, & a good supply of powder & ball, & if our men were not treacherous, could probably drive them off,—as they do not like to fight for-eigners. No other course is open to us, as no men of war are bound that way, nor foreign vessels.

We make ourselves comfortable in our junk, by mats & blankets, wh. we take with us, & enjoy highly the delightful scenery of the archipelago. Dr. L. says it is like a Swiss Lake. We are, all the while, among islands, some rocky & high, & some undulating & cultivated to the tops, & all green with vegetation. The sea has the yellow muddy color of all the seas near the great river, wh. mars the beauty of the scene.

Otherwise, it might be a lake of Switzerland or Northern Italy. Fleets of junks, by scores at a time, pass & repass, bound to & from the Continent, chiefly Ning Po. There are so many that an attack by pirates by day would be impossible, if they had any courage. These junks are loaded, chiefly with stone, & the industrious Chinese are cutting the stones on the passage. Our junk is light & outsails all. She has a head man (lauder) & six men, large cotton sails on bamboos, in the junk style. The Chinese sing at the ropes & windlass, a word or two & chorus, as our sailors do, but more often & more generally.

We are fortunate in our day & wind & weather. Fair, strong breese, smooth sea, & rapid sailing, & favorable tide for six hours, & reach the entrance to Ching Hae, by the middle of the afternoon, pass the high citadel of Shing Hae, & long before dark are at anchor at Ning Po, where lies one of those ubiquitous English gunboats, & by 5 o'ck., I am at the house of Dr. C. W. Bradley, the Am. Consul, his guest, in a nice room, filled with books, on open shelves, with that delightful library smell that open shelves give one, & windows looking out on the ivy grown walls of Ning Po, said to be 700 years old, wh. form the limit of Dr. Bradley's garden.

Walk in the garden. Varieties of flowers & shrubs. Handsome house, & full of books. Dr. Bradley very kind & attentive. In the vol. of poets of America, find my father's face, & spend some time over it. Dr. B. offers to cut it out & give me, —but must decline it. It is the best face in the volume, though I say it &c.

Dr. B. says there are no antiquities in China,—scarcely anything over 6 or 800 years. Their buildings are not durable. The walls of Ning Po are said to be 700 years old. The oldest monument in China is Christian,—thot to be of the Nestorians. Dr. B. is hardly over an attack of fever & ague, the 3d he has had in 6 mos. He says they are very subject to it in Ning Po. (Have I mentioned that at Shanghai? There is a great deal of it there. Several persons had it while I was there).

Sunday. May 20. Although there are 4 clergymen of the Ch. of Engl. here, there is no service. They are all very low churchmen, &, on Sundays join with the Presb. & Baptists for an Engl. service,—a unity in wh. they yield all. An Am. or

Engl. layman cannot have his service, tho' there are 4 clergy-men here,—even on Easter or Whitsunday. This is wrong. They can be *compelled* to give the service.

Went with Dr. B, (who is a Churchman, & dislikes this course) to the Presb. Chapel. Sermon in wh. the preacher, a Baptist, named Lord, gave up the whole doctrine of death as a consequence of the fall, to what he called the results of Modern Science. Called at house of Mr. Rankin, a Presb. Mis-sionary, & then to the Chinese Chapel of the Presbyterians. They have about 150 in attendance, men & women. The Mis-sionary said it was hard to teach the Chinese to sit still & listen for a long time. A quiet, still meeting was unnatural to them. This is a proof in favor of liturgical worship. All the singing is of metrical hymns, wh. is also unnatural to the Chinese. They know only melody, & sing chants naturally. They would sing well in unison. I believe their women never sing in meetings.

There are 3 missions here—Ch. of England, Am. Presb. (Old School) & Baptist. The Presbyterians live together, on the river bank, outside the city, in a very pretty place, good houses. The others are scattered. Saw houses of two Ch. missionaries, Gough & Russell, in the city, large handsome houses.

Church Missionaries.	Gough, Russell, Mole.
Presbyterian " .	Rankin, Nevius, & Dr. McCarty.
Baptist " .	Lord, Knowlton.

Talked with Dr. Bradley about China. He says Williams had not seen the N. of China, nor even the city of Canton, when he wrote his Middle Kingdom, & that his generalisations are often wrong, but thinks it the best treasury. Dr. Morrison had no ear for sounds, & made great mistakes, in consequence, so that his translation of the Bible is worse than useless, & is abandoned—also he translated phrases directly, making unin-telligible stuff. A new translation is now going forward, on wh. there has been a long continued & rather bitter feud, as to the word to be used for God. Some contend for *Shang Ti*, & others for *Shin*, or *Sin*. Each party thinks the other fatally wrong, & wd. suffer martyrdom rather than use their word. The translation leaves it blank, & there are two sets printed, one by each party, or rather by the Boards. Each makes it a conscience not to use the other. Bishop Boone is of the Sin party,—wh. the other side call the *sinners*. The Engl. Ch. Miss. are Shang Ti men, & the Presb. are divided.

Dr. B says that the deaths among the Miss women, here, in China, especially in child-bed, are frequent, & they fail under the climate. They are obstructions to work, & do very little themselves. The Chinese, also, are offended by much publicity in the action of women. He thinks the Miss. should not marry.

I think, myself, that these missions are temptations to second rate young men & to women who have little chance of marriage. They can not only marry, but have a relay of wives, & live pretty well, keep servants, & become gentlemen. I have seen no Miss. yet in China, except B. Boone, who has not bettered his condition by coming here. They are in many cases inferior men. Some of the women are ladies, & have made sacrifices in coming—Mrs. B is sister of Bishop Elliott, Mrs. Smith is d. of Dr. Sparrow, Miss Jones is d. of Gen. Jones of Wash., & Mrs. Gough is a lady of fortune, & so with Mrs. Bonney at Canton. But the men are mostly of a lower type, & would do little at home. All persons I have seen here, of all nations & religions & of no religions,—if disconnected fr. the Missions —speak with more respect of the R. Cath. than of the Prot. Missions.

Bayard Taylor is spoken very lightly of here. His China is said to be a sham.—Rev. Mr. Gough & wife, of the Eng. Ch. Miss., are persons of independent fortune, & spend all their income on the Mission—much respected.

Monday. May 21.   Called on Rev. Messers. Russell & Gough of the Ch. of Engl. mission, & on Bishop Delaplasse, the R. Cath. bishop. The R. Cath. have 2 schools, 1 of boys & 1 of girls, of about 100 scholars each,—the latter under charge of Sisters of Charity. There are 11 Sisters here, 3 died last year, of cholera, & 6 are coming out. They have a small hospital & a pharmacy, fr. wh. they dispense med. to the poor daily. Four of the Sisters came in & shewed us their chief rooms—of course as neat as possible. Boys' dormitories, Chapel, apothecary room &c. Bishop have 6 or 8 Chinese youth preparing for orders. He & his clergy dress in Chinese costume.

Visited the Pagoda. Seven stories. The galleries are gone,

but the stairs, inside, are entire. View of city & suburbs. Ning Po is walled, uniformly, & with some 6 or 8 gates. Walls about 40 f. high, & thus —— thro' the whole length—so are all city walls I have seen,—& with moats. Population about 350,000.

Great number of beggars at the city gates,—dreadful objects, some very sick, & all ragged & lousy. Chief temple seems to be used as a furniture shop. They are very liberal in allowing selling, gambling & working at trades in & about the temples. Here was also a play going on, in the usual artificial falsetto voice, with the usual preposterous dresses & coarse painting of faces. Actors are outcasts. For 5 generations their descendants cannot become scholars,—so of barbers.

Those innumerable little huts we saw, coming up the river, with thatched roofs, are ice-houses. The Chinese use ice to preserve meat & fish, & not for drinking. Dr. B tells me there are 5000 ice houses in this district.

The U. States Govt. furnish to the Consulates here no jails nor jailors nor Marshal. By the treaty the jur. to punish Am. citisens is surrendered by China to our Consuls. Having none of these means, our Consuls can neither arrest, detain nor coerce. In short, Am. offenders go unpunished, unless we borrow, as sometimes we do, the Engl. jails. The Chinese complain, our Consuls admit the justice of the complaint, write despatches home, but nothing is done.

This ev. (Mond. 21 May) we start on an excursion to the Snowy Valley, Siueh Tau. Our party is Dr. Bradley, Rev. Mr. Nevius & myself, with 3 house servants, the chief of whom is Filial Piety. We have two Chinese boats, one for cooking & servants, & one for ourselves, & take cots, bedding, food &c. Start at 7 o'ck., & glide along the canal, under the wall of the silent city, for 2 hours, the canal crowded with boats, & the suburb lighting up its shops & houses.

Now comes the open country. By the side of the canal is a river, into wh., in due time, we slide, by what is called the Mud Slide,—where boats are pulled up an inclined plane of slimy mud by capstans, & slide down into the river. The jam of boats at these slides is great, & we buy off our predecessors by a few *kas*. Now, in the river, retire to our cots. Here, as on our Su Chau expedition, we have service in our boats.

Tuesd. May 22. Wake up. Boat still & fast. Daybreak. At a village, Su Fau, tau, where we leave the boats. Crowd gathers, & large concourse of spectators to see us wash, & free criticisms of our combs, brushes, towels &c.

Here hire 3 chairs, & 6 bearers, & 10 burden carriers, & start for the mountain. Ride on the plain, & walk up the ascent. Very hot, but have umbrellas & pith hats, & the free perspiration is the safest thing in such climates—only keep off the direct rays of the sun, & you do well eno'—wearing flannel.

The endless cultivation! Rice fields everywhere. Water is raised by the endless chain pump,—a Chinese invention, small ones worked by hand, & large ones by cattle,—buffaloes & bullocks. These rice fields, or rice *ponds*, one might call them, go to the very mountain tops, & into the deepest ravines, always on a plumb level, & terraced. On a sharp hill they look like low fortifications. The wheat is nearly ripe, & its yellow alternates with the green of the rice. This is the time of transplanting the rice—& the paddy fields are full of laborers, picking up, putting in baskets, setting out, & raising water. Every hill top discloses miles of industry. From them, the paddy fields look like vats of all colors of water, placed side by side all over the country.

The camphor trees are in flower, & have much the effect of the Chestnut trees in an Am. forest. And we have evergreens of the cedar sort, the weeping cypress, the Sihu willow, daphne odora, camellia Japonica &c., & all kinds of creepers & climbers, many in full blow. One old tree has its trunk covered with roses.

Reach the monastery, Siueh Tau S'z', Snowy Valley Monastery, by 11 o'ck., when Mr. Bradley, who has hardly got over his fever, is too weak to go to the falls, & here we leave our chairs, luggage & coolies, & Mr. Nevius & I go on. We mount to the top & view the falls fr. above, & force our way, where no path is, thro' thickets & over rocks, to the foot. This celebrated fall, She Hu Gau, is in a chasm formed by flat perpend. rocks, of not less than 400 feet in height, opening like a half opened book, the fall coming down at the angle. Below, the valley opens into the plain & discloses a noble landscape. The falls are one sheet, small & broken into silvered drops, falling in a basin,—a direct fall of at least 400 feet, & plenty of trees, shrubs & grass & creepers.

Wound up the rocks on the other side, & stopped a while at a woodcutter's hut, & reached the monastery, the Siueh Tau Sz', just before dark. On our return, passed another fall, smaller, with less extensive views, but dark, deep & romantic, Lung Yin Tan (Dragon's Shady Dell).

At the monastery, the monks give us house room, tables, chairs & bedsteads, fuel & use of kitchen,—but we find victuals, cooks, table furniture, & bed furniture. We have good dinner, prepared by our cook, with wine, tea & all the usual luxuries, & a good night's sleep, after a walk of not less than 8 hours, mostly up & down steep hills.

The idols in this temple are gigantic, & look rather fearful in the large dingy rooms, by the flicker of candles, & there is a huge new drum, the recent gift of some votaries, whose names are inscribed on a tablet, & a large bell, struck, as usual, by a wooden hammer, on the outside, the end of a stick suspended in air. While we are at dinner, the drum, the bell & the gong are all at work for the ev. service. But all is decay & neglect. Except the votive drum, nothing is repaired or supplied. The priests are mere ignorant drones. In China, there are three unlearned professions,—or rather, the priests & physicians are illiterate, & lawyers or jurists there are not.

Wed. May 23d. Rise early, walk about the monastery, the lower courts of wh. are filled by our servants, & then breakfast, & take an early start, sending the burden bearers off to their village, & our servants to the boat, all but Filial Piety, who, true to his name, gets leave to go & visit his parents in a neighboring village.

To-day we visit the falls of Tsien Chang Gau (the chasm of 10,000 feet) wh. is an exaggeration, it being about 500 feet, but a romantic scene, perpendicular rocks, a deep ravine, a broken fall of about 500 feet, & a closed-in view.

All our way down to the boats is this endless succession of rice fields & grain fields, & here & there tea fields, & some tea picking I saw. At noon, passing thro' a village, being hungry & thirsty, & our provisions gone on, stopped at Chinese shop & had eggs boiled & some tea, wh. we found or thought excellent, & wh. we drank in the sight of as large a crowd as could get into the two rooms, leaving us elbow room,—Mr.

Nevius making a short sermon, in wh. he had to encounter a quick witted scoffer, & Dr. Bradley refusing to eat or drink anything fr. the unclean kitchen of the Chinese.

Here we left our chairs, & sent the bearers to the boats, & got the variety of a passage down the river on a raft. These rafts are of bamboos lashed together, bent up for a prow before, loaded, & drawing not over 6 inches, the river being very shallow here. This is a pleasant mode of travelling, in fine weather. It is noiseless, gentle & with variety of river scenery. These rafts carry a large commerce down to the head of boat navigation. We placed our chairs on the rafts, spread our umbrellas, & enjoyed a drift of 2 or 3 hours very much, wh. took us to our boats at Sa Fau Tau, & there we begin our course down the river, homeward. Stopped, however, just at night-fall, at a pagoda on a hill that overlooks the village of Kiang Kau fr. wh. there is a good view, tho' we were a little too late for it.

(Mr. Bradley's excited state. Not over his fever, talking in sleep for hours, but he is a generous, hospitable man. Nevius tells me B.'s story, his marriage, separation, insanity, recovery, holy orders, scholarship &c. N. is an ordinary man, of no philosophy or theology.)

Thursd. May 24.   Reached the crenalated walls of Ning Po, at daybreak, drop down the canal, under the walls for 2 hours, amid a throng & jam of early boats, & reach home in the early morning.

Rev. Mr. J. Knowlton, Baptist Missionary, calls. Gives me statistics &c. The Southern Baptists have missions at Canton & Shanghai. The Am. Bapt. Board, here & at Hong Kong. There are three clergymen, 28 Chinese Christians, all told, & one native Assistant. They have 2 day schools of about 45 pupils in all. He tells me that all the Prot. Missions pay the girls to come to school, for the parents do not care to have girls taught, & their time at home is of some value. The R.C. bishop had told me this, but I thought him mistaken. Mr. K. says it is necessary to do so. Mr. K. is a dull man, imperfectly educated.

Being the Queen's Birth Day, Mr. Bradley & I, dressed in our best, he in consular gold lace, & I in dress coat & kids, under a hot sun, & called on the Br. Consul. The gun boat Restive fired salutes.

Walked round the city, on the walls, with Mr. B. Very pretty views. A river & a canal nearly surround the city, under the walls. The walls are wide & furnish a pleasant walk, but the beggars, in filth & rags, lying at the Gate houses, are a distress & disgust. The city abounds with little stone, close houses for burying babies. The babies are not killed, as many supposed, but no baby is *buried* in China, but merely wrapped in matting & thrown away. These tombs have small holes in the tops, just big eno' to admit a little body, & the people tumble them in until they are full to the top, & then new ones are built. Mr. B. pointed out one, now full & overflowing, wh. had not been built 3 mos., & yet there were 4 built at that time.

Rev. Mr. Rankin calls. He is of the Presb. Mission, & was once settled in Rochester N.Y., & knows Mr. Daggett well, & talked of Canandaigua.

The complication of Prot. Missionaries here is increased by a New Engl. Society, called the Soc. for Evangel China, wh. has sent two open Communion Baptists here. Tried to learn the mystery of the Prot. translations of Scriptures. There are so many, & none are confided in, & then there is the Shang Ti & Shin controversy, & the Baotigio controversy, & all seems a chaos. I wonder they have *one* convert. The Presbyterians are doing pretty well, & have some 75 or 100 communicants, & 2 boarding schools, boys & girls, of about 30 each, & sev. day schools.

This ev. Rev. Mr. Russell, of the Engl. Ch. Miss. Soc., called & spent an hour or so. He is an Irishman, of the Univ. of Dublin, & a very polite man, faithful, & of good sense,—a very, very low churchman. Yet I found him decided in favor of the superiority, indeed almost necessity, of a liturgy for the Chinese. The Ch. of Engl. Mission at Ning Po was established in 1848. There are now 4 missionaries & their wives, & (including the out-lying station of San Pâ) 160 baptised Chinese, 100 adult communicants, & 3 schools for boys & 3 for girls, in all about 60 scholars of each sex.

He entirely denies the *extension* of learning among the Chinese. He says thus—The Chinese written language is so difficult that only scholars can read it to any advantage, & it is forgotten if not constantly kept up. The common people know only a few characters, for necessary purposes, & do not read at all. In Ning Po, of 350,000 people, & one of the best cities of China, there are only 4 small book-shops, & in the entire district, in all the 15 or 20 towns, of from 5 to 50,000 inhab. each, there are no book-shops, & no peddlers of books. The poor have no books in their houses, not a new book is produced in this province in 20 years. Literature is *deified* in China, because it is so difficult & rare. The Chinese character has no sound known to the spoken dialect. The *sounds* attached to the characters give no idea to the hearer. Reading aloud is never done, & wd. be useless. It is the eye only that gives the idea, & the characters are by myriads. They must be translated into the spoken dialects, as we would translate Cicero, & this can only be done *orally*, for the spoken dialects have no characters to represent their sounds. It is like latin books among a people who have no written language, but learned scholars who can read latin. Now, the object of the Roman letters is to make the spoken dialects written languages. This they cannot be, by using the Chinese characters, & the making of new Chinese characters, added to the myriads, would be worse than useless. They translate foreign books into the dialects, & print them with the Roman letters, on the phonetic principle,—just as if the Chinese had only unwritten dialects. As to the book language, the ——, that is to stand. All Christian Chinese are to learn that also, if they wish, & to read the classics in those characters. It is hardly practicable to translate the Classics into the dialects, & the prejudices of centuries must be respected. (Qu. If the prevalence of the Roman letters, & the making the dialects written, will not result in burying the ancient literature of China?) A Chinese can learn to read by Roman letters, any book, quite as quick as our boys at home,—while to read the character requires a teacher for every word & sound, years of study, & then an imperfect result.

Friday. May 25.   Called on Rev. Russell. Saw there a blind Chinese girl, a foundling, who had been made blind to use her as a beggar,—no unusual thing, & saved by Dr. Gützlaff, sent to England when very young, carefully educated there by a benev. Engl. lady, & now lives with the Engl. Ch. Missionaries here, & teaches the Chinese girls orally. She reads English, on raised type, beautifully. She read to us a passage fr. St. John's Gospel, with a justness of emphasis & delicacy of intonation I have rarely known equalled, & with no sign of foreign accent. She also played to us pieces from Handel,—on a very disagreeable melodeon, but well.

Mrs. Russell has a school of 7 blind Chinese girls, who plait straw, & are taught orally, chiefly by this girl, Agnes.

Called on Mr. & Mrs. Nevius, Mr. & Mrs. Rankin, Dr. & Mrs. McCarty, of the Presb. Mission, & Mr. Knowlton of the Bapt. Mission, & exd. the printing press of the Pr. Mission. They print the Chinese character fr. types, & the number of characters being thousands, setting up is slow work.

Take leave of my kind host, Mr. Bradley, & go on board the lorcha Rosina, to sail to-night for Shanghai. Bradley loads a basket of prog for me, & seems really sorry to have me leave him.

Our boat I call a lorcha, for she is as much that as anything, of about 50 tons burden, commanded by an Englishman with a crew of 8 Chinese sailors & 3 Manilla men. The latter, one of whom is the gunner, live apart fr. the Chinese, & are the guard, as well as sailors, & are relied upon to do the fighting, in case of an attack by pirates, for the Chinese will not risk their lives to defend foreign property ag. Chinese. We have two long six pounders, & a quantity of rifles, musketoons & pistols, and are in good order, for the pirates have been bold of late, & the news has just come of the capture of a Ning Po boat by them & the murder of all hands,—one Smith, a European residing in Ning Po, being master. Dr. Lindau is with me, & so we muster 3 foreigners & 3 Manilla men, but the captain says the pirates have never, of late years, attacked a boat belonging to one of the great Engl. houses, (the Rosina is Dent & Co.'s) although they know how much opium & treasure they carry as well as the owners themselves, for fear of the consequences,—the gunboats being sent to break them all up.

Decent cabin, Chinese cook & steward, & fair living.

Sat. May 26. At day light are going down the river, passing Ching Hae, & the junks, & the citadel, & with a leading wind & fine weather are just able to stand our course. Dr. L. & I lounge & read & sleep & talk, in our small quarters, or sit on deck with the crew. Afternoon & ev. rainy & thick. The Chinese are good pilots & go on, see or no see.

Late in P.M., make the Rugged Islands, & at midnight then make Gutslaff, & then the Light Ship, as true as the needle. Weather rough, & seas come on board, & crew bailing a little. Racing with the Heather Bell, wh. sailed at same time. She outsails us.

Sund. May 27.   In the Yang Ts' Kiang, & reached Wosung by 8 A.M., & obliged to lie there at anchor nearly all day, until 2 P.M., within 8 m. of Shanghai, wind & tide adverse, & see the steamers Yang Tse & Aden, former with the mails fr. Europe, go up. At turn of tide, in heavy rain, with thunder & lightening & close hot air, we scull up to the anchorage, & in a few minutes I am, for the fourth time, instated at Russell & Co.'s, in my old quarters, where a bath & change are agreeable. My China boy seems pleased to see me, tho' they say the Chinese have no emotion or attachments. (Mr. Nevius denies this, & thinks they have gratitude & affection, but are not treated by most Europeans in a way to draw them out).

Gordon Dexter is here, also a guest of Russell & Co. He has been at Manila, since Japan. He says that Commodore Tattnall & the Capt. of the Powhatan traded in itsebus & purchase of kobans, as well as the junior officers. The Am. merchants in China sent great quantities of specie to Japan in the Powhatan, on freight, wh. freight goes to the Com. & Capt., & with this & borrowed money they bought kobans. The junior officers bought with money borrowed of the Am. & Engl. merchants. Only 2 officers were clear of it. This was when the Jap. Govt. had forbidden the exp. of kobans,—& the Naval officers were exempt fr. Cu. Hs. examination.

Mond. May 28.   The Yang Tse is chartered to take down the Chinese Gov. Gen. to Fu Chau, who seems to be flying from the rebels, so I cannot go in her. The rebels are making head again, after their success at Hang Chau, & have greatly alarmed our good friends at Su Chau, & its neighborhood. I wonder how our magnificent Mandarin with the 3 plumes feels about it?

Called on Mr. Ward, who arrived Sat. last in the Hartford.

He is justly angry with Ld. Palmerston for his reference to him in his speech of M'ch. last, & has written to Sir M. Seymour to thank him for his correction of Ld. P. on that head, & a full expln. to Mr. Cass. Ward also thinks Harris did very shabbily not to invite me to Yedo, & wishes to resent it.

Marten, in the Roebuck, has been here & gone again to Chusan. The Hartford & Saganaw lie opp. us here, & the river is full of ships of war, transports & despatch boats.

(Read Seward's Speech, at Ning Po. Admirable!)

This afternoon walked into the city with Mr. Lyle. The alarm at Su Chau has spread here, & numerous fugitives are on their way. The Govt. have yesterday beheaded some 20 as deserters. The deserters fr. the Imp. Army are feared as robbers, & usually executed when caught. Bruce & de Bourbulon have posted proclamations, in Chinese, all about the city, assuring the people that the foreign forces will protect them. This satisfies many, but the panic exists, increased by the recollection of the horrors of the rebel occupation of Shanghai 5 years ago, & there is a steady exodus of the people, all day, through the N. & E. gates, with their little stocks of furniture & household goods & gods, hurrying out into the distant villages. They have a proverb to the effect that "in little troubles, go to the city; in great troubles, go to the country". But one cannot wonder. What must a panic be in a city of sev. hundr. thous. inhab., with streets so narrow & choked that no communication can be had betw. diff. parts by the officers, & where the houses are so frail & consumable! As I walked the streets, I cd. not but think what suicides by scores—nay, by hundreds—what famine, plunder, distress wd. be enacted here, if the rebels shd. reach the walls.

Went with Mr. L. to his house for the blind. Here are about 60 blind people, mostly women, adults, who are employed all day in braiding straw, & get the diff. betw. the cost of the straw & the price of the rope or twist. It keeps them in food & clothing. The land & house are held by Mr. L. in trust, & the foreign merch. contribute about $1000 annually for it. (Mr. L. says the for. merch. here are truly liberal in all cases of charity well approved to them). Of the 60, over 20 are Christians.

To the chapel, where Mr. L. got a collection of 20 persons, talked a while, & distributed books.

At an open door, heard music & went in. Had been a marriage three days before, & the wedding feast was still going on. It usually lasts 3 to 7 days, & often involves the party in burdensome expenses. This is a house of mod. pretensions, but there are 8 pieces of music, mostly played by children, & tables are standing, set out with confectionary, cakes, tea & sugarwater, & some 6 or 8 solemn guests are tasting & smoking. The bridegroom, who has a broad piece of gold leaf on his breast, comes forward, & receives us politely, though strangers & intruders, makes us sit down, sits with us, devotes himself to conv. with us, & has sweetmeats & sugar-water served. He thinks little of the rebels, & sees only happiness & security before him. Of course, the wife is out of sight, in some hidden room within.

Per contra, Mr. L. takes me to a small hut of a poor Chinese Xtian,—a blind old crone, who has 2 blind old crones visiting her. L. says she is a model woman, for sense & kindness. One story is that these people cry themselves blind, by immod. weeping.

To a vapor-bath, or sweating house. The Chinese do not use much water, but here the poor go into a steam room, & sweat themselves & wipe off, & then take tea & a pipe. The cost of the bath, towel, tea & pipe is, in all, only about four cents!

Tuesd. May Visit on board the Hartford, to Commodore Stribling. Then to Capt. Lowndes, & then to the wardroom. Fine looking ship. Ward room very large—steerage too small, Com.'s cabin small. Stribling says the ship was an outrageously costly job, among politicians in Yard, & so was the little Saganaw. Jobs to keep voters in pay. All the officers, in cabin & ward-room alike, deplore the condit. of our Navy—the political jobbing, the negl. & indif. of Toucey (Sec. of Navy) to the interests of the Navy, & number of incompetent officers, & the slowness of promotion. Lowndes is a white haired old man. 1st. lieut. is Barnet. A midsh. named Greene is neph. of Gen. Dana of Charlestown.

Dined with Webb, present, Hon. Col. Foley, of Br. army, Capt. Barnard of the P.&O. steamer Aden (a grad. of Cambr. Univ.) who talks of latin & German authors, Dr. Lindau & myself. Col. F. thinks I *can* do India in July. Lindau thinks the

Chinese character, as used by the Japanese, does *not* give the image or idea it does in Chinese, but is used only to express a sound, & that sound diff. fr. its Chinese sound. (Qu.?)

The Chinese are beginning to believe that they can have junks without eyes painted on the bows. They see foreign ships make long voyages safely without them, & are slowly beginning to be willing to sail in small vessels without them.

Wed. May 30. Called on the Capt. Schenck of the Saganaw. Pleasant man. His 1st lieut., ——, is almost imbecile in mind & body. The 2d & 3d, Wardell & Campbell, are excellent men, — the latter a scholarly man. But absurd to have 3 lieuts., & a Master, to so small a craft. She is a success, as a steamer, excellent machinery, steams fast,—but cost 3 times her value.

Thence to my friend Jones, of the Furious, who is receiving Com. Stribling, manning yards for him, &c. Pleasant call. He thinks highly of Marten, & that he will get promotion soon. Introduced to Capt. Windgard, of the Nimrod, a twin of the Roebuck.

This ev. Mr. Ward called & spent an hour or so.

Thursday. May 31. Last day at Shanghai. Take leave early, & at 8 A.M. am under way for Hong Kong, in the P.&O. steamer Aden, Barnard, master. At Wosung, a fleet of Fr. men of war & transports full of troops, ready to start for the North. Boat fr. Fr. Adm, comes alongside & puts letters on board. The Hartford does not look so well head on. Rises too much.

Sat. June 2. At sea. How marvelous content I am at sea! Believe I was intended for a sailor. State-room to myself, usual routine of hours & duties. Discipline the same here as in the Peking. But this is a screw, & what a terrible noise, what beating & thumping of the ship's bottom a screw makes. It seems to be breaking thro' keel, keelson, floor & all. I wonder that delicate passengers can endure it. It would drive crasy some persons I know.

A little boy passenger about 7 years old, looks & acts so much like little Dick, that can't keep away fr. him. Has his figure, complexion, lay of hair & eyes. Find him to be Robert Olyphant, son of Mr. O. the China merchant. His parents on board. Make acq. of Mr. O., Mrs. O. seasick. Mr. O. is a strong Presbyterian, lives in Shanghai, & tells me that the Presb. Mission there is large & successful—regrets I did not make acq. of its clergy. Also, the Ch. Miss. Soc. (Engl.) has 2 missionaries there. He thinks very highly of Bishop B's mission. Says there have been 2 "Seventh Day Baptists" missionaries in Shanghai —who are returning there, to complicate matters & confound the Chinese. They make it a principle to work on Sunday.

Another passenger is a Mr. F. D. Williams, formerly of Boston, now of Wetmore & Co. He has large B acq.—rather of the Cadet & fast order, I think.

Mr. Cheney, who knew Ned slightly in Heidelberg. Campbell, agt. of Oriental B'k. Cheney is a silk merchant, nephew of Seth & John Cheney, & acts as agt. for his br. & uncle who are silk manuf. in Manchester, Conn. Mrs. Olyphant is a d. of Mr. Wm. Vernon, of Newport R.I., & talked with me about the Newport people, Aunt Phily, Hasards, Perrys, Vernons & Ellerys. Master Bob is like Dick in his manners, also. Olyphant tells me that sev. of the Miss at Shanghai whom I did not see, are able men, who gave up high situations at home, & are here at a sacrifice,—some of the Presb. B'd., & one of the Engl. Ch. Miss. Soc., & that the Presb. have 3 chapels in Shanghai & suburbs.

Rainy & windy, rolling sea & ports shut down.

Sund. June 3. At anchor, in Hong Kong, at 7 A.M. Ashore at Russell & Co.'s, at breakfast. Mr. Delano not returned. Mr. Beckwith at Canton. Most news is that no letters have come for me fr. Calcutta.

To the Engl. Church at 11 o'ck. Large, handsome church, well filled, good share of red coats. No singing, in this great & rich congregation! The preacher a puppy! Sorry to say so—but no other phrase meets his case.

A Mr. Ellis calls, who is friend of C. F. Adams, Fr. Palfrey &c. &c.

Flowers, trees & shrubs in Bradley's garden, at Ning Po— Pride of China, Woodbine, Maiden's bower, honeysuckle, yellow jasmine, chrysanthimum, spirla, tree peony, hyperacum, banana, rhododendron max., Camellia Japonica, althea, magnolia, weeping cypress, sika willow, daphne ordora, camphor tree, China astor, tree hybiscus, moutan, & 15 kinds of roses.

Mond. June 4. Call on Mr. & Mrs. Olyphant, Mr. Heard, Mr. Dent, & on Père Libois, the director of those R. C. missionaries in China who are supported by the Fr. Soc. des Missions étrangères. He has an intellectual head. Tells me there are 8 bishops & 56 European missionaries of his Society, in China, & about 40 native priests. This is excl. of the Jesuits, & the missionaries of the Propaganda. At Hong Kong is the Head Quarters, station house & bureau of the Two Societies, the Miss. Etrang. & the Propaganda. The Propaganda directs ultimately all the Missions, but some miss. go directly fr. it, supported by it. Père Ambrosi, an Italian, represents the Propaganda here.

Grand looking fellows, the Sikhs. Proud of step, flashing eye, reg. features, but black as black can be. Look at the Sepoy soldiers, in black glased hats, without front-pieces, looking into the glaring, burning sun without blinking! How picturesque, too, is the white turban, with the dangling white robe & half bare legs & dainty step!

Tuesd. June 5. Last night, dined at Heard's, with Mr. Greene of Manilla, (Russell Sturgis & Co.).

To-day, called on Gen. Keenan, the Am. Consul, a tall, well made, rather Westernish man, illiterate, pleasant & natural. Then, on Sir Hercules Robinson, the Gov. of H.K. Sir H. is a thoroughly well bred man, intelligent & young looking for his post—an Irishman. Then, on the Sisters of St. Paul de Chartres. The Superior is very ill, & affairs not in so good order as usual, as there is only one sister for all the establishment, in wh. there are a great number of children, all orphans or children abandoned by their parents. It is called La Sainte Enfance & is a charity, very highly spoken of. Then called on Speidon, at the U.S. Naval Store Hs., where met Rev. Mr. Johnson, Bapt. Missionary, & wife. J. says no *mission* strictly here, & are going to Swatow. Thinks they have 30 Chinese here, whom they can rely upon as converts, & from 4 to 6 native preachers.

Letter from Mr. Nye, at Macao, respecting the portrait he is to send me, probably by the ship Judge Shaw. Spent ev. at Mrs. Beckwith's;—sister of P. S. & Rev. Dr. Forbes.

Wed. June 6. Call on Father Ambrosi. His title is Procurator of the Propaganda Fide in China, & Prefect Apostolic of Hong Kong. He is repr. & ag't. of that Soc. & head of its missionaries here. The missionaries of the Fr. Soc. des M. Etrangères are under a head at Paris, who is under the Propaganda at Rome. The Prop. Soc. has in China 5 bishops, 36 Europ. missionaries, & 40 native missionaries. The Lasarists have bishops & clergy. In all,—Jesuits, Prop. Lasarists & Miss. Etrangeres, are abt. 20 bishops & 120 Europ. priests. Each b. has his province.

He tells me that the sisters I saw yesterday are to go to Macao, & that an Italian order of Daughters of Charity, is to come here & have a convent, school, hospital &c.

The Cath. clergy originally adopted the "Shang Ti", for God, but after long & patient investig. (so says Père Ambrosi) they discarded it. The objection was that it signified Supreme Governor, & is applied by the Chinese to the Emperor & to powers supreme in part. They then, 200 years ago, adopted T'ien Chu, wh. means *Coali Dominus*, Heavenly Lord, & have been united on that ever since. The first Protestants took Shang Ti. They later discarded it for S'in. On this is the Prott. controversy. The Bishop of Victoria has adopted the Cath. word "T'ien Chu", & it is placed on the Br. Ch. College in H. Kong.

Spent all day, after 11 o'ck., alone, in this great house, no one but Chinese servants near, & a hot Chinese sun out of doors, & Chinese locusts murmuring, & I reading Webster's correspondence. Read the 2d vol. He does not put his *mind* into *these* letters. Has not Mr. Everett weeded out the strength of them, or left out the strongest?

Singapore, Ceylon, India, Egypt,
and Europe: June–September 1860

Saturday. June 9. Westward & Homeward, at last! Left Hong Kong, Th. 7th, at 2 P.M. in the P.&O. steamer "Madras". She is a large screw steamer, one of the best of the line. The last three days in H. Kong were hot,—the regular summer heat, & we dined under punkahs, wh. are worked by men out of sight, the lines going thro' the walls, so that the luxurious diners need not be heated by seeing the labor of others. But I have liked this heat, so far. I like the clean white clothes one wears, the slow gait, & the gentle perspiration, & the indolence. Pith hats abound, & other hats & caps with all sorts of puckenys. How cool are the naked feet, the loose dangling white robes & the gause turbans of the E. Indian races! One meets 6 or 7 races, in a walk up the street of H. Kong— Chinese, Europeans, Parsees, Malays, Hindoos, Negroes &c. &c. & ev. subdivision of those.

Mr. Greene (of Russell Sturgis & Co. of Manilla) has been extremely kind—done more than all the rest, as a mere volunteer.

When I told Beckwith I wanted an introduction to the Capt. & purser, as my comfort depended on it,—he gave a long dissertation on steamers, & sneered at all officers thereof, & all arrangements,—but Greene quietly wrote to the captain, whom he knows well, & got a Director of the company to speak to the purser for me, & thus I got a stateroom to myself, & a seat at the head of the table, & all proper attentions.

Just as we steamed out of H. Kong, Jardine's steamer fr. Calcutta steamed in,—I fear, having my letters on board.

The expenses of exchange & of getting money available among the Chinese are so great, that one gets just about 65 cents for every dollar he draws for. My total expenses in China have been about $300, of wh. $200 are for steamer passages. For this $300, I have been obliged to draw on London for nearly 100 £. At Shanghai, I had to pay 26½ per cent for money. Including my passage home in the P.&O. steamers, I shall lose on exchange about $500!! This is hard to bear. It wd. have been cheaper to pay full board for 6 mos. than to pay exchange.

Still, China & Japan have been a great experience, & a constant pleasure, & I must not grumble!

So far, I have liked the universally abused P.&O. steamers. There is most excellent discipline on deck, & cleanliness, & I have found only civility among the officers. Hours are regular, & cooking, so far, good. The heat does not trouble me. I rather like the tropical routine. Perhaps I shall feel it more in time.

Routine. Made interest & got my steward to spread my mat on the transom in the large cabin, at 10 o'ck. ev. night, & there I lie down in pajamas, with head on a hard China pillow & sleep comfortably. At abt. 5.30, stewards begin to move. Turn out & get a salt-water bath, in a comfortable bathing room. At 6, stewards serve tea or coffee to those who wish it. Gentlemen lounge about in pajamas & China slippers & take coffee, until about 8 o'ck. I take fruit, instead, so long as it lasts. (Delicious fruit is the lychee of China!). At 8, or 8½, go to state room & dress—slippers, loose clothes & straw hat all morning. Breakfast at 9 o'ck. Lunch at 12. Dinner at 4. Tea at 7. In hot weather, at sea, best rule is to take a little at each meal. Never be hungry at sea, or in the tropics, & never be full!

Dress a little for dinner,—a waistcoat, new-collar, &c., & shoes. After tea, I walk deck for 2 hours or more. I believe in exercise in the tropics. It makes perspiration. How wretched are the hours at H. Kong & Shanghai! Dinner under hot lamps at 8 o'clk., & no exercise. The young men say it is hurtful,—& they all drink too much, & of too many kinds. The steamer hours are better.

(Beckwith tells me that the silk trade of China is rapidly increasing, & is now greater than the tea trade, & that much of the raw silk goes to France, but it goes via England. If France took home her silk in her own vessels, & pd. by drafts on Paris, there wd. be a large Fr. commerce, but London does all).

No distinguished passengers. Three or four invalided young officers, going home—rather ordinary persons. Two Sp. gentl. fr. Manila, one a Lt. Col. of the Sp. army,—the other has wife & 2 children, & none of them speak a word of Eng. or French,

& have great difficulty. El Señor sits next me, & I help him all I can,—but my stock is small. Still, I gain in Spanish, daily.

Punkahs over all the tables, & swarthy boys in turbans to pull them,—*punkah-wallahs*. Our punkah-wallah has large languid eyes, turban, fes & cap—picturesque!

Last night, heard a song so much like some of our genuine negro songs, that I went forward to see if it was possible that lascars or Malays had learned the negro minstrel melodies. But the song came from the gang of Abysinnian negroes, who are the stokers of the ship,—and it was one of their native melodies. Singular that it should so resemble the melody of the N. Am. negroes that I should mistake it! Proof of unity of negro race. Capt. B. tells me these Abys. negroes are always singing at their work, & are light hearted,—while the Malays & Lascars never sing. The language of the Lascars is all ábrakadábraka, Káraktaŕaktarak.

Sund. June 10. Coast of Cochin China in sight all day. High, with some mountains. At 10 A.M., crew mustered, in neat dresses. Officers & stewards, engineers & petty officers Europeans. Seamen are Lascars & Malays. Firemen & stokers are Abysinnian negroes—"sidis". Some are Mahommedan, with turbans, feses & sashes. Officers have blue coats, uniform caps & buttons, & the Europ. petty officers have white trowsers & frocks—all very neat.

At 10.30, the Church service, read by the Captain, at the capstan. Officers, the Engl. part of the crew, & most of the passengers present. How respectable & proper is this usage of all the ships of the Engl. companies, the world over!

Dead calm, & sun very hot. Even under the awning, it is hardly safe to sit uncovered. An officer told me his head was a little affected, being uncovered. Hence the Eastern custom of covering the head—necessity.

Reading Sir J. Bowring's Philippine Islands. In this, he says that China now clothes her 300 millions with cotton of her own production.

Delightful nights! Great Bear & North Star, in the North, & Southern Cross in the South, both visible together here, in Northern Tropics.

Thursd. 14.   Islands off the Coast of Malacca in sight all day. Towards night, saw the P.&O. steamer Peking, bound to China. She has the Eng. & Fr. ensigns set. Ld. Elgin & Baron Gros must be on board. Hove to. Boat comes alongside. Crowd gathers round the officer. The "Malabar" was lost in Point de Galle harbour, having Ld. E. & Baron G. on board, all lives saved, but all or nearly all luggage, & all cargo lost. After delay of 2 weeks, the passengers come on in the Peking. Govt. had great amt. of money on board the M. Ld. E. & Baron G. are on board.

Arrive at Singapore at 10 P.M., & can only see a few lights on shore, some elevated,—said to be on the Government Hill. Gun & rocket.

Frid. June 15.   At daylight, on deck, & Singapore lies about us. Land is level, but not low, with one or two eminences, & rising into undulating country in rear of the town. Large Govt. establishments & Br. flag waving fr. them. Good deal of shipping in port, of all nations, & numerous Malay, Chinese & Siamese junks. Malay boats come off—long, sharp bows. Malays have broad faces, broad & flat noses, & expression not kindly, nor particularly intelligent. Boat loads of pine-apples going by.

Steam up, & go to the new harbor, where P.&O. Co. has a coaling yard, & we all go ashore, with liberty to 2 P.M. of Sat.

To Hotel de l'Esperance, &—first thing in a tropical voyage—, get washing taken, on promise to return tomorrow at 10 o'ck. This hotel is on the Esplanade,—an open ground, with walks & trees, on the sea shore, pretty & cool—open sea, sea-breeze, & needed, as this is almost directly under the Equator.

Town is English, in plan & construction,—large buildings of stone & brick, wide, straight streets. ⅔ of the people you meet are Chinese. Shops, shops, shops, & all kinds of work, by the endless industry of these strange people. They come here without women, by the thousands, have children of Malay & Madras mothers, grow rich, & absorb the business & merch. trades. Next to the Chinese, are the "Klings", or Madras men. They are nearly black, but with reg. features—blacker than most negroes. They, too, supersede the Malays, where the

Chinese do not, & the Malays, go to the wall, & diminish in numbers.

Sun hot, of course, but air agreeable, & effect of all you see & feel is pleasing. Plenty of trees & shade, & open country abt. the town is rich with grass & trees—palms of all sorts, mango, nutmeg, cocoa nut tree, & bamboo groves & hedges. Pine apples, oranges & bananas in abundance, & the celebrated mangosteen is in its finest condition.

Get carriage—no one walks, as too hot, at noon—& drive to Boustead & Co. to see if my letters have been sent here fr. Calcutta, as I directed. The junior partner says "No" positively. Great disappointment. Let out some of my grief & surprise to the Senior, who sends for the file, looks it over & finds a complete budget for me, fr. Calcutta, & I sit right down & read them all—dates are fr. Dec. to Feb. & fr. all the family, & all are alive & safe. Three letters fr. Dick,—dear little fellow. [—] Write & spell them correctly. Mr. Brown invites me to dine. Meet Mr. . . . O'Sullivan. He invites me, also, but too late—sorry—think shd. have preferred him & his wife, who is sd. to be a pretty Wallachian woman.

At Hodgdon's, Hasen's partner. He was out. At the R. Cath. Convent, to see Miss Spooner. Sister Joseph, I think is her name—came in with the Lady Superior. She is thin & rather pale, & was moved at seeing me & speaking of her Boston friends. Asked her to write to Charlotte, & offered to call for the letter tomorrow. "May I write to Miss Dana?" "Oh yes, certainly", says the Superior. This is a Convent & School. Here are about 60 scholars, girls, & of all races & mixtures of races, educated here at exp. of parents or friends if rich, otherwise *gratis*. Grounds handsome, & houses large & airy. Miss Spooner says she likes the climate, has perfect health, & is happy. Is also a day-school connected with the institution.

In Singapore, is the large & handsome Engl. church, not yet finished, & one R. Cath., & one American. The American was closed, or I shd. have entered it. It is in handsome style, & has a cross on the spire.

The variety of races is greater here than in China, if possible. Europeans, of all races, Chinese, Malays, Parsees, Hindoos, Klings &c. &c. Chinese keep to their costume, & the E. Indians wear turbans of all colors, with white dangling robes. The drivers running beside their horses when in full trot. The Klings "fr. Madras" are well formed, active men, & run beautifully,— thin arms & legs, but very straight, & well set about the hips.

Anderson, to whom Greene gave me a letter, comes in & invites me to breakfast. Just before dark, Brown drives me to his "box" in the country, 3 miles or so out of town. Ground rises, & fine views of the ocean. Delightful ev. breese. House large, rooms lofty, beds large & stately, with rich mosquito nets,—baths & all appliances, large piassas, grass lawn in front, & palm trees, bananas, orange trees, nutmeg, &c. &c.

Company all Scotch. One lady, a Mrs. Davidson—& we have Scotch political talk, Scotch landscapes &c. They are all Jacobites. Arise at day-break, & enjoy cool morning mist. Anderson sends buggy to drive me to his house to breakfast. It is some 3 miles off. Thence, to the river, to see a Malay river. Water dark & deep, & shores lined with jungle. Jungle by the road side, & stories of tigers. Sometimes, the tigers come in towards the settlements, & an average of a man a week is taken off by them.

Surface undulating, & scenery tropical. Pepper fields, on all sides. Pepper grows like hops, on poles, & looks like it. Pineapples grow in ridges, on low bushes.

Anderson has a huge house, with plenty of ventilation & distant views. In the goodness of his heart, he took pains to get me an American breakfast, with salt mackerel, balls of salt cod fish, & such things, when I wished only to eat the products of the place. But he ended with some excellent mangos from Bombay—much better than the mango of Singapore. Taste is something betw. a peach & a muskmellon. The mangosteen has a thick dark red rind, within wh. is a small fruit as white as milk, which melts on your mouth & is delicious, tho' not piquant. Hardly know wh. to prefer the mangosteen, or the lychee of China. They are the most etherial of fruits.

Passed a rajah's house, built in Europ. style, large & sumptuous.

Lucky in getting my washing back safe & in season—wh. all steamer passengers do not. To the Convent, to get Miss Spooner's letter. She says—"tell my friends I am happy here, much engaged in teaching, like the climate better than ours at home, & am in good health"—& desired me to call on her mother, & to remember her to our family, Metcalfs, Judge Bigelow, Sister Jane &c. Leave to shake hands with her. Happening to turn back, saw tears & a h'd'kf.,—but not much.

Anderson drives me to the boat, & gives me loaf of cake, & letters of introdn. to Bombay. Going out, drift into the big steamer Coromandel troop ship,—no damage & Capt. not blamed, as pilot directing. On the whole, much pleased with Singapore. Tell me climate healthy, temperature uniform, always hot,—but tolerable, & showers & rains, but no dangerous blows. Harbor open, but safe, for the season of no storms. Is the greatest *place of call* in the East, & has consid. trade of its own, in pepper fr. the Main, & tea fr. China &c., spices, &c.

Sund. June 17. At sea again, & in the good routine. Glad to find that I can bear the heat as well as others, & better than many, & can sleep when most must sit up in chairs, for want of air. Again, the good responses in the service, as general & loud as in the best churches. My home letters give me constant pleasure. Having no letters of introdn. to E. India fr. England settle the little doubt I had about going there—added to expense, loss of time & midsummer heat.

A passenger, bound to Siam, named Allen. Introduces himself to me as a Mass. man, knowing the Salters, under obligations to them for much kindness in Boston. He is in business in the capital of Siam.

Monday. June 18th. *Penang* is the most beautiful place I have seen in the East. It is a large island separated by a wide still bay from the main land of Malacca,—the town level, dry & not low, & hills immediately behind it, sloping gradually up, & rising to small mountains, with a waterfall & picturesque scenery. The town is healthy, free fr. malaria, though hot, the temperature & weather being the same through the year. The only bad effect is debility & lassitude. Those who can afford it live part of the time on the hills, in bungalows. The streets are straight & wide, & the whole town is under shade,—the shade of cocoa nut trees, (fr. wh. the name comes), with an interspersing of other palms, of Pride of India & Weeping Cypress. The houses are large, airy & with large yards. How very hot the sun is at noon!—for as we stay here but 6 hours, I must be about at noon, if at all. A double umbrella, linen over silk, & a pith hat covered, hardly defend one. Yet the air is pure, & a gentle sea breese blows all the time, & the sensations are delightful. The Eng. Ep. Ch., & the Presb. are large & handsome, & stand in large yards, under trees.

The mixed races who do the labor here, are very slightly clad, merely white long cloths thrown over the shoulders, & the hard workers not that. The E. Indians, the turban. The drivers of carriages run by the side of their horses. Mine ran so all the morning. Cook, acting Am. Consul, head of Currier & Co. He is generally said to be accomplished, but as ev. man in Penang is writing letters for the mail, I cannot ask him or any one else to do more than direct me.

Remembered that this was the place where George Channing died & was buried. Mr. Cook thot was a grave stone to a Mr. Channing, but not sure. Drove to the cemetery. In outskirts of town, in good condition, handsome monuments, shaded with trees. In the multitude of tombs hardly expected to find what I sought, when saw a small foot-stone, with letters G.E.C. At the other end of the grave was the head stone, of marble, in good condition, on wh. was the perfectly legible inscription—

> George E. Channing.
> born in Boston,
> United States of America,
> August 10, 1815,
> Died in Penang,
> July 20, 1837,
> from a fever contracted
> on the West Coast of Sumatra.

This was, perhaps, the most interesting incident of my travels in the East,—the more so from its being unexpected. George Channing, & our youth, our College days, our separation to go East & West in 1834, & his coming down to the ship to meet me on my return from California,—these have been in my mind all day. I hope, too, it will gratify his family, & I plucked some grass & leaves wh. were growing on the grave, to take home to them,—& a piece of brick wh. had crumbled off the arch wh. lies over the grave. I am glad, too, to get rid of the associations I had had with Penang,—of deadly fevers, miasmas, Malays & low damp soil, & to see his grave amid so much beauty of nature & so much care of art.

No Am. missionaries here. Called on the rector of the Engl. Church. He lives at a beaut. spot, a mile out of town, high one story house, roomy, airy, blinds, punkahs, verandahs, trees, & the garden running to the bay, with view of the sky-piercing mountain tops of Queda, across the still blue bay. He has gone to town with his letters, but his wife receives me. His name is McKay, a Scotchman, was sev. years assistant to Dr. Harry Croswell of N. Haven, then in Scotland, then chaplain in India, now has this desirable post—wh. is, in fact, a Br. Govt. Chaplaincy.

The chief institutions here are the R.C. College for education of Chinese, & the Convent & School for girls. Called at the Convent. Lady Superior gave me a few minutes. Same order with that of Miss Spooner at Singapore,—"Saint Enfant Jesus". There are 8 sister, & 240 scholars, all girls, few of rich parents, who pay, but chiefly foundlings, orphans or abandoned by parents, & of all those mixtures of races wh. the Oriental life of Europeans results in. Buildings, & grounds large & handsome. Lady Superior a bright Fr. woman, & praises Penang, except for debility & lassitude from heat. "Have you no bungalow, on the hills?" "Oh no. Expense of two establishments too great".

Disappointed by not seeing the Chinese College. The Bishop was away, & the priest in charge evidently busy, & I did not wait for the B., as his return was uncertain. The priest told me they had about 120 Chinese, all studying for Holy Orders. Prefer this place for ed. of Chinese, as safe, & remote fr. unfav. influences.

Did I not eat, here, on my way back to the boat, thirsty & hot, the most delicious of pine-apples! It needed no chewing, but melted in the mouth,—completely ripened in the tropical sun.

On board again at 1 o'ck., as we sail at 2. Find the cabin table set out with the fruits of Penang,—Mangosteens, pine apples, mangoes, lychees, oranges, custard apples & bananas. Those called lychees are not the same, nor so good as those of China, —they have prickers on the rind, like a chestnut. Custard apple is pleasant, but insipid. The pine apple can be *imagined* by one who has eaten them at home. Mangosteen is a little pearl of a fruit.

Punctual in starting at 2 P.M. Take lesson fr. the engineer on the action of the screw, in going forward & backing. Backing, turns the vessel round rapidly. Capt. much prefers screw to paddles for working ship.

Leave the little, shady silent town, behind. But the well wooded hills, wooded to their tops, are still in sight, & across the bay, the mountains of Queda, the highest, a slanting wedge, piercing the deep, deep blue of the tropical sky! I cannot take my eyes off from it. What stupidity called it Elephant Mountain? It is like Chocorua Peak in N. H., seen fr. Conway, only a sharper wedge, & more slanting.

Tu. June 19.   High lands of Sumatra in sight. We are steering now due West, for Ceylon, & soon shall be in the Bay of Bengal.

Capt. Brown of P.&O.S.N. Co's ship Madras, pronounces, from the head of his table, that Poe is worth all the Lake Poets put together, ten times over!

We have one Musselman passenger, who has his separate cooking stove, poultry, cook & table, eats by himself, & his cook kills all his poultry. He is a dignified man with long gray silk dress & white turban.

Sat. June 23.   Very heavy seas the last 3 days, with squalls. Carried away foretopmast. Most passengers sea-sick. S.W. Monsoons, wh. are light in the China Sea, are very heavy in Bay of Bengal.

Mond. Afternoon, June 25, 1860.   The island of Ceylon,— that dream of the poet,—that isle of romance, of aromatic perfumes, in sight all day. Indeed it is very beautiful. There are high mountains in the interior, & undulations of hills & valleys all along the coast, & a dense vegitation of trees. The trees come to the water's edge, as in a lake, but the white surf that lines the shore, & the small rim of beach show it is no lock or mere, but the great ocean that surrounds it. There are few breaks to this close approach of trees & salt sea,—here & there, at long distances, a broken gravelly side of a hill. With our glasses we see a few houses wh. look large & well built, as

if of Europeans, standing among the trees. This is the S. Eastern coast we see, between Trincomalee & Galle. We shall be at
an anchor in Galle before dark.

Came to anchor at Point de Galle, Island of Ceylon, at about
4 o'ck. this afternoon. A water-spout follows us for a while,
outside, in the dim half rainy sky, but soon dissipates. This
place is at the S. end of Ceylon, an open harbor, with a surf
always rolling, & merely a little sheltered spot for boats to
land, under the lee of the fort. The fort is large, of dingy yellow, with high parapets & numerous bastions, over wh. sweeps
whatever of sea breese may be blowing, & within its limits are
the light house, the churches, & most of the houses of the foreign residents. The view in all directions is delightful,—truly &
thoroughly tropical. Nine trees in ten are cocoa nuts,—tall,
gaunt, perverse & whimsical in the course their trunks take,
with the large tuft at the top of long leaves or branches,
swaying about in fantastic directions in the wind, rustling like
so many silk banners, & the little knots of fruit, lying half hid
at the top of the trunk. There are also the other tropical trees,
plaintain, breadfruit, mango & soursop, but the cocoa nut is
the feature. The land is high enough, undulating, rising into
high hills, & then into mountains, in the interior, & everywhere wooded,—covered with verdure. Hardly anywhere on
the globe will you see so much verdure at one glance,—one
circumspection—as in Ceylon, & it is high, healthful & not
low, dank, pestilential luxuriance.

The native boats that come alongside, & the pilot boat that
boarded us, are canoes with outriggers, like those in wh. I
skirted Hawaii by moonlight. The native boatmen are naked,
except a cloth wrapped about the waist, & wear semi-circular
combs to keep back their hair, like our school girls.

Landed, & went to Lorette's hotel, where is large piassa,
opening on a large yard full of cocoa nut trees, swaying in the
cool afternoon breese. It is delightful. We are nearly under the
Equator & the direct ray of the sun is severely hot, but there is
a delicious airy balminess, with a gentle roll of surf, & the
rustling of the long palm leaves,—& I am on the Island of
Ceylon! It feels like it! All looks like it, as I lie for an hour or
more, languidly, at length on a couch, in the piassa.

Call on Mr. John Black, to whose wife I have a letter of

introduction with a parcel of Japanese charms from Greene of
Manilla,—the universal favorite Greene, to whom every one
seems to be under obligations. Black is a Scotchman, acting
Am. Consul, & a merchant, & most Americans of note visit
him *en route* to & fr. India & China. Mrs. B. is English, well
educated, agreeable & lively. Family of 3 small children,—
betw. 12 & 5 yrs. old,—all born in Ceylon.

Surprised to hear them talk of *telegrams*! "Is it possible?"
"Yes. We have a telegraph direct to Madras, where it goes to
Bombay & Calcutta". The communication to those places is
immediate, & to England only 6 or 7 days. The island is close
to the main. Plenty of Engl. & European news here, but scanty,
jumbled & hardly intelligible accounts of Am. politics,—the
two Nat. Conventions. The "Overland Mail" & "Home News"
gives as much space to America as to Hessi Casel, & what they
give is often unimportant & untrue & sometimes unintelligible. Tea at the Blacks. "Assam" tea, a product of Bengal, very
strong, goes twice as far as Chinese tea (*on dit*) & bears high
price in England. Like it very well. Conversation about Ceylon
& its people. B been here 20 & Mrs. B. 10 years. They say the
natives are gentle, amiable, reasonably intelligent, but inefficient. They have no power of organisation, & no civilisation or
social order except what the Europeans put over them. All
authority & organisation & learning is exotic,—British. The
natives are merely individual subjects, & take what is given
them. Offices are open to them, but few rise above the laborer,
servant, small trader or small yeoman. The Br. Govt. maintains
excellent native schools, in wh. Engl. & Ceylonese are taught,
& the people learn generally & readily up to the point of ord.
school edn. A few have risen to be magistrates, & one, who I
believe, however, is a half-caste, is a judge of the Supreme
Court. You may travel through the interior of Ceylon, in all directions, without weapons. The natives are as inoffensive as
women. (They call themselves & are called,—not Ceylonese,
but Cingalese, tho' they call the island Ceylon).

They learn to speak English easily & well. All the servants,
the laborers, the men one meets in the streets speak English,
much more correctly & intelligibly than the natives of most
countries under English control. The clerks at the hotels &
shops,—who are usually natives, speak it as a mother tongue.

The climate is uniform,—always hot, never cold enough for a change or recruiting of the system, yet agreeable & free from malaria; but the effect on the Northern constitution is debilitating. The women fade & the men run down. The mountain climate is bracing, & has not its superior in the world. There is no special rainy or dry season.

Fruits are oranges, limes, pómiloses, mangoes, breadfruit, plantain & banana, cocoa nut, pine apple, custard apple &c. &c. Pómilo has a rind like a lemon, is about twice the sise of the largest oranges, divided & formed inside precisely like the orange, but with tougher & stronger pulp, & the juice is in little red vessels. It must be torn open & not cut, & the pulp not swallowed. Taste is pleasant, slightly acid, like Deacon Brown's "Good family oranges"—& healthful. Natives live mostly on breadfruit & yams, with a little rice. The rice is more cultivated of late, since the volunteer E. I. coolie emigration of coffee planters. Coffee is a large article of growth. These coolies come overland, & on their own hook.

Invited to take an early drive into the country, before sun well up. Mr. & Mrs. B. cannot go, & their eldest child, Miss Lissy, a girl of about Rosamund's age, is to be my guide.

Tuesd. June 26.   Rise at day-break, bath, coffee, & at Black's door in good season, where the carriage & Miss Lissy are ready. We drive along the esplanade, through the gates (by the way, the usual tantanana of trumpets of a garrison town is going on here all the time) & into the country. Lissy knows everything, & talks like a book,—is very clever & observing & self-possessed. She could not do better at fifty. She tells me the names & history of everything; & I tell her she may travel the world over (she has never been out of Ceylon) & never see a richer landscape than she showed me from the mount we drove to, about 5 miles out of town. The Serpentine river winds for miles, the green hills & green vales are everywhere, the high mountains in the distance, the soft tropical clouds, that always seem to be ready to drop water, floating over all, & the waving palms & rich scents & perfumes! But the citronella is a little too strong in its perfume. It almost stifles one to ride past it, after it is bruised & crushed to be made into oil. At the Mount is a house, occupied only by servants, who get us fresh cocoa nuts, to drink the milk, & mangoes. Lissy tells me they never drink the cocoa nut milk after the sun is well up, of choice, as it is then a little rank.

I am struck with the excellence of the roads. They are as good as in the suburbs of Boston or London. Lissy says they were made under direction of an engineer, & are kept in good repair by the Govt., & that the road to Columbo is the same, all the way,—some 60 miles,—& that Sir Henry Ward, the Governor, is to be transferred to Madras, & that Sir Ch. Trevelyan is recalled, & much other news & information for a girl of ten,—& that the natives' jewelry wh. they try to sell me at every stop is "glass & brass".

The native life here seems to me to be more truly that of the tropical aborigines, than I have yet seen anywhere, as I see the simple Ceylonese in their open-thatched huts, under the groves of cocoa-nut trees, in their scanty clothing, with their simple inoffensive, gentle manners & expression of countenance.

The girls tie their hair in behind, but the men wear it short, kept back by combs. The usual dress is white, tho' there are some gay colors,—a dangling robe, sometimes drawn over the shoulders, but oftener merely tied about the waist, the women always (I speak only, of course, of the neighborhood of the Engl. settlement) with a decent jacket or short tunic of white.

We see several trees about the sise & shape of an American walnut tree, covered all over with the most brilliant scarlet flowers, as thick as leaves. Indeed, they obscure & eclipse the leaves, & you see only their flaming mass. Unfortunately my Lissy-peadia balked only at that,—she could not recall the name, nor could her mother,—tho' they know it. The sensitive plant grows along the road side as common as grass. A touch shuts it up for the day.

Along these excellent roads, the Govt. has considerably built, at intervals, "Rest Houses", decent covered buildings, with seats. These the Chinese have had fr. time immemorial.

Parrots & paroquets abound in Ceylon, & so do pearls & many kinds of precious stones.

Returned to Black's to breakfast, at 9 o'ck. Call on a Mr. Toppan, agt. for Mr. Tudor's ice business, & get some odd numbers of the D. Advertiser. Visited two Govt. schools. The buildings are large & airy, & the boys are not compelled to sit confined to benches, as in China & Japan, but, with books in hand, walk up & down the piassas studying aloud. The boys look, ordinarily, intelligent, but effeminate. They are to be the gentle inefficient men their ancestors have been. The teachers were all natives, full blood or half-caste, speaking Engl. perfectly well. In these schools the boys were decently dressed from the shoulders.

A tolerable library of periodicals & books, to wh. I was admitted by Mr. Black, maintained by subscribers.

Sailed at 5 P.M., for Bombay, leaving all our passengers behind, to take the expected boat fr. Calcutta to Aden. We have the boat almost to ourselves, the officers & the Musselman & myself, with Capt. King & the officers of the P.&O. steamer Oriental, condemned.

At Galle, saw the wreck of the Malabar. Ld. Elgin is said to have shown great self possession & coolness in the danger, when many were rushing from the ship.

Long lingering last looks at this beautiful island, as it recedes, in the fading sun of the late afternoon, its deep green hills & vales growing dim, & the white surf that rolls all around its shores less & less audible. Good Night!

Rather a rough & disagreeable passage of six days, from Galle to Bombay, rolling sea, rain & head winds all the way. The last day, Sunday, I was thrown violently, by the pitching of the vessel, & over a wet deck, against a stancheon, receiving a very heavy blow on the ribs that knocked me down & took the breath from my body, leaving it doubtful for some seconds whether I ever breathed again. I fainted dead away for a minute or two, & could not breathe freely for a long time. I struck the right side. Nearly at the same time the Second Steward was thrown down & dislocated his shoulder bone.

It is interesting, Sundays, to see the crew drawn up, for quarters—the Engl. stewards & waiters, in their neat white trowsers & blue jackets, the Engl. seamen, who are all petty officers, in neat white trowsers & white shirts with blue collars, & then the Abysiannian negroes, & the Lascars,—Bengales, Hindoos & of all classes, with robes & turbans, & to hear them answer to their names—the British John Brown, Tom

Adams, William Jones, & the Oriental Ismad Mahommed, Ali Abdullah, Mahommed Ali, Daused Sulimanji, Hoosenboy Hoosenji, &c.

Of a rainy night, when the decks are wet & dreary, & the passengers have left the cabin for their berths, how cheerful it looks to go into the engine room, & see the engine working away briskly, the fires gleaming & the oil lamps burning bright. It reminds one of boyhood, when you come home & find the parlor deserted & cold, & take refuge in the kitchen, where there is a cheerful fire, & the preparations for tea, & the smell of newly ironed clothes, & the sight of busy people.

Monday. July 2, 1860.   Early to-day we make Bombay, but I see nothing of the passage, being laid up in my state-room by my hurt of yesterday. I only hear the jabber of strange voices alongside, & see the red masts of the pilot's boat through my port.

When I am up, it is so rainy & cloudy that I see but little. We are at anchor opposite the company's dock, about 3 miles beyond the city, & the decks are half full of P.&O. officers & clerks,—for Bombay is the seat of the P.&O. power.

The surgeon is very kind, & sees me safe ashore, & goes with me to my hotel, the Adelphi, kept by a Parsee, named Palanjee. I have a nice room in a bungalow, in the yard, opening out towards the sea. Too stiff & painful from my injury to enjoy much. But I am in Br. India, & the servants call me *Sahib*, & say "Salaam" & touch their turbans. My room is long & bare, but with good ventilation, & I have a servant to stay in the room all the time, or about the door. This is the Indian custom.

One of the firm of Dossabhoy Merwanjee & Co., a Parsee house, calls on me, with offers of civilities, in conseq. of letters from Anderson in Singapore. He sits an hour or so, in his cherry colored silk trowsers, white robe & Parsee hat, & declines an invitation to dine, alleging that Parsees never dine with strangers, as cannot eat our meats, beef & pork. Letter fr. Mr. Stearns, an Am. merchant, inviting me to his house.

It rains all the time, being the S.W. Monsoon, wh. is the rainy season, & is rather dreary. Proof that my health must be good, that I can be so cheerful in solitude & dull weather, confined to my room by a hurt.

Tuesd. July 3. In my room all day, finishing "Friends in Council", & reading the Am. newspapers my friends the Parsees have sent me. My heart sinks at the nomination of "Abe" Lincoln & Hannibal Hamlin, instead of Seward.

At 4 o'ck., Mr. Stearns comes for me, in carriage. He turns out to be son of Prest. Stearns of Amherst College, & his wife is a niece of Kittredge of Roxbury. Very kind of him. Request him to call in a good surgeon, & sends for Dr. Meade, Surgeon of the Gen. Hosp. to meet me at his house. Ride in the rain through Bombay. See but little. Much is European, or European modified by tropical necessities, & some is native. Here are tanks, where the water is collected in the rainy season, & women carrying pitchers on their heads, & oxen drawing water fr. the tanks. What strikes me most is the free, graceful, queenly carriage of the women,—even the poor women that carry water on their heads. It is a delight to see them move. A white robe drawn over the shoulder hangs gracefully about them, allowing perfect freedom of motion, & showing the shape & movements, while they step off with a proud, dainty step, each a duchess,—but no duchess that I ever saw walked so well. Sutherland is a waddle to them.

This place has the greatest conglomeration of races, sects & castes, of perhaps any place in the world,—everything that Africa, Europe & Asia, & all their intermixtures, can produce.

Stearns has a pretty bungalow on Malabar Hill, some 2 or 3 miles fr. the fort. Here most Europeans live. There is a view of the sea, wh. opens at the foot of the hill, & we can both see & hear the breakers. The house is one story, with piassas all round, & long projecting thatched roof, like all bungalows, & is airy & shady, with large, high rooms. I have three rooms *en suite*, a sleeping, sitting & bathing room assigned me, & a native servant. This is very agreeable, & a most pleasant change fr. my hotel. Mrs. Stearns is a pleasing woman, in appearance & manners, with good sense, apparently. They are young, married at home last year, & have their first child, only 6 weeks old,—a boy.

Accident no. 3! Dr. Meade comes & makes a thorough examination, & discovers that I have broken a rib. It is a small rib, & a simple transverse fracture, with no unpleasant attendant circumstances. The break is just over the liver, on the right side, & if I had not been strong in the chest might have given me trouble through the liver, sickness, fever, cough &c. But I am very well, good appetite, no fever & he says I have nothing to fear. Indeed, I can go on in the "Madras" next Sat., if I must, but he rather recommends my staying over one steamer, until I can move about freely, without bandage. Now, he has girded me up as they do a poor saddle horse. But I am allowed to walk about the house & yard, sit at table &c. I take no medicine & not diet.

A good Providence has decreed me an accident, but mercifully made it light, & all its circumstances as favorable as possible, a pleasant home & kind friends, a good surgeon, & above all the good health that gives good spirits & sleep.

In this connexion, Friends in Council quotes fr. Nat. Hist. of Enthousiasm,—to the effect that "the world of nature affords no instances of complicated & exact contrivances comparable to that wh. so arranges the vast chaos of contingencies as to produce, with unerring precision, a special order of events as adapted to the character of every individual of the human family. Amid the whirl of myriads of fortuities, the means are selected & combined for constructing as many independent machineries of moral discipline as there are moral agents in the world; & each apparatus is at once complete in itself, & complete as part of a universal movement".

July 4, 1860 Wed.   Early this morning, my Parsee friend, Dossabhoy Merwanjee, sends me, after the pretty Eastern fashion, a basket of fruit & flowers, in commemoration of our American holiday, with an invitation to dine to meet some Am. residents. The latter I must decline, with thanks for the former. The dinner is to be at the house of Bomanjee Tramjee Camajee! This afternoon, Mr. —— calls, & brings his Hindoo friend, Dr. Bhow Dajee, a scholar & physician, who offers to be my cicerone as soon as I get out. There they sit talking with me, the best of friends, but they cannot eat together! They would loose caste forever. Ask Dr. Bhow Dajee if he was going to Europe. He said it was difficult for a Hindoo to travel out of India, for if he ate with one not a Hindoo, even at a public table, under any circumstances, even of necessity, he was no longer a Hindoo, & could have no dealings with his race & family as an equal ever after. He kindly brought me some photographs of scenes & persons in India, to examine. He inquired about Prof. Dana, the great chemist & geologist, & said his book was thought here to be the best treatise on chemistry extant. How glad I am these people keep to their costumes,—their robes & turbans, while they speak Engl. & read our books! A barber shaves me every morning, dressed in a maroon turban & white robe, & my servant wears a red turban.

All parties, races & persons in India agree in giving Sir Ch. Trevelyan the credit of being the ablest civil ruler India has seen in this generation, however much they differ about his course in publishing his minutes. For insight into the native character, energy & administrative genius, & influence over the natives, he has had no equal.

July 5. Dr. Meade says I am doing very well. Think of that stupid, negligent surgeon of the Madras, having me two days in charge, & not discovering that I had a broken rib, but setting a man to rub me,—to *knead* me, for a bruise! I wonder the fellow did not break it in, or effect a displacement, at least,—right over the liver, too! Dr. Meade is an attentive careful man, & says I have been fortunate both in the nature of the orig. injury, & in escaping the effects of bad treatment. The fact is that throughout the East, I have experienced the benefits of two good habits, *first*, that I have not, in my youth, "'plied hot & rebellious liquors to my blood"—& second, that I have the habit, of years, of drinking nothing, not even water, between meals. In the steamers & hotels, & private houses, when almost every one is contriving cooling drinks, & some take soda bottles to bed with them, I drink nothing & have no thirst. And I have the inestimable advantage of a body untouched by anything injurious, blood & marrow as pure as in boyhood.

Fr. July 6. As it is now the 5th day since my accident, & I am in excellent health, & sleep soundly all night, I may congratulate myself; &, now, I have no pain in my side. Dr. M. thinks I had better not go on in the boat tomorrow, as the weather is rough in this monsoon, & to be obliged to keep still & watch ev. step & roll is not agreeable. I agree to this, fully. Beside, it would be absurd to leave here without seeing anything of Br. India except from this bungalow. This next boat is the 23d July. This loses me two weeks, but patience, amid so many blessings, is not great virtue.

Sunday. July 15. I have now been in the house for 14 days;—well all the time, & in good spirits, but advised to be careful about moving suddenly, lest rib be displaced. To-day, Dr. Meade says rib has closed well, & may be risked. Ride to Church this P.M. with Mr. & Mrs. Stearns, & get my (really) first view & notion of Bombay. It is a picturesque & interesting spectacle—that of the E. Indian races, in their marked costumes—Hindoos, Musselmans & Parsees, & here & there an Arab or Persian or negro, each cognisable by his dress,—all, or nearly all with turbans,—but differing in form & color, as much as a 'prentice cap differs from a grenadier's hat. Then, too, of the Hindoos, the divisions of race & region, the Mahrattas, the Gussarattas, the occasional mountaineer from the Scinda & Rohilla country,—& then the marks of caste in the forehead, the caballistic dots & streaks of white or red or yellow; for wh. they will give up their lives—at any time,—that caste wh. will not let a Brahmin beggar take a cup of water from a king of the second caste,—wh. keeps ev. man & woman in India in relations with 9 in every 10, not indeed of hostility, but of separation & abomination.

It is the middle of the"Rains",—the S.W. Monsoon, & everything is green, & rich, & dank & mouldy. The mould affects all the houses, making them look as dull & dingy as St. Paul's. Our woolen clothes, books, shoes, gloves—all are mouldy, & servants are employed in wiping & drying, day after day. This is not the most unhealthy season, tho' it is so damp & warm. There is but little cholera, & not a great deal of dysentery. My phys is down with dysentery & fever, & about half the Europeans you hear of are sick, in one way or another, —yet there is no epidemic.

The tanks are pretty places. They are of all sises,—some as

large as the Brooklyn Reservoir, others as the Frog Pond, & so
down to the sise of dry docks & small basins. They are little
lakes or reservoirs, open, edged with stone or grass, & in them
the water is collected during the rains, for all the year. They are
built by benevolent persons, & usually bear their names. They
are free to all, to "come & draw freely, without money or
price". Now, I see the force of the Scripture figure,—in these
dry hot lands. And there are the poor, drawing water freely! &
by the banks they wash. And how graceful are these water
bearers,—the women, I mean! Here are a thousand swarthy
Dianas, Hebes & Charites. I cannot keep my eyes from
them—there is such grace, freedom & ease in their movements & attitudes. No credit to the Greek sculptors, for their
female figures, if they had such before them. These women
wear a short, low-necked, short sleeved waistcoat or boddice,
just eno' to cover the chest, & then fold about them a piece of
cloth, usually of a gay color, wh. falls to the figure, & is gathered up at the knee or thigh, like the pictures of Diana. When
they stand to rest or talk, they fall into the attitudes of the an-
tique Greek statues.

The Church we go to is called the Byculla,—fr. the quarter
of the town in wh. it stands,—an Engl. Ch. It is curious to see
it fitted with punkahs, 6 on each side & one over the Chancel,
& an Engl. Congr. inside, & the poor heathen, to whom the
Gospel is sent, standing outside pulling the punkahs. As it is
dark before the service ends, each pew has a light, at the corner, a candle in a glass globe, & all are lighted,—but the
waving punkahs keep us cool. Then, almost ev. one rides to
church, & the garra-wallahs & drivers, hang round outside. I
fear the congr. of heathen servants outside is greater than that
of Europeans inside.

On our way, passed a group of Bedouin Arabs. The heathen
might as well be outside. The stupid Chaplain had such a thick,
lolloping tongue & bad elocution, that I could not tell what
he was reading about, in the lessons, & the sermon, scarcely
more articulate, had nothing to do with the text, & the parts
of the sermon no connexion with each other. The Stearnses
say the Engl. chaplains & preachers here are intolerably dull.

While I was laid up, my friends Dr. Bhawoo Dajee, the learned
Hindo, & Dhunjeebhoy Merwanjee, the Parsee merchant,

called & offered services, brot books &c. I delivered no Engl.
letters & made no calls,—as I had little time, & preferred to
give what I had to natives.

Mond. July 16th.   Rode to town, & called on Merwanjee &
Co. & Dr. Bhawoo Dajee. The streets in the "Fort", where all
the business is done, & where most of the natives live, are very
narrow, with high walls, 5 & 6 stories high, & crowded with
passers, & hot & close. How can these people live there, day &
night, for years! No wonder they are so yellow & bloodless.
Passed the Basaar at wh. the stock brokers congregate, all in
white robes, & white or red turbans.

Bombay is built on an island, or series of islands, connected
by causeways. The harbor lies betw. these & the Main. On the
rear, & open to the sea, is Malabar Hill, where the bungalows
are, in wh. the Europeans live who can afford it. The Parsees
own the hill, or rather hire of the Govt., & no bungalows can
be got but fr. them, & rents are very high. The next best section is Byculla, but it is low, & the next is Colába. In the centre is the Fort & esplanade. The Fort has walls & gates & a
ditch, & is guarded; but within its straightened limits is all the
business of Bombay, wh. is now or soon is to be, the largest in
India.

At Bhawoo Dajee's, introduced to sev. venerable old Brahmins, & at Merwanjee's to some Persians, with long beards &
long white robes.

Dined with us to-day Rev. Mr. Harding, Miss. of Am. Board,
& his wife, & Rev. Mr. Bowen. H. is rather a flat,—no match
for a Hindoo. Mr. Bowen is a character. Was a rich, fashionable
New Yorker, of liberal education, European travel &c., love
affair, death, change of life, Missionary, renounces all "Boards"
& denominations, supports himself, lives among the natives,
in their closest streets & among their meanest houses. Yet,
when he does go out among the Europeans, he is prised above
all men for his convers. powers & manners.

Bowen tells me there are as many as 100 castes now, & that
they have little power in regulating the callings & occupations,
little being left but their exclusiveness, wh. continues unabated.

Tuesd. July 17th.   Call on Bhawoo Dajee, by appointment.
Shows me his library & cabinet &c. he took the prises at

Elphinstone College, & studied 6 years at the Grant Med. College, in all branches of Nat. science, & was distinguished. He has large practice & consid. influence, both with natives & Europeans. Shows me a Ms. on palm leaves, 500 years old, & the title deeds to an estate engraved on plates of copper, bound together by chain & key.

B.D. took me to Sir Jamsetjee's Hospital. This was founded by Sir Jamsetjee Jijibhai, the Parsee merchant. He gave a lac of rupees (100,000) & the Govt. as much more. Much has been added since & its entire cost, to this time, has been about 700,000 rupees. Large stone building, long & low, in large yard, & well ventilated. Wards for leprosy & small pox. Prevalent diseases (chronic) are elephantiasis, opthalmia, leprosy & dysentery, & (acute) small pox & cholera. Next, went to the Grant Med. College, an admirable institution, where all the nat. sciences are taught, with good apparatus, museum of comp. anat., cabinets of minerals &c. Rather an imposing building. Then, saw outsides of the Elphinstone College & the Byculla School, & Sir Jamsetjee's Charity School. (Sir J. was made a baronet, in 1858, & died soon after). His son, Sir Custeebjee, is now in Engl. Sir J. is said to have given away 100,000 £ sterling.

To the Bot. Garden. Saw there a strychnine tree, every leaf a deadly poison, sev. banyan trees, & the cinnamon, frankinsence, tamarind, nutmeg & teak. The common laboring coolie, half naked (& more) who followed us to climb the trees & cut flowers, knew the names of all the rare trees & shrubs.

On our way, stopped at the cottage of a laboring Parsee, to taste the toddy, made from the wild date tree. A naked coolie went up the tree, like a monkey, with a hoop of pliable bamboo round his waist & round the tree, to keep him to it, & then bore off by his feet—hatchet & pitcher in hand,—tapped the tree & brot down the pitcher full of juice. When allowed to ferment, it becomes intoxicating, & is the *arrak*. But when fresh, it is pleasant & healthful, slightly acid.

B.D. takes me to the house of a wealthy Hindoo, perhaps the wealthiest in Bombay. His son is in, & does the honors, —a most sensual & gorged looking chap, of about five & twenty, turning into an animal, fast, as in the fable. His house is very large, halls & rooms large & high, & a great deal of the black-wood furniture, for wh. Bombay is celebrated. But this is a waste of taste or experience, for cheap & commonplace Europ. prints, plaster casts & furniture are mixed with it. Gardens large, level, exquisitely neat & carefully attended. Low, open-work walls of porcelain, on each side of the walks. Servants in troops, 4 or 5 dusting one room. Sepoys at the door. Sepoys in mil. dress are the Suiss, the door keepers, of the great houses in India.

In a carriage saw a man having a full sised crown on his head, with high points, gold or gilded. Bhawoo Dajee tells me he is one of the lineal descendants of Mahommed, who are known by that crown, everywhere, & are treated with honor or worship—descendants of his daughter. His sons died without children. It is worth coming to Bombay, to see a lineal descendant of Mahommed!

Bhawoo Dajee rejects Hindooism, & abhors the system of castes, & receives all the moral teachings of X'tianity, but has doubts abt. the X'n Revelation. In this state, he conforms outwardly to Hindooism, wears the caste mark on his forehead &c., but is doing all he can indirectly by aiding the dissemn. of knowledge & education among Hindoos & intercourse with Europeans, to break in on the system.

Wed. July 18. Called, by appointement, on Merwanjee & Co., who have promised to show me the ladies of their households, in full dress. In the third story of their house, is a large drawing room, with richly carved blackwood furniture. Here the ladies & children were seated. The women were most richly dressed. Short low tunics, & long robes, of bright colors, & jeweled rings in the ears, at top & bottom, in one nostril, on neck & wrists & fingers & ankles & toes, barefooted, of course, except that they have ornamented slippers, into wh. they sometimes thrust their feet. Hair black, eyes black or dark, complexions—the best a fair olive, but ordinarily yellow, noses aquiline & sharp, & a kind of Jewess look,—usually very thin,—tho' I have seen fat Parsee women. None of them spoke Engl., & I believe none of them can read or write. A Parsee has but one wife, but divorce is allowed in case of having no child. The Parsees are the Jews of India, excluded fr. other occupations, have taken to trade & become very rich. They live by themselves, never eat or marry with others. No Parsee woman in Bombay ever became a public woman. Their rigid system prevents it. When I rose to leave, they gave me a bouquet & showered me with rosewater, from a silver censer, & brot me paun soparees on a waiter,—these are little mixtures of spicery rolled up in a betel leaf, wh. the natives are fond of chewing. They are agreeable. I have become fond of them. Betel nut is an ingredient & alspice, cloves &c.

Nearly all the men of this large family were present. The family name is Lowjee, but that is not in use ordinarily. They use two names, as Dossabhoy Merwanjee, Dhunjeebhoy Merwanjee, Cursetjee Dhurjeebohy &c.

This ev. at abt. 8 o'ck., set off, with Mr. Stearns, for Poonah, in the Deccan, the ancient capital of the Mahratta Empire, the headquarters of the Brahmin power in S. India. The great enterprise of the rail road has brot Poonah within attainable distance, & only the Ghats Mts. are to be crossed on foot. Went up by night, because Mr. S. cd. only give two whole days.

Rail road carriages large & commodious & as it was dark & raining, had only to lie down on the benches & sleep. At stopping places, heard jackals, close to the cars, & occasional other distant cries, wh. *may* have been tigers.

About midnight, reached Kampoolie, where the road stops, at the foot of the Ghats, & we take palkees (palanquins), to ascend the Ghats by torch light. It is dark & rainy, & we see nothing but high hills ag. the sky, & the flash of torches, along the steep winding ascent. I get a palkee, a kind of palanquin, in wh. one lies nearly at length,—not high eno' for sitting up, with sliding doors on each side, borne on men's shoulders, 2 before & 2 behind. I have seen no sedans in India, & saw no palanquins in China. My palanquin had 10 men, & I suppose each had the same, 4 bearers, 4 reliefs, & 2 torch bearers. The carriage of all the passengers & freight up the Ghats, by night, in this style, makes an array—but the freight, I believe, is carried in gharreys, or bullock carts.

I dosed away most of my time, & about 3 o'ck. in the morning we reached Khandála, whence the rail road begins again, & half sleeping, half awake, were precipitated along to Poonah, wh. we reached just at dawn. I believe the distance is 130 miles fr. Bombay.

Look out of our carriage just eno' to see that Poonah is on a wide spread of high table land, with mountains in the distance, & are driven to a hotel, called the Queen's, owned by Parsees, kept by a Hindoo, where we have a bed-room & washing room a piece, & after washing & a cup of tea, & ordering breakfast at 9 o'ck., Stearns & I walk out to get our first fair view of Poonah.

Thursday. July 19th.   The ancient city of Poonah is about a mile below us, the Br. garrison about 2 m. off, on the high plain. All the space abt. the garrison & betw. that & the city is called the Camp. We walked thro' the Camp Basaar, wh. is a town of natives, laid out by the Br. in reg. streets & built mostly of native houses. Here are the Fish Basaar, the Meat Basaar, the Fruit Basaar, & the Vegit. Basaar, & the usual varieties of mango, pineapple, pómelo, pomegranite, banana, custard apple &c. &c., & the usual sprinkling of Parsees & Mussulmans among the Hindoos. Out of the basaars, the streets are wide & straight, & lined with bungalows of Europeans, each having the occupant's name on a sign at the gate—"Capt. Barker, 19th N.I.", "Lt. Jones, 4 E. Cavalry" &c. These bungalows are pretty, with grass & trees. The roads are hard & well kept, & the horses & carriages in good Europ. style.

All the ground betw. the city & garrison, or nearly all, is occupied by Europeans. Soldiers abound. Red coats & topees (pith hats) & pugrees & Sepoys in the half Europ. uniform.

After breakfast, called on Rev. Mr. Gell, Army Chaplain, to whom Mr. Bowen gave me a letter, & Stearns called on a Mr. Mitchell, a Presb. Miss., whom he knew. No tropical vegitation visible on the high plain of Poona,—that is, no palms, cocoas, or palms of any kind. It might be England, or N. England. Yet many of the trees are tropical & aromatic, like the mango, nutmeg &c., but do not look peculiar to the tropics.

It rains ev. hour or two. Gells have a pretty house. Mrs. G. is young & pretty, & Mr. G. has the University Gentleman look. But they are going out on a visit to sick friends, & I beg not to detain them. While they are gone, Stearns comes in with an invitation fr. Mr. Mitchell to go in his carriage to see the famous old Hindoo temples on Parvutti Hill. Leave note for the Gells, & go to Mitchell's. M. & wife, & a Rev. Robertson & wife, all invalids, & all drinking ale or wine, at tiffin, under advice of physicians. Mrs. R. too ill to come to table. The heats of May & June, wh. are terrible on this plain, have done them all up. Both R. & M. are scholars, & talk of Greek & Modern Greek &c.

After tiffin, ride to Parvutti Hill. Get out at foot, & walk up. Broad stone steps all the way up, 20 f. wide or more. Temples & fort in one. Well fortified, for old times. Temples in the Saracenic style, with numerous little domes & minarets, richly colored. Not permitted to enter—profanation. Several Brahmins to wh. Mitchell talks freely ag. their idols. They say they do not worship the idol, but only reverence the representation of a Divine Power or agency. They are all beggars & stipendiaries, & the British Government pays an annual sum for the maintenance of this Heathen Temple! The defence is that they succeed to the custom of the Hindoo Govt. they subverted, & policy requires its support. The temple is decaying & the Brahmins diminished in number, & but for the Govt. support, I think the whole wd. fall to the ground.

(Parvutti is a daughter of Vishnu.) From the battlements of the temple, fine view of the great plain & distant empire. There lies the ancient city of Poona, the capital of the Mahratta Empire. Hyder Ali took it once, Wellington was here, but not as conqueror, I believe, & there, only 3 or 4 miles fr. the city, just below where the two rivers join, is Kirkee, where the battle was fought, in 1817, that ended the power of the Peshwar, & placed Poona in the hands of the English. Mountstuart Elphinstone was residing near there, the "Resident" at the court of Poona, & the Peshwar went out to take him prisoner by subtlety, but E. got notice, swam the river on his horse, reached the Engl. camp at Kirkee, & the Br. sallied out, & the battle ended the Mahratta Empire.

Returned slowly through the ancient city. The great palace is converted into a jail & hospital. Several of the old palaces frown upon the streets, looking like store houses, four storied, mouldy stone buildings, in plain style. The streets are narrow, & so crowded, so dense with people, who all look so hot, & sweaty & bilious, as if they never breathed fresh air. Here, too, are some very pretty tanks, & women bearing water on their heads, & bullock with leathern panniers filled with water,

& monetary looking Parsees, with long receeding hats, & Hindoos with the patch of "caste" on the forehead, & the grave Mussulman, & turbans of red & yellow & white & green, & dangling robes of all colors, & the common people naked to a mere hand breadth,—making the greater number of all you meet. Naked men lie on the floor & ag. the sides of houses, & all wear as little as possible, & of a form to drop off as easily as possible. Here, too, the common women are bangled & spangled & ringed like the richest Hindoo matron, the only difference being that the one wear real gold & jewels, & the other glass & brass; but, at a distance, the common woman is the counterpart, with her nose rings, & ear rings, necklaces & bracelets, finger rings, anklets & rings on her toes. How proudly & daintily she steps off, barefooted, bare headed & bare armed, with the water vessel on her head, & her glitter & jangle of glass & brass!

Spent the night quietly at the inn, where were a party of three commonplace Englishmen, who had been drunk all day, & were sick, & one thought he had cholera, & made a sad scene of it. The next day they looked wretched eno'. The wonder is that they stand these excesses in such a climate as long as they do.

Friday. July 20th.   Took rail-road at 9.45 A.M. for Bombay. Stopped at Kirkee, wh. is a cavalry station, & where there are red coats & spurs & pugrees on the platform; & then at Campowlee, where we took palkees (palenquins) to descend the Ghats.

This descent, wh. occupies about 2½ hours, is glorious! The road, cut by the native princes, centuries ago, to connect the upper Deccan with the sea coast, winds down the mountains, as steep as men or bullocks can safely walk, while above, below & around are the high tops, the deep ravines & gorges, & the opening, far stretching plains; & now, in the midsts of the rains, the mountain sides are alive with cascades. Water falls fr. all points, & in all forms & quantities. The bearers sing all the way, a rude line with a short chorus of 2 or 3 words.

Khandala. Tiffin at the "Victoria Hotel", a hut of 2 rooms & no furniture but chairs & plain tables. Still, got a decent lunch, for the natives can cook,—all people can cook but the Yankee

& Englishman. Reached Bombay at dark, where Stearns' faithful garra wallahs & coach were waiting for us.

It rained nearly all the way after we left the Ghats. The laborers in the field wear a curious rain coat, a mat with a top like a hood, partly surrounding them. They put it on & stand with the back to the rain, as if they were looking out of a mat cabin that had no door. Most of the laborers in the fields are men. The women, if they work at all, do light work. In the heavy rain, & up to their ankles in mud & water, the natives are ploughing & weeding. The plough is the scratch plough, wh. goes lightly over, & the animals are the Indian bullock, wh. has a high hump ag. wh. the yoke rests, or the water buffalo, an animal as common here as in China, & always rolling in the water or sand when it can.

(On our way down, stopped at Tannah, wh. was a Portuguese fort & settlement. Some Portuguese are there still). (At Poonah, saw great abnormal, towering awkward camels, with riders, passing through the streets).

Saturday. July 21. An Anglo Indian household has a great many servants. The native servants do but one thing each. One sweeps, one cleans furniture, one takes care of the lamps, another waits on table, & in the stables no man takes care of more than one horse. Their pay is very small & they find themselves —food, lodging & clothing. The rules of their religions & the rules of caste keep them from the food of Europeans & often fr. the tables of each other. They sleep on mats under the verandahs, or, if they have families, in huts of their own in the compound (yard). Some have as little as $2 a month, feeding themselves. Mr. Stearns has a reasonable establishment for a successful young merchant with only a wife & child; yet he has, in all, 17 servants. The butler is the chief officer of every household, a kind of steward & housekeeper. He presides over the servants, & all complaints on discipline are thro' him. Mr. S.'s butler has $7 a month. The other servants are bobajee (cook), cook's coolie, 2 table boys, musaul (lamps), hamaul (furniture cleaner), 3 gorawallahs (grooms), shobee (laundry man), parree wallah (water carrier), dirsee (tailor & seamstress), sweeper, gardener, watchman, & coolie. These are men. Then there is the ayah (child's nurse), Mrs. S. is thot very self denying not to have an amah, or waiting woman for herself, & when the pair of horses is out in the carriage, one of the gora wallahs is coachman, wh. is an economy. Each gora wallah sticks to his horse, & either drives him or sits behind or runs by his side. No coach goes without at least one footman, & often two. They run before, when coming to a corner, to warn & give notice, & stand by the horse's head when the coach stops.

Mr. Stearns' broker is a liberal Hindoo, a disbeliever in Hindooism, & inclined to X'tianity, a very clever young man named Kársandros Madhavadras. Knowing that I wished to see Hindoo ladies, he prevailed on a friend to have his wife dressed in her full dress, & sent his own wife & sister to join them, at a certain hour, when I was to be introduced, secretly, for, if known, they would be considered as polluted. We drove to the house, & after a while I was presented to the ladies. They were richly decked. Rings in ears & noses, on fingers & toes, & necklaces, bracelets & anklets. Their dress was a small tunic just eno' to cover the breast, feet, arms & neck bare, & a mantle of silk or cotton wrapped about the figure, coming down to the knee & looped up. It is very graceful, & very cool. They are of sallow complexions, & without the sharp features of the Parsee women. They sat on sofas, & gathered their feet up, or one foot, & bent the knee, as small children would do. They spoke no English. Karsandros' wife was fat,—the others lean & sickly.

Thence to Bhawoo Dajee's. My good friend has taken great pains to entertain me. Several Hindoo friends of rank come in & are presented. The first entertainment is a juggler. He sits on the floor of the verandah, & we sit in chairs directly before him, & he has no table or accomplice, or long sleeves, or any means of concealment, except a small coarse bag wh. lay by him. He is a Mahommedan & has grave & decorious manners, salaaming to us before & after each trick. He produced a small mango tree with flowers from nothing, & brought sev. cooing doves from nowhere, & burned out the insides of his mouth, & performed inexplicable tricks with cups & balls. B.D. apologised for not getting a snake-charmer. They are not here in "the rains". Next came a man with two bears, who performed creditable tricks, salaamed, wrestled, were thrown &c. Then came a man with monkeys & goats, who acted little farces, taking parts of soldiers, old women &c., he singing all the time, & shaking a little drum wh. was thus beaten by two balls on the ends of strings.

Now we adjourned to the parlor, & minstrels came. One played an instrument like a guitar with a bow. The other played a lute & sang. The songs were in Hindostanee, Mahratta, Gussaratta & Persian. The singer is said to be the best in Bombay. I liked the Persian songs best. They had more air & the words were more articulate. They were like Spanish airs. Next a boy of 14 or 15 sang, the most celebrated boy singer in Bombay. B.D. says the Hindoos have little notion of harmony, & make no direct attempts at it; but he thinks the Hindoo music fully equal to the European in melody. In his *omnifacent* way, he is arranging some Hindoo airs with the harmonies.

The next & last entertainment was a mimic. He gave imitations of Brahmin pundits disputing on a nice point of metaphysics, of Parsees chanting their prayers, & of a Brahmin reading passages of Sanscrit & expounding them. The latter caused great merriment among our grave friends, for B.D. says the Sanscrit was mere sound & the interpretation mere jumbles of great words. Then he imitated Arabs singing, in deep, hoarse voices, ending almost in a bray, & the sharp, high-voiced people of the Carnatic. I called for an imitation of English. They declined, but when I insisted, he gave one, but seemed embarrassed & drew it mildly. But I could get their notion of us. He rubbed his chin, rubbed his knees, worked his face, turned his head on one side & the other, talked in a thick voice, often too low to be heard, & as it were by jerks, with awkward attitudes & motions. It is evident that the native notion of the Englishman is not of a lion or tiger, but of a wild boar.

After this very agreeable entertainment, we drove out. Drove to a beautif. Mahomn. mosque, very large, of white stone, with numerous domes. Then to the chief Parsee Fire Temple. This is a clean, quiet house, in a clean quiet yard, with a verandah at each end, & rooms with books & pictures, & a few white robed Parsees lounging there to read or pray. In the centre, where I cannot enter, is a room with a kind of altar on wh. burns the perpetual fire. It is a clear hot afternoon, & from the walk we see the broad Back Bay, & the Parsees making their evening worship to the sea. Bhawoo Dajee gives me his expln. of what we call worship of sun & sea. He says the Oriental habit is reverential & worshipful. They bow down before parents, elders & benefactors & they honor by outward reverence all great manifestations of goodness & power. In theory, the sea & sun have no being, no soul, no power to will or do, & are not treated as persons, but the people declare & speak out, by outward reverence, their admiration of the greatness & benefits of the Sun & Sea.

Stopped at place where four streets met, & sat in our carriage while B.D. pointed out to me the races, castes, nationalities & occupations of the thronged passers by. He knew them all—by dress & feature—Mahommedan, Parsee, Hindoo, Persian, Arab, Nubian, & the Mahrattas, Gussarattas, Sikhs, Bengales, Rohilla &c. Among them were devotees, fakihrs, one who lived under a log by the wayside, & wore his hair to the waist uncombed, & lived on charity. He was a traveling fakihr, & had seen all parts of India, going fr. temple to temple.

Then to the dense basaars,—where one can hardly breathe from the closeness. At an ivory carver's shop, he selected an ivory music box, & insisted on making it a present to my wife in America, & added to it two carved paper folders of sandal wood. A Mahommedan beggar stands in the middle of the street, with a fan, & gives a single stroke of the fan toward each passer by. B.D. says the theory is that every benefit, however slight, calls for a return, & a whiff of a fan in the heat, is a benefit, & he is to be compensated. But very few seemed to notice him.

My friend B.D. had got me an invitation to a party at the house of a Parsee millionaire, one Byranjee Hormuejee Camagee, said to be worth 25 laco, & head of the house of Cama & Co. of Bombay, having a branch in London. At 10.30 P.M., B.D. came for me in his brougham, for, as an M.D. he drives in a brougham; but, *mem.* that the natives all keep to their costumes. It was a dark rainy night, & the monsoon blew half a gale, but all houses here have a vestibule to drive under, a protector ag. sun & rain. Here were numbers of servants & lights, & going up the broad steps, we came into the hall. We were very late, & the guests were just going into supper. I was duly presented to Byranjee, & recd. with elaborate but kindly politeness, & placed near him at the table. In the supper room, a long table is set, with fruits, flowers & cakes,—no meats or fish—& an abundance of wine. Byranjee took the head of the table, & all the Europeans sat down, but no Hindoo sat at the table, or ate anything, for that is an abomination to the Hindoos. The Parsees, too, ate nothing, but took wine. The party was given to a Mr. Fleming, an Engl. merchant, who takes leave of India on Monday, having made a consid. fortune, & is much respected. Byranjee, in a simple, straight-forward speech, in good English, proposed Mr. F.'s health, spoke of his kind & just conduct toward the natives, & their respect for him & regret at parting with him, & added a few proper words about the amity & intercourse of the races in India. This was done in a diffident but dignified & graceful way. Thereupon the English drank Mr. F.'s health, standing, with hip, hip, hurrah & 3 cheers. Mr. F. made a few remarks in reply, with good feeling, & propriety, but not so well as the Parsee. Then followed a long awkward silence. I spoke to my neighbor & asked if no one was to propose the health of our host. I suspect all the company were merchants & traders, & not used to such occasions, for no one spoke, & my neighbor was a nobody. At length poor Byranjee rose, & begged his European friends to excuse him if he omitted anything that became a host, as he was unacquainted with our usages, & proposed the health of all his guests. His guests drank their own healths, & then came another silence. I was strongly tempted to get up & thank & compliment our host, & lead the way,—but I was an entire stranger, & it might be thot an Am. interference, besides, I expected some one to rise ev. moment & do the proper thing. But no,—all rose & left the table, without a word. Byranjee seemed to think it all right, & they thanked him privately for his hospitality &c.—but how stupid it was! So some of them admitted after it was too late.

From the dining room, we went into the large saloon, where seats are ranged against the wall, on three sides, the outer doors being the fourth side. At the head of the room are the seats of honor, & there the guests shaded down to those of the lower degrees near the doors. There were occasional pressures to "go up higher", (see Scripture), & having taking a low seat, not intentionally, but in ignorance of the order & to be nearer the musicians & dancers, I was eventually carried up.

The entertainment consisted of music & dancing by Nautch girls. This is the usual entertainment at Parsee & Hindoo parties, for their own ladies never are present, & they never dance themselves,—neither men nor women,—the accomplishment being confined to girls who live by it & by its usual accessories. The guests sit round the 3 sides of the square, the Parsees in high receeding hats, red loose trowsers & white cassocks, & the Hindoos in turbans of all shapes & colors, tunics & togas wrapped or draped about them, & all without stockings, & some without shoes, & conforming to the European custom of sitting in chairs, they still ease themselves occasionally by gathering up one or both legs.

At the other end, by a pile of shawls & cushions, on the floor, sit two Nautch girls, & two grave musicians, playing on stringed instruments.

The gravity & even sadness of the countenances of these girls was most striking. It fascinated you. What can it mean? What hidden grief? What concealed sickness?

Presently the elder, who is perhaps 18 or 20, rises & begins the dance. She is dressed as a Persian, in a rich gown, coming to the knees, with pantaloons below. It is not so graceful a dress as the Hindoo, but it is perfectly proper & decent. The dance is as slow & dull & meaningless as I have seen it described,— more like a funeral solemnity than a social entertainment. She is a Mahratta girl, of that warlike race that so long ruled the Carnatic & the Deccan, & gave so much trouble to the English, a race of natural politicians & soldiers, as the Gujaratas are natural traders. She is very, very, thin, very, very sallow, with damp black hair parted & drawn back from her ears, & deep, deep dark eyes. How fixed, sad, serious is their look! Is this all mere color, or is it character?

Now the girls retire, & come in again in their native Hindoo dress. The graceful mantle, or wrapper, gathered across the shoulders & falling as drapery to the figure. She looks larger, & less thin in this, & the yellow hue suits her face better. But her features are irregular, & she has no beauty,—yet there is a charm in the gravity & seriousness of mien & the *capabilities* of that eye. Now the girls sit & only sing. The other girl is only

12 or 13, & does not dance at all, & only sings to accompany the elder. The songs, wh. B.D. translates to me, are all light, fanciful love songs, & here—as I believe almost always in E. Indian love songs, the woman is the lover, the adorer & the sufferer. One song was that calling on her dear rajah to take her to Calcutta. Marajah.

Fleming & his friends having taken leave, & it being late, I followed, leaving the Nautch girls & some 20 or 30 Parsees & Hindoos still there. I am told that the dancing is often more animated at the small hours, if the host encourages it. Before leaving we had bouquets, paun soparees (spices, & betel nuts in a soparee leaf) & were sprinkled with rose water.

Sunday. July 22. To the Engl. Church at Colába. It is a truly beautiful church, large, cruciform, of yellow stone, with clerestory & very deep Chancel. Large part of the congr. were soldiers & officers & red-coats prevailed. The high roof & open windows make the church a resort for sparrows, who twitter distractingly all the time, &, though the parson is, no doubt, of more value than many sparrows, he did not make as much noise, & we could hardly distinguish what he read or said. Besides, he kept his voice up at the same key with the twitter. If he had pitched it as low as possible he would have been heard.

Rode home fr. church over Malabar Hill from the Back Bay, a picturesque scene, of high rocks, deep dells, & a climbing carriage way. All along this hill, across it & on the W. slope are the bungalows of all who can afford to live out of the town,— that is, afford the necess. horses, carriages & servants.

Spent the ev. quietly with my kind host & hostess, for to-morrow I leave India.

S is a true N. Engl. youth, alert, quick, fond of trade & enterprising, with respect for learning & talents, moral, supposes himself Orthodox, & attached to his wife, to whom he was engaged before he came here. Came to India as an adventurer, with nothing but a good merc. education at Weld & Co.'s Boston, & good letters. In less than 3 years, he was able to go home & marry & bring his wife to a handsome home & a position of respectability. Mrs. S. was edd. at the High School at Cambr., & has excellent sense, self respect & an unaffected taste for good reading & for the best of culture,—& natural kind manners. Stearns is lucky in his wife,—who is his superior in all the essentials. They have been extremely kind to me, & my visit has been made very agreeable to me.

Mond. July 23.   Dr. Meade's bill is 100 rupees, more than S. thot. This & other inev. exp. of a 3 weeks delay, cut in on me again.

Take leave. Ride to town. Send notes of thanks & farewell to Merwanjee & Co., & to Bhawoo Dajee,—as no time to call, & go on board the steamer China, a screw of 2000 tons, P.&O. line, bound to Aden & Sues. Stearns goes with me to the pier, over wh. the monsoon is pitching the waves in wild confusion, & going off is no little trouble. Merwanjee & Co. send me off a letter of intense politeness, & a present of an E. I. inkstand of papier machee.

At 5 P.M. steam out of the bay,—wh. is a truly noble harbor, of vast dimensions, yet safe, & in the dim cloudy monsoon, leave the far outreaching reefs, over wh. the seas are tossing, behind us,—& steam directly out into the dull, leaden ocean, & dull leaden evening sky, the tossing sea, & whistling monsoon.

Wed. Aug. 1.   My birth day. Nine days out. Passed Socotra Island. It is high, with sand beach for its shore. The W. end breaks off in a precipice, called Ras Kattanie, 1455 f. of nearly perp. height,—one of the most striking points of sea scenery I have ever met with.

I have a state room to myself, & am entirely comfortable on board. My rib & trunk get better daily. I can now lie on my side, & have no pain except a little, in particular *junctures*, as Prest. Benson of Liberia would say. Company better than in the Madras. Henry, the commander, an Irishman,—with the goods & ills of a Hibernian,—the former predominating. A Mr. Pollock, a solicitor of Bombay, who goes home at 45 with an impaired constitution & a handsome property—a nephew of Sir Fred. & Sir Geo. Pollock, & son of Sir David, late Ch. J. of Bombay. He is rather of the fast & superficial order. Mrs. P. is pleasant & well mannered, my chief friend on board. Mr. Fleming (supra). He has made a plum, & goes home to be head of the Engl. branch of his house. He is sensible & upright, &

well informed,—but no more. Mrs. F. is young & pretty. Col.
Brown, of the Royal Artillery, I am inclined to like the best of
the men. Lt. Col. Cleaveland, ditto, is amiable, but a flat. Then
there are some 8 or 10 returning lieuts. & ensigns, mostly on
sick leave,—some on duty. There are 60 soldiers forward, all
going home at the expiration of their terms. One is dying of
dysentery, & must be left at Aden, if he lives to get there.
Capt. Miller of the Boston ice ship Squantum, wrecked, is on
board, 2d class, with his wife. I have been kind to him, & Capt.
Henry & I have waited upon Mrs. M. to a seat on the qu.
deck, wh. she now uses, & wh. has made their lives on board
much more tolerable. M. felt bound to save expense.

At Bombay, read Mill's India, the dullest book on the most
interesting of subjects—a sister piece with Williams' china.

Saturday. Aug. 4. At daylight, the high, dry, treeless, verdureless mountains of the peninsula of Aden are in sight, &
the low sandy waste of the isthmus that connects it with the
main land of Arabia. Soon we can see lines of fortifications
curving along over the rocks, & then a telegraph station &
small houses. We wind round the rock, & see masts of ships, &
then come to anchor, in the harbor, where are two P.&O.
steamers, a sch of the E. I. Navy, & some merchantmen.

After breakfast, go on shore. Capt. Trumbull, agent for the
Salem merchants, (who have the Am. trade here in their
hands) to whom Stearns gave me a letter, has gone home very
ill, & his successor, a Mr. Webb, died a few days ago, so there
is no Am. merch. or consul here. Threw myself on the kindness of a Parsee, who got me a covered chaise & negro driver,
wh. was an accommodation, for, being the Sabbath, the Jews,
who own nearly all the carriages, will let none. My turn-out &
driver were $2 for the day. It is scorching hot. Many of the pas-
sengers are afraid to tempt the shore. But I am armed, as to
the head, in a double ventilating felt helmet, over wh. are a ½
dos. folds of a Japanese pugree, & I have a double umbrella,
when in the sun, & my carriage has a white cotton cover over
the leather. There is a good breese. It is only the sun & rocks
that give the trouble.

My driver speaks English. He is a negro from the African
coast of Sobaya (?). He tells me there is no water, wood or

grass in Aden, & no vegitable or fruit grown there. All are brought on camels from the Arabian shore, across the isthmus; & we are passing streams of the strange creatures, bearing leather bags of water, large piles of fuel, & fodder, & baskets of vegitables. A camel's load of water sells for from 1½ to 3 rupees. It rains here about once in two years, or 18 mos., & then usually in torrents, for a few hours, making cataracts fr. the mountains. If the time goes by without the rain, they may have to wait 18 mos. more. Lately some very ancient tanks were discovered, filled with rubbish, wh. indicate that there must have been a consid. city here centuries ago. The Br. Govt. are digging these out, & find the cement unbroken, in sev. of them. To these they have added two, & now there is, or soon will be, a series of tanks, as large as dry docks. It is thot that one of these bi-ennial torrents will fill them, with, as a Br. officer told me, 80,000 rupees worth of water.

Passed the village of straw & mud huts, where the Africans live, along the shore, along costly cause ways, thro' gates guarded by Sepoys, to the Turkish Wall, as it is called, wh. extends across the isthmus, & guards the landward side of the Peninsula. There are two high hills, of volcanic stone, rising fr. the water on each side, & betw. them is the passage. The hills & the passage are alike fortified, & guns mounted. A seige of Aden must be a short matter, for no army can subsist before it long. It wd. be capture or retreat very soon. All the peninsula is volcanic stone, & mountainous, with valleys & little plains, lying like little ovens betw. the broken sides of the hot rocks; & this volcanic rock gives no water, at any attainable depth, except brackish water fr. the sea, nor does it admit of vegitation. Nothing can be more dreary, or, as an officer said to me —heart breaking. It is perhaps the most undesired station in the Br. dominions. It is, moreover, often unhealthy, with fevers & dysentery, & the usual chances of cholera, while opthalmic disorders are almost inevitable, from the fine dust as well as the reflected sun.

Called at the Guard House, on the Isthmus, & sent in my card. The officer in charge is Lt. Wm. Melville Lane, 29th B. N. Inf., & he has two juniors, lieuts. of the 4th, King's Own. They receive me kindly, explain the works in sight, & Lane offers to take me to the camp & tanks, & to tiffin at the Mess.

Lane has been here nearly 3 years, & expects to be relieved in 4 mos. The others are new comers, & have a long term in expectn.

We drive along the ramparts, thro' a very long dark tunnel, & emerge into the town & camp. This is in the extinct crater of a volcano, with dry crumbly, pummice stone, hot, hot hot hills, on all sides, & rising almost perp. fr. the outer edges of the volcanic crater.

The town is larger than I expected to find it. They say there are 20,000 Arabs, with a sprinkling of Parsees & Jews, & sev. thousand Africans, who live in the village outside the walls. No Europ. who can escape, live in the town, & the officers have bungalows high up the hills, outside, where they go for a week or two, on furloughs. I think this camp at Aden is the hottest place I have ever seen, & the fine dust is extremely annoying. The Sepoys do the exposed duty: the Africans the servile labor, & the Europ. are kept in the shade as much as possible. The drills & parades are fr. 5 to 6 A.M.

Lane said I must see the tanks & if I wd. risk the sun, he wd. go with me. It was just noon, but we went. We rode to the foot, in my chaise, & then walked up. They are a series of dry docks, in the hills (if those can be called hills, on wh. there is not a spade full of earth), cemented, with stairs leading into them to the bottom. The ancient tanks, recently excavated, are in whimsical forms, like some intricate sea shells, & the lining is as white as marble, in this dry hot climate.

They are well worth seeing. The last rain, some 14 mos. ago, tho' it lasted but 6 hours, was such a terrific torrent that it bore along rocks, broke the walls of the tanks, & let out the water, 80,000 rupees' worth. Now the engineers have guarded ag. the recurrence, as they hope.

Returned to the Mess Room of the 29th, very hot, & glad to wash, & sit in the high room, where the mats keep the heat fr. the doors, & windows, & the punkahs give free air. There I find one Engl. weekly paper, of July 18, wh. gives the arrival of the Gr. Eastern at N. York, & the nomn. of Douglas.

Absences at sanitariums, returns to Engl. on "sick leave", or absence on staff duty, have thinned the Mess down to 5. They tell me that 2 years at Aden makes almost entire changes in the Mess. The officers seem well mannered, intelligent men, of good connexions at home, tho' their talk is almost exclusively of the service. Yet, to me, the anecdotes of the late mutiny are as interesting as any thing of the sort can be. With these gentlemen, Sir Jas. Outram is the favorite of living officers. Of the dead, Havelock, the Lawrences, Nicholson & Wheeler. Rose, Grant & Mansfield are thot the ablest of the Gen. officers.

After a long rest & a very good dinner under the name of tiffin, where our soda (*cum* claret) was cooled by saltpetre, we drove back to the point, in what is called the "cool" of the evening—when the therm. is perhaps at 94°.

Certainly this Aden is a place to be seen. But great exigencies only will warrant a man's living here. Some of the fortifications are as high as the eagle flies, & one covered way is at a dissy height.

Walk round to the Point, where the houses of the chief officers, & the retiring places of others are perched on rocks to get the sea breeses. There are the grave yards, & an Engl. & a R.C. chapel.

Returned on board at 7 o'ck., & Lane came & took tea with me.

At 9 P.M., steamed off fr. Aden, leaving the dull hot rocks in their picturesque outlines, broken, jagged, sharp, standing dry & stiff in the moonlight.

Sund. Aug. 5. At 8.30 A.M. passed the straights of Babel Mandeb, & are in the Red Sea, Arabia on our right, & the mountains of Africa on our left. My first view of the Continent of Africa. At the straights is the Island of Perrin, wh. the Br. have occupied, & on wh. there is a light hs. & a few simple works. It has no water, nor a blade of grass.

Met two large ships, coming down Sues or Medina, with returning pilgrims fr. Mecca, bound to India. Sev. ship loads go in this way ev. year.

(The people at Aden see rain storms pass over the Arabian coast, a few miles fr. them, frequently, but they never come to them).

Friday. Aug. 10. This is the 6th day fr. Aden, & we expect to reach Sues by mid-night. Our fears of extreme heat have not been entirely met. The passage up the Red Sea in mid summer, in a steamer, is commonly thot to be the extreme limit of human endurance. Feeble persons die of mere heat, sometimes. For three days it was intensely hot. The scene was this, & no more nor less—a burning sun, a smooth sea, a dead calm or very light breese, & a hot hase lying over the African or Arabian mountains. We sleep on deck, wherever we can lay a mat & pillow, for the cabins are too hot. The thick awning of sailcloth is but little defense ag. the sun, & under it we are obliged to wear pugrees & double hats as if we were in open air, & fr. 10 to 4 it is cooler in the saloon, under deck, the punkahs waving. I live light & am perfectly well. But there is great deal of drinking,—the thirst tempting so much. There is much sickness,—tho' none dangerous, & only among persons who have had disease before,—the victims of E.I. fevers & dysenteries. My friend Col. Brown has been very ill, of return of jungle fever, but is better to-day. The sick soldier died before getting to Aden, & was buried at sea. He had served 20 years, had 3 good service marks, & was going home with his discharge & a pension. My steward was sun struck yesterday, by standing in sun without cap a few minutes—brot to by throwing buckets of cold water over his head, & putting feet in cold water. He is at work to-day—stroke must have been slight. Cold water on his head is the E.I. remedy now, & no bleeding.

Yesterday was a little more comfortable, & to-day is delightful. We are betw. the Egypt. & Arab. mountains, in a smooth sea, with fresh breese. How aerial those mountains do look— how barren, hot & deserted! On the Arabian coast we see the range that lies about Sinai, & is called after it, & some say that solitary peak is Sinai itself, but no one seems sure. It begins to become exciting as we draw near these ancient long honored scenes of the world's history, Egypt, Sinai!

Saturd. Aug. 11.   Last night we came to anchor at Sues, & this morning we are lying in the narrow top of the Red Sea, with a sand plain on one side & barren hills on the other. The sunset last night, disclosed the *beauty of desolation.* I can now believe that the hues in Hunt's picture of the Scape Goat may be in nature. The sands are not white but reddish brown, & so are the hills, & the flush of sunset makes them red. The hills are not hills, but the ruins of hills. They have been *pared*, below the roots of all vegitation, & then sliced off, leaving bare the gravel & stones, & then gouged & hacked & sliced, after every wild fashion. They are not only irregular in outline at the tops, but in the sides & at the bases. They have as little shape as a boy's lump of crystal. I attribute this—being no naturalist —to the entire absence of rain & all water-shed, to smooth things off.

Landed at Sues, at 10 o'ck. I remained until the 3 P.M. train. Got lunch & cup of Turkish coffee, full of grounds & no milk. It is too hot to go about, so I lounge in the inn. While I am at the Transit Co.'s office, the clerk, an Englishman, has occasion to speak, & does so, with apparent fluency, Greek, Italian, & Arabic. My trunks are exd. by an Egyptian Custom Hs. officer, dressed just like the pictures of Joseph & his brethern.

Took train at 3 P.M. for Cairo. Have a car (carriage) to myself. Our course lies thro' the desert,—& it *is* a desert,—miles & miles of mere sand, but not white, a kind of brown or yellow sand, & those strange, shapeless, verdureless hills! No one can live on them. I should think no one could climb them. They must exist for some meteriological purpose. The poorer Egyptians live in mere pens on pounds,—enclosures of mud or stone, with little or no roof, & that flat, mere covers of straw, & open holes for doors or windows. They look like little cattle pens. Here & there are tents, & men & women standing at the tent doors, at close of day.

I am now in Africa, have set foot on all the continents, unless Australia be one, wh. I will not admit;—this is old Egypt, & hereabouts the children of Jacob came to buy corn, & hereabouts they passed out of Egypt, a disenthralled multitude! But what a country to dwell in & to travel in,—so hot, & no rain ever! There is not a tree or blade of grass betw. Sues & Cairo!

The sun goes down, in a hot flush, & the stars come out, & soon there are distant lights, & now a row of trees & houses, & then close streets, & a great "Station", & we come to a stand. It is nearly 9 o'ck., there is no light in the station, but a small fire of faggots burning at the end of a long stick, & not a European in the station, but a crowd of howling Arabs. It is with great difficulty I secure two carriers, & have to wait for the men to beat off the cleats from the baggage crates by bits of soft stone, & can find no carriage—as my train was not expected, & start off into an unknown city, in the dark, with two

Arabs. But we find the hotel, at last, & after bath & dinner, I am at home in my room, with my red striped luggage about me,—nothing lost.

Sund. Aug. 12th.   Took donkey & guide & rode to find the British Consul. This is the oddest place I have seen yet—more picturesque than a Chinese city, or even than Bombay or Poonah. In the old parts of the town, the streets are as narrow as in Canton, & the houses are of stone, with thick walls & 3 stories high. To see a street roofed over some 40 or 50 f. above the ground, with great rafters & occasional open spaces, has something of the fearful. It is a city of back entries. This cannot be a street. It must be a paved back passage of a house. But here & there are open spaces & gardens kept alive by artificial irrigation.

Donkeys, donkeys everywhere, & camels! There are Joseph's brethren, ambling down the street, each riding his ass, & the asses bearing provender & corn; & there are the Midianites with their camels, bearing spicery.

The Br. Consul, Mr. Calvert, is also acting Am. Consul, & promises to send off my letters this afternoon, to Alex.

The Engl. service is given up, in the midsummer heat, & so is that of the Am. Presb. missionaries.

Called on Rev. Wm. Barnett, of Am. Pr. Board, with letter of introdn. from Mr. Prime. He has had an Arab class, but says there is no Engl. Prot. service, & I am too late for the Coptic service, & the Greek Ch., both of wh. I should much like to have seen. The Copts are the descendants of the early Egyptian Christians, converted in the Apostles' times, & soon after, Mr. Barnett says, and have kept aloof fr. all European X'tians, whether Greek Ch., R. Cath. or Protestant. Their faith & forms of worship closely resemble the R. Catholic. The Coptic language has become a dead language, & is not even understood, when read, by one in a thousand. All Egyptians speak Arabic, & all but the Copts became Mahommedans. The religions here are Mahommedan, & Coptic, Greek & R.C. Christians. Mr. Barnett has been very kind in instructing my dragoman (guide, valet & interpreter) as to my desires in the way of Pyramids, Sphynxes &c., & I am to start off tomorrow morning, at 3 o'ck., by moonlight, for Memphis, to see the upper pyramids, a two days' journey, on donkeys, with my dragoman, one Mahmond ——, to return by Old Cairo & Persepolis, & Thursday, 16th, I expect to go to Alexandria, & hope to sail for Trieste on the 17th or 18th.

Monday, Aug. 13th. This Cairo is a grand, ponderous, solemn old city. It is as far before the E. Indian cities in romantic interest, as they are before the Chinese. There is something great as well as old & quaint about it. And now, by moonlight, of this Monday morning, Aug. 13th, I am traversing its great shadows, & threading my way, donkey-back, among its narrow streets, betw. its high, thick prison looking walls, on my march out to Memphis,—every now & then in danger of treading on some sleeper;—for in this dry, hot climate, they sleep out of doors all night. We pass by high walls of gardens & high walls of palaces, &, to ev. inquiry, my dragoman says the garden, the palace of Achmet Pacha, or Ibrahim Pacha's sons, or Seid Pacha's daughter, or Suliman Pacha, or the hareem of the Pacha. These few Pachas, of the reigning family, descendants of Mohammed Ali, seem to own everything in the grasp of their sensual despotism. At last, we are in the open fields, & can see the stars, in their last glimmer.

To Old Cairo, where we take a boat & cross the Nile by sails. It is here & now a turbid & rapid river, but the all in all of Egypt! They drink the Nile, cook with the Nile, wash in the Nile, give the Nile to their cattle to drink, & where the Nile does not go they carry it, by canal & aqueducts.

Pass Roda Island, in the Nile, where is the Nilometer, & the Palace & hareem of Seid Pacha, & one of Ibrahim Pacha's sons, & in the open country, in the grey of the morning, miles & miles off, we see the great Pyramids!

Stop under a grove of date-tree palms & get breakfast. This sounds very fine, but a grove of dates, at early day, gives as much shade as a grove of liberty-poles.

My dragoman is Mohammed Hossayn. He has taken many parties to Upper Egypt & Syria, & has their certificates;— among others, last year, Lord Dufferin. He charges me 4 shillings a day, & does everything as a bodyservant as well as interpreter & guide. He makes good Turkish coffee.

Our first visit is to the ruins of Memphis.

The sand of the desert has covered all. Only where this is dug off & down is anything reached. (Metrahineh is the present name). Visited the recumbent statue, some 40 f. long, all fr. one block of stone, & then the bits & reliques wh. have been gathered in the tents of the excavators, who are acting under the Pacha.

Then to Sakkára, where is an underground temple, the walls of alabaster & black granite, & the inscriptions on them as plain as if written yesterday. There are remains of vermillion paintings on the figures. It is called El Biar.

It is now about 11 o'ck., & the sun, on this sand plain, in August, intensely hot, & notwithstanding my double helmet & pugree, I am relieved to reach the tombs of Serapion, where the sarcophagi of the bulls were kept, & to get under ground. Here we were, under ground, myself, 3 Arabs & 3 donkeys, & here we rested. They spread my mat, & lay themselves on the sand,—& we rested, with a lunch of meat & wine & water, until 4 o'ck., when we explored the tombs. They are vast & deep, & doubtless built to hold the stone coffins of the Sacred Bulls. These sarcophagi are enormous, all but the cover being of one piece of stone, & that as big as it would seem possible to get to its place. The tombs are in high galleries, & each sarcophagus has its tomb at the side.

Thence to Kanéseh, where is a newly discovered temple, in wh. the paintings are still bright. Rev. Mr. Barnett says Kanéseh will serve as a substitute for going to Upper Egypt.

The afternoon sun is still hot, & the breese from the desert still warm, when we issue from our subterranean cavern, & a ride of two hours (have I said we were on donkeys? The *sina qua non* of Egyptian life, & neither obstinate nor sure footed) brings us to the great Pyramids of Gezeh, & the Pyramid of Cheops, & the Sphynx. All the way they loom before us, sharp, high & wide, looking about as large 15 miles off as close by.

Here (at Gezeh) 3 pyramids stand near together, 2 large & 1 small. Of the large, Cheops is the larger, & the only one that can be entered. But these have been too minutely described & too often! I need only say that they are built of large blocks of stone, of diff. sises, & irregular, but resulting in rows, each receeding, so as to form something like stairs, fr. top to bottom. By climbing & a little aid from lifting by others, any person of ord. strength of body & steadiness of head can go to the top. Perpend. height, little less than 500 f., about double Bunker Hill M't. The stones are not white, grey or black, but of a yellow color. Some of the blocks are huge, so that it excites your wonder how they got there. The dreary look of all around the pyramids & sphynx is first to be noted. The sands of the desert have blown over & submerged temples, palaces, tombs,—all but pyramids. Imagine a long Northern snowstorm, of yellow snow, only rock-tops peering above, & the open channels & lagoons of the great river.

The Sphynx disappoints—being in a scooped out hollow, & dwarfed by the pyramid. You have to stimulate your wonder by remembering that it is one block of stone, & was once a kind of face.

Before dark, we entered the tomb discovd. by Col. Vyse, & the temple under ground, or under sand. The latter is in good order, with no arches, but only the Egyptian upright pillars & flat top stone—but very large & heavy.

It is now sundown, & here, in this dreary magnificent spot, I am to pass the night. My dragoman makes me up a bed of blankets & my mat on the hard stone forming the lower range of the pyramid, & with moon & stars bright overhead, in this clear dry sky, with a congregation of a dosen Arabs, disputing & howling & praying towards Mecca, kneeling on carpets, & as many donkeys eating out of bags, myself trying to look up & realise the place & the scene, I dropped asleep, having been up since 4 o'ck. & much of the time on the road. The great dispute was betw. my dragoman & a huge Arab, who insisted on letting himself to us as guard for the night, & I dropped off when it was at the highest.

Once in the night, I awoke. Stars & moon bright,—sky cloudless, & the Arabs lying in the sand, but the pyramid receedes too fast for me to see the top, where I lie.

Tuesd. 14th. Aug.   Dragoman calls me at 4 o'ck. Coffee & bread, & my 3 Arab guides take me inside the Pyramid, entering a small door, up several ranges of stones, insignificant,—the door, I mean, showing that the pyramids were never built for *use*, & following low passages, often bending to the ground, visit the well known & often described recesses & chambers.

Then, just at clear day dawn, begin the ascent outside. It is not extremely difficult, & I reach the summit a few minutes before sunrise, & have the great gratifn. of seeing, from the top of the highest pyramid, the blood red African sun rise over this vast expanse,—this expanse now of sand & water, of scattered villages, the illimitable Lybian desert on the West, & glittering in the East the citadel of Cairo.

The Nile spreads itself & winds itself everywhere, in branches & off shoots, in lagoons & pools, in parallel streams & artificial canals, & the agriculture of Egypt is exactly coextensive with the Nile & its influences.

The Second Pyramid has a part of its casing of hewn smooth stone still at the top, & all antiquarians agree that the great pyramid had also once a similar casing, wh. has been removed for use in building the palaces of Cairo. If so, it was not intended to be ascended without, any more than within.

Descent, & take our asses for Old Cairo, following the dikes all the way, as the Nile has begun to rise. This more than doubles the journey, but we reach the river by 9 o'ck., & crossing close by the island of Roda, where are the palace & hareem of a great pacha, are in Old Cairo.

Irrigation is the great subject, in lower Egypt. Canals, sluices, dikes, culverts & tide gates, give the people the control of the waters of the Nile,—& this is their all.

The Citadel of Cairo is a grand object, for miles around— one of the grandest imaginable;—dominating as it does over all the region about, high, dome-filled, & glittering, mosque, palace & fortress in one.

In Old Cairo, after breakfast of bread, grapes & coffee, went to an ancient Coptic Church. It is thro' a close alley, thro' a deep gate way, up flights of stairs, & in the 3d story of a house are the several rooms, separated by wooden screens, dark, dingy, dusty, ratty, mousy, wormy,—old—very old—making the place of worship of the Copts. The walls are lined with very old & quaint pictures of saints, with extraord. legends attached. There is a Chancel, altar, candles, & the Chancel is separated so as to let people only look in, or peep in, as at the small door of a stage. They have a few books, as I understood, in Coptic, now a dead language. All Egyptians having adopted the Arabic of their conquerors. They seemed very poor. Mr.

Barnett tells me the R. Cath. have drawn many of them into union, & the Gr Ch. press them, & Prot. have little sympathy with them, so they seem destined to extinction. Yet they are the successors & representatives of the Christians of Egypt in the Apostles' days, when St. Mark planted X'tianity there.

Visited also a Greek Ch. An intelligent priest showed me the building, wh. is also, I believe, a monastery, but as he spoke no Engl. or French or Sp., we could get on only by writing Greek, —for the pronunciation of Mod. Greek is unintelligible to me—, & by guessing at Italian. This Church is rather full of paintings & seems prepared for a good deal of ceremony.

To the Mosque of Amer, said to be the oldest in Egypt. This is built round four sides of a square, the enclosed square being open to the sky & paved with flat stone, & capable of holding an immense multitude. There is no central dome. The four sides are high roofed, with rows of pillars to sustain the roofs. At one end is the tomb of Amer. While I was there, two women were admitted to kiss it. They embraced & kissed, with a loud smack & unction each corner of the tomb, & really seemed to enjoy the process. I thought the younger one looked at us rather wilfully—as much as to say—what would you give?

Next, to the grand Mosque or whatever it may be called, built to contain the tombs of the descendants of Mohammed Ali. It is stately & sumptuous. Over each tomb is a dome, & the various rooms in wh. the tombs lie, open into each other. The light is dim & from above, & the entire flooring of all is covered with rich Turkey carpets. The faithful come & go freely, & the rooms seem to be used as resting, sleeping, reading & smoking places for whomever chooses & is decently dressed. All that was required of us was to put on slippers. The tombs are large costly structures, of marble, inlaid with gold, & in much better taste than the costlier monumental architecture with us—no effigies, all images being prohibited by the Mahom. faith. Lying about, on the carpeted floors, were lasy Turks, sleeping & smoking, & avoiding the heat of the outer sun.

The tombs of the Mamelukes, was the last place we visited to-day,—& it was now nearly noon, & the sun intensely hot. I was glad to get back to my hotel, & have a warm bath & change of linen, & lie down to rest. I had done & seen a good deal since 4 A.M. of Monday.

Rev. Mr. Barnett, & Mr. Calvert, the Br. Consul, called. Barnett is of the Scotch Presb. Ch. of the U.S. (Rev. Blaikie's connexion), a well meaning man, but dull & half taught, & I suspect the Mission is feebleness itself. His associate, Mr. Mc—, goes home in feeble health.

The great Square of Cairo is very gay at night. Cafés & other places of entertainment are open, & bands of music play in the open air, & it is in open air that all sit & take refreshments. One band was fr. Damascus, playing on Damascene instruments, among wh. were 2 or 3 harps with some 50 strings each, running across a nearly flat board. The musicians sang a good deal with their playing. The Turkish bands used European (as we now call them, at least) instruments.

The system of polygamy & concubinage does not prevent tho' it may diminish public harlotry. I saw sev. Egyptian harlots, most sumptuously decked & perfumed, in the square, & had the offers of services of sev. men in Italian & French, to act as brokers. It seems this is the usage, & direct address is not the custom; & so a worthy class of men get a pittance in this way & are encouraged. Mr. Barnett told me that the public women are numerous & have sections of the city where they are known to be. They were all banished by the late pacha, but have been silently tolerated by the present pacha. It may be that they get their support from foreigners,—not Mahommedans.

I am, to-day, the only guest at Shepherd's enormous hotel. In midsummer, Egypt is deserted by travelers, & the transit passengers, to & fr. India, are much fewer in summer.

Wed. Aug. 15. Off early, on donkeys, to see the remaining sights. The sight to-day, & the great sight of Cairo, is the Citadel. It is the highest point, dominating over all the city & country round, & a splendid group of buildings,—castle, palace & mosque, together! The color of the stone is beautiful, a reddish brown. The great building is the Mosque of Mohammed Ali. Here is something that may truly be called magnificent!— I mean one of the magnificencies of the world. I think, for gorgeousness, it surpasses all I have ever seen. The marble court is surmounted by a dome, from wh. comes the most delicious light, fr. the stained glasses. Marble, alabaster, polished stone, stained glass & gold, above, below & on all sides, & smaller domes, rising from the sides, each beautiful & rich.

The view fr. the Citadel is noble. Cairo is a city of domes & minarets & towers, & the great Nile, with its canals, lakes, lagoons, ditches, & its separating channels, lies before us, & the steep Citadel-hill, & the boundless Lybian desert stretching westward, & the lonely pyramids, rising out of the desolation of sand. The whole presents a scene wh. no where else I think can be matched, for interest. The Pacha being away, at Alexandria, with all his hareem, & officers, the palace was open to me. I made the circuit of all but the hareem, wh., tho' unoccupied, is closed. The palace is very costly & sumptuous— marble, gold, alabaster & precious stones. The great halls of reception & audience are very large & imposing, & the luxury of the old wretch's couches, divans, beds, baths & smoking rooms, is unspeakable. He is so large that it is diff. for him to mount, so he has a dumb waiter, by wh. he ascends & descends. It has a very mysterious & treacherous look, in a dungeon-like closet. Mohammed Ali is the favorite of the common Egyptian. Everything great is attributed to his times. My dragoman's eyes glisten as he tells stories of the power & splendor & great doings of Mohammed Ali, & if anything is in a bad state now, it has become so since Mohammed Ali's time.

One of the most extraordinary things in the Citadel, &, indeed, in Egypt, is the Great Well, called Joseph's Well,—said to have been built (tho' that is doubted) by the Soldan Josef, known to us as Saladin, the Conqueror. It is an enormous work. Not a mere well, but a stone room, some 20 or 30 feet square, descending more than 200 f. into the ground, to water, wh. is drawn up by the perpetual chain & buckets, worked by oxen. (The oxen of Egypt are chiefly the water bison, as in India & China). There is access nearly to the foot of the well, outside the wall, down a wet, spiral passage of mud, perfectly dark, along wh. guides take you with torches.

The Mosque of Sultan Hassan is the next sight in order,—a large, plain, grave structure, in extreme contrast with that of Mohammed Ali, & with the Sit Teinab, a light, modern, showy mosque, from wh. the worshippers were pouring in a throng as I went by. Then, too, I went to the Tayloon,—but for the life of me, cannot recall it, or how it differed from the Mosque of Sultan Hassan.

This ended my early morning excursion. Returned to late breakfast—& at 10.30, am to go, in a carriage, with Mr. Barnett, to visit Shubra palace & gardens,—the sumptuous pleasure grounds of the Haleem Pacha.

There is a straight avenue to Shubra, lined on each side with trees, affording a good shade, & kept watered. The trees are pine, cedar, acasia, & sycamore,—Mr. B. says the sycamore of Scripture.

At the gate of the Shubra gardens is a new palace, now finished. It is of blue, with cornice & outworks of white. Mr. Barnett said, well, that it was like coming upon a cloud in the sky —the blue & white. The gardens occupy about 100 acres, & all under full cultivation. The gardens seemed to me as costly as any I saw in India or China, & in better taste. Shade is appreciated, & all the walks & avenues are well lined with trees, among wh. the pines & cedars abound,—with sycamores. The flowers & shrubs I cannot specify, except that they took pains to show me the sensitive plant.

In the gardens, is a second palace, or pleasure house. It encloses an open space wh. is filled artificially with water & lined with marble, & a marble island in the middle. The palace runs round the four sides of this small lake, consisting of broad marble walks, beautifully roofed & supported by pillars, with here & there rooms,—& at each corner a suite of rooms. These rooms are furnished in the most costly style of the Eastern & Western luxury—as Burke says—"uniting the vivid satisfactions of Europe, with the torpid blandishments of Asia"—such divans, such carpets, such couches, such gilding & precious stones, such mirrors & such Cashmere coverings! An evening party, a ball, given here, with a band of music on the island, would be unsurpassed. But, poor creatures, what is all their style, without women! A few prisoners in the hareem, & all this show & style is for the heavy men alone.

Thursd. Aug. 16.   Took train at 8.30 for Alexandria. The officers of the road seem to be natives, but it is said that the chief engineers are Fr. or Engl.

The Delta of the Nile seems very fertile. So far as the fertilising effects of the overflow goes, there seems to be abundant productiveness. For sev. miles the scene reminded me of the bottom lands of the Connecticut, trees, rich fields,—only the cuts & canals for irrigation, & the constant occurrence of wheels to raise water, were Egyptian. But lower down, towards Alexandria, sandy plains occur again. The common people live in mere cots, or pens of mud, while here & there are great houses of big men, usually of yellow stone, but sometimes plastered & painted blue & white. Now, the country is perfectly flat, & there—that long, low blue ridge is the Mediterranean,—my first sight of the Mediterranean! & houses thicken, streets show themselves, & we are in Alexandria.

Alexandria is a Europeanised city. The streets are wide & straight (mostly) & the houses of white stone. Seen from an eminence, it is a city of white stone—solely. The signs are in Italian, Greek, French, Arabic & English. European women, in crinoline & retreating bonnets are frequent in the streets, & all mixtures of costumes, from the pure Turk to the pure Frank, abound.

Took lodgings at the Hotel Abbot, where we sat at table,— Turk, French, Greek, Italian, I the only Anglo Saxon.

Frid. Aug. 17. Gave the day to sight seeing,—that is the morning & ev., for it is here the noon in wh. no man can labor. Pompey's Pillar—(nothing to do with Pompey, more than Cleopatra's Needle has to do with Cleopatra). All know its form. Its material is brown stone & one piece. Cleopatra's Needle, of wh. only one is standing, is of darker stone.

Visited a Synagogue, built of white stone, handsome & in good repair, a handsome Jew girl showing it to me, & taking her fee—the eternal *backshish*, the one word of Egypt. Then a Coptic Church, in wh. service was going on,—a baptismal service. The Chancel is screened off entirely, & the child is handed in to the priest, as at a parcel's delivery office. The women were behind another screen, making almost a separate room. Four or five men were standing & chanting, & the congregation, beside the invisible women, consisted of some dosen men & boys. Three children were baptised. They seemed to me to use chrysm as well as water. The boys demanded bakshish of me, after the service, & they & the older girls, now emerged, scrambled for what my dragoman threw to them, on the church floor.

There is a handsome Engl. Ch. of white stone, & sev. R. Cath. & Greek churches.

The Syrian massacres excite great interest among the foreigners here. Many X'tian refugees are here, at the house of the Lasarists.

At 5 P.M. took a Turkish bath. Rooms with marble floor, vapor, so that one can hardly breathe, wrapped in dry clothes, rubbed, put into warm bath, rubbed & kneaded, cooler water poured on, soaped & washed again, slowly dried, let into a breathable air, dried more, laid down on couch. Pipe (water) & coffee, & bakshish & Adieu.

Rode down to the point between the two harbors, & visited the Pacha's palace. It is very large, & finely situated, with one sea front, & one on each harbor. I was not admitted. The soldiers on guard seemed careless, & sat at their posts, & an air of languor & disorder was spread about the palace.

Strange there should be so few objects of historical interest in so ancient & distinguished a city—but so it is. It is probably the most cosmopolitan city in the world,—having little character of its own, but made up of all nations, races, religions & languages. The French influence seems to prevail. They furnish more high officers in the Pacha's service than any nation. (By the way, Mr. Fleming told me that the Engl. merchants & others in Bombay, leased the stations & built the buildings for the land route between Sues & Alexandria, & when the rail road superceded the stations, instead of surrendering them to the Egyptian Govt., these merchants made them over to the British Govt., & they are now maintained by the Foreign Office).

Sat. 18. Aug. 9 A.M., took Austrian Lloyd's steamer "Bombay" for Trieste. Mr. & Mrs. Pollock, Major & Mrs. Russell, & Mr. Kenshaw, of the "China", are on board. Alexandria looks well in going out. It is low & level, but the buildings are striking, the palaces, mosques, minarets, domes, & towers. A great many vessels of all flags, in the harbor. Long rows of windmills! City of white stone!

Now, we are out on the blue Mediterranean—my first experience of it, & it is not long before the low shores of Africa are out of sight, & we are at sea. It is smooth, & very pleasant, & a gentle breese. In the afternoon, the ladies say it is really cool & they send below for shawls. One of us has the curiosity to look at the thermometer. It is at 84°! Such is the effect of India & the Red Sea on the blood. But there is a difference in the *sun*. Even at 84°, it is cooler than in Asia or Africa, for the sun has not that peculiar power. We sit under the awning at noon, without feeling the sun striking through it & our hats too.

Sunday. Aug. 19.   4 P.M., made island of Candia. Weather comfortable, & a change at night, tho' still very hot. Plenty of fruit on board,—grapes, melons, peaches & figs,—& variety of vegitables.

Mond. Aug. 20.   The Peloponnesus! Made the S.W. end of the Morea, & all day are coasting the Morea, close on board, & going between it & the islands. Here is Navarino Bay! The captain points out the place where the Turkish fleet lay at anchor, & where the allied squadrons came in. There is a fortified town just at the mouth of the Straits, above Navarino, now abandoned.

How deeply interesting is the sight of Greece,—the Peloponessus,—tho' it be of a part little known to fame! Yet it is Greece! And these are the

> Isles of Greece—the Isles of Greece
> Where burning Sappho loved & sung,
> Where grew the arts of war & peace.

and we are to see Ithica, the isle of Ulysses! And worthy of Greece is the outline & figure of the land & the islands as seen from the sea! There are no flat marshes or sand wastes. Everywhere the hills & mountains come to the water's edge, the hills crowned with forests, & breaking into dells & glens & ravines, & small plains. It is picturesque, everywhere. Nowhere strikingly rich or fertile, in appearance, but a land of diversity & interest, hill, mountain, grove, valley, shore. We are all enthousiastic Greeks, & wish to wander about the shores. We pass the entrance to the Gulf of Corinth by night.

Tuesd. Aug. 21. Pass between the main land of Albania, & the islands of Zante, Cephalonia, & Corfu, & at 10 A.M. are at anchor in the beautiful harbor of Corfu. What a romantic & beautiful spot! Those who have seen Malta put this far before it. The rocks run up to sharp points, overlooking all, & crowned with forts, & the tall houses, all of white stone, & some of 3 & 4 & 5 stories in height, seen like watch towers & fortresses. And how beautifully the blue sea lies all about the islands, & away up in the little bays!

We are ashore, amid Greek signs, & Greek faces & Greek speech! How odd to see the language of your school & college, your Homer & New Testament, on placards & signs, & applied to modern things. I buy a daily paper, ''Συνοπσίσ Είδησεων'' Έν Κερκυρα τη 9 Αυγουττσυ 1860, (Πωλείται 'οβολούση), with news of the Αποβασισ Γαραβαλδη, ending in Τηλεγράφημα.

It struck me that in this hot climate, there should be no verandahs, piassa or porticos. The houses have flat fronts, with wooden shutters. Drove to the town palace & the country palace of the Br. Governor. Large & sufficiently stately buildings. The country about is beautifully diversified with hill & dale, & all has a healthful, variegated, romantic air. How much of this is fancy? But who can resist it, in the isles of Greece, amid olive trees & vineyards, & where the Greek of the world's poetry, eloquence, philosophy & art is domesticated. We fancy, too, that the women have a *castey* look. See the low forehead, full temple, straight nose, & chiseled lip! And the men,—how keen they look, & active! Certainly, they are neither a dull nor an oppressed people. They look independent & clever. Among these faces, is a sprinkling of what must be Austrian, sunburnt yellow complexions, large foreheads & brown hair. The red coats of the Engl. *protectorate* soldiery, are the only signs of a present subjection, mild as it is, & the Venetian lion, carved on the gateways, tells of that of years gone by.

What delicious grapes are these purple grapes of the open vineyards! And these fresh figs, so cooling & soft! And how full are the basaars of melons, peaches & all manner of vegitables!

Went into the Church of San Spiridion, sumptuous & burning with candles,—the body of the Saint being on exhibition, & paying one shilling I get a sight of it. The face is entire, in a glass case, while the legs are exhibited & open to the touch, but cased in painted cloth. A Greek girl, a cripple, sits by it, with a truly beautif. & classic face, & fair complexion.

(It must not be supposed that Greek is the only language. On the contrary, Italian is perhaps even oftener met with on the signs. French & Engl. are occasionally seen, & a good deal of Engl. is spoken, on acct. of the Engl. protectorate & commerce).

But our 2½ hours' leave is up, & we must take our feet from off the classic soil, to the sooty deck of the steamer,—newly coaled & well stored with fruits & vegitables. We are all on deck, & delighting ourselves with the views as we steam out of the harbor. What a place for yatching! What drives & walks! What shooting mountains opposite, & so near! We are so glad we avoided commonplace routes by Marseilles or Southampton. We turn the corner, & the castle, forts, palace, towers, & towering stone houses are hidden, & Adieu to Corfu!

All the afternoon we are skirting the Albanian shores, often within a mile of the beach. Here again, thro' its whole length, there are no reaches of sand, or of low marsh, but always a bold shore, & hills & mountains, with opening valleys, & the blue sea washing their feet.

All day Wed. (22d) the coast in sight on the right hand, — the coast of Dalmatia & the Austrian-Turkish provinces. Delightful sailing.

Thursday. Aug. 23rd.   The entrance to Trieste in sight, early this morning, & at 8 A.M., we are at anchor in the port, the slopes of the hills, well dotted with pleasure houses, villages & churches, & the close built city before us. Custom Hs. officers easy & civil, & by 9 o'ck., I am in my room at my hotel— Hotel de la Villa,—& all my luggage safe, & my sea-voyage ended.

I am in Europe! It is an exciting thought, & one calling for gratitude. I have been carried across the Pacific, through all the seas, & inland journeys & changes of climate, & heats & dangers, of China & Japan, & of the Eastern seas, & British India, & Egypt,—without so much as a hair of my head injured. I am, & have been, in perfect health, & have apparently escaped every danger & ev. inconvenience of the hot climates, in midsummer, & am now on European soil. I feel almost as if my journey were ended, & these European customs seem so homelike,—no more Chinese, Hindoos or Arabs. How much I have seen & how constantly I have enjoyed! Can I expect the same in Europe? Yet, why not? *Nec temere, nec timide.*

Venice! Venice! Venice! All my resolutions broke down, & my principles gave way! I left Trieste with a virtuous resolve to spend one day only in Venice. But it was impossible. I can allow for anything a man may do in Venice. It took me as much by surprise as if I had never heard of it. I did not really believe that things were as I had read. People may be divided into two classes, those who have seen Venice & can believe in the actualising of the imagination, & those who have not seen it, & may not so believe.

And how strange it all is! Here, in the midst of the banks & shoals of the Adriatic, not only off the land, but *out of sight of* hard ground,—where only coral insects would think of beginning, they build a magnificent, sumptuous city,—a city of marble & gold & precious stones, of palaces, churches, monasteries, courts, bridges, columns, arsenals, & prisons,—where every stone had to be brought from a distant *terra firma*, & gardens, where every morsel of earth was imported; and there they led about the sea, in canals, as they wished for it, & excluded it, by breakwaters, where they did not desire it; and on the weakest foundations of mud & sand, they built the heaviest & loftiest structures, & undertook to rule the Mediterranean world. The wonders of the place, the never ceasing charm of canal & gondola, front-door steps washed by the tide, & overlooking balconies, & noiseless motion, of a city without wheel or shod hoof,—so seised on me, that after going all Friday to sights, & finding them not half finished, I gave way, & sacrificed another day,—wh., indeed involved a third, for that was Sunday, & I did not wish to travel all that day, as I must—if I did not stay over.

I shall not attempt to *describe*. I will only *catalogue*.

But, first, have I said that we arrived in Trieste, Thursd. morning, Aug. 23d, & spent the day there? Trieste is beautifully situated, on the gentle slope of hills that run to the Adriatic; with every variety of inclination, & is well built of white stone, the houses large, streets generally wide, & a good deal given up to public uses, squares, promenades, drives &c. Left at midnight for Venice, in a A.L. steamer. Waked up at daylight, about an hour fr. Venice, & came into the city, or *among* the city, at sunrise,—& could not have had a more beautiful entrance. Passed the Lido, where Byron used to ride, & the open port where the Doges wedded the sea, & came to anchor nearly opp. the piassa de San Marco—(the Square of St. Mark).

Stopped at the hotel Danieli, wh. was a palace, & has 2 doors on canals, & balconies, & marble floors & marble halls, & the arms of the old family cut into the walls.

The first day, I saw the Piassa de San Marco, with its campanile, its clock tower, the 2 marble columns, one surmounted by the winged lion, the facade of San Marco, & the ducal Palace. I ascended the Campanile, & got a gen. view of the city,—all white houses & brown roofs, with towers & domes, canals & bridges.

Next, the Palace of the Doges, the giant stair case, standing on the spot, at its head, where Marino Faliero was beheaded, —the hall of the Senate, the hall of the Council of forty, & the hall of the terrible Council of Ten, & the Sentence room, where the 3 masked Senators, unknown to each other & to the accused, gave sentence,—& saw the Lion's Mouths, where anonymous accusations were furtively dropped, &

> "I stood in Venice, in the Bridge of Sighs,
> A palace & a prison on each hand"

& saw the statues & the pictures,—the Titians, & Tintorettos, & P. Veroneses, &c. &c. & got a notion no book can give of the splendor, the taste, the grandeur of idea, the luxury, of this remorseless, despotic oligarchy.

Next, the Church of St. John & St. Paul. (S. S. Giovanni & Paulo),—splended, vast, gorgeous! "The Venetian pantheon" —full of chapels, altars, monuments, tombs, statues & pictures, & frescoed from floor to dome, & Titian's Martyrdom of St. Peter, the Dominican, & Paul Veronica's Adoration of the Shepherds &c. &c.

Next, the S. Maria dei Frari, (commonly called the Frari, to distinguish it fr. the other Marias) where is the tomb of Titian, & pictures & statues by all the great Venetian artists, & altars & chapels, & tombs & fresco & mosaics.

And, last, the Academy of Fine Arts, (Academia di Belli

Arti), where I spent hours, in the various halls of this wonderful collection, & could well have spent days.

An hour of rest, a late dinner in the Square of St. Marc, & an evening of strolling about the Square, in the clear Italian summer moonlight, & hanging over the railing of the bridges, & walking under the shadows of the columns & porticoes, & listening to the music of violins & guitars & voices, of wh. the Square was full,—& so ends my first day in Venice!—& I lie with my window opening on a canal, & hear an occasional cry of a gondolier, & can hardly sleep fr. the fascinating music of a violin & guitar from across the water.

My second day in Venice (Sat. Aug. 25th—wh. I also observed as my wedding day). Breakfast in Sq. of S. Mark, wh. is lined with the best of restorants & cafés, where people eat & read, at tables, in the open air,—where fruits are abundant & cheap—grapes, peaches, figs & melons.

Order of Sights.

1. San Biagio, a Mariner's Church.

2. The Arsenal,—full of trophies of the Venetian Republic, & curious models of galleys & of armor. Among other trophies is the Turkish Admiral's flag taken at Lepanto. Model of the Bucentaur, &c.

3. The Jesuati Church (Real name is S. Maria del Rosario).

4. The Palace of the Giovanelli family, said to be as good a specimen as Venice affords. (Family now on *Terra Firma*,—wh. is the natural phrase here for going into the country). And exquisite,—exquisite, it is, in every part! No people ever equalled the Italians for maintaining exquisite taste & refinement in their pomps, pleasures, luxuries & pride. With them "vice lost all its grossness", & pride & pomp seemed elevated to an angelic state. Our vulgar modern shoes are unfit to tread these marble floors, & our mean French costumes make us look fit only to be the servitors of a race who planned & lived up to such refined splendor.

Passed the Palace that Byron occupied, on the Grand Canal, the palaces now owned by the Duchess de Beni, her son, the Count de Chanbourg, the Duchess of Parma, of the (late) Taglioni, & the ancestral palaces of those great Venetian names, Fóscari, Faliéro, Contárni, Cappello, Donato, Rimini, Giustiniani, &c. &c.—all splendid monuments of those high, wide, refined minds that gave Italy its place at the head of art. Each palace fronts on a canal, & each has a back or side door on a canal. The sea washes the marble steps, & the balconies overlook the sea. And it seems a city of palaces. Were there any poor? Where did they live? But, on what terrible terms, of a secret, oligarchal despotism, they held their lives & fortunes!

5. Church degle Scabze, (S. Maria in Nasaret), not one of the largest or most costly, yet it cost 1,200,000 francs, & one Chapel alone, of the Giovanelli family, cost 18000 ducats.

6. Church of San Rocco, one of the finest in the world, & full of the works of Titian, Tintoretto & Michael Angelo, & lined by chapels of great Venetian families.

7. The Rialto (Ponte de Rialto). How much more real & natural are the characters of Shakespeare, than the shadowy, *masky* characters wh. historians give us! "On the Rialto" one looks to see where Shylock trod, & watched & bargained, & where Antonio "rated" him, about his "monies & his usanses". It is larger & wider than I supposed—has three passages along & one across, & shops—little brokers' dens, & notaries', between. The Exchange is now removed to the floor of the Ducal Palace, & the Rialto is becoming a market.

8. Church of the Redentore, erected by the State, in pursuance of a vow, at the termination of the Plague, in 1577. It is immensely costly, with fine pictures, statues, bas reliefs, frescoes & mosaics,—& all a public gift.

9. Church of San Giorgio Maggiore—also large & costly, but situated on a small island, remote, & deserted, & service in it only kept up by 2 or 3 Benedictines (?). But all the world visits it.

10. Last of all—the Basilica of St. Mark! Here I saw all that is to be seen of this wonder of the world, built over the body of St. Mark, the Evangelist, who lies under its High Altar. I cannot recall one thing in ten, except a shoe of St. Charles Boromeo. But the wonder is that a church of five domes, all the walls & ceilings alive with scenes & figures, & yet not a touch of a pencil—all is *Mosaic*! One can hardly believe it! Those pictures, of all forms & colors,—all made by bits of colored marble! And then the bronses, the bas reliefs, the marble statues, monuments & columns, the gorgeousness of all! It cannot be exaggerated.

After dinner, joined my friends, the Pollocks, (who have just arrived fr. Trieste) in an evening row about the city, by moonlight, in a gondola. We passed thro' the Grand Canal, under the Rialto, & by the famous palaces,—whole streets (or canals) of fronts equal to Whitehall, & many superior,—& ended in seats in the Square of St. Mark's, with passing crowds, moonlight & music.

Sunday. Aug. 26. Church at St. Marc's. Succession of masses, from 9 A.M. to 12 M. & Vespers beginning at 2½ P.M. I spent some 3 hours in the basilica, dreaming, looking about on the crowds at the different altars, & hearing the music, & understanding next to nothing of the Services.

Kept quiet the rest of the day, writing this, in my room, dropping bits of paper into the canal. Every moment I have been in Italy has been exquisite weather,—neither hot nor cool,—that is, not hot, to an escaped E. Indian,—& clear & pure, & I have seen few mosquitos & meet few bad smells, wh. we were told would plague our lives.

Tomorrow morning, I leave for Milan. People here are excited & uneasy. All minds are turned towards Garibaldi. The city is full of Austrian soldiers, & said to be full of spies, 10,000 Austrian regulars—ft. & cannon planted so as to command the square & great avenues. The soldiers on guard & post are behind railings, caged in.

Another moonlight evening, & music in St. Mark's Place, by a mil. band of 36 instruments. Pretty to watch the parties coming to the stairs, in their gondolas, so still, so swift, so dream like!

Mond. Aug. 27. Took leave of Venice by early morning, going to the R.R. Station, in a gondola, under the Bridge of Sighs, by the Rialto, & passed the palaces on the Grand Canal,—&, Adieu to the most interesting & incredible creation of men's hands in the form of town or city on the Earth's surface!

All day on the R.R. fr. Venice to Milan;—a delightful day it has been—finest of weather, few clouds, clear sun, & this peculiar Italian scenery. The peculiarity, I think, is that the hills have the characteristics of mountains,—the breaks, the peaks, the irregular & picturesque outlines. The country is under high cultivation, every foot of it, as in England, & the roads & bridges are admirable, & the fields are separated by rows of trees or high shrubbery, or hedges, & almost every road, lane or foot-path has its double border of trees or high shrubbery. Then, there are so many churches, & relig. buildings of other sorts, castles, towers, watch-towers, bell towers, fortresses, & so many of these buildings are on the summits of the hills. In the ext. face of the country there is no sign of poverty or oppression. The *gravamen* is the subjugation of Italians to Austrians, & necessarily severe, often cruel, & always harassing & irritating regulations, enforced by soldiers, who are *everywhere*.

Passed thro' Padua, Vicensa, Verona, Peschiera, Desensano, Brescia, Bergamo & Treviglio,—"names that bear a perfume in the mention"—& along the beautiful Largo di Garda, wh. looked, all the afternoon, as if it were lying there waiting to be sketched by Claude. These towns all look historical, & like collegiate or ecclesiastical cities, adorned by the residence also of a peaceful & cultivated nobility.

We find the usual delays for exn. of passports & luggage, & fee-ing of officials, &—did any one *ever* see a polite German? —except as you may see a blossom on a graffed limb. Their language, by the side of the Italian, sounds Hyrcinian & hirsute. If I were an Italian, I would conspire to cut their throats over tubs, as Leonard did his hogs.

Reached Milan at 10 o'ck. P.M. In the dominions of Victor Emmanuel, regenerated Northern Italy; & ancient Milan,— the Milan of Attila & Charles V, of St. Ambrose, St. Augustin & St. Ch. Borromeo, of the Iron Crown of the Lombards! Hotel de la Villa, my window opens on a huge dome,—at least it looks so against the stars,—the Church of St. Charles Borromeo. A warm bath & bottle of German ale,—having had no dinner, & too late now, & bed, & waked up at 9.30 A.M. of—

Tuesday. Aug. 28th,   to the beautiful light of another day, & to hear a party of English women, at breakfast, making themselves wretched about beds & coffee & inns, in such a "glorious birth" as this country is to a newly arrived person of any reading or thought or feeling!

To-day, I devoted chiefly to the Cathedral. One should not begin too strong to talk of Italy. I called St. Mark's a wonder of the world. So it is. But what is the Cathedral at Milan? No words are adequate for the dedication of such a structure but *Gloria in excelsis Deo*. It is overpowering. I really believe that if a sensitive & imaginative person, who had seen nothing but N. England (say Miss Lydia Marsh) were transported into the interior of that church the effect might be too great for the brain to bear. And the prodigality of riches in the architecture & sculpture without! It is endless. The marble (white) keeps its color so beautifully in this climate. Most parts,—the upper especially are snow white, & the slight yellow tint the ceilings get, in the interior, is beautiful, & gives the fine work of the marble ceilings the look of old lace. One feeling, & a constant one is—is it possible? Is this the work of men's hands? I can imagine an excitable person, if out of sight, doing anything— rolling on the pavement, jumping up into the air & yelling, gasping for breath, or clapping hands to head & running until out of sight.

I mounted to the top, passing lines,—crowds—of statues, all the way,—for the ascent is over the exterior, in a way only a view can explain.

Milan lies in the great plain of Lombardy, wh. looks as green with grass & trees as the richest valleys. The charm of an Italian city is that it is *finished*. There are no vacant lots, no prepared streets unbuilt on, no pulling down & altering. Centuries have done the work, & the present accepts it. From the top of the Cathedral is a sea of brown roofs & white stone houses, avenues & patches of deep green, for gardens & public grounds, within the city, & a flat circumference of deep green extending to the distant hills. Not England is greener.

From the top to the crypt. Down to the tomb of St. Charles Borromeo. This is in a small chapel, where light always burns, & the sacrifice of the Mass is daily offered, the altar being over the tomb. This is the richest tomb in Christendom. Everything about it seems to have cost hundreds of thousands, & all gifts. The cross of emeralds, the gift of Maria Theresa, is the richest & most beautiful I ever saw. The affect. devotion to the mem. of this man is unlimited. I was pleased to see that the priest, when he opens the tomb, puts on a surplice. The golden side of the tomb is lowered by machinery, & the interior is disclosed, thro' pure & genuine crystal—all the side is crystal. There is his body, in robes of office, but the face is open to view, being enclosed in hermetically sealed crystal.

Lingered about the Cathedral until I had barely time to go to the incredibly ancient Ch. of St. Ambrose. Some service or other seems to be going on nearly all the time, in the Cathedral, & there are always people sitting or kneeling, reading or praying, somewhere.

Ch. of St. Ambrose. A curiosity. His body is there, under the altar, & there is the verit. pulpit in which he & St. Augustin preached, & the altar where St. Aug. renounced his errors.— (But, see Murray for dates). It is a quaint old place, & must not be suffered to decay.

Milan is very military—not only the regular army, but the Nat. Guard, the Militia, is in constant training, & nearly half the men one meets are in uniform. They mean to be prepared for Austria, if necessary. All the talk is "Garibaldi". I cannot understand them, but his name is in all mouths, & the speech is apparently always earnestly in his favor.

I like the open-air habits of the Italians, in the evenings. Walked about Milan from 9 to 10 P.M.—a well ordered, quiet, sober decent people, & no external signs of vice. In Venice, there were a few signs, as in Boston,—but Milan is better.

Wed. 29, Aug.   Left Milan for Arona, by rail. On our way out, saw handsome boulevards & walks, & numerous large public buildings.

Train passes thro' Magenta, the scene of the dreadful battle of 1859. They say that hardly a house is without shot marks; for the latter part of the battle was fought in the streets.

To Arona, at foot of Largo Maggiori, is about 4 hours. We stopped a half hour at Novara, & I walked about the town, to its cathedral & market &c. I like very much these middle sised Italian towns. They look solid, finished, ancient & tasteful, & the niches, oratories, frescoes out of doors, give an air of art to them.

(Selfish, hard headed, wiley priest, maneuvering to keep a double seat. Three Franciscans, in full garb, in my carriage).

At Arona, took steamer, on Largo Maggiori, for Farioli. Sail up the lake is one of those scenes to be remembered for life, especially the Isola Bella, & the other islands of the Borromeo

family; & there, at Arona, in full view, out "in the open", overlooking the lake, is the colossal bronse statue of St. Charles
Borromeo, erected by the city of Milan.

At Farioli, took diligence for Domo D' Ossola, where
passed the night. The way was directly up the Alps, & I had an
outside seat, with the driver, & commanded the whole view. It
was the height of harvest, & laborers were out in all the valleys
& green spots—& the laborers were mostly the women &
girls, carrying heavy loads of grass & wheat on their backs, &
often no hats or bonnets, & the sun very hot. The verdure is
intense, as great as in England, in the valleys & slopes, & vines,
fruit trees & cultivated grounds are everywhere. The mountains are tipped with perpet. snow, & snow & glaciers go far
down their sides, & in great prairies across & between them.
Nothing in America is to be compared with the Alps. All the
mountains in N.H. might be taken fr. a single range of the
Alps & not missed. And, besides being double their height &
more, the Alps have wild, broken, surprising outlines,—wh.
our mountains have not. Then, in the midst of this prodigality
of grandeur, there are the sweetest scenes of quiet industry &
peaceful life, for the valleys & nooks & slopes, wh. with us are
unoccupied, here centuries of labor & civilisation have peopled & cultivated, & spotted with Chapels, towers, quaint
churches, & hospices or monasteries. The road over the Simplon (Bonaparte's work) is solid & smooth as any road about
London, & the walls that support it as good as any of Ben.
Bussey's. It is a miracle of human skill & labor.

Now, imagine the roads & viaducts of Ancient Rome, & the
cultivation of the best counties in England, & the architecture
of Tuscany, spread among & over the wildest parts of the Himalayas & Andes, & you can get some notion of the Alps. But
you must add that water is everywhere, cascades & rushing
streams, wh. the everlasting snows never permit to fail. In one
place the Simplon road passes under the sheet of a torrent.

(Have I remarked the prevalence of blue eyes, yellow or
flaxen hair, & red hair, in Northern Italy? In Venetia, & Lombardy, very generally, & in Piedmont more. The blonds &
auburns & light brunettes almost equal the dark hair & eyes,
in numbers, on the plains, & exceed them as you ascend the
mountains).

This diligence traveling is delightful, if you are outside—air, view, & sight of all the people, on the road, & in the street of the little hamlets.

Night at Domo D'Osola, window looking out on the snow covered mountains, & sleeping by the sound of the rushing water.

Thursd. 30th. Aug.   From Domo D'Ossola, over the summit of the Simplon Pass, to Brienz for the night. At the summit, stopped at the Hospice, where were four monks of the St. Bernard Monastery, in charge, with some noble dogs, of the true breed, dark brown color with white spots. The monks gave us wine & bread, & we put a gift in the box in the Chapel. (The St. Bernard monks are all of the Augustine order, & not of the order of St. Bernard,—if there be such).

At the Swiss border, stopped at a little, humble inn, kept by a Swiss woman, who had five daughters, from 4 to 12 years old, all healthy, pretty, well behaved children, & where we got good bread & wine. (Good bread everywhere but in America).

This has been a glorious day—a day for a life time—a succession of wonders & delights. How the Himalayas or Andes compare with the Alps I know not, but it is certain they have not the presence of ruined castles, towers & hospices, still-used hospices & churches, villages & vineyards, close in upon the snows. The constant presence of water is a great feature. Think of poor, dry volcanic Mauna Loa, without a drop of water fr. summit to base!

Frid. 31. Aug.   Diligence (outside, always) fr. Brienz to Sion, rail road from Sion to St. Maurice. Diligence from St. Maurice to Bex. Rail Road from Bex to Villeneuve, on the banks of the Lake of Geneva—Lake Leman,—which we reached at night, & saw the moon shine over the "pure, placid Leman". The road all day has been by the side of the rushing Rhone, & through the valley of the Rhone,—a stupendous valley, or chain of valleys, & everywhere the Rhone a torrent of clay colored water. Between Martiguy & Bex is a famous cascade, the ——. Everything is dwarfed & ordinary in comparison with the Alps & their peaks & vale & torrents. Europe is *the continent*, after all.

Sat. Sep. 1.   Steamer from Villeneuve to Geneva. This is the charm of charms! First the dull white, sullen walls of Chillon, foundations sunk in the lake, & then Vevey, Lausanne, Nyon, Coppet, &c., & the succession, all the way to Geneva, of castles, towers, villas, simple country houses, churches, chapels, cities, towns, hamlets, washed by the Lake, or lying on its slopes, & in the distance, the towering Alps, & Jura in its "misty shroud". I should think that no small portion of the world had country seats upon the Lake of Geneva. And, now, we approach the high walls of Old Geneva. Here the narrow, rushing Rhone divides the city, bridged across by many bridges, but no longer of a clay color, but of a beautiful light green, as it hurries past the arches & along the walls.

Sat. afternoon, I am sitting at the window of my chamber in the hotel, looking out upon the Rhone, the island with Rousseau's statue, & the great bridges & opposite streets, & towers of the cathedral. This may be called a stage in my progress round the world.

Sunday. Sep. 2, 1860.   At Geneva went first to the old cathedral, & saw the pulpit in wh. John Calvin preached. The Church is still used by a Calvinistic society, filled with pews, & no altar. Next went to morning service at the Engl. Church. Stone, good sise, well designed, built & supported by vol. contributions. One of the best,—perhaps the best, congregation I ever saw, in quality,—picked people—Engl. & Am. travellers, decent eno' to stay over Sunday & go to service,—or with means & taste eno' to have permanent residences here. So many healthy sensible looking Engl. girls, & mothers & fathers. Church crowded—seats in the aisles. The Am. Consul (one Giles, of Md., son of Dist. judge, a flat) tells me there are 200 Am. boys at school within a day's journey of Geneva. So many Americans attend the Eng. Ch. here, that they add a prayer for the Prest. of U.S. to that for the Queen, in the Liturgy.

In afternoon, walked with Giles & Mr. Peters, son of Peters the U.S. Reporter, to the confluence of the Rhone & Arve,— beautiful spot. Rhone is dark green, & Arve is muddy. At sundown walked, alone, on the high grounds of Geneva, & saw clouds & openings here & there, where Mt. Blanc lies, but not sure whether got a glimpse of the Mt. or no. It is seen plainly in clear weather. The rushing of the Rhone past the bridges, at night, is fearful. It is a torrent, & by day, of a dark emerald color.

Swiss troops are mustering & drilling everywhere, to preserve the integrity & neutrality of the poor little republic.

Geneva is a large place now, & growing,—a centre of travel & pleasure residence. Population abt. equally Cath. & Prot. Houses built of light colored stone, & high, 5 & 6 stories, & let by stories, as in Paris. Adds to style of place.

Monday. Sep. 3. Rail Road, along the Lake of Geneva, towards Neufchatel. Skirted the pretty Lake of Neufchatel, had a good view of the town, where we stopped a few minutes, & then across country, to Landeron at the foot of Lake Biel (Fr., *Bienne*), & there took steamer through the length of the lake, to the town of Biel (Bienne), & thence, by rail again, through Solence, Aarburg, Hertogenbuchsee, & Olen, to Basle, where passed the night. At Basle, first view of the Rhine, wh. is here a broad, shallow, rapid, turbid river. Reached Basle in season to visit the cathedral before dark. It is a large, respectable looking edifice, of red sandstone, with roof of colored tiles. In it is the tomb & monument of Erasmus. I had the satisfaction of reading the latin epitaph in the manner he succeeded in banishing from England, but wh. is now regaining its place among English & Am. scholars. Here is a nemesis for you, after centuries,—to have an Am. standing over his ashes & reading his epitaph in the Roman manner! In the Chapter House, is the desk or chest used by Erasmus,—also a chest (very old) wh. contained the records of the Chapter before the Reformation. In the rear of the church, is a platform wh. overlooks the Rhine & all the town, planted with trees & grass. Here I walked, in the beautiful twilight & moonlight, for an hour or more.

As one comes North, from the Oriental, tropical regions,— the gradual changes are curious. First, in Switzerland & Upper Germany, began to notice the blowing of noses, coughing, sneesing, spitting, & other signs of regions of phlegm & saliva. Then, the increasing fairness of skin, prevalence of blue & grey eyes & fair hair—increasing breadth of jaw, thickness of lips, bigness of head; &, in Germany, a cowlike heaviness of tread & width of foot. The gradual mixture of French with Italian, in Piedmont, French with German, in Switzerland, & the ceasing of French in Germany. In nature, you notice the length of twilight, the coming in of turf, grass plots, thick shade trees & hedges.

Tuesday Morning, Sep. 4.   Rail fr. Basle to Heidelberg, by the Black Forest. Next me, in the car, made an acquaintance in young James M. Crafts, gr. son of Jeremiah Mason, a capital fellow, good looking, strong, intelligent, manly,—been on a tramp over Tyrol, & bound to Heidelberg, where he is to study chemistry & geology.

Reached Heidelberg by 1 P.M., & gave the afternoon to the Castle, with young Crafts. Went all over it. It is a noble—not quite *ruin*, but memorial or monument of feudal & chivalric times, & the grounds & walks about it are more varied & beautif. than I have seen connected with any such place. View of Neckar, & distant white stripe of the Rhine, & the level Palatenate, is grand. Heidelberg stands just where the hills cease.

In ev., walked about the town, to do honor to memories of Ned's eight year residence. Called at Wittermaden's—but he was *ex re*, & it is vacation. Looked at the University, Museum, bridge over Neckar & chief churches. It is a nice quiet, old town, & with its numerous shady hill-side walks, well adapted for resid. of people who love such things.

Lodged at the "Prins Karl".

Wed. Sep. 5.   Heidelberg, by rail, to Mayence, & there took steamer down the Rhine, to Cologne. Passed, by rail, through Darmstadt, where large body of Hessian troops were parading, to receive the King of the Belgians.

Will not describe Rhine. Trite. Was not disappointed. Scenery is not (& I did not expect to find it) on a gigantic scale, like the Saguenay, or Yosemete,—nor impending & perpendicular, but often very high, sharp, ragged & wild, & interspersed among exquisite beauties, & everywhere the imagn. & feelings are touched by the ruins of successive ages—Roman, Dark Ages, feudal, ages of chivalry, Religious wars of Reformation,

& abbeys, convents & churches, among the castles & towns. Passed & saw the usual most marked objects—Johannisberg, Rüdesheim, Bingen, Rheinstein (a rebuilt castle, occupied by Prince Fr. of Prussia) the island rock of Pfalz, The Seven Maidens, St. Goar, Boppard, Stolzenfels, Coblens, Ehrenbreitstein (wh. is not, as I expected, a castle, but a great series of towers & walls, making a long & very extensive fortification, on the high hill-top, with a noble position, & almost unrivalled *outlook*), Rheineck castle, Drachenfels, & Bonn.

As far as Coblens, we had beautif. weather. From Cleins to Cologne rain, & chilly weather. This cold rain is new to me, & rather gloomy, but the scene & sights interest me eno' to keep off dullness.

Yankee face, gold specs,—Yankee voice,—loud, *platform* conversation—"Professor in a college—New England—knew Wayland, of course,—He was my chief. Yes Sir, Frank Wayland & I . . . Shoulder to Shoulder. Yes, Sir—shoulder to shoulder, 30 years—all the influences—Abolition—Now, there, Sir . . . Brown Univ. . . . Minister of the Gospel. Baptist. So offended that made acq. of no Baptist clergyman in England. Know was wrong, &c. &c.". He saw none of the scenery. When could not get an auditor, sat with back to the house, eyes shut, meditating more talk. Could it be Gammell? He had a wife with him,—been pretty. "When other boys playing, I was digging into hard theol. controversy".

Reached Cologne in dark rainy, chilly night. Hotel Hollande. With my topee & red stripes on luggage, was taken for a returning E. Indian officer, & got the best rooms.

(Noticed the entire absence of *animal* life in Germany. No cattle in the fields,—neither sheep, nor cows, nor oxen. High cultivation, but all inanimate nature).

Thursday. Sep. 6.   At Cologne. Spent the morning at the Cathedral. It is a stupendous structure, even now, & when completed, will be, probably, the largest cathedral in Christendom. But it is not interesting or agreeable now; for the work going on interferes with the effects. False roofs, low & plain, destroy the chief effect of a cathedral—height & elegance of roof, & vistas are cut off. Moreover, it must be said that the German Prot. Church can do nothing with a cathedral. As well might the Temple in Jerusalem, after it had been consecrated by Solomon, have been handed over to the Moravians. All looks cheerless & unused & misapplied & merely a show. There is R. Cath. worship held in some side chapels, & in one aisle, & was going on, at the time,—but it filled little space. I went to the top, & got lost in coming down, & wandered among dark passages ending in closed doors, & went up & down, for about a half an hour, until a workman coming along gave me a clue. I had taken no guide, I hate them so, in a Cathedral. The day was beautiful, & the view of Cologne & the Rhine, well repays the labor of ascent. Absurd bank of *Sunflowers*, around the Chancel, outside.

Geo. F. Hoar. "Why do men hate Geo. T. Curtis so?"

Mr. Choate. "Why, Mr. Hoar, some men we hate for cause, but him we hate peremptorily".

In the afternoon, took the train for Antwerp. A beautiful journey this—fr. Cologne to Antwerp! It is lower Prussia from Cologne to Aix La Chapelle, (or, more strictly, Verviers) & thence it is Belgium. I am charmed with Belgium. Here is a sight that comes home,—cattle grasing in the fields, under the trees,—cows, oxen, sheep,—everywhere,—& English hedges, & shrubbery, & thick trees, & groves, & such nice houses,— all so neat & tasteful—a good medium between the Dutch & French.

All the way, I should say, from Cologne to Antwerp, the rail road is lined, on each side, by a hedge. The towns & villages are delightful. The better classes speak French, the lower, Flemish,—& tho' the German is a far greater language than the French, for poetry, theology, oratory & metaphysics,—yet, after the popularly spoken German, it is a pleasure to hear the French again,—so *genteel* & facile a language,—so civilised, urbane & complaisant.

(The train starts by a trumpet, instead of a bell, at each station).

Liège (French, & in 2 syllables —the German being Lüttich) is a beautiful town, & the watering-place of Chaudefontaine, as pretty as need be. From Cologne to Liège the country is hilly, well diversified, & picturesque & abounding in water, as well as rich & populous & highly cultivated. After Liège, comes the "Low Country",—Netherlands,—of the Flemings

& Netherlanders proper. No longer picturesque, but as pretty as art & industry can make a level country.

At Malines (Mecklin) trams separate, to Brussels & Antwerp. Reached Antwerp at 10 P.M.,—so the last three hours, we saw nothing. Lodged at a capital hotel, the Hotel St. Antoine,—such beds & sheets & pillows & curtains!

Friday. Sep. 7.   Took guide, this time, & made a pretty active campaign, from 8.30 P.M. until 12 M. *Cathedral.* Large, high rich & especially rich in Rubens' pictures. Such is genius—Rubens is a revenue to the Cathedral. All the world pays to see his pictures. They are the Descent from the Cross, the Elevation of the Cross, the Resurrection & the Assumption. My remark is that the pictures seemed alive,—full of work. The way they are shown, by drawing up a curtain & keeping it up a few minutes, for each set of comers, at so much a head, is not agreeable. While the beadle was drawing the curtain over the Assumption, & I was contemplating it, he breaks in, to a man before me,—"that is not 5 shillings, only 4 s. & 6 d". "That is the Virgin Mary", said he, to a common-place, diffident English woman—"Who is that *other lady?*" said she.

Went to the top of the spire, 466 feet high. Can see Bergen op Zoom, & the spires of a town in Holland, at the North, & the spires of Ghent, in the South. Perfectly level country, thickly populated & richly cultivated, & no signs of poverty or neglect anywhere, in city or country.

Next, to Church of Saint Jacques (St. James). This is more curious & extraordinary than the Cathedral, tho' smaller—also richer & more beautiful. There are no less than 22 chapels, each of marble. The whole church seems inlaid with beautif. stones,—roofs, floor & walls. One chapel of the Rubens family, with marble groups & effigies. Both here & in the cathedral a great deal of exquisite oak carving. (Omitted to mention the picture of St. Francis, by Murillo, in the Cathedral, wh. struck me very much).

Church of St. Paul's—also large & rich, full of marble & oak & gold, with a renowned picture of the Scourging of Jesus, by Rubens, & of the bearing of the Cross, by Van Dyke,—the latter in bad light at this hour. In the close of this church is a famous representation of the garden, Mt. Calvary, & Purgatory, in the grotto form. My guide explained the figures to me, & as he turned to go out, I asked "What are all those other figures?". "Oh, only Twelve Apostles, four Evangelists, & Angels, —that's all".

Visited a private collection of the late Mr. Nuyts—who died 2 years ago, & gave the collection for the benefit of the poor. It is in excellent order, & each visitor pays a small fee, for the good object. Here are master pieces of Van Dyck, Teniers, Rubens, Jordaens, Guido & Murillo, &, I believe, one of Claude. Murillo's (?) St. Anthony, looks like Father.

All the great churches here—Cathedral, St. Paul's, & St. James, are Catholic, & worship was going on, & people reading & praying, in the usual manner, & at some altars lights burning, & the smell of incense, & the sounds of voices. To my surprise, my guide told me that Antwerp was entirely a Catholic city, & that there were no Protestant churches, except of foreigners.

Took leave of this clean, orderly, wealthy, respectable city, with regret,—& took steamer, at 1 P.M., for London, & took my latest step on the *Continent* of Europe. Passage down the Scheldt, by the neatest little villages, with red roofs, & by night were out at sea,—on the German Ocean. So natural is it now to me, to be on the deck of a ship! I am at home, at once.

Saturday. Sep. 8. Here I am, in dear old London, again! At the house of the Bithneys, too,—tho' they have moved fr. 19 Regent st., to 7 Bury st. St. James. They received me most cordially,—& in half an hour, my trunks were unpacked, my clothes sorted in drawers & shelves, & I sat down to read my letters from home, (wh. I got at the Barings)—not having heard from home, a word—for six months,—and when I found all well,—all living,—it seemed that my cup of blessing was full. Here, in England, in perfectly good health, in vigor of health—with no loss even of an umbrella, from my luggage,— escaped all dangers of sea & land, of violence & sickness,—in all climates & countries. If I am not grateful, it is because gratitude is not in me.

Sturgis was very cordial & kind, & got me the last berth to

be had in the Persia, on the 15th, & sent a line to F. E. Parker, by extra mail, *via* Cork, to notify my arrival. Mr. Baring, also, interested & cordial.

None of my great friends are in town,—my friends of 1856,—as all the world that can leave London has gone. Called at houses (or clubs) of Parkes, Senior, Sir Wm. Heathcote, Mr. Gladstone, &c. & left cards or notes,—& the papers announced that the Duke of Argyll, the Sutherlands, Lord Lansdowne, Ld. Campbell, Ld. Cranworth, &c. are in the country. Better so,—for I have no clothes to make visits in. Have seen no washer woman since Cairo, & Mrs. Bithney has a large bag to deal with,—& tho' I have a superabundance of tropical clothing, have hardly a decent suit for Engl. climate. Turn up Henry T. Parker, who is full of kindness & introduces me to a proper tailor, who is to get me in order before I sail.

How pleasant are the old London sights! And the parks— Hyde, Green, St. James',—are more beautiful, after all I have seen elsewhere, than my recollection held them.

Sunday, Sep. 9.   What could I do but go to the Abbey, to the early Communion Service, at 8 o'ck.? How still! How solemn! The high roof, the dim sunset colored stone,—so much more agreeable to the eye than the white & red of most of the Continental churches—& the still statues of the great dead,—statesmen, orators, soldiers, poets, scholars. In this early service there is no music, & the whole company—in deserted West End—did not exceed twenty.

After breakfast H.T.P. called & took me to the morning service at the church of All Saints, Margaret st. This is the most perfectly finished, rich & exquisite religious structure, for its sise,—it is not large, in England,—& probably not exceeded in Europe. Beresford Hope gave 10,000 £. towards it, & a London banker gave 30,000 £., & it cost much more. The outside is of dark red & black brick. The interior is a masterpiece of color & arrangement. Yet not a touch of paint, or stucco,—all is marble & stone, inlaid! It is a wonder of skill & beauty. Yet, this exquisite Church —not for the rich & fashionable, but a Free Church,—open to all,—a *gift* to the public, & in a poor neighborhood, & its congregations made up much of the poor. It has a rector & four curates, who all live in the Church Yard, & its services, schools, charities &c. are constant. The order of services is this—

Every day in the week.
    Holy Communion at 7 A.M.
    Morning Prayer at 8 A.M.
    Evening Prayer at 5 P.M.
Sundays
    Holy Communion at 7 A.M.
    Morning Prayer Sermon & Communion at 11 A.M.
    Litany 12 M.
    Evening Prayer 5 P.M.
    Evening Prayer & Sermon 7 P.M.
Other Holy Days
    Holy Communion 7 A.M.
    Morning Prayer, Sermon & Commn. 11 A.M.
    Evening Prayer 5 P.M.

And the Church is always open for persons to sit & read, or meditate or for private devotions. And this has been entirely successful. The clergy & active parishoners are even over-worked. The church, this morning, was so full we could scarcely get a seat, & many could not sit. The service was choral, throughout. When the Communion office begins, they light the candles on the altar, as in the Eastern Greek & Roman Churches,—& I think, too, but am not sure—the Lutheran.

Went to Parker's to dine (3 Ladbroke Gardens, Kensington Park, Notting Hill). Mrs. P. & children well, & nice house with good country view.

At 6 ½ P.M., went to Ev. Service at a nice, half rural, half city church of St. Stephen's, Notting Hill,—where the service was choral, half the seats free, &—tho' a beautif. Sunday twilight, —the church was crowded. Respectable sermon. To-day, all the clergy preach on the Harvest, & have prayers,—at request of Bishop of London,—as has been danger of losing it. The Harvest & Garibaldi, are the two topics, in all men's mouths, Parliament being adjourned.

Monday. Sep. 10.   In my rooms, writing & reading, all A.M. by a sea-coal fire. Memories of Egypt & Aden & Red Sea!
    Parker calls & takes me to the British Museum, to see the

Reading Room, wh. has been built since 1856. It is the room where students & readers have their desks, & consult the text books, cyclopaedias, catalogues &c., & from wh. they send orders for books to the Library,—the Library not being visited, at all, for study. There is no such room as this in Europe. It is a circle, with dome, lighted from above, & its diameter is 4 feet greater than that of the dome of St. Paul's.

The autographs are now open to view of all, spread out in glass cases,—as well as many other lit. curiosities. This is the grandest Literary & Scientific institution (not for instruction) in the world. The Reading Room, I told Parker, was a temple to the deification of Bibliology.

In the ev., called on Mrs. Leslie, (widow of C. R. Leslie, the artist, who was so attentive to me in 1856,—the friend of my father & Mr. Allston) at 2 Abercom Pl.—far out. She was evidently touched by my attention, & I was glad to pay it. Her son-in-law Fletcher, was there—daughters in Scotland. She gave me a photograph of a portrait of Leslie by himself in early life.

Tuesd. Sep. 11.   Kind letter fr. Sir Wm. Heathcote, inviting me to Hursley. Cannot go,—as no clothes fit. *Au lieu*, shall go to York, Boston &c., to pass the time until Friday, when pack up & go to Liverpool.

Weather has been clear & fine, now, for four days—good for me,—but almost a salvation of the harvest.

From Trieste to Antwerp, inclusive—Austrian Italy, *Italian* Italy, Piedmont, Lombardy, Switzerland, Southern Germany, Prussia, Northern-Germany, and Belgium—have seen no signs of poverty, pauperism, beggary, idleness, drunkenness, obtrusive vice, decay or wanting. The signs of industry, prosperity, advance, growth, progress, content, are as general as with us. I saw, in no city, anything so bad as New York & Boston & London present,—(& N. York worst of all) in the regions of the abject poor, & the abandoned vicious. Other travelers tell me that those things not only are not seen, but are not. External, offensive vice & pauperism are suppressed & controlled.

But *industry* & *decent provision for life*,—are general,—as in New England,—& more than in many parts of Old England, Scotland,—far before Ireland—& more than in California, &

many parts of middle & Western America. Doubtless, *change of condition* is rare, the ruts are deep, & routine governs,—but order, industry, sobriety, outward decency prevail also on the Continent of Europe as I saw it.

Tuesday. Sep. 11. Drove to Barings & settled accts. Spent morning in Chamber, before sea-coal fire, writing journal & letters.

At 5 P.M. took train for York, at King's Cross station. (I have traveled 2d class throughout the continent of Europe & in England. On the continent, the 2d class are generally excellent, —as good as our cars at home, but in England they are not quite good eno' for a long journey,—stiff, straight backs. The company is mixed,—sometimes the best of people, that is, scholars, professional men, &c., & with them a good many lower & disagreeable persons, but the chance for view is about as good as fr. the first class).

Stopped 5 minutes at Peterboro', & got a view of the out-side of the cathedral, but over the tops of low houses, &, of course, not satisfactory.

The long rains have kept everything green, & now the clear, fine weather, wh. has relieved the mind of the whole kingdom fr. fear of an entire loss of harvest, seems to take everybody out of doors. The number of boys playing cricket in the green fields, as we hurry by (for it is vacation, now, at the schools) would surprise one. They seemed to have been arranged for a show,—& the girls are walking about & looking on, & women sitting under the trees, sewing or reading, or tending babies,— & all the working people are at the harvest,—cutting, gathering, binding or "carrying". After all the world seen,—there is no land like England, for a home!

After Peterboro', it is too dark to see, & we are thundered through Grantham, Dorcester, in the dark, &c. &c., & reach York at a little after 10 P.M., & I am soon in a comfortable chamber, in this most ancient of towns,—the scene of great events in British history.

Wed. Sep. 12. Rose early, & walked the circuit of the walls, round the half of the city on the S. side of the river. The walls are in excellent preservation, & a walk of about 6 f. in width is carried along them, bringing the parapet breast high. This preservation of the walls of the old walled towns has the advantage, not only of antiquarian interest, & effect on the imagn., but it gives an open space for healthful air & exercise, & if the towns grow, they can build outside the walls as well as inside. At York, the gates are preserved, & have a heavy, sombre, feudal look about them, & the chief streets are named from the gates, which are called "bars", as well, or in addition—as in Petergate Bar, Micklegate Bar, Bootharn Bar, Monk Bar &c.

The river Ouse divides the town, & over it is one stone bridge & two ferries. Spent the chief part of the morning at the "Minster"—(no one calls it the "Cathedral"). It is very grand & large. The stone is not so dark & agreeable to my eye as Westmin. Abbey, but more so than the chief cathedrals on the continent. The interior has a hollow & deserted look. There are no frescoes, no paintings, & the choir is shut off by screens & organ, so that the vista is interrupted. The chapter-house is handsome & in good order. On the whole, I am not disappointed in York Minster as regards sise, & grandeur, but it does not *interest* me; & in mere sise, & especially in height of roof, it is entirely eclipsed by Milan. No cathedral that I have seen, anywhere, approaches Milan for effect of height & vistas, & then it is warmed & alive with color & paintings, burning candle, praying people, moving priests, & the smell of incense. The few marble monuments & effigies, in York Minster, have a peculiarly cold & desolate look.

Walked round the castle, wh., like most of the castles in the English country towns, is used as a prison, & in good repair, & visited the ruins of St. Mary's Abbey, & the Manor House, & looked at some of the quaint old churches, St. Helen's, St. Sampson's (*what* St. Sampson, for the δγουιστ was an evil liver,) & went into one—St. Mary's something,—and an odd old place eno' it was,—everything where you did not expect to find it, & black with time, & rather damp for comfort, I should say. Attended morning service at the Minster. Choral, with two choirs, & pretty well done.

After lunch, took train for Doncaster, learning that I have just time to see the Doncaster races,—the great race of the St. Leger,—wh. ranks next to the Derby,—&, as I have never seen a race in England, I am fortunate to catch this, unexpectedly.

Reach Doncaster at 2 P.M. Great crowds, pouring out to

"The Leger". Thicken as we go on. Great open fields, roofs of the few houses abt. it covered with people,—& there is the "Grand Stand", a large house, with piassas &c. A guinea admits to the Grand Stand & Betting Ring,—but I do not afford it, & take my chance in the crowd. The horses that are to run, —some 15, are walking & prancing & running about, in the course,—& their riders in gay dresses, marked on the cards wh. nearly all spectators carry.

1. Lord A.'s ch. m. Firefly, red coat & black cap.

2. Col. B.'s b. h. Swiftrune, blue coat & red cap.

3. Mr. C.'s b. s. Onward. Yellow coat & black sash. &c. &c.

The most observed among the horses are the winner of the Derby of this year, "Thormanby", the American horse "Umpire", and one named "Wisard". It was a pretty sight, & the horses seemed to me to be brought to the pitch of the combination of strength & fleetness.

They made several false starts, until people got tired & vexed, & one of the Stewards, Lord Coventry, came down & took part in getting them off. It was said that the false starts among the horses, especially if they get far off &c., & are obliged to come back, as was the case with "Wisard" are harmful. They came in at a lightning pace. The pictures do not exagg. the appearance of speed & effort in the horses. To the surprise of nearly all, the race is won by St. Albans, a horse that was not a favorite, & the favorite, "Thormanby", came in 4th, & "Umpire" 5th & "Wisard" 3d, & the 2d being "High Treason", not highly betted on.

There were 2 more races, a Sweepstakes & a handicap, & beautifully run, but the intense interest died out with the "Leger".

The crowd seemed to me decent & orderly,—much more so than wd. have been one near either N. York or Philad., & the desperate rowdies of our large crowd,—the fighters, do not exist, or appear. About ¼ of the crowd were women, & apparently, the greater part, even in the open ground, decent people, the d. & wives of yeomen & laborers. The upper classes are in carriages or in the stands. Lord Derby ran a horse, but, as usual, failed to win. A man I met in the evening at the inn, said the reason Ld. Derby does not win is that he will not cheat, or combine to defraud, & the others oust him. This man thought nearly all the races were frauds. Others, however, tell me they are generally fair. (A man who has once failed to pay a lost bet is not admitted within the betting ring. In some cases, like insolvency, where the man has retrieved himself & paid up in full, he has been restored).

Great crowds at the station, bound up to London, & to all quarters of the kingdom. But good order preserved. I take train for Boston. As go out, get good view of the tower & spire of the large church of Doncaster,—said to be one of the best in the North of England. Reach Boston at about 10 P.M., & "put up" at the Peacock Inn.

Thursday. Sep. 13.   In Old Boston,—(St. Botolf's town),— & a nice old town it is—not walled, nor with a castle, or a cathedral,—yet an old & important place,—the 2d town in dignity in Lincolnshire, & quite equal to Lincoln in trade & population. All abt. Boston the country is flat,—a dead level— the Fens of Lincolnshire. Yet, it *is* rich, highly cultivated, thickly settled, well wooded & well watered. The Chirwall, a small, slow stream divides Boston nearly equally, & handsome stone bridges span it, & barges, luggers, & even vessels of consid. burden lie in its channel. Boston is closely built, of brick, with red tiled roofs,—the streets irregular but clean & paved, & lighted with gas. (I walked abt. a little, before going to bed, & heard a man & woman sing Byron's "Maid of Cadis", at an inn door, for sixpences,—or rather, pennies & ha'pennies). The only thing to be seen here is the great church of St. Botolf. In this, there is no disappointment. It is not a cathedral, nor an abbey or collegiate church,—but simply a parish church, of the largest sise & highest style. The tower is its chief beauty, & how could a tower be more beautiful? You can stand & look at it for hours. It has *parts*, that interest & please you, as well as its whole. It is at once simple & rich. And high too, for its height is —— feet, half as high again as Bunker Hill Mon't. It is the largest church in England without a transept. I ascended to the top, & got a fine view of Lincolnshire. Col. Sibthorp's house, & Mr. Humphrey Sibthorp's hospital are the chief objects in the neighborhood. The town looks very pretty beneath, & the rooks fly & bother about the coins &

buttresses, & in & out of the open work of the upper tower & lantern.

The interior is plain, & without color or ornament, except some oak carving & stained glass. It had been grossly out of repair, utterly neglected, but was restored by subscription & reopened some 7 years ago. It holds conveniently 3000 persons, &, being a great favorite, is often full, or nearly so. A marriage service took place, while I was here, & I attended & took part, so as to be able to say & feel that I had worshipped in the old parent church.

The Chancel is very large. Within the choir sit the Mayor & town corporation on one side, & the singers on the other, each Alderman & Councilman having his stall & his worshipful seat & worshipful stamped book.

The Cotton Chapel, which was restored by subscriptions among the descendants of John Cotton in Boston, U.S., is used to keep the records & for a vestry. They think a good deal of the fact here, & were quite pleased by the attention & interest. The tablet in latin (Mr. Everett's composition), is of brass & makes a good show.

At noon, took the train for Lincoln, which I reached at a little after 1 P.M. & after lunch, walked out to the cathedral.

The chief object of interest betw. Boston & Lincoln is Tattershall Castle, a ruin, but one or two towers of full height. It now belongs to the Earl Fortescue.

Was surprised to find Lincoln standing on elevated ground, a good deal of a hill, & the cathedral really on the top of a hill of some pretensions, & seen at a great distance over the level country of Lincolnshire. It has the highest site & most commanding of any cathedral in England,—unless it be Durham, —which I have not seen & cannot compare with it.

Macaulay was right. He told me, in 1856, to see Lincoln. The question was to wh. cathedrals I should go, having then seen none but St. Paul's & the Abbey. Some said Salisbury, some York & some Canterbury &c. &c. but Macaulay said—"Lincoln, Lincoln. See Lincoln. That is the best of all". I attributed this to some accidental prejudice, & did not go, but I sympathise with him. If I must choose among all,—taking inside & outside, form & color, beauty, sise & interest,—all into account

—give me Lincoln. (*Mem.* that I have not seen Canterbury, Durham & Gloucester & Exeter). For interest in the interior, I will not yield the Abbey, nor for beauty of color & form in the exterior, Salisbury; but the interior of Salisbury is nothing & less than nothing. In exterior, Lincoln has an agreeable color, —not the exquisite touch of the russet of Salisbury, but still, satisfactory, & with its nave, choir, chancel, double transepts, aisles, chapter house, & towers, it has the look of a town of buildings. The color of the interior is beautiful,—a dark buff, —& there is a great deal of black oak, richly carved. There is a look of warmth & richness, in strong contrast with the cold, deserted look of York minster. The evening service began soon after I entered, & I remained through it. The afternoon sun on the "storied windows, richly dight", the charm of the color of the ancient stone, relieved by dark oak, the frequent monuments, the resounding organ & the full voiced choir, made it just what an evening in a rural cathedral should be. I ascended the tower,—the central tower, & stood up inside the "Great Tom of Lincoln" whose tongue is six feet long. The view from the top gives you the hill country of Rutland & Leicestershire, close by, & the fens—the level of Lincolnshire, stretching to the sea. Belvoir Castle can be seen, of a clear day.

In the Close, is a piece of Roman pavement, wh. is housed over & carefully protected.

The ruins of the Bishop's Palace, destroyed by Cromwell, but with much remaining, & venerable with ivy, are among the best pieces of ruins I have seen. They are in the Close, concealed by a high wall, from the casual passer, & hard by the cathedral. The houses of the Dean, Subdean, &c. in the Close, are in the usual cathedral style of beauty, exquisite order, & repose. The description of the Deanery, in the "Angel in the House" (?) applies to almost all of them.

The town of Lincoln, too, I like well. It has diversity of service, hollow, hillside & hill top, irreg. streets, but neat, a river to cross by stone bridges, ancient gateways, cathedral & castle. The castle is large, & now altered for a county prison.

Left at about 6 P.M. & reached London at 10.30, & drove, for the last time, along the miles of streets by flaming gas light, Bloomsbury Sq., Russell Sq., & the wide, straight well built

streets that fashion has deserted, into the crowd of Regent st.,
& home to my quiet little room at Bithney's.

Friday. Sep. 14. H.T.P. called, & we went out for a short
walk. He took me to two objects of interest I had never seen
before, tho' near,—the house of Sir Isaac Newton, in St. Martin's st., & that of Sir Joshua Reynolds, 47 Leicester Sq. Newton's house has still the observatory on its roof, wh. he put
there & used. Then we walked down Parliament st., through
Whitehall Gardens, past the house of Peel, into St. James'
Park, & took our seats in the mall, with a view of the towers of
the Abbey just over the trees,—as rural a view as you would
get in the Midland Counties.

Rest of the noon in packing, or superintending Bithney in
so doing, (except a call on Hon. A Kinnaird, who came to
town this morning, who, by the way, is now heir presumptive
to the title & estates,—his brother's only son, the "Master of
Kinnaird", being dead)—& took train for Liverpool at 5 P.M.
Short stops at Rugby, Stafford & Warrington,—mostly after
dark, & reached Adelphi Hotel, Liverpool at 9.45 P.M.

Saturday. Sep. 15. Took steamer Persia, for N. York, wh. got
under way at 9 o'ck. The old views of the fortress-like docks,
the low shores of Lancashire, & the high coast of Cheshire &
Wales,—the light at Holyhead, & then the open sea. Some 180
passengers. Know no one on board.

Sunday. Sep. 16. Service, well attended, & singing. Judkins
is famed for his good reading. Reads better than almost any
Engl. clergyman I have heard. At about noon, make the harbor of Queenstown, (Cove of Cork) & come to anchor in the
Cove. This is an admirable harbor,—perhaps the best I ever saw.
Easy of access, landlocked, & large eno' for the ships of the
world—one would say. Went ashore, in order to say & feel that
I have stood upon the shores of Ireland. Town of Queenstown
is small,—all the merchants residing at Cork, 7 miles above, &
the population eminently Irish, in look & manner,—the better
classes pretty (women, I mean) & all healthy looking, & many
barefooted, & some begging, & numerous gin shops, & a
look of untidiness & unthrift everywhere. I was surprised to

find that of the three churches, one is Ch. of England & large, & another Scotch Presb. (tho' small) & only one—tho' the largest, R. Catholic. Still, nearly all the pop. must be R. Cath.

Harbor is well fortified, & the country about richly green, with plenty of hedges & shrubbery, & few trees. Sailed, again, with mails, at about 5 P.M.

Passage across, is about as usual. 180 passengers, chiefly very common-place persons. Large proportion of Germans trading in U.S., & cotton dealers fr. the Southern states. About half way across, find out a young Parkman, from Savannah, who was at Cambridge 3 or 4 years ago. The last day but two, Eustis, late M.C. from New Orleans, introduces himself, & I make acquaintance of his wife, d. of Corcoran of Washington, the banker. Eustis is son of late Ch. J. of Louisiana. And the last day, make acq. of Bancroft Davis (formerly I knew him at Cambr.) son of "Honest John", late Sec. of Legation at London, now lawyer in N. York, & his wife, a d. of James Gore King, & a cousin, a d. of John A. King. These were pleasant people. But, as no list of passengers published, & many were sea-sick the first half of the passage, strangers who ought to know one another, do not find one another out.

No incidents. Weather pretty good. But the Atlantic is heavy & dull after the Pacific & the Oriental seas.

Reached Fire Island & Neversink after 10 P.M. & went up N.Y. harbor by moonlight, & anchored at 1 A.M.

Thursday, Sep. 27.   This day opens in America—home. Been absent 433 days, of wh. spent about 233 on the water & 200 on land. New York completes the circumnavigation of the globe!

CHRONOLOGY

NOTE ON THE TEXTS

NOTES

Chronology

1815   Born August 1 in Cambridge, Massachusetts, the second child of Ruth Charlotte Smith Dana and Richard Henry Dana. (Father's family is descended from Richard Dana, a laborer who settled in Cambridge in 1640 and died in 1690, leaving an estate valued at over £300. Great-grandfather Richard Dana was a prominent opponent of the Stamp Act and remained active in the colonial cause until his death in 1772. Grandfather Francis Dana, born 1743, served in the Continental Congress and as an envoy to Russia before becoming a justice of the Massachusetts supreme judicial court in 1785 and its chief justice in 1791; a conservative Federalist, he served until 1806 and died in 1811. Uncle Francis Dana Jr., born 1777, mortgaged many of the family's landholdings in 1804 in order to build wharves along the Charles River. When the new docks failed to attract shipping, the family lost much of its land, Francis Dana Sr. was forced to sell his mansion, and Francis Jr. went to Russia to avoid his creditors. Father Richard Henry Dana, born 1787, attended Harvard, then studied law and was admitted to the bar in 1812. He married Ruth Charlotte Smith, born 1787, a schoolteacher from Providence, Rhode Island, on May 11, 1813; their first child, Ruth Charlotte, was born on February 28, 1814.)

1817   Father begins to contribute literary essays to *The North American Review*.

1818   Brother Edmund Trowbridge (Ned) born August 29.

1819   Father ends his association with *The North American Review* after being passed over for its editorship and closes his legal practice.

1820   Sister Susan born June 8.

1821   Father founds literary journal *The Idle Man*, contributing essays and stories while paying its publication costs. Mother falls ill, possibly with tuberculosis.

1822   Mother dies February 10. (Dana later writes that his father experienced grief "which no description we have read of agony short of madness has equalled.") Sister Susan dies April 27 after being injured in a fall. *The Idle Man* ceases publication after six issues. Despite his mother's death, Dana later remembers having a happy early childhood, describing himself as "active & hardy . . . though not stout built," and writing, "I went where I was told not to go, played with boys whom I was warned against as vulgar . . . followed soldiers, droves of cattle, showmen, & anything else that was attractive & noisy."

1823   Begins studying Latin grammar at a school in Cambridgeport (a village that became part of Cambridge in 1846) where pupils are regularly flogged with a pine ferrule.

1824   Withdraws from school because of a recurring fever and is tutored for a few weeks by George Ripley (later the founder of Brook Farm) before being sent in May to an academy in the country town of Westford, 25 miles northwest of Cambridge. Develops an interest in geography and neglects his other studies to the point that the schoolmaster names him the "Day-Dreamer." Sees the Marquis de Lafayette during his visit to Boston in August and begins reading Revolutionary War histories and biographies.

1825   Leaves Westford in August and returns to grammar school in Cambridgeport.

1826   In the spring Dana begins attending a school in Cambridge taught by Ralph Waldo Emerson, whom he will later describe as "a very pleasant instructor . . . although he had not system or discipline enough to ensure regular & vigorous study." Continues at Cambridge school after Emerson is succeeded in the fall by other teachers.

1827–29 Father publishes *The Buccaneer and Other Poems* in 1827. After Dana leaves school one day during recess while ill, a teacher flogs his hands 36 times; Dana protests to the school's trustees, and the teacher is dismissed.

1830   Begins preparing for college examinations as day student at a boarding school in Cambridge. Attends sermons of the Rev. Nehemiah Adams, a prominent conservative Congregationalist opposed to liberal Unitarianism. Although convinced of the truth of his doctrines, Dana later writes that he was unable at the time to commit himself to a religious life. Aunt Martha Dana marries the painter and poet

Washington Allston, whose Cambridgeport studio Dana will frequently visit.

1831   Passes Harvard examinations in July and enters college in August. Studies plane geometry, in which he excels, Latin, and Greek.

1832   In March Dana is suspended for six months after joining a protest during prayer assembly against what he considered the unfair disciplining of a fellow student. During his suspension he is tutored in Andover by Leonard Woods Jr., a resident scholar at the theological seminary (later president of Bowdoin College), whom Dana admires for his love of learning, religious faith, and "heart full of kind & noble sentiments." Reads Horace in Latin, Demosthenes in Greek, and the shorter poetry of Schiller and Goethe in German with Woods and studies solid and spherical geometry with a friend of Woods. After his "most delightful & improving" study in Andover, Dana returns in the fall to "college recitations, college rank, college gossips, & college *esprit du corps* as a slave whipped to his dungeon." Enjoys class in German taught by Charles Follen and reads Boswell's *Life of Johnson* and Carlyle's *Life of Schiller*.

1833–34   Stands seventh in his class at the end of his sophomore year. Father publishes *Poems and Prose Writings*. An attack of measles during the summer leaves Dana's eyes so weakened that he is unable to read and he is forced to leave Harvard before the start of his junior year. Remains at home, "a useless, pitied & dissatisfied figure," and worries that he is a burden on his financially pressed father, then decides "to make a long voyage, to relieve myself from ennui, to see new places & modes of life, & to effect if possible a cure of my eyes." Ships as an ordinary seaman on board the *Pilgrim*, bound for California. Departs Boston August 14, 1834 and rounds Cape Horn in November.

1835   Arrives in Santa Barbara on January 14, 1835. Spends the year collecting and curing cattle hides along the coast from San Francisco to San Diego and falls "into all the bad habits of sailors."

1836   Sails from San Diego on board the *Alert*, May 8, and rounds Cape Horn in July. Lands in Boston on September 22 and enjoys his "first wash with fresh water & soap in a basin for 2 years." While preparing to re-enter Harvard, Dana learns that a young woman he had known before his voyage had prayed for his salvation on her deathbed; believing the incident to have been "especially contrived of God, as a last call, to touch me in the most sensitive points," he undergoes a religious conversion. (The woman, not identified by Dana, was probably a sister of Leonard Woods Jr., Sarah Woods, who had died on September 3, 1836, aged 19.) Passes examination in December for admittance to the senior class at Harvard.

1837   Receives high marks in moral and intellectual philosophy, rhetoric, themes, and forensics, and is awarded Bowdoin prize for a dissertation on Edward Bulwer's novels *Pelham*, *Paul Clifford*, and *Eugene Aram*. Graduates on August 30, delivering a commencement dissertation on Wordsworth's ode "Intimations of Immortality." Enters the Dane Law School at Harvard, where he studies with Joseph Story, an associate justice of the U.S. Supreme Court, and Simon Greenleaf, the Royall Professor of Law at Harvard; his fellow students include two future U.S. attorneys general, William M. Evarts and Ebenezer Hoar. Begins writing a narrative of his voyage to California.

1838   In April Dana is confirmed in the Protestant Episcopal Church at St. Paul's in Boston. Hears Emerson deliver his controversial address at the Harvard Divinity School on July 15. Meets Sarah Watson (b. 1814), the niece of a family friend, on July 20, and corresponds with her after she returns in August to her home in Wethersfield, Connecticut. (Watson lives with her widowed mother; her father, a merchant, had gone bankrupt before his death.) Completes manuscript of his narrative by Christmas.

1839   Appointed instructor in elocution at Harvard in January, "an exceedingly pleasant office" in which he assists his cousin, professor of rhetoric Edward Channing. Washington Allston and Dana's father encourage Dana to publish his narrative; after William Cullen Bryant, a friend of his father, reads the manuscript, Bryant and the elder Dana offer it to Harpers and several other publishers. Dana visits Sarah Watson in August.

1840   Becomes engaged to Sarah Watson in early February. Resigns his instructorship and leaves law school to complete his legal training in the office of Charles Loring in Boston. When Harpers shows interest in his narrative, Dana adds a preface and new concluding chapter, and in March Harpers agrees to buy the copyright from him for $250. Dana is admitted to the bar in September and opens his own office at 20 Court Street in Boston. *Two Years Before the Mast* is published by Harper and Brothers on September 18 and sells well, though Dana receives no royalties. (Dana later estimates that the book earned Harpers $10,000 by 1842 and $50,000 over the 28 years the firm held the copyright.)

1841   Helped by the success of his book, Dana builds law practice specializing in claims by seamen against dishonest shipmasters and captains. Edward Moxon publishes an English edition of *Two Years Before the Mast* in February and pays Dana $500 for the work. Receives letter in March from his former shipmate Ben Stimson, who writes that he failed to mention in his book "*the beautiful Indian lasses*, who so often frequented your humble abode in the *hide house* . . ." Dana writes a manual for sailors with chapters on seamanship, maritime law, and the customs and practices of the merchant service. Marries Sarah Watson in Hartford on August 25. After a short trip to Rockport, Massachusetts, they take rooms in a Boston hotel. In October *The Seaman's Friend* is published in Boston by Little and Brown and by Moxon in London as *The Seaman's Manual.* Dana works on a long autobiographical sketch (completed in 1842), then begins writing a journal on December 17 that he will keep until 1860.

1842   Meets Charles Dickens several times during his visit to Boston; Dana writes that Dickens is "the *cleverest* man I ever met," while also recording "the impression that he is a low bred man." Delivers lectures on his experiences at sea and "Knowledge Is Power." (Will continue to make lyceum tours in the Northeast for more than a decade in order to supplement his income; other subjects will include "The Sources of Influence" and "American Loyalty.") Reads *The Old Curiosity Shop* and experiences "several hours of the purest & most delightful melancholy & virtuous feeling . . ." In April Dana and Sarah move to rented rooms in Roxbury. Their first child, Sarah Watson Dana, is born June 12. Exhausted by long hours of work, Dana sails for Nova Scotia on July 16 while his wife and daughter remain in Roxbury. Enjoys sailing and fishing off Halifax during the day, then dresses in sailor's clothes and explores the rough district near the barracks at night. Visits dance houses and befriends a young prostitute, giving her money and urging her to reform. Returns to Roxbury on July 29 shortly before Sarah and the baby go to Wethersfield for a six-week stay. Dana admits his brother Ned to his law practice on October 1. Wins a succession of civil and criminal cases and acquires a reputation for careful legal work, though he is annoyed by "the slurs or open opposition of masters & owners of vessels whose seamen I undertake to defend or look after." Family moves into a rented house in Boston in November. Reads and is disappointed by Dickens' *American Notes*. His friend Henry Wadsworth Longfellow tells Dana that the English poet Samuel Rogers has described *Two Years Before the Mast* as "the best book of the age." Continues to follow news of his former shipmates.

1843   Visits New York City in early January, where he attends the court of inquiry investigating Commander Alexander Slidell Mackenzie, captain of the U.S. brig *Somers*, who had summarily hanged three alleged mutineers, including the son of the Secretary of War, while at sea on December 1, 1842. Makes a nighttime tour of the notorious Five Points district of lower Manhattan, where he talks with a prostitute in her room, then writes in his journal: "Am I any better in the sight of an *all*-seeing God than these filthy wretches? I have done things worse *in me*, than brought some of them to that condition . . ." Returns to Boston and writes a 5,000 word letter defending Mackenzie that appears in the *New York Evening Post* and is reprinted in several New York and Boston newspapers. Attends meetings held by Millerites, who believe the Second Coming will occur by March 22, 1843, and by Mormons; concludes that both sects are fanatical and deluded. Visits the *Alert* when she docks in Boston. Attends the New England Anti-Slavery Convention, May 31–June 1, where he hears speeches by Frederick Douglass and Charles Lenox Remond ("conceited, shallow-pated negro youths") and William Lloyd Garrison ("a fanatic . . . an infidel & a socialist"). Listens to Daniel Webster deliver his oration at the Bunker Hill monument on June 17 ("the great man of the age, with a voice, action & presence almost god-like"). Uncle Washington Allston dies July 9. With the assistance of Samuel F. B. Morse, who had studied under Allston, Dana oversees the disposition of Allston's studio and helps arrange for the exhibition of his unfinished painting "Belshazzar's Feast." Writes to Sarah, who is spending the summer in Wethersfield, urging her to economize on expenses after he is forced to borrow $1,000. Publishes two letters in the *Boston Courier* defending Mackenzie, who was acquitted at court-martial in March. Goes sailing and fishing in the Isles of Shoals off New Hampshire for a week in August. Experiences one of his brief periodic fits of depression in early September, able to "do nothing without tears and sighings" and longing to be free of "the business & petty things of this world."

1844   Continues to move in elite Boston social circles. Travels to New York in late February, where he again tours the Five Points, then goes to Washington, D.C., where he attends Congress and the Supreme Court. Visits Mount Vernon, where he meets Robert E. Lee, then a captain in the army. Calls on former president John Quincy Adams, who is now serving in the House. Visits Baltimore and Philadelphia before returning to Boston in mid-March. Second child, Ruth Charlotte Dana, born June 30. Travels in the White Mountains and Maine, August 16–September 2. Having previously considered the theater as "an assignation house, & a sink of iniquity," Dana attends his first stage performance, a production of *Hamlet* with the English actor William Macready, and later sees him perform in *The Merchant of Venice* and *Macbeth*. Speaks at Whig campaign meetings. Leaves St. Paul's, where he was confirmed, to help found the Church of the Advent, formed on High Church principles.

1845   Keeps up an intense schedule of legal work and lecturing, driven by an increasing need for income as his father, aunts, uncles, and unmarried sister Charlotte require his aid, while his brother Ned proves to be an undependable law partner. Sarah continues to spend excessively as she tries to keep up with wealthy society, and quarrels and reconciliations become a pattern of their married life. Observes Lent for the first time, finding himself "freed from those temptations & sins of the flesh wh. easily beset me." Purchases property in Manchester, Massachusetts, in May, where he builds a house to serve as a summer residence for his sister and father and a retreat for his own family. Tours upstate New York with Sarah in July, visiting Niagara Falls and Ontario.

1846   Third child, Elizabeth Ellery Dana, born April 3. Writes to his father in June that he has handled only three sailors' cases in the past year as he concentrates on more lucrative work.

1847   Serves as attorney for Dr. William Morton in his dispute with Dr. Charles Jackson over credit for the discovery of the anesthetic uses of ether. In July the educator Horace Mann suggests to Dana that he rewrite *Two Years Before the Mast* for use as a school text; Dana replies that he would not change the narrative even if he owned the copyright to the work. Meets Herman Melville in early July and again in August when Melville is in Boston for his wedding. Experiences another episode of depression during a period of serious marital tension, writing to Sarah in Connecticut on July 22 that he fears he is falling into "a kind of insanity."

1848   Dissolves partnership with his "entirely uncertain and unreliable" brother Ned in February and sends him to Germany to study civil law. Forms new partnership with Francis E. Parker, an experienced lawyer who is able to bring wealthy clients to the firm. (Dana will do almost all of the trial work for the partnership, while Parker handles the office work.) Serves as chairman of a meeting held in Boston on July 7 to oppose the extension of slavery into territory gained in the Mexican War and is later chosen as a delegate to the first convention of the Free Soil Party, a coalition of "Conscience" Whigs, antislavery "Barnburner" Democrats, and supporters of the Liberty Party. Travels to Buffalo, New York, where the convention meets on August 9. When his candidate, U.S. Supreme Court Justice John McLean, withdraws, Dana supports the nomination of former president Martin Van Buren, the leader of the "Barnburners," for president and Charles Francis Adams, son of John Quincy Adams, for vice-president. Dana speaks in support of the Free Soil ticket at Faneuil Hall in Boston and in several Massachusetts towns afterward. Fourth child, Mary Rosamond Dana, is born on September 1; Sarah suffers a nearly fatal hemorrhage during the delivery. Dana publicly criticizes Daniel Webster for supporting Zachary Taylor, the Whig nominee. Taylor wins the presidential election on November 7 and carries Massachusetts; Van Buren receives 10 percent of the national popular vote, but fails to carry any states.

1849   In March Dana dines twice with Melville and writes to Ned that Melville is "incomparable in dramatic story telling." Suffers attack of dyspepsia in June that is attributed to overwork and lack of exercise. Leaves Boston on June 18 for an extended trip through the Green Mountains, the White Mountains, and the Adirondacks. Climbs Mt. Washington and has breakfast one morning in the backwoods farmhouse of John Brown, the future leader of the Harpers Ferry raid. Returns to Boston July 23. Writes in August that an ongoing cholera outbreak "has impressed upon my mind the frailty & uncertainty of human life, the certainty of death & eternity." Sends Melville a letter of introduction to his English publisher, Edward Moxon, in September and urges him to write about his experiences on a man-of-war. In his reply, Melville tells Dana that his book *White-Jacket* is already in proof and asks him to support the book if it is treated unfairly by the critics; he signs the letter "a sea-brother." Dana continues his active support of the Free Soil Party while maintaining a busy lecture schedule (will earn over $1,000 a year from speaking fees in 1849–50). Sarah and the children return to Boston in November after spending several months in Wethersfield.

1850   During a visit to Concord in February Dana stays at Emerson's house and listens as his former teacher describes his meetings with Wordsworth, Carlyle, and Tennyson, and his impressions of Disraeli and Gladstone. In a speech in the Senate on March 7, Webster calls for compromise with the South over slavery; Dana writes to Ned: "He will run no personal risk for a principle. . . . He has a gigantic frame, but is weak in the knees." In the early spring Dana writes to Melville, praising *Redburn* and *White-Jacket* and advising him to make similar use of his whaling experiences. In his reply of May 1, Melville recalls the "strange, congenial feelings, with which after my first voyage, I for the first time read 'Two Years Before the Mast,' and while so engaged was, as it were, tied & welded to you by a Siamese link of affectionate sympathy," then writes: "About the 'whaling voyage,'—I am half way in the work, & am very glad that your suggestion so jumps with mine." Dana edits *Lectures on Art, and Poems by Washington Allston.* Tours Saratoga, the Catskills, and West Point with Sarah in July and early August. Congress passes a new federal Fugitive Slave Law on September 18. Dana denounces the law as both inhumane and unconstitutional at a mass meeting held in Boston on October 14, but opposes efforts to form a Democratic-Free Soil coalition during the fall election campaign.

1851 Fifth child, Richard Henry Dana III, born January 3. Dana agrees on February 15 to appear in court on behalf of Frederick "Shadrach" Minkins, a fugitive slave arrested under the 1850 law. After Dana leaves the courthouse, Shadrach is rescued by a group of African-Americans and escapes to Canada; Dana writes in his journal: "How can any right minded man do else than rejoice at the rescue of a man from the hopeless, endless slavery to wh. a *recovered fugitive* is always doomed." Helps defend Charles G. Davis, a white attorney who is the first of a series of men accused of aiding the rescue. After Dana delivers a closing argument he considers "the best thing I ever did," the charges against Davis are dismissed on February 26. Dana and his friend Charles Sumner draft a "personal liberty" law designed to prevent the enforcement of the Fugitive Slave Act in Massachusetts, but the measure is rejected by the state legislature. After Thomas Sims, another fugitive slave, is arrested in Boston on April 3, Dana joins his defense, unsuccessfully seeking a writ of habeas corpus from the Massachusetts supreme judicial court before obtaining one from federal judge Levi Woodbury, but a hearing in another legal matter prevents him from participating further in the case. Woodbury orders Sims returned to slavery on April 11, and he is taken onboard a ship under heavy guard the following day. Dana is criticized in the press by pro-Webster "Cotton Whigs," some of who call for a boycott of his legal practice, but he is encouraged by the election of Sumner to the U.S. Senate by the state legislature on April 24. Along with John P. Hale, a Free Soil senator from New Hampshire, Dana defends James Scott and Lewis Hayden, black Bostonians charged with participation in the "Shadrach Rescue"; both trials end in hung juries. Purchases house lot in Cambridge on July 22, then sails the following day for Halifax, where he visits British warships in the harbor. Tours Nova Scotia and New Brunswick and successfully hunts moose in Maine before returning to Boston on August 15. Defends Robert Morris, a black attorney charged in Shadrach Rescue, and wins an acquittal.

1852 Family moves on March 16 into their new house at 4 Berkeley Street, Cambridge, where for the first time Dana has his own study. Reads *Uncle Tom's Cabin* while traveling by train and notices that "four persons were reading this book, each unconnected with the other, in one car." Daniel Webster dies October 24; Dana writes "all men agree to mourn his death." Wins acquittal of Elizur Wright, a white newspaper editor charged in the Shadrach Rescue (the government later drops all remaining charges in the case). Attends Webster's public funeral on October 29. Dismayed by the election to the presidency on November 2 of Franklin Pierce, a pro-Southern Democrat; John P. Hale, the Free Soil candidate, receives only five percent of the national popular vote. Writes lecture on Edmund Burke in December and begins delivering it in towns around Boston.

1853 Dines with William Makepeace Thackeray, Longfellow, and James Russell Lowell. Builds reputation in maritime salvage and insurance cases and begins defending ship officers accused of assaulting seamen. Elected as a Free Soil delegate from Manchester to convention called to consider revisions to the Massachusetts state constitution. Rents out house in Cambridge for six months in attempt to bolster finances. Convention meets in Boston on May 4. Dana serves on the committee charged with revising the bill of rights and takes a generally conservative role in the convention debates, opposing measures to elect state judges and defending the existing legislative apportionment system that strongly favors rural townships over cities. Joins former governor George Boutwell in drafting the final text of the revised constitution submitted by the convention to the voters for ratification. Convention adjourns August 1. Dana travels in Quebec and the White Mountains, August 16–September 9, while Sarah takes a "water cure" in Vermont. Despite his reservations regarding the new constitution, Dana speaks in support of its ratification throughout eastern Massachusetts in October and November. After the voters reject the document on November 14, he writes: "I do not find it easy to determine whether I am most pleased or disappointed with the result."

1854   On May 25 Dana offers to defend Anthony Burns, the first fugitive slave arrested in Boston since 1851, and persuades U.S. commissioner Edward G. Loring to delay hearing the case for two days. Dana writes in his journal that conservative Whigs who had shunned him in 1851 now support his legal efforts on behalf of fugitives. An unsuccessful attempt to rescue Burns from the courthouse on May 26 results in the fatal wounding of a special guard hired by the U.S. marshal to guard the fugitive. In hearings before Loring, May 29–31, Dana and co-counsel Charles Ellis succeed in challenging the claimant's legal standing in the case and rebutting the testimony of his main witness; during his closing argument Dana alludes disparagingly to the criminal backgrounds of many of the "specials" hired to guard the courtroom. On June 2 Loring orders Burns returned to slavery, and he is taken onto a federal revenue cutter under the guard of several hundred soldiers and marines. That night Dana is struck on the head near his office by Henry Huxford, a former prize fighter and gang enforcer who had served as a "special" during the hearings (Huxford is later given a two-year prison sentence for the assault). Travels with Sarah in the White Mountains, July 5–15. Appears before the Maine supreme court in *Donahoe v. Richards*, defending a public school committee that expelled a Catholic girl for refusing to be present when the King James Version of the Bible was read aloud. In a widely reported decision, the court rules for the school committee and adopts Dana's argument that the King James Bible was being taught for nonsectarian reasons. Sails along the Maine coast in a schooner while accompanying an army engineer officer on an inspection tour of lighthouses in late August. ("The sea has a charm for me . . . a languid, dreamy idle state comes on, wh. is a kind of bath to tired nature, & with the freshening breese & the long swinging seas, & hurrying foam, the wake, the dashing of foam from the bows, there is an exhileration that nothing else equals.") In the *Osprey* case, the U.S. district court adopts Dana's argument and establishes a rule in admiralty law that a sailing ship on collision course with a steamship should maintain its heading while the steamer takes evasive action.

1855   Dana opposes attempt by the legislature to remove Edward G. Loring, the commissioner in the Burns case, from his position as a state probate judge. Meets with Burns, whose freedom had recently been purchased by Massachusetts supporters, on March 30. Begins attending the monthly dinners of the "Saturday Club," whose members include Louis Agassiz and Emerson (later members will include Lowell, Longfellow, John Lothrop Motley, Oliver Wendell Holmes Sr., John Greenleaf Whittier, and Nathaniel Hawthorne). Participates in several meetings in August aimed at bringing Free Soilers, antislavery Democrats, and nativist Know-Nothings into the new Republican Party. At the Republican convention held in Worcester on September 20, Dana secures the adoption of a strong antislavery platform and defeats an attempt to nominate Henry Gardner, the Know-Nothing incumbent, for governor; the convention instead chooses Julius Rockwell, an antislavery Whig, as its candidate. Dana campaigns vigorously for Rockwell, but Gardner is reelected in November.

1856   Defends Benjamin Dalton, charged with manslaughter for killing his wife's lover, in a widely publicized case that ends with Dalton receiving a five-month sentence for assault and battery. Presides over protest meeting held in Cambridge after Charles Sumner is badly beaten on the Senate floor by South Carolina congressman Preston Brooks on May 22. Sails on July 2 to begin a long-contemplated trip to England. Lands at Liverpool on July 13 and notes "the sense of stability and repose" provided by its brick and stone buildings. Arrives in London on July 14 and goes sightseeing throughout the city. Meets prominent aristocrats, including the Duke of Argyll and Lord Lansdowne, tours the British Museum with Lord Elgin as his guide, and has dinner with the historian Thomas Babington Macaulay. Hears Gladstone, Disraeli, and Palmerston speak in the House of Commons and sees Queen Victoria during a military review at Aldershot. Attends sessions of various trial, appeals, and chancery courts, and meets Lord Campbell, the lord chief justice, and Lord Cranworth, the lord chancellor. Sees his brother Ned for the first time in eight years. Visits Windsor Castle, Eton College, Cambridge, Ely Cathedral, Oxford, Warwick Castle, Stratford-on-Avon, Kenilworth, Shrewsbury, Wroxeter (the home of the English Danas), Winchester, Salisbury, and Portsmouth. Meets Charlotte M. Yonge, whose novel *The Heir of Redclyffe* had deeply affected him. Visits Paris and Versailles, August 19–21, before sailing from Liverpool on August 23. During the fall Dana speaks in Connecticut, Rhode Island, Massachusetts, and New Hampshire in support of Republican presidential candidate John C. Frémont. Although Frémont is defeated in November, his strong showing encourages Dana.

1857   Sixth child, Angela Henrietta Channing Dana, born February 22. Defends the Rev. Isaac Kalloch, a popular Baptist preacher, in a widely publicized adultery case that ends in a hung jury (Kalloch later serves as mayor of San Francisco, 1879–81). Represents Benjamin Dalton when Dalton sues his wife for adultery. Opposed by the celebrated attorney Rufus Choate, Dana delivers a 12-hour closing address; the trial ends in a hung jury. Witnesses a deadly battle in lower Manhattan between the "Bowery Boys" and "Dead Rabbits" street gangs during a visit to New York on July 4. Takes a two-week vacation in upstate New York, Vermont, and the Berkshires. Finds himself under increasing financial pressure brought about by interest on his outstanding debts, school fees for his children, expensive treatments for Sarah's nervous disorders, and the needs of his father, sister, and brother, who has returned from Europe as a semi-invalid. Gives up lecturing as insufficiently profitable, reduces his political activities, and concentrates on his legal work.

1858   Spends three weeks at his shore house in Manchester in lieu of a vacation trip. Writes only one entry for the year in his journal, noting that "my duties are so constant."

1859   Takes advantage of interval between court sessions to sail for Cuba, arriving in Havana on February 18. Visits Matanzas and a sugar plantation in Limonar before sailing from Havana on March 2. *To Cuba and Back: A Vacation Voyage* is published in May by Ticknor and Fields and sells well. Faints in early summer while in the midst of arguing a complex maritime insurance case. Borrows money from Frank Parker and sails from New York on July 20; writes in his journal: "I have over-worked for the last ten years— undertaking to do everything & study everything . . . my physician is satisfied, & so am I that my system is out of order, both nervous & bilious, & that I need long rest & recreation. Of all plans proposed, none suits me so well as a voyage round the world. This has been the dream of my youth & maturer years, & I am actually happy in being able to realise it." Arrives on August 1 at Aspinwall (Colón), crosses the Isthmus of Panama by train, and embarks for California. Lands at San Francisco on August 13 and revisits the sites along the California coast that he had known in 1835–36. Sails for Hawaii on September 10 in the clipper ship *Mastiff*, which catches fire five days out; all but one of the passengers and crew are rescued by the nearby *Achilles* and reach Honolulu on September 27. Dana sends an account of the fire and rescue to the San Francisco *Daily Alta California* and the Boston *Daily Advertiser*. Leaves Honolulu on November 16 and arrives at San Francisco on December 11.

1860   Sails for Asia from San Francisco on January 11. Arrives at Hong Kong on March 8 and visits Canton (Guangzhou), Macao, and Shanghai. Lands in Japan at Nagasaki on April 9 and visits Yokohama and Hakodate. Returns to Shanghai on April 30 and travels to Soochow (Suzhou), Chusan (Zhoushan), and Ningbo. Sails from Hong Kong on June 9 for Suez, stopping at Singapore, Penang, and Ceylon. During a storm in the Indian Ocean, Dana is thrown against a stanchion and breaks a rib. Recuperates in Bombay, where he is disappointed to learn that Abraham Lincoln has defeated William Seward for the Republican presidential nomination. Resumes his journey on July 23 and reaches Suez on August 10. Travels by train to Cairo and visits Alexandria before sailing on August 18 for Trieste. Travels to Venice, Milan, Geneva, Heidelberg, Cologne, Antwerp, and London. Sails from Liverpool and lands in New York on September 27. After Lincoln wins election on November 6, Dana writes to a friend: "We live in a new country!" South Carolina secedes on December 20. Dana writes to Charles Francis Adams on December 26 that he would support a "reasonable Fugitive Slave Law" in order to preserve the Union.

1861   In a speech delivered at Cambridge on February 11 Dana calls for "faithfully" honoring the fugitive slave clause in the Constitution but opposes any new constitutional concessions to the South. At Melville's request, Dana writes to Sumner in support of his bid to become consul at Florence (Melville does not receive the appointment). With the support of Sumner and Adams, Dana is appointed U.S. district attorney for Massachusetts on April 12. Takes office on April 26 and becomes responsible for prosecuting cases of customs embezzlement, postal theft, counterfeiting, crimes against seamen, and maritime slave trading (duties will later include prosecution of draft and tax evaders). Establishes a prompt system for handling prize claims involving vessels captured under the blockade and brought to Boston. Considers running for the House of Representatives when the member for his district resigns in September, but decides that he cannot financially afford to serve in Congress.

1862   Successfully argues two prize cases in U.S. district court involving the legality of the Union blockade of the Confederacy. In the *Revere* case, the court adopts Dana's argument that the United States has both "sovereign and belligerent rights" against rebels and under international law can impose a blockade without recognizing the Confederacy as a sovereign nation, while in the *Amy Warwick* case, the court accepts his definition of "enemies' property" subject to capture. Drafts federal legislation governing the treatment of prize cases (will also draft additional legislation in 1864). Dana's financial situation improves after new regulations allow him to keep $6,000 in prize fees annually in addition to his $6,000 salary. Opposes Sumner and other Republicans who seek to make emancipation a Union war aim, and unsuccessfully attempts to keep the Republican convention held at Worcester on September 9 from endorsing Sumner for a third Senate term. After Lincoln issues the preliminary Emancipation Proclamation on September 22, Dana writes in a letter that he fears "it is to be a *dead failure.*"

1863   Appears before the U.S. Supreme Court as the lead government attorney in the *Prize Cases*, a consolidated hearing of the *Amy Warwick* and three other cases. Defends the legality of the blockade proclamations issued by Lincoln in April 1861, arguing that the president has the constitutional power to defend the country in the absence of congressional action. After returning from Washington, Dana describes Lincoln in a letter to Charles Francis Adams as "an unutterable calamity to us where he is." On

March 10 the Supreme Court rules 5–4 for the government in the *Prize Cases*, accepting Dana's definition of "enemies' property" and his broad construction of presidential war-making power.

1864　Publishes pamphlet "Enemy's Territory and Alien Enemies: What the Supreme Court Decided in the Prize Causes" in response to William Beach Lawrence and other legal writers who argued that the decision acknowledged the right of secession. Meets General Ulysses Grant during a visit to Washington in April and describes him in a letter to his wife as "an ordinary, scrubby-looking man, with a slightly seedy look," but with a "clear blue eye and a look of resolution . . ." Writes after meeting Lincoln at the White House: "You can't help feeling an interest in him, a sympathy and a kind of pity; feeling, too, that he has some qualities of great value, yet fearing that his weak points may wreck him or wreck something." Agrees to request by the widow of Henry Wheaton to edit a new edition of his *Elements of International Law* (1836), the standard American work on the subject. Speaks in favor of Lincoln's reelection in the Midwest.

1865　Writes to his son after Lincoln's assassination: "The last time I saw him, he put his arms round me, as if he had been my father, and seemed to want to keep me." Gives speech on Reconstruction in Boston on June 21, arguing that its military victory gives the Union the right to require Southern states to abolish slavery and allow freemen to own land, testify in court, and, if literate, vote. His increased earnings allow him to settle his debts, hire new servants, and buy property in Boston.

1866　Sails for Europe in June with Sarah, beginning three-month tour of England, France, Switzerland, and Italy. Granted Doctor of Laws degree by Harvard. New edition of Wheaton's *Elements of International Law*, containing 250 notes by Dana, is published in July by Little, Brown. William Beach Lawrence, the editor of the 1855 and 1863 editions, publicly accuses Dana of plagiarizing his notes. Dana returns from Europe and resigns as U.S. attorney on September 29. In October Lawrence sues Dana in U.S. circuit court for infringement of copyright. Unable to run for Congress because the seat for Cambridge is held by a Republican, Dana is elected by a wide margin to the Massachusetts house of representatives in November. Gives course of 12 lectures on international law at the Lowell Institute in Boston.

1867   Devotes himself to his legislative duties and to answering Lawrence's charges. Serves as chairman of the committee on harbors and wins repeal of usury law limiting interest payments to six percent. Agrees in October to join William M. Evarts as government counsel in the treason case against Jefferson Davis, although he opposes prosecution on both legal and political grounds. Refuses to support repeal of the rarely enforced state prohibition law and is narrowly reelected to the legislature. Travels to Richmond, Virginia, in late November to obtain a postponement in the Davis case.

1868   Serves as chairman of the Massachusetts house judiciary committee. Secures new treason indictment against Davis in March but continues to postpone trial. Opposes the impeachment of President Andrew Johnson. Regains copyright of *Two Years Before the Mast* for a 14-year period. Decides to challenge Benjamin F. Butler, the former Union general and Radical Republican who represents the Essex district (which includes Manchester) in Congress. After Butler is renominated by the Republican organization he controls, Dana accepts nomination on October 5 by a group of conservative Republicans opposed to Butler's fiscal policies. In his campaign speeches Dana criticizes Butler for proposing to redeem government bonds with legal tender notes instead of gold, while Butler's supporters accuse Dana of being an aristocrat "of the snobbiest sort" and a "political Beau Brummel . . . with his kid gloves on." Dana responds by citing his years "before the mast" and his legal defense of mistreated seamen and fugitive slaves. In the election on November 3, Butler receives 13,081 votes; Democrat Otis P. Lord, 4,941; and Dana, 1,818. Dana appears in court in Richmond on November 30 to oppose a defense motion to dismiss the indictment against Davis on constitutional grounds. On December 25 President Johnson issues a general amnesty that covers Davis, ending the case.

1869   Dana resumes his private legal practice and attracts increasingly lucrative civil cases, many involving admiralty law. Sells his Cambridge house and moves to Marlborough Street in Boston. As a member of the Board of Overseers, Dana opposes the hiring of Charles William Eliot as the new president of Harvard. Fields, Osgood, & Co. publishes a revised edition of *Two Years Before the Mast* that includes a new chapter, "Twenty-Four Years After," describing Dana's return to California in 1859–60. (Editions with further revisions are published in 1872 and 1876.) Brother Ned dies on May 18. The U.S. circuit court rules on September 20 that some of Dana's notes in the Wheaton edition "do infringe the equitable rights" of Lawrence and appoints Henry Paine, a Boston attorney, to assist the court in determining the extent of the infringement. Paine begins detailed study of the lengthy depositions and pleadings in the case.

1870 Sails for Great Britain in late July after experiencing symptoms of ill health and overwork. Lands in Liverpool in early August and tours Scotland for a month; delighted by its scenery and history, he writes Sarah: "though in nothing else, I am lucky as a traveller." Visits Oxford and London, where he dines with Gladstone and John Lothrop Motley, before sailing from Liverpool on September 15. Son Richard enters Harvard College.

1871 Sends Sarah and three of their daughters to Europe for an extended stay. Moves to 361 Beacon Street in Boston. Publishes article in *American Law Review* on the history of admiralty jurisdiction in the United States. Hopes for appointment to the international tribunal arbitrating American claims against Great Britain for losses caused by Confederate raiders built in British ports, but President Ulysses Grant and Secretary of State Hamilton Fish instead choose Charles Francis Adams for the position. Unsuccessfully seeks appointment as a government attorney appearing before the tribunal, and blames his failure on the active opposition of Lawrence, who continues to denounce Dana as a plagiarist.

1872 Prospers as building boom increases the value of his Cambridge landholdings. Despite misgivings about the administration, writes public letter during the presidential campaign urging black voters in Boston to support Grant over his Liberal Republican opponent Horace Greeley.

1873 Writes in March to Sarah, who is still in Europe: "I have given up all expectation of public employment . . . our

politics look low and dark. They seem to be drifting off
beyond the reach of the moral opinion of society." In
April he writes to Sarah: "my life has been a failure, compared with what I might and ought to have done. My
great success—my book—was a boy's work, done before
I came to the Bar." Expresses hope that he can "give
myself to a work on international law, as the work of my
life . . . before I am too old to do my best."

1874–75   Speaks at memorial meeting held after Sumner's death on
March 11, 1874, but declines offer to become his official
biographer. Continues to take active role on the Harvard
Board of Overseers. Sends son Richard on a 15-month European tour in 1875, urging him to "do all you can *to fit
yourself* for the career of a jurist and statesman."

1876   Grant nominates Dana on March 7 to succeed Robert
Schenck as American minister to Great Britain after
Schenck is forced to resign because of his involvement in
an alleged silver mine stock fraud. Dana writes to Sarah's
aunt that the post will give him "precedence of all the
nobility of England" and consults with Charles Francis
Adams regarding diplomatic protocols. Benjamin F. Butler
and Lawrence appear before the Senate foreign relations
committee in executive session on March 14 and accuse
Dana of plagiarism and of committing perjury in his de-
position in the Wheaton case. Senator Simon Cameron,
the committee chairman and leader of the Pennsylvania
Republican Party, asks for the nomination to be withdrawn, but Grant and Secretary of State Fish refuse. Dana
decides not to testify on his own behalf and writes to
George Boutwell, now a senator, on March 16: "there is
nothing in the gift of the government which would induce
me to go to Washington and submit a question touching
my honor to a committee which has taken the course
which has been taken by the Senate Committee on Foreign Relations." His letter angers Cameron, who calls
Dana "one of those damn literary fellers," and the committee votes against the nomination, which is then rejected, 31–17, by the Senate on April 4. In June Dana
attends the Republican convention in Cincinnati as a
Massachusetts delegate-at-large. Supports Secretary of the
Treasury Benjamin H. Bristow, who had uncovered the
"whiskey rings" defrauding the government of excise
taxes, for six ballots before joining other Bristow dele-

gates in voting for Ohio governor Rutherford P. Hayes, an advocate of civil service reform. Campaigns for Hayes in the fall. Daughter Ruth marries Francis Lyman on December 27.

1877   Publishes article in *The North American Review* calling for civil service reform and the abolition of the electoral college. Henry Paine files his report in the plagiarism case on June 2, finding that Dana had technically infringed copyright in only 14 of the 146 instances alleged by Lawrence. Both Lawrence and Dana file exceptions to the report. Dana hopes to receive a diplomatic appointment from the Hayes administration, but in June is instead asked to serve as government counsel before the fishery commission meeting in Halifax to determine the amount owed by the United States to Great Britain for fishing rights in Canadian waters. Spends summer and fall preparing his case in Halifax with Sarah and their daughter Henrietta, who serves as his secretary. Dana argues that the United States has already compensated Britain for the fishing rights through import concessions, but on November 23 the commission awards $5.5 million to Great Britain. In a letter to William Evarts, now Secretary of State, Dana blames the decision primarily on the "worse than useless" American commissioner Ensign Kellogg.

1878   Son Richard marries Edith Longfellow, daughter of Henry Wadsworth Longfellow, on January 10. Dana turns his law practice over to Richard as a wedding present and decides to move to Europe and begin work on his long-planned treatise on international law. Daughter Mary Rosamond marries Henry Wild on August 26. Dana, Sarah, and two of their daughters travel to Europe and eventually take an apartment on the Rue Keppler in Paris. Settles into routine of studying international law for four hours in the morning, then spending afternoons on social calls and sightseeing.

1879   Father dies February 2. Dana returns to Boston to settle his father's estate. Granddaughter Rosamond Dana Wild born July 9. Makes his final courtroom appearance in hearings on Paine's report, which begin July 31 and continue through August; writes in a letter: "To my surprise, I really enjoyed it—the old war-cry and the cuts and slashes of the 'heady fight' excited and interested me." Grandson

Richard Henry Dana IV born September 1. Dana returns to Paris in September and resumes his study of international law.

1880   The final version of Paine's report is submitted on January 14, and neither Dana nor Lawrence file further appeals in the case. (Lawrence dies on March 26, 1881.) Dana and Sarah spend five weeks at Versailles, then go to Geneva and Aix-les-Bains before settling in Rome for the winter. Publishes an article in the August *North American Review* arguing that Lincoln lacked the legal authority to issue the Emancipation Proclamation. Granddaughter Ruth Charlotte Lyman born December 22.

1881   Grandson Henry Wadsworth Longfellow Dana born January 26. Dana writes of Italy in a letter, "It is a dream of life." Spends six months touring Campania, the Apennines, and Tuscany with Sarah before returning to Rome in early November. Writes the introduction to his treatise and begins work on the first chapter. Falls ill after Christmas.

1882   Develops pneumonia and slips into delirium. Dies on January 6 and is buried on January 8 in the Protestant Cemetery in Rome.

Note on the Texts

This volume collects three travel narratives by Richard Henry Dana, Jr.: *Two Years Before the Mast: A Personal Narrative of Life at Sea* (1840), *To Cuba and Back: A Vacation Voyage* (1859), and the journal Dana kept during his voyage around the world in 1859–1860, which was first published in its complete form in 1968 and is presented here under the title *Journal of a Voyage Round the World, 1859–1860*.

In 1833 Dana suffered an attack of measles that weakened his eyes and left him unable to read without experiencing severe pain. He was forced to leave Harvard College and to live at home, "a useless, pitied & dissatisfied creature" who felt himself to be a financial burden on his father. "This consideration," Dana later wrote in an autobiographical manuscript, "added to the loss of all employment & any prospect of advancement in life, added to a strong love of adventure which I had always with difficulty repressed, & which now broke out in full force, determined me upon making a long voyage, to relieve myself from ennui, to see new places & modes of life, & to effect if possible a cure of my eyes, wh. no medicine had helped, & wh. nothing but a change of my system seemed likely to ensure." Dana sailed from Boston on August 14, 1834, and arrived at Santa Barbara on January 14, 1835. He spent the next 15 months collecting and curing cattle hides along the California coast, then sailed from San Diego on May 8, 1836, and landed in Boston on September 22. During his trip Dana kept a detailed journal, which was lost shortly after his arrival in Boston, and a 20-page logbook, which survived.

Dana returned to Harvard College and, after graduating in 1837, entered the Dane Law School at Harvard. During his first year in law school he began writing an account of his trip, using the title *Two Years Before the Mast: A Narrative of a Voyage to the Pacific Ocean* and drawing upon his logbook and the letters he had written to his family. He completed a draft by Christmas of 1838 and then revised the manuscript, making both deletions and interleaved additions. Some of the revisions eliminated retrospective observations, and others removed references to swearing, drunkenness, and venereal disease. ("From that book," Dana later wrote, "I studiously kept out most of my reflections, & much of the wickedness which I was placed in the midst of.") The manuscript was read by his father, the essayist and poet Richard Henry Dana, Sr., and by his uncle, the painter and poet Washington Allston, both of whom recommended that Dana publish the work. Dana agreed, in part because he hoped that its publication would help bring maritime cases to his future law practice.

Richard Henry Dana, Sr., in May 1839 then asked his friend, the poet and editor William Cullen Bryant, for help in finding a publisher for the narrative. At the same time the elder Dana sent the manuscript to the firm of Harper and Brothers. James Harper initially expressed interest in the work and offered a 10 percent royalty on sales after the first 1,000 copies, but when Bryant visited the firm in June seeking better terms, he was told by two of the other Harper brothers that they were too busy to publish the work in the immediate future. Bryant then wrote to Carey, Lea and Blanchard in Philadelphia and approached Wiley & Putnam and Samuel Colman in New York. These overtures also proved unsuccessful, and Bryant was told by Colman that the current "hard times and dull sales" in the publishing trade made it too risky to publish unknown authors.

In January 1840 Richard Henry Dana, Sr., and Bryant visited Harper and Brothers together. Although the firm now expressed interest in publishing the narrative, Harpers insisted that Dana sell them the copyright for a fixed sum. He agreed, believing that if Harpers owned the copyright they would be more likely to promote his book and reprint it in the future. On February 21 Dana sent his father a revised manuscript containing a newly written preface and concluding chapter, and proposed using the title *Two Years Before the Mast: A Personal Narrative of Sea Life*. Bryant then offered Harpers the copyright for $500, but the firm insisted on paying only $250, and held to that sum even after Bryant asked for only $300. Dana eventually agreed to sell the copyright for $250 and 25 free copies of the book. *Two Years Before the Mast: A Personal Narrative of Life at Sea* was published in New York by Harper and Brothers on September 18, 1840, the same month that Dana was admitted to the bar and opened his law practice in Boston. The book sold well, and in August 1842 Dana wrote in his journal that he had been told "on excellent authority" that it had already earned Harpers $10,000. *Two Years Before the Mast* was reprinted several times by Harpers during the 28 years that they controlled the copyright, but no changes were made in these printings.

In 1868 the copyright reverted for a period of 14 years to Dana, who by this time was a prominent Boston attorney and a leading figure in the conservative wing of the Massachusetts Republican Party. He prepared a new edition of *Two Years Before the Mast*, published in Boston in 1869 by Fields, Osgood, & Co., adding a new preface and replacing the original "Concluding Chapter" (pp. 347–63 in this volume), which addressed the harsh living and working conditions of merchant seamen, with a new chapter, "Twenty-Four Years After," describing his return to California in 1859–1860. Dana also incorporated into the new edition almost 400 changes in wording that had been marked in a family copy of the 1840 edition by him, his father, and his brother Edmund. For example, "I had taken no sustenance for three days" was changed to "I had taken no food for three days" (11.29–30); "we again kept off before the wind, leaving the land on our quarter" became "we again stood out to sea, leaving the land on our quarter" (24.17–18); and "Add to this the never-failing cloak, and you have the dress of the Californian" was replaced by "Add to this the never-failing poncho, or the serapa, and you have the dress of the Californian" (73.14–15). Further alterations in wording were made by Dana in editions published by James R. Osgood and Company in 1872 and 1876, and the original preface to the 1840 edition was omitted from the 1876 edition.

This volume prints the text of the 1840 Harper and Brothers edition of *Two Years Before the Mast* because it contains the original "Concluding Chapter" and because its style and diction reflect the younger Dana. The text of "Twenty-Four Years After" is printed in this volume as an appendix (pp. 365–95) to *Two Years Before the Mast* and is taken from the 1876 Osgood edition, the last edition that Dana made revisions in. Dana's corrections of 14 errors that appeared in the 1840 edition have been accepted and incorporated into the text printed here: at 12.40, "stern" becomes "stem"; at 44.8, "tripped" replaces "tipped"; at 78.27, 78.30, and 80.5, "alcaldis" becomes "alcaldes"; at 85.10, "kedge" replaces "hedge"; at 86.22, "drown" becomes "down"; at 157.28, "'A regular" replaces "A regular"; at 164.2, "together with" replaces "together"; at 206.2–3, "merchantmen" becomes "merchantman"; at 211.4, "and the order" replaces "and order"; at 220.25, "Gaudaloupe" becomes "Guadaloupe"; at 282.6, "*26th*" becomes "*27th*"; at 358.19, "Notwithstanding" replaces "Notwitstanding."

Dana visited Cuba from February 18 to March 2, 1859, during an interval between court sessions. After his return to Boston he prepared an account of his trip using a journal he had kept during his travels. *To Cuba and Back: A Vacation Voyage* was published in Boston in May 1859 by Ticknor and Fields. Dana made no changes in the several reprintings of the book that appeared during his lifetime. This volume prints the text of the 1859 Ticknor and Fields edition of *To Cuba and Back*.

On July 20, 1859, Dana wrote in his journal: "I have over-worked for the last ten years—undertaking to do everything & study everything . . . my physician is satisfied, & so am I that my system is out of order, both nervous & bilious, & that I need long rest & recreation. Of all plans proposed, none suits me so well as a voyage round the world. This has been the dream of my youth & maturer years, & I am actually happy in being able to realise it." He sailed from New York that same day and returned there on September 27, 1860, after traveling to California, Hawaii, China, Japan, India, Egypt, and Europe. The original version of the travel journal that Dana began when he left New York was lost on September 15, 1859, when his clipper ship, the *Mastiff,* burned at sea while sailing from San Francisco to Hawaii. He continued to keep his journal, sending completed sections home at intervals, and later rewrote the missing section (541.1–557.2 in this volume), drawing on his notes, letters, and recollections. The journal of his voyage remained unpublished during his lifetime; it is possible that Dana considered publishing a narrative of his circumnavigation, but abandoned the idea after the outbreak of the Civil War. Charles Francis Adams printed excerpts from Dana's journal, including passages written during his 1859–1860 voyage, in *Richard Henry Dana: A Biography* (2 vols., 1890), and a portion of the travel journal appeared as "A Voyage on the Grand Canal of China" in *Atlantic Monthly,* May 1891.

The complete text of the journal kept by Dana from 1841 to 1860 was published in *The Journal of Richard Henry Dana, Jr.,* edited by Robert F. Lucid (3 vols., Cambridge: The Belknap Press of Harvard University Press, 1968). In *The Journal of Richard Henry Dana, Jr.,* the 1859–1860 travel journal appeared in Volume III under the title *A Voyage Round the World—1859–1860* and was divided into seven chapters; the present volume uses the title *Journal of a Voyage Round the World, 1859–1860* and retains the chapter divisions of the Lucid edition but provides different chapter headings. Lucid printed the text of the journal with only minor alterations in punctuation, number, and tense, and corrected the spelling of some proper names.

This volume prints the text of the 1859–1860 travel journal as it appeared in *The Journal of Richard Henry Dana, Jr.,* but with a few alterations in editorial procedure. Bracketed editorial conjectural readings in *The Journal of Richard Henry Dana, Jr.,* in cases where the original manuscript was damaged or difficult to read, are accepted without brackets in this volume when that reading seems to be the only possible one; but when it does not, or when no conjecture was made, the missing word or words are indicated by a bracketed two-em space, i.e., [   ]. In cases where *The Journal of Richard Henry Dana, Jr.* supplied in brackets letters or words that were omitted from the manuscript by an obvious slip of the pen, this volume removes the brackets and accepts the editorial emendation. Bracketed editorial insertions used in *The Journal of Richard Henry Dana, Jr.* to expand contractions, abbreviations, and proper names, or to clarify meaning, have been deleted in this volume. The list of Hawaiian words printed at 589.22–590.35 in this volume was preceded in the Lucid edition by a bracketed editorial insertion: "[Here Dana inserted the following vocabulary, with the notation 'Words in common use here—for a mem.']." In this volume, the brackets and the editorial comment have been deleted and Dana's notation is printed at 589.21 at the head of the list. The list of Japanese words printed at 738.1–9 in this volume appeared as a footnote in *The Journal of Richard Henry Dana, Jr.*, preceded by an editorial note: "Here Dana inserted the following catalog of words into the text." In this volume the list has been inserted into the text at the place indicated by the footnote in the Lucid edition. The editorial "[*sic*]" that appears in *The Journal of Richard Henry Dana, Jr.* following "each genius" at 675.28 has been deleted in this volume, and "genius" has been accepted as a variant singular form of "genii." At 604.13, "tubes, [?]" has been treated as a transcription error and replaced by "tribes," and at 718.32, "suspected Chinese" has been treated as a slip of the pen and corrected as "suspected Christians," even though it was not corrected in *The Journal of Richard Henry Dana, Jr.*

This volume presents the texts of the original printings chosen for inclusion here, but it does not attempt to reproduce nontextual features of their typographic design. The texts are presented without alteration except for the changes previously discussed and for the correction of typographical errors. Spelling, punctuation, and capitalization are often expressive features and are not altered, even when inconsistent or irregular. The following is a list of typographical errors corrected, cited by page and line number: 448.7, Conception; 509.8, in done; 532.17, star; 560.19, Mr. Cifford's; 599.10, funiture; 604.18, follows; 611.14, trial; 617.36, d'houneur"; 617.37, of Am.; 620.18, Boston]"; 622.9, *tem*; 629.3, & Latham, & Latham,; 632.5, a double; 640.36, angel; 641.6, angel; 653.3, Wahmpoa; 660.26, passenger; 661.16, weighted; 664.2, materal; 665.14, offf; 671.29, is his; 677.29, priest; 679.17, on; 692.33, coolies; 704.16, pasengers; 707.31, Catherdral; 710.16, The are; 718.7, even that; 734.15, permsision; 735.29, beautfiully; 743.25, Matchless, Mountain; 750.32, No quite; 755.3, Ksohun; 769.9, youngs; 771.13, liturigical; 774.30, out; 777.1, called in; 779.32, greal; 785.14, Sihks; 786.5, Progaganda; 790.21, boat; 793.21, Intoduces; 798.21, natvies; 799.37, two; 806.19, 'prentice; 809.19, Byaulla; 817.8, Persians; 818.15, Sihks; 822.34, consitution; 844.36, Maria die; 860.13, cilmate.

Notes

In the notes below, the reference numbers denote page and line of this volume (the line count includes headings). No note is made for material included in the eleventh edition of *Merriam-Webster's Collegiate Dictionary*. Biblical quotations are keyed to the King James Version. Quotations from Shakespeare are keyed to *The Riverside Shakespeare*, ed. G. Blakemore Evans (Boston: Houghton Mifflin, 1974). For further biographical background, more detailed notes, and references to other studies, see Samuel Shapiro, *Richard Henry Dana, Jr.: 1815–1882* (East Lansing: Michigan State University Press, 1961); Robert L. Gale, *Richard Henry Dana* (New York: Twayne Publishers, Inc., 1969); *The Journal of Richard Henry Dana, Jr.*, edited by Robert F. Lucid (3 vols., Cambridge: The Belknap Press of Harvard University Press, 1968).

TWO YEARS BEFORE THE MAST

1.4–8 Crowded in . . . rude voyage] Cf. Samuel Taylor Coleridge, *The Piccolomini; or, The First Part of Wallenstein* (1800), I.vi.126–27, 130–33, translated from the German of Friedrich Schiller.

3.4 Mr. Cooper's Pilot and Red Rover] *The Pilot* (1824) and *The Red Rover* (1827), James Fenimore Cooper's first and second sea novels.

3.8–10 Mr. Ames' . . . "Mariner's Sketches"] *A Mariner's Sketches* (1830) by Nathaniel Ames (1796–1835).

4.17–18 the escape . . . British channel] In *The Pilot*.

5.35 "With all . . . my head,"] *Hamlet*, I.v.79.

18.17–19 "Wherein the . . . furs dry;—"] *King Lear*, III.i.12–14.

18.34 "Philadelphia Catechism"] The catechism adopted by the Philadelphia Baptist Association in 1742.

20.10–11 hermaphrodite brig] A brig with a square-rigged foremast and a fore-and-aft-rigged mainmast.

23.17 *Mahon soger*] Mahon soldier, an epithet for a shirker and malingerer. It originated in the Royal Navy and referred to the British garrison at Mahón on Minorca that surrendered to the French in 1756.

34.6–7 Dublin frigate . . . Ann M'Kim] H.M.S. *Dublin* cruised in South American waters under the command of Lord James Townshend

(1785–1842) from 1831 to 1834. The *Ann McKim*, one of the first clipper ships, was launched in 1833 and visited Peru on her maiden voyage.

35.32 "the mourners go about the streets;"] Ecclesiastes 12:5.

42.14 Lord Anson] A British squadron commanded by Commodore George Anson (1697–1762) visited Juan Fernández in 1741.

43.2 *paseo*] Stroll.

44.15–17 the associations . . . Robinson Crusoe] Alexander Selkirk (1676–1721), the model for Daniel Defoe's Robinson Crusoe, was stranded on Juan Fernández from 1704 to 1709.

49.28–29 wars and rumors of wars] Matthew 24:6.

54.39 the battle] Peruvian revolutionary forces led by Simón Bolívar defeated the Spanish at Ayacucho on December 9, 1824.

63.35 the Royal George] A 100-gun British ship of the line that sank off Portsmouth in 1782 with the loss of at least 800 lives. Its foundering was attributed by some to a sudden breeze.

72.9 "Father Taylor,"] Edward Thompson Taylor (1793–1871), chaplain of the Seamen's Bethel in Boston and a model for Father Mapple in *Moby-Dick*.

73.17 *"gente de razón,"*] Literally, "people of reason," a phrase originally applied to those who could speak Spanish.

78.28 corregidores] Magistrates.

88.30 nolens volens] Willy-nilly.

89.38 "linementa laborum;"] Liniments for the pains of toil.

94.14 "no quiero"] I don't want to.

100.35–36 "sweethearts and wives."] A traditional Saturday night toast at sea, to which was sometimes added "and may they never meet."

102.23 "trienta uno,"] Thirty-one.

102.23–24 "everlasting."] A cardgame that ends when one player has all the cards.

102.27 coati] Here and elsewhere Dana refers not to the coati, a near relative of the raccoon, but to the coyote.

103.7 Scott's Pirate] Walter Scott's novel *The Pirate* (1821).

110.37 "Pulperia."] Grocery, general store.

111.16 *bon gré, mal gré*] With good grace or bad grace.

113.3–4 Grey Friars] Monks of the Franciscan order.

113.15 "Hay algunas . . . comer?"] Do you have anything to eat?

113.16 "Que gusta usted?"] What would you like?

113.32–33 "Dios se lo pague."] May God reward you.

118.20 Tom Cringle] The hero of *Tom Cringle's Log* (1829–33), an episodic novel about the Royal Navy in the West Indies, by Michael Scott (1789–1835).

119.12 Robinson's Alley] In Boston's North End.

119.16 Leander] In Greek legend, Leander would swim across the Hellespont every night to visit Hero, a priestess of Aphrodite.

125.24–25 Garrick, between tragedy and comedy] Title of a painting (1761) by Sir Joshua Reynolds (1723–1779) in which the actor David Garrick (1717–1779) is placed between feminine figures representing tragedy and comedy, each of whom is trying to draw the actor to her side.

127.3 "No importe!"] It doesn't matter.

127.26 veni-vidi-vici] I came, I saw, I conquered.

127.29 "*caballos*" and "*carréra*,"] Horses; race.

128.19 "Otra vez!"] One more time!

130.33–36 "For the . . . harshest clime."] William Wordsworth, "On the Power of Sound" (1835), stanza IV, ll. 53–56.

133.14 "world of waters!"] John Milton, *Paradise Lost*, III, 11.

134.14–17 "That walked . . . for sight"] Cf. *King Lear*, IV.vi.17–20.

136.1 pearls before swine] Matthew 7:6.

136.22 "mollia tempora fandi,"] Favorable times for speaking.

140.5 Tamahamaha] Kamehameha I (c.1758–1819), who unified the Hawaiian Islands under his rule.

140.6–7 ate Captain Cook] British explorer James Cook was killed on the island of Hawaii on February 14, 1779.

140.22–23 Riho Riho . . . Byron] Liholiho (1797–1824) succeeded his father as Kamehameha II before dying of measles during a visit to England; his body was returned to Oahu in 1825. George Anson Byron (1789–1868) inherited the title Lord Byron following the death of his cousin, the poet Byron, in 1824.

148.38 the Tower] The Tower of London.

153.21 Otaheitan] Tahitian.

153.36 aquadiente and annisou] Aguardiente and anisado (brandy and anisette).

156.16   Bowditch's Navigator] *The New American Practical Navigator* by Nathaniel Bowditch (1773–1838). First published in 1802, the treatise went through seven editions by 1833 and served as the standard American work on navigation throughout the 19th century.

156.27–28   "Mandeville . . . Godwin] *Mandeville* (1817), a novel by the English writer William Godwin (1756–1836).

158.29   "Tityre, tu . . . tegmine fagi."] Virgil, *Eclogues*, I, 1: "Tityrus, you who lie under cover of the spreading beech-tree."

163.24   the loaves and fishes] A colloquial expression for the emoluments of office. Cf. Matthew 14:14–21.

168.24   "equal to either fortune,"] Byron, *Marino Faliero* (1821), IV, 628.

171.21   seventy-four] A warship with 74 guns.

175.28   Bulwer's Paul Clifford] A novel published in 1830 by Edward Bulwer, later Bulwer-Lytton (1803–1873).

176.39–40   Hingham . . . "Bucket-maker."] The town of Hingham, Massachusetts, was known for the manufacture of buckets.

179.37   a voice like a young lion] Cf. Psalm 104:21: "The young lions roar after their prey."

186.29–30   Falconer's Shipwreck] *The Shipwreck* (1762), a narrative poem in three cantos by William Falconer (1732–1769). A purser in the Royal Navy, Falconer was lost at sea when H.M.S. *Aurora* disappeared in the Indian Ocean.

187.30–31   the Corn Laws] The laws governing the import and export of grain in Great Britain.

196.18–19   Ladrone and Pelew Islands] The Mariana and Palau islands.

198.36–37   governments . . . payment of a debt] A treaty signed in 1831 required France to pay the United States $5 million for spoliation claims from the Napoleonic wars. After the chamber of deputies failed to appropriate the necessary funds, President Andrew Jackson called in December 1834 for French property to be seized if the indemnity was not paid. France then recalled its minister from the U.S., and the dispute continued until February 1836, when Jackson accepted British assurances that France would pay the indemnity.

199.22   "soup meagre,"] *Soupe maigre*, meatless soup.

212.12–13   not so large as a man's hand] Cf. 1 Kings 18:44: "Behold, there ariseth a little cloud out of the sea, like a man's hand."

214.15   Asitka] Sitka on Baranof Island, the seat of government of Russian Alaska.

214.28–29   Nova Zembla] Novaya Zemlya, two large islands in the Arctic Ocean in northeastern Russia.

220.18   eleven days before] Due to the difference between the Julian and Gregorian calendars, Orthodox Christmas would have been celebrated on January 6, while the Feast of St. Nicholas (December 6) would have fallen on December 18, seven days before.

222.4   the ex-governor] Baron Ferdinand von Wrangel, who was relieved as governor of Russian Alaska on October 29, 1835.

222.24   *intermedios*] Points between.

228.29   Gil Blas] A picaresque novel (1715–35) by Alain-René Lesage, first translated into English by Tobias Smollett in 1749.

226.40–227.1   Santa Ana . . . Tampico] Centralist troops loyal to President Antonio López de Santa Ana (1794–1876) defeated Federalist rebels and their American supporters at Tampico on November 15, 1835.

227.6   Bustamente] Anastasio Bustamente (1780–1853) was president of Mexico, 1830–32, before being ousted by Santa Ana.

227.8   "Santa Ana no quiere religion."] Santa Ana has no fondness for religion.

227.15–16   Taney . . . Marshall?] Following the death of John Marshall on July 6, 1835, President Jackson made clear his intention to appoint Roger B. Taney (1777–1864) as chief justice of the Supreme Court, and the nomination was formally submitted to the Senate on December 28, 1835.

227.17–21   "El Vizconde Melbourne" . . . Wellington?] William Lamb, Viscount Melbourne (1779–1848), a Whig, became prime minister on April 18, 1835, succeeding a minority Tory ministry led by Sir Robert Peel in which the Duke of Wellington, prime minister from 1828 to 1830, served as foreign secretary. Melbourne had previously been prime minister from July 16 to November 17, 1834, when he was dismissed by William IV and replaced by Peel. Earl Grey was prime minister of a Whig government from 1830 until 1834, when he retired and was succeeded by Melbourne.

231.22–23   Espiritu Santu] Holy Ghost.

237.31–32   "Capitán de . . . la casa,"] Captain of the beach; master of the house.

238.4   paseár] Stroll.

239.35   *Bullknop* 'treet] Belknap Street in Boston, now Joy Street.

241.33   Pope to back him] Cf. Alexander Pope, *Moral Essays*, "Epistle II: Of the Characters of Women" (1735), ll. 1–2: "Nothing so true as what you once let fall, / 'Most Women have no Characters at all.'"

242.22　"Old Wilson"]　Jimmy Wilson (d. 1841), the last Boston town crier.

242.37　President]　Josiah Quincy (1772–1864), president of Harvard from 1829 to 1845.

242.38　"auctoritate mihi commissâ,"]　By the authority entrusted in me.

245.6　"Forsitan et hæc olim,"]　Cf. Vergil, *Aeneid*, I, 203: "Forsan et haec olim meminisse iuvabit." (Perhaps someday it will be pleasant to remember even this.)

247.6　Woodstock]　*Woodstock; or, The Cavalier* (1826), a novel by Sir Walter Scott.

251.8　Dr. Graham]　Sylvester Graham (1794–1851), a popular lecturer and writer on health who advocated a diet of fruits, vegetables, and bread made from coarsely ground wheat.

253.35　Ann street]　A street in the waterfront district lined with disorderly houses, later renamed North Street.

254.7–9　"All in . . . ye landsmen!"]　Song (1720) by John Gay (1685–1732), also known as "Black-Eyed Susan"; song (1789) by Charles Dibdin (1745–1814), also known as "Tom Bowling"; song (c. 1805) by Andrew Cherry (1762–1812); song by George A. Stevens (1720–1784), also known as "The Storm."

254.18–19　"Oh no . . . mention him."]　A song by Thomas Haynes Bayly (1797–1839).

256.9–10　"raised my . . . them a'."]　Cf. Robert Burns, "The Author's Earnest Cry and Prayer" (1786), ll. 35–36.

256.13　"vi et armis,"]　By force of arms.

259.28–29　"the cry . . . meaning knew."]　Walter Scott, *Marmion* (1808), VI.xxv.5.

267.12　live dog . . . dead lion]　Cf. Ecclesiastes 9:4.

271.15　New Holland]　Australia.

271.21　Professor N——]　Thomas Nuttall (1786–1859), who had resigned his position at Harvard to join the expedition under Nathaniel Wyeth that traveled overland from Missouri to the Oregon coast in 1834.

272.5　Old South]　Old South Meeting House in Boston.

274.33　long. 166° 45' W.]　This figure places the *Alert* to the west of the Hawaiian Islands. Although both the notebook that Dana kept on the voyage and the manuscript of *Two Years Before the Mast* appear to give the longitude as 106° 45' W., the more plausible figure is 116° 45' W.

276.6–7   "stemming nightly toward the pole."]   John Milton, *Paradise Lost*, II, 642.

276.27   Ducie's Island]   A small uninhabited atoll, located at 24° 40′ S., 124° 48′ W., 290 miles east of Pitcairn Island.

282.2   lunar observation]   A complex method of determining longitude without the use of a chronometer.

294.30   plagues of Egypt]   See Exodus 7–12.

300. 3–4   Cape of Pillars]   Cape Pilar on Desolación Island off southern Chile.

302.35   "thrilling regions of thick-ribbed ice,"]   *Measure for Measure*, III.i.122.

307.14   Cowper's Castaway]   "The Castaway" (1799), a poem by William Cowper (1731–1800) about a sailor washed overboard in a storm, is based on an incident in *Voyage Round the World* (1748) by the British naval officer George Anson (1697–1762).

307.20–21   "Ille et nefasto" . . . Erl King]   *Odes*, II, xiii; "Erlkönig" (1782).

311.17–18   Long wharf]   The principal wharf on the Boston waterfront.

333.5   Jack Downing]   Seba Smith (1792–1868), the editor of the Portland (Maine) *Courier*, created the character "Jack Downing," a Down East Yankee, in 1830 and used his "letters" to satirize politics in the Jacksonian era.

334.16–17   "With over-weathered . . . strumpet wind."]   *The Merchant of Venice*, II.vi.18–19.

334.36   swifted]   Brought closer together.

339.6   St. Peters]   The dome of St. Peter's Basilica in Rome is 404 feet high.

340.14   the Home]   The Sailors' Home in Quincy, Massachusetts, a boarding house run on religious principles.

343.12   the Castle.]   Castle Island in Boston Harbor.

344.14–16   "the first . . . sullen bell—"]   *2 Henry IV*, I.i.100–2.

346.2   Topliff's agent]   Samuel Topliff (1789–1864) was the proprietor of the Merchants' Reading Room in Boston and a supplier of foreign news to newspapers.

350.6–7   the sea shall . . . dead.]   Revelation 20:13.

353.27   *in terrorem*]   As a warning.

361.35   Godwin, though . . . his novels]   In *Mandeville* (1817), volume I, chapter V.

363. 33–34   laid his hand upon its mane]   Cf. Byron, *Childe Harold's Pilgrimage*, Canto IV (1818), CLXXXIV.

TWENTY-FOUR YEARS AFTER

367.32–33   "worlds not realized."]   William Wordsworth, "Intimations of Immortality from Recollections of Early Childhood" (1807), stanza IX.

368.7   Bishop Kip's church]   Grace Church, then located on Powell Street. William I. Kip (1811–1893) served as the missionary Episcopal Bishop of California, 1854–57, and as its elected Diocesan Bishop, 1857–93.

369.8–9   the Vigilance Committee]   A vigilance committee with more than 6,000 enrolled members was formed in San Francisco in 1856. It publicly hanged four men and banished dozens more from the city before disbanding. An earlier vigilance committee formed in 1851 also hanged four men.

369.13   Lies]   Jacob Primer Leese (1809–1892), who built the first house in San Francisco in 1836.

378.22   Fugit, interea fugit irreparabile tempus.]   Vergil, *Georgics*, III, 284: "Time meanwhile is flying, flying beyond recall."

379.3–5   "When for . . . and unknown."]   Byron, *Childe Harold's Pilgrimage*, Canto IV (1818), CLXXIX.

379.31–32   *sub Jove*]   In the open air.

381.15   "The legislature of a thousand drinks,"]   During the first session of the California state legislature (1849–50), Senator Thomas Jefferson Green (1802–1863) is reported to have frequently cried out at adjournment, "Let's have a drink! Let's have a thousand drinks!"

381.23–24   "*the* Colonel . . . Mrs. Fremont]   John C. Frémont (1813–1890), an army officer and explorer, led a military surveying party in 1845 to California, where he joined American settlers in their 1846 rebellion against Mexican rule. He resigned from the army in 1848 and was the Republican candidate for president in 1856. Jessie Benton Frémont (1824–1902), the daughter of Senator Thomas Hart Benton of Missouri, joined her husband in California in 1849.

382.28   *auri sacra fames*]   Vergil, *Aeneid*, III, 57: "accursed hunger for gold."

383.29   Mr. Latham]   Milton S. Latham (1827–1882), a pro-slavery Democrat, was inaugurated on January 9, 1860. He resigned five days later after the legislature elected him to the U.S. Senate to fill the vacancy caused in September 1859 by the death of David C. Broderick in a duel. Latham served in the Senate until 1863.

383.40   Kearney]   Stephen Watts Kearney (1794–1848), commander of the U.S. overland expedition to New Mexico and California in 1846 and military governor of California in 1847.

384.11   Mr. Edward Stanley]   Edward Stanly (1810–1872), a Whig, served
in Congress, 1837–43 and 1849–53. He moved to San Francisco in 1853 to practice law.

384.33–36   the old Independent]   The *Independent*, a 54-gun frigate, was
launched in 1814.

385.7   the Donner Party]   A party of settlers from Illinois who were
trapped by snow in the Sierra Nevada in the winter of 1846–47. Only 45 of
the 81 people who were snowbound survived, and more than half of the survivors resorted to cannibalism.

388.33–34   Mr. Channing]   George Edward Channing (1815–1837).

391.21   *cun*]   Ken; range of vision.

392.37–38   the victim . . . criminal law.]   Dr. George Parkman (1790–
1849), a wealthy physician, landlord, and money lender, disappeared on
November 23, 1849. Dr. John White Webster (1793–1850), a professor of chemistry at Harvard who owed Parkman a large sum of money, was convicted of
his murder and hanged. (George Parkman was the uncle of the historian
Francis Parkman.)

393.34   Hurd's Island]   Heard Island in the southern Indian Ocean, discovered in 1853.

395.1   the "Alabama Claims"]   Damages sought by the United States
from Great Britain for losses caused by Confederate commerce raiders built
in British shipyards. An Anglo-American treaty on the settlement of outstanding claims was overwhelmingly rejected by the Senate on April 13, 1869,
because it did not include any admission of regret or liability by Great
Britain. In 1871 a new treaty was signed and ratified that submitted the
wartime claims to arbitration, and in 1872 an international tribunal awarded
the United States $15.5 million in gold for losses inflicted by the *Alabama* and
two other raiders.

TO CUBA AND BACK

398.1   the SATURDAY CLUB]   See Chronology, 1855.

403.5   Robinson-street]   The street, later renamed Park Place, no longer
extends to the Hudson River.

403.18   the process of the Sibyl]   According to Roman legend, the
Cumaean Sibyl offered Lucius Tarquinius Superbus, the last king of Rome,
nine volumes of prophecies at a price he refused to pay. She then burned
three volumes and offered the remainder at the same price; when he refused
again, she burned three more, and the king bought the remaining three volumes at the initial price.

403.33   Captain Bullock]   James Dunwody Bulloch (1823–1901), a former officer in the U.S. Navy. In 1861 he became the Confederate naval agent in Great Britain and arranged for the construction and outfitting of the *Alabama* and several other commerce raiders. His half-sister Martha (1835–1884) was the mother of Theodore Roosevelt.

404.32   The Heights of Neversink]   Along the New Jersey coast, south of Sandy Hook.

407.20   Bache]   Lieutenant George Mifflin Bache (1811–1846), a great-grandson of Benjamin Franklin, was swept off the coastal survey brig *Washington*, along with 10 of his men, on September 8, 1846. His brother Alexander Dallas Bache (1806–1867) was the superintendent of the U.S. Coastal Survey, 1844–67.

408.6   "in wavering morrice move;"]   Milton, *Comus* (1637), l. 116.

409.14   the old Commodore]   John Rodgers (1773–1838), a naval officer who fought in the undeclared naval war with France; in North Africa against the Barbary pirates; and in the War of 1812.

409.36   "Billy Bowlegs"]   Holata Micco (c. 1810–c. 1864), a leader in the second (1835–42) and third (1855–58) Seminole Wars, surrendered in May 1858 and was sent with 122 other Seminoles to the Indian Territory.

415.36   "posada," "tienda,"]   Inn; shop.

417.1   "Every prospect pleases, and only man is vile."]   Reginal Heber (1783–1826), "Missionary Hymn" (1819).

420.28   Mr. Parker is here for his health]   Theodore Parker (1810–1860), a Unitarian minister and abolitionist, was forced by illness to retire from public life in January 1859. He died in Florence, Italy, on May 10, 1860.

420.32–33   Dr. Howe . . . benefactor of his race]   Dr. Samuel Gridley Howe (1801–1876) was the founding director of the Perkins School for the Blind and an advocate for prison reform, abolition, and better care for the mentally ill and disabled.

420.34   since Kane died]   Elisha Kent Kane (1820–1857), an American naval officer who explored the Arctic, 1850–51 and 1853–55.

420.35   Bishop of Havana]   Francisco Fleix Soláus (1804–1870) was bishop of Havana from 1846 to 1864.

421.3   my hero's wife]   Julia Ward Howe (1819–1910), a poet and editor of the abolitionist newspaper *The Commonwealth*.

421.18–21   The Opera . . . Miss Ada Phillips]   The New York Italian opera company managed by the Moravian impresario and conductor Max Maretzek (1821–1897). Its members included Marietta Gazzaniga (1824–1884), an Italian soprano; Louise Lamoureux, a ballet dancer; and Adelaide Phillips (1833–1882), an American contralto.

421.29–30   "With wanton . . . mazes running"]   Milton, *L'Allegro* (c. 1631), ll. 141–42.

426.14–15   "What is . . . of him!"]   Psalm 8:4.

426.27   *hic jacet . . . sic itur*]   Here lies; this is the way.

428.21   St. Nicholas . . . or Meurice's]   Elegant hotels in New York, Boston, London, and Paris, respectively.

430.7   Gil Blas]   See note 228.29.

430.31–32   "And, poured . . . melancholy waste"]   William Cullen Bryant, "Thanatopsis" (1817), ll. 42–43.

431.2   "with handmaid lamp attending"]   Milton, *Hymn on the Morning of Christ's Nativity* (1629), XXVII.

431.4   "strumpet winds,"]   Cf. *The Merchant of Venice*, II.vi.16.

431.28   Tacon]   Miguel Tacon (1777–1855), Spanish governor-general of Cuba, 1834–38.

433.16   Concha]   Jose Gutierrez de la Concha (1809–1895) was governor general of Cuba, 1850–52, 1854–59, and 1874–75.

433.39   Maria de Rohan]   Tragic opera by Gaetano Donizetti (1797–1848), first performed in 1843.

436.19–20   Bishop of Puebla de los Angelos]   Pelagio Antonio de Labastida y Dávalos (1816–1891) was Bishop of Puebla de los Angeles from 1855 until 1863.

436.36–37   "Thirty Millions Bill" of Mr. Slidell]   Senator John Slidell (1793–1871) of Louisiana had recently introduced a bill appropriating $30 million for the purchase of Cuba by the United States. The bill was approved by the Senate foreign relations committee in February 1859, but Republican opposition prevented the full Senate from voting on it before the 35th Congress adjourned on March 3, 1859.

437.17   Brownson]   Orestes Brownson (1803–1876), a Unitarian minister who converted to Roman Catholicism in 1844.

437.23   Propaganda or St. Sulpice]   The Collegio di Propaganda Fide in Rome, founded by Urban VIII in 1627 for the training of missionaries; the Seminaire Saint-Sulpice in Paris, founded by Jean-Jacques Olier in 1641.

442.13   "must give us pause,"]   *Hamlet*, III.i.67.

442.14–15   they live in cedar . . . rests in curtains]   Cf. 2 Samuel 7:2.

442.32–33 "a sword shall . . . soul also."] Luke 2:35.

443.5 Faber] Pierre Favre (1506–1546), French theologian and a co-founder of the Society of Jesus in 1539.

444.8–16 "In much . . . all things."] 2 Corinthians 6:4–6 and 8–10.

450.5 *lusus naturæ*] Freak of nature.

452.17 Señor C——] Juan Chartrand.

453.17 Miss Bremer . . . New World] *The Homes of the New World* (1853), a travel book by the Swedish novelist Frederika Bremer (1801–1865).

454.35 "Evenings in Boston,"] A children's reader that was published anonymously in 1827; it has been attributed to John Lauris Blake (1788–1857), a prolific writer of school textbooks.

455.7 the dreadful insurrection] The Haitian slave insurrection of 1791.

462.3–5 Mr. Butler . . . Governor Banks] Benjamin F. Butler (1818–1893) was a prominent Lowell attorney who later served as a Union general, 1861–65; as a member of Congress, 1867–75 and 1877–79; and as governor of Massachusetts, 1883–84. (For Butler's later opposition to Dana, see Chronology, 1868 and 1876.) Josiah G. Abbott (1814–1891) served in the state legislature and as a superior court justice for Suffolk County, 1855–58. Tappan Wentworth (1802–1875), a Lowell attorney, served in Congress, 1853–55. Rufus Choate (1799–1859) served in Congress, 1831–34, and in the Senate, 1841–45; he was considered to be the leader of the Boston bar. Nathaniel P. Banks (1816–1894) served in Congress, 1853–57, and was governor of Massachusetts, 1858–61; he later became a Union general and served another seven terms in Congress after the Civil War.

485.3 "I say . . . to me."] Walter Scott, *The Lay of the Last Minstrel* (1805), II.xxii.16.

485.14 a Montalembert trial] In November 1858 Charles Forbes, comte de Montalembert (1810–1870), a prominent liberal Catholic statesman, was sentenced to six months imprisonment for publishing a pamphlet contrasting English civil liberty with the repressive regime of Napoleon III. His sentence was remitted by Napoleon in December 1858.

487.3 Countess Villanueva] The countess was the widow of Claudio Martinez de Pinillos, count of Villanueva (1789–1853), who was general treasurer of Cuba from 1825 to 1851.

489.10 vomito] Yellow fever.

491.25 battle of the Boyne] The Protestant army led by William of Orange crossed the Boyne River near Drogheda and defeated the Irish-French army of James II on July 1 (O.S.), 1690.

493.27–28   his Prussian prison]   Howe was arrested in Berlin in 1832 for distributing funds to Polish refugees who had fled the suppression of the 1831 uprising in Russian Poland. He was imprisoned for six weeks and then expelled from Prussia.

494.18–19   "more sinned . . . sinning,"]   *King Lear*, III.ii.60.

502.3   *lege soluti*]   Freed from the law.

504.31   the Lucumí]   The Yorubas of southwestern Nigeria and Benin.

506.18–19   the Lopez expedition]   Narciso López (1799–1851), a former Spanish army officer, landed in Cuba on August 11, 1851, with 450 Cuban exiles and American volunteers. The expedition failed to start a general uprising, and 51 of the American filibusters were captured and shot on August 16. Lopez was publicly executed on September 1.

510.35–36   "I Puritani"]   *I Puritani di Scozia* (1825), an opera by Vincenzo Bellini (1801–1835) set during the English Civil War.

510.36   Lealtà]   Loyalty.

510.38–40   Facciolo . . . garroted]   Eduardo Facciolo was executed in 1852.

525.1–2   but one neck . . . tyrant]   The historian Suetonius quoted the Emperor Caligula (A.D. 12–41) as saying: "Would that the Roman people had but one neck!"

529.36–37   the Black Warrior]   The steamship ran aground on Rockaway Bar off Long Island on February 20, 1859, and broke up during a gale on February 24.

533.18   Chief Justice Eustis]   George Eustis (1796–1858) was born in Boston and educated at Harvard College. He later moved to Louisiana and served as chief justice of its state supreme court from 1846 to 1852. Eustis died at his home in New Orleans on December 22, 1858.

533.25   Morrissey . . . Heenan]   John Morrissey (1831–1878) defended his heavyweight championship by knocking out John C. Heenan (1835–1873) in the eleventh round of a prizefight held at Long Point, Ontario, on October 20, 1858.

535.15   Sickles and Key tragedy]   Daniel Edgar Sickles (1819–1914), a Democratic congressman from New York City, shot and killed Philip Barton Key (1818–1859), the U.S. attorney for the District of Columbia and the son of Francis Scott Key, in Washington on February 27, 1859, shortly after he learned that Key was having an affair with his wife. Sickles was acquitted of murder in April 1859, becoming the first defendant to successfully use the defense of temporary insanity in an American court. He later served as a Union general in the Civil War and lost a leg at Gettysburg.

JOURNAL OF A VOYAGE ROUND THE WORLD, 1859–1860

541.9   Capt. Bulloch] See note 403.33.

542.5   Le Grand's] The hotel where Dana stayed during his first visit to Cuba; see pp. 418–19 in this volume.

542.21–22   "It may . . . be forever"] Julia Crawford (1799–1860), "Kathleen Mavourneen"; the poem is also attributed to Anne Crawford (1734–1801) and Louisa Macartney Crawford (1790–1858).

542.24–26   "Sweet Nellie . . . any more"] Cf. Benjamin Russell Hanby (1833–1867), "Darling Nelly Gray" (1856).

544.13–14   Morissey prise . . . McKinley] John Morrissey (1831–1878) defeated George Thompson in a prizefight held at Mare Island on August 31, 1852. John McKinley (1780–1852) served on the U.S. Supreme Court from 1837 until his death on July 9, 1852.

544.27   Bishop Kip] See note 368.7.

545.3   Archb. Alemany] Joseph Sadoc Alemany (1814–1888) was the Archbishop of San Francisco from 1853 to 1884.

545.31–32   the Vigilence Committee] See note 369.8–9.

546.15   Alfred Robinson] Robinson (1806–1895) was the purchasing agent for the *Pilgrim* during Dana's first voyage to California.

546.35   Henry Mellus] Mellus became the mayor of Los Angeles on May 9, 1860, and served until his death on December 26, 1860.

548.17   Capt. Hancock] Winfield Scott Hancock (1824–1886), later a corps commander in the Union army and the Democratic candidate for president in 1880.

548.18–19   Major Armistead] Lewis A. Armistead (1817–1863) defeated a party of Mohave Indians near Fort Mohave in Arizona Territory on August 5, 1859. Armistead joined the Confederacy in 1861 and was mortally wounded leading his brigade in Pickett's Charge at Gettysburg.

550.11   Mrs. Frémont] See note 381.23–24.

551.14   Clark's] Clark's Station at Palachum (now Wawona), a log cabin built by Galen Clark (1815–1910), an early explorer and guardian of the Yosemite Valley.

551.28   Dr. Gwin] William McKendree Gwin (1805–1885), Democratic senator from California, 1850–61.

553.18   Joaquin] Joaquín Murietta, a notorious outlaw killed by California Rangers in the San Joaquin Valley on July 25, 1853. His severed head was later displayed in a jar filled with spirits.

553.36   Mary *Collins*] One of several women with whom Dana lived while on the California coast in 1835–36.

554.2   his conflict with the Merced Co.] In July 1858 Frémont and his supporters were involved in an armed confrontation with miners and gunmen backed by the Merced Mining Company as part of a long-running dispute over mining rights on the Mariposa County land Frémont had purchased in 1847. The standoff ended without bloodshed after the state militia was called out.

555.4   "People's Party"] Organized by members of the Vigilance Committee, the party won the 1856 elections and controlled the city for the next decade.

556.7–8   Gov. Clifford . . . Chas. C. Harris] John Henry Clifford (1809–1876), a Whig, was governor of Massachusetts, 1853–54. Charles Coffin Harris (1822–1881) later served as attorney general of Hawaii, 1863–66; as its minister of finance, 1865–69; as its minister of foreign affairs, 1869–72; and as chief justice of its supreme court, 1877–81.

556.25   Donald McKay's best manner] McKay (1810–1880), a Boston shipyard director, began designing and building clipper ships in 1850.

559.11   mourning of David over Absalom] 2 Samuel 18:33, 19:4.

561.3–4   King . . . shooting Mr. ——] King Kamehameha IV (1834–1863) drank heavily and shot his private secretary Henry A. Neilson after hearing rumors that he was having an affair with Queen Emma (1836–1885). Neilson died from his wounds in 1861.

561.5   Lot Kamehameha] Prince Lot Liholiho Kapuaiwa Kamehameha (1830–1872), who succeeded his brother to the throne as Kamehameha V.

561.18   R. Cath. Bishop] Louis Maigret (1804–1882), bishop of Hawaii from 1847 to 1882.

562.31   Prest. Woods] Leonard Woods (1807–1878), a friend and former tutor of Dana (see Chronology, 1832), was president of Bowdoin College, 1839–66.

564.6   F.P.B.] Francis Preston Blair (1791–1876), editor of the Washington *Globe*.

565.3   Lt. Reynolds] William Reynolds (1815–1879), who had served with the Wilkes Expedition that explored the Antarctic and the Pacific Northwest, 1838–42, was sent to Honolulu as a naval storekeeper to recover his health.

568.2   Am. B.C.F.M.] American Board of Commissioners for Foreign Missions.

568.4   W. Cedar st.] Dana rented a house at 7 West Cedar Street in Boston in November 1842 and lived there for the next seven years.

576.12–14   Hebron, Dedham . . . Old Hundred] Hymn tunes by Lowell Mason (1792–1872), William Gardiner (1770–1853), and Louis Bourgeois (1510–1561) respectively.

576.15–18   "The day . . . draw near"] Cf. "The Day Is Past and Gone," hymn (1792) with words by John Leland (1754–1841) and music by Louis Bourgeois.

580.25   the Governess] Princess Ruth Luka Keanolani Kanahoahoa Ke'elikolani (1826–1883).

583.7   Tom Comer] Thomas Comer (1790–1862), a composer, performer, and theatrical music director in Boston.

583.21   Ockotsk] The Sea of Okhotsk.

584.16   Encycl. Brittanica] The article was published in the eighth edition of the *Britannica* (1852–60).

585.1–2   "Bossuet's Exposition de la doctrine Catholique"] Jacques Bénigne Bossuet (1627–1704), *Exposition de la doctrine de l'Église catholique* (1671).

585.22   the Alert] The ship Dana returned from California on in 1836.

586.27–28   "If I . . . for me"] From the traditional ballad "The Saracen."

587.20   Sleeper of Roxbury] John Sherburne Sleeper (1794–1878), a Massachusetts shipmaster and newspaper editor, was mayor of Roxbury, 1856–58, and wrote sea stories under the name "Hawser Martingale."

591.11   Anderson, the magician] John Henry Anderson (1814–1874), a Scottish magician who first toured the United States in 1851.

593.38   De Tocqueville's U. States] The first volume of Alexis de Tocqueville's *Democracy in America* was published in the United States in 1838, the second in 1840.

596.24–25   church in Boston . . . 15th anniversary] See Chronology, 1844.

596.27   Kane] Elisha Kent Kane (1820–1857), author of *Arctic Explorations* (1856), an account of the expedition Kane led in the Canadian Arctic and Greenland in 1853–55.

596.34   "From the . . . the Sun &c."] Malachi 1:11, used as a reading in "The Order for Daily Morning Prayer" of the Anglican *Book of Common Prayer*.

599.16–18   Said Scripture . . . were equal] Luke 8:5–13.

600.3   Rockwood] Ebenezer Rockwood Hoar (1816–1895) studied law with Dana at Harvard.

600.4   Sargent Prentiss]   Seargent Prentiss (1808–1850), born in Maine, was a lawyer and Whig orator in Mississippi known for his heavy drinking and gambling.

601.14   Crabbe]   The English poet George Crabbe (1754–1832).

601.23   lines on his 36th birthday]   "On This Day I Complete my Thirty-Sixth Year" (1824).

601.24–27   "I am . . . for me &c."]   2 Timothy 4:6–8.

602.4   Kossuth hats]   Broad-brimmed slouch hats of the style popularized by the Hungarian patriot Louis Kossuth.

602.7–8   John Adams . . . fired]   Although opponents of the Vigilance Committee persuaded the navy to anchor the sloop *John Adams* off San Francisco, the federal government refused to intervene further.

602.16   Gov.-elect Latham]   See note 383.29.

603.15   Fred. Billings]   Frederick Billings (1823–1890) later helped found the Northern Pacific Railroad.

603.24   *ore tenus*]   Delivered orally.

605.8   the Advent]   The church Dana helped found in Boston.

606.1–2   Quitman . . . Shields]   John Anthony Quitman (1799–1858), brigadier general in the Mississippi militia; Persifor F. Smith (1798–1858) of Louisiana, brigadier general; James Shields (1806–1879), brigadier general of Illinois volunteers.

606.6   Mr. Parker]   Francis E. Parker (1821–1886), Dana's law partner.

606.9   Mr. Edw. Stanly]   See note 384.11.

609.12   "Donner Party"]   See note 385.7.

612.8   Glass]   Hugh Glass (c. 1783–c. 1833), a fur trader and mountain man, was mauled by a grizzly bear in 1823 while serving on an expedition commanded by Major Andrew Henry (1775?–1833).

612.10–11   man & boy]   John Fitzgerald and Jim Bridger (1804–1881), later a famous mountain man.

613.16–19   John Randolph . . . she replied]   In 1809 Gouverneur Morris married Nancy (Anne Cary) Randolph (1774–1837), whose sister Judith had been married to their cousin Richard Randolph (1770–1796), the brother of the politician John Randolph of Roanoke. John Randolph wrote a letter to Nancy in 1814 in which he accused her of murdering her newborn child in 1792, poisoning Richard, and supporting herself by prostitution. In her reply Nancy admitted to having given birth to a stillborn child, but denied his other charges.

613.35   the new Bishop]   George Hills (1816–1895) was bishop of British Columbia from 1859 to 1892.

614.16   Dr. Bushnell says]   Horace Bushnell (1802–1876), a Congregational clergyman and theologian, in his pamphlet *California: Its Characteristics and Prospects* (1858).

619.29   *coram omnibus*]   In the presence of everybody.

620.9   Broderick's place]   Senator David C. Broderick (1820–1859) was mortally wounded on September 13, 1859, in a duel with David S. Terry (1823–1889). Terry, the chief justice of the California supreme court, 1856–59, resigned from the bench and challenged Broderick after the senator questioned his honesty. He was indicted for killing Broderick but was acquitted. In 1889 Terry was shot to death by a U.S. marshal after he assaulted Supreme Court Justice Stephen J. Field, who had ruled against him while sitting as a circuit judge the previous year.

620.28–29   Chief Just. Field]   Stephen J. Field (1816–1899), who succeeded David S. Terry as chief justice of the California supreme court, was an associate justice of the U.S. Supreme Court, 1863–97. His brother David Dudley Field (1805–1894) was a prominent New York lawyer.

621.18   Horace Gray]   Gray (1828–1902) was the reporter for the Massachusetts supreme judicial court, 1853–61; a justice of the supreme judicial court, 1864–73; its chief justice, 1873–82; and an associate justice of the U.S. Supreme Court, 1882–1902.

622.9   *pro re nata . . . in rem* or *in personam*]   As the situation required; against a thing; against a person.

623.35–36   *Ex.* Lt. Gov. Purdy]   Samuel Purdy, a Democrat, was lieutenant governor of California, 1852–56.

623.39   the Alta]   The *Daily Alta California* newspaper.

624.24   Andrés Pico]   Pico (1810–1876) commanded the Mexican forces at the battle of San Pasqual on December 6, 1846. He signed the surrender of the Mexican army in California on January 13, 1847.

625.20–21   Johnson]   J. Neely Johnson (1825–1872), a Know-Nothing, was governor of California, 1856–58.

626.25   Marshal Tukey]   Francis Tukey was Boston city marshal in 1851 during the Shadrach and Sims fugitive slave cases; see Chronology.

626.29   Weller]   John B. Weller (1812–1875), a Democrat, was governor of California, 1858–60.

629.24–25   Lt. Gov. Downie]   John G. Downey (1826–1894) succeeded Latham and served as governor, 1860–62.

629.37   Ned McGowan] Edward McGowan (1813–1893), a Democratic politician, fled San Francisco in 1856 after being accused by the Vigilance Committee of complicity in murder. He published the *Narrative of Edward McGowan* in 1857.

630.12–14   "A few . . . Mother Earth"] Byron, *Childe Harold's Pilgrimage*, Canto I (1812), XIII.

631.6–7   S. Wells Williams . . . History of China] Samuel Wells Williams (1812–1884), an American missionary and author of *The Middle Kingdom* (1848).

634.37–38   "Adieu, Adieu . . . waters blue . . ."] Cf. Byron, *Childe Harold's Pilgrimage*, Canto I, XIII.

635.33   Bowditch] See note 156.16.

636.29   Huc's Travels in China] Evariste R. Huc (1813–1860), *A Journey through the Chinese Empire* (1855). Huc was a French missionary.

637.35   Thoms' book on navigation] William Thoms, *A New Treatise on the Practice of Navigation at Sea* (1854).

642.39   birth day of my little daughter] Angela Henrietta Channing Dana, who was born in 1857.

643.3–4   I confess . . . regimentals notwithstanding] Dana alludes to a joke he had recorded in his journal on December 18, 1851: "A Yankee countryman was looking at a copy of Canova's 'dancing girl,' & exclaimed—'I had rather sleep with that gal, without a rag on her, than to sleep with Gen. Washington in all his regimentals.'"

643.4–5   "If that . . . of it."] Cf. Patrick Henry's speech on the Stamp Act, May 29, 1765.

643.9   Hildreth's Japan] Richard Hildreth (1807–1865), *Japan As It Was and Is* (1855).

643.14–15   John Halifax, gentleman] Title of a novel (1856) about a poor English orphan by Dinah Maria Mulock (1826–1887), writing as "Mrs. Craik."

643.18   life of Charlotte Brontë] Biography (1857) by Elizabeth C. Gaskell (1810–1865).

643.39   Mr. Everett's Address] Edward Everett (1794–1865), "The Uses of Astronomy," delivered in Albany, New York, in 1856 and published as a pamphlet that same year.

644.14   Shirley] Novel (1849) by Charlotte Brontë.

648.1   Russell & Co.] A Boston trading firm.

648.4   Adele] Adele Watson, the wife of Dana's brother-in-law William Watson.

648.6   Warren Delano] A senior partner in Russell & Co., Delano (1809–1898) was the maternal grandfather of Franklin Delano Roosevelt.

648.15   Aug. Hurd & Co.] Augustine Heard & Co., a Boston trading firm.

648.27   Ned] Dana's brother, Edmund Trowbridge Dana (1818–1869).

649.29   Reed] William Bradford Reed (1806–1876), U.S. minister to China, 1857–59.

650.17–18   Mr. Ward . . . Bowring] John Elliott Ward (1814–1902), U.S. minister to China, 1859–60; Sir John Bowring (1792–1872), governor of Hong Kong, 1854–59.

650.39   Hartford] A steam-powered sloop of 2,900 tons, launched in Boston in 1859. It later served as the Union flagship at the battle of Mobile Bay in 1864.

652.4   Sir Hope Grant] James Hope Grant (1808–1875), commander of British troops in China, 1860–61. Dana visited China during the later phases of the Second China War, 1857–60, waged by Great Britain and France to protect and expand their trade concessions in China.

652.14–15   English guns . . . *present* war] The British had bombarded the Bogue forts during the Opium War, 1839–42.

653.35   Com. Foote] An American squadron commanded by Andrew Hull Foote (1806–1863) captured the four forts, November 20–22, 1858, after the Chinese opened fire on an unarmed American boat.

654.22   the Back Bay Commnrs.] Under the supervision of the Commissioners of Public Lands, Boston began filling in the Back Bay tidal flats in 1857.

665.2–3   Mr. Parkes] Harry Smith Parkes (1828–1885), British diplomat and one of three commissioners appointed to govern Canton.

671.2   John P. Cushing] John Perkins Cushing (1787–1862), a Boston merchant who traded in China from 1803 to 1830.

672.12   Commissioner Yeh] Ye Mingchen, viceroy of Canton, whose refusal to release the British ship *Arrow* in 1856 led to the outbreak of the Second China War. He was captured by the British in 1858 and exiled to Calcutta, where he died in 1859.

673.35   Hughes & Fitzpatrick] John Joseph Hughes (1797–1864), Roman Catholic archbishop of New York, 1850–64, and John Bernard Fitzpatrick (1812–1866), Roman Catholic bishop of Boston, 1846–66.

683.34   height . . . Blue Hill, Milton] The hill, ten miles south of Boston, is 635 feet high.

686.40   Dr. Kerr] John Glasgow Kerr (1824–1901), American missionary physician and director of a hospital in Canton.

691.12   Chesterfield was born] Philip Stanhope, fourth earl of Chesterfield (1694–1773), wrote a series of letters to his son on manners that were published in 1774.

692.37   its ponderous & *iron* jaws] Cf. *Hamlet*, I.iv.50: "his ponderous and marble jaws."

693.5–6   2d relief . . . Sir C. Campbell] A force commanded by Sir Colin Campbell (1792–1865) relieved the besieged Lucknow residency on November 17, 1857, during the Indian Mutiny.

694.7   red button] A red coral button that signified the highest rank attainable by one not in public office.

695.23   *en garcon*] As a bachelor.

697.19   Theodore Parker] See note 420.28.

698.1–2   Dom Isadoro Guimaiaes] Isidoro Francisco Guimaraes, governor of Macao, 1851–63.

698.23–24   Camoens . . . Lusiad] *Os Lusiades* (1572), an epic poem by Luis de Camoëns (1524–1580).

698.31   Dr. Morrison] Robert Morrison (1782–1834), an English missionary who translated the Bible into Chinese.

699.2   Mr. Cushing] Caleb Cushing (1800–1879), American minister to China in 1844 and attorney general of the United States, 1853–57. Cushing negotiated the first Chinese-American treaty, which he signed at Wanghia in 1844.

699.10   Lord Elgin] James Bruce, earl of Elgin (1811–1863), was appointed envoy plenipotentiary to China in 1857. After a series of British victories he negotiated the treaty of Tianjin in 1858 under which the Chinese made further political and commercial concessions. Elgin returned to China in 1860 to enforce the terms of the treaty.

699.28   Motley's book] John Lothrop Motley (1814–1877), *The Rise of the Dutch Republic* (1856).

699.29   Chinnery] George Chinnery (1774–1852), an English painter.

701.32   death of Mrs. Russell] Lydia Smith Russell (1789–1859) was the mother of Jonathan Russell (1825–1875) and a first cousin of Dana's mother.

701.35–36   more sinned . . . sinning] *King Lear*, III.ii.60.

703.29   Dominick Lynch] Lynch (d. 1884) was a U.S. naval officer and brother of Adele Watson (see note 648.4).

705.28   Mr. Bruce]   Frederick William Bruce (1814–1867), younger brother of Lord Elgin, was named minister to China in 1858. He was superseded by his brother when Lord Elgin returned in 1860.

705.26   Bishop Boone]   William Jones Boone (1811–1864), Episcopal missionary bishop to China from 1844 to 1864.

708.15   M. de Bornier]   Pierre André Borgniet (1811–1862).

708.34   Commodore Tattnall]   Despite U.S. neutrality in the Second China War, Josiah Tattnall (1795–1871) came to the aid of a disabled British ship during an attack on the Dagu forts guarding Tianjin on June 25, 1859. In a dispatch to Washington, Tattnall explained his actions by citing the adage "blood is thicker than water."

709.3   his 2 vols.]   Richard Henry Dana, Sr., *Poems and Prose Writings*. The collection first appeared in 1833, and then in an enlarged edition in 1850.

709.7   Gen. Walter Jones]   Walter Jones (1776–1861), a prominent Washington lawyer and general of the District of Columbia militia.

709.34   yamuns]   Buildings used for government offices or as official residences.

714.4   the Bishop of Victoria]   George Smith (1815–1871), consecrated as the Anglican bishop of Victoria (Hong Kong) in 1847.

714.20   Meadows . . . Wade]   Thomas Taylor Meadows, secretary and translator for the British consulate in Canton and author of *The Chinese and Their Rebellions* (1856); Thomas Francis Wade (1818–1895), British diplomat and linguist.

718.19–20   Father Valignano]   Alessandro Valignano (1539–1606), leader of the Jesuit missions in Asia.

725.27   props]   Cowrie shells that were shaken and thrown like dice in a gambling game much in vogue in New England in the mid-19th century.

726.1   the Japanese embassy]   An official Japanese delegation visited the United States from May 14 to June 30, 1860.

726.12–13   "a bed of heaped Elysian flowers"]   Milton, *L'Allegro* (c. 1631), ll. 146–47.

728.30–31   Oliphant's China & Japan]   Laurence Oliphant (1829–1888), *Narrative of a Mission to China and Japan in 1857-8-9* (1859).

732.6   "garniture & screen"]   Richard Henry Dana, Sr. (1787–1879), "The Moss supplicateth for the Poet," l. 24.

732.23–24   "wee, modest"]   Robert Burns, "To a Mountain Daisy" (1786).

734.14   Mr. Harris]   Townsend Harris (1804–1878) was American consul general to Japan, 1855–59, and minister to Japan, 1859–62. He negotiated the Japanese-American treaties of 1857 and 1858.

734.26–27   the assassination . . . of Mito]   Ii Naosuke (1815–1860), who negotiated and signed the 1858 treaty with the United States, was killed on March 3, 1860, by samurai sent by Tokugawa Nariaki (1800–1860), lord of the Mito clan.

739.26   Goble]   Jonathan Goble (1827–1898), who had served as a Marine in Perry's squadron, later became the first person to translate portions of the New Testament into Japanese and was one of the inventors of the jinrikisha.

739.30–31   be called *Rabbi, Rabbi*]   Cf. Matthew 23:7.

739.37   Irvingite]   Name popularly given to members of the Catholic Apostolic Church, an apocalyptic sect that originated in England under the leadership of Edward Irving (1792–1834).

742.8   Miss Porter]   Sarah Porter (1813–1900), founder of Miss Porter's School, which Dana's daughters attended.

750.12   the Mississippi & Powhatan]   Small U.S. Navy paddle steamers.

750.30–31   I'm on . . . ever be!]   Barry Cornwall (pseudonym of Brian Waller Procter, 1787–1874), "The Sea," ll. 7–8.

751.18   Baron Gros]   Jean Baptiste Louis Gros (1793–1870), French envoy plenipotentiary to China.

752.17–18   Bayard Taylor's book on China]   *A Visit to India, China, and Japan in the Year 1853* (1855).

753.6   *Quien Sabe?*]   Who knows?

758.31   Dr. Hobson's work on anatomy]   *Quanti xin lun (Outline of Anatomy and Physiology)*, published in 1850 by the British medical missionary Benjamin Hobson (1816–1873). The work was originally written in Chinese by Hobson and his Chinese collaborators.

760.25   Nan King . . . the rebels]   The city was held by Taiping rebels from 1853 to 1864.

762.7   gingall]   A light gun mounted on a swivel.

766.21   Sir. Wm. Peel]   Peel (1824–1858) led a naval brigade during the Indian Mutiny, 1857–58.

768.29   Charles Lever novels stamp]   Lever (1806–1872) was a popular Irish novelist.

769.26   "Flapped in . . . pirate's sheet"]   Richard Henry Dana, Sr., "The Buccaneer," l. 21.

772.28   Bishop Delaplasse]   Louis-Gabriel Delaplace (1820–1884).

773.3   40 f. high, & thus]   At this point in the manuscript Dana drew a picture of a crenellated wall.

773.18   the treaty]   The Treaty of Wanghia, signed in 1844.

777.16   Mr. Daggett]   Oliver Ellsworth Daggett (1810–1880), a Congregational minister in Canandaigua, New York, was married to Dana's sister-in-law, Elizabeth Watson Daggett (1812–1891).

779.15   lorcha]   A light coastal vessel having a European-type hull and a Chinese rig.

781.1   Ld. Palmerston]   Viscount Palmerston (1784–1865) served as prime minister, 1855–58 and 1859–65.

781.4   Mr. Cass]   Lewis Cass (1782–1866) was secretary of state, 1857–60.

781.18   the rebel occupation of Shanghai]   The Chinese district of Shanghai was occupied from September 1853 to February 1855 by the "Small Swords," an underground society allied with the Taiping. In 1860 the city was directly threatened by the Taiping rebels.

782.31   Toucey]   Isaac Toucey (1792–1869) was secretary of the navy, 1857–60.

782.34   Greene]   Samuel Dana Greene (1840–1884), a distant relative of Dana, would later serve as gunnery officer of the Union ironclad *Monitor*.

783.35   little Dick]   Richard Henry Dana III, born January 3, 1851.

787.4   P&O]   The Peninsular & Oriental Steamship Navigation Company.

789.33   Sir J. Bowring's Philippine Islands]   John Bowring, *A Visit to the Philippine Islands* (1859).

790.5–6   The "Malabar" . . . Point de Galle]   The wreck occurred on May 11, 1860, at the southern Ceylonese (Sri Lankan) port of Galle.

791.25   Charlotte]   Dana's sister.

794.13–14   George Channing]   Dana's cousin and friend.

799.21   Rosamund's age]   Dana's daughter Mary Rosamund was 11.

800.38   Mr. Tudor's ice business]   Frederick Tudor (1783–1864) had been exporting ice cut from Massachusetts ponds, including Walden, to the tropics since 1806.

803.3–4   "Friends in Council"]   Sir Arthur Helps (1813–1875), *Friends in Council, A Series of Readings and Discourse Thereon* (1847), a collection of dialogues between imaginary characters on social and moral questions.

804.18–19   Nat. Hist. of Enthousiasm] Isaac Taylor (1787–1865), *Natural History of Enthusiasm* (1830).

805.7–9   Prof. Dana . . . chemistry extant] Possibly a conflation of James Dwight Dana (1813–1895), a geologist, with James Freeman Dana (1793–1827), author of *An Epitome of Chymical Philosophy* (1825). Both men were distant cousins of Dana.

805.15–17   Trevelyan . . . publishing his minutes] Charles Edward Trevelyan (1807–1866) was recalled for having provided the press with a memorandum critical of the Legislative Council of India.

805.30   "'plied hot . . . my blood"] *As You Like It*, II.iii.48–49.

807.1   the Frog Pond] On Boston Common.

807.6–7   "come & . . . or price"] Cf. Isaiah 55:1.

807.11   Charites] The three graces of Greek mythology, Aglaea, Euphrosyne, and Thalia.

819.40   "go up higher"] Luke 14:10.

822.30   Prest. Benson] Stephen Allen Benson (1816–1865), second president of Liberia, 1855–63.

823.13   Mill's India] James Mill (1773–1836), *The History of British India* (1817).

825.36   Gr. Eastern . . . Douglas] The 19,000 ton British steamship *Great Eastern*, which was six times larger than any previous vessel, reached New York on her maiden voyage on June 17, 1860. Senator Stephen A. Douglas was nominated for president by the Democratic national convention in Baltimore on June 23, 1860. Southern delegates then withdrew and nominated John C. Breckinridge as their candidate. The Democrats previously had met in Charleston, South Carolina, April 23–May 3, but were unable to choose a candidate.

827.35   Hunt's picture of the Scape Goat] "The Scapegoat" (1854), painting by Holman Hunt (1827–1910).

830.19   Mohammed Ali] Muhammad Ali Pasha (1769–1849), viceroy of Egypt, 1805–48.

832.15   Col. Vyse] Richard W. H. Vyse (1784–1853), a British military officer who explored the Pyramids, 1835–37.

835.4   Rev. Blaikie's] William Garden Blaikie (1820–1899), editor of the *North British Review* and a leader of the Scottish Presbyterian Church.

839.6   The Syrian massacres] Thousands of Christians were killed in Syria during the spring and summer of 1860.

840.18–20   Naviron Bay]   Combined British, French, and Russian naval forces destroyed the Turkish-Egyptian fleet in Naviron Bay on October 20, 1827, during the Greek War of Independence.

840.26–28   Isles of . . . & peace.]   Byron, *Don Juan*, Canto III (1821), LXXXVI.

841.13–16   [΄Συνοπσίσ . . . Τηλεγράφημα.]   Dana gives the name, place of publication, date, and price of the newspaper, which contains a story on Garibaldi's invasion of Sicily based on a report transmitted by telegraph.

843.5   *Nec temere, nec timide.*]   Neither rashly nor timidly.

844.24–25   "I stood . . . each hand"]   Byron, *Childe Harold's Pilgrimage*, Canto IV (1818), I.

845.30   "vice lost all its grossness"]   Cf. Burke, *Reflections on the Revolution in France* (1790): "Vice itself lost half its evil by losing all its grossness."

846.17   Antonio "rated" . . . his usanses"]   See *The Merchant of Venice*, I.iii.107–8.

848.13–14   "names that bear . . . the mention"]   Cf. Charles Lamb (1775–1834), "Detached Thoughts on Books and Reading" (1833): "the sweetest names, and which carry a perfume in the mention."

848.35–36   "glorious birth"]   William Wordsworth, "Intimations of Immortality from Recollections of Early Childhood" (1807), stanza II.

849.5   Miss Lydia Marsh]   An aunt of Dana's wife.

850.11   Murray]   A guidebook published by John Murray.

850.26   the dreadful battle of 1859]   Fought on June 4, the battle ended in a French victory over the Austrians.

851.26–27   Ben Bussey's]   Benjamin Bussey (1757–1842), a wealthy Boston merchant and philanthropist who built a number of roads in eastern Massachusetts.

852.31   "pure, placid Leman"]   Cf. Byron, *Childe Harold's Pilgrimage*, Canto III, LXXXV: "Clear, placid Leman!"

853.8   "misty shroud"]   *Childe Harold's Pilgrimage*, Canto III, XCII.

853.35–36   Peters the U.S. Reporter]   Richard Peters (1780–1848), reporter of the U.S. Supreme Court from 1828 to 1843.

856.16   Frank Wayland]   Francis Wayland (1796–1865), president of Brown University, 1827–55.

856.23   Gammell]   William Gammell (1812–1889), professor of theology at Brown.

857.13–14   *Geo. F. Hoar . . . Mr. Choate*]   The exchange between George F. Hoar (1826–1904) and Rufus Choate (1799–1859) concerned George Ticknor Curtis (1812–1894); all three men were active in Massachusetts politics.

859.38   Sturgis]   Russell Sturgis, American-born senior partner of the banking house of Baring Brothers.

860.14   Henry T. Parker]   Henry Tuke Parker (1824–1890), a wealthy Bostonian who moved to London in 1855.

864.30–31   the . . . was an evil liver]   Dana refers to the Samson portrayed in Milton's *Samson Agonistes*.

866.24   Byron's "Maid of Cadis"]   "The Girl of Cadiz" (1809).

867.16   John Cotton]   Cotton (1584–1652), a leading minister of the Massachusetts Bay Colony, had been vicar of St. Botolph's Church, 1612–32.

868.32–33   "Angel in the House"]   A sequence of narrative poems (1854–63) by Coventry Patmore (1823–1896). The description of the deanery appears in Book 1, Canto 1, "The Cathedral Close," stanza 2.

870.11–12   Eustis]   George R. Eustis, Jr. (1828–1872), was a Know-Nothing congressman from Louisiana, 1855–59.

870.15   Bancroft Davis]   John Chandler Bancroft Davis (1822–1907); his father, John Davis (1787–1854), a Whig, was governor of Massachusetts, 1834–35 and 1841–43.

Library of Congress Cataloging-in-Publication Data

Dana, Richard Henry, 1815–1882.
  Two years before the mast and other voyages / Richard
Henry Dana.
        p. cm.—(Library of America ; 161)
    Includes bibliographical references.
    Contents: Two years before the mast—To Cuba and back:
a vacation voyage—Journal of a voyage round the world
1859–1860.
    ISBN 1–931082–83–9 (alk. paper)
    1. Dana, Richard Henry, 1815–1882—Travel. 2. Voyages and
travels. 3. Seafaring life. 4. Cuba—Description and travel.
I. Title. II. Series.

G540.D2   2005
910.4′5—dc22   2005045094

THE LIBRARY OF AMERICA SERIES

The Library of America fosters appreciation and pride in America's literary heritage by publishing, and keeping permanently in print, authoritative editions of America's best and most significant writing. An independent nonprofit organization, it was founded in 1979 with seed money from the National Endowment for the Humanities and the Ford Foundation.

*This book is set in 10 point Linotron Galliard,
a face designed for photocomposition by Matthew Carter
and based on the sixteenth-century face Granjon. The paper
is acid-free Domtar Literary Opaque and meets the requirements
for permanence of the American National Standards Institute. The
binding material is Brillianta, a woven rayon cloth made by
Van Heek-Scholco Textielfabrieken, Holland. Composition by Dedicated Business Services. Printing by
Malloy Incorporated. Binding by Dekker Book-
binding. Designed by Bruce Campbell.*

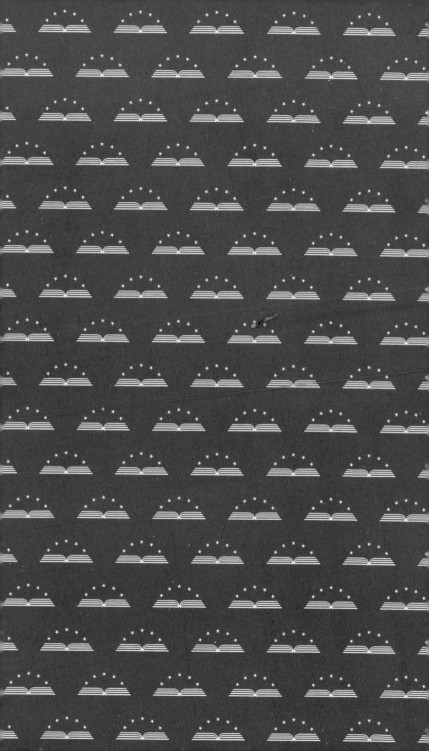